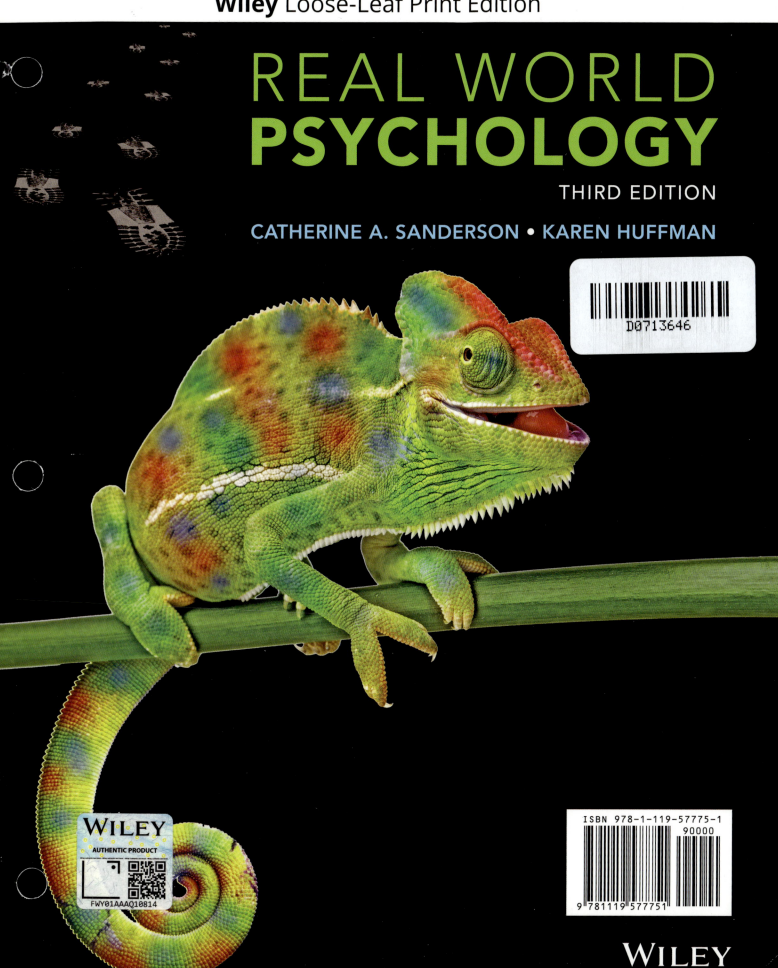

Wiley Loose-Leaf Print Edition

REAL WORLD
PSYCHOLOGY

THIRD EDITION

CATHERINE A. SANDERSON • KAREN HUFFMAN

ISBN 978-1-119-57775-1
90000

9 781119 577751

WILEY

WileyPLUS

WileyPLUS gives you the freedom of mobility and provides a clear path to your course material and assignments, helping you stay engaged and on track.

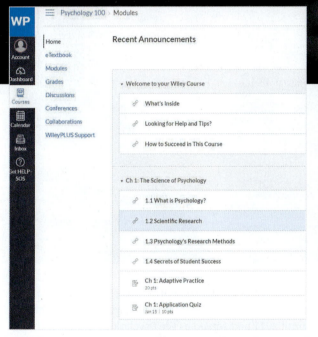

When course materials are presented in an organized way, you are more likely to stay focused, develop mastery, and participate in class. WileyPLUS provides you a clear path through the course material.

Starting with Wiley's quality curated content and adaptive practice questions, you can quickly access material most relevant to your course and understand topics that are most challenging to you. This easy-to-use, intuitive interface saves you time, helps you stay on track, and keeps you motivated throughout your course.

Customized Content

Your course has been customized with videos, documents, pages, and relevant links to keep you motivated.

Interactive eTextbook

You can easily search content, highlight and take notes, access instructor's notes and highlights, and read offline.

Adaptive Practice Questions

Quickly identify areas that are most challenging for you and then focus on material most relevant to your needs.

Linear Design and Organization

Course modules organized by learning objective include eTextbook content, videos, animations, interactives, and practice questions.

Calendar

The course calendar syncs with other features—like assignments and syllabus—so any updates from your instructor will immediately appear.

Student App

You can view due dates, submit assignments, read material, and communicate with your instructor all from your phone.

www.wileyplus.com/student-register

WILEY

About the Authors

CATHERINE A. SANDERSON is the Manwell Family Professor of Life Sciences (Psychology) at Amherst College. She received a bachelor's degree in psychology, with a specialization in health and development, from Stanford University, and received both masters and doctoral degrees in psychology from Princeton University. Professor Sanderson's research examines how personality and social variables influence health-related behaviors such as safer sex and disordered eating, the development of persuasive messages and interventions to prevent unhealthy behavior, and the predictors of relationship satisfaction. This research has received grant funding from the National Science Foundation and the National Institutes of Health. Professor Sanderson has published over 25 journal articles and book chapters, five college textbooks, and middle school and high school health textbooks. Her most recent book, *The Positive Shift*, examines the link between happiness, health, and longevity. In 2012, she was named one of the country's top 300 professors by the Princeton Review.

KAREN HUFFMAN is an emeritus professor of psychology at Palomar College, San Marcos, California, where she taught full-time until 2011 and served as the Psychology Student Advisor and Co-Coordinator for psychology faculty. Professor Huffman has received the Excellence in Teaching and Outstanding Research Awards at Palomar College and the National Teaching Award for Excellence in Community/Junior College Teaching given by the American Psychological Association (APA), along with other awards and accolades. She is also the author and co-author of several textbooks, including *Real World Psychology, Psychology in Action*, and *Visualizing Psychology*. Professor Huffman's special research and presentation focus is on active learning and critical thinking. She has been an invited speaker and conducted numerous presentations, online web seminars, and teaching workshops throughout the United States, Spain, Canada, and Puerto Rico.

Photo by Jo Chattman

Courtesy of Karen Huffman

Real World Psychology

Third Edition

CATHERINE A. SANDERSON

Amherst College

KAREN HUFFMAN

Palomar College

WILEY

VICE PRESIDENT AND DIRECTOR	Veronica Vistentin
EXECUTIVE EDITOR	Glenn A. Wilson
SENIOR MARKETING MANAGER	Carolyn Wells
PRODUCT DESIGN	Karen Staudinger
SENIOR CONTENT MANAGER	Dorothy Sinclair
SENIOR PRODUCTION EDITOR	Sandra Rigby
SENIOR DESIGNER	Wendy Lai

Cover photos: Kuttelvaserova Stuchelova/Shutterstock.com; iStock.com/TPopova

This book was set in Source Sans Pro 9.5/12.5 pts by Lumina Datamatics, Inc., and printed and bound by Quad Graphics/Versailles.

Founded in 1807, John Wiley & Sons, Inc. has been a valued source of knowledge and understanding for more than 200 years, helping people around the world meet their needs and fulfill their aspirations. Our company is built on a foundation of principles that include responsibility to the communities we serve and where we live and work. In 2008, we launched a Corporate Citizenship Initiative, a global effort to address the environmental, social, economic, and ethical challenges we face in our business. Among the issues we are addressing are carbon impact, paper specifications and procurement, ethical conduct within our business and among our vendors, and community and charitable support. For more information, please visit our website: www.wiley.com/go/citizenship.

Evaluation copies are provided to qualified academics and professionals for review purposes only, for use in their courses during the next academic year. These copies are licensed and may not be sold or transferred to a third party. Upon completion of the review period, please return the evaluation copy to Wiley. Return instructions and a free-of-charge return shipping label are available at www. wiley.com/go/return label. If you have chosen to adopt this textbook for use in your course, please accept this book as your complimentary desk copy. Outside of the United States, please contact your local representative.

ePub ISBN: 978-1-119-57773-7

The inside back cover will contain printing identification and country of origin if omitted from this page. In addition, if the ISBN on the back cover differs from the ISBN on this page, the one on the back cover is correct.

Printed in the United States of America

SKY10030758_102221

Brief Contents

Contents

Preface

Kuttelvaserova Stuchelova/Shutterstock.com

Have you ever wondered why certain images (like this chameleon) are chosen for the cover of a book? Given that many students come to their first psychology class with far too many misconceptions and limited notions about psychology, themselves, and human nature in general, our core mission is to demonstrate how psychological science can expand and change their minds, hearts, and views of the world around them. Therefore, we chose a chameleon as our "brand image" because of its well-known ability to change color, and for its 360-degree range of vision!

Why did we choose "Real World Psychology" as the title of our book? Although students may have numerous misconceptions about psychology, we know that most of them are truly interested in the field. However, in our fast-paced, modern society, they also face enormous pressures from their work, families, friends, and life in general. To capture and hold their attention, we cover all the essentials of psychology, while emphasizing "hot topics" based on fascinating scientific research with practical applications to their everyday lives, hence our title—*Real World Psychology!*

Thankfully, our readers seem to really enjoy our approach. Both students and professors have written emails and letters expressing how much they appreciate our writing style and how they feel like the book spoke directly to them. Two of their most frequent, and our most treasured, compliments were:

Dave Coverly/The Cartoonist Group

"The real-life examples and FUN activities and visuals (see cartoon) in Real World Psychology made the material easy to understand and helped me apply the information to my personal situations."

"It's clear that the authors really love their field and truly care about their readers."

As you can see, we feel passionate about our third edition and we're eager to hear from all instructors and students. If you have suggestions or comments, please feel free to contact us directly: Catherine Sanderson (casanderson@amherst.edu) and Karen Huffman (khuffman@palomar.edu).

Note to Instructors

Welcome to the third edition of *Real World Psychology*! If you are reading this, and have used one or more of our previous editions, or are considering an adoption for the first time, we want to offer our sincere appreciation. We've received emails and texts from many of you, and we're honored by the enthusiastic responses to our text.

In response to your questions, and the continuing challenges of teaching, we'll address three of the most common and pressing issues, and how we've addressed them in this third edition.

1. "How can using *Real World Psychology* increase active learning, student engagement, and motivation?"

Research clearly shows that active learning, student engagement and motivation are essential to student (and professor success). And, beginning with our first edition, these three items have always been our primary goal! As you'll see throughout the text, we've done everything we can to promote active learning and to engage and inspire our readers. For example:

- Each chapter begins with six, intriguing **[AQ]** *Application Questions* that are directly related to that chapter's specific content. Reviewer and student comments agree that they are a great way to grab student interest and motivation for reading the chapter's material. Special icons (e.g., **[AQ1]**) appear in the text to alert readers where answers to the questions are addressed. See the sample below.

Kuttelvaserova Stuchelova/Shutterstock.com

CHAPTER **1**

The Science of Psychology

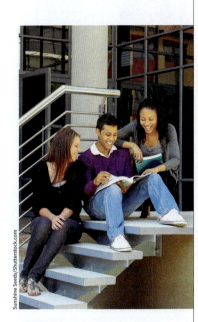
Sunshine Seeds/Shutterstock.com

Real World Application Questions [AQ]

Things you'll learn in Chapter 1

[AQ1] Does your ethnicity affect the type of questions you're asked in a job interview?

[AQ2] Can strength training decrease depression?

[AQ3] Can a diet high in fats and sugars impair learning and memory?

[AQ4] Does spending more time on Instagram decrease your psychological well-being?

[AQ5] Is there a correlation between years of education and physical health?

[AQ6] What are the best study techniques for improving your exam performance?

Throughout the chapter, look for [AQ1]–[AQ6] icons. They indicate where the text addresses these questions.

- Given the well-known student interest and motivation related to practical applications, as well as the increasing public demand for increased scientific thinking, we include four special features in each chapter dedicated to these two topics. See the samples below.

PP **Practical Application: PositivePsych**

What Makes Us Happy?

(APA Goal 1.3) Describe applications of psychology

One of the most consistent findings in positive psychology is that other people make us happy. "Simply" building and maintaining relationships tends to significantly improve our overall happiness and well-being (Diener & Tay, 2015; Galinha et al., 2016; Lee & Kawachi, 2019). As shown in the photo, even just talking with strangers leads to higher levels of happiness. Researchers who asked riders on trains and buses to either quietly sit alone or talk to a stranger found that those who talked to a stranger reported more positive feelings than those who sat alone (Epley & Schroeder, 2014).

In addition, contrary to the popular belief that "money buys happiness," research shows that once we have enough income to meet our basic needs, additional funds do not significantly increase our levels of happiness and well-being (Kushlev et al., 2015; Whillans & Macchia, 2019). Furthermore, when adults are given money and told to spend it on others, they experience higher levels of happiness than do those who are told to spend it on themselves (Dunn et al., 2008).

kali9/E+/Getty Images

STH **Scientific Thinking Highlight**

Have Women Really "Come a Long Way, Baby"?

(APA Goal 2.1) Use scientific reasoning to interpret psychological phenomena

In the 1960s, when the feminist movement was gaining in strength and popularity, and attitudes toward women's rights were shifting, the Virginia Slims tobacco company attempted to capitalize on that change. Using their own form of cognitive retraining and classical conditioning (Chapter 6), they created clever ads that paired smoking their brand of cigarettes with being independent, stylish, confident, and liberated. Their campaign line, "You've come a long way, baby," remains one of the most famous in U.S. history (see photo).

But is this true? Women have definitely made considerable gains, including laws protecting them from domestic violence and laws providing family medical leave. There are also more women in the halls of political power than ever before. Yet they still have a long way to go before reaching equality with men. Consider the following examples based on recent research.

Within the United States:

- Given that men and women have different work histories, experiences, and career opportunities, it's difficult to pinpoint the exact pay gap between the sexes, but one common estimate is that for full-time, year-round workers, women still earn far less that their White male counterparts. Specifically, for every dollar earned by White men: Asian women earn $0.85, White women $0.77, Black women $0.61, Native American women $0.58, and Latina women $0.53 (AAUW, 2019; Graf et al., 2019; Hegewisch, 2019).

- Women who speak up in meetings, or during participation in the "wild," are much less likely to be considered leaders, even when the ideas they share are the same as a man's in the same setting (McClean et al., 2018).

- As discussed in Chapter 10, female attorneys who express anger in the courtroom are seen as shrill and obnoxious, whereas male attorneys who express similar anger are seen as powerful and full of conviction (Salerno et al., 2018).

- When asked to draw a scientist, a meta-analysis of 78 studies found that children are still far more likely to draw a man versus a woman, and the difference is the greatest among older children (Miller et al., 2018).

Around the world:

- The economic participation and opportunity gap between men and women is currently 41.9 percent among the 149 countries studied, and experts predict it will take more than a hundred years for this gap to close (The Global Gender Gap, 2018).

- Among these same 149 countries, only 17 currently have women as heads of state, and women hold only 34 percent of all managerial positions (The Global Gender Gap, 2018).

- Out of 15 countries, including the United States, women are at far greater risk of gender-based violence than men (Blum et al., 2017).

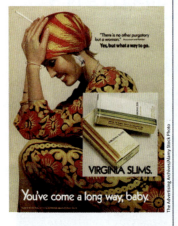

"There is no other purgatory but a woman." *Baccaccio and Petrarch*
Yes, but what a way to go.

VIRGINIA SLIMS.
You've come a long way, baby.

The Advertising Archives/Alamy Stock Photo

Q **Test Your Scientific Thinking**

As you recall from Chapter 1, scientific thinking is an approach to information that combines a high degree of *skepticism* (questioning what "everybody knows") with *objectivity* (using empirical data to separate fantasy from reality) and with *rationalism* (practicing logical reasoning).

1. **Skepticism** Given the title and topic of the report cited at the beginning of this highlight "Have Women Really 'Come a Long Way, Baby'?" were you predisposed to believe or discount the information? Did the cited research change your attitudes? Why or why not?

2. **Objectivity** Imagine you are talking to someone who is a strong believer or denier of sexism within the United States and around the world. Using the objective research and statistics cited above, how could you use the information to have a meaningful conversation on these topics with these two individuals? How might this type of dialogue be helpful to both of you?

3. **Rationalism** Given the serious national and international challenges that we all face, solving these problems logically demands innovative engineering solutions (Roscoe et al., 2019), as well as the input of all people—regardless of gender, ethnicity, age, and so on. What can (and should) we do to correct this persistent sexism?

(Compare your answers with those of your fellow students, family, and friends. Doing so will improve your scientific thinking and your media savvy.)

PAH **Practical Application Highlight**

Tips for Grade Improvement

(APA Goal 1.3) Describe applications of psychology

In combination with the previous study habit and time management tips, the following strategies are virtually guaranteed to improve your overall grade point average (GPA) in all your college classes and your mastery of the material.

1. **Refuse to multitask on new or complex material.** Are you one of the many students who believe that doing more than one task at a time makes you more effective? If so, you'll be surprised to know that this so-called "multitasking" is actually just "task-switching," and that it clearly decreases overall performance and productivity—particularly for new or complex tasks (Aagaard, 2019; Bender et al., 2017; Ralph et al., 2019). As you discovered earlier in the section on active reading and the *Test Yourself* Stroop test, switching from one task to another (reading a word while trying to state its color) greatly increased your response time—and errors.

   Can you see how this explains why texting and driving (or walking) is so dangerous (Chapter 5), and how casually listening to the professor, while also texting, playing computer games, or talking to other classmates, is largely a waste of time? In fact, a study in an introductory psychology class found that Internet use during lectures was *negatively correlated* with student performance, which means, as you learned earlier in this chapter, that as Internet usage went up performance went down (Ravizza et al., 2017). A good rule to remember is that one hour of full attention in class is generally worth about four hours on your own outside of class. In addition to paying full attention, taking detailed notes by hand during each class session is one of the most efficient and profitable uses of your time (Mueller & Oppenheimer, 2014).

2. **Maximize the value of each class session.** As you know, the authors of this text are both college professors, so this advice may sound biased. However, solid psychological research (e.g., Putnam et al., 2016) recommends that all students do the following:

   - **Prepare ahead of time.** Be sure to study the assigned material ahead of each class.

   - **Attend every class.** Most instructors provide unique ideas and personal examples that are not in the text, and even when they do repeat what is covered in the text, we all need to have multiple exposures to new material. Also, pay close attention to what your professor emphasizes in class, as this material is likely to appear on exams. Think of your professor's lecture as you would tips from your coach or an employer who was going out of his or her way to tell you what you needed to know to maximize your performance or paycheck.

3. **Improve your general test-taking skills.** Virtually all students can improve their performance on exams by taking additional courses designed to develop their reading speed and comprehension. During exams, expect a bit of stress but don't panic. Pace yourself and focus on what you know. Skip over questions when you don't know the answers, and then go back if time allows. On multiple-choice exams, carefully read each question and all the alternative answers, before responding. Answer all questions

and make sure you have recorded your answers correctly.

Also, bear in mind that information relevant to one question is often found in another test question. Do not hesitate to change an answer if you get more information—or even if you simply have a better guess about an answer. Contrary to the belief held by many students (and faculty) that "your first hunch is your best guess," research suggests this is NOT the case (Benjamin et al., 1984; Lilienfeld et al., 2010, 2015). Changing answers is far more likely to result in a higher score (Figure 1.20).

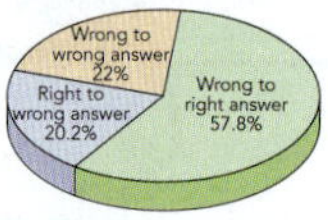

Wrong to wrong answer 22%
Right to wrong answer 20.2%
Wrong to right answer 57.8%

FIGURE 1.20 **Should you change your answers?** Research clearly shows that answer changes that go from a wrong to a right answer (57.8 percent) greatly outnumber those that go from a right to a wrong answer (20.2 percent). **Source:** Benjamin et al., 1984.

4. **[AQ6] Distribute your practice and practice test taking.** Research has firmly established that these last two techniques—*distributed practice* and *practice testing*—are the MOST important keys to grade improvement—see photo (Carpenter & Yeung, 2017; Gagnon & Cormier, 2018; Trumbo et al., 2016). Why? Spreading your study sessions out over time (distributed practice) and practice testing are far more efficient than waiting until right before an exam and cramming in all the information at once (massed practice) (Chapter 7). If you were a basketball player, you wouldn't wait until the night before a big play-off game to practice. Just as you need to repeatedly practice your free throw shot to become a good basketball player, you need to repeatedly practice your test-taking to become a good student.

   Based on this growing body of research and our own teaching success with frequent testing, we've designed this text to include numerous, distributed practice opportunities sprinkled throughout each chapter. As you're actively reading and studying, be sure to complete all these self-tests. When you miss a question, it's very helpful, and important, to immediately go back and reread the sections of the text that correspond to your incorrect response. You can also easily access the free flashcards and other forms of self-testing provided with the purchase of this text.

5. **Adjust your attitude.** We've saved our best tip—*attitude adjustment*—for last. You have the power to decide that you can, and will, improve your academic skills. Instead of focusing on negative thoughts, such as "I can't go to the party because I have to study" or "Going to class feels like a waste of time," try counter statements, like "I'm going to learn how to study and make better use of my class time, so that I can have more free time." Similarly, rather than thinking or saying "I never do well on tests," do something constructive like taking a study skills and/or test preparation course at your college.

Olga_Danylenko/iStock/Getty Images

RC **Scientific Thinking: Research Challenge**

Is Happiness Defined by Your Social Class?

(APA Goal 2.4) Interpret, design, and conduct basic psychological research

Earlier in this chapter, we discussed research in positive psychology showing that once we have enough income to meet our basic needs, additional funds won't significantly increase our levels of happiness. In short, money doesn't buy happiness. However, now that you've studied the basics of psychological research and are applying your scientific and critical thinking skills, do you wonder how happiness was identified and defined? Researchers interested in the emotional components of happiness, and how these components might vary among people in different socioeconomic classes, recruited a large nationally representative U.S. sample of 1,519 individuals (Piff & Moskowitz, 2018). Participants were asked to self-report on their tendencies to experience seven different positive emotions that are core to happiness—amusement, awe, compassion, contentment, enthusiasm, love, and pride.

Can you predict their findings? Interestingly, wealthier participants (as measured by household income) were more likely to report *self-focused* emotions, such as amusement, contentment, and pride. Conversely, the lower social class participants reported more *other-oriented* emotions, like compassion and love. There were no class differences in enthusiasm.

How would you explain the results? The researchers suggested that the class differences may reflect varying social concerns and priorities of the higher versus lower social classes. The self-oriented feelings of the upper-class participants may result from their specific upbringing and desires for independence and self-sufficiency. In contrast, the other-oriented emotions of the lower-class may follow from growing up in more threatening

environments, which possibly led to a greater desire for compassion, love, and more interdependent bonds. What do you think? Given that you may be attending college hoping to secure a high-paying job, how can you apply this research to your own career and relationship aspirations?

Identify the Research Method

1. Based on the information provided, did this study (Piff & Moskowitz, 2018) use descriptive, correlational, and/or experimental research?

2. If you chose:
   - *descriptive research*, is this a naturalistic or laboratory observation, survey/interview, case study, and/or archival research?
   - *correlational research*, is this a positive, negative, or zero correlation?
   - *experimental research*, label the IV, DV, experimental group(s), and control group. (Note: If participants were not randomly assigned to groups, list the design as *quasi-experimental*.)
   - both *descriptive* and *correlational*, answer the corresponding questions for both.

Check your answers by clicking on the answer button or by looking in Appendix B.

Note: The information provided in this study is admittedly limited, but the level of detail is similar to what is presented in most textbooks and public reports of research findings. Answering these questions, and then comparing your answers to those provided, will help you become a better scientific and critical thinker and consumer of scientific research.

- Recognizing the growing interests and diversity of our students, we embed numerous examples of diversity throughout the text, along with more inclusive photos, figures, and tables. In addition, we have added a special, NEW feature **GCD** **Gender** and **Cultural Diversity** to each chapter, which expands on cultural issues related to that chapter's academic content. See the sample below.

GCD Gender and Cultural Diversity

Biopsychosocial Forces and Acculturative Stress

(APA Goal 2.5) Incorporate sociocultural factors in scientific inquiry

Have you ever lived in or dreamed of emigrating to another country? If so, you probably imagine yourself fully enjoying all the excitement and adventure. But have you considered the stress and stressors that come with adapting to and surviving in a new culture?

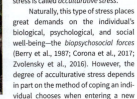

International travelers, military personnel, immigrants, refugees, individuals who move from one social class to another, and even the native-born may fall victim to the unspoken and unforeseen stressors of adjusting their personal and family values, their cultural norms, and maybe their style of dress to the new or dominant culture (like the young Native American woman in these two photos). These required adjustments are referred to as *acculturation*, whereas the associated stress is called *acculturative stress*.

Courtesy of Linda Locklear

Naturally, this type of stress places great demands on the individual's biological, psychological, and social well-being—the *biopsychosocial forces* (Berry et al., 1987; Corona et al., 2017; Zvolensky et al., 2016). However, the degree of acculturative stress depends in part on the method of coping an individual chooses when entering a new society. Researchers have identified four major approaches to acculturation (Berry & Ataca, 2010; Urzúa et al., 2017):

1. **Integration** As you might expect, a choice toward *integration* typically leads to the lowest levels of acculturative stress. People who have a high desire to maintain their original cultural identity, while also having a strong motivation to learn from and seek positive relations mainly with the new culture are pursuing the path to integration. However, stress will still be a factor if the person has been forced to emigrate, or if the new country is reluctant to accept newcomers and distrustful of ethnic and cultural diversity.

2. **Assimilation** People who choose to *assimilate* typically have a low identification with their culture of origin and a high desire to identify with the new culture. They tend to have the next lowest level of stress, but there are still many problems, presumably due to the loss of cultural support from other members of the original culture who do not assimilate.

3. **Separation** Individuals who choose to *separate* often place high value on their original culture and do not want to adapt to the new one. They generally have the next to highest level of acculturative stress, which is most likely due to being separated from the new or dominant culture. Their stress levels are even higher for those who are forcibly separated by prejudice and discrimination than for those who separate voluntarily.

4. **Marginalization** People who have a low identification with both the new culture and their culture of origin are likely to be *marginalized* from the dominant culture. This pattern normally leads to the highest levels of acculturative stress, presumably due to the fact that they tend to live on the "margins" and lack the connections and support of either the old or new cultures.

To check your understanding of these four patterns, see the following **Test Yourself**.

Q Test Yourself: Cultural Reactions to Stress

Picture yourself as a college graduate who's been offered a high-paying job that will allow you to move from a lower socio-economic class to the middle or upper class. What you don't know is that your change in status will likely lead to considerable acculturative stress. In anticipation of this change, will you:

- Adopt the *majority* culture and seek positive relations with the new or dominant culture?
- Maintain your original cultural identity and avoid relations with the dominant culture?

Your responses to these two questions tend to place you into one of the four major approaches to acculturation—and will likely predict your level of stress.

As an example of acculturative stress, consider Malala Yousafzai, the famous activist (see photo), who, at the age of 17, was the youngest person ever to win the Nobel Peace Prize. The path to this honor began when she was an 11-year-old writing a courageous blog describing her life under the Taliban and her desire for all girls to have the chance to be educated. Tragically, her courage led to her being shot in the head at the age of 15 by the Taliban as she was on her way to school. After surviving the attempted murder, Malala went on to become an international activist who's traveled all over the world. Malala also recently published a book describing her experiences visiting refugee camps and the tens of millions of people who are currently displaced (Yousafzai, 2019).

Although Malala and her family emigrated to the UK after the attack on her life, she plans to return to the home she loves in Pakistan after completing her education at Oxford University. Which of the four approaches to acculturation do you think she has followed while living in the UK?

Take-Home Message Later in this chapter, we will introduce the topic of *ethnocentrism*, believing that one's culture is typical of all cultures and/or that one's own culture is the "correct" one. Can you see how ethnocentrism would logically increase acculturative stress if you decide to relocate or even just when you're traveling? Perhaps the most important question is how can we as individuals and citizens of the world help reduce the anxiety, depression, alienation, and physical illnesses associated with forced and voluntary emigration, and the inevitable acculturative stress?

---

2. "Our administrators are pressing for better retention, accountability, and improved learning outcomes, how does *Real World Psychology* meet those demands?"

As you'll note throughout the text, and in the upcoming section describing all our teaching and learning resources, we the authors, along with all the hard-working specialists at Wiley, have strived to ensure better retention, accountability, and improved learning outcomes. In addition, see the following information, including Table 1, which demonstrate how our text meets the national standards set by the American Psychological Association (APA).

Real World Psychology's Connections to APA Undergraduate Learning Goals and Outcomes

"The *APA Guidelines for the Undergraduate Psychology Major: Version 2.0* represents a national effort to describe and develop high-quality undergraduate programs in psychology." APA Guidelines Executive Summary, August 2013. Retrieved from http://www.apa.org/ed/precollege/about/psymajor-guidelines.pdf

Table 1 demonstrates how the third edition of *Real World Psychology* connects directly with the APA guidelines to help instructors and their students meet the five goals set forward by the APA.

TABLE 1	**APA Guidelines and Related Coverage in *Real World Psychology*, 3rd ed. [RWP(3e)]**

Goal 1. Knowledge Base in Psychology

APA Learning Objectives:

1.1 *Describe key concepts, principles, and overarching themes in psychology*
1.2 *Develop a working knowledge of psychology's content domains*
1.3 *Describe applications of psychology*

PAH **Practical Application Highlight**—NEW feature in RWP(3e). Includes topics such as Secrets of Student Success, Tips for Improved Problem Solving, Self-Efficacy in Daily Life, Myths, Stigma, and Discrimination in Mental Illness, and What Are the Secrets to Enduring Love?

PP **Practical Application: PositivePsych**—NEW feature in RWP(3e). Includes topics such as, What Makes Us Happy?, Promoting Resilience, Why Talk or Read to Babies?, and Would You Donate a Kidney to a Stranger?

Real World Psychology offers full coverage of the knowledge base in psychology, including all the major subject areas in psychology: history and research methods, biological psychology, stress and health psychology, sensation and perception, and so on. We also offer comprehensive, up-to-date psychological research in each chapter (over 1,000 new citations). Regarding practical applications, we provide TWO NEW special features in each chapter (see the descriptions of the **PAH** and **PP** in left column), along with numerous embedded applications throughout the text. As our title implies, *Real World Psychology* focuses on applications to our everyday life and *real world* examples.

The knowledge base in psychology is also emphasized in the Instructor's Resource Guide, WileyPlus, and other Wiley website assets that can be found at **www.wiley.com/college/sanderson**, and more.

Goal 2. Scientific Inquiry and Critical Thinking

APA Learning Objectives:

2.1 *Use scientific reasoning to interpret psychological phenomena*
2.2 *Demonstrate psychology information literacy*
2.3 *Engage in innovative and integrative thinking and problem solving*
2.4 *Interpret, design, and conduct basic psychological research*

STH **Scientific Thinking Highlight**—NEW feature in RWP(3e). Includes topics such as Psychology and the Replication Crisis, Do We All Have ADHD?, Vaccination and Herd Immunity, and Have Women Really "Come a Long Way, Baby"?

RC **Scientific Thinking: Research Challenge**—NEW feature in RWP(3e). Includes topics such as Does Retrieval Practice Help?, Can Head Injuries Increase the Risk for Depression and Other Psychological Disorders?, and Can a 10-Minute Conversation Reduce Prejudice?

Throughout the entire text, *Real World Psychology* emphasizes the importance of scientific inquiry and critical thinking. Along with the TWO NEW special features focusing on scientific thinking, the **STH** and **RC**, we also include a special embedded (non-boxed) feature— **S&P** **Scientific Thinking and Practical Application**—which focuses on critical topics and questions, such as Science Versus

Pseudoscience, Is Schizophrenia the Same as Multiple Personalities?, and Can Gender Differences Lead to Differential Diagnoses?

In addition, each chapter begins with six Application Questions [AQ1–AQ6] designed to immediately engage the reader, with answers embedded throughout the chapter (e.g., Does spending more time on Instagram decrease your psychological well-being? Does your ethnicity affect the type of questions you're asked in a job interview? Can reading *Harry Potter* books increase positivity towards gay people?)

2.5 *Incorporate sociocultural factors in scientific inquiry*

Regarding sociocultural factors, in addition to comprehensive coverage throughout, we also offer a **GCD** **Gender and Cultural Diversity**—NEW feature in RWP(3e). Includes topics such as Biopsychosocial Forces and Acculturative Stress, Avoiding Ethnocentrism, and How Does Culture Affect Our Personal Space?

Scientific inquiry and critical thinking are also highlighted in the Instructor's Resource Guide, WileyPlus, and other Wiley website assets that can be found at **www.wiley.com/college/sanderson**, and more.

Goal 3. Ethical and Social Responsibility in a Diverse World

APA Learning Objectives:

3.1 *Apply ethical standards to evaluate psychological science and practice*
3.2 *Build and enhance interpersonal relationships*
3.3 *Adopt values that build community at local, national, and global levels*

Throughout the entire text, *Real World Psychology* highlights ethical and social responsibility, such as Psychology's Research Ethics (Chapter 1), Can Growing Up in Poverty Cause Changes in Your Brain? (Chapter 3), Patients' Race and Quality of Medical

Care (Chapter 4), i Can Meditation Increase Helping Behaviors? (Chapter 5), Can Diversity Affect Moral Development? (Chapter 9), Preventing Sexual Violence (Chapter 10), What Parenting Skills Are Associated with Marital Satisfaction? (Chapter 12), Avoiding Ethnocentrism (Chapter 13), and Promoting Resilience in Children and Adults (Chapter 13).

Ethical and social responsibility is also emphasized in the Instructor's Resource Guide, WileyPlus, and other Wiley website assets that can be found at **www.wiley.com/college/sanderson**, and more.

Goal 4. Communication

APA Learning Objectives:

4.1 *Demonstrate effective writing for different purposes*
4.2 *Exhibit effective presentation skills for different purposes*
4.3 *Interact effectively with others*

Each chapter of *Real World Psychology* affirms the importance of communication with special topics and sections such as Helping Someone with PTSD (Chapter 3), Can Maximizing Your Consciousness Save Lives? (Chapter 5), Using Reinforcement and Punishment Effectively (Chapter 6), The Impressive Powers of Prosocial Media (Chapter 6), Negative Effects of Smartphones (Chapter 7), Understanding Verbal and Nonverbal Language (Chapter 8), Differentiating Fake News from Real News (Chapter 8), Sexual Communication (Chapter 10), Conflict Resolution (Chapter 10), Tips for Finding a Therapist (Chapter 14), Can a 10-Minute Conversation Reduce Prejudice (Chapter 15)?

Communication is also a key feature in the Instructor's Resource Guide, WileyPlus, and other Wiley website assets that can be found at **www.wiley.com/college/sanderson**, and more.

Goal 5. Professional Development

APA Learning Objectives:

5.1 *Apply psychological content and skills to career goals*
5.2 *Exhibit self-efficacy and self-regulation*
5.3 *Refine project management skills*

Throughout the entire text, *Real World Psychology* emphasizes professional development with special topics and sections such as Where Psychologists Work and What Psychologists Do (Chapter 1), Using your Frontal Lobes to Train Your Brain (Chapter 2), Coping with Job Stress and Technostress (Chapter 3), Vocational ver-sus Academic Interests and the FFM (Chapter 12), Self-Efficacy in Daily Life (Chapter 13), and Tips for a Great Interview (Chapter 15).

Professional development is also highlighted in the Instructor's Resource Guide, WileyPlus, and other Wiley website assets that can be found at **www.wiley.com/college/sanderson**, and more.

3. "I want my students to come to class better prepared and able to perform better on exams. How can *Real World Psychology* help me?"

Real World Psychology, Third Edition, is completely integrated with WileyPLUS, featuring a suite of teaching and learning resources. With WileyPLUS, you can provide students with a personalized study plan that gives access to the content and resources needed to master the material, and assess their progress along the way. WileyPLUS provides an immediate understanding of students' strengths and problem areas with reports and metrics that provide insight into each student's performance, allowing you to identify and address individual needs in a timely manner. Many dynamic resources are integrated into the course to help students build their knowledge and understanding, stay motivated, and prepare for decision making in a real world context.

WileyPLUS also includes integrated adaptive practice that helps students build proficiency and use their study time most effectively. Additional features of the WileyPLUS course include:

For Each Learning Objective

- **What the Authors Say** videos, featuring Catherine Sanderson and Karen Huffman, provide a lively discussion, introducing key terms and concepts to give students a better understanding of the topic they are about to study.

- **In the Classroom** videos show author Catherine Sanderson illustrating the concepts presented in the chapter section with an example. In many cases, a Student Voices segment is also featured, showing a student discussion group.

Throughout the Course

- More than 40 **Wiley Psychology Animations** illustrate difficult-to-learn concepts from a real world perspective.

- More than 30 **Tutorial Videos**, featuring author Karen Huffman and Katherine Dowdell of Des Moines Area Community College, provide students with explanations and examples of some of the most challenging concepts in psychology. These 3- to 5-minute videos reflect the richness and diversity of psychology, from the steps of the experimental method to the interaction of genes and our environment, to the sources of stress.

- 20 **Virtual Field Trips** allow students to view psychology concepts in the real world as they've never seen them before. These 5- to 10-minute virtual field trips include visits to places such as a neuroimaging center, a film studio where 3-D movies are created, and a sleep laboratory, to name only a few.
- More than 20 **Visual Drag-and-Drop and Interactive Graphics** provide students with a different, and more interactive, way to visualize and label key illustrations from the text.

Practice and Assessment

WileyPLUS features adaptive practice, video quizzes, and more. Two highlights of the practice and assessment content in this edition are:

- With approximately 150 questions per chapter, the Test Bank is available in two modes. Word file is available for review in the Instructor Resources. In addition, all questions have been programmed for WileyPLUS, where they can now be filtered by APA standards, as well as learning objective, section, Bloom's level, and level of difficulty for use in custom assignments. A carefully designed assignment using these questions, a Quick Start Text Bank Assignment, is also provided. This gathers the most popular questions from the prior edition, based on user data from WileyPLUS.
- A specific, ready-made assignment is also now available with all new Application questions. In keeping with the theme of this revision, these questions ask students to use the knowledge they have acquired in an applied setting.

Acknowledgments

To the professors who care as much as we do about good teaching, and have given their time and constructive criticism, we offer our sincere appreciation. We are deeply indebted to the following individuals and trust that they will recognize their contributions throughout the text.

Kojo Allen, *Metropolitan Community College of Omaha*
Patrick Allen, *College of Southern Maryland*
Dennis Anderson, *Butler Community College, Andover Campus*
Roxanna Anderson, *Palm Beach State College*
Sheryl Attig, *Tri-County Technical College*
Pamela Auburn, *University of Houston–Downtown*
Jeannine Baart, *Westchester Community College*
Christine Bachman, *University of Houston–Downtown*
Linda Bajdo, *Macomb Community College*
Michelle Bannoura, *Hudson Valley Community College*
Marina Baratian, *Eastern Florida State College*
Elizabeth Becker, *Saint Joseph's University*
Amy Beeman, *San Diego Mesa College*
Karen Bekker, *Bergen Community College*
Shannon Bentz, *Northern Kentucky University*
Vivian Bergamotto, *Manhattan College*
Jamie Borchardt, *Tarleton State University*
Debi Brannan, *Western Oregon University*
Alison Buchanan, *Henry Ford College*
Donald Busch, *Bergen Community College*
Carrie Carmody, *California State University Fullerton*
Elizabeth Casey, *SUNY Onondaga Community College*

Amber Chenoweth, *Hiram College*
April Cobb, *Macomb Community College*
Jennifer Cohen, *Metropolitan Community College of Omaha*
Frank Conner, *Grand Rapids Community College*
Lisa Connolly, *Ivy Tech Community College–Bloomington*
Katrina Cooper, *Bethany College*
Kristi Cordell-McNulty, *Angelo State University*
Kristen Couture, *Manchester Community College*
Stephanie Ding, *Del Mar College*
Maureen Donegan, *Delta College*
Lauren Doninger, *GateWay College Community*
Denise Dunovant, *Hudson County Community College*
Judith Easton, *Austin Community College*
Daniella Errett, *Pennsylvania Highlands Community College*
Gary Freudenthal, *Florida Southwestern State College*
Betty Jane Fratzke, *Indiana Wesleyan University*
Lenore Frigo, *Shasta College*
Adia Garrett, *University of Maryland, Baltimore County*
Michael K. Garza, *Brookhaven College*
Nichelle Gause, *Clayton State University*
Bryan Gibson, *Central Michigan University*
Jeffrey Gibbons, *Christopher Newport University*
Kim Glackin, *Metropolitan Community College–Blue River*
Jonathan Golding, *University of Kentucky*
Cameron Gordon, *University of North Carolina, Wilmington*
Peter Gram, *Pensacola State College*
Justin Hackett, *University of Houston–Downtown*

Keith Happaney, *CUNY Lehman College*
Sidney Hardyway, *Volunteer State Community College*
Brett Heintz, *Delgado Community College*
Jaime Henning, *Eastern Kentucky University*
Carmon Hicks, *Ivy Tech Community College*
Karen Hoblit, *Del Mar College*
Sandra Holloway, *Saint Joseph's University*
Amy Houlihan, *Texas A&M University Corpus Christi*
Cory Howard, *Tyler Junior College*
Mildred Huffman, *Virginia Western Community College*
Sayeedul Islam, *Farmingdale State College*
Nita Jackson, *Butler Community College, Andover Campus*
Michael James, *Ivy Tech Community College–Bloomington*
Judy Jankowski, *Grand Rapids Community College*
Margaret Jenkins, *Seminole State College of Florida*
Andrew Johnson, *Park University*
James Johnson, *Illinois State University*
Deana Julka, *University of Portland*
Kiesa Kelly, *Tennessee State University*
Dana Kuehn, *Florida State College at Jacksonville*
Elizabeth Laurer, *Owens Community College*
Anthony Lauricella, *Suny Old Westbury*
Robert Lawyer, *Delgado Community College*
Juliet Lee, *Cape Fear Community College*
Marvin Lee, *Tennessee State University*
Robin Lewis, *California Polytechnic State University*
Ashlee Lien, *SUNY Old Westbury*
Shayn Lloyd, *Tallahassee Community College*
Christine Lofgren, *University of California Irvine*
Wade Lueck, *Mesa Community College*
Lisa Lynk-Smith, *College of Southern Maryland*
Mike Majors, *Delgado Community College*
Claire Mann, *Coastline Community College*
Haili Marotti, *Florida Southwestern State College Online*
Monica Marsee, *University of New Orleans*
Jason McCoy, *Cape Fear Community College*
Bradley McDowell, *Madison Area Technical College of Florida*
Valerie Melburg, *SUNY Onondaga Community College*
Jan Mendoza, *Golden West College*
Steven Mewaldt, *Marshall University*
Yesimi Milledge, *Pensacola State College*
Joseph Miller, *Pennsylvania College of Technology*
Dennis Miller, *University of Missouri Columbia*
Tal Millet, *Bergen Community College*
Kristie Morris, *Rockland Community College*
Brendan Morse, *Bridgewater State University*
Elizabeth Moseley, *Pensacola State College*

Ronald Mulson, *Hudson Valley Community College*
Dan Muhwezi, *Butler Community College, Andover Campus*
Paulina Multhaupt, *Macomb Community College*
Michael Ofsowitz, *Monroe Community College*
Jennifer Ortiz-Garza, *University of Houston–Victoria*
Bill Overman, *University Of North Carolina, Wilmington*
Justin Peer, *University of Michigan–Dearborn*
Yopina Pertiwi, *University of Toledo*
Alexandr Petrou, *CUNY Medgar Evers College*
Andrea Phronebarger, *York Technical College*
Susan Pierce, *Hillsborough Community College*
Harvey Pines, *Canisius College*
Lydia Powell, *Vance Granville Community College*
Sandra Prince-Madison, *Delgado Community College*
Sadhana Ray, *Delgado Community College*
Vicki Ritts, *St. Louis Community College*
Brendan Rowlands, *College of Southern Idaho*
Angela Sadowski, *Chaffey College*
Spring Schafer, *Delta College*
Monica Schneider, *SUNY Geneseo*
John Schulte, *Cape Fear Community College*
Mary Shelton, *Tennessee State University*
Kelly Schuller, *Bethany College*
Randi Shedlosky-Shoemaker, *York College of Pennsylvania*
Barry Silber, *Hillsborough Community College*
Peggy Skinner, *South Plains College Levelland*
Deirdre Slavik, *Northwest Arkansas Community College*
Theodore Smith, *University of Louisiana, Lafayette*
Jonathan Sparks, *Vance Granville Community College*
Jessica Streit, *Northern Kentucky University*
William Suits, *Seminole State College of Florida*
Griff in Sutton, *University of North Carolina, Wilmington*
Rachelle Tannenbaum, *Anne Arundel Community College*
Laura Thornton, *University of New Orleans*
Virginia Tompkins, *The Ohio State University at Lima*
Regina Traficante, *Community College of Rhode Island*
Kirsten Treadwell, *Columbus State Community College*
Rebekah Wanic, *Grossmont College*
Mark Watman, *South Suburban College*
Molly Wernli, *College of Saint Mary*
Khara Williams, *University of Southern Indiana*
Keith Williams, *Oakland University*
Michelle Williams, *Holyoke Community College*
Carl Wilson, *Ranken Technical College*
Stacy Wyllie, *Delgado Community College*
Gary Yarbrough, *Arkansas Northeastern College*
Anthony Zoccolillo, *Texas A&M University Corpus Christi*

Acknowledgments from the Authors

We'd like to offer our very special thank you to the superb editorial and production teams at Wiley, who enjoy a well-deserved reputation for producing high-quality college textbooks and supplements. Like any cooperative effort, writing a book requires an immense support team, and we are deeply grateful to this remarkable group of people: Sandra Rigby, Senior Production Editor; Dorothy Sinclair, Senior Content Manager; Wendy Lai, Senior Designer; Karen Staudinger; and a host of others. Each of these individuals helped enormously throughout the production of this third edition.

- Our deepest gratitude also goes out to Glenn Wilson, our Executive Editor, for his unique insights and unfailing support of this third edition. We're also deeply indebted to Carolyn Wells, who handles all the ins and outs of marketing with great patience, talent, and an unflappable sense of humor.

- *Real World Psychology* would simply not exist without a great ancillary author team. We gratefully acknowledge the expertise and immense talents of the following people: Jason Spiegelman, The Community College of Baltimore County (Test Bank); Vicki Ritts, St. Louis Community College (Instructor's Manual); Joe S. Miller, Clarks Summit University (PowerPoint), and Marc Genztler, Valencia College (Practice and Assessments).

- We'd also like to express our heartfelt appreciation to the hundreds of faculty across the country who contributed their constructive ideas to this third edition and to our many students over all the years. They've taught us what students want to know and inspired us to write this book.

- Finally, we'd like to acknowledge that all the writing, producing, and marketing of this book would be wasted without an energetic and dedicated Wiley support team! We wish to sincerely thank all the account managers for their tireless efforts and good humor. It's a true pleasure to work with such a remarkable group of people.

Authors' Personal Notes

- The writing of this text has been a group effort involving the input and support of all our wonderful families, friends, and colleagues. To each person we offer our sincere thanks: Sky Chafin, Haydn Davis, Tom Frangicetto, Mike Garza, Teresa Jacob, Jim Matiya, Lou Milstein, Kandis Mutter, Tyler Mutter, Roger Morrissette, Katie Townsend-Merino, Maria Pok, Fred Rose, and Kathy Young. They provided careful feedback and a unique sense of what should and should not go into an introduction to psychology text.

- *From Catherine Sanderson:* Thank you to my husband, Bart Hollander, who supported me in taking on this immense challenge, even though he understood it would require considerable late-night writing, a (very) messy study, and even more take-out dinners. I also want to express my appreciation to my children—Andrew, Robert, and Caroline—who sometimes allowed me peace and quiet with which to write.

- *From Karen Huffman:* A big hug and continuing appreciation to my family, friends, and students who supported and inspired me. I also want to offer my deepest gratitude to Richard Hosey. His careful editing, constructive feedback, professional research skills, and shared authorship were essential to this revision. Having saved the truly best for last, I want to thank my dear friend and beloved husband, Bill Barnard—may the magic continue.

What's New in *Real World Psychology,* Third Edition?

ParabolStudio/Shutterstock.com

Science knows no country, because knowledge belongs to humanity, and is the torch which illuminates the world.
—Louis Pasteur

NEW THEME: *Scientific Thinking and Practical Applications*

Why did we choose this particular theme for our third edition? Introductory psychology is a fascinating and popular college class, but most students taking this course will not go on to be psychology majors. However, what they learn in the course, combined with our emphasis on scientific thinking and practical applications, will have an impact in other ways. As you can see in the photo above and the quote by Pasteur, we believe that our current global climate crisis is the single most important issue of our time—there simply is "No Planet B!" However, there are still some who believe "climate change is not real or is a hoax," "the science around climate change is not settled," or "humans are not the main contributors to climate change." They maintain these beliefs despite overwhelming evidence to the contrary. For example, multiple studies published in peer-reviewed scientific journals clearly show that 97 percent or more of actively publishing climate scientists agree that humans are the dominant cause of today's climate change.

Given the urgent need for consensus and action on the climate crisis, increasing global political divisions and racial tensions, poverty, income inequality, and other pressing problems, we thought we might help students to influence positive change by emphasizing the importance of scientific thinking and practical applications throughout this edition. We also believe that scientific thinking, combined with the ability to apply psychological science principles to our everyday life, are key to student understanding and personal success—not only in this introductory psychology course, but also in simply getting along well in life.

General Changes

The changes in this edition center around aligning our features to our new theme, as well as our ongoing desire to maintain currency and refine our content. The following outlines these general changes.

NEW and Revised Core Features

To reflect our theme, **Scientific Thinking** and **Practical Applications**, along with our increased focus on **APA Goals** for the undergraduate psychology major (which was discussed earlier in this preface), we added three NEW features to each chapter and revised two other continuing features. All of these features are highlighted in the outline at the beginning of each chapter. They are:

- NEW **STH** **Scientific Thinking Highlight** (APA GOAL 2.1)
- NEW **PAH** **Practical Application Highlight** (APA GOAL 1.3)
- NEW **GCD** **Gender** and **Cultural Diversity** (APA GOAL 2.5)
- REVISED and updated previous PsychScience feature, which is now **RC** **Scientific Thinking/Research Challenge** (APA GOAL 2.4)
- REVISED and updated previous PositivePsych feature, which is now **PP** **Practical Application/PositivePsych** (APA GOAL 1.3)

Other Changes

The most *significant general changes* that we incorporated throughout this edition include:

- Each chapter contains one or more NEW sections, called **PAN** **Practical Applications of Neuroscience**, which focus on high interest topics in neuroscience and their real world applications.
- Over **1,200 new research citations**; a fresh design and layout; and numerous new photos, figures, and tables.
- Several chapter reorganizations have been made, the most important of which is the inclusion of the updated chapter on gender and human sexuality in the main text (Chapter 10).
- Many new **Real World Application Questions [AQ1–AQ6]** have been added to the chapter opener and to each section's Learning Objectives. The answers to these questions are then embedded within the chapter content and identified by special icons **[AQ1-AQ6]**.
- Learning objectives for each chapter have been updated and expanded.
- Each chapter has one or more unique study tips, identified with this icon **TIP**, which clarify difficult or particularly confusing terms and concepts.
- To enhance readability and highlight our new theme, we updated and revised the previous *Psychology and You* and *Real World Psychology* boxes, and embedded them within the text with these two titles: **S&P** **Scientific Thinking/Practical Application** and **PA** **Practical Application/Test Yourself**.
- We added several NEW key terms and updated or fine-tuned several previous definitions.
- We expanded details within each of the end-of-chapter narrative summaries.

Specific Changes

Following, you will find a listing of the specific content changes for each chapter of *Real World Psychology*, Third Edition.

Chapter	New Research	New and Revised Features	Other Updates
Chapter 1 The Science of Psychology (new title)	• scientific thinking, ethnicity and job interviews, strength training and depression, co-sleeping with pets, psychology's replication crisis, quasi-experimental design, strategies for student success	• **PP** What Makes Us Happy? • **GCD** Biopsychosocial Forces and Acculturative Stress • **STH** Psychology and the Replication Crisis • **RC** Is Happiness Defined by Your Social Class? • **PAH** Tips for Grade Improvement • **PAN** Why Are Genes Important to Psychologists?	• 9 new key terms: confounding variable, demand characteristic, functionalism, random sample, replicate, scientific attitude, scientific thinking, structuralism, variable • new or revised: 8 figures, 3 photos, 2 process diagrams, 1 table
Chapter 2 Neuroscience and Biological Foundations	• effect of exercise on memory, oxytocin, dMRI new brain imaging, executive functions, athletes and traumatic brain injuries, dangers of high-fat foods	• **PP** How Does Positivity Affect Your Brain? • **STH** Can Neuroscience Help Kids (and Adults) Make Better Choices? • **RC** Phineas Gage—Myths versus Facts • **PAH** Can You Use Your Frontal Lobes to Train Your Brain? • **PAN** Stem Cell Transplants and Spinal Cord Injuries	• 1 new key term: executive functions (EFs) • new or revised: 4 figures, 2 process diagrams, 1 table
Chapter 3 Stress and Health Psychology	• social media and stress, chronic pain, social integration, placebos and personality differences, mindfulness-meditation, job stressors and acute/chronic stress	• **PP** Mindfulness and Your GPA • **PAH** Helping Someone with PTSD • **RC** Exercise, Mental Health, and Team Sports • **GCD** Can Job Stress be Fatal? • **PAN** Stress and Cortisol Effects on Memory	• 1 new key term: chronic pain • new or revised: 2 figures, 1 Test Yourself
Chapter 4 Sensation and Perception	• global increase in myopia, kangaroo care, priming and its effects on trust, depth perception taste preferences for cannabis users, how helmets increase risky behaviors	• **PP** Can Bouncing a Baby Increase Helping Behaviors? • **PAH** Why Do So Many People Believe in ESP? • **RC** Perceptual Set, Patients' Race, and Quality of Medical Care • **GCD** Are the Gestalt Laws Universally True? • **STH** Can Your Astrological Sign Predict Crime? • **PAN** Practical Importance of Rods and Cones Sensitivity • **PAN** Why Taste and Smell Receptors are Continually Replaced	• new or revised: 4 figures and 1 table
Chapter 5 States of Consciousness	• inattentional blindness, "catching up" on sleep, benefits of caffeine, repair and restoration theory of sleep, Facebook's efforts to increase addiction, sexsomnia (sleep sex), meditation and pain relief, marijuana's effects on cognitive functions	• **GCD** Dream Similarities and Variations • **STH** The Dangers of Distraction • **PP** Can Meditation Increase Helping Behaviors? • **PAH** Hidden Costs of Addiction • **RC** Can Alcohol Improve Your Foreign Language Skills? • **PAN** Why Teens Need More Sleep	• new or revised: 3 figures, 1 table, 1 Test Yourself

Chapter	New Research	New and Revised Features	Other Updates
Chapter 6 Learning	• positive images and relationship satisfaction, emotional eating, taxes on soda consumption, mirror neurons, taste aversion, enriched environments and older adults, generalization and relationship satisfaction, human cognitive maps	• **GCD** Learning, Scaffolding, and Culture • **STH** Wealth, Affirmative Action, and College Admission • **PP** The Impressive Powers of Prosocial Media • **PAH** Using Reinforcement and Punishment Effectively • **RC** Should You Use Food or Praise to Train Your Dog? • **PAN** Mirror Neurons and Learning	• new or revised: 5 figures, 2 cartoons, 1 table, 1 Test Yourself, 1 process diagram
Chapter 7 Memory	• how phones affect memory, physical fitness and dementia, parallel distributed processing (PDP), difference between Alzheimer disease (AD) and dementia, eyewitness testimony and police lineups, negative effects of smartphones, false memories	• **STH** Why False versus Repressed Memories Matter • **GCD** Can Culture Affect Our Memories? • **PP** Memory and Age-Related Happiness • **PAH** Tips for Memory Improvement • **RC** Can Taking Photos Impair Our Memories? • **PAN** Diagnosing and Preventing Alzheimer's Disease (AD)	• 2 new key terms: parallel-distributing processing (PDP) model, repression • new or revised: 7 figures, cartoons, 1 process diagram
Chapter 8 Thinking, Language, and Intelligence	• phone effects on problem solving, sexual attractiveness and creativity, identifying fake news, effects of brain size, artificial intelligence, genetic effects on educational attainment, cognitive offloading, divergent and convergent thinking, mind-wandering and creativity, extremes in intelligence	• **PAH** Tips for Improved Problem Solving • **STH** Should We Teach EI in Schools? • **GCD** Can Your Nonverbal Language Reveal Your Roots? • **PP** Why Talk or Read to Babies? • **RC** Is Creativity Linked with Psychological Disorders? • **PAN** Why Can't We Ignore a Crying Baby?	• 3 new key terms: artificial intelligence (AI), cognitive offloading • new or revised: 5 figures, 2 photos, 1 process diagram
Chapter 9 Development	• transmission of parents' early emotional trauma to unborn child, differences in teen brain, foreign travel effects on morality, "good touch" versus "bad touch," theory of mind (ToM)	• **STH** Vaccination and Herd Immunity • **GCD** Should Diversity Affect Research? • **PAH** Aging—It's Mostly Good News • **PP** Adults Need Hugs Too • **RC** Deprivation and Development • **GCD** Can Diversity Affect Moral Development? • **PAN** Puberty's Effects on Teen Sleep Pattern	• deleted section on sex and gender influences (moved to the NEW Chapter 10) • 5 new key terms: age-related positivity effect, autism spectrum disorder (ASD), herd immunity, morality, theory of mind (ToM) • new: 4 figures, 1 cartoon

Chapter	New Research	New and Revised Features	Other Updates
Chapter 10 Sex, Gender, and Sexuality (formerly an optional chapter, now part of the core content)	• AI voice assistants and gender-role stereotypes, myths of "stranger danger," normal variations in biological sex and gender, gender roles and sexual problems, assertiveness, sexual assault and harassment, rape myths	• **PAH** Preventing Sexual Violence • **STH** Can Political Affiliation Predict Sexual Behavior? • **GCD** Sexuality Across Cultures • **PP** Can Good Moods Lead to Safer Sex? • **RC** Why Do Men and Women Lie About Sex? • **PAN** Biology and Sexual Orientation	• 13 new key terms: double standard, excitement phase, gender expression, intersex, orgasm phase, pair bonding, plateau phase, resolution phase, sexual assault, sexual harassment, sexual response cycle, sexuality, sexually transmitted infections (STIs) • new or revised: 3 figures, 1 table
Chapter 11 Motivation and Emotion	• arousal effects on performance, social media and eating disorders, brain imaging and emotions, cognitive expectancies and alcohol consumption, rankings of America's happiness	• **STH** Do Losers Sometimes Actually Win? • **GCD** Does Your Smile Tell Others Where You're From? • **PAH** Five Tips for Increased Happiness • **PP** Can Long-Distance Relationships Survive? • **RC** Can Fake Smiling Lead to Heavy Drinking? • **PAN** How Can Some People Eat All They Want and Not Gain Weight?	• deleted the discussion of Sex and Motivation (moved to the NEW Chapter 10) • 1 new key term: display rules • new or revised: 3 figures, 2 tables, 2 Test Yourselves
Chapter 12 Personality	• cooperation and eating from a shared plate, using social media to measure personality, the FFM, vocational versus academic interests and the five-factor model (FFM), agreeableness and neuroticism and the FFM, myths of introversion and extraversion, parenting skills and marital satisfaction, travel effects on personality	• **GCD** Can Culture Affect Your Personality? • **STH** Could You Pass the Stanford Marshmallow Test? • **PAH** Can (and Should) We Improve Our Personality Traits? • **PP** Self-Efficacy in Daily Life • **RC** Do Non-Human Animals Have Unique Personalities? • **PAN** Neurochemistry Effects on Personality	• 4 new key terms: character, interactionism, situationism, temperament • new: 2 figures, 1 Test Yourself
Chapter 13 Psychological Disorders	• insanity defense in criminal trials, variations in psychological disorders around the world, myths, stigma, and mental illness, "trigger warnings" and anxiety disorders, mental health and electronic devices, biological factors and bipolar disorder, neurodevelopmental disorders, worldwide prevalence of schizophrenia, suicide, adverse childhood experiences (ACEs)	• **GCD** Avoiding Ethnocentrism? • **STH** Do We All Have ADHD? • **PAH** Myths, Stigma, and Discrimination in Mental Illness • **PP** Promoting Resilience in Children and Adults • **RC** Head Injuries and Depression • **PAN** Why has the usage of ADHD medication dramatically increased?	• 10 new key terms: adverse childhood experiences (ACEs), attention-deficit/hyperactivity disorder (ADHD), autism spectrum disorder (ASD), avoidance learning, major depressive disorder (MDD), mania, neurodevelopmental disorder, nonsuicidal self-injury (NSSI), psychological disorder, psychology student syndrome (PSSS) • new: 8 figures, 4 tables
Chapter 14 Therapy	• accepting versus eliminating fears and PTSD, using modeling and imitation for phobias, dangers of media and itportrayals of suicide, ketamine as a treatment for depression, effectiveness of teletherapy, power of self-compassion	• **GCD** How Do Culture and Gender Affect Psychotherapy? • **STH** Do Psychedelic Drugs Lead to Psychosis? • **PAH** Tips for Finding a Therapist • **PP** Using Psychology to Promote Mental Health • **RC** Can Simple Self-Compassion Improve Your Mental and Physical Health? • **PAN** Why Lobotomies Gained Such a Bad Reputation	• 5 new key terms: evidence-based practice in psychology (EBPP), mindfulness-based cognitive therapy (MBCT), therapeutic alliance, token economy, transcranial direct current stimulation (tDCS) • new: 8 figures, 2 tables, 2 cartoons

Chapter	New Research	New and Revised Features	Other Updates
Chapter 15 Social Psychology	• Harry Potter and prejudice reduction, tips for great job interview, conformity and neighbor's conservation efforts, problems with Zimbardo's prison study, affirmative action, explicit and implicit attitudes and racism, conformity and who defied the majority in Asch's study, deindividuation, social facilitation, social loafing, how engaging in the arts increases cooperation and prosocial behavior	• **STH** Have Women Really "Come a Long Way, Baby"? • **PAH** What Are the Secrets to Enduring Love? • **GCD** How Does Culture Affect Our Personal Space? • **PP** Would You Donate a Kidney to a Stranger? • **RC** Can a 10-Minute Conversation Reduce Prejudice? • **PAN** Can Genetics Affect Our Political Attitudes?	• briefly explained the deletion of Zimbardo's prison study • 7 new key terms: assertiveness, compliance, dehumanization, person perception, self-fulfilling prophecy, social facilitation, social loafing • new: 8 figures, 5 photos, 1 cartoon, 1 table

Kuttelvaserova Stuchelova/Shutterstock.com

The Science of Psychology

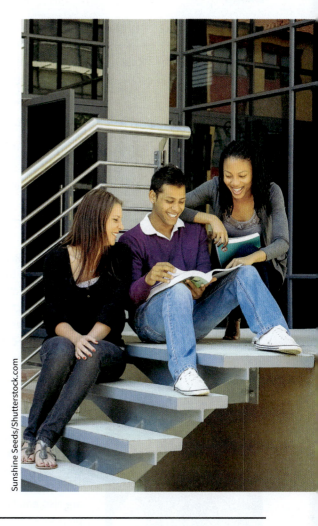

Sunshine Seeds/Shutterstock.com

Real World Application Questions [AQ]

Things you'll learn in Chapter 1

[AQ1] Does your ethnicity affect the type of questions you're asked in a job interview?

[AQ2] Can strength training decrease depression?

[AQ3] Can a diet high in fats and sugars impair learning and memory?

[AQ4] Does spending more time on Instagram decrease your psychological well-being?

[AQ5] Is there a correlation between years of education and physical health?

[AQ6] What are the best study techniques for improving your exam performance?

Throughout the chapter, look for [AQ1]–[AQ6] icons. They indicate where the text addresses these questions.

CHAPTER OUTLINE

1.1 | What Is Psychology?

LEARNING OBJECTIVES

Retrieval Practice   While reading the upcoming sections, respond to each Learning Objective in your own words.

Summarize psychology, its past and present.

- **Define** psychology, pseudoscience, and scientific thinking.
- **Review** structuralism, functionalism, and the psychoanalytic perspectives.

- **Discuss** modern psychology's seven major perspectives, the contributions of women and people of color, and the biopsychosocial model.
- **Summarize** psychology's major career options and specialties.

Real World Application Question

[AQ1] Does your ethnicity affect the type of questions you're asked in a job interview?

Welcome to **Real World Psychology!** As our title suggests, we believe psychology's unique contributions to the scientific world are best shown through every day, real-life examples. Given that this first chapter is an overview of the entire field of psychology, we begin with a formal definition of psychology, followed by its brief history as a scientific discipline. Then, we explore the basics of science, the scientific method, and how psychologists apply them when conducting research. We close with a section on Secrets of Student Success based on psychological science that will help you master the material in this and all your other college textbooks and courses.

Psychology   The scientific study of behavior and mental processes.

Psychology and Scientific Thinking

What is **psychology**? The term derives from the roots *psyche*, meaning "mind," and *logos*, meaning "word." Modern psychology is most commonly defined as the *scientific study of behavior and mental processes*. *Scientific* is a key feature of the definition because psychologists follow strict scientific procedures to collect and analyze their data. *Behaviors* (crying, hitting, sleeping) are also emphasized because they can be directly observed and measured. Although *mental processes* cannot be directly observed (feelings, thoughts, memories), they can be studied scientifically. Keep in mind that psychology encompasses humankind as well as our non-human compatriots—from rats and pigeons to cats and chimps.

Psychology versus Pseudoscience
Why is the scientific foundation so important in psychology? Since ancient times, people have always been interested in the fascinating topics we study in psychology. Unfortunately, psychological science is often confused with faulty, non-scientific claims of psychic powers, horoscopes, mediums, and "pop psych" statements such as "I'm mostly right brained" or "We use only ten percent of our brains."

For many people, reading their horoscope or going to a palmist to have their fortunes told may be simple entertainment. However, fervent believers have been known to waste large sums of money on charlatans purporting to know the future or to speak with their deceased relatives (e.g., M. Wilson, 2015). Broken-hearted families have also lost valuable time, money, and emotional energy on psychics claiming they could locate their missing children.

How can we spot the difference between true psychological science and this type of *pseudoscience*, which is based on fantasy, folk wisdom, or superstitions? First of all, note that *pseudo* means "false." Second, although pseudoscientific claims often give the appearance of science, they do not follow the basics of the scientific method, which will be covered in depth later in this chapter.

To offset the dangers of pseudoscience, organizations and websites, like Skeptical Inquirer and Snopes, and some individuals, like James Randi (see photo), have dedicated their lives to revealing the many problems posed by these beliefs (Arkowitz & Lilienfeld, 2017; Gordin, 2017; Loftus, 2010). If you'd like to test your own possible misconceptions about psychology, try the following **Test Yourself**.

Magic versus pseudoscience
The magician James Randi has dedicated his life and his skills as a magician to educating the public about fraudulent paranormal, psychic, and pseudoscientific claims. Although his foundation offered a prize of $1 million for many years to "anyone who proves a genuine psychic power under proper observing conditions," the money was never collected (Randi, 2014; The Amazing Meeting, 2011). For more information, check out https://web.randi.org/home/jref-status

PA Practical Application

Test Yourself: True or False?

_____ 1. Hypnosis improves the accuracy of our memories.

_____ 2. Advertisers and politicians often use subliminal persuasion to influence our behavior.

_____ 3. Most brain activity stops when we're asleep.

_____ 4. Punishment is the most effective way to permanently change behavior.

_____ 5. Our personalities are "set in plaster" by age 30.

_____ 6. The best way to learn and remember information is to "cram," or study it intensively during one concentrated period.

_____ 7. Vaccination is a leading cause of autism.

_____ 8. Polygraph ("lie detector") tests can reliably detect when a person is lying.

_____ 9. Violent offenders generally have a diagnosis of mental illness.

_____ 10. People with schizophrenia have multiple personalities.

_____ 11. Opposites attract and make better and more long-lasting romantic partners.

_____ 12. In an emergency, the more people who are present the more likely you are to get help.

Answers: As you'll discover by reading this text, all 12 of these statements are _false_. We include them to demonstrate how common sense beliefs about psychology are often not backed by scientific facts, and to increase your interest in becoming a more informed consumer of psychological science.

Why Study Psychology?

If you've taken other science courses, you know that physicists explain the physical world in terms of mathematics, chemists explain processes at the atomic level, and biologists examine organisms at a cellular level. Unlike these scientists and their science courses, psychologists study non-physical phenomena—behavior and mental processes. However, like all scientists, psychologists follow the scientific method (fully discussed later in this chapter), and our research findings help us understand why other people (and even non-human animals) think, feel, and act in the ways they do.

As an example, we all experience minor and significant choices and problems in our relationships, school, and work life, but few (if any) would simply flip a coin to choose a romantic partner or career. Thankfully, the psychological principles you'll discover in this course will maximize your chances of choosing and maintaining successful romantic and career relationships. They'll also demonstrate how applying these general principles can improve overall human life. In addition, given that psychology is an integral part of today's political, social, and economic world, studying it will broaden your general knowledge and increase your academic and personal success as a global citizen.

Scientific Thinking

Now that we've defined psychology, how it differs from pseudoscience, and why we should study it, let's explore why psychology emphasizes **scientific thinking**. As you know, our world is filled with controversial ideas, so-called "fake news," and unreliable personal beliefs and opinions. How do we evaluate this abundance of information and the competing claims of advertisers and politicians? To separate scientific facts from "alternative facts," scientific theories from "personal theories," and sense from nonsense, we need scientific thinking (see **Figure 1.1**). This approach to information combines a high degree of _skepticism_ (questioning what "everybody knows"), followed by _objectivity_ (using empirical data to separate fantasy from reality) and _rationalism_ (practicing logical reasoning). Let's carefully examine these three steps:

Scientific thinking An approach to information that combines a high degree of skepticism with objectivity and rationalism.

- **Step 1: Skepticism** Many people mistake skepticism for harsh, unthinking attacks on all claims. Instead, the term "skepticism" comes from the Greek word _skeptikos_, which means "to consider carefully." Skepticism encourages curiosity and an open-minded approach to what "everybody knows," while also delaying judgment until persuasive, empirical data is available.

- **Step 2: Objectivity** The persuasive empirical data required in Step 1 is based on objectivity. The source, author, and evidence must be carefully evaluated for bias and reliability. Using empirical data, scientific thinkers can separate _facts_ from pseudofacts or so-called "alternative facts," and scientific _theories_ from opinions and hunches. A _fact_ for scientists is a statement backed by direct, verifiable evidence, whereas a _theory_ is a tool that predicts facts. In short, scientific thinking will help us separate fantasy from reality.

The Advertising Archives/Alamy Stock Photo

Snake oil is wonderful stuff!

a.

Scientific thinking

Step 1: Skepticism
(curiosity + open mind + delayed judgment)

Step 2: Objectivity
(source, author, and evidence must be unbiased and reliable)

Step 3: Rationalism
(logic + reason versus opinion and emotion)

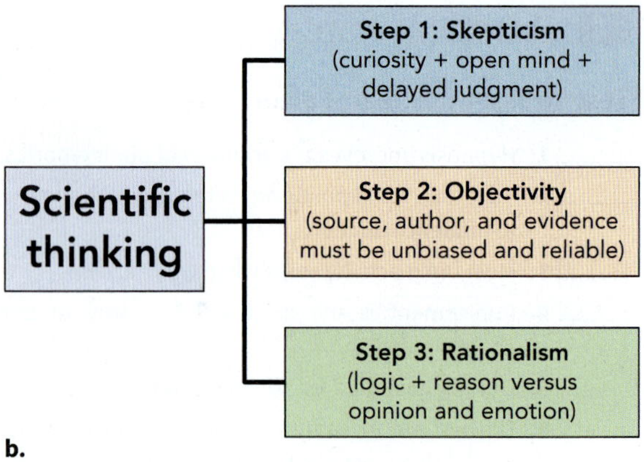

b.

FIGURE 1.1 **Scientific thinking versus "snake oil"**
(a) In the 19ᵗʰ century, ads like these were used to sell cure-all elixirs designed for all kinds of ailments. Today, the term "snake oil" is a euphemism for deceptive, fraudulent marketing and "fake news." **(b)** Try using these three steps to evaluate the "snake oil" ad. Can you see how this type of scientific thinking can also be applied when assessing modern ads for "miracle drugs" and political claims for "miracle solutions"?

- **Step 3: Rationalism**   Even when we've successfully practiced skepticism and objectivity, we may still require logic and reason to overcome opinions and emotions. For instance, many people continue to text and drive despite overwhelming evidence documenting its dangers. Rationalism requires us to logically value truth and to follow established scientific facts and warnings.

Critical thinking The process of objectively evaluating, comparing, analyzing, and synthesizing information.

Scientific versus Critical Thinking   How does scientific thinking differ from **critical thinking**, *the process of objectively evaluating, comparing, analyzing, and synthesizing information* (Caine et al., 2016; Halpern, 2014)? Critical thinking is closely linked with theoretical philosophy, pedagogy, and the social sciences, and over the years it has evolved into an umbrella-type term with numerous components and skills. In contrast, scientific thinking is narrower and focused more on empiricism and the processes underlying scientific research (e.g., generating and systematically testing hypotheses).

Given psychology's scientific emphasis, we've chosen scientific thinking as the general theme embedded throughout this text, as well as in special features, like the **STH** *Scientific Thinking Highlight* and the **RC** *Scientific Thinking: Research Challenge*. As you'll also see throughout this text, scientific thinking is closely linked with practical applications that can be a valuable asset to your academic and personal life. For example, you're almost guaranteed to receive higher grades on all your assignments if you consult reliable sources, like those in **Table 1.1**, and when you practice the three steps of scientific thinking—skepticism, objectivity, and rationalism. Employing scientific thinking will likewise improve your personal life by helping you evaluate new ideas and avoid making hasty and costly decisions.

Take-Home Message   Scientific and critical thinking are both vital skills and components of becoming an educated person. When facing life's inevitable problems, having the ability to think objectively and rationally is essential to personal growth and understanding.

Psychology's Origins

Ancient scholars asked many of the same questions about human nature that modern psychologists are still examining. However, psychology is a relative newcomer to the scientific world—less than 150

TABLE 1.1   Sample Reliable Resources for Scientific Thinking

American Psychological Association [apa.org]	Research Digest [digest.bps.org.uk]	PsyBlog [spring.org.uk]
Association for Psychological Science [psychologicalscience.org]	PsychINFO [apa.org/pubs/databases/psycinfo/]	Snopes [snopes.com]
American Psychiatric Association [psychiatry.org]	We're Only Human [psychologicalscience.org/news/were-only-human]	Neuroskeptic [realclearscience.com/authors/neuroskeptic/]
Association for Behavior Analysis International [abainternational.org]	ScienceAlert [sciencealert.com]	Skeptical Inquirer [skepticalinquirer.org]
Canadian Psychological Association [cpa.org]	PsychCentral [psychcentral.com]	Skeptic magazine [skeptic.com]
British Psychological Society [bps.org.uk]	Scientific American Mind [scientificamerican.com/mind/]	TED Talks [ted.com/topics/psychology]
National Institute of Mental Health [nimh.nih.gov/news]	Public Library of Science [plos.org]	Google Scholar [scholar.google.com]
The Psychonomic Society [psychonomic.org]	Mindhacks [mindhacks.com]	

years old. In this section, we will explore the beginnings of psychological science, and how as interest in the new field grew, psychologists adopted various perspectives on the "appropriate" topics for psychological research and the "proper" research methods. These diverse viewpoints and subsequent debates molded and shaped modern psychological science.

Early Pioneers—Wundt, Titchener, and James

Psychology's history as a science began in 1879, when Wilhelm Wundt [VILL-helm Voont], generally acknowledged as the "father" of psychology, established the first psychological laboratory in Leipzig, Germany. Wundt and his followers were primarily interested in conscious experiences—how we form sensations, images, and feelings. Their chief methodology was termed "introspection," and it relied on participants' self-monitoring and reporting on conscious experiences (Freedheim & Weiner, 2013; Weger et al., 2019).

A student of Wundt's, Edward Titchener, brought his ideas to the United States. Titchener's approach, now known as **structuralism**, sought to identify the basic building blocks, or "structures," of mental life through introspection and then to determine how these elements combine to form the whole of experience. Because introspection could not be used to study animals, children, or more complex mental disorders, however, structuralism failed as a working psychological approach. But it did establish a model for studying mental processes scientifically.

Structuralism's intellectual successor, **functionalism**, examined the way mental and behavioral processes function to enable humans and other animals to adapt to their environment. William James was the leading force in the functionalist school (**Figure 1.2**). Although functionalism also eventually declined, it expanded the scope of psychology to include research on emotions and observable behaviors, initiated the psychological testing movement, and influenced modern education and industry. Today, James is widely considered the "father" of American psychology.

Psychoanalytic Perspective

During the late 1800s and early 1900s, while functionalism was prominent in the United States, the **psychoanalytic perspective** was forming in Europe. Its founder, Austrian physician Sigmund Freud, believed that a part of the human mind, the unconscious, contains unresolved desires and conflicts, as well as memories of past experiences that lie outside personal awareness—yet still exert great influence. According to Freud, a man who is cheating on his wife might slip up and say, "I wish you were her," when he consciously planned to say, "I wish you were here." Such seemingly meaningless so-called Freudian slips supposedly reveal a person's true unconscious desires and motives.

Freud also believed many psychological problems develop from unconscious sexual or aggressive motives and conflicts between "acceptable" and "unacceptable" behaviors. His theory led to an influential theory of personality and a system of therapy known as *psychoanalysis* (Chapters 12 and 14).

Structuralism Wundt's and Titchener's approach that used introspection to study the basic elements (or structures) of the mind.

Functionalism James's approach that explored how mental and behavioral processes function to enable organisms to adapt to the environment.

Psychoanalytic perspective An approach to psychology developed by Sigmund Freud, which focuses on unconscious processes, unresolved conflicts, and past experiences.

Bettmann/Getty Images

FIGURE 1.2 William James (1842–1910) William James founded the perspective known as functionalism and established the first psychology laboratory in the United States, at Harvard University. In modern times, he is commonly referred to as the "father" of American psychology, whereas Wundt is considered the "father" of *all* psychology.

Modern Psychology

As summarized in **Table 1.2**, contemporary psychology reflects seven major perspectives: *psychodynamic*, *behavioral*, *humanistic*, *cognitive*, *biological*, *evolutionary*, and *sociocultural*. Although there are numerous differences among these seven perspectives, most psychologists recognize the value of each orientation and agree that no one view has all the answers.

TABLE 1.2 **Modern Psychology's Seven Major Perspectives**

Perspectives	Major Emphases	Sample Research Questions
Psychodynamic	Unconscious dynamics, motives, conflicts, and past experiences	How do adult personality traits or psychological problems reflect unconscious processes and early childhood experiences?
Behavioral	Objective, observable, environmental influences on overt behavior; stimulus–response (S-R) relationships and consequences for behavior	How do reinforcement and punishment affect behavior? How can we increase desirable behaviors and decrease undesirable ones?
Humanistic	Free will, self-actualization, and human nature as naturally positive and growth seeking	How can we promote a client's capacity for self-actualization and understanding of his or her own development? How can we promote international peace and reduce violence?
Cognitive	Mental processes used in thinking, knowing, remembering, and communicating	How do our thoughts and interpretations affect how we respond in certain situations? How can we improve how we process, store, and retrieve information?
Biological	Genetic and biological processes in the brain and other parts of the nervous system	How might changes in neurotransmitters, or damage to parts of the brain, lead to psychological problems and changes in behavior and mental processes?
Evolutionary	Natural selection, adaptation, and reproduction	How does natural selection help explain why we love and help certain people, but hurt others? Do we have specific genes for aggression and altruism?
Sociocultural	Social interaction and the cultural determinants of behavior and mental processes	How do the values and beliefs transmitted from our social and cultural environments affect our everyday psychological processes?
	Why do we need multiple perspectives? What do you see in this figure? Is it two profiles facing each other, a white vase, or both? Your ability to see both figures is similar to a psychologist's ability to study behavior and mental processes from a number of different perspectives.	

Psychodynamic Perspective
Freud's non-scientific approach and his emphasis on sexual and aggressive impulses have long been controversial, and today there are few strictly Freudian psychoanalysts left. However, the broad features of his theory remain in the modern **psychodynamic perspective**. The general goal of psychodynamic psychologists is to explore unconscious *dynamics*—internal motives, conflicts, and past experiences—while focusing more on social and cultural factors and less on sexual drives.

Behavioral Perspective
In the early 1900s, another major perspective appeared that dramatically shaped the course of modern psychology. Unlike earlier approaches, the **behavioral perspective** emphasizes objective, observable environmental influences on overt behavior. Behaviorism's founder, John B. Watson (1913), rejected the practice of introspection and the influence of unconscious forces. Instead, Watson adopted Russian physiologist Ivan Pavlov's concept of *conditioning* (Chapter 6) to explain behavior as a result of observable stimuli (in the environment) and observable responses (behavioral actions).

Most early behaviorist research was focused on learning and non-human animals were ideal participants for this research. One of the best-known behaviorists, B. F. Skinner, was convinced that behaviorist approaches could be used to "shape" both human and non-human animal behavior (**Figure 1.3**). As you'll discover in Chapters 6 and 14, therapeutic techniques rooted in the behavioristic perspective have been most successful in treating observable behavioral problems, such as those related to phobias and alcoholism (Anker et al., 2016; Coates et al., 2018; Yoshinaga et al., 2019).

Humanistic Perspective
Although the psychoanalytic and behavioral perspectives dominated U.S. psychology for some time, in the 1950s a new approach emerged—the **humanistic perspective**, which stresses *free will* (voluntarily chosen behavior) and *self-actualization* (an inborn drive to develop all of one's talents and capabilities). According to Carl Rogers and Abraham Maslow, two central figures within this perspective, all individuals are born with free will and naturally strive to develop and move toward self-actualization. Like the psychoanalytic perspective, the humanistic approach developed an influential theory of personality and its own form of psychotherapy (Chapters 12 and 14).

The humanistic approach also led the way to a contemporary research specialty known as **positive psychology**—the study of optimal human functioning (Diener & Tay, 2015; Sanderson, 2019; Seligman, 2003, 2018). For an example of how this research has direct, practical applications, see the **PP PositivePsych**. (Recognizing the increasing research focus on positive psychology, as well as its direct applicability to the real world and your everyday life, we have included a special *PositivePsych* feature in each chapter of this text. We hope you enjoy them.)

Cognitive Perspective
One of the most influential modern approaches, the **cognitive perspective**, emphasizes the mental processes we use in thinking, knowing, remembering, and communicating (Farmer & Matlin, 2019; Greene, 2016). These mental processes include perception,

FIGURE 1.3 **B. F. Skinner (1904–1990)** B. F. Skinner was one of the most influential psychologists of the 20th century.

Psychodynamic perspective
A modern approach to psychology that emphasizes unconscious dynamics—motives, conflicts, and past experiences; based on the psychoanalytic approach.

Behavioral perspective
A modern approach to psychology that emphasizes objective, observable environmental influences on overt behavior.

Humanistic perspective
A modern approach to psychology that perceives human nature as naturally positive and growth seeking; it emphasizes free will and self-actualization.

Positive psychology The study of optimal human functioning; emphasizes positive emotions, traits, and institutions.

Cognitive perspective
A modern approach to psychology that focuses on the mental processes used in thinking, knowing, remembering, and communicating.

PP Practical Application: **PositivePsych**

What Makes Us Happy?

(APA Goal 1.3) Describe applications of psychology

One of the most consistent findings in positive psychology is that other people make us happy. "Simply" building and maintaining relationships tends to significantly improve our overall happiness and well-being (Diener & Tay, 2015; Galinha et al., 2016; Lee & Kawachi, 2019). As shown in the photo, even just talking with strangers leads to higher levels of happiness. Researchers who asked riders on trains and buses to either quietly sit alone or talk to a stranger found that those who talked to a stranger reported more positive feelings than those who sat alone (Epley & Schroeder, 2014).

In addition, contrary to the popular belief that "money buys happiness," research shows that once we have enough income to meet our basic needs, additional funds do not significantly increase our levels of happiness and well-being (Kushlev et al., 2015; Whillans & Macchia, 2019). Furthermore, when adults are given money and told to spend it on others, they experience higher levels of happiness than do those who are told to spend it on themselves (Dunn et al., 2008).

memory, imagery, concept formation, problem solving, reasoning, decision making, and language. Many cognitive psychologists also use an *information-processing approach*, likening the mind to a computer that sequentially takes in information, processes it, and then produces a response.

Biological Perspective
During the past few decades, scientists have explored the role of biological factors in almost every area of psychology. Using sophisticated tools and technologies, psychologists who adopt this **biological perspective** examine behavior through the lens of genetics and biological processes in the brain and other parts of the nervous system.

Biological perspective
A modern approach to psychology that focuses on genetics and biological processes.

PAN Practical Application of Neuroscience

Why are genes so important to psychologists? Research shows that genes influence many aspects of our behavior, including how kind we are to other people, whom we vote for in elections, and even whether or not we decide to purchase a handgun (Barnes et al., 2014; Ksiazkiewicz et al., 2016; D. S. Wilson, 2015). Recent research even shows that our genes may predict dog ownership. A study examining 35,035 twin pairs found that genes explain more than half of the variation in dog ownership, showing that the choice of owning a dog is heavily influenced by our genetic make-up (Fall et al., 2019).

Evolutionary Perspective
The **evolutionary perspective** stresses natural selection, adaptation, and reproduction (Buss, 2011, 2015; Dawkins, 2016; Goldfinch, 2015). This perspective stems from the writings of Charles Darwin (1859), who suggested that natural forces select traits that aid an organism's survival. This process of **natural selection** occurs when a particular genetic trait gives an organism a reproductive advantage over others. Because of natural selection, the fastest, strongest, smartest, or otherwise most fit organisms are more likely to live long enough to reproduce and thereby pass on their genes to the next generation. According to this perspective, there's even an evolutionary explanation for the longevity of humans over other primates—it's grandmothers. Without them, a mother who has a two-year-old and then gives birth would have to devote her time and resources to the newborn at the expense of the older child. Grandmothers act as supplementary caregivers.

Evolutionary perspective
A modern approach to psychology that stresses natural selection, adaptation, and reproduction.

Natural selection Darwin's principle of an evolutionary process in which heritable traits that increase an organism's chances of survival or reproduction are more likely to be passed on to succeeding generations.

Sociocultural Perspective
Finally, the **sociocultural perspective** emphasizes social interactions and cultural determinants of behavior and mental processes. Although we are often unaware of their influence, factors such as ethnicity, religion, occupation, and socioeconomic class all have an enormous psychological impact on our mental processes and behavior.

Sociocultural perspective
A modern approach to psychology that emphasizes social interaction and the cultural determinants of behavior and mental processes.

[AQ1] For instance, a study involving three separate experiments found that professional recruiters tend to ask different questions of job applicants depending on their ethnicity (Wolgast et al., 2018). When job applicants were of the same ethnicity as that of the potential employer (called the ingroup), professional recruiters tended to help prepare applicants for interviews by focusing on questions pertaining to the match between the applicants' abilities and the job demands (person-job fit). However, when the applicants were of different ethnicities (called the outgroup), the job recruiters helped prepare applicants for questions related to how well they had integrated the cultural norms (person-culture fit) and how well they matched their potential work team (person-culture fit). As you might expect, the ingroup applicants who were trained toward person-job fit were seen as more suitable for employment (see photo). Can you see how research like this and the sociocultural perspective could highlight and potentially reduce some of the unconscious biases that perpetuate racism and discrimination?

DW labs Incorporated/Shutterstock.com

In connection with the sociocultural perspective, during the late 1800s and early 1900s, most colleges and universities provided little opportunity for women and people of color, either as students or as faculty members. One of the first women to be recognized in the field of psychology was Mary Calkins. Her achievements are particularly noteworthy considering the significant discrimination that she overcame. For example, married women could not be teachers or professors in co-educational settings during this time in history. In Mary Calkins's case, even after she completed all the requirements for a Ph.D. at Harvard University in 1895 and was described by William James as his brightest student, the university refused to grant the degree to a woman. Nevertheless, Calkins went on to perform valuable research on memory, and in 1905 served as the first female president of the American Psychological Association (APA). The first woman to receive her Ph.D. in psychology was Margaret Floy Washburn in 1894. She wrote several influential books and served as the second female president of the APA.

Francis Cecil Sumner became the first Black person in the United States to earn a Ph.D. in psychology in 1920. Dr. Sumner later chaired one of the country's leading psychology departments, at Howard University. In 1971, one of Sumner's students, Kenneth B. Clark, became the first person of color to be elected APA president. Clark's research with his wife, Mamie Clark, documented the harmful effects of prejudice and directly influenced the Supreme Court's landmark 1954 ruling against racial segregation in schools, *Brown v. Board of Education* (**Figure 1.4**).

Calkins, Washburn, Sumner, and Clark, along with other important people of color and women, made significant and lasting contributions to psychology's development. Today, women earning doctoral degrees in psychology greatly outnumber men, but, unfortunately, people of color are still underrepresented (American Psychological Association, 2014; Willyard, 2011).

Biopsychosocial Model   The seven major perspectives have all made significant contributions to modern psychology. This explains why most contemporary psychologists do not adhere to one single intellectual perspective. Instead, a more integrative, unifying theme—the **biopsychosocial model**—has gained wide acceptance. This model views biological processes (genetics, neurotransmitters, and evolution), psychological factors (learning, personality, and motivation), and social forces (family, culture, gender, and ethnicity) as interrelated. It also sees all three factors as influences inseparable from the seven major perspectives (**Figure 1.5**).

Why is the biopsychosocial model so important? As the old saying goes, "A fish doesn't know it's in water." Similarly, as individuals living alone inside our own heads, we're often unaware of the numerous interacting factors that affect us—particularly cultural forces. For a look at how biopsychosocial forces affect some Native Americans and other individuals who are not from the dominant culture, see the **GCD** **Gender and Cultural Diversity**.

Careers and Specialties in Psychology

Many people think of psychologists only as therapists, and it's true that the fields of clinical and counseling psychology do make up the largest specialty areas. However, many psychologists' jobs or careers have little or no direct connection with therapy. Instead, they work as researchers, teachers, or consultants in academic, business, industry, and government settings or in a combination of settings. As you can see in **Table 1.3**, a bachelor's degree in psychology equips you with valuable life skills and opens up several career paths. Of course, your options are even greater if you go beyond the bachelor's degree and earn your master's degree, Ph.D., or Psy.D.; see **Table 1.4**. For more information about what psychologists do—and how to pursue a career in psychology—check out the websites of the American Psychological Association (APA) and the Association for Psychological Science (APS).

TABLE 1.3 What Can I Do with a Bachelor's Degree in Psychology?
Top Careers with a Bachelor's Degree in Psychology
Management and administration
Sales
Social work
Labor relations, personnel and training
Real estate, business services, insurance
Sample Skills Gained from a Psychology Major
Improved ability to predict and understand behavior
Better understanding of how to use and interpret data
Increased communication and interpersonal skills
Increased ability to manage difficult situations and high-stress environments
Enhanced insight into problem behavior
Note that the U.S. Department of Labor predicts only an average rate of growth for psychologists in the next decade. However, the good news is that a degree in our field, and this course in general psychology, will provide you with invaluable lifetime skills.

FIGURE 1.4   Kenneth Clark (1914–2005) and Mamie Phipps Clark (1917–1985)   Kenneth Clark and Mamie Phipps Clark conducted experiments with Black and White dolls to study children's attitudes about race. This research and their expert testimony contributed to the U.S. Supreme Court's ruling that racial segregation in public schools was unconstitutional.

Biopsychosocial model
Modern psychology's theme that sees biological, psychological, and social processes as interrelated and interacting influences.

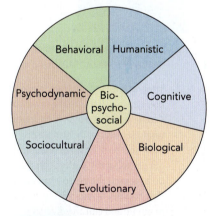

FIGURE 1.5   The biopsychosocial model   The biopsychosocial model recognizes that there is usually no single cause for our behavior or our mental states. Our moods and feelings, for instance, are often influenced by genetics and neurotransmitters (biological), our learned responses and patterns of thinking (psychological), and our socioeconomic status and cultural views of emotion (sociocultural).

GCD Gender and Cultural Diversity

Biopsychosocial Forces and Acculturative Stress

(APA Goal 2.5) Incorporate sociocultural factors in scientific inquiry

Have you ever lived in or dreamed of emigrating to another country? If so, you probably imagine yourself fully enjoying all the excitement and adventure. But have you considered the stress and stressors that come with adapting to and surviving in a new culture?

Courtesy of Linda Locklear

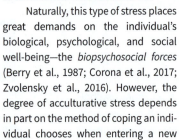

Courtesy of Linda Locklear

International travelers, military personnel, immigrants, refugees, individuals who move from one social class to another, and even the native-born may fall victim to the unspoken and unforeseen stressors of adjusting their personal and family values, their cultural norms, and maybe their style of dress to the new or dominant culture (like the young Native American woman in these two photos). These required adjustments are referred to as *acculturation*, whereas the associated stress is called *acculturative stress*.

Naturally, this type of stress places great demands on the individual's biological, psychological, and social well-being—the *biopsychosocial forces* (Berry et al., 1987; Corona et al., 2017; Zvolensky et al., 2016). However, the degree of acculturative stress depends in part on the method of coping an individual chooses when entering a new society. Researchers have identified four major approaches to acculturation (Berry & Ataca, 2010; Urzúa et al., 2017):

1. **Integration** As you might expect, a choice toward *integration* typically leads to the lowest levels of acculturative stress. People who have a high desire to maintain their original cultural identity, while also having a strong motivation to learn from and seek positive relations mainly with the new culture are pursuing the path to integration. However, stress will still be a factor if the person has been forced to emigrate, or if the new country is reluctant to accept newcomers and distrustful of ethnic and cultural diversity.

2. **Assimilation** People who choose to *assimilate* typically have a low identification with their culture of origin and a high desire to identify with the new culture. They tend to have the next lowest level of stress, but there are still many problems, presumably due to the loss of cultural support from other members of the original culture who do not assimilate.

3. **Separation** Individuals who choose to *separate* often place high value on their original culture and do not want to adapt to the new one. They generally have the next to highest level of acculturative stress, which is most likely due to being separated from the new or dominant culture. Their stress levels are even higher for those who are forcibly separated by prejudice and discrimination than for those who separate voluntarily.

4. **Marginalization** People who have a low identification with both the new culture and their culture of origin are likely to be *marginalized* from the dominant culture. This pattern normally leads to the highest levels of acculturative stress, presumably due to the fact that they tend to live on the "margins" and lack the connections and support of either the old or new cultures.

To check your understanding of these four patterns, see the following **Test Yourself**.

Q Test Yourself: Cultural Reactions to Stress

Picture yourself as a college graduate who's been offered a high-paying job that will allow you to move from a lower socioeconomic class to the middle or upper class. What you don't know is that your change in status will likely lead to considerable acculturative stress. In anticipation of this change, will you:

- **Adopt the *majority* culture and seek positive relations with the new or dominant culture?**
- **Maintain your original cultural identity and avoid relations with the dominant culture?**

Your responses to these two questions tend to place you into one of the four major approaches to acculturation—and will likely predict your level of stress.

As an example of acculturative stress, consider Malala Yousafzai, the famous activist (see photo), who, at the age of 17, was the youngest person ever to win the Nobel Peace Prize. The path to this honor began when she was an 11-year-old writing a courageous blog describing her life under the Taliban and her desire for all girls to have the chance to be educated. Tragically, her courage led to her being shot in the head at the age of 15 by the Taliban as she was on her way to school. After surviving the

SOPA Images Limited/Alamy Stock Photo

attempted murder, Malala went on to become an international activist who's traveled all over the world. Malala also recently published a book describing her experiences visiting refugee camps and the tens of millions of people who are currently displaced (Yousafzai, 2019).

Although Malala and her family emigrated to the UK after the attack on her life, she plans to return to the home she loves in Pakistan after completing her education at Oxford University. Which of the four approaches to acculturation do you think she has followed while living in the UK?

Take-Home Message Later in this chapter, we will introduce the topic of *ethnocentrism*, believing that one's culture is typical of all cultures and/or that one's own culture is the "correct" one. Can you see how ethnocentrism would logically increase acculturative stress if you decide to relocate or even just when you're traveling? Perhaps the most important question is how can we as individuals and citizens of the world help reduce the anxiety, depression, alienation, and physical illnesses associated with forced and voluntary emigration, and the inevitable acculturative stress?

TABLE 1.4   **Sample Careers and Specialties in Psychology**

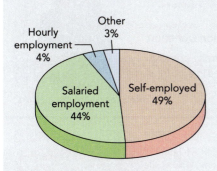

a. **Where psychologists work/primary employment settings**

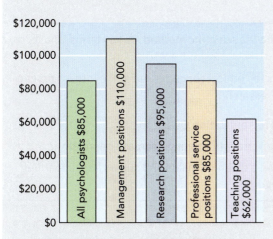

b. **Employment arrangement**

c. **Median annual reported salaries 2015**

Where psychologists work, their employment arrangements, and median salaries   Note that all data are compiled from self-reported information.

Source: American Psychological Association (2016).

Career/Specialty	Description
Biopsychologist/ neuroscientist	Investigates the relationship between biology, behavior, and mental processes, including how physical and chemical processes affect the structure and function of the brain and nervous system
Clinical psychologist	Specializes in the evaluation, diagnosis, and treatment of psychological disorders
Cognitive psychologist	Examines "higher" mental processes, including thought, memory, intelligence, creativity, and language
Comparative psychologist	Studies the behavior and mental processes of non-human animals; emphasizes evolution and cross-species comparisons
Counseling psychologist	Overlaps with clinical psychology, but generally works with less seriously disordered individuals and focuses more on social, educational, and career adjustment
Cross-cultural psychologist/psychological anthropologist	Studies similarities and differences in and across various cultures and ethnic groups
Developmental psychologist	Examines the course of human growth and development from conception to death
Educational psychologist	Studies the processes of education and works to promote the academic, intellectual, social, and emotional development of children in the school environment
Environmental psychologist	Investigates how people affect and are affected by the physical environment
Experimental psychologist	Researches processes such as learning, conditioning, motivation, emotion, sensation, and perception in humans and other animals (Note that psychologists working in almost all other areas of specialization also conduct research.)
Forensic psychologist	Applies principles of psychology to the legal system, including jury selection, psychological profiling, assessment, and treatment of offenders
Gender and cultural psychologists	Investigates how men and women and different cultures vary from one another and how they are similar
Health psychologist	Studies how biological, psychological, and social factors affect health, illness, and health-related behaviors
Industrial/organizational psychologist	Applies principles of psychology to the workplace, including personnel selection and evaluation, leadership, job satisfaction, employee motivation, and group processes within the organization
Personality psychologist	Studies the unique and relatively stable patterns in a person's thoughts, feelings, and actions
Positive psychologist	Examines factors related to optimal human functioning
School psychologist	Collaborates with teachers, parents, and students within the educational system to help children with special needs related to a disability and their academic and social progress; also provides evaluation and assessment of a student's functioning and eligibility for special services
Social psychologist	Investigates the role of social forces in interpersonal behavior, including aggression, prejudice, love, helping, conformity, and attitudes
Sport psychologist	Applies principles of psychology to enhance physical performance

Retrieval Practice 1.1 | What Is Psychology?

Self-Test   Completing this self-test, and then checking your answers by clicking on the answer button or by looking in Appendix B, will provide immediate feedback and helpful practice for exams.

1. Psychology is defined as the _____.
   a. science of conscious and unconscious forces
   b. empirical study of the mind and behavior
   c. scientific study of the mind
   d. scientific study of behavior and mental processes

2. _____ relies on common beliefs, folk wisdom, or even superstitions and does not follow the basics of the scientific method.
   a. Pseudoscience
   b. Astrophysics
   c. Astronomy
   d. None of these options

3. _____ is generally acknowledged to be the father of psychology.
   a. Sigmund Freud
   b. B. F. Skinner
   c. Wilhelm Wundt
   d. William Tell

4. Which of the following terms do not belong together?
   a. structuralism, unconscious behavior
   b. behaviorism, observable behavior
   c. psychoanalytic, unconscious conflict
   d. humanism, free will

Q Test Your Critical Thinking

1. Psychologists are among the least likely to believe in psychics, palmistry, astrology, and other paranormal phenomena. Why might that be?

2. Which of the seven modern perspectives of psychology do you most agree with? Why?

3. How might the biopsychosocial model explain difficulties or achievements in your own life?

Real World Application Question

[AQ1]   Does your ethnicity affect the type of questions you're asked in a job interview?

DW labs Incorporated/Shutterstock.com

Hint: Look in the text for **[AQ1]**

1.2   Scientific Research

LEARNING OBJECTIVES

Retrieval Practice   While reading the upcoming sections, respond to each Learning Objective in your own words.

Discuss the key principles underlying the science of psychology.

- **Review** psychology's four main goals.
- **Compare and contrast** the fundamental goals of basic and applied research.

- **Describe** the scientific method, its key terms, and its six steps.
- **Discuss** the ethical concerns and guidelines for psychological research.

Real World Application Questions

[AQ2] Can strength training decrease depression?

[AQ3] Can a diet high in fats and sugars impair learning and memory?

Psychology's Four Main Goals

When conducting their research, psychologists have four major goals—to *describe*, *explain*, *predict*, and *change* behavior and mental processes:

1. **Description**   Description tells what occurred. In some studies, psychologists attempt to *describe*, or name and classify, particular behaviors and mental processes by making careful scientific observations. Description is usually the first step in psychological research. For example, if someone says, "Boys are more aggressive than girls," what does that mean? The speaker's definition of aggression may differ from yours. Science requires specificity.

2. **Explanation**   An explanation tells why a behavior or mental process occurred. One of the most enduring debates in science is the **nature–nurture controversy**. Are we controlled by biological and genetic factors (the nature side) or by the environment and learning (the nurture side)? As you will see throughout the text, psychology generally avoids "either-or" positions and focuses instead on *interactions*. Today, almost all scientists agree that most psychological, and even physical, traits reflect an interaction between nature and nurture. As expected, research suggests numerous interacting causes or explanations for aggression, including culture, learning, and other biopsychosocial factors (Bushman, 2016; Rodriguez-Hidalgo et al., 2018; Salimi et al., 2019).

3. **Prediction**   Psychologists generally begin with description and explanation (answering the "whats" and "whys"). Then they move on to the higher-level goal of *prediction*, identifying when and under what conditions a future behavior or mental process is likely to occur. For instance, knowing that alcohol leads to increased aggression (Denson et al., 2018; Woodin et al., 2016; Zinzow & Thompson, 2015), we can predict that more fights will erupt in places where alcohol is consumed than in places where it isn't.

4. **Change**   For some people, change as a goal of psychology brings to mind evil politicians or cult leaders brainwashing unknowing victims. However, to psychologists, *change* means applying psychological science to prevent unwanted outcomes or bring about desired goals. In almost all cases, change as a goal of psychology is positive. Psychologists help people improve their work environments, stop addictive behaviors, become less depressed, improve their family relationships, and so on. Furthermore, as you may know from personal experience, it is very difficult (if not impossible) to change someone's attitude or behavior against her or his will. (*Here is an old joke*: Do you know how many psychologists it takes to change a light bulb? *Answer*: None. The light bulb has to want to change.)

Basic and Applied Research

In science, research strategies are generally categorized as either *basic* or *applied*. **Basic research** is most often conducted to advance core scientific knowledge, whereas **applied research** is generally designed to solve practical (real-world) problems (**Figure 1.6**). As you'll see in Chapter 6, classical and operant conditioning principles evolved from numerous *basic research* studies designed to advance the general understanding of how human and non-human animals learn. In Chapters 13 and 14, you'll also discover how *applied research* based on these principles has been used to successfully treat psychological disorders, such as phobias. Similarly, in Chapter 7, you'll see how basic research on how we create, store, and retrieve our memories has led to practical applications in the legal field, such as a greater appreciation for the fallibility of eyewitness testimony.

Keep in mind that basic and applied research approaches are not polar opposites. Instead, they frequently share similar goals, and their outcomes interact, with one building on the other.

The Scientific Method

In contrast to the previously discussed problems with *pseudoscience*, which relies on unsubstantiated beliefs and opinions, psychological science is based on rigorous, systematic scientific methods. Psychologists follow strict, standardized procedures so that others can understand, interpret, and repeat or test their findings. During both basic and applied research, most scientific investigations consist of six basic steps, collectively known as the **scientific method** (**Process Diagram 1.1**).

Nature–nurture controversy An ongoing dispute about the relative contributions of nature (biological and genetic factors) and nurture (environment and learning) in behavior and mental processes.

Basic research   A type of research primarily conducted to advance core scientific knowledge; most often conducted in universities and research laboratories.

Applied research   A type of research primarily conducted to solve practical, real-world problems; generally conducted outside the laboratory.

Scientific method   The cyclical and cumulative research process used for gathering and interpreting objective information in a way that minimizes error and yields dependable results.

Leigh Green/Alamy Stock Photo

FIGURE 1.6 **Applied research in psychology**   Can you see how this billboard advertisement is a good example of both basic and applied research? Scientific findings on the global climate crisis and its resulting prolonged droughts has led to later studies and approaches to deal with the real-world water shortage problem—restricted times and alternating days for watering outdoors in California.

STOP! This Process Diagram contains essential information NOT found elsewhere in the text, which is likely to appear on quizzes and exams. Be sure to study it CAREFULLY! Research has shown that having diagrams showing how a process works results in higher performance on tests than having no diagrams at all, or just a text outline of the process (Bui & McDaniel, 2015). This and other research, along with our own experiences as educators, explains why we've included process diagrams throughout this text.

PROCESS DIAGRAM 1.1 **The Scientific Method** Although there is no one, official "scientific method" that is accepted by all scientists, scientific investigations do follow a progression of logical steps while collecting data, like those in this diagram. Note also that scientific knowledge is constantly evolving and self-correcting—as shown by the arrows connecting the steps in this diagram. As soon as one research study is published, the cycle almost always begins again. The scientific method's ongoing, cyclical nature often frustrates students. In most chapters, you will encounter numerous, and sometimes conflicting, scientific theories and research findings. You'll be tempted to ask: "Which one is right?" But, as with most aspects of behavior, the "correct" answer is almost always a combination and interaction of multiple theories and competing findings. The good news is that such complex answers lead to a fuller and more productive understanding of behavior and mental processes. (Note the dotted line from Step 5 to Step 6. It indicates that theories may develop after a combination of repeated testing and numerous supportive publications.)

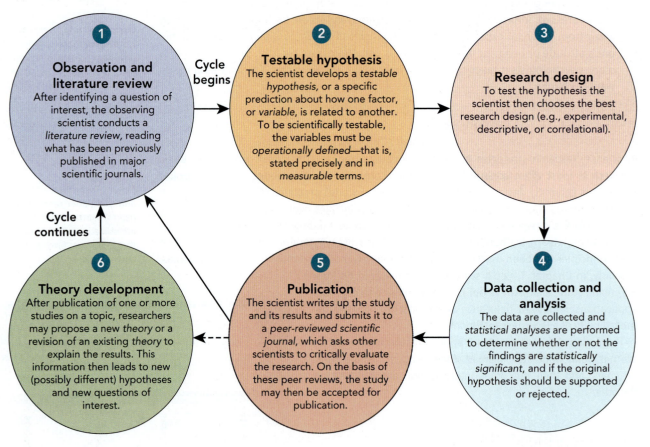

Step 1: Observation and Literature Review Do you recall from the beginning of this chapter that *scientific thinking* is characterized by curiosity—an eager willingness to question and explore the world around us? Curious psychologists, much like professional journalists, begin with a "simple" *observation* and questions about who, what, when, where, why, or how something is happening. For instance, have you observed all the *Retrieval Practice* exercises sprinkled throughout each chapter of this text, including those at the ends of sections and those within the Learning Objectives and Key Terms? As a curious student, thinking

scientifically and critically, are you wondering whether completing these activities is worth your time? Or whether doing so will help you do better on exams?

If so, let's conduct an imaginary exercise that will answer these questions about retrieval practice, while helping you also master key terms and concepts within the six steps of the scientific method. Beginning with Step 1 of your research, you'll need to clarify the specific factors you want to observe and measure—in this case, retrieval practice and exam grades. (Note that these specific factors are officially referred to as **variables**, which are simply any factors that can vary or change and can be observed, measured, and verified.) After completing this first part of Step 1, you would perform a *literature review*, which involves consulting professional journals and studying previous research findings on retrieval practice and exam grades.

Step 2: Testable Hypothesis

To complete Step 2, you need to create a tentative and testable **hypothesis**, which is a statement and/or possible explanation of the relationship you've observed between two or more variables. This hypothesis should be based on the information you gathered during your literature review in Step 1, and it should provide predictions about the outcome of your study that can be tested in some way. To make such predictions, you'll need to explicitly state how each of the variables in your hypothesis will be **operationally defined** (observed, manipulated, and measured).

Returning to the retrieval practice exercise, a better grade on your exams might be operationally defined as earning a grade one letter higher than the one you earned on your previous exam. Your combined hypothesis and operational definition might be: "Students who spend two hours studying Chapter 1 in this text and one hour completing the Retrieval Practice will earn higher scores on a standard academic exam than students who spend three hours studying Chapter 1 without completing the Retrieval Practice."

Steps 3 and 4: Research Design/Data Collection and Analysis

For Step 3, you would most likely choose an experimental research design. To begin the data collection and analysis of your experiment (Step 4), you might recruit 100 volunteers from various classes on your college campus. Of these, you would then **randomly assign** 50 to Group 1 (Retrieval Practice) and the other 50 to Group 2 (no Retrieval Practice). After allowing both groups to study for three hours, you would present and score a 20-point quiz on the material. Then you would record and compare the scores of the two groups.

Another important approach to data collection and analysis is required when psychologists want to reveal overall trends that may not show up in individual studies, or when different researchers report contradictory findings. When facing this dilemma, psychologists employ a popular statistical technique called **meta-analysis**, which averages or combines the results of many studies to reach conclusions about the overall weight of the evidence.

[AQ2] For example, a meta-analysis of 33 studies and over 2,000 participants found that resistance exercise training significantly reduced the incidence of depression (Gordon et al., 2018). Surprisingly, even when participants saw few physical changes from this type of strength training, they still tended to see improvements in their overall mood (see photo).

Step 5: Publication

In this step, you would submit your research for possible publication, assuming your results were *statistically significant*. Before accepting your findings for publication, most scientific journals will send your paper to reputable scientists for *peer review*. These reviewers will evaluate and comment on the quality, significance, and originality of your research. If the reviews are positive and the suggested corrections are minor, you will have the opportunity to make corrections and your paper will likely be accepted for publication.

The journal editors will then decide what month and year to publish your article. Note that authors and peer reviewers are NOT paid for their work. Their free services are all part of the ethical standards of the academic community—members share their findings and contribute their work for the general advancement of science.

In addition to making a contribution to science, one small payoff for authors/researchers is that they may be cited in other journal articles or in textbooks like this one. As you've

Variable Any factor that can vary or change and can be observed, measured, and verified.

Hypothesis A tentative and testable statement and possible explanation about the relationship between two or more variables; an educated guess about the outcome of a scientific study.

Operational definition A precise description of how the variables in a study will be observed, manipulated, and measured.

Random assignment A research technique for assigning participants to experimental or control conditions so that each participant has an equal chance of being in either group; minimizes the possibility of biases or preexisting differences within or between the groups.

Meta-analysis A statistical technique for combining and analyzing data from many studies in order to determine overall trends.

lightfieldstudios/123RF

Theory A broad explanation for a set of observations or facts that have been substantiated through repeated testing.

Replicate To repeat or duplicate the essence of a research study using different situations or participants to determine if the basic findings can be reproduced; replication helps demonstrate reliability of research findings.

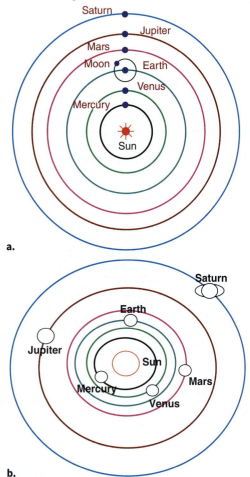

a.

b.

FIGURE 1.8 **Opinions versus facts—science to the rescue** Early experiments, conducted primarily by Nicolaus Copernicus (1473–1543), led to a collection of facts and ultimately to the theory that the Earth was not the center of the universe, as generally assumed at the time. Instead, it was thought to rotate around the sun with the other planets in concentric circles (**a**). Later scientists (astronomers Johannes Kepler and Tycho Brahe) built on this Copernican (heliocentric) theory with additional experiments that led to a revised theory, in which the orbits were not circular, but rather elliptical (**b**). Today, researchers have expanded the theory even further by demonstrating that our sun is not the center of the universe, but only a part of a galaxy that in turn is only one of many billions of galaxies. Can you see how these incremental changes illustrate the value of scientific theories and their ever-changing—and self-correcting nature?

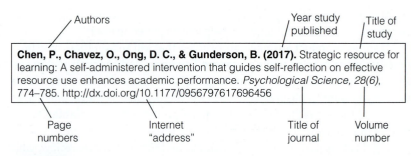

FIGURE 1.7 **How to interpret a scientific journal reference** Note that the citation for this particular reference would appear in the chapter as (Chen et al., 2017), with the et al. indicating multiple authors. However, as shown in this figure, the names of all four authors, along with the article title, and the journal, book, or other reference work in which the article was published are included in the full journal reference. The citation also includes the doi (digital object identifier), which is a string of letters, numbers, and symbols allowing easy access to that specific article on the Internet. Although instructors rarely expect you to memorize the names and dates in parentheses, as a scientific and crititcal thinker you may want to use this set of full references (found at the end of this text) to double-check our citations, as a reliable source for research projects, and for additional information on a topic of interest.

noticed throughout this text, citations to publications appear in parentheses at the end of many sentences. These citations, such as (Aagaard, 2019; Yong, 2018), list just the authors' names and the dates of their publications. However, **Figure 1.7** shows what a complete reference looks like and how to interpret its various parts.

Step 6: Theory Development

Once you've published your research findings, you (and other researchers) might discover additional findings on effective study techniques. After many related findings have been collected and confirmed, scientists can sometimes develop a **theory**, which is a broad explanation for a set of observations or facts that have been substantiated through repeated testing. Theories are particularly helpful because they often lead to new hypotheses, other research, important predictions, and even all-new refined theories. In sum, *science is the cumulative, cyclical process of developing accurate theories using the scientific method.*

Unfortunately, the term *theory* is also commonly (and mistakenly) used to refer to a simple guess, a hunch, or even just personal opinion. In fact, *theory* has been listed as one of the seven most commonly misused scientific terms (Ghose, 2013). As mentioned in our discussion of scientific thinking, theories are tools that predict facts and facts are statements backed by direct verifiable evidence. Far too often, valid scientific findings and widespread agreement on issues like the climate crisis are ignored or diminished by those who claim that these results are "just a theory." Can you see why it's so important to understand that scientific theories are based on empirical evidence, not just simple hunches or opinions? The value of facts over opinions and science's self-correcting nature are further explained in **Figure 1.8**.

Before leaving this section on the six steps of the scientific method, be sure to carefully study the following **STH Scientific Thinking Highlight**, which alerts you to possible benefits and problems that may occur when other researchers attempt to repeat, or **replicate**, the original research. Also, given that we began this section on the scientific method by asking you to imagine yourself as a researcher interested in the effectiveness of retrieval practice exercises, you'll be interested to know that actual published research does, in fact, support the power of retrieval practice in improving retention and exam scores (Carpenter & Yeung, 2017; Schuetze et al., 2019). This and other research

STH Scientific Thinking Highlight

Psychology and the Replication Crisis

(APA Goal 2.1) Use scientific reasoning to interpret psychological phenomena

As you might expect, publication (Step 5 in the research method) and replication are core to scientific research. Unfortunately, psychology, medicine, and other sciences have recently come under heavy fire for a serious lack of replication of their original research findings (Diener & Biswas-Diener, 2019; Open Science Collaboration, 2017). This so-called *replication crisis* first began when scientists revisited a large collection of previous publications, and found that only about one-third to just under two-thirds of all psychological studies could be replicated (Camerer et al., 2018; Open Science Collaboration, 2015; Yong, 2018).

Given that psychologists are justifiably alarmed by this crisis, let's examine the importance of replication using the three principles of scientific thinking. Recall from earlier in this chapter, *scientific thinking* is an approach to information that combines a high degree of *skepticism* (questioning what "everybody knows") with *objectivity* (using empirical data to separate fantasy from reality) and *rationalism* (practicing logical reasoning).

1. **Skepticism** As mentioned earlier, skepticism requires us to open-mindedly evaluate all claims, while also requiring persuasive evidence before we accept the claim. If numerous researchers, using different procedures or different participants in varied settings, can successfully replicate a study's results, the study is considered more persuasive and there is increased scientific confidence in the findings. Without replication, scientists might rely on research findings that wouldn't be found again because they result from a unique set of participants or a very specific procedure. For these reasons, replication helps satisfy the *skepticism* requirement of scientific thinking.

2. **Objectivity** Replication also helps address the need for *objectivity*. Only when scientists do the same thing and arrive at the same conclusion can we create a shared knowledge that we call objective. Using empirical data to separate fantasy from reality also allows psychological scientists to more successfully *describe, explain, predict*, and *change* behavior and mental processes—the four goals of psychology. Objectivity requires that if specific findings cannot be replicated, researchers cannot meet these core psychological goals, and we must look for other explanations and/or conduct further studies.

3. **Rationalism** There are sometimes logical and legitimate reasons why replication attempts fail. For instance, a series of studies started in the late 1960s and early 1970s found that children who were able to delay immediate gratification—

by not eating a marshmallow placed right in front of them— showed better life outcomes, including greater academic achievement, lower levels of substance abuse, and so on, even 40 years later (Mischel, 2014; Mischel et al., 2011; Mischel & Ebbesen, 1970). Unfortunately, later studies reported results that were much weaker than those from the original series of studies (Watts et al., 2018).

One rational, logical explanation for the relative lack of replication of this so-called "Marshmallow study" could be that nowadays more young children attend preschool, which may help teach skills in delaying gratification. Furthermore, rather than measuring delay of gratification, the researchers might have inadvertently assessed the children's reaction to authority and whether or not they trusted adults.

Considering this and other studies and their lack of replication, researchers suggest that attempted replications may not have accurately recreated the original studies, the newer sample size might have been too small to produce significant results, or the replication of certain topics is difficult and unrealistic in current times (Diener & Biswas-Diener, 2019; Van Bavel et al., 2016).

Take-Home Message   This *replication crisis* is very important and psychologists are responding to the challenge with a greater emphasis on transparency, better outlets for investigating and storing replication attempts, and even sharing data with other researchers to verify findings. Note also that psychological science has several built-in tools for self-correction. For example, as you discovered earlier in Process Diagram 1.1, the scientific method is cyclical and cumulative, which means that scientific progress results from repeatedly challenging and revising existing research.

Q Test Your Scientific Thinking

Imagine you are talking to someone who is a strong believer in or denier of climate change, and then to someone who is a strong proponent or opponent of childhood vaccinations.

1. Describe how you could use the three key principles of scientific thinking—*skepticism, objectivity,* and *rationalism*—to have a meaningful conversation on these topics with these two individuals. How might this type of dialogue be helpful to both of you?

2. Try applying the three scientific principles to your personal beliefs and positions on climate change and childhood vaccinations. Did this type of scientific thinking help clarify or modify your own beliefs and positions? Why or why not?

(Compare your answers with those of fellow students, family, and friends. Doing so will improve your scientific thinking and your media savvy.)

---

explains why self-testing is so often emphasized throughout this text. As you'll see in Chapter 3, practice testing can even reduce the negative effects of stress (Smith et al., 2016).

Psychology's Research Ethics

So far, we've discussed applied versus basic research, the scientific method, and the four basic goals of psychology. Now we need to examine the general ethics that guide psychological research. The two largest professional organizations of psychologists, the American

Psychological Association (APA) and the Association for Psychological Science (APS), both recognize the importance of maintaining high ethical standards in research, therapy, and all other areas of professional psychology. The preamble to the APA's publication *Ethical Principles of Psychologists and Code of Conduct* (2016) requires psychologists to maintain their competence, to retain objectivity in applying their skills, and to preserve the dignity and best interests of their clients, colleagues, students, research participants, and society. In addition, colleges and universities have institutional review boards (IRBs) that carefully evaluate the ethics and methods of research conducted at their institutions.

Respecting the Rights of Human Participants

The APA and APS have developed rigorous guidelines regulating research with human participants, including the following:

Informed consent   A participant's agreement to take part in a study after being told what to expect.

- **Informed consent**   Researchers must obtain an **informed consent** agreement from all participants *before* initiating an experiment. Participants are made aware of the nature of the study, what to expect, and significant factors that might influence their willingness to participate, including all physical risks, discomfort, and possibly unpleasant emotional experiences.

- **Voluntary participation**   Participants must be told that they're free to decline to participate or to withdraw from the research at any time.

- **Restricted use of deception, followed by debriefing**   If participants knew the true purpose behind certain studies, they might not respond naturally. In one of psychology's most famous, and controversial, studies (Milgram, 1963), researchers ordered participants to give electric shocks to another participant, who was really a confederate of the researcher, and was not actually receiving any shocks (Chapter 15). Although they were told that the study was examining the use of shocks to assist with learning, the researchers were actually testing participants' willingness to follow orders. Obviously in this case, participants' behavior could not be accurately measured if they were told the true focus of the study. Therefore, researchers occasionally need to temporarily deceive participants about the actual reason for the experiment.

Debriefing   A discussion procedure conducted at the end of an experiment or study; participants are informed of the study's design and purpose, possible misconceptions are clarified, questions are answered, and explanations are provided for any possible deception.

    On the limited and rare occasions when deception is necessary, ethical guidelines and restrictions still apply. One of the most important is **debriefing**. After data collection has been completed, participants are provided with a full explanation of the research, including its design and purpose and any deception used. During this debriefing, researchers also address participants' misconceptions, questions, or concerns.

- **Confidentiality**   Whenever possible, participants are provided anonymity. All personal information acquired during a study must be kept private, and not published in such a way that an individual's right to privacy is compromised.

Respecting the Rights of Non-human Animals

Although they are used in only seven to eight percent of psychological research (American Psychological Association [APA], 2009; Institute for Laboratory Animal Research [ILAR], 2010; Market Opinion Research International [MORI], 2005), non-human animals—mostly rats and mice—have made significant contributions to almost every area of psychology, including the brain and nervous system, health and stress, sensation and perception, sleep, learning, memory, motivation, and emotion.

[AQ3]   For instance, one study found that rats who are fed a diet high in fats and sugars show impairment in their learning and memory (Tran & Westbrook, 2015). This study could have critical, real-world implications for people, but do you see why this type of research would be unethical and impossible to conduct using human subjects?

    Non-human animal research also has produced significant gains for some animal populations, such as the development of more natural environments for zoo animals and more successful breeding techniques for endangered species.

pedalist/Shutterstock.com

Despite the advantages, using non-human animals in psychological research remains controversial (see cartoon). Although debate continues about ethical issues in such research, psychologists take great care in handling research animals. Researchers also actively search for new and better ways to minimize any harm to the animals (APA Congressional Briefing, 2015; Morling, 2015; Pope & Vasquez, 2011).

Respecting the Rights of Psychotherapy Clients

Professional organizations, such as the APA and APS, as well as academic institutions and state and local agencies, all require that therapists, like researchers, maintain the highest ethical standards. Therapists must also uphold their clients' trust. All personal information and therapy records must be kept confidential. Furthermore, client records are made available only to authorized persons, and with the client's permission. However, therapists are legally required to break confidentiality if a client threatens violence to himself or herself or to others, if a client is suspected of abusing a child or an elderly person, and in other limited situations (Adi & Mathbout, 2018; Kress et al., 2013; Rabelo et al., 2019).

"He says he wants a lawyer."

Tom Chalkley/The New Yorker Collection/The Cartoon Bank

Take-Home Message

What about ethics and beginning psychology students? Once friends and acquaintances know you're taking a course in psychology, they may want you to interpret their dreams, help them discipline their children, or even advise them on whether they should start or end their relationships. Although you will learn a great deal about psychological functioning in this text and in your psychology class, take care that you do not overestimate your expertise. Also remember that the theories and findings of psychological science are cyclical and cumulative—and continually being revised.

David L. Cole, a recipient of the APA Distinguished Teaching in Psychology Award, reminds us, "Undergraduate psychology can, and I believe should, seek to liberate the student from ignorance, but also the arrogance of believing we know more about ourselves and others than we really do" (Cole, 1982, p. 24).

Retrieval Practice 1.2 | Scientific Research

Self-Test Completing this self-test, and then checking your answers by clicking on the answer button or by looking in Appendix B, will provide immediate feedback and helpful practice for exams.

1. The goal of _____ is to tell what occurred, whereas the goal of _____ is to tell when.

   a. health psychologists; biological psychologists

   b. description; prediction

   c. psychologists; psychiatrists

   d. pseudopsychologists; clinical psychologists

2. If you conducted a study on areas of the brain most affected by drinking alcohol, it would be _____ research.

   a. unethical   c. pseudopsychology

   b. basic   d. applied

3. A(n) _____ provides a precise definition of how the variables in a study will be observed and measured.

   a. meta-analysis   c. independent observation

   b. theory   d. operational definition

4. A participant's agreement to take part in a study after being told what to expect is known as _____ .

   a. psychological standards

   b. an experimental contract

   c. debriefing

   d. informed consent

Q Test Your Critical Thinking

1. What is the difference between a scientific theory, an opinion, and a hunch?

2. If you had a million dollars to contribute to either basic or applied research, which one would you choose? Why?

Real World Application Questions

[AQ2] Can strength training decrease depression?

lightfieldstudios/123RF

[AQ3] Can a diet high in fats and sugars impair learning and memory?

pedalist/Shutterstock.com

Hint: Look in the text for **[AQ2]** and **[AQ3]**

1.3 Psychology's Research Methods

LEARNING OBJECTIVES

Retrieval Practice   While reading the upcoming sections, respond to each Learning Objective in your own words.

Summarize psychology's three major research methods.

- **Review** descriptive research and its four key methods.
- **Discuss** correlational research and the correlation coefficient.
- **Identify** the key terms and components of experimental research.

- **Review** the major research problems and biases, along with the possible safeguards against them.

Real World Application Questions

[AQ4] Does spending more time on Instagram decrease your psychological well-being?

[AQ5] Is there a correlation between years of education and physical health?

Having studied the scientific method and psychology's four main goals, we can now examine how psychologists conduct their research. Psychologists generally draw on three major research methods—*descriptive*, *correlational*, and *experimental* (**Figure 1.9**). As you'll see in the upcoming section, each of these approaches has advantages and disadvantages, and psychologists often use variations of all three methods to study a single problem. In fact, when multiple approaches lead to similar conclusions, scientists have an especially strong foundation for concluding that one variable does affect another in a reliable and predictable way.

Descriptive Research

Descriptive research   A type of research that systematically observes and records behavior and mental processes without manipulating variables; designed to meet the goal of *description*.

Almost everyone observes and describes others in an attempt to understand them, but in conducting **descriptive research**, psychologists do so systematically and scientifically. The key types of descriptive research are *observation*, *survey/interview*, *case study*, and *archival research*.

Observation   A descriptive research technique that assesses and records behavior and mental processes in natural, real-world and/or laboratory settings.

Observation   When conducting **observation**, researchers systematically assess and record participants' behavior in their natural, real-world and/or laboratory settings, without interfering. Many settings lend themselves to *naturalistic observation*, from supermarkets to airports to outdoor settings. Jane Goodall's classic naturalistic observations of wild chimpanzees provided invaluable insights into their everyday lives, such as their use of tools, acts of aggression, demonstrations of affection, and, sadly, even the killing of other chimps' babies (infanticide). In Chapter 15, you'll read about an observational study of the human animal that examined whether Uber and Lyft drivers take longer to respond to ride requests from Black travelers than from White travelers (Ge et al., 2016). Can you guess what they found?

Survey/interview   A descriptive research technique that questions a large sample of people to assess their behaviors and mental processes.

The chief advantage of observation in a natural setting is that researchers can obtain data about real-world behavior rather than about behavior that is a reaction to an artificial experimental situation. But naturalistic observation can be difficult and time-consuming, and the lack of control by the researcher makes it difficult to conduct observations of behavior that occurs infrequently.

For a researcher who wants to observe behavior in a more controlled setting, *laboratory observation* has many of the advantages of naturalistic observation, but with greater control over the variables (**Figure 1.10**).

Survey/Interview   Psychologists use **surveys/interviews** to ask people to self-report on

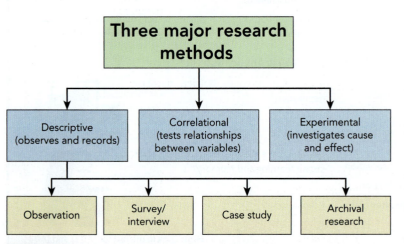

FIGURE 1.9   **An overview of psychology's major research methods**

their behaviors, opinions, and attitudes (see cartoon). In Chapter 3, you'll read about survey research showing that even a single close childhood friendship can protect vulnerable children in lower socioeconomic circumstances from several psychological risk factors (Graber et al., 2016).

One key advantage of this approach is that researchers can gather data from many more people than is generally possible with other research designs. Unfortunately, most surveys/interviews rely on self-reported data, and not all participants are honest. As you might imagine, people are especially motivated to give less-than-truthful answers when asked about highly sensitive topics, such as infidelity, drug use, and illegal behavior.

Case Study
What if a researcher wants to investigate photophobia (fear of light)? In such a case, it would be difficult to find enough participants to conduct an experiment or to use surveys/interviews or observation. For rare disorders or phenomena, researchers try to find someone who has the problem and then study him or her intensively. This type of in-depth study of a single research participant, or a small group of individuals, is called a **case study**. In Chapter 9, we'll share a fascinating case study that examined the impact of severe neglect during childhood on language acquisition. Research like this obviously could not be conducted using another method, for ethical reasons, and because of the rarity of such severe deprivation.

Archival Research
The fourth type of descriptive research is **archival research**, in which researchers study previously recorded data. Interestingly, archival data from 30,625 Himalayan mountain climbers from 56 countries found that expeditions from countries with hierarchical cultures, which believe that power should be concentrated at the top and followers should obey leaders without question, had more climbers reach the summit than did expeditions from more egalitarian cultures (Anicich et al., 2015). Sadly, they also had more climbers die along the way. The researchers concluded that hierarchical values impaired safety by preventing low-ranking team members from sharing their valuable insights and perspectives. (If you're wondering, American climbers ranked a little below midpoint in hierarchical values.)

Correlational Research

As you've just seen, data collected from descriptive research provide invaluable information on behavior and mental processes. The findings typically describe the dimensions of a phenomenon or behavior in terms of who, what, when, and where it occurred. However, if we want to know *whether* and *how* two or more variables change together, we need **correlational research**. As the name implies, the purpose of this approach is to determine whether any two variables are *co-related*, meaning a change in one is accompanied by a change in the other. If one variable increases, how does the other variable change? Does it increase or decrease?

[AQ4] For example, a disturbing link has been found between Instagram and psychological well-being (Sherlock & Wagstaff, 2019). For women between 18 and 35 years of age, frequency of Instagram use (see photo) was correlated with lower self-esteem, higher depressive symptoms, increased general and physical appearance anxiety, and higher body dissatisfaction. Researchers have also found a correlation between age and job satisfaction (Dobrow Riza et al., 2018). In this

FIGURE 1.10   **Laboratory observation**   In this type of observation, the researcher may bring participants into a specially prepared room in the laboratory, with one-way mirrors, or hidden cameras and microphones. Using such methods, the researcher can observe school children at work, families interacting, or other individuals and groups in various settings.

Education & Exploration 1/Alamy Stock Photo

"Hi. I'm doing a survey. Do you have a few minutes to answer some questions?"

Joe Dator/The New Yorker Collection/The Cartoon Bank

Case study   A descriptive research technique involving an in-depth study of a single research participant or a small group of individuals.

Archival research   A descriptive research technique that studies existing data to find answers to research questions.

Correlational research   A type of research that examines possible relations between variables; designed to meet the goal of *prediction*.

alexey malkin/123RF

longitudinal study (research conducted over a long period), participants reported feeling less satisfied with their jobs over the years, but as they aged (and often changed jobs) their satisfaction increased. How can we explain this apparent contradictory finding? Job satisfaction appears to follow a cyclical pattern. When first employed, we go through a "honeymoon period," but our satisfaction tends to decline the longer we stay in that particular job. However, when we move on to another organization, with generally higher wages, our satisfaction increases.

As you can see, correlational research allows us to make predictions about one variable based on knowledge of another. Suppose scientists noted a relationship between hours of television viewing and performance on exams. They could then predict exam grades based on the amount of TV viewing. The researchers could also determine the direction and strength of the relationship using a statistical formula that gives a **correlation coefficient**, which is a number from −1.00 to +1.00 that indicates the direction and strength of a relationship between two variables. Understanding what all of this means is crucial to becoming an educated consumer of research. As shown in **Figure 1.11**, one clear "payoff" for understanding correlations is that it can prevent problems, such as the link between a

Correlation coefficient A number from −1.00 to +1.00 that indicates the direction and strength of the relationship between two variables.

FIGURE 1.11 **Interpreting a correlation coefficient**

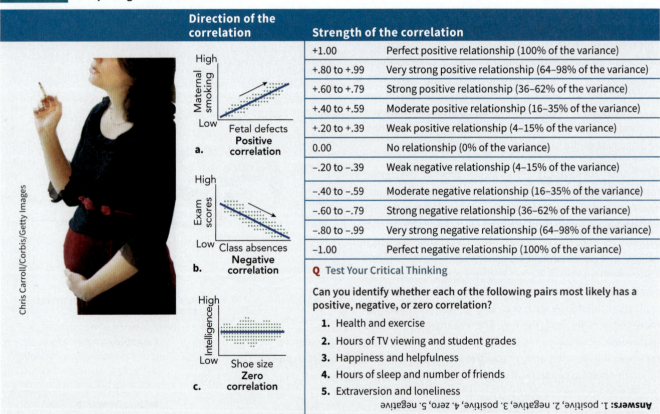

Chris Carroll/Corbis/Getty Images

Direction of the correlation	Strength of the correlation	
	+1.00	Perfect positive relationship (100% of the variance)
	+.80 to +.99	Very strong positive relationship (64–98% of the variance)
	+.60 to +.79	Strong positive relationship (36–62% of the variance)
	+.40 to +.59	Moderate positive relationship (16–35% of the variance)
	+.20 to +.39	Weak positive relationship (4–15% of the variance)
	0.00	No relationship (0% of the variance)
	−.20 to −.39	Weak negative relationship (4–15% of the variance)
	−.40 to −.59	Moderate negative relationship (16–35% of the variance)
	−.60 to −.79	Strong negative relationship (36–62% of the variance)
	−.80 to −.99	Very strong negative relationship (64–98% of the variance)
	−1.00	Perfect negative relationship (100% of the variance)

Q Test Your Critical Thinking

Can you identify whether each of the following pairs most likely has a positive, negative, or zero correlation?

1. Health and exercise
2. Hours of TV viewing and student grades
3. Happiness and helpfulness
4. Hours of sleep and number of friends
5. Extraversion and loneliness

Answers: 1. positive, 2. negative, 3. positive, 4. zero, 5. negative

---

There are three major forms of correlation and they're often depicted in graphs called scatterplots (shown in the left column of this figure). Each dot on these graphs represents one participant's score on both variables, such as maternal smoking and fetal defects. The pattern (or "scattering") of the dots (upward, downward, or horizontal) reveals the direction of the correlation (positive, negative, or zero).

- **Direction of the correlation** (left-hand column)   The + or − sign in the correlation coefficient indicates the *direction* of the correlation, either positive or negative. Note in Figure a that when two factors vary in the same direction, meaning they increase or decrease together, the correlation is called a *positive correlation*. In contrast, when two factors vary in opposite directions, one increasing as

the other decreases, it's known as a *negative correlation* (Figure b). When there is NO relation between the two variables, it is called a *zero correlation* (Figure c).

- **Strength of the correlation** (right-hand column)   Look again at the scatterplots in the left column, and note how the various dots cluster around the three solid dark lines. The closer the dots are together, the stronger the relationship—little scatter (more clustering) indicates a high correlation. Correlations of +1.00 and a −1.00 magnitude both indicate the strongest possible relationship. As the number decreases and gets closer to 0.00, the relationship weakens. We interpret correlations close to zero as representing NO relationship between the variables—like the "relationship" between intelligence and shoe size.

pregnant woman's use of drugs—like nicotine and alcohol—and serious birth defects (e.g., Denny et al., 2019; Maessen et al., 2019).

Limits of Correlations

Unfortunately, correlations are sometimes confusing, misleading, and sometimes not particularly useful. In addition, a mathematical correlation can be found between two events or variables that have no direct connection—yet people may wrongly infer that they do. Therefore, it's very important to note these two major cautions concerning correlations:

1. **Correlation does NOT prove causation!** Correlational studies can detect whether or not two variables are related. However, they cannot tell us which variable is the cause or the effect—or whether other known or unknown factors may explain the mathematical relationship. As an example, studies show that cities with a higher total number of police officers have a higher crime rate. Does this mean that an increase in police officers leads to more crime? Of course not. Instead, a *third variable* (increased population) is the most logical source of the link between more officers and more crime. A similar confusion occurs with the correlational finding that sales of ice cream are higher when the rate of drownings is highest (**Figure 1.12**).

   This mistake of confusing correlation with causation is sometimes referred to as the **third-variable problem**, which identifies a situation in which a variable that has not been measured accounts for a relationship between two or more other variables. Would you like another example? See **Figure 1.13**.

2. **Correlations are sometimes illusory—meaning they don't exist.** In this second problem, there is NO factual connection between two variables; the supposed correlation is the result of random coincidence and/or misperception. Popular beliefs, such as that infertile couples are more likely to conceive after an adoption, or that certain slot machines are more likely to pay off than others, or that strange behaviors increase during a full moon, are called **illusory** (false) **correlations** (Ernst et al., 2019; Lilienfeld et al., 2015).

TIP Are you confused about the difference between third variables and illusory correlations? If so, note that with the *third-variable problem*, a correlation does exist between two or more variables, but a third factor might be responsible for their relationship. In contrast, with an *illusory correlation* there is NO actual connection between two variables—the apparent connection is totally FALSE.

Superstitions, such as the idea that breaking a mirror will lead to seven years of bad luck or that wearing your lucky team jacket will bring the team good luck, are additional examples of illusory correlations. We mistakenly perceive an association that factually does not exist. Unfortunately, these and other well-known superstitions persist despite logical reasoning and scientific evidence to the contrary (**Table 1.5**).

Why are beliefs in illusory correlations so common? As you'll discover in upcoming chapters, we tend to focus on the most noticeable (salient) factors when explaining the potential causes of behavior. For example, focusing attention on the dramatic (but very rare) instances when infertile couples conceive after adoption or when a gambler wins a large payout are both examples of illusory correlations, as well as what is called the *saliency bias* (see Chapter 15). We also more often note and remember events that confirm our expectations and ignore the "misses." This is known as the *confirmation bias* (Chapter 8).

The important thing to remember while reading research reports in the media or any textbook is that observed correlations may be illusory and that correlational research can NEVER provide a clear cause and effect relationship between variables. Always consider that a third factor might be a better explanation for a perceived correlation. To find causation, we need the experimental method, which is discussed in the next section.

Third-variable problem A situation in which a variable that has not been measured affects (confounds) a relationship between two or more other variables; also known as a problem of confounding.

Illusory correlation A mistaken perception that a relationship exists between variables when no such relationship actually exists.

aslysun/Shutterstock.com

Sarocha_S/Shutterstock.com

FIGURE 1.12 **Revisiting correlation versus causation** Ice cream consumption and drowning are highly correlated. Obviously, eating ice cream doesn't *cause* people to drown. A third factor, such as high temperatures, increases both ice cream consumption and participation in water-based activities.

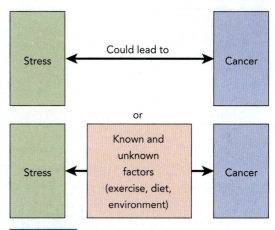

FIGURE 1.13 **Correlation versus causation—The third-variable problem** Research has found a strong correlation between stress and cancer (Chapter 3). However, this correlation does not tell us whether stress causes cancer, whether cancer causes stress, or whether other known and unknown factors, such as smoking, drinking, or poverty, could contribute to both stress and cancer. Can you think of a way to study the effects of stress on cancer that is not correlational—and still ethical?

TABLE 1.5 **Superstitions as Illusory Correlations**

	Behavior	Superstition
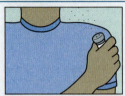	**Wedding plans:** Why do brides wear something old, and something borrowed?	The something old is usually clothing that belongs to an older woman who is happily married. Thus, the bride will supposedly transfer that good fortune to herself. Something borrowed is often a relative's jewelry. This item should be golden, because gold represents the sun, which was once thought to be the source of life.
	**Spilling salt:** Why do some people throw a pinch of salt over their left shoulder?	Years ago, people believed good spirits lived on the right side of the body, and bad spirits on the left. If someone spilled salt, it supposedly meant that a guardian spirit had caused the accident to warn him or her of evil nearby. At the time, salt was scarce and precious. Therefore, the person was advised to bribe the bad spirits with a pinch of salt thrown over his or her left shoulder.
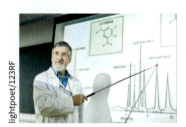	**Knocking on wood:** Why do some people knock on wood when they're speaking of good fortune or making predictions?	Down through the ages, people have believed that trees were homes of gods, who were kind and generous—if approached in the right way. A person who wanted to ask a favor of the tree god would touch the bark. After the favor was granted, the person would return to knock on the tree as a sign of thanks.

The Value of Correlations   After discussing the limits of correlational research, it's important to point out that this research method is still incredibly valuable, offering at least three major advantages:

lightpoet/123RF

1. **Prediction**   A correlation can tell us if a relationship exists between two variables, allowing us to use one variable to predict scores on another. **[AQ5]** Consider the findings of a positive correlation between years of education and health outcomes—see photo (e.g., Frakt, 2019). This correlation means that we can successfully predict that, as your educational level increases, your overall health and life expectancy will also increase. In fact, the age-adjusted mortality rate of high school dropouts ages 25–64 is more than twice that of those with some college (Cutler & Lleras-Muney, 2006; Picker, 2016). This large and persistent correlation between education and health has been observed many times and in many countries. Although there are several possible explanations for this finding, researchers in this area suggest the results are most likely due to better access to health care among the more highly educated, along with improved thinking and decision-making patterns. (Keep this correlation in mind if someone questions you about why you're going to college.)

2. **Real-world settings**   A second value to correlational studies is that, like descriptive studies, they can be conducted in real-world settings to examine relationships that would otherwise be impossible or unethical to study. As mentioned earlier, smoking cigarettes and drinking alcohol while pregnant are highly correlated with birth defects and other poor birth outcomes, and conducting experiments on pregnant women with cigarettes and alcohol would obviously be immoral and illegal. Fortunately, evidence from this strong correlation, along with other research, has helped convince many women to avoid these harmful substances while pregnant—likely preventing many birth defects. Similarly, correlational findings that drunk driving and distracted driving are highly linked with serious and fatal car accidents have led to strict laws that have reduced these practices.

   On a lighter note, research described in Chapter 3 validates a long-suspected link between high stress levels and reduced odds of conception (Akhter et al., 2016). Do you recognize how this type of correlational data offers encouraging news and pleasant options for those trying to conceive—like taking a vacation?

These real-world correlations offer other practical applications. For instance, many parents, professionals, and researchers (mentioned earlier) have repeatedly expressed concerns about the potential ill effects of Facebook and other social media sites on young people. However, when 12 million Facebook users were compared to non-users, researchers found that people with moderate levels of online social interaction and high levels of offline social interaction actually have a lower short-term mortality risk (Hobbs et al., 2016). Research has long showed that people who have strong social networks live longer, but this is the first large-scale study showing that online relationships may be good for our mental and physical health—when used in moderation.

3. **Directions for future research**   Correlational research, like descriptive studies, offers data and ideas for future research. Even though correlation does NOT prove causation, it can point to *possible* causation, which can then become the subject of later experiments (which can prove causation)—the topic of our next section.

Experimental Research

As you've just seen, both descriptive and correlational studies are important because they reveal important data, insights, and practical applications. However, to determine *causation* (what causes what), we need **experimental research**. This method is considered the "gold standard" for scientific research because only through an **experiment** can researchers manipulate and control variables to determine cause and effect.

If you've ever followed a recipe to cook a new dish or tried various methods of dating to see what works best, you're already familiar with the basics of an *experiment*. You manipulated and controlled the variables and then noticed the cause and effect of your efforts. Now, to further help you understand all the important key terms and the general set-up for an experiment, imagine yourself as a psychologist interested in determining how texting while driving a car might affect the number of traffic accidents.

You begin by reviewing the very simple experimental set-up in **Process Diagram 1.2**. Your first task is to develop your *hypothesis* (Step 1), which we defined earlier as a tentative and testable explanation about the relationship between two or more variables.

Next, you solicit volunteers for your experiment (Step 2). To minimize critical differences between participants, you'll need to avoid **sample bias**, which occurs when the researcher recruits and selects individuals who do not accurately reflect the composition of the larger population from which they are drawn. Interestingly, some critics suggest that psychological literature is biased because it too often uses college students as participants. Psychologists counteract potential sample bias by selecting participants who constitute a **random sample** of the entire population of interest, which allows each member of that group an equal chance of being selected.

After randomly sampling, it's important to randomly assign participants to one or more research group(s)—either the **experimental group** or the **control group**—using chance procedures (such as a coin toss or a random numbers table). As defined earlier, random assignment helps ensure that all participants have an equal opportunity to be in either group. Note that having at least two groups allows the performance of one group to be compared with that of another.

Then, both the experimental group and the control group will be assigned to a driving simulator (Step 3). Participants assigned to the *experimental group* receive one level of the **independent variable (IV)**, which is the treatment under study, and the variable being manipulated by you—the experimenter. Those assigned to the *control group* will be treated in every way just like the experimental group. The only difference is that they will NOT text while driving.

In Step 4, while all participants drive for a given amount of time (e.g., 30 minutes in the driving simulator), you, the experimenter, will record the number of simulated traffic accidents—the **dependent variable (DV)**. Note that the goal of any experiment is to learn how the dependent variable is *affected by* (depends on) the independent variable.

Experimental research
A type of research that involves the manipulation and control of variables to determine cause and effect; designed to meet the goal of *explanation*.

Experiment   A careful manipulation of one or more independent variables to measure their effect on other dependent variables; allows the determination of cause-and-effect relationships.

Sample bias   A bias that may occur when research participants are unrepresentative of the larger population or population of interest.

Random sample   A sample that allows each member of the population of interest an equal chance of being selected.

Experimental group   The group that is manipulated (i.e., receives treatment) in an experiment; participants who are exposed to the independent variable (IV).

Control group   The group that is not manipulated (i.e., receives no treatment) during an experiment; participants who are NOT exposed to the independent variable (IV).

Independent variable (IV)   The variable that is manipulated and controlled by the experimenter to determine its causal effect on the dependent variable; also called the treatment variable.

Dependent variable (DV)   The variable that is observed and measured for change; the factor that is affected by (or dependent on) the independent variable.

STOP! This Process Diagram contains essential information NOT found elsewhere in the text, which is likely to appear on quizzes and exams. Be sure to study it CAREFULLY.

PROCESS DIAGRAM 1.2 **Experimental Research Design**   When designing an experiment, researchers must follow certain steps to ensure that their results are scientifically meaningful. In this example, you, as the imaginary experimenter, will be examining whether people texting on phones while driving have more traffic accidents than those who don't text while driving.

Step ❶ The experimenter begins by identifying the hypothesis.

Step ❷ Next, the experimenter solicits volunteers for the experiment. In order to avoid sample bias, the experimenter first attempts to select a random sample of the entire population of interest. Then, the experimenter randomly assigns these participants to two different groups—either the experimental group, which receives the treatment, or the control group, which does not receive the treatment. Having two groups allows a baseline comparison of responses between the two groups.

Step ❸ Both the experimental and the control groups are assigned to a driving simulator. The experimental group then texts while driving, whereas the control group does not text. Texting or not texting are the two levels of the independent variable (IV).

Step ❹ The experimenter counts the number of simulated traffic accidents for each group and then analyzes the data. The number of simulated traffic accidents is the dependent variable (DV). [Note that the DV is called "dependent" because the behavior (or outcome) exhibited by the participants is assumed to *depend* on manipulations of the IV.]

Step ❺ If the differences between the two groups are statistically significant, the experimenter writes up his or her report and submits it to scientific journals for possible publication.

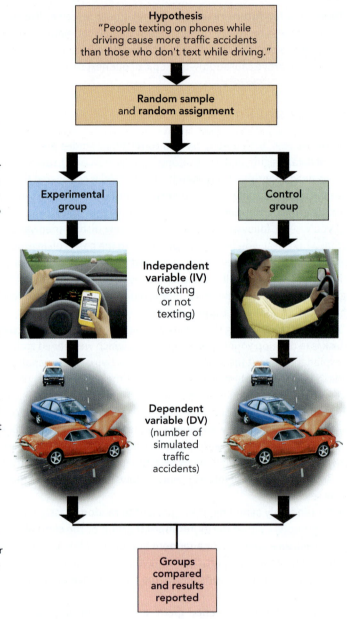

Hypothesis
"People texting on phones while driving cause more traffic accidents than those who don't text while driving."

Random sample and random assignment

Experimental group

Control group

Independent variable (IV) (texting or not texting)

Dependent variable (DV) (number of simulated traffic accidents)

Groups compared and results reported

TIP Are you confused about the difference between independent and dependent variables (IV and DV)? If so, carefully study the "puppet" and "ruler" illustrations, which help illustrate the differences, while also creating a lasting visual picture in your own mind of how:

The experimenter "manipulates" the IV to determine its causal effect on the DV.

The experimenter "measures" the DV, which "depends" on the IV.

Finally, in Step 5, you'll compare the results from both groups. If the differences are significant, you may want to report your findings to a peer-reviewed scientific journal like the ones found in the References section provided at the end of this text. Keep in mind that because the control group was treated exactly like the experimental group, except for the differing levels of the IV, any significant difference in the number of traffic accidents (the DV) between the two groups would be the result of the level of the IV. In contrast, if you found little or no difference between the groups, you would conclude that texting does not affect traffic accidents.

Take-Home Message   Research clearly shows that phone use, particularly texting, while driving leads to increased accidents, and potentially serious or fatal consequences (e.g., Federal Communications Commission, 2019; National Highway Traffic Safety Administration, 2019). In other words: "Let's all just put down our phones and drive."

General Research Problems and Safeguards

As you've seen, descriptive, correlational, and experimental research methods are valuable sources of scientific information, but they also have serious limits and potential biases. To offset these problems, researchers have created several safeguards to protect against potential sources of error on the part of both the researcher and the participants.

Potential Researcher Issues   In addition to the potential biases mentioned earlier (e.g., sample bias and lack of random assignment), during experiments the researcher must be aware of and control for extraneous **confounding variables** (such as time of day, lighting conditions, and room temperature). These variables must be held constant across both experimental and control groups. Otherwise, these variables might contaminate (or confound) the research results (**Figure 1.14**).

Researchers also need to be alert for signs of their own personal beliefs and expectations. Imagine what might happen if an experimenter inadvertently breathed a sigh of relief when a participant gave a response that supported the researcher's hypothesis. This type of behavior, known as **experimenter bias**, can easily influence the research results in the experimenter's expected direction. A closely related type of bias, **demand characteristics**, refers to any aspect of a study that unknowingly communicates to the participants how the experimenter wants them to behave. Rather than influencing the results in an expected direction (experimenter bias), the researcher, or subtle cues or signals within the study, create an implicit *demand* for how participants should behave.

A good example of both experimenter bias and demand characteristics is provided by the case of *Clever Hans*, the famous mathematical "wonder horse"(**Figure 1.15**). One way to prevent such biases from destroying the validity of participants' responses is to establish objective methods for collecting and recording data, such as using computers to present stimuli and record responses.

Experimenters can also skew their results if they assume that behaviors typical in their own culture are typical of all cultures—a bias known as **ethnocentrism**. One way to avoid this problem is to have researchers from two cultures each conduct the same study twice, once with participants from their own culture and once with participants from at least one other culture. This kind of *cross-cultural sampling* isolates group differences in behavior that might stem from any researcher's personal ethnocentrism.

Confounding variable   An extraneous factor that, if not held constant, may contaminate, or confound, the experimental results; also known as the third-variable problem in correlational research.

Experimenter bias   A problem that occurs when the experimenter's behavior and/or expectations inadvertently influence (bias) the outcome of the research.

Demand characteristics   Any aspect of a study that unknowingly communicates to participants how the experimenter wants them to behave; either the researcher or subtle cues or signals within the study, create an implicit *demand* for how participants should behave.

Ethnocentrism   The belief that one's culture is typical of all cultures; also, viewing one's own ethnic group (or culture) as central and "correct" and judging others according to this standard.

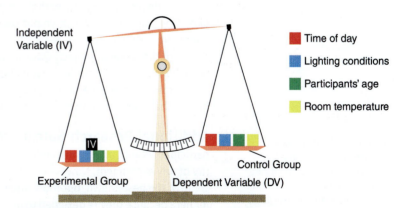

FIGURE 1.14   **Controlling for confounding variables**   Recognizing that certain extraneous variables, like time of day, lighting conditions, etc., may affect their experimental findings, researchers work to make sure the variables are the same for both the experimental group and the control group. Once a particular level of the independent variable (IV) is added to the experimental group, the experimenters check to see if the scale's balance is significantly disrupted. If so, they can then say that the IV *caused* the change. However, if the IV is not "heavy" enough to make a significant difference, then the experiment "failed," and experimenters go back to further refine their approach, start over, or go on to a new project.

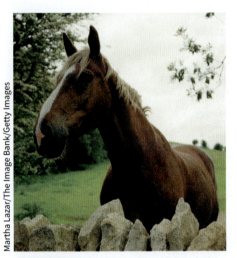

FIGURE 1.15 **Can a horse add, multiply, and divide?** Clever Hans and his owner, Mr. Von Osten, convinced many people that this was indeed the case (Rosenthal, 1965). When asked to multiply 6 times 8, minus 42, Hans would tap his hoof 6 times. Or if asked to divide 48 by 12, add 6, and take away 6, he would tap 4 times. Even when Hans's owner was out of the room and others asked the question, he was still able to answer correctly. How did he do it? Researchers eventually discovered that all questioners naturally lowered their heads to look at Hans's hoof at the end of their question. And Hans had learned that this was a signal to start tapping. When the correct answer was approaching, the questioners also naturally looked up, which signaled Hans to stop. Can you see how this provided an early example of both experimenter bias and demand characteristics?

FIGURE 1.16 **Participant bias and co-sleeping with pets** Research shows that a little over half of all pet owners share their bed with their pets, with about 40 percent reporting that it helps or doesn't significantly interfere with their sleep (Krahn et al., 2015). Interestingly, the researchers noted that pet owners appeared eager to report their sleeping arrangements but reluctant to reveal any undesirable consequences. Can you see how this type of potential participant bias might unintentionally affect research results?

Participant bias A problem that occurs when a research participant's behavior and/or expectations inadvertently influence (bias) the outcome of the research.

Potential Participant Issues

An error similar to researcher bias but produced by participants is called **participant bias**. It may arise if researchers use surveys as their main research method. When participants are asked to self-report on sensitive topics, such as their sexual behaviors, alcohol and other drug consumption, or even their sleeping arrangements with pets, they often distort their own behaviors (**Figure 1.16**).

How do researchers deal with this type of participant bias, also known as *social-desirability bias*? One way is to offer anonymous participation, along with guarantees of privacy and confidentiality. When necessary, researchers can temporarily deceive participants about the true nature of the research project. Obviously, this is a controversial approach, but there are times when it's necessary. In studies examining when and how people help others, participants may not be told the true goal of the study because they might try to present themselves as more helpful than they actually would be in real life.

Single-blind study An experimental technique in which only the participants are unaware of (blind to) who is in the experimental and control groups.

Double-blind study An experimental technique in which both the participants and the researcher(s) are unaware of (blind to) who is in the experimental and control groups.

Placebo An inactive substance or fake treatment used as a control technique in experiments; often used in drug research.

Additional Research Safeguards

So far we've discussed several researcher and participant issues, along with methods for preventing these problems and protecting the integrity of any experiment. Now we'd like to offer a few additional safeguards, which are actually some of the best-known, but most-often confused, types of research controls. We saved them for here because they're designed to minimize both experimenter and participant issues.

Let's begin with **single-blind** and **double-blind studies**. As you can see in **Figure 1.17**, this approach requires experimenters to keep themselves and/or their participants blind to (unaware of) of the treatment or condition to which the participants have been assigned.

Imagine yourself in an experiment in which you are told that the pill you're taking for eight weeks will stop your headaches. Can you see how it's critical that you as a participant, and possibly the experimenter who collects your data, should be blind as to whether you are in the control or experimental group? In this example, this means that if you were a participant you wouldn't know if you were being given the actual, experimental drug or an inactive **placebo** pill that had no physiological effects. Researchers do this because your expectations or beliefs, rather than the experimental treatment, can produce a particular outcome, called a **placebo effect**. Giving members of the control group a placebo, while giving the experimental group a pill with the active ingredients, allows researchers to determine whether changes are due to the pill that's being tested or simply to the participants' expectations.

Quasi-Experimental Design

Given the numerous limits to and problems with the experimental method, some researchers turn to alternative methods called *quasi-experimental designs*. The prefix *quasi-* means "sort of," and in this case the research looks sort of like a true experiment. But it lacks a key ingredient—*random assignment to groups*—because in many situations random assignment is impossible or unethical. Imagine that you wanted to study how a father's later attachment to his child was affected by his presence or absence at that child's birth. You obviously could not randomly assign fathers to either the present-at-birth condition or the absent-at-birth condition.

Knowing that assessing the differences between the two groups still might provide important information, experimenters can compare the two groups without random assignment, and the research method would then be a quasi-experimental design. Why can't these designs make the same strong claims for causation that can be made based on true experiments? Without random assignment, uncontrolled third variables might skew the results.

Summing Up

Recognizing that we've offered a large number of research problems and safeguards associated with the various research methods (descriptive, correlational, and experimental), we've gathered them all into **Figure 1.18**. Be sure to study it carefully.

Given all these problems, should we simply pack our bags and go home? Of course not. As you can see in **Table 1.6**, there are advantages and disadvantages to each method, and psychological research does have its limits. Nevertheless, having a general understanding of research methods will help guide you through the often conflicting claims made in newspapers, in television ads, and by our friends and neighbors. Research findings have also offered solutions to practical problems, led us to significant improvements in our personal and interpersonal lives, and provided invaluable guidelines that will help us make more informed decisions. If you'd like additional information about research methods and statistical analyses, see Appendix A. Note also that each chapter of this text offers an in-depth analysis of a hot topic in research, along with its own, built-in, self-grading quiz (see the following **RC Research Challenge**).

Participants   **Researcher**

Single-blind procedure
Only the participants are unaware of (blind to) who is in the experimental or control groups.

Double-blind procedure
Both the participants and researcher(s) are unaware of (blind to) who is in the experimental or control groups.

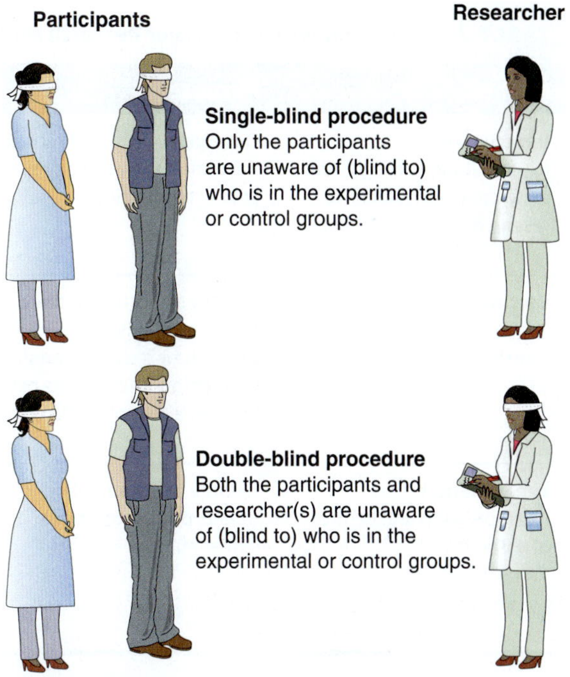

FIGURE 1.17 **A single- or double-blind experimental design**   To scientifically evaluate the effectiveness of something like a new drug, researchers administering the experimental drug, and the participants taking the drug, must be unaware of (or "blind" to) who is receiving a *placebo* (a fake pill), and who is receiving the drug itself. Placebos are necessary because researchers know that participants' beliefs and expectations can change their responses and the experimental outcome—the so-called "placebo effect" (Leibowitz et al., 2019; Yanes et al., 2019).

Placebo effect   A change that occurs when a participant's expectations or beliefs, rather than the actual drug or treatment, influences the experimental outcome.

Researcher

Potential problems
Sample bias, third and confounding variables, experimenter bias, ethnocentrism

Potential solutions
Representative sampling, random assignment, computers (input, score data), cross-cultural sampling, double-blind studies, and placebos

Participant

Potential problems
Participant bias, social desirability response

Potential solutions
Single- and double-blind studies, placebos, anonymity, privacy, confidentiality, and deception

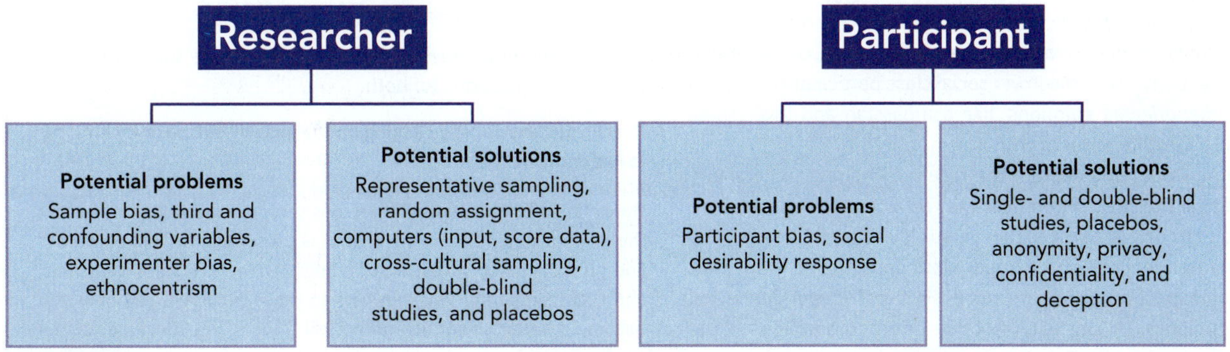

FIGURE 1.18   **Potential research problems and solutions**

TABLE 1.6 Psychology's Three Major Research Methods

Method	Purpose	Advantages	Disadvantages	
Descriptive (observation, survey/interview, case study, archival research)	Observe, collect, and record data (meets psychology's goal of description)	Minimizes artificiality, makes data collection easier, allows description of behavior and mental processes as they occur	Little or no control over variables, potential biases, cannot identify cause and effect	
Correlational (statistical analyses of relationships between variables)	Identify strength and direction of relationships, and assess how well one variable predicts another (meets psychology's goal of prediction)	Allows prediction and helps clarify relationships between variables that cannot be examined by other methods	Little or no control over variables, cannot identify cause and effect, possible illusory correlation and third-variable problem, and potential biases	
Experimental (manipulation and control of variables)	Identify cause and effect (meets psychology's goal of explanation)	Allows researchers more precise control over variables, and provides explanation of the causes of behavior and mental processes	Ethical concerns, practical limitations, artificiality of lab conditions, uncontrolled variables may confound results, and potential biases	

RC Scientific Thinking: **Research Challenge**

Is Happiness Defined by Your Social Class?

(APA Goal 2.4) Interpret, design, and conduct basic psychological research

Earlier in this chapter, we discussed research in positive psychology showing that once we have enough income to meet our basic needs, additional funds won't significantly increase our levels of happiness. In short, money doesn't buy happiness. However, now that you've studied the basics of psychological research and are applying your scientific and critical thinking skills, do you wonder how happiness was identified and defined? Researchers interested in the emotional components of happiness, and how these components might vary among people in different socioeconomic classes, recruited a large nationally representative U.S. sample of 1,519 individuals (Piff & Moskowitz, 2018). Participants were asked to self-report on their tendencies to experience seven different positive emotions that are core to happiness—amusement, awe, compassion, contentment, enthusiasm, love, and pride.

Can you predict their findings? Interestingly, wealthier participants (as measured by household income) were more likely to report *self-focused* emotions, such as amusement, contentment, and pride. Conversely, the lower social class participants reported more *other-oriented* emotions, like compassion and love. There were no class differences in enthusiasm.

How would you explain the results? The researchers suggested that the class differences may reflect varying social concerns and priorities of the higher versus lower social classes. The self-oriented feelings of the upper-class participants may result from their specific upbringing and desires for independence and self-sufficiency. In contrast, the other-oriented emotions of the lower-class may follow from growing up in more threatening environments, which possibly led to a greater desire for compassion, love, and more interdependent bonds. What do you think? Given that you may be attending college hoping to secure a high-paying job, how can you apply this research to your own career and relationship aspirations?

Identify the Research Method

1. Based on the information provided, did this study (Piff & Moskowitz, 2018) use descriptive, correlational, and/or experimental research?

2. If you chose:

   ○ *descriptive research*, is this a naturalistic or laboratory observation, survey/interview, case study, and/or archival research?

   ○ *correlational research*, is this a positive, negative, or zero correlation?

   ○ *experimental research*, label the IV, DV, experimental group(s), and control group. (Note: If participants were not randomly assigned to groups, list the design as *quasi-experimental*.)

   ○ both *descriptive* and *correlational*, answer the corresponding questions for both.

Check your answers by clicking on the answer button or by looking in Appendix B.

Note: The information provided in this study is admittedly limited, but the level of detail is similar to what is presented in most textbooks and public reports of research findings. Answering these questions, and then comparing your answers to those provided, will help you become a better scientific and critical thinker and consumer of scientific research.

Retrieval Practice 1.3 | Psychology's Research Methods

Self-Test   Completing this self-test, and then checking your answers by clicking on the answer button or by looking in Appendix B, will provide immediate feedback and helpful practice for exams.

1. When a researcher observes or measures two or more variables to find relationships between them, without directly manipulating them or implying a causal relationship, he or she is conducting _____ .
   - **a.** experimental research
   - **c.** non-causal metrics
   - **b.** a correlational study
   - **d.** a meta-analysis

2. When participants are not exposed to any amount or level of the independent variable, they are members of the _____ group.
   - **a.** control
   - **b.** experimental
   - **c.** observation
   - **d.** out-of-control

3. If researchers gave participants varying amounts of a new memory drug and then gave them a story to read and measured their scores on a quiz, the _____ would be the IV, and the _____ would be the DV.
   - **a.** response to the drug; amount of the drug
   - **b.** experimental group; control group
   - **c.** amount of the drug; quiz scores
   - **d.** researcher variables; extraneous variables

4. When both the researcher and the participants are unaware of who is in the experimental or control group, the research design can be called _____ .
   - **a.** agnostic
   - **b.** double-blind
   - **c.** valid
   - **d.** quasi-experimental

Q Test Your Critical Thinking

1. Which form of research would you most trust: descriptive, correlational, experimental, or a meta-analysis? Why?

2. Cigarette companies have suggested that there is no scientific evidence that smoking causes lung cancer. How would you refute this claim?

Real World Application Questions

[AQ4] Does spending more time on Instagram decrease your psychological well-being?

[AQ5] Is there a correlation between years of education and physical health?

Hint: Look in the text for **[AQ4]** and **[AQ5]**

1.4 | Secrets of Student Success

LEARNING OBJECTIVES

Retrieval Practice   While reading the upcoming sections, respond to each Learning Objective in your own words.

Review the key strategies for student success.

- **Describe** the four steps you can take to improve your study habits.

- **Discuss** ways to improve your time management.
- **Identify** the key factors in grade improvement.

Real World Application Question

[AQ6] What are the best study techniques for improving your exam performance?

In this closing section, you will find several important, well-documented study tips and techniques guaranteed to make you a more efficient and successful college student. In fact, an experiment with randomly assigned college students found that the group of students who were asked to self-reflect and to identify and use learning resources wisely improved their class performance by an average of one-third of a letter grade compared to the group that did not self-reflect (Chen et al., 2017). For an example of this type of self-reflection, and an overview of the major topics in this section, be sure to **Test Yourself** by completing the following checklist.

PA Practical Application

Test Yourself: Student Success Checklist

Answer true or false to each item. Then for each item that you answered "True," pay particular attention to the corresponding heading in this *Secrets of Student Success* section.

Study Habits

_____ **1.** While reading, I often get lost in all the details and can't pick out the most important points.

_____ **2.** When I finish studying a chapter, I frequently can't remember what I've just read.

_____ **3.** I generally study with either the TV or music playing in the background.

_____ **4.** I tend to read each section of a chapter at the same speed, instead of slowing down on the difficult sections.

Time Management

_____ **5.** I can't keep up with my reading assignments given all the other demands on my time (see photo).

_____ **6.** I typically wait to study, and then "cram" right before a test.

_____ **7.** I go to almost all my classes, but I generally don't take notes and often find myself texting, playing games on my computer, or daydreaming.

Freddy Cahyono/123RF

Grade Improvement

_____ **8.** I study and read ahead of time, but during a test I frequently find that my mind goes blank.

_____ **9.** Although I study and read before tests and think I'll do well, I often find that the exam questions are much harder than I expected.

_____ **10.** I wish I could perform better on tests and read faster or more efficiently.

_____ **11.** Going to class is a waste of time.

_____ **12.** I just can't do well on tests.

Study Habits

If you answered "True" to one or more of questions 1–4, try these four ways to improve your study habits and to more successfully read (and remember) information in this and most other texts:

1. **Familiarization**   The first step to good study habits is to familiarize yourself with the text so that you can take full advantage of its contents. Scanning through the Chapter Outline will give you a bird's-eye view of each chapter. Also, be sure to note the various tables, figures, photographs, and special feature boxes, all of which will enhance your understanding of the chapter content.

2. **Active Reading**   The next step is to make a conscious decision to *actively* read and learn the material (Putnam et al., 2016). Reading a text is *not* like reading a novel or fun articles on the Internet. You must tell your brain to slow down, focus on details, and save the material for future recall (see the **Test Yourself**).

SQ4R method   A study technique based on six steps: Survey, Question, Read, Recite, Review, and wRite.

Perhaps the most effective way to practice reading actively is to use the **SQ4R method**, which was developed by Francis Robinson (1970). The initials stand for six steps in effective reading: Survey, Question, Read, Recite, Review, and wRite (**Process Diagram 1.3**). Taking notes (wRite) while you're reading and studying can be particularly helpful. Ask yourself, "What is the

PA Practical Application

Test Yourself: Demonstrating the Importance of Active Reading

a. Using a stopwatch, test to see how fast you can name the color of each rectangular box.

GREEN   RED   BROWN   RED

BROWN   GREEN   GREEN   BLUE

GREEN   BROWN   RED   BLUE

b. Now, time yourself to see how fast you can state the color of ink used to print each word, ignoring what each word says.

After timing yourself on both tasks, how did you do? Interestingly, young children who have learned their colors, but have not yet learned to read, easily name the colors in both sections in about the same amount of time. However, virtually every adult takes more time, and makes more errors on (b) than on (a). This is because, over time, our well-learned ability to read words has become a *passive* task, which interferes with the less common *active* task of naming the color rather than the words.

We include this demonstration, known as the *Stroop effect*, here because it helps illustrate the importance of active reading. If you passively read a chapter in a text once, or even several times, you'll still do poorly on an exam. Just as it takes more time to state the color in part (b), it will take you more time and effort to override your well-learned passive reading, and focus on the details to truly learn and master the material.

> **STOP!** This Process Diagram contains essential information NOT found elsewhere in the text, which is likely to appear on quizzes and exams. Be sure to study it CAREFULLY.

PROCESS DIAGRAM 1.3   **Using the SQ4R Method**   Follow these steps to improve your reading efficiency.

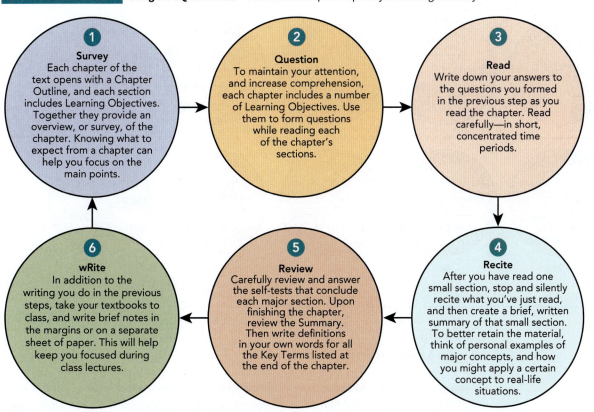

1 Survey
Each chapter of the text opens with a Chapter Outline, and each section includes Learning Objectives. Together they provide an overview, or survey, of the chapter. Knowing what to expect from a chapter can help you focus on the main points.

2 Question
To maintain your attention, and increase comprehension, each chapter includes a number of Learning Objectives. Use them to form questions while reading each of the chapter's sections.

3 Read
Write down your answers to the questions you formed in the previous step as you read the chapter. Read carefully—in short, concentrated time periods.

6 wRite
In addition to the writing you do in the previous steps, take your textbooks to class, and write brief notes in the margins or on a separate sheet of paper. This will help keep you focused during class lectures.

5 Review
Carefully review and answer the self-tests that conclude each major section. Upon finishing the chapter, review the Summary. Then write definitions in your own words for all the Key Terms listed at the end of the chapter.

4 Recite
After you have read one small section, stop and silently recite what you've just read, and then create a brief, written summary of that small section. To better retain the material, think of personal examples of major concepts, and how you might apply a certain concept to real-life situations.

main idea?" Then write down key ideas and supporting details and examples. As you might have guessed, this text was designed to incorporate each of the six steps in the SQ4R method.

3. **Avoid highlighting and rereading** Marking with a yellow highlighter, or underlining potentially important portions of material, and rereading text material after initial reading,

are common techniques students frequently use while studying. Unfortunately, they are almost always a waste of time. Research clearly shows that highlighting and rereading are among the LEAST effective of all the major study techniques, whereas *distributed practice* and *practice testing* (explained later in the grade improvement section) are the MOST effective. As previously discussed, you need to actively focus on your reading. Highlighting and rereading generally encourage passive reading.

4. **Overlearn** Many students tend to study new material just to the point where they can recite the information, without attempting to understand it more deeply. For best results, however, you should overlearn. In other words, be sure you fully understand how key terms and concepts are related to one another and can generate examples other than the ones in the text. Overlearning also involves carefully reviewing the material (by visualizing the phenomena that are described and explained in the text and by rehearsing what you have learned) until the information is firmly locked in place. This is particularly important if you suffer from test anxiety. Would you like a quick demonstration of why we sometimes need to overlearn? See the following **Test Yourself**.

PA Practical Application

Test Yourself: Demonstrating the Importance of Overlearning

Can you identify which one of these 10 pennies is an exact duplicate of a real U.S. penny? Unless you're a coin collector, you probably can't easily choose the correct one without comparing it to a real coin—despite having seen thousands of pennies. Why? As you will discover later in the text

(Chapter 7), you must encode (or process) the information in some way before it will be successfully stored in your long-term memory. Given that most of us don't need to carefully study and overlearn the details of what a penny looks like, because we can function in our everyday world with a superficial glance at the coin, why are we providing this demo? The point is that if you're going to take a test on pennies, or any material, you need to carefully study to the point of overlearning in order to do well.

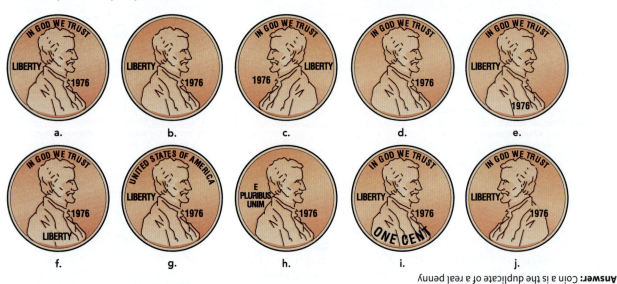

Answer: Coin a is the duplicate of a real penny

Time Management

If you answered "True" to one or more of the questions 5–7 in the Student Success Checklist at the start of this section, and find that you aren't always good at budgeting your time, here are four basic time-management strategies:

- **Establish a baseline.** Before attempting any changes, simply record your day-to-day activities for one to two weeks (see the sample in **Figure 1.19**). You may be surprised at how you spend your time.

	Sunday	Monday	Tuesday	Wednesday	Thursday	Friday	Saturday
7:00		Breakfast		Breakfast		Breakfast	
8:00		History	Breakfast	History	Breakfast	History	
9:00		Psychology	Statistics	Psychology	Statistics	Psychology	
10:00		Review History and Psychology	Campus Job	Review History and Psychology	Statistics Lab	Review History and Psychology	
11:00		Biology		Biology		Biology	
12:00		Lunch / Study		Exercise	Lunch	Exercise	
1:00		Bio Lab	Lunch	Lunch	Study	Lunch	
2:00			Study	Study			

FIGURE 1.19 **Sample record of daily activities**   To help manage your time, draw a grid similar to this, and record your daily activities in appropriate boxes. Then fill in other necessities, such as daily maintenance tasks and downtime.

- **Set up a realistic schedule.**   Make a daily and weekly "to do" list, including all required activities, basic maintenance tasks (like laundry, cooking, child care, and eating), and a reasonable amount of downtime. Then create a daily schedule of activities that includes time for each of these. To make permanent time-management changes, shape your behavior, starting with small changes and building on them.

- **Reward yourself.**   Give yourself immediate, tangible rewards for sticking with your daily schedule, such as calling a friend, getting a snack, or checking your social media.

- **Maximize your time.**   To increase your efficiency, begin by paying close attention to the amount of time you spend on true, focused studying versus the time you waste worrying, complaining, and fiddling around getting ready to study ("fretting and prepping").

Time experts point out that people often overlook important *time opportunities*—spare moments that normally go to waste that you might use productively. When you use public transportation, review notes or read your textbook. While waiting for doctor or dental appointments or to pick up your kids after school, take out your text or electronic device and study for 10 to 20 minutes. Hidden moments count. See the following **PAH** **Practical Application Highlight** for a general overview and specific techniques for improving your grades and furthering your student success.

Final Take-Home Message   Success in college, and in virtually all parts of life, is
within your control. Given that you've read this *Secrets of Student Success* section, we're confident that you will do well. Our final tip is to *write out your goals* for success in this course and all other important parts of your life. Research shows that making a habit of writing down your goals definitely leads to higher performance (Murphy, 2018; Stringer, 2017; van der Hoek et al., 2018). Why? The writing process helps us focus on relevant versus irrelevant activities, while increasing our effort and persistence.

PAH   **Practical Application Highlight**

Tips for Grade Improvement

(APA Goal 1.3) Describe applications of psychology

In combination with the previous study habit and time management tips, the following strategies are virtually guaranteed to improve your overall grade point average (GPA) in all your college classes and your mastery of the material.

1. **Refuse to multitask on new or complex material.**   Are you one of the many students who believe that doing more than one task at a time makes you more effective? If so, you'll be surprised to know that this so-called "multitasking" is actually just "task-switching," and that it clearly decreases overall performance and productivity—particularly for new or complex tasks (Aagaard, 2019; Bender et al., 2017; Ralph et al., 2019). As you discovered earlier in the section on active reading and the *Test Yourself* Stroop test, switching from one task to another (reading a word while trying to state its color) greatly increased your response time—and errors.

    Can you see how this explains why texting and driving (or walking) is so dangerous (Chapter 5), and how casually listening to the professor, while also texting, playing computer games, or talking to other classmates, is largely a waste of time? In fact, a study in an introductory psychology class found that Internet use during lectures was *negatively correlated* with student performance, which means, as you learned earlier in this chapter, that as Internet usage went up performance went down (Ravizza et al., 2017). A good rule to remember is that one hour of full attention in class is generally worth about four hours on your own outside of class. In addition to paying full attention, taking detailed notes by hand versus a laptop during each class session is one of the most efficient and profitable uses of your time (Mueller & Oppenheimer, 2014).

2. **Maximize the value of each class session.**   As you know, the authors of this text are both college professors, so this advice may sound biased. However, solid psychological research (e.g., Putnam et al., 2016) recommends that all students do the following:

    - **Prepare ahead of time.**   Be sure to study the assigned material ahead of each class.

    - **Attend every class.**   Most instructors provide unique ideas and personal examples that are not in the text, and even when they do repeat what is covered in the text, we all need to have multiple exposures to new material. Also, pay close attention to what your professor emphasizes in class, as this material is likely to appear on exams. Think of your professor's lecture as you would tips from your coach or an employer who was going out of his or her way to tell you what you needed to know to maximize your performance or paycheck.

3. **Improve your general test-taking skills.**   Virtually all students can improve their performance on exams by taking additional courses designed to develop their reading speed and comprehension. During exams, expect a bit of stress but don't panic. Pace yourself and focus on what you know. Skip over questions when you don't know the answers, and then go back if time allows. On multiple-choice exams, carefully read each question and all the alternative answers, before responding. Answer all questions

and make sure you have recorded your answers correctly.

Also, bear in mind that information relevant to one question is often found in another test question. Do not hesitate to change an answer if you get more information—or even if you simply have a better guess about an answer. Contrary to the belief held by many students (and faculty) that "your first hunch is your best guess," research suggests this is NOT the case (Benjamin et al., 1984; Lilienfeld et al., 2010, 2015). Changing answers is far more likely to result in a higher score (**Figure 1.20**).

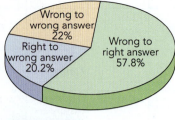

FIGURE 1.20 **Should you change your answers?**   Research clearly shows that answer changes that go from a wrong to a right answer (57.8 percent) greatly outnumber those that go from a right to a wrong answer (20.2 percent).

Source: Benjamin et al., 1984.

4. **[AQ6]** **Distribute your practice and practice test taking.**   Research has firmly established that these last two techniques—*distributed practice* and *practice testing*—are the MOST important keys

to grade improvement—see photo (Carpenter & Yeung, 2017; Gagnon & Cormier, 2018; Trumbo et al., 2016). Why? Spreading your study sessions out over time (distributed practice) and practice testing are far more efficient than waiting until right before an exam and cramming in all the information at once (massed practice) (Chapter 7). If you were a basketball player, you wouldn't wait until the night before a big play-off game to practice. Just as you need to repeatedly practice your free throw shot to become a good basketball player, you need to repeatedly practice your test-taking to become a good student.

    Based on this growing body of research and our own teaching success with frequent testing, we've designed this text to include numerous, distributed practice opportunities sprinkled throughout each chapter. As you're actively reading and studying, be sure to complete all these self-tests. When you miss a question, it's very helpful, and important, to immediately go back and reread the sections of the text that correspond to your incorrect response. You can also easily access the free flashcards and other forms of self-testing provided with the purchase of this text.

5. **Adjust your attitude.** We've saved our best tip—*attitude adjustment*—for last. You have the power to decide that you can, and will, improve your academic skills. Instead of focusing on negative thoughts, such as "I can't go to the party because I have to study" or "Going to class feels like a waste of time," try counter statements, like "I'm going to learn how to study and make better use of my class time, so that I can have more free time." Similarly, rather than thinking or saying "I never do well on tests," do something constructive like taking a study skills and/or test preparation course at your college.

Before going on, be sure to complete the final Retrieval Practice quiz 1.4 below, and then answer the critical thinking questions in the following **Test Your Critical Thinking**.

Retrieval Practice 1.4 | Secrets of Student Success

Self-Test   Completing this self-test, and then checking your answers by clicking on the answer button or by looking in Appendix B, will provide immediate feedback and helpful practice for exams.

1. Which of the following is NOT one of the recommended study habits?

   a. active reading   c. highlighting

   b. familiarization   d. note taking

2. One of the clearest findings in psychology is that _____ practice is a much more efficient way to study and learn than _____ practice.

   a. spaced (distributed); massed   c. applied; basic

   b. active; passive   d. none of these options

3. _____ is particularly important if you suffer from test anxiety.

   a. Overlearning   c. Active studying

   b. Hyper-soma control   d. Passive listening

4. Research suggests that _____ might be two of the most important keys to improving your grades.

a. highlighting and rereading

b. personal control and better time management

c. active studying and the SQ4R method

d. distributed practice and practice testing

Q Test Your Critical Thinking

1. What topic or secret for student success do you consider most valuable? Why?

2. What prevents you or other students you know from fully employing the strategies for student success presented in this chapter?

Real World Application Question

[AQ6]   What are the best study techniques for improving your exam performance?

Olga_Danylenko/iStock/Getty Images

Hint: Look in the text for **[AQ6]**

Q Test Your Critical Thinking

We began this chapter with six intriguing, chapter opening questions, and you were asked to revisit these questions at the end of each section. Questions like these have an important and lasting impact on all of our lives. See if you can answer these additional critical thinking questions related to real-world examples. Did you notice and wonder why we provided six Real Word Application Questions [AQ1–AQ6] throughout the chapter? We've found that they not only help you to engage with and master the material, but also have an important and lasting impact on your critical thinking skills. For additional mastery and enrichment, consider the following questions:

1. Non-human animals, like the mice in this photo, are sometimes used in psychological research when it would be impractical or unethical to use human participants. Do you believe non-human animal research is ethical? Why or why not?

2. What research questions might require the use of non-human animals? How would you ensure the proper treatment of these animals?

3. Imagine you designed an experiment to test whether watching violent TV might increase aggression in children. Assuming that you did find a significant increase, can you think of reasons the findings might not generalize to real-world situations?

Jonathan Selig/The Image Bank/Getty Images

4. You may have heard that dog owners are healthier than cat owners, which leads some to believe that getting a dog would improve their health. Given this chapter's repeated warning that "correlation does not prove causation," can you think of an alternative explanation for why dog owners might be healthier?

5. How does psychology's emphasis on scientific thinking and the scientific method contribute to critical thinking?

Summary

1.1 What Is Psychology?   2

- **Psychology** is the scientific study of *behavior* and *mental processes*. The discipline places high value on **scientific thinking** and **critical thinking**. *Pseudosciences*, such as belief in psychic powers, are not based on scientific evidence.

- Wilhelm Wundt, considered the father of psychology, and his followers were interested in studying conscious experience. Their approach, **structuralism**, sought to identify the basic structures of mental life through introspection.

- The **functionalism** perspective, promoted by William James, considered the father of American psychology, studied the way the behavior and mental processes function to enable humans and non-human animals to adapt to their environment.

- The **psychoanalytic perspective**, founded by Sigmund Freud, emphasized unconscious processes, unresolved conflicts, and past experiences.
- Contemporary psychology reflects the ideas of seven major perspectives: **psychodynamic, behavioral, humanistic, cognitive, biological, evolutionary,** and **sociocultural**.
- Despite early societal limitations, women and people of color have made important contributions to psychology. Pioneers include Mary Calkins, Margaret Floy Washburn, Francis Cecil Sumner, and Kenneth and Mamie Clark.
- Most contemporary psychologists embrace a unifying perspective known as the **biopsychosocial model**.
- Psychologists work as therapists, researchers, teachers, and consultants, in a wide range of settings.

1.2 Scientific Research   12

- Psychology's four basic goals are to *describe, explain, predict,* and *change* behavior and mental processes. One of psychology's most enduring debates is the **nature–nurture controversy**.
- **Basic research** is conducted to advance core scientific knowledge, whereas **applied research** works to address practical, real-world problems.
- Most scientific investigations consist of six basic steps, collectively known as the **scientific method,** which is the cyclical and cumulative research process used for gathering and interpreting objective information in a way that minimizes error and yields dependable results. Scientific progress comes from repeatedly challenging and revising existing **theories** and building new ones.
- Psychologists must maintain high ethical standards, including respecting the rights of therapy clients and research participants (both human and non-human). **Informed consent**, voluntary participation, restricted deception (followed by **debriefing**), and confidentiality are critical elements of research using human participants. U.S. researchers and clinicians are held professionally responsible by the APA and APS, their research institutions, and local and state agencies.

1.3 Psychology's Research Methods   20

- **Descriptive research** systematically observes and records behavior and mental processes to meet the goal of *description*, without manipulating variables. The four major types of descriptive research are **observation, survey/interview, case study,** and **archival research**.
- **Correlational research** examines the possible relationship between variables, and it provides important information about those relationships and valuable predictions. Researchers analyze their results using a **correlation coefficient**. Correlations can be *positive*, when they vary in the same direction, or *negative*, meaning they vary in opposite directions. A *zero* correlation occurs when there is no relationship between the variables. A correlation between two variables does not necessarily mean that one causes the other. There could be a **third-variable problem** or an **illusory correlation**. It's important to remember that *correlation does not prove causation.*
- **Experimental research** manipulates and controls variables to determine cause and effect. An experiment has several critical components: **hypothesis, independent** and **dependent variables,** and **experimental** and **control groups**. A good scientific experiment protects against potential sources of *bias* (or error), including **sample bias, experimenter bias, ethnocentrism, and participant bias**. Good experiments also provide rigorous experimental controls, including **representative sampling, random assignment, single- and double-blind studies, placebos**, privacy and confidentiality.

1.4 Secrets of Student Success   31

- To improve your study habits, try familiarization, active reading (including the SQ4R method) and overlearning, while avoiding highlighting and rereading.
- For better time management, establish a baseline, set up a realistic schedule, reward yourself, and maximize your time.
- To improve your grades, refuse to multitask on new material, maximize each class session, improve your general test-taking skills, distribute your study sessions, practice testing, and adjust your attitude.

Key Terms

Retrieval Practice   Write your own definition for each term before turning back to the referenced page to check your answer.

- applied research   13
- archival research   21
- basic research   13
- behavioral perspective   7
- biological perspective   8
- biopsychosocial model   9
- case study   21
- cognitive perspective   7
- confounding variable   27
- control group   25
- correlation coefficient   22
- correlational research   21
- critical thinking   4
- debriefing   18
- demand characteristic   27
- dependent variable (DV)   25
- descriptive research   20
- double-blind study   28
- ethnocentrism   27

- evolutionary perspective   8
- experiment   25
- experimental group   25
- experimental research   25
- experimenter bias   27
- functionalism   5
- humanistic perspective   7
- hypothesis   15
- illusory correlation   23
- independent variable (IV)   25
- informed consent   18
- meta-analysis   15
- natural selection   8
- nature–nurture controversy   13
- observation   20
- operational definition   15
- participant bias   28
- placebo   28
- placebo effect   29

- positive psychology   7
- psychoanalytic perspective   5
- psychodynamic perspective   7
- psychology   2
- random sample   25
- random assignment   15
- replicate   16
- sample bias   25
- scientific method   13
- scientific thinking   3
- single-blind study   28
- sociocultural perspective   8
- SQ4R method   32
- structuralism   5
- survey/interview   20
- theory   16
- third-variable problem   23
- variable   15

CHAPTER 2

Kuttelvaserova Stuchelova/Shutterstock.com

Neuroscience and Biological Foundations

Caiaimage/Paul Bradbury/OJO+/Getty Images

Real World Application Questions [AQ]

Things you'll learn in Chapter 2

[AQ1] Can singing or dancing make you feel closer to strangers, while also raising your pain threshold?

[AQ2] Why does eye contact with your dog make you feel good?

[AQ3] Would stem cell injections have saved "Superman"?

[AQ4] Could gently riding a bike for ten minutes affect your memory and hippocampus?

[AQ5] Why are some professional athletes at increased risk of depression, dementia, and suicide?

[AQ6] Can high-fat foods decrease your cognitive efficiency?

Throughout the chapter, look for [AQ1]–[AQ6] icons. They indicate where the text addresses these questions.

CHAPTER OUTLINE

2.1 | Neural and Hormonal Processes

LEARNING OBJECTIVES

Retrieval Practice While reading the upcoming sections, respond to each Learning Objective in your own words.

Describe the key features and functions of the nervous and endocrine systems.

- **Describe** the neuron's key components and their respective functions.
- **Explain** how neurons communicate throughout the body.

- **Describe** the roles of hormones and the endocrine system.

Real World Application Questions

[AQ1] Can singing or dancing make you feel closer to strangers, while also raising your pain threshold?

[AQ2] Why does eye contact with your dog make you feel good?

The brain is the last and grandest biological frontier, the most complex thing we have yet discovered in our universe. It contains hundreds of billions of cells interlinked through trillions of connections. The brain boggles the mind.

—James Watson (Nobel Prize winner)

We begin this chapter with a look at the neuron, hormones, and the endocrine system. Following this, we discuss the overall organization and key functions of the nervous system. We conclude with a brief tour of the major structures of the brain.

Understanding the Neuron

Stop for a moment and consider your full human body. Did you know that your brain and nervous system are responsible for receiving, transmitting, and interpreting all the sensory information from both your internal and the external environment? Are you surprised to learn that your body is composed of about ten trillion cells divided into about 200 different types—muscle cells, heart cells, etc.? For psychologists, the approximately one trillion nerve cells, called **neurons,** are the most important of all these cells because they receive, integrate, and transmit information throughout the entire nervous system. This intricate system of communication is responsible for all your thoughts, feelings, and actions.

Neurons are held in place and supported by **glial cells**, which make up about 90 percent of the brain's total cells. They supply nutrients and oxygen, perform cleanup tasks, and insulate one neuron from another so that their neural messages are not scrambled. In addition, they play a direct role in nervous system communication, your immune system, and even in the initiation and progression of neurodegenerative diseases like Alzheimer's disease (AD) (Geyer et al., 2019; Lee & Chung, 2019; Sénécal et al., 2016). In short, neurons simply could not function without glial cells. However, the "star" of the communication show is still the neuron.

Structure of the Neuron It's important to recognize that there are different types of neurons, but they generally share three basic features: **dendrites**, the **cell body**, and an **axon** (**Figure 2.1**). *Dendrites* look like leafless branches of a tree. In fact, the word *dendrite* means "little tree" in Greek. Each neuron may have hundreds or thousands of dendrites, which act like antennas to receive electrochemical information from other nearby neurons. The information then flows into the *cell body*, or *soma* (Greek for "body"). If the cell body receives enough information/stimulation from its dendrites, it will pass the message on to a long, tubelike structure, called the *axon* (from the Greek word for "axle"). The axon then carries information away from the cell body to the *terminal buttons*.

Just as skin covers your body, the **myelin sheath**, a white, fatty coating (or "skin") surrounds the axons of some neurons. Also like your skin, this membrane separates the inside of the neuron from the outside environment. This sheath is not considered one of the three key features of a neuron, but it plays the essential roles of insulating and speeding neural impulses.

Neuron The basic building block (nerve cell) of the nervous system; responsible for receiving, integrating, and transmitting electrochemical information.

Glial cells The cells that provide structural, nutritional, and other functions for neurons; also called glia or neuroglia.

Dendrites The branching fibers of a neuron that receive information (signals) from other neurons and convey impulses toward the cell body.

Cell body The part of a neuron that contains the cell nucleus and other structures that help the neuron carry out its functions; also known as the soma.

Axon A long, tubelike structure that conveys impulses away from a neuron's cell body toward other neurons or to muscles or glands.

Myelin sheath The layer of fatty insulation wrapped around the axon of some neurons that increases the rate at which neural impulses travel.

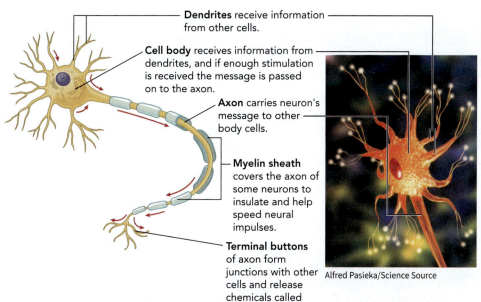

Dendrites receive information from other cells.

Cell body receives information from dendrites, and if enough stimulation is received the message is passed on to the axon.

Axon carries neuron's message to other body cells.

Myelin sheath covers the axon of some neurons to insulate and help speed neural impulses.

Terminal buttons of axon form junctions with other cells and release chemicals called neurotransmitters.

Alfred Pasieka/Science Source

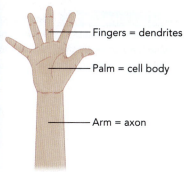

TIP Want an easy way to learn the three key parts of a neuron? Visualize your hand and arm, with your fingers as the dendrites, your palm as the cell body, and your arm as the axon.

Fingers = dendrites

Palm = cell body

Arm = axon

FIGURE 2.1 **Key parts and functions of a neuron** Red arrows in the figure indicate the direction of information flow: dendrites → cell body → axon → terminal buttons of axon. To understand how information travels through the neuron, think of the three key parts in reverse alphabetical order: Dendrite → Cell Body → Axon (D, C, B, A).

As you'll discover in the next section, the human body is essentially an information-processing system dependent upon electrical impulses and chemical messengers. Like the wires in data cables, which are insulated from one another by plastic, the myelin sheath provides insulation and separation for the numerous axons that travel throughout your body. Similarly, data cable wires are bundled together into larger cables, just as your myelin-coated axons are bundled together into "cables" called *nerves.*

The importance of myelin sheaths becomes readily apparent in certain diseases, such as *multiple sclerosis,* in which myelin progressively deteriorates and the person gradually loses muscular coordination. Fortunately, the disease often goes into remission, but it can be fatal if it strikes the neurons that control basic life-support processes, such as breathing or heartbeat. Myelin is also very important in the first few weeks and months of life. Research shows that social isolation during these critical periods (as occurs for babies who are neglected in some orphanages, see photo) prevents cells from producing the right amount of myelin. Sadly, this loss of normal levels of myelin can lead to long-term problems in cognitive functioning (Makinodan et al., 2012; Turner, 2019).

Having described the structure, function, and importance of the neuron itself, we also need to explain that we have two general types of neurons—sensory and motor. *Sensory neurons* respond to physical stimuli by sending neural messages to your brain and nervous system. In contrast, *motor neurons* respond to sensory neurons by transmitting signals that activate muscles and glands. For example, light and sound waves from the text messages that we receive on our phones are picked up by our sensory neurons, whereas our motor neurons allow our fingers to type reply messages.

fred goldstein/Shutterstock.com

Communication Within the Neuron

As we've just seen, the basic function of neurons is to transmit information throughout the nervous system. But exactly how do they do it? Neurons "speak" selectively with certain other neurons in a type of electrical and chemical language. The communication begins within the neuron itself, when the dendrites and cell body receive electrical signals from our senses (sight, sound, touch) or from chemical messages from other nearby neurons. If the message is sufficiently strong, it will instruct the neuron to "fire"—to transmit information to other neurons (see **Process Diagram 2.1**).

STOP! This Process Diagram contains essential information NOT found elsewhere in the text, which is likely to appear on quizzes and exams. Be sure to study it CAREFULLY.

PROCESS DIAGRAM 2.1 **Communication *Within* the Neuron**   The process of neural communication begins within the neuron itself, when the dendrites and cell body receive information and conduct it toward the axon. From there, the information moves down the entire length of the axon via a brief traveling electrical charge called an *action potential,* which can be described in the following three steps:

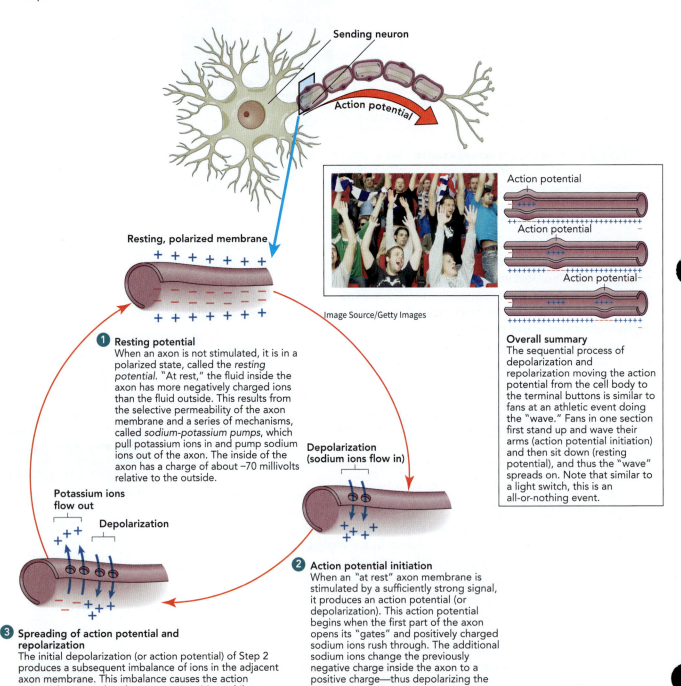

Sending neuron

Action potential

Image Source/Getty Images

Resting, polarized membrane

Action potential
Action potential
Action potential
Action potential

Overall summary
The sequential process of depolarization and repolarization moving the action potential from the cell body to the terminal buttons is similar to fans at an athletic event doing the "wave." Fans in one section first stand up and wave their arms (action potential initiation) and then sit down (resting potential), and thus the "wave" spreads on. Note that similar to a light switch, this is an all-or-nothing event.

1 **Resting potential**
When an axon is not stimulated, it is in a polarized state, called the *resting potential.* "At rest," the fluid inside the axon has more negatively charged ions than the fluid outside. This results from the selective permeability of the axon membrane and a series of mechanisms, called *sodium-potassium pumps,* which pull potassium ions in and pump sodium ions out of the axon. The inside of the axon has a charge of about –70 millivolts relative to the outside.

Depolarization (sodium ions flow in)

Potassium ions flow out

Depolarization

2 **Action potential initiation**
When an "at rest" axon membrane is stimulated by a sufficiently strong signal, it produces an action potential (or depolarization). This action potential begins when the first part of the axon opens its "gates" and positively charged sodium ions rush through. The additional sodium ions change the previously negative charge inside the axon to a positive charge—thus depolarizing the axon.

3 **Spreading of action potential and repolarization**
The initial depolarization (or action potential) of Step 2 produces a subsequent imbalance of ions in the adjacent axon membrane. This imbalance causes the action potential to spread to the next section. Meanwhile, "gates" in the axon membrane of the initially depolarized section open and potassium ions flow out, allowing the first section to repolarize and return to its resting potential.

As you can see, this type of electrical communication within the neuron is somewhat confusing. Therefore, we'll briefly explain it here in narrative form:

Step 1   Resting potential   Neurons are normally at rest and ready to be activated, which explains why this stage is called the *resting potential.*

Step 2   Acting potential initiation   If a resting neuron receives a combined signal (from the senses or other neurons) that exceeds the minimum threshold, it will be activated and "fire," thus transmitting an electrical impulse (called an **action potential**). (Note that in Process Diagram 2.1, we're only demonstrating how an action potential "fires," also known as excitation. However, this resting neuron also receives simultaneous messages telling it NOT to fire, a process called inhibition. Given these contradictory messages, the neuron does something simple—it goes with the majority. If it receives more excitatory messages than inhibitory messages, it fires—and vice versa.)

Step 3   Spreading of action potential and repolarization   The beginning action potential then spreads and travels down the axon. As the action potential moves toward the terminal buttons, the areas on the axon left behind return to their resting state. Note that this firing of an action potential is similar to the operation of a light switch, where once you apply the minimum amount of pressure needed to flip the switch, the light comes on. There is no "partial firing" of a neuron. It's either on or off. This neural reaction of either firing with a full-strength response or not firing at all is known as the **all-or-nothing principle**. But if this is true, how do we detect the intensity of a stimulus, such as the difference between a rock or a butterfly landing on our hand? A strong stimulus (like the rock) causes more neurons to fire and to fire more rapidly when the rock falls on our hand versus a butterfly's soft landing.

Now that we have seen how communication occurs within the neuron, we need to look at how it works between neurons.

Communication Between Neurons

As you discovered in the text description and Process Diagram 2.1, neural transmission (via action potentials) *within* the neuron can be compared to the behavior of a crowd doing the "wave" in a stadium. The analogy helps explain how the action potential travels down the axon in a "wavelike" motion. However, the comparison breaks down when we want to know how the message moves from one neuron to another—or how the "wave" in a stadium gets across the aisles. The answer is that within the neuron messages travel electrically. In contrast, messages between neurons travel across the **synapse** (the space between neurons) via chemicals called **neurotransmitters**—see **Process Diagram 2.2**.

Like Process Diagram 2.1, this procedure is complicated, so we'll also briefly summarize it in narrative form here:

Beginning with Step 1, note how the *action potential* travels down the axon and on to the knoblike terminal buttons. These buttons contain small tiny vesicles (sacs) that store the neurotransmitters. These neurotransmitters then travel across the *synapse*, or space between neurons, to bind to receptor sites on the dendrites (or less common, on the cell body) of the nearby receiving neurons. (The neuron that delivers the neurotransmitter to the synapse is called a *pre-synaptic neuron*.)

Then in Step 2, like a key fitting into a lock, the neurotransmitters unlock tiny channels in the receiving neuron and send either excitatory ("fire") or inhibitory ("don't fire") messages. (The receiving neuron is called a *post-synaptic neuron*.)

Finally, in Step 3, after delivering their message, the neurotransmitters must be removed from the receptor sites before the next neural transmission can occur. Note how some of the neurotransmitters are used up in the transmission of the message. However, most of the "leftovers" are reabsorbed by the axon and stored until the next neural impulse—a process known as *reuptake*. In other cases, the "leftovers" are dealt with through enzymes that break apart the neurotransmitters to clean up the synapse.

Appreciating Neurotransmitters
While researching how neurons communicate, scientists discovered numerous neurotransmitters with differing effects, which will be

---

Action potential   A neural impulse, or brief electrical charge, that carries information along the axon of a neuron; movement is generated when positively charged ions move in and out through channels in the axon's membrane.

All-or-nothing principle   The principle that a neuron's response to a stimulus is either to fire with a full-strength response or not to fire at all; also known as the all-or-none law.

Synapse   The space between the axon tip of the sending neuron and the dendrite and cell body of the receiving neuron; during an action potential, neurotransmitters are released and flow across the synapse.

Neurotransmitter   A chemical messenger released by neurons that travels across the synapse allowing neurons to communicate with one another.

STOP! This Process Diagram contains essential information NOT found elsewhere in the text, which is likely to appear on quizzes and exams. Be sure to study it CAREFULLY.

PROCESS DIAGRAM 2.2 **Communication *Between* Neurons** Within the neuron, messages travel electrically (see Process Diagram 2.1). Between neurons, messages are transmitted chemically. The three steps shown here summarize this chemical transmission.

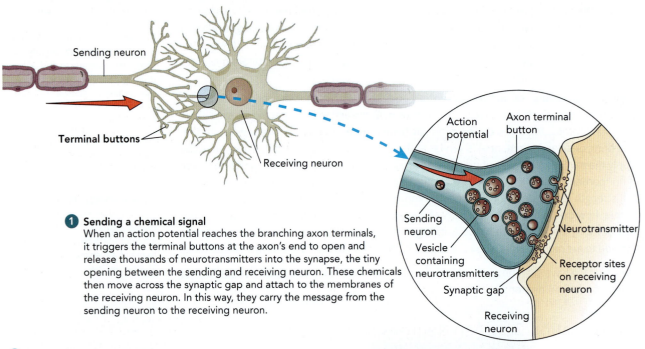

1 Sending a chemical signal
When an action potential reaches the branching axon terminals, it triggers the terminal buttons at the axon's end to open and release thousands of neurotransmitters into the synapse, the tiny opening between the sending and receiving neuron. These chemicals then move across the synaptic gap and attach to the membranes of the receiving neuron. In this way, they carry the message from the sending neuron to the receiving neuron.

2 Receiving a chemical signal
After a chemical message flows across the synaptic gap, it attaches to the receiving neuron. It's important to know that the dendrites or cell body of each receiving neuron gets multiple neurotransmitter messages. As you can see in this close-up photo, the axon terminals from thousands of other nearby neurons almost completely cover the cell body of the receiving neuron. It's also important to understand that neurotransmitters deliver either excitatory ("fire") or inhibitory ("don't fire") messages. The receiving neurons will produce an action potential and pass along the message only if the number of excitatory messages exceeds the number of inhibitory messages.

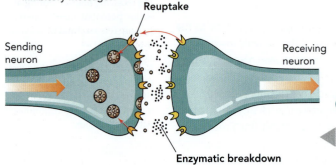

OMIKRON/Science Source

3 Dealing with leftovers
Given that some neurons have thousands of receptors, which are responsive only to specific neurotransmitters, what happens to excess neurotransmitters or to those that do not "fit" into the adjacent receptor sites? The sending neuron normally reabsorbs the excess (called reuptake), or they are broken down by special enzymes.

Agonist drug A substance that binds to a receptor and mimics or enhances a neurotransmitter's effect.

Antagonist drug A substance that binds to a receptor and blocks or inhibits a neurotransmitter's effect.

discussed here and in later chapters. For instance, we now know that **agonist drugs** enhance or mimic the action of particular neurotransmitters, whereas **antagonist drugs** block or inhibit the effects (**Figure 2.2**).

In addition to knowing how drugs and other chemicals can alter neurotransmission, we also know that neurotransmitters play important roles in certain medical problems. Decreased levels of the neurotransmitter dopamine, for example, are associated with Parkinson's disease

FIGURE 2.2 **How poisons and drugs affect neural transmission** Foreign chemicals, such as poisons and drugs, can mimic or block ongoing actions of neurotransmitters, thus interfering with normal functions.

Most snake venom and some poisons, like *botulinum toxin* (Botox®), seriously affect normal muscle contraction. Ironically, these same poisons are sometimes used to treat certain medical conditions involving abnormal muscle contraction—as well as for some cosmetic purposes. Here, this man is receiving botox injections to reduce wrinkles resulting from facial muscle contractions.

Normal neurotransmission

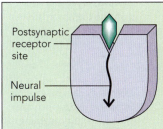

Somewhat like a key fitting into a lock, receptor sites on receiving neurons' dendrites recognize neurotransmitters by their particular shape. When the shape of the neurotransmitter matches the shape of the receptor site, a message is sent.

Postsynaptic receptor site

Neural impulse

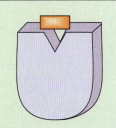

Neurotransmitters without the correct shape won't fit the receptors, so they cannot stimulate the dendrite. Therefore, normal neurotransmission and that neurotransmitter's message are blocked.

a. Normal neurotransmitter activation

b. Blocked neurotransmitter activation

How poisons and drugs affect neurotransmission

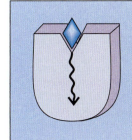

Some *agonist drugs*, like the nicotine in cigarettes (and the poison from a black widow spider bite), are similar enough in structure to a specific neurotransmitter (in this case, acetylcholine) that they mimic its effects on the receiving neuron, and a message is sent.

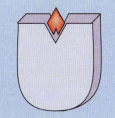

Some *antagonist drugs or poisons* (like curare) block neurotransmitters such us acetylcholine, which is vital in muscle action. Blocking it paralyzes muscles, including those involved in breathing, which can be fatal.

c. Agonist drug mimics neurotransmitter

d. Antagonist drug fills receptor space and blocks neurotransmitter

(PD), whereas excessively high levels of dopamine appear to contribute to some forms of schizophrenia. **Table 2.1** presents additional examples of how some of the most common neurotransmitters affect us.

Perhaps the best-known neurotransmitters are the endogenous opioid peptides, commonly known as **endorphins** (a contraction of *endogenous* [self-produced] and *morphine*). These chemicals mimic the effects of opium-based drugs such as morphine: They elevate mood and reduce pain (Antunes et al., 2016; Choi & Lee, 2019).

Interestingly, drinking alcohol leads to endorphins being released in parts of the brain that are responsible for feelings of reward and pleasure (Mitchell et al., 2012). Endorphins, along with several other neurotransmitters, are also believed to be responsible for the so-called runner's high—the euphoric response to endurance running (e.g., Hicks et al., 2019).

[AQ1] Surprisingly, researchers have found that even when we sing in choirs or move in synchrony with others (e.g., dancing, see photo) our pain thresholds are higher (Tarr et al., 2016; Weinstein et al., 2016). We also tend to feel closer to others—even if the other singers or dancers are strangers. The researchers attributed these findings to the release of endorphins. They also hypothesized that singing and dancing may have evolved over time because they encourage social bonding.

Endorphin A chemical substance in the nervous system similar in structure and action to opiates; involved in pain control, pleasure, and memory.

TABLE 2.1 **How Neurotransmitters Affect Us**

Neurotransmitter (Molecule's illustration)	Neurotransmitter (Functions)	Sample Agonist/ Antagonist Acting Drugs	Known or Suspected Effects
	Acetylcholine (ACh) (learning, attention, sleeping, memory, muscle contraction)	Nicotine, amphetamines, LSD, PCP, marijuana	Neurons producing ACh deteriorate; decreased ACh plays a suspected role in Alzheimer's disease
	Dopamine (DA) (movement, emotion, learning, attention)	Cocaine, methamphetamine, LSD, GHB, PCP, marijuana, Ecstasy (MDMA), L-Dopa (treatment for Parkinson's disease), chlorpromazine (treatment for schizophrenia)	Oversupply linked with schizophrenia; undersupply linked with Parkinson's disease; key role in addiction and the reward system
	Endorphins (pain perception, positive emotions)	Heroin, morphine, oxycodone (treatments for pain)	Decreases pain perception; improves and/or increases mood, memory, learning, blood pressure, appetite, sexual activity
	Epinephrine (or adrenaline) (emotional arousal, memory)	Amphetamines, Ecstasy (MDMA), cocaine	Increases metabolism of glucose necessary for energy release
	GABA (gamma-aminobutyric acid) (learning, anxiety regulation, major role in inhibitory messages)	Alcohol, GHB, rohypnol, valium (treatment for anxiety)	Undersupply linked to seizures and insomnia; tranquilizing drugs, like Valium, increase inhibitory effects and thereby decrease anxiety
	Glutamate (learning, movement, memory, major role in excitatory messages)	Alcohol, phencyclidine (PCP) (mind-altering drug), ketamine (an anesthetic)	Improves learning and memory; low levels linked to anxiety, depression, migraines, and seizures

(Continued)

TABLE 2.1	How Neurotransmitters Affect Us (*continued*)

Neurotransmitter (Molecule's illustration)	Neurotransmitter (Functions)	Sample Agonist/ Antagonist Acting Drugs	Known or Suspected Effects
	Norepinephrine (NE), or noradrenaline (NA) (attention, arousal, learning, memory, dreaming, emotion, stress)	Cocaine, methamphetamine, amphetamine, Ecstasy (MDMA), Adderall (treatment for ADHD)	Low levels associated with depression; high levels linked with agitated, manic states
	Serotonin (emotional states, dreaming, impulse control, appetite, sensory perception, arousal, temperature regulation, pain suppression)	Ecstasy (MDMA), LSD, cocaine, SSRIs, like Prozac (treatment for depression)	Linked with impulsivity; undersupply associated with depression

In contrast to all the positive effects of endorphins, their connection to appetite enhancement leads to at least one potential downside. Researchers have found that rats injected with an endorphinlike chemical ate considerably more M&Ms than they would under normal conditions, consuming as much as 17 grams—more than five percent of their body weight (DiFeliceantonio et al., 2012). Although this may not seem like a lot of chocolate to you, it is the equivalent of a normal-sized adult eating 7.5 pounds (or 71 standard packages) of M&Ms in a single session. Another study with humans found that eating leads to endorphin release and increased feelings of satiety and pleasure, which suggests that overeating may overstimulate endorphin release and contribute to the development of obesity (Tuulari et al., 2017).

Hormones and the Endocrine System

We've just seen how the nervous system uses neurotransmitters to transmit messages. We also have a second type of communication system that uses **hormones** as its messengers. This second system is made up of a network of glands, called the **endocrine system** (**Figure 2.3**).

Why do we need two communication systems? Neurotransmitters are like emails that we send only to certain people—they deliver messages only to certain receptors. Hormones, in contrast, are like a global email message that we send to everyone in our address book.

Another difference between the two communication systems is that neurotransmitters are released from a neuron's terminal buttons into the synapse, whereas hormones are released from endocrine glands directly into our bloodstream. These slower hormonal messages are then carried by the blood throughout our bodies to any cell that will listen. Like our global email recipients, who may forward our message on to other people, messages from hormones are often forwarded on to other parts of the body. For example, a small part of the brain called the hypothalamus releases hormones that signal the pituitary gland, which in turn stimulates or inhibits the release of other hormones.

Hormone   Chemical messengers manufactured and secreted by the endocrine glands, which circulate in the bloodstream to produce bodily changes or maintain normal bodily functions.

Endocrine system   A network of glands located throughout the body that manufacture and secrete hormones into the bloodstream.

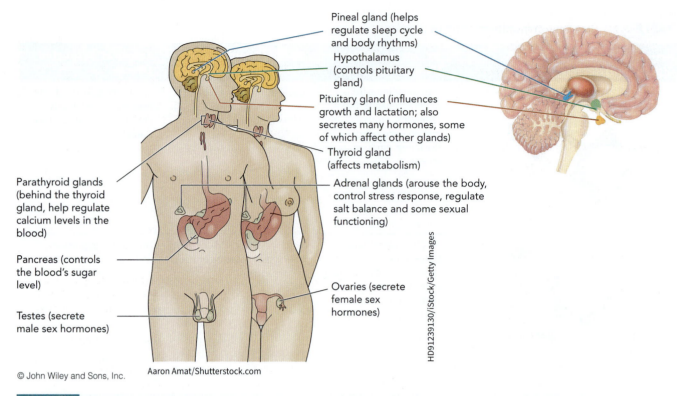

Pineal gland (helps regulate sleep cycle and body rhythms)

Hypothalamus (controls pituitary gland)

Pituitary gland (influences growth and lactation; also secretes many hormones, some of which affect other glands)

Thyroid gland (affects metabolism)

Adrenal glands (arouse the body, control stress response, regulate salt balance and some sexual functioning)

Parathyroid glands (behind the thyroid gland, help regulate calcium levels in the blood)

Pancreas (controls the blood's sugar level)

Testes (secrete male sex hormones)

Ovaries (secrete female sex hormones)

HD91239130/iStock/Getty Images

© John Wiley and Sons, Inc.   Aaron Amat/Shutterstock.com

FIGURE 2.3 The endocrine system   This figure shows the major endocrine glands, along with some internal organs to help you locate the glands.

Our hormone-releasing endocrine system has several important functions. It helps regulate long-term bodily processes, such as growth and the development of sexual characteristics, while also changing or maintaining short-term processes, such as digestion and elimination.

Before going on, it's important to know that in spite of the previously mentioned differences between the nervous system and the endocrine system, they're actually close relatives that are intricately interconnected. In times of crisis, the hypothalamus sends messages through two pathways—the neural system and the endocrine system (primarily the pituitary gland). The pituitary sends hormonal messages to the adrenal glands (located right above the kidneys). As you'll discover in Chapter 3, the adrenal glands then release *cortisol*, a stress hormone that boosts energy and blood sugar levels, *epinephrine* (commonly called adrenaline), and *norepinephrine* (or noradrenaline). (Note that these same chemicals also can serve as neurotransmitters.)

The pituitary gland also releases another important hormone (and neurotransmitter), *oxytocin*, which is thought to play a very interesting role in love, attachment, and social bonding. Oxytocin enables contractions during birth and sexual orgasm, and high oxytocin levels are also found during hugging, cuddling, and emotional bonding with romantic partners. One study even discovered that men who receive an intranasal spray of the hormone oxytocin rate their female partners as more attractive than unfamiliar women—thus suggesting oxytocin may increase faithfulness (Scheele et al., 2013).

[AQ2]   Perhaps even more intriguing is research showing that dogs who stare at their owners show elevated levels of oxytocin (see photo), and after a human receives these dog gazes, the human's level of oxytocin also increases (Nagasawa et al., 2015). Can you see how this might explain why we feel so good after sharing eye contact with our dogs?

As you'll discover in Chapters 14 and 15, oxytocin may even increase empathy and social learning (De Dreu & Kret, 2016; Geng et al., 2018; Xu et al., 2019). Considering the importance of empathy, check out the following **STH** **Scientific Thinking Highlight**. Also, be sure to complete the Retrieval Practice.

Yuttana Jaowattana/ Shutterstock.com

STH **Scientific Thinking Highlight**

Can Neuroscience Help Kids (and Adults) Make Better Choices?

(APA Goal 2.1) Use scientific reasoning to interpret psychological phenomena

Did you know that:

- Empathy scores among American college students have significantly declined since 2000 (Konrath et al., 2011)?
- Creativity and critical thinking have declined in the last 20 years—especially among kindergartners through third graders (Kim, 2011)?
- Self-control in young children has regressed by about 2 years since the 1940s (Kim, 2011)?

These are the headlines and research cited in a recent article (Divecha, 2019), which discusses neuroscientist Erin Clabough's new book *Second Nature: How Parents Can Use Neuroscience to Help Kids Develop Empathy, Creativity, and Self-Control.*

The author claims that by following the tips in her book, parents will actually be reinforcing synaptic connections and shaping and remodeling neural circuits, while their children will learn greater self-regulation. Thanks to the improved self-regulation, children will then supposedly become more altruistic, kind, and connected with their community. They also can expect greater academic success, a "career boost," and greater competitiveness in a global economy.

What do you think? Based on what you know from other sources and other texts, and after reading the first part of this chapter, *Neuroscience and Biological Foundations*, are you more or less willing to buy believe the claims made in Erin Clabough's new book?

Q **Test Your Scientific Thinking**

As you may recall from Chapter 1, scientific thinking is an approach to information that combines a high degree of *skepticism* (questioning what "everybody knows") with *objectivity* (using empirical data to separate fantasy from reality) *and rationalism* (practicing logical reasoning). Using these three principles, consider the following questions:

1. **Skepticism**   Given the title and topic of this report, "Can Neuroscience Help Kids (and Adults) Make Better Choices?" were you predisposed to believe or discount the information? Can children (or adults) really become more altruistic, kind, and so on simply from developing self-regulation? Scientific thinkers approach claims like these with skepticism.

2. **Objectivity**   Are the author's assumptions supported by the data? Did you notice that the author is a neuroscientist? Does her academic and professional training increase your trust in the objectivity of her findings? Can you check the original research to see if its findings are correctly interpreted? Scientific thinkers carefully analyze data for value and content. Also, could her data and claims, if verified, be an example of confusing correlation with causation, the third-variable problem, or an illusory correlation? Scientific thinkers gather information and delay judgment until adequate data are available.

3. **Rationalism**   Aside from possible problems with the data, can we logically explain how teaching self-regulation could produce all the positive outcomes the author is claiming? Can you think of any other logical explanations for these findings?

(Compare your answers with those of fellow students, family, and friends. Doing so will improve your scientific thinking and your media savvy.)

Retrieval Practice 2.1 | Neural and Hormonal Processes

Self-Test   Completing this self-test, and then checking your answers by clicking on the answer button or by looking in Appendix B, will provide immediate feedback and helpful practice for exams.

1. The three major parts of a neuron are the _____.
   a. glia, dendrites, and myelin
   b. myelin, dendrites, and axon
   c. dendrites, cell body, and axon
   d. axon, glia, and myelin

2. An action potential is _____.
   a. the likelihood that a neuron will take action when stimulated
   b. the tendency for a neuron to be potentiated by neurotransmitters

   c. the firing of a nerve, either toward or away from the brain
   d. a neural impulse that carries information along the axon of a neuron

3. According to the all-or-nothing principle, the _____.
   a. neuron cannot fire again during the refractory period
   b. neurotransmitter either attaches to a receptor site or is destroyed in the synapse
   c. neuron either fires completely or does not fire at all
   d. none of these options

4. Chemical messengers that are released by neurons and travel across the synapse are called _____.
   a. chemical agonists
   b. neurotransmitters
   c. synaptic transmitters
   d. neuroactivists

5. Chemicals manufactured and secreted by endocrine glands and circulated in the bloodstream to change or maintain bodily functions are called _____.

   a. vasopressors

   b. neurotransmitters

   c. hormones

   d. chemical antagonists

Q Test Your Critical Thinking

1. Why is it valuable for scientists to understand how neurotransmitters work at a molecular level?

2. What are some examples of how hormones affect your daily life?

Real World Application Questions

[AQ1] Can singing or dancing make you feel closer to strangers, while also raising your pain threshold?

[AQ2] Why does eye contact with your dog make you feel good?

Caiaimage/Paul Bradbury/ OJO+/Getty Images

Yuttana Jaowattana/ Shutterstock.com

Hint: Look in the text for **[AQ1]** and **[AQ2]**

2.2 | Nervous System Organization

LEARNING OBJECTIVES

Retrieval Practice While reading the upcoming sections, respond to each Learning Objective in your own words.

Summarize the major divisions and functions of our nervous system.

- **Explain** the key features and role of our central nervous system (CNS).

- **Define** neuroplasticity and neurogenesis.

- **Describe** the key components and role of our peripheral nervous system (PNS).

Real World Application Question

[AQ3] Would stem cell injections have saved "Superman"?

Central nervous system (CNS)
The part of the nervous system consisting of the brain and spinal cord.

Peripheral nervous system (PNS)
The part of the nervous system composed of the nerves connecting the central nervous system (CNS) to the rest of the body.

Have you heard the expression "Information is power"? Nowhere is this truer than in the human body. Without information, we could not survive. Neurons within the nervous system must take in sensory information from the outside world and then pass it along to the entire human body. Just as the circulatory system handles blood, which conveys chemicals and oxygen, the nervous system uses chemicals and electrical processes to convey information.

The nervous system is divided and subdivided into several branches (**Figure 2.4**). The main branch includes the brain and a bundle of nerves that form the spinal cord. Because this system is located in the center of the body (within the skull and spine), it is called the **central nervous system (CNS)**. The CNS is primarily responsible for processing and organizing information.

The second major branch of the nervous system includes all the nerves outside the brain and spinal cord. This **peripheral nervous system (PNS)** carries messages (action potentials) to and from the CNS to the periphery of the body. Now, let's take a closer look at the CNS and the PNS.

Central Nervous System (CNS)

The central nervous system (CNS) is what makes humans unique. Most other animals can smell, run, see, and hear far better than we can. But thanks to our CNS, we can process information and adapt to our environment in ways that no other animal can. Unfortunately, our CNS is also incredibly fragile. Unlike neurons in the PNS, which can regenerate and require less protection, neurons in the CNS can suffer serious and permanent damage. As

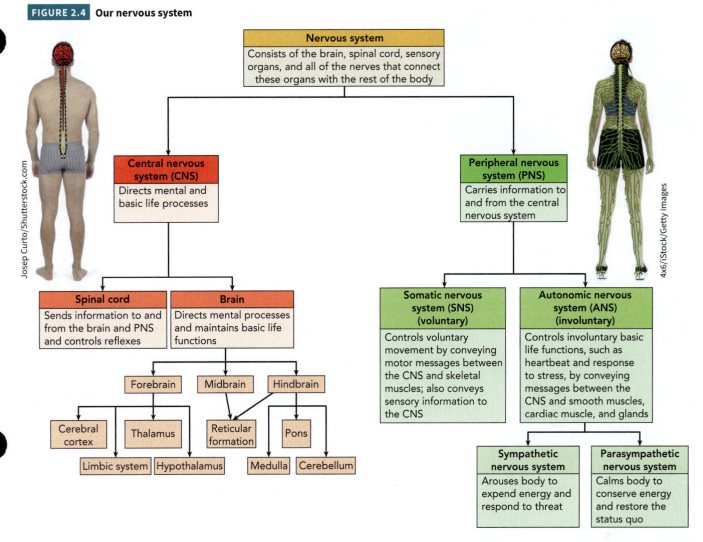

FIGURE 2.4 **Our nervous system**

Josep Curto/Shutterstock.com

4x6/iStock/Getty Images

Nervous system
Consists of the brain, spinal cord, sensory organs, and all of the nerves that connect these organs with the rest of the body

Central nervous system (CNS)
Directs mental and basic life processes

Peripheral nervous system (PNS)
Carries information to and from the central nervous system

Spinal cord
Sends information to and from the brain and PNS and controls reflexes

Brain
Directs mental processes and maintains basic life functions

Forebrain   Midbrain   Hindbrain

Cerebral cortex   Thalamus   Reticular formation   Pons

Limbic system   Hypothalamus   Medulla   Cerebellum

Somatic nervous system (SNS) (voluntary)
Controls voluntary movement by conveying motor messages between the CNS and skeletal muscles; also conveys sensory information to the CNS

Autonomic nervous system (ANS) (involuntary)
Controls involuntary basic life functions, such as heartbeat and response to stress, by conveying messages between the CNS and smooth muscles, cardiac muscle, and glands

Sympathetic nervous system
Arouses body to expend energy and respond to threat

Parasympathetic nervous system
Calms body to conserve energy and restore the status quo

TIP Are you overwhelmed with all these terms and divisions and subdivisions?   If so, remember that when attempting to learn a large set of new terms and concepts, such as those in this chapter, organization is the best way to master the material and get it "permanently" stored in long-term memory (Chapter 7). A broad overview like this figure provides the big picture to help you organize and file specific details. Just as you need to see a globe of the world showing all the continents to easily place individual countries, you need a map of the entire nervous system to effectively study its individual parts.

we'll see later in this chapter, repeated head trauma, particularly when associated with loss of consciousness, can lead to debilitating and potentially fatal illnesses (see photo of Lou Gehrig).

Lou Gehrig's disease or repeated head trauma?   Lou Gehrig was a legendary player for the New York Yankees from 1925 to 1939. Tragically, he had to retire while still in his prime when he developed symptoms of *amyotrophic lateral sclerosis (ALS)*, a neurological disease caused by degeneration of motor neurons (later commonly called Lou Gehrig's disease).

In fact, Lou Gehrig may not have had ALS. Instead, he may have developed symptoms that were similar to those of ALS because he was so often hit in the head with baseballs. (Gehrig played before batting helmets were required.) Modern research and medical professionals now believe that many athletes, including football players, soccer players, and boxers, may have been similarly misdiagnosed with ALS, Parkinson's disease, early onset dementia, or Alzheimer's disease (AD). Like Lou Gehrig, their symptoms are most likely the result of repeated concussions (Falcon et al., 2019; Lim et al., 2019; Tharmaratnam et al., 2018).

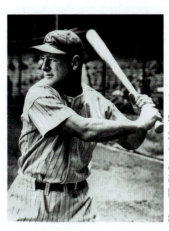

Photo File/Hulton Archive/Getty Images

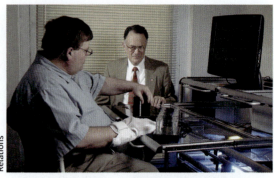

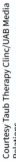
Courtesy Taub Therapy Clinc/UAB Media Relations

A breakthrough in neuroscience By immobilizing the unaffected arm or leg and requiring rigorous and repetitive exercise of the affected limb, psychologist Edward Taub and colleagues "recruit" stroke patients' intact brain cells to take over for damaged cells (Taub, 2004; Taub et al., 2014). The therapy has restored function in some patients as long as 21 years after their strokes.

Dan Piraro/King Features Syndicate

However, the brain may not be as "hardwired" and fragile as we once thought. In the past, scientists believed that after the first two or three years of life damaged neurons within the brain or spinal cord of most animals, including humans, were impossible to repair or replace. Today, we know that the brain is capable of lifelong *neuroplasticity* and *neurogenesis*.

Neuroplasticity Modern research has shown that, rather than being a fixed, solid organ, the brain is capable of changing its structure and function as a result of usage and experience (Mateos-Aparicio & Rodriguez-Moreno, 2019; Presti, 2016). This "rewiring," officially known as **neuroplasticity**, is what makes our brains so wonderfully adaptive. For example, when infants suffer damage to the speech area of their left hemisphere, the right hemisphere can reorganize and pick up some language abilities. Remarkably, this rewiring has even helped "remodel" the adult brain following strokes (see photo).

Neurogenesis Unlike *neuroplasticity*, which refers to the brain's ability to restructure itself, **neurogenesis** is achieved through the formation (generation) of new neurons in the brain. The source of these newly created cells is **stem cells**—rare, immature cells that can grow and develop into any type of cell (see cartoon). Their fate depends on the chemical signals they receive.

Fortunately, experiments and clinical trials using stem cells for bone marrow transplants and to repopulate or replace cells devastated by injury or disease, have provided successful treatment and hope to patients suffering from strokes, Alzheimer's, Parkinson's, epilepsy, stress, and depression (Belkind-Gerson et al., 2016; Cuartero et al., 2019; Kim et al., 2016). In addition, stem cell injections into the eyes of patients with untreatable eye diseases and severe visual problems have led to dramatic improvements in vision (Chucair-Elliott et al., 2015; Fahnehjelm et al., 2016; Song & Bharti, 2016).

Neuroplasticity The brain's lifelong ability to reorganize and change its structure and function by forming new neural connections.

Neurogenesis The formation (generation) of new neurons.

Stem cells Immature (uncommitted) cells that have the potential to develop into almost any type of cell, depending on the chemical signals they receive.

PAN Practical Application of Neuroscience

Will stem cell transplants allow people paralyzed from spinal cord injuries to walk again? Scientists have had some success transplanting stem cells into spinal cord–injured animals (Raynald et al., 2016; Sandner et al., 2015). When the damaged spinal cord was viewed several weeks later, the implanted cells had survived and spread throughout the injured area. More important, the transplant animals also showed some improvement in previously paralyzed parts of their bodies. Medical researchers are testing the safety of embryonic stem cell therapy for human paralysis patients, and future trials may determine whether these cells will repair damaged spinal cords and improve sensation and movement in paralyzed areas (Jin et al., 2019; Kamelska-Sadowska et al., 2019; Presti, 2016).

Before going on, it's important to note that neuroplasticity and neurogenesis are NOT the same as *neuroregeneration*, which refers to the regrowth or repair of neurons, glia, or synapses. This process is fairly common within the peripheral nervous system (PNS). You've undoubtedly watched a cut heal on your skin and known of someone who slowly regained his or her feeling and function after a serious motor vehicle accident or severe fall.

Although regeneration after damage within the central nervous system (CNS) is far less common, scientists have made significant advances in promoting axon growth, preventing scar formation, and enhancing compensatory growth on uninjured neurons. **[AQ3]** Actor Christopher Reeve's well-publicized partial recovery after serious damage to his spinal cord following a horse riding accident in 1995 is a likely example of this type of regeneration (Kaiser et al., 2019). Sadly, "Superman" Christopher Reeve (see photo) never regained full mobility and died in 2004, reportedly due to sepsis ("blood poisoning") or a fatal reaction to an antibiotic (Clifford, 2015; Petty, 2018).

Now that we've discussed neuroplasticity and neurogenesis within the central nervous system, let's take a closer look at the spinal cord. Because of its central importance for psychology and behavior, we'll discuss the brain in more detail in the next major section.

Spinal Cord   Beginning at the base of our brains and continuing down our backs, the spinal cord carries vital information from the rest of the body into and out of the brain. But the spinal cord doesn't simply relay messages. It can also initiate certain automatic behaviors on its own. We call these involuntary, automatic behaviors **reflexes**, or *reflex arcs*, because the response to the incoming stimuli is automatically sent to the spinal cord and then "reflected" back to the appropriate muscles. This type of "shortcut" allows an immediate action response without the delay of routing signals first to the brain (see **Process Diagram 2.3**).

We're all born with numerous reflexes, many of which fade over time (**Figure 2.5**). But even as adults, we still blink in response to a puff of air in our eyes, gag when something touches the back of the throat, and urinate and defecate in response to pressure in the bladder and rectum.

AF archive/Alamy Stock Photo

Reflex   An innate, automatic response to a stimulus that has a biological relevance for an organism (e.g., the knee-jerk reflex).

STOP!   This Process Diagram contains essential information NOT found elsewhere in the text, which is likely to appear on quizzes and exams. Be sure to study it CAREFULLY.

PROCESS DIAGRAM 2.3   **How the Spinal Reflex Operates**   In a simple reflex arc, a sensory receptor responds to stimulation and initiates a neural impulse that travels to the spinal cord. This signal then travels back to the appropriate muscle, which reflexively contracts. Note that the reflex response is automatic and immediate because the signal travels **only** as far as the spinal cord before action is initiated, not all the way to the brain. The brain is later "notified" when the spinal cord sends along the message, which, in this case of the hot pan, leads to a perception of pain. What might be the evolutionary advantages of the reflex arc?

1
In a simple reflex circuit, like this withdrawal reflex, skin receptors in the fingertips detect heat from the hot handle of the sauce pan. These receptors then send neural messages to sensory neurons.

2
Sensory neurons then send messages to interneurons, in the spinal cord, which in turn connect with motor neurons.

6
Finally, an area of the brain, known as the somatosensory cortex, receives the message from the thalamus and interprets it as PAIN!

5
A small structure in the brain, the thalamus, then relays incoming sensory information to the higher, cortical areas of the brain.

4
While the simple reflex is occurring within the spinal cord, messages are also being sent up the spinal cord to the brain.

3
Next, motor neurons send messages to hand muscles, causing a withdrawal reflex away from the hot handle of the pan—and possibly the dropping of the sauce pan. (This occurs before the brain perceives the actual sensation of pain.)

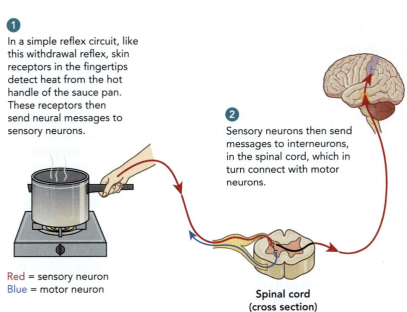

Red = sensory neuron
Blue = motor neuron

Spinal cord (cross section)

FIGURE 2.5 **Testing for reflexes** If you have a newborn or young infant in your home, you can easily (and safely) test for these simple reflexes. (Most infant reflexes disappear within the first year of life. Interestingly, if they reappear in later life, it generally indicates damage to the central nervous system.)

Q Test Your Critical Thinking

1. What might happen if infants lacked these reflexes?

2. Can you explain why most infant reflexes disappear within the first year?

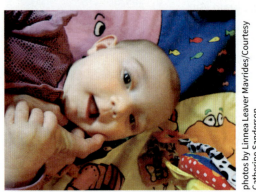
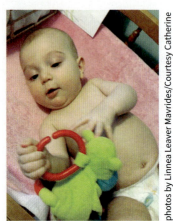
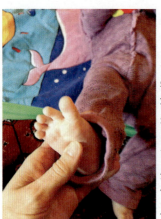

photos by Linnea Leaver Mavrides/Courtesy Catherine Sanderson

a. Rooting reflex
Lightly stroke the cheek or side of the mouth and watch how the infant automatically (reflexively) turns toward the stimulation and attempts to suck.

b. Grasping reflex
Place your finger or an object in the infant's palm and note his or her automatic grasping reflex.

c. Babinski reflex
Lightly stroke the sole of the infant's foot, and the big toe will move toward the top of the foot, while the other toes fan out.

PA Practical Application

Do spinal cord reflexes also affect our sexuality? Certain stimuli, such as the stroking of the genitals, can lead to arousal and the reflexive muscle contractions of orgasm in both men and women. However, in order for us to have the passion, thoughts, and emotion we normally associate with sex, the sensory information from the stroking and orgasm must be carried on to the appropriate areas of the brain that receive and interpret these specific sensory messages.

Peripheral Nervous System (PNS)

The peripheral nervous system (PNS) is just what it sounds like—the part that involves nerves *peripheral* to (or outside) the brain and spinal cord. The chief function of the peripheral nervous system is to carry information to and from the central nervous system. It links the brain and spinal cord to the body's sense receptors, muscles, and glands.

Looking back at Figure 2.4, note again that the PNS is subdivided into the somatic nervous system and the autonomic nervous system. The **somatic nervous system (SNS)** consists of all the nerves that connect to sensory receptors and skeletal muscles. The name comes from the term *soma*, which means "body," and the somatic nervous system plays a key role in communication throughout the entire body. In a kind of two-way street, the somatic nervous system (also called the skeletal nervous system) first carries sensory information to the brain and spinal cord (CNS) and then carries messages from the CNS to skeletal muscles.

The second subdivision of the PNS, the **autonomic nervous system (ANS)**, is responsible for involuntary tasks, such as heart rate, digestion, pupil dilation, and breathing. Like an automatic pilot, the ANS can sometimes be consciously overridden. But as its name implies, the autonomic system normally operates on its own (autonomously).

The ANS is further divided into two branches, the *sympathetic* and *parasympathetic*, which tend to work in opposition to each other to regulate the functioning of such target organs as

Somatic nervous system (SNS)
A subdivision of the peripheral nervous system (PNS) that connects the central nervous system (CNS) to sensory receptors and controls skeletal muscles.

Autonomic nervous system (ANS) The subdivision of the peripheral nervous system (PNS) that controls the body's involuntary motor responses by connecting the central nervous system (CNS) and the smooth muscles, cardiac muscle, and glands.

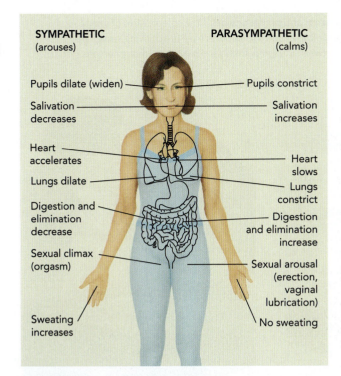

SYMPATHETIC (arouses)

PARASYMPATHETIC (calms)

Pupils dilate (widen) — Pupils constrict

Salivation decreases — Salivation increases

Heart accelerates — Heart slows

Lungs dilate — Lungs constrict

Digestion and elimination decrease — Digestion and elimination increase

Sexual climax (orgasm) — Sexual arousal (erection, vaginal lubrication)

Sweating increases — No sweating

designer491/Alamy Stock Photo

wang Tom/123 RF

FIGURE 2.6 **Actions of the autonomic nervous system** The ANS is responsible for a variety of independent (autonomous) activities, such as salivation and digestion. It exercises this control through its two divisions, the sympathetic and parasympathetic branches.

the heart, intestines, and lungs. Like two children on a teeter-totter, one will be up while the other is down, but they essentially balance each other out. **Figure 2.6** illustrates the functions of the ANS, and provides a familiar example of the interaction between the sympathetic and parasympathetic nervous systems.

During stressful times, either mental or physical, the **sympathetic nervous system** arouses and mobilizes bodily resources to respond to the stressor. This emergency response is often called the "fight or flight" response. (This response, which has recently been expanded and relabeled as the "fight-flight-freeze" response, will be fully discussed in Chapter 3.) If you noticed a dangerous snake coiled and ready to strike, your sympathetic nervous system would increase your heart rate, respiration, and blood pressure; stop your digestive and eliminative processes; and release hormones, such as cortisol, into the bloodstream. The net result of sympathetic activation is to get more oxygenated blood and energy to the skeletal muscles, thus allowing you to cope with the stress—to fight, flight, or freeze.

In contrast to the sympathetic nervous system, the **parasympathetic nervous system** is responsible for calming our bodies and conserving energy. It returns our bodies to normal functioning by slowing our heart rate, lowering our blood pressure, and increasing our digestive and eliminative processes.

Can you see how the sympathetic nervous system provides an adaptive, evolutionary advantage? At the beginning of human evolution, when we faced a dangerous bear or other threat, there were only three reasonable responses—fight, flight, or freeze. This automatic mobilization of bodily resources can still be critical, even in modern times. However, less life-threatening events, such as traffic jams, also activate our sympathetic nervous system. As the next chapter discusses, ongoing sympathetic system response to such chronic daily stress can become detrimental to our health. For a look at how the autonomic nervous system affects our sexual lives, see **Figure 2.7**.

Sympathetic nervous system The subdivision of the autonomic nervous system (ANS) that is responsible for arousing the body and mobilizing its energy during times of stress; also called the "fight-flight-freeze" system.

Parasympathetic nervous system The subdivision of the autonomic nervous system (ANS) that is responsible for calming the body and conserving energy.

FIGURE 2.7 **Autonomic nervous system and sexual arousal** The complexities of sexual interaction—and, in particular, the difficulties couples sometimes have in achieving sexual arousal or orgasm—illustrate the balancing act between the sympathetic and parasympathetic nervous systems.

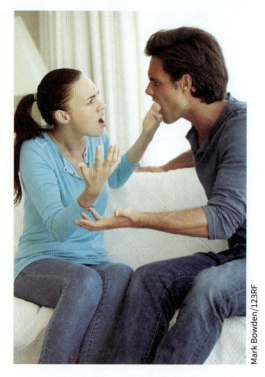

a. Parasympathetic dominance Sexual arousal and excitement require that the body be relaxed enough to allow increased blood flow to the genitals—in other words, the nervous system must be in *parasympathetic dominance*. Parasympathetic nerves carry messages from the central nervous system directly to the sexual organs, allowing for a localized response (increased blood flow and genital arousal).

b. Sympathetic dominance During strong emotions, such as anger, anxiety, or fear, the body shifts to *sympathetic dominance*, which causes blood flow to the genitals and other organs to decrease because the body is preparing to fight, flight, or freeze. As a result, the person is unable (or less likely) to become sexually aroused. Any number of circumstances—performance anxiety, fear of unwanted pregnancy or disease, or tensions between partners—can trigger sympathetic dominance, and thereby block sexual arousal and orgasm.

Retrieval Practice 2.2 | Nervous System Organization

Self-Test Completing this self-test, and then checking your answers by clicking on the answer button or by looking in Appendix B, will provide immediate feedback and helpful practice for exams.

1. The major divisions of the nervous system are the _____.

    a. sympathetic and parasympathetic

    b. somatic and autonomic

    c. gray matter and white matter

    d. central and peripheral

2. The central nervous system _____.

    a. consists of the brain and spinal cord

    b. is responsible for the fight, flight, or freeze response

    c. includes the autonomic and somatic nervous systems

    d. all these options

3. The peripheral nervous system is _____.

    a. composed of the spinal cord and peripheral nerves

    b. less important than the central nervous system

    c. contained within the skull and spinal column

    d. a combination of all the nerves and neurons outside the brain and spinal cord

4. The _____ nervous system is responsible for the fight, flight, or freeze response, whereas the _____ nervous system is responsible for maintaining or restoring calm.

    a. central; peripheral

    b. parasympathetic; sympathetic

    c. sympathetic; parasympathetic

    d. autonomic; somatic

5. If you are startled by the sound of a loud explosion, the _____ nervous system will become dominant.

   a. semiautomatic
   b. afferent
   c. parasympathetic
   d. sympathetic

Q Test Your Critical Thinking

1. If human stem cells could be used to create a fully-formed and functional human fetus, do you believe this specific form of research should be limited? If so, how and why?

2. What are some everyday examples of neuroplasticity—that is, of the way the brain is changed and shaped by experience?

Real World Application Question

[AQ3]   Would stem cell injections have saved "Superman"?

AF archive/Alamy Stock Photo

Hint: Look in the text for **[AQ3]**

2.3 | A Tour Through the Brain

LEARNING OBJECTIVES

Retrieval Practice   While reading the upcoming sections, respond to each Learning Objective in your own words.

Review the tools used in biological research, along with the brain's key structures and functions.

• **Identify** the tools neuroscientists use to study the brain and nervous system.

• **Describe** the major structures of the hindbrain, midbrain, and forebrain, as well as their respective functions.

Real World Application Question

[AQ4]   Could gently riding a bike for ten minutes affect your memory and hippocampus?

We begin our exploration of the brain with a discussion of the tools that neuroscientists use to study it. Next, we offer a quick tour of the brain, beginning at its lower end, where the spinal cord joins the base of the brain, and then moving upward, all the way to the top of the skull. As we move from bottom to top, "lower," basic processes, such as breathing, generally give way to more complex mental processes.

Biological Tools for Research

How do we know how the brain and nervous system work? Beginning in early times, scientists have *dissected* the brains and other body parts of human and non-human animals. They've also used *lesioning* techniques (systematically destroying bodily tissue to study the effects on behavior and mental processes). By the mid-1800s, this research had produced a basic map of the nervous system, including some areas of the brain. Early researchers also relied on clinical observations and case studies of living people who had experienced injuries, diseases, and disorders that affected brain functioning.

Recent advances in brain science have led to various types of brain-imaging scans, which can be used in both clinical and laboratory settings. Most of these methods are relatively *non-invasive*—that is, their use does not involve breaking the skin or entering the body. Modern researchers still use these and other techniques to examine biological processes that underlie our behavior (**Table 2.2**). For an example of how this research has direct, practical applications, see the following **PP** **PositivePsych**.

TABLE 2.2 **Sample Tools for Biological Research**

	Tool	Description	Purpose
dblight/E+/Getty Images	**Electrical recordings** Electrical activity throughout the brain sweeps in regular waves across its surface, and the electroencephalogram (EEG) is a read-out of this activity.	Using electrodes attached to the skin or scalp, brain activity is detected and recorded on an EEG.	Reveals areas of the brain most active during particular tasks or mental states, such as reading or sleeping; also traces abnormal brain waves related to brain malfunctions, such as epilepsy or tumors.
Mehau Kulyk/ Science Source	**CT (computed tomography) scan** This CT scan used X-rays to locate a brain tumor, which is the deep purple mass at the top, slightly to the left.	Computer-created cross-sectional X-rays of the brain or other parts of the body produce 3-D images. The least expensive type of imaging, it is widely used in research.	Reveals the effects of strokes, injuries, tumors, and other brain disorders.
N.I.H/Science Source	**PET (positron emission tomography) scan** The red and yellow colors in these two PET scans highlight where the highest level of neural firing is taking place.	A radioactive form of glucose is injected into the bloodstream; a scanner records the amount of glucose used in particularly active areas of the brain and produces a computer-constructed picture of the brain.	Originally designed to detect abnormalities, now used to identify brain areas active during ordinary activities (such as reading or singing).
Scott Camazine/ Science Source	**MRI (magnetic resonance imaging)** Note the fissures and internal structures of the brain. The throat, nasal airways, and fluid surrounding the brain are dark.	Using a powerful magnet and radio waves linked to a computer, a scanner creates detailed cross-sectional images.	Produces high-resolution 3-D pictures of the brain useful for identifying abnormalities and mapping brain structures and function.
Philippe Psaila/ Science Source	**fMRI (functional magnetic resonance imaging)** The yellow highlighted areas in this fMRI are "lit up," which tells us that oxygen from the blood is being heavily used in this region.	Newer, faster version of MRI that detects blood flow by picking up magnetic signals from blood, which has given up its oxygen to activate brain cells.	Measures blood flow, which indicates areas of the brain that are active and inactive during ordinary behaviors or responses (like reading or talking); also shows changes associated with various disorders.
Michael Braham/Shutterstock. com	**dMRI (diffusion magnetic resonance imaging)** This dMRI image is of the whole brain—as if you were looking down through the top of the skull of a person who is looking straight ahead. The bright colors are highlighting axons and dendrites.	Latest scanning technique that tracks the movement of molecules as they travel in the brain.	Produces 3-D images of the brain's neural pathways.
	Other methods: a. Cell body or tract (myelin) staining, b. Microinjections, and c. Intrabrain electrical recordings	a. Colors/stains selected neurons or nerve fibers. b. Injects chemicals into specific areas of the brain. c. Records activity of one or a group of neurons inside the brain.	a. and b. Increase overall information on structure and function through direct observation and measurement. c. Intrabrain wire probes allow scientists to "see" individual neuron activity.

PP Practical Application: **PositivePsych**

How Does Positivity Affect Your Brain?

(APA Goal 1.3) Describe applications of psychology

Have you ever watched coaches harshly yelling at their young athletes and wondered how those children felt? If so, you'll be happy to know that the tools we regularly use to study the brain can provide valuable information and insights. In one study, researchers used fMRI brain-imaging scans (see again Table 2.2) to study which parts of the brain are most active during interviews (Jack et al., 2013). All participants underwent two distinct types of interviews. One interview focused on positive messages, such as: "If everything worked out ideally in your life, what would you be doing in ten years?" The other interview focused on negative messages, such as "What challenges have you encountered or do you expect to encounter in your experience here? How are you doing with your courses? Are you doing all of the homework and readings?"

As you might expect, during the positive interview, participants showed more brain activity in the parts of the brain associated with positive emotions, including empathy, positive affect, and emotional security. In contrast, during the negative interview, they showed more activity in brain areas linked with the sympathetic nervous system (fight-flight-freeze response) and negative feelings. Can you see how this research has powerful implications

Blend Images/Getty Images

for coaches (see photo), instructors, and parents, as well as in management and organizational practices? As the authors of this research suggest, "effective coaching and mentoring is crucial to the success of individuals and organizations."

What's the take-home message? For the best emotional responses in all our interactions, we need to emphasize positive messages. The value and effectiveness of reinforcement compared to the limits and serious problems with punishment is further detailed in Chapter 6.

Brain Organization

Having studied the tools scientists use for exploring the brain, we can now begin our tour. Let's talk first about brain size and complexity, which vary significantly from species to species (**Figure 2.8**). In the following section, we offer an in-depth look at what researchers now know about you and your human brain. While studying this section, keep in mind that your various brain structures are specialized to perform certain tasks, a process known as *localization of function*. However, most parts of the brain perform integrating, overlapping functions.

As you can see in **Figure 2.9**, scientists typically divide and label the human brain into three major sections: the *hindbrain, midbrain,* and *forebrain.* The hindbrain and midbrain are primarily responsible for basic survival, whereas your forebrain controls your thoughts, motivations, and emotions.

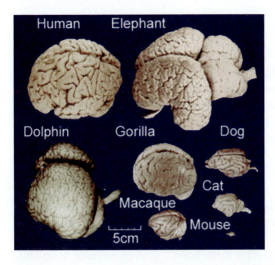

FIGURE 2.8 **Brain comparisons**
In general, the largest and most complex brains belong to higher mammals (such as dogs, elephants, dolphins, gorillas, chimps, and humans). Lower species (such as fish and reptiles) tend to have smaller and less complex brains.

Reproduced (or adapted) with permission from Caution-Caution-http://brainmuseum.org, Specimens used for this publication are from the Department of Health Affairs Neuroanatomical Collections Division of the National Museum of Health and Medicines the University of Wisconsin and Michigan State Comparative Mammalian Brain Collections supported by the US National Science Foundation.

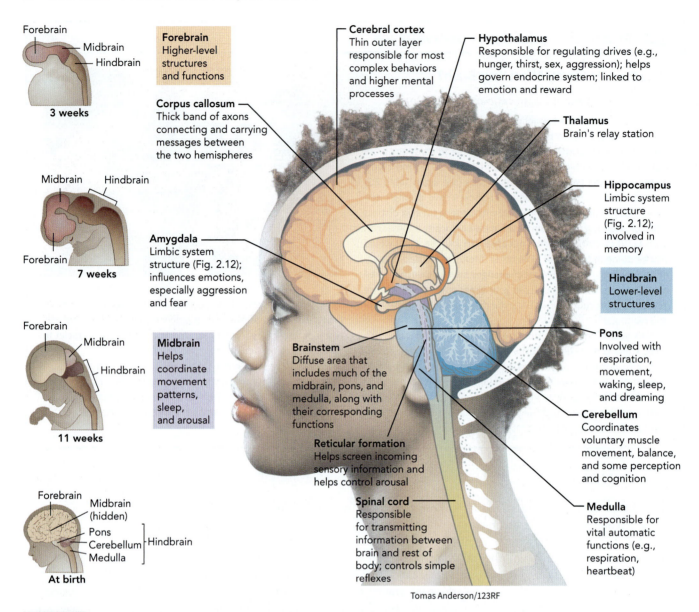

Forebrain
Midbrain
Hindbrain

3 weeks

Forebrain
Higher-level structures and functions

Midbrain   Hindbrain

Forebrain

7 weeks

Forebrain
Midbrain
Hindbrain

11 weeks

Midbrain
Helps coordinate movement patterns, sleep, and arousal

Forebrain
Midbrain (hidden)
Pons
Cerebellum — Hindbrain
Medulla

At birth

Corpus callosum
Thick band of axons connecting and carrying messages between the two hemispheres

Amygdala
Limbic system structure (Fig. 2.12); influences emotions, especially aggression and fear

Cerebral cortex
Thin outer layer responsible for most complex behaviors and higher mental processes

Brainstem
Diffuse area that includes much of the midbrain, pons, and medulla, along with their corresponding functions

Reticular formation
Helps screen incoming sensory information and helps control arousal

Spinal cord
Responsible for transmitting information between brain and rest of body; controls simple reflexes

Hypothalamus
Responsible for regulating drives (e.g., hunger, thirst, sex, aggression); helps govern endocrine system; linked to emotion and reward

Thalamus
Brain's relay station

Hippocampus
Limbic system structure (Fig. 2.12); involved in memory

Hindbrain
Lower-level structures

Pons
Involved with respiration, movement, waking, sleep, and dreaming

Cerebellum
Coordinates voluntary muscle movement, balance, and some perception and cognition

Medulla
Responsible for vital automatic functions (e.g., respiration, heartbeat)

Tomas Anderson/123RF

FIGURE 2.9 **The human brain** Note on the left side of this figure how the forebrain, midbrain, and hindbrain radically change in their size and placement during prenatal development. The profile drawing in the middle highlights key structures and functions of the right half of the adult brain. As you read about each of these structures, keep this drawing in mind and refer to it as necessary. (The diagram shows the brain structures as if the brain were split vertically down the middle and if the left hemisphere were removed.)

Hindbrain The lower or hind region of the brain; a collection of structures including the medulla, pons, and cerebellum.

Medulla The hindbrain structure responsible for vital automatic functions, such as respiration and heartbeat.

Pons The hindbrain structure involved in respiration, movement, waking, sleep, and dreaming.

Cerebellum The hindbrain structure responsible for coordinating fine muscle movement, balance, and some perception and cognition.

Hindbrain
Picture this: You're asleep and in the middle of a frightening nightmare. Your heart is racing, your breathing is rapid, and you're attempting to run away but find you can't move! Suddenly, your nightmare is shattered by a buzzing alarm clock. All your automatic behaviors and survival responses in this scenario are controlled or influenced by parts of the hindbrain. The **hindbrain** includes the medulla, pons, and cerebellum.

The **medulla** is essentially an extension of the spinal cord, with many neural fibers passing through it carrying information to and from the brain. Because the medulla controls many essential automatic bodily functions, such as respiration and heart rate, serious damage to this area is most often fatal.

The **pons** is involved in respiration, movement, sleeping, waking, and dreaming (among other things). It also contains axons that cross from one side of the brain to the other (*pons* is Latin for "bridge").

The cauliflower-shaped **cerebellum** (Latin for "little brain") is, evolutionarily, a very old structure. It is primarily responsible for coordinating fine muscle movement and balance.

PAN Practical Application of Neuroscience

Why is the cerebellum important? As shown in **Figure 2.10**, your cerebellum controls several important functions related to fine muscle movement and balance. It also plays a role in perception, cognition, social behavior, and even "multitasking" (e.g., Carta et al., 2019; Ng et al., 2016; Presti, 2016).

Interestingly, researchers have found that people who play video games for 30 minutes a day for two months show increases in gray matter in the cerebellum—along with other brain areas (Kühn et al., 2014). Gray matter is critical for higher cognitive functioning, and we'll study more about it in the next section. For now it's enough to know that the cerebellum is largely responsible for spatial navigation, strategic planning, and fine motor skills in the hands, which suggests that playing video games may actually be good for your brain.

Tom Wood/Alamy Stock Photo

FIGURE 2.10 Walk the line
Asking drivers to perform tasks like walking the white line is a common part of a field sobriety test for possible intoxication. Why? The cerebellum, responsible for smooth and precise movements, is one of the first areas of the brain to be affected by alcohol.

Midbrain The collection of structures in the middle of the brain responsible for coordinating movement patterns, sleep, and arousal.

Reticular formation (RF) The set of neurons that helps screen incoming information and helps control arousal.

Brainstem An area of the brain that includes much of the midbrain, pons, and medulla; responsible for automatic survival functions, such as respiration and heartbeat.

Forebrain The collection of upper-level brain structures including the cerebral cortex, limbic system, thalamus, and hypothalamus.

Limbic system The interconnected group of forebrain structures involved with emotions, drives, and memory; its two most important structures are the hippocampus and amygdala.

Amygdala A part of the limbic system linked to the production and regulation of emotions—especially aggression and fear.

Hippocampus The seahorse-shaped part of the limbic system involved in forming and retrieving memories.

Midbrain As mentioned earlier, the hindbrain and midbrain are primarily responsible for basic survival. To do this, the **midbrain** helps us orient our eye and body movements to visual and auditory stimuli, and it works with the pons to help control sleep and level of arousal. It also contains a small structure, the *substantia nigra*, that secretes the neurotransmitter dopamine. Deterioration of neurons in the substantia nigra and the subsequent loss of dopamine causes abnormal brain activity, leading to symptoms of Parkinson's disease.

Running through the core of the hindbrain and midbrain is the **reticular formation (RF)**. This finger-shaped network of neurons helps screen incoming sensory information and alert the higher brain centers to important events. It also plays a central role in arousal. Without our reticular formation, we would not be alert or perhaps even conscious.

Before going on, it's important to note that the reticular formation also passes through the **brainstem**, which includes much of the midbrain, pons, and medulla in the hindbrain (see again Figure 2.9). At its lower end, the brainstem connects with the spinal cord, and at its upper end it attaches to the thalamus.

Forebrain The **forebrain** is the largest and most prominent part of the human brain. It includes four key structures—the cerebral cortex, limbic system, thalamus, and hypothalamus (**Figure 2.11**). The last three are located near the top of the brainstem. The cerebral cortex (discussed separately, in the next section) is wrapped above and around them. (*Cerebrum* is Latin for "brain," and *cortex* is Latin for "covering" or "bark.")

Limbic System An interconnected group of forebrain structures, known as the **limbic system**, is located roughly along the border between the cerebral cortex and the lower-level brain structures (**Figure 2.12**). Although the limbic system is generally responsible for emotions, drives, and memory, one of it's most important structures, the **amygdala**, is particularly linked with aggression and fear (Cohen et al., 2016; Doré et al., 2019; Schönfeld & Wojtecki, 2019).

In Chapter 7, you'll discover how the seahorse-shaped **hippocampus**, the second key part of the limbic system, is involved in forming and retrieving our memories. **[AQ4]** Experimenters interested in the effects of exercise on the hippocampus and memory asked 36 college students to sit quietly on a stationary bicycle for ten minutes while their brains were being studied inside a MRI machine (Suwabe et al., 2018). Then, in a second session of the same length also within the MRI machine, the same students were asked to pedal the bike so gently that their heart rates were barely raised (see photo). After both sitting and slowly pedaling, the students were given several memory tasks to complete. The MRI scans of the gentle pedalers showed that portions of their hippocampus lit up in synchronized fashion with various parts of the brain associated with learning. Interestingly, the greater the coordination between the disparate parts of the brain, the better the gentle pedalers performed on the memory test.

monkeybusinessimages/iStock/Getty Images

FIGURE 2.11 **Structures of the forebrain**

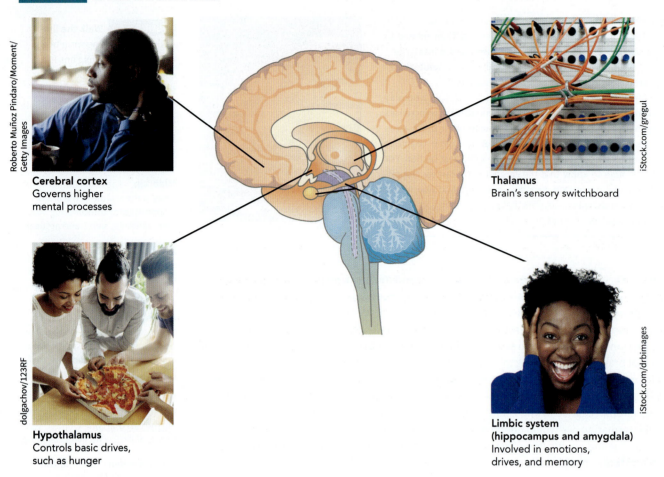

Cerebral cortex
Governs higher
mental processes

Hypothalamus
Controls basic drives,
such as hunger

Thalamus
Brain's sensory switchboard

**Limbic system
(hippocampus and amygdala)**
Involved in emotions,
drives, and memory

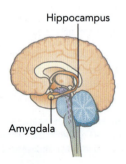

Hippocampus

Amygdala

FIGURE 2.12 **Key brain structures commonly associated with
the limbic system**

Thalamus The forebrain structure at the top of the brainstem
that relays sensory messages to
and from the cerebral cortex.

Do you see the exciting practical implications of this research? It suggests that even
very simple and short exercise can change our brains in minutes (rather than weeks or
months) of working out. Moreover, the equipment and exertion were so minor that almost
anyone could complete the exercise, even those who are out of shape or are disabled in
some way.

Thalamus In addition to the cerebral cortex and the limbic system, the third major
structure of the forebrain, the **thalamus**, is located at the top of the brainstem. It integrates
input from the senses, and it may also function in learning and memory. The thalamus
receives input from nearly all sensory systems, except smell, and then directs the information to the appropriate cortical areas. The thalamus also transmits some higher brain
information to the cerebellum and medulla. Think of the thalamus as the switchboard in
an air traffic control center that receives information from all planes and directs them to
appropriate landing or takeoff areas.

Because the thalamus relays sensory impulses from receptors located throughout the
body to the cerebral cortex, damage or abnormalities in the thalamus might lead to the cortex
misinterpreting or not receiving vital sensory information. As you'll discover in Chapter 13,
brain-imaging research links thalamus abnormalities to schizophrenia, a serious psychological disorder characterized by problems with sensory filtering and perception (Buchy et al.,
2015; Steullet, 2019; Wolff & Vann, 2019).

Hypothalamus   Beneath the thalamus lies the forebrain's fourth major structure, the kidney bean–sized **hypothalamus** (*hypo-* means "under"). This organ controls the body's internal environment, including temperature, which it accomplishes by regulating the endocrine system. It has also been called the "master control center" for many basic motives or drives, such as hunger, thirst, sex, and aggression, along with being linked to emotions and the reward system.

Hypothalamus   The small forebrain structure beneath the thalamus that helps govern the endocrine system (e.g., temperature), motives or drives (e.g., hunger, thirst, sex), and is linked to emotions and the reward system.

S&P Scientific Thinking and Practical Application

Have you ever gone on a diet and successfully lost weight, but then struggled to maintain the loss?
One of the reasons long-term weight loss is so hard for many people is that eating a high-fat diet can lead to long-term changes in the hypothalamus (Lizarbe et al., 2019; Stamatakis et al., 2016; Zhang et al., 2015). These changes make it harder for the body to regulate its weight, meaning that you will continue to feel hungry even when you have just eaten plenty of food. Sadly, this process makes it hard to stick to a diet and thereby increases the risk of obesity (Miller & Spencer, 2014).

Another well-known function of the hypothalamus is its role as part of the so-called pleasure center, a set of brain structures whose stimulation leads to highly enjoyable feelings (Lazaridis et al., 2019; Naneix et al., 2016; Olds & Milner, 1954). The hypothalamus also directly influences some important aspects of behavior, such as eating and drinking patterns.

Hanging down from the hypothalamus, the *pituitary gland* is usually considered the master endocrine gland because it releases hormones that activate the other endocrine glands. The hypothalamus influences the pituitary through direct neural connections and through the release of its own hormones into the blood supply of the pituitary.

Retrieval Practice 2.3 | A Tour Through the Brain

Self-Test   Completing this self-test, and then checking your answers by clicking on the answer button or by looking in Appendix B, will provide immediate feedback and helpful practice for exams.

1. Damage to the medulla can lead to loss of _____.

   a. vision

   b. respiration

   c. hearing

   d. smell

2. The pons, cerebellum, and the medulla are all _____.

   a. higher-level brain structures

   b. cortical areas

   c. association areas

   d. a part of the hindbrain

3. The brainstem is primarily involved with your _____.

   a. sense of smell and taste

   b. sense of touch and pain

   c. automatic survival functions

   d. emotional behavior

4. An interconnected group of forebrain structures particularly responsible for emotions is known as the _____.

   a. subcortical center

   b. homeostatic controller

   c. limbic system

   d. master endocrine gland

Q Test Your Critical Thinking

1. Which tool for biological research do you consider the least invasive and damaging? Which would be the most dangerous?

2. Given that the limbic system is largely responsible for our emotional arousal and expression, do you think people with significant damage to this section of the brain should be held less responsible for violent crimes? Why or why not?

Real World Application Question

[AQ4]   Could gently riding a bike for ten minutes affect your memory and hippocampus?

monkeybusinessimages/
iStock/Getty Images

Hint: Look in the text for **[AQ4]**

The Cerebral Cortex

LEARNING OBJECTIVES

Retrieval Practice While reading the upcoming sections, respond to each Learning Objective in your own words.

Summarize the key features and major divisions of the cerebral cortex.

- **Discuss** the location and functions of the eight lobes of the cerebral cortex.

- **Describe** the brain's two specialized hemispheres and split-brain research.

Real World Application Questions

[AQ5] Why are some professional athletes at increased risk of depression, dementia, and suicide?

[AQ6] Can high-fat foods decrease your cognitive efficiency?

Cerebral cortex The thin surface layer on the cerebral hemispheres that regulates most complex behavior, including sensations, motor control, and higher mental processes.

Avpics/Alamy Stock Photo

Damage to the brain Cyclist Kelly Catlin was part of the U.S. women's cycling team that won a silver medal in the 2016 Rio Olympic Games, along with three world championships in cycling between 2016 and 2018. Unfortunately, she suffered several crashes on her bike and sustained at least one serious concussion, which led to bouts of severe depression and most likely to her heart-breaking death by suicide in 2019 at the age of 23 (Ingber, 2019; Oates, 2019).

The gray, wrinkled **cerebral cortex**, the surface layer of the cerebral hemispheres, is responsible for most complex behaviors and higher mental processes. It plays such a vital role that many consider it the essence of life itself. The full cerebral cortex and the two cerebral hemispheres beneath it closely resemble an oversized walnut. The division, or *fissure*, down the center marks the separation between the left and right *hemispheres* of the brain, which make up about 80 percent of the brain's weight. The hemispheres are mostly filled with axon connections between the cortex and the other brain structures. Each hemisphere controls the opposite side of the body (**Figure 2.13**).

Although the cerebral cortex is only about one-eighth of an inch thick, it's made up of approximately 30 billion neurons and nine times as many glial cells. Its numerous wrinkles, called *convolutions*, significantly increase its surface area.

Damage to the cerebral cortex is linked to numerous problems, including suicide, substance abuse, and dementia (Fralick et al., 2019; Lim et al., 2019; Tharmaratnam et al., 2018). **[AQ5]** Evidence suggests that such trauma is particularly common in professional athletes who experience head injuries in sports like football, ice hockey, boxing, soccer, and even cycling, as in the case of Olympic cyclist Kelly Catlin (see photo). Her tragic suicide highlights the need for greater support and public awareness of both the physical and mental health issues of athletes.

Lobes of the Brain

The cerebral hemispheres are each divided into four distinct areas, or lobes (**Figure 2.14**). Like the lower-level brain structures, each lobe specializes in somewhat different tasks, another example of localization of function. However, some functions overlap two or more lobes.

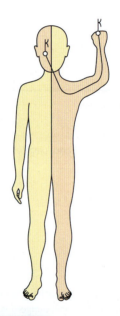

FIGURE 2.13 Information crossover Our brain's right hemisphere controls the left side of our body, whereas the left hemisphere controls the right side.

Frontal lobes The two lobes at the front of the brain that govern motor control, speech production, and higher cognitive processes, such as executive functions, intelligence, and personality.

Executive functions (EFs) A set of higher-order cognitive processes controlled by the brain's frontal lobes.

Frontal Lobes By far the largest of the cortical lobes, the two **frontal lobes** are located at the top front portion of the two brain hemispheres—right behind the forehead. The frontal lobes are generally what we think of as "our mind," and they receive and coordinate messages from all other lobes of the cortex, while also being responsible for at least three additional functions:

1. **Higher cognitive processes** The frontal lobes control most of our complex cognitive processes, including **executive functions (EFs)**, intelligence, and personality. Research suggests that EFs are composed of three major abilities—*cognitive flexibility* ("thinking outside the box"), *working memory*, and *impulse control*. It is also believed that EFs are crucial for success in all parts of life. Moreover, work with very young children has shown that EFs can be identified, developed, and improved with practice (Diamond, 2013, 2016; Kraybill et al., 2019).

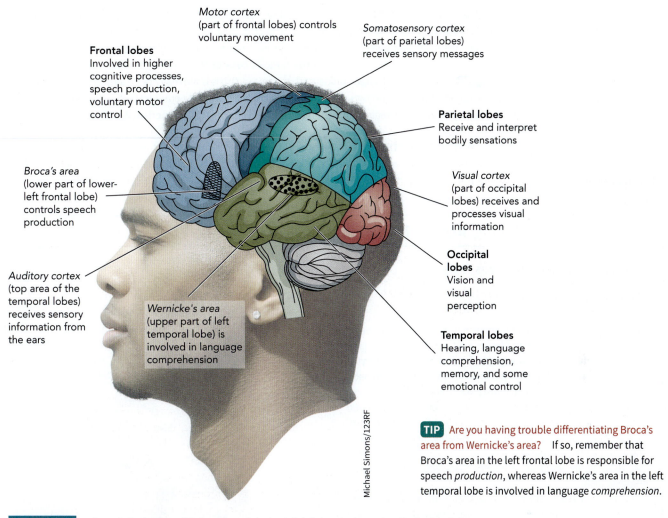

Motor cortex
(part of frontal lobes) controls
voluntary movement

Somatosensory cortex
(part of parietal lobes)
receives sensory messages

Frontal lobes
Involved in higher
cognitive processes,
speech production,
voluntary motor
control

Parietal lobes
Receive and interpret
bodily sensations

Broca's area
(lower part of lower-
left frontal lobe)
controls speech
production

Visual cortex
(part of occipital
lobes) receives and
processes visual
information

**Occipital
lobes**
Vision and
visual
perception

Auditory cortex
(top area of the
temporal lobes)
receives sensory
information from
the ears

Wernicke's area
(upper part of left
temporal lobe) is
involved in language
comprehension

Temporal lobes
Hearing, language
comprehension,
memory, and some
emotional control

Michael Simons/123RF

TIP Are you having trouble differentiating Broca's
area from Wernicke's area?   If so, remember that
Broca's area in the left frontal lobe is responsible for
speech *production*, whereas Wernicke's area in the left
temporal lobe is involved in language *comprehension*.

FIGURE 2.14   **Lobes of the brain**   This is a view of the brain's left hemisphere showing its four lobes—
frontal, parietal, temporal, and *occipital*. The right hemisphere has the same four lobes. Divisions between
the lobes are marked by visibly prominent folds. Keep in mind that Broca's and Wernicke's areas occur
only in the left hemisphere.

2. **Speech production**   Broca's area, located in the *left* frontal lobe near the bottom of the
motor control area, plays a crucial role in speech production. In 1865, French physician Paul
Broca discovered that damage to this area is linked with difficulty in speech, but not language
comprehension. This type of impaired language ability is known as *Broca's aphasia*.

3. **Voluntary motor control**   At the very back of the frontal lobes lies the *motor cortex*, which
sends messages to the various muscles that instigate voluntary movement. When you want
to text a new friend on your phone, the motor control area of your frontal lobes guides your
fingers to press the desired sequence of numbers and letters to form your message.

As you might imagine, damage to the frontal lobes can be very serious because they are largely
responsible for motivation, drives, creativity, self-awareness, initiative, and reasoning. Individuals suffering from schizophrenia (Chapter 13) often show loss of tissue and abnormal brain
activity in the frontal lobes (Allen et al., 2019; Lake et al., 2017; Watsky et al., 2016).

[AQ6]   Researchers have even found that a high-fat diet can negatively affect synapses
in the frontal lobes (see photo), which in turn appears to increase the chances of cognitive and
psychiatric problems in later life—especially if these foods are consumed during the teenage
years (Labouesse et al., 2017). Why? Apparently, these foods deplete levels of a key protein that
helps synapses in the frontal lobes function properly.

Kiattikhun Nilsophon/123RF

At this point in the chapter, you may be feeling overwhelmed with all the new terms and functions of the brain and nervous system. If so, please note that this information is essential to understanding every chapter of this text and the entire field of psychology. More importantly, recognizing

that your brain is YOU—all your personality, your thoughts, and your very life—will undoubtedly increase your motivation to study and protect it. Just as we routinely wear shoes to protect our feet, we need seat belts and helmets to protect our far more fragile brains. On a more encouraging note, updated information on the famous case of Phineas Gage, which is discussed in the **RC** **Research Challenge**, indicates that damage to the brain may not be as permanent as we once thought, thanks to the two processes we discussed earlier—*neuroplasticity* and *neurogenesis*. For further good news regarding your frontal lobes, see the **PAH** **Practical Application Highlight**.

Temporal lobes The two lobes above the ears, one on each side of the brain, that are involved in audition (hearing), language comprehension, memory, and some emotional control.

Temporal Lobes
The **temporal lobes** are responsible for audition (hearing), language comprehension, memory, and some emotional control. The *auditory cortex*, which processes sound, is located at the top front of each temporal lobe. This area is responsible for receiving

---

RC Scientific Thinking: **Research Challenge**

Phineas Gage—Myths Versus Facts

(APA Goal 2.4) Interpret, design, and conduct basic psychological research

In 1848, a 25-year-old railroad foreman named Phineas Gage had a metal rod (13½ pounds, 3 feet 7 inches long, and 1¼ inches in diameter) accidentally blown through the front of his face, destroying much of his brain's left frontal lobe. Amazingly, Gage was immediately able to sit up, speak, and move around, and he did not receive medical treatment until about 1½ hours later. After his wound healed, he tried to return to work, but reportedly was soon fired. The previously friendly, efficient, and capable foreman was now "fitful, impatient, and lacking in deference to his fellows" (Macmillan, 2000). In the words of his friends, "Gage was no longer Gage" (Harlow, 1868).

This so-called American Crowbar Case is often cited in current texts and academic papers as one of the earliest in-depth studies of an individual's survival after massive damage to the brain's frontal lobes. The evidence is clear that Gage did experience several dramatic changes in his behavior and personality after the accident, but the extent and permanence of these changes are in dispute (e.g., Damasio, 2018). Most accounts of post-accident Gage report him as impulsive and unreliable until his death. However, more recent evidence finds that Gage spent many years driving stage-coaches—a job that required high motor, cognitive, and interpersonal skills (Griggs, 2015; Macmillan & Lena, 2010).

So why bother reporting this controversy? As you'll note throughout this text, we discuss several popular misconceptions in psychology in order to clarify and correct them. Phineas Gage's story is particularly important because it highlights how a small set of reliable facts can be distorted and shaped to fit existing beliefs and scientific theories. At the time of Gage's accident, for instance, little was known about how the brain functions, and damage to it was believed to be largely irreversible. Can you see how our current research techniques, along with our new understanding of *neurogenesis* and *neuroplasticity*, might now explain the previously ignored evidence of Gage's significant recovery in later life?

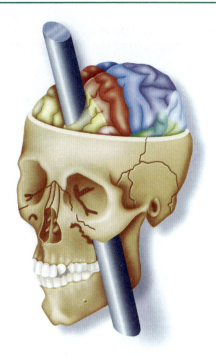

Identify the Research Method

1. Based on the information provided, did the researchers in this study of Phineas Gage use descriptive, correlational, and/or experimental research?

2. If you chose:
   - *descriptive research*, is this a naturalistic or laboratory observation, survey/interview, case study, and/or archival research?
   - *correlational research*, is this a positive, negative, or zero correlation?
   - *experimental research*, label the IV, DV, experimental group(s), and control group. (Note: If participants were not randomly assigned to groups, list the design as *quasi-experimental*.)
   - both *descriptive* and *correlational*, answer the corresponding questions for both.

Check your answers by clicking on the answer button or by looking in Appendix B.

Note: The information provided in this study is admittedly limited, but the level of detail is similar to what is presented in most textbooks and public reports of research findings. Answering these questions, and then comparing your answers to those provided, will help you become a better scientific and critical thinker and consumer of scientific research.

PAH Practical Application Highlight

Can You Use Your Frontal Lobes to Train Your Brain?

(APA Goal 1.3) Describe applications of psychology

Being a college student, you probably make resolutions at the beginning of each new year, such as studying more, partying less, and so on. But did you know that most New Year's resolutions made in January have been broken by the beginning of February? Why? The general answer is faulty brain training. The good news is that by understanding your frontal lobes, you now have the power to create positive brain training that leads to lasting, healthy changes in your life.

As you can see in **Process Diagram 2.4**, making a change in your life begins within your brain's frontal lobes. Using your *executive functions*, first identify the problem you want to solve (a behavior you want to change). Next, develop a plan for implementing the desired change. Then activate an "I can do it" attitude by reminding yourself of your abilities and potential for change and improvement. For example, if your identified problem is that you need to study more to achieve your long-term goals, you might start by self-monitoring and keeping careful notes of what you do throughout a typical day. If, as a result of the self-monitoring, you notice that you watch television every night instead of studying, decide what you need to do to increase your impulse control and delay your gratification (Chapter 11), and then implement the new behavior.

One way to accomplish all of this might be to create a rule that you cannot turn on your television until you've studied for at least one hour. You can later expand on this rule by thinking flexibly and maybe adding another rule that you can only check your email or social media after studying for ten minutes. Keep in mind that these rewards should be small, immediate, and presented AFTER the appropriate behavior (Chapter 6). Keep in mind that it takes time to develop new behaviors. We all need time, repeated practice, and continued reinforcement to successfully train our brains.

> **STOP!** This Process Diagram contains essential information NOT found elsewhere in the text, which is likely to appear on quizzes and exams. Be sure to study it CAREFULLY.

PROCESS DIAGRAM 2.4 **Brain Training—A "Virtuous" Cycle** Note the arrows joining the three steps. They signal that with repeated practice the new behavior becomes self-reinforcing. Research has shown that healthy behaviors, exercise in particular, actually improve your brain's frontal lobes and executive functions, including cognitive flexibility, impulse control, and other higher cognitive processes (Allan et al., 2016; Diamond, 2013, 2016). By pushing through the first few weeks of a behavior change, you'll be ultimately rewarded with stronger frontal lobes and enhanced executive functions, which will transfer to all areas of your life.

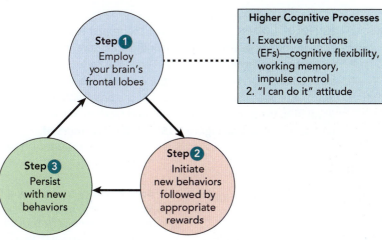

Higher Cognitive Processes

1. Executive functions (EFs)—cognitive flexibility, working memory, impulse control
2. "I can do it" attitude

Step 1 Employ your brain's frontal lobes

Step 2 Initiate new behaviors followed by appropriate rewards

Step 3 Persist with new behaviors

incoming sensory information and sending it on to the parietal lobes, where it is combined with other sensory information.

A part of the left temporal lobe called *Wernicke's area* aids in language comprehension. About a decade after Broca's discovery, German neurologist Carl Wernicke noted that patients with damage in this area could not understand what they read or heard, but they could speak quickly and easily. However, their speech was often unintelligible because it contained made-up words, sound substitutions, and word substitutions. This syndrome is now referred to as *Wernicke's aphasia*.

Occipital Lobes   The **occipital lobes** are responsible for, among other things, vision and visual perception. Damage to the occipital lobes can produce blindness, even if the eyes and their neural connection to the brain are perfectly healthy.

Occipital lobes The two lobes at the back of the brain that are primarily responsible for vision and visual perception.

FIGURE 2.15 **Body representation of the motor cortex and somatosensory cortex** This drawing shows a vertical cross section taken from the left hemisphere's motor cortex and right hemisphere's somatosensory cortex. If body areas were truly proportional to the amount of tissue on the motor and somatosensory cortices that affected them, our bodies would look like the oddly shaped human figures draped around the outside edge of the cortex.

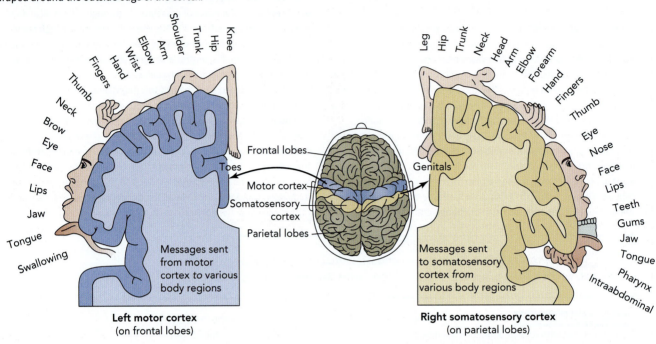

Left motor cortex
(on frontal lobes)

a. Note how larger areas of the *motor cortex* are devoted to body parts that need to be controlled with great precision, such as the hands, face, and tongue.

Right somatosensory cortex
(on parietal lobes)

b. Similar areas of the *somatosensory cortex* are also disproportionately large because these body parts contain a high number of sensory receptors, which makes them particularly sensitive.

Parietal lobes The two lobes located at the top of the brain in which bodily sensations are received and interpreted.

Parietal Lobes At the back of the frontal lobes, lies the **parietal lobes**, which receive and interpret bodily sensations including pressure, pain, touch, temperature, and location of body parts (see again Figure 2.14). The *motor cortex*, which is in the rear portion of the frontal lobe, is immediately adjacent to the *somatosensory cortex*, which receives information about touch in different body areas. Areas of the body with more somatosensory and motor cortex devoted to them (such as the hands and face) are most sensitive to touch and have the most precise motor control (**Figure 2.15**). See the **Test Yourself**.

PA Practical Application

Test Yourself: Understanding Your Motor Cortex and Somatosensory Cortex

1. **Motor cortex** Try wiggling each of your fingers one at a time. Now try wiggling each of your toes. Noting in Figure 2.15 how the area of your motor cortex is much larger for your fingers than for your toes, can you see how this explains why it's so much easier to wiggle each of your fingers versus your toes?

2. **Somatosensory cortex** Ask a friend to close his or her eyes. Using a random number of fingers (one to four), press down on the skin of your friend's back for 1 to 2 seconds. Then ask, "How many fingers am I using?" Repeat the same procedure on the palm or back of the hand. Note the increased accuracy of responses to pressing on the hand. The fact that the area of the somatosensory cortex is much larger for the hands than for the back explains why our hands have much greater sensitivity than our backs.

Association areas The "quiet" areas in the cerebral cortex involved in interpreting, integrating, and acting on information processed by other parts of the brain.

Association Areas One of the most popular myths in psychology is that we use only ten percent of our brains. This myth might have begun with early research which showed that approximately three-fourths of the cortex is "quiet" (with no precise, specific function responsive to electrical brain stimulation). Later research, however, found that these association areas are clearly engaged in interpreting, integrating, and acting on information processed by other parts of the brain. They are called **association areas** because they *associate*, or connect, various areas and functions of the brain. Association areas in the frontal lobes, for example, help in decision making and planning. Similarly, the association area right in front of the motor cortex aids in the planning of voluntary movement.

Two Brains in One?

We mentioned earlier that the brain's left and right cerebral hemispheres control opposite sides of the body. Each hemisphere also has separate areas of specialization, which is an example of localization of function or *lateralization*.

Early researchers believed the right hemisphere was non-dominant or subordinant to the left, with few special functions or abilities. However, in the 1960s, landmark **split-brain surgeries** began to change this view. In some rare cases of severe epilepsy, when other forms of treatment have failed, surgeons sometimes perform split-brain surgeries, which involve cutting through the **corpus callosum** (**Figure 2.16**), to stop (or severely limit) the spread of epileptic seizures from one hemisphere to the other.

Given that the corpus callosum (Figure 2.16) is the primary connection between the two cerebral hemispheres, cutting through it stops the flow of messages between the two hemispheres, which not only lessens the frequency and severity of the epilepsy seizures but also reveals what each half of the brain can do in isolation from the other.

Although most split-brain surgery patients show very few outward changes in their behavior, the surgery does create a few unusual responses. One split-brain patient reported that when he dressed himself, he sometimes pulled his pants down with his left hand and up with his right (Gazzaniga, 2009). The subtle changes in split-brain patients normally appear only with specialized testing. See **Figure 2.17** for an illustration and description of this type of specialized test. Keep in mind that in actual split-brain surgery on live patients, only some fibers within the corpus callosum are cut (*not* the lower brain structures). Furthermore, with advances in modern drug treatments, this type of surgery has become extremely rare.

The resulting research has profoundly improved our understanding of how the two halves of the brain function. For example, when someone has had a brain stroke and loses his or her language comprehension or ability to speak, we know this generally points to damage in the left hemisphere, because this is where *Wernicke's area*, which is responsible for language comprehension, and *Broca's area*, which controls speech production, are located (refer back to Figure 2.14). Note however, that we now know that when specific regions of the brain are injured or destroyed, their functions can sometimes be picked up by a neighboring region—even the opposite hemisphere.

S&P Scientific Thinking and Practical Application

Have you heard people referring to their "neglected right brain" or how they're "right-brain dominant"?   Popular accounts of split-brain research have led to some exaggerated claims and unwarranted conclusions about differences between the left and right hemispheres. As an example, courses and books directed at "right-brain thinking" and "drawing on the right side of the brain" often promise to increase our intuition, creativity, and artistic abilities by "waking up" our neglected and underused right brain. Contrary to this myth, research has clearly shown that the two hemispheres work together in a coordinated, integrated way, each making important contributions (Garrett, 2015; Kaufman, 2019; Lilienfeld et al., 2015).

If you are a member of a soccer or basketball team, you can easily understand this principle. Just as you and your teammates often specialize in different jobs, such as offense and defense, the hemispheres also somewhat divide their workload. However, like good team players, each of the two hemispheres is generally aware of what the other is doing.

FIGURE 2.16 **Views of the corpus callosum**   **a.** This photo of the "half-brain" on the blue background, is a view of a human brain that was sliced vertically from the top to the bottom to expose the corpus callosum, which conveys information between the two hemispheres of the cerebral cortex. **b.** This top-down illustration of a brain with portions of the right hemisphere removed, which shows how fibers, or axons, of the corpus callosum link to both right and left hemispheres. Note: The deep, extensive cuts shown in these images are to reveal the corpus callosum. In split-brain surgeries on live patients, only some fibers within the corpus callosum itself are cut.

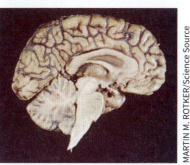

a. Side-view of the left hemisphere

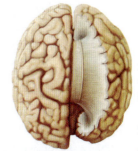

b. Top-down view of the left hemisphere

Split-brain surgery   The cutting of some fibers within the corpus callosum to separate the brain's two hemispheres; used medically to treat severe epilepsy; provides information on the functions of the two hemispheres.

Corpus callosum   A bundle of neural fibers that connects the brain's two hemispheres.

FIGURE 2.17 **Split-brain research** Experiments on split-brain patients often present visual information to only the patient's left or right hemisphere, which leads to some intriguing results.

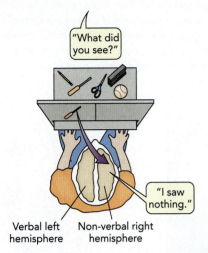

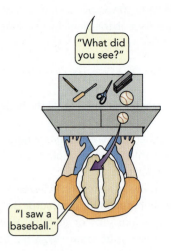

a. When a split-brain patient is asked to stare straight ahead while a photo of a screwdriver is flashed only to the right hemisphere, he will report that he "saw nothing."

b. However, when asked to pick up with his left hand what he saw, he can reach through and touch the items hidden behind the screen and easily pick up the screwdriver.

c. When the left hemisphere receives an image of a baseball, the split-brain patient can easily name it.

- -

Assuming you have an intact, non-severed corpus callosum, if the same photos were presented to you in the same way, you could easily name both the screwdriver and the baseball. Can you explain why? The answers lie in our somewhat confusing visual wiring system (as shown in Figures D and E below).

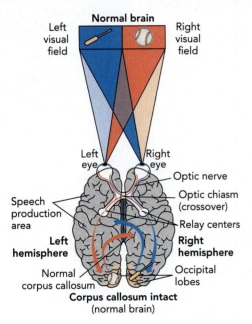

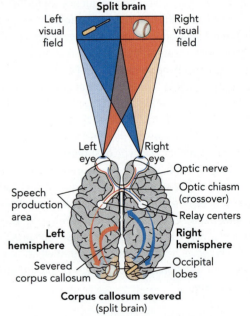

d. As you can see, our eyes normally connect to our brains in such a way that, when we look straight ahead, information from the left visual field travels to our right hemisphere (the blue line). In contrast, information from the right visual field travels to our left hemisphere (the red line). The messages received by either hemisphere are then quickly sent to the other across the corpus callosum (the red and blue arrows).

e. When the corpus callosum is severed (note the white line down the middle of the two hemispheres), a split-brain patient cannot state out loud the name of what he sees in the left visual field (in this case "screwdriver"). Why? It's because the image from the left visual field is sent to both eyes, but only to the right side of the brain. For most people, the speech-control center is in the left hemisphere, and information from either hemisphere is normally passed quickly to the other hemisphere across the corpus callosum. However, in the split-brain patient, the corpus callosum is severed and communication between the two hemispheres is blocked. (Compare how the red and blue arrows cross over to the opposite hemisphere in Figure D versus how the same arrows are limited to only one hemisphere here in Figure E.)

In our tour of the nervous system, the principles of localization of function, lateralization, and specialization recur: Dendrites receive information, the occipital lobes specialize in vision, and so on. On the other hand, it's also important to remember that all parts of the brain and nervous system also play overlapping and synchronized roles. Before going on, be sure to complete the final Retrieval Practice, and then answer the critical thinking questions in the **Test Your Critical Thinking** feature.

Retrieval Practice 2.4 | The Cerebral Cortex

Self-Test   Completing this self-test, and then checking your answers by clicking on the answer button or by looking in Appendix B, will provide immediate feedback and helpful practice for exams.

1. The _____ lobes are largely responsible for voluntary motor control, speech production, and higher cognitive processes, such as thinking, personality, and memory.

   a. cortical   **c.** parietal

   b. frontal   **d.** occipital

2. Specialization of the left and right hemispheres of the brain for particular operations is known as _____.

   a. centralization   **c.** normalization of function

   b. asymmetrical processing   **d.** lateralization

3. Although the left and right hemispheres sometimes perform different, specialized functions, they are normally in close communication and share functions, thanks to the _____.

   a. thalamus system   **c.** corpus callosum

   b. sympathetic nervous system **d.** cerebellum

4. Split-brain research has indicated that, in most people, the left hemisphere is largely responsible for our abilities in _____.

   a. athletic and spatial   **c.** speech and language

   b. music and artistic   **d.** none of these options

Q Test Your Critical Thinking

1. Imagine that you are giving a speech. Name the cortical lobes involved in the following behaviors:

   a. Seeing faces in the audience

   b. Hearing questions from the audience

   c. Remembering where your car is parked when you are ready to go home

   d. Noticing that your new shoes are too tight and hurting your feet

2. What are some everyday examples of the different functions of the two hemispheres?

Real World Application Questions

[AQ5] Why are some professional athletes at increased risk of depression, dementia, and suicide?

[AQ6] Can high-fat foods decrease your cognitive efficiency?

Avpics/Alamy Stock Photo

Kiattikhun Nilsophon/123RF

Hint: Look in the text for **[AQ5]** and **[AQ6]**

Q Test Your Critical Thinking

Did you notice or wonder why we provided six Real World Application Questions [AQ1–AQ6] throughout this chapter? We've found that they not only help you to engage with and master the material, they also have an important and lasting impact on your critical thinking skills. For additional mastery and enrichment, consider the following questions:

1. If you were one of the parents in this photo, what might you do to protect and maximize your infant's brain development?

2. Given that neglect in the first few months of life leads to lasting problems, what can we do as a society to increase parental bonding and infant security?

3. If neuroscientists were able to use brain scans to determine what a person was thinking, what might be the ethical considerations associated with this type of research?

4. Imagine that your friend Juan has suffered a major automobile accident, and now has right-sided paralysis. Given that he has lost his ability to speak, can you identify the specific section of the brain and which hemisphere was most likely damaged in the accident?

Kei Uesugi/Getty Images

5. Some research suggests that women are better than men at multitasking. In what part(s) of the brain would you expect to find gender based differences as a possible explanation?

Summary

2.1 Neural and Hormonal Processes 40

- **Neurons**, supported by **glial cells**, receive and send electrochemical signals to other neurons and to the rest of the body. Their major components are **dendrites**, a **cell body**, and an **axon**.

- Within a neuron, a neural impulse, or **action potential**, moves along the axon. Neurons communicate with each other using **neurotransmitters**, which are released at the **synapse** and attach to the receiving neuron. Neurons receive input from many synapses. Hundreds of different neurotransmitters regulate a wide variety of physiological processes. Many **agonist** and **antagonist drugs** and poisons act by mimicking or interfering with neurotransmitters.

- The **endocrine system** uses **hormones** to broadcast messages throughout the body. The system regulates long-term bodily processes, maintains ongoing bodily processes, and controls the body's response to emergencies.

2.2 Nervous System Organization 50

- The **central nervous system (CNS)** includes the brain and spinal cord. The CNS allows us to process information and adapt to our environment in ways that no other animal can. The spinal cord transmits information between the brain and the rest of the body, and it initiates involuntary **reflexes**. Although the CNS is very fragile, research shows that the brain is capable of lifelong **neuroplasticity** and **neurogenesis**. Neurogenesis is made possible by **stem cells**.

- The **peripheral nervous system (PNS)** includes all the nerves outside the brain and spinal cord. It links the brain and spinal cord to the body's sense receptors, muscles, and glands. The PNS is subdivided into the **somatic nervous system (SNS)**, which controls voluntary movement, and the **autonomic nervous system (ANS)**, which is responsible for automatic behaviors.

- The ANS includes the **sympathetic nervous system** and the **parasympathetic nervous system**. The sympathetic nervous system mobilizes the body's fight-flight-freeze response. The parasympathetic nervous system returns the body to its normal functioning.

2.3 A Tour Through the Brain 57

- Neuroscientists have developed several tools to explore the human brain and nervous system. Early researchers used dissection and other methods like clinical observation and case studies of living people. Recent scientific advances include new brain-imaging scans, which have improved scientists' ability to examine these processes and to do so non-invasively.

- The brain is divided into the **hindbrain**, **midbrain**, and **forebrain**. Certain brain structures are specialized to perform certain tasks thanks to *localization of function*.

- The hindbrain, including the **medulla, pons,** and **cerebellum**, controls automatic behaviors and survival responses.

- The midbrain helps us orient our eye and body movements, helps control sleep and arousal, and is involved with the neurotransmitter dopamine. The **reticular formation (RF)** runs through the core of the hindbrain, midbrain, and brainstem, and is responsible for screening information and managing our levels of alertness.

- Forebrain structures, including the **cerebral cortex, limbic system, thalamus**, and **hypothalamus**, integrate input from the senses, control basic motives, regulate the body's internal environment, and regulate emotions, learning, and memory.

2.4 The Cerebral Cortex 64

- The **cerebral cortex**, part of the forebrain, governs most higher processing and complex behaviors. It is divided into two hemispheres, each controlling the opposite side of the body. The **corpus callosum** links the hemispheres.

- Each hemisphere is divided into **frontal, parietal, temporal**, and **occipital lobes**. Each lobe specializes in somewhat different tasks, but a large part of the cortex, the **association areas**, are devoted to integrating actions performed by different brain regions.

- **Split-brain surgery** has shown that each hemisphere performs somewhat different functions, although they work in close communication.

Key Terms

Retrieval Practice Write your own definition for each term before turning back to the referenced page to check your answer.

Kuttelvaserova Stuchelova/Shutterstock.com

Stress, Coping, and Health Psychology

Real World Application Questions [AQ]

Things you'll learn in Chapter 3

[AQ1] How does social media affect stress?

[AQ2] Can the stress of growing up in poverty lead to significant changes in the brain?

[AQ3] Why are some chronic pain sufferers more susceptible to placebos than others?

[AQ4] Does watching televised coverage of natural disasters increase symptoms of posttraumatic stress disorder?

[AQ5] Can social integration with peers during childhood and adolescence help protect against high blood pressure and obesity in adulthood?

[AQ6] Are people with stressful jobs at increased risk of experiencing a heart attack?

Throughout the chapter, look for [AQ1]–[AQ6] icons. They indicate where the text addresses these questions.

CHAPTER OUTLINE

3.1 Understanding Stress

LEARNING OBJECTIVES

Retrieval Practice While reading the upcoming sections, respond to each Learning Objective in your own words.

Summarize the major issues and discoveries concerning stress.

- **Define** stress and stressors.
- **Identify** the major sources of stress.

- **Describe** our physical and cognitive reactions to stress.
- **Review** the benefits of stress.

Real World Application Questions

[AQ1] How does social media affect stress?

[AQ2] Can the stress of growing up in poverty lead to significant changes in the brain?

Stress The interpretation of specific events, called *stressors*, as threatening or challenging; the physical and psychological reactions to stressors are known as the *stress response*.

Stressor A trigger or stimulus that induces stress.

We begin this chapter with a general description of stress, along with its sources, effects, and surprising benefits. Next we explore how we cope with stress, and then close with a discussion of the field of health psychology.

Did you know that the latest APA annual stress report found that people currently between the ages of 15 and 21 are the most likely of all generations to report poor mental health (American Psychological Association, 2018)? This report also revealed that high-profile issues, like gun violence and sexual harassment, were among the most significant factors associated with this high level of stress.

Everyone experiences **stress**, and we generally know what a person means when he or she speaks of being "stressed." But scientists typically define stress as *the interpretation of specific events*, called **stressors**, *as threatening or challenging*. The resulting physical and psychological reactions to stressors are known as the *stress response* (Becker & Rohleder, 2019; Sanderson, 2013; Selye, 1936, 1983). Using these definitions, can you see how the gun violence and sexual harassment problems listed above would be called stressors, whereas their physical and psychological reactions would be their stress response? In this section, we'll discuss the key sources of stress and how it affects us. Before going on, test your general knowledge of stress and health in the **Test Yourself**.

PA Practical Application

Test Yourself: Stress—Myths and Misconceptions

Answer true or false to each item.

_____ **1.** Even positive events, like landing your first great job or getting married, are major sources of stress.

_____ **2.** Small, everyday hassles can impair your immune system functioning.

_____ **3.** Police officers, nurses, doctors, social workers, and teachers are particularly prone to "burnout."

_____ **4.** Stress causes cancer.

_____ **5.** Having a positive attitude can prevent cancer.

_____ **6.** Optimistic personality types may cope better with stress.

_____ **7.** Ulcers are caused primarily or entirely by stress.

_____ **8.** Friendship is one of your best health resources.

_____ **9.** Prolonged stress can lead to death.

_____ **10.** You can control, or minimize, most of the negative effects of stress.

Pablo Calvog/Shutterstock.com

Answers: Three out of the 10 questions are false. Looking for the false answers, while reading the chapter, will improve your mastery of the material.

Sources of Stress

Although literally hundreds of things can cause stress in all of our lives, psychological science has focused on seven major sources (**Figure 3.1**).

Life Changes   Early stress researchers Thomas Holmes and Richard Rahe (1967) believed that any *life change* that required some adjustment in behavior or lifestyle could cause some degree of stress. They also believed that exposure to numerous stressful events in a short period could have a direct, detrimental effect on health.

To investigate the relationship between change and stress, Holmes and Rahe created the Social Readjustment Rating Scale (SRRS), which asks people to check off all the life events they have experienced in the previous year (see the **Test Yourself** which is based on the SRRS). The SRRS is an easy and popular tool for measuring stress (e.g., Fabre et al., 2013), and cross-cultural studies have shown that most people rank the magnitude of their stressful events similarly (Bagheri et al., 2016; Loving & Sbarra, 2015; Noone, 2017). (As a scientific and critical thinker, did you note that like all surveys this is an example of correlational research? It only shows a *correlation* between stress and illness. It does not prove that stress actually *causes* illnesses.)

FIGURE 3.1   **Major sources of stress**

Conflict   A forced choice between two or more incompatible alternatives.

PA Practical Application

Test Yourself: Student Stress Scale

See how many of the following changes in your life as a student have occurred in the past year. Check all those that apply and then add up your score to see what your stress level is.

Life Events	Life Change Units	Life Events	Life Change Units
Death of a close family member	100	Increased workload at school	37
Death of a close friend	73	Outstanding personal achievement	36
Divorce between parents	65	First quarter/semester in college	35
Jail term	63	Change in living conditions	31
Major personal injury or illness	63	Serious argument with instructor	30
Marriage	58	Lower grades than expected	29
Fired from job	50	Change in sleeping habits	29
Failed important course	47	Change in social activities	29
Change in health of a family member	45	Change in eating habits	28
Pregnancy	45	Chronic car trouble	26
Sex problems	44	Change in number of family get-togethers	26
Serious argument with close friend	40	Too many missed classes	25
Change in financial status	39	Change of college	24
Change in academic major	39	Dropped more than one class	23
Trouble with parents	39	Minor traffic violations	20
New girlfriend or boyfriend	38	Total:	_____

Scores of 300 and higher indicate a relatively high health risk, whereas scores of 150 to 299 indicate a 50/50 chance of serious health problems within two years.

Source: Adapted from de Meuse, 1985; Holmes & Rahe, 1967; Insel & Roth, 1985.

Conflict   Stress can also arise when we experience **conflict**—that is, when we are forced to make a choice between at least two incompatible alternatives. There are three basic types of conflict: **approach–approach**, **approach–avoidance**, and **avoidance–avoidance** (**Table 3.1**).

Generally, approach–approach conflicts are the easiest to resolve and produce the least stress. Avoidance–avoidance conflicts, on the other hand, are usually the most difficult and take the longest to resolve because either choice leads to unpleasant results. As expected, the longer any conflict exists, or the more important the decision, the more stress a person will experience.

Approach–approach conflict
A forced choice between two options, both of which have equally desirable characteristics.

Approach–avoidance conflict
A forced choice involving one option with equally desirable and undesirable characteristics.

Avoidance–avoidance conflict
A forced choice between two options, both of which have equally undesirable characteristics.

TABLE 3.1 Types of Conflict

Conflict	Description/Resolution	Example/Resolution	
Approach–approach ➕ ➕	Forced choice between two options, both of which have equally desirable characteristics Generally easiest and least stressful conflict to resolve	Two equally desirable job offers, but you must choose one of them You make a pro/con list and/or "flip a coin"	+ Great job offer #1 ? + Great job offer #2 **a.** Approach–approach conflict
Approach–avoidance ➕ ➖	Forced choice involving one option with equally desirable and undesirable characteristics Moderately difficult choice, often resolved with a partial approach	One high-salary job offer that requires you to relocate to an undesirable location away from all your friends and family You make a pro/con list and/or "flip a coin"; if you take the job you decide to only live in the new location for a limited time (a partial approach)	+ Great job offer but − have to relocate ? **b.** Approach–avoidance conflict
Avoidance–avoidance ➖ ➖	Forced choice between two options, both of which have equally undesirable characteristics Difficult, stressful conflict, generally resolved with a long delay and considerable denial	Two equally undesirable options— bad job or no job—and you must choose one of them You make a pro/con list and/or "flip a coin" and then delay the decision as long as possible, hoping for additional job offers	− Bad job offer ? − No job offer **c.** Avoidance–avoidance conflict

Q Test Your Critical Thinking

The expression on this man's face indicates that he's experiencing some form of conflict.

1. Can you explain how this could be both an avoidance–avoidance and an approach–avoidance conflict?

2. What might be the best way resolve this conflict?

Riccardo Piccinini/123RF

Hassles The small problems of daily living that may accumulate and become a major source of stress.

Burnout A state of physical, mental, and emotional exhaustion resulting from chronic exposure to high levels of stress, with little personal control.

Hassles

We all share numerous minor **hassles** of daily living, such as time pressures and financial concerns, but our reactions to them vary. Persistent hassles, particularly when combined with little personal control, can lead to a form of physical, mental, and emotional exhaustion known as **burnout** (Koutsimani et al., 2019; Zysberg et al., 2017). This is particularly true for people in chronically stressful professions, such as firefighters, police officers, doctors, and nurses. Their exhaustion and "burnout" then lead to more work absences, reduced productivity, and increased risk of illness.

Some authorities believe hassles can be more significant than major life events in creating stress (Keles et al., 2017; Stefanek et al., 2012). Divorce is extremely stressful, but it may be so because of the increased number of hassles it brings—changes in finances, child-care arrangements, longer working hours, and so on.

Frustration

Frustration   Like hassles, **frustration**, a negative emotional state resulting from a blocked goal, can also cause stress. And the more motivated we are, the more frustrated we become when our goals are blocked. After getting stuck in traffic and being five minutes late to an important job interview, we may become very frustrated. However, if the same traffic jam forces us to be five minutes late showing up to a casual party, we may experience little or no frustration.

Frustration   A negative emotional state resulting from a blocked goal.

Cataclysmic Events

Cataclysmic Events   Mass shootings and natural disasters that cause major damage and loss of life are what stress researchers call **cataclysmic events**. They occur suddenly and generally affect many people simultaneously. Politicians and the public often imagine that such catastrophes inevitably create huge numbers of seriously depressed and permanently scarred survivors, and relief agencies often send large numbers of counselors to help with the psychological aftermath. Surprisingly, researchers have found that because the catastrophe is shared by so many others, the coping skills of survivors may be improved due to the mutual social support from those with firsthand experience with the same disaster (Aldrich & Meyer, 2015; Ginzburg & Bateman, 2008).

Cataclysmic event   A stressful occurrence that happens suddenly and generally affects many people simultaneously.

On the other hand, cataclysmic events are still clearly devastating. In fact, people who experience extreme stress, such as a natural disaster like the 9.0 magnitude earthquake that hit Japan and caused devastating tsunami waves, show changes in the brain as long as one year later (Sekiguchi et al., 2014). Specifically, the hippocampus and orbitofrontal cortex are smaller following stress. Some survivors may even develop a prolonged and severe stress reaction, known as *posttraumatic stress disorder (PTSD)*, which we discuss later in this chapter.

Job Stress

Job Stress   For many people, job stressors, such as being denied a promotion, loss of employment, underemployment, or forced retirement, are highly stressful. Other common sources of job stress are *role conflict*, being forced to take on separate and incompatible roles, and *role ambiguity*, being uncertain about the expectations and demands of your role (Din et al., 2019; Lu et al., 2016). A mid-level manager who reports to many supervisors, while also working among the people he or she is expected to supervise, is a prime example of someone who experiences both role conflict and role ambiguity. You'll discover more about job stress, technostress, and coping with stress later, in the *Gender and Cultural Diversity* and *Research Challenge* features at the end of this chapter.

Acute/Chronic Stress

Acute/Chronic Stress   When considering specific sources of stress, it's important to note that many stressors can fit into multiple categories. For example, life changes generally also include conflicts and frustrations. Furthermore, stressors can be either acute or chronic—and sometimes both. **Acute stress** is generally severe but short term and with a definite endpoint, such as narrowly avoiding a bike or car accident or missing a critical deadline. In modern times, this type of immediate, short-term arousal is almost a daily occurrence, and it often leads to unhealthy emotions (anxiety, tension, irritability) and physical reactions (transient increases in blood pressure and heart rate, dizziness, chest pains).

Acute stress   A short-term state of arousal, in response to a perceived threat or challenge that has a definite endpoint.

Thankfully, because acute stress is short term, it generally doesn't lead to the type of extensive damage associated with long-term **chronic stress**. Ongoing wars, a bad marriage, domestic violence, poor working conditions, poverty, prejudice, and discrimination (**Figure 3.2**) can all be significant sources of chronic stress (Benner et al., 2018; Koutsimani et al., 2019; Simons et al., 2016). This type of stress is widely recognized as a major factor in psychological disorders, such as major depressive disorder (MDD), posttraumatic stress disorder (PTSD), and anxiety disorders (e.g., Anderson et al., 2019; Song et al., 2019). Surprisingly, chronic stress can even suppress sexual functioning in both men and women (Hamilton & Julian, 2014). Confirming what many have long suspected, chronic stress can even reduce the probability of conception (Akhter et al., 2016). It can also contribute to low birth weight in infants, negatively affect the structure and maturation of the adolescent brain, and lead to depression across the life span (Colman et al., 2014; Romeo, 2017; Witt et al., 2016). Finally, as you well know, academic life can be both an acute and chronic stressor.

Chronic stress   A continuous state of arousal in which demands are perceived as greater than the inner and outer resources available for dealing with them.

fizkes/Shutterstock.com

FIGURE 3.2 **Prejudice and discrimination as chronic stressors**   Research has found that the chronic stress resulting from prejudice and discrimination is linked to serious physical and mental problems, including a higher risk of heart disease, inflammation, substance abuse, depression, relationship strain, and suicide (Brewer et al., 2018; Leventhal et al., 2018; Wofford et al., 2019).

Studies have found that academic stress can reduce your subjective well-being, along with leading to dropped courses and lowered life satisfaction and grades (Karaman et al., 2019; Watson & Watson, 2016).

Although social support can help buffer the negative effects of stress (e.g., Keneski et al., 2018), our social lives can be chronically stressful as well. Making and maintaining friendships requires considerable thought and energy (Ehrlich et al., 2016; Flannery et al., 2017; Sriwilai & Charoensukmongkol, 2016). For example, research suggests that your stress level increases with the number of social media "friends" you have and the amount of time you spend on social networking sites (APA Press Release, 2017; Bevan et al., 2014; Wegmann & Brand, 2016). In fact, higher cortisol levels were found in teens with more than 300 friends on Facebook (Morin-Major et al., 2016). However, teens who acted in support of their Facebook friends—for example, by liking what they posted—had less stress, as measured by decreased cortisol levels.

TIP What is cortisol?   As mentioned in Chapter 2 and discussed throughout this chapter, cortisol is the so-called stress hormone released from our adrenal glands when we're under physical or emotional stress. Cortisol releases glucose and fatty acids that provide energy for fast action, but as you'll see, it also suppresses our immune system. Cortisol levels are commonly measured in stress research.

[AQ1]   Research also shows that people who spend more time on social media (see photo) experience lower levels of day-to-day happiness, lower overall feelings of life satisfaction, and higher levels of loneliness, social isolation, and depression, which are all due, at least in part, to social comparison (Hunt et al., 2018; Primack et al., 2019; Rosenthal et al., 2016). Why is social comparison stressful? People may feel excluded from social events that are described and posted on social media, while also experiencing pressure to be entertaining when they post, along with worrying that they are missing vital information if they don't check in repeatedly (e.g., Beyens et al., 2016). (As you may know, this fear of missing out is so common that it has its own acronym—FOMO.) The good news is that limiting how often you check your social media accounts and email has been shown to decrease stress and increase overall well-being (Hunt et al., 2018; Kushlev & Dunn, 2015; Shaw et al., 2015).

alexey malkin/123RF

Reactions to Stress

It's not stress that kills us—it's our reaction to it.
—Hans Selye (Austrian endocrinologist, "father" of stress research)

As we've just seen, there are numerous factors that contribute to stress, and while it may strike without warning, it can also be a chronic, lifelong condition. In this section, we'll take a close look at four ways the human body typically responds to both short- and long-term stress—the GAS, the SAM and HPA axis, changes in the immune system, and alterations in our cognitive functioning.

Stress and the GAS   When we're mentally or physically stressed, our bodies undergo several biological changes that can be detrimental to our health. In 1936, Canadian physician Hans Selye (SELL-yay) described a generalized physiological reaction to a continuing stressor, which he called the **general adaptation syndrome (GAS)**. The GAS occurs in three phases—*alarm*, *resistance*, and *exhaustion*—activated by efforts to adapt to any stressor, whether physical or psychological (**Process Diagram 3.1**).

Most of Selye's ideas about the GAS pattern have proven to be correct. For example, studies have found that the primary behavioral response to stress is to fight or flee–the classic

General adaptation syndrome (GAS)   Selye's three-stage (alarm, resistance, exhaustion) reaction to chronic stress; a pattern of non-specific, adaptational responses to a continuing stressor.

> **STOP!** This Process Diagram contains essential information NOT found elsewhere in the text, which is likely to appear on quizzes and exams. Be sure to study it CAREFULLY.

PROCESS DIAGRAM 3.1   **General Adaptation Syndrome (GAS)**   The three phases of Selye's syndrome (alarm, resistance, and exhaustion) focus on the biological response to stress—particularly the "wear and tear" on the body that results from prolonged stress.

1 Alarm phase
When surprised or threatened, your body enters an alarm phase during which your sympathetic nervous system (SNS) is activated (e.g., increased heart rate and blood pressure) and blood is diverted to your skeletal muscles to prepare you for the "fight-flight-freeze" response (Chapter 2).

2 Resistance phase
As the stress continues, your body attempts to resist or adapt to the stressor by summoning all your resources. Physiological arousal remains higher than normal, and there is an outpouring of stress hormones. During this resistance stage, people use a variety of coping methods. For example, if your job is threatened, you may work longer hours and give up your vacation days.

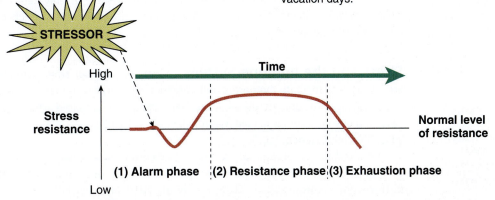

3 Exhaustion phase
Unfortunately, your body's resistance to stress can only last so long before exhaustion sets in. During this final phase, your reserves are depleted and you become more susceptible to serious illnesses, as well as potentially irreversible damage to your body. Selye maintained that one outcome of this exhaustion phase for some people is the development of *diseases of adaptation*, including asthma and high blood pressure. Unless a way of relieving stress is found, the eventual result may be complete collapse and death.

Art Resource, NY

FIGURE 3.3 **Stress in ancient times** As shown in these ancient cave drawings, the automatic "fight-flight-freeze" response was adaptive and necessary for early human survival. However, in modern society, it occurs as a response to many situations that require other, more flexible responses. Think of your own situation. Like many students, you're probably working while going to school and you cannot fight, flight, or freeze when your instructor assigns another exam, your boss changes your work schedule, your car breaks down, or you're constantly worried about money. This type of uncontrollable stress and chronic worry leads to repeated arousal that can be detrimental to your health.

SAM system Our body's initial, rapid-acting stress response, involving the sympathetic nervous system and the adrenal medulla; also called the sympatho–adreno–medullary (SAM) system.

HPA axis Our body's delayed stress response, involving the hypothalamus, pituitary, and adrenal cortex; also called the hypothalamic–pituitary–adrenocortical (HPA) axis.

Homeostasis Our body's tendency to maintain equilibrium, or a steady state of internal balance.

"fight-or-flight" response. However, this two-option response does not include situations in which we become immobile and freeze in the face of stress. Therefore, many researchers have now replaced the previous label of "fight-or-flight" with a new three-option response, called *fight-flight-freeze* (Corr & Cooper, 2016; Friedman, 2015; Maack et al., 2015).

Beyond this shared, primary fight-flight-freeze response, it's important to note that different stressors evoke different responses. Women, for instance, are more likely to "tend and befriend" (Israel-Cohen & Kaplan, 2016; Taylor, 2006, 2012; von Dawans et al., 2012). This means that when under stress women more often take care of themselves and their children (tending), while also forming strong social bonds with others (befriending). Other research has found that after being administered oxytocin, the so-called "love hormone," which is believed to increase bonding, attachment, and empathy, both men and women participants showed enhanced compassion toward women but not toward men (Palgi et al., 2015). These researchers suggest that the females' "tend and befriend" behaviors may have evolved from a socially constructed desire to help vulnerable individuals, and because the oxytocin administrations affected both sexes it may not be a true biological difference.

What is Selye's most important take-home message? **Our bodies are relatively well designed for temporary stress but poorly equipped for prolonged stress.** In other words, and as noted in **Figure 3.3**, the same biological processes that were adaptive historically and in the short run, such as the fight-flight-freeze response, can be hazardous in the long run (Papathanasiou et al., 2015; Russell et al., 2014).

Stress, the SAM System, and the HPA Axis To understand how stress can be damaging, we need to first describe a normal, healthy response to stress. As you can see in **Process Diagram 3.2**, once our brains identify a stressor, our **SAM** (sympatho–adreno–medullary) **system** and **HPA** (hypothalamic–pituitary–adrenocortical) **axis** work together to increase our arousal and energy levels to deal with the stress (Brannon et al., 2018; Dieleman et al., 2016; Garrett, 2015). Once the stress is resolved, these systems turn off, and our bodies return to normal, baseline functioning, known as **homeostasis**.

Unfortunately, given our increasingly stressful modern lifestyle, our bodies are far too often in a state of elevated, chronic arousal, which can wreak havoc on our health. Some of the most damaging effects of stress are on our immune system and our cognitive functioning.

Stress and the Immune System When we're under stress, our immune systems are less able to regulate the normal inflammation system, which makes us more susceptible to diseases, such as bursitis, colitis, Alzheimer's disease, rheumatoid arthritis, periodontal disease, and even the common cold (Campbell et al., 2015; C. Cohen et al., 2012; S. Cohen et al., 2003; O'Farrell & Harkin, 2017).

As noted earlier, prolonged, excessive, and chronic stress also contributes to hypertension, depression, posttraumatic stress disorder (PTSD), drug and alcohol abuse, and low birth weight (Guardino et al., 2016; Kim et al., 2016; Li et al., 2019). Severe or prolonged stress can even lead to premature aging and death (Lohr et al., 2015; Prenderville et al., 2015; Song et al., 2019).

How does this happen? *Cortisol*, a key element of the HPA axis, plays a critical role in the long-term, negative effects of stress. Although increased cortisol levels initially help us fight stressors, if these levels stay high, as they do when stress continues over time, the body's disease-fighting immune system is suppressed. For example, studies have found that people who are lonely have

STOP! This Process Diagram contains essential information NOT found elsewhere in the text, which is likely to appear on quizzes and exams. Be sure to study it CAREFULLY.

PROCESS DIAGRAM 3.2 **The SAM System and HPA Axis—Two Co-Actors in Our Stress Response**
Faced with stress, our sympathetic nervous system prepares us for immediate action—fight-flight-freeze. Our slower-acting HPA axis maintains our arousal. Here's how it happens.

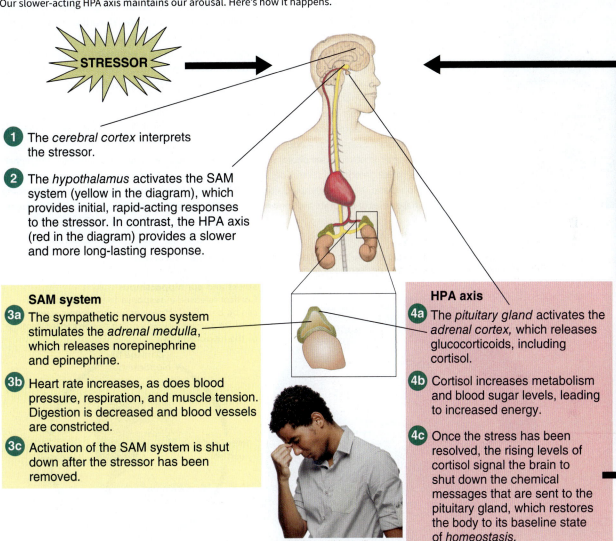

STRESSOR

1 The *cerebral cortex* interprets the stressor.

2 The *hypothalamus* activates the SAM system (yellow in the diagram), which provides initial, rapid-acting responses to the stressor. In contrast, the HPA axis (red in the diagram) provides a slower and more long-lasting response.

SAM system

3a The sympathetic nervous system stimulates the *adrenal medulla,* which releases norepinephrine and epinephrine.

3b Heart rate increases, as does blood pressure, respiration, and muscle tension. Digestion is decreased and blood vessels are constricted.

3c Activation of the SAM system is shut down after the stressor has been removed.

HPA axis

4a The *pituitary gland* activates the *adrenal cortex,* which releases glucocorticoids, including cortisol.

4b Cortisol increases metabolism and blood sugar levels, leading to increased energy.

4c Once the stress has been resolved, the rising levels of cortisol signal the brain to shut down the chemical messages that are sent to the pituitary gland, which restores the body to its baseline state of *homeostasis.*

iStock.com/Aldo Murillo

an impaired immune response, leaving their bodies vulnerable to infections, allergies, and many of the other illnesses cited above (Drake et al., 2016; Zilioli et al., 2017).

Knowledge that psychological factors have considerable control over infectious diseases has upset the long-held assumption in biology and medicine that these diseases are strictly physical. The clinical and theoretical implications are so important that a new interdisciplinary field, called **psychoneuroimmunology**, studies the effects of psychological and other factors on the immune system.

Psychoneuroimmunology The interdisciplinary field that studies the effects of psychological and other factors on the immune system.

Stress and Cognitive Functioning
What happens to our brains and thought processes when we're under immediate stress? As we've just seen, cortisol helps us deal with immediate dangers by mobilizing our energy resources, but stress and cortisol can also affect cognitive functions, such as language, thinking, and memory.

PAN   Practical Application of Neuroscience

How do stress and cortisol affect our memories?   As you'll discover in Chapter 7, short-term stress can solidify our memories for highly emotional, "flashbulb" events. But it can also be detrimental to our memory because it may interfere with the creation of new memories and general information processing (Lukasik et al., 2019; Paul et al., 2016; Rubin et al., 2016). This interference with cognitive functioning helps explain why you forget important information during a big exam, and why people often become danger-ously confused during a fire and are unable to find the fire exit. The good news is that once the cortisol washes out, memory performance generally returns to normal levels.

What happens during prolonged stress? Long-term exposure to cortisol can permanently damage cells in the hippocampus, a key part of the brain involved in memory (Chapter 7). Furthermore, once the hippocampus has been damaged, it cannot provide proper feedback to the hypothalamus. Without proper feedback and control, cortisol continues to be secreted, thereby creating a vicious cycle (**Figure 3.4**). Per-haps even more alarming is the finding that long-term stress in mice not only disturbs their short-term memory, but also leads to changes in parts of the brain that closely resemble that of humans—a part linked to depression and social avoidance (McKim et al., 2016).

[AQ2]   To make matters even worse, living below the poverty line (a chronic type of stressor) can literally make it harder to learn. How? Researchers have found that poverty leads to differences in certain surface areas of the brain essential for academic success (Noble et al., 2015). In addition, when MRI brain scans of children growing up in poverty (see photo) were compared to those of children from middle- and higher-income families, researchers found several important differences in brain structures, including in the frontal and temporal lobes and the hippocampus, along with less overall gray matter (Harden et al., 2016; Wang et al., 2016). These areas of the brain are known to be among the most crucial for academic achievement.

Oleksiy Rezin/Shutterstock.com

Stress and our prefrontal cortex
Chronic stress results in a reduction in the size and number of neurons in the prefrontal cortex and a diminished performance during cognitive tasks.

Stress and our hippocampus
Cortisol released in response to immediate stress can be beneficial. However, under chronic stress it can produce a vicious cycle leading to permanent damage to the hippocampus.

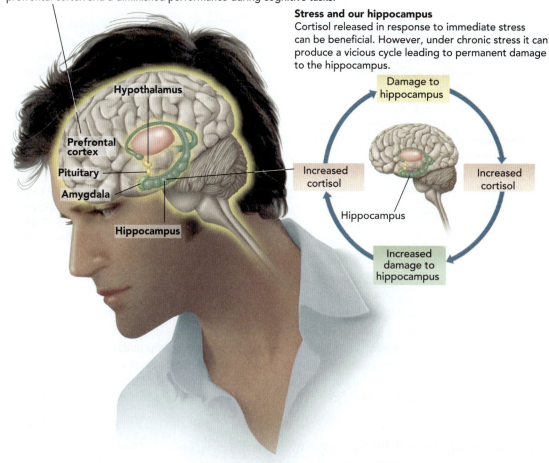

FIGURE 3.4   **Our brain under chronic stress**

Benefits of Stress

So far in our discussion, we've focused primarily on the harmful, negative side of stress. But not all stress is bad. In this section, we'll define the difference between "good" and "bad" stress and then focus on how to maximize the positive aspects.

Eustress versus Distress
As you recall from the start of the chapter, our bodies are nearly always in some state of stress, whether pleasant or unpleasant, mild or severe. *Anything* placing a demand on the body can cause stress. Stress that is unpleasant, undesirable and caused by aversive conditions is generally referrred to as **distress** (Selye, 1974).

When stress is pleasant, desirable, and arouses us to persevere and accomplish challenging goals, it's called **eustress**. Physical exercise provides a clear example of the benefits of eustress. When we're working out at a gym, or even just walking in a park, we're placing some level of stress on our bodies. However, this stress encourages the development and strengthening of all parts of our body, particularly our muscles, heart, lungs, and bones. Exercise also releases endorphins (Chapter 2), which help lift depression and overall mood.

Distress The unpleasant, undesirable stress caused by aversive conditions.

Eustress The pleasant, desirable stress that arouses us to persevere and accomplish challenging goals.

Task Complexity
Keep in mind that the benefits of stress generally require considerable effort and an optimal level of arousal depending on task complexity. As shown in **Figure 3.5**, during well-learned, simple tasks we typically need a higher level of stress to perform at our best. This is why athletes more often break their "personal best" during high-stakes competition—when their stress levels are higher. However, these same athletes need a moderate level of stress while practicing and learning new skills. In contrast, if you're like most students, you'll need a really low level of stress during a hard, complex exam in your psychology class (unless you're well prepared thanks to all the practice tests provided in this text and its accompanying website).

Stress and Social Support
Given enough social support, even highly stressful events can, in some cases, be somewhat beneficial. Researchers compared data on psychological adjustment, including anxiety and depression, collected from female students before

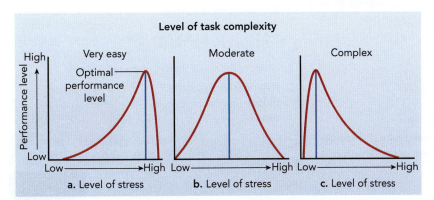

FIGURE 3.5 **Stress and task complexity** As you can see in this figure, stress can benefit performance. However, the level of stress should match the complexity of the task. **a. Level of stress** Note how a higher level of stress helps keep us focused during well-learned, very easy tasks, but we may need to deliberately raise our stress levels to better focus our attention when the easy task demands it. **b. Level of stress** During moderate tasks, we need a medium level of stress for maximum performance. **c. Level of stress** Note that during complex, demanding tasks, we need to lower our stress level. For example, during difficult exams your performance will benefit from deep breathing and other methods of relaxation.

the 2007 shooting at Virginia Tech (as part of an already ongoing study), and then again after the event (Mancini et al., 2016). They found that some students suffered continued distress after the shooting, while others showed relatively long-lasting psychological improvement and resilience. On the face of it, this sounds absurd. However, numerous studies have shown that the outpouring of social support after mass traumas can promote greater cooperation, sharing, solidarity, and bonding among the survivors. One researcher described it as "a paradise built in hell" (Solnit, 2009).

Sadly, the opposite is generally true after individual-level traumas, like rape and other forms of sexual assault. In these cases, survivors often suffer in silence, due to the tragic (and ongoing) stigma associated with those crimes, and the fact that when they report the crime they're too often not believed. Can you see then why group therapy is often so helpful for rape and assault survivors (Chapter 14)? Or why we all need to remember to offer strong social support to survivors of both mass and individual traumas—and to actively seek it for ourselves during stressful times?

Retrieval Practice 3.1 | Understanding Stress

Self-Test Completing this self-test, and then checking your answers by clicking on the answer button or by looking in Appendix B, will provide immediate feedback and helpful practice for exams.

1. When John saw his girlfriend kissing another man at a party, he became very upset. In this situation, watching someone you love kissing a competitor is _____, and becoming upset is _____.

   a. a stressor; a biological imperative

   b. distressing; a life change event

   c. a cataclysmic event; evidence of a burnout

   d. a stressor; a stress response

2. In an approach–approach conflict, we must choose between two or more goals that will lead to _____, whereas in an avoidance–avoidance conflict, we must choose between two or more goals that will lead to _____.

   a. less conflict; more ambivalence

   b. frustration; hostility

   c. a desirable result; an undesirable result

   d. effective coping; ineffective coping

3. A state of physical, emotional, and mental exhaustion resulting from chronic exposure to high levels of stress, with little personal control is called _____.

   a. primary conflict

   b. technostress

   c. burnout

   d. secondary conflict

4. As Michael watches his instructor pass out papers, he suddenly realizes that this is the first major exam, and that he is unprepared. Which phase of the GAS is he most likely experiencing?

   a. resistance

   b. alarm

   c. exhaustion

   d. phase out

5. Stress that is pleasant and motivates us to accomplish challenging goals _____.

   a. can be beneficial

   b. is called eustress

   c. both a and b

   d. none of these options

Q Test Your Critical Thinking

1. What are the major sources of stress in your life?

2. How does chronic stress threaten our immune system?

Real World Application Questions

[AQ1] How does social media affect stress?

[AQ2] Can the stress of growing up in poverty lead to significant changes in the brain?

Oleksiy Rezin/Shutterstock.com   alexey malkin/123RF

Hint: Look in the text for [AQ1] and [AQ2]

3.2 | Stress and Illness

LEARNING OBJECTIVES

Retrieval Practice While reading the upcoming sections, respond to each Learning Objective in your own words.

Review how stress contributes to major illnesses.

- **Explain** how stress affects gastric ulcers.
- **Describe** the role of stress in cancer.
- **Discuss** how the development of cardiovascular disorders is affected by stress.
- **Describe** how chronic pain is affected by stress.

- **Explain** the role of stress in PTSD, and the methods used to cope with this disorder.

Real World Application Questions

[AQ3] Why are some chronic pain sufferers more susceptible to placebos than others?

[AQ4] Does watching televised coverage of natural disasters increase symptoms of posttraumatic stress disorder?

As we've just seen, stress has dramatic effects on our bodies. This section explores how stress is related to five serious illnesses—gastric ulcers, cancer, cardiovascular disorders, chronic pain, and posttraumatic stress disorder (PTSD).

Gastric Ulcers

Gastric ulcers are lesions in the lining of the stomach (and duodenum—the upper section of the small intestine) that can be quite painful. In extreme cases, they may even be life-threatening. Beginning in the 1950s, psychologists reported strong evidence that stress can lead to ulcers. Studies found that people who live in stressful situations have a higher incidence of ulcers than people who don't. In addition, numerous experiments with laboratory animals have shown that stressors, such as shock, water-immersion, or confinement to a very small space, can produce ulcers in a few hours (e.g., Landeira-Fernandez, 2015; Sun et al., 2016).

The relationship between stress and ulcers seemed well established until researchers identified a bacterium (*Helicobacter pylori*, or *H. pylori*) that appeared to be associated with ulcers. Later studies confirmed that this bacterium clearly damages the stomach wall, and that antibiotic treatment helps many ulcer patients. However, approximately 75 percent of normal, healthy people's stomachs also have the bacterium. This suggests that the bacterium may cause the ulcer, but only in people who are compromised by stress. Furthermore, behavior modification and other psychological treatments, used alongside antibiotics, can help ease ulcers. In other words, although stress *by itself* does not cause ulcers, it is a contributing factor, along with biological factors (Jaul et al., 2016; Wang et al., 2017).

TIP Have you heard from others that ulcers are "psychosomatic" and therefore imaginary? In scientific terms, *psychosomatic* (*psyche* means "mind" and *soma* means "body") refers to symptoms or illnesses that are caused or aggravated by psychological factors, especially stress. Most researchers and health practitioners believe that almost all illnesses are, at least in part, psychosomatic.

Cancer

Cancer is among the leading factors in the untimely death of adults in the United States and more than 100 types of cancer have been identified. They appear to be caused by an

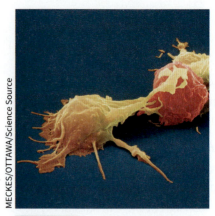

FIGURE 3.6 **The immune system**
The actions of a healthy immune system are shown here. The round red structures are leukemia cells. Note how the yellow killer cells are attacking and destroying the cancer cells.

interaction between environmental factors (such as diet, smoking, and pollutants) and inherited predispositions. Generally, cancer occurs when a particular type of primitive body cell begins rapidly dividing and then forms a tumor that invades healthy tissue. Unless destroyed or removed, the tumor eventually damages organs and ultimately leads to death.

Note that research does *not* support the popular myths that stress directly *causes* cancer or that positive attitudes can prevent or cure it (Chang et al., 2015; Coyne & Tennen, 2010; Lilienfeld et al., 2010, 2015).

In a healthy person, whenever cancer cells start to multiply, the immune system checks the uncontrolled growth by attacking the abnormal cells (**Figure 3.6**). Prolonged stress, however, prompts the adrenal glands to release hormones that negatively affect the immune system, and a compromised immune system is less able to resist infection or to fight off cancer cells (Cao et al., 2019; Jung et al., 2015; Kokolus et al., 2014). Stress may also contribute to cancer's progression and to the spread of cancer cells to other organs (Klink, 2014; Obradović et al., 2019).

PA Practical Application

How can we use this information in our daily life?   Think about a time when you were experiencing stress, such as studying for a difficult exam, having a fight with a loved one, or struggling to pay your bills. Both minor and major stressors can decrease the effectiveness of your immune system and thereby lead to both short- and long-term health problems. Given the previous discussion of all the ill effects of stress, can you see why it's so important to not only reduce your stress levels but to also improve your personal coping skills? (Tips for improving these skills are provided later in this chapter.)

Cardiovascular Disorders

Cardiovascular disorders contribute to over half of all deaths in the United States (American Heart Association, 2013). Understandably, health psychologists are concerned because stress is a major contributor to these deaths (Marchant, 2016; Orth-Gomér et al., 2015; Taylor-Clift et al., 2016).

Heart disease is a general term for all disorders that eventually affect the heart muscle and lead to heart failure. *Coronary heart disease* occurs when the walls of the coronary arteries thicken, reducing or blocking the blood supply to the heart. Symptoms of such disease include *angina* (chest pain due to insufficient blood supply to the heart) and *heart attack* (death of heart muscle tissue).

How does stress contribute to heart disease? Recall that one of the major brain and nervous system autonomic reactions to stress is the release of epinephrine (adrenaline) and cortisol into the bloodstream. These hormones increase heart rate and release fat and glucose from the body's stores to give muscles a readily available source of energy. If no physical fight-flight-freeze action is taken (and this is most likely the case in our modern lives), the fat that was released into the bloodstream is not burned as fuel. Instead, it may adhere to the walls of blood vessels. These fatty deposits are a major cause of blood-supply blockage, which, in turn, leads to heart attacks. Of course, the stress-related buildup of fat in our arteries is not the only risk factor associated with heart disease. Other factors include smoking, obesity, a high-fat diet, and lack of exercise (Carbone et al., 2019; Diaz et al., 2016; Orth-Gomér et al., 2015).

Chronic Pain

Have you ever wished that you could skateboard, race cars, downhill ski, and/or go to the dentist without ever worrying about pain? It may sound good but pain is essential to the survival and well-being of humans and all other animals. It alerts us to dangerous or harmful situations and forces us to rest and recover from injury.

On the other hand, **chronic pain**, the type that comes with a lingering illness or continues long past the healing of a wound, generally does not serve a useful function. Sadly, studies find that more than 20 percent of all people around the world suffer from chronic pain, which leads to a serious reduction in each individual's quality of life (Dahlhamer et al., 2018; Djordjevic, 2019).

Even when psychological factors are not the source of chronic pain, they frequently intensify the related anxiety, depression, fatigue, and disability (Kerns et al., 2011; Miller-Matero et al., 2017; Vlaeyen et al., 2016). Traumatic childhood experiences, such as physical and emotional abuse and exposure to stressful family environments, have a strong link to chronic pain (e.g., Ortiz, 2019; Ranjbar & Erb, 2019; Schrepf et al., 2018). These *adverse childhood experiences (ACEs)* are further discussed in Chapter 9.

To treat chronic pain, medical professionals often prescribe strong pain medications, like opioids, which too often lead to serious side effects, such as epidemic forms of addiction (see Chapter 5). Instead, health psychologists emphasize psychologically oriented treatments, such as behavior modification, biofeedback, and relaxation.

- **Behavior modification** You'll discover in Chapters 6 and 14 that behavior modification programs often emphasize "well behaviors" such as exercise, which is known to produce an increase in endorphins and a resulting decrease in pain (Chapter 2).

- **Biofeedback** This non-invasive, non-drug treatment is used to help pain sufferers learn how to control one or more of their involuntary bodily functions by monitoring their own brain waves, heart rate, blood pressure, degree of muscle tension, etc. (see **Figure 3.7**). Such feedback helps reduce some types of chronic pain.

- **Relaxation and mindfulness-based meditation techniques** Because the pain is always unabating and constantly recurring, chronic pain sufferers tend to talk and think about their pain whenever they are not thoroughly engrossed in an activity. Watching movies or television, attending parties, or performing any activity that diverts attention from the pain seems to reduce discomfort. As you'll discover later in this chapter, attention might also be diverted with mindfulness-based stress reduction (MBSR) meditation programs and special relaxation techniques like those taught in some childbirth classes. These techniques focus the birthing mother's attention on breathing and relaxing the muscles, which helps distract her attention away from the fear and pain of the birthing process. Similar techniques can also be helpful for chronic pain sufferers. Remember, however, that these techniques do not completely eliminate the pain. They merely allow the person to ignore it for a time.

[AQ3] Did you notice anything missing from these three forms of psychological treatment for chronic pain? What about individual differences in personality? Researchers who

Chronic pain A continuous or recurrent pain experienced over a period of 6 months or longer.

FIGURE 3.7 Biofeedback and pain control Most biofeedback with chronic pain patients is done with the *electromyograph (EMG)*, which measures muscle tension by recording electrical activity in the skin. The EMG is most helpful when the pain involves extreme muscle tension, such as tension headaches and lower back pain. Electrodes are attached to the site of the pain, and the patient is instructed to relax. When sufficient relaxation has been achieved, the machine signals with a tone or a light. The signal serves as feedback, enabling the patient to learn how to relax. Research shows that biofeedback is helpful and sometimes as effective as more expensive and lengthier forms of treatment (Jensen et al., 2009; Urban, 2016). Apparently, it is successful because it teaches patients to recognize patterns of emotional arousal and conflict that affect their physiological responses. This self-awareness, in turn, enables them to learn self-regulation skills that help control their pain.

Malt Digital Agency/Shutterstock.com

Pablo Calvog/Shutterstock.com

studied a group of patients with chronic back pain (see photo) found that some patients were more likely than others to see a significant reduction in pain after taking placebo pain pills (Vachon-Presseau et al., 2018). Compared to the non-responders, the "placebo responders" found a reduction of about 30 percent, which is similar to the effect of real painkillers. Furthermore, using MRI and fMRI brain imaging, the researchers found differences in brain structures between the two groups. Can you see how this type of study could be very helpful in predicting who will respond best to placebo treatments?

Posttraumatic Stress Disorder (PTSD)

Posttraumatic stress disorder (PTSD) A long-lasting, trauma- and stressor-related disorder that overwhelms an individual's ability to cope.

One of the most powerful examples of the effects of severe stress is **posttraumatic stress disorder (PTSD)** (American Psychiatric Association, 2013; Brannon et al., 2018; Levine, 2015). PTSD is a long-lasting, trauma- and stressor-related disorder that overwhelms an individual's ability to cope. It can occur in both adults and children.

PTSD's essential feature is the development of characteristic symptoms (**Table 3.2**) following exposure to one or more traumatic events (American Psychiatric Association, 2013). These symptoms may continue for months or even years after the event. Unfortunately, some victims of PTSD turn to alcohol and other drugs to cope, which generally compounds the problem (Goldstein et al., 2016; McLean et al., 2015; Smith et al., 2016).

Have you ever been in a serious car accident or been the victim of a violent crime? According to the National Institute of Mental Health (NIMH) (2014), it's natural to feel afraid when in danger. But for some people suffering from PTSD, the normal fight-flight-freeze response is modified or damaged. This change helps explain why people with PTSD continue to experience extreme stress and fear, even when they're no longer in danger. Research shows that approximately 40 percent of all children and teens will experience a traumatic stressor and that the lifetime prevalence for trauma is between 50 percent and 90 percent (Brown et al., 2013; J. Cohen et al., 2014). However, the vast majority will not go on to develop PTSD.

Sadly, one of the most dangerous problems associated with PTSD is the increased risk for suicide (e.g., Lewis et al., 2019; Stanley et al., 2019). Did you know that the number of suicides among young male veterans under the age of 30 jumped by 44 percent between 2009 and

Bob Collet/Alamy Stock Photo

2011, while the rate for female vets increased by 11 percent in the same time period? The precise cause for this astronomically high and climbing rate of suicides is unknown, but experts point to PTSD, along with combat injuries, and the difficulties of readjusting to civilian life (Ashrafioun et al., 2016; Finley et al., 2015; Legarreta et al., 2015).

[AQ4] In case you think PTSD develops only from military experiences, it's important to note that victims of natural disasters, physical violence or sexual assault, and mass shootings, may also develop PTSD. In addition, research shows that simply watching televised coverage of major natural disasters, such as hurricanes, earthquakes, and tornados (see photo), can increase the number of PTSD symptoms, especially in children who are already experiencing symptoms (Holman et al., 2014; Weems et al., 2012).

TABLE 3.2 Key Characteristics of PTSD

1. *Direct exposure to trauma* through personal experience, witnessing it, or discovering that it happened to others. Also, direct, ongoing exposure to traumatic events, such as that experienced by first responders, can lead to PTSD.

2. *Recurrent, intrusive symptoms*, including thoughts, feelings, memories, and bad dreams. Also, re-experiencing the trauma over and over through *flashbacks*.

3. *Avoidance symptoms*, such as feeling emotionally numb, losing interest in previously enjoyable activities, and avoiding memories of the trauma and stimuli associated with the traumatic event.

4. *Chronic heightened arousal and reactivity*, including irritability, being easily startled, sleep disturbances, angry outbursts, and reckless/self-destructive behaviors.

MediaPunch Inc/Alamy Stock Photo

FIGURE 3.8   **Stress and PTSD**   People who experience traumatic events, such as the survivors of the shooting massacre in 2018 at Stoneman Douglas High School in Parkland, Florida, may develop symptoms of PTSD.

PTSD is not a new problem. During the Industrial Revolution, workers who survived horrific railroad accidents sometimes developed a condition very similar to PTSD. It was called "railway spine" because experts thought the problem resulted from a twisting or concussion of the spine. Later, doctors working with combat veterans referred to the disorder as "shell shock" because they believed it was a response to the physical concussion caused by exploding artillery. Today, we know that PTSD is generally a response to exposure to extraordinary stress (**Figure 3.8**).

What can we do to help? Professionals have had success with various forms of therapy and medications for PTSD (e.g., Castillo et al., 2016; Dunsmoor et al., 2019; Watts et al., 2016). They've also offered several constructive tips for anyone helping others deal with general crisis and trauma (see **Table 3.3** and the **PAH** **Practical Application Highlight**).

TABLE 3.3   **Seven Important Tips for Coping With Crisis**
1. If you have experienced a traumatic event, recognize your feelings about the situation, and talk to others about your fears. Know that these feelings are a normal response to an abnormal situation.
2. If you know someone who has been traumatized, be willing to patiently listen to their account of the event, pay attention to their feelings, and encourage them to seek counseling, if necessary.
3. Be patient and kind to yourself and others. It's natural to feel anxious, helpless, and frustrated, but give yourself a break. Also, tempers are short in times of crisis, and others may be feeling as much stress as you.
4. Recognize normal crisis reactions, such as sleep disturbances and nightmares, withdrawal, reversion to childhood behaviors, and trouble focusing on work or school.
5. Be mindful of your time. Feel free to say "NO" to others. Limit your news watching—except when it's necessary to do so, as in a national emergency. Take time with your children, spouse, life partner, friends, and co-workers to do something you enjoy.
6. Get plenty of sleep and avoid alcohol and other drugs. We all need a good night's sleep, especially during times of crisis. Alcohol and other drugs interfere with sleep and good decision making.
7. Study and adopt stress management skills, such as the ones discussed in this chapter.

Source: Adapted from Pomponio, 2002; Stress in College Students, 2019; Tips for Coping with Crisis, 2015.

PAH Practical Application Highlight

Helping Someone with PTSD

(APA Goal 1.3) Describe applications of psychology

If you have friends or loved ones with PTSD, it may feel as if you're walking through a minefield when you're attempting to comfort and help them. What do the experts suggest that you say (or NOT say)? Here are a few general tips:

What Not To Do?

1. **Don't trivialize the disease.** Like cancer or heart disease, PTSD, and its associated anxiety and depression, is a critical, life-threatening illness. Asking someone, "What do you have to be depressed about?" is akin to asking cancer patients why they have cancer, or why they don't just smile and exercise more?

2. **Don't be a cheerleader or a Mr. or Ms. Fix-It.** You can't pep-talk someone out of PTSD, and offering cheap advice or solutions is the best way to ensure that you'll be the last person he or she will turn to for help.

What Can You Do?

Educate yourself. Your psychology instructor, college library, book stores, the Internet, and Chapters 13 and 14 of this text can all provide a wealth of information.

Be Rogerian. Carl Rogers's four important qualities of communication (*empathy, unconditional positive regard, genuineness*, and *active listening*, discussed in Chapter 12) are probably the best, and safest, approaches for any situation—including talking with someone who's suffering from PTSD.

JOHNGOMEZPIX/iStock/Getty Images

Get help! The most dangerous problem associated with PTSD, and its commonly associated serious depression, is the high risk of suicide. If a friend or loved one mentions suicide, or if you believe he or she is considering it, get professional help fast. Consider calling the police for emergency intervention, the person's trusted friend or family member, or the toll-free 7/24 hotline 1-800-SUICIDE.

Retrieval Practice 3.2 | Stress and Illness

Self-Test   Completing this self-test, and then checking your answers by clicking on the answer button or by looking in Appendix B, will provide immediate feedback and helpful practice for exams.

1. The term *"psychosomatic"* means that some illnesses are _____.

   a. imaginary
   b. influenced by psychological factors
   c. caused by stress
   d. none of these options

2. Which of the following is true?

   a. Stress is a leading cause of cancer
   b. Positive attitudes alone can prevent cancer.
   c. Both of these options.
   d. None of these options.

3. Stress may contribute to heart disease by releasing _____ and _____, which increase the level of fat in the blood.

   a. angina; cortisol
   b. hormones; GABA
   c. cynical hostility; hormones
   d. epinephrine (adrenaline); cortisol

4. Someone who experiences flashbacks, nightmares, and other forms of recurring intrusive symptoms following a life-threatening or other horrifying event may be _____.

   a. suffering from a substance abuse disorder
   b. experiencing symptoms of posttraumatic stress disorder (PTSD)
   c. having a psychotic breakdown
   d. none of these options

5. _____ is one of the key characteristics of PTSD identified in the text.

   a. Exposure to serious trauma
   b. Persistent avoidance of stimuli related to traumatic event
   c. Marked changes in arousal and reactivity
   d. All of these options

Q Test Your Critical Thinking

1. How is stress a contributing factor to gastric ulcers?
2. Has stress contributed to your own illnesses? If so, what can you do to avoid or decrease future illnesses?

Real World Application Questions

[AQ3] Why are some chronic pain sufferers more susceptible to placebos than others?

[AQ4] Does watching televised coverage of natural disasters increase symptoms of posttraumatic stress disorder?

Pablo Calvog/Shutterstock.com

Bob Collet/Alamy Stock Photo

Hint: Look in the text for **[AQ3]** and **[AQ4]**

3.3 # Stress Management

LEARNING OBJECTIVES

Retrieval Practice   While reading the upcoming sections, respond to each Learning Objective in your own words.

Review the major factors involved in managing and coping with stress.

- **Discuss** the role of cognitive appraisal in coping with stress.

- **Describe** how personality and individual differences affect stress responses.
- **Summarize** the major resources for healthy living.

Real World Application Question

[AQ5] Can social integration with peers during childhood and adolescence help protect against high blood pressure and obesity in adulthood?

As noted at the beginning of this chapter, stress is a normal, and necessary, part of our lives. Therefore, *stress management* is the goal—not stress elimination. Although our initial, bodily responses to stress are largely controlled by non-conscious, autonomic processes, our higher brain functions can help us avoid the serious damage from chronic overarousal. The key is to consciously recognize when we are overstressed and then to choose resources that activate our parasympathetic, relaxation response. In this section, we'll first discuss the role of cognitive appraisal in coping with stress. Then we'll explore how personality and individual differences affect our coping responses. Finally, we'll present several important resources for healthy living and stress management.

Cognitive Appraisal

Because we can't escape stress, we need to learn how to effectively cope with it. Our first approach to stress management generally begins with a cognitive appraisal of the stressor (**Process Diagram 3.3**). One of the biggest challenges with this approach to stress management is deciding whether to try to change the stressor itself or our emotional reaction to it.

Problem-focused coping strategies work to deal directly with a stressor in order to eventually decrease or eliminate it (Delahaij & van Dam, 2016; Dixon et al., 2016; Mayordomo-Rodríguez et al., 2015). We tend to choose this approach, and find it most effective, when we have some control over a stressful situation. Although you may feel as if you have little or no control over exams and other common academic stressors, our students have found that by using the various study tools provided throughout this text and on our text's website, they increased their personal control and success, while also decreasing their stress levels. Do you see how this approach of studying and adopting new study skills would be a good example of *problem-focused coping*?

Many times, however, it seems that little or nothing can be done to alter the stressful situation, so we turn to **emotion-focused coping**, in which we attempt to relieve or regulate our emotional reactions. If you're dealing with the death of a loved one, the pain and stress are out of your control. To cope with your painful emotions, you might try distraction, meditation, journaling, or talking to a friend and/or therapist, which are all healthy forms of *emotion-focused coping*.

According to psychoanalyst Sigmund Freud, when facing uncomfortable or painful stressors we commonly turn to another type of cognitive appraisal and response, known as **defense mechanisms**, in which we unconsciously distort reality to protect our egos and to avoid anxiety (see Chapter 12). These defense mechanisms can sometimes act as a beneficial type of emotion-focused coping. For example, when you're really angry at your boss, and realize that you can't safely express that anger, you may take out your frustration by aggressively hitting a punching bag at the gym. This would be a healthy use of defense mechanisms. But if taken too far, defense mechanisms can be destructive. If we fail to get a

Problem-focused coping   The strategies we use to deal directly with a stressor to eventually decrease or eliminate it.

Emotion-focused coping   The strategies we use to relieve or regulate our emotional reactions to a stressful situation.

Defense mechanisms   Freud's term for the strategies the ego uses to reduce anxiety, which distort reality and may increase self-deception.

> **STOP!** This Process Diagram contains essential information NOT found elsewhere in the text, which is likely to appear on quizzes and exams. Be sure to study it CAREFULLY.

PROCESS DIAGRAM 3.3 **Cognitive Appraisal and Stress Management** Research suggests that when facing a serious stressor, we begin with a *primary appraisal* process to evaluate the threat, and decide whether it's harmless or potentially harmful. Next, during *secondary appraisal*, we assess our available and potential resources for coping with the stress. Then, we generally choose either *emotion-* or *problem-focused* methods of coping. When attempting to resolve complex stressors, or a stressful situation that is in flux, we often combine both emotion- and problem-focused approaches.

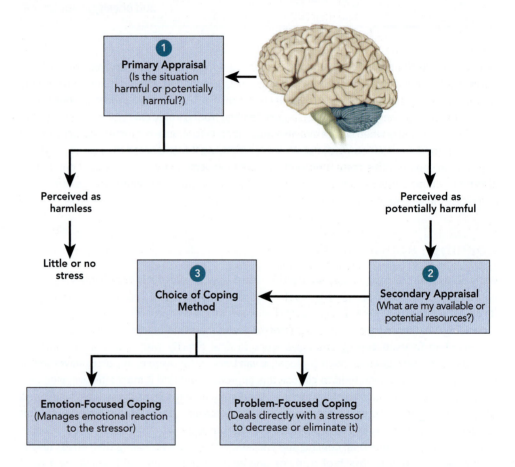

promotion, and then resort to elaborate excuses (rationalizations) for our failure, this may block us from seeing the situation clearly and realistically, which in turn can prevent us from developing valuable skills.

Take-Home Message The occasional use of defense mechanisms can be beneficial, as long as it's not excessive (Hertel et al., 2015; Levine, 2015). Also, keep in mind that emotion-focused forms of coping can't change the problem, but they do make us feel better about the stressful situation. As an example, teenagers who are asked to think about the "silver lining" benefits of a recent stressful event—such as having a traffic accident or losing a valued relationship—show increases in positive mood and decreases in negative mood (Rood et al., 2012). Instant messaging (IM) also helps distressed teenagers share their emotions, and receive immediate social support and advice (Dolev-Cohen & Barak, 2013).

Personality and Individual Differences

We've just seen how problem- and emotion-focused coping, as well as defense mechanisms, are used in stress management. Research has also found that personality types and individual differences directly affect how we cope with stress. In this section, we discuss the various effects of *locus of control*, *positive affect*, and *optimism*.

Locus of Control   Perhaps one of the most important personal resources for stress management is a sense of personal control. People who believe they are the "masters of their own destiny" have what is known as an **internal locus of control**. Believing they control their own fate, they tend to make more effective decisions and healthier lifestyle choices, are more likely to follow treatment programs, and more often find ways to positively cope with a situation.

In contrast, people with an **external locus of control** believe that chance or outside forces beyond their control determine their fate. Therefore, they tend to feel powerless to change their circumstances, are less likely to make effective and positive changes, and are more likely to experience high levels of stress (e.g., Au, 2015; Reknes et al., 2019; Rotter, 1966).

Positive Affect   Why do some people survive in the face of great stress (personal tragedies, demanding jobs, or an abusive home life) while others do not? One answer may be that these "survivors" have a unique trait called **positive affect**, meaning they more often experience and express positive emotions, including feelings of happiness, joy, enthusiasm, and contentment (e.g., Katana et al., 2019). People who are high in positive affect also tend to have lower levels of inflammation, fewer colds and auto accidents, better sleep, and an enhanced quality of life (Brannon et al., 2018; Tavernier et al., 2016).

Positive states are also sometimes associated with longer life expectancy. One study of 600 patients with similar forms of heart disease found that those with more positive attitudes were less likely to die during a 5-year follow-up period (Hoogwegt et al., 2013). Specifically, only 9 percent of those with positive attitudes had died five years later, compared to 16.5 percent of those with less positive attitudes. This study provides intriguing evidence for the mind-body link. Positive affect is also associated with a lower risk of mortality in patients with diabetes, which is a leading cause of death in the United States (Cohn et al., 2014; Moskowitz et al., 2008). Interestingly, this well-established link between higher levels of positive affect and better health within Western cultures doesn't hold up in Asian countries (Yoo et al., 2017). Why? The researchers suggest that Asian cultures tend to de-emphasize positive emotions.

Can you see how having positive affect is closely associated with a good sense of humor? Humor is one of the best methods you can use to reduce stress. The ability to laugh at oneself and at life's inevitable ups and downs allows us to relax and gain a broader perspective (**Figure 3.9**). In addition, "laughter therapy" has been linked to a significant reduction in heart rate and systolic blood pressure (e.g., Yoshikawa et al., 2018).

Optimism   Positive affect is also closely associated with **optimism**, the expectation that good things will happen in the future and bad things will not. If you agree with statements such as, "I tend to expect the best of others," or, "I generally think of several ways to get out of a difficult situation," you're probably an optimist. If you tend to disagree with these statements, you're more likely to be a pessimist.

As you might expect, optimists are generally much better at stress management. Rather than seeing bad times as a constant threat and assuming personal responsibility for them, they generally assume that bad times are temporary and external to themselves. Optimists also tend to have better overall physical and psychological health, and typically have longer and overall happier lives, along with better odds of achieving "exceptional longevity"—living to the age of 85 or beyond (Denovan & Macaskill, 2017; Hernandez et al., 2015; Lee et al., 2019).

Internal locus of control   The belief that we control our own fate.

External locus of control   The belief that chance or outside forces beyond our control determine our fate.

Positive affect   The experience or expression of positive feelings (affect), including happiness, joy, enthusiasm, and contentment.

Optimism   A tendency to expect the best and to see the best in all things.

Dean Drobot/Shutterstock.com

FIGURE 3.9   Positive affect in action   Based on his smile and cheery "thumbs up," it looks as if this patient may be one of those lucky people with a naturally positive outlook on life. Can you see how this approach might help him cope and recuperate from his serious injuries?

S&P Scientific Thinking and Practical Application

Why are optimists healthier? To test this question, researchers in one study tracked 135 older adults (aged 60+) over 6 years (Jobin et al., 2014). Participants were asked about the level of stress they perceived in their day-to-day lives and whether they would rate themselves as optimists or pessimists. Saliva samples were then collected from each individual to measure his or her current level of cortisol. The results revealed that, compared to self-described optimists, people who described themselves as pessimists had higher cortisol levels, a higher baseline level of stress, and more difficulty coping with challenging life events. Can you see why optimists tend to experience better overall health? Their lower cortisol levels and better coping strategies reduce the "wear and tear" of the biological effects of stress on their bodies.

The good news is that according to Martin Seligman, a leader in the field of positive psychology, optimism can be learned (Seligman, 2011). In short, he believes optimism requires careful monitoring and challenging of our thoughts, feelings, and self-talk. For example, if you don't get a promotion at work or you receive a low grade on an exam, don't focus on all the negative possible outcomes and unreasonably blame yourself. Instead, force yourself to think of alternative ways to meet your goals and develop specific plans to improve your performance. Chapter 14 offers additional help and details for overcoming faulty thought processes.

Resources for Healthy Living

As we've just seen, various cognitive appraisal techniques and personality and individual differences have significant effects on our stress management. In this section, we'll provide specific, evidence-based resources and personal tips for managing your stress.

Mindfulness-based stress reduction (MBSR) A stress reduction strategy based on developing a state of consciousness that attends to ongoing events in a receptive and non-judgmental way.

Mindfulness-Based Stress Reduction
Perhaps the most interesting approach to stress reduction comes from the recent **mindfulness-based stress reduction (MBSR)** programs, which are focused on developing a state of consciousness that attends to ongoing events in a receptive, non-judgmental way. The practice of MBSR has proven to be particularly effective in managing stress and treating mood disturbances, and it's even been linked to increased positive emotions, as well as with positive, and perhaps permanent, cell and brain changes (Creswell et al., 2016; Lindsay et al., 2018). For an example of how this research has direct, practical applications, see the following PP **PositivePsych**.

Social Support
When we're faced with stressful circumstances, our friends and family often help us take care of our health, listen, hold our hands, make us feel important, and provide stability to offset the changes in our lives.

PP Practical Application: **PositivePsych**

Mindfulness and Your GPA

(APA Goal 1.3) Describe applications of psychology

Researchers interested in the potential usefulness of mindfulness training in academic settings assigned students either to a 7-week mental training program designed to tame mind wandering and increase focus, or to a control group that received no training (Morrison et al., 2013). Students in the two groups did not differ at the start of the semester on levels of attention and mind wandering (two factors that lead to lower academic performance). However, by the end of the semester, people in the control group showed diminished attention and increased mind wandering. In contrast, those who participated in the mindfulness program showed significant improvements in attention and no increases in reported mind wandering.

Related studies with college students who engage in mindfulness-based stress reduction (MBSR) programs show improvements in reading comprehension and working memory capacity, as well as overall better adjustment to the college environment (Mrazek et al., 2013; Ramler et al., 2016). For younger children, a school-based mindfulness program, which includes breathing and movement exercises, helps many elementary school students better manage their stress, and become more optimistic, helpful, caring, better liked by peers, and even better at math (Schonert-Reichl et al., 2015).

David Malan/Photographer's Choice/Getty Images

Social support can also help offset the stressful effects of chronic illness, pregnancy, physical abuse, job loss, and work overload. For instance, individuals who have greater social support experience better health outcomes, including greater psychological well-being, greater physical well- being, faster recovery from illness, and a longer life expectancy (Crittenden et al., 2018; Keneski et al., 2018; Martínez-Hernáez et al., 2016). Another study found that even one single close childhood friendship seems to protect children in lower socioeconomic circumstances (which is an ongoing stressor) from several negative psychological risk factors (Graber et al., 2016). **[AQ5]** A longitudinal study of 267 men also found that greater social integration in childhood (see photo) and adolescence led to lower blood pressure and body mass index readings two decades later (Cundiff & Matthews, 2018).

Ariel Skelley/DigitalVision/Getty Images

Unfortunately, when people experience the numerous and often serious effects of stress, some of the negative physical and psychological consequences also carry over to their family, friends, and even to others nearby (Sterley et al., 2018; Wofford et al., 2019). So what is the important take-home message from this emphasis on social support? As a helper to individuals suffering from stress, be aware of potentially "catching" their same symptoms, but don't be afraid to offer help and support to others—or to ask for the same for yourself.

The six major resources for healthy living and stress management are summarized in **Table 3.4**. The exceptional benefits from exercise are also explored in the **RC Research Challenge**.

RC Scientific Thinking: **Research Challenge**

Exercise, Mental Health, and Team Sports

(APA Goal 2.4) Interpret, design, and conduct basic psychological research

The mental and physical benefits of exercise are generally well known and well-documented. However, did you know that participating in team sports may be particularly helpful? A study of 1.2 million people in the United States found that people who exercise report having 1.5 fewer days of poor mental health a month than people who do not exercise (Chekroud et al., 2018).

Participants were asked to recall their past 30 days and then to estimate on how many of those days they would rate their mental health as 'not good' based on stress, depression, and emotional problems. They were then asked how often they took part in exercise in the past 30 days outside of their regular job, how many times a week or month they did this exercise, and for how long. Compared to people who reported doing no exercise, those who exercised reported 1.5 fewer days of poor mental health each month.

Note that exercising for 30–60 minutes three to five times a week was associated with the biggest reduction in poor mental health days. On the other hand, exercising for more than three hours a day was associated with worse mental health than not exercising at all. The authors note that people doing extreme amounts of exercise might have obsessive characteristics which could place them at greater risk of poor mental health.

Interestingly, almost all types of exercise were associated with improved mental health. However, the strongest associations were seen for team sports: "Our finding that team sports are associated with the lowest mental health burden may indicate that social activities promote resilience and reduce depression by reducing social withdrawal and isolation, giving social sports an edge over other kinds."

Identify the Research Method

1. Based on the information provided, did this study (Chekroud et al., 2018) use descriptive, correlational, and/or experimental research?

2. If you choose:

   o *descriptive research*, is this a naturalistic or laboratory observation, survey/interview, case study, and/or archival research?

   o *correlational research*, is this a positive, negative, or zero correlation?

   o *experimental research*, label the IV, DV, experimental group(s), and control group. (Note: If participants were not randomly assigned to groups, list the design as *quasi-experimental*.)

   o both *descriptive* and *correlational*, answer the corresponding questions for both.

Check your answers by clicking on the answer button or by looking in Appendix B.

Note: The information provided in this study is admittedly limited, but the level of detail is similar to what is presented in most textbooks and public reports of research findings. Answering these questions, and then comparing your answers to those provided, will help you become a better scientific and critical thinker and consumer of scientific research.

TABLE 3.4 **Six Key Stress Resources**

Exercise	Exercising and keeping fit help minimize anxiety and depression, relieve muscle tension, improve cardiovascular efficiency, and increase strength, flexibility, and stamina. Those who do not find time for exercise will have to find time for illness. —Edward Smith-Stanley	 Wavebreak Media Ltd/123RF
Social skills	People who acquire social skills (such as knowing appropriate behaviors for certain situations, having conversation starters up their sleeves, and expressing themselves well) suffer less anxiety than people who do not. Social skills not only help us interact with others but also communicate our needs and desires, enlist help when we need it, and decrease hostility in tense situations.	 Caiaimage/Paul Bradbury/Getty Images
Behavior change	When under stress, do you smoke, drink, overeat, zone out in front of the TV or computer, sleep too much, procrastinate, or take your stress out on others? If so, you can substitute these activities with healthier choices, such as listening to your favorite podcast.	 Jozef Polc/123RF
Stressor control	Stress is a part of life and cannot be eliminated, but you can recognize and avoid unnecessary stress by: analyzing your schedule and removing non-essential tasks, avoiding people and topics that increase your stress, finding a less stressful job, and/or giving yourself permission to say "no" to extra tasks and responsibilities.	 izusek/E+/Getty Images
Material resources	Money increases the number of options available for eliminating sources of stress or reducing the effects of stress. When faced with the minor hassles of everyday living, acute or chronic stressors, or major catastrophes, people with more money, and the skills to effectively use it, generally fare better. They experience less overall stress, and can "buy" more resources to help them cope with what stressors they do have.	 famveldman/123RF
Relaxation	There are a variety of relaxation techniques. *Biofeedback* is often used in the treatment of chronic pain, but it is also useful in teaching people to relax and manage their stress. *Progressive relaxation* helps reduce or relieve the muscular tension commonly associated with stress (see the following **Test Yourself**).	 dolgachov/123RF

PA Practical Application

Test Yourself: Practicing Progressive Relaxation

You can use progressive relaxation techniques anytime and anywhere you feel stressed, such as before or during an exam. Here's how:

1. Sit in a comfortable position, with your head supported.
2. Start breathing slowly and deeply.
3. Let your entire body relax. Release all tension. Try to visualize your body getting progressively more relaxed with each breath.

4. Systematically tense and release each part of your body, beginning with your toes. Curl them tightly while counting to 10. Now, release them. Note the difference between the tense and relaxed states. Continue upward with your calves, thighs, buttocks, abdomen, back muscles, shoulders, upper arms, forearms, hands, neck, jaw, facial muscles, and forehead. Try practicing progressive relaxation twice a day for about 15 minutes each time. You will be surprised at how quickly you can learn to relax—even in the most stressful situations.

Retrieval Practice 3.3 | Stress Management

Self-Test   Completing this self-test, and then checking your answers by clicking on the answer button or by looking in Appendix B, will provide immediate feedback and helpful practice for exams.

1. Emotion-focused forms of coping are based on relieving or regulating your _____ when faced with stressful situations.
   a. feelings
   b. behavior
   c. dreams
   d. all these options

2. Freud's term for the strategies the ego uses to reduce anxiety by unconsciously distorting reality is known as _____.
   a. "rose-colored glasses" syndrome
   b. defense mannerisms
   c. ego-denial apparatus
   d. defense mechanisms

3. Research suggests that people with a(n) _____ have less psychological stress than those with a(n) _____.
   a. external locus of control; internal locus of control
   b. internal locus of control; external locus of control
   c. attributional coping style; person-centered coping style
   d. none of these options

4. Demonstrating positive emotions, including feelings of happiness, joy, enthusiasm, and contentment, is known as _____.
   a. positive defect
   b. the positivity principle

   c. the Rogerian technique
   d. positive affect

5. Which of the following is *not* one of the ways to cope with stress outlined in the chapter?
   a. exercise
   b. sense of humor
   c. social support
   d. stimulant drugs

Q Test Your Critical Thinking

1. Do you generally prefer an emotion-focused style of coping or a problem-focused style of coping when faced with a stressful situation? Why?

2. Which of the various personality styles discussed in this section best describes you? How could you use this information to improve your stress management.

Real World Application Question

[AQ5] Can social integration with peers during childhood and adolescence help protect against high blood pressure and obesity in adulthood?

Ariel Skelley/DigitalVision/Getty Images

Hint: Look in the text for **[AQ5]**

3.4 Health Psychology

LEARNING OBJECTIVES

Retrieval Practice   While reading the upcoming sections, respond to each Learning Objective in your own words.

Summarize the field of health psychology, and the role of stress in health psychology.

- **Identify** health psychology.

- **Describe** the work of health psychologists.

- **Discuss** how health psychology can be used in the workplace.

Real World Application Question

[AQ6] Are people with stressful jobs at increased risk of experiencing a heart attack?

Health psychology   A subfield of psychology that studies how biological, psychological, and social factors influence health, illness, and health-related behaviors.

Health psychology is the branch of psychology that studies how biological, psychological, and social factors influence health, illness, and health-related behaviors. It emphasizes wellness and the prevention of illness, as well as the interplay between our physical health and our psychological well-being. In this final section, we'll discuss the work of health psychologists and then explore stress in the workplace.

What Does a Health Psychologist Do?

As researchers, health psychologists are particularly interested in how changes in behavior can improve health outcomes (Brannon et al., 2018; Straub, 2014). They also emphasize the relationship between stress and the immune system. As we discovered earlier, a normally functioning immune system helps defend against disease. On the other hand, a suppressed immune system leaves the body susceptible to a number of illnesses.

As practitioners, health psychologists can work as independent clinicians or as consultants alongside physicians, physical and occupational therapists, and other health care workers. The goal of health psychologists is to reduce psychological distress and unhealthy behaviors. They also help patients and families make critical decisions and prepare psychologically for surgery or other treatment. Health psychologists have become so involved with health and illness that medical centers are one of their major employers (Considering a Career, 2011). Health psychologists also educate the public about illness *prevention* and health *maintenance*. For example, they provide public information about the effects of stress, smoking, alcohol, lack of exercise, and other health issues.

Tobacco use is of particular concern because it endangers both smokers and those who breathe secondhand smoke. Thanks in large part to comprehensive mass media campaigns warning about the dangers associated with smoking, along with smoke-free policies, restrictions on underage access to tobacco, and high taxes on cigarettes, adult smoking rates have declined in recent years, but cigarette smoking remains the leading cause of preventable death in the U.S. and worldwide (Centers for Disease Control and Prevention, 2019).

Given the well-known dangers of cigarette smoking, an increasing number of people are now switching to e-cigarettes (also known as "e-cigs," "vapes," etc.). Originally marketed as a safer alternative to cigarettes because it doesn't emit the same cancer-causing tar and toxins of burning tobacco leaves, vaping still delivers nicotine, which is highly addictive. Recent research also shows that vaping is linked with possible respiratory illnesses, heart attacks, coronary artery disease, and depression (American College of Cardiology, 2019; American Heart Association, 2018; Kaplan and Richtel, 2019). As a result of these serious illnesses and several fatalities, the sale of e-cigarettes has been banned in some cities, and medical personnel are warning about vaping's growing list of possible health risks—particularly for teens and young adults.

FIGURE 3.10 Understanding nicotine addiction

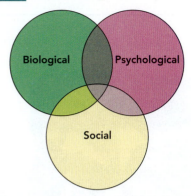

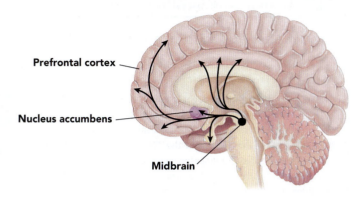

Prefrontal cortex

Nucleus accumbens

Midbrain

a. The biopsychosocial model of addiction

As you'll see throughout this text, the biopsychosocial model helps explain almost all human behavior, including nicotine addiction. From a psychological and social perspective, smokers learn to associate smoking with pleasant things, such as good food, friends, and sex. People also form such associations from seeing smoking in the movies, which is one reason researchers believe that requiring all movies with characters who smoke to be rated R would reduce smoking among teenagers by 20 percent (Sargent et al., 2012). From a biological perspective, nicotine is highly addictive. Once a person begins to smoke, there is a biological need to continue—as explained in part b of this figure.

b. The biology of addiction

Nicotine quickly increases the release of acetylcholine and norepinephrine in our brains, thereby increasing alertness, concentration, memory, and feelings of pleasure. Nicotine also stimulates the release of dopamine, the neurotransmitter most closely related to our brains' reward centers (shown in the figure above). This so-called "pleasure pathway" extends from an area in the midbrain, to the nucleus accumbens, and on to other subcortical structures and the prefrontal cortex. Nicotine addiction appears to be very similar to heroin, cocaine, and alcohol addiction, and all four drugs are commonly associated with depression (Müller & Homberg, 2015; Torrens & Rossi, 2015; Wu et al., 2014).

Given that almost everyone recognizes the serious consequences of smoking, and that the first puff is rarely pleasant, why do people start smoking? The answer can be found in the biopsychosocial model and the biology of addiction (**Figure 3.10**). In addition to encouraging smokers to stop, or to never start, health psychologists help people cope with conditions such as chronic pain, diabetes, and high blood pressure, as well as unhealthful behaviors such as inappropriate anger and lack of assertiveness. If you're interested in a career in this field, check with your college's counseling or career center.

Health Psychology at Work

[AQ6]   Have you ever dragged yourself home from work so tired you feared you couldn't make it to your bed? Do you think your job may be killing you? You may be right. Some research suggests that job stress and overwork (see photo) can seriously affect both your mental and physical health—even increasing your risk of dying from heart disease and stroke (Greenberg, 2018; Weston et al., 2019; Xiao et al., 2019). In fact, a large meta-analysis of the correlation between job strain and coronary heart disease found that people with stressful jobs are 23 percent more likely to experience a heart attack than those without stressful jobs (Kivimäki et al., 2012). The Japanese even have a specific word for this type of extreme job stress. It's known as "karoshi" [KAH-roe-she], which is translated literally as "death from overwork." See the following **GCD** **Gender and Cultural Diversity**.

Caiaimage/Paul Bradbury/Getty Images

Technostress   If you're not suffering from overwork, are you hassled and stressed by the ever-changing technology at your workplace? Do the expensive machines employers install to "aid productivity" create stress-related problems instead? Does technology in your daily life lead you to suffer from modern-day problems, such as *FOMO* (fear of missing out in social media), *phantom vibration syndrome* (feeling your phone vibrating even though it

---

GCD Gender and Cultural Diversity

Can Job Stress Be Fatal?

(APA Goal 2.5) Incorporate sociocultural factors in scientific inquiry

The term *karoshi* was first brought to public awareness in 1969 when a 29-year-old Japanese worker died of a stroke following long hours working under stressful conditions (Sullivan, 2014). During Japan's "Boom Years" of the 1980s and the "Lost Decade" of the 1990s, work-related deaths and illnesses increased, and Japanese health personnel officially recognized karoshi as a valid and potentially lethal condition. Despite growing knowledge of the problem, and a law passed in Japan in 2018 that caps overtime at 100 hours a month, the problem persists. Working under stressful conditions 10 or 15 hours a day, 6 or 7 days a week, year after year also increases the risk of death or serious disabilities from strokes and diabetes (Caputo, 2019).

Andriy Popov/123RF

Similar issues with deaths, disabilities, and psychological problems from overwork have spread to other Eastern countries, and things are not much better in the United States and Western Europe. Economic globalization appears to be making jobs more stressful for workers, with characteristics such as additional and changing demands, low job control, effort-reward imbalances, job insecurity, and long work hours. Larger-scale employer and economic factors, including precarious employment, downsizing/restructuring, privatization, and lean production, further exacerbate these problems (Nishiyama & Johnson, 1997; Schnall et al., 2016; Takahashi, 2019).

You may be surprised to discover that Americans work longer hours and have more stress-related illnesses than other people in most of the world's developed nations (American Time Use Survey, 2018; Roser, 2019; Smith, 2018). In addition to suffering from more stress-related illnesses and overwork, employers are constantly requiring more education, training, and experience from their workers. According to the Pew Research Center, more than half of American adults believe they need continuous training throughout their work life, and that they currently don't have the necessary skills to advance in their job (State of American Jobs, 2016).

Another serious concern is that job stress can contribute to serious mental health issues, including death by suicide (Ito &

Aruga, 2018; Weston et al., 2019). Studies of first responders and people in other high-risk professions, such as police officers, firefighters, paramedics, and military and medical personnel, have found an elevated risk of suicide, suicidal thoughts and behaviors, and posttraumatic stress disorder (PTSD) (Jones, 2017; Lynn, 2019; Stanley et al., 2016). In addition, studies have found that job stress is higher in occupations that have little job security and make great demands on performance and concentration, with little or no allowance for creativity or opportunity for advancement (Bauer & Hämmig, 2014; Dawson et al., 2016; Sarafino & Smith, 2016).

Intense job stressors reportedly not only increase the risk of potentially lethal physical and psychological problems, but also leave some workers disoriented and suffering from serious stress even when they're not working (Calderwood & Ackerman, 2016; Tayama et al., 2016; Tetrick & Peiró, 2016). Stress at work can also cause serious stress at home, not only for the worker but for other family members as well. Unfortunately, in our global economy, pressures to reduce costs and to increase productivity will undoubtedly continue, and job stress is a serious and growing health risk. What do you think? How can you use this information to control your stress and perhaps influence your lifestyle and career choices?

Technostress A feeling of anxiety or mental pressure from overexposure to or involvement with technology; stress caused by an inability to cope with modern technology.

isn't nearby), or *nomophobia* (fear of being without a cellphone or cellular service)? If so, you may be suffering from the well-documented, ill-effects of **technostress**, a feeling of anxiety or mental pressure from overexposure to or involvement with technology (Brivio et al., 2018; Hauk et al., 2019; Joo et al., 2016).

PA Practical Application

What do experts recommend for coping with job stress and technostress? First, evaluate each new technology on its usefulness for you and your lifestyle. It isn't a yes or no, "technophobe" or "technophile," choice. If something works for you, invest the energy to adopt it. Second, establish clear boundaries. Technology came into the world with an implied promise of a better and more productive life. But, for many, the servant has become the master. Like any healthy relationship, our technology interactions should be based on moderation and balance (Ashton, 2013).

Of course, technostress is not the only source of job-related stress. In the following **Test Yourself**, you can score your past, current, and potential future careers on several additional factors to assess job-related stress.

Test Yourself: Workplace Stress

Start by identifying what you like and don't like about your current (and past) jobs. With this information in hand, you'll be prepared to find jobs that will better suit your interests, needs, and abilities—which, in turn, will likely reduce your stress. To start your analysis, answer *Yes* or *No* to these questions:

1. Is there a sufficient amount of laughter and sociability in my workplace?
2. Does my boss notice and appreciate my work?
3. Is my boss understanding and friendly?
4. Am I embarrassed by the physical conditions of my workplace?
5. Do I feel safe and comfortable in my place of work?
6. Do I like the location of my job?
7. If I won the lottery and were guaranteed a lifetime income, would I feel truly sad if I also had to quit my job?
8. Do I watch the clock, daydream, take long lunches, and leave work as soon as possible?
9. Do I frequently feel stressed and overwhelmed by the demands of my job?
10. Compared to others with my qualifications, am I being paid what I am worth?
11. Are promotions made in a fair and just manner where I work?
12. Given the demands of my job, am I fairly compensated for my work?

Now score your answers. Give yourself one point for each answer that matches the following: 1. No; 2. No; 3. No; 4. Yes; 5. No; 6. No; 7. No; 8. Yes; 9. Yes; 10. No; 11. No; 12. No.

The questions you just answered are based on four factors that research shows are conducive to increased job satisfaction and reduced stress: supportive colleagues, supportive working conditions, mentally challenging work, and equitable rewards (Robbins, 1996). Your total score reveals your overall level of dissatisfaction. A look at specific questions can help identify which of these four factors is most important to your job satisfaction—and most lacking in your current job.

1. **Supportive colleagues (items 1, 2, 3)**   For most people, work fills valuable social needs. Therefore, having friendly and supportive colleagues and superiors leads to increased satisfaction.
2. **Supportive working conditions (items 4, 5, 6)**   Not surprisingly, most employees prefer working in safe, clean, and relatively modern facilities. They also prefer jobs close to home.
3. **Mentally challenging work (items 7, 8, 9)**   Jobs with too little challenge create boredom and apathy, whereas too much challenge creates frustration and feelings of failure.
4. **Equitable rewards (items 10, 11, 12)**   Employees want pay and promotions based on job demands, individual skill levels, and community pay standards.

Before going on, be sure to complete the final Retrieval Practice quiz and then answer the critical thinking questions in the **Test Your Critical Thinking**.

Retrieval Practice 3.4 | Health Psychology

Self-Test   Completing this self-test, and then checking your answers by clicking on the answer button or by looking in Appendix B, will provide immediate feedback and helpful practice for exams.

1. Which of the following is *true* of health psychology?
    a. It studies the relationship between psychological well-being and physical health.
    b. It studies the relationship between social factors and illness.
    c. It emphasizes wellness and the prevention of illness.
    d. All these statements are true.

2. According to the Centers for Disease Control and Prevention (CDC), _____ is the leading cause of preventable death in the U.S. and worldwide.
    a. cigarette smoking
    b. lack of exercise
    c. overeating
    d. heart disease

3. An increase in acetylcholine and norepinephrine is associated with _____.
    a. nicotine use
    b. any alcohol consumption
    c. binge drinking
    d. stress

4. Once you begin smoking, you continue because _____.
    a. nicotine is addictive
    b. it increases alertness
    c. it stimulates the release of dopamine
    d. all of these options

5. Technostress can be defined as _____.
    a. a feeling of euphoria from exposure or involvement with technology
    b. anxiety or mental pressure from overexposure to loud "techno" style music.
    c. stress caused by an inability to cope with modern technology.
    d. none of these options

Q Test Your Critical Thinking

1. Why is it so difficult for people to quit smoking?
2. Would you like to be a health psychologist? Why or why not?

Real World Application Question

[AQ6]   Are people with stressful jobs at increased risk of experiencing a heart attack?

Caiaimage/Paul Bradbury/Getty Images

Hint: Look in the text for **[AQ6]**

Q Test Your Critical Thinking

Did you notice and/or wonder why we provided six Real World Application Questions [AQ1–AQ6] throughout the chapter? We've found that they not only help you to engage with and master the material, but also have an important and lasting impact on your critical thinking skills. For additional mastery and enrichment, consider the following questions: We began this chapter with six intriguing, chapter opening questions, and you were asked to revisit these questions at the end of each section. Questions like these have an important and lasting impact on all of our lives.

1. How might the child in this photo be affected biologically, psychologically, and socially (the biopsychosocial model) by her mother's drinking?

2. Are you more of an internal or external locus of control type of person? What are the advantages and disadvantages to each type?

3. What could a health psychologist do to improve the well-being of the mother and child in this photo?

Dmytro Zinkevych/Shutterstock.com

4. Health psychologists often advise us to make lifestyle changes to improve our health and longevity. Do you think this is important? If so, what do you plan to change in your own life?

Summary

3.1 Understanding Stress   74

- **Stress** is the interpretation of specific events, called **stressors**, as threatening or challenging.

- The seven major sources of stress are life changes, conflict, hassles, frustration, cataclysmic events, job stressors, and acute/chronic stressors. *Life changes* require adjustment in our behaviors that cause stress. **Conflicts** are forced choices between two or more competing goals or impulses. They are often classified as **approach–approach, avoidance–avoidance,** or **approach–avoidance. Hassles** are little everyday life problems that pile up to cause major stress, and possibly **burnout. Frustration** refers to blocked goals. **Cataclysmic events** are disasters that occur suddenly and generally affect many people simultaneously. Work-related **job stressors** include role conflict and/or role ambiguity. **Acute stressors** refer to a short-term state of arousal in response to a perceived threat or challenge. **Chronic stressors** produce a state of continuous physiological arousal, in which demands are perceived as greater than available coping resources.

- Hans Selye's **general adaptation syndrome (GAS)** describes our body's three-stage reaction to stress: the initial alarm reaction, the resistance phase, and the exhaustion phase (if resistance to stress is not successful). If stress is resolved, our bodies return to normal, baseline functioning, called **homeostasis**.

- The **SAM system** and the **HPA axis** control significant physiological responses to stress. The SAM system prepares us for immediate action; the HPA axis responds more slowly but provides a response that lasts longer.

- Prolonged stress suppresses the immune system, which increases the risk for many diseases (e.g., colds, colitis, cancer). The new field of **psychoneuroimmunology** studies the effects of psychological and other factors on the immune system.

- During acute stress, cortisol can prevent the retrieval of existing memories, as well as the laying down of new memories and general information processing. Under prolonged stress, cortisol can permanently damage the hippocampus, a key part of the brain involved in memory.

- Our bodies are nearly always under stress, some of which has beneficial effects. **Eustress** is pleasant, desirable stress, whereas **distress** is unpleasant, undesirable stress. Stress is also beneficial depending on task complexity, and social support is invaluable for coping with stress.

3.2 Stress and Illness   85

- Scientists once believed that stress, or the *H. pylori* bacterium, acting alone, could cause gastric ulcers. Current psychological research shows that biopsychosocial factors, including stress, interact to increase our vulnerability to the bacterium, which may then lead to gastric ulcers.

- Cancer appears to result from an interaction of heredity, environmental factors (such as smoking), and immune system deficiencies. Although stress is linked to a weakened immune response, research does *not* show that it *causes* cancer, or that a positive attitude alone will prevent cancer.

- Increased stress hormones can cause fat to adhere to blood vessel walls, increasing the risk of cardiovascular disorders, including heart attacks.

- **Chronic pain** is a type of continuous or recurrent pain, generally experienced over a period of 6 months or longer. To treat chronic pain, health psychologists emphasize psychologically oriented treatments, such as behavior modification, biofeedback, and relaxation.

- Exposure to extraordinary stress can cause **posttraumatic stress disorder (PTSD)**, a type of trauma- and stressor-related disorder characterized by the persistent re-experiencing of traumatic events, which resulted from war, natural disasters, sexual assault, and so on.

3.3 Stress Management   91

- Stress management generally begins with a three-step cognitive appraisal. Step 1 is **primary appraisal** (deciding if a situation is harmless or potentially harmful), and Step 2 is **secondary appraisal** (assessing our resources and choosing a coping method). In Step 3, we tend to choose either **emotion-focused coping** (managing emotional reactions to a stressor) or **problem-focused coping** (dealing directly with the stressor to decrease or eliminate it). Freud also proposed that we commonly cope with stress with **defense mechanisms**, which are strategies the ego uses to protect itself from anxiety, but they often distort reality and may increase self-deception.

- Personality and individual differences also affect stress management. Having an **internal locus of control** (believing that we control our own fate), as opposed to an **external locus of control** (believing that chance or outside forces beyond our control determine our fate), is an effective personal strategy for stress management. People with a **positive affect** and **optimism** tend to live longer and to deal better with stress.

- **Mindfulness-based stress reduction (MBSR)** and social support are two important keys to stress management. Six additional resources are exercise, social skills, behavior change, stressor control, material resources, and relaxation.

3.4 Health Psychology   98

- **Health psychology** is a branch of psychology that studies how biological, psychological, and social factors influence health, illness, and health-related behaviors.

- Health psychologists focus on how changes in behavior can improve health outcomes. They often work as independent clinicians, or as consultants to other health practitioners, to educate the public about illness prevention and health maintenance.

- Health psychologists also study job stress and how to reduce it.

Key Terms

Retrieval Practice   Write your own definition for each term before turning back to the referenced page to check your answer.

Kuttelvaserova Stuchelova/Shutterstock.com

Sensation and Perception

Noriko Cooper/123RF

Real World Application Questions

Things you'll learn in Chapter 4

[AQ1] Do athletes have a higher pain tolerance than non-athletes?

[AQ2] Can looking at a photograph of a loved one lead you to feel less pain?

[AQ3] Does a lack of direct sunlight contribute to nearsightedness?

[AQ4] Can using a lower-pitched voice affect your perceived influence and power?

[AQ5] Why do babies (and adults) need skin-to-skin contact?

[AQ6] Can wearing a helmet actually increase risky behaviors?

Throughout the chapter, look for [AQ1]–[AQ6] icons. They indicate where the text addresses these questions.

CHAPTER OUTLINE

4.1 Understanding Sensation

LEARNING OBJECTIVES

Retrieval Practice   While reading the upcoming sections, respond to each Learning Objective in your own words.

Review the key features and processes of sensation.

- **Differentiate** sensation from perception.
- **Describe** how raw sensory stimuli are processed and converted to signals sent to our brains.
- **Discuss** how and why we reduce the amount of sensory information we receive and process.

- **Explain** psychophysics and subliminal stimuli.
- **Summarize** the factors involved in sensory adaptation and pain perception.

Real World Application Questions

[AQ1] Do athletes have a higher pain tolerance than non-athletes?

[AQ2] Can looking at a photograph of a loved one lead you to feel less pain?

Psychologists are keenly interested in our senses because they are our mind's window to the outside world. We're equally interested in how our mind perceives and interprets the information it receives from the senses. In this chapter, we separate the discussion of sensation and perception, but in our everyday life the two normally blend into one apparently seamless process. We'll start with an explanation of how they differ.

Sensation versus Perception

Sensation begins with specialized receptor cells located in our sense organs (eyes, ears, nose, tongue, skin, and internal body tissues). When sense organs detect an appropriate stimulus (light, sound, smell), they convert it into neural impulses (action potentials) that are transmitted to our brains (**Figure 4.1**).

Through the process of **perception**, the brain then assigns meaning to this sensory information. **Table 4.1** summarizes our five major senses—their energy sources, receptor cells, sense organs, and organs for perception.

Sensation   The process of detecting, and converting, raw sensory information from the external and internal environments and transmitting it to the brain.

Perception   The process of selecting, organizing, and interpreting sensory information into meaningful objects and events.

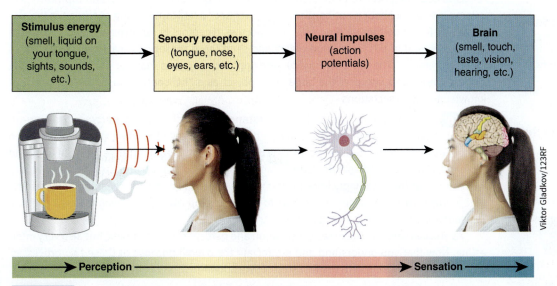

FIGURE 4.1   **Understanding how sensation becomes perception**   Note how the stimulus energy (in this case, smell, liquid on your tongue, sights, sounds, etc.) from your brewing coffee first travels to your sensory receptors (tongue, nose, eyes, ears, etc.). Neural impulses then carry the neural messages to appropriate areas of your brain (smell, touch, taste, vision, hearing, etc.). Your brain then receives and interprets these messages, while you relax and enjoy the delicious coffee.

TABLE 4.1 How We Sense and Perceive the World Around Us

	Vision	Audition (Hearing)	Olfaction (Smell)	Gustation (Taste)	Body Senses
Stimulus energy source	Light waves	Sound waves	Chemical (molecules dissolved on nose's mucous membranes)	Chemical (molecules dissolved on tongue)	Mechanical (variety of stimuli)
Sensory receptor cells	 Light sensitive rods and cones in eye's retina	 Pressure-sensitive hair cells in ear's cochlea	 Receptors in nose's olfactory epithelium	 Taste buds on tongue's surface	 Variety of receptors (this drawing is of a cell for touch)
Sense organ	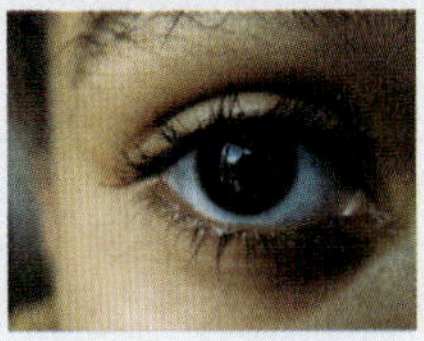	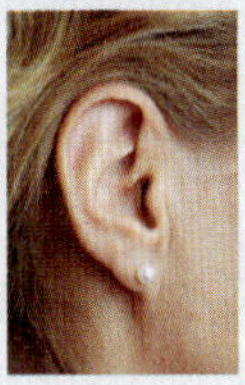		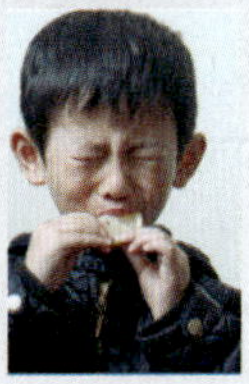	
Organs for perception	Visual cortex in occipital lobes	Auditory cortex in temporal lobes	Olfactory bulb, limbic system	Limbic system, somatosensory cortex, frontal lobes	Motor cortex in frontal lobe, somatosensory cortex in parietal lobes

How do we unknowingly and automatically combine sensation and perception? At least two processes are involved (Ciria et al., 2019; Sussman et al., 2016; van Ommen et al., 2016):

- In **bottom-up processing**, information processing starts at the "bottom" with an analysis of smaller features and then builds on them to create complete perceptions. In other words, processing begins at the sensory level and works "up."
- During **top-down processing**, our brains create useable perceptions from the sensory messages based on prior knowledge and expectations. In this case, processing begins at the "top," our brain's higher-level cognitive processes, and works "down."

One additional way to understand the difference between bottom-up and top-down processing is to think about what happens when we "see" a helicopter flying overhead in the sky. According to the *bottom-up processing* perspective, receptors in our eyes and ears record the sight and sound of this large, loud object and send these sensory messages on to our brains for interpretation. The top-down processing approach suggests that our brains quickly make a "best guess" and interpret the large, loud object as a "helicopter," based on our previous knowledge and expectations.

TIP Are you having difficulty understanding the distinction between bottom-up and top-down processing? If so, think about the process of reading (**Figure 4.2**). When most of us first learned to read, we initially discovered that certain arrangements of lines and "squiggles" represented specific letters—an example of *bottom-up processing*. Only later did we realize that these squiggly lines (letters) made up words that have meaning—an example of *top-down processing. Now, yuor aiblity to raed uisng top-dwon prcessoing mkaes it psosible to unedrstnad this sntenece despite its mnay mssipllengis.*

As you can see, the processes of sensation and perception are complex, but also very interesting. Now that you understand and appreciate the overall purpose of these two processes, let's dig deeper, starting with the first step of sensation—*processing*.

Bottom-up processing Information processing that starts at the "bottom" with an analysis of smaller features and then builds on them to create complete perceptions; data-driven processing that moves from the parts to the whole.

Top-down processing Information processing that starts at the "top" with higher-level analysis (prior knowledge and expectations) and then works "down" to recognize individual features as a unified whole; conceptually driven processing that moves from the whole to the parts.

FIGURE 4.2 Bottom-up versus top-down processing

Processing

Looking again at Table 4.1, note that our eyes, ears, skin, and other sense organs all contain special cells called receptors, which receive and process sensory information from the environment. For each sense, these specialized cells respond to a distinct stimulus, such as sound waves or odor molecules. Next, during the process of **transduction**, the receptors convert the energy from the specific sensory stimulus into neural impulses, which are then sent on to the brain. In hearing, for example, tiny receptor cells in the inner ear convert mechanical vibrations from sound waves into electrochemical signals. Neurons then carry these signals to the brain, where specific sensory receptors detect and interpret the information.

How does your brain differentiate between sensations, such as sounds and smells? Through a process known as **coding**, the brain interprets different physical stimuli as distinct sensations because their neural impulses travel by different routes and arrive at different parts of the brain (**Figure 4.3**).

We also have structures that purposefully reduce the amount of sensory information we receive. In this process of *sensory reduction*, we analyze and then filter incoming sensations before sending neural impulses on for further processing in other parts of our brains. Without this natural filtering of stimuli, we would constantly hear blood rushing through our veins and feel our clothes brushing against our skin. Some level of filtering is needed to prevent our brains from being overwhelmed with unnecessary information.

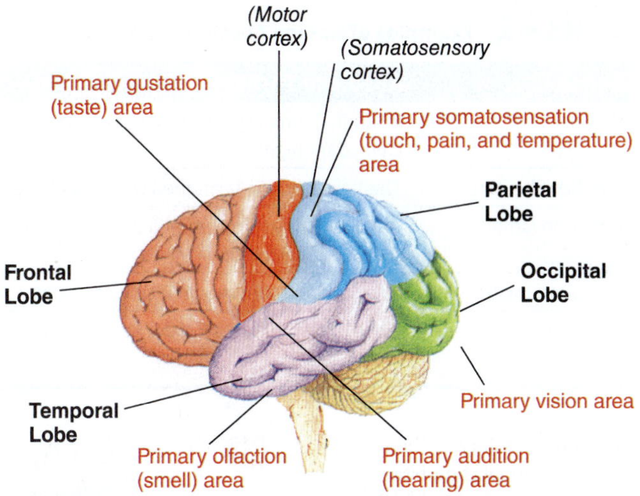

All species have evolved selective receptors that suppress or amplify information for survival. Humans, for example, cannot sense ultraviolet light, electric or magnetic fields, the ultrasonic sound of a dog whistle, or infrared heat patterns from warm-blooded animals, as some other animals can.

FIGURE 4.3 **Sensory processing within the brain**   Neural messages from the various sense organs must travel to specific areas of the brain in order for us to see, hear, smell, and so on. Shown here with the red-colored labels are the primary locations in the cerebral cortex for vision, hearing, taste, smell, and somatosensation (which includes touch, pain, and temperature sensitivity).

Transduction   The process of converting sensory stimuli into neural impulses that are sent along to the brain (e.g., transforming light waves into neural impulses).

Coding   The process in which neural impulses travel by different routes to different parts of the brain; it allows the brain to detect various physical stimuli as distinct sensations.

Psychophysics   The study of the link between the physical characteristics of stimuli and the psychological experience of them.

Difference threshold   The smallest physical difference between two stimuli that is consciously detectable 50 percent of the time; also called the *just noticeable difference (JND)*.

Psychophysics

How can scientists measure the exact amount of stimulus energy it takes to trigger a conscious experience? The answer comes from the field of **psychophysics**, which studies and measures the link between the physical characteristics of stimuli and the psychological experience of them.

One of the most intriguing insights from psychophysics is that what is out there is not directly reproduced inside our bodies. At this moment, there are light waves, sound waves, odors, tastes, and microscopic particles touching us that we cannot see, hear, smell, taste, or feel. We are consciously aware of only a narrow range of stimuli in our environment.

Difference and Absolute Thresholds   German scientist Ernst Weber (1795–1878) was one of the first to study the smallest difference between two weights that could be detected (Foley & Bates, 2019; Schwartz & Krantz, 2016). This **difference threshold**, also known as *Weber's law of just noticeable differences (JND)*, is the minimum difference that is consciously detectable 50 percent of the time (**Figure 4.4**).

FIGURE 4.4 **Why is our difference threshold important?**   This radiologist is responsible for detecting the slightest indication of a tumor in this mammogram of a female breast. The ability to detect differences between stimuli (like the visual difference between normal and abnormal breast tissue) can be improved by special training, practice, and instruments. However, it's still limited by our basic sensory difference thresholds.

BSIP/Universal Images Group/Getty Images

TABLE 4.2	Examples of Human Absolute Thresholds
Sense	**Absolute Threshold**
Vision	A candle flame seen from 30 miles away on a clear, dark night
Audition (hearing)	The tick of an old-fashioned watch at 20 feet
Olfaction (smell)	One drop of perfume spread throughout a six-room apartment
Gustation (taste)	One teaspoon of sugar in 2 gallons of water
Body senses	A bee's wing falling on your cheek from a height of about half an inch

Another scientist, Gustav Fechner (1801–1887), expanded on Weber's law to determine what is called the **absolute threshold**, the minimum stimulation necessary to consciously detect a stimulus 50 percent of the time. See **Table 4.2** for a list of absolute thresholds for our various senses.

To measure your senses, an examiner presents a series of signals that vary in intensity and asks you to report which signals you can detect. In a hearing test, the softest level at which you can consistently hear a tone is your absolute threshold. The examiner then compares your threshold with those of people with normal hearing to determine whether or not you have hearing loss (**Figure 4.5**).

Absolute threshold The minimum amount of stimulation necessary to consciously detect a stimulus 50 percent of the time.

PA Practical Application

Did you know that many non-human animals have higher and lower thresholds than humans? A dog's absolute and difference thresholds for smell are far more sensitive than those of a human. This exceptional sensitivity allows specially trained dogs to provide invaluable help in sniffing out dangerous plants, animals, drugs, and explosives; tracking criminals; and assisting in search-and-rescue operations (Concha et al., 2019; MacLean & Hare, 2018; Porritt et al., 2015). Some researchers believe dogs can even detect hidden corrosion, fecal contamination, and chemical signs of certain illnesses (such as diabetes or cancer), and possibly even predict seizures in humans (Rooney et al., 2019; Schoon et al., 2014; Urbanová et al., 2015). In addition, other research found that when dogs were presented with five different scents from humans and dogs, sensory receptors in the dogs' noses easily picked up all five scents (Berns et al., 2015). However, only the human scents activated a part of the dog's brain (the caudate nucleus) that has a well-known association with positive expectations. The researchers concluded that this brain activation, and the dog's positive association with human scents, points to the importance of humans in dogs' lives. A related study has shown that dogs can even discriminate among many emotional expressions on human faces (Muller et al., 2015).

Subliminal perception The detection of stimuli below the absolute threshold for conscious awareness.

Priming A form of memory activation that supposedly occurs when exposure (often unconscious) to previously stored information predisposes (or *primes*) our response to related stimuli.

Subliminal Perception Have you heard some of the wild rumors about subliminal messages? During the 1970s, it was said that rock songs contained demonic messages, which could be heard only when the songs were played backwards. Similarly, in the 1990s, some suggested that certain Disney films contained obscene subliminal messages. In the film *Aladdin*, the lead character supposedly whispered, "all good teenagers take off your clothes," and *The Lion King* reportedly showed close-up shots of the dust with a secret spelling out of the word "sex." In addition, at one time movie theaters were reportedly flashing messages like "Eat popcorn" and "Drink Cola-Cola" on the screen. Even though the messages were so brief that viewers weren't aware of seeing them, it was believed they increased consumption of these products (Smarandescu & Shimp, 2015; Vokey & Read, 1985).

Can subliminal stimuli really affect our behavior? Experimental studies on **subliminal perception** have clearly shown that we *can* detect stimuli and information below our level of conscious awareness (Lucini et al., 2019; Rabellino et al., 2016; Urriza et al., 2016). These studies commonly use an instrument, called a *tachistoscope*, to flash images too quickly for conscious recognition, but slowly enough to be registered by the brain. How does this happen? As we've just seen, our "absolute threshold" is the point at which we can detect a stimulus half the time. *Subliminal stimuli* are just stimuli that fall below our 50 percent absolute threshold, and they can be detected without our awareness.

Related studies on **priming** suggest that certain subliminal or unnoticed stimuli can reach our brains and predispose (*prime*) us to make it easier or more difficult to recall related information already in storage (Elgendi et al., 2018;

FIGURE 4.5 Measuring the absolute and difference thresholds for hearing

iStock.com/carmen Martinez Banu

Ohtomo, 2017; Sassenberg et al., 2017). If a researcher shows you the words "red" and "fire engine," you'll be slightly faster to recognize the word "apple" because all of these words have been previously stored and closely associated in your memory. Note that some early studies on priming have failed to be replicated, which has led to considerable controversy. However, others have conducted studies and meta-analyses that support priming, and some have suggested that the criticism may be overblown and based on faulty logic (e.g., Dijksterhuis, 2014; Lodder et al., 2019; Payne et al., 2016).

Even if we assume that *subliminal stimuli* and *priming* do occur, it doesn't mean that such processes lead to significant behavioral changes. Subliminal stimuli are basically weak stimuli. In one experiment that used priming, for example, researchers offered participants implicit primes as well as direct, overt warnings about the danger of cyberattacks (Junger et al., 2017). Surprisingly, almost 80 percent of the participants nevertheless were willing to provide personal information, such as their e-mail addresses, and over 40 percent willingly provided 9 digits from their 18-digit bank account numbers. Apparently, our tendency to trust one another overrides priming, direct warnings, and even our common sense.

Sensory Adaptation

Imagine that friends have invited you to come and visit their beautiful new baby kitten. As they greet you at the door, you are overwhelmed by the odor of the kitten's overflowing litter box. Why don't your friends do something about that smell? The answer lies in the previously mentioned sensory filtering and reduction, combined with **sensory adaptation**, which occurs when receptors in our sensory system become less sensitive to ongoing, unchanging stimuli. In other words, they get "tired" and actually fire less frequently.

Sensory adaptation   The sensory receptors' innate tendency to fatigue and stop responding to ongoing and unchanging stimuli; an example of bottom-up processing.

Sensory adaptation can be understood from an evolutionary perspective. We can't afford to waste attention and time on unchanging, normally unimportant stimuli. "Turning down the volume" on repetitive information helps the brain cope with an overwhelming amount of sensory stimuli and enables us to pay attention to change. Sometimes, however, adaptation can be dangerous as when people stop paying attention to a small gas leak in the kitchen.

Although some senses, like smell and touch, adapt quickly, we never completely adapt to visual stimuli or to extremely intense stimuli, such as the odor of ammonia or the pain of a bad burn. From an evolutionary perspective, these limitations on sensory adaptation may improve our odds for survival by reminding us to keep a watch out for dangerous predators, avoid strong odors and heat, and take care of that burn. Interestingly, there are at least four factors that help explain pain perception—*endorphins, distraction, gate control,* and *phantom limb pain*.

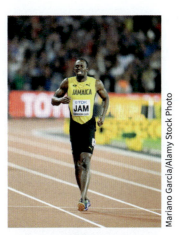

Endorphins   [AQ1] If we don't adapt to pain, how do athletes keep playing despite painful injuries? In certain situations, including times of physical exertion, the body releases natural, pain-killing neurotransmitters, called *endorphins* (Chapter 2), which inhibit pain perception. This is the so-called "runner's high," which may help explain why athletes tend to have a higher pain tolerance than non-athletes—see photo (Tesarz et al., 2012). (As a scientific and critical thinker, do you think it is possible that individuals with a naturally high pain tolerance are just more attracted to athletics? Or might the experience of playing sports change your pain tolerance?)

Distraction   Along with the power of endorphins, the pain of athletes, soldiers, firefighters, and others is sometimes diminished when they're distracted by factors such as duty, competition, or fear. Similarly, surgical patients who listen to music—even while under anesthesia—have less anxiety, report a 20 percent reduction in postsurgery pain, and need less pain medication during recovery (Hole et al., 2015). **[AQ2]** Studies have even shown that simply holding the hand of a loved one—or just looking at a photograph of them (see photo)—can help reduce pain during a medical procedure (Master et al., 2009). Similarly, having a larger social network also tends to increase our pain tolerance (Johnson & Dunbar, 2016).

Gate control theory of pain
The theory that pain sensations are processed and altered by certain cells in the spinal cord, which act as gates to interrupt and block some pain signals while sending others on to the brain.

Gate Control Theory   In addition to endorphin release and distraction, one of the most widely accepted explanations of pain perception is the **gate control theory of pain**, first proposed by Ronald Melzack and Patrick Wall (1965). According to this theory, the experience of pain depends partly on whether the neural message gets past a "gatekeeper" in the spinal cord. Normally, the gate is kept shut, either by impulses coming down from the brain or by messages being sent from

Mariano Garcia/Alamy Stock Photo

PeopleImages/E+/Getty Images

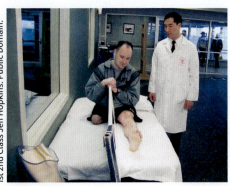

Source: Navy Mass Communication Specialist 2nd Class Jeff Hopkins. Public Domain.

FIGURE 4.6 **Treating phantom limb pain** Using mirror therapy, this amputee patient places his intact limb on one side of the mirror, and the amputated limb on the other side. He then concentrates on looking into the mirror on the side that reflects the intact limb, creating the visual impression of two complete undamaged limbs. The patient then attempts to move both limbs. Thanks to the artificial feedback provided by the mirror, the patient sees the complete limb, and the reflected image of the complete limb, moving. He then interprets this as the phantom limb moving.

large-diameter nerve fibers that conduct most sensory signals, such as touch and pressure. However, when body tissue is damaged, impulses from smaller pain fibers open the gate (Price & Prescott, 2015; Rhudy, 2016; Zhao & Wood, 2015). Can you see how this gate control theory helps explain why massaging an injury or scratching an itch can temporarily relieve discomfort? It's because pressure on large-diameter neurons interferes with pain signals. In addition, studies suggest that the pain gate may be chemically controlled. A neurotransmitter called *substance P* opens the pain gate, and endorphins close it (Deer et al., 2019; Fan et al., 2016; Wu et al., 2015).

In sum, endorphins, distraction, listening to music, and holding a loved one's hand may all provide soothing comfort and pain reduction, especially for those who are very anxious (Dickie et al., 2019; Gardstrom & Sorel, 2015).

Phantom Limb Pain (PLP)
Did you know that when normal sensory input is disrupted, the brain can also generate pain and other sensations entirely on its own, which is the case with *phantom limb pain (PLP)* (Fan et al., 2016; Limakatso et al., 2019; Melzack, 1999)? After an amputation, people commonly report detecting their missing limb as if it were still there with no differences at all. In fact, up to 80 percent of people who have had amputations sometimes "feel" pain (and itching, burning, or tickling sensations) in the missing limb, long after the amputation. Numerous theories attempt to explain this type of PLP, but one of the most widely accepted theories suggests that there is a mismatch between the sensory messages sent and received in the brain.

Can you explain how this may be an example of our earlier description of how *bottom-up processes* (such as the sensory messages sent from our limbs to our brains) combine with our *top-down processes* (our brain's reception and interpretation of these messages)? Messages are no longer being transmitted from the peripheral nerves and the missing limb to the brain (bottom up). However, areas of the brain responsible for receiving and interpreting messages are still intact (top down). The brain's attempt to interpret the confusing messages (seeing the missing limb and missing the sensory feedback) may explain the resulting perceptions of pain and other sensations.

In line with this idea of mismatched signals, when amputees wear prosthetic limbs, or when *mirror visual therapy* is used, phantom pain often disappears. In mirror therapy (see **Figure 4.6**), pain relief apparently occurs because the brain is somehow tricked into believing there is no longer a missing limb (Thieme et al., 2016; Villa-Alcázar et al., 2019). Others believe that mirror therapy works because it helps the brain reorganize and incorporate this phantom limb into a new nervous system configuration (Guo et al., 2016).

Now that we've studied how we perceive pain, how we might ignore or "play through" it, and how we might misperceive it with phantom limb pain, it's important to point out that when we get anxious or dwell on our pain, we can intensify it (Burston et al., 2019; Miller-Matero et al., 2017; Ray et al., 2015). Ironically, well-meaning friends or anxious parents who ask pain sufferers about their pain may unintentionally reinforce and increase it.

Before leaving this section on pain, check out the following **Test Yourself**, for an assessment and strategies for your personal pain management.

PA Practical Application

Test Yourself: How Well Do You Manage Your Pain?

Score yourself on how often you use one or more of these strategies, to manage your pain, using the following scale: 0 = never, 1 = seldom, 2 = occasionally, 3 = often, 4 = almost always, 5 = always.

_____ **1.** I do something I enjoy, such as watching TV or listening to music.

_____ **2.** I try to be around other people.

_____ **3.** I do something active, like household chores or projects.

_____ **4.** I try to feel distant from the pain, almost as if I'm floating above my body.

_____ **5.** I try to think about something pleasant.

_____ **6.** I replay in my mind pleasant experiences from the past.

_____ **7.** I tell myself that I can overcome the pain.

_____ **8.** I don't think about the pain.

These questions are based on effective pain management techniques, such as distraction, ignoring pain, and reinterpreting it. Review those items that you checked as "never" or "seldom" and consider adding them to your pain management skills.

Retrieval Practice 4.1 | Understanding Sensation

Self-Test   Completing this self-test, and then checking your answers by clicking on the answer button or by looking in Appendix B, will provide immediate feedback and helpful practice for exams.

1. _____ starts at the "bottom" with an analysis of smaller features.

   a. Perception   **c.** Sensation

   b. Bottom-up processing   **d.** Integration

2. Transduction is the process of converting _____.

   a. sensory stimuli into neural impulses that are sent along to the brain

   b. receptors into transmitters

   c. a particular sensory stimulus into a specific perception

   d. receptors into neural impulses

3. The _____ is the minimum stimulation necessary to consciously detect a stimulus 50 percent of the time.

   a. threshold of excitation   **c.** absolute threshold

   b. difference threshold   **d.** low point

4. Experiments on subliminal perception have _____.

   a. supported its existence, but shown that it has little or no effect on behavioral change

   b. shown that subliminal perception occurs only among children and some adolescents

   c. shown that subliminal messages affect only people who are highly suggestible

   d. failed to support the phenomenon

5. The _____ theory of pain helps explain why it sometimes helps to rub or massage an injured area.

   a. sensory adaptation   **c.** just noticeable difference

   b. gate control   **d.** Lamaze

Q Test Your Critical Thinking

1. Sensation and perception are closely linked. What is the central distinction between the two?

2. If we sensed and attended equally to each stimulus in our environment, the amount of information would be overwhelming. What sensory and perceptual processes help us lessen the din?

Real World Application Questions

[AQ1] Do athletes have a higher pain tolerance than non-athletes?

[AQ2] Can looking at a photograph of a loved one lead you to feel less pain?

Mariano Garcia/ Alamy Stock Photo

PeopleImages/E+/ Getty Images

Hint: Look in the text for **[AQ1]** and **[AQ2]**

4.2

How We See and Hear

LEARNING OBJECTIVES

Retrieval Practice   While reading the upcoming sections, respond to each Learning Objective in your own words.

Summarize the key components and processes of vision and audition.

- **Identify** the key characteristics of light and sound waves.
- **Explain** the visual process, the key parts and functions of the human eye.
- **Identify** vision's major problems and peculiarities, along with color vision.

- **Describe** audition, the key parts and functions of the human ear, and pitch perception.
- **Summarize** the two major types of hearing problems and what we can do to protect our hearing.

Real World Application Questions

[AQ3] Does a lack of direct sunlight contribute to nearsightedness?

[AQ4] Can using a lower-pitched voice affect your perceived influence and power?

Many people mistakenly believe that what they see and hear is a copy of the outside world. In fact, vision and hearing are the result of what our brains create in response to light and sound waves, which vary in wavelength and frequency—much like ocean waves (**Figure 4.7**).

In addition to wavelength/frequency, waves also vary in height (technically called *amplitude*). This wave height/amplitude determines the intensity of sights and sounds. Finally, waves

FIGURE 4.7 **Waves of light and sound** Ocean waves have a certain distance between them (the *wavelength*), and they pass by you at intervals. If you counted the number of passing waves in a set amount of time (e.g., 5 waves in 60 seconds), you could calculate the *frequency* (the number of complete wavelengths that pass a point in a given time). Longer wavelength means lower frequency and vice versa.

Wavelength
The distance between successive peaks.

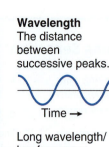

Time →

Long wavelength/
low frequency =
Reddish colors/
low-pitched sounds

Short wavelength/
high frequency =
Bluish colors/
high-pitched sound

Wave amplitude
The height from peak to trough.

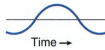

Time →

Low amplitude/
low intensity =
Dull colors/
soft sounds

High amplitude/
high intensity =
Bright colors/
loud sounds

Range of wavelengths
The mixture of waves.

Time →

Small range/
low complexity =
Less complex colors/
less complex sounds

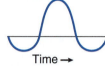

Time →

Large range/
high complexity =
Complex colors/
complex sounds

FIGURE 4.8 **Properties of light and sound**

also vary in range, or complexity, which mixes together waves of various wavelength/frequency and height/amplitude (**Figure 4.8**).

Vision

Did you know that professional baseball players can hit a 90-miles-per-hour fastball four-tenths of a second after it leaves the pitcher's hand? How can the human eye receive and process information that fast? To understand the marvels of vision, we need to start with the basics—that light waves are a form of electromagnetic energy and only a small part of the full *electromagnetic spectrum* (**Figure 4.9**).

To fully appreciate how our eyes turn these light waves into the experience we call *vision*, we need to first examine the various structures in our eyes that capture and focus the light waves. Then, we need to understand how these waves are transformed (transduced) into neural messages (action potentials) that our brains can process into images we consciously (see **Process Diagram 4.1**).

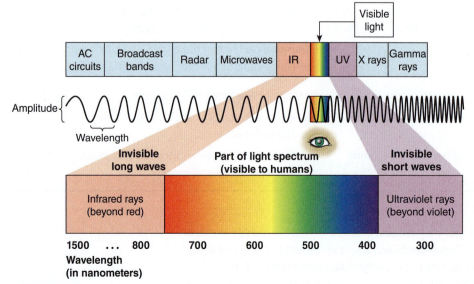

a. Waves of the electromagnetic spectrum Note that each type of wave has a different name and wavelength. Unlike sound waves, which need air to travel, these waves are vibrations of magnetic and electric fields, and they can move in a vacuum. The fact that light waves travel nearly 900,000 times faster than sound waves explains why we see a flash of lightning before we hear the thunder.

b. What we see Only the light waves in the middle of the electromagnetic spectrum, can be seen by the human eye. Note that we perceive the longer visible wavelengths as red, whereas the shortest are seen as blue, with the rest of the colors in between.

FIGURE 4.9 **The electromagnetic spectrum for vision**

STOP! This Process Diagram contains essential information NOT found elsewhere in the text, which is likely to appear on quizzes and exams. Be sure to study it CAREFULLY.

PROCESS DIAGRAM 4.1 **How Our Eyes See** Various structures of your eye work together to capture and focus the light waves from the outside world. Receptor cells in your retina (rods and cones) then convert these waves into messages that are sent along the optic nerve to be interpreted by your brain.

3 The muscularly controlled lens then focuses incoming light into an image on the light-sensitive *retina*, located on the back surface of the fluid-filled eyeball.

2 The light then passes through the *pupil*, a small adjustable opening. Muscles in the *iris* allow the *pupil* to dilate or constrict in response to light intensity or emotional factors.

4 In the **retina**, light waves are detected and transduced into neural signals by vision receptor cells (rods and cones). Note how the image of the flower is inverted when it is projected onto the retina. Our brains later reverse the visual input into the final image that we perceive.

1 Light first enters through the *cornea*, which helps protect the eye and focus incoming light rays.

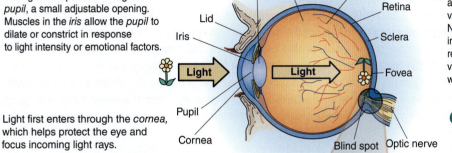

Lens · Vitreous humor · Retinal blood vessels · Retina · Lid · Iris · Sclera · Light · Light · Fovea · Pupil · Cornea · Blind spot · Optic nerve

5 The **fovea**, a tiny pit filled with cones, is responsible for our sharpest vision.

Have you noticed your blind spot? At the back of the retina lies an area that has no visual receptors at all and absolutely no vision. This **blind spot** is where blood vessels and nerves enter and exit the eyeball. To find yours, hold this book about one foot in front of you, close your right eye, and stare at the X with your left eye. Very slowly, move the book closer to you. You should see the worm disappear and the apple become whole.

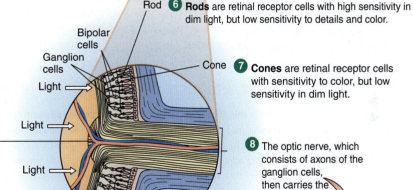

Rod · Bipolar cells · Ganglion cells · Light · Cone · Light · Light

6 **Rods** are retinal receptor cells with high sensitivity in dim light, but low sensitivity to details and color.

7 **Cones** are retinal receptor cells with sensitivity to color, but low sensitivity in dim light.

8 The optic nerve, which consists of axons of the ganglion cells, then carries the message on to the brain.

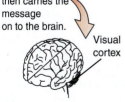

Visual cortex

Blind spot The point at which the optic nerve leaves the eye, which contains no receptor cells for vision—thus creating a "blind spot."

Vision Problems

As shown in Process Diagram 4.1, visual images are normally focused directly on the **retina** at the back of the eye. However, if you've been diagnosed as being *nearsighted* (*myopic*), you have normal vision close-up (like when you're using a computer), but you find it hard to focus on distant objects (such as looking at the front of the classroom). This is because your eyeball is "too long" and images are focused in front of your retina.

Whereas images are focused in front of the retina in nearsightedness (myopia), the images are focused behind the retina in *farsightedness* (hyperopia). This condition occurs when the eyeball is "too short," but it may also be related to irregularity in the shape of the cornea or lens. This irregularity results in close objects appearing blurry, while vision is normal for distant objects.

Retina The light-sensitive inner surface of the back of the eye, which contains the receptor cells for vision (rods and cones).

Towfiqu Photography/ Moment/Getty Images

Alexey Emelyanov/123RF

TIP Are you having trouble remembering the difference between myopia and hyperopia? If so, note that the names focus on what the person CAN do—nearsighted people can see nearby objects, whereas farsighted people can see far off.

[AQ3] Interestingly, research conducted in the year 2000 found that about 25 percent of the world's population was nearsighted/myopic (see photo), and by the year 2050, it's estimated that about half the people on Earth will be myopic (Bailey, 2018). Although many experts believe this increase is related to the long hours young people spend staring at computers and other screens, other researchers have found that the increase in myopia is actually linked with the amount of time children spend outdoors—see photo (Williams et al., 2017). After giving vision exams to more than 3,100 older European men and women, researchers found strong correlations between current eyesight and the volunteers' childhood and lifetime exposure to sunlight.

What do you think? Can you see how this may be an example of confusing correlation with causation? Could simply being outdoors (regardless of the amount or intensity of the sunlight) have caused the better eyesight? Or maybe sunlight wasn't the issue. Perhaps being outdoors gave certain children more opportunities to develop their long-distance vision? Can you think of other third-variable possibilities? Given the well-established risks of skin cancer, can you also see how some people might try to balance the dangers of skin cancer with the potential risk of myopia?

In contrast to the visual problems of myopia and hyperopia related to the shape of the eyeball, the third major visual acuity problem for most people occurs during middle age. The lenses of people in this age group typically lose elasticity and the ability to accommodate for near vision, a condition known as *presbyopia*. Fortunately, corrective lenses or laser surgery can often correct all three of these visual acuity problems.

Rods Retinal receptor cells with high sensitivity in dim light, but low sensitivity to details and color.

Cones Retinal receptor cells with high sensitivity to color and detail, but low sensitivity in dim light.

Vision Peculiarities In addition to these three vision problems, which vary among individuals, we also have at least two visual peculiarities that we all share. As demonstrated in Process Diagram 4.1, there are no receptor cells in the area where the optic nerve exits the eyeball—thus resulting in a "blind spot." A second peculiarity exists in the retina's vision receptor cells (the rods and cones). The **rods** are highly sensitive in dim light, but are less sensitive to detail and color. The reverse is true for the **cones**, which are highly sensitive to color and detail, but are less sensitive in dim light.

PAN Practical Application of Neuroscience

Why is the difference in sensitivity between rods and cones important? Understanding this distinction helps explain why you're cautioned to look away from bright headlights when driving or biking at night. Staring into the bright lights activates your cones, which are less effective in dim light. In contrast, looking away activates the rods in your peripheral vision, which are more sensitive at night. Have you noticed that when you walk into a dark movie theater on a sunny afternoon, you're almost blind for a few seconds? The reason is that in bright light, the pigment inside the *rods* (refer to Process Diagram 4.1) is bleached, making them temporarily non-functional. It takes a second or two for the rods to become functional enough again for you to see. This process of *dark adaptation* continues for 20 to 30 minutes.

In contrast, *light adaptation*, the adjustment that takes place when you go from darkness to a bright setting, takes about 7 to 10 minutes and is the work of the *cones*. This is because a region in the center of the retina, called the **fovea**, has the greatest density of cones, which are most sensitive in brightly lit conditions. They're also responsible for color vision and fine detail.

Fovea A tiny pit in the center of the retina that is densely filled with cones; it is responsible for sharp vision.

Color Vision Our ability to perceive color is almost as remarkable and useful as vision itself. Humans may be able to discriminate among seven million different hues, and research conducted in many cultures suggests that we all seem to see essentially the same colored world (He et al., 2019; Ozturk et al., 2013). Furthermore, studies of infants old enough to focus and move their eyes show that they are able to see color nearly as well as adults and have color preferences similar to those of adults (Bornstein et al., 2014; Yang et al., 2015).

Trichromatic theory of color The theory that color perception results from three types of cones in the retina, each of which is most sensitive to either red, green, or blue; other colors result from a mixture of these three.

Although we know color is produced by different wavelengths of light, the actual way in which we perceive color is a matter of scientific debate. Traditionally, there have been two theories of color vision: the trichromatic (three-color) theory and the opponent-process theory. The **trichromatic theory of color** (from the Greek words *tri*, meaning "three," and *chroma*, meaning "color") suggests that we have three "color systems," each of which is maximally sensitive to red, green, or blue (Young, 1802). The proponents of this theory demonstrated that mixing lights of these three colors could yield the full spectrum of colors we perceive (**Figure 4.10**).

However, trichromatic theory doesn't fully explain color vision, and other researchers have proposed alternative theories. The **opponent-process theory of color** agrees that we have three color systems, but it says that each system is sensitive to two opposing colors—blue and yellow, red and green, black and white—in an "on/off" fashion. In other words, each color receptor responds either to blue or yellow, or to red or green, with the black-or-white system responding to differences in brightness levels. This theory makes a lot of sense because when different-colored lights are combined, people are unable to see reddish greens and bluish yellow. In fact, when red and green lights or blue and yellow lights are mixed in equal amounts, we see white. This opponent-process theory also explains *color afterimages*, a fun type of optical illusion in which an image briefly remains after the original image has faded (**Test Yourself**).

FIGURE 4.10 **Primary colors** Trichromatic theory found that the three primary colors (red, green, and blue) can be combined to form all colors. For example, a combination of green and red creates yellow.

PA Practical Application

Test Yourself: Do You See the Afterimage?

Try staring at the dot in the middle of this color-distorted U.S. flag for 60 seconds. Then stare at a plain sheet of white paper. You should get interesting color afterimages—red in place of green, blue in place of yellow, and white in place of black: a "genuine" U.S. flag. (If you don't see the afterimage, blink once or twice and try again.)

What happened? As you stared at the green, black, and yellow colors, the neural systems that process those colors became fatigued. Then when you looked at the plain white paper, which reflects all wavelengths,

a reverse opponent process occurred: Each fatigued receptor responded with its opposing red, white, and or blue colors. This is a good example of color afterimages—and further support for the opponent-process theory.

Today we know that both trichromatic and opponent-process theories are correct—they just operate at different levels in visual processing. Color vision is processed in a trichromatic fashion in the retina. In contrast, color vision during opponent processing involves the retina, optic nerve, and brain.

Color-Deficient Vision Most people perceive three different colors—red, green, and blue—and are called *trichromats*. However, a small percentage of the population has a genetic deficiency in the red–green system, the blue–yellow system, or both. Those who perceive only two colors are called *dichromats*. People who are sensitive to only the black–white system are called *monochromats*, and they are totally color blind. If you'd like to test yourself for red–green color blindness, see **Figure 4.11**.

Hearing

The sense or act of hearing, known as **audition**, has a number of important functions, ranging from alerting us to dangers to helping us communicate with others. To understand audition, we need to first discuss the properties of sound waves and ear anatomy. Then we'll explore pitch perception, softness versus loudness, and hearing problems.

Like the visual process, which transforms light waves into vision, the auditory system is designed to convert sound waves into hearing. Sound waves are produced by air molecules moving in a particular wave pattern. Vibrating objects like vocal cords or guitar strings create waves of compressed and expanded air resembling ripples on a lake that circle out from a tossed stone. Our ears detect and respond to these waves of small air pressure changes, our brains then interpret the neural messages resulting from these waves, and we hear.

Opponent-process theory of color The theory that all color perception is based on three systems, each of which contains two color opposites (red versus green, blue versus yellow, and black versus white).

Audition The sense or act of hearing.

FIGURE 4.11 **Are you color blind?** People who suffer red–green color deficiency have trouble perceiving the number in this design. Although we commonly use the term *color blindness*, most problems are color confusion rather than color blindness. Surprisingly, most people who have some color blindness are not even aware of it.

PROCESS DIAGRAM 4.2 **How Our Ears Hear** The **outer ear** captures and funnels sound waves into the eardrum. Next, three tiny bones in the **middle ear** pick up the eardrum's vibrations and transmit them to the **inner ear**. Finally, the snail-shaped **cochlea** in the inner ear transforms (transduces) the sound waves into neural messages (action potentials) that our brains process into what we consciously hear.

1 The **outer ear** captures and funnels sound waves onto the tympanic membrane (ear drum).

2 Vibrations of the tympanic membrane strike the **middle ear's** ossicles (hammer, anvil, and stirrup). Then the stirrup hits the oval window.

3 Vibrations of the oval window create waves in the **inner ear's** cochlear fluid which deflect the basilar membrane. This movement bends the hair cells.

4 The hair cells communicate with the auditory nerve, which sends neural impulses to the brain.

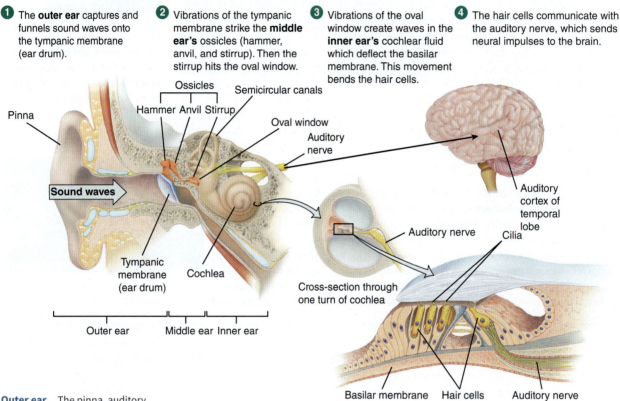

Outer ear The pinna, auditory canal, and eardrum structures, which funnel sound waves to the middle ear.

Middle ear The hammer, anvil, and stirrup structures of the ear, which concentrate eardrum vibrations onto the cochlea's oval window.

Inner ear The semicircular canals, vestibular sacs, and cochlea, which generate neural signals that are sent to the brain.

Cochlea [KOK-lee-uh] The fluid-filled, coiled tube in the inner ear that contains the receptors for hearing.

Place theory for hearing The theory that pitch perception is linked to the particular spot on the cochlea's basilar membrane that is most stimulated.

Frequency theory for hearing The theory that pitch perception depends on how often the auditory nerve fires.

To fully understand this process, pay close attention to the step-by-step diagram in **Process Diagram 4.2**.

Pitch Perception

How do we determine that certain sounds are from a child's voice, and not from an adult's? We distinguish between high- and low-pitched sounds by the *frequency* of the sound waves. The higher the frequency, the higher the pitch. There are three main explanations for how we perceive *pitch*:

- According to the **place theory for hearing**, we hear different pitches because different sound waves stimulate different sections (or *places*) on our cochlea's basilar membrane (see again Process Diagram 4.2). Our brains figure out the pitch of a sound by detecting the position of the hair cells that sent the neural message. High frequencies produce large vibrations near the start of the basilar membrane—next to the oval window. However, this theory does not predict well for low frequencies, which tend to excite the entire basilar membrane.

- The **frequency theory for hearing** differs from place theory because it states that we hear pitch by the *frequency* of the sound waves traveling up the auditory nerve. High-frequency sounds trigger the auditory nerve to fire more often than do low-frequency sounds. The problem with this theory is that an individual neuron cannot fire faster than 1,000 times per second, which means that we could not hear many of the notes of a soprano singer.

- The **volley principle for hearing** solves the problem of frequency theory, which can't account for the highest pitched sounds. It states that clusters of neurons take turns firing in a sequence of rhythmic *volleys*. Pitch perception depends upon the frequency of volleys, rather than the frequency carried by individual neurons.

Interestingly, as we age, we tend to lose our ability to hear high-pitched sounds but are still able to hear low-pitched sounds. Young people can hear a phone ringtone that sounds at 17 kilohertz—too high for most adult ears to detect—and so they can take advantage of this age-related hearing difference to call or text one another during class (see photo). Ironically, the stealth ringtone that most adults can't hear is an offshoot of another device, called the Mosquito, which was originally designed to help shopkeepers annoy and drive away loitering teens.

Now that we've explored the mechanics of pitch and pitch perception, would you like another real-world example that you can apply to your everyday life? **[AQ4]** If so, one study found that research participants who lowered the pitch of their voices were seen as being more influential, powerful, and intimidating (Cheng et al., 2016). This finding also held true in a second experiment in which the people only listened to audio recordings of various voices. Can you see why the famous deep-voiced actor James Earl Jones was chosen as the voice of Darth Vader in the *Star Wars* films (see photo)? Given that women generally tend to have higher-pitched voices, can you also see how this research might help explain why women often find it harder to gain leadership positions?

Softness versus Loudness

How we detect a sound as being soft or loud depends on its amplitude (or wave height). Waves with high peaks and low valleys produce loud sounds; waves with relatively low peaks and shallow valleys produce soft sounds. The relative loudness or softness of sounds is measured on a scale of *decibels* (dBs) (**Figure 4.12**).

Hearing Problems

What are the types, causes, and treatments of hearing loss? **Conduction hearing loss**, also called conduction deafness, results from problems with the mechanical system that conducts sound waves to the cochlea. Hearing aids that amplify the incoming sound waves, and some forms of surgery, can help with this type of hearing loss.

"Thanks" to age-related hearing loss, this student can respond to a text that her older teacher cannot detect.

Volley principle for hearing An explanation for pitch perception suggesting that clusters of neurons take turns firing in a sequence of rhythmic volleys, and that pitch depends on the frequency of these volleys.

Conduction hearing loss A type of hearing loss that results from damage to the mechanical system that conducts sound waves to the cochlea; also called conduction deafness.

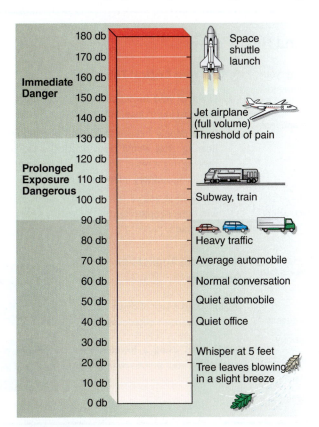

180 db	Space shuttle launch
170 db	
160 db	
150 db	
140 db	Jet airplane (full volume)
130 db	Threshold of pain
120 db	
110 db	Subway, train
100 db	
90 db	
80 db	Heavy traffic
70 db	Average automobile
60 db	Normal conversation
50 db	Quiet automobile
40 db	Quiet office
30 db	
20 db	Whisper at 5 feet
10 db	Tree leaves blowing in a slight breeze
0 db	

Immediate Danger — Prolonged Exposure Dangerous

FIGURE 4.12 **Beware of loud sounds** The higher a sound's decibel (dB) reading, the more damaging it is to the ear.

FIGURE 4.13 **Preventing hearing loss** Given the limited ability of medicine or technology to improve hearing following damage, it's important to protect our sense of hearing. We can do this by avoiding exceptionally loud noises, wearing earphones or earplugs when we cannot avoid such stimuli, and paying attention to bodily warnings of possible hearing loss, including a change in our normal hearing threshold and *tinnitus*, a whistling or ringing sensation in the ears. These relatively small changes can have lifelong benefits.

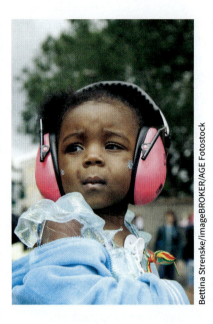

Bettina Strenske/imageBROKER/AGE Fotostock

Sensorineural hearing loss
A type of hearing loss resulting from damage to the cochlea's receptor (hair) hearing cells or to the auditory nerve; also called nerve deafness.

In contrast, **sensorineural hearing loss**, also known as nerve deafness, results from damage to the cochlea's receptor (hair) cells or to the auditory nerve. Disease and biological changes associated with aging can result in sensorineural hearing loss. But the most common (and preventable) factor in sensorineural hearing loss is continuous exposure to loud noise, which can damage hair cells and lead to permanent hearing loss. Even brief exposure to really loud sounds, like a stereo or headphones at full blast, a jackhammer, or a jet airplane engine, can cause permanent nerve deafness (see again Figure 4.12). In fact, a high volume on earphones can reach the same noise level as a jet engine! All forms of high-volume noise can damage the coating on nerve cells, making it harder for the nerve cells to send information from the ears to the brain (Fagelson & Baguley, 2016; Jiang et al., 2016; Nyarubeli et al., 2019).

Although most hearing loss is temporary, damage to the auditory nerve or receptor cells is generally considered irreversible. The only treatment for auditory nerve damage is a small electronic device called a *cochlear implant*. If the auditory nerve is intact, the implant bypasses hair cells to stimulate the nerve. Existing cochlear implants produce only a crude approximation of hearing, but the technology is improving. For the simplest form of hearing protection, see **Figure 4.13**.

Retrieval Practice 4.2 | How We See and Hear

Self-Test Completing this self-test, and then checking your answers by clicking on the answer button or by looking in Appendix B, will provide immediate feedback and helpful practice for exams.

1. A visual acuity problem that occurs when the cornea and lens focus an image in front of the retina is called _____.
   a. farsightedness   **c.** myopia
   b. hyperopia   **d.** presbyopia

2. The _____ theory of color vision states that there are three systems of color opposites (blue-yellow, red-green, and black-white).
   a. trichromatic   **c.** tri-receptor
   b. opponent-process   **d.** lock-and-key

3. Unlike the visual process, which transforms _____ waves into vision, the auditory system is designed to convert _____ waves into hearing.
   a. slow; fast   **c.** amplitude; frequency
   b. light; sound   **d.** all of these options

4. Chronic exposure to loud noise can result in permanent _____ .
   a. auditory illusions   **c.** nerve deafness
   b. auditory hallucinations **d.** conduction deafness

Q **Test Your Critical Thinking**

1. Which of your sensations, vision or hearing, would you most and least like to lose? Why?

2. Many people believe that blind people have supernatural hearing. How would brain plasticity explain how enhanced hearing might result from greater reliance on hearing or from just using auditory information more effectively?

3. Using what you've learned about pitch perception, explain why older people often find it easier to hear a man's voice than a woman's.

Real World Application Questions

[AQ3] Does a lack of direct sunlight contribute to nearsightedness?

[AQ4] Can using a lower-pitched voice affect your perceived influence and power?

Towfiqu Photography/Moment/Getty Images

Dorset Media Service/Alamy Stock Photo

Hint: Look in the text for **[AQ3]** and **[AQ4]**

4.3 # Our Other Important Senses

LEARNING OBJECTIVES

Retrieval Practice   While reading the upcoming sections, respond to each Learning Objective in your own words.

Review the processes involved in smell, taste, and the body senses.

- **Explain** the key factors in olfaction and gustation, and how the two senses interact.

- **Describe** how the body senses (skin, vestibular, and kinesthesis) work.

Real World Application Question

[AQ5] Why do babies (and adults) need skin-to-skin contact?

Vision and audition may be the most prominent of our senses, but the others—smell, taste, and the body senses—are also important for gathering information about our environment.

Smell and Taste

Smell and taste are sometimes called the *chemical senses* because they both rely on chemo-receptors that are sensitive to certain chemical molecules. Have you wondered why we have trouble separating the two sensations? Smell and taste receptors are located near each other and closely interact (**Figure 4.14**).

Our sense of smell, **olfaction**, which results from stimulation of receptor cells in the nose, is remarkably useful and sensitive. We possess more than 1,000 types of olfactory receptors, which allow us to detect more than 10,000 distinct smells. The nose is more sensitive to smoke than any electronic detector, and because people who are blind rely more on their sense of smell, they often learn to recognize other people by their unique odors.

Some research on **pheromones**—chemicals released by organisms that trigger certain responses, such as aggression or sexual mating, in other members of the same species—also affect human sexual responses (Beny & Kimchi, 2016; Kupferschmidt, 2019; Plush et al., 2016). However, other research suggests that human sexuality is far more complex than that of other animals (Chapters 10 and 15).

Today, the sense of taste, **gustation**, which results from stimulation of receptor cells in the tongue's taste buds, may be the least critical of our senses, but in the past it probably contrib-uted significantly to our survival. For example, humans and other animals have a preference for sweet foods, which are generally non-poisonous and are good sources of energy. Furthermore, taste (aided by smell) helps us avoid eating or drinking harmful substances. Because many plants that taste bitter contain toxic chemicals, an animal is more likely to survive if it avoids bitter-tasting plants (Foley & Bates, 2019; French et al., 2015; Tuwani et al., 2019).

Olfaction   The sense or act of smelling; receptors are located in the nose's nasal cavity.

Pheromones [FARE-oh-mones] Chemical signals released by organisms that trigger certain responses, such as aggression or sexual mating, in other members of the same species.

Gustation   The sense or act of tasting; receptors are located in the tongue's taste buds.

PAN ## Practical Application of Neuroscience

Did you know that our taste and smell receptors normally die and are replaced every few days?   This probably reflects the fact that these receptors are directly exposed to the environment, whereas our vision receptors are protected by our eyeball and our hearing receptors are protected by the eardrum. However, as we grow older, the number of taste cells diminishes, which helps explain why adults enjoy spicier foods than do infants. Scientists are particularly excited about the regenerative capabilities of the taste and olfactory cells because they hope to learn how to transfer this regeneration to other types of cells that are currently unable to self-replace when damaged.

Did you also know that it was once believed that we had only four distinct tastes: sweet, sour, salty, and bitter. However, we now know that we also have a fifth taste sense, *umami*, a word that means "delicious " or "savory" and refers to sensitivity to an amino acid called glutamate (Feeney et al., 2019; Lease et al., 2016). Glutamate is found in meats, meat broths, and monosodium glutamate

(MSG). Scientists also once believed that specific areas of the tongue were dedicated to detecting bitter, sweet, salty, and other tastes. Today we know that the major taste receptors—taste buds—are distributed all over our tongues within little bumps called papillae (see again Figure 4.14). The taste receptors, like smell receptors, respond differentially to the varying shapes of food and liquid molecules.

FIGURE 4.14 **Why we enjoy eating pizza: olfaction plus gustation** When we eat pizza, the crust, cheese, sauce, and other food molecules activate taste receptor cells on our tongue, while the pizza's odors activate smell receptor cells in our nose. This combined sensory information is then sent on to our brain where it is processed in various association regions of the cortex. Taste and smell also combine with sensory cells that respond to touch and temperature, which explains why cold, hard pizza "tastes" and "smells" different than hot, soft pizza.

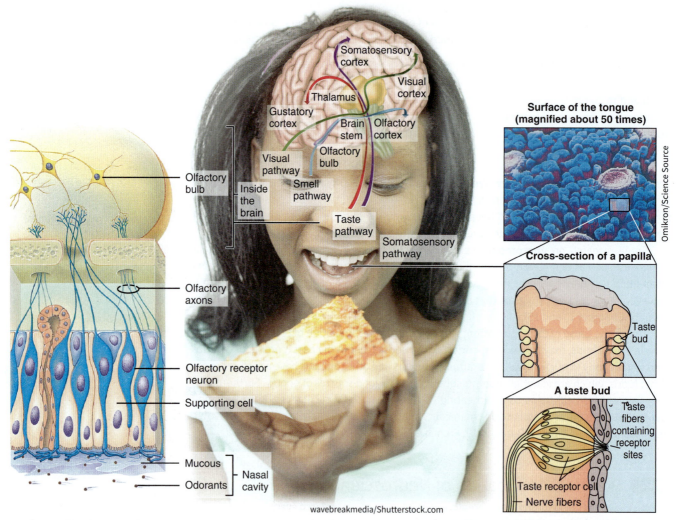

wavebreakmedia/Shutterstock.com

Omikron/Science Source

a. The smell pathway Olfactory receptor neurons (shown here in blue) transduce information from odorant molecules that enter the nose. The olfactory nerve carries this information into the olfactory bulb, where most information related to smell is processed before being sent on to other parts of the brain. (Note that olfaction is the only sensory system that is NOT routed through the thalamus.)

b. The taste pathway While during eating and drinking, liquids and dissolved foods flow over the tongue's papillae (the lavender circular areas in the top photo) and into their pores. This activates the taste receptor cells, which then send messages on to the nerve fibers, which carry information on to the brain stem, thalamus, gustatory cortex, and somatosensory cortex.

Learning and Culture   Many food and taste preferences are learned from an early age and from personal experiences (Myers, 2018; Nekitsing et al., 2018; Nicklaus, 2016). Researchers have found that multiple-drug users, for instance, have a higher preference for salty and sour tastes, whereas daily tobacco and cannabis users have a higher preference for sweet and spicy tastes (Dovey et al., 2016). Other studies have revealed that adults who are told a bottle of wine costs $90 (rather than its real price of $10) report that it tastes better than the wine that they were told costs only $10 (Plassmann et al., 2008). Ironically, these false expectations actually trigger areas of the brain that respond to pleasant experiences. This means that in a neuro-chemical sense, the wine we believe is better does, in fact, taste better.

Along with learning, the culture we live in also affects our taste preferences. Many Japanese children eat raw fish, and some Chinese children eat chicken feet as part of their normal diet. Although most U.S. children would consider these foods "yucky," they tend to love cheese, which children in many other cultures find repulsive.

The Body Senses

In addition to the chemical senses of smell and taste, we have three important body senses that help us navigate our world—skin, vestibular, and kinesthesis (**Figure 4.15**).

FIGURE 4.15 Our body senses—skin, vestibular, and kinesthesis

a. Skin senses
The tactile senses rely on a variety of receptors located in different parts of the skin. Both human and non-human animals are highly responsive to touch.

b. Vestibular sense
Part of the "thrill" of amusement park rides comes from our vestibular sense of balance becoming confused. The vestibular sense is used by the eye muscles to maintain visual fixation and sometimes by the body to change body orientation. We can become dizzy or nauseated if the vestibular sense becomes "confused" by boat, airplane, or automobile motion. Children between ages 2 and 12 years have the greatest susceptibility to motion sickness.

iStock.com/Philip Dyer

Pain and temperature
Free nerve endings for pain (sharp pain and dull pain)
Free nerve endings for temperature (heat or cold)

Fine touch and pressure
Meissner's corpuscle (touch)
Merkel's disc (light to moderate pressure against skin)
Ruffini's end organ (heavy pressure and joint movements)
Hair receptors (flutter or steady skin indentation)
Pacinian corpuscle (vibrating and heavy pressure)

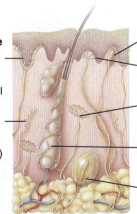

RubberBall/Alamy Stock Photo

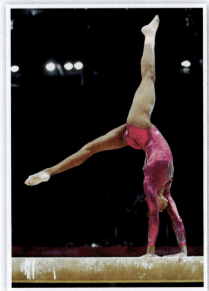
Mike Blake/Reuters

c. Kinesthesis
This athlete's finely tuned behaviors are the result of information provided by receptors in her muscles, joints, and tendons that detect the location, orientation, and movement of her individual body parts relative to each other.

FIGURE 4.16 [AQ5] **Infant benefits from kangaroo care** This type of skin-to-skin touch helps babies in several ways, including providing warmth, reducing pain (lower levels of arousal and stress increase pain tolerance and immune functioning), and better sleep quality. Other research, including a meta-analysis (which combines results from multiple studies), found that babies who receive kangaroo care have a 36 percent lower likelihood of death—as well as a lower risk of blood infection and other positive long-term effects beyond infancy (Boundy et al., 2016; Gayen et al., 2019; Mekonnen et al., 2019). As we discovered earlier in this and in other chapters of this text, skin-to-skin contact, including holding hands and hugs, provides numerous physical and mental benefits for people of all ages.

Blend Images - Mike Kemp/Getty Images

Skin Senses

Our skin is uniquely designed for the detection of touch (or pressure), temperature, and pain (Figure 4.15a). The concentration and depth of the receptors for each of these stimuli vary (Hsiao & Gomez-Ramirez, 2013; Ruzzoli & Soto-Faraco, 2014). For example, touch receptors are most concentrated on the face and fingers and least concentrated in the back and legs. Getting a paper cut can feel so painful because we have many receptors on our fingertips. Some receptors respond to more than one type of stimulation. For example, itching, tickling, and vibrating sensations seem to be produced by light stimulation of both pressure and pain receptors.

The benefits of touch are so significant for human growth and development that the American Academy of Pediatrics recommends that all mothers and babies have skin-to-skin contact in the first hours after birth. This type of contact, which is called *kangaroo care*, is especially beneficial for preterm and low birthweight infants, who then experience greater weight gain, fewer infections, and improved cognitive and motor development. How does kangaroo care lead to these improvements in infant health? See **Figure 4.16**.

Vestibular sense The sense that provides information about balance and movement; receptors are located in the inner ear.

Vestibular Sense

Our sense of balance, the **vestibular sense**, informs our brains of how our bodies are oriented with respect to gravity and three-dimensional space. When our head tilts, liquid in the *semicircular canals*, located in our inner ear, moves and bends hair cell receptors. In addition, at the end of the semicircular canals are *vestibular sacs*, which contain hair cells sensitive to our body's acceleration relative to gravity (as shown in the amusement park ride examples in Figure 4.15b). Information from the semicircular canals and the vestibular sacs is converted to neural impulses that are then carried to our brains.

Kinesthesis The sense that provides information about the location, orientation, and movement of individual body parts relative to each other; receptors are located in muscles, joints, and tendons.

Kinesthesis

The sense that provides the brain with information about the location, orientation, and movement of individual body parts is called **kinesthesis** (Figure 4.15c). Kinesthetic receptors are found throughout the muscles, joints, and tendons of our body. They tell our brains which muscles are being contracted or relaxed, how our body weight is distributed, where our arms and legs are in relation to the rest of our body, and so on. For an intriguing example of the unusual power of kinesthesis in young babies, see the following **PP** **PositivePsych**.

PP   Practical Application: **PositivePsych**

Can Bouncing a Baby Increase Helping Behaviors?

(APA Goal 1.3) Describe applications of psychology

Researchers in a clever study examined whether 14-month-old babies who bounced to music with another person were then more likely to assist that person (see photo) (Cirelli et al., 2014). To test this question, two researchers worked in pairs: one held a baby in a forward-facing carrier—not like the baby being held in this photo—while the second researcher stood across and facing the baby. When music started to play, both researchers gently bounced up and down (with the baby being automatically bounced as it was held in the forward-facing carrier).

Some babies were bounced at the same tempo as the researcher across from them, whereas other babies were bounced at a different tempo. When the song finished, the babies were removed from the carriers and stood on the floor. The baby then watched while the researcher, who previously stood in front of the baby in the carrier, starting drawing a picture. The researcher then "accidentally" dropped the marker she was using to draw, to see if the baby would toddle over to pick up the object and hand it back to her. (This is a standard task used to measure altruism in babies.)

Can you predict what the researchers found? Surprisingly, compared to the babies who were bounced at an asynchronous, different tempo, babies who had been bounced in sync with the researcher were much more likely to toddle over, pick up the object,

Oldos/RooM/Getty Images

and pass it back to the researcher. These synchronous babies also responded more quickly to the dropped pen.

How would you explain these results? The researchers suggest that engaging in synchronous movement leads to feelings of shared social bonds between people, which in turn may lead to more prosocial behavior.

Q Test Your Critical Thinking

1. Could these research findings also help explain why we generally feel closer to someone after dancing with him or her?

2. Would members of a band, a dance troop, or the military feel more bonded, and thus be more likely to help? Why or why not?

Retrieval Practice 4.3 | Our Other Important Senses

Self-Test   Completing this self-test, and then checking your answers by clicking on the answer button or by looking in Appendix B, will provide immediate feedback and helpful practice for exams.

1. _____ results from stimulation of receptor cells in the nose.
   a. Audition
   b. Gustation
   c. Olfaction
   d. None of these options

2. Chemical signals released by organisms that may affect behavior, such as aggression and sexual mating, are known as _____.
   a. olfactory attractants
   b. sexual odorifants
   c. pheromones
   d. olfactory hormones

3. Most of our taste receptors are found on the _____.
   a. olfactory bulb
   b. gustatory cells
   c. frenulum
   d. taste buds

4. The skin senses include _____.
   a. pressure
   b. pain
   c. warmth and cold
   d. all of these options

5. The _____ sense is located in the inner ear and is responsible for our sense of balance.
   a. auditory
   b. vestibular
   c. kinesthetic
   d. olfactory

Q Test Your Critical Thinking

1. From an evolutionary perspective, which is more important—smell or taste?

2. From a personal perspective, which sense is most important to you—your sense of smell, taste, skin senses, vestibular sense, or kinesthesis?

Real World Application Question

[AQ5]   Why do babies (and adults) need skin-to-skin contact?

Blend Images - Mike Kemp/Getty Images

Hint: Look in the text for **[AQ5]**

Understanding Perception

LEARNING OBJECTIVES

Retrieval Practice   While reading the upcoming sections, respond to each Learning Objective in your own words.

Summarize the three processes involved in perception.

- **Explain** illusions and why they're important.
- **Discuss** the process of selection and its three major factors.

- **Describe** the three ways we organize sensory data.
- **Review** the main factors in perceptual interpretation.
- **Discuss** the research findings on ESP and why so many people believe in it.

Real World Application Question

[AQ6] Can wearing a helmet actually increase risky behaviors?

Having studied sensation, we're now moving on to *perception*, the process of selecting, organizing, and interpreting incoming sensations into useful mental representations of the world.

Normally, our perceptions agree with our sensations. When they do not, the result is called an **illusion**, a false or misleading impression produced by errors in the perceptual process or by actual physical distortions, as in desert mirages. Illusions provide psychologists with a tool for studying the normal process of perception (**Figure 4.17**).

Illusion   A false or misleading perception shared by others in the same perceptual environment.

Selection

In almost every situation, we confront more sensory information than we can reasonably pay attention to. Three major factors help us focus on some stimuli while ignoring others: *selective attention*, *feature detectors*, and *habituation*.

FIGURE 4.17   **Understanding perceptual illusions**   As you may have noticed, this text highlights numerous popular *myths* about psychology because it's important to understand and correct our misperceptions. For similar reasons, you need to know how illusions mislead our normal information processing and recognize that "seeing is believing, but seeing isn't always believing correctly" (Lilienfeld et al., 2010, p. 7).

a. Müller-Lyer illusion   Which vertical line is longer? In fact, the two vertical lines are the same length, but psychologists have learned that people who live in urban environments normally see the one on the right as longer. This is because they have learned to make size and distance judgments from perspective cues created by right angles and horizontal and vertical lines of buildings and streets.

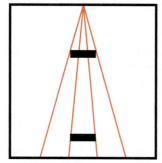

b. Ponzo illusion   Which of the two horizontal lines is longer? In fact, both lines are the exact same size, but the converging, vertical lines provide depth cues telling you that the top dark horizontal line is farther away than the bottom line and therefore much longer.

c. The horizontal-vertical illusion   Which is longer, the horizontal (flat) or the vertical (standing) line? People living in areas where they regularly see long straight lines, such as roads and train tracks, perceive the horizontal line as shorter because of their environmental experiences.

TIP   Are you confused about the word "illusions" versus *hallucinations* or *delusions*? If so, it's important to note their distinct differences. *Hallucinations* are false sensory experiences that occur without external stimuli, such as hearing voices during a psychotic episode or seeing particular images after using some type of hallucinogenic drug, like LSD or hallucinogenic mushrooms. *Delusions* refer to false beliefs, often of persecution or grandeur, that may accompany drug or psychotic experiences.

Q Test Your Critical Thinking

1. Can you see how illusions like these might create real-world dangers for our everyday lives?

2. When you watch films of moving cars, the wheels appear to go backward. Can you explain this common visual illusion?

d. Shepard's tables   Do these two table tops have the same dimensions? Get a ruler and check it for yourself.

Phillip Suddick/The Image Bank/Getty Images

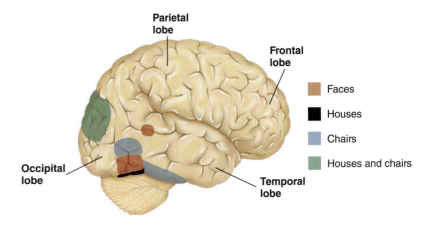

FIGURE 4.18 **Selective attention**   Have you noticed that when you're at a noisy party, you can still select and attend to the voices of people you find compelling, or that you can suddenly pick up on another group's conversation if someone in that group mentions your name? These are prime examples of *selective attention*, also called the "cocktail party phenomenon."

FIGURE 4.19 **Location of feature detectors**   Recall from Chapter 2 that during fMRI scans, specific areas of the brain are activated (they "light up"). In this case, researchers identified areas that are activated when people look at specific objects, such as faces, houses, chairs, and even combinations like houses and chairs. Given that our brains are not designed to waste time or processing power, can you see why humans have developed specific cells designed to recognize lines and angles of different orientations, as well as for more complex stimuli, such as faces?

Certain basic mechanisms for perceptual selection are built into the brain. For instance, we're able to focus our conscious awareness on a specific stimulus, while filtering out other stimuli, thanks to the process of **selective attention** (**Figure 4.18**). This type of focused attention and concentration allows us to select only information that is important to us and discard the rest (Chen et al., 2016; Howell et al., 2016; Reuter et al., 2019).

In addition to exhibiting selective attention, the brains of humans and other animals contain specialized cells, called **feature detectors**, which respond only to specific characteristics of visual stimuli, such as shape, angle, or movement. For example, frogs are known to have specific "bug detector" cells that respond to small, dark, moving objects. Humans also have specific cells for detecting general motion in our peripheral vision.

Interestingly, studies with humans have found feature detectors in the temporal and occipital lobes that respond maximally to faces (**Figure 4.19**). Problems in these areas can produce a condition called *prosopagnosia* (*prosopon* means "face" and *agnosia* means "failure to know"). Surprisingly, people with prosopagnosia can recognize that they are looking at a face. But they cannot say whose face is reflected in a mirror, even if it is their own or that of a well-known friend or relative (Jiahui et al., 2018; Lohse et al., 2016; Wegrzyn et al., 2019).

Additional examples of the brain's ability to filter experience occur with **habituation**, the brain's learned tendency to ignore or stop responding to unchanging information. Apparently, the brain is "prewired" to pay more attention to changes in the environment than to stimuli that remain constant. As you'll discover in Chapter 9, developmental psychologists often use measurements of habituation to tell when a stimulus can be detected and discriminated by infants who are too young to speak. When presented with a new stimulus, infants initially pay attention, but with repetition they learn that the stimulus is unchanging and their responses weaken.

Selective attention   The process of focusing conscious awareness on a specific stimulus, while filtering out a range of other stimuli occurring simultaneously.

Feature detectors   Neurons in the brain's visual system that respond to specific characteristics of stimuli, such as shape, angle, or movement.

Habituation   The brain's learned tendency to ignore or stop responding to unchanging information; an example of top-down processing.

PA Practical Application

Can you see why attention and compliments from a stranger are generally more exciting than those from a long-term romantic partner?   Unfortunately, some people (who haven't taken psychology courses or understand the concept of habituation) may misinterpret and overvalue this new attention. They may even leave good relationships, not realizing that they will also soon habituate to the new person.

TIP Are you confused about the distinction between *sensory adaptation*, which we discussed earlier, and *habituation?* If so, recall that adaptation refers to the *sensory receptors' innate* tendency to fatigue and stop responding to unchanging stimuli. In contrast, habituation is our *brain's learned* tendency to stop responding to unchanging stimuli. The first is innate and at the sensory receptor level, whereas the second is within the brain itself and learned. Here's a simple example: If someone pulled the fire alarm at your college, you'd initially jump up and try to evacuate. However, if your instructor told you that this was a false alarm, which couldn't be immediately turned off, the loud noise of the alarm would slowly start to fade because your sensory receptors would automatically adapt to the unchanging noise. In contrast, if students keep pulling the fire alarm as a dangerous prank, you and others will soon learn to ignore the sound and stop trying to evacuate.

S&P Scientific Thinking and Practical Application

Have you noticed how advertisers and politicians can manipulate our perceptual processes to their advantage? Advertisers and politicians know that children, adults, and apparently even dogs quickly adapt and habituate to unchanging, constant stimuli, but will pay more attention to stimuli that are intense, novel, moving, and contrasting, such as ads on television (see photo). The good news is that your awareness of the psychological factors behind these persuasive techniques may help you become a more informed consumer.

Tetra Images, LLC/Tom Grill/ Alamy Stock Photo

Also keep in mind that understanding the essentials of sensory adaptation and habituation can literally save your life! If you ignore the smell of leaking gas in your apartment, you'll eventually adapt—and may die from the fumes. Similarly, repeated "prank" fire alarms, lock-down drills at schools, and national "red alert" terrorist warnings may lead all of us to become habituated, complacent, and less vigilant. Ideally, your increased understanding of sensory adaptation and habituation will better prepare you for a proper response when a true need arises.

FIGURE 4.20 **Form perception and "impossible figures"**

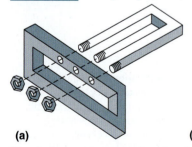

Fine Art Images/AGE Fotostock

(a) **(b)**

What do these two images teach us about form perception? When you first glance at figure **(a)** and the famous painting by M. C. Escher in figure **(b)**, you detect specific features of the stimuli, and judge them as sensible figures. But as you try to sort and organize the different elements into a stable, well-organized whole, you realize they don't add up—they're illogical or "impossible." The point of the illustration is that there is no one-to-one correspondence between your actual sensory input and your final perception. The same stimuli looked at from another perspective can lead to very different perceptions. Can you also see how this is another example of top-down versus bottom-up processing? We see both (a) and (b) as representing normal three-dimensional (3-D) figures. So we have trouble interpreting them because we're using our "higher," top-down cognitive processes or previous knowledge and expectations with normal drawings of 3-D. Our brain can only interpret (perceive) these deliberately misdrawn figures as being "impossible."

Source: M.C. Escher's "Concave and Convex" © 2012 The M.C. Escher Company-Holland. All rights reserved

Organization

In the previous section, we discussed how we select certain stimuli in our environment to pay attention to and not others. The next step in perception is to organize this selected information into useful mental representations of the world around us. Raw sensory data are like the parts of a watch—the parts must be assembled in a meaningful way before they are useful. We organize visual sensory data in terms of *form*, *depth*, and *constancy*.

Form Perception Look at **Figure 4.20a**. What do you see? Can you draw a similar object on a piece of paper? This is known as an "impossible figure." Now look at **Figure 4.20b**, which shows a painting by M. C. Escher, a Dutch painter who created striking examples of perceptual distortion. Although drawn to represent three-dimensional objects or situations, the parts don't assemble into logical wholes. Like the illusions studied earlier, impossible figures and distorted paintings help us understand perceptual principles— in this case, the principle of *form perception*.

Figure–Ground:
Objects (the *figure*) are seen as distinct from the surroundings (the *ground*). (Here the red objects are the figure and the yellow background is the ground.)

Proximity:
Objects that are physically close together are grouped together. (In this figure, we see 3 groups of 6 hearts, not 18 separate hearts.)

Continuity:
Objects that continue a pattern are grouped together. (When we see line **a**, we normally see a combination of lines **b** and **c** — not **d**.)

When we see this,

a.

we normally see this

b.

plus this.

c.

Not this.

d.

Closure:
A finished unit (triangle, square, or circle) is formed from an is formed incomplete stimulus.

Similarity:
Similar objects are grouped together (the green colored dots are grouped together and perceived as the number 5).

FIGURE 4.21 Understanding Gestalt principles of organization Gestalt principles are based on the notion that we all share a natural tendency to force patterns onto whatever we see. Although the examples of the Gestalt principles in this figure are all visual, each principle applies to other modes of perception as well. For example, the Gestalt principle of *contiguity* cannot be shown because it involves nearness in time, not visual nearness. Similarly, the aural (hearing) effects of figure and ground aren't shown in this figure, but you've undoubtedly experienced them in a movie theater. Despite nearby conversations in the audience, you can still listen to the voices on the film because you make them your focus (the figure) versus the ground.

Gestalt psychologists were among the first to study form perception and how the brain organizes sensory impressions into a *gestalt*—a German word meaning "form" or "whole." They emphasized the importance of organization and patterning in enabling us to perceive the whole stimulus rather than perceive its discrete parts as separate entities. The Gestaltists proposed several laws of organization that specify how people perceive form (**Figure 4.21**).

The most fundamental Gestalt principle of organization is our tendency to distinguish between the *figure* (our main focus of attention) and *ground* (the background or surroundings). Your sense of figure and ground is at work in what you are doing right now—reading. Your brain is receiving sensations of black lines and white paper, but your brain is organizing these sensations into black letters and words on a white background. You perceive the letters as the figure and the white as the ground. If you make a great effort, you might be able to force yourself to see the page reversed, as though a black background were showing through letter-shaped-holes in a white foreground.

There are times, however, when it is very hard to distinguish the figure from the ground, as you can see in **Figure 4.22**.

This is known as a *reversible figure*. Your brain alternates between seeing the light areas as the figure and seeing them as the ground. As a scientific and critical thinker, are you wondering if these Gestalt laws might not apply in other cultures? If so, check out the **GCD Gender and Cultural Diversity**.

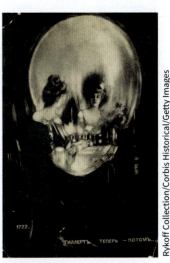

Rykoff Collection/Corbis Historical/Getty Images

FIGURE 4.22 Understanding reversible figures This so-called *reversible figure* demonstrates alternating figure–ground relations. It can be seen as a woman looking in a mirror or as a skull, depending on what you see as figure or ground.

GCD Gender and Cultural Diversity

Are the Gestalt Laws Universally True?

(APA Goal 2.5) Incorporate sociocultural factors in scientific inquiry

Gestalt psychologists conducted most of their work with formally educated people from urban European cultures. A. R. Luria (1976) was one of the first to question whether their laws held true for all participants, regardless of education and cultural setting. Luria recruited a wide range of participants living in what was then the U.S.S.R. He included Ichkeri women from remote villages (with no formal education), collective farm activists (who were semiliterate), and female students in a teachers' school (with years of formal education).

Luria found that when presented with the stimuli shown in **Figure 4.23**, the formally trained female students were the only ones who identified the first three shapes by their categorical name of "circle." Whether circles were made of solid lines, incomplete lines, or solid colors, they called them all circles. However, participants with no formal education named the shapes according to the objects they resembled. They called a circle a watch, a plate, or a moon, and referred to a square as a mirror, a house, or an apricot-drying board. When asked if items 12 and 13 from Figure 4.23 were alike, one woman answered, "No, they're not alike. This one's not like a watch, but that one's a watch because there are dots."

One interpretation of Luria's findings is that the Gestalt laws of perceptual organization are valid only for people who have been schooled in geometric concepts. But an alternative explanation has also been suggested. Luria's study, as well as most research on visual perception and optical illusions, relied on two-dimensional presentations—either on a piece of paper or projected on a screen. It may be that experience with pictures and photographs (not formal education in geometric concepts) is necessary for learning to interpret two-dimensional figures as portraying three-dimensional forms. Westerners who have had years of practice learning to interpret two-dimensional drawings of three-dimensional objects may not remember how much practice it took to learn the cultural conventions for judging the size and shape of objects drawn on paper (Berry et al., 2011; Keith, 2010).

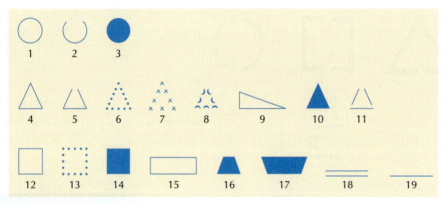

FIGURE 4.23 **Luria's stimuli** When you see these shapes, you readily identify them as circles, triangles, and other geometric forms. According to cross-cultural research, this is due to your formal educational training. If you were from a culture without formal education, you might identify them instead as familiar objects in your environment—"the circle is like the moon."

Sources: Reprinted by permission of the publisher from, *Cognitive Development: Its Cultural and Social Foundations* by A.R. Luria, translated by Martin Lopez-Morillas and Lynn Solotaroff, edited by Michael Cole, p. 33, Cambridge, Mass.: Harvard University Press Copyright © 1976 by the President and Fellows of Harvard College.

Depth perception The ability to perceive three-dimensional space and to accurately judge distance.

Depth Perception In our three-dimensional world, the ability to perceive the depth and distance of objects—as well as their height and width—is essential. **Depth perception** is learned primarily through experience. However, research using an apparatus called the *visual cliff* (**Figure 4.24**) suggests that very young infants can perceive depth, and will actively avoid it.

Some have suggested that this visual cliff research proves that depth perception, and an avoidance of heights, is inborn. The modern consensus is that infants are, indeed, able to perceive depth. But the idea that infants' fear of heights causes their avoidance is not supported by research (Adolph et al., 2014). Instead, researchers found that infants display a flexible and adaptive response at the edge of a drop-off. They pat the surface, attempt to reach through the glass, and even rock back and forth at the edge. They decide whether or not to cross or avoid a drop-off based on previous locomotor experiences, along with gained knowledge of their own muscle strength, balance, and other criteria. In short, infants perceive depth, but their fear of heights apparently develops over time, like walking or language acquisition.

Although we do get some sense of distance based on hearing and even smell, most depth perception comes from several visual cues, which are summarized in **Figure 4.25**. The first mechanism we use is the interaction of both of our eyes, which produces **binocular cues** (**Figure 4.26**). We also have several **monocular cues**, which need only one eye to work (**Figure 4.27**).

- **Linear perspective**   Parallel lines converge, or angle toward one another, as they recede into the distance.
- **Interposition**   Objects that obscure or overlap other objects are perceived as closer.
- **Relative size**   Close objects cast a larger retinal image than distant objects.
- **Texture gradient**   Nearby objects have a coarser and more distinct texture than distant ones.
- **Aerial perspective**   Distant objects appear hazy and blurred compared to close objects because of intervening atmospheric dust or haze.
- **Light and shadow**   Brighter objects are perceived as being closer than darker objects.
- **Relative height**   Objects positioned higher in our field of vision are perceived as farther away (see cartoon).

Two additional monocular cues for depth perception, *accommodation* and *motion parallax*, cannot be used by artists and are not shown in Figure 4.27. In accommodation, muscles that adjust the shape of the lens as it focuses on an object send neural messages to the brain, which uses these signals to interpret and perceive distance. For near objects, the lens bulges; for far objects, it flattens. Motion parallax (also known as *relative motion*) refers to the fact that close objects appear to race by, whereas farther objects seem to move more slowly or remain stationary.

Constancies Perception
To organize our sensations into meaningful patterns, we develop **perceptual constancies**, the learned tendency to perceive the environment as stable, despite changes in an object's *size*, *color*, *brightness*, or *shape*. Without perceptual constancy, things would seem to grow as we got closer to them, change shape as our viewing angle changed, and change color as light levels changed (Albright, 2015; Fleming, 2014; Foley & Bates, 2019).

- **Size constancy**   Regardless of its distance from us (or the size of the image it casts on our retina), *size constancy* allows us to interpret an object as always

FIGURE 4.24 **Visual cliff**   Given the desire to investigate depth perception, while also protecting infants and other experimental participants from actual falls, psychologists E. J. Gibson and R. D. Walk (1960) created a clever miniature cliff with a protected drop-off covered by glass. Infants were placed on the glass surface that covered the entire table, and then encouraged (usually by their mothers) to crawl over either the shallow or the deep side. Research has shown that most crawling infants hesitate or refuse to move to the "deep end" of the visual cliff, indicating that they perceive the difference in depth.

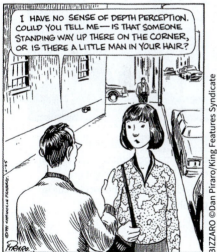

Binocular cues   Visual input from two eyes, which allows perception of depth or distance.

Monocular cues   Visual input from a single eye alone that contributes to perception of depth or distance.

Perceptual constancy   The tendency to perceive the environment as stable, despite changes in the sensory input.

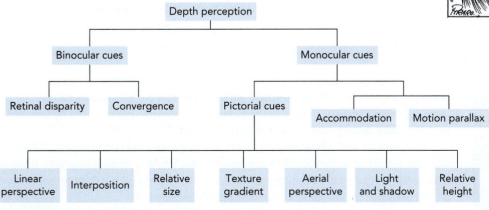

FIGURE 4.25   **Visual cues for depth perception**

FIGURE 4.26 **Binocular depth cues** How do we perceive a three-dimensional world with a two-dimensional receptor system? One mechanism is the interaction of both eyes to produce binocular cues.

a. Retinal disparity Did you know that your left eye and your right eye normally see slightly different images? Or that the larger the difference (or greater *disparity*) between the image each eye has of the same object the closer it is to you? If you'd like a demonstration of this *retinal disparity*, stare at your two index fingers a few inches in front of your eyes with their tips half an inch apart. Do you see the "floating finger"? Move it farther away and the "finger" will shrink. Move it closer and it will enlarge. Because our eyes are about 2½ inches apart, objects at different distances (such as the "floating finger") project their images on different parts of the retina, an effect called *retinal disparity*. Far objects project on the retinal area near the nose, whereas near objects project farther out, closer to the ears.

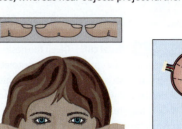

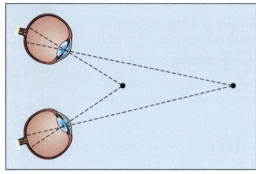

b. Convergence When we want to focus on nearby objects, our two eyes tend to rotate inward toward each other in a coordinated manner. For an example of this binocular cue of *convergence*, hold your index finger at arm's length in front of you and watch it as you bring it closer until it is right in front of your nose. The amount of strain in your eye muscles created by the *convergence*, or turning inward of the eyes, is used as a cue by your brain to interpret distance.

soul_studio/Shutterstock.com

FIGURE 4.27 **Monocular depth cues** Imagine yourself as an artist and think about how you might use each individual tree as a monocular cue in this photo.

being the same size. Note that the image of the leaf in the foreground of the photo (**Figure 4.28**) is larger on our retina than the image of the woman behind it. However, thanks to size constancy, we perceive the woman to be of normal size—just further away from the camera. Without this constancy, we would perceive people as "shrinking" when they moved away from us and "growing" when they moved toward us.

Although researchers have found evidence of size constancy in newborns, it also develops from learning and experience. Case studies of people who have been blind since birth, and then have their sight restored, find that they initially have little or no size constancy (Sacks, 2015).

- **Color and brightness constancies** Our perceptions of color and brightness remain the same even when the light conditions change. Look at the obvious variations in the woman's hair color in **Figure 4.29**. We perceive the color and brightness of her hair as constant despite the fact that the wavelength of light reaching our retina may vary as the light changes.

- **Shape constancy** One additional perceptual constancy is the tendency to perceive an object's shape as staying constant even when the angle of our view changes (**Figure 4.30**).

Interpretation

In the previous two sections, we discussed how we select and organize all the available and incoming sensory information. Now we'll explore how our brains work to interpret this large database. This final stage of perception—*interpretation*—is influenced by several factors, including sensory adaptation and perceptual set.

Imagine that your visual field has suddenly been inverted and reversed. Things you normally expect to be on your right are now on your left, and those above your head are now below it. How would you ride a bike, read a book, or even walk through your home? Do you think you could ever adapt to this upside-down world?

To answer that question, psychologist George Stratton (1896) invented, and for 8 days wore, special prism goggles that flipped his view of the world from up to down and right to

Paul Mansfield photography/ Moment/Getty Images

FIGURE 4.28 **Size constancy**

left. For the first few days, Stratton had a great deal of difficulty navigating in this environment and coping with everyday tasks. But by the third day, he noted:

> Walking through the narrow spaces between pieces of furniture required much less care than hitherto. I could watch my hands as they wrote, without hesitating or becoming embarrassed thereby.

By the fifth day, Stratton had almost completely adjusted to his strange perceptual environment, but when he later removed the headgear, he quickly readapted.

Sensory Adaptation   What does this experiment have to do with our everyday life? Stratton's study illustrates the critical role that *sensory adaptation* plays in the way we interpret the information that our brains gather. Without the ability to adapt his perceptions to a skewed environment, Stratton would not have been able to function. His brain's ability to retrain itself to interpret his new surroundings allowed him to create coherence from what would otherwise have been chaos.

Perceptual Set   As you can see in **Figure 4.31**, our previous experiences, assumptions, and expectations also affect how we interpret and perceive the world by creating a **perceptual set,** or a readiness to perceive in a particular manner, based on expectations (Dye & Foley, 2017; Sella et al., 2017). In other words, we largely see what we expect to see. For example, our strong perceptual set for seeing faces leads virtually everyone to see a face on the moon—despite the fact that the darker and lighter spots are actually craters and mountains. But this is not the case cross-culturally. Observers in Japan most often see a rabbit making rice cakes, whereas people in India see two giant hand prints. These differences reflect varying cultures, as well as the contrasting views of the moon from the Northern and Southern Hemispheres.

[AQ6]   Perceptual sets may also have a surprising influence on our behavior. As an example, some research finds that wearing protective devices, like helmets (see photo), actually leads

FIGURE 4.29 **Color and brightness constancies**

Perceptual set   The readiness to perceive in a particular manner, based on expectations.

Note how as the coin is rotated, it changes shape, but we still perceive it as the same coin—thanks to shape constancy.

 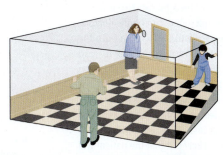

FIGURE 4.30 **Shape constancy**   This Ames room illusion (shown in the two figures above) is found in many amusement parks. It's also been used in films, such as *The Lord of the Rings* trilogy, to make Gandalf appear much larger than the hobbits. In the first diagram, the child on the right appears to be almost the same size as his adult mother on the left. How does this illusion work? To a viewer peering through the peephole (diagram on the right), the room appears to be a normal cubic shape. In fact, it's an artificially constructed, trapezoid-shaped room. The walls are slanted to the right, and the floor and ceiling are placed at an angle facing forward. Note also how the right corner of the room is much closer to the observer. If you're the person looking through the peephole, can you now understand why the mother and child appear to be almost the same size? If so, you'll also understand, but still be amazed, that when the two individuals walk across to exchange places, they will appear to be growing and/or shrinking!

While mind-challenging and fun, this illusion illustrates what happens when our normal perceptual processes of size constancy, shape constancy, and depth perception are disrupted. We have no perceptual experience with trapezoid-shaped rooms, so we compensate by distorting the relative sizes of the human figures.

FIGURE 4.31 **What is the middle figure?**   If you look at the letters from left to right, you see the middle figure as a B. However, if you look at it from top to bottom, you see the number 13. Can you see how the "environment" created a perceptual set that affected how you interpreted the visual stimulus in the middle of the figure?

many people to *increase* their risky behaviors (Fyhri & Phillips, 2013; Gamble & Walker, 2016; Phillips et al., 2011). Although a large meta-analysis of several studies found evidence that helmet wearing was actually associated with safer cycling behaviors, other studies supported the link between helmets and increased risky behaviors (Esmaeilikia et al., 2019). Why? Apparently, wearing or using safety devices unconsciously primes us to expect greater levels of protection, so we then feel freer to ski, bike, or drive motorcycles faster than we otherwise would!

In addition, researchers have examined how perceptual sets regarding race may influence judgments of football players (Hall & Livingston, 2012). In this study, participants read a scenario in which a Black or White NFL football player scored a touchdown and then either celebrated that touchdown (by spiking the ball and then doing his signature dance) or showed no reaction to scoring. They were then asked to rate the player's level of arrogance, and to say whether the player deserved a salary bonus for this touchdown. Perhaps not surprisingly, all players who celebrated after touchdowns were perceived as more arrogant than those who did not celebrate (regardless of race). Sadly, White players were seen as equally deserving of a bonus whether or not they had celebrated their touchdown, whereas Black players were judged as deserving a bonus only if they had *not* celebrated. These findings, termed the "hubris penalty," show that the same celebratory behavior is seen in different—and biased—ways as a function of the athlete's race or gender (see photos).

Before going on, would you like another practical application of a perceptual set? If so, check out the **RC** Research Challenge.

Racism and sexism in celebrations? Research shows that Black football players (see photo) versus White players are judged differently for celebrating after scoring a touchdown. Others have suggested that the criticism of soccer star Megan Rapinoe's "arrogant" pose (see photo) is an example of sexism. What do you think about both of these issues?

RC Scientific Thinking: **Research Challenge**

Perceptual Set, Patients' Race, and Quality of Medical Care

(APA Goal 2.4) Interpret, design, and conduct basic psychological research

Does a patient's race influence his or her medical care? To examine this important question, researchers recruited clinicians—doctors, nurses, physician assistants, and medical students—from both the United States and France, and randomly assigned them to read doctor's notes about a hypothetical male patient who had been diagnosed with hypertension (Khosla et al., 2018). The notes were identical with the exception of race, which was noted as either Black or White. The clinicians then gave their perceptions of the patients' expected improvement and adherence to medical recommendations by answering questions, such as "How likely is it that the patient will take the recommended prescriptions?" and "How likely is it that the patient's condition will improve?"

Can you predict their findings? Clinicians in France showed no differences in their responses as a function of the patient's race. But American clinicians rated the hypothetical White patient as significantly more responsible for his health and more likely to adhere to his treatment than the hypothetical Black patient. They also saw the White patient as significantly more likely to improve.

Given what you've learned about perceptual sets—our readiness to perceive in a particular manner based on expectations—can you imagine the potential dangers of this type of racial bias? If clinicians expect Black patients to be less likely to follow instructions,

like taking their recommended prescriptions, wouldn't that logically affect how they might treat these patients, and, in turn, have a lasting, damaging impact on their patients' health?

Identify the Research Method

1. Based on the information provided, did this research (Khosla et al., 2018) use descriptive, correlational, and/or experimental research?

2. If you chose:
   - *descriptive research*, is this a naturalistic or laboratory observation, survey/interview, case study, and/or archival research?
   - *correlational research*, is this a positive, negative, or zero correlation?
   - *experimental research*, label the IV, DV, experimental group(s), and control group. (Note: If participants were not randomly assigned to groups, list the design as *quasi-experimental*.)
   - both *descriptive* and *correlational*, answer the corresponding questions for both.

Check your answers by clicking on the answer button or by looking in Appendix B.

Note: The information provided in this study is admittedly limited, but the level of detail is similar to what is presented in most textbooks and public reports of research findings. Answering these questions, and then comparing your answers to those provided, will help you become a better scientific and critical thinker and consumer of scientific research.

Science and ESP

So far in this chapter, we have talked about sensations provided by our eyes, ears, nose, mouth, and skin. What about a so-called sixth sense? Can some people perceive things that cannot be perceived with the usual sensory channels, by using **extrasensory perception (ESP)**? Those who claim to have ESP profess to be able to read other people's minds (*telepathy*), perceive objects or events that are inaccessible to their normal senses (*clairvoyance*), or see and predict the future (*precognition*). (Psychokinesis, the ability to move or change objects with mind power alone, such as bending a spoon or levitating a table, is generally not considered a type of ESP because, unlike the other three alleged abilities, it does not involve the senses, like "seeing the future.")

As we discussed in Chapter 1, each of these claims falls in the category of *pseudoscience*. Although a large number of people around the world tend to believe in ESP, virtually all reports and so-called studies of ESP either have been successfully debunked or have produced weak or controversial results (Branković, 2019; Lilienfeld et al., 2015; Schick & Vaughn, 2014). Furthermore, findings of ESP are notoriously "fragile" in that they do not hold up to scientific scrutiny.

Perhaps the most serious weakness of studies supporting ESP is their lack of replication in independent laboratories, which is a core requirement for scientific acceptance (Francis, 2012; Hyman, 1996; Rouder et al., 2013). (Recall from Chapter 1 that magician James Randi and the MacArthur Foundation offered $1 million to "anyone who proves a genuine psychic power under proper observing conditions." But even after many years, the money was never collected.)

For even more explanations and critical thinking exercises for why we tend to believe in ESP, see the **PAH** **Practical Application Highlight** and **STH** **Scientific Thinking Highlight**.

Extrasensory perception (ESP)
The perceptual, so-called "psychic," abilities that supposedly go beyond the known senses (e.g., telepathy, clairvoyance, and precognition).

PAH Practical Application Highlight

Why Do So Many People Believe in ESP?

(APA Goal 1.3) Describe applications of psychology

As we discussed in Chapter 1, belief in *pseudoscience* claims can be both psychologically and financially dangerous. To improve your understanding of why the belief in ESP is so popular, consider the following four types of faulty reasoning. Doing so will improve your chances of avoiding costly decisions associated not only with ESP claims, but also with other pseudoscientific phenomena.

1. **Willingness to suspend disbelief**—*disengaging one's normal critical thinking skills because of wishful thinking, out of a personal need for power and control, or simply for entertainment.* ESP satisfies some of our deepest fantasies. We want to believe that there is something "more" out there—outside our normal avenues of sensation and perception. Also, given today's fast-paced technological world and rapid scientific progress, it's tempting to believe that virtually anything is possible. Furthermore, a belief in ESP gives us an illusion of higher personal powers and control. Finally, for some, believing in ESP is like going to the movies. They're willing to suspend disbelief in exchange for momentary entertainment.

2. **Confirmation bias (or fallacy of positive instances)**—*the preference for information that confirms preexisting positions or beliefs while ignoring or discounting contradictory evidence (in other words, remembering the "hits" and ignoring the "misses").* Like the "psychic," who quickly reinforces and elaborates on any chance connections that the person acknowledges and quickly moves on from any misses, most Internet search engines now track our computer requests and then tailor all our later searches to present what they think we want to see. Can you see any danger in this practice? If we end up seeing only things that confirm our prior beliefs, will this limit our world view, and further solidify our confirmation biases?

3. **Innumeracy**—*failing to recognize chance occurrences for what they are due to a lack of training in statistics and probabilities.* Unusual events are misperceived as statistically impossible, and extraordinary explanations, such as ESP, are seen as the logical alternative.

4. **The saliency bias**—*focusing on the most noticeable (salient) factors.* Human information processing and memory storage and retrieval are often based on the initial "vividness" or most noticeable events or information. Sincere personal testimonials, theatrical demonstrations, and detailed anecdotes easily capture our attention and tend to be remembered better than rational, scientific descriptions of events. This is the heart of most stories about extraterrestrial visitations.

STH Scientific Thinking Highlight

Can Your Astrological Sign Predict Crime?

(APA Goal 2.1) Use scientific reasoning to interpret psychological phenomena

What's your astrological sign? Do you believe that your personal astrological, zodiac sign, which is supposedly based on the relative positions of the stars and planets at the time of your birth, accurately describes your unique personality traits and personal future? Or are you someone who reads horoscopes just for fun and entertainment? Members of both groups may be surprised to find that the scientific community considers astrology a *pseudoscience*, since it gives a false appearance of being scientific (Chapter 1). How would a scientist explain the following news report?

> After searching their official criminal files, the police department of Chatham-Kent, Ontario, Canada discovered that for the almost 2,000 crimes committed between January and November 2011 criminals born under the sign of Aries were arrested most often (203), followed by Libra (189) and Virgo (183). Sagittarius (139), Aquarius (142), Taurus (146), and Cancer (147) were the signs least likely to have been arrested (Kuitenbrouwer, 2011).

Q Test Your Scientific Thinking

As you may recall from Chapter 1, scientific thinking is an approach to information that combines a high degree of *skepticism* (questioning what "everybody knows") with *objectivity* (using empirical data to separate fantasy from reality) and *rationalism* (practicing logical reasoning). Using these three principles, consider the following questions:

1. **Skepticism** Given the title and topic of this report, "Astrology and Crime," were you predisposed to believe or discount the information? Scientific thinkers approach claims like these with deep skepticism.

2. **Objectivity** Are the author's assumptions supported by the data? Although scientific studies suggest that any

relationship between crime and astrology is almost certainly due to chance or coincidence (e.g., von Eye et al., 2003), proponents of astrology suggest that the conflicting data resulted from an incomplete understanding of astrology. They claim that it is much more complex than just the month and date of birth, and all measurements must include factors such as the time of day and the year of birth, as well as the positions of planets.

Scientific thinkers carefully analyze data for value and content. Could this be an example of confusing correlation with causation, the third-variable problem, or an illusory correlation? Scientific thinkers gather information and delay judgment until adequate data are available.

3. **Rationalism** Setting aside the conflicting data from other research, can we logically explain the police report's apparent connection between astrological signs and criminality? One important thing to note is that births are not evenly distributed throughout the year. In the United States, more babies are born between May and October, which covers the three signs cited as having higher crime rates in the police report (Aries, Libra, and Virgo). Can you see how, statistically speaking, we're more likely to find higher numbers of people doing almost anything (committing crimes, getting married, or winning the lottery) within those same zodiac signs?

Did the police report contain any other demographic data, such as height, gender, or educational level? Might any of those factors also show a relationship to crimes? Although a spokesperson for the police department cautioned the public about drawing any conclusions from the data, the report didn't offer any alternative explanations or conclusions. Can you think of any other logical explanations for these findings? (*Compare your answers with those of fellow students, family and friends. Doing so will improve your scientific thinking and your media savvy.*)

Before going on, be sure to complete the final Retrieval Practice quiz 4.4 below, and then answer the critical thinking questions in the following **Test Your Critical Thinking**.

Retrieval Practice 4.4 | Understanding Perception

Self-Test Completing this self-test, and then checking your answers by clicking on the answer button or by looking in Appendix B, will provide immediate feedback and helpful practice for exams.

1. _____ are false impressions of the environment, whereas _____ are false sensory perceptions that occur without external stimuli.
   a. Delusions; illusions
   b. Hallucinations; delusions

   c. Illusions; hallucinations
   d. Illusions; delusions

2. The tendency for the environment to be perceived as remaining the same even with changes in sensory input is called _____.
   a. perceptual constancy
   b. the constancy of expectation
   c. an illusory correlation
   d. Gestalt's primary principle

3. A readiness to perceive in a particular manner is known as
_____.

   a. sensory adaptation

   b. perceptual set

   c. habituation

   d. frame of reference

4. Scientists sometimes find that one person will supposedly demonstrate ESP in one laboratory but not in another. This suggests that _____.

   a. replication of studies is useless

   b. one or both of the studies were probably flawed

   c. the researcher or the participant was biased against ESP

   d. ESP abilities have been scientifically proven to exist

Q Test Your Critical Thinking

1. Can you explain how your own perceptual sets might create prejudice or discrimination?

2. How has reading this chapter's information about ESP influenced your beliefs about this topic?

3. Why do you think no one ever collected the $1 million dollar award that had been offered for a provable case of ESP?

Real World Application Question

[AQ6] Can wearing a helmet actually increase risky behaviors?

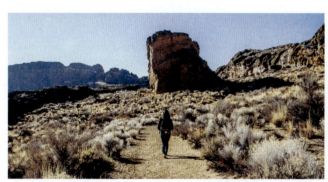
John P Kelly/Stockbyte/Getty Images

Hint: Look in the text for **[AQ6]**

Q Test Your Critical Thinking

Did you notice and wonder why we provided six Real World Application Questions [AQ1–AQ6] throughout the chapter? We've found that they not only help you to engage with and master the material, but also have an important and lasting impact on your critical thinking skills. For additional mastery and enrichment, consider the following questions:

1. Imagine yourself as a hiker who happens upon an unusual structure in the middle of the desert (as shown in this photo). How might information from this chapter help you capture this structure in a painting?

2. How has sensory adaptation been both advantageous and disadvantageous in your own life?

3. Why is it important to test all young children's vision and hearing capabilities?

Noel Dong/EyeEm/EyeEm/Getty Images

4. If scientists could improve your sensory capabilities (such as vision and hearing) far beyond the normal range, would you volunteer for this treatment? What might be the advantages and disadvantages?

Summary

4.1 Understanding Sensation   105

- **Sensation** is the process by which we detect, and convert raw sensory data from the environment and transmit it to our brain. Through the process of **perception**, our brain then selects, organizes, and interprets this sensory information.

- Although sensation and perception are an interrelated, continuous process, the particular combination of **bottom-up processing** and **top-down processing** affects our interpretation of what we sense and perceive.

- **Transduction** is the process by which we convert sensory stimuli into neural signals that are sent to the brain. During **coding**, the neural impulses generated by different physical stimuli travel by separate routes and arrive at different parts of the brain. In *sensory reduction*, we filter and analyze incoming sensations.

- **Psychophysics** studies the link between physical characteristics of stimuli and our psychological experience. The **difference threshold**, or just noticeable difference (JND), is the smallest physical difference between two stimuli that is consciously detectable 50 percent of the time. The **absolute threshold** is the minimum stimulation necessary to consciously detect a stimulus 50 percent of the time.

- **Subliminal perception**, the detection of stimuli below conscious awareness, is a fact, and unconscious stimuli can **prime** certain responses. However, these processes don't lead to significant behavioral change.

- In **sensory adaptation**, sensory receptors fatigue and stop responding to unchanging stimuli. We never completely adapt to visual stimuli, strong stimuli like the smell of ammonia, or pain.

- Because our body releases natural painkillers called endorphins, we can persist in spite of pain. In addition, according to the **gate control theory**, our experience of pain depends partly on whether the neural message gets past a "gatekeeper" in the spinal cord, which researchers believe is chemically controlled.

4.2 How We See and Hear 111

- Light waves are a form of electromagnetic energy, and sound waves are produced when air molecules move in a particular wave pattern.

- Light enters the eye at the front of the eyeball. The cornea protects the eye and helps focus light rays. The lens further focuses light, adjusting to allow focusing on objects at different distances. At the back of the eye, incoming light waves reach the **retina**, which contains light-sensitive **rods** and **cones**. A network of neurons in the retina transmits neural information to the brain. There are two theories of color vision—the **trichromatic** theory and the **opponent process** theory.

- The sense of hearing is known as **audition**. The ear has three parts: the **outer ear** gathers sound waves, the **middle ear** amplifies and concentrates the sounds, and the **inner ear** changes the mechanical energy of sounds into neural impulses. The frequency of sounds determines how we distinguish among sounds of different pitches, and there are three explanations for pitch perception—**place theory**, **frequency theory**, and the **volley principle**. The amplitude of sound waves determines the softness or loudness of sounds.

4.3 Our Other Important Senses 119

- Smell and taste, sometimes called the chemical senses, involve chemoreceptors that are sensitive to certain chemical molecules. In **olfaction**, odor molecules stimulate receptors in the olfactory epithelium, in the nose. The resulting neural impulse travels to the olfactory bulb, where the information is processed before being sent elsewhere in the brain. Our sense of taste (**gustation**) involves five tastes: sweet, sour, salty, bitter, and umami (which

means "savory" or "delicious"). The taste buds are distributed on our tongues within the papillae.

- The body senses—the skin senses, the **vestibular sense**, and **kinesthesis**—tell the brain what it's touching or being touched by, how the body is oriented, and where and how it is moving.

4.4 Understanding Perception 124

- **Illusions** are false or misleading perceptions that can be produced by actual physical distortions, as in desert mirages, or by errors in perception. These errors allow psychologists insight into normal perceptual processes.

- **Selective attention** allows us to filter out unimportant sensory messages. **Feature detectors** are specialized cells that respond only to certain sensory information. **Habituation** refers to our brain's learned tendency to stop responding to unchanging information.

- To be useful, sensory data must be organized in a meaningful way—in terms of form, depth, and constancy. Gestalt principles are based on the notion that we all share a natural tendency to force patterns onto whatever we see.

- Interpretation, the final stage of perception, can be influenced by *sensory adaptation* and **perceptual set**.

- Research on **extrasensory perception (ESP)**, the supposed ability to perceive things that go beyond the normal senses, has produced notoriously "fragile" results that do not hold up to scientific scrutiny; they lack experimental controls and replicability.

Key Terms

Retrieval Practice   Write your own definition for each term before turning back to the referenced page to check your answer.

- absolute threshold   108
- audition   115
- binocular cues   129
- blind spot   113
- bottom-up processing   106
- cochlea [kok-lee-uh]   116
- coding   107
- conduction hearing loss   117
- cones   114
- depth perception   128
- difference threshold   107
- extrasensory perception (esp)   133
- feature detectors   125
- fovea   114
- frequency theory for hearing   116

- gate control theory of pain   109
- gustation   119
- habituation   125
- illusion   124
- inner ear   116
- kinesthesis   122
- middle ear   116
- monocular cues   129
- olfaction   119
- opponent-process theory of color   115
- outer ear   116
- perception   105
- perceptual constancy   129
- perceptual set   131
- pheromones [fare-oh-mones]   119

- place theory for hearing   116
- priming   108
- psychophysics   107
- retina   113
- rods   114
- selective attention   125
- sensation   105
- sensorineural hearing loss   118
- sensory adaptation   109
- subliminal perception   108
- top-down processing   106
- transduction   107
- trichromatic theory of color   114
- vestibular sense   122
- volley principle for hearing   117

States of Consciousness

ferli/123RF

Real World Application Questions

Things you'll learn in Chapter 5

[AQ1] Under what conditions, would you fail to notice a clearly visible brutal assault (or a person in a gorilla suit)?

[AQ2] Can being distracted and multitasking sometimes be beneficial?

[AQ3] Will sleeping in on the weekends make up for sleep deprivation during the week?

[AQ4] Does Facebook deliberately try to create addiction?

[AQ5] Can using marijuana decrease your IQ?

[AQ6] Can meditation be an effective painkiller?

Throughout the chapter, look for the [AQ1–AQ6] icons. They indicate where the text addresses these questions.

CHAPTER OUTLINE

5.1 Understanding Consciousness

Retrieval Practice While reading the upcoming s ections, respond to each Learning Objective in your own words.

Summarize how selective attention and levels of awareness affect consciousness.

- **Define** consciousness and altered states of consciousness (ASCs).
- **Describe** the key factors in selective attention.

- **Review** how consciousness exists on various levels of awareness.

Real World Application Questions

[AQ1] Under what conditions, would you fail to notice a clearly visible brutal assault (or a person in a gorilla suit)?

[AQ2] Can being distracted and multitasking sometimes be beneficial?

We begin this chapter by exploring our understanding of consciousness. What is consciousness? Is it simple awareness? What would it be like to be unaware? How can we study and understand the contents of our own consciousness when the only tool of discovery is consciousness itself?

Consciousness Our awareness of ourselves and our environment.

Most psychologists define **consciousness** as a two-part awareness of both ourselves and our environment (W. O. Li, 2016; Thompson, 2015). This dual-natured awareness explains how we can be deeply engrossed in studying or a conversation with others and still hear the ping of an incoming message on our phone. However, if we're deeply asleep, we probably won't hear this same message ping due to the fact that sleep is an **altered state of consciousness (ASC)**, which is defined as a temporary mental state other than ordinary waking consciousness. Later in this chapter, we will fully discuss the ASCs of sleep, dreaming, psychoactive drugs, meditation, and hypnosis. But we first need to explore the general nature of consciousness.

Altered state of consciousness (ASC) A temporary mental state, other than ordinary waking consciousness, that includes sleep, dreaming, psychoactive drug use, meditation, and hypnosis.

Selective attention The process of focusing conscious awareness onto a specific stimulus, while filtering out a range of other stimuli occurring simultaneously.

Selective Attention

As you may recall from Chapter 1, the "father" of American psychology, William James, likened *consciousness* to a stream that's constantly changing yet always the same. It meanders and flows, sometimes where the person wills and sometimes not. The process of **selective attention** (Chapter 4) allows us to control this *stream of consciousness* through deliberate concentration and full attention. When you are listening to a classroom lecture, your attention may drift away to thoughts of a computer you want to buy, or an attractive classmate. But you can catch and control this wandering stream of consciousness and willingly go back to selectively attending to the lecture.

Inattentional blindness The failure to notice a fully visible, but unexpected, stimulus when our attention is directed elsewhere; also known as perceptual blindness.

There's another aspect of selective attention that you may find fascinating. **[AQ1]** Sometimes when we're fully focused and selectively attending, we can fail to notice clearly visible stimuli, particularly if they're unexpected and we're otherwise distracted. A Boston police officer chasing a shooting suspect on foot ran right past a brutal assault, but later claimed no memory of seeing the assault (Lehr, 2009). Nevertheless, a jury convicted him of perjury and obstruction of justice. Can you see how you might also fail to see such an assault if you were otherwise distracted?

4x6/iStock/Getty Images

Another example of this surprising phenomenon, known as **inattentional blindness**, can be found in the popular YouTube videos in which observers fail to notice a grown man dressed in a gorilla costume as he repeatedly passes through a group of people (see photo). These videos are based on a clever experiment that first asked participants to count the number of passes in a videotaped basketball game (Simons & Chabris, 1999). Researchers then sent an assistant, dressed in a full gorilla suit, to walk through the middle of the ongoing game. Can you predict what happened? The participants were so focused on their pass-counting task that they failed to notice the person in the gorilla suit. When the participants later watched the video without having to count the basketball passes, most could not believe they had missed seeing the gorilla.

Does this research help explain why magicians ask us to focus on a distracting element, such as a deck of cards or beautiful assistant, while they manipulate the real object of their magic—removing an unsuspecting volunteer's wallet or watch? On a more important note, this type of inattentional blindness can lead to serious problems for pilots focused on landing their plane who might fail to see a flock of birds, or a driver texting on a phone who fails to see the red light. In case you're wondering, this type of "blindness" also occurs in some of our other senses, such as *inattentional deafness*—failing to notice unexpected auditory stimuli when focusing on another task (Kreitz et al., 2016).

Levels of Awareness

As this example of inattentional blindness demonstrates, our *stream of consciousness* varies in its level of awareness. Consciousness is not an all-or-nothing phenomenon—conscious or unconscious. Instead, it exists along a continuum, ranging from high awareness and sharp, focused alertness at one extreme, to middle levels of awareness, to low awareness or even non-consciousness and coma at the other extreme (**Figure 5.1**).

As you can see from Figure 5.1, this continuum of levels of awareness involves *controlled* and *automatic* processes. When you're working at a demanding task or learning something new, such as how to drive a car, your consciousness is at the high end of the continuum. These **controlled processes** demand focused attention and generally interfere with other ongoing activities.

In sharp contrast to the high awareness and focused attention required for controlled processes, **automatic processes** require minimal attention, and generally do not interfere with other ongoing activities. Think back to your teen years when you were first learning how to drive a car and it took all of your attention (controlled processing). The fact that you can now effortlessly steer a car and work the brakes all at once (with little or no focused attention) is thanks to automatic processing. In short, learning a new task requires complete concentration and *controlled processing*. Once that task is well-learned, you can switch to *automatic processing*.

TIP Is there a problem with using automatic processes while reading? Although reading is a well-learned, automatic process for most college students, you can't casually (automatically) read complex new material (like this text). If you want to do well on upcoming quizzes and exams, be sure to use highly focused, controlled processing while reading and studying this and other essential material.

The following **STH** Scientific Thinking Highlight offers further insights and practical applications on the importance of selective attention and levels of awareness.

Before moving on, let's look at how several key concepts in this section have direct, real-world applications. For example, understanding and maximizing your consciousness can literally save your own life and those of others! How? First, shifting your *selective attention* back and forth between what's on your phone versus what's on the road or in your walking path helps explain the dangers of texting while driving or walking. Similarly, recalling how people failed to see someone dressed in a gorilla suit, it's easy to see how inattentional blindness also makes us less attentive to dangerous hazards. In addition, as shown in the Scientific Thinking Highlight, EEG scans of

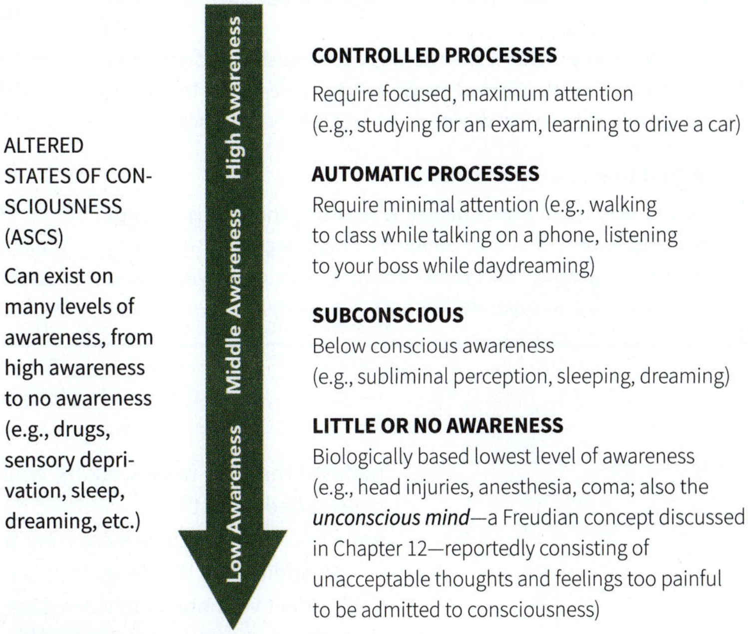

Controlled processes The mental activities that require focused attention and generally interfere with other ongoing activities.

Automatic processes The mental activities that require minimal attention and generally have little impact on other activities.

ALTERED STATES OF CONSCIOUSNESS (ASCS)

Can exist on many levels of awareness, from high awareness to no awareness (e.g., drugs, sensory deprivation, sleep, dreaming, etc.)

High Awareness

Middle Awareness

Low Awareness

CONTROLLED PROCESSES
Require focused, maximum attention (e.g., studying for an exam, learning to drive a car)

AUTOMATIC PROCESSES
Require minimal attention (e.g., walking to class while talking on a phone, listening to your boss while daydreaming)

SUBCONSCIOUS
Below conscious awareness (e.g., subliminal perception, sleeping, dreaming)

LITTLE OR NO AWARENESS
Biologically based lowest level of awareness (e.g., head injuries, anesthesia, coma; also the *unconscious mind*—a Freudian concept discussed in Chapter 12—reportedly consisting of unacceptable thoughts and feelings too painful to be admitted to consciousness)

FIGURE 5.1 Levels of awareness

STH Scientific Thinking Highlight

The Dangers of Distraction

(APA Goal 2.1) Use scientific reasoning to interpret psychological phenomena

Did you know that using your phone while:

- *driving*, including dialing, talking, texting, reaching for the phone, etc., greatly increases your risk of accidents and near collisions (Hill et al., 2019; Tucker et al., 2015), and

- *walking* leads to impaired judgment and accidents, with pedestrian fatalities increasing 46 percent in the last decade (Courtemanche et al., 2019; National Safety Council, 2018, 2019)?

We've all received repeated warnings about the dangers of texting while driving, and these dangers explain why it's against the law in many states. However, we've also seen pedestrians walking along the sidewalk and even crossing the street with their eyes on their phones instead of their surroundings, and some cities around the world are considering passing laws against walking while using your phone (e.g., Anthony, 2019; Knutson, 2019).

Why is this type of *distracted walking* so problematic and dangerous? To find out, an enterprising journalist, Jeff Rossen, decided to perform his own informal experiment involving volunteers from *Today*, a popular TV program (Rossen & Ferguson, 2018). The participants were asked to walk and text while cameras recorded their behaviors. Unfortunately, some participants almost tripped over a curb or ran into rocks, others went diagonal inside a crosswalk, and most didn't look up while crossing the street.

To better understand what was happening, Rossen then asked a neuroscientist, David Putrino, to use an EEG headset to monitor his brain waves while he walked without using his phone and then while he was texting. What happened? As you might expect, Rossen's brain scans were normal when he walked without his phone. But when walking while texting, the EEG scans showed that his brain was "completely overloaded." The take-home message was: "The next time you're out for a walk, put away the phone."

What do you think? After seeing these statistics and considering the journalist's informal study, are you more willing to give up using your phone while driving or walking? Why or why not?

Q Test Your Scientific Thinking

As you may recall from Chapter 1, scientific thinking is an approach to information that combines a high degree of *skepticism* (questioning what "everybody knows") with *objectivity* (using empirical data to separate fantasy from reality) and *rationalism*

AP Images/M. Spencer Green

(practicing logical reasoning). Using these three principles, consider the following questions:

1. **Skepticism** Given just the title and topic of this report, "The Dangers of Distraction," are you more or less likely to believe the information? Scientific thinkers approach claims like these with mild to deep skepticism.

2. **Objectivity** Are the claims and assumptions supported by the data? How would you check the statistics regarding the dangers of driving and walking to see if the findings were correctly cited and interpreted? Scientific thinkers carefully analyze data for value and content. Also, could the journalist's informal experiment be an example of *experimenter bias or demand characteristics* (Chapter 1)? Did the volunteers possibly exaggerate their walking and texting behaviors due to the fact they were being videotaped or because they picked up on subtle cues and wanted to help confirm Rossen's belief in the dangers of distraction? Scientific thinking requires unbiased, persuasive evidence.

3. **Rationalism** Aside from possible problems with the data, can you rationally explain why given the grim statistics so many people continue to text and drive or text and walk? After reading the first part of this chapter, *States of Consciousness*, can you logically explain why distracted driving and walking are so dangerous?

(Compare your answers with those of fellow students, family and friends. Doing so will improve your scientific thinking and your media savvy.)

---

pedestrians who were walking while texting showed that their brains were "completely overloaded," and they committed dangerous errors like failing to look up from their phones and check for cars before crossing the street.

In addition to the dangers of texting while driving or walking, distractions can also negatively affect your ability to learn. Like texting, many people mistakenly believe they can safely and efficiently *multitask*. However, in a Stanford University study involving 100 college students, researchers ran a series of three tests with the participants divided into two groups—those who regularly multitasked and those who didn't (Ophir et al., 2009). You may be surprised to discover that compared to participants who preferred doing only one task at a time, on all three tests the self-described multitaskers paid less attention to detail, displayed poorer memory, and had more trouble switching from one task to another. A related study found that heavy media multitasking among adolescents, such as watching TV while texting, was associated with lower scores on statewide standardized achievement tests in math and English, poorer performance on behavioral measures of executive function (working memory capacity), and greater impulsivity (Cain et al., 2016).

Can you see how this explains why trying to listen to a lecture and simultaneously texting or playing games on a smartphone may threaten your GPA? Or how even your own life is threatened when you text while driving or walking? In short, the ability to multitask is largely a myth. Although most people believe they're capable of successfully doing two things at once, the truth is that they're not paying full attention to either task. They're simply doing both with divided attention.

What's the good news? **[AQ2]** Being distracted and multitasking isn't always bad. In fact, listening to music while exercising at the gym (see photo), or fixing dinner while watching TV, can be somewhat beneficial and productive. Just remember that when you're in a potentially dangerous situation or trying to learn something that you will want to later recall, you need to focus and use your *controlled processes*.

Retrieval Practice 5.1 | Understanding Consciousness

Self-Test   Completing this self-test, and then checking your answers by clicking on the answer button or by looking in Appendix B, will provide immediate feedback and helpful practice for exams.

1. An organism's awareness of its own self and surroundings is known as _____.

   a. awareness
   b. consciousness
   c. alertness
   d. central processing

2. Mental states other than ordinary waking consciousness, such as sleep, dreaming, or hypnosis, are known as _____.

   a. altered states of consciousness
   b. intentional blindness
   c. automatic processes
   d. none of these options

3. Mental activities that require minimal attention, and have little impact on other activities are called _____ processes.

   a. controlled
   b. peripheral
   c. conscious
   d. automatic

4. For optimal learning as you read this text, you should _____.

   a. be in an altered state of consciousness (ASC)
   b. employ controlled processing
   c. let your stream of consciousness take charge
   d. employ automatic processing

5. Which of the following is TRUE?

   a. Consciousness exists on a continuum.
   b. Selective attention allows us to control our stream of consciousness.
   c. Our consciousness varies in its level of awareness.
   d. All of these options.

Q Test Your Critical Thinking

1. Can you see how selective attention and inattentional blindness might explain why some arguments with friends and love partners are impossible to resolve?

2. How would automatic processing explain how you can walk all the way from one end of your college campus to the other and not remember anything you did or saw along the way?

Real World Application Questions

[AQ1]   Under what conditions, would you fail to notice a clearly visible brutal assault (or a person in a gorilla suit)?

[AQ2]   Can being distracted and multitasking sometimes be beneficial?

Hint: Look in the text for **[AQ1]** and **[AQ2]**

5.2 | Understanding Sleep and Dreams

LEARNING OBJECTIVES

Retrieval Practice While reading the upcoming sections, respond to each Learning Objective in your own words.

Review the major processes that occur while we sleep and dream.

- **Describe** circadian rhythms and how they affect our lives.
- **Review** what happens during the various stages of sleep.

- **Compare and contrast** the key factors and theories involved in sleep and dreams.

- **Describe** the major sleep-wake disorders and their possible treatment.

Real World Application Question

[AQ3] Will sleeping in on the weekends make up for sleep deprivation during the week?

Having explored the definition and description of everyday, waking consciousness and its properties of selective attention and levels of awareness, we now can turn to two of our most common *altered states of consciousness* (ASCs)—sleep and dreaming. These ASCs are fascinating to both scientists and the general public. Why are we born with a mechanism that forces us to sleep and dream for approximately a third of our lives? How can an ASC that requires reduced awareness and responsiveness to our environment be beneficial in an evolutionary sense? What are the functions and role of sleep and dreams? To answer these questions and fully understand sleep and dreaming, we need to first discuss circadian rhythms.

Circadian Rhythms and Sleep

Circadian rhythm The internal, biological clock governing bodily activities, such as the sleep/wake cycle, and temperature, that occur on a 24- to 25-hour cycle. (*Circa* means "about," and *dies* means "day.")

Most animals have adapted to our planet's cycle of days and nights by developing a pattern of bodily functions that wax and wane over each 24-hour period. For humans, sleep cycles, attention, core body temperature, moods, learning efficiency, blood pressure, metabolism, immune responses, and pulse rate all follow these **circadian rhythms** (Goh et al., 2016; Gumz, 2016; Valdez, 2019). See **Figure 5.2**.

FIGURE 5.2 **Explaining circadian rhythms**

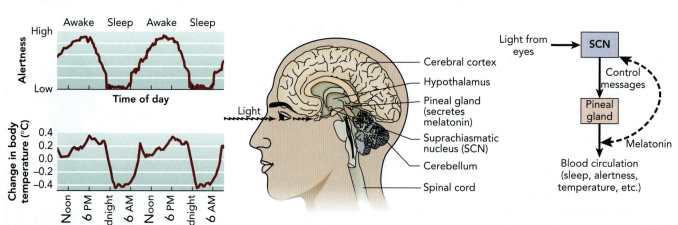

a. Why are circadian rhythms important? Note how the 24-hour daily circadian rhythm affects our degree of alertness and core body temperature, and how they rise and fall in similar ways.

b. What controls our circadian rhythms? A part of the hypothalamus, the suprachiasmatic nucleus (SCN), receives information about light and darkness from our eyes, and then sends control messages to our *pineal gland,* which releases the hormone *melatonin.*

c. What regulates the melatonin? As in other feedback loops in the body, the level of melatonin in the blood is sensed by the SCN, which then adjusts the output of the pineal gland to maintain the "desired" level.

PAN Practical Application of Neuroscience

During your teen years, do you remember having a really difficult time getting up in the morning (see photo)? This common pattern of staying up late at night and then sleeping longer in the morning appears to be a result of the natural shift in the timing of circadian rhythms that occurs during puberty (Carskadon et al., 1998; McGlinchey, 2015; Paiva et al., 2015). This shift is due to a delay in the release of the hormone melatonin. In adults, this hormone is typically released around 10 p.m., signaling the body that it is time to go to sleep. But in teen-

agers, melatonin isn't released until around 1 a.m.—thus explaining why it's more difficult for teenagers to fall asleep as early as adults or younger children do. Recognition of this unique biological shift in circadian rhythms among teenagers has led some school districts to delay the start of school in the morning. Research shows that even a 25- to 50-minute delay allows teenagers to be more alert and focused during class, contributes to improvements in their moods and overall health, and results in a significant decrease in driving accidents (Bin-Hasan et al., 2019; Bryant & Gómez, 2015; Weintraub, 2016). When a Seattle, WA high school delayed their opening time 55 minutes, researchers found a significant increase in student grades and attendance (Dunster et al., 2018).

In addition to the problems of disrupted circadian cycles during your teen years, as a college student are you skipping a lot of sleep due to your academic courses, job, family responsibilities, and/or studying? **[AQ3]** Do you believe you can make up for the deficit by sleeping extra hours on the weekends (see photo)? If so, you'll be disappointed by a recent study that debunks that myth (Depner et al., 2019). In this 2-week sleep lab study, participants in the experimental group were limited to 5 hours of sleep on weekdays, and then allowed complete freedom to sleep in and nap during the weekends. Compared to the control group, which had no sleep deprivation, participants in the experimental group had increased insulin levels, more weight gain, slower metabolism, and greater changes in circadian timing. The authors of the study claim that

Can sleeping in help make up sleep deficits?

just as you can't "make up" for a junk diet all week by eating healthy only on the weekends, you can't make up your sleep deprivation by sleeping in on the weekend. One author also recommended that "people should prioritize sleep…just as we do a healthy diet and exercise [and] cut out the optional 'sleep stealers,' such as watching television shows or spending time on electronic devices" (cited in Johnson, 2019).

Flying across several time zones also disrupts your circadian rhythms and sleeping patterns, which in turn can lead to fatigue and irritability, decreases in your alertness and mental agility, as well as possibly exacerbating certain physical and psychological disorders (Hassan et al., 2018; Selvi et al., 2015; Srinivasan et al., 2014). Do you know why this so-called "jet lag" tends to be worse when we fly eastward rather than westward? Our bodies adjust more easily to going to bed later compared to trying to sleep earlier than normal.

Sleep Deprivation   Disturbances in circadian rhythms are clearly an important problem because they lead to sleep deprivation, which increases the risk of serious health issues, including heart disease, obesity, and sleep disorders, along with increased accidents and problems with memory, concentration and productivity (e.g., McAlpine et al., 2019; Ratcliff & Van Dongen, 2018; Situala et al., 2016).

Sleep deprivation is also linked with impairments in the immune system, which is one reason why adults who get fewer than 7 hours of sleep a night are four times as likely to develop a cold as those who sleep at least 8 hours a night (CDC, 2016; Dimitrov et al., 2019; Prather et al., 2015). Surprisingly, when we're sleep deprived, we're also more likely to "remember" things that did not actually happen, a phenomenon you'll learn more about in Chapter 7 (Frenda et al., 2014).

Those who suffer the most immediate and obvious ill effects from these sleep and circadian disturbances tend to be physicians, nurses, police, and others—about 20 percent of employees in the United States—whose occupations require rotating "shift work" schedules. Typically divided into a first shift (8 a.m. to 4 p.m.), second shift (4 p.m. to midnight), and a third shift (midnight to 8 a.m.), these work shifts often change from week to week, and clearly disrupt the workers' circadian rhythms (Ganesan et al., 2019; Resuehr et al., 2019). Some research suggests that productivity and safety increase when shifts are rotated every 3 weeks instead of every week, and napping is allowed. In fact, recent research finds that afternoon napping is generally healthy and helpful for almost everyone (Boukhris et al., 2019; Häusler et al., 2019).

Perhaps the most frightening and immediate danger from sleep deprivation is that lapses in attention among drivers, physicians, pilots, and other workers contribute to serious and fatal accidents (see photo) (Bougard et al., 2016; M. L. Lee et al., 2016a; Tefft, 2018). The good news is that greater enforcement of safety regulations for pilot flight times and hours of service for truck drivers and other public personnel could offset many of these public dangers. If you're concerned about your own levels of sleep deprivation, take the two-part test in the following **Test Yourself**.

Paul Hennessy/NurPhoto/Getty Images

PA Practical Application

Test Yourself: Sleep Deprivation

Take the following test to determine whether you are sleep deprived.

Part 1 Set up a small mirror next to this text and trace the black star pictured here, using your non-dominant hand, while watching your hand in the mirror. The task is difficult, and sleep-deprived people typically make many errors. If you are not sleep deprived, it still may be difficult to trace the star, but you'll probably do it more accurately.

Part 2 Give yourself one point each time you answer yes to the following:

_____ **1.** To wake up in the morning, I generally need an alarm clock or my phone alarm.

_____ **2.** I sometimes fall asleep unintentionally in public places.

_____ **3.** Because it's so hard for me to wake up early, I try to take only late morning or early afternoon college classes.

_____ **4.** People often tell me that I look tired and sleepy.

_____ **5.** I often struggle to stay awake during class, especially in warm rooms.

_____ **6.** While studying, I often nod off or find it hard to concentrate.

_____ **7.** I often feel sluggish and sleepy in the afternoon.

_____ **8.** I need several cups of coffee or other energy drinks to make it through the day.

_____ **9.** My friends often tell me I'm less moody and irritable when I've had enough sleep.

Pixtal/AGE Fotostock

Effects of sleep deprivation Insufficient sleep can seriously affect your college grades, as well as your physical health, motor skills, and overall mood.

_____ **10.** I tend to get lots of colds and infections, especially around final exams.

_____ **11.** When I get in bed at night, I generally fall asleep within 4 minutes.

_____ **12.** I try to catch up on my sleep debt by sleeping as long as possible on the weekends.

The average student score is between 4 and 6. The higher your number, the greater your level of sleep deprivation.

Sources: Bianchi, 2014; Howard et al., 2014; National Sleep Foundation, 2012; M. Smith et al., 2012.

Stages of Sleep

> The woods are lovely, dark and deep. But I have promises to keep, and miles to go before I sleep.
> —Robert Frost

Having discussed our daily circadian cycle, and the problems associated with its disruption, we now turn our attention to our cyclical patterns and stages of sleep. We begin with an exploration

FIGURE 5.3 **Scientific study of sleep and dreaming** Data collected in sleep labs have helped scientists understand the stages of sleep.

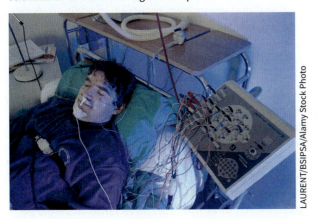

a. What happens in a sleep lab? Participants in sleep research labs wear electrodes on their heads and bodies to measure brain and bodily responses during the sleep cycle. An electroencephalogram (EEG) detects and records brain-wave changes by means of small electrodes on the scalp. Other electrodes measure muscle activity and eye movements.

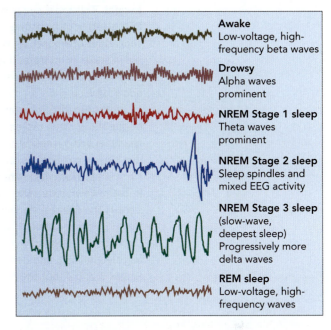

Awake
Low-voltage, high-frequency beta waves

Drowsy
Alpha waves prominent

NREM Stage 1 sleep
Theta waves prominent

NREM Stage 2 sleep
Sleep spindles and mixed EEG activity

NREM Stage 3 sleep
(slow-wave, deepest sleep)
Progressively more delta waves

REM sleep
Low-voltage, high-frequency waves

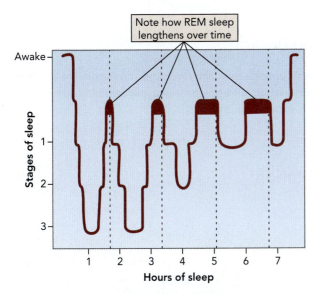

Note how REM sleep lengthens over time

b. Why do they measure brain waves? The various stages of sleep are defined by telltale changes in brain waves, as indicated by the jagged lines. The compact brain waves of alertness gradually lengthen as you descend downward through NREM Stages 1–3. The final stage in the 90-minute sleep cycle is called REM sleep, which as you can see involves compact, faster brain waves.

c. How do the stages of sleep change while we sleep? Your first sleep cycle generally lasts about 90 minutes from awake and alert, downward through NREM Stages 1–3, and then reverses back up through NREM Stages 3–1, followed by a period of REM sleep. If you sleep 8 hours, you'll typically go through approximately four or five sleep cycles (as shown by the vertical dotted lines). Note how the overall amount of REM sleep increases as the night progresses, while the amount of deep sleep (Stage 3) decreases.

of how scientists study sleep. Surveys and interviews can provide general information, but for more detailed and precise data researchers in sleep laboratories use a number of sophisticated instruments (**Figure 5.3**). Imagine that you are a participant in a sleep experiment. When you arrive at the sleep lab, you are assigned one of several bedrooms. The researcher hooks you up to various physiological recording devices, which will require a night or two of adaptation before the researchers can begin to monitor your typical night's sleep (**Figure 5.3a**). After this adaptation, if you're like most sleepers, you'll begin the sleep cycle with a drowsy, presleep state followed by several distinct stages of sleep, each progressively deeper (**Figure 5.3b**). Then the sequence begins to reverse.

Note that we don't necessarily go through all sleep stages in this exact sequence (**Figure 5.3c**). But during the course of a night, people usually complete four to five cycles of light to deep sleep and then back up to light sleep. Each of these down and up cycles lasts about 90 minutes. Also note the two important divisions of sleep shown in Figures 5.3b and 5.3c: **non-rapid-eye-movement (NREM) sleep** (Stages 1, 2, and 3) and **rapid-eye-movement (REM) sleep**.

Non-rapid-eye-movement (NREM) sleep The sleep stages (1 through 3) during which a sleeper does not show rapid eye movements.

Rapid-eye-movement (REM) sleep The fourth stage of sleep, marked by rapid eye movements, irregular breathing, high-frequency brain waves, paralysis of large muscles, and often dreaming.

REM and NREM Sleep

During REM sleep, your brain's wave patterns are similar to those of a relaxed wakefulness stage, and your eyeballs will move up and down and from left to right. This rapid eye movement is a signal that dreaming is occurring. In addition, during REM sleep your breathing and pulse rates become fast and irregular, and your genitals may show signs of arousal. Yet your musculature is deeply relaxed and unresponsive, so many people mistakenly interpret it as being the deepest stage of sleep when actually it is the lightest stage of sleep. Given these contradictory qualities, REM sleep is sometimes referred to as *paradoxical sleep.*

Although dreams occur most frequently during REM sleep, they also sometimes occur during NREM sleep (Askenasy, 2016; Jones & Benca, 2013). Note how *Stage 1* of NREM sleep is characterized by theta waves and drowsy sleep. During this stage, many people experience sudden muscle movements called *myoclonic jerks* accompanied by a sensation of falling. In *Stage 2 sleep*, muscle activity further decreases and sleep spindles occur, which involve a sudden surge in brain wave frequency. Stages 1 and 2 are relatively light stages of sleep, whereas *Stage 3 sleep* is the deepest stage of sleep, often referred to as *slow wave sleep (SWS)* or simply *deep sleep.* Sleepers during this deep sleep are very hard to awaken, and if something does wake them, they're generally confused and disoriented at first. This is also a time that sleepwalking, sleeptalking, and bedwetting occur. (Note that Stage 3 sleep was previously divided into Stages 3 and 4, but the American Academy of Sleep Medicine [AASM] recently removed the Stage 4 designation.)

Why Do We Sleep and Dream?

There are many myths and misconceptions about why we sleep and dream (see the **Test Yourself**). Fortunately, scientists have carefully studied what sleep and dreaming do for us and why we spend approximately 25 years of our life in these ASCs.

S&P Scientific Thinking and Practical Application

Test Yourself: Fact or Fiction?

Before reading the facts about each statement below, answer "true" or "false" is the space provided:

_____ 1. Drinking alcohol before you go to bed helps you get a good night's sleep.

_____ 2. Watching television before going to sleep is unhealthy for children, but has little or no effect on the quality of sleep of adults.

_____ 3. Most young adults need 8 hours of sleep each night to maintain sound mental and physical health

_____ 4. Dreams often have special or symbolic meaning.

_____ 5. Some people never dream.

_____ 6. Dreams last only a few seconds and occur only in REM sleep.

_____ 7. When genital arousal occurs during sleep, it means the sleeper is having a sexual dream.

_____ 8. Most people dream only in black and white, and blind people don't dream.

_____ 9. It's easy to learn new, complicated things, like a foreign language, while asleep.

_____ 10. Dreaming of dying can be fatal.

"No, Smith, that's NOT why they're called 'spreadsheets'."

Shaun McCallig/Cartoon Stock

Facts:

1. **False:** Alcohol reduces your ability to achieve deeper levels of sleep, which are necessary for proper functioning (Nicholls, 2018; Robbins et al., 2019).

2. **False:** Both children and adults who watch television in their bedrooms have shorter and worse sleep patterns (Helm & Spencer, 2019; Nicholls, 2018).

3. **True:** Sleep experts say that most adults need between 7 and 9 hours of sleep each night, and that we can't "pay back" the deficit by sleeping in on the weekends (Johnson, 2019; Robbins et al., 2019).

4. **False:** Many people mistakenly believe that dreams can foretell the future, reflect unconscious desires, have secret meaning, reveal the truth, or contain special messages. But scientific research finds little or no support for these beliefs (Domhoff, 2010; Hobson et al., 2011; Lilienfeld et al., 2010, 2015).

5. **True:** In rare cases, adults with certain brain injuries or disorders do not dream (Solms, 1997). But otherwise, virtually all adults regularly dream for a total of about 2 hours per night. However, many people don't remember doing so. Even people who firmly believe they never dream report dreams if they are repeatedly awakened during an overnight study in a sleep laboratory. Children also dream regularly. Between ages 3 and 8, they dream during approximately 25 percent of their sleep time (Foulkes, 1993, 1999; Nicholls, 2018).

6. **False:** Research shows that most dreams occur in real time. A dream that seemed to last 20 minutes probably did last approximately 20 minutes (Dement & Wolpert, 1958). Dreams also sometimes occur in NREM sleep (Askenasy, 2016; Jones & Benca, 2013; Oudiette et al., 2012).

7. **False:** When sleepers are awakened during this genital arousal, sleepers are no more likely to report sexual dreams than at other times.

8. **False:** People frequently report seeing color in their dreams. Those who are blind do dream, but they report visual images only if they lost their sight after approximately age 7 (Bakou et al., 2014; Nicholls, 2018).

9. **False:** Although some learning can occur during the lighter stages (1 and 2) of sleep, processing and retention of this material is minimal (Chambers & Payne, 2015; Lilienfeld et al., 2010, 2015). Wakeful learning is much more effective and efficient.

10. **Fact or Fiction?:** This is a good opportunity to exercise your scientific and critical thinking skills. Although many people have personally experienced and recounted a fatal dream, how would we scientifically prove or disprove this belief?

Four Sleep Theories
How do scientists explain our shared need for sleep? There are four key theories:

1. **Adaptation/protection theory** Sleep evolved due to the human and non-human animals need to conserve energy and protect themselves from predators by keeping us inactive and quiet when the danger is greatest—normally at night (Drew, 2013; Tsoukalas, 2012). As you can see in **Figure 5.4**, animals with the highest likelihood of being eaten by others, a higher need for food, and the lowest ability to hide tend to sleep the least.

2. **Repair/restoration theory** Sleep helps us recuperate not only from physical fatigue but also from emotional and intellectual demands (Blumberg, 2015). Essential chemicals and bodily tissues are repaired or replenished while we sleep, and the brain repairs and cleans itself of potentially toxic waste products that accumulate (Iliff et al., 2012; Konnikova, 2014; Xie et al., 2013).

    A study offering support for repair/restoration theory found that synapses in the brains of sleeping mice were 18 percent smaller than in their awake brains (De Vivo et al., 2017). The researchers suggest our brains get overloaded while we're awake, and the role of sleep is to pare down the synapses. This decrease in synapses allows important signals to be lifted over the excess "noise." The fact that when we're deprived of REM sleep most people "catch up" later by spending more time than usual in this state (the so-called REM rebound) further supports this theory.

3. **Growth/development theory** The percentage of REM versus NREM sleep changes over the life span and coincides with changes in the structure and organization of the brain, as well as the release of growth hormones from the pituitary gland—particularly in children. As we age, our brains change less, and we release fewer of these hormones, grow less, and sleep less.

4. **Learning/memory theory** Sleep is important for learning and the consolidation, storage, and maintenance of memories (Bennion et al., 2015; Chambers & Payne, 2015; Vorster & Born, 2015). This is particularly true for REM sleep, which increases after periods of stress or intense learning. For instance, infants and young children, who generally are learning more than adults, spend far more of their sleep time in REM sleep (**Figure 5.5**).

Adaptation/protection theory of sleep The theory that sleep evolved to conserve energy and provide protection from predators.

Repair/restoration theory of sleep The theory that sleep allows organisms to repair their bodies or recuperate from depleting daily waking activities.

Growth/development theory of sleep The theory that sleep is correlated with changes in the structure and organization of the brain due to growth and development.

Learning/memory theory of sleep The theory that sleep is important for learning and for the consolidation, storage, and maintenance of memories.

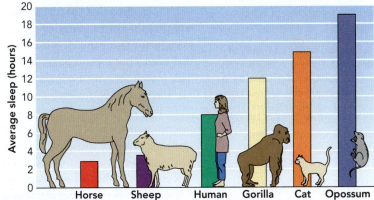

FIGURE 5.4 **Average daily hours of sleep for different mammals** According to the adaptation/protection theory, differences in diet and number of predators affect different species' sleep habits. Given that opossums are relatively safe in their environment and easily find food and shelter, they can sleep many hours each day. In comparison, sheep and horses sleep very little because their diets require almost constant foraging for food in more dangerous open grasslands.

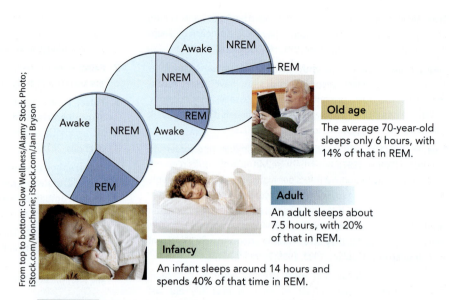

From top to bottom: Glow Wellness/Alamy Stock Photo; iStock.com/Moncherie; iStock.com/Jani Bryson

Old age
The average 70-year-old sleeps only 6 hours, with 14% of that in REM.

Adult
An adult sleeps about 7.5 hours, with 20% of that in REM.

Infancy
An infant sleeps around 14 hours and spends 40% of that time in REM.

FIGURE 5.5 **Aging and the sleep cycle** Our biological need for sleep changes throughout our life span. The pie charts in this figure show the relative amounts of REM sleep, NREM sleep, and awake time the average person experiences as an infant, an adult, and an older adult.

Three Dream Theories

Now let's look at three theories of why we dream—and whether dreams carry special meaning or information.

One of the oldest and most scientifically controversial explanations for why we dream is Freud's **wish-fulfillment view of dreams**. Freud proposed that unacceptable desires, which are reportedly normally repressed, rise to the surface of consciousness during dreaming. We avoid anxiety, Freud believed, by disguising our forbidden unconscious needs (what Freud called the dream's **latent content**) as symbols (**manifest content**). A journey supposedly symbolizes death; horseback riding and dancing could symbolize sexual intercourse; and a gun might represent a penis.

Most modern scientific research does not support Freud's view (Domhoff, 2003, 2010; Sándor et al., 2014). Critics also say that Freud's theory is highly subjective and that the symbols can be interpreted according to the particular analyst's view or training.

In contrast to Freud's theory, a biological view called the **activation–synthesis theory of dreams** suggests that dreams are a by-product of random, spontaneous stimulation of brain cells during sleep, which the brain combines (synthesizes) into coherent patterns known as dreams (Hobson, 1999, 2005; Wamsley & Stickgold, 2010). Alan Hobson and Robert McCarley (1977) proposed that specific neurons in the brain stem fire spontaneously during REM sleep and that the cortex struggles to "synthesize," or make sense of, this random stimulation by manufacturing dreams. This is *not* to say that dreams are totally meaningless. Hobson suggests that even if our dreams begin with essentially random brain activity, our individual personalities, motivations, memories, and life experiences guide how our brains construct the dream.

Have you ever dreamed that you were trying to run away from a frightening situation but found that you could not move? The activation-synthesis hypothesis might explain this dream as random stimulation of the amygdala. As you may recall from Chapter 2, the amygdala is a specific brain area linked to strong emotions, especially fear. If your amygdala is randomly stimulated and you feel afraid, you may try to run. However, in this dream you can't move. This is due to the fact that your major muscles are temporarily paralyzed during REM sleep. Can you see how your brain might try to make sense out of this strange conflict by making up a dream about a fearful situation in which you were trapped in heavy sand or someone was holding onto your arms and legs?

Finally, other researchers support the **cognitive view of dreams**, which suggests that dreams are simply another type of information processing that helps us organize and interpret our everyday experiences. This view of dreaming is supported by research showing strong similarities between dream content and waking thoughts, fears, and concerns (Domhoff, 2003, 2010; Malinowski & Horton, 2014; Weinstein et al., 2018). Like most college students, you've probably experienced what

Wish-fulfillment view of dreams The Freudian belief that dreams provide an outlet for unacceptable desires.

Latent content According to Freud, a dream's unconscious, hidden meaning is disguised in symbols within the dream's manifest content (story line).

Manifest content In Freudian dream analysis, the "surface," or remembered, story line, which contains symbols that mask the dream's latent content (the true meaning).

Activation–synthesis theory of dreams The theory that dreams are a by-product of random, spontaneous stimulation of brain cells during sleep, which the brain combines (synthesizes) into coherent patterns, known as dreams.

Cognitive view of dreams The perspective that dreaming is a type of information processing that helps us organize and interpret our everyday experiences.

GCD Gender and Cultural Diversity

Dream Similarities and Variations

(APA Goal 2.5) Incorporate sociocultural factors in scientific inquiry

Are there differences in dream content between cultures or between men and women? Researchers have found both similarities and differences. Dreams about basic human needs and fears (like sex, aggression, and death) seem to be found in all cultures, and children around the world frequently dream about large, threatening monsters or wild animals. Interestingly, dreams in most cultures typically include more misfortune than good fortune, and the dreamer is more often the victim of aggression than the cause of it (Dale et al., 2016; Domhoff, 2003, 2010; Krippner, 2015).

    With regard to gender differences, research has found that men and women tend to share many of the common dream themes shown in **Table 5.1**. But women are more likely to report dreams about children, family members and other familiar people, household objects, and indoor events. In contrast, men tend to report dreams about strangers, violence, weapons, sexual activity, achievement, and outdoor events (Dale et al., 2016; Mathes et al., 2014; Mazandarani et al., 2013).

    As a scientific and critical thinker, can you see how attitudes toward "proper" male and female gender roles might have affected what the participants were willing to report? For instance, might a male hesitate to report dreaming about caring for children? Might a female think it was inappropriate for her to report dreaming about guns and violence? Interestingly, a study of World War II prisoners of war found that their dreams contained less sexuality and even less aggression than the male norms (Barrett et al., 2014).

TABLE 5.1   Top 10 Common Dream Themes

1. Being attacked or pursued
2. Falling
3. Sexual experiences
4. Being lost
5. Being paralyzed
6. Flying
7. Being naked in public
8. School, teachers, studying
9. Arriving too late
10. Death of a loved one or dead people as alive

Q Test Your Critical Thinking

1. Given that these 10 dream themes are found worldwide, what might be the evolutionary advantage of such dreams?
2. Imagine that someone marketed a drug that provided complete rest and recuperation with only 1 hour of sleep, however, it did stop you from dreaming. Would you take the drug? Why or why not?

Sources: Domhoff 2003, 2010; Weinstein et al., 2018.

are called "examination anxiety" dreams. You can't find your classroom, you're running out of time, your pen or pencil won't work, or you've completely forgotten a scheduled exam and show up totally unprepared. Sound familiar? Can you see how this type of dream fits best with the cognitive view of dreams? For more information on dreams, see the GCD **Gender and Cultural Diversity** feature.

Sleep–Wake Disorders

In any given year, an estimated 40 million Americans suffer from chronic sleep disorders, and another 30 million experience occasional sleep disorders serious enough to disrupt their daily activities (Larzelere & Campbell, 2016; Morin & Edinger, 2015; Ng et al., 2015).

    Judging by these statistics, and your own experiences, you probably won't be surprised to learn that almost everyone has difficulty sleeping at some point in his or her lifetime. The most common and serious of these disorders are summarized in **Table 5.2**.

TABLE 5.2   Sleep-Wake Disorders

Label	Characteristics
Insomnia	Persistent difficulty with falling or staying asleep, or waking up too early
Narcolepsy	Sudden, irresistible onset of sleep during waking hours, characterized by sudden sleep attacks while standing, talking, or even driving
Breathing-Related Sleep Disorder (Sleep apnea)	Repeated interruption of breathing during sleep, causing loud snoring or poor-quality sleep and excessive daytime sleepiness
Nightmare	Bad dream that significantly disrupts REM sleep
NREM Sleep Arousal Disorder (Sleep terror)	Abrupt awakening with feelings of panic that significantly disrupts NREM sleep

Insomnia A sleep disorder characterized by persistent problems in falling asleep, staying asleep, or awakening too early.

Insomnia

Although it's normal to have trouble sleeping before an exciting event, as many as 1 person in 10 may suffer from **insomnia**. Those who suffer from this disorder have persistent difficulty with falling or staying asleep, or waking up too early. Nearly everybody has insomnia at some time; a telltale sign is feeling poorly rested the next day (Morin et al., 2013; Williamson & Williamson, 2015). Most people with serious insomnia have other medical or psychological disorders as well (American Psychiatric Association, 2013; Ashworth et al., 2015; Primeau & O'Hara, 2015). As a college student, you'll be particularly interested to know that students who send a high number of text messages are more likely to experience symptoms of insomnia (Murdock, 2013). Why? Researchers believe that most students feel pressured to immediately respond to texts and may be awakened by alerts from incoming texts, which can reduce both sleep quality and quantity. On a related note, another study found that 10 to 30 percent of Americans experience long-term, *chronic* insomnia, compared to only 2 percent of hunter gatherers living in Africa and South America (Yetish et al., 2015). Could it be that our American culture, filled with smart phones, television, and a hectic pace of modern life, is interfering with our ability to get good-quality sleep?

S&P Scientific Thinking and Practical Application

Can sleeping pills help people sleep? To cope with insomnia, many people turn to non-prescription, over-the-counter sleeping pills, which may have more risks than benefits. Although prescription tranquilizers and barbiturates do help people sleep, they decrease Stage 3 and REM sleep, seriously affecting sleep quality. In the short term, limited use of drugs such as Ambien, Dalmane, Xanax, Halcion, and Lunesta may be helpful in treating sleep problems related to anxiety and acute, stressful situations. However, chronic users run the risk of psychological and physical drug dependence (Maisto et al., 2015; Mehra & Strohl, 2014; Taylor et al., 2016). In addition, a recent study of prescription sleeping pill users found that half of the participants slept through a fire alarm, which clearly shows that the use of sleeping pills impairs the ability to wake up in response to danger signals (Iwakawa et al., 2019).

Given that prescription sleeping pills may have serious side effects, it's important to note that there are healthier alternatives, such as removing all electronic devices from your bedroom. Research shows that watching television or using electronic devices, like your computer, iPad, eReader, or phone, around bedtime makes it much harder to get to sleep (Chang et al., 2015; van der Lely et al., 2015). Why? Exposure to the light from the screens on these devices disrupts the circadian rhythm and reduces the level of melatonin in the body by about 22 percent, which leads to shorter and worse sleep patterns (Helm & Spencer, 2019; Nicholls, 2018). Interestingly, rather than taking prescription or over-the-counter sleep aids, the hormone *melatonin* may provide a safer alternative. Some research suggests that taking even a relatively small dose (just .3 to .4 milligrams) can help people fall asleep and stay asleep (Hajak et al., 2015; Paul et al., 2015).

See the **Test Yourself** for additional recommendations about getting to sleep and staying asleep.

PA Practical Application

Test Yourself: Natural Sleep Aids

The Internet is filled with common remedies and advice for sleep problems, like counting sheep or imagining peaceful scenes, such as waterfalls (see cartoon). If you'd like more scientific and research-based sleep hygiene tips and behaviors that will provide consistent benefits that you can easily apply. For example, when you're having a hard time going to sleep, don't keep checking the clock and worrying about your loss of sleep. In addition, remove all TVs, stereos, and books from your bedroom, and limit it to sleep rather than reading, watching movies, checking e-mail, and the like. If you need additional help, try some of the following suggestions.

Joe Benintende/Cartoon Stock

During the Day

- **Exercise.** Daily physical activity works away tension. But don't exercise vigorously late in the day, or you'll get fired up instead.
- **Keep regular hours.** An erratic schedule can disrupt biological rhythms. Get up at the same time each day.

- **Avoid stimulants.** Coffee, tea, soft drinks, chocolate, and some medications contain caffeine. Nicotine may be an even more potent sleep disrupter.
- **Avoid late meals and heavy drinking.** Overindulgence can interfere with your normal sleep pattern.
- **Stop worrying.** Focus on your problems at a set time earlier in the day.
- **Use presleep rituals.** Follow the same routine every evening: listen to music, write in a diary, meditate.
- **Practice yoga.** These gentle exercises help you relax.

In Bed

- **Use progressive muscle relaxation.** Alternately tense and relax various muscle groups.
- **Use fantasies.** Imagine yourself in a tranquil setting. Feel yourself relax.
- **Use deep breathing.** Take deep breaths, telling yourself you're falling asleep.
- **Try a warm bath.** This can induce drowsiness because it sends blood away from the brain to the skin surface.

Narcolepsy

Have you seen the TV ads showing people falling asleep in movies and even while driving a car? The ads are highlighting the previously little known sleep disorder called **narcolepsy**. This disorder, characterized by uncontrollable sleep attacks, afflicts about 1 person in 2,000 and generally runs in families (Ivanenko & Johnson, 2016; Kotagal & Kumar, 2013; Williamson & Williamson, 2015). During an attack, REM-like sleep suddenly intrudes into the waking state of consciousness. Victims may experience sudden, incapacitating attacks of muscle weakness or paralysis (known as cataplexy). They may even fall asleep while walking, talking, or driving a car. Although long naps each day and stimulant or antidepressant drugs can help reduce the frequency of attacks, both the causes and cure of narcolepsy are still unknown (**Figure 5.6**).

Sleep Apnea

Perhaps the most serious sleep disorder is **sleep apnea**. People with sleep apnea may fail to breathe for a minute or longer and then wake up gasping for breath. When they do breathe during their sleep, they often snore. Sleep apnea seems to result from blocked upper airway passages or the brain's failure to send signals to the diaphragm, causing breathing to stop.

Unfortunately, people with sleep apnea are often unaware they have this disorder, and fail to understand how their repeated awakening during the night leaves them feeling tired and sleepy during the day. More importantly, they should know that sleep apnea is linked with high blood pressure, strokes, cancer, depression, and heart attacks (Kendzerska et al., 2014; Larzelere & Campbell, 2016; Pataka et al., 2019).

Treatment for sleep apnea depends partly on its severity. If the problem occurs only when you're sleeping on your back, sewing tennis balls to the back of your pajama top may help remind you to sleep on your side. Because obstruction of the breathing passages is related to obesity and heavy alcohol use (X. Tan et al., 2015; Yamaguchi et al., 2014), dieting and alcohol restriction are often recommended. For other sleepers, surgery, dental appliances that reposition the tongue, or CPAP machines that provide a stream of air to keep the airway open may provide help.

Research suggests that even "simple" snoring (without the breathing stoppage characteristic of sleep apnea) is associated with heart disease and possible death (Deeb et al., 2014; Jones & Benca, 2013). Although occasional mild snoring is fairly normal, chronic snoring is a possible warning sign that should prompt people to seek medical attention.

Nightmares and Night Terrors

Two additional sleep disturbances are nightmares and night terrors. **Nightmares** are anxiety-arousing dreams that occur near the end of the sleep cycle and during REM sleep. In contrast, **sleep terrors** involve abrupt awakenings from NREM sleep (**Figure 5.7**). *Sleepwalking*, which sometimes accompanies sleep terrors, usually occurs during NREM sleep. (Recall that large muscles are paralyzed during REM sleep, which explains why sleepwalking normally occurs

Narcolepsy A sleep disorder characterized by uncontrollable sleep attacks. (*Narco* means "numbness," and *lepsy* means "seizure.")

Sleep apnea A sleep disorder of the upper respiratory system resulting from a repeated interruption of breathing during sleep; it also leads to loud snoring, poor-quality sleep, and excessive daytime sleepiness.

Nightmares The anxiety-arousing dreams that generally occur near the end of the sleep cycle, during REM sleep.

Sleep terrors The abrupt awakenings from NREM (non-rapid-eye-movement) sleep accompanied by intense physiological arousal and feelings of panic.

Juniors/SuperStock

FIGURE 5.6 **Narcolepsy in action** Research on specially bred narcoleptic dogs has found degenerated neurons in certain areas of the brain (J. M. Siegel, 2000). Whether human narcolepsy results from similar degeneration is a question for future research. Note how this hungry puppy has lapsed suddenly from alert wakefulness to deep sleep even when offered his preferred food.

ekramar/123RF

FIGURE 5.7 **Nightmare or sleep terror?** Nightmares, or bad dreams, occur toward the end of the sleep cycle, during REM sleep. Less common but more disturbing are sleep terrors, which occur late in the cycle, during Stage 3 of NREM sleep. Like the child in this photo, the sleeper may sit bolt upright, screaming and sweating. They also may walk around, and talk incoherently and be almost impossible to awaken.

during NREM sleep.) An estimated 4 percent of U.S. adults—meaning over 8 million people—have at least one episode of sleepwalking each year (Ohayon et al., 2012). *Sleeptalking* can occur during any stage of sleep, but it appears to arise most commonly during NREM sleep. It can consist of single, indistinct words or long, articulate sentences. It is even possible to engage some sleep talkers in a limited conversation.

Nightmares, sleep terrors, sleepwalking, and sleep talking are all more common among young children, but they can also occur in adults, usually during times of stress or major life events (Carter et al., 2014; Ivanenko & Johnson, 2016). Patience and soothing reassurance at the time of the sleep disruption are usually the only treatment recommended for both children and adults. However, some people, such as those with *posttraumatic stress disorder (PTSD)*, suffer from such disabling and frightening nightmares that they may have suicidal thoughts or attempts, which generally requires professional intervention (Littlewood et al., 2016). See Chapters 3 and 14.

Before going on, you're probably wondering about sexsomnia, commonly known as "sleep sex," in which an individual engages in sexual acts while in NREM sleep (Contreras et al., 2019; Dubessy et al., 2017; Schenck, 2019). Unlike sexual dreams that normally do not include physical actions (aside from arousal and possible ejaculation), sexsomnia typically involves masturbation, fondling, and attempts or actual occurrences of sexual intimacy with others followed by morning amnesia. Given that NREM occurs randomly during the night, it's very difficult to study scientifically (e.g., Mioč et al., 2018).

Retrieval Practice 5.2 | Understanding Sleep and Dreams

Self-Test Completing this self-test, and then checking your answers by clicking on the answer button or by looking in Appendix B, will provide immediate feedback and helpful practice for exams.

1. The circadian rhythm is _____ .

   a. patterns that repeat themselves on a twice-daily schedule

   b. physical and mental changes associated with the cycle of the moon

   c. circulating sleep processes in your brain

   d. the biological clock governing activities that occur on a 24- to 25-hour cycle

2. The sleep stage marked by irregular breathing, eye movements, high-frequency brain waves, and dreaming is called _____ sleep.

   a. beta   **c.** REM

   b. hypnologic   **d.** transitional

3. The _____ theory says that sleep allows us to replenish what was depleted during daytime activities.

   a. repair/restoration   **c.** supply-demand

   b. evolutionary/circadian   **d.** conservation of energy

4. The _____ theory suggests dreams are by-products of random stimulation of brain cells.

   a. activation-synthesis   **c.** wish fulfillment

   b. manifest-content   **d.** information processing

5. A sleep disorder characterized by uncontrollable sleep attacks is known as _____ .

   a. dyssomnia   **c.** narcolepsy

   b. parasomnia   **d.** sleep apnea

Q Test Your Critical Thinking

1. How are you affected by sleep deprivation and disruption of your circadian rhythms?

2. Which of the major theories of dreaming best explains your own dreams?

Real World Application Question

[AQ3] Will sleeping in on the weekends make up for sleep deprivation during the week?

AfricaImages/iStock/Getty Images

Hint: Look in the text for **[AQ3]**

Psychoactive Drugs

LEARNING OBJECTIVES

Retrieval Practice   While reading the upcoming sections, respond to each Learning Objective in your own words.

Summarize the major issues and concepts associated with psychoactive drugs.

- **Identify** psychoactive drugs and the key terms associated with them.

- **Explain** how agonist and antagonist drugs produce their psychoactive effects.

- **Discuss** the four major categories of psychoactive drugs.

- **Review** the problems with club drugs.

Real World Application Questions

[AQ4] Does Facebook deliberately try to create addiction?

[AQ5] Can using marijuana decrease your IQ?

Virtually everyone routinely experiences the altered states of consciousness found in sleep and dreams. The vast majority of us also use *psychoactive drugs* (legal and illegal) to alter our moods, memory, concentration, and perception on a regular daily basis. As a busy college student, do you start your day with a routine cup of coffee (see **Figure 5.8**)? How about that glass of wine or beer used to relax at a party? If you're like most people, you manage to use these substances in moderation and without creating problems in your life. Therefore, you may be wondering why we're including these common drinks as "drug use." If so, you'll be particularly interested in the next section.

Understanding Psychoactive Drugs

> I don't do drugs, my dreams are frightening enough.
> —M. C. Escher (Dutch Graphic Artist)

In our society, where the most popular **psychoactive drugs** are caffeine, tobacco, and ethyl alcohol, people often become defensive when these drugs are grouped with illicit drugs such as marijuana and cocaine. Similarly, marijuana users are disturbed that their drug of choice is grouped with "hard" drugs like heroin. Most scientists believe that there are good and bad uses of almost all drugs. The way drug use differs from drug abuse and how chemical alterations in consciousness affect a person, psychologically and physically, are important topics in psychology.

Alcohol, for example, has a diffuse effect on neural membranes throughout the nervous system. Most psychoactive drugs, however, act in a more specific way: by enhancing or reducing a particular neurotransmitter's effect. As you may recall from Chapter 2, an *agonist* is a molecule that binds to a receptor and mimics or enhances of a neurotransmitter. In contrast, an *antagonist* also binds to a receptor, but it blocks the neurotransmitter's effect. Similarly, in the case of psychoactive drugs and neurotransmitters, an **agonist drug** binds to a receptor and mimics or enhances the effects, whereas an **antagonist drug** blocks them (**Process Diagram 5.1**). Examples of agonist drugs are heroin and oxycodone, whereas naloxone is an example of an antagonist drug that is sometimes used to reverse a heroin overdose.

PeopleImages/E+/Getty Images

FIGURE 5.8   **Surprising benefits of caffeine**   As a college student, you're probably well aware of the many benefits of coffee—particularly its wonderful taste and stimulating effects. But did you know one study found that older women who drink more than an average amount of coffee are less likely to develop dementia or cognitive impairment (Driscoll et al., 2016)? Furthermore, another study found that participants who drank coffee before an assigned discussion of a controversial political topic rated themselves and their co-discussants more positively than did those who drank the coffee afterwards (Unnava et al., 2018). Are you wondering why we're offering this positive research on caffeine? We're hoping to offset the stereotypes of a "drug user" and the upcoming research on all psychoactive drugs, which is primarily negative. We want to remind you that there are both good and bad uses of most drugs.

Psychoactive drug   A chemical that changes mental processes, such as conscious awareness, mood, and perception.

Agonist drug   A substance that binds to a receptor and mimics or enhances a neurotransmitter's effect.

Antagonist drug   A substance that binds to a receptor and blocks a neurotransmitter's effect.

STOP!   This Process Diagram contains essential information NOT found elsewhere in the text, which is likely to appear on quizzes and exams. Be sure to study it CAREFULLY.

PROCESS DIAGRAM 5.1   **Agonist and Antagonist Drugs and Their Psychoactive Effects**   Most psychoactive drugs produce their mood, energy, and perception-altering effects by changing the body's supply of neurotransmitters. Note how they can alter the synthesis, storage, or release of neurotransmitters: (1). They also can change the neurotransmitters' effects on the receiving site of the receptor neuron; (2). After neurotransmitters carry their messages across the synapse, the sending neuron normally deactivates the excess, or leftover, neurotransmitter; (3). However, when agonist drugs block this process, excess neurotransmitters remain in the synapse, which prolongs the effect of the psychoactive drug.

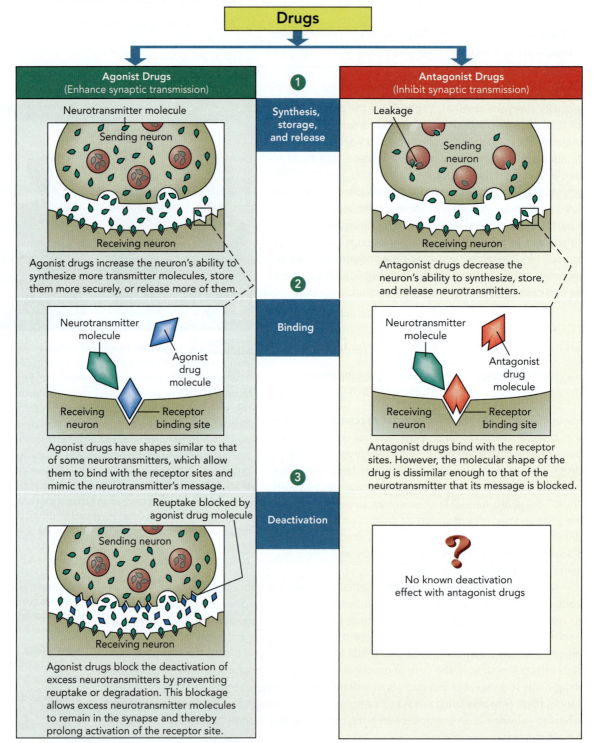

Abuse versus Addiction   How does drug abuse differ from drug addiction? The term **drug abuse** generally refers to drug taking that leads to emotional or physical harm to oneself or others. Drug consumption among abusers is typically compulsive, frequent, and intense. **Addiction** is a broad term that refers to a condition in which a person feels compelled to use a specific drug, or engage in almost any type of compulsive activity, from working to surfing the Internet (Maisto et al., 2019; Sdrulla et al., 2015). In fact, the latest version of the *Diagnostic and Statistical Manual (DSM-5)*, which officially classifies mental disorders, now includes *gambling disorders* as part of their substance-related and addictive disorders category (American Psychiatric Association, 2013). But other disorders, like "sex addiction" or "exercise addiction," were not included due to insufficient evidence at this time.

Evidence shows that we can even become addicted to social media. In addition to the self-reported "fear of missing out" (FOMO), researchers have found that using social media can create a high that's indistinguishable from that experienced during risky trading in the financial markets or with drug addiction (Buglass et al., 2017; Hong & Chiu, 2016; Suissa, 2015).

[AQ4]   Have you heard that Facebook (see photo) deliberately attempts to addict its users? In this case the rumor is true. Facebook personnel have created programs that systematically withhold the number of "likes" that appear on your postings. They then release them on a variable reward schedule of reinforcement (Chapter 6) in order to increase intermittent surging feelings of reward and the odds of addiction (Haynes, 2018; Newman, 2018). As one columnist put it: "All social media is addictive by design. Maximizing engagement is in their business model" (Wågström, 2018).

Drug abuse A type of drug taking that leads to emotional or physical harm to the drug user or others.

Addiction A broad term that describes a condition in which the body requires a drug (or specific activity) in order to function without physical and psychological reactions to its absence; it is often the outcome of tolerance and dependence.

Nikada/iStock Unreleased/Getty Images

Psychological Dependence versus Physical Dependence   In addition to distinguishing between drug abuse and addiction, many researchers use the term **psychological dependence** to refer to the mental desire or craving to achieve a drug's effects. In contrast, **physical dependence** describes changes in bodily processes that make a drug necessary for minimum daily functioning. Physical dependence appears most clearly when the drug is withheld and the user undergoes **withdrawal** reactions, including physical pain and intense cravings.

Keep in mind that psychological dependence may be as damaging as physical dependence. The craving in psychological dependence can be strong enough to keep the user in a constant drug-induced state—and to lure an addict back to a drug habit long after he or she has overcome physical dependence. After repeated use of a drug, many of the body's physiological processes adjust to higher and higher levels of the drug, producing a decreased sensitivity called **tolerance**.

Tolerance leads many users to escalate their drug use and experiment with other drugs in an attempt to re-create the original pleasurable altered state. Sometimes using one drug increases tolerance for another, a result known as *cross-tolerance*. Developing tolerance or cross-tolerance, however, does not prevent drugs from seriously damaging the brain, heart, liver, and other organs.

Finally, note that some psychoactive drugs may induce symptoms of psychosis, which involves varying degrees of loss of contact with reality (see Chapter 13). Individuals who abuse high doses of amphetamines for an extended period of time may develop *amphetamine psychosis* and compulsively pick at their skin, believing bugs are burrowing beneath the outer layer. In addition to this type of *hallucination* (a false, imaginary sensory perception), some individuals may become paranoid and extremely afraid of others, even those they've known for a long time. You can clearly see that someone who is experiencing these types of *delusions* (false, imaginary beliefs) or hallucinations is out of touch with reality and possibly extremely dangerous. Therefore, be very careful not to upset or antagonize such a person. The best way to help is to call 911. For more on how psychoactive drugs, and in particular, addiction, could affect your own life, see the **PAH** **Practical Application Highlight**.

Psychological dependence The psychological desire or craving to achieve a drug's effect.

Physical dependence The changes in bodily processes that make a drug necessary for minimal functioning.

Withdrawal The discomfort and distress, including physical pain and intense cravings, experienced after stopping the use of an addictive drug.

Tolerance The bodily adjustment to continued use of a drug in which the drug user requires greater dosages to achieve the same effect.

> **PAH** Practical Application Highlight
>
> ### Hidden Costs of Addiction
>
> **(APA Goal 1.3) Describe applications of psychology**
>
> As previously noted, addiction is a broad term referring to a compulsive craving for a substance, thing, or activity despite harmful consequences. Sadly, for both the addict and those who love him or her, it's most often heartbreaking. In this section, we will examine the serious negative effects addiction can have on your academic and job success in at least five major areas:
>
> - **Time management**   Virtually all compulsive behaviors are "time gobblers." If you notice that your GPA is lower than you expected or that you're not advancing in your career, check out how much time you're spending on your various hobbies/addictions. Many college students and employees feel unreasonably compelled to check and use social media throughout the day and even late at night—the so-called "fear of missing out" (FOMO).
> - **Quality and quantity of sleep**   Heavy TV viewing, alcohol and other drug use, gambling, or pursuit of any other addiction can slowly disrupt or destroy your career and academic life by leading to sleep deprivation. As described earlier, lack of sleep is associated with numerous problems, including reduced cognitive and motor performance, which in turn affects your quality of work, productivity, and overall safety (e.g., McAlpine et al., 2019; Ratcliff & Van Dongen, 2018). The lack of attention and concentration and slower reaction time associated with sleep deprivation also lead to many work-related injuries, accidents, and economic losses (Bougard et al., 2016; Tefft, 2018).
> - **Interpersonal relationships**   Due to the time-gobbling effect and the sleep losses associated with addictions, you may find it difficult to maintain successful social relationships with your family, classmates, coworkers, or employers.
> - **Impression management**   Having a criminal record of illegal drug abuse or DUIs will obviously negatively affect potential employers' perceptions of you. What you may not know is that many employers commonly use Facebook and other social media sites to recruit, evaluate, and potentially fire employees (e.g., Baert, 2018; Cappelli, 2019). The safest rule is to never post anything you don't want your current or future bosses to see.
> - **Overall performance**   Aside from caffeine, most psychoactive drug use is associated with inconsistent work quality, increased absenteeism, lessened concentration, and lack of focus, all of which have a negative effect on overall academic and professional achievement.

Take-Home Message   Successful students and employees have discovered that they need to prioritize their studies and work in order to achieve. Each of us is allotted only 24 hours each day, and how we choose to spend this time is critical to our long-term success. What is more important to you—your addictions or your academic and professional life? If you need help, talk with your psychology instructor, college counselor, or other professionals.

Four Drug Categories

Psychologists generally divide psychoactive drugs into four broad categories: *depressants, stimulants, opiates/opioids,* and *hallucinogens* (**Table 5.3**).

Depressant   A drug that decreases bodily processes and overall responsiveness.

Depressants   The group of drugs known as **depressants**, sometimes called "downers," act on the central nervous system to suppress or slow bodily processes and reduce overall responsiveness. Due to the fact that tolerance and both physical and psychological dependence are rapidly acquired with these drugs, there is strong potential for abuse.

Given alcohol's reputation as a popular "party drug," you may be surprised to see it listed as a depressant in Table 5.3. This positive view is understandable if you're considering only low doses and the column of "desired effects"—reduced stress, social anxiety, etc. However, as consumption increases, the potential for undesirable and potentially fatal effects also increases. It's important to note that reactions to alcohol are determined primarily by the amount that reaches the brain (**Table 5.4**).

TABLE 5.3   Effects of the Major Psychoactive Drugs

	Category	Desired Effects	Undesirable Effects
RICHARD NOWITZ/ National Geographic Image Collection	**Depressants (sedatives)** Alcohol, barbiturates, anxiolytics (antianxiety or tranquilizing drugs), alprazolam (Xanax), flunitrazepam (Rohypnol, "date-rape drug," "roofies"), ketamine (special K), gamma-hydroxybutyrate (GHB)	Reduced social anxiety, self-consciousness, stress, and depression, increased confidence, happiness, carefree feelings, and disinhibition	Impaired cognition, perception (especially vision and hearing), reflexes, and motor functioning, increased blood pressure and heart rate, nausea, vomiting, disorientation, shallow or irregular breathing, mood swings, amnesia, loss of consciousness, shallow respiration, convulsions, coma, death
TAYLOR S. KENNEDY/ National Geographic Image Collection	**Stimulants** Cocaine, amphetamine, ("crystal meth," "speed"), 3,4-methylenedioxymethamphetamine (MDMA, ecstasy, "molly")	Exhilaration, euphoria, high physical and mental energy, reduced appetite, perceptions of power, sociability	Irritability, anxiety, sleeplessness, paranoia, hallucinations, psychosis, elevated blood pressure and body temperature, convulsions, death
SAM ABELL/ National Geographic Image Collection	Caffeine	Increased alertness	Insomnia, restlessness, increased pulse rate, mild delirium, ringing in the ears, rapid heartbeat
	Nicotine	Relaxation, increased alertness, sociability	Irritability, increased blood pressure, stomach pains, vomiting, dizziness, cancer, heart disease, emphysema
TIERBILD OKAPIA KG/ Science Source	**Opiates/opioids (narcotics)** Morphine, heroin ("H," "smack," "horse"), codeine, oxycodone	Euphoria, "rush" of pleasure, pain relief, prevention of withdrawal, sleep	Nausea, vomiting, constipation, painful withdrawal, shallow respiration, convulsions, coma, death
JOEL SARTORE/ National Geographic Image Collection	**Hallucinogens (psychedelics)** Lysergic acid diethylamide (LSD), mescaline (extract from the peyote cactus), psilocybin (extract from mushrooms)	Heightened aesthetic responses, euphoria, mild delusions, hallucinations, distorted perceptions and sensation	Panic, nausea, longer and more extreme delusions, hallucinations, perceptual distortions ("bad trips"), psychosis
	Marijuana	Relaxation, mild euphoria, nausea relief	Perceptual and sensory distortions, hallucinations, fatigue, increased appetite, lack of motivation, paranoia, possible psychosis

TABLE 5.4   Alcohol's Effect on the Body and Behavior

Number of Drinks[a] in 2 Hours	Blood Alcohol Content (%)[b]	Effect
(2)	0.02 to 0.05	Relaxed state, increased sociability, impaired judgment, lowered willpower
(3)	0.05 to 0.10	Increased confidence and feelings of euphoria, but balance, coordination, speech, vision, and hearing somewhat impaired
(4)	0.10 to 0.15	Distinct impairment of mental faculties (judgment, concentration, reasoning, memory), slurred speech, poor coordination, and delayed reaction time
(7)	0.15 to 0.20	Obvious intoxication, bloodshot eyes, and major loss of balance and coordination, along with major impairment of mental faculties
(12)	0.20 to 0.40	Difficult to wake up, severe intoxication, minimal control of mind and body, unconsciousness
(15)	0.40 to 0.50	High possibility of coma and death at the upper limit of 0.40 to 0.50

[a]A drink refers to one 12-ounce beer, a 4-ounce glass of wine, or a 1.25-ounce shot of hard liquor.
[b]In the U.S., the legal blood alcohol level for "drunk driving" varies from 0.05 to 0.12.

AP Images/Eric Risberg

FIGURE 5.9 **Alcohol and rape** In January 2016, 20-year-old Brock Turner was caught in the act and later convicted of sexually assaulting an unconscious woman he had met earlier at a fraternity party. It was estimated that at the time of the assault, Turner's blood alcohol concentration was 0.17 and the victim's level was 0.24. Turner was found guilty of *assault with intent to rape an intoxicated victim* but only served 3 months in jail. Turner was also required to register as a sex offender and later expelled from Stanford University.

Q Test Your Critical Thinking

1. As you can see in the photo, numerous protests erupted following the judge's sentencing of Brock Turner to six months. Many believed that such a short jail term was inappropriate in light of his crime. What do you think?

2. Given alcohol's widely accepted social role in many college functions, what could we do to decrease its link with sexual assault?

Given that the liver breaks down alcohol at the rate of about 1 ounce per hour, the number of drinks and the speed of consumption are both very important. People can die after drinking large amounts of alcohol in a short period of time. In addition, men's bodies are more efficient than women's at breaking down alcohol. Even after accounting for differences in weight and muscle-to-fat ratio, women have a higher blood alcohol level than men after consuming equal doses of alcohol.

One of the most common, but seldom mentioned, risks with alcohol is that college students are more likely to have unprotected sex on days they binge drink, which may lead to serious problems such as STIs and unplanned pregnancies (Kerr et al., 2015). Sadly, overuse of alcohol and binge drinking are also linked with major sexual crimes (**Figure 5.9**).

Keep in mind that alcohol can also be very dangerous when combined with certain other drugs. For example, combining alcohol and barbiturates—both depressants—can relax the diaphragm muscles to such a degree that the person suffocates (Marczinski, 2014). Does this information surprise you? Take the quiz in the **Test Yourself** to discover if some of your other ideas about alcohol are really misconceptions.

PA Practical Application

Test Yourself: What's Your Alcohol IQ?

True or False?

_____ 1. Alcohol increases sexual desire.

_____ 2. Alcohol helps you sleep.

_____ 3. Alcohol kills brain cells.

_____ 4. It's easier to get drunk at high altitudes.

_____ 5. Switching among different types of alcohol is more likely to lead to drunkenness.

_____ 6. Drinking coffee and taking a cold shower are great ways to sober up after heavy drinking.

_____ 7. Alcohol warms the body.

_____ 8. You can't become an alcoholic if you drink only beer.

_____ 9. Alcohol's primary effect is as a stimulant.

_____ 10. People experience impaired judgment after drinking only if they show obvious signs of intoxication.

Answers: All these statements are false. Detailed answers are provided in this chapter and in Lilienfeld et al., 2010.

Given all the negative information and warnings we've just presented about the dangers of alcohol, we want to end this section with a small bit of "good news." See the **RC Research Challenge**.

Stimulant A drug that increases overall activity and general responsiveness.

Stimulants Whereas depressants suppress central nervous system activity, **stimulants,** or "uppers," increase the overall activity and responsiveness of the central nervous system. Like depressants, stimulants also have the potential for abuse.

RC   Scientific Thinking: **Research Challenge**

Can Alcohol Improve Your Foreign Language Skills?

(APA Goal 2.4) Interpret, design, and conduct basic psychological research

Have you heard the phrase "Dutch courage"—meaning increased confidence gained by drinking alcohol? How can that be, given that alcohol slurs speech and impairs cognition, including the ability to remember and pay attention? This apparent contradiction was tested when researchers randomly assigned native German speakers who had recently learned a new language (Dutch) to drink either a beverage containing a low level of alcohol or a control beverage with no alcohol (Renner et al., 2018). All participants then chatted for a few minutes in Dutch with an experimenter. These conversations were audiotaped and then rated by two native Dutch speakers, who assessed the participants' foreign language skills. Participants also rated their own Dutch language skills during the conversation.

Can you predict the findings? Individuals who had consumed alcohol were rated by the native speakers as having significantly better language fluency, and specifically better pronunciation, than those who had not consumed alcohol. Unexpectedly, alcohol consumption did not influence participants' self-ratings of their Dutch language skills. Keep in mind that the participants in this study consumed only a small amount of alcohol. As the researchers themselves pointed out, consumption of higher amounts of alcohol might not have had such beneficial effects on foreign language pronunciation.

Izabela Habur/E+/Getty Images

2. If you chose:

- *descriptive research*, is this a naturalistic or laboratory observation, survey/interview, case study, and/or archival research?
- *correlational research*, is this a positive, negative, or zero correlation?
- *experimental research*, label the IV, DV, experimental group(s), and control group. (Note: If participants were not randomly assigned to groups, list the design as *quasi-experimental*.)
- both *descriptive* and *correlational*, answer the corresponding questions for both.

Check your answers by clicking on the answer button or by looking in Appendix B.

Note: The information provided in this study is admittedly limited, but the level of detail is similar to what is presented in most textbooks and public reports of research findings. Answering these questions, and then comparing your answers to those provided, will help you become a better scientific and critical thinker and consumer of scientific research.

Identify the Research Method

1. Based on the information provided, did this study (Renner et al., 2018) use descriptive, correlational, and/or experimental research?

Cocaine is a powerful central nervous system stimulant extracted from the leaves of the coca plant. It produces feelings of alertness, euphoria, well-being, power, energy, and pleasure. But it also acts as an *agonist drug*, blocking the reuptake of our body's natural neurotransmitters that produce these same effects. As you can see in **Figure 5.10**, cocaine's ability to block reuptake allows neurotransmitters to stay in the synapse longer than normal—thereby artificially prolonging the effects and depleting the user's natural supply of such neurotransmitters.

FIGURE 5.10   **Cocaine: an agonist drug in action**

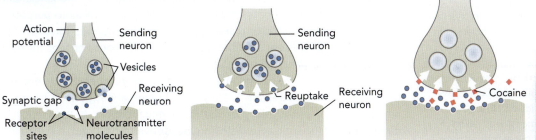

Todd Gipstein/National Geographic Image Collection

a. Normal neurotransmitter reuptake   The two figures above depict how after releasing neurotransmitter into the synapse, the sending neuron normally reabsorbs (or reuptakes) excess neurotransmitters back into the vesicles, called terminal buttons.

b. Cocaine blocks normal neurotransmitter uptake   This figure shows that when cocaine is present in the synapse, it will block the reuptake of dopamine, serotonin, and norepinephrine, and levels of these substances will increase. The result is overstimulation and a brief euphoric high. When the drug wears off, the depletion of the normally reabsorbed neurotransmitters may cause the drug user to "crash."

Although cocaine was once considered a relatively harmless "recreational drug," even small initial doses can be fatal. It interferes with the electrical system of the heart, causing irregular heartbeats and, in some cases, heart attacks, hypertension, and strokes by temporarily constricting blood vessels (e.g., Kim & Park, 2019). The most dangerous form of cocaine is the smokable, concentrated version known as "crack," or "rock." Its lower price makes it affordable and attractive to a large audience. Its greater potency also makes it more highly addictive.

Even legal stimulants can lead to serious problems. Cigarette smoking, for example, is considered to be among the most preventable causes of death and disease in the United States, and the second leading cause of death worldwide (Fast Facts, 2019; Goodchild et al., 2018). Chewing tobacco and vaping from electronic cigarettes that heat a nicotine-containing liquid, as well as the "heat-not-burn" (IQOS) devices that directly heat the tobacco itself, are also extremely dangerous, and may be no less toxic to bodily cells than ordinary cigarette smoke (Glantz, 2019; Shukla et al., 2019; Sohal et al., 2019). Sadly, in 2014 fans mourned the loss of Hall of Fame baseball player Tony Gwynn, who died of mouth cancer, which he attributed to his lifelong use of chewing tobacco. Gwynn's family later filed a wrongful-death lawsuit against the tobacco industry on the grounds of negligence, fraud, and product liability (Kepner, 2016).

Given these well-known health hazards and the growing stigma against tobacco users, why do people ever start using tobacco? One of the most compelling reasons is that nicotine is highly addictive and it offers significant cognitive rewards (Castaldelli-Maia et al., 2016; Herman et al., 2014; X. Li et al., 2014). In fact, nicotine's effects—relaxation, increased alertness, and diminished pain and appetite—are so powerfully reinforcing that some people continue to smoke even after having a cancerous lung removed.

Opiate/opioid A drug derived from opium that numbs the senses and relieves pain.

Hallucinogen A drug that produces sensory or perceptual distortions.

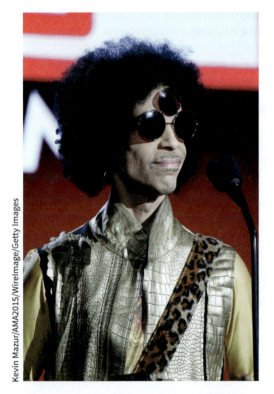

Kevin Mazur/AMA2015/WireImage/Getty Images

The high cost of drug abuse Even 3 years after the death of musician Prince, he is still remembered and celebrated for the massive impact he made on music and the wider culture (Waite, 2019). Music fans around the world were shocked when Prince died at the age of 57—reportedly due to an opioid overdose and possible addiction to painkillers (Eldred & Eligon, 2016; Eligon et al., 2016). Prince earned the reputation of being a clean-living musician, but he suffered chronic pain from a hip surgery. His death was supposedly from a counterfeit drug containing fentanyl, a synthetic opioid, which is estimated to be up to a hundred times stronger than morphine. The opioid epidemic has been recently called the worst drug crisis in American history (NIDA, 2019; Piana, 2019).

Opiates/Opioids

The drugs found within our third category, **opiates/opioids**, or narcotics, are given this name because they're derived from the opium poppy. Given that these drugs depress the central nervous system (CNS), they're generally classified as depressants. However, they also excite areas of the CNS. In addition, they're sometimes used medically to relieve pain because they mimic the brain's natural endorphins (Chapter 2), which numb pain and elevate mood. This creates a dangerous pathway to drug abuse, however (see photo). After repeated flooding with opiates/opioids, the brain eventually reduces or blocks the production of its own natural, pain-reducing endorphins. If the user later attempts to stop, the brain lacks both the artificial and the normal level of painkilling chemicals, and withdrawal becomes excruciatingly painful (**Figure 5. 11**).

Hallucinogens

Our fourth category of drugs, **hallucinogens**, produce sensory or perceptual distortions, including visual, auditory, and kinesthetic hallucinations. Some cultures have used hallucinogens for religious purposes, as a way to experience "other realities" or to communicate with the supernatural. However, in Western societies, most people use hallucinogens for their reported "mind-expanding" potential.

Hallucinogens are commonly referred to as *psychedelics* (from the Greek for "mind manifesting"). They include mescaline (derived from the peyote cactus), psilocybin (derived from mushrooms), PCP (phencyclidine), and LSD (lysergic acid diethylamide, derived from ergot, a rye mold). LSD, or "acid," produces dramatic alterations in sensation and perception, including an altered sense of time, synesthesia (blending of the senses), and spiritual experiences. Perhaps because the LSD experience is so powerful, few people "drop acid" on a regular basis. Nevertheless, LSD can be an extremely dangerous drug. Bad LSD "trips" can be terrifying and may lead to accidents, deaths, or suicide. One 32-year-old man, with no known

FIGURE 5.11 **How opiates/opioids help create physical dependence** The U.S. is currently in the midst of an opioid epidemic (National Institute of Health (NIH) (2019). Psychoactive drugs such as opiates/opioids lead to addiction because they affect the brain and body in a variety of ways.

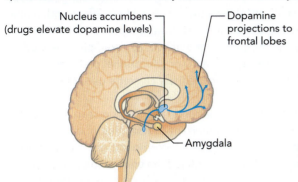

a. Our brain's reward system helps initiate and perpetuate addiction Most researchers believe that increased dopamine activity in this so-called *reward pathway* of the brain accounts for the reinforcing effects of most addictive drugs.

b. Strong withdrawal symptoms discourage attempts to stop drug use Absence of the drug triggers intense pain and cravings.

psychiatric disorder, intentionally removed his own testes after his first and single use of LSD combined with alcohol (Blacha et al., 2013).

Marijuana, also called cannabis, is generally classified as a hallucinogen even though it has some properties of a depressant—it induces drowsiness and lethargy—and some of a narcotic—it acts as a weak painkiller. The active ingredient in marijuana is THC, or tetrahydrocannabinol, which attaches to receptors that are abundant throughout the brain. In low doses, marijuana produces mild euphoria; moderate doses may lead to an intensification of sensory experiences and the illusion that time is passing slowly. High doses may produce hallucinations, paranoia, and distortions of body image (Maisto et al., 2019; Spindle et al., 2018). As expected, marijuana can be habit forming, although few users experience the intense cravings associated with cocaine or opiates/opioids. Withdrawal symptoms are generally mild because the drug dissolves in the body's fat and leaves the body very slowly, which also explains why a marijuana user can test positive for days or weeks after the last use.

Interestingly, research has found that the greater access to marijuana in the U.S., as a result of recent changes in its legal status, is linked to a reduced annual death from opioid use by 20 to 35 percent (Chan et al., 2019). Death reduction is always good news, but as you recall from Chapter 1, correlation doesn't necessarily mean causation. Can you think of other third variables that might also explain the reduction in opioid deaths?

Other encouraging research has found marijuana to be therapeutic in alleviating the nausea and vomiting associated with chemotherapy, and reducing chronic pain, insomnia, and other health problems, such as treatment-resistant epilepsies (Bachhuber et al., 2019; Freeman et al., 2019; Wilkie et al., 2016). In response to these potential medical benefits, and to free up police resources for fighting crime, many states have passed laws legalizing marijuana for medical and/or recreational use.

On the other hand, marijuana remains relatively controversial for a variety of reasons. For example, marijuana has been widely touted as a treatment for glaucoma (an eye disease) because it was found to lower pressure in the eye. However, a study found that the use of highly-concentrated CBD, the non-psychoactive ingredient in cannabis commonly marketed in oil, gummies, creams, and health food, in combination with THC blocked this effect (Miller et al., 2018). In addition, some researchers have reported several negative effects of marijuana, such as increased throat and respiratory disorders, impaired lung functioning and immune response, declines in testosterone levels, reduced sperm count, and disruption of the menstrual cycle and ovulation (e.g., Harley et al., 2016; Rajanahally et al., 2019; Spindle et al., 2018). Other research, however, has found higher sperm counts and testosterone among those who have smoked marijuana (Nassan et al., 2019).

JOEL SARTORE/National
Geographic Image Collection

[AQ5]   One area of particular concern to psychologists has to do with cognitive functioning. Some studies report that even moderate use of marijuana (see photo) may lead to decreases in IQ, educational achievement, and overall cognitive functioning (Cyr et al., 2019; deShazo et al., 2019; Suerken et al., 2016). However, studies of marijuana with human subjects are virtually all correlational, and as you recall from Chapter 1 this means that their results may be confounded by the *third-variable problem*. For example, one study of adolescents found marijuana was not associated with IQ or educational performance once adjustments were made for potential confounds, particularly cigarette use—the third variable (Mokrysz et al., 2016).

At this point, marijuana remains a controversial drug and more research is needed. While we wait for more conclusive research, it's important to note that marijuana use by pregnant women, like virtually all drugs, can lead to serious complications for the growing fetus. Furthermore, during adolescence and early adulthood the brain is still developing, so regular and/or heavy use of marijuana and other psychoactive drugs is particularly hazardous and may lead to permanent changes in the brain (e.g., deShazo et al., 2019).

Club Drugs

As you may know from television or newspapers, psychoactive drugs like Rohypnol (the "date rape drug," also called "roofies"), MDMA (3,4-methylenedioxymethylamphetamine, or Ecstasy), GHB (gamma-hydroxybutyrate), ketamine ("special K"), methamphetamine ("ice" or "crystal meth"), synthetic cathinones ("bath salts"), and LSD ("acid"), are all sometimes called "club drugs." This name reflects the fact that they're often used by teenagers and young adults at parties, bars, and nightclubs (NIDA, 2016). Unfortunately, these drugs can have very serious consequences, including potentially fatal damage to hippocampal cells in the brain, as well as a reduction in the neurotransmitter serotonin, which can lead to memory, sleep, mood, and appetite problems (Adulterants in Drugs, 2019; NIDA, 2016; Pereira et al., 2018). Perhaps the most graphic example of the dangers associated with club drugs and general drug addiction are the before and after images of users (see photos).

In contrast, the club drug ketamine, "special K," shows promise as a potential treatment for major depression, suicidal behaviors, and bipolar disorders. Research has found that it appears to have an immediate and positive effect on parts of the brain responsible for executive function and emotion regulation (Hirota & Lambert, 2018; Traynor, 2019).

Despite the potentially positive benefits of ketamine, and the subjective positive reports of some users, it's important to note that club drugs, like all illicit drugs, are particularly dangerous given that there are no truth-in-packaging laws to protect buyers from unscrupulous practices. Sellers often substitute unknown cheaper, and possibly even more dangerous, substances for the ones they claim to be selling. Also, club drugs (like most psychoactive drugs) can seriously affect the motor coordination, perceptual skills, and reaction time necessary for overall safety.

Impaired decision making is a serious problem as well. Just as "drinking and driving don't mix," club drug use may lead to risky behaviors, such as impaired driving and engaging in unsafe sexual practices, which leads to dangerous and deadly sexually transmitted infections (STIs). Add in the fact that some drugs, like Rohypnol, are odorless, colorless, and tasteless, and can easily be added to beverages by individuals who want to intoxicate or sedate others, and you can see that the dangers of club drug use go far beyond the drug itself.

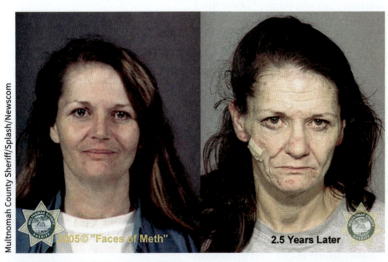

Multnomah County Sheriff/Splash/Newscom

2005© "Faces of Meth"   2.5 Years Later

The visible cost of drug abuse   The facial sores and scabs, tooth decay, and rapid aging shown in this woman before starting methamphetamine use and then 2.4 years later are common among drug abusers. Photos like these are released to the public to help raise awareness about the dangers of drug abuse.

Retrieval Practice 5.3 | Psychoactive Drugs

Self-Test Completing this self-test, and then checking your answers by clicking on the answer button or by looking in Appendix B, will provide immediate feedback and helpful practice for exams.

1. Psychoactive drugs _____.

   a. change conscious awareness, mood, or perception

   b. are addictive, mind altering, and dangerous to your health

   c. are illegal unless prescribed by a medical doctor

   d. all these options

2. Drug taking that leads to emotional or physical harm to the drug user or others is known as _____.

   a. addiction   c. psychological dependence

   b. physical dependence   d. drug abuse

3. _____ drugs inhibit or block a neurotransmitter's effect, whereas _____ drugs increase a neurotransmitter's effect.

   a. Antagonist; agonist   c. Protagonist; agonist

   b. Agonist; antagonist   d. Protagonist; co-agonist

4. _____ act on the brain and nervous system to increase overall activity and responsiveness.

   a. Stimulants   c. Depressants

   b. Opiates/opioids   d. Hallucinogens

5. Depressants include all the following *except* _____.

   a. antianxiety drugs   c. tobacco

   b. alcohol   d. Rohypnol

Q Test Your Critical Thinking

1. Which is more important in creating addiction—physical dependence or psychological dependence?

2. Do you think marijuana use should be legal in all states? Why or why not?

Real World Application Questions

[AQ4] Does Facebook deliberately try to create addiction?

[AQ5] Can using marijuana decrease your IQ?

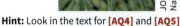

Nikada/iStock Unreleased/Getty Images

JOEL SARTORE/ National Geographic Image Collection

Hint: Look in the text for **[AQ4]** and **[AQ5]**

5.4 Meditation and Hypnosis

LEARNING OBJECTIVES

Retrieval Practice While reading the upcoming sections, respond to each Learning Objective in your own words.

Review the major features of meditation and hypnosis.

• **Describe** meditation and its major effects.

• **Identify** hypnosis, its key features, and its major myths.

Real World Application Question

[AQ6] Can meditation be an effective painkiller?

As we have seen, factors such as sleep, dreaming, and psychoactive drug use can create altered states of consciousness (ASCs). Changes in consciousness can also be achieved by means of meditation and hypnosis.

Meditation

Suddenly, with a roar like that of a waterfall, I felt a stream of liquid light entering my brain through the spinal cord . . . I experienced a rocking sensation and then felt myself slipping out of my body, entirely enveloped in a halo of light. I felt the point of consciousness that was myself growing wider, surrounded by waves of light

(Krishna, 1999, pp. 4–5).

This is how spiritual leader Gopi Krishna described his experience with **meditation**, a group of techniques generally designed to focus attention, block out distractions, and produce an ASC (**Figure 5. 12**). Most people in the beginning stages of meditation report a simpler,

Meditation A group of techniques generally designed to focus attention, block out distractions, and produce an altered state of consciousness (ASC); it's believed to enhance self-knowledge and well-being through reduced self-awareness.

FIGURE 5.12 **Benefits of meditation**

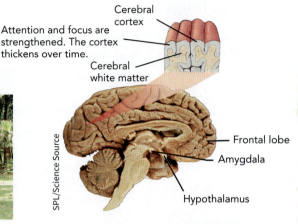

Attention and focus are strengthened. The cortex thickens over time.

Cerebral cortex

Cerebral white matter

Frontal lobe

Amygdala

Hypothalamus

SPL/Science Source

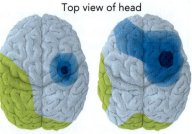

Top view of head

Before meditation   During meditation

Phil Date/123RF

a. Varieties of meditation Some meditation techniques, such as tai chi and hatha yoga, include body movements and postures. In other techniques, the meditator remains motionless, chanting or focusing on a single point, like a candle flame.

b. Positive effects of meditation Over time, meditation leads to a thickening of the cortex and increased attention and focus. In addition, the hypothalamus diminishes the sympathetic response and increases the parasympathetic response. Limiting the fight-flight-freeze response in this way allows for deep rest, slower respiration, and overall health improvement.

c. Additional effects of meditation Researchers have found that a larger area of the brain responds to sensory stimuli during meditation, suggesting that meditation enhances the coordination between the brain hemispheres (Kilpatrick et al., 2011; Kurth et al., 2014). Note how much the blue-colored areas enlarged and spread from the right to the left hemisphere during meditation.

mellow type of relaxation, followed by a mild euphoria and a sense of timelessness. Some advanced meditators report experiences of profound rapture, joy, and strong hallucinations.

How can we explain these effects? Brain imaging studies suggest that meditation's requirement to focus attention, block out distractions, and concentrate on a single object, emotion, or word, reduces the number of brain cells that must be devoted to the multiple competing tasks normally going on within the brain's frontal lobes. This narrowed focus thus explains the feelings of timelessness and mild euphoria.

Research has also verified that meditation can produce dramatic changes in basic physiological processes, including heart rate, oxygen consumption, sweat gland responses, and brain activity. In addition, it's been somewhat successful in lowering blood pressure, anxiety, and stress, and improving overall cognitive functioning and mental health (Adams et al., 2018; Heffner et al., 2016; Taylor & Abba, 2015). In fact, a meta-analysis (which combines results from multiple studies) revealed that 30 minutes of meditation once a day may provide as much relief from anxiety and depression as antidepressants (Goyal et al., 2014).

[AQ6] Fortunately, research suggests meditation may even be an effective method of pain relief (see photo). In a very simple experiment, one group of healthy young people was asked to meditate for just 10 minutes, while the control group sat quietly (Tashani et al., 2017). Both groups then plunged their hands first into warm water and then into ice water for as long as they could. The fact that the meditating group demonstrated a significantly higher pain tolerance is potentially very important—especially given the high number of worldwide chronic pain sufferers and the growing concern over traditional pain killers, like opioids, and their risks of addiction.

sk_koh/Shutterstock.com

As shown in **Figures 5. 12b** and **c**, studies have also found that meditation can change the body's sympathetic and parasympathetic responses, and increase structural support for the sensory, decision-making, emotion regulation, and attention-processing centers of the brain (Esch, 2014; Tang et al., 2014; Xue et al., 2014).

A number of elite athletes even use meditation to help prepare for competition. To help control arousal and pregame "jitters," NBA coach Phil Jackson led his LA Lakers team in meditation before games, former MLB star Derek Jeter meditated for an hour each day on non-game days, and marathon runner Deena Kastor meditates to reduce anxiety before a big race. If you'd like more information on the positive effects of meditation, see the following **PP** **PositivePsych** feature.

PP   **Practical Application: PositivePsych**

Can Meditation Increase Helping Behaviors?

(APA Goal 1.3) Describe applications of psychology

To answer this question, research participants were randomly assigned to a 3-week, mobile-app training course in either mindfulness meditation or cognitive skills (Lim et al., 2015). After the training, the participants arrived at a lab to complete a supposed measure of their cognitive abilities. Upon arrival, each participant was invited to sit down in a waiting room with two other individuals, who were already seated. Another person using crutches, and appearing to be in great physical pain, then entered the room. As she did, the two previously seated individuals ignored her obvious need for a chair by fiddling with their phones, or opening a book. (The woman who entered with crutches, and the two seated individuals who ignored her, were all actually *confederates*, secret accomplices, of the experimenter.)

Zdenka Darula/123RF

As you probably suspect, the researchers were actually interested in whether the participants who took part in the meditation classes would be more likely than the non-meditators to come to the aid of the person in pain, even in the face of everyone else ignoring her. Interestingly, only about 15 percent of the non-meditators acted to help the woman on crutches, compared to about 50 percent of those who were trained in meditation. This strong helping response from the meditation group was particularly impressive given that they had just watched the two other people in the room ignore the woman's need for a chair.

What do you think? Given all the previously described physical and mental health benefits of meditation, along with this positive finding on increased helping behaviors, you may want to try this simple meditation/relaxation technique developed by Herbert Benson (2000):

1. Pick a focus word or short phrase that is calming and rooted in your personal value system (such as love, peace, one, shalom).

2. Sit quietly in a comfortable position, close your eyes, and relax your muscles.

3. Focusing on your breathing, breathe through your nose, and as you breathe out, say your focus word or phrase silently to yourself. Continue for 10 to 20 minutes. You may open your eyes to check the time, but do not use an alarm. When you have finished, sit quietly for several minutes, first with closed eyes and later with opened eyes.

4. Maintain a passive attitude throughout the exercise—permit relaxation to occur at its own pace. When distracting thoughts occur, ignore them and gently return to your repetition.

5. Practice the technique once or twice daily, but not within 2 hours after a meal—the digestive processes seem to interfere with a successful relaxation response.

Hypnosis

> Relax . . . your eyelids are so very heavy . . . your muscles are becoming more and more relaxed . . . your breathing is becoming deeper and deeper . . . relax . . . your eyes are closing . . . let go . . . relax.

Hypnotists use suggestions like these to begin **hypnosis**, a trance-like state of heightened suggestibility, deep relaxation, and intense focus. Once hypnotized, some people can be convinced that they are standing at the edge of the ocean, listening to the sound of the waves and feeling the ocean mist on their faces. Invited to eat a "delicious apple" that is actually an onion, the hypnotized person may relish the flavor. Told they are watching a very funny or sad movie, hypnotized people may begin to laugh or cry at their self-created visions.

From the 1700s to modern times, entertainers and quacks have used (and abused) hypnosis (**Table 5.5**), but physicians, dentists, and therapists have also long employed it as a respected clinical tool. Modern scientific research has removed much of the mystery surrounding hypnosis. A number of features characterize the hypnotic state (Huber et al., 2014; Spiegel, 2015; Yapko, 2015):

- Narrowed, highly focused attention (ability to "tune out" competing sensory stimuli)
- Increased use of imagination and hallucinations
- A passive and receptive attitude
- Decreased responsiveness to pain
- Heightened suggestibility, or a greater willingness to respond to proposed changes in perception ("This onion is an apple")

Hypnosis An altered state of consciousness (ASC) characterized by deep relaxation and a trance-like state of heightened suggestibility and intense focus.

TABLE 5.5   Hypnosis Myths and Facts

Myth	Fact
Faking Hypnosis participants are "faking it" and playing along with the hypnotist.	There are conflicting research positions about hypnosis. Although most participants are not consciously faking hypnosis, some researchers believe the effects result from a blend of conformity, relaxation, obedience, suggestion, and role playing. Other theorists believe that hypnotic effects result from a special ASC. A group of "unified" theorists suggests that hypnosis is a combination of both relaxation/role playing and a unique ASC.
Forced hypnosis People can be hypnotized against their will or hypnotically "brainwashed."	Hypnosis requires a willing, conscious choice to relinquish control of one's consciousness to someone else. The best potential subjects are those who are able to focus attention, are open to new experiences, and are capable of imaginative involvement or fantasy.
Unethical behavior Hypnosis can make people behave immorally or take dangerous risks against their will.	Hypnotized people retain awareness and control of their behavior, and they can refuse to comply with the hypnotist's suggestions.
Superhuman strength Under hypnosis, people can perform acts of special superhuman strength.	When non-hypnotized people are simply asked to try their hardest on tests of physical strength, they can do anything that a hypnotized person can do.
Exceptional memory Under hypnosis, people can recall things they otherwise could not.	Although the heightened relaxation and focus that hypnosis engenders improves recall for some information, it adds little (if anything) to regular memory. Hypnotized people are just more willing to guess. Given that memory is normally filled with fabrication and distortion (Chapter 7), hypnosis generally increases the potential for error.

Sources: Arkowitz & Lilienfeld, 2017; Heid, 2018; Hilgard, 1978, 1992; Jensen et al., 2017.

Today, even with available anesthetics, hypnosis is occasionally linked with other treatment modalities and sometimes used during surgery, as well as with the treatment of cancer, pain, and sleep disorders (e.g., Chamine et al., 2018; Jensen et al., 2017; Kaiser et al., 2018). Hypnosis has found its best use in medical areas such as dentistry and childbirth, where patients have a high degree of anxiety, fear, and misinformation. Also, because tension and anxiety strongly affect pain, any technique that helps the patient relax is medically useful.

Final Take-Home Message
Before going on to the next chapter, we'd like to take an unusual step for authors. We'd like to offer you, our reader, a piece of caring, personal and professional advice about altered states of consciousness (ASCs). The core problem while you're in any ASC is that you're less aware of external reality, which places you at a significantly higher risk for serious physical and psychological dangers (e.g., accidents from distracted driving, sexual assaults, and so on). Most people are aware the serious risks of ASC when they're driving on a long trip and start to feel sleepy, so they typically stop for coffee, walk around, or rent a hotel room before allowing themselves to fall asleep.

Our simple advice to you is to follow this same "sleepy driver" logic and standards. If you decide to meditate, undergo hypnosis, use psychoactive drugs, or engage in any other form of altered consciousness, carefully research their potential effects and risks. Then, just as you set up a designated driver before you drink alcohol, plan ahead for the best options for dealing with your chosen ASC. Take care and best wishes,

Cathrine A. Sanderson   Karen R. Huffman

Be sure to complete the final Retrieval Practice quiz 5.4 below, and then answer the critical thinking questions in the **Test Your Critical Thinking**.

Retrieval Practice 5.4 | Meditation and Hypnosis

Self-Test   Completing this self-test, and then checking your answers by clicking on the answer button or by looking in Appendix B, will provide immediate feedback and helpful practice for exams.

1. Altered states of consciousness (ASCs) can be achieved in which of the following ways?

   a. during sleep and dreaming

   b. via chemical channels

   c. through hypnosis and meditation

   d. all these options

2. _____ is a group of techniques designed to focus attention, block out all distractions, and produce an ASC.

   a. Hypnosis
   c. Parapsychology

   b. MDMA
   d. Meditation

3. Research on the effects of meditation has found a(n) _____.

   a. increase in blood pressure

   b. reduction in stress

   c. lack of evidence for changes in any physiological functions

   d. all of these options

4. _____ is an ASC characterized by deep relaxation and a trance-like state of heightened suggestibility and intense focus.

   a. Meditation
   c. Hypnosis

   b. Amphetamine psychosis
   d. Daydreaming

5. Which of the following is NOT associated with hypnosis?

   a. the use of imagination

   b. exceptional memory

   c. a passive, receptive attitude

   d. decreased pain

Q **Test Your Critical Thinking**

1. Why is it almost impossible to hypnotize an unwilling participant?

2. Describe the possible health benefits of hypnosis and meditation.

Real World Application Question

[AQ6]   Can meditation be an effective painkiller?

sk_koh/Shutterstock.com

Hint: Look in the text for **[AQ6]**

Q Test Your Critical Thinking

Did you notice or wonder why we provided six Real World Application Questions [AQ1–AQ6] throughout this chapter? We've found that they not only help you to engage with, and master the material, they also have an important and lasting impact on your critical thinking skills. For additional mastery and enrichment, consider the following questions:

1. In which stage of sleep is the kitten in each photo, and how do you know?

2. Why might REM sleep serve an important adaptive function for cats?

3. Why do you think Freud's dream theory remains so popular, despite serious scientific questions and alternative modern theories?

4. Why do you think alcohol is more popular and culturally acceptable than the other drugs discussed in this chapter?

5. What are some possible ethical considerations of using hypnosis?

age fotostock/Alamy Stock Photo

Jena Ardell/Moment/Getty Images

Summary

5.1 Understanding Consciousness   **138**

- **Consciousness**, an organism's awareness of internal events and the external environment, varies in its depth. We spend most of our time in waking consciousness, but also spend time in various **altered states of consciousness (ASCs)**, such as sleep and dreaming.

- **Selective attention** allows us to focus our conscious awareness on specific stimuli, whereas **inattentional blindness** blocks us from seeing unexpected stimuli.

- Consciousness varies and exists along a continuum of awareness. **Controlled processes**, which require focused attention, are at the highest level of the continuum. **Automatic processes**, which require minimal attention, are found in the middle. And, unconsciousness and coma are at the lowest level.

5.2 Understanding Sleep and Dreams 142

- Many physiological functions follow 24-hour **circadian rhythms**. Disruptions in these rhythms, as well as long-term sleep deprivation, lead to increased fatigue, cognitive and mood disruptions, and other health problems.

- During a normal night's sleep, we progress through several distinct stages of **non-rapid-eye-movement (NREM) sleep**, with periods of **rapid-eye-movement (REM) sleep** generally occurring at the end of each sleep cycle. Both REM and NREM sleep are important for our biological functioning.

- There are four major theories about why we sleep. **Adaptation/ protection theory** proposes that sleep evolved to conserve energy and to provide protection from predators. The **repair/ restoration theory** suggests that sleep helps us recuperate from the day's events. The **growth/development theory** explains that deep sleep is particularly important during times of physical development. The **learning/memory theory** says that we use sleep for consolidation, storage, and maintenance of memories.

- Three major theories about why we dream are Freud's **wish fulfillment view,** the **activation–synthesis hypothesis**, and the **cognitive view**. Researchers have found many similarities and differences in dream content between men and women and across cultures. How people interpret and value their dreams also varies across cultures.

- Sleep–wake disorders include **insomnia**, **narcolepsy**, **sleep apnea**, **nightmares**, and **sleep terrors**.

5.3 Psychoactive Drugs 153

- **Psychoactive drugs** influence the nervous system in a variety of ways. Alcohol affects neural membranes throughout the entire nervous system. Most psychoactive drugs act in a more specific way, by either increasing a particular neurotransmitter's effect—an **agonist drug**—or inhibiting it—an **antagonist drug**.

- The term **drug abuse** refers to drug-taking behavior that leads to emotional or physical harm to oneself or others. **Addiction** refers to a condition in which a person feels compelled to use a specific drug. **Psychological dependence** refers to the mental desire or craving to achieve a drug's effects. **Physical dependence** refers to biological changes that make a drug necessary for minimum daily functioning, so as to avoid **withdrawal** symptoms (pain and intense cravings experienced after stopping the use of an addictive drug). Repeated use of a drug can produce decreased sensitivity, or **tolerance**. Sometimes, using one drug increases tolerance for another (*cross-tolerance*).

- Psychologists divide psychoactive drugs into four categories: **depressants** (such as alcohol, barbiturates, Rohypnol, and Ketamine), **stimulants** (such as caffeine, nicotine, cocaine, and amphetamines), **opiates/opioids** (such as morphine, heroin, and codeine), and **hallucinogens** (such as marijuana and LSD). Almost all psychoactive drugs may lead to serious health problems and, in some cases, even death.

- Club drugs are popular due to their desirable effects, but they can also create serious health problems and impair decision making.

5.4 Meditation and Hypnosis 163

- **Meditation** refers to techniques designed to focus attention, block out distractions, and produce an altered state of consciousness (ASC).

- Modern research has removed the mystery surrounding **hypnosis**, a trance-like state of heightened suggestibility, deep relaxation, and intense focus.

Key Terms

Retrieval Practice Write a definition for each term before turning back to the referenced page to check your answer.

- activation–synthesis theory of dreams 148
- adaptation/protection theory of sleep 147
- addiction 155
- Agonist drug 153
- altered state of consciousness (ASC) 138
- Antagonist drug 153
- automatic processes 139
- circadian rhythm 142
- cognitive view of dreams 148
- consciousness 138
- controlled processes 139
- depressant 156
- drug abuse 155

- growth/development theory of sleep 147
- hallucinogen 160
- hypnosis 165
- inattentional blindness 138
- insomnia 150
- latent content 148
- learning/memory theory of sleep 147
- manifest content 148
- meditation 163
- narcolepsy 151
- nightmares 151
- non-rapid-eye-movement (NREM) sleep 145
- opiate/opioid 160

- physical dependence 155
- psychoactive drug 153
- psychological dependence 155
- rapid-eye-movement (REM) sleep 145
- repair/restoration theory of sleep 147
- selective attention 138
- sleep apnea 151
- sleep terrors 151
- stimulant 158
- tolerance 155
- wish-fulfillment view of dreams 148
- withdrawal 155

Learning

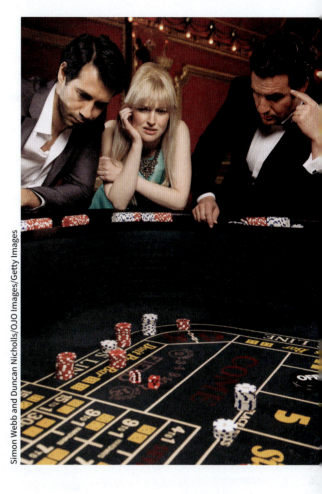

Simon Webb and Duncan Nicholls/OJO Images/Getty Images

Real World Application Questions

Things you'll learn in Chapter 6

[AQ1] Why can simply hearing the sound of a drill in a dentist's office—even if that drill is nowhere near you—make you feel anxious?

[AQ2] Can simply looking at positive images increase your relationship satisfaction?

[AQ3] Why do gamblers have such trouble quitting, even when they continue to lose money?

[AQ4] Can children learn anti-fat prejudice and math anxiety from their parents?

[AQ5] Do humans have specific neurons responsible for empathy and imitation of others?

[AQ6] Why can even young children recognize a picture of a snake much faster than a picture of a frog or caterpillar?

Throughout the chapter, look for [AQ1]–[AQ6] icons. They indicate where the text addresses these questions.

CHAPTER OUTLINE

6.1 Classical Conditioning

LEARNING OBJECTIVES

Retrieval Practice   While reading the upcoming sections, respond to each Learning Objective in your own words.

Summarize the key terms and findings in classical conditioning.

- **Define** learning and classical conditioning.
- **Describe** Pavlov's and Watson's contributions to classical conditioning.
- **Discuss** the six principles and applications of classical conditioning.

- **Identify** how classical conditioning is used in every day life.

Real World Application Questions

[AQ1] Why can simply hearing the sound of a drill in a dentist's office—even if that drill is nowhere near you—make you feel anxious?

[AQ2] Can simply looking at positive images increase your relationship satisfaction?

Associative learning   Learning that two stimuli or events occur or happen together.

Learning   A relatively permanent change in behavior or mental processes resulting from experience.

As you can see in **Figure 6.1**, we learn about ourselves and the world around us in many ways. Within this chapter we'll focus on the two most basic forms of associative learning—classical and operant conditioning. Then we discuss the various cognitive-social and biological factors involved in learning.

Note that both classical and operant conditioning are generally classified as **associative learning**. As the name implies, they occur when an organism makes a connection, or *association*, that two stimuli or events occur or happen together. During classical conditioning an association is made that one stimuli or event predicts another, whereas in operant conditioning the association is made between a response and its consequences.

Although most people think of learning as something formal that occurs between teachers and students, psychologists see the term as much broader. We define **learning** as a *relatively permanent change in behavior or mental processes resulting from experience*. This relative permanence applies to bad habits, like texting while driving or procrastinating about studying, as well as to useful behaviors and emotions, such as finding new ways to protect the environment, training guide dogs for the blind, or falling in love.

Change is the key feature of this definition. Without the ability (and willingness) to modify their behavior and mental processes, all animals, including humans, simply would not survive. Learning not only alerts us to the dangers in our environment, but also how to succeed and

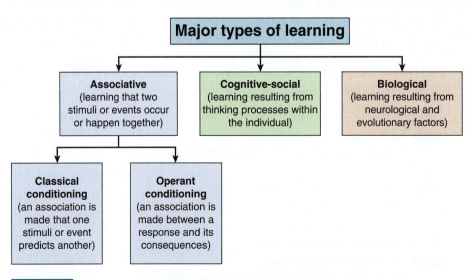

FIGURE 6.1   **Major types of learning**   Why do we provide this overview? Having a "big picture" or road map is helpful to understanding complex material. It also highlights the major differences and relationships between the various forms of learning discussed in this chapter.

prosper from our personal experiences. For example, you may have learned that you "can't do well on essay exams" or that you "can't stop yourself from talking on the phone or texting while driving." The good news is that since learning is only "relatively" permanent, with new experiences, like practicing the study skills sprinkled throughout this text and actively practicing turning off your phone in the car, mistaken beliefs and dangerous habits can be replaced with new, more adaptive ones (Bönstrup et al., 2019; Gardner et al., 2016).

Now that we've defined and examined the major components of learning, let's explore one of its earliest forms, *classical conditioning*, made famous by Pavlov's salivating dogs.

FIGURE 6.2 **Pavlov's experimental setup**

SPUTNIK/Alamy Stock Photo

Beginnings of Classical Conditioning

Why does your mouth water when you stare at a large slice of delicious cake or a juicy steak? The experimental answer to this was accidentally discovered in the laboratory of Russian physiologist Ivan Pavlov (1849–1936). Interested in the role of saliva in digestion, Pavlov created an apparatus that measured the amount of saliva dogs produced when given different types of foods (**Figure 6.2**). During these experiments, one of Pavlov's students noticed that even before receiving the actual food, many dogs began salivating at the mere sight of the food or the food dish, the smell of the food, or even just the sight of the person who normally delivered the food.

Pavlov's genius was in recognizing the importance of this "unscheduled" salivation. Unlike innate, automatic reflexes, such as salivating when actually tasting the food, the dogs were salivating as a result of experience or learning. They had learned to pair up the sight of the food or food dish with the food itself. This is believed to be the first example of what came to be known as *associative learning*—that two stimuli or events occur or happen together.

Excited by this accidental discovery, Pavlov and his students conducted several additional experiments, including sounding a tone on a tuning fork just before food was placed in the dogs' mouths. After several pairings of the tone and food, dogs in the laboratory began to salivate on hearing the tone alone. In fact, Pavlov and later researchers found that many things can become conditioned stimuli for salivation if they are paired with food—a bell, a buzzer, a light, and even the sight of a circle or triangle drawn on a card. This type of learning, called **classical conditioning**, develops through involuntary, paired associations (McSweeney & Murphy, 2017).

To fully understand classical conditioning and how it applies to our everyday life, the first step is to recognize that **conditioning** is simply another word for learning. Next, we need to explain that classical conditioning is a three-step process—*before*, *during*, and *after conditioning*. This process is explained in detail below and visually summarized in **Process Diagram 6.1**.

Step 1 Before conditioning, the sound of the tone does NOT lead to salivation, which makes the tone a **neutral stimulus (NS)**. Conversely, food naturally brings about salivation, which means that food is an *unlearned*, **unconditioned stimulus (US)**. The initial reflex of salivation also is *unlearned*, so it is called an **unconditioned response (UR)**.

Step 2 During conditioning, the tuning fork is repeatedly sounded right before the presentation of the meat (US).

Step 3 After conditioning, the tone alone will bring about salivation. At this point, we can say that the dog has been *classically conditioned*. The previously neutral stimulus (NS), the tone, has now become a *learned*, **conditioned stimulus (CS)** that produces a *learned*, **conditioned response (CR)**, the dog's salivation.

In sum, the overall goal of Pavlov's classical conditioning was for the dog to learn to associate the tone with the unconditioned stimulus (meat) and then to show the same response (salivation) to the tone as to the meat.

Classical conditioning Learning that develops through involuntarily paired associations; a previously neutral stimulus (NS) is paired (associated) with an unconditioned stimulus (US) to elicit a conditioned response (CR).

Conditioning The process of learning associations between stimuli and behavioral responses.

Neutral stimulus (NS) A stimulus that, before conditioning, does not naturally bring about the response of interest.

Unconditioned stimulus (US) A stimulus that elicits an unconditioned response (UR) without previous conditioning.

Unconditioned response (UR) An unlearned reaction to an unconditioned stimulus (US) that occurs without previous conditioning.

Conditioned stimulus (CS) A previously neutral stimulus (NS) that, after repeated pairings with an unconditioned stimulus (US), comes to elicit a conditioned response (CR).

Conditioned response (CR) A learned reaction to a conditioned stimulus (CS) that occurs after previous repeated pairings with an unconditioned stimulus (US).

STOP! This Process Diagram contains essential information NOT found elsewhere in the text, which is likely to appear on quizzes and exams. Be sure to study it CAREFULLY.

PROCESS DIAGRAM 6.1 The Beginnings of Classical Conditioning and a Real-World

Application Although Pavlov's initial experiment used a metronome, a ticking instrument designed to mark exact time, and later experiments used a bell, his best-known method (depicted here) involved a tone from a tuning fork. As you can see, the basic process of classical conditioning is simple. Just as you've been classically conditioned to respond to your phone's chimes or vibrations, or possibly to just the sight of a pizza box, Pavlov's dogs learned to respond to a tuning fork's tone.

TIP Are you having trouble mastering all these new terms and abbreviations? If so, this figure will help you visualize and organize the three major stages of classical conditioning, along with all their major terms. For further help, keep in mind that *conditioning* is essentially the same as "learning."

	Pavlov example	Modern-day example

① Before conditioning
The neutral stimulus (NS) produces no relevant response. The unconditioned (unlearned) stimulus (US) elicits the unconditioned (unlearned) response (UR).

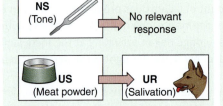

② During conditioning
The neutral stimulus (NS) is repeatedly paired with the unconditioned (unlearned) stimulus (US) to produce the unconditioned (unlearned) response (UR).

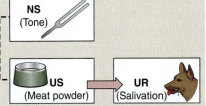
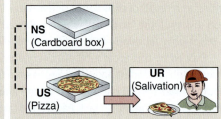

③ After conditioning
The neutral stimulus (NS) has become a conditioned (learned) stimulus (CS). This CS now produces a conditioned (learned) response (CR), which is usually similar to the previously unconditioned (unlearned) response (UR).

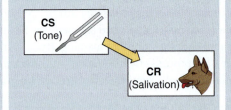
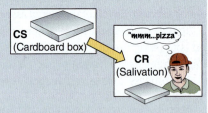

Summary
An originally neutral stimulus (NS) becomes a conditioned (learned) stimulus (CS), which elicits a conditioned (learned) response (CR). Note that both the CR and the UR are the same—salivation. The key difference is that through classical conditioning, the dog has learned to salivate at the sound of the tone, and the young boy has learned to salivate at the sight of the cardboard pizza box!

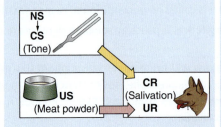
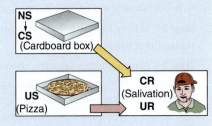

Practical Application

How can you use this information in your everyday life?   Classical conditioning is a fundamental way that all animals, including humans, learn. Just as you may have learned to salivate at the sight of a pizza box (see again Process Diagram 6.1), smokers often report cravings to smoke after watching a cigarette commercial on TV—or even after a quick glance at an ashtray. Laboratory experiments show that smokers can even be trained to develop cravings for a cigarette after seeing a simple geometric design if it was previously paired with cigarette-related cues (Deweese et al., 2016). The human compulsion to gamble, the common experience of emotional eating (**Figure 6.3**), and the almost universal fear of public speaking all result largely from classical conditioning.

"I think we need to have a chat about your 'support team'..."

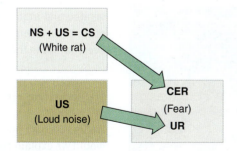

How do we learn to be afraid of public speaking or of typically harmless things like mice and elevators? In a now-famous experiment, John B. Watson and Rosalie Rayner (1920) demonstrated how a fear of rats could be classically conditioned.

In this study, a healthy 11-month-old child, later known as Little Albert, was first allowed to play with a white laboratory rat. Like most other infants, Albert was curious and reached for the rat, showing no fear. Knowing that infants are naturally upset by loud noises, Watson stood behind Albert and banged a steel bar with a hammer when he reached for the rat. The loud noise obviously frightened the child and made him cry (**Figure 6.4**). The rat was paired with the loud noise only seven times before Albert became classically conditioned and demonstrated fear of the rat even without the noise. The rat had become a CS that brought about the CR (fear).

Although this deliberate experimental creation of what's now called a **conditioned emotional response (CER)** remains a classic in psychology, it has been heavily criticized and would never be allowed under today's experimental guidelines (Antes, 2016; Avieli et al., 2016; Ethical Principles of Psychologists and Code of Conduct, 2016). The research procedures used by Watson and Rayner violated several ethical guidelines for scientific research (Chapter 1). The researchers not only deliberately created a serious fear in a child, but also ended their experiment without *extinguishing* (removing) it. In addition, the researchers have been criticized for not measuring Albert's fear objectively. Their subjective evaluation raises doubt about the degree of fear conditioned.

FIGURE 6.3 **Classical conditioning and emotional eating (EE)** As shown in this cartoon and documented in an experiment (Bongers & Jansen, 2017), negative emotions can act as conditioned stimuli (CS) that lead to the conditioned response (CR) of hunger. This is particularly true for so-called comfort foods—in this case, wine and cakes.

Conditioned emotional response (CER) An emotion, such as fear, that becomes a learned, conditioned response to a previously neutral stimulus (NS), such as a loud noise.

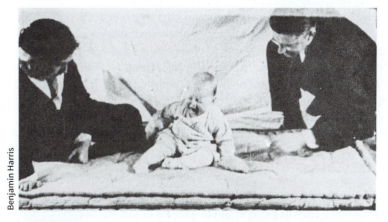

FIGURE 6.4 **Conditioning Little Albert's fears** Watson and Rayner's famous Little Albert study demonstrated how some fears can originate through conditioning. Using classical conditioning terms, we would say that the white rat (a neutral stimulus/NS) was initially paired with the loud noise (an unconditioned stimulus/US) to produce a conditioned stimulus (CS)—the white rat. Then, just the appearance of the white rat (CS) would elicit Little Albert's conditioned emotional response (CER)—his fear of the rat. Note again that just as the CR and UR (salivation) were the same for Pavlov's dogs, the CER and UR (fear) are the same for Little Albert. The key difference is that through classical conditioning the infant learned to fear just the sight of the white rat.

FIGURE 6.5 Real-world applications of classical conditioning

a. Prejudice How do children, like the one wearing the KKK uniform and holding the wooden cross in this photo, develop prejudice at such an early age? Research shows that prejudice may arise from a combination of biological and cultural factors (Hughes et al., 2016; Mallan et al., 2013). As shown in the diagram, children are naturally upset and fearful (UR) when they see that their parents are upset and afraid (US). Over time, they may learn to associate their parents' reaction with all members of a disliked group (CS), thus becoming prejudiced like their parents.

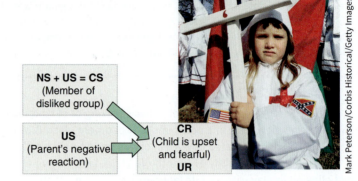

NS + US = CS
(Member of disliked group)

US
(Parent's negative reaction)

CR
(Child is upset and fearful)
UR

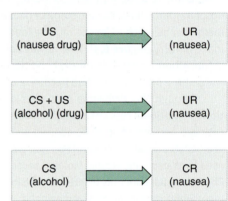

Mark Peterson/Corbis Historical/Getty Images

dennizn/123RF

b. Advertising Magazine ads, TV commercials, and business promotions often use emotional strategies based on classical conditioning to pair their products or company logo, the neutral stimulus (NS), with previously conditioned pleasant images like those of celebrities, the conditioned stimulus (CS). These images then trigger desired behaviors such as purchasing their products, the conditioned response (CR) (Poels & Dewitte, 2019; van der Pligt & Vliek, 2016).

c. Medicine Classical conditioning also is used in the medical field. A well-known treatment designed for alcohol-addicted patients pairs alcohol with a nausea-producing drug. Afterward, just the smell or taste of alcohol makes the person sick. Some, but not all, patients have found this treatment helpful.

US
(nausea drug)

UR
(nausea)

CS + US
(alcohol) (drug)

UR
(nausea)

CS
(alcohol)

CR
(nausea)

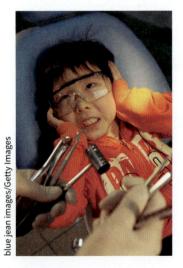

blue jean images/Getty Images

Despite such criticisms, this study of Little Albert and follow-up research led to our current understanding that many of our likes, dislikes, prejudices, and fears are examples of *conditioned emotional responses (CERs)*. As an example, if your romantic partner always uses the same shampoo, simply the smell of that shampoo may soon elicit a positive response. In Chapter 14 you'll discover how Watson's research later led to powerful clinical tools for eliminating exaggerated and irrational fears of a specific object or situation, known as *phobias* (Abramowitz et al., 2019; Cheng et al., 2017). For more examples of how classical conditioning applies to our everyday life in the real world, see **Figure 6.5**.

Principles of Classical Conditioning

We've just seen how a loud noise was used to condition Little Albert's fear of rats. But how would we explain common fears, such as being afraid of dentists or just the sound of a dentist's drill? How did they develop? **[AQ1]** Imagine being seated in a dental chair and finding that, even though the drill is nowhere near you, its sound immediately makes you feel anxious. Your anxiety is obviously not innate. Little children don't cringe at the sight of dental instruments or at the sound of a dental drill unless it's very loud (see photo). Your fear of the drill and maybe dentistry in general are learned responses, which developed from one or more of the classical conditioning principles summarized in **Table 6.1**. Each of these six

TABLE 6.1   **Six Principles and Applications of Classical Conditioning**

Process	Description	Example
Acquisition	Learning occurs (is acquired) when an organism involuntarily links a neutral stimulus (NS) with an unconditioned stimulus (US), which in turn elicits the conditioned response (CR) and/or conditioned emotional response (CER)	You learn to fear (CER) a dentist's drill (CS) after you associate it with the pain of your tooth extraction (US).
Generalization	A conditioned response (CR) and/or a conditioned emotional response (CER) comes to be involuntarily elicited not only by the conditioned stimulus (CS), but also by stimuli similar to the CS; the opposite of discrimination	You generalize your fear of the dentist's drill to your dentist's office and other dentists' offices.
Discrimination	Learned ability to distinguish (discriminate) between similar stimuli so as NOT to involuntarily respond to a new stimulus as if it were the previously conditioned stimulus (CS); the opposite of generalization	You are not afraid of your physician's office after you've learned to differentiate it from your dentist's office.
Extinction	Gradual diminishing of a conditioned response (CR) and/or a conditioned emotional response (CER) when the unconditioned stimulus (US) is withheld or removed	You return several times to your dentist's office for routine checkups, with no dental drill; your fear of the dentist's office (CER) gradually diminishes.
Spontaneous recovery	Reappearance of a previously extinguished conditioned response (CR) and/or conditioned emotional response (CER)	While watching a movie depicting dental drilling, your previous fear (CER) suddenly returns.
Higher-order conditioning	A new conditioned stimulus (CS) is created by pairing it with a previously conditioned stimulus (CS)	You fear the sign outside your dentist's office, an originally neutral stimulus (NS). Why? It has become a conditioned stimulus (CS), associated with the previously conditioned stimulus (CS) of the dental drill.

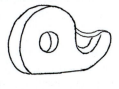

Which of the six basic principles of classical conditioning summarized in this table best explain(s) this cartoon?

Answer: generalization

"I don't care if she is a tape dispenser. I love her."

Sam Gross/Conde Nast/The Cartoon Bank

principles is fully discussed in the following pages. (Note that dental fears and even serious dental phobias can be successfully treated—see Chapters 13 and 14.)

1. **Acquisition**   After Pavlov's original (accidental) discovery of classical conditioning, he conducted numerous experiments beyond the basic **acquisition** phase, which is a general term for learning that occurs (is acquired) when an organism involuntarily links a neutral

Acquisition (in classical conditioning)   Learning occurs (is acquired) when an organism involuntarily links a neutral stimulus (NS) with an unconditioned stimulus (US), which in turn elicits the conditioned response (CR).

Motortion Films/Shutterstock.com

Generalization and the real world Experimenters have found that attitudes and relationship satisfaction can be affected by generalization (McNulty et al., 2017). **[AQ2]** In one study, participants were shown various images of their marital partners, which were paired with either positive or neutral stimuli. Surprisingly, just this simple passive pairing of positive images with their respective partners led to more positive attitudes and increased relationship satisfaction. Can you see how the positive images generalized and spread to the marital partners, and why it's so important to build-in positive associations within your own relationships?

Generalization (in classical conditioning) A conditioned response (CR) spreads (generalizes) and comes to be involuntarily elicited not only by the conditioned stimulus (CS) but also by stimuli similar to the CS; the opposite of discrimination.

Discrimination (in classical conditioning) A learned ability to distinguish (discriminate) between similar stimuli so as NOT to involuntarily respond to a new stimulus as if it were the previously conditioned stimulus (CS); the opposite of generalization.

Extinction (in classical conditioning) The gradual diminishing of a conditioned response (CR) when the unconditioned stimulus (US) is withheld or removed.

Spontaneous recovery The reappearance of a previously extinguished conditioned response (CR).

Higher-order conditioning A new conditioned stimulus (CS) is created through pairing with a previously conditioned stimulus (CS); also known as second-order conditioning.

stimulus (NS) with an unconditioned stimulus (US). This acquisition in turn elicits the conditioned response (CR).

2. **Generalization** One of Pavlov's most intriguing findings was that stimuli similar to the original conditioned stimulus (CS) can also elicit the conditioned response (CR). After first conditioning dogs to salivate to the sound of low-pitched tones, Pavlov later demonstrated that the dogs would also salivate in response to higher-pitched tones. Similarly, after Watson and Rayner's conditioning experiment, Little Albert learned to fear not only rats, but also a rabbit, a dog, and a bearded Santa Claus mask. This process by which a conditioned response (CR) spreads (generalizes) and comes to be involuntarily elicited not only by the conditioned stimulus (CS) but also by stimuli similar to the CS is called stimulus **generalization** (El-Bar et al., 2017; Rehman et al., 2019). (See photo.)

3. **Discrimination** In contrast to Pavlov's dogs learning to generalize and respond to similar stimuli in a similar way, they also learned how to *discriminate* between similar stimuli. When Pavlov or his assistants gave the dogs food following a high-pitched tone, but not following a low-pitched tone, they found that the dogs quickly learned the difference between the two tones and salivated only to the high-pitched one. Likewise, Little Albert learned to recognize differences between rats and other stimuli and presumably overcame his fear of them. This learned ability to distinguish (discriminate) between similar stimuli so as NOT to involuntarily respond to a new stimulus as if it were the previously conditioned stimulus (CS) is known as stimulus **discrimination**.

4. **Extinction** What do you think happened when Pavlov repeatedly sounded the tone without presenting food? The dogs' salivation gradually declined, a process Pavlov called **extinction**. This term is defined as the gradual diminishing of a conditioned response (CR) when the unconditioned stimulus (US) is withheld or removed. Without continued association with the US, the CS loses its power to elicit the CR.

5. **Spontaneous recovery** It's important to note that extinction is not complete unlearning. It does not fully "erase" the learned connection between the stimulus and the response (González et al., 2016; Oyarzún et al., 2019). Pavlov found that sometimes, after a CR had apparently been extinguished, if he sounded the tone once again, the dogs would occasionally still salivate. This reappearance of a previously extinguished conditioned response (CR) is called **spontaneous recovery**.

6. **Higher-order conditioning** The phenomenon of **higher-order conditioning** takes basic classical conditioning one step higher. Also known as "second-order conditioning," this process refers to a situation in which a previously neutral stimulus (NS), like a tone, was first made into a conditioned stimulus (CS) through pairing with an unconditioned stimulus (US), such as food. The next step of higher-order (or second-order) conditioning then uses that previous CS as a basis for creating a *new* CS (like a flashing light) that produces its own conditioned response (CR). In short, a new CS is created through pairing with a previously created CS (**Process Diagram 6.2**).

STOP!   This Process Diagram contains essential information NOT found else-where in the text, which is likely to appear on quizzes and exams. Be sure to study it CAREFULLY.

PROCESS DIAGRAM 6.2   **Real-World Higher-Order Conditioning**   Have you noticed how cats learn to salivate and come running at the sound of an electric can opener, and then later to the sound of the squeaky drawer that houses the electric can opener? They're obviously not born with this response. Running toward the sound of the can opener was learned through first-order, classi-cal conditioning. Afterwards, learning to run just to the sound of the squeaky drawer was learned through higher-order conditioning, which occurs when a new conditioned stimulus (CS) is paired with a previously conditioned stimulus (CS).

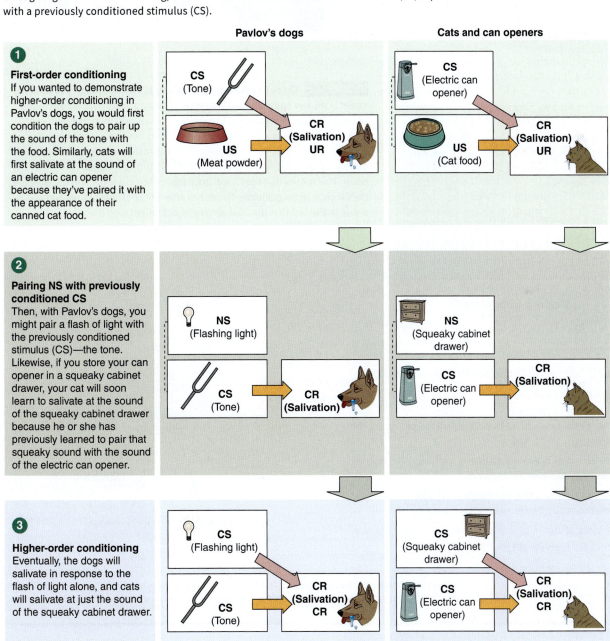

1

First-order conditioning
If you wanted to demonstrate higher-order conditioning in Pavlov's dogs, you would first condition the dogs to pair up the sound of the tone with the food. Similarly, cats will first salivate at the sound of an electric can opener because they've paired it with the appearance of their canned cat food.

2

Pairing NS with previously conditioned CS
Then, with Pavlov's dogs, you might pair a flash of light with the previously conditioned stimulus (CS)—the tone. Likewise, if you store your can opener in a squeaky cabinet drawer, your cat will soon learn to salivate at the sound of the squeaky cabinet drawer because he or she has previously learned to pair that squeaky sound with the sound of the electric can opener.

3

Higher-order conditioning
Eventually, the dogs will salivate in response to the flash of light alone, and cats will salivate at just the sound of the squeaky cabinet drawer.

PA Practical Application

How can we use this information in our daily life? Have you ever felt renewed excitement at the sight of a former girlfriend or boyfriend, even though years have passed, you have a new partner, and extinction has occurred? This may be an example of *spontaneous* recovery (see photo). It also may help explain why people sometimes misinterpret a sudden flare-up of feelings and are tempted to return to unhappy relationships. To make matters worse, when a conditioned stimulus is reintroduced after extinction, the conditioning occurs much faster the second time around—a phenomenon known as *reconditioning*.

The good news is that those who have taken general psychology (or are currently reading this book) are (we hope) far less likely to make this mistake. Looking at **Figure 6.6**, you can see that even if you experience spontaneous recovery, your sudden feelings for the old love partner will gradually return to their previously extinguished state. So don't overreact. As a final review of the six principles of classical conditioning, try the **Test Yourself**.

avemario/123RF

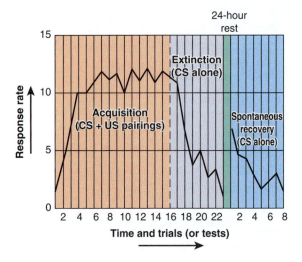

FIGURE 6.6 **Three key principles of classical conditioning—acquisition, extinction, and spontaneous recovery** During acquisition, the strength of the conditioned response (CR) rapidly increases and then levels off near its maximum. During extinction, the CR declines erratically until it is extinguished. After a "rest" period in which the organism is not exposed to the conditioned stimulus (CS) (the green-colored column), spontaneous recovery may occur. This means that the CS will once again elicit a (weakened) CR. Note that the CR once again gradually diminishes after the spontaneous recovery. This is due to the fact that the CS is alone and not paired with the US.

Test Yourself: Identifying the Six Principles of Classical Conditioning

_____ **1.** The mere smell of coffee helps wake me up in the morning.

_____ **2.** The sound of ocean waves makes me cringe, but hearing raindrops falling makes me smile.

_____ **3.** I used to enjoy eating hamburgers, but after months on a vegetarian diet, I no longer want to eat meat.

_____ **4.** Pictures of my ex-girlfriend on Facebook made me suddenly sad even though we broke up months ago.

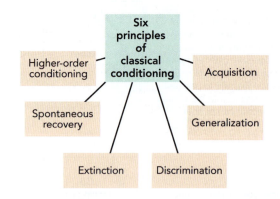

Answers: (1) acquisition, (2) discrimination, (3) extinction, (4) spontaneous recovery. Note that adding additional examples from your personal life will further help you understand, appreciate, and master the principles of classical conditioning.

Retrieval Practice 6.1 | Classical Conditioning

Self-Test   Completing this self-test, and then checking your answers by clicking on the answer button or by looking in Appendix B, will provide immediate feedback and helpful practice for exams.

1. _____ conditioning occurs when a neutral stimulus becomes associated with an unconditioned stimulus to elicit a conditioned response.

   a. Reflex
   b. Instinctive
   c. Classical
   d. Basic

2. A young child learns to fear dogs after being bitten. In this situation, the unconditioned RESPONSE (UR) is the _____.

   a. dog
   b. bite
   c. fear
   d. none of these options

3. In John Watson's demonstration of classical conditioning with Little Albert, the unconditioned stimulus was _____.

   a. symptoms of fear
   b. a rat
   c. a bath towel
   d. a loud noise

4. A baby is bitten by a small dog and then is afraid of all small animals. This is an example of _____.

   a. discrimination
   b. extinction
   c. reinforcement
   d. generalization

5. Extinction in classical conditioning occurs when the _____.

   a. conditioned stimulus is no longer paired with the unconditioned response
   b. unconditioned stimulus is withheld or removed
   c. conditioned response is no longer paired with the unconditioned stimulus
   d. unconditioned stimulus is ambiguous

Q Test Your Critical Thinking

1. How might Watson and Rayner, who conducted the famous Little Albert study, have designed a more ethical study of conditioned emotional responses (CERs)?

2. Most classical conditioning is involuntary. Considering this, is it ethical for politicians and advertisers to use classical conditioning to influence our thoughts and behavior? Why or why not?

Real World Application Questions

[AQ1]   Why can simply hearing the sound of a drill in a dentist's office—even if that drill is nowhere near you—make you feel anxious?

[AQ2]   Can simply looking at positive images increase your relationship satisfaction?

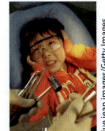

blue jean images/Getty Images

Motortion Films/ Shutterstock.com

Hint: Look in the text for **[AQ1]** and **[AQ2]**

6.2 Operant Conditioning

LEARNING OBJECTIVES

Retrieval Practice   While reading the upcoming sections, respond to each Learning Objective in your own words.

Discuss the key terms and findings in operant conditioning.

- **Define** operant conditioning, reinforcement, and punishment.
- **Describe** Thorndike's and Skinner's contributions to operant conditioning.
- **Explain** how reinforcement and punishment influence behavior.
- **Review** the six key principles in operant conditioning.
- **Identify** how operant conditioning is used in everyday life.
- **Summarize** the major similarities and differences between classical and operant conditioning.

Real World Application Question

[AQ3]   Why do gamblers have such trouble quitting, even when they continue to lose money?

Operant conditioning Learning through voluntary behavior and its subsequent consequences; consequences that are reinforcing increase behavioral tendencies, whereas consequences that are punishing decrease them.

Reinforcement Adding or removing a stimulus following a response and thereby increasing the likelihood that the response will be repeated.

Punishment Adding or removing a stimulus following a response and thereby decreasing the likelihood that the response will be repeated.

FIGURE 6.7 **Classical versus operant conditioning** Classical conditioning is based on involuntary behavior, whereas operant conditioning is based on voluntary behavior.

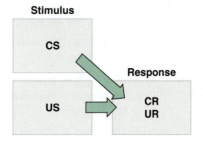

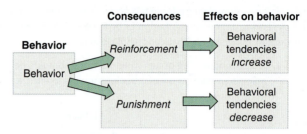

a. Classical conditioning The subject is passive while the previously neutral stimulus (NS) is paired with an unconditioned stimulus (US). After repeated pairings, the NS becomes a conditioned stimulus (CS) that leads to a conditioned response (CR).

b. Operant conditioning The subject is active and voluntarily "operates" on the environment. The consequences (reinforcement or punishment) that follow the behavior determine whether the behavioral tendencies will increase or decrease.

As we've just seen, classical conditioning is based on what happens *before* we *involuntarily* respond: Something happens to us, and we learn a new response. In contrast, **operant conditioning** is based on what happens *after* we *voluntarily* perform a behavior (Cooper et al., 2019; Pear, 2016). We do something and learn from the consequences. Be sure to note that when a behavior is followed by reinforcement, it increases. When it's followed by punishment, it decreases (**Figure 6.7**).

"WATCH THIS... I HAVE HiM TRAINED TO GIVE Me A TREAT every Time I SHAKE HiS HAND."

The key point to remember is that *consequences* are the heart of operant conditioning (see cartoon). In classical conditioning, consequences are irrelevant—Pavlov's dogs still got to eat whether they salivated or not. But in operant conditioning, the organism voluntarily performs a behavior (an operant) that produces a consequence—either reinforcement or punishment—and the behavior either increases or decreases.

It's also very important to note that **reinforcement** is the process by which *adding* or *taking away* a stimulus following a response increases the likelihood that the response will be repeated. **Punishment**, in contrast, is the process by which *adding* or *taking away* a stimulus following a response decreases the likelihood that the response will be repeated.

The power and problems with reinforcement and punishment will be explored later in this section. For now we want to highlight how they can be used to improve your everyday life. For example, allowing yourself to watch TV only while exercising is a form of reinforcement that will improve your general physical health. Similarly, stop-smoking programs that offer reinforcement in the form of cash incentives, such as requiring a $150 deposit that is returned only to people who have successfully quit smoking six months later, are nearly twice as effective at helping people stop as other approaches, such as counseling and nicotine replacement therapy (Halpern et al., 2015). In one Pennsylvania city, using a form of punishment—increasing the taxes on sugared beverages—led to a 38 percent decrease in soda consumption (Zhong et al., 2018).

Law of effect Thorndike's rule that any behavior followed by pleasant consequences is likely to be repeated, whereas any behavior followed by unpleasant consequences is likely to be reduced.

Beginnings of Operant Conditioning

Edward Thorndike, a pioneer of operant conditioning, was the first to identify that the frequency of a behavior is controlled by its consequences (Thorndike, 1911). This law, known today as Thorndike's **law of effect**, clarifies that any behavior followed by pleasant consequences is likely to be repeated, whereas any behavior followed by unpleasant consequences is likely to be reduced. Thorndike's findings were based on his study of cats in puzzle boxes (**Figure 6.8**).

B. F. Skinner later extended Thorndike's law of effect to more complex behaviors. However, he carefully avoided Thorndike's use of terms like *pleasant* and *unpleasant* because they are subjective and not directly observable. Furthermore, Skinner argued that such words make unfounded assumptions about what an organism feels or wants and imply that behavior is due to conscious choice or intention. Skinner believed that to understand behavior, we should consider only external, observable stimuli and responses. We must look outside the learner, not inside.

Skinner also talked about reinforcement and punishment in terms of *increasing* or *decreasing* the likelihood of the response being repeated. If a toddler whines for candy and the parent easily gives in, the child's whining will likely increase. But what if the parent initially refuses and yells at the child for whining, yet eventually gives in and gives him or her the lollipop? The child might feel both happy to get the candy and sad because the parent is upset. Given that we don't know the full extent of the child's internal, mixed feelings, it's cleaner (and more scientific) to limit our focus to observable behaviors and consequences. If the child's whining for lollipops increases, we can say that whining was reinforced. If it decreases, then it was punished.

Can you see why Skinner emphasized that reinforcement and punishment should always be presented *after* the targeted behavior has occurred? He believed that the only way to know how we have influenced an organism's behavior is to check whether it increases or decreases. As Skinner pointed out, we too often think we're reinforcing or punishing behavior when we're actually doing the opposite (see **Figure 6.9**).

Reinforcement versus Punishment

So far, we've discussed reinforcement and punishment only in general terms. Now it's important to clarify under what conditions they either increase or decrease behavior. To begin, you need to understand that psychologists group reinforcers into two types, primary and secondary. A **primary reinforcer** is any unlearned, innate stimulus (like food, water, or sex) that reinforces a response and thus increases the probability that it will recur. A **secondary reinforcer** is any learned, not innate, stimulus (like money, praise, or attention) that reinforces a response and thus increases the probability that it will recur. The key point is that *primary* is another word for unlearned, whereas *secondary* means learned. Note that the term *primary* may seem to imply that primary reinforcers are the most critical or powerful kind. But as you'll see in this section, that's not always the case.

It's also important to note that both primary and secondary reinforcers can produce **positive reinforcement** or **negative reinforcement**, depending on whether certain stimuli are added or taken away. *Positive reinforcement* is a process by which adding (or presenting) a stimulus following a response increases the likelihood that the response will be repeated. *Negative reinforcement* is a process by which taking away (or removing) a stimulus following a response increases the likelihood that the response will be repeated (**Table 6.2**).

The terminology used with reinforcement can be confusing. *Positive* normally means something "good" and *negative* generally means something "bad." But recall that Skinner cautioned us to avoid subjective terms like *good* and *bad* or *pleasant* and *unpleasant* because they are not external and directly observable. Instead, he used *positive* and *negative*, in line with standard scientific terminology. You'll find this section much easier if you

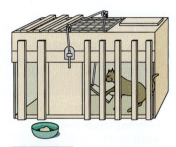

FIGURE 6.8   Thorndike's law of effect   In his most famous experiment, Thorndike put a cat inside a specially built puzzle box. When the cat stepped on a pedal inside the box (at first by chance), the door opened, and the cat could get out and eat. Then, through trial and error, the cat learned what specific actions led to opening the door. With each additional success, the cat's actions became more purposeful, and it soon learned to open the door immediately (Thorndike, 1898).

Primary reinforcer   Any unlearned, innate stimulus (like food, water, or sex) that reinforces a response and thus increases the probability that it will recur.

Secondary reinforcer   Any learned stimulus (like money, praise, or attention) that reinforces a response and thus increases the probability that it will recur.

Positive reinforcement A process by which adding (or presenting) a stimulus following a response increases the likelihood that the response will be repeated.

Negative reinforcement   A process by which taking away (or removing) a stimulus following a response increases the likelihood that the response will be repeated.

Stockbroker/MBI/Alamy Stock Photo

FIGURE 6.9   Unintended consequences   A professor may think she is encouraging shy students to talk by repeatedly praising them each time they speak up in class. But what if you are one of those shy students and are embarrassed by this extra attention? If so, you may actually decrease the number of times you talk in class. Can you see why it's important to always check to see if the target behavior is increasing or decreasing? What is reinforcing or punishing for one person may not be so for another.

TABLE 6.2	How Reinforcement Increases (or Strengthens) Behavior	
	POSITIVE REINFORCEMENT Stimulus Added (+) and Behavior Increases	**NEGATIVE REINFORCEMENT** Stimulus Taken Away (–) and Behavior Increases
Primary Reinforcers Unlearned, innate stimuli that reinforce and increase the probability of a response	You put money in the vending machine, and a snack comes out. The addition of the snack makes it more likely that you will put money in the vending machine in the future. You hug your baby and he smiles at you. The addition of his smile increases the likelihood that you will hug him again when he smiles.	You switch from formal dress shoes to sneakers, and your foot pain goes away. The removal of your pain makes it more likely that you will wear sneakers or other casual shoes in the future. Your baby is crying, so you hug him, and he stops crying. The removal of crying increases the likelihood that you will hug him again when he cries. 
Secondary Reinforcers Learned stimuli that reinforce and increase the probability of a response	Completing a quest in your video game increases your score, and unlocks desirable game items. The addition of these items increases your video game playing behavior. You study hard and receive a good grade on your psychology exam. The addition of the good grade makes it more likely that you'll study hard for future exams.	You mention all the homework you have to do, and your partner offers to do the dinner dishes. The removal of this chore increases the likelihood that you will again mention your homework the next time it's your turn to do the dishes. You're allowed to skip the final exam because you did so well on your unit exams. The removal of the final exam makes it more likely that you'll work hard to do well on unit exams in the future. 

Alen thien/Shutterstock.com

daisydaisy/123RF

Primary punisher Any unlearned, innate stimulus, such as hunger or thirst, that punishes a response and thus decreases the probability that it will recur.

Secondary punisher Any learned stimulus, such as poor grades or a parking ticket, that punishes a response and thus decreases the probability that it will recur.

Positive punishment A process by which adding (or presenting) a stimulus following a response decreases the likelihood that the response will be repeated.

Negative punishment A process by which taking away (or removing) a stimulus following a response decreases the likelihood that the response will be repeated.

always remember that *positive* is simply adding something [+] and *negative* is taking something away [–].

As with reinforcement, there are two kinds of punishers—primary and secondary. A **primary punisher** is any unlearned, innate stimulus, such as hunger or thirst, that punishes a response and thus decreases the probability that it will recur. In contrast, a **secondary punisher** is any learned, not innate, stimulus, such as poor grades or a parking ticket, that punishes a response and thus decreases the probability that it will recur.

Also, as in reinforcement, there are two kinds of punishment—positive and negative. **Positive punishment** is a process by which adding (or presenting) a stimulus following a response decreases the likelihood that the response will be repeated. **Negative punishment** is a process by which taking away (or removing) a stimulus following a response decreases the likelihood that the response will be repeated (**Table 6.3**).

At this point, it's very important to emphasize that negative reinforcement is NOT punishment. In fact, the two concepts are actually the complete opposite of each other. Reinforcement (both positive and negative) *increases* a behavior, whereas punishment (both positive and negative) *decreases* a behavior. (To check your understanding of the principles of reinforcement and punishment, see **Figure 6.10**.)

Problems with Punishment   As you've seen, punishment is tricky to use appropriately and effectively. We often think we're punishing, yet the behavior continues.

TABLE 6.3 **How Punishment Decreases (or Weakens) Behavior**

	POSITIVE PUNISHMENT Stimulus Added (+) and Behavior Decreases (or Weakens)	NEGATIVE PUNISHMENT Stimulus Taken Away (–) and Behavior Decreases (or Weakens)	
Primary Punishers Unlearned, innate stimuli that punish and decrease the probability of a response	You were late to practice, therefore you must run four extra laps. Adding the four extra laps makes it less likely that you'll be late for soccer practice in the future. You forget to apply sunscreen, and as a consequence you later suffer a painful sunburn. The addition of the sunburn makes it less likely that you'll forget to apply sunscreen in the future.	You lose sleep for several nights "cramming" for your final exams. The loss of sleep makes it less likely that you'll try last-minute "cramming" for your future final exams. A hungry child is denied dessert because she refused to eat her dinner. The removal of the dessert option decreases the likelihood of the child refusing to eat her dinner in the future.	 Nattakorn_Maneerat/ Shutterstock.com
Secondary Punishers Learned stimuli that punish and decrease the probability of a response	You text on your phone while driving, and receive a ticket. The addition of the ticket for texting makes it less likely you will text while driving in the future. You study hard for your psychology exam, and still receive a low grade. The addition of the low grade after studying hard decreases the likelihood that you will study hard for future exams.	A parent takes away a teen's phone following a poor report card. The removal of the phone makes it less likely that the teen will earn poor grades in the future. You argue aggressively with your friend, and he or she goes home. The removal of your friend's presence decreases the likelihood that you'll argue aggressively in the future.	 inhauscreative/E+/Getty Images

FIGURE 6.10 **Using the "Skinner box" for both reinforcement and punishment** To test his behavioral theories, Skinner created an operant conditioning chamber, popularly known as a "Skinner box." Using this device, experimenters can teach subjects (like rats or pigeons) to perform specific behaviors, such as pressing a lever or pecking at a disk, in response to specific signals, such as a light or sound. In many experiments, the subject's responses also are mechanically recorded. Do you see how this highly controlled environment helps reduce potential experimental errors?

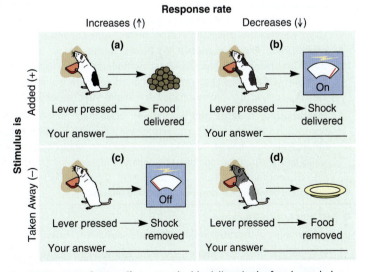

a. The classic Skinner box In Skinner's basic experimental design, an animal (such as a rat) could press a lever and food pellets or shocks (administered through an electric grid on the cage floor) could be used to administer reinforcement or punishment.

b. Test your understanding Use the blank lines in the four boxes below to fill in the label of the correct learning principle—*positive reinforcement*, *negative reinforcement*, *positive punishment*, or *negative punishment*.

Answers: (a) positive reinforcement, (b) positive punishment, (c) negative reinforcement, (d) negative punishment

Similarly, we often mistakenly think we're reinforcing when we're actually punishing. The key thing to remember is that punishment, by definition, is a process that adds or takes away something, causing a behavior to decrease. If the behavior does not decrease, it's NOT punishment. In addition to these problems, there are at least seven other potential side effects (**Table 6.4**).

TABLE 6.4   **Potential Side Effects of Punishment**

1. **Undesirable emotional responses**   For the recipient, punishment often leads to fear, anxiety, frustration, anger, and hostility—obviously, not the responses most punishers intend. For example, modern parents generally disapprove of physical punishment. But how often have you seen a parent threaten to leave a child in the store if he or she doesn't hurry and catch up? The parent may see this as a simple way to obtain compliance, whereas the child may interpret it as a threat of abandonment, and experience one or more of these unintended, undesirable emotional responses.

2. **Passive aggressiveness**   Most of us have learned from experience that retaliatory aggression toward a punisher (especially one who is bigger or more powerful) is often followed by more punishment. So instead, we may resort to subtle techniques, called *passive aggressiveness*, in which we deliberately show up late, "forget" to do an assigned chore, or complete the chore in a half-hearted way.

3. **Lying and avoidance behavior**   No one likes to be punished, so we naturally try to avoid the punishment by lying, or by avoiding the punisher. Can you see how this is an example of negative reinforcement, which will actually increase the behavior? If lying gets you out of trouble, you'll be more likely to do it again in the future. Similarly, if every time you come home, your parent or spouse starts yelling at you, you'll learn to delay coming home—or you'll find another place to go.

4. **Inappropriate modeling**   Have you ever seen a parent spank or hit his or her child for hitting another child? Ironically, the punishing parent may unintentionally serve as a "model" for the same behavior he or she is attempting to stop.

5. **Temporary suppression versus elimination**   Punishment generally suppresses the behavior only temporarily, while the punisher is nearby. In addition, the recipient only learns what NOT to do, but not necessarily what he or she SHOULD do.

6. **Learned helplessness**   Early researchers theorized that non-human animals, when faced with uncontrollable aversive events, learned that nothing they did mattered, which, in turn, undermined their attempts to escape. However, studies suggest that this passivity is not learned, but is instead a biologically based response that inhibits escape. Regardless of whether the helplessness response was learned or unlearned, can you see how this phenomenon, known as *learned helplessness*, might explain, in part, why some people stay in abusive relationships? Or why some students who've experienced many failures in academic settings might passively accept punishingly low grades or engage in self-defeating behaviors, such as procrastination or minimal effort responses?

7. **Inappropriate rewards and escalation**   Given that punishment often produces a decrease in undesired behavior, at least for the moment, the punisher is in effect rewarded for applying punishment. To make matters worse, a vicious cycle may be established in which both the punisher and the recipient are reinforced—the punisher for punishing, and the recipient for being fearful and submissive. This side effect may partially explain the escalation of violence in domestic abuse and bullying.

PeopleImages/E+/Getty Images

Time out   Is using "time out" an example of positive or negative punishment? What might be some of the unintended consequences? (Answer is below.)

Answer: It depends on the circumstances and the individual. This type of negative punishment ("time out") is often considered more ethical than positive punishment, and it's often used by parents and preschool teachers as a consequence for unwanted behavior. Time out does remove children from what the punisher considers a pleasurable environment, and it allows them quiet time to think about the situation. However, if the child was acting out to gain attention, being placed in a special chair may be unintentionally reinforcing the very behavior the punisher is trying to decrease.

Q Test Your Critical Thinking

Using one or more of these seven side effects of punishment, answer the following questions:

1. Why do you think roommates, children, and spouses refuse to load the dishwasher despite repeated nagging?

2. Why do drivers quickly slow down when they see a police car following behind, and then quickly resume speeding once the police officer is out of sight?

Sources: Gershoff et al., 2019; Lapré & Marsee, 2016; Maier & Seligman, 2016; McSweeney & Murphy, 2017; Miller et al., 2012; Seligman & Maier, 1967; Walker & Gresham, 2016.

After considering all these potential problems with punishment, you may be feeling a bit overwhelmed and wondering what to do instead. For specific tips on the effective use of both reinforcement and punishment, see the **PAH** **Practical Application Highlight**, and the **RC** **Research Challenge**.

PAH Practical Application Highlight

Using Reinforcement and Punishment Effectively

(APA Goal 1.3) Describe applications of psychology

These five suggestions can be helpful if you are managing employees, raising children, or in any other situation in which you're attempting to change another's behavior.

1. **Provide clear and concise directions and feedback.** Have you noticed how frustrating it is when a boss (or an instructor) asks you to do something but doesn't give you clear directions or helpful feedback on your work? When using either reinforcement or punishment, be sure to provide these, along with a sample or demonstration of the desired response. We all need to know precisely what to do, as well as what NOT to do.

2. **Use immediate and appropriate timing.** Reinforcers and punishers should be presented as close in time to the response as possible (see cartoon). If you're a manager, don't offer your staff a large party at the end of the year if they reach a significant goal. Instead, reward them with immediate compliments and small bonuses. Similarly, if your child hits another child, it's best to immediately stop the behavior and explain in no uncertain terms that "hitting is not allowed." In short, reinforcement and punishment should be applied as soon as possible. In addition, both reinforcement and punishment should be provided when the timing is right and the audience is most receptive.

3. **Follow correct order of presentation.** As a teenager, did you ever ask for a few extra dollars as an advance on your allowance or promise to mow the grass before the end of the week? Did you later conveniently "forget" the advance or your promise? As a manager, you can understand why providing reinforcement before the desired response occurs generally leads to increased requests for advances and broken promises. At the same time, imagine how an employee might feel if he or she asked to telecommute (work from home) and you immediately denied the request simply because you believe all employees "slough off if they're not being watched." Here, refusing the request before the negligent behavior occurs is likely to lead to frustration, resentment, and lowered productivity. In short, both reinforcement and punishment should come *after* the behavior, never *before*.

4. **Be consistent.** To be effective, both reinforcement and punishment must be consistent. Have you noticed how some children or even college students gain attention by complaining or begging? As mentioned earlier, parents often start out saying "no" to a child whining for candy but ultimately

"I like to reward my employees for doing a good job. That's why I keep treats in my pockets when I walk past the cubicles."

Marty Bucella/Cartoon Stock

give in. Why? When the parent gives in and the begging or complaining is removed, the parent is *negatively reinforced*. At the same time, the begging or whining pays off and the child is *positively reinforced*. Given that both the parent and child are reinforced, can you see why these behaviors typically escalate and become even more resistant to extinction? In sum, effective punishment requires consistent responses and almost constant surveillance. Consequently, it's impossible to be a "perfect punisher." It's best (and easiest) to use consistent reinforcement for good behavior and extinction for bad behavior.

5. **Combine key learning principles.** Police officers cannot immediately and consistently stop all drivers each and every time they speed nor reward them every time they obey the laws. Similarly, parents can't immediately and consistently scold their children every time they curse nor reward them each time they brush their teeth. Therefore, the overall best method for changing behavior seems to be a combination of the major learning principles: Reinforce appropriate behavior, extinguish inappropriate behavior, and save punishment for the most extreme cases (such as when a child is running into a busy street or hitting another child or one employee is bullying or abusing another). Key take-home message? Punishment teaches us what not to do, whereas reinforcement teaches us what to do.

RC Scientific Thinking: **Research Challenge**

Should You Use Food or Praise to Train Your Dog?

(APA Goal 2.4) Interpret, design, and conduct basic psychological research

Did you know that dogs were the first domesticated species? Or that they're currently the most loved household pets around the world, with the United States having the largest population of dogs, followed by Brazil and China (A Guide to Worldwide Pet Ownership, 2016)?

Both humans and dogs have clearly benefited from their shared social bonding. But how do we explain why dogs have become so uniquely gifted at attending to and interpreting social cues from humans (e.g., Müller et al., 2015)? Is it because humans generally provide dogs with food, a *primary reinforcer*? Or are dogs more interested in *secondary reinforcers*, like praise and human social interactions?

Previous studies attempting to answer such questions have found it difficult to separate food and social rewards during training, or to measure their relative contributions to learning. Fortunately, advances in fMRI brain scans now allow scientists to examine the precise neural mechanisms, such as those involved in the bond between humans and dogs (e.g., Andics et al., 2016).

Using this type of brain scans, researchers monitored the brains of 15 dogs of various breeds while their owners praised them or provided food (Cook et al., 2015, 2016). When dogs received praise alone, 13 of the 15 dogs showed levels of brain activity that were equal to or higher than levels shown when they just received food. To confirm that the differences were driven solely by the value of social praise, the researchers then conducted a follow-up brain-scan study in which the praise was withheld on some trials, and the findings strongly supported those of the first study.

Wondering how the dogs might respond outside the brain-imaging equipment, the researchers then used a Y-shaped maze, placing the dogs' owners on one side of the Y and a bowl of treats on the other. As predicted, the same 13 of the 15 canines preferred to go in the direction of their owner rather than to the food. In contrast, the other two dogs that preferred food over praise during the brain scans also chose food in the maze.

Can you see why this research is important? Millions of dogs are currently serving as guide dogs for people who are blind, as companions or therapy animals, and as herders, hunters, and trackers. They also assist in search-and-rescue operations and in the detection of drugs and dangerous explosives. Given these multiple roles and invaluable services, the scientists in this study suggest that brain scans could be used to better match certain dogs or specific breeds of dogs with carefully matched service assignments. For example, therapy jobs requiring close human contact might be better for dogs with a higher preference for praise. In

svetikd/E+/Getty Images

contrast, dogs with a lower need for praise might do better in more independent settings like herding and hunting, in which they normally receive a treat after successfully completing a task.

How does this apply to those of us who only want our dogs to "serve" as our loyal companions, protectors, and playmates? Should we use food or praise? The authors of this study suggest that "social reinforcement is at least as effective as food—and probably healthier too" (Cook et al., 2016, p. 17).

Identify the Research Method

1. Based on the information provided, did the second follow-up study using the Y-shaped maze (Cook et al., 2016) use descriptive, correlational, and/or experimental research?

2. If you chose

   - *descriptive research,* is this a naturalistic or laboratory observation, survey/interview, case study, and/or archival research?

   - *correlational research,* is this a positive, negative, or zero correlation?

   - *experimental research,* label the IV, DV, experimental group(s), and control group. (Note: If participants were not randomly assigned to groups, list the design as *quasi-experimental.*)

   - both *descriptive* and *correlational,* answer the corresponding questions for both.

Check your answers by clicking on the answer button or by looking in Appendix B.

Note: The information provided in this study is admittedly limited, but the level of detail is similar to what is presented in most textbooks and public reports of research findings. Answering these questions, and then comparing your answers to those provided, will help you become a better scientific and critical thinker and consumer of scientific research.

Principles of Operant Conditioning

Earlier, we discussed the six principles of classical conditioning. In this section, we explore six principles of operant conditioning: *acquisition, generalization, discrimination, extinction, shaping,* and *schedules of reinforcement* (**Figure 6.11**). (Note that the first four of these principles are very similar to those in classical conditioning, except that in classical conditioning the response is involuntary, whereas it is voluntary in operant conditioning.)

1. **Acquisition** Recall that *acquisition (in classical conditioning)* refers to learning that occurs (is acquired) when an organism involuntarily links a neutral stimulus (NS) with an unconditioned stimulus (US). This acquisition then elicits the conditioned response (CR) and/or conditioned emotional response (CER). However, during **acquisition (in operant conditioning)**, learning occurs (is acquired) when an organism voluntarily links a response with a consequence, such as a reward (see cartoon).

2. **Generalization** *Generalization (in classical conditioning)* occurs when the CR is involuntarily elicited not only by the CS but also by stimuli similar to the CS. In comparison, **generalization (in operant conditioning)** refers to voluntarily responding to a new stimulus as if it were the original, previously conditioned stimulus (CS). A pigeon that's been trained to peck at a green light might also peck at a red light, and a young child who is rewarded for calling her father "Daddy" might generalize and call all men "Daddy" (Sturdy & Nicoladis, 2017).

   TIP How does the CR differ in classical versus operant conditioning? Note that in classical conditioning the CR is *involuntarily elicited,* whereas in operant conditioning the CR is a *voluntary response.*

3. **Discrimination** *Discrimination (in classical conditioning)* refers to the learned ability to involuntarily distinguish (discriminate) between stimuli that differ from the CS. Likewise, **discrimination (in operant conditioning)** refers to the learned ability to distinguish (discriminate) between similar stimuli based on whether the response to the stimuli is reinforced or punished, and then to voluntarily respond accordingly. A pigeon might be punished after pecking at a green light, and not after pecking at a red light. As a result, it would quickly learn to peck only at red and to stop pecking at green. Similarly, a child who is reinforced only for calling her father "Daddy" will quickly learn to quit calling all men "Daddy."

4. **Extinction** Recall that *extinction (in classical conditioning)* involves a gradual diminishing of the conditioned response (CR) when the unconditioned stimulus (US) is withheld or removed. Similarly, **extinction (in operant conditioning)** refers to a gradual diminishing of a response when it is no longer reinforced. Skinner quickly taught pigeons to peck at a certain stimulus using food as a reward (Bouton & Todd, 2014; van den Akker et al., 2015). However, once the reinforcement stopped, the pigeons soon quit pecking. How does this apply to human behavior? If a local restaurant stops serving our favorite dishes, we'll soon quit going to that restaurant. Similarly, if we routinely ignore compliments or kisses from a long-term partner, he or she may soon stop giving them.

5. **Shaping** How do seals in zoos and amusement parks learn how to balance beach balls on their noses or to clap their flippers together on a command from the trainers? For new and complex behaviors such as these, which aren't likely to occur naturally, **shaping** is the key. Skinner believed that shaping, or *rewarding successive approximations,* explains a variety of abilities that each of us possess, from eating with a fork to playing a musical instrument. Parents, athletic coaches, teachers, therapists, and animal trainers all use shaping techniques (Diefenbach et al., 2017; Fonger & Malott, 2018). See **Figure 6.12**.

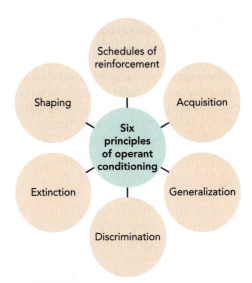

FIGURE 6.11 Major principles of operant conditioning

Acquisition (in operant conditioning) Learning occurs (is acquired) when an organism voluntarily links a response with a consequence, such as a reward.

Generalization (in operant conditioning) Voluntarily responding to a new stimulus as if it were the original, previously conditioned stimulus (CS); the opposite of discrimination.

Discrimination (in operant conditioning) A learned ability to distinguish (discriminate) between similar stimuli based on whether the response to the stimuli is reinforced or punished, and then to voluntarily respond accordingly; the opposite of generalization.

Extinction (in operant conditioning) The gradual diminishing of a conditioned response when it is no longer reinforced.

Shaping Reinforcement is delivered for successive approximations of the desired response.

"Look—we'll whistle when it's fifteen dollars an hour."

KUPER

Kuper, Peter/Cartoon Stock

FIGURE 6.12 **Shaping in action** How do gorillas learn to have their teeth brushed? Zookeepers use simple shaping techniques. They first place the toothbrush at a safe distance and then bring it closer so that they can hold it near the gorilla. Next, they reward the gorilla with grapes, apples, or popcorn if it opens its mouth while the toothbrush is near. Finally, they reward it again if it allows brushing (Wollan, 2015).

Continuous reinforcement A pattern in which every correct response is reinforced.

6. Schedules of Reinforcement Now that we've discussed how we learn complex behaviors through shaping, you may want to know how to maintain them. When Skinner was training his animals, he found that learning was most rapid if the correct response was reinforced every time it occurred—a pattern called **continuous reinforcement**.

Although most effective during the initial training/learning phase, continuous reinforcement unfortunately also leads to rapid *extinction*—the gradual diminishing of a response when it is no longer reinforced. Furthermore, in the real world, continuous reinforcement is generally not practical or economical. When teaching our children, we can't say, "Good job—you brushed your teeth," every morning for the rest of their lives. As employers, we can't give a bonus for every task our employees accomplish. For pigeons in the wild and people in the real world, behaviors are almost always reinforced only occasionally and unpredictably—a pattern called **partial (or intermittent) reinforcement**.

Partial (intermittent) reinforcement A pattern in which some, but not all, correct responses are reinforced.

Given the impracticality, and near impossibility, of continuous reinforcement, let's focus on the good news regarding partially reinforced behaviors—they're highly resistant to extinction. Skinner found that pigeons that were reinforced on a continuous schedule would continue pecking approximately 100 times after food was removed completely, indicating extinction. In contrast, pigeons reinforced on a partial schedule continued to peck thousands of times (Skinner, 1956). Moving from pigeons to people, consider the human behavior of persistent gambling (**Figure 6.13**).

Schedules of reinforcement Specific patterns of reinforcement (either fixed or variable) that determine when a behavior will be reinforced.

When using partial reinforcement, it's also important to note that some partial **schedules of reinforcement** are better suited for maintaining or changing behavior than others (Cooper et al., 2019; Jessel & Borrero, 2014; Thrailkill & Bouton, 2015). There are four

FIGURE 6.13 **Gambling—a partial schedule of reinforcement** **[AQ3]** Given that gamblers most often lose far more than they win, gambling should be a punishing situation, and easily extinguished. However, the fact that they occasionally, and unpredictably, win keeps them "hanging in there." In addition to being subjected to this dangerous *partial schedule of reinforcement*, which is highly resistant to extinction, some research demonstrates that pathological gamblers are less able to make an association between negative events (such as losing lots of money) and the stimuli that cause those events (such as gambling) (Stange et al., 2016; Templeton et al., 2015; Yücel et al., 2018). As a scientific and critical thinker, can you see how this inability to see connections between losses and gambling might also be an example of the *confirmation* bias (discussed in Chapters 1 and 8)? Most gamblers are far more likely to note and remember their wins—and ignore their losses.

TABLE 6.5   **Four Schedules of Partial (Intermittent) Reinforcement**

	Definitions	Response Rates	Examples
Ratio Schedules (Response Based)			
Fixed Ratio (FR)	Reinforcement occurs after a fixed, predetermined number of responses	High response rate with a brief pause after the delivery of the reinforcer	Piecework—you receive a free flight from your frequent flyer program after accumulating a given number of flight miles.
Variable Ratio (VR)	Reinforcement occurs after a varying number of responses	High and steady response rate after an unpredictable number of responses; variability also makes it resistant to extinction	Gambling—slot machines are designed to pay out after an average number of responses (maybe every 10 times), but any one machine may pay out on the first response, then the seventh, then the twentieth.
Interval Schedules (Time Based)			
Fixed Interval (FI)	Reinforcement occurs after the first response, following a fixed period (interval) of time	Responses increase near the time for the next reinforcement, but drop off after reinforcement and during intervals	You receive a monthly paycheck. Health inspectors visit a restaurant every 6 months.
Variable Interval (VI)	Reinforcement occurs after the first response, following varying periods (intervals) of time	Slow, steady, response rates because respondents cannot predict when reward will come; variability also makes it resistant to extinction	You're intermittently reinforced by "likes" when you check your Facebook. Your professor gives extra credit points at random times throughout the course.

schedules—**fixed ratio (FR)**, **variable ratio (VR)**, **fixed interval (FI)**, and **variable interval (VI)**. **Table 6.5** defines these terms, compares the respective response rates, and provides examples. As you can see in **Figure 6.14**, fixed and variable ratios lead to the highest overall response rate. But each of the four types of partial schedules has different advantages and disadvantages (as shown in Table 6.5).

How do we know which schedule to choose? The type of partial schedule to select depends on the type of behavior being studied and on the speed of learning desired. In general, when you're trying to teach a new behavior, it's best to start with a continuous schedule of reinforcement. Once the behavior is well learned, it's better (and often more practical) to switch to a partial schedule. Suppose you want to teach your dog to sit. First, you could reinforce your dog with a cookie every time he sits (continuous reinforcement). To make his training more resistant to extinction, you then could switch to a partial reinforcement schedule.

Before going on, look at **Figure 6.15**, which offers even more examples of how operant conditioning applies to your everyday life. If you're feeling a bit overwhelmed with all the terms and concepts for both classical and operant conditioning, carefully study the summary provided in **Table 6.6**.

Fixed ratio (FR) schedule   A pattern in which a reinforcer is delivered for the first response made after a fixed number of responses.

Variable ratio (VR) schedule A pattern in which a reinforcer is delivered for the first response made after a variable number of responses whose average is predetermined.

Fixed interval (FI) schedule A pattern in which a reinforcer is delivered for the first response made after a fixed period of time.

Variable interval (VI) schedule A pattern in which a reinforcer is delivered for the first response made after a variable period of time whose average is predetermined.

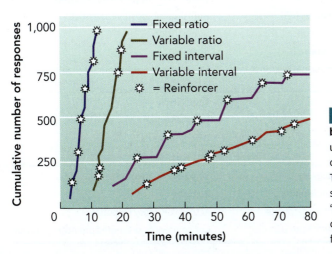

FIGURE 6.14   **Which schedule is best?**   Each of the different schedules of *reinforcement* produces its own unique pattern of response. The best schedule depends on the specific task—see Table 6.5. (The "stars" on the lines represent the delivery of a reinforcer.) (Adapted from Skinner, 1958.)

FIGURE 6.15 **Real-world applications of operant conditioning** Reinforcement and punishment shape behavior in many aspects of our everyday lives.

a. Prejudice and discrimination Although prejudice and discrimination show up early in life, children are not born believing others are inferior. How might posters like this one discourage children and adults from developing and perpetuating prejudice and discrimination?

b. Superstition Like prejudice and discrimination, we are not born with superstitions. These attitudes are learned—partly through operant conditioning. Knocking on wood for good fortune, a bride wearing "something old" at her wedding, and this French soccer player, Laurent Blanc, kissing the bald head of his teammate, goalkeeper Fabien Barthez, are all examples of superstitious behaviors that developed from accidental reinforcement. This particular kissing ritual first began when Blanc jokingly kissed his gamekeeper before each game in the 1998 World Cup finals, which they happened to win. The ritual continues despite occasional losses.

c. Biofeedback Biofeedback relies on operant conditioning to treat ailments such as anxiety and chronic pain. As an example, chronic pain patients are sometimes connected to electrodes and instructed to either watch a monitor with flashing lights or listen to different beeps, which display changes in their internal bodily functions. The patients then use the machine's feedback, flashing lights or beeps, to gauge their progress as they try various relaxation strategies to gain relief from the pain of muscle tension.

TABLE 6.6 **Comparing Classical and Operant Conditioning**

	Classical Conditioning	**Operant Conditioning**
Example	Cringing at the sound of a dentist's drill	A baby cries and you pick her up
Pioneers	Ivan Pavlov	Edward Thorndike
	John B. Watson	B. F. Skinner
Key Terms	Neutral stimulus (NS)	Reinforcers and punishers (primary/secondary)
	Unconditioned stimulus (US)	Reinforcement (positive/negative)
	Conditioned stimulus (CS)	Punishment (positive/negative)
	Unconditioned response (UR)	Superstition
	Conditioned response (CR)	Shaping
	Conditioned emotional response (CER)	Schedules of reinforcement (continuous/partial)
Key Principles and Major Similarities	Acquisition	Acquisition
	Generalization	Generalization
	Discrimination	Discrimination
	Extinction	Extinction
Major Differences	Spontaneous recovery	Schedules of reinforcement
	Higher-order conditioning	Shaping
	Passive/involuntary response	Active/voluntary response
	NS presented *before* the US	Consequences presented *after* the behavior

STH   Scientific Thinking Highlight

Wealth, Affirmative Action, and College Admission

(APA Goal 2.1) Use scientific reasoning to interpret psychological phenomena

Do you recall the college admission scandal in 2019? The public was alarmed and outraged when the press revealed that several prominent families and Hollywood stars had contributed huge donations to specific universities (see cartoon), and/or paid bribes to coaches and test proctors to increase the chances that their children would gain admission to elite American universities. In the aftermath of this scandal, many people claimed that wealthy families have always enjoyed an unfair advantage and that college admissions should be based on a level playing field.

What do you think? If you agree, how would you define what makes a "level playing field"? Setting aside the scandal in 2019 involving possibly criminal acts, most people agree that existing, legal admissions practices (either intentionally or by chance) tend to favor the rich. Only families in the upper economic brackets can afford to pay for expensive college consultants, ACT and SAT test prep courses, professional editing of college essays, and advice on how to produce the perfect application (Medina et al., 2019). Furthermore, well-off alumni often give money to their alma maters, and nearly half of all private colleges and universities (and even some public institutions) give extra consideration to donors and family members of alumni—so called "legacy admissions"(Jaschik, 2018; Lombardo, 2019).

What do you think? American students, and those around the world, have long believed that every applicant had an equal opportunity for college admission. But the recent scandal involving wealthy contributors has seriously damaged this belief, along with the reputation of first-class American universities. On the other hand, if we remove the privilege of wealth out of the admission process, some have suggested we likewise end affirmative action, meaning that colleges and universities should also remove considerations of race or ethnicity when making college admission decisions (Baker, 2019; Goodkind, 2019).

What would happen if we did ban affirmative action in college admissions? Consider the case of Justice Sonia Sotomayor. Despite being born to immigrant parents, including an alcoholic father, and being raised in a public housing project, she attended two of our nation's finest universities—thanks to affirmative action. Sotomayor proudly states: "I am the perfect affirmative action baby. My test scores were not comparable to my colleagues at Princeton and Yale…[but] I came to accept during my freshman year that many of the gaps in my knowledge and understanding were simply limits of class and cultural background, not lack of aptitude or application as I'd feared." When addressing the belief of some that "disadvantaged people just make bad choices," Sotomayor has noted on several occasions that the central purpose of affirmative action was "to create conditions whereby students from disadvantaged backgrounds could be brought to the starting line of a race many were unaware was even being run" (Sotomayor, 2014, p. 135).

"I SEE YOU HAVE A RICH AND GENEROUS FATHER. YOU'RE IN."

Schwadron, Harley/Cartoon Stock

Q Test Your Scientific Thinking

As you may recall from Chapter 1, scientific thinking is an approach to information that combines a high degree of *skepticism* (questioning what "everybody knows") with *objectivity* (using empirical data to separate fantasy from reality) and *rationalism* (practicing logical reasoning). Using these three principles, consider the following questions:

1. **Skepticism**   Given the title and topic of this Scientific Thinking Highlight, and your own experience with college admissions, were you predisposed to believe or discount the information? Scientific thinkers attempt to carefully evaluate their own biases and to value truth above self-interest. They also approach contrary positions and information with open-minded curiosity and delay judgment until adequate data and persuasive evidence are available.

2. **Objectivity**   Earlier in this section we discussed the latest objective, scientific research on operant conditioning, and how reinforcement and punishment (by definition) always increase or decrease behavior. In this highlight, we've also provided additional information about the 2019 college admissions scandal. How can you decide whether or not wealth and/or affirmative action should play a role in admission decisions? Scientific thinkers carefully analyze and compare data and questions on both sides of a controversy for their comparative value and content.

3. **Rationalism**   What would you logically recommend regarding the 2019 scandal and the current policies for college admissions? Can you think of other rational alternatives to existing policies that would truly level the playing field for all applicants, regardless of their race, ethnicity, or socioeconomic background?

(Compare your answers with those of fellow students, family, and friends. Doing so will improve your scientific thinking and your media savvy.)

Retrieval Practice 6.2 | Operant Conditioning

Self-Test Completing this self-test, and then checking your answers by clicking on the answer button or by looking in Appendix B, will provide immediate feedback and helpful practice for exams.

1. Learning in which voluntary responses are controlled by their consequences is called _____.
   a. self-efficacy
   c. classical conditioning
   b. operant conditioning
   d. involuntary pairing

2. An employer's giving his or her employees a cash bonus after they've done a good job is an example of _____.
   a. positive reinforcement
   c. classical conditioning
   b. incremental conditioning
   d. bribery

3. _____ reinforcers normally satisfy an unlearned biological need.
   a. Positive
   c. Primary
   b. Negative
   d. None of these options

4. The overall best method for changing behavior is to _____.
   a. reinforce appropriate behavior
   b. extinguish inappropriate behavior
   c. save punishment for extreme cases
   d. all of these options

5. Gamblers become addicted partially because of a _____.
   a. previously generalized response discrimination
   b. previously extinguished response recovery
   c. partial (intermittent) reinforcement
   d. behavior being learned and not conditioned

Q Test Your Critical Thinking

1. You observe a parent repeatedly yelling "No!" to his or her child who is screaming for candy in a supermarket, but ultimately gives in to the child's demands. Given what you've learned about operant conditioning, can you predict how both the parent and the child will respond in similar future situations?

2. Can you think of a better alternative to yelling "No!"?

Real World
Application Question

[AQ3] Why do gamblers have such trouble quitting, even when they continue to lose money?

Adam Gault/Photographer's Choice RF/Getty Images

Hint: Look in the text for **[AQ3]**

Cognitive-Social Learning

LEARNING OBJECTIVES

Retrieval Practice While reading the upcoming sections, respond to each Learning Objective in your own words.

Summarize the key terms and findings in the cognitive-social theory of learning.

- **Describe** insight learning, cognitive maps, and latent learning.

- **Discuss** observational learning and Bandura's four key factors.

Real World Application Question

[AQ4] Can children learn anti-fat prejudice and math anxiety from their parents?

> He who learns but does not think is lost. He who thinks but does not learn is in great danger.
> —Confucious (Chinese philosopher, teacher, politician)

Cognitive-social learning theory
A theory that emphasizes the roles of thinking and social learning.

So far, we have examined learning processes that involve associations between a stimulus and an observable behavior—the key to both classical and operant conditioning. Although some behaviorists believe that almost all learning can be explained in such stimulus–response terms, cognitive psychologists disagree. **Cognitive-social learning theory** (also called cognitive-social learning or cognitive-behavioral theory) incorporates the general concepts of conditioning. But rather than relying on a simple S–R (stimulus and response) model, this theory emphasizes the cognitive processes (thinking) that occur within the organism: S–O–R (stimulus–organism–response).

According to this view, humans have attitudes, beliefs, expectations, motivations, and emotions that affect learning. Furthermore, humans and many non-human animals are social creatures that are capable of learning new behaviors through the observation and imitation of others (e.g., Meyer et al., 2019). In this section, we look first at insight and latent learning, followed by observational learning.

Insight and Latent Learning

Early behaviorists likened the mind to a "black box" whose workings could not be observed directly. German psychologist Wolfgang Köhler (1887–1967) wanted to look inside the box. He believed that there was more to learning—especially learning to solve a complex problem—than responding to stimuli in a trial-and-error fashion. In one of his best known classic experiments, Köhler placed a piece of fruit and a long stick just outside the reach of one of his brightest chimpanzees, named Sultan (Köhler, 1925). He also placed a short stick inside Sultan's cage. Sultan then quickly picked up the stick and tried to rake the fruit into his reach outside the cage, but the stick was too short. Köhler noticed that the chimp did not solve the problem in a random trial-and-error fashion. Instead, he seemed to sit and think about the situation for a while. Sultan then suddenly picked up the shorter stick and used it to drag the longer stick within his reach, and then used the longer stick to rake in the fruit.

Köhler called this sequence of events **insight learning** because some internal mental process, which he could only describe as *insight*, or an "aha" experience, went on between the presentation of the fruit and the use of the two sticks to retrieve it. (See **Figure 6.16** for another example of how Köhler's chimps solved a similar "out-of-reach banana" problem.)

Like Köhler, Edward C. Tolman (1898–1956) believed that previous researchers had underestimated human and non-human animals' cognitive processes and cognitive learning. He noted that when allowed to roam aimlessly in an experimental maze with no food reward at the end, rats seemed to develop a **cognitive map**, or mental representation of the maze.

To test the idea of cognitive learning, Tolman allowed one group of rats to aimlessly explore a maze, with no reinforcement, while a second group was reinforced with food whenever they reached the end of the maze (Tolman & Honzik, 1930). A third group was not rewarded during the first 10 days of the trial, but starting on day 11 they found food at the end of the maze.

As expected from simple operant conditioning, the first and third groups were slow to learn the maze, whereas the second group, which had reinforcement, showed fast, steady improvement. However, when the third group started receiving reinforcement (on the 11th day), their learning quickly caught up to that of the group that had been reinforced every time. This showed that the non-reinforced rats had been thinking and building cognitive maps of the area during their aimless wandering and that their **latent learning** showed up only when there was a reason to display it (the food reward).

Cognitive maps and latent learning are not limited to rats. A chipmunk will pay little attention to a new log in its territory (after initially checking it for food). When a predator comes along, however, the chipmunk will head directly for and hide beneath the log. Scientific experiments provide additional clear evidence of latent learning and the existence of internal cognitive maps in both human and non-human animals (Boccara et al., 2019; Geronazzo et al., 2016; Leising et al., 2015). See **Figure 6.17**. Do you remember your first visit to your college campus? You probably just wandered around checking out the various buildings, without realizing you were engaged in "latent learning" and building your own "cognitive maps." This exploration undoubtedly came in handy when you later needed to find your classes or the student center.

FIGURE 6.16 **Cognitive-social learning** In a second Köhler experiment, chimpanzees were placed in a room with several scattered boxes, none of which was high enough to enable them to reach a suspended banana. They initially ran around and unproductively jumped for the banana. Then, all of a sudden, they saw the solution—they stacked the boxes and used them to climb up and grab the banana. (Also, note how the chimp in the background is engaged in observational learning, our next topic.)

Insight A sudden understanding or realization of how a problem can be solved.

Cognitive map A mental image of a three-dimensional space that an organism has navigated.

Latent learning Hidden learning that exists without behavioral signs.

Stephen Zeigler/Taxi/Getty Images

FIGURE 6.17 **Cognitive maps** This skateboarder enjoys simply riding around her neighborhood. Without realizing it, she's also developing her own internal cognitive maps, and could probably easily return to the local park. Have you developed similar cognitive maps of your local area?

Observational Learning

Observational learning The learning of new behaviors or information by watching and imitating others (also known as social learning or modeling).

In addition to classical and operant conditioning and cognitive processes (such as insight and latent learning), we learn many things through **observational learning**, which is also called *imitation* or *modeling*. From birth to death, observational learning is very important to our biological, psychological, and social survival (the *biopsychosocial model*). Watching others helps us avoid dangerous stimuli in our environment, teaches us how to think and feel, and shows us how to act and interact socially (Carcea & Froemke, 2019; Meyer et al., 2019). Toddlers typically go through a picky eating phase, but research shows that toddlers who watched their parents eating a novel food were far more likely to try that food than toddlers who were only repeatedly prompted by parents (Edelson et al., 2016).

[AQ4] Unfortunately, observational learning may also lead to negative outcomes. Research finds that even very young toddlers will show a clear preference for looking at average-sized rather than obese-sized figures (Ruffman et al., 2016). Noting that the toddlers' responses were correlated with their mothers' anti-fat attitudes and were unrelated to parental BMI or education or the child's television viewing time, the researchers concluded that the toddlers' prejudices most likely resulted from modeling and observational learning. A similar example of bad modeling comes from research on math-anxious parents who help with their child's math homework (see photo). A study found that the children of these parents actually learn less math over a school year and are more likely to develop math anxiety themselves (Maloney et al., 2015).

On a happier note, longitudinal analyses of children who grew up with mothers who held more pro-environmental attitudes later engaged in more pro-environmental behaviors as young adults (Evans et al., 2018). Furthermore, researchers have even found that 15-month-old infants who watch adults model persistence in achieving a goal will observe and imitate this persistence (Leonard et al., 2017).

Bandura's "Bobo doll" Studies
Much of our appreciation for observational learning initially came from the work of Albert Bandura and his colleagues (Bandura, 2011; Bandura et al., 1961; Bandura & Walters, 1963). Wanting to know whether children learn to be aggressive by watching others be aggressive, Bandura and his colleagues set up several experiments in which children watched a live or televised adult model punch, throw, and hit a large inflated "Bobo doll" (**Figure 6.18**).

Later, the children were allowed to play in the same room with the Bobo doll. As Bandura hypothesized, children who had watched the live or televised aggressive model were much more aggressive with the Bobo doll than children who had not seen the modeled aggression (see again Figure 6.18). Thanks to the Bobo doll studies and his other experiments, Bandura established that observational learning requires at least four separate processes: *attention*, *retention*, *reproduction*, and *motivation* (**Figure 6.19**).

Real-World Applications of Cognitive-Social Learning
We use cognitive-social learning in many ways in our everyday lives, yet one of the most powerful examples is frequently overlooked—*media influences*. Experimental and correlational research clearly show that when we watch television, go to movies, and read books, magazines, or websites that portray people of color, women, and members of other groups in demeaning and stereotypical roles, we often learn to expect these behaviors and to accept them as "natural." Exposure of this kind initiates and reinforces the learning of prejudice (Graf et al., 2019; Scharrer & Ramasubramanian, 2015; van der Pligt & Vliek, 2016).

Watching popular media also teaches us what to eat, what toys to buy, what homes and clothes are most fashionable, and what constitutes "the good life." When a TV commercial shows children enjoying a particular cereal and beaming at their parent in gratitude (with mom smiling back), both children and parents in the audience are participating in a form of observational learning. The children learn how to manipulate the parents, while the parents learn that they can make their children happy by purchasing the advertised products. The good news is that research has found that media may also offer several benefits to viewers (see **PP PositivePsych**).

golero/E+/Getty Images

Albert Bandura

Albert Bandura

FIGURE 6.18 **Bandura's Bobo doll study**

FIGURE 6.19 **Bandura's four key factors in observational learning** A child wanting to become a premier ballerina—or you, if you wanted to learn to paint, ski, or play a musical instrument—would need to incorporate these four factors to maximize learning.

a. Attention Observational learning requires attention. This is why teachers insist on having students watch their demonstrations.

b. Retention To learn new behaviors, we need to carefully note and remember the model's directions and demonstrations.

c. Reproduction Observational learning requires that we imitate the model.

Tetra Images - Erik Isakson/Getty Images

d. Motivation We are more likely to repeat a modeled behavior if the model is reinforced for the behavior, e.g., with applause or other recognition.

PP **Practical Application: PositivePsych**

The Impressive Powers of Prosocial Media

(APA Goal 1.3) Describe applications of psychology

Parents, educators, and politicians have long complained about media portrayals of teenage sexuality, and many teens are transfixed by reality television shows featuring pregnant teenagers, such as *16 and Pregnant* and *Teen Mom*. But could these programs, which *accurately* portray the realities of teen pregnancy, have a positive effect on adolescent sexual behavior? To answer this and other questions, researchers examined national teenage birth rates and collected data from Nielsen ratings of these programs, along with measurements of Google and Twitter searches conducted by viewers (Kearney & Levine, 2015). Surprising to some, the results showed that reality television shows featuring pregnant teenagers led to an estimated 5.7 percent decline in teen births in the 18 months following the reality shows' first broadcast.

Further good news regarding prosocial media comes from a cross-cultural study that tested levels of empathy and helpfulness in thousands of adolescents and young adults in seven different

kali9/E+/Getty Images

countries (Australia, China, Croatia, Germany, Japan, Romania, and the United States) (Prot et al., 2014). Happily, researchers found that greater exposure to *prosocial media*—meaning video games, movies, or TV programs showing helpful, caring, and cooperative behaviors— led to higher levels of helping behavior among the viewers.

How do learning principles apply to your personal life? The **Test Yourself** provides a quick, helpful way to review the three major forms of learning, while also improving your student success skills. See also the **GCD** **Gender and Cultural Diversity**.

PA Practical Application

Test Yourself: Using Learning Principles to Succeed in College

Having studied the principles of classical, operant, and cognitive-social learning, see if you can apply this new information to your overall educational goals.

1. **Classical conditioning** If you're overly anxious when taking exams and you can see that this might be a conditioned emotional response (CER), describe how you could use the principle of extinction to weaken this response.

2. **Operant conditioning** List three ways you can positively reinforce yourself for studying, completing assignments, and attending class.

3. **Cognitive-social learning** Discuss with friends what they do to succeed in college classes and how participating in club and campus activities can reinforce your commitment to education.

GCD Gender and Cultural Diversity

Learning, Scaffolding, & Culture

(APA Goal 2.5) Incorporate sociocultural factors in scientific inquiry

Learning in the real world is often a combination of classical conditioning, operant conditioning, and cognitive-social learning. This is especially evident in informal situations in which an individual acquires new skills under the supervision of a master teacher. The ideal process used by teachers in these situations is known as *scaffolding*. Like the temporary platform on which construction workers stand, a cognitive *scaffold* provides temporary assistance while a learner acquires new skills. During this type of cognitive scaffolding, a more experienced person adjusts the amount of guidance to fit the learner's current performance level. In most cases, scaffolding also combines *shaping* and *modeling*, where the teacher selectively reinforces successes of the student and models more difficult parts of the task.

Patricia Marks Greenfield (1984, 1994) has described how scaffolding helps young girls learn to weave in Zinacantán, Mexico. Weaving is an important part of the culture of the Zinacantecos, who live in the highlands of southern Mexico. Greenfield videotaped 14 girls at different levels of learning to weave. Each girl was allowed to complete what she was able to do with ease, and then a more experienced weaver created a scaffold by reinforcing correct weaving and modeling more difficult techniques. Surprisingly, the teachers appear oblivious to their teaching methods and to the fact that they are teaching at all. Most of the Zinacanteco women believe that girls learn to weave by themselves. Similarly, in our Western culture, many believe that children learn to talk by themselves and ignore how often children are reinforced and scaffolded by others.

Retrieval Practice 6.3 | Cognitive-Social Learning

Self-Test Completing this self-test, and then checking your answers by clicking on the answer button or by looking in Appendix B, will provide immediate feedback and helpful practice for exams.

1. _____ emphasizes the roles of thinking and social learning.
   a. Classical conditioning
   b. Operant conditioning
   c. Patent learning
   d. Cognitive-social learning theory

2. Insight is _____.
   a. based on unconscious classical conditioning
   b. an innate human reflex
   c. a sudden flash of understanding
   d. an artifact of operant conditioning

3. When walking to your psychology class, you note that the path you normally take is blocked for construction, so you quickly choose an alternative route. This demonstrates that you've developed _____ of your campus.
   a. a neural map
   b. insight into the layout
   c. a cognitive map
   d. none of these options

4. Latent learning occurs without being rewarded and _____.
   a. remains hidden until a future time when it is needed
   b. is easily extinguished
   c. serves as a discriminative stimuli
   d. has been found only in non-human species

5. Bandura's observational learning studies focused on how _____.

    a. rats learn cognitive maps through exploration

    b. children learn aggressive behaviors by observing aggressive models

    c. cats learn problem solving through trial and error

    d. chimpanzees learn problem solving through reasoning

Q Test Your Critical Thinking

1. What are some examples of how insight learning has benefited you in your life?

2. Are there instances in which observational learning has worked to your advantage?

Real World Application Question

[AQ4] Can children learn anti-fat prejudice and math anxiety from their parents?

golero/E+/Getty Images

Hint: Look in the text for **[AQ4]**

Biology of Learning

LEARNING OBJECTIVES

Retrieval Practice   While reading the upcoming sections, respond to each Learning Objective in your own words.

Review the biological factors in learning.

- **Explain** how learning changes our brains.
- **Describe** how experiences and enriched environments affect our brains.
- **Discuss** the importance of mirror neurons.

- **Summarize** the role of evolution in learning.

Real World Application Questions

[AQ5] Do humans have specific neurons responsible for empathy and imitation of others?

[AQ6] Why can even young children recognize a picture of a snake much faster than a picture of a frog or caterpillar?

Having discussed how we learn through classical conditioning, operant conditioning, and cognitive-social learning, we can now explore the key biological factors in all forms of learning. In this section, we will examine both neurological and evolutionary influences on learning.

Neuroscience and Learning

Did you know that each time we learn something, either consciously or unconsciously, that experience creates new synaptic connections and alterations in a wide network of our brain's structures, including the cortex, cerebellum, hippocampus, hypothalamus, thalamus, and amygdala? Interestingly, research shows that both love AND money involve similar neural circuits and reward systems within the human brain (Gu et al., 2019). It also appears that somewhat different areas of our brains respond to reinforcement and punishment (Correia & Goosens, 2016; Cubillo et al., 2019; Ollmann et al., 2015). See **Figure 6.20**.

Evidence that learning changes brain structure first emerged in the 1960s, from studies of animals raised in *enriched* versus *deprived* environments. Compared with rats raised in a stimulus-poor environment, those raised in a colorful, stimulating "rat Disneyland" had a thicker cortex, increased nerve growth factor (NGF), more fully developed synapses, more dendritic branching, and improved performance on many tests of learning and memory (Bergendahl et al., 2016; Hong et al., 2016; Lima et al., 2014).

FIGURE 6.20 **How our brains respond to reinforcement versus punishment**

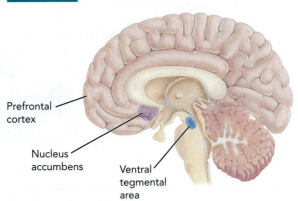

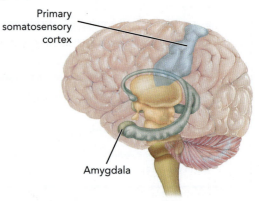

a. Brain areas responsive to reinforcement Learning from reinforcement primarily involves sections of the ventral tegmental area, nucleus accumbens, and prefrontal cortex.

b. Brain areas responsive to punishment Learning from punishment involves some of the same brain regions as reinforcement, but the amygdala and primary somatosensory cortex are particularly responsive, due to their role in fear and pain.

Mirror neurons Neurons that fire (or are activated) when an action is performed, as well as when the actions or emotions of another are observed; believed to be responsible for empathy, imitation, language, and the deficits of some mental disorders.

Research suggests that the human brain also responds to environmental conditions (**Figure 6.21**). For instance, older adults who are exposed to stimulating environments generally perform better on intellectual and perceptual tasks than those in restricted environments (Leon & Woo, 2018; Rohlfs Domínguez, 2014; Schaeffer et al., 2014). Similarly, babies who spend their early weeks and months of life in an orphanage, receiving little or no one-on-one care or attention, show deficits in the cortex of the brain, indicating that early environmental conditions may have a lasting impact on cognitive development (Behen & Chugani, 2015; Moutsiana et al., 2015; Perego et al., 2016).

The good news, however, is that children who are initially placed in an orphanage but later move on to foster care—where they receive more individual attention—show some improvements in brain development. Further good news comes from research showing that enriching the environment of older adults can reverse the decline in sensory systems, which, in turn, may aid in improving cognitive functioning (Leon & Woo, 2018).

Mirror Neurons Research has identified another neurological influence on learning processes. **[AQ5]** Studies using fMRIs and other brain-imaging techniques have identified specific **mirror neurons** believed to be responsible for observational learning, human empathy, and imitation of others (Carrillo et al., 2019; Lim & Okuno, 2015; Livi et al., 2019). When we see another person in pain, one reason we empathize and "share their pain," while seemingly unconsciously imitating their facial expressions, may be that our mirror neurons are firing (see photo).

FIGURE 6.21 **Environmental enrichment and brain devlopment** Given that environmental conditions play such an important role in enabling learning, can you see why it's so important to a child's brain development that he or she have the opportunity to attend classrooms like the one in this photo, which is filled with stimulating toys, games, and books? Similarly, how might an "enriched" cage environment, like the one these mice seem to be enjoying, also encourage brain development in non-human animals?

Mirror neurons were first discovered by neuroscientists who implanted wires in the brains of monkeys to monitor areas involved in planning and carrying out movement (Bruni et al., 2018; Rizzolatti, 2014; Rizzolatti et al., 1996, 2008). When these monkeys moved and grasped an object, specific neurons fired, but they also fired when the monkeys simply observed another monkey performing the same or similar tasks.

PAN Practical Application of Neuroscience

While watching athletes like the one in the photo, have you ever found yourself moving your arms or legs slightly in synchrony with the athletes? Mirror neurons may be the underlying biological mechanism for this imitation, and may help explain certain psychological disorders. For example, the emotional deficits of children and adults with autism or schizophrenia, who often misunderstand the verbal and non-verbal cues of others, may be linked to deficiencies in mirror neurons (Brown et al., 2016; Hillus et al., 2019; Jeon & Lee, 2018).

On the other hand, some of the research findings on mirror neurons may have been overstated. Have you heard proud parents claiming that when they stick their tongue out, their baby will quickly mimic the same gesture? Early research did, in fact, find that when an adult displayed a certain facial expression, even very young infants seemed to respond with a similar expression (e.g., Heimann & Meltzoff, 1996) (**Figure 6.22**). However, a comprehensive and longitudinal investigation of this type of early infant imitation failed to replicate (repeat) the original findings (Oostenbroek et al., 2016). As you may recall from Chapter 1, certain studies from psychology and other sciences have been criticized and are now part of the so-called "replication crisis." In this case of infant imitation, researchers now believe that the initial findings lacked sufficient controls, were methodologically limited, and should be modified or abandoned.

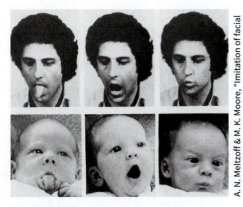

A. N. Meltzoff & M. K. Moore, "Imitation of facial and manual gestures by human neonates," Science, 1977, 198, 75–78.

FIGURE 6.22 Infant imitation—true evidence of mirror neurons? In a series of well-known studies, Andrew Meltzoff and M. Keith Moore (1977, 1985, 1994) supposedly found that newborns could easily imitate such facial movements as tongue protrusion, mouth opening, and lip pursing. Why do we say "supposedly"? As noted in the text, these findings have not been sufficiently replicated.

Take-Home Message Despite the lack of replication of infant imitation of facial expressions, scientists remain excited about the promising links between mirror neurons and the thoughts, feelings, and actions of both humans and non-humans. But we do not yet know the full extent of the influence of mirror neurons, how they develop, and if they are present at birth or develop later due to observational learning. However, we do appreciate that, thanks to our mirror neurons, we're able to successfully imitate and empathize with others, skills that are essential to survival in our complex, highly developed social world.

Evolution and Learning

In addition to being born with brains that adapt and change with learning, humans and other animals are born with various innate reflexes and instincts that help ensure their survival. However, these evolutionary responses are inherently inflexible, whereas learning allows us to more flexibly respond to complex environmental cues such as spoken words and written symbols, which in turn enables us to survive and prosper in a constantly changing world. As we've seen, learning even enables non-human animals to be classically conditioned to salivate to tones and operantly conditioned to perform a variety of novel behaviors, such as a seal balancing a ball on its nose.

Classical Conditioning Evolutionary and learning theorists initially believed that the fundamental laws of conditioning would apply to almost all species and all behaviors. However, researchers have discovered that some associations are much more readily learned than others. As an example, when a food or drink is associated with nausea or vomiting, that particular food or drink readily becomes a conditioned stimulus (CS) that triggers a conditioned **taste aversion**. Like other classically conditioned responses, taste aversions develop involuntarily (see the **Test Yourself**).

Taste aversion A classically conditioned dislike for, and avoidance of, a specific food whose ingestion is followed by illness.

PA Practical Application

Test Yourself: Taste Aversion

Years ago, a young woman named Rebecca unsuspectingly bit into a Butterfinger candy bar (see photo) filled with small, wiggling maggots. Horrified, she ran gagging and screaming to the bathroom.

iStock.com/robtek

Q Test Your Critical Thinking

1. After many years, Rebecca still feels nauseated when she even sees a Butterfinger candy bar. Can you use the term *discrimination* to explain why she doesn't feel similarly nauseated by the sight of a Snickers candy bar?

2. Under what conditions would a taste aversion be evolutionarily maladaptive?

Harris, Sidney/Cartoon Stock

"OF COURSE IT TASTES TERRIBLE. IT'S A DUNG BEETLE."

amwu/iStock/Getty Images

Biological preparedness The built-in (innate) readiness to form associations between certain stimuli and responses.

The initial discovery of taste aversions is credited to psychologists John Garcia and Robert Koelling (1966). They produced a taste aversion in lab rats by pairing sweetened water (NS) and a shock (US), which produced nausea (UR). After being conditioned and then recovering from the illness, the rats refused to drink the sweetened water (CS) due to the conditioned taste aversion. Remarkably, however, Garcia and Koelling discovered that only certain stimuli could produce aversions. Their rats developed aversions to tastes but not to sights or sounds.

Taste aversion illustrates an important evolutionary process (see cartoon). Being biologically prepared to quickly associate nausea with food or drink is obviously adaptive. It helps us avoid that specific food or drink, and similar ones, in the future (Buss, 2015; Goldfinch, 2015; Shepherd, 2017).

[AQ6] Similarly, perhaps because of the more "primitive" evolutionary threat posed by snakes, darkness, spiders, and heights, people tend to develop phobias of these stimuli more easily than they do phobias of guns, knives, and electrical outlets. Research also shows that both adults and very young children around the world appear to have an innate predisposition to detect and respond quickly to snakes, compared to other (non-life-threatening) objects, including a caterpillar, flower, or frog (see photo) (Landová et al., 2018; Thrasher & LoBue, 2016; Young et al., 2012). We apparently inherit a built-in (innate) readiness to form associations between certain stimuli and responses—but not others. This is known as **biological preparedness**. Note, however, that this predisposition to pay more attention to certain stimuli might make fear learning easier later on—but fears and phobias are NOT innate and hardwired (Thrasher & LoBue, 2016). In other words, even these evolutionarily based fears are learned, and therefore can be unlearned.

Operant Conditioning

As we've just seen, there are biological, evolutionary limits on classical conditioning. The same is true of operant conditioning. Just as Garcia and Koelling couldn't produce noise–nausea associations, other researchers have found that an animal's natural behavior pattern can interfere with the learning of certain operant responses. For instance, early researchers tried to teach a chicken to play a modified form of baseball (Breland & Breland, 1961). Through shaping and reinforcement, the chicken first learned to pull a loop that activated a swinging bat and then learned to time its response to actually hit the ball. Surprisingly, the researchers had more difficulty training the chicken to run to first base. Instead, it would often chase the moving ball as if it were food. Regardless of the lack of reinforcement for chasing the ball, the chicken's natural predatory behavior of chasing moving objects took precedence. This tendency for a conditioned behavior to revert (drift back) to innate response patterns is known as **instinctive drift**.

Instinctive drift The tendency for conditioned responses to revert (drift back) to innate response patterns.

Final Take-Home Message

In this chapter, we've discussed three general types of learning: classical, operant, and cognitive-social. We've also examined several biological effects on learning. What is the most important thing to remember? As humans, *we have the ability to learn and change*. Using what you've discovered in this chapter, we hope you'll remember to avoid using punishment whenever possible and "simply" reinforce desired behaviors. This basic principle can also be successfully applied on a national and global scale.

Be sure to complete the final Retrieval Practice quiz, and then answer the critical thinking questions in the **Test Your Critical Thinking**.

Retrieval Practice 6.4 | Biology of Learning

Self-Test Completing this self-test, and then checking your answers by clicking on the answer button or by looking in Appendix B, will provide immediate feedback and helpful practice for exams.

1. Rats _____ had a thicker cortex, more fully developed synapses, and improved test performances.
   a. given a restricted diet
   b. injected with nerve growth factor (NGF)
   c. raised in an enriched environment
   d. none of these options

2. _____ neurons may be responsible for human empathy and imitation.
   a. Motor
   b. Sensitivity
   c. Efferent
   d. Mirror

3. Rebecca's story of becoming nauseated and vomiting after eating a spoiled candy bar is a good example of _____.
   a. a biological imperative
   b. a taste aversion
   c. learned empathy
   d. negative reinforcement

4. Being innately predisposed to form associations between certain stimuli and responses is called _____.
   a. biological readiness
   b. vicarious learning
   c. superstitious priming
   d. biological preparedness

5. The fact that chickens trained to play baseball tend to chase the ball, rather than running to first base, is an example of _____.
   a. latent learning
   b. biological unpreparedness
   c. instinctive drift
   d. low salaries for professional ball players

Q Test Your Critical Thinking

1. If mirror neurons explain human empathy, could they also explain why first responders (like police and firefighters) are more vulnerable to job burnout? Why or why not?

2. Do you have any taste aversions? If so, how might you use information in this chapter to remove them?

Real World Application Questions

[AQ5] Do humans have specific neurons responsible for empathy and imitation of others?

[AQ6] Why can even young children recognize a picture of a snake much faster than a picture of a frog or caterpillar?

amwu/iStock/ Getty Images / Prostock-studio/ Shutterstock.com

Hint: Look in the text for **[AQ5]** and **[AQ6]**

Q Test Your Critical Thinking

Did you notice or wonder why we provided six Real World Application Questions [AQ1–AQ6] throughout this chapter? We've found that they not only help you to engage with and master the material, but also have an important and lasting impact on your critical thinking skills. For additional mastery and enrichment, consider the following questions:

1. What principles of learning best explain why politicians kiss babies (as shown in the photo)?

2. What other stimuli or symbols do politicians use in their campaigns that are based on learning principles?

3. Have you ever used learning principles to get others to do what you want? Was it ethical?

4. How could the media be used to promote desirable traits and behaviors in the viewing public?

Joe Mahoney/Stringer/Getty Images News/ Getty Images

Summary

6.1 Classical Conditioning 170

- **Learning** is a relatively permanent change in behavior or mental processes resulting from experience. Pavlov discovered a fundamental form of **conditioning** (learning) called **classical conditioning**, which develops through involuntarily paired associations. A previously **neutral stimulus (NS)** becomes associated with an **unconditioned stimulus (US)** to elicit a **conditioned response (CR)**.

- In the Little Albert study, Watson and Rayner demonstrated how many of our likes, dislikes, prejudices, and fears are examples of a **conditioned emotional response (CER)**.

- **Acquisition**, the first of six key principles of classical conditioning, is the initial learning when an organism involuntarily links an NS with a US, which then elicits the CR. **Generalization (in classical conditioning)** occurs when a CR is involuntarily elicited not only by the CS but also by stimuli similar to the CS. In contrast, **discrimination** (in classical conditioning) is the learned ability to involuntarily distinguish (discriminate), and to NOT respond to a new stimulus as if it were the previous CS. **Extinction (in classical conditioning)** is a gradual diminishing of a CR when the US is withheld or removed. However, if a CS is reintroduced after extinction, an extinguished response may **spontaneously recover. Higher-order conditioning** occurs when a new CS is created through pairing with a previous CS.

6.2 Operant Conditioning 179

- Both classical and operant conditioning are forms of **associative learning**. In **operant conditioning**, an organism learns as a result of voluntary behavior and its subsequent consequences. **Reinforcement** increases the response, while **punishment** decreases the response.

- Thorndike developed the **law of effect**, saying that any behavior followed by pleasant consequences is likely to be repeated, whereas any behavior followed by unpleasant consequences is likely to be stopped. Skinner extended Thorndike's law of effect to more complex behaviors, with a special emphasis on external, observable behaviors.

- **Primary reinforcers** and **primary punishers** are innate, whereas **secondary reinforcers** and **secondary punishers** are learned. Each type of reinforcer can produce **positive reinforcement** or **negative reinforcement,** and both of these forms of reinforcement increase the response they follow. Negative reinforcement is NOT punishment. Both **positive punishment** and **negative punishment** decrease a response.

- Punishment can have serious side effects: undesirable emotional responses, passive aggressiveness, lying and avoidance behavior, inappropriate modeling, temporary suppression versus elimination, learned helplessness, inappropriate rewards, and escalation.

- **Acquisition (in operant conditioning)**, the first of six key principles of operant conditioning, occurs when an organism voluntarily links a response with a consequence, such as a reward. **Generalization (in operant conditioning)** refers to voluntarily responding to a new stimulus as if it were the original, previously conditioned stimulus (CS). In contrast, **discrimination (in operant conditioning)** is the learned ability to distinguish (discriminate) between similar stimuli based on whether the response to the stimuli is reinforced or punished, and then to voluntarily respond accordingly. **Extinction (in operant conditioning)** refers to a gradual

diminishing of a response when it is no longer reinforced. **Shaping** involves delivering reinforcement for successive approximations of the desired response. **Schedules of reinforcement** refer to patterns of reinforcement (fixed or variable) that determine when a behavior is reinforced. Most behavior is rewarded and maintained through one of four partial schedules of reinforcement: fixed ratio (FR), variable ratio (VR), fixed interval (FI), or variable interval (VI).

- Both classical and operant conditioning share terms, including acquisition, generalization, discrimination, and extinction. The key difference is that classical conditioning is learning through passive, involuntary paired associations, whereas operant conditioning is learning through active, voluntary behavior and its subsequent consequences.

- Note that almost all behaviors result from a combination of both classical and operant conditioning.

6.3 Cognitive-Social Learning 192

- **Cognitive-social learning theory** emphasizes the roles of thinking and social learning. Köhler discovered that animals sometimes learn through sudden **insight**, rather than through trial and error. Tolman provided evidence of hidden **latent learning** and internal **cognitive maps**.

- Bandura's research found that children who watched an adult behave aggressively toward an inflated Bobo doll became more aggressive themselves. **Observational learning** requires attention, retention, reproduction, and motivation.

6.4 Biology of Learning 197

- Learning creates structural changes in the brain (e.g., different areas of our brains respond to reinforcement and punishment). Early evidence for such changes came from research on animals raised in enriched environments versus deprived environments. Another neurological influence on learning comes from **mirror neurons**, which fire when an action is performed, as well as when the actions or emotions of others are observed.

- Learning responses such as a **taste aversion** are an evolutionary adaptation that enables organisms to survive and prosper in a constantly changing world. In addition, there are biological constraints that may alter or limit conditioning, such as **biological preparedness** and **instinctive drift**.

Key Terms

Retrieval Practice Write your own definition for each term before turning back to the referenced page to check your answer.

Kuttelvaserova Stuchelova/Shutterstock.com

CHAPTER 7

Memory

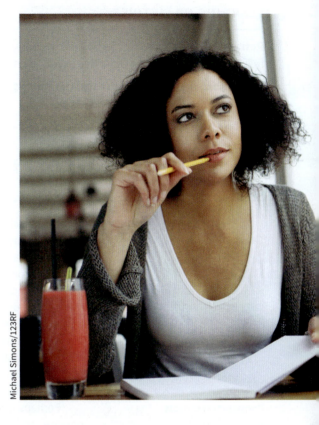

Michael Simons/123RF

Real World Application Questions

Things you'll learn in Chapter 7

[AQ1] Can your phone affect your memory—even when it's turned off?

[AQ2] How can taking a nap improve your memory?

[AQ3] Why do we remember President Lincoln better than President Truman?

[AQ4] How might exposure to pornography interfere with memory?

[AQ5] Can physical fitness help prevent dementia?

[AQ6] Could someone falsely convince you as an adult that you had committed a serious crime as a teenager?

Throughout the chapter, look for AQ1–AQ6 icons. They indicate where the text addresses these questions.

CHAPTER OUTLINE

7.1	The Nature of Memory

LEARNING OBJECTIVES

Retrieval Practice   While reading the upcoming sections, respond to each Learning Objective in your own words.

Summarize the key factors, research findings, and major models of memory.

- **Define** memory and its constructive process.
- **Discuss** the four major memory models.
- **Explain** the function and process of each stage of the three-stage memory model.

- **Describe** the core features, functions, and various types of long-term memory (LTM) and how to improve it.

Real World Application Questions

[AQ1] Can your phone affect your memory—even when it's turned off?

[AQ2] How can taking a nap improve your memory?

We begin this chapter with a look at the nature of memory. Then we explore the basic factors in forgetting and the biological bases of memory. We close with a look at how, when, and why we sometimes distort our memories, and a summary of the best memory improvement tools for student success.

Memory   The persistence of learning over time; the process by which information is encoded, stored, and retrieved.

We all commonly use the term *memory*, but what exactly do we mean? Is it simply remembering? What would it be like to have no memories? Most psychologists define **memory** as learning that persists over time. It allows us to learn from our experiences and to adapt to ever-changing environments. Without it, we would have no past or future. Yet our memories are also highly fallible. Although some people think of memory as a gigantic library or an automatic video recorder, our memories are not exact recordings of events. Instead, memory is highly *selective* (Baddeley et al., 2015; Bäuml, 2019; Wan et al., 2017). As discussed in Chapter 5, we pay attention to and remember only a small fraction of the information we're exposed to each day.

Constructive process   The process of organizing and shaping information during encoding, storage, and retrieval of memories.

Perhaps most important, memory is a **constructive process** through which we actively organize and shape information as it is being encoded, stored, and retrieved (e.g., Schacter, 2019). As expected, this construction often leads to serious errors and biases, which we'll discuss throughout the chapter. Would you like personal proof of the constructive nature of your own memory? See the **Test Yourself**.

PA Practical Application

Test Yourself: Do You Have a Good Memory?

Carefully read through all the words in the following list.

Sour	Chocolate	Pie	Bitter
Nice	Heart	Honey	Good
Honey	Cake	Candy	Taste
Artichoke	Tart	Sugar	Tooth

Now cover the list and write down all the words you remember. *Scoring:*

15 to 16 words = excellent

10 to 14 words = average

5 to 9 words = below average

4 or fewer words = you might need a nap

How did you do? Did you recall seeing the words "sour" and "tooth"? Most students do, and it's a good example of the *serial-position effect*—the first and last words in the list are more easily remembered than

those in the middle. Did you remember the words "artichoke" and "honey"? If you recalled "artichoke" it illustrates the power of *distinctiveness*, whereas if you remembered seeing "honey" it's because it was repeated twice. These examples demonstrate how distinctive or repeated material is more easily encoded, stored, and recalled.

Finally, did you see the word "sweet"? If so, look back over the list. That word is not there, yet students commonly report seeing it. Why? As mentioned above, memory is not a faithful duplicate of an event; it is a *constructive process*. We actively shape and build on information as it is encoded and retrieved.

Q Test Your Critical Thinking

1. Other than seeing the word "sweet," can you think of an example of a situation in which you may have created a false memory?

2. How might constructive memories create misunderstandings at work and in our everyday relationships?

Memory Models

To understand memory (and its constructive nature), you need a model of how it operates. Over the years, psychologists have developed numerous models for memory, and **Figure 7.1** provides a visual comparison of the four most popular models.

1. Encoding, Storage, Retrieval (ESR)

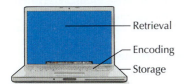

Retrieval
Encoding
Storage

Memory is *a process*, roughly analogous to a computer, where information goes through three basic processes—*encoding*, *storage*, and *retrieval*.

2. Levels of Processing

Memory Bits

Shallow = poor memory

Deeper = better memory

The more deeply material is processed, the better we are at remembering it.

3. Parallel Distributed Processing (PDP)

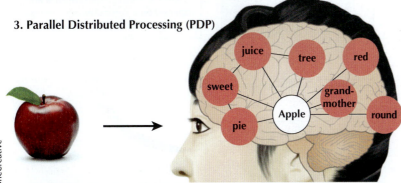

juice, tree, red, sweet, grand-mother, Apple, pie, round

Memory is distributed across a wide network of interconnected neorons located throughout the brain. When activated, this network works simultaneously (in a *parallel* fashion) to process information.

4. Three-Stage Memory

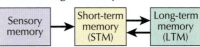

Sensory memory → Short-term memory (STM) → Long-term memory (LTM)

Memory requires three different storage boxes or stages to hold and process information for various lengths of time.

FIGURE 7.1 Four major memory models

istock.com/ZoneCreative

1. Encoding, Storage, and Retrieval (ESR) Model

According to the **encoding, storage**, and **retrieval (ESR) model**, the barrage of information that we encounter every day goes through three basic operations: *encoding, storage*, and *retrieval*. Each of these processes represents a different function that is closely analogous to one performed by a computer (**Process Diagram 7.1**).

To input data into a computer, you begin by typing letters and numbers on the keyboard. The computer then translates these keystrokes into its own electronic language. In a roughly similar fashion, our brains **encode** sensory information (sound, visual images, and other senses) into a neural code (language) it can understand and use. Once information is *encoded*, it must be **stored**. Computer information is normally stored on a flash drive or hard drive, whereas human information is stored in our brains. Finally, information must be **retrieved**, or taken out of storage. We retrieve stored information by going to files on our computer or to "files" in our brains.

Keep this model in mind. To do well in college or almost any other pursuit, you must successfully encode, store, and retrieve a large amount of facts and concepts. Throughout this chapter, we'll discuss ways to improve your memory during each of these steps.

2. Levels of Processing Model

Fergus Craik and Robert Lockhart (1972) were the first to suggest that encoding can be influenced by how *deeply* we process and store information. Their **levels of processing model** is based on a continuum ranging from shallow to intermediate to deep, with deeper processing leading to improved encoding, storage, and retrieval (Amlien et al., 2019; Craik & Tulving, 1975; Dinsmore & Alexander, 2016).

How can we "deep process" information? The most efficient way is to link the new material to previously stored information, which is why your instructors (and we, the authors of this text) use so many analogies and metaphors to introduce new material. As an example, we created Process Diagram 7.1 to clarify that the ESR model of memory is analogous to the workings of a computer knowing that most of our readers have previous knowledge about the basic functions of computers. Another way to deeply process new information is by putting it into your own words or talking about it with others. Have you ever wondered why college instructors so often object to students using their phones during class lectures? Instructors know that this type of distraction seriously interferes with selective attention and a *deeper level of processing*. But what

Encoding, storage, and retrieval (ESR) model A memory model that involves three processes: *encoding* (getting information in), *storage* (retaining information for future use), and *retrieval* (recovering information).

Encoding The first step of the ESR memory model; the process of moving sensory information into memory storage.

Storage The second step of the ESR memory model; retention of encoded information over time.

Retrieval The third step of the ESR memory model; recovery of information from memory storage.

Levels of processing model A model of memory based on a continuum of memory processing ranging from shallow to intermediate to deep, with deeper processing leading to improved encoding, storage, and retrieval.

> **STOP!** This Process Diagram contains essential information NOT found elsewhere in the text, which is likely to appear on quizzes and exams. Be sure to study it CAREFULLY.

PROCESS DIAGRAM 7.1 Encoding, Storage, and Retrieval (ESR) Model vs. a Computer

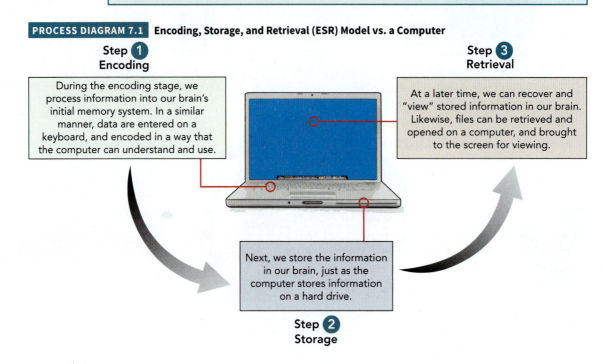

Step 1
Encoding

During the encoding stage, we process information into our brain's initial memory system. In a similar manner, data are entered on a keyboard, and encoded in a way that the computer can understand and use.

Step 3
Retrieval

At a later time, we can recover and "view" stored information in our brain. Likewise, files can be retrieved and opened on a computer, and brought to the screen for viewing.

Next, we store the information in our brain, just as the computer stores information on a hard drive.

Step 2
Storage

about other activities like taking pictures during important events? Does being a photographer have similar negative effects? See the following **RC** **Research Challenge**.

[AQ1] Along with the possible negative effects of taking photos, did you know that your phone can also interfere with your levels of processing, and thereby negatively affect your learning and memory—even when it's turned off (see photo)? Researchers who were interested in measuring the brain's ability to hold and process data at any given time asked participants to take a series of tests requiring full concentration (Ward et al., 2017). Before they began, randomly assigned groups of participants were first asked to turn their phones off, and then to place their phones either on the desk facedown, in their pocket or personal bag, or in another room.

Can you predict what happened? Although participants believed they were giving full concentration to the difficult tasks, their phones' location had a significant effect. The group that performed best was the one with the phone in another room, and the second best performers were those with their phones in their pockets or personal bag, whereas those with their phones on the desk were the worst performers. Remember that all phones were turned off and the one on the desk was facedown. Apparently just the mere presence of our phones can reduce our cognitive capacity and impair our overall cognitive functioning. Do you see how the presence of phones might interfere with deeper levels of processing and the concentration necessary not only for classroom lectures, but also for full engagement with our friends and family? (See cartoon.)

3. Parallel Distributed Processing (PDP) Model

A third way of thinking about memory is the **parallel distributed processing (PDP) model**, also known as *connectionism* (McClelland, 2011; Saxe et al., 2019). As its name implies, this model also uses a computer metaphor but proposes that memory processes are *parallel* operations performed simultaneously throughout the brain rather than sequential operations processed one at a time. In addition, memory is spread out, or *distributed*, throughout the brain in a web-like network of processing units.

For example, if you're swimming in the ocean and see a large fin nearby, your brain does not conduct a one-by-one search of all fish with fins before urging you to begin a rush to shore. Instead, you conduct a mental *parallel* search. You note the color of the fish, the shape of the fin, and the potential danger all at the same time. Because the processes are parallel, you can quickly process the information—and possibly avoid being eaten by a shark!

Parallel distributed processing (PDP) model The theory that memory is stored throughout the brain in web-like connections among interacting processing units operating simultaneously, rather than sequentially; also known as connectionism.

RC Scientific Thinking: **Research Challenge**

Can Taking Photos Impair Our Memories?

(APA Goal 2.4) Interpret, design, and conduct basic psychological research

Researchers interested in this and related questions set up two studies in which participants were led on a guided tour of an art museum (Henkel, 2014). During the tour, participants were randomly assigned to groups and asked to take note of certain objects, either by photographing them or by simply observing them. The next day their memory for the specific objects was tested. As you may have suspected, participants were less accurate in recognizing the objects they had photographed than those they had only observed, and they weren't able to answer as many questions about the objects' details.

However, when participants were asked to zoom in and photograph a specific part of the object, their subsequent recognition and detail memory was not impaired. Furthermore, participants' memories for features that were NOT zoomed in on were just as strong as their memories for features that were zoomed in on. Can you see how this finding suggests that the selective attention and deeper levels of processing engaged by this focused activity improve overall encoding and may eliminate the photo-taking-impairment effect?

This research has important implications. Given that it's difficult to always be paying full focused attention, we need to remember that while we're mindlessly taking numerous "selfies" and other photos we may encode fewer details. This means that taking photos the whole time we're on vacation or during a child's dance recital may interfere not only with our full enjoyment of the event but also with our actual memories of that special occasion.

TIP In addition to the possible memory impairment resulting from "simply" taking photos, can you see how this research may also apply to your academic life?   While reading this and other college texts or listening to lectures, you can improve your learning and memory by consciously directing your brain to pay focused, selective attention to important details. You can also process the material at a deeper level by "zooming in" on important details.

Identify the Research Method

1. Based on the information provided, did this study (Henkel, 2014) use descriptive, correlational, and/or experimental research?

Fabio Michele Capelli/Shutterstock.com

2. If you chose

   o *descriptive research*, is this a naturalistic or laboratory observation, survey/interview, case study, and/or archival research?

   o *correlational research*, is this a positive, negative, or zero correlation?

   o *experimental research*, label the IV, DV, experimental group(s), and control group. (Note: If participants were not randomly assigned to groups, list the design as *quasi-experimental*.)

   o both *descriptive* and *correlational*, answer the corresponding questions for both.

Check your answers by clicking on the answer button or by looking in Appendix B.

Note: The information provided in this study is admittedly limited, but the level of detail is similar to what is presented in most textbooks and public reports of research findings. Answering these questions, and then comparing your answers to those provided, will help you become a better scientific and critical thinker and consumer of scientific research.

Can you see how this PDP model allows a faster response time to threats to our survival, while also being consistent with neurological information about brain activity (Chapter 2)? Thanks to our richly interconnected synapses, activation of one neuron can influence many other neurons. This model has also been useful in explaining perception (Chapter 4), language (Chapter 8), and decision making (Chapter 8).

4. **Three-Stage Memory Model**   Since the late 1960s, the most highly researched and widely used memory model has been the **three-stage memory model** (Atkinson & Shiffrin, 1968; Eichenbaum, 2013; Li, 2016). It remains the leading paradigm in memory research because it offers a convenient way to organize the major findings. Like the previous ESR model, the three-stage memory model has been compared to a computer, with an input, process, and output. However, unlike in the ESR model, the three different storage "boxes," or memory stages, that store and process information each have a different purpose, duration, and capacity (**Process Diagram 7.2**). Let's discuss each stage in more detail.

Three-stage memory model
A memory model based on the passage of information through three stages (sensory, short-term, and long-term memory).

> **STOP!** This Process Diagram contains essential information NOT found elsewhere in the text, which is likely to appear on quizzes and exams. Be sure to study it CAREFULLY.

PROCESS DIAGRAM 7.2 **Updating the Traditional Three-Stage Memory Model** Each "box" represents a separate memory storage system that differs from the others in purpose, duration, and capacity. When information is not transferred from sensory memory or short-term memory, it is assumed to be lost. Information stored in long-term memory can be retrieved and sent back to short-term memory for use. In addition to the three traditional stages, modern research has discovered other routes to memory formation, such as *automatic encoding*. As shown by the dotted line and as you may know from personal experience, some information from the environment bypasses Steps 1 and 2 and gets into our long-term memory without our conscious awareness.

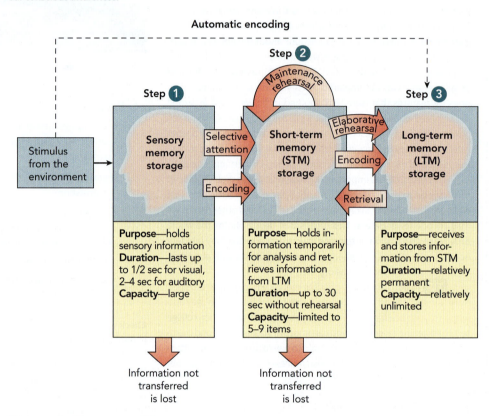

Stage 1: Sensory Memory

Sensory memory The initial memory stage, which holds sensory information; it has relatively large capacity, but the duration is only a few seconds.

Everything we see, hear, touch, taste, and smell must first enter our **sensory memory**. Once it has entered, the information remains in sensory memory just long enough for our brain to locate relevant bits of data and transfer them on to the next stage of memory. For visual information, known as *iconic memory*, the visual image (icon) stays in sensory memory only about one-half of a second before it fades away.

In an early study of iconic sensory memory, George Sperling (1960) flashed an arrangement of 12 letters like the ones in **Figure 7.2** for 1/20 of a second. Most people, he found, could recall only four or five of the letters. Sperling then instructed participants to report just the top, middle, or bottom row, depending on whether they heard a high, medium, or low tone, which was played immediately after the flashed letters. In this condition, participants reported the letters of whichever row was called for more accurately and consistently than before. Apparently all 12 letters are held in sensory memory right after they are viewed, but only those that are immediately attended to are noted and processed.

Like the fleeting visual images in iconic memory, auditory stimuli (what we hear) are temporary, but a weaker "echo," or *echoic memory*, of this auditory input lingers for up to 4 seconds (Erviti et al., 2015; Kojima et al., 2014; Neisser, 1967). Why are visual and auditory memories so fleeting? We cannot process all incoming stimuli, so lower brain centers need only a few seconds

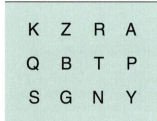

FIGURE 7.2 **Sperling's test for iconic memory**

to "decide" if the information is important enough to promote to conscious awareness (**Figure 7.3**).

Early researchers believed that sensory memory had an unlimited capacity. However, later research suggests that sensory memory does have limits and that stored images are fuzzier than once thought (Cohen, 2014; Franconeri et al., 2013; Howes & O'Shea, 2014.)

Stage 2: Short-Term Memory (STM)

The second stage of memory processing, **short-term memory (STM)**, temporarily stores and processes sensory stimuli. If the information is judged to be important, STM organizes and sends it along to long-term memory (LTM); otherwise, information decays and is lost. STM also retrieves stored memories from LTM.

Improving Your STM The capacity of STM is limited to five to nine bits of information and the duration to less than 30 seconds (Bankó & Vidnyánsky, 2010; Nairne & Neath, 2013). To extend the *capacity* of STM, you can use a technique called **chunking**, which involves grouping separate pieces of information into larger, more manageable units (Miller, 1956; Portrat et al., 2016; Thalmann et al., 2019). Have you noticed that credit card, social security, and telephone numbers are almost always grouped into three or four distinct units (sometimes separated by hyphens)? This is another example of the many practical applications of psychology. Whenever you want to remember a long list of information—not just numbers—you can break the list into bit size chunks. For example, if you have ten items to buy at a grocery store, you might organize your list into three chunks—bakery items, frozen foods, fruits and vegetables.

Chunking even helps in sports. What do you see when you observe the arrangement of players shown in **Figure 7.4**, from a football playbook? To the novice eye of a person with little or no understanding or appreciation of the cognitive skills required in football, it looks like a random assembly of lines and arrows. But for experienced players and seasoned fans who recognize the standard plays, the scattered lines form meaningful patterns—classic arrangements that recur often. Just as you group the letters of this sentence into meaningful words and remember them long enough to understand the meaning of the sentence, football experts group the different football plays into easily recalled patterns (or chunks).

In addition to chunking information, you can extend the *duration* of your STM almost indefinitely by consciously "juggling" the information—a process called **maintenance rehearsal**. You are using maintenance rehearsal when you mentally repeat your attractive classmate's phone number over and over until you type it into your phone.

People who are good at remembering names know how to take advantage of maintenance rehearsal. They repeat the name of each person they meet, aloud or silently, to keep it active in STM. They also make sure that other thoughts (such as their plans for what to say next) don't intrude.

STM versus Working Memory Short-term memory is more than just a passive, temporary "holding area." Given that active processing of information occurs in STM, many researchers prefer the term **working memory** (Baddeley, 1992, 2007; Lin et al., 2019). All our conscious thinking occurs in this "working memory," and the manipulation of information that takes place here helps explain some of the memory errors and false constructions described in this chapter.

As you can see in **Figure 7.5**, working memory is composed of a *visuospatial sketchpad*, a *phonological loop*, and a *central executive*. To understand this three-part system, consider what's happening when we "channel surf." As we all know, this "simply" involves pushing the channel selector on our television's remote control to quickly switch from channel to

FIGURE 7.3 **Demonstrating iconic and echoic memories**

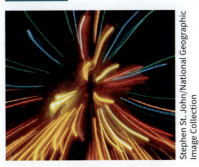 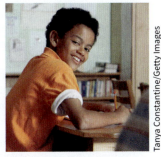

a. Visual images—iconic memory imagine yourself at a fireworks' display and quickly shutting your eyes after one of the most colorful explosions (like one in this photo). The fact that the image, or icon, of the explosion will linger for a fraction of a second in your "mind's eye" is a good demonstration of the duration of visual memory, or *iconic memory*.

b. Auditory stimuli—echoic memory Think back to a time when someone asked you a question while you were deeply absorbed in a task. Did you ask "What?" and then immediately answer without hearing a repeat of the question? Now you know why. A weaker "echo" (echoic memory) of auditory information is available for up to four seconds.

Short-term memory (STM) The second memory stage, which temporarily stores sensory information and sends information to and receives information from long-term memory (LTM); its capacity is limited to five to nine items, and it has a duration of about 30 seconds.

Chunking A memory technique involving grouping separate pieces of information into larger, more manageable units (or chunks).

Maintenance rehearsal The act of repeating information over and over to maintain it in short-term memory (STM).

Working memory A newer term for short-term memory (STM) that emphasizes the active processing of information.

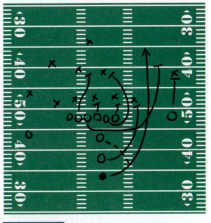

FIGURE 7.4 **Chunking in football**

FIGURE 7.5 **Working memory as a three-part system** The *central executive* supervises and coordinates two subsystems, the *phonological loop* and the *visuospatial sketchpad*, while also sending information to and retrieving information from LTM. Picture yourself as a food server in a busy restaurant. A couple has just given you a complicated food order. When you mentally rehearse the food order (the phonological loop) and combine it with a mental picture of your customers, their food orders, and the layout of plates on their table (the visuospatial sketchpad), you're using your central executive.

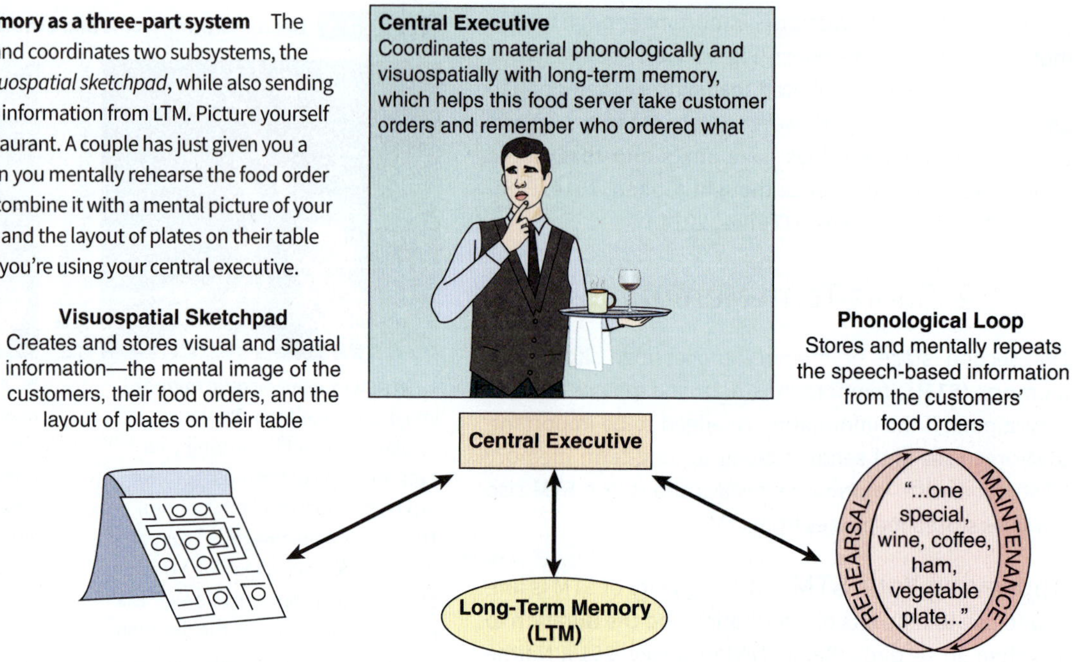

Central Executive
Coordinates material phonologically and visuospatially with long-term memory, which helps this food server take customer orders and remember who ordered what

Visuospatial Sketchpad
Creates and stores visual and spatial information—the mental image of the customers, their food orders, and the layout of plates on their table

Phonological Loop
Stores and mentally repeats the speech-based information from the customers' food orders

Central Executive

Long-Term Memory (LTM)

REHEARSAL — MAINTENANCE — "...one special, wine, coffee, ham, vegetable plate..."

channel until we find something interesting to watch. But did you know that this process actually requires a complex interaction among all parts of our working memory system?

During this "surfing," the visuospatial sketchpad allows us to keep a brief mental image of each channel in mind, while the phonological loop enables us to continually mentally rehearse the auditory information. Even more amazing is the fact that we're simultaneously actively retrieving previously stored information from our LTM. We then use all of this information to decide whether or not we like the particular program we're briefly seeing on each channel.

Stage 3: Long-Term Memory (LTM)

After information has been transferred from STM, it is organized and integrated with other information in **long-term memory (LTM)**. LTM serves as a storehouse for information that must be kept for long periods. When we need the information, it is sent back to STM for our conscious use. Compared with sensory memory and short-term memory, long-term memory has relatively unlimited *capacity* and *duration* (Eichenbaum, 2013). But, just as with any other possession, the better we label and arrange our memories, the more readily we'll be able to retrieve them.

Long-term memory (LTM)
The third stage of memory, which stores information for long periods of time; the capacity is virtually limitless, and the duration is relatively permanent.

Explicit/declarative memory
A subsystem within long-term memory (LTM) that involves conscious, easily described (declared) memories; it consists of semantic memories (facts) and episodic memories (personal experiences).

Semantic memory A subsystem of long-term memory (LTM) that stores general knowledge; a mental encyclopedia or dictionary.

Episodic memory A subsystem of long-term memory (LTM) that stores autobiographical events and the contexts in which they occurred; a mental diary of a person's life.

Various Types of LTM How do we store the vast amount of information we collect over a lifetime? Several types of LTM exist (**Figure 7.6**). **Explicit/declarative memory** involves intentional learning or conscious knowledge. If asked to remember your phone number or your mother's name, you can easily state (*declare*) the answers directly (*explicitly*). Explicit/declarative memory can be further subdivided into two parts. **Semantic memory** is memory for general knowledge, rules, events, facts, and specific information. It is our mental encyclopedia. In contrast, **episodic memory** is like a mental diary. It records the major events (*episodes*) in our lives. Some of our episodic memories are short-lived, whereas others last a lifetime.

Have you ever wondered why most adults can recall almost nothing of the years before they reached age 3? Research suggests that a concept of self, sufficient language development, and growth of the frontal lobes of the cortex (along with other structures) may be necessary for us to encode early events and retrieve them many years later (Bauer & Larkina, 2014; Feldman, 2014; Pathman & Bauer, 2013). Interestingly, older adults describe their most important memories as occurring between the ages of 17 and 24, in part because many major life transitions—such as attending college, starting a first job, and possibly getting married—happen during this period of time (Steiner et al., 2014). Contrary to stereotypes about "grumpy old people," psychological research consistently finds an increase in happiness and well-being as we grow older (Riediger & Luong, 2016; Sutin et al., 2013). Why? See the **PP** **PositivePsych** feature.

FIGURE 7.6   **LTM is divided and subdivided into various types**

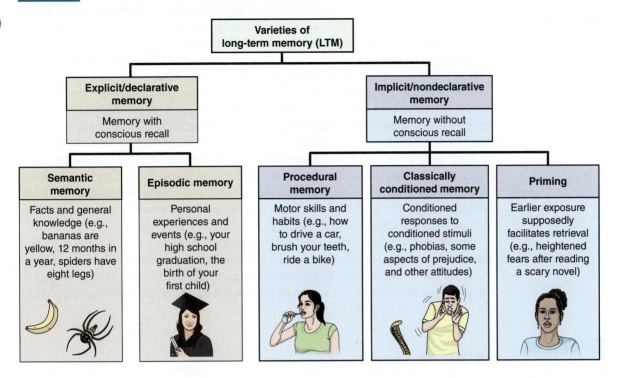

```
                          Varieties of
                       long-term memory (LTM)

        Explicit/declarative                      Implicit/nondeclarative
             memory                                      memory

         Memory with                                 Memory without
        conscious recall                            conscious recall
```

Semantic memory	**Episodic memory**	**Procedural memory**	**Classically conditioned memory**	**Priming**
Facts and general knowledge (e.g., bananas are yellow, 12 months in a year, spiders have eight legs)	Personal experiences and events (e.g., your high school graduation, the birth of your first child)	Motor skills and habits (e.g., how to drive a car, brush your teeth, ride a bike)	Conditioned responses to conditioned stimuli (e.g., phobias, some aspects of prejudice, and other attitudes)	Earlier exposure supposedly facilitates retrieval (e.g., heightened fears after reading a scary novel)

Practical Application: PositivePsych

Memory and Age-Related Happiness

(APA Goal 1.3) Describe applications of psychology

Why are older people generally happier? Research finds that this age group tends to have stronger relationships, value time more than money, and become more selective with their time and friendships as they age (Birditt & Newton, 2016; McFall et al., 2019; Whillans et al., 2016). In addition, according to the **age-related positivity effect**, older adults generally prefer and pay more sustained attention to positive than negative information. They also remember more positive events than negative events (Carstensen, 1993, 2006; English & Carstensen, 2015; Mikels & Shuster, 2016).

To test possible neural changes underlying this positive attention and memory bias, researchers asked both younger adults (ages 19–31) and older adults (ages 61–80) to look at a series of photographs with positive and negative themes, such as a skier winning a race and a wounded soldier, and to remember as much as they could about the photographs (Addis et al., 2010). While participants viewed these images, researchers measured their brain activity through the use of functional magnetic resonance imaging (fMRI) scans (Chapter 2). Surprisingly, they found no difference between younger and older adults in brain activity associated with the encoding of information while watching the negative images. However, when older adults were viewing the positive images, areas of their brains that process emotions (the amygdala and the ventromedial prefrontal cortex) directly affected the hippocampus. (As you may recall, the hippocampus is responsible for encoding and

Blend Images - Rolf Bruderer/
Brand X Pictures/Getty Images

storage of memories.) In contrast, in the younger adults' brains, the thalamus (a "simple" relay station) had a bigger influence on the hippocampus. This suggests that older adults may be better at sustaining attention on positive information, and remembering good times, because areas of their brains that process positive emotions are instructing the hippocampus to "remember this."

Q **Test Your Critical Thinking**

1. Can you think of possible reasons why our brains might become more alert to positive information as we age?

2. As emphasized throughout this text, we have considerable control over our brains—at almost any age. Given this type of personal control, how can you use this information to increase your own level of happiness?

Age-related positivity effect   The relative preference in older adults for positive over negative information in attention and memory.

Implicit/nondeclarative memory
A subsystem within long-term memory (LTM) that contains memories independent of conscious recall; it consists of procedural motor skills, priming, and simple classically conditioned responses.

Implicit/nondeclarative memory involves unintentional learning or unconscious knowledge. Try telling someone how you tie your shoelaces without demonstrating the actual behavior. Given that the memory of this skill is unconscious and hard to describe (*declare*) in words, this type of memory is sometimes referred to as *nondeclarative*.

Implicit/nondeclarative memory consists of *procedural* motor skills, like tying your shoes or riding a bike, as well as *classically conditioned emotional responses* (CERs), such as fears and prejudices (Chapter 6). Implicit/nondeclarative memory also includes *priming*, in which exposure (often unconscious) to previously stored information supposedly predisposes (or primes) one's response to related stimuli (Cesario, 2014; Schacter, 2019). As you may recall from Chapter 4, research on *subliminal perception* finds that certain unconscious (unnoticed) stimuli can reach our brains and supposedly predispose (*prime*) us to find it easier or more difficult to recall related information already in storage (Elgendi et al., 2018; Ohtomo, 2017; Sassenberg et al., 2017). If a researcher shows you the words "yellow" and "sun," you're likely to be slightly faster to recognize the word "banana" because those words are already stored and the three words are closely associated in your memory.

Why do we say "supposedly" when referring to priming? As discussed in Chapter 4, some studies of priming have failed to be replicated, which questions the validity of the concept. However, other researchers have conducted studies and meta-analyses that supported priming, and have suggested that the criticism may be based on faulty logic (e.g., Dijkesterhuis, 2014; Lodder et al., 2019; Payne et al., 2016).

PA Practical Application

Can our emotions also be primed? Have you ever felt nervous being home alone while reading a scary novel, experienced sadness after hearing about a tragic event in the news, or developed amorous feelings while watching a romantic movie? These are all examples of how the situation we are in may influence our mood, in conscious or unconscious ways. Given this new insight into how priming can "set you up" for certain emotions, can you see how those who haven't studied psychology might possibly mislabel or overreact to their feelings?

Improving LTM There are three major ways to improve long-term memory—*organization*, *rehearsal* (or repetition), and *retrieval*.

Organization To successfully encode information for LTM, we need to *organize* material into hierarchies. This means arranging a number of related items into broad categories that we further divide and subdivide. (This organizational strategy for LTM is similar to the strategy of chunking material in STM.) For instance, by grouping small subsets of ideas together (as subheadings under larger main headings and within diagrams, tables, and so on), we hope to make the material in this book more understandable and *memorable*.

[AQ2] Admittedly, organization takes time and work. But you'll be happy to know that some memory organization and filing is done automatically while you sleep or nap (Adi-Japha & Karni, 2016; Cona et al., 2014; Nielsen et al., 2015). In fact, people who rest and close their eyes for as little as 10 minutes (see photo) show greater memory for details of a story they've just heard (Dewar et al., 2012). Unfortunately, despite claims to the contrary, research shows that we can't recruit our sleeping hours to memorize new material, such as a foreign language.

Rehearsal Like organization, *rehearsal* improves encoding for both STM and LTM. If you need to hold information in STM for longer than 30 seconds, you can simply keep repeating it (maintenance rehearsal). But storage in LTM requires *deeper levels of processing*, called **elaborative rehearsal**.

The immediate goal of elaborative rehearsal is to *understand*—not to memorize. Fortunately, the attempt to understand is one of the best ways to encode new information into long-term memory. Elaborative rehearsal involves forming a number of different connections to new material and linking them to previously stored information (e.g., Amlien et al., 2019). It's

ONOKY - Eric Audras/Brand X Pictures/Getty Images

Elaborative rehearsal A process of forming numerous connections of new information to material already stored in long-term memory (LTM); a memory improvement technique that makes information more meaningful and the memory more durable and lasting.

obviously easier to remember something if we associate it with something we already know. This is why we use so many analogies in this text.

Elaborative rehearsal was first proposed by Craik and Lockhart (1972) in their *levels of processing* model of memory. As discussed earlier, the term refers to the fact that we process our memories on a continuum from shallow, to intermediate, to deep, and that deep levels of processing result in improved encoding, storage, and retrieval. How does this apply to your everyday life?

A surprising study found that students who took notes on laptops performed worse on conceptual questions than students who took notes on paper (Mueller & Oppenheimer, 2014). Why? The researchers suggested that students who take notes using a laptop tend to just transcribe lectures verbatim (*shallow processing*), rather than reframing lecture material in their own words (*deeper processing*). (Additional tips for improving elaborative rehearsal, and deeper levels of processing, are provided in the following **Test Yourself**.)

PA Practical Application

Test Yourself: Improving Your Elaborative Rehearsal

Think about the other students in your college classes. Have you noticed that older students tend to get better grades? This is, in part, because they've lived longer and can tap into a greater wealth of previously stored material. If you're a younger student (or an older student just returning to college), you can learn to process information at a deeper level and build your elaborative rehearsal skills by doing the following:

- **Expanding (or elaborating on) the information** The more you elaborate, or try to understand something, the more likely you are to remember the information. One experiment found that participants who have a chance to reflect on a task show better learning/memory than those who don't (Schlichting & Preston, 2014). This study has clear implications for teachers. Asking students to reflect on what they've just learned helps them to remember that information better. As a student, you can discuss the major points of a lecture with your study group or practice repeating or reading something aloud—another form of *elaborative rehearsal* (Lafleur & Boucher, 2015).

- **Linking new information to yourself** All humans think about and store memories about themselves many times each day.

Therefore, creating links between new information and our own experiences, beliefs, and memories will naturally lead to more lasting memories. In addition to applying new information to your personal life, which is known as the *self-reference effect,* research shows that the use of *visual imagery* (such as the numerous figures, photos, and tables we've added to this text and the personal images you create while listening to lectures or reading this text) greatly improves LTM and decreases forgetting (Collins et al., 2014; Leblond et al., 2016; Paivio, 1995).

- **Finding meaningfulness** When studying new terms in this book and other college textbooks, try to find meaning. For example, if you want to add the term *iconic memory* to your LTM, ask yourself, "What does the word *iconic* mean"? By looking it up on your smartphone, you'll discover that it comes from the Greek word for "image" or "likeness," a piece of information that adds meaning to the word and thereby increases your retention. Similarly, when you meet people at a party, don't just maintenance-rehearse their name. Ask about their favorite TV shows, career plans, political beliefs, or anything else that requires deeper analysis. You'll be much more likely to remember their names.

Retrieval Finally, effective *retrieval* is critical to improving long-term memory. There are two types of **retrieval cues**. *Specific* cues require you only to *recognize* the correct response. *General* cues require you to *recall* previously learned material by searching through all possible matches in LTM—a much more difficult task. Can you see how this helps explain why multiple-choice exams are generally easier than essay exams? (See **Figure 7.7**.)

Information present at the time of encoding or learning can serve as an important retrieval cue, whether the goal is recognition or recall (Gao et al., 2016; Gibbons et al., 2018; Wheeler & Gabbert, 2017). Have you noticed that you tend to do better on exams when you take them in the same seat and classroom in which you originally studied the material? If so, you've stumbled upon the **encoding-specificity principle** (Tulving & Thompson, 1973). This principle simply means that you're able to remember better when you attempt to recall information in the *same* context in which you learned it (**Figure 7.8**).

Retrieval cues A prompt or stimulus that aids recall or retrieval of a stored piece of information from long-term memory (LTM).

Encoding-specificity principle The principle that retrieval of information is improved if cues received at the time of recall are consistent with those present at the time of encoding.

Sergiy Zavgorodny/Shutterstock.com

FIGURE 7.7 **Retrieval cues and the environment** In a classic study, researchers gave scuba divers lists of words to remember—some on land and some underwater (Godden & Baddeley, 1975). As the encoding-specificity principle would predict, recall was best when the divers recalled the list of words in the same environment in which they learned them. Can you see how this also explains why you may not remember your instructor's name when you meet him or her outside of the classroom?

Antonio M. Rosario/Photographer's Choice/ Getty Images

FIGURE 7.8 **Retrieval cues and recall versus recognition** Can you *recall*, in order, the names of the planets in our solar system? If not, it's probably because this question, like questions on an essay exam, requires retrieval using only general, nonspecific cues. In contrast, multiple-choice exams provide specific cues, which require you only to identify the correct answer. Notice how much easier it is to recognize the names of the planets when you're provided a specific retrieval cue—in this case, the first three letters of each planet: Mer-, Ven-, Ear-, Mar-, Jup-, Sat-, Ura-, Nep-, Plu-. (Note that in 2006 Pluto was officially reclassified and is now considered a "dwarf planet.")

Mnemonic A strategic device that makes use of familiar information during the encoding of new information to enhance later recall.

In this section, we've discussed how organization, rehearsal, and retrieval are important factors in improving your LTM. Now we want to add one additional well-known memory technique, which involves using **mnemonic** devices to encode items in a special way (see the **Test Yourself**). Notice that these devices take practice and time, and some students report that they get better results using the other well-researched principles discussed throughout this chapter.

PA Practical Application

Test Yourself: Mnemonics and Memory Improvement

Before your next speech or class exam, try one or more of these four mnemonic devices. They improve your memory by tagging information to physical locations (*method of loci*), organizing information into main and subsidiary topics (an *outline*), using familiar information to remember the unfamiliar (*acronyms*), and creating a diagram that depicts relationships between concepts (*concept maps*).

a. Method of loci Greek and Roman orators developed the *method of loci* to keep track of the many parts of their long speeches. Orators

would imagine the parts of their speeches attached to places in a courtyard. If the opening point in a speech was the concept of *justice,* they might visualize a courthouse placed in the back corner of their garden. Continuing this imaginary garden walk, the orator might see a prison for the second point, about the prison system, and a set of scales, symbolizing the need for balance in government, for the third point.

b. Outline organization When listening to a lecture or reading this text, create an outline by drawing a vertical line approximately 3 inches from the left margin of your notebook paper. Write main topics from the lecture or headings from the chapter outline to the left of the line, and add specific details and examples from the lecture or text on the right, as in this example:

Outline	Details and Examples from Lecture and Text
1. Nature of Memory	_____
a. Memory Models	_____
b. Sensory Memory	_____
c. Short-Term Memory (STM)	_____

c. Acronyms   To use the *acronym method*, create a new code word from the first letters of the items you want to remember. For example, to recall the names of the Great Lakes, think of *HOMES* on a *great lake* (*H*uron, *O*ntario, *M*ichigan, *E*rie, *S*uperior). Visualizing homes on each lake will help you remember the acronym *HOMES*.

d. Concept map   When facing numerous interrelated concepts that you need to recall, create a concept map visually depicting the relationships. (This sample depicts how you might diagram the components and functions of the concept map itself.) Research suggests that this method improves memory by promoting elaborative, pictorial, and motor codes (Fernandes et al., 2018).

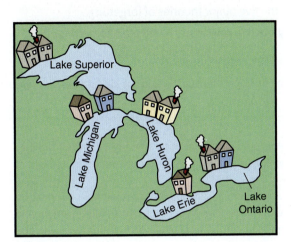

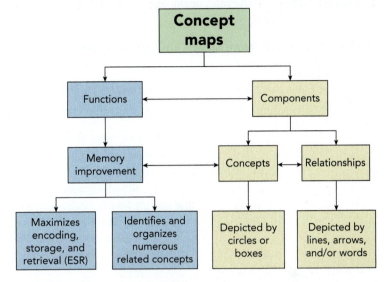

Q Test Your Critical Thinking

1. How could you use the method of loci to remember several items on your grocery shopping list?

2. How would you use the acronym method to remember the names of the last seven presidents of the United States?

Retrieval Practice 7.1 | The Nature of Memory

Self-Test   Completing this self-test, and then checking your answers by clicking on the answer button or by looking in Appendix B, will provide immediate feedback and helpful practice for exams.

1. According to the ESR model, memory is a process that can be compared to the workings of _____.
   a. a board of executives
   b. a flashbulb memory
   c. redintegration
   d. a computer

2. Information in _____ lasts only a few seconds or less and has a relatively large (but not unlimited) storage capacity.
   a. perceptual processes
   b. working memory
   c. short-term storage
   d. sensory memory

3. _____ is the process of grouping separate pieces of information into a single unit.
   a. Chunking
   b. Collecting
   c. Conflation
   d. Dual-coding

4. In answering this question, the correct multiple-choice option may serve as a _____ for recalling accurate information from your long-term memory.
   a. specificity code
   b. retrieval cue
   c. priming pump
   d. flashbulb stimulus

5. The encoding-specificity principle says that information retrieval is improved when _____.
   a. both maintenance and elaborative rehearsal are used
   b. reverberating circuits consolidate information
   c. conditions of recovery are similar to encoding conditions
   d. long-term potentiation is accessed

Q Test Your Critical Thinking

1. What are some of the possible advantages and disadvantages of memory being a constructive process?

2. If you were forced to lose one type of memory—sensory, short-term, or long-term—which would you select? Why?

Real World Application Questions

[AQ1]   Can your phone affect your memory—even when it's turned off?

[AQ2]   How can taking a nap improve your memory?

leungchopan/ Shutterstock.com

ONOKY - Eric Audras/Brand X Pictures/Getty Images

Hint: Look in the text for **[AQ1]** and **[AQ2]**

7.2 | Forgetting

LEARNING OBJECTIVES

Retrieval Practice While reading the upcoming sections, respond to each Learning Objective in your own words.

Review the research, key theories, and important factors in forgetting.

• **Describe** Ebbinghaus's research on learning and forgetting.

• **Review** the five major theories of forgetting.

• **Identify** the five key factors involved in forgetting.

Real World Discovery Question

[AQ3] Why do we remember President Lincoln better than President Truman?

Have you ever been at a family get-together and found yourself arguing with your siblings over whether something did or did not happen? Or have you ever misremembered important details (**Figure 7.9**)?

We've all had numerous experiences with *forgetting*—the inability to remember information that was previously available. We misplace our keys, forget the name of a familiar person, and even miss important exams. Although forgetting can be annoying and sometimes even catastrophic, it's generally adaptive. If we remembered everything we ever saw, heard, or read, our minds would be overwhelmed with useless information.

Ebbinghaus's Forgetting Curve

Hermann Ebbinghaus first introduced the experimental study of learning and forgetting in 1885. As you can see in **Figure 7.10**, his research revealed that forgetting occurs soon after we learn something and then gradually tapers off (Ebbinghaus, 1885).

If this dramatic "curve of forgetting" discourages you from studying, note that meaningful material is much more memorable than Ebbinghaus's nonsense syllables. Furthermore, after some time had passed and Ebbinghaus thought he had completely forgotten the material, he discovered that *relearning* it took less time than the initial learning took. The good news is that if your college requires you to repeat some of the math or foreign language courses you took in high school, you'll be happily surprised by how much you recall and how much easier it is to relearn the information the second time around.

FIGURE 7.9 **The high price of forgetting** In 2015, Brian Williams was removed from his NBC news anchor position following allegations that he had misrepresented his own involvement in various wars and current events that he had covered (e.g., Koblin & Steel, 2015). In particular, he implied that he had faced far more dangerous circumstances than in reality he had. He later apologized to viewers, noting, "I made a mistake in recalling the events of 12 years ago." As you read this section on forgetting, see if you can identify factors explaining how and why Brian Williams misrepresented himself.

Ray Tamarra/FilmMagic/Getty Images

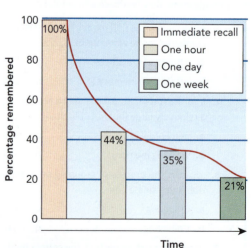

FIGURE 7.10 **How quickly we forget** Using himself as a research participant, Ebbinghaus calculated how long it took to learn a list of three-letter nonsense syllables, such as *SIB* and *RAL*. He found that 1 hour after he knew a list perfectly, he remembered only 44 percent of the syllables. A day later, he recalled 35 percent, and a week later only 21 percent.

Theories of Forgetting

Psychologists have developed several theories to explain why forgetting occurs (**Figure 7.11**): *decay*, *interference*, *motivated forgetting*, *encoding failure*, and *retrieval failure*. Each theory focuses on a different stage of the memory process or a particular type of problem in processing information.

- *Decay theory* focuses on the way memory is processed and stored in a physical form—for example, in a network of neurons. Connections between neurons may deteriorate over time, leading to forgetting. This theory explains why skills and memory degrade if they go unused ("use it or lose it").

- According to *interference theory*, forgetting results from two competing memories, and particularly memories with similar qualities. At least two types of interference exist: *retroactive*

Mick Stevens/CartoonStock

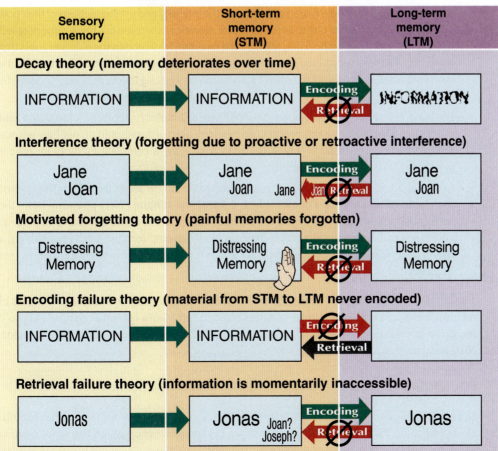

FIGURE 7.11 **Theories of forgetting** Which of these five theories of forgetting best applies to this cartoon?

TIP Are you having trouble remembering these five theories? If so, think of how forgetting involves memories that grow "dimmer," and note that the acronym created from the first letter of each theory has almost the same spelling—D-I-M-E-R.

FIGURE 7.12 Retroactive interference and proactive interference

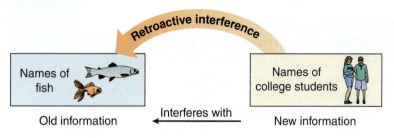

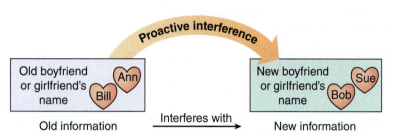

a. Retroactive (backward-acting) **interference** occurs when new information interferes with old information. This example comes from a story about an absent-minded ichthyology professor (fish specialist) who refused to learn the names of his college students. Asked why, he said, "Every time I learn a student's name, I forget the name of a fish."

b. Proactive (forward-acting) **interference** occurs when old information interferes with new information. Have you ever been in trouble after you used an old romantic partner's name to refer to your new partner? You now have a guilt-free explanation—proactive interference.

Retroactive interference
A memory problem that occurs when new information disrupts (*interferes* with) the recall of old "retro" information; backward-acting interference.

Proactive interference
A memory problem that occurs when old information disrupts (*interferes* with) the recall of new information; forward-acting interference.

and *proactive* (**Figure 7.12**). When new information disrupts (*interferes* with) the recall of old "retro" information, the problem is called **retroactive interference** (acting backward in time). Learning your new home address may lead you to forget your old home address (prior "retro" information is forgotten). Conversely, when old information disrupts (*interferes* with) the recall of NEW information, the problem is called **proactive interference** (acting forward in time). Old information (like the Spanish you learned in high school) may interfere with your ability to learn and remember material from your new college course in French.

- *Motivated forgetting theory* is based on the idea that we forget some information for a reason. According to Freudian theory, people forget unpleasant or anxiety-producing information, such as the box of cookies they ate last night, either consciously or unconsciously. Surprisingly, people who have just finished a marathon often rate the intensity and unpleasantness of their pain at about a 5.5 on a scale of one to 10 (Babel, 2016). However, when you ask these same people 3 to 6 months later to report how they felt after the race, they've forgotten the pain and guess that it was about a three. Do you see how the runners, having enjoyed the overall experience of the event, are motivated to forget the pain? This motivated forgetting theory may help explain why all children aren't only children—mothers tend to forget the actual pain of childbirth.

- *Encoding failure theory* focuses on how our sensory memory receives information and passes it to STM. If, during this process, we overlook precise details and do not fully encode the information, the result will be a failure to pass along a complete memory for proper storage in LTM (see the **Test Yourself**).

- According to *retrieval failure theory*, memories stored in LTM aren't forgotten. They're just momentarily inaccessible. For example, the **tip-of-the-tongue (TOT) phenomenon**—the feeling that a word or an event you are trying to remember will pop out at any second—is known to result from interference, faulty cues, and high emotional arousal. Interestingly, a recent study found that physically fit older adults had fewer TOT experiences than the less fit (Segaert et al., 2018).

Tip-of-the-tongue (TOT) phenomenon A strong, confident feeling of knowing something, while not being able to retrieve it at the moment.

Take-Home Message Stress can interfere with encoding and increase your chances of retrieval failure and forgetting. However, stress can also sometimes enhance memory—as you'll see in the later section on flashbulb memories (e.g., Bolton & Robinson, 2017; Cadle & Zoladz, 2015; Ramirez et al., 2017).

Factors Involved in Forgetting

Since Ebbinghaus's original research, scientists have discovered numerous factors that contribute to forgetting. Five of the most important are the *misinformation effect*, the *serial-position effect*, *source amnesia*, *spacing of practice,* and *culture*.

PA Practical Application

Test Yourself: Can You Identify the Actual Apple Logo?

For a simple (but fascinating) example of encoding failure, try to iden-tify which of the six examples shown in the drawing is the closest match to the actual Apple Inc. logo. Despite having seen the Apple logo thou-sands of times in our lives, most of us have difficulty recognizing the details. In fact, the Apple logo has several distinguishing characteristics (the size of the bite, the direction the stem faces, the curve at the bot-tom of the Apple, and so on). Furthermore, this logo, like all others, was carefully designed to be memorable and distinctive, in order to increase consumer sales and brand loyalty. However, in a study with 85 under-graduates, fewer than half of all participants correctly identified the logo (Blake et al., 2015). Even more surprising, only one student was able to correctly reproduce the logo when asked to draw it on a blank sheet of paper. Ironically, participants indicated HIGH levels of confidence in both their recognition and their recall abilities.

How does this apply to your everyday life? Have you ever taken an exam and felt fairly confident that you did well, yet later received a low score? Most participants in this study felt similarly confident that they could easily identify the correct Apple logo. However, in both cases—identifying logos and taking exams—we may fail to succeed when we don't encode the fine details and pass them along for storage in our

LTM. Why is it important to remember how you did on this logo iden-tification test when studying for exams? Just as most people cannot identify the correct logo due to encoding failure, you may not recog-nize correct answers on a multiple-choice test or recall the import-ant details required for an essay exam because you failed to carefully study and encode important details from your textbook. Keep in mind that you can't read a textbook the way you read articles on the Internet or a novel. You must slow down and encode the details.

Answers: 1. For copyright reasons, the researchers could not show the actual Apple logo, so none of the choices exactly matches the real logo. However, the bottom middle figure was considered by the researchers to be the *closest to the actual logo, which has the leaf facing the opposite way.*

---

1. **Misinformation Effect** As mentioned earlier, our memories are highly fallible and filled with personal constructions that we create during encoding, storage, and retrieval. Research on the **misinformation effect** shows that misleading information presented *after an event* may further alter and revise those constructions. Can you see how this is another example of *retroactive interference*? Our original memories are forgotten or altered due to misleading post-event information.

   In one study, participants completed an interview in one room and then answered questions about it in another room (Morgan et al., 2013). Participants who received neutral questions like "Was there a telephone in the room?" answered accurately for the most part, making errors on only 10 percent of the interview questions. However, other participants were asked questions such as "What color was the telephone?" which falsely implied that there had been a telephone in the room. Of these respondents, 98 percent "remembered" a telephone. Other experiments have created false memories by showing participants doc-tored photos of themselves taking a completely fictitious hot-air balloon ride or by asking participants to simply imagine an event, such as having a nurse remove a skin sample from their finger. In these and similar cases, a large number of participants later believed that the misleading information was correct and that the fictitious or imagined events actually occurred (Kaplan et al., 2016; Kirk et al., 2015; Takarangi & Loftus, 2016).

2. **Serial-Position Effect** Stop for a moment and write down the names of all the U.S. presi-dents that you can immediately recall. How did you do?

   [AQ3]   Research shows that most people recall presidents from the beginning of American history (e.g., Washington, Adams, Jefferson) and the more recent ones (e.g., Bush, Obama, Trump) (DeSoto & Roediger, 2019). This is known as the **serial-position effect** (**Figure 7.13**). We tend to recall items at the beginning (*primacy effect*) and the end (*recency effect*) better than those in the middle of the list. When asked to remember presi-dents in the middle of the list, we're more likely to recall Lincoln and not Truman (see pho-tos) because Lincoln is associated with significant events, such as the Civil War.

3. **Source Amnesia** Each day we read, hear, and process an enormous amount of infor-mation, and it's easy to get confused about how we learned who said what to whom and

Misinformation effect A mem-ory error resulting from mislead-ing information being presented after an event, which alters mem-ories of the event itself.

Serial-position effect A char-acteristic of memory retrieval in which information at the beginning and end of a series is remembered better than material in the middle.

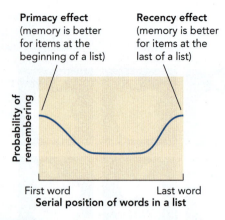

Primacy effect (memory is better for items at the beginning of a list)

Recency effect (memory is better for items at the last of a list)

Probability of remembering

First word · Last word
Serial position of words in a list

FIGURE 7.13 **The serial-position effect** When we try to recall a list of similar items, we tend to remember the first and last items best. Can you see how you can use this information to improve your chances of getting a job? If a potential employer calls you to set up an interview, you can increase the person's memory of you (and your application) by asking to be either the first (*primacy effect*) or the last (*recency effect*) candidate.

Jeff Morgan 08/Alamy Stock Photo

FIGURE 7.14 **Source amnesia and negative political ads** Think back to a recent political election. What type of political advertisement comes most readily to mind? Research shows that we're more likely to recall ads that rely on creating negative feelings about one of the candidates (Lariscy & Tinkham, 1999). They stick in our memory even if we initially have negative feelings about them. In addition, over time the negative "facts" stay in our memory, and we forget the source—*source amnesia*. The good news for politicians, and you in your personal life, is that direct rebuttals of negative ads are generally effective and do not backfire (Weeks & Garrett, 2014).

Source amnesia A memory error that occurs when we forget the origin of a previously stored memory; also called source confusion or source misattribution.

in what context. Forgetting the origin of a previously stored memory is known as **source amnesia** (Allen, 2018; Ferrie, 2015; Leichtman, 2006). (See **Figure 7.14**.)

4. **Spacing of Practice** Have you heard about software programs and websites, such as *Lumosity*, heavily promoted on the Internet and in television ads, that promise to dramatically decrease forgetting and improve memory, while revolutionizing the way we learn? Interestingly, most of these "new" programs are based on the older, well-established principle of **distributed practice**, in which studying or practice is broken up into a number of short sessions spaced out over time to allow numerous opportunities for "drill and practice." As you first discovered in the *Strategies for Student Success* at the end of Chapter 1, this type of spaced learning is widely recognized as one of the very best tools for learning and grade improvement (Dunlosky et al., 2013; Feng et al., 2019; Gagnon & Cormier, 2019). In response to research findings on the superiority of distributed practice, we've built in numerous opportunities for distributed practice and *self-tests* throughout this text. Unfortunately, many students do the exact opposite. They put off studying and believe they're better off using **massed practice**, or "cramming," right before an exam, which has proven to be far less effective than distributed practice.

Distributed practice A learning strategy in which studying or practice is broken up into a number of short sessions over a period of time; also known as spaced repetition.

Massed practice A study technique in which time spent learning is grouped (or massed) into long unbroken intervals; also called "cramming."

5. **Culture** As illustrated in the following **GCD** Gender and Cultural Diversity, cultural factors play a role in memory and how well people remember what they have learned (Gutchess & Huff, 2016; Wang, 2011).

GCD **Gender and Cultural Diversity**

Can Culture Affect Our Memories?

(APA Goal 2.5) Incorporate sociocultural factors in scientific inquiry

Have you heard the famous saying *A fish doesn't know it's in water*? Like fish, we humans often forget (or ignore) the powerful influences of culture, and this is particularly true for how culture might affect what we store in both our short-term and long-term memory. As you'll see in Chapter 12, culture also affects our personalities. People raised in *individualistic cultures*, such as Americans and Western Europeans, tend to value the needs and goals of the individual. In comparison, people who grow up in collectivistic cultures, such as most Asians and West Africans, more often emphasize the needs and goals of the group.

Why is this important? Research has revealed several cross-cultural differences between these two groups, including variations in cognitive biases, memory for objects versus background, episodic memory, and even emotional memories evoked by music (Gutchess & Huff, 2016; Juslin et al., 2016; Schwartz et al., 2014). These variations clearly illustrate that culture helps shape our memories.

Ross and Millson (1970) designed a cross-cultural study comparing American and Ghanaian college students' abilities to remember stories that were read aloud. Students listened to the stories without taking notes and without being told they would be tested. Two weeks later, all students were asked to write down as much as they could remember. The Ghanaian students had better recall than the Americans. Their superior performance was attributed to their culture's long oral tradition, which requires developing greater skill in encoding oral information.

Does this mean that people from cultures with an oral tradition simply have better memories? Recall from Chapter 1 that a core requirement for scientific research is further testing and generation of related hypotheses and studies. In this case, when other researchers orally presented African participants without formal schooling with lists of words instead of stories, they did *not* perform better (Cole et al., 1971). However, when all participants' memory for lists of words were tested, the African college students performed better than the American college students (Scribner, 1977). This suggests that formal schooling helps people develop memory strategies for things like lists of words. Participants without formal schooling may see such lists as unrelated and meaningless (Berry et al., 2011).

Wagner (1982) conducted a study with Moroccan and Mexican children that helps explain the effect of formal schooling. Participants were first presented with seven cards that were placed face down in front of them, one at a time. They were then shown a card and asked to point out which of the seven cards was its duplicate. Everyone, regardless of culture or amount of schooling, was able to recall the latest cards presented (the *recency effect*). However, the amount of schooling significantly affected overall recall and the ability to recall the earliest cards presented (*primacy effect*).

Wagner suggests that the primacy effect depends on *rehearsal*—the silent repetition of things you're trying to remember—and that this strategy is strongly related to schooling. As a child in a typical classroom, you were expected to memorize letters, numbers, multiplication tables, and a host of other basic facts. This type of formal schooling provides years of practice in memorization

and in applying these skills in test situations. According to Wagner, memory has a "hardware" section that does not change across culture. But it also contains a "software" part that develops particular strategies for remembering, which are learned.

Take-Home Message In cultures in which communication relies on oral tradition, people develop good strategies for remembering orally presented stories (**Figure 7.15**). In cultures in which formal schooling is the rule, people learn memory strategies that help them remember lists of items. From these studies, we can conclude that, across cultures, people tend to develop memory skills to match the demands of their environment.

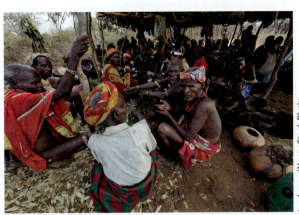

FIGURE 7.15 **Oral transmission of memories?** In some societies, leaders pass down vital information through stories related orally. Children living in such cultures tend to have better memories for this type of information than children of other cultures.

ton koene/Alamy Stock Photo

Retrieval Practice 7.2 | Forgetting

Self-Test Completing this self-test, and then checking your answers by clicking on the answer button or by looking in Appendix B, will provide immediate feedback and helpful practice for exams.

1. According to the _____ theory of forgetting, memory is processed and stored in a physical form, and connections between neurons may deteriorate over time.

   a. decay **c.** motivated forgetting
   b. interference **d.** retrieval failure

2. The _____ theory suggests that forgetting results from two competing memories, particularly memories with similar qualities.

   a. decay **c.** motivated forgetting
   b. interference **d.** encoding failure

3. The _____ effect suggests that people will recall information presented at the beginning and end of a list better than information from the middle of a list.

   a. recency **c.** serial position
   b. latency **d.** primacy

4. Distributed practice is a learning technique in which _____.

   a. students are distributed (spaced) equally throughout the room

   b. learning periods are broken up into a number of short sessions over a period of time

   c. learning decays faster than it can be distributed

   d. several students study together, distributing various subjects according to their individual strengths

5. Which of the following is NOT one of the key factors that contribute to forgetting outlined in the text?

   a. misinformation effect **c.** consolidation
   b. serial-position effect **d.** source amnesia

Q **Test Your Critical Thinking**

1. Briefly describe an example from your own life of source amnesia.

2. Why might advertisers of shoddy services or products benefit from channel surfing, especially if the television viewer is skipping from news programs to cable talk shows to infomercials?

Real World Application Question

[AQ3] Why do we remember President Lincoln better than President Truman?

Hint: Look in the text for **[AQ3]**

Source: W.F. Crummer/ Library of Congress. Public Domain

Source: Chase-Statler/ Library of Congress. Public Domain

Biological Bases of Memory

Retrieval Practice   While reading the upcoming sections, respond to each Learning Objective in your own words.

Summarize the biological factors involved in memory.

• **Describe** the synaptic and neurotransmitter changes that occur when we learn and remember.

• **Review** how our memories are processed and stored.

• **Explain** how emotional arousal affects memory.

• **Discuss** the biological factors in memory loss.

Real World Application Questions

[AQ4] How might exposure to pornography interfere with memory?

[AQ5] Can physical fitness help prevent dementia?

Having discussed the nature of memory and the various models of how it is organized, now we'll explore the biological bases of memory—the synaptic and neurotransmitter changes, where memories are processed and stored, the effects of emotional arousal, and the biological factors in memory loss.

Synaptic and Neurotransmitter Changes

Do you recall from Chapters 2 and 6 how learning and memory modify our brains' neural networks? When you are learning to play a sport like tennis, for example, repeated practice builds specific neural pathways that make it progressively easier for you to get the ball over the net. These same pathways later enable you to remember how to play the game.

Long-term potentiation (LTP)
A long-lasting increase in neural sensitivity; a biological mechanism for learning and memory.

These changes, called **long-term potentiation (LTP)**, happen in at least two ways. First, early research with rats raised in enriched environments found that repeated stimulation of a synapse strengthens it by causing the dendrites to grow more spines (Rosenzweig et al., 1972). This repeated stimulation further results in more synapses and receptor sites, along with increased sensitivity.

Second, when learning and memory occur, there is a measurable change in the amount of neurotransmitter released, which increases the neuron's efficiency in message transmission. Research with *Aplysia* (sea slugs) clearly demonstrates this effect (**Figure 7.16**).

Further evidence comes from research with genetically engineered "smart mice," which have extra receptors for a neurotransmitter named NMDA (N-methyl-d-aspartate). These mice perform significantly better on memory tasks than do normal mice (Lin et al., 2014; Plattner et al., 2014; Tsien, 2000).

Although it is difficult to generalize from sea slugs and mice, research on long-term potentiation (LTP) in humans supports the idea that LTP is one of the major biological mechanisms underlying learning and memory and certain cognitive impairments in humans (Baddeley et al., 2015; Biss & Collingridge, 2019; Camera et al., 2016).

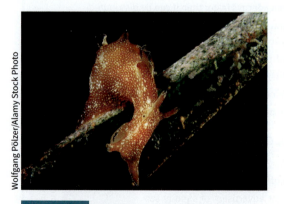

Wolfgang Pölzer/Alamy Stock Photo

FIGURE 7.16 **How does a sea slug learn and remember?**   After repeated squirting with water, followed by a mild shock, the sea slug *Aplysia* releases more neurotransmitters at certain synapses. These synapses then become more efficient at transmitting signals that allow the slug to more quickly withdraw its gills when squirted (presumably to minimize the pain from the shock). As a scientific and critical thinker, can you explain why this ability might provide an evolutionary advantage?

Memory Processing and Storage

How and where are our memories processed? Encoding begins with a focusing of our attention, which is controlled by our *thalamus* and *frontal lobes*. The encoded neural messages are then decoded (interpreted) in various areas in our cerebral cortex. Next, they're sent along to the *hippocampus*, which "decides" which of these messages will be stored in LTM. As you will see, emotional arousal tends to increase attention, and those messages and resulting memories are processed primarily in the *amygdala*, a brain structure involved in emotion. Note that memory is not a single process. Different types of memory involve different neural systems. As an example, the *basal ganglia* are important in implicit/nondeclarative memory (motor skills and habits, conditioned responses, and priming). In contrast, the *temporal lobes* are key to explicit/declarative memory (facts and general knowledge, as well as personal experiences).

Early memory researchers believed that memory was *localized*, or stored in a particular brain area. Later research suggests that, in fact, memory tends to be localized not in a single area but in many separate areas throughout the brain. In support of this, research shows that training with mnemonic devices (discussed earlier) induced new neural connections within several areas of the brain (e.g., Dresler et al., 2017).

Research techniques today are so advanced that we can identify specific brain areas that are activated or changed during memory processes by using functional magnetic resonance imaging (fMRI) brain scans. In one study, researchers used fMRI imaging to examine the brains of passengers of Air Transit Flight 236 to locate areas of the brain responsible for storing memories of a near-fatal crash (McKinnon et al., 2015; Palombo et al., 2015). The survivors were shown videos of the potential disaster, the September 11, 2001 attack, and a comparatively non-emotional (neutral) event. The fMRI scans showed that traumatic memory enhancement was associated with activation in the amygdala, medial temporal lobe, anterior and posterior midline, and visual cortex in these passengers. This pattern was not observed in a comparison group of non-traumatized individuals who were also scanned.

Emotional Arousal and Memory

When stressed or excited, we naturally produce neurotransmitters and hormones that arouse the body, such as *epinephrine* and *cortisol* (Chapter 3). These chemicals also affect the amygdala (a brain structure involved in emotion) and other brain areas, such as the hippocampus and cerebral cortex (parts of the brain that are important for memory). Research has shown that these chemicals can interfere with, as well as enhance, how we encode, store, and retrieve our memories (Jiang et al., 2019; Quas et al., 2016).

[AQ4] Surprisingly, some research suggests that exposure to pornography (see photo) can disrupt memory. Researchers in one study asked men to view a series of either pornographic or non-pornographic images and judge whether they had previously seen each image (Laier et al., 2013). Men who saw the nonsexual images gave 80 percent correct answers, whereas men who saw the pornographic images gave only 67 percent correct answers. Can you see how sexual arousal interferes with working memory and how it may help explain these findings?

On the other hand, emotional arousal can sometimes lead to memory enhancement, as shown by **flashbulb memories (FBMs)**—vivid, detailed, and near-permanent memories of emotionally significant moments or events (Brown & Kulik, 1977). During important historical, public, or autobiographical events, such as the U.S. presidential election in 2016 (**Figure 7.17**) or the Parkland, Florida mass shooting, it appears that our minds automatically create FBMs. We tend to remember incredible details, such as where we were, what was going on, and how we and others were feeling and reacting at that moment in time. FBMs are also long-lasting. In fact, researchers have found that people have retained their FBMs of the 9/11 attacks for as long as 10 years, and that their confidence in these memories has remained high (Hirst et al., 2015). We also sometimes create uniquely personal (and happy) FBMs (see the **Test Yourself**).

morrbyte/iStock/Getty Images

Flashbulb memory (FBM)
A vivid, detailed, and near-permanent memory of an emotionally significant moment or event; memory resulting from a form of automatic encoding, storage, and later retrieval.

Allen J. Schaben/Los Angeles Times/Getty Images

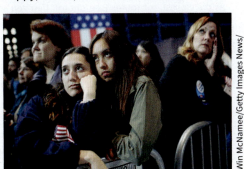

Win McNamee/Getty Images News/Getty Images

FIGURE 7.17   Politics and FBMs   Do you have a vivid flashbulb memory of the moment in 2016 when it was first announced that Donald Trump had been elected President of the United States? This election was very emotional for voters on both sides of the political divide.

Practical Application

Courtesy of Catherine Sanderson and Bart Hollander

Test Yourself: Common FBMs

Why do most people clearly remember their college graduation or wedding ceremony? Due to the extraordinary level of emotionality that most of us experience during these happy occasions, as shown in this photo of your author, Catherine Sanderson and her husband on their wedding day, we tend to automatically create detailed, long-lasting memories of our thoughts, feelings, and actions during exciting and momentous events.

Q Test Your Critical Thinking

1. Do your personal memories of highly emotional events fit with what flashbulb memory (FBM) research suggests?

2. Despite documented errors with FBMs, most people are very confident in their personal accuracy. What problems might result from this overconfidence?

de Vries, Conan/Cartoon Stock

"I remember that game of Spin-the-Bottle like it was yesterday. It was love at first spin."

How do FBMs happen? It's as if our brains command us to take "flash pictures" of highly emotional events in order for us to "pay attention, learn, and remember." As we've just seen, a flood of neurotransmitters and hormones helps create strong, immediate memories. Specifically, as discussed in Chapter 3, the flood of the hormone cortisol that happens during traumatic events has been studied as a contributor to long-lasting memories and, sadly, to PTSD (Drexler et al., 2015). In addition to experiencing these chemical changes, we actively replay the memories in our minds again and again (see cartoon), which further encourages stronger and more lasting memories.

Note that research shows that our FBMs for specific details, particularly the time and place the emotional event occurred, are fairly accurate (Rimmele et al., 2012). However, these FBMs suffer the same alterations and decay as all other forms of memory. They're NOT perfect recordings of events (El Haj et al., 2016; Hirst & Phelps, 2016; Lanciano et al., 2018). In one study, researchers asked participants shortly after the death of Michael Jackson to report on their FBMs and other reactions to the news of his death (Day & Ross, 2014). When these same people were interviewed again 18 months later, researchers found that, despite several discrepancies in their memories, confidence in their personal accuracy remained high.

Practical Application

Have you wondered why some people get seriously or fatally injured in certain situations, whereas others safely escape? News reports are filled with stories of people becoming fatally confused during fires or other emergencies because they panic and forget important survival tips, such as the closest exit routes (see photo). Can you see why airlines and fire departments routinely provide safety and evacuation drills, or why it's dangerous to drive when we're arguing with a loved one or to discipline our children when we're very angry? Recognizing that we're sometimes "not in our right minds" during times of high emotional arousal may save our lives—and our relationships.

Thongden Studio/Shutterstock.com

Take-Home Message FBMs, like other forms of memory, are subject to alterations. What separates them from ordinary, everyday memories is their vividness and our subjective confidence in their accuracy. But confidence is not the same as accuracy—an important point we'll return to in the last part of this chapter. We all need to remember that our memory processes are sometimes impaired during high emotional arousal.

FIGURE 7.18 **The brain and memory**   Note the location and names of the major areas of the brain responsible for encoding, storage, and retrieval of memories.

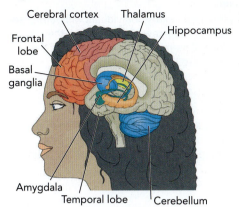

Q **Test Your Critical Thinking**

1. What effect might damage to the amygdala have on a person's relationships with others?

2. How might damage to your thalamus affect your day-to-day functioning?

Area of the Brain	Effects on Memory
Amygdala	Emotional memories
Basal ganglia and cerebellum	Creation and storage of basic memory and implicit/nondeclarative LTM (such as skills, habits, and simple classically conditioned responses)
Hippocampal formation (hippocampus and surrounding area)	Explicit/declarative and implicit/nondeclarative LTM, as well as sequences of events
Thalamus	Formation of new memories and spatial and working memory; implicit/nondeclarative and explicit/declarative LTM
Cerebral cortex	Encoding, storage, and retrieval of explicit/declarative and implicit/nondeclarative LTM

Source: Allen, 2018; Baddeley et al., 2015; Gao et al., 2018; Lacagnina et al., 2019; Wolff & Vann, 2019.

The Biology of Memory Loss

So far in this section, we've discussed the neuronal and synaptic changes that occur when we learn and remember, memory processing and storage, and how emotional arousal affects memory. As noted earlier, memory researchers once believed that memory was *localized*, or stored in a particular area of the brain. We now believe that memory tends to be localized not in a single area but in many separate areas throughout the brain. See **Figure 7.18** for a summary of the areas of the brain responsible for various memory functions.

Now that we know where memory is located, we can better explain how injury and disease affect our memory processes. In this section, we will explore the specific and devastating effects of *traumatic brain injury (TBI)*, *amnesia, dementia*, and *Alzheimer's disease (AD)*.

Traumatic Brain Injury (TBI)   One of the leading factors in neurological disorders—including memory loss—among U.S. men and women between the ages of 15 and 25 is *traumatic brain injury* (TBI). These injuries most commonly result from car accidents, falls, blows, and gunshot wounds.

TBI happens when the skull suddenly collides with another object. Compression, twisting, and distortion of the brain inside the skull all lead to serious and sometimes permanent damage to the brain. The frontal and temporal lobes often take the heaviest hit because they directly collide with bony ridges inside the skull.

Perhaps the most troubling, and controversial, factor in TBIs is the number of severe or repeated blows to the head that occur during sports participation (Centers for Disease Control and Prevention, 2016; Falcon et al., 2019; Lim et al., 2019). Sadly, both professional and non-professional athletes frequently experience *concussions*, a form of TBI, and multiple concussions can lead to *chronic traumatic encephalopathy (CTE)*. To make matters worse, the frequency of sports-related brain injuries may have been grossly underestimated (Baugh et al., 2015), and a growing body of research connects these multiple brain injuries to diseases and disorders like Alzheimer's, depression, and even suicide (see **Figure 7.19**).

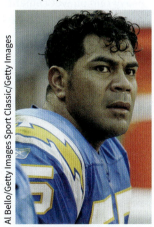

FIGURE 7.19 **Professional sports and brain damage**   Junior Seau (photo of the player in the blue jersey) was a famous, 10-time all-pro linebacker in the National Football League (NFL), who died by suicide in 2012—at the age of 43. Experts later concluded that Seau suffered from chronic traumatic encephalopathy (CTE), a serious neurological disease linked to concussions, which is also seen in the injuries and deaths of other athletes (Lim et al., 2019; Thamaratnam et al., 2018). Due to his personal concerns over concussions, San Francisco 49ers (NFL) linebacker Chris Borland (photo of player in the white jersey), one of the league's top rookies quit playing in 2015—despite being in the prime of his athletic career.

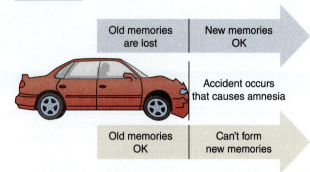

FIGURE 7.20 Two types of amnesia

a. Retrograde amnesia

After an accident or other brain injury, individuals with *retrograde amnesia* have no trouble forming new memories, but they do experience *amnesia* (loss of memories) for segments of the past—old, "retro" memories are lost.

b. Anterograde amnesia

In contrast, people with *anterograde amnesia* have no trouble recovering old memories, but they do experience *amnesia* (cannot form new memories) after an accident or other brain injury.

Retrograde amnesia The inability to retrieve information from the past; backward-acting amnesia.

Consolidation The process by which LTM memories become stable in the brain; neural changes that take place when a memory is formed.

Anterograde amnesia The inability to form new memories; forward-acting amnesia.

Amnesia Now that we know a little more about brain injuries and how they're related to memory loss (or amnesia), let's examine some common misunderstandings. For example, it's important to note that, although being completely amnesic about your past and not knowing who you are is a common plot in movies and television, real-life amnesia generally doesn't lead to a specific loss of self-identity. Instead, the individual typically has trouble retrieving more widespread and general old memories or forming new ones (Allen, 2018). These two forms of amnesia are called *retrograde* and *anterograde* (**Figure 7.20**).

In **retrograde amnesia** (acting backward in time), the person has no memory (is amnesic) for events that occurred *before* the brain injury because those memories were never stored in LTM. However, the same person has no trouble remembering things that happened after the injury. As the name implies, only the old "retro" memories are lost.

What leads to retrograde amnesia? Recall from our earlier discussion that during long-term potentiation (LTP) our neurons change to accommodate new learning. In addition, we know that it takes a certain amount of time for these neural changes to become fixed and stable in long-term memory, a process known as **consolidation**. Like heavy rain on wet cement, the brain injury "wipes away" unstable memories because the cement has not had time to harden (*retrograde amnesia*). In cases where the individual is amnesic only for the events right before the brain injury, it may be due to a failure of consolidation.

In contrast to retrograde amnesia, in which people lose memories for events *before* a brain injury, **anterograde amnesia** (acting forward in time) involves losing memory for events that occur *after* a brain injury. This type of amnesia generally results from a surgical injury or from diseases such as chronic alcoholism. Continuing our analogy with cement, having anterograde amnesia would be like having permanently hardened cement, which prevents the laying down of new memories.

Remember that retrograde amnesia is normally temporary and is somewhat common, such as what happens to football players after a head injury. In contrast, anterograde amnesia is relatively rare and most often permanent. However, patients often show surprising abilities to learn and remember procedural motor skills, such as how to mow a lawn. Also note that some individuals have both forms of amnesia.

Consider the famous case of H.M., who underwent brain surgery at the age of 27 to correct severe epileptic seizures (Augustinack et al., 2014; Corkin, 2013; Mauguière & Corkin, 2015). Although the surgery improved his medical problem, his family and doctors soon recognized that something was wrong with H.M.'s long-term memory. When his uncle died, he grieved in a normal way. But soon after, he began to ask why his uncle never visited him. H.M. had to be repeatedly reminded of his uncle's death, and each reminder would begin a new mourning process. H.M. lived another 55 years not recognizing the people who cared for him daily. Each time he met his caregivers, read a book, or ate a meal, it was as if for the first time. H.M. died in 2008, never having regained his long-term memory. Can you see how H.M. suffered from anterograde amnesia, as well as mild memory loss for events in his life that happened the year or two before the operation (retrograde amnesia) (Allen, 2018)? What should we make of this real-life example? What would it be like to be H.M.—existing only in the present moment, unable to learn and form new memories?

Dementia and Alzheimer's Disease (AD)
Like the brain injuries from concussions and/or surgeries, which may lead to amnesia, various diseases can also alter the physiology of the brain and nervous system and thereby disrupt memory processes. For example, *dementia* is a progressive mental deterioration that occurs most commonly in old age. What is the difference between dementia and Alzheimer's disease (AD)? Dementia is an umbrella term for a variety of progressive memory-related brain disorders, including Huntington's disease, Parkinson's disease, and Alzheimer's disease (AD). We'll focus our attention on AD, given that it is the most common form of dementia (**Figure 7.21**).

Alzheimer's does not attack all types of memory equally. A hallmark of the disease is an extreme decrease in *explicit/declarative memory*—failing to recall facts, information, and personal life experiences (Howes & O'Shea, 2014; Müller et al., 2014; Redondo et al., 2015). However, those who suffer from AD still retain some *implicit/nondeclarative* memories, such as of simple classically conditioned responses and procedural tasks like brushing their teeth.

What are the possible causes of AD? Brain autopsies of people with Alzheimer's show unusual *tangles* (structures formed from degenerating cell bodies) and *plaques* (structures formed from degenerating axons and dendrites). Hereditary Alzheimer's generally strikes its victims between the ages of 45 and 55 (see again Figure 7.21). Some experts believe Alzheimer's is primarily genetic and age related. However, like many other diseases, it undoubtedly results from a mixture of multiple factors (Cook Maher et al., 2017; Schaffert et al., 2018; Solomon et al., 2018).

FIGURE 7.21 The effect of Alzheimer's disease (AD) on the brain

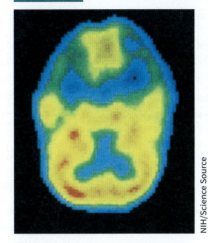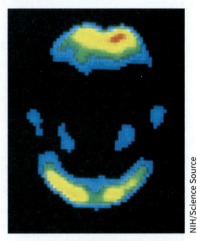

a. Normal brain In this PET scan of a normal brain, note the high amounts of the red and yellow colors (signs of brain activity).

b. Brain of a person with AD In this PET scan of a person with AD, note how the reduced activity in the brain is most significant in the temporal and parietal lobes (the mostly black areas in the center and on the sides of this AD patient's brain). These are the key areas for storing memories.

PAN Practical Application of Neuroscience

How can we diagnose and possibly prevent AD? Unfortunately, there is currently no effective way to diagnose early Alzheimer's, but there is promising new research based on telltale changes in the retina of the human eye (Tsai et al., 2014). **[AQ5]** Regarding prevention, research shows that AD individuals may benefit from a strong social network and a healthy diet and exercise program (e.g., Cook Maher et al., 2017; Solomon et al., 2018). In one study, researchers who measured the fitness levels of 191 middle-aged women (see photo), and then followed them for over four decades, found that 32 percent of the women at the low fitness level, 25 percent of those at the medium level, and 5 percent of those at the high level eventually developed dementia (Hörder et al., 2018). Surprisingly, even those in the high fitness level who eventually did develop dementia were diagnosed 11 years later than those in the medium-fitness group.

Retrieval Practice 7.3 | Biological Bases of Memory

Self-Test Completing this self-test, and then checking your answers by clicking on the answer button or by looking in Appendix B, will provide immediate feedback and helpful practice for exams.

1. The long-lasting increase in neural sensitivity believed to be a biological mechanism for learning and memory is called _____.
   a. maintenance rehearsal
   b. adrenaline activation
   c. long-term potentiation (LTP)
   d. the reverberating response

2. Your vivid memory of what you were doing when you were first informed about your parents' impending divorce might be an example of _____.
   a. encoding specificity   c. latent learning
   b. long-term potentiation (LTP)   d. a flashbulb memory (FBM)

3. The leading factor in memory loss among U.S. men and women between the ages of 15 and 25 is _____.
   a. age-related amnesia (ARA)
   b. long-term potentiation (LTP)
   c. Alzheimer's disease (AD)
   d. traumatic brain injury (TBI)

4. Ralph can't remember anything that happened to him before he fell through the floor of his tree house. His lack of memory of events before his fall is called _____ amnesia.
   a. retroactive   c. retrograde
   b. proactive   d. anterograde

5. A progressive mental deterioration characterized by severe memory loss that occurs most commonly in elderly people is called _____.
   a. retrieval loss syndrome deterioration
   b. prefrontal cortex disease (PCD)
   c. Alzheimer's disease (AD)
   d. age-related amnesia (A-RA)

Q Test Your Critical Thinking

1. What might be the evolutionary benefit of flashbulb memories?
2. How might anterograde amnesia affect a person's relationships with others?

Real World Application Questions

[AQ4] How might exposure to pornography interfere with memory?

morrbyte/iStock/ Getty Images

[AQ5] Can physical fitness help prevent dementia?

Monkey Business Images/ Shutterstock.com

Hint: Look in the text for **[AQ4]** and **[AQ5]**

7.4 | Memory Distortions and Improvement

LEARNING OBJECTIVES

Retrieval Practice While reading the upcoming sections, respond to each Learning Objective in your own words.

Summarize how our memories get distorted and the resulting problems.

- **Discuss** how our need for logic, consistency, and efficiency contributes to some memory distortions.

- **Describe** the memory problems associated with eyewitness testimony.

- **Discuss** false versus repressed memories.

- **Review** the 10 tips for memory improvement.

Real World Application Questions

[AQ6] Could someone falsely convince you as an adult that you had committed a serious crime as a teenager?

Remembrance of things past is not necessarily the remembrance of things as they were.
—Marcel Proust

At this point in your life, you've undoubtedly experienced a painful breakup of a serious love relationship or witnessed such breakups among your close friends. During these breakups, did you wonder how the reported experiences of two people in the same partnership could be so different? Why would each partner reconstruct his or her own personal memory of the relationship? How can we explain such common memory distortions?

Understanding Memory Distortions

There are several reasons why we shape, rearrange, and distort our memories. One of the most common is our need for *logic* and *consistency*. When we're initially forming new memories or sorting through old ones, we fill in missing pieces, make "corrections," and rearrange information to make it logical and consistent with our previous experiences or personal desires. For instance, if you left a relationship because you preferred a new partner, you might rearrange your memories to suit your belief that you are just a weak-willed person who can't stay faithful or that you were mismatched from the beginning. However, if you were the one left behind, you might reconstruct your memories so that you now believe that you're doomed to lose people you love or that your partner was a manipulative "player" from the beginning.

We also edit, summarize, and augment new information and tie it into previously stored LTM for the sake of *efficiency*. Unfortunately, this type of "efficient" shaping and constructing sometimes results in a loss of specific details, which we need later on. For instance, when taking notes during lectures, you can't (and shouldn't) record every word. Instead, you edit, summarize, and augment information and (hopefully) tie it into other related material. However, your note taking may occasionally miss important details that later trip you up during exams.

Despite all their problems and biases, our memories are normally fairly accurate and serve us well in most situations. They have evolved to encode, store, and retrieve general and vital information, such as the location of dangerous cliffs or the smell of nutritious foods. However, when faced with tasks that require encoding, storing, and retrieving precise details like those in a scholarly text, or recalling dates like birthdays or anniversaries, our brains are not as well-equipped.

Eyewitness Testimony

When our memory errors come into play in the criminal justice system, they may lead to wrongful judgments of guilt or innocence, with possible life or death consequences.

In the past, one of the best forms of trial evidence a lawyer could have was an *eyewitness*— "I was there; I saw it with my own eyes." Unfortunately, research has identified several problems with eyewitness testimony (Gustafsson et al., 2019; Loftus, 1993, 2011; Michael & Garry, 2016). As an example, if multiple eyewitnesses talk to one another after a crime, they may "remember" and corroborate erroneous details that someone else reported, which is why police officers try to separate eyewitnesses while taking their reports.

As a scientific and critical thinker, can you see how the problems we discussed earlier with respect to flashbulb memories (FBMs) might apply to eyewitness testimony? Traumatic events, like watching a crime, often create FBMs for eyewitnesses. Despite high confidence in their personally vivid memories, they can make serious errors, such as identifying an innocent person as the perpetrator (**Figure 7.22**).

Problems with eyewitness recollections are so well established that judges now allow expert testimony on the unreliability of eyewitness testimony and routinely instruct jurors on its limits (Pozzulo, 2017; Safer et al., 2016). If you serve as a member of a jury or listen to accounts of crimes in the news, remind yourself of these problems. Also, note that participants in eyewitness studies generally report their inaccurate memories with great self-assurance and strong conviction (DeSoto & Roediger, 2019; Kaplan et al., 2016; Morgan & Southwick, 2014).

Fortunately, research now finds that eyewitness statements taken at the time of the initial identification of a suspect are quite reliable (Wixted et al., 2015). The overall accuracy of eyewitness testimony can also be improved if people are asked to make very fast judgments (Brewer et al., 2012). In fact, giving people only a few seconds to identify the culprit in a lineup increases the accuracy of such identifications by 20 to 30 percent over rates obtained when people are allowed to take as long as they want to make a decision. In addition, simply asking people to close their eyes when they're trying to remember leads to greater accuracy in both audio and visual details (Nash et al., 2016). **Figure 7.23** offers further insights into eyewitness testimony.

Courtesy of the Innocence Project, New Orleans

FIGURE 7.22 **Dangerous eyewitness testimony** Malcolm Alexander (pictured here) was wrongly convicted of rape—in large part because of mistaken eyewitness testimony (Ollove, 2018). Thankfully, DNA evidence later proved his innocence and he was released from prison in 2018. However, he still served 38 years for a crime he did not commit.

FIGURE 7.23 **Understanding and improving eyewitness testimony**

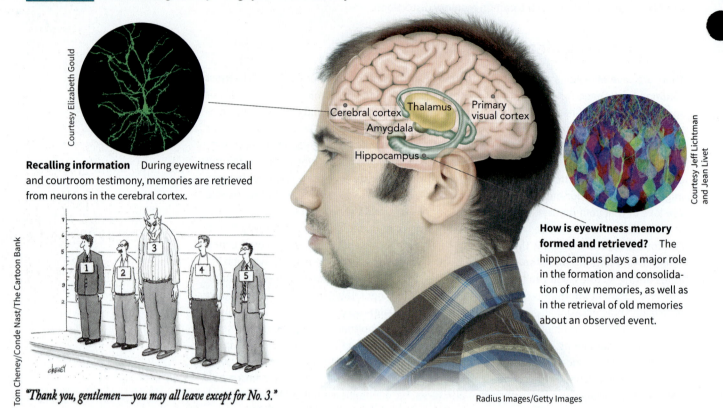

Courtesy Elizabeth Gould

Recalling information During eyewitness recall and courtroom testimony, memories are retrieved from neurons in the cerebral cortex.

Cerebral cortex
Thalamus
Primary visual cortex
Amygdala
Hippocampus

Tom Cheney/Conde Nast/The Cartoon Bank

"Thank you, gentlemen—you may all leave except for No. 3."

Eyewitnesses and police lineups As humorously depicted in this cartoon, officials now recommend that suspects never "stand out" from the others in a lineup. Witnesses also are cautioned not to assume that the real criminal is in the lineup and never to "guess" when asked to make an identification. Some states now require police lineups to be conducted by administrators who do not know which lineup member is the suspect (Kovera & Evelo, 2017; Ollove, 2018).

Courtesy Jeff Lichtman and Jean Livet

How is eyewitness memory formed and retrieved? The hippocampus plays a major role in the formation and consolidation of new memories, as well as in the retrieval of old memories about an observed event.

Radius Images/Getty Images

False versus Repressed Memories

> We invent memories. Without thinking. If we tell ourselves something happened often enough, we start to believe it, and then we can actually remember it.
>
> —S. J. Watson

Like eyewitness testimony, false memories can have serious legal, personal, and social implications. Have you heard the true-life story of the famous memory expert and psychologist Elizabeth Loftus? When she was 14, her mother drowned in the family's pool. Decades later, a relative told Elizabeth that she, Elizabeth, had been the one to find her mother's body. Despite her initial shock, Elizabeth's memories slowly started coming back. Her recovery of these gruesome childhood memories, although painful, initially brought great relief. It seemed to explain why she had always been fascinated by the topic of memory. The relative who told Elizabeth that she had been the one to discover her mother's body later remembered—and other relatives confirmed—that it had actually been Aunt Pearl, not Elizabeth. Loftus, a world-renowned expert on memory distortions, had unknowingly created her own *false memory*.

Confirming Loftus's own personal experience, extensive research has shown that it's relatively easy to create false memories, and under some circumstances adults are more suggestible than children (Kaplan et al., 2016; Lynn et al., 2015; Otgaar et al., 2018).

[AQ6] Interestingly, even innocent adult participants can be convinced, over the course of a few hours, that as teenagers they had committed serious crimes (Shaw & Porter, 2015). Researchers brought college students to the lab for three 40-minute interviews that took place about a week apart. In the first interview, the researchers told each student about two events he or she had experienced as a teen, only one of which actually happened. These false events were serious, such as an assault, theft (see photo), personal injury, or

Universal Images Group/Getty Images

attack by a dog. (The false event stories included some true details about that time in the student's life, which they obtained from talking to the student's parent or guardian.) Participants were then asked to explain what happened in each of the two events. When they had difficulty explaining the false event, the interviewer encouraged them to try anyway, explaining that if they used specific memory strategies they might be able to recall more details. In the second and third interviews, the researchers again asked the students to recall as much as they could about both the true and the false event. Over half of the students were classified as having developed a false memory of the event, and many included elaborate details about their false experience.

Understanding False Memories   Do you recall our earlier discussion of the *misinformation effect* and how experimenters created a false memory of seeing a telephone in a room? Participants who were asked neutral questions such as "Was there a telephone in the room?" made errors on only 10 percent of the queries (Morgan et al., 2013). In contrast, when participants were asked, "What color was the telephone?" falsely implying that a telephone had been in the room, 98 percent "remembered" it being there.

To make matters worse, once false memories have been formed, they can multiply over time—and last for years. Researchers in one study showed participants pictures of an event, such as a girl's wallet being stolen (Zhu et al., 2012). Participants then read a series of statements about the event, which included both accurate information (for instance, the person who took the girl's wallet was a man) and false information (the person who took the girl's wallet put it in his pants pocket). (In reality, the picture showed him hiding the wallet in his jacket.) Initially after reading these statements, participants identified only 31 percent of the false events as having occurred. However, when participants were asked 1½ years later which events had occurred, they identified 39 percent of the false statements as true. This indicates that false memories not only last but can even multiply over time.

As you can see, research like this has serious and compelling implications for the legal system. The good news is that recent studies using brain scans have shown that different areas of the brain are activated during true and false memories, which may lead to more reliable tests of memory (**Figure 7.24**).

Are you wondering how all this research applies to our everyday life? In addition to producing serious legal problems in the case of eyewitness testimony, false memories

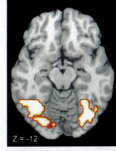
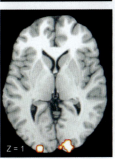

Courtesy of Roberto Cabeza, Duke University. From Cabeza, cerebral cortex, 2007, Figure 4. Reproduced with permission of Oxford University Press.

FIGURE 7.24 **Brain scans detecting true versus false memories**   The orange/white areas on these brain scans reveal activity in the primary visual cortex part of the brain. Comparing the larger sections of activity in these two brain scans, note that the individual with the larger orange/white area was recalling both true and false memories, whereas the individual in the other scan was recalling only true memories.

PA Practical Application

Would you like a less depressing and simpler example of false memories?   Consider the following real world personal story:

One of the co-authors of this book, Karen Huffman, is a dear friend of *mine (see photo), and we* co-taught intro psych for many years. During our times together in the classroom, we've often told stories about our own children to provide real-life examples of various psychological principles. Ironically, in working on the chapter on memory, we suddenly realized that some of the stories we were currently telling our students about our respective daughters were becoming blended in our own minds. We couldn't remember whether certain events happened to one of my three daughters or to Karen's only daughter. For us, this became a perfect personal example of both the constructive nature of memory and source amnesia.

Courtesy of Katie Townsend-Merino

Professor Katie Townsend-Merino
Palomar College
San Marcos, CA

may affect our interpersonal relationships. It's important to remember that everyone is vulnerable to creating and believing false memories. Just because something feels true doesn't mean that it is.

Understanding Repressed Memories

Repression According to Freud's psychoanalytic theory, a basic coping or defense mechanism that prevents anxiety-provoking thoughts, feelings, and memories from reaching consciousness.

Creating false memories may be somewhat common, but what about so-called *repressed memories?* Can we recover true memories that were previously buried in childhood? There is a great deal of debate regarding this question (Boag, 2012; Brodsky & Gutheil, 2016; Goldfarb et al., 2019). **Repression** is the supposed unconscious coping mechanism by which we prevent anxiety-provoking thoughts from reaching consciousness.

According to some research, repressed memories are *actively* and *consciously* "forgotten" in an effort to avoid the pain of their retrieval (Anderson et al., 2004; Boag, 2012). Other researchers suggest that some memories are so painful that they exist only in an *unconscious* corner of the mind, making them inaccessible to the individual (Haaken, 2010; Mancia & Baggott, 2008). In these cases, therapy supposedly would be necessary to unlock the hidden memories.

Repression is a complex and controversial topic in psychology. No one doubts that some memories are forgotten and later recovered. What some question is the idea that *repressed memories* of painful experiences (especially childhood sexual abuse) are stored in the unconscious mind, especially since these memories may play an important role in legal proceedings (Howe & Knott, 2015; Lampinen & Beike, 2015; Loftus & Cahill, 2007). Critics suggest that most people who have witnessed or experienced a violent crime or have survived childhood sexual abuse have intense, persistent memories. They have trouble *forgetting*, not remembering. Other critics wonder whether therapists sometimes inadvertently create false memories in their clients during therapy. For more information on both false and repressed memories, see the **STH** **Scientific Thinking Highlight**.

While the debate over false versus repressed memories continues, we must be careful not to ridicule or condemn people who recover true memories of abuse. In the same spirit, we must protect innocent people from wrongful accusations that come from false memories. Ideally, with continued research (and perhaps new technology) we may someday better protect the interests of both the victim and the accused.

To close on another encouraging note, see the following **PAH** **Practical Application Highlight**, which provides a handy list of the key tips for memory improvement. One of the many beauties of our human brain is that we can recognize the limits and problems of memory and then develop appropriate coping mechanisms. Just as our ancestors domesticated wild horses and cattle to overcome the physical limits of the human body, we can develop similar approaches to improve our mental limits—especially those responsible for fine detail.

Take-Home Message

As we've seen throughout this chapter, our memories are remarkable—yet highly fickle. Recognizing our commonly shared frailties of memory will make us better jurors in the courtroom, more informed consumers, and more thoughtful and open-minded parents, teachers, students, and friends. Unfortunately, sometimes our memories are better than we would like. Traumatic and extremely emotional memories can persist even when we would very much like to forget. Though painful, these memories can sometimes provide important insights. As Elizabeth Loftus suggests in a letter to her deceased mother:

> I thought then [as a 14-year-old] that eventually I would get over your death. I know today that I won't. But I've decided to accept that truth. What does it matter if I don't get over you? Who says I have to? David and Robert still tease me: "Don't say the M word or Beth will cry." So what if the word mother affects me this way? Who says I have to fix this? Besides, I'm too busy (Loftus, 2002, p. 70).

STH Scientific Thinking Highlight

Why False versus Repressed Memories Matter

(APA Goal 2.1) Use scientific reasoning to interpret psychological phenomena

The notion of false versus repressed memories continues to be a complex and controversial topic in psychology (Goodman et al., 2019; Lampinen & Beike, 2015; Loftus & Cahill, 2007). It also remains a subject of current scientific research. For example, a recent study of 1,082 participants found that 122 reported having recovered a memory of abuse during psychotherapy (Patihis & Pendergrast, 2019). In cases where the therapist discussed the possibility of repressed memories, participants were 20 times more likely to report the recovery of such memories.

What do you think? Although some critics suggest that therapists are at fault for creating false or recovered memories, can you see how, if a clinician simply mentions the possibility of abuse, the client's own *constructive processes* may lead him or her to create a false memory? Even without prompting from a therapist, some clients might start to incorporate portrayals of abuse from movies and books into their own existing memories. They might then go on to forget their original sources (a form of *source amnesia*), and eventually come to believe them as reliable. Furthermore, some cases of repressed memories may be an example of *motivated forgetting,* which we discussed earlier. In this case, the client may be motivated to forget the early trauma because it is so painful or anxiety-producing.

What is the general consensus among psychologists? Most agree that:

- False memories can be created and certain memories can be forgotten and later recovered.
- Sexual abuse of both children and adults is a serious and historically underreported and unacknowledged problem around the world.
- The ability to reliably distinguish real memories from false memories and to identify inaccurate and repressed memories is extremely difficult—particularly if those memories are recovered through hypnosis.

Psychologists also recognize that egregious problems and potential tragedies surround the question of false and repressed memories—especially those of sexual assault. Abuse survivors may never reveal the abuse and silently suffer the consequences of recurring or repressed painful memories, they may tell others and not be believed, or they may tell others and never see legal action taken or justice done. For those who are falsely accused, consequences may include losing their reputation, job, family, and even their freedom.

Q Test Your Scientific Thinking

As you may recall from Chapter 1, scientific thinking is an approach to information that combines a high degree of *skepticism* (questioning what "everybody knows") with *objectivity* (using empirical data to separate fantasy from reality) and *rationalism* (practicing logical reasoning). Using these three principles, consider the following questions:

1. **Skepticism** Given your likely preexisting knowledge and beliefs about false and repressed memories, were you predisposed to believe or discount claims of recovered memories (particularly of childhood sexual assault)? Scientific thinkers approach controversies like these with considerable skepticism and an open mind.

2. **Objectivity** In the study cited above (Patihis & Pendergrast, 2019), how would you verify the statistics regarding the number of recovered memories and whether or not the therapist actually suggested the recovered memory? Could this survey be an example of *representative, participant,* or *sample bias* or *demand characteristics* (Chapter 1)? Scientific thinkers gather information and delay judgment until adequate data are available. Scientific thinkers also carefully analyze and compare data and questions on both sides of a controversy for their comparative value and content.

3. **Rationalism** Setting aside the question of whether recovered memories are real, false, inaccurate, or repressed, what are the potential dangers and logical consequences of believing them? Recovered memories of sexual abuse in childhood often result in long-term damage to family relationships, with some members completely cutting off contact with other family members. On the other hand, what are the costs of not believing a true victim of abuse? Can you think of positive outcomes and how some of the problems could be eliminated or diminished if cases of abuse were reported and investigated immediately rather than years later?

(Compare your answers with those of fellow students, family, and friends. Doing so will improve your scientific thinking and your media savvy.)

PAH **Practical Application Highlight**

Tips for Memory Improvement

(APA Goal 1.3) Describe applications of psychology

The following ten suggestions for memory improvement were discussed earlier in this chapter and in the *Strategies for Student Success* at the end of Chapter 1. We've summarized and repeated them here because they're particularly helpful for increasing college success and reducing wasted time. Given that the three key steps in memory are *encoding, storage,* and *retrieval* (the ESR model), we've arranged these tips accordingly.

To get the maximum benefits, first read through the list, placing a check mark (✓) in the blank space next to items you're currently using, a + mark by the tips you want to add, and a − mark by those strategies you don't plan to try. After adding the new skills to your daily study habits, look back and reconsider those items with a − mark. We'd like to hear how these strategies work out for you (casanderson@amherst.edu, khuffman@palomar.edu).

Encoding   As discussed earlier, the first step in memory is successful *encoding*. To improve your study skills and exam performance, try these encoding tips:

_____ 1. **Pay attention and reduce interference.**   When you really want to remember something, you must *selectively attend* to the information you want to encode and ignore distractions. During class, focus on the instructor, and sit away from distracting people or views outside. When studying, choose a place with minimal interference. Also, recall from earlier chapters that *multitasking* while studying or listening to lectures greatly increases interference and reduces your ability to pay attention.

_____ 2. **Strive for a deeper level of processing.**   Some students try to study important terms or concepts by highlighting, rereading, or simply repeating the information over and over to themselves. As you may recall from Chapter 1, highlighting and rereading are the LEAST effective study techniques. While repeating information (maintenance rehearsal) does extend the duration of STM beyond the normal limit of about 30 seconds, this type of rehearsal, highlighting, and rereading are all forms of *shallow processing*. They're not efficient for LTM or for preparing for exams. If you want to effectively encode (and later successfully retrieve) information, you need a deeper level of processing, which involves active reading and taking notes. Another way to deeply process is *elaborative* rehearsal, which involves thinking about the material and relating it to other previously stored information. We hope you've noticed that we formally define each key term immediately in the text and generally give a brief explanation with one or two examples for each term. While studying this text, use these tools to help your elaborative rehearsal—and ensure a deeper level of processing. In addition, try making up your own examples. The more elaborate the encoding of information, the more memorable it will become.

_____ 3. **Counteract the serial-position effect.**   Given that we tend to remember information that occurs at the beginning or end of a sequence, spend extra time with information in the middle. When reading or reviewing the text, start at different places—sometimes at the second section, sometimes at the fourth.

Storage   The second step in successful memory is *storage*. The best way to create an effective storage system, in either your brain or your computer, is through logical filing and good organization. Try these two helpful strategies:

_____ 4. **Use chunking.**   Although the storage capacity of STM is only around five to nine items, you can expand it by chunking information into groups. If you need to remember a 12-digit number, try grouping it into four groups of three numbers.

_____ 5. **Create hierarchies.**   An efficient way to organize and store a large body of information is to create hierarchies, which involves grouping concepts from most general to most specific. Chapter outlines and the tables and figures in this text are examples of hierarchies. Be sure to study them carefully—and make up your own versions whenever possible.

Retrieval   The third and final stage of successful memory is *retrieval*. As you know, your grades in most courses are determined primarily by some form of quizzing or exams, both of which rely exclusively on retrieval. Here are five tips for improving retrieval:

_____ 6. **Engage in practice testing.**   Recall from Chapter 1 that research clearly shows practice testing is one of the best ways to improve your retrieval—and course grades (Aziz et al., 2014; Dunlosky et al., 2013; Gagnon & Cormier, 2019). Taking tests is not a favorite pastime for most people. However, if you think of it as practice, then it becomes more attractive and logical. Just as we need to practice our skateboarding tricks, golf swing, or dance routine, we need to practice testing ourselves—BEFORE any exam. This is why we provide so many self-testing options within this text (the learning objective questions that start each section, the self-test at the end of each major section, and the key term review at the end of each chapter). We also offer numerous additional free tests on our website. Be sure to take advantage of these options.

_____ 7. **Distribute your practice.**   *After* practice testing, the next best way to improve your memory is through distributed practice. Researchers have found that we encode, store, and retrieve information better when our study sessions are distributed (or spaced out) over time (Dunlosky et al., 2013; Feng et al., 2019; Gagnon & Cormier, 2019). Although *massed practice* (cramming) can produce speedy short-term learning, it's far less effective than distributed practice. There are at least two other major problems with staying up late or "pulling an all-nighter" to cram for exams: (1) Being drowsy while studying or taking an exam negatively affects overall performance, and (2) during sleep we process and store most of the new information we acquired when awake (Chapter 5).

_____ 8. **Remember the encoding-specificity principle.**   When we form memories, we store them with links to the way we thought about them at the time. Therefore, the closer the retrieval cues are to the original encoding situation, the better the retrieval (**Figure 7.25**). Knowing that you encode a lot of material during class time, avoid "early takes" or makeup exams, which are generally scheduled in other classrooms. The *context* will be different, and your retrieval may suffer. Similarly, when you take a test, try to reinstate the same psychological and physiological state that you were in when you originally learned the material.

_____ 9. **Employ self-monitoring.** When studying a text, you should periodically stop and test your understanding of the material using the built-in self-testing throughout each chapter. This type of self-monitoring is a common strategy used by successful students. Even when you are studying a single sentence, you need to monitor your understanding. Poor readers tend to read both easy and difficult material at the same speed. Good readers (and more successful students) tend to monitor themselves and slow down for or repeat difficult material. Keep in mind that if you evaluate your learning only while you're reading the material, you may overestimate your understanding (because the information is still in STM). However, if you delay for at least a few minutes and then test your understanding, your evaluation will be more accurate.

_____ 10. **Overlearn.** Successful students know that the best way to ensure their full understanding of material (and success on an exam) is through *overlearning*—studying information even after you think you already know it. Don't just study until you *think* you know it. Work hard until you *know* you know it.

Slonov/E+/Getty Images

FIGURE 7.25 **What's wrong with this picture?** Many students claim that they study best while listening to music or in a noisy environment. However, as you may recall from Chapter 1, this type of multitasking almost always decreases overall performance, and that's particularly true when you're attempting to learn something new. Just as people are trained to do public speaking in front of an audience and deep-sea divers practice their diving underwater, you should, when you study, try to re-create the academic environment under which you initially learn and will later perform. Similarly, when taking a test, most instructors will generally not allow you to wear headphones and will attempt to keep the room as quiet as possible. Therefore, this is the environment you need to re-create while studying.

Be sure to complete the final Retrieval Practice quiz, and then answer the critical thinking questions in the **Test Your Critical Thinking**.

Retrieval Practice 7.4 | Memory Distortions and Improvement

Self-Test Completing this self-test, and then checking your answers by clicking on the answer button or by looking in Appendix B, will provide immediate feedback and helpful practice for exams.

1. Problems with eyewitness recollections are so well established and important that judges now _____.

   a. allow expert testimony on the unreliability of eyewitness testimony

   b. routinely instruct jurors on the limits and unreliability of eyewitness recollections

   c. both the above

   d. none of the above

2. Researchers have demonstrated that it is _____ to create false memories.

   a. relatively easy   c. moderately difficult

   b. rarely possible   d. never possible

3. Dave was told the same childhood story of his father saving his neighbor from a fire so many times that he is now sure it is true, but all the evidence proves it never happened. This is an example of _____.

   a. a repressed memory   c. a false memory

   b. deluded childhood   d. early-onset juvenile
      fantasies   dementia

4. _____ memories are related to anxiety-provoking thoughts or events that are supposedly prevented from reaching consciousness.

   a. Suppressed   c. Flashback

   b. Flashbulb   d. Repressed

5. To improve your encoding, you should _____.

   a. pay attention and reduce interference

   b. strive for a deeper level of processing

   c. counteract the serial-position effect

   d. all of these options

Q Test Your Critical Thinking

1. As an eyewitness to a crime, how could you use information in this chapter to improve your memory for specific details?

2. If you were a juror, what would you say to the other jurors about the reliability of eyewitness testimony?

Real World Application Question

[AQ6] Could someone falsely convince you as an adult that you had committed a serious crime as a teenager?   **Hint:** Look in the text for **[AQ6]**

Universal Images Group/Getty Images

Q Test Your Critical Thinking

Did you notice or wonder why we provided six Real World Application Questions [AQ1–AQ6] throughout this chapter? We've found that they not only help you to engage with and master the material but also have an important and lasting impact on your critical thinking skills. For additional mastery and enrichment, consider the following questions:

1. Many people think they can perfectly recall elaborate memories about how they felt or what they said when they first learned about devastating events, like the mass shooting at the high school in Parkland, Florida in 2018? What do you recall about this particular event? Do your memories fit with what flashbulb memory (FBM) research suggests?

2. Despite documented errors with FBMs, most people are very confident in their personal accuracy. What problems might result from this overconfidence?

3. Human memory is often compared to the workings of a computer. Based on your own experience, what are the advantages and limits of this comparison?

4. Amnesia is a common theme for Hollywood movies and television. How might these portrayals, which are often inaccurate, negatively influence the public's perception?

5. What memory improvement techniques described in this chapter have you found to be helpful in your everyday life? What new strategies do you plan to try?

MediaPunch Inc/Alamy Stock Photo

Summary

7.1 The Nature of Memory 204

- **Memory** is an internal representation of some prior event or experience. It's also a **constructive process** that organizes and shapes information as it's being processed, stored, and retrieved.

- Major perspectives on memory include the **encoding, storage, and retrieval (ESR) model**, the **levels of processing model**, the **parallel distributed processing (PDP) model**, and the **three-stage memory model**. This last approach, which is the dominant model, proposes that information is stored and processed in **sensory memory**, **short-term memory (STM)**, and **long-term memory (LTM)**. The three stages differ in purpose, duration, and capacity.

- Sensory memory has a relatively large capacity, but the duration is only a few seconds. Visual sensory memory **(iconic memory)** holds for only about one-half of a second, whereas auditory sensory memory **(echoic memory)** lasts for up to 4 seconds.

- Short-term memory (STM) has a limited capacity and duration. Material is retained for as long as 30 seconds, but capacity is limited to five to nine bits of information.

- **Chunking** and **maintenance rehearsal** improve STM's duration and capacity. Researchers now call the active processing of STM **working memory.**

- LTM is an almost unlimited storehouse for information that must be kept for long periods. The two major types of LTM are **explicit/declarative memory** and **implicit/nondeclarative memory.** Organization and **elaborative rehearsal** improve encoding. **Retrieval cues** help stimulate retrieval of information from LTM. According to the **encoding-specificity principle,** retrieval is improved when conditions of recovery are similar to encoding conditions.

7.2 Forgetting 216

- Early research by Ebbinghaus showed that we tend to forget newly learned information quickly, but we relearn the information more readily the second time.

- Researchers have proposed five major theories to explain forgetting—decay, **retroactive** and **proactive interference,** motivated forgetting, encoding failure, and retrieval failure. The **tip-of-the-tongue phenomenon** is an example of the retrieval failure theory.

- There are several major factors that help explain why we forget: the **misinformation effect,** the **serial-position effect, source amnesia,** spacing of practice, and culture.

7.3 Biological Bases of Memory 222

- Learning modifies the brain's neural networks through **long-term potentiation (LTP),** strengthening particular synapses and affecting the ability of neurons to release their neurotransmitters.

- Memory formation begins with attention to certain stimuli. This attention then results in encoding, which, in turn, produces neural messages that are processed and stored in various areas of the brain.

- Emotional arousal increases neurotransmitters and hormones that affect several parts of the brain. Heightened arousal can also increase the encoding and storage of new information and the formation of **flashbulb memories (FBMs).**

- Research using advanced techniques, such as the fMRI, has indicated that several brain regions are involved in encoding, storing, and retrieving memories.

- Traumatic brain injuries and diseases such as Alzheimer's disease (AD) can lead to memory loss. Two major types of amnesia are **retrograde** and **anterograde amnesia.** The lack of **consolidation** may help explain retrograde amnesia.

7.4 Memory Distortions and Improvement   228

- People shape, rearrange, and distort their memories in order to create logic, consistency, and efficiency. Despite all their problems and biases, our memories are normally fairly accurate and usually serve us well.

- When memory errors occur in the context of the criminal justice system, they can have serious legal and social consequences. Problems with eyewitness testimony are so well established that judges often allow expert testimony on the unreliability of eyewitnesses.

- False memories, a well-established phenomenon, are relatively common and easy to create. However, memory repression (especially of childhood sexual abuse) is a complex and controversial topic.

- How can we improve our memory? During *encoding*, pay attention and reduce interference, strive for a deeper level of processing, and counteract the serial-position effect. During *storage*, use chunking and hierarchies. During *retrieval*, practice test taking (in-text quizzes, website quizzes, etc.), use distributed rather than massed practice, remember the encoding-specificity principle, and, finally, employ self-monitoring and overlearning.

Key Terms

Retrieval Practice   Write a definition for each term before turning back to the referenced page to check your answer.

- age-related positivity effect   211
- anterograde amnesia   226
- chunking   209
- consolidation   226
- constructive process   204
- distributed practice   220
- elaborative rehearsal   212
- encoding   205
- encoding-specificity principle   213
- encoding, storage, and retrieval (ESR) model   205
- episodic memory   210
- explicit/declarative memory   210

- flashbulb memory (FBM)   223
- implicit/nondeclarative memory   212
- levels of processing model   205
- long-term memory (LTM)   210
- long-term potentiation (LTP)   222
- maintenance rehearsal   209
- massed practice   220
- memory   204
- misinformation effect   219
- mnemonic   214
- parallel distributed processing (PDP) model   206
- proactive interference   218

- repression   232
- retrieval   205
- retrieval cues   213
- retroactive interference   218
- retrograde amnesia   226
- semantic memory   210
- sensory memory   208
- serial-position effect   219
- short-term memory (STM)   209
- source amnesia   220
- storage   205
- three-stage memory model   207
- tip-of-the-tongue (TOT) phenomenon   218
- working memory   209

Kuttelvaserova Stuchelova/Shutterstock.com

CHAPTER 8

Thinking, Language, and Intelligence

Fran Polito/Moment/Getty Images

Real World Application Questions

Things you'll learn in Chapter 8

[AQ1] Can phones damage our ability to solve problems?

[AQ2] Are creative people judged to be more sexually attractive?

[AQ3] Does speaking multiple languages make you smarter?

[AQ4] Why is it so hard to ignore a crying baby?

[AQ5] Can personal traits and character strengths predict achievement better than IQ?

[AQ6] Will watching TV dramas increase your emotional intelligence?

Throughout the chapter, look for [AQ1]–[AQ6] icons. They indicate where the text addresses these questions.

CHAPTER OUTLINE

8.1 | Thinking

LEARNING OBJECTIVES

Retrieval Practice   While reading the upcoming sections, respond to each Learning Objective in your own words.

Summarize thinking, cognition, problem solving, and creativity.

- **Explain** cognitive building blocks and how they affect thinking.
- **Describe** the three stages of problem solving, including algorithms and heuristics.

- **Review** the five potential barriers to problem solving.
- **Identify** the major characteristics of creativity.

Real World Application Questions

[AQ1] Can phones damage our ability to solve problems?

[AQ2] Are creative people judged to be more sexually attractive?

Economists who have studied the relationship between education and economic growth confirm what common sense suggests: The number of college degrees is not nearly as important as how well students develop cognitive skills, such as critical thinking and problem-solving ability.

—Derek Bok

If you go on to major in psychology, you'll discover that researchers often group thinking, language, and intelligence under the larger umbrella of **cognition**, the mental activities of acquiring, storing, retrieving, and using knowledge (Ellis, 2019; Goldstein, 2019). We also discuss cognition throughout this text (e.g., the previous chapters on sensation and perception, consciousness, learning, and memory). We begin this first section on thinking with a focus on what it is and where it's located. Then, we probe the nature of thinking (cognitive building blocks), followed by problem solving and creativity.

Every time we take in information and mentally act on it, we're thinking. These thought processes are both localized and distributed throughout our brains in networks of neurons. During decision making, our brains are most active in the *prefrontal cortex*. This region associates complex ideas; makes plans; forms, initiates, and allocates attention; and supports multitasking. In addition to serving as the locale of thinking processes, the prefrontal cortex links to other areas of the brain, such as the limbic system (Chapter 2), to synthesize information from several senses.

Cognition   The mental activities involved in acquiring, storing, retrieving, and using knowledge.

Cognitive Building Blocks

Having established where thinking occurs, we now need to discuss its basic components. Imagine yourself lying, relaxed, in the warm gritty sand on an ocean beach. Do you see palms swaying in the wind? Can you smell the salty sea and taste the dried salt on your lips? Can you hear children playing in the surf? What you've just created is a *mental image*, a mental representation of a previously stored sensory experience, which includes visual, auditory, olfactory, tactile, motor, and gustatory imagery (McKellar, 1972). We all have a mental space where we visualize and manipulate our sensory images (see **Figure 8.1**). Surprisingly, research shows that when we create mental images and thoughts about "healthy foods," we tend to consider them less filling and actually order larger portions and eat more (Suher et al., 2016).

Along with mental images, thinking also requires the ability to form *concepts*, or mental representations of a group or category. Concepts can be concrete (like car and concert) or abstract (like intelligence and beauty). They are essential to thinking and communication because they simplify and organize information. Normally, when you see a new object or encounter a new situation, you relate it to your existing conceptual structure and categorize it according to where it fits. If you see a metal box with four wheels driving on the highway, you know it is a car, even if you've never seen that particular model before.

FIGURE 8.1 **Fun with mental images**   Can you identify how the two yellow figures are the same and how the two blue figures are different? Solving this problem requires mental imagery and manipulation. If you want to check your answers, compare your solutions with those at the end of the chapter.

FIGURE 8.2 **Concepts** When learning concepts, we most often use prototypes, artificial concepts, and hierarchies to simplify and categorize information. For instance, when we encounter a bird, we fit it into our existing concept of a bird.

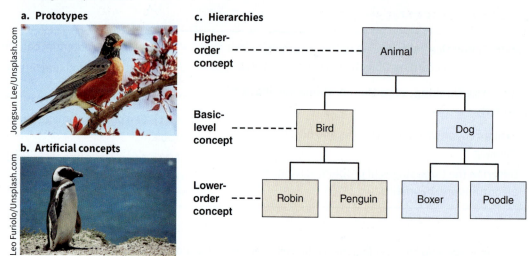

a. Prototypes

b. Artificial concepts

c. Hierarchies

Higher-order concept — — — — — — — — — — — Animal

Basic-level concept — — — — — — — Bird   Dog

Lower-order concept — — — — Robin   Penguin   Boxer   Poodle

How do we learn concepts? They typically develop through the environmental interactions of three major building blocks—prototypes, artificial concepts, and hierarchies (see **Figure 8.2**).

Prototype A mental image or best example that embodies the most typical features of a concept or category.

- **Prototypes** When initially learning about the world, a young child develops a general natural concept based on a typical representative, or **prototype**. Children typically form the concept of *bird* after a parent or caregiver points out a number of examples. Once the child has developed the prototype of a *bird*, he or she then is able to quickly classify all flying animals, such as the robin in Figure 8.2a, correctly.

- **Artificial concepts** We create *artificial* (or formal) *concepts* from logical rules or definitions. When an example doesn't quite fit the prototype, like the penguin in Figure 8.2b, we must review our artificial concept of a bird: warm-blooded animals that fly, have wings and beaks, and lay eggs. Although the penguin doesn't fly, it has wings, a beak, and lays eggs. So it must be a bird.

- **Hierarchies** Creating *hierarchies*, or subcategories within broader concepts, helps us master new material more quickly and easily. Note, however, that we tend to begin with basic-level concepts (the middle row in Figure 8.2c) when we first learn something (Rosch, 1978). For example, a child develops the basic-level concept for *bird* before learning the higher-order concept *animal* or the lower-order concept *robin*.

PA Practical Application

Why are these cognitive building blocks important? It's easy to see why children might need to develop separate categories for birds and dogs. What's less obvious is that this same kind of understanding may be a lifesaver for adults. Consider the widespread prototype of a heart attack—sharp, sudden pains in the chest (see photo). Can you see how using this limited, and somewhat faulty, prototype might discourage us from seeking help because we ignore other equally serious common symptoms, such as fatigue, nausea, sudden dizziness, shortness of breath, and tightness in the

chest? Similarly, many forms of dangerous prejudice result from expectations of how a "legitimate" proto-typical citizen differs from an immigrant. On a more encouraging note, researchers have found that most people can effectively differentiate so-called fake news from real news regardless of their political ideology (Pennycook & Rand, 2019). The fact that falling for fake news is more reflective of lazy thinking than hard-core biased partisanship is heartening given that it offers potential avenues for combating it.

Problem Solving

Our lives are filled with problems. Many we solve through simple *trial and error* (**Figure 8.3**). In contrast to this "hit or miss" approach, formal problem solving involves a logical progression from a given state (the problem) to a goal state (the solution), which usually has three steps: *preparation, production,* and *evaluation* (Bourne et al., 1979).

Note in **Process Diagram 8.1** that during the preparation stage, we begin by defining our ultimate goal, and then we identify and separate relevant and irrelevant facts. Next, during the production stage, we generate possible solutions, called hypotheses, by using *algorithms* and *heuristics.* **Algorithms** are logical, step-by-step procedures that, if followed correctly, will always lead to an eventual solution. But they are not practical in many situations. **Heuristics**, or simplified rules based on experience, are much faster but do not guarantee a solution. Finally, during the evaluation stage, we judge the hypotheses generated during the production stage against the criteria established in the preparation stage.

In addition, we sometimes solve problems with a sudden flash of *insight,* like that of Köhler's chimps when they stacked boxes to reach the bananas (Chapter 6). Keep in mind that the sudden understanding in these "aha" moments often leads to more accurate solutions than those found through logical reasoning and analysis (Salvi et al., 2016). However, insight is somewhat unconscious and automatic so it can't be rushed. When a problem has you stumped, it sometimes helps to mentally set the problem aside for a while, in an *incubation period;* the solution may then come to mind without further conscious thought.

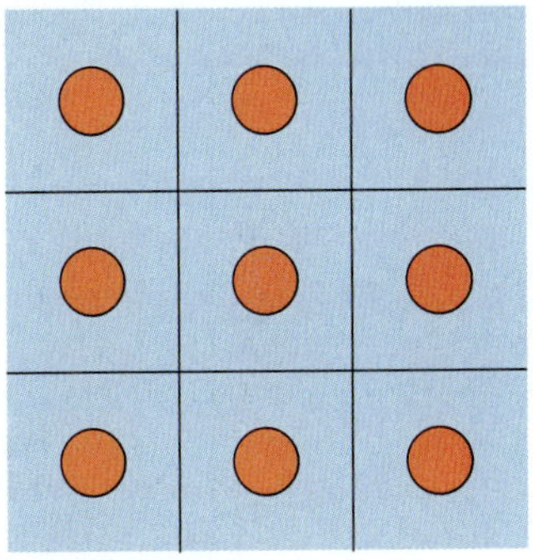

Six Potential Barriers to Problem Solving

As we've just seen, algorithms, heuristics, and insight all help us solve problems in our daily life. In this section, we'll discuss six potential barriers to effective problem solving. Why do we say "potential"? It's because most of these factors have both positive and negative influences.

1. **Mental sets**   Why are some problems so difficult to solve? The reason may be that we often stick to problem-solving strategies that have worked in the past, called **mental sets**, rather than trying new, possibly more effective ones (**Figure 8.4**).

2. **Functional fixedness**   We sometimes fail to see solutions to our problems when we view objects as functioning only in the usual or customary way—a phenomenon known as **functional fixedness** (Chrysikou et al., 2016; Ho & Shu, 2019; Wright et al., 2015). When a child uses sofa cushions to build a fort and you use a table knife instead of a screwdriver to tighten a screw, you have both successfully avoided functional fixedness. Similarly, the individual who discovered a way to retrofit diesel engines to allow them to use discarded restaurant oil as fuel overcame functional fixedness—and may become very wealthy. For practice with functional fixedness, see **Figure 8.5**.

FIGURE 8.3 **Trial-and-error learning**
This infant is developing his thinking abilities through repeated trials and errors. As adults, we're still using similar processes when we're stuck in a traffic jam, having trouble sleeping, or trying to lose weight. We "simply" try several different solutions until we succeed—or give up.

FIGURE 8.4 **The nine-dot problem**   Can you connect all nine dots without lifting your pencil or using more than four lines? If not, the reason may be that you're trying to use *mental sets*—problem-solving strategies that have worked well for you in the past. Try "thinking outside the box," and then compare your answer to the solution presented at the end of the chapter.

Algorithm   A logical, step-by-step procedure that, if followed correctly, will always eventually solve the problem.

Heuristic   An educated guess, or "rule of thumb," often used as a shortcut for problem solving; it does not guarantee a solution to a problem but does narrow the alternatives.

Mental set   A fixed-thinking approach to problem solving that sees only solutions that have worked in the past.

Functional fixedness   A barrier to problem solving that comes from thinking about objects as functioning only in their usual or customary way.

FIGURE 8.5 **Testing your functional fixedness**
Imagine that you are left in a room with a chair and a pair of pliers, and your task is to join together two strings that are hanging from the ceiling—ten feet apart. Obviously, you can never reach both strings at the same time because they are too far away from each other. What can you do? Try to solve this problem, and then compare your answer to the solution presented at the end of the chapter.

STOP! This Process Diagram contains essential information NOT found elsewhere in the text, which is likely to appear on quizzes and exams. Be sure to study it CAREFULLY.

PROCESS DIAGRAM 8.1   **Three Steps to the Goal**   There are three stages of problem solving that help you attain a goal, such as choosing a satisfying career.

1 Preparation

Begin by clarifying the problem using these three steps in preparation.

• Define the ultimate goal.

Finding a satisfying lifetime career.

Choosing a satisfying career.
✓ Personal values and interests—what's most important to me and what do I naturally like to do?
✓ Personality—do I want to work with others, travel for work, etc.?
✓ Personal skills—what are my special talents and limitations?
✓ Lifestyle requirements—where do I want to live, how much money do I want to make, etc.

• Outline your limits and/or desires.

• Separate the non-negotiable from the negotiable.

✓ Personal values and interests
✓ Personality
* Meeting a potential lifetime mate
* Pleasing your parents

2 Production

Next, test your possible paths and solutions with one or both of these methods.

• Use an **algorithm**, a logical step-by-step procedure that, if followed correctly, will eventually solve the problem. Note that algorithms may take a long time—especially for complex problems.

Going to your college library, counseling center, and/or doing your own Internet research will provide a wealth of information about various jobs.

• Use a **heuristic**, a simple rule for problem solving that does not guarantee a solution, but offers a likely shortcut to it.

Work backwards from the solution—visit two or more professionals currently working in the field of your choice, and ask for their advice and guidance regarding your personal career plans.

3 Evaluation

Did your possible solutions solve the problem?

• If no, then you must return to the production and/or preparation stages.

• If yes, then take action to achieve your goal.

a. Plane crash versus car accident   We fear flying, yet Americans are far more likely to die from car accidents. In fact, in an average lifetime, your chance of dying in a plane crash is about one in 190,000, whereas the odds of dying in a car crash are around one in 100 (Mazzei, 2019).

b. Shark attack versus drowning   Despite popular media and movies portraying sharks as human-eating monsters, your actual chance of dying from a shark attack is around one in 3.7 million compared to your chance of drowning, which is about one in 1000 (Madden, 2019; Midway et al., 2019).

FIGURE 8.6   Why do we fear the wrong things?   Thanks to the availability heuristic, we fear what's most vivid and most readily available in our memories.

3. **Availability heuristic**   Thanks to multiple public announcements celebrating the latest lottery winners, many people grossly overestimate their personal chance of winning the jackpot (the availability heuristic). Before buying lottery tickets, however, we need to consider the fact that any one individual's odds of winning either the MegaMillions or the Powerball jackpot are about 300 million to one, which is roughly equal to one person being randomly picked a winner among the entire U.S. population (Begley, 2017; McDonald, 2019). Can you see how the availability heuristic helps explain some of our most irrational fears (see **Figure 8.6**)? These are just a few of the many examples of the **availability heuristic**, in which we take a mental shortcut and make estimates of the frequency or likelihood of an event based on the information that is most vivid and readily *available* in our memories. In other words, we give greater credence to information and examples that readily spring to mind (Tversky & Kahneman, 1974, 1993; Vis, 2019).

4. **Representativeness heuristic**   Have you ever been walking in the woods and suddenly frozen or jumped away thinking you saw a dangerous snake, when in fact it was just a curled stick on the ground? This may be an example of the **representativeness heuristic**, in which we estimate the probability of an event based on how well something matches (or *represents*) an existing prototype or stereotype in our minds (Alkhars et al., 2019; Kulkarni et al., 2019; Peteros & Maleyeff, 2015). We all have a prototype of a snake in our mind and the curled stick readily matches our preexisting prototype. Can you see how this is also an example of the *availability heuristic*? While walking in the woods, you're primed to look out for snakes, and the sight of the twisted stick immediately brings images of a snake to your mind.

5. **Cognitive offloading**   When lost in a new area of town or curious about the definition of a new word, what do you do? Most of us immediately turn to our phones for answers (see photo). The general idea of **cognitive offloading** is that we tend to use external resources to decrease the information processing requirements of a task in order to reduce the cognitive demand. As we discovered in Chapter 7, we can hold only a limited amount of information active in our memory. Therefore, rather than cognitively processing entirely in

Availability heuristic
A cognitive strategy (or shortcut) that involves estimating the frequency or likelihood of an event based on information that is readily available in our memory.

Representativeness heuristic
A cognitive strategy (or shortcut) that involves making judgments based on how well something matches (represents) an existing prototype or stereotype.

Cognitive offloading   The use of external resources to decrease the information processing requirements of a task in order to reduce the cognitive demand.

marctran/123RF

our head, we're likely to "off-load" information and problem solving out into the world via online resources or just writing down the information (Gilbert, 2015; Hu et al., 2019).

[AQ1] Given our increasing (and almost automatic) reliance on the Internet and our phones (see photo), it may distress you to discover that these helpful resources may have negative effects on our problem solving, recall, and general learning. In an interesting study, participants were first asked to answer challenging trivia questions, with one group being allowed to use Google while the other group used only their memory (Storm et al., 2017). On the second round, all participants were allowed to choose either method to answer even easier trivia questions. As expected, participants who had first used Google for the challenging questions were significantly more likely to use it again and to use it more quickly. More surprising, 30 percent of those who were allowed to use Google in the first round failed to even attempt to answer a single simple question without it on the second round.

Noting that cognitive offloading will undoubtedly increase over time, some researchers conclude that our memory and problem-solving abilities will suffer accordingly. Does this mean that if we "don't use it, we lose it"? What do you think?

6. **Confirmation bias**   Do you wonder why the U.S. Congress can't seem to solve serious national problems, like fixing our deteriorating bridges and highways? Or why we can't resolve ongoing disputes with our roommates or spouses? It may be that we too often seek confirmation of our preexisting positions or beliefs and tend to ignore or discount contradictory evidence. As discussed in Chapters 1 and 4, this type of faulty thinking and barrier to problem solving is known as the **confirmation bias** (Meppelink et al., 2019; Nickerson, 1998; Webb et al., 2016).

Like gamblers who keep putting coins into slot machines, we all have preexisting beliefs and biases that may lead us to focus only on our "hits" and ignore our "misses." Unfortunately, this type of confirmation bias may lead to consequences ranging from the small (see the **Test Yourself**) to the catastrophic (the U.S. war against Iraq based on the belief that there were weapons of mass destruction).

Unfortunately, we not only seek out and "cherry pick" information (the confirmation bias) when searching our memories, we also tend to recall evidence that readily springs to mind, which further reinforces our original position (the availability heuristic). To make matters worse, confirmation bias is also closely related to what's called *belief perseverance*— our tendency to stick to our positions and beliefs even when we acknowledge the contrary information. Real-world examples of the confirmation bias (coupled with the availability heuristic and belief perseverance) are all around us—people who believe (or don't believe) that the climate crisis is primarily caused by human factors, that gun control can (or cannot) save lives, and that immigration helps (or hurts) our economy. For practical strategies for overcoming this confirmation bias and the other five barriers to problem solving, see the **PAH** **Practical Application Highlight**.

Confirmation bias   The tendency to prefer information that confirms our preexisting positions or beliefs and to ignore or discount contradictory evidence; also known as remembering the "hits" and ignoring the "misses."

PA Practical Application

Test Yourself: Sports Fans and Superstitious Beliefs

Have you heard of *Sports Illustrated* magazine's "cover jinx"? This belief is that once a team or person appears on the cover of this magazine, something bad will soon befall that team or person. After Oklahoma Sooners guard Buddy Hield appeared on the cover hyping Oklahoma's appearance in the 2016 NCAA Basketball Tournament, the Sooners were blown out by the Villanova Wildcats 95–51 as Hield was held to just nine points. Similarly, three NFL players, Aaron Rodgers, J. J. Watt, and David Johnson, were featured on the cover in 2017, and then suffered injuries serious enough to end

their playing seasons. Can you see how this is another example of confirmation bias? Those who believe in the "jinx" might tend to look for examples to support it but fail to see examples that don't. Consider the fact that the New York Yankees, Michael Jordan, and Muhammad Ali have all been repeatedly featured on the cover of the magazine, yet their exceptional winning histories are anything but "jinxed."

iStock.com/Willard

PAH Practical Application Highlight

Tips for Improved Problem Solving

(APA Goal 1.3) Describe applications of psychology

Are you feeling overwhelmed by all these *potential* barriers to problem solving? If so, keep in mind that, as we mentioned earlier, each of these factors has both positive and negative effects. As an example, the availability and representativeness heuristics provide mental shortcuts that are generally far more helpful than damaging to problem solving because they allow immediate "inferences that are fast, frugal, and [often] accurate" (Pohl et al., 2013; Todd & Gigerenzer, 2000, p. 736). If you're shopping for a new apartment and note that several windows in a building have safety bars, images of burglars climbing through windows might readily pop up in your mind (the availability heuristic) and you might decide not to rent in that building. Likewise, if you're hiking in the woods and see a curled stick that looks like your prototype of a snake (the representativeness heuristic), it's smart to initially freeze or jump away. When faced with an immediate decision, we often don't have time to investigate all the options. We need to make quick decisions based solely on the currently available information.

What about long-term decisions, such as choosing your college major and your future career, that don't require immediate resolution? How can you use the material we've been discussing to improve your personal success? You obviously can't try all possible options using algorithms. Instead, the three heuristics presented in **Table 8.1** may help focus your search and attain your desired outcomes.

TABLE 8.1   Three Problem-Solving Heuristics and Your Career

Problem-Solving Heuristics	Description	Example
Working Backward	Start with the solution, a known condition, and work backward through the problem. Once the search has revealed the steps to be taken, the problem is solved.	Deciding you want to be an experimental psychologist, you ask your psychology professor to recommend graduate programs at various colleges and universities. Then you contact these institutions for information on their academic requirements and admission policies. Next, you adapt your current college courses to fit those institutional requirements and policies.
Means–end Analysis	Determine what measures would reduce the difference between the existing state and the end goal. Once the means to reach the goal have been determined, the problem is solved.	You know you need a high GPA to get into a good graduate school for experimental psychology. Therefore, you ask your professors for study suggestions and interview several "A" students to compare their study habits to your own. You then determine the specific means (the number of hours and study techniques) required to meet your end goal of a high GPA.
Creating Subgoals	Break large, complex problems down into a series of small subgoals. These subgoals then can serve as a series of stepping stones, which can be taken one at a time to reach the end goal.	Getting a good grade in many college courses requires subgoals, like writing a successful term paper. To do this, you first choose a topic and then go to the library and Internet to locate information related to that topic. Once you have the information, you organize it, create an outline, write the paper, review the paper, rewrite, rewrite again, and then submit the final paper, on or before the due date.

Creativity

According to legend, many years ago in Los Angeles, a 12-foot-high tractor-trailer got stuck under a bridge that was 6 inches too low. After hours of fruitless towing, tugging, and pushing, the police and transportation workers were stumped. Then a young boy happened by and asked, "Why don't you let some air out of the tires?" It was a simple, creative suggestion—and it supposedly worked.

Everyone exhibits a certain amount of creativity in some aspects of life. Even when doing ordinary tasks, like planning an afternoon of errands, you are being somewhat creative. And if you've ever used a plastic garbage bag as a temporary rain jacket or placed a thick college textbook on a chair as a booster seat for a child, you've found a creative solution to a problem.

Despite the fact that we're all creative in our own personal and varied ways, many people think creativity applies only to artists, musicians, or writers. Most people also believe that we're at our creative peak when we're young. However, a recent study revealed at least two peaks in creativity—early in life and then later in life (Weinberg & Galenson, 2019). **[AQ2]** Interestingly, research also finds many people judge creative people to be more sexually attractive (see photo)

than less creative individuals (Geher & Kaufman, 2013; Lange & Euler, 2014). A case in point: One survey of 815 undergraduates found that Bill Gates would be considered sexy based on his applied/technological creativity, whereas others might be considered sexy based on their ornamental/aesthetic or everyday/domestic creativity (Kaufman et al., 2016).

How Do We Define Creativity?

Conceptions of creativity are obviously personal and influenced by culture, but most psychologists agree that a creative solution or performance produces original, appropriate, and valued outcomes in a novel way. Three characteristics are generally associated with **creativity**: *originality*, *fluency*, and *flexibility*. Famed engineer and inventor Nikola Tesla (1856-1943), with his numerous technological developments, offers a prime example of each of these characteristics (**Table 8.2**).

Creativity The ability to produce original, appropriate, and valued outcomes in a novel way; it has three characteristics—originality, fluency, and flexibility.

TABLE 8.2   **Three Elements of Creative Thinking**

	Explanations	Nikola Tesla Examples
Originality	Seeing unique or different solutions to a problem	After noting the limitations of Thomas Edison's direct current (DC) transmission system, Tesla devised a means of transmitting power via an alternating current (AC), which greatly reduced power loss over long distances.
Fluency	Generating a large number of possible solutions	Tesla developed numerous alternating current (AC) systems, including generators, motors, and transformers.
Flexibility	Shifting with ease from one type of problem-solving strategy to another	Tesla was a prolific inventor who held over 300 patents worldwide. He played a key role in developing fluorescent bulbs, neon signs, X-rays, the radio, lasers, remote controls, robotics, and even the technology used in modern cell phones.

1. Can you identify which of the three characteristics of creativity (originality, fluency, or flexibility) best explains your personal experiences with being creative?

2. Creativity is usually associated with art, poetry, and the like. What are other areas in which creativity should be highly valued?

Researchers have also found that creativity requires the coming together of at least seven interrelated resources (**Table 8.3**).

TABLE 8.3   **Resources of Creative People**

Affective Processes	Emotional intelligence and joy in creative expression	Which of these seven resources do you think best explains Lady Gaga's phenomenal success? Interestingly, research shows that audiences like art more when they perceive the artist as eccentric—which certainly applies to Lady Gaga (Van Tilburg & Igou, 2014).
Intellectual Ability	Enough intelligence to see problems in a new light	
Knowledge	Sufficient basic knowledge of the problem to effectively evaluate possible solutions	
Thinking Style	Novel ideas, divergent thinking, and ability to distinguish between the worthy and the worthless	
Personality	Conscientiousness, openness, and willingness to grow and change, take risks, and work to overcome obstacles	
Motivation	Sufficient motivation to accomplish the task and more internal than external motivation	
Environment	An environment that supports creativity	

WENN Rights Ltd/Alamy Stock Photo

Sources: Geher et al., 2017; Khalil et al., 2019; Sternberg, 2014, 2015.

How Do We Measure Creativity?   Most tests focus on **divergent thinking**, a type of thinking in which we develop many possibilities from a single starting point (Forthmann et al., 2019; Palmiero et al., 2016; van de Kamp et al., 2015). Divergent thinking is open-ended and focused on generating multiple novel solutions. You're using divergent thinking when you're brainstorming or thinking of various ways to decorate your dorm, apartment, or home. Psychologists have developed several methods to test for divergent thinking. For example, the *Unusual Uses Test* requires you to think of as many uses as possible for an object such as a brick. In the *Anagrams Test*, you're asked to reorder the letters in a word to make as many new words as possible.

Divergent thinking   A type of thinking that produces many solutions to the same problem.

Convergent thinking is the opposite of divergent thinking. Instead of looking for numerous solutions, it looks for the one single best answer. You're using convergent thinking when you search for the answer to a math problem or a multiple-choice question.

Convergent thinking   A type of thinking that seeks the single best solution to a problem.

Although divergent thinking and convergent thinking are very different, we generally use both to successfully problem solve. "Thinking outside the box" and generating many ideas (divergent thinking) increase the odds of finding a solution. But then you need convergent thinking to bring all the differing ideas together and identify (or *converge* on) the single best solution. For a fun example of divergent thinking, try the activities in the **Test Yourself**.

PA Practical Application

Test Yourself: Are You Creative?

- Find 10 coins and arrange them in the configuration shown here. By moving only two coins, form two rows that each contains six coins. One solution is offered at the end of the chapter.

- In five minutes, see how many words you can make using the letters in the word *hippopotamus*.

- In five minutes, list all the things you can do with a paper clip.

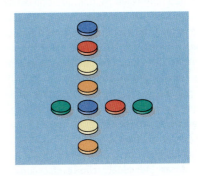

How Can We Increase Creativity?   Outdoor activities—such as climbing, jumping, and exploring—have a positive effect on children's creativity (Brussoni et al., 2015). Why? One reason might be that unstructured free play time (both indoors and outdoors) helps children to feel, express, regulate, and think about their own and others' emotions (Russ, 2014; Russ & Wallace, 2013). Play also appears to build the skills essential to success in the arts, entrepreneurship, and even fields like science and engineering. Researchers suggest that play allows safe practice of the skills that provide an evolutionary advantage to both human and non-human animals (Holmes et al., 2015; Kuczaj, 2017; Yogman et al., 2018).

Given that outdoor activities (see photo) and free play time for children increases creativity, could a simple walk do the same for adults? Researchers asked adult participants to think about alternative ways of using a common object (Oppezzo & Schwartz, 2014). For the word "button," a person might say "as a doorknob on a dollhouse." Half the participants did this task while sitting at a desk facing a blank wall, whereas the other half did it while walking on a treadmill facing a blank wall. Next, researchers repeated the study with participants walking outside, and the walkers in both conditions outperformed the sitters in creativity.

In addition to walking in nature and other outdoor activities, researchers have also found that just letting your mind wander may play a role in creativity (Gable et al., 2019; Williams et al., 2018). Surveying people who work in creative fields, like screenwriters, novelists, and writers, these researchers found that some of our most inventive ideas occur when our minds are relaxed, rather than directly focused on working on a solution. So, the next time you need to be creative, maybe take a walk and let your mind wander.

So far we've presented only the positive side of creativity. What about the famous stories of creative geniuses who suffer from psychological disorders? Are these stories based on myths or on reality? See the RC **Research Challenge**.

kali9/E+/Getty Images

Play and creativity   Can you see how outdoor activities and free play time might be particularly important given the increasing pressure on parents and schools to emphasize science, math, and more structured activities?

RC Scientific Thinking: **Research Challenge**

Is Creativity Linked with Psychological Disorders?

(APA Goal 2.4) Interpret, design, and conduct basic psychological research

Marvista Entertainment/Everett Collection

Who do you picture when you think of a creative genius? Thanks to movies, television, and novels, many people share the stereotypical image of an eccentric inventor (Nikola Tesla), a deranged artist (Vincent Van Gogh), or the lead character with bipolar disorder in the movie *The Ghost and the Whale* (see photo).

Thinking back to Chapter 1 and *illusory correlations*, such as the mistaken belief that a full moon leads to more crime, can you see how believing that creativity is linked to psychological disorders might simply be a mistaken perception? Or could there be a small kernel of truth?

Researchers interested in this question analyzed years of stored data on more than a million people, including their professions, whether they had ever been diagnosed with or treated for a psychological disorder, and, if so, what type of disorder (Kyaga et al., 2012). The researchers found that individuals in generally creative professions (scientific or artistic) were no more likely to suffer from most psychiatric disorders than those in other professions. However, one illness, *bipolar disorder*—which is characterized by extreme high and low mood swings (Chapter 13)—*was* found to be significantly more common in artists and scientists, and particularly in authors.

But could an individual's choice of occupation have confounded these results? As you'll discover in Chapter 13, there is a strong genetic component in bipolar disorders. Furthermore, we all have a high likelihood of entering a profession similar to those of our parents due to familiarity, access, and modeling. Given that children of artists, scientists, and authors often choose the same professions as their parents, might it be that the modest link between creativity and bipolar disorder is actually due to kinship—and the profession is incidental?

How would you explain this intriguing association between certain types of creativity and bipolar disorder? If there is a true link, does the manic phase increase the energy levels of artists, scientists, and authors, giving them greater access to creative ideas than they would otherwise have? What about the "tortured artist" stereotype? Could the depressive phase of bipolar disorder somehow benefit the creative process? What do you think?

Identify the Research Method

1. Based on the information provided, did this study (Kyaga et al., 2012) use descriptive, correlational, and/or experimental research?

2. If you chose:
   - *descriptive research*, is this a naturalistic or laboratory observation, survey/interview, case study, and/or archival research?
   - *correlational research*, is this a positive, negative, or zero correlation?
   - *experimental research*, label the IV, DV, experimental group(s), and control group. (Note: If participants were not randomly assigned to groups, list the design as *quasi-experimental*.)
   - both *descriptive* and *correlational*, answer the corresponding questions for both.

Check your answers by clicking on the answer button or by looking in Appendix B.

Note: The information provided in this study is admittedly limited, but the level of detail is similar to what is presented in most textbooks and public reports of research findings. Answering these questions, and then comparing your answers to those provided, will help you become a better scientific and critical thinker and consumer of scientific research.

Retrieval Practice 8.1 | Thinking

Self-Test Completing this self-test, and then checking your answers by clicking on the answer button or by looking in Appendix B, will provide immediate feedback and helpful practice for exams.

1. The mental activities involved in acquiring, storing, retrieving, and using knowledge are collectively known as _____.
   a. perception
   c. cognition
   b. consciousness
   d. awareness

2. _____ is a logical step-by-step procedure that, if followed, will always eventually solve the problem.
   a. An algorithm
   c. A heuristic
   b. A problem-solving set
   d. Brainstorming

3. Rosa is shopping in a new supermarket and wants to find a standard type of mustard. Which problem-solving strategy would be most efficient?
   a. algorithm
   c. instinct
   b. heuristic
   d. mental set

4. _____ is a fixed-thinking approach to problem solving that sees only solutions that have worked in the past.

   a. Problem-solving set   **c.** Mental set

   b. Functional fixedness   **d.** Incubation

Q Test Your Critical Thinking

1. During problem solving, do you use primarily algorithms or heuristics? What are the advantages of each?

2. Would you prefer to be highly creative or highly intelligent? Why?

Real World Application Questions

[AQ1] Can phones damage our ability to solve problems?

marctran/123RF

[AQ2] Are creative people judged to be more sexually attractive?

wavebreakmedia/ Shutterstock.com

Hint: Look in the text for **[AQ1]** and **[AQ2]**

Language

LEARNING OBJECTIVES

Retrieval Practice While reading the upcoming sections, respond to each Learning Objective in your own words.

Summarize the key characteristics and theories of language.

- **Identify** the major building blocks of language.

- **Describe** the prominent theories of language and thinking and how they interact.

- **Discuss** the major stages of language development, including the language acquisition device (LAD).

- **Review** the evidence and controversy surrounding non-human animals' acquisition and use of language.

Real World Application Questions

[AQ3] Does speaking multiple languages make you smarter?

[AQ4] Why is it so hard to ignore a crying baby?

Using **language** enables us to mentally manipulate symbols, thereby expanding our thinking. Whether it's spoken, written, or signed, language also allows us to communicate our thoughts, ideas, and feelings (Harley, 2014; Jandt, 2016).

Language Characteristics

How do children learn to produce language? They first build words using **phonemes** [FO-neems] and **morphemes** [MOR-feems]. Next, they string words into sentences (see cartoon) using rules of **grammar**, such as _syntax_ and _semantics_ (**Figure 8.7**).

What happens in our brains when we produce and comprehend language? Language, like our thought processes, is both localized and distributed throughout our brains (**Figure 8.8**). For example, the amygdala is active when we engage in a special type of language—cursing or swearing. Why? Recall from Chapter 2 that the amygdala is linked to emotions, especially fear and rage. So it's logical that the brain regions activated by cursing or hearing swear words would be the same as those for fear and aggression.

As shown in Figure 8.8, additional parts of the brain are involved in language, including _Broca's area_ (which is responsible for speech generation) and _Wernicke's area_ (which controls language comprehension). Keep in mind that several additional areas of the brain not shown on this figure are activated during different types of language generation and listening.

How do we know which parts of the brain are involved with language? Scientists can track brain activity through a colored _positron emission tomography (PET) scan_. Injection

Language A form of communication using sounds or symbols combined according to specified rules.
Phoneme The smallest basic unit of speech or sound in any given language.
Morpheme The smallest meaningful unit of language, formed from a combination of phonemes.
Grammar The set of rules (syntax and semantics) governing the use and structure of language.

"GOT IDEA. TALK BETTER. COMBINE WORDS, MAKE SENTENCES."

Sidney Harris/ScienceCartoonPlus.com

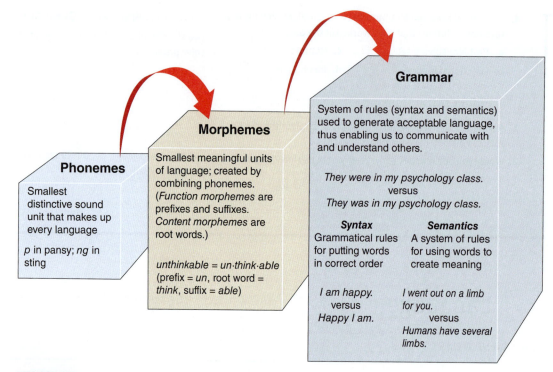

Phonemes

Smallest distinctive sound unit that makes up every language

p in pansy; *ng* in sting

Morphemes

Smallest meaningful units of language; created by combining phonemes. (*Function morphemes* are prefixes and suffixes. *Content morphemes* are root words.)

unthinkable = un·think·able (prefix = *un*, root word = *think*, suffix = *able*)

Grammar

System of rules (syntax and semantics) used to generate acceptable language, thus enabling us to communicate with and understand others.

They were in my psychology class.
versus
They was in my psychology class.

Syntax
Grammatical rules for putting words in correct order

I am happy.
versus
Happy I am.

Semantics
A system of rules for using words to create meaning

I went out on a limb for you.
versus
Humans have several limbs.

FIGURE 8.7 **The three major building blocks of language**

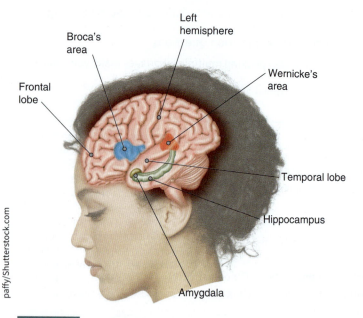

Left hemisphere

Broca's area

Frontal lobe

Wernicke's area

Temporal lobe

Hippocampus

Amygdala

paffy/Shutterstock.com

FIGURE 8.8 **Key parts of the brain involved in language**

of the radioactive isotope oxygen-15 into the participant's bloodstream makes areas of the brain with high metabolic activity light up in red and orange on the scan (**Figure 8.9**).

Language Theories

Does the fact that you speak English instead of German—or Chinese instead of Swahili—determine how you reason, think, and perceive the world? Linguist Benjamin Whorf (1956) believed so. As evidence for his *linguistic relativity hypothesis*, Whorf offered a now classic example: Because Inuits (previously known as Eskimos) supposedly have many words for snow (*apikak* for "first snow falling," *pukak* for "snow for drinking water," and so on), they can reportedly perceive and think about snow differently from English speakers, who have only one word—*snow*.

Though intriguing, Whorf's hypothesis has not fared well. He apparently exaggerated the number of Inuit words for snow and ignored the fact that English speakers also have a number of terms to describe various forms of snow, such as *slush*, *sleet*, *hard pack*, and *powder* (Pullum, 1991). Other research has directly contradicted Whorf's theory. Eleanor Rosch (1973) found that although people of the Dani tribe in New Guinea possess only two color names—one indicating cool, dark colors and the other describing warm, bright colors—they discriminate among various hues as well as English speakers do.

Whorf apparently overstated his belief that language *determines* thought. But there is no doubt that language *influences* thought (Caldwell-Harris, 2019; Yang, 2016; Zhong et al., 2015). For example, simply replacing the term *climate change* with "climate crisis" better emphasizes the urgency of the need for immediate action.

FIGURE 8.9 **Using PET scans to study language and the brain**

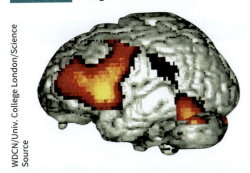

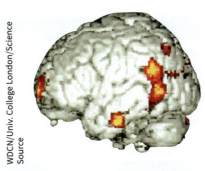

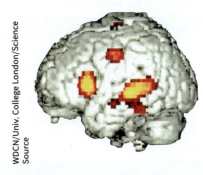

a. Language generated in the frontal lobe (center left) has its cognition checked in the temporal lobe (lower right).

b. Working out the meaning of heard words makes areas of the temporal lobe light up.

c. Repeating words increases activity in Broca's area and Wernicke's area, as well as a motor region responsible for the pronunciation of words (reddish area at the top).

Interestingly, people who speak multiple languages report that the language they're currently using affects their sense of self and how they think about events (Berry et al., 2011; Lai & Narasimhan, 2015). But what about the fact that English speakers have a word for those who have lost their spouse (widower and widow) and a word for children who have lost their parents (orphan), but no word for parents who have lost a child (Burton, 2018). That doesn't mean that we cannot think of these parents. **[AQ3]** Research also shows that speaking several languages, and even just learning one new language (see photo), offers a wide range of benefits, including improved job opportunities, better communication skills, and more gray matter in key brain regions (Alvear, 2019; Bak et al., 2016). However, other research has suggested there may be some disadvantages for bilinguals and/or that the advantages possibly do not stem from bilingualism (e.g., Antón et al., 2019; Bright & Filippi, 2019; Sörman et al., 2019).

Language Development

Although children's language development varies in timing, virtually all children follow a similar sequence (see **Table 8.4**). The various stages within this table are believed to be universal, meaning that all children progress through similar stages regardless of what culture they're born into or what language(s) they ultimately learn to speak.

Prelinguistic Stage
From birth, a child communicates through facial expressions, eye contact, and body gestures (**Figure 8.10**). Babies only hours old begin to "teach" their caregivers when and how they want to be held, fed, and played with. Babies even start to learn language before they are born. Researchers in one study played sounds from two different languages—English and Swedish—to babies at hospitals in both the United States and Sweden shortly after birth (Moon et al., 2013). These babies were given special pacifiers that were hooked up to a computer, and the more times they sucked on the pacifier, the more times they heard the vowels. Half the babies heard sounds from the language they had been exposed to in utero, whereas the others heard vowels from a different language. In both countries, the babies who heard the foreign vowels sucked more frequently than those who heard sounds from their native language, suggesting that babies have already become familiar—through listening to their mother's voice—with the sounds in their native language and are now more interested in hearing novel sounds.

Linguistic Stage
After the prelinguistic stage, infants quickly move toward full language acquisition (see again Table 8.4). By age 5, most children have mastered basic grammar and typically use about 2,000 words (a level of mastery considered adequate for getting by in any given culture). Past this point, vocabulary and grammar gradually improve throughout the life span (Levey, 2014; Oller et al., 2014).

FIGURE 8.10 **Can you identify this facial expression?** Infants as young as 2.5 months can non-verbally express emotions such as joy, surprise, or anger.

TABLE 8.4 **Language Acquisition**

Birth to 12 Months

Kevin Liu/Moment/Getty Images

Features	Examples
Crying (reflexive in newborns) becomes more purposeful	hunger cry, anger cry, and pain cry
Cooing (vowel-like sounds) at 2–3 months	"ooooh," "aaaah"
Babbling (consonants added) at 4–6 months	"bahbahbah," "dahdahdah"

12 Months to 2 Years

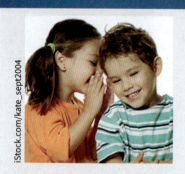

Niamh Baldock/Alamy Stock Photo

Features	Examples
Babbling resembles language of the environment, and child understands that sounds relate to meaning	"Mama," "Da Da"
Speech consists of one-word utterances	"Juice," "Up"
Expressive ability more than doubles once words are joined into short phrases	"Daddy milk," "no night-night"
Overextension (using words to include objects that do not fit the word's meaning)	all men = "Daddy," all furry animals = "doggy"

2 Years to 5 Years

iStock.com/kate_sept2004

Features	Examples
Telegraphic speech (like telegrams, omits non-essential connecting words)	"Me want cookie," "Grandma go bye-bye?"
Vocabulary increases at a phenomenal rate	
Child acquires a wide variety of grammar rules	adding -ed for past tense, adding -s to form plurals
Overgeneralization (applying basic rules of grammar even to cases that are exceptions to the rule)	"I goed to the zoo," "Two mans"

TIP Are you having difficulty differentiating between overextension and overgeneralization? Remember the "g" in overgeneralize as a cue that this term applies to problems with grammar.

PAN Practical Application of Neuroscience

BFG Images/Gallo Images ROOTS RF collection/Getty Images

Have you ever wondered why a crying baby on a plane is so stressful for all passengers? Research shows that mammals tend to cry when they're upset, in pain, or alone, with a pitch and sound specifically designed to attract attention and responses from their caregivers (Lingle et al., 2015). Thanks to evolution, it appears that crying is a primitive behavior shared by most mammals that plays a crucial role in infant survival (Darwin, 1872; Raine, 2016). In fact, the sounds of infant mammals are highly similar, which may explain why both children and adults respond to the cries of kittens and puppies and why deer will respond to the cries of infant humans, seals, and cats (Lingle & Riede, 2014).

[AQ4] Why is it so hard to ignore these cries (see photo)? Although some parents seem to be able to distinguish between their baby's different cries, the overall function of crying may be to signal infant distress. This distress signal, in turn, creates distress and discomfort in others, which then triggers their helping response (Esposito et al., 2017; Lin et al., 2016). Specifically, research has shown that infant cries modulate our hormone levels and activate specific areas of our brains responsible for attention and empathy (Quintana et al., 2016; Riem & Karreman, 2019; Swain & Ho, 2012). In short, In short, everyone on the plane wants someone to comfort and quiet the crying baby.

For unique insights on the effects of nonverbal language, see the following **GCD** **Gender and Cultural Diversity**.

Can Your Nonverbal Language Reveal Your Roots?

(APA Goal 2.5) Incorporate sociocultural factors in scientific inquiry

If English is not your native language, are you amused (or annoyed) by how often people ask where you're from? Just as a Spanish accent, an Irish brogue, or a Minnesota lilt brings to light one's background, facial expressions and body language (our *nonverbal language*) often reveal our cultural origins. Nonverbal language and behavior are sometimes considered to be universal—wherever you go, a groan sounds like a groan and a smile looks like a smile. However, a growing body of research suggests that where we live shapes both how we display emotion and how we perceive it in others. In one study, researchers found that American volunteers could distinguish American from Australian faces when the faces were photographed smiling, but not when they were photographed with neutral expressions (Marsh et al., 2007). In addition, the way Americans and Australians walk or wave in greeting not only telegraphs their nationality but also apparently triggers stereotypes about the two groups. In this particular study, Americans were judged more dominant (think, "Carry a big stick") and Australians more likable (think, "G'day, mate.").

What explains cultural variations in nonverbal communication? Research suggests that some differences may be the result of *historical heterogeneity*—the degree to which a country's present-day population descended from migrants who came from diverse nations over a period of 500 years (Rychlowska et al., 2015). To test this hypothesis, the researchers carefully analyzed existing data on cultural rules for displaying emotions from 32 countries (Matsumoto et al., 2008). As predicted, countries with lower migration tended to be less expressive. Why? The researchers propose that over time homogeneous countries—those with less diversity—develop stronger rules for how openly emotions should be expressed. In relatively homogeneous Japan, for instance, when subordinates are upset around their bosses, they're likely to conceal these feelings with smiles. In countries with a more diverse past, though, people needed to beef up their facial expressions, perhaps to overcome cultural and language barriers.

In their follow-up research, the team zeroed in on a particular kind of facial expression: the smile (Rychlowska et al., 2015). They conducted a new study of 726 people in nine countries, including the United States, Japan, and France. Participants were asked to complete a questionnaire regarding cultural rules for emotional expression. But in this case, they were asked to consider what constituted a good reason for someone else to smile, such as

Jennifer Lam/Shutterstock.com

that he or she "is a happy person," "wants to sell you something," or "feels inferior to you." The participants rated each reason to smile on a scale from Strongly Disagree to Strongly Agree. The researchers then compared the results for each country with their migration numbers. In further support of their initial hypothesis, participants from countries with less migration and less diversity thought smiles were related to the social hierarchy—people smile because they "feel inferior to you." In contrast, participants from countries with greater and more diverse immigration over the past 500 years were more likely to interpret smiles as friendly gestures.

Other research suggests that people from different cultures are attuned to different nonverbal cues. Americans, who tend to express their emotions more overtly, look to the mouth to interpret others' true feelings (Yuki et al., 2007). However, Japanese people, who tend to be more emotionally guarded, give greater weight to the eyes, which are less easily controlled.

"These studies show both that people can be sensitive to cultural cues that they are barely aware of, and also that their own cultural norms can lead them astray," comments Judith Hall, who studies nonverbal communication at Northeastern University. "Americans who think the Japanese are unexpressive mistake subtlety for lack of expression. These Americans would misjudge facial cues that Japanese might be very successful at interpreting." Do you recognize how such judgments can lead to cross-cultural misunderstandings? Or why improving our awareness of these differences might go a long way toward improving cross-cultural interactions?

Source: Sections of this feature were originally published in *Scientific American Mind*, August/September 2007, p. 13. Reprinted with permission of author, SIRI CARPENTER.

Before going on, it's important to note that children vary greatly in the ages and ways in which they acquire language, and parents often needlessly worry if their child is a "late talker." Atypical language development can sometimes be a sign of certain problems, but there are numerous reasons why some children talk sooner than others. For example, one recent study found that children with an older sister have better language abilities than those with an older brother—particularly when there is a large age gap between the siblings (Havron et al., 2019). How would you explain these results?

Theories of Language Development
Some theorists believe that language capability is innate, primarily a matter of maturation. Noam Chomsky (1968, 1980) suggests that children are "prewired" with a neurological ability within the brain, known as a

Language acquisition device (LAD) According to Chomsky, an innate mechanism within the brain that enables a child to analyze language and extract the basic rule of grammar.

language acquisition device (LAD), that enables them to analyze language and to extract the basic rules of grammar. This mechanism needs only minimal exposure to adult speech to unlock its potential. As evidence for this *nativist position*, Chomsky observes that children everywhere progress through the same stages of language development at about the same ages. He also notes that babbling is the same in all languages and that deaf babies babble just like hearing babies.

Nurturists argue that the nativist position doesn't fully explain individual differences in language development. They hold that children learn language through a complex system of rewards, punishments, and imitation. For example, parents smile and encourage any vocalizations from a very young infant. Later, they respond even more enthusiastically when the infant babbles "mama" or "dada." In this way, parents unknowingly use *shaping* (Chapter 6) to help babies learn language. Unfortunately, as discussed in the following **PP PositivePsych**, researchers have found wide variability in how much parents talk or read to their children, and this difference leads to serious gaps in the children's language development skills (Hirsh-Pasek et al., 2015; Hutton et al., 2015; Ockerman, 2016).

Human and Non-Human Animal Language

Without question, non-human animals communicate. They regularly send warnings, signal sexual interest, share locations of food sources, and so on. But can non-human animals master the complexity of human language? Since the 1930s, many language studies have attempted to answer this question by probing the language abilities of chimpanzees, gorillas, and other animals (Fitch, 2018; Scott-Phillips, 2015; Zuberbühler, 2015).

PP Practical Application: PositivePsych

Why Talk or Read to Babies?

(APA Goal 1.3) Describe applications of psychology

Have you seen the public service ads on TV emphasizing talking and reading to babies and toddlers? Did you know that the number of words and amount of talking babies hear (or don't hear) from their caregivers play a fundamental role in the development of their critical language skills? To identify the specific factors that influence language acquisition, researchers examined babies living in two communities—a relatively wealthy college town and a low-income area nearby (Fernald et al., 2013). They found that parents and caregivers from the wealthier community talked to their children much more frequently, which gave them a chance to learn new words and to form better vocabularies. A similar study reported that low-income children hear a lower quantity and variety of words, which affects their language expression ability (Hirsh-Pasek et al., 2015).

Hero Images/DigitalVision/Getty Images

Recognizing the importance of talking to babies, an enterprising company developed a word-tracking device, called *Starling*, that parents attach to their babies to record the number of verbal exchanges experienced by their children (Ockerman, 2016). Interestingly, fMRI brain scans done on children during a story-listening task showed that there was more activation in Broca's area of children's brains—the area largely responsible for language—during verbal exchanges between adults and children (Romeo et al., 2018). This study, along with other similar research (e.g., Gilkerson et al., 2018), confirms that the number of conversational turns with adults is more important for a child's language development than the sheer quantity of words heard, and these results apply regardless of the family's socioeconomic status (SES).

Like talking, reading to babies and toddlers has been revealed to have numerous benefits. Reading books is particularly

important given that they contain more unique words than children hear in everyday speech (Montag et al., 2015). Research also shows that reading activates important areas of the child's brain (Hutton et al., 2015). Using fMRI scans of brain activity in 3- to 5-year-old children as they listened to age-appropriate stories, the researchers found that children whose parents reported more reading at home and more books in the home showed significantly greater activation of the parietal-temporal-occipital association cortex, which is responsible for integrating sound and visual stimulation. Even though the children in the fMRI scanner were just listening to a story and could not see any pictures, they were actively integrating the sound of the words and imagining what they were hearing. The greater levels of brain activation in children who are read to more often and have more books at home suggests that they gain more practice in developing visual images, which helps in overall language acquisition.

Ron Cohn/Gorilla Foundation/Koko.org

FIGURE 8.11 **Signing**   According to her teacher, Penny Patterson, Koko used ASL to converse with others, talk to herself, joke, express preferences, and even to lie (Linden, 1993; P. Patterson, 2002).

MICHAEL NICHOLS/National Geographic Image Collection

FIGURE 8.12 **Computer-aided communication**   Apes lack the necessary anatomical structures to vocalize the way humans do. For this reason, language research with chimps and gorillas has focused on teaching the animals to use sign language or to "speak" by pointing to symbols on a keyboard.

One of the most successful early studies was conducted by Beatrice and Allen Gardner (1969), who recognized chimpanzees' manual dexterity and ability to imitate gestures. The Gardners used American Sign Language (ASL) with a chimp named Washoe. By the time Washoe was four years old, she had learned 132 signs and was able to combine them into simple sentences such as "Hurry, gimme toothbrush" and "Please tickle more." The famous gorilla Koko also used ASL to communicate; she reportedly used more than 1,000 signs (**Figure 8.11**).

In another well-known study, a chimp named Lana learned to use symbols on a computer to get things she wanted, such as food, a drink, and a tickle from her trainers, and to have her curtains opened (Rumbaugh et al., 1974). See **Figure 8.12**.

Dolphins have also been the subject of interesting language research (see cartoon) (Christie, 2018; Melo-Santos et al., 2019; Pack, 2015). Communication with dolphins is typically conducted with hand signals or audible commands transmitted through an underwater speaker system. In one typical study, trainers gave dolphins commands made up of two- to five-word sentences, such as "Big ball—square—return," which meant that they should go get the big ball, put it in the floating square, and return to the trainer (Herman et al., 1984). By varying the syntax (for example, the order of the words) and specific content of the commands, the researchers showed that dolphins are sensitive to these aspects of language.

Scientists generally disagree about how to interpret the findings on chimps, apes, and dolphins. Most believe that non-human animals definitely communicate, but

"ALTHOUGH HUMANS MAKE SOUNDS WITH THEIR MOUTHS AND OCCASIONALLY LOOK AT EACH OTHER, THERE IS NO SOLID EVIDENCE THAT THEY ACTUALLY COMMUNICATE WITH EACH OTHER."

Sidney Harris/ScienceCartoonPlus.com

that they're not using true language because they don't convey subtle meanings, use language creatively, or communicate at an abstract level. Critics suggest that these animals do not truly understand language, but are simply operantly conditioned (Chapter 6) to imitate symbols to receive rewards. Finally, many language scientists contend that data regarding animal language has not always been well documented (Beran et al., 2014; Savage-Rumbaugh, 1990; Terrace, 1979).

Proponents of animal language respond that apes can use language creatively and have even coined some words of their own. Koko the gorilla supposedly signed "finger bracelet" to describe a ring and "eye hat" to describe a mask (Patterson & Linden, 1981). Proponents also argue that, as demonstrated by the dolphin studies, animals can be taught to understand basic rules of sentence structure. As you can see, the jury is still out on whether non-human animals use "true" language or not. Stay tuned.

Retrieval Practice 8.2 | Language

Self-Test   Completing this self-test, and then checking your answers by clicking on the answer button or by looking in Appendix B, will provide immediate feedback and helpful practice for exams.

1. _____ is the set of rules (syntax and semantics) that govern the use and structure of language.
   a. Syntax
   b. Semantics
   c. Pragmatics
   d. Grammar

2. The _____ rule of English is violated by this sentence: *The girl Anne is.*
   a. deep structure
   b. phonemic structure
   c. semantics
   d. syntax

3. "I goed to the zoo" and "I hurt my foots" are examples of _____.
   a. prelinguistic verbalizations
   b. overexposure to adult "baby talk"
   c. overgeneralization
   d. Noam Chomsky's theory of language acquisition

4. According to Chomsky, the innate mechanism that enables a child to analyze language is known as a(n) _____.
   a. telegraphic understanding device (TUD)
   b. language acquisition device (LAD)
   c. language and grammar translator (LGT)
   d. overgeneralized neural net (ONN)

5. Some researchers believe non-human animals are not using true language because they don't _____.
   a. convey subtle meanings
   b. use language creatively
   c. communicate at an abstract level
   d. all of these options

Q Test Your Critical Thinking

1. Describe a personal example of language influencing your thinking.

2. Review the evidence that nonhuman animals are able to learn and use language. Do you think apes and dolphins have true language? Why or why not?

Real World Application Questions

[AQ3]   Does speaking multiple languages make you smarter?

[AQ4]   Why is it so hard to ignore a crying baby?

Sean Prior/Alamy Stock Photo

BFG Images/Gallo Images ROOTS RF collection/Getty Images

Hint: Look in the Text for **[AQ3]** and **[AQ4]**

8.3   Intelligence

LEARNING OBJECTIVES

Retrieval Practice   While reading the upcoming sections, respond to each Learning Objective in your own words.

Summarize the nature and measurement of intelligence and the factors that influence it.

• **Define** intelligence.

• **Compare** the different forms and theories of intelligence.

• **Describe** how intelligence is measured and the groups that fall at the extremes.

Real World Application Question

[AQ5]   Can personal traits and character strengths predict achievement better than IQ?

> Intellectual growth should commence at birth and cease only at death.
>
> —Albert Einstein

What is intelligence and what does it mean to say someone is "intelligent"? People and cultures vary in the ways they define intelligence. For example, the Mandarin word that corresponds most closely to the word *intelligence* is a character meaning "good brain and talented" (Matsumoto, 2000). In other cultures, intelligence is associated with traits like imitation, effort, and social responsibility (Keats, 1982). An experiment carried out in seven countries found that even whether or not people smiled affected judgments of intelligence (Krys et al., 2014). Surprisingly, German respondents perceived smiling individuals as being more intelligent, whereas Chinese participants judged smilers as less intelligent.

Even among Western psychologists there is considerable debate over the definition of intelligence. In this discussion, we rely on a formal definition of **intelligence** as the global capacity to think rationally, act purposefully, profit from experience, and deal effectively with the environment (Wechsler, 1944, 1977).

The Nature of Intelligence

In the 1920s, British psychologist Charles Spearman first observed that high scores on separate tests of mental abilities tend to correlate with each other. Spearman (1923) thus proposed that intelligence is a single factor, which he termed **general intelligence (*g*)**. He believed that *g* underlies all intellectual behavior, including reasoning, solving problems, and performing well in all areas of cognition. Spearman's work laid the foundations for today's standardized intelligence tests (Bouchard, 2016; Woodley of Menie & Madison, 2015).

About a decade later, L. L. Thurstone (1938) proposed seven primary mental abilities: verbal comprehension, word fluency, numerical fluency, spatial visualization, associative memory, perceptual speed, and reasoning. J. P. Guilford (1967) later expanded the number, proposing that as many as 120 factors are involved in the structure of intelligence.

Around the same time, Raymond Cattell (1963, 1971) reanalyzed Thurstone's data and argued against the idea of multiple intelligences. He believed that two subtypes of *g* exist:

- **Fluid intelligence (*gf*)** refers to the ability to think speedily and abstractly and to solve novel problems. Fluid intelligence is relatively independent of education and experience, and like most biological capacities, it declines with age (Gazes et al., 2016; Gerstorf et al., 2015; Klein et al., 2015).

- **Crystallized intelligence (*gc*)** refers to the store of knowledge and skills gained through experience and education (Santos, 2016; Sternberg, 2014, 2015). Crystallized intelligence tends to increase over the life span.

Measuring Intelligence

Different IQ tests approach the measurement of intelligence from different perspectives (see cartoon). However, most are designed to predict grades in school. Let's look at the most commonly used IQ tests.

The *Stanford-Binet Intelligence Scale* is loosely based on the first IQ tests developed in France around the turn of the twentieth century by Alfred Binet. In the United States, Lewis Terman (1916) developed the Stanford-Binet (at Stanford University) to test the intellectual ability of U.S.-born children ages three to 16. The test has been revised periodically—most recently in 2003. The test is administered individually and consists of such tasks as copying geometric designs, identifying similarities, and repeating number sequences.

After administering the individual test to a large number of people, researchers discovered that their scores typically are distributed in a **normal distribution** that forms a symmetrical, bell-shaped curve (**Figure 8.13**). This means that a majority of the scores fall in the middle of the curve and a few scores fall on the extremes. In addition to intelligence, measurements of many physical traits, like height and weight, form a similar "bell curve" normal distribution.

In the original version of the Stanford-Binet, results were expressed in terms of a **mental age (MA)**, which refers to an individual's level of mental development relative to that of others. If a 7-year-old's score equaled that of an average 8-year-old, for example, the child was considered to have a mental age of 8. To determine the child's **intelligence quotient (IQ)**, mental age was divided by the child's chronological age (actual age in years) and multiplied by 100.

Intelligence The global capacity to think rationally, act purposefully, profit from experience, and deal effectively with the environment.

General intelligence (*g*) Spearman's term for a common skill set that underlies all intellectual behavior.

Fluid intelligence (*gf*) The ability to think speedily and abstractly and to solve novel problems; it tends to decrease over the life span.

Crystallized intelligence (*gc*) The store of knowledge and skills gained through experience and education; it tends to increase over the life span.

Normal distribution A statistical term used to describe how traits are distributed within a population; IQ scores usually form a symmetrical, bell-shaped curve, with most scores falling near the average, and fewer scores near the extremes.

Mental age (MA) An individual's level of mental development relative to that of others; it was initially compared to chronological age (CA) to calculate IQ.

Intelligence quotient (IQ) An index of intelligence initially derived from standardized tests, computed by dividing mental age (MA) by chronological age (CA) and then multiplying by 100; it is now derived by comparing individual scores with the scores of others of the same age.

Gradisher, Martha/Cartoon Stock

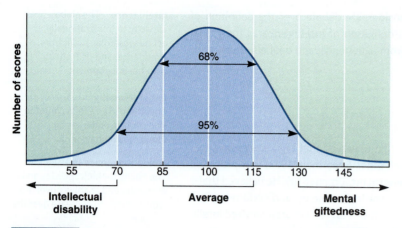

FIGURE 8.13 **The normal distribution (bell curve) of scores on intelligence tests** The term *bell curve* refers to the fact that the graph used to depict the normal distribution of scores (shown here) is shaped like a bell. The highest point at the top of the bell represents the most probable score (100 points); all the other scores are equally distributed around this center point. Note that 68 percent of people score 15 points above or below the national average, which is 100 points.

The most widely used intelligence test today, the *Wechsler Adult Intelligence Scale (WAIS)*, was developed by David Wechsler in the early 1900s. He later created a similar test for school-aged children. Like the Stanford-Binet, Wechsler's tests yield an overall intelligence score, in addition to separate index scores related to four specific areas: *verbal comprehension, perceptual reasoning, working memory,* and *processing speed.* See **Figure 8.14** for samples of the Wechsler's perceptual reasoning test items.

Today, most intelligence test scores are expressed as a comparison of a single person's score to scores of a national sample of similar-aged people (see again Figure 8.13). Even though the IQ is no longer calculated using the original formula comparing mental and chronological ages, the term *IQ* remains as a shorthand expression for intelligence test scores.

Principles of Test Construction
What makes a good test? How are the tests developed by Binet and Wechsler any better than those published in popular magazines and presented on websites? To be scientifically acceptable, all psychological tests must fulfill three basic requirements (Dombrowski, 2015; Jackson, 2016; Suzuki et al., 2014):

Standardization Establishing a set of uniform procedures for administering and scoring a test; also, establishing norms based on the scores of a pretested group.

Reliability The degree to which a test produces similar scores each time it is used; stability or consistency of the scores produced by an instrument.

- **Standardization** in intelligence tests (as well as personality, aptitude, and most other tests) involves following a certain set of uniform procedures when administering the test. First, every test must have *norms*, or average scores, developed by giving the test to a representative sample of people (a diverse group of people who resemble those for whom the test is intended). Second, testing procedures must be standardized. All test takers must be given the same instructions, questions, and time limits, and all test administrators must follow the same objective scoring standards.

- **Reliability** is usually determined by retesting participants to see whether their test scores change significantly. Retesting can be done via the *test–retest method*, in which participants' scores on two separate administrations of the same test are compared, or via the

FIGURE 8.14 **Items similar to those on the Wechsler Adult Intelligence Scale (WAIS)** These simulated items resemble those found on the Wechsler Adult Intelligence Scale, Fourth Edition (WAIS-IV). Previous editions of the WAIS included sections such as Picture Arrangement, Block Design, and Object Assembly, which were dropped to increase reliability and user friendliness. The WAIS-IV also takes less time to administer, and the results show smaller differences based on level of education or racial/ethnic group membership. Answers to the two puzzles provided in this figure can be found at the end of this chapter.

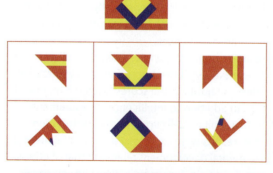

a. Visual puzzles The test administrator asks: "Which three pieces go together to make this puzzle?"

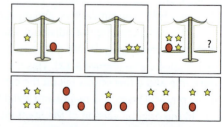

b. Figure weights The test administrator asks: "Which one of these works to balance the scale?"

Source: Based on simulated items from the Wechsler Adult Intelligence Scale, Fourth Edition (WAIS-IV).

split-half method, in which a test is split into two equivalent parts (such as odd and even questions) and the degree of similarity between the two halves is measured.

- **Validity** is the ability of a test to measure what it is designed to measure. The most important type of validity is *criterion-related validity*, or the accuracy with which test scores can be used to predict another variable of interest (known as the criterion). Criterion-related validity is expressed as the *correlation* (Chapter 1) between the test score and the criterion. If two variables are highly correlated, then one can be used to predict the other. Thus, if a test is valid, its scores will be useful in predicting an individual's behavior in some other specified situation. One criterion that might be used for intelligence test scores is their ability to predict grades in college.

Do you see why a test that is standardized and reliable but not valid is worthless? For example, a test for skin sensitivity might be easy to standardize (the instructions specify exactly how to apply the test agent), and it might be reliable (similar results are obtained on each retest). But it certainly would not be valid for predicting college grades.

Extremes in Intelligence

One of the best methods for judging the validity of a test is to compare people who score at the extremes. Despite the uncertainties discussed in the previous section, intelligence tests provide one of the major criteria for assessing mental ability at the extremes—specifically, for diagnosing *intellectual disability* and *mental giftedness*.

Intellectual Disability The clinical label *intellectually disabled* (previously referred to as *mentally retarded*) is applied when someone has significant deficits in general mental abilities such as reasoning, problem solving, academic learning, and adaptive functioning, including communication, social participation, and personal independence (American Psychiatric Association, 2013; Kumin, 2015).

Fewer than three percent of people are classified as having an intellectual disability (see **Table 8.5**). Of this group, 85 percent have only mild intellectual disability, and many become self-supporting, integrated members of society. Furthermore, people can score low on some measures of intelligence and still be average or even gifted on others (Hughes et al., 2018; Miller et al., 2016; Treffert, 2014). The most dramatic examples are people with *savant syndrome*. People with savant syndrome generally score very low on IQ tests (usually between 40 and 70), yet they demonstrate exceptional skills or brilliance in specific areas, such as rapid calculation, art, memory, or musical ability (**Figure 8.15**).

Validity The degree to which a test measures what it is intended to measure.

Justin Sutcliffe/Eyevine/Redux Pictures

FIGURE 8.15 Savant syndrome—an unusual form of intelligence Derek Paravicini, a musical savant, was born premature, blind, and with a severe learning disability. In spite of these challenges, he plays the concert piano entirely by ear and has a repertoire of thousands of memorized pieces.

TABLE 8.5   **Degrees of Intellectual Disability**

	Level of Disability	IQ Scores	Characteristics
General population / Intellectually disabled 1–3% / 85% Mild / 1–2% Profound / 3–4% Severe / 10% Moderate	**Mild (85 percent)**	50–70	Usually able to become self-sufficient; may marry, have families, and secure full-time jobs in low-skilled occupations
	Moderate (10 percent)	35–49	Generally able to perform simple, low-skilled tasks; may contribute to a certain extent to their livelihood
	Severe (3–4 percent)	20–34	Generally able to follow daily routines, but need supervision; with training, may learn basic communication skills
	Profound (1–2 percent)	below 20	Generally able to perform only the most rudimentary behaviors, such as walking, feeding themselves, and saying a few phrases

Some forms of intellectual disability stem from genetic abnormalities, such as Down syndrome, fragile-X syndrome, and phenylketonuria (PKU). Possible contributing factors are environmental, including prenatal exposure to alcohol and other drugs, extreme deprivation or neglect in early life, and brain damage from physical trauma such as car accidents or sports injuries. However, in many cases, there is no known cause of the intellectual disability.

Mental Giftedness At the other end of the intelligence spectrum are people with especially high IQs (typically defined as being in the top one or two percent). In the early 1900s, Lewis Terman identified 1,500 gifted children—affectionately nicknamed the Termites—with IQs of 140 or higher (Terman, 1925). He and his colleagues then tracked their progress through adulthood. The number who became highly successful professionals was many times the number a random group would have produced (Kreger Silverman, 2013; Plucker & Esping, 2014; Terman, 1954).

Researchers noted, however, that those who were most successful tended to have extraordinary motivation, and typically had someone at home or school who was especially encouraging (Goleman, 1980). Also, as you might expect, some "Termites" became alcoholics, got divorced, and died as a result of suicide at rates similar to the general population (Campbell & Feng, 2011; Leslie, 2000; Terman, 1954).

In sum, a high IQ is no guarantee of success in every endeavor. In fact, research has found a strong correlation between having a high IQ and an increased risk for affective disorders, ADHD, and ASD (Chapter 13), as well as allergies, asthma, and autoimmune disease (Karpinski et al., 2018). **[AQ5]** Furthermore, as shown by the Termites study and the problem-solving research mentioned earlier, personal traits and character strengths, like self-control, motivation, and perseverance, may be the strongest predictors of overall achievement and well-being (see photo). Although critics have questioned the research on having a *growth mindset,* the belief that intelligence can be developed over time, it may also be important to intellectual achievement (Dweck, 2012; Dweck & Yeager, 2019; Sisk et al., 2018).

> You have to be careful if you're good at something. Because I've been very successful at software development, people come in and expect that I have wisdom about topics that I don't.
> —Philanthropist Bill Gates

Andersen Ross Photography Inc/DigitalVision/Getty Images

Retrieval Practice 8.3 | Intelligence

Self-Test Completing this self-test, and then checking your answers by clicking on the answer button or by looking in Appendix B, will provide immediate feedback and helpful practice for exams.

1. The formal definition of intelligence stresses the global capacity to _____.

   a. successfully adapt to and perform well within relationships, in school, and on the job

   b. read, write, and do computations at home and at work

   c. perform verbally and physically within the environment

   d. think rationally, act purposefully, profit from experience, and deal effectively with the environment

2. The store of knowledge and skills gained through experience and education is known as _____ intelligence.

   a. crystallized   c. general

   b. fluid   d. specific

3. If a test gave you the same score each time you took it, that test would be _____.

   a. reliable   c. standardized

   b. valid   d. none of these options

4. Validity refers to the ability of a test to _____.

   a. return the same score on separate administrations of the test

   b. measure what it is designed to measure

   c. avoid discrimination between different cultural groups

   d. give a standard deviation of scores

Q Test Your Critical Thinking

1. Do you believe IQ tests are more reliable than valid? Explain.

2. Do you think IQ tests are culturally biased? Why or why not?

Real World Application Questions

[AQ5] Can personal traits and character strengths predict achievement better than IQ?

Andersen Ross Photography Inc/DigitalVision/Getty Images

Hint: Look in the text for **[AQ5]**

8.4 | Intelligence Controversies

LEARNING OBJECTIVES

Retrieval Practice   While reading the upcoming sections, respond to each Learning Objective in your own words.

Review the major controversies surrounding intelligence.

- **Discuss** the relative contributions of nature and nurture to IQ.
- **Describe** how and why groups differ on mental ability tests.

- **Identify** the various theories and controversies over multiple intelligences.
- **Evaluate** the importance of artificial intelligence (AI) and emotional intelligence (EI).

Real World Application Question

[AQ6] Will watching TV dramas increase your emotional intelligence?

Psychologists have long debated several important questions related to intelligence: Is IQ mostly inherited or is it molded by our environment? Do men and women or people in different ethnic groups differ in mental abilities? If so, how and why? Is intelligence a general ability or a number of specific talents and aptitudes?

Nature, Nurture, and IQ

How is brain functioning related to intelligence? What factors—environmental or hereditary—influence an individual's intelligence? These specific questions, and the controversies surrounding them, are discussed in this section.

The Brain's Influence on Intelligence   A basic tenet of neuroscience is that all mental activity (including intelligence) results from neural activity in the brain. Most recent research on the biology of intelligence has focused on brain anatomy and functioning. For example, neuroscientists have found that people who score highest on intelligence tests have noticeable differences in the anatomy of their brain cells, and also respond more quickly on tasks requiring perceptual judgments (Miller & Sherwood, 2019; Sternberg, 2014, 2015; Wagner et al., 2014).

In addition, research using positron emission tomography (PET) scans to measure brain activity (Chapter 2) suggests that intelligent brains work smarter, or more efficiently, than less-intelligent brains (Jung & Haier, 2007; Neubauer et al., 2004; Posthuma et al., 2001). See **Figure 8.16**.

Does size matter? It seems logical that bigger brains would be smarter. As predicted, imaging studies have found a significant correlation, in humans, between brain size (adjusted for body size) and intelligence (Bouchard, 2016; Goriounova & Mansvelder, 2019; Herculano-Houzel, 2017). Surprisingly, Albert Einstein's brain was no larger than normal (Lepore, 2018; Witelson et al., 1999). In fact, some of Einstein's brain areas were actually smaller than average, but the area responsible for processing mathematical and spatial information was 15 percent larger than average.

As expected, some animals, such as whales and dolphins, have larger brains than humans. However, our brains are larger relative to our body size. Interestingly, some bird species have brain-to-body size ratios greater than humans, and the tiny shrew has the highest ratio of all.

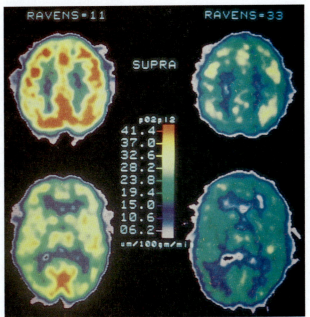

FIGURE 8.16   **Do intelligent brains work more efficiently?**   In PET scan images, red and yellow indicate more activity in relevant brain areas. Note how, during problem-solving tasks, low-IQ brains (left) show more activity than high-IQ brains (right). This research suggests that lower-IQ brains actually work harder, although less efficiently, than higher-IQ brains.

Courtesy of Richard J. Haier, University of California-Irvine

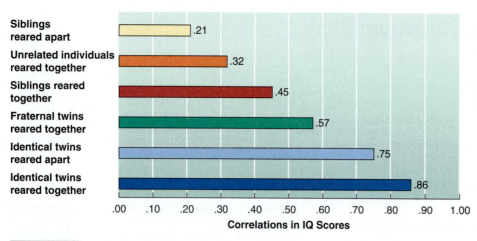

FIGURE 8.17 **Genetic and environmental influences on IQ** Note the higher correlations between identical twins' IQ test scores than all other pairs. Genes no doubt play a significant role in intelligence, but these effects are difficult to separate from environmental influences.

Sources: Based on Bouchard, 2016; Bouchard & McGue, 1981; Plomin & von Stumm, 2018.

Genetic and Environmental Influences on Intelligence

Are similarities in intelligence between family members due to a combination of heredity (shared genetic material) or to the environment (similar living arrangements and experiences)? Researchers who are interested in the role of heredity in intelligence often focus on identical (monozygotic) twins, given that they share 100 percent of their genetic material (see **Figure 8.17**). The long-running Minnesota Study of Twins, an investigation of identical twins raised in different homes and reunited only as adults, found that genetic factors appear to play a surprisingly large role in the IQ scores of identical twins (Bouchard, 2016; Plomin & von Stumm, 2018).

However, those who emphasize the environmental influences on intelligence would say that these twin study results are not conclusive. Adoption agencies tend to look for similar criteria in their choice of adoptive parents. Therefore, the homes of these "reared apart" twins were actually quite similar. In addition, these twins shared the same 9-month prenatal environment, which might have influenced their brain development and intelligence (Felson, 2014; White et al., 2002).

Additional evidence of the environmental influences on intelligence comes from studies on the numerous effects of abuse in childhood, as well as from brain scans of children who have been seriously neglected (**Figure 8.18**). Likewise, early malnutrition, which affects over 113 million children worldwide, can retard a child's intellectual development, curiosity, and motivation for learning (Peter et al., 2016; Schoenmaker et al., 2015; Venables & Raine, 2016). Interestingly, research has found a measurable difference between the gray matter volume in the brains of only versus non-only children in areas related to creativity and agreeableness, which further supports the importance of the family environmental factors (Yang et al., 2016).

S&P Scientific Thinking and Practical Application

What are some of the other effects of neglect and abuse? In addition to permanent brain changes, children who lack reliable care and stable attachment—or who experience deliberate abuse in the first few years of life—show not only lower intelligence but also less empathy for others and a greater vulnerability to later substance abuse and addiction (Luby et al., 2012). In contrast, children who are enrolled in high-quality preschool programs and are regularly read to by their parents show increases in IQ. These studies provide further evidence that the environment, for better or worse, has a major impact (Protzko et al., 2013).

FIGURE 8.18 **Neglect and IQ** These images illustrate the negative impact of neglect on the developing brain. The brain on the left is from a normal developing child, whose brain size is in the 50th percentile. The brain on the right is from a child suffering from severe sensory deprivation neglect, whose brain size is in the 3rd percentile. Photo supplied with kind permission from Springer Science+Business Media: Perry, B. D. Childhood experience and the expression of genetic potential: what childhood neglect tells us about nature and nurture. *Brain and Mind* 3: 79–100, 2002.

In short, genetics and environment play interacting and inseparable roles. Intelligence is like a rubber band. Heredity equips each of us with innate intellectual capabilities, our personal rubber band. But our environment helps deteriorate or stretch this band, which significantly influences whether or not we reach our full intellectual potential.

Group Differences in IQ Scores

Although genetics play a significant role in intelligence, it's VERY important to recognize that heritability cannot explain *between*-group differences. Note the overall difference between the average height of the plants on the left and those on the right in **Figure 8.19**. Just as we cannot say that the difference *between* these two groups of plants is due to genetics, we cannot say that differences in IQ *between* any two groups of people are due to heredity.

Note also the considerable variations in height *within* the group of plants on the left and those *within* the group on the right. Just as some plants are taller than others, there are individuals who score high on IQ tests and others who score low. Always remember that the greatest differences in IQ scores occur when we compare individuals *within* groups—not *between* groups.

What about the controversial differences between the sexes, such as those in verbal and math skills? For instance, after analyzing 27 years of standardized test scores from more than 3.4 million students, researchers found that girls scored significantly higher in both reading and writing (Reilly et al., 2019). Research using brain scans, autopsies, and volumetric measurements has also found several differences between the brains of men and women (**Figure 8.20**). Two areas in the frontal and temporal lobes associated with language skills are generally larger in women than in men. In contrast, a region in the parietal lobes correlated with manipulating spatial relationships and mathematical abilities is typically larger in men than in women (Garrett, 2015; Ingalhalikar et al., 2014). **Table 8.6** illustrates the tasks researchers have used to explore possible sex differences.

How do we explain these differences? Evolutionary psychologists often suggest that sex differences like these may be the product of gradual genetic adaptations (Buss, 2015; Ingalhalikar et al., 2014). In ancient societies, men were most often the "hunters," while women were almost always the "gatherers." Therefore, the male's superiority on many spatial tasks and target-directed motor skills (see again Table 8.6) may have evolved from the adaptive demands of hunting, whereas activities such as food gathering, childrearing, and domestic tool construction and manipulation may have contributed to the female's language superiority and fine motor coordination.

Some critics, however, suggest that evolution progresses much too slowly to account for this type of behavioral adaptation. Furthermore, there is wide cross-cultural variability in gender differences, and explanations of these differences are difficult to test scientifically (Halpern, 2014; Miller & Halpern, 2014; Newcombe, 2010).

In addition to the debate over possible gender differences in verbal and math skills, there is an ongoing debate over the reported differences in IQ scores between various ethnic groups. Unfortunately, some of the strongest proponents of the "heritability of intelligence" argument seem to ignore the "fertile soil" background of the groups who score highest on IQ tests. As an open-minded scientific and critical thinker, carefully consider these important research findings:

- **Environmental and cultural factors may override genetic potential and later affect IQ test scores.**   Like plants that come from similar seeds but are placed in poor rather than enriched soil, children of color are more likely to grow up in stressful, lower socioeconomic conditions, which may hamper their true intellectual potential. Furthermore, in some ethnic groups and economic classes, a child who excels in school may be ridiculed for trying to be different from his or

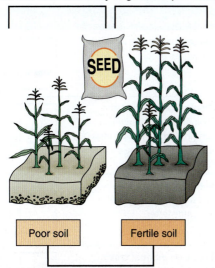

Differences *within* groups are due almost entirely to genetics (the seed).

Poor soil   Fertile soil

Differences *between* groups are due almost *entirely* to environment (the soil).

FIGURE 8.19   **Genetics versus environment** Note that even when you begin with the same package of seeds (genetic inheritance), the average height of corn plants in fertile soil will be greater than the average height of corn plants in poor soil (environmental influences). Therefore, no valid or logical conclusions can be drawn about the overall genetic differences between the two groups of plants given the two environments (soils) are so different. Similar logic must be applied to intelligence scores between groups.

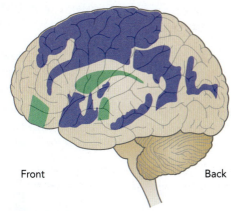

Front   Back

FIGURE 8.20   **Brain differences by sex** Note that the areas in purple are, on average, larger in women, whereas the areas in green are, on average, larger in men.

TABLE 8.6 Problem-Solving Tasks Generally Favoring Women and Men

Problem-Solving Tasks Generally Favoring Women		Problem-Solving Tasks Generally Favoring Men	
Perceptual speed: As quickly as possible, identify matching items.		**Spatial tasks:** Mentally rotate the 3-D object to identify its match.	
Displaced objects: After looking at the middle picture, tell which item is missing from the picture on the right.		**Spatial tasks:** Mentally manipulate the folded paper to tell where the holes will fall when it is unfolded.	
Verbal fluency: List words that begin with the same letter.	B – – – Bat, big, bike, bang, bark, bank, bring, brand, broom, bright, brook, bug, buddy, bunk	**Target-directed motor skills:** Hit the bull's eye.	
Precision manual tasks: Place the pegs in the holes as quickly as possible.		**Disembedding tests:** Find the simple shape on the left in the more complex figures.	
Mathematical calculation: Compute the answer.	72 6 (18+4)−78+$^{36}/_2$	**Mathematical reasoning:** What is the answer?	5½ If you bicycle 24 miles a day, how many days will it take to travel 132 miles?

her classmates. Moreover, if children's own language and dialect do not match the language of their education system or the IQ tests they take, they are obviously at a disadvantage (Davies et al., 2014; Suzuki et al., 2014; von Stumm & Plomin, 2015). In addition, environmental stress can lead to short-term decreases in test scores. The good news is that positive environmental messages can help offset some of these problems. Simply including aspects of Black culture—*The Color Purple*, BET, Black History Month—within a university setting has been linked to positive academic outcomes for Black students (Brannon et al., 2015).

Perhaps even more important to you as a college student is the research showing that individual gene variants have very little predictive value for educational attainment (Lee et al., 2018). Researchers studied datasets from more than 1.1 million participants from 15 countries and found that ambition, family situation, socioeconomic status, and other factors play a significantly bigger role than genes.

- **Traditional IQ tests may be culturally biased.** If standardized IQ tests contain questions that reflect White middle-class culture, they will discriminate against test takers with differing language, knowledge, and experience (Chapman et al., 2014; Stanovich, 2015). Researchers have attempted to create a *culture-fair* or *culture-free* IQ test, but they have found it virtually impossible to do so. Past experiences, motivation, test-taking abilities, and previous experiences with tests are powerful influences on IQ scores.

- **Intelligence (as measured by IQ tests) is not a fixed trait.** Around the world, IQ scores have increased over the past half century, although there has been a slowdown or reversal of this trend in recent years (Bratsberg & Rogeberg, 2018). This well-established phenomenon, known as the *Flynn effect*, may be due to improved nutrition, better public education, more proficient test-taking skills, and rising levels of education among a greater percentage of the world's population (Flynn, 1987, 2019; Flynn et al., 2014; Woodley of Menie et al., 2016).

- **Race and ethnicity, like intelligence itself, are almost impossible to define.** Depending on the definition we use, there are between three and 300 races, and no race is pure in a biological sense (Humes & Hogan, 2015; Kite, 2013). Furthermore, like former President Barack Obama, Olivia Munn, and Kamala Harris, many people today self-identify as multiracial.

Stereotype Threat   Perhaps one of the hottest controversies in group differences in IQ scores involves negative stereotypes about women and people of color, which can lead some group members to doubt their abilities. This phenomenon, called **stereotype threat**, may, in turn, reduce their intelligence test scores and other abilities (Boucher et al., 2015; Kaye & Pennington, 2016; Steele & Aronson, 1995). In the first study of stereotype threat, Claude Steele and Joshua Aronson (1995) recruited Black and White college students with similar ability levels to complete a difficult verbal exam. In the group of students who were told that the exam was diagnostic of their intellectual abilities, Black students underperformed in relation to White students. However, in the second group, where students were told the exam was not diagnostic of their abilities, there were no differences between the scores of the Black and White students.

Stereotype threat The awareness of a negative stereotype directed toward a group, which leads members of that group to respond in a self-fulfilling way that impairs their performance.

Given the potential lasting impact of stereotype threat, let's explore it in more depth. First, why did the Black students in the first group underperform and not those in the second group? It appears that members of stereotyped groups are anxious that they will fulfill their group's negative stereotype. This anxiety, in turn, hinders their performance on tests. Some people cope with stereotype threat by *disidentifying*, telling themselves they don't care about the test scores (Major et al., 1998; Rothgerber & Wolsiefer, 2014). Unfortunately, this attitude reduces motivation and leads to decreased performance (**Figure 8.21**).

It's important to note that some studies have found it difficult to replicate these effects and even revealed contradictory findings (e.g., Pennington et al., 2019). However, other researchers have found substantial evidence for adverse effects of stereotype threat among many social groups, including those who are low-income, elderly, people of color, and women. Researchers in one study examined high school girls' interest in computer science after they were given descriptions and photographs of both a stereotypical and a nonstereo-typical classroom (Master et al., 2016). The stereotypical classroom contained objects such as *Star Wars* items, tech magazines, and science fiction books. The non-stereotypical classroom had objects such as nature pictures, general magazines, and plants. On average, the girls expressed significantly more interest in taking a computer science class after seeing the nonstereotypical classroom. The boys' interest, in comparison, did not differ by classroom. Studies like this suggest that when women are underrepresented in particular fields, like computer science, it may be due not to the females' lack of ability in such areas, but rather to subtle social and environmental factors.

Other research has found that simply using action words can significantly increase girls' interest in science—and thereby help overcome the gender disparity in science (Rhodes et al., 2019). In this study, young girls and boys were first introduced to the scientific method using terms of action (e.g., "Let's do science") or words of identity (e.g., "Let's be scientists"). Next, all children were asked to solve science games. While the wording had little or no effect on the young boys, the young girls exposed to the action words more often chose to continue solving problems—thus showing more engagement.

Can you see how this type of research can suggest strategies to help overcome the persistent gender disparity in science training and careers? This research also helps explain some group differences in intelligence and achievement tests. Furthermore, it

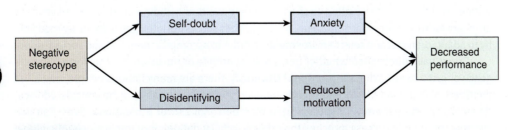

FIGURE 8.21   **How stereotype threat may lead to decreased performance**

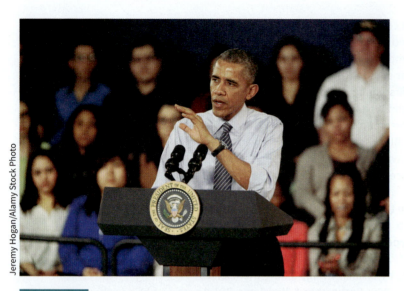

FIGURE 8.22 **"Obama effect" versus stereotype threat** Some research has found a so-called Obama effect, which reportedly offsets problems related to the stereotype threat (Barker, 2016; Dillon, 2009; Meirick & Schartel Dunn, 2015). However, other studies found either no relationship between test performance and positive thoughts about Obama or mixed results (Aronson et al., 2009; Stricker & Rock, 2015).

underscores why relying solely on such tests to make critical decisions affecting individual lives—for example, in hiring, college admissions, or clinical application—is unwarranted and possibly even unethical.

What's the good news? First, some research found that having Barack Obama as president improved the academic performance of people of color, thus offsetting stereotype threat (Marx et al., 2009). (See **Figure 8.22**.) Second, people who have the opportunity to self-affirm, or validate, their identities in some meaningful way are less likely to experience the negative effects of stereotype threat (e.g., Albalooshi et al., 2019; Goyer et al., 2017). As an example, Black middle school students who participated in a brief values affirmation intervention were more likely to enroll in college seven to nine years later and to attend relatively more selective colleges (Layous et al., 2017). Similarly, in England, where socioeconomic status (SES) is a stronger predictor of academic success than is ethnicity, researchers found that just having students complete three brief writing exercises reduced their level of stress (Hadden et al., 2019).

Multiple Intelligences

While some researchers in the field of intelligence have focused on the controversies over nature or nurture and group differences, others have debated whether intelligence is a general ability or a collection of separate abilities (e.g., Kovacs & Conway, 2019). Earlier we discussed the history of the concept of "g," an abbreviation for the general measure of intelligence—at least in terms of "academic smarts." In this section, we'll explore why many contemporary cognitive theorists believe we all possess different types of intelligence.

Gardner's and Sternberg's Theories
According to *Gardner's theory of multiple intelligences* (1983, 2008), people have several independent forms of intelligence and they are stronger in some areas than others (**Table 8.7**). They also use their intelligences differently to learn new material, perform tasks, and solve problems. Moreover, Gardner's research suggests that most people possess one or more natural intelligences important to success in various occupations. Carefully consider each of the multiple intelligences in Table 8.7 and how it might help guide you toward a satisfying career.

Triarchic theory of intelligence
Sternberg's theory that intelligence involves three forms: analytical, creative, and practical.

Robert Sternberg's **triarchic theory of intelligence** also assumes multiple abilities. As shown in **Table 8.8**, Sternberg believes there are three separate learned aspects of intelligence: (1) *analytical*, (2) *creative*, and (3) *practical* (Sternberg, 1985, 2015).

Sternberg emphasizes the process underlying thinking, rather than just the product. In addition, he stresses the importance of applying mental abilities to real-world situations, rather than testing mental abilities in isolation. In short, Sternberg avoids the traditional idea of intelligence as an innate form of "book smarts." Instead, he emphasizes successful intelligence as the learned ability to adapt to, shape, and select environments in order to accomplish personal and societal goals.

Critics have questioned whether being a great athlete or musician is a true form of intelligence or just a talent. What do you think? Obviously, there are many famous people, as well as members of your own family and friends, or even yourself, who may not be considered "academically smart," yet are very successful in their personal and/or professional lives. Can you see how this type of success matches the original, official definition of intelligence—the global capacity to think rationally, act purposefully, profit from experience, and deal effectively with

TABLE 8.7 **Gardner's Multiple Intelligences**

Type of Intelligence	Possible Careers
Linguistic Language, such as speaking, reading a book, or writing a story	Novelist, journalist, teacher
Spatial Mental maps, such as figuring out how to pack a variety of presents in a box or how to draw a floor plan	Engineer, architect, pilot
Bodily/kinesthetic Body movement, such as dancing, soccer, or football	Athlete, dancer, ski instructor
Intrapersonal Understanding oneself, such as setting achievable goals or recognizing self-defeating behaviors	Increased success in almost all careers
Logical/mathematical Problem solving or scientific analysis, such as following a logical proof or solving a mathematical problem	Mathematician, scientist, engineer
Musical Musical skills, such as singing or playing a musical instrument	Singer, musician, composer
Interpersonal Social skills, such as managing diverse groups of people	Salesperson, manager, therapist, teacher
Naturalistic Being attuned to nature, such as noticing seasonal patterns or using environmentally safe products	Biologist, naturalist
Spiritual/existential Attunement to the meaning of life and death and other conditions of life	Philosopher, theologian

NASA Photo/Alamy Stock Photo

samuiarzt/PHUCHONG CHOKSAMAI/123RF

chris piason/Shutterstock.com

Source: Adapted from Gardner, 1983, 2008.

TABLE 8.8 **Sternberg's Triarchic Theory of Successful Intelligence**

	Analytical Intelligence	Creative Intelligence	Practical Intelligence
Sample skills	Good at analysis, evaluation, judgment, and comparison skills	Good at invention, coping with novelty, and imagination skills	Good at application, implementation, execution, and utilization skills
Methods of assessment	Intelligence tests assess the meaning of words based on context and how to solve number-series problems	Open-ended tasks, writing a short story, creating a piece of art, solving a scientific problem requiring insight	Tasks requiring solutions to practical personal problems

the environment? The idea of multiple intelligences is important because it recognizes that individuals have unique capabilities and skills, that individuals can be intelligent in different ways, and that diversity strengthens us as a whole.

Artificial Intelligence (AI) and Emotional Intelligence (EI)

Artificial Intelligence (AI)

As you may know, scientists in the field of **artificial intelligence (AI)** have struggled for decades to create machines that can simulate human intelligence, thought processes, and performance. So far, they've successfully developed computers that can outperform humans on several complex information processing tasks, skills, and

Artificial intelligence (AI) The scientific field concerned with creating machines that can simulate human thought processes and performance.

Nancy Ney/DigitalVision/Getty Images

FIGURE 8.23 **How do we develop emotional intelligence?**
The mother in this photo appears to be empathizing with her young daughter and helping her to recognize and manage her own emotions. According to Goleman, this type of modeling and instruction is vital to the development of emotional intelligence.

Q **Test Your Critical Thinking**

1. Should preschools and elementary schools be required to teach children emotional intelligence? Why or why not?

2. What is the role of emotional intelligence in business? Should it be a factor in hiring and promotions? What might be the advantages and drawbacks if it were?

Emotional Intelligence (EI) The ability to perceive, understand, manage, and utilize emotions accurately and appropriately.

games—particularly those that require speed, perseverance, and a huge memory (Abeywardena et al., 2019; Jee, 2017; Vincent, 2019). In addition, they're uniquely valuable given that they never get tired, distracted, or take a break.

Science fiction novels and movies often portray AI as robots that serve as helpful companions to humans or as evil monsters trying to take over the world. In reality, this field offers great benefits to business, industry, health care, and our personal lives. Thanks to AI research, we have seen incredible advances, such as Google's *Deep Learning* and IBM's *Watson*, as well as personal assistants like Apple's *Siri*, Google's *Assistant,* and Microsoft's *Cortana*. Will AI someday match human cognition in flexibility, emotional capacity, and consciousness? Some have estimated that computers will soon surpass human brains. What do you think?

Emotional Intelligence (EI)
Have you ever wondered why some people who are very intelligent in terms of "book smarts" still experience frequent conflicts and repeated failures in their friendships and work situations? Daniel Goleman's research (1995, 2000, 2008) and best-selling books have popularized the concept of emotional intelligence, based on original work by Peter Salovey and John Mayer (1990). **Emotional intelligence (EI)** is generally defined as *the ability to perceive, understand, manage, and utilize emotions accurately and appropriately*. Proponents of EI have suggested that traditional measures of human intelligence ignore a crucial range of abilities that characterize people who are high in EI and tend to excel in real life: self-awareness, impulse control, persistence, zeal and self-motivation, empathy, and social deftness (Garg et al., 2016; O'Connor et al., 2019; Stein & Deonarine, 2015). These proponents have also said that parents can play an instrumental role in the development of EI, as shown in **Figure 8.23**. If you'd like a brief self-test of your own emotional intelligence, see the **Test Yourself**.

PA Practical Application

Test Yourself: Key Traits for Emotional Intelligence (EI)

Decide whether each statement is true or false.

_____ 1. Some of the major events of my life have led me to re-evaluate what is important and not important.

_____ 2. I can tell how other people are feeling just by looking at them.

_____ 3. I seek out activities that make me happy.

_____ 4. I am aware of my emotions as I experience them.

_____ 5. I am aware of the nonverbal messages I send to others.

_____ 6. I compliment others when they have done something well.

Scoring: Each of these items represents one or more of the traits of an emotionally intelligent person. A higher number of "True" responses indicates a higher level of overall EI.

Moviestore collection Ltd/Alamy Stock Photo

[AQ6] Surprisingly, research has even shown that people who watch televised dramas—such as *Mad Men* (see photo)—show greater increases in emotional intelligence than those who watch documentaries (Black & Barnes, 2015). This suggests that just viewing such dramas exposes us to different emotions, which increases our awareness of emotions. Recent research also finds that emotional intelligence may help buffer the effects of acute stress (Lea et al., 2019).

Although the idea of emotional intelligence is very appealing, critics caution that a handy term like EI invites misuse. Their strongest reaction is to Goleman's proposals for widespread teaching of EI (see the **STH** **Scientific Thinking Highlight**).

STH Scientific Thinking Highlight

Should We Teach EI in Schools?

(APA Goal 2.1) Use scientific reasoning to interpret psychological phenomena

Building on his contention that traditional measures of human intelligence ignore a crucial range of abilities that characterize people who excel in real life (self-awareness, impulse control, persistence, zeal, self-motivation, empathy, and social deftness), Goleman proposes that many societal problems, such as domestic abuse and youth violence, can be attributed to low EI. Therefore, he argues, EI should be fostered and taught to everyone. In line with this view, researchers in one study found that elementary schools in which emotional intelligence is taught show higher levels of warmth between students and teachers, more leadership among students, and a greater focus among teachers on students' interests and motivations (Rivers et al., 2013).

One of Goleman's critics, Paul McHugh, director of psychiatry at Johns Hopkins University, contends that Goleman is "presuming that someone has the key to the right emotions to be taught to children. We don't even know the right emotions to be taught to adults" (cited in Gibbs, 1995, p. 68). What do you think?

Q Test Your Scientific Thinking

As you may recall from Chapter 1, scientific thinking is an approach to information that combines a high degree of *skepticism* (questioning what "everybody knows") with *objectivity* (using empirical data to separate fantasy from reality) and *rationalism* (practicing logical reasoning). Using these three principles, consider the following questions:

1. **Skepticism**   Given Goleman's claims that many societal problems, like domestic abuse and youth violence, can

be attributed to low EI, were you predisposed to believe or discount the proposal that EI should be fostered and taught to everyone? Scientific thinkers approach ideas and proposals like these with deep skepticism.

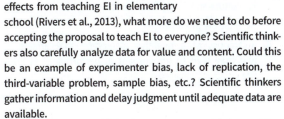

iStock.com/Michaeljung

2. **Objectivity**   Are the authors' assumptions supported by the data? Although the cited research study found positive effects from teaching EI in elementary school (Rivers et al., 2013), what more do we need to do before accepting the proposal to teach EI to everyone? Scientific thinkers also carefully analyze data for value and content. Could this be an example of experimenter bias, lack of replication, the third-variable problem, sample bias, etc.? Scientific thinkers gather information and delay judgment until adequate data are available.

3. **Rationalism**   Setting aside the limited data from other research, can we logically support putting more demands on teachers and students? Most American elementary schools are currently emphasizing STEM courses (science, technology, engineering, and math) and have eliminated or sharply decreased extracurricular activities like art and music. Should we spend the already limited class time teaching EI? Can you think of any other logical problems with and consequences of teaching EI to everyone?

(Compare your answers with those of fellow students, family, and friends. Doing so will improve your scientific thinking and your media savvy.)

Take-Home Message   In this chapter, we've explored three cognitive processes (*thinking, language*, and *intelligence*), each of which is greatly affected by numerous interacting factors. Solving problems, being creative, communicating with others, and adapting to our environment requires various mental abilities, most of which are not genetic and can be easily learned. Be sure to complete the final Retrieval Practice quiz, and then answer the critical thinking questions in the **Test Your Critical Thinking**.

Retrieval Practice 8.4 | Intelligence Controversies

Self-Test   Completing this self-test, and then checking your answers by clicking on the answer button or by looking in Appendix B, will provide immediate feedback and helpful practice for exams.

1. Does brain size matter?

    a. Yes; some animals, such as whales and dolphins, have larger brains than humans, but our brains are larger relative to our body size.

    b. Yes; brain-imaging studies have found a significant correlation between brain size (adjusted for body size) and intelligence.

    c. No; men have larger brains, relative to body size, but both sexes have similar IQs.

    d. Yes, all of these options are true.

2. Which of the following people would be most likely to have similar IQ test scores?

    a. identical twins raised apart

    b. identical twins raised together

    c. fraternal twins raised apart

    d. brothers and sisters from the same parents

3. By examining identical twins raised in different homes and reunited only as adults, _____ found that genetic factors appear to play a surprisingly large role in the IQ scores of identical twins.

   a. the Minnesota Study of Twins

   b. Lewis Terman's Termites research

   c. the Stanford-Binet Intelligence Studies

   d. David Wechsler's research

4. Howard Gardner proposed a theory of _____.

   a. language development

   b. fluid and crystallized intelligence

   c. culture specificity intelligence

   d. multiple intelligences

5. Awareness of a negative stereotype that affects oneself and may lead to impairment in performance is known as the _____.

a. Flynn effect

b. Obama effect

c. bell curve

d. stereotype threat

Q Test Your Critical Thinking

1. Do you believe IQ tests are biased against certain groups? Why or why not?

2. How would someone with exceptionally low or high emotional intelligence behave?

Real World Application Question

[AQ6] Will watching TV dramas increase your emotional intelligence?

Moviestore collection Ltd/ Alamy Stock Photo

Hint: Look in the text for **[AQ6]**

Q Test Your Critical Thinking

Did you notice or wonder why we provided six Real World Application Questions [AQ1–AQ6] throughout this chapter? We've found that they not only help you to engage with and master the material but also have an important and lasting impact on your critical thinking skills. For additional mastery and enrichment, consider the following questions:

1. Jerry Levy and Mark Newman, the two men shown in this photo, are identical twins who were separated at birth and first met as adults at a firefighter's convention. Research shows that IQ tends to be highly correlated for identical twins, but do you believe identical twins share a special connectedness? Why or why not?

2. Does the brothers' choosing the same uncommon profession seem like a case of special "twin telepathy"? How might *confirmation bias* contribute to the perception of twin telepathy?

3. Would you prefer to be high in emotional intelligence or high in musical intelligence? Why?

Thomas Wanstall/The Image Works

4. How might being bilingual or multilingual be more of an asset in business than having a high IQ?

5. Which of the barriers to problem solving described in this chapter are the biggest problems for you? How will you work to overcome them?

Summary

8.1 Thinking 239

- Thinking is a central aspect of **cognition**. Thought processes are distributed throughout the brain in neural networks. Mental images and concepts aid our thought processes. There are three major building blocks for concepts—**prototypes**, artificial concepts, and hierarchies.

- **Problem solving** usually has three steps: *preparation, production,* and *evaluation.* **Algorithms** are logical step-by-step procedures that eventually solve the problem. **Heuristics** are a cognitive strategy, or "rule of thumb," for problem solving.

- Barriers to problem solving include **mental set, functional fixedness,** the **availability heuristic,** the **representativeness heuristic, cognitive offloading,** and **confirmation bias.**

- **Creativity** is the ability to produce original, appropriate, and valued outcomes in a novel way. Creative thinking involves *originality, fluency,* and *flexibility.* Tests of creativity usually focus on **divergent thinking,** which involves generating as many alternatives or ideas as possible. In contrast, **convergent thinking**—or conventional thinking—works toward a single correct answer.

8.2   Language   249

- **Language** supports thinking and enables us to communicate. To produce language, we use **phonemes**, **morphemes**, and **grammar** (syntax and semantics). Several different parts of our brains are involved in producing and listening to language.

- According to Whorf's *linguistic relativity hypothesis*, language determines thought. Generally, this hypothesis is not supported, but it's clear that language does strongly influence thought.

- Children communicate non-verbally from birth. Their language development proceeds in stages: *prelinguistic*, which includes crying, cooing, and babbling, and *linguistic*, which includes single utterances, telegraphic speech, and acquisition of the basic rules of grammar.

- According to nativists like Chomsky, humans are "prewired" with a **language acquisition device (LAD)** that enables language development with minimal environmental input. Nurturists believe that children learn language through rewards, punishments, and imitation. Most psychologists hold an intermediate, interactionist view.

- Research with chimpanzees, gorillas, and dolphins suggests that these animals can learn and use basic rules of language. However, critics suggest that non-human animal language is less complex, less creative, and not as rule laden as human language.

8.3   Intelligence   256

- There is considerable debate over the meaning of **intelligence**. But it's commonly defined by psychologists as the global capacity to think rationally, act purposefully, profit from experience, and deal effectively with the environment.

- Spearman proposed that intelligence is a single factor, which he termed **general intelligence (*g*)**. Thurstone and Guilford argued that intelligence includes numerous distinct abilities. Cattell proposed two subtypes of *g*: **fluid intelligence (*gf*)** and **crystallized intelligence (*gc*)**.

- Early intelligence tests computed a person's **mental age (MA)** to arrive at an **intelligence quotient (IQ)**. Today, two of the most widely used intelligence tests are the *Stanford-Binet Intelligence Scale* and the *Wechsler Adult Intelligence Scale (WAIS)*. Intelligence tests commonly compare the performance of an individual with that of other individuals of the same age. The distribution of test scores is typically a **normal distribution**, represented by a symmetrical bell-shaped curve.

- To be scientifically acceptable, all psychological tests must fulfill three basic requirements: **standardization**, **reliability**, and **validity**.

- Intelligence tests provide one of the major criteria for assessing **intellectual disability** and **mental giftedness**, both of which exist on a continuum. Studies of people who are intellectually gifted found that they had more intellectual opportunities and tended to excel professionally. However, a high IQ does not guarantee success in every endeavor.

8.4   Intelligence Controversies   261

- Most research suggests that nature and nurture are interacting influences on intelligence. Research on the biology of intelligence has focused on brain functioning, not size, and it indicates that intelligent people's brains respond especially quickly and efficiently.

- Studies of group differences and how gender and ethnicity affect IQ suggest that heredity and the environment are always interacting, inseparable factors.

- Rather than being a single factor, many contemporary cognitive theorists, including Gardner and Sternberg, believe that intelligence is a collection of many separate specific abilities. Goleman believes that **emotional intelligence (EI)**, the ability to empathize and manage our emotions and relationships, is just as important as any other kind of intelligence.

- The field of **artificial intelligence (AI)** has created machines that can, to some degree, simulate human intelligence, thought processes, and performance.

Key Terms

Retrieval Practice   Write your own definition for each term before turning back to the referenced page to check your answer.

Solutions

Fun with mental images (Figure 8.1) solution

To solve this problem, mentally rotate one of the objects and then compare the rotated image with the other object to see whether they matched or not. The figures in (b) are more difficult to solve because they require a greater degree of mental rotation. This also is true of real objects in physical space. It takes more time and energy to turn a cup 150 degrees to the right, than to turn it 20 degrees.

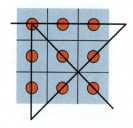

Nine-dot problem (Figure 8.4) solution

Many people find this puzzle difficult because they see the arrangement of dots as a square—a mental set that limits possible solutions.

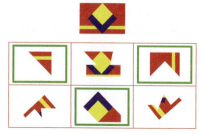

Two-strings problem (Figure 8.5—Test your functional fixedness) solution

To overcome functional fixedness, you need to recognize that the pliers can be used as a weight for a pendulum. You can tie it to one of the strings and then push it away toward the other string. While holding onto the "non-plier" string, wait for the first one to move toward you. If necessary, you can climb on the chair to better reach the second string.

Coin problem (Test Yourself—Are you creative?) solution

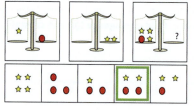

Move this coin to the other row.

Stack this coin on top of the middle coin so that it is in both rows.

Items similar to those on the Wechsler Adult Intelligence Scale (Figure 8.14) solution

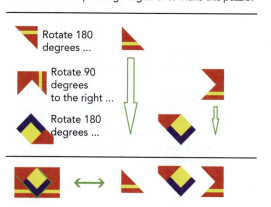

a. "Which three pieces go together to make this puzzle?"

Rotate 180 degrees ...

Rotate 90 degrees to the right ...

Rotate 180 degrees ...

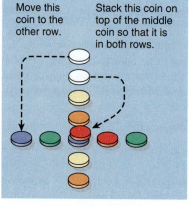

b. "Which one of these works to balance the scale?"

From the middle image, we deduce an empty scale would be out of balance, since we need two stars added to the right just to be in balance.

From the first image, since we know that the scale is two stars heavy on the left, if adding one star to the already heavier left side balances with one ball, a ball must equal three stars.

☆ ☆ ☆ = ●

The final image shows three stars and one ball on the left. To balance on the right, we match what is shown on the left AND ADD two stars since we know the scale, by itself, is two stars heavy on the left.

Therefore we need one ball and five stars to balance. But that is NOT one of the answers. But we know one ball equals three stars. Looking at the possible answers, we see that two stars and two balls (1+1+3+3=8 stars) is the same as one ball and five stars (3+1+1+1+1+1=8 stars)—and that is the answer.

CHAPTER 9

Kuttelvaserova Stuchelova/Shutterstock.com

Life Span Development

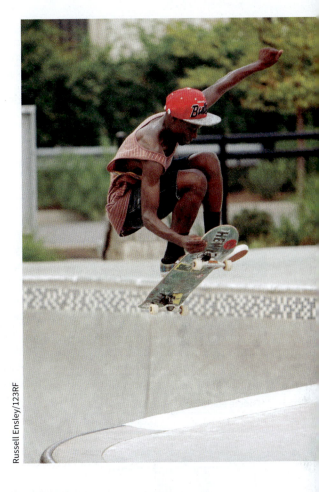

Russell Ensley/123RF

Real World Application Questions [AQ]

Things you'll learn in Chapter 9

[AQ1] Why are young people more supportive of gay marriage?

[AQ2] Can parents' early emotional trauma be passed on to their unborn children?

[AQ3] How is the teenage brain different from that of an adult?

[AQ4] Do babies learn faster when they're sitting up versus lying down?

[AQ5] Does the taking and posting of self-portraits ("selfies") increase narcissism?

[AQ6] Can foreign travel lead to moral flexibility and immoral behaviors?

Throughout the chapter, look for the AQ1–AQ6 icons. They indicate where the text addresses these questions.

CHAPTER OUTLINE

9.1 Studying Development

LEARNING OBJECTIVES

Retrieval Practice While reading the upcoming sections, respond to each learning objective in your own words.

Review developmental psychology's theoretical issues and key research approaches.

• **Define** developmental psychology.

• **Discuss** the three key theoretical issues in developmental psychology.

• **Contrast** the cross-sectional research design with the longitudinal research design.

• **Discuss** cultural psychology's four research guidelines.

Real World Application Question

[AQ1] Why are young people more supportive of gay marriage?

TABLE 9.1	Life Span Development
Stage	**Approximate Age**
Prenatal	Conception to birth
Infancy	Birth to 18 months
Early childhood	18 months to 6 years
Middle childhood	6 to 12 years
Adolescence	12 to 20 years
Young adulthood	20 to 45 years
Middle adulthood	45 to 60 years
Late adulthood	60 years to death

Are you one of the lucky individuals who grew up with loving parents who documented every stage of your development with photos, videos, and journals—starting with your birth, first smile, first day of school, and all the way to your high school graduation? Just as some parents carefully document their child's progress throughout his or her life, the field of **developmental psychology** studies age-related behavior and mental processes—from conception to death, or "womb to tomb" (**Table 9.1**).

As you might expect, studying development across the entire life span is a monumental task, so we've organized this chapter into three major sections—*physical*, *cognitive*, and *social-emotional development*. Before we begin, we need to briefly examine the research issues and methods psychologists use to study development. These studies have led to three key theoretical issues.

Theoretical Issues

Almost every area of research in human development frames questions around three major issues:

1. **Nature or nurture** (see cartoon)? This is one of the oldest philosophical debates in psychology. Even today, the so-called *naturists* believe that our genes and other hereditary factors have the greatest influence on development, whereas the *nurturists* suggest that learning and other influences from the environment are most important. Given that the nature position is the least understood, let's focus on it. According to the *nature position*, development is largely governed by automatic, genetically predetermined signals in a process known as *maturation*. Just as a flower unfolds in accord with its genetic blueprint, humans crawl before we walk, and walk before we run. In addition, naturists believe there are **critical periods**, or windows of opportunity, that occur early in life when exposure to certain stimuli or experiences is necessary for proper development. For example, many newborn animals, and theoretically humans, form rigid attachments to particular stimuli shortly after birth, a process called **imprinting**.

Human children may also have critical periods for normal development. When doctors operate on infants who are born with *cataracts*, a condition in which the eye's lens is cloudy and distorts vision, they're able to see much better than if they're operated on after the age of 8. In addition, research has shown that appropriate social interaction with adults in the first few weeks of life is essential for creating normal cognitive, mental, and social development (Chopik & Edelstein, 2019; Harker et al., 2016; Nelson et al., 2019). These and other similar studies provide suggestive evidence for critical periods in human development—at least in the early years (see the **RC** **Research Challenge**).

2. **Stages or continuity?** Some developmental psychologists suggest that development generally occurs in *stages* that are discrete and qualitatively different from one another,

Philip Berkin/Cartoon Stock

"Trevor was rasied in the wild by sloths."

Developmental psychology The study of age-related behavior and mental processes from conception to death.

Critical period A specific time during which an organism must experience certain stimuli in order to develop properly in the future.

Imprinting The process by which attachments are formed during critical periods in early life.

| **RC**   **Scientific Thinking: Research Challenge** |

Deprivation and Development

(APA Goal 2.4) Interpret, design, and conduct basic psychological research

What happens if a child is deprived of appropriate stimulation during a critical period of development? Consider the story of Genie, the so-called "wild child." From the time she was 20 months old until authorities rescued her at age 13, Genie was locked alone in a tiny, windowless room. By day, she sat naked and tied to a child's toilet with nothing to do and no one to talk to. At night, she was immobilized in a kind of straitjacket and "caged" in a covered crib. Genie's abusive father forbade anyone to speak to her for those 13 years. If Genie made noise, her father beat her while he barked and growled like a dog.

Genie's tale is a heartbreaking account of the lasting scars from a disastrous childhood. In the years after her rescue, Genie spent thousands of hours receiving special training, and by age 19 she could use public transportation and was adapting well to special classes at school. Genie was far from normal, however. Her intelligence scores were still close to the cutoff for intellectual disability. Sadly, although linguists and psychologists worked with her for many years, she was never able to master grammatical structure, and was limited to sentences like "Genie go" (Rymer, 1993).

These findings suggest that due to her extreme childhood isolation and abuse, Genie, like other seriously neglected or environmentally isolated children, missed a necessary critical period for language development (Curtiss, 1977; Raaska et al., 2013; Sylvestre & Mérette, 2010). To make

AP Images

matters worse, she was also subjected to a series of foster home placements, some of which were emotionally and physically abusive. According to the latest information, Genie now lives in a privately run facility for adults who are mentally underdeveloped (James, 2008).

Identify the Research Method

1. Based on the information provided, did this study (Rymer, 1993) use descriptive, correlational, and/or experimental research?

2. If you chose:

   o *descriptive research*, is this a naturalistic or laboratory observation, survey/interview, case study, and/or archival research?

   o *correlational research*, is this a positive, negative, or zero correlation?

   o *experimental research*, label the IV, DV, experimental group(s), and control group. (**Note:** If participants were not randomly assigned to groups, list the design as *quasi-experimental.*)

   o both *descriptive* and *correlational*, answer the corresponding questions for both.

Check your answers by clicking on the answer button or by looking in Appendix B.

Note: The information provided in this study is admittedly limited, but the level of detail is similar to what is presented in most textbooks and public reports of research findings. Answering these questions, and then comparing your answers to those provided, will help you become a better scientific and critical thinker and consumer of scientific research.

---

whereas others believe it follows a *continuous pattern*, with gradual, but steady and quantitative (measurable) changes (**Figure 9.1**).

3. **Stability or change?** Which of our traits are stable and present throughout our life span, and what aspects will change? Psychologists who emphasize *stability* hold that measurements of personality taken during childhood are important predictors of adult personality; those who emphasize *change* disagree.

Which of these positions is most correct? Psychologists generally do not take a hard line either way. Rather, they prefer an interactionist perspective or the biopsychosocial model. For instance, in the nature-versus-nurture debate, psychologists agree that development emerges from unique genetic predispositions *and* environmental experiences (Barlow, 2019; Gallagher & Jones, 2016; Wedow et al., 2018).

FIGURE 9.1 **Stages versus continuity in development**   There is an ongoing debate about whether development is better characterized by discrete stages or by gradual, continuous development.

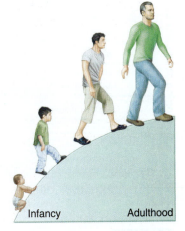

a. Stage theorists think development results from discrete, qualitative changes.

b. Continuity theorists believe development results from gradual, quantitative (incremental) changes.

CROSS-SECTIONAL RESEARCH

Different participants of various ages are compared at one point in time to determine age-related *differences*

Group One
20-year-old participants

Group Two
40-year-old participants

Group Three
60-year-old participants

Research done in 2020

Advantages	Disadvantages
• Provides information about age differences • Quick and less expensive • Typically larger sample	• Cohort effects difficult to separate • Restricted generalizability (measures behaviors and mental processes at only one point in time)

LONGITUDINAL RESEARCH

The **same** participants are studied at various ages to determine age-related *changes*

Study One
Participants are 20 years old

Research done in 2020

Study Two
Same participants are now 40 years old

Research done in 2040

Study Three
Same participants are now 60 years old

Research done in 2060

Advantages	Disadvantages
• Provides information about age changes • Increased confidence in results • More in-depth information per participant	• More expensive and time consuming • Restricted generalizability (typically smaller sample due to participant dropouts over time)

FIGURE 9.2 **Cross-sectional versus longitudinal research** To study development, psychologists may use a cross-sectional research design, a longitudinal research design, or both.

Research Approaches

Cross-sectional design In developmental psychology, a research technique that measures individuals of various ages at one point in time and provides information about age differences.

Longitudinal design In developmental psychology, a research design that measures individuals over an extended period and gives information about age changes.

To answer these three controversies and other questions, developmental psychologists typically use all the research methods discussed in Chapter 1. However, to study the entire human life span, they also need two additional techniques—*cross-sectional* and *longitudinal* (**Figure 9.2**).

The **cross-sectional design** measures individuals of various ages at a single point in time to provide information about age differences. For example, one cross-sectional study of U.S. adults conducted by the Pew Research Center (2019) found significant differences between various age groups in their reported use of the *Instagram* social media platform. In 2019, 75 percent of those between the ages of 18–24 used this platform, compared to 57 percent of those ages 25–29, and 8 percent of those over age 65.

In contrast, a **longitudinal design** takes repeated measures of one person or a group of same-aged people over a long period of time to see how the individual or the group changes over time. One group of developmental researchers wondered if peer ratings of personality taken during childhood might be better predictors of later adult personality than self-ratings (Martin-Storey et al., 2012). To explore this question, they designed a longitudinal study that began when they first asked grade school children in 1976–1978 to rate themselves and their peers on several personality factors, such as likeability, aggression, and social withdrawal. In 1999–2003, the researchers returned and asked the same participants, now in mid-adulthood, to complete a second series of personality tests. As hypothesized, the peer ratings were better than self-ratings in predicting adult personality. Does this finding surprise you? If so, try contacting some of your childhood peers and then compare notes on how you remember one another's personality as children and now as adults.

Now that you have a better idea of these two types of research, if you were a developmental psychologist interested in studying intelligence in adults, which design would you choose—cross-sectional or longitudinal? Before you decide, note the different research results shown in **Figure 9.3**.

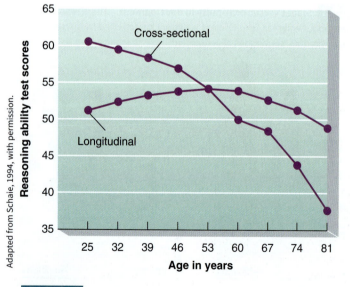

Adapted from Schaie, 1994, with permission.

FIGURE 9.3 **Which results are true?** Cross-sectional studies have shown that reasoning and intelligence reach their peak in early adulthood and then gradually decline. In contrast, longitudinal studies have found that a marked decline does not begin until about age 60.

Why do the two methods show such different results? Cross-sectional studies sometimes confuse genuine age differences with *cohort effects*—differences that result from specific histories of the age group studied. As shown in the top line in Figure 9.3, the 81-year-olds measured by the cross-sectional design have dramatically lower scores than the 25-year-olds. But is this due to aging, or perhaps to broad environmental differences, such as less formal education or poorer nutrition?

[AQ1]   A prime example of possible environmental effects on cross-sectional studies was found in research on attitudes towards gay marriage, which revealed that young people are much more in favor of gay marriage than older adults (Pew Research Center, 2016). So, does this mean that people grow more opposed to gay marriage as they age? Probably not. These differences are most likely a reflection of cohort and generational effects. Young people today are generally more liberal and positive toward different sexual orientations, and therefore more likely to support gay marriage (see photo).

The key thing to remember is that the different age groups, called *cohorts*, grew up in different historical periods. Therefore, the results may not apply to people growing up at other times. With the cross-sectional design, age effects and cohort effects are sometimes inextricably tangled. (As a scientific and critical thinker, can you see how *cohort effects* are a unique research problem for cross-cultural studies, just as the *third-variable problem* poses a unique threat to correlational studies—discussed in Chapter 1?)

Longitudinal studies have their own share of limits and disadvantages. They are expensive in terms of time and money, and it is difficult for us to generalize their results. Given that participants often drop out or move away during the extended test period, the experimenter may end up with a self-selected sample that differs from the general population in important ways. Each method of research has strengths and weaknesses (as you recall from the right side of Figure 9.2). Keep these differences in mind when you read the findings of developmental research.

Combining Cross-Sectional and Longitudinal Design   Before we go on, it's important to point out that modern researchers sometimes combine both cross-sectional and longitudinal designs into one study. For example, when researchers examined both cross-sectional and longitudinal data from two independent samples taken over 30 years, they initially found that well-being *declined* with age. However, when they then controlled for the fact that older cohorts started out with lower levels of well-being, they found that well-being among all cohorts *increased* rather than decreased with age (Sutin et al., 2013). They suggested that the reversal in findings was likely due to the fact that the older group of people had experienced instances of major turmoil in their younger years, including America's Great Depression during the 1930s. This means that this group started out with lower levels of well-being—yet their levels still increased over time.

Why is this combination of two research designs important? It offers a more accurate and reliable view of well-being in old age than what was indicated in either the cross-sectional design or the longitudinal design. It also suggests some troubling possibilities for today's young adults. As the study's authors say, "economic turmoil may impede [their] psychological, as well as financial, growth even decades after times get better" (Sutin et al., 2013, p. 384). If you're a young adult in today's stagnant and uncertain economy, you may be comforted by other research findings that individuals who enter their teens and early 20s during a recession are less narcissistic than those who come of age in more prosperous times (Bianchi, 2014, 2015). In fact, CEOs who were in their teens and early 20s during bad economic times later paid themselves less compared to other top executives.

The **PAH** Practical Application Highlight later in this chapter offers additional positive findings for all ages, and the following **GCD** **Gender and Cultural Diversity** offers intriguing insights on how culture may affect human development.

GCD Gender and Cultural Diversity

Should Diversity Affect Research?

(APA Goal 2.5) Incorporate sociocultural factors in scientific inquiry

How would you answer the following question: "If you wanted to predict how a human child anywhere in the world was going to grow up—what his or her behavior was going to be like as an adult—and you could have only one fact about that child, what fact would you choose to have?" According to cultural psychologists, the answer to this question should be "culture" (**Figure 9.4**).

Developmental psychology has traditionally studied people (children, adolescents, and adults) with little attention given to the sociocultural context. In recent times, however, psychologists are paying increasing attention to the following points:

FIGURE 9.4 **Cultural influences on development** As you're reading this chapter, ask yourself how culture might affect the life span development of these two groups of adolescents.

- **Culture may be the major determinant of development.** If a child grows up in an individualistic/independent culture (such as those of the United States, Canada, and most countries in Western Europe), we can predict that this child will probably be competitive and question authority as an adult. Were this same child reared in a collectivist/interdependent culture (common in Africa, Asia, and Latin America), she or he would most likely grow up to be cooperative and respectful of elders (Berry et al., 2011; Greenfield, 2012; Manago & Greenfield, 2011).

- **Human development cannot be studied outside its sociocultural context.** In parts of Korea, most teenagers see a strict, authoritarian style of parenting as a sign of love and concern (Kim & Choi, 1995). Korean American and Korean Canadian teenagers, however, see the same behavior as a sign of rejection. Thus, rather than studying any general response to "authoritarian parenting styles," discussed later in this chapter, researchers in child development prefer to study children only within their *developmental niche* (Hewlett & Roulette, 2014; Narvaez et al., 2019). A developmental niche has three components: the physical and social contexts in which the child lives, the rearing and educational practices of the child's culture, and the psychological characteristics of the caretakers (Bugental & Johnston, 2000; Harkness et al., 2007).

- **Each culture's ethnotheories are key determinants of behavior.** Within every culture, people have a prevailing set of ideas and beliefs that attempt to explain the world around them (an *ethnotheory*) (Kartner et al., 2013; Srivastava et al., 2019). In the area of child development, for example, cultures have specific ethnotheories about how children should be trained. As a scientific and critical thinker, you can anticipate that differing ethnotheories can lead to problems between cultures. In fact, the very idea of "critical thinking" is part of our North American ethnotheory regarding education, and it, too, can produce culture clashes. Concha Delgado-Gaitan (1994) found that Mexican immigrants from a rural background have a difficult time adjusting to U.S. schools, which teach children to question authority and think for themselves. In their culture of origin, these children are trained to respect their elders, be good listeners, and participate in conversation only when their opinion is solicited. Children who argue with adults are reminded not to be *malcriados* (naughty or disrespectful).

- **Culture is largely invisible to its participants.** Culture consists of ideals, values, and assumptions that are widely shared among a given group and that guide specific behaviors (Hamedani & Markus, 2019; Lamm, 2015; Ratner, 2011). Precisely because these ideals and values are widely shared, they are seldom discussed or directly examined. We take our culture for granted and operate within it almost automatically. In short, most cultural influences are largely invisible—yet they still have a big impact on our behaviors. See the following **Test Yourself**.

PA Practical Application

Test Yourself: Culture Invisibility

If you'd like a personal demonstration of the invisibility of culture and its prescribed norms for proper behavior, try this simple experiment: The next time you walk into an elevator, don't turn around. Remain facing the rear or even toward a side wall, and then watch how others respond when you don't turn around. Think about all the invisible rules we've learned for the "right way" to ride in an elevator (see photo). Although there is some logic to turning around to face the elevator doors, how would you react if you were alone on the elevator and a new passenger entered and stood right next to you,

rather than going to the other side of the elevator? Every culture has thousands of rules that prescribe the "proper" behavior for not only riding elevators, but also for greeting strangers versus family, the proper eating utensils to use for various foods, and so on. As you'll learn if you

try this elevator "experiment," people become very uncomfortable when those invisible rules are violated.

Retrieval Practice 9.1 | Studying Development

Self-Test   Completing this self-test, and then checking your answers by clicking on the answer button or by looking in Appendix B, will provide immediate feedback and helpful practice for exams.

1. _____ studies age-related changes in behavior and mental processes from conception to death.
   a. Thanatology
   b. Teratogenology
   c. Human development
   d. Developmental psychology

2. _____ is governed by automatic, genetically predetermined signals.
   a. The cohort effect   c. Thanatology
   b. Secondary aging   d. Maturation

3. A specific time during which an organism must experience certain stimuli in order to develop properly in the future is known as _____ .
   a. the cohort years   c. the thanatology phase
   b. a critical period   d. maturation

4. What three major questions are studied in developmental psychology?
   a. nature versus nurture, stages versus continuity, and stability versus change
   b. nature versus nurture, "chunking" versus continuity, and instability versus change

   c. nature versus nurture, stages versus continuity, and stagnation versus instability
   d. none of these options

5. _____ studies are the most time-efficient method, whereas _____ studies provide the most in-depth information per participant.
   a. Latitudinal; longitudinal
   b. Neogerontology; longitudinal
   c. Cross-sectional; longitudinal
   d. Class-racial; longitudinal

Q Test Your Critical Thinking

1. Which of the three important debates or questions in developmental psychology do you find most valuable? Why?

2. Based on what you have learned about critical periods, can you think of a circumstance in your own development, or that of one of your friends, when a critical period might have been disrupted or lost?

Real World Application Question

[AQ1]   Why are young people more supportive of gay marriage?

SoumenNath/iStock Unreleased/Getty Images

Hint: Look in the text for [AQ1]

9.2 Physical Development

LEARNING OBJECTIVES

Retrieval Practice   While reading the upcoming sections, respond to each Learning Objective in your own words.

Summarize the major physical changes that occur throughout our life span.

- **Discuss** how genetic material passes from one generation to the next.
- **Identify** the three phases of prenatal physical development.

- **Summarize** physical development during early childhood.
- **Describe** the physical changes that occur during adolescence and adulthood.

Real World Application Questions

[AQ2]   Can parents' early emotional trauma be passed on to their unborn children?

[AQ3]   How is the teenage brain different from that of an adult?

After studying the photos of your two authors as they've aged over the life span (**Figure 9.5**), or after reviewing your own similar photos, you may be amused and surprised by all the dramatic changes in physical appearance. But have you stopped to appreciate the incredible underlying process that transforms all of us from birth to death? In this section, we will explore the fascinating processes of physical development from conception through childhood, adolescence, and adulthood.

Courtesy of Catherine Sanderson

Courtesy of Karen Huffman

FIGURE 9.5 **Changes in physical development over the life span** As this series of photos of your two textbook authors shows, physical changes occur throughout our lives. Our cognitive, social, and emotional processes, as well as our personalities, also are continually changing, but the changes aren't as visible. (The top row is Catherine Sanderson at ages 1, 5, 10, 30. The bottom row is Karen Huffman at ages 1, 10, 30 and 60.)

Chromosome A thread-like molecule of DNA (deoxyribonucleic acid) that carries genetic information.

DNA The main constituent of chromosomes found in all living organisms, which transmits hereditary characteristics from parents to children; short for *deoxyribonucleic acid*.

Gene A segment of DNA (deoxyribonucleic acid) that occupies a specific place on a particular chromosome, and carries the code for hereditary transmission.

Behavioral genetics The study of the relative effects of heredity and the environment on behavior and mental processes.

Epigenetics The study of how non-genetic factors, such as age, environment, lifestyle, or disease, affect how (and if) genes are expressed.

Prenatal Development

At the moment of your conception, your biological mother and father each contributed 23 **chromosomes**, which are thread-like, linear strands of **DNA** (deoxyribonucleic acid) encoded with their **genes** (**Figure 9.6**). Interestingly, DNA of all humans (except identical twins) has unique, distinguishing features, much like the details on our fingerprints. This uniqueness is commonly used in forensics to exclude or identify criminal suspects. In addition, DNA analysis is often used for genetic testing during prenatal development to identify existing or potential future disorders.

Note that *genes* are the basic building blocks of our entire biological inheritance. Each of our human characteristics and behaviors is related to the presence or absence of particular genes that control the transmission of traits. In some traits, such as blood type, a single pair of genes (one from each parent) determines what characteristics we will possess. When two genes for a given trait conflict, the outcome depends on whether the gene is *dominant* or *recessive*. A dominant gene reveals its trait whenever the gene is present. In contrast, the gene for a recessive trait is normally expressed only if the other gene in the pair is also recessive.

Unfortunately, there are numerous myths and misconceptions about traits supposedly genetically *determined* by dominant genes. For example, we once assumed that characteristics such as eye color, hair color, and height were the result of either one dominant gene or two paired recessive genes. But modern geneticists now believe that these characteristics are *polygenic*, meaning they are controlled by multiple genes. One of the major goals of the new field of **behavioral genetics**, which studies the interplay of heredity and the environment, is to identify and study these polygenic traits.

Another new and related field of research, known as **epigenetics**, studies how non-genetic factors can dramatically affect how (and if) inherited genes are expressed throughout our lives (Brody et

FIGURE 9.6 **Conception and your hereditary code**

Francis Leroy/Science Source

Thierry Berrod, Mona Lisa Production/Science Source

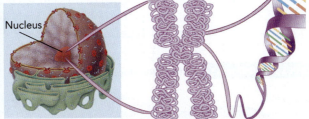

Nucleus

a. Before conception
Millions of sperm are released when a man ejaculates into a woman's vagina, but only a few hundred sperm survive the arduous trip up to the egg.

b. During conception
Although a joint effort is required to break through the outer coating, only one sperm will actually fertilize the egg. At the moment of conception, a father's sperm and a mother's egg each contribute 23 chromosomes, for a total of 46.

c. Cell nucleus
Each cell in the human body (except red blood cells) contains a nucleus.

d. Chromosomes
Each cell nucleus contains 46 chromosomes, which are thread-like molecules of DNA (deoxyribonucleic acid).

e. DNA and genes
Each DNA molecule contains thousands of genes, which are the most basic units of heredity.

al., 2016; Cortes et al., 2019; Wallack & Thornburg, 2016). Unlike simple genetic transmission, which is based on changes in the DNA sequence, changes in gene expression can result from other factors, such as age, environment, lifestyle, or disease. (The term "epi" means "above" or "outside of.")

In other words, nurture can shape nature. Epigenetic factors can switch genes "On" or "Off." For example, abuse or even malnutrition suffered by the mother as a child or during her pregnancy can lead to her children failing to reach their full potential genetic height or maximum genetic intelligence, and even predispose her children to obesity and metabolic disorders, such as Type 2 diabetes, in adulthood (Li, 2018; Vaiserman & Lushchak, 2019; Venables & Raine, 2016).

TIP Are you confused by the term *epigenetics?* If so, try picturing genetics as this text (either print or digital format) and epigenetics as you, the reader. Like traditional genetic inheritance, once this text is published, the information is "hard wired" and will be passed along to all readers in the same fashion. But how this information is later interpreted will vary depending on you and all other readers—some might leave their mark using highlighters to color certain passages, whereas others might take notes on their laptops. The important thing to remember is that epigenetic factors in human development, like pollution and a poor diet, can affect all of us throughout our life span.

Three Stages of Prenatal Development
Now that we've discussed the general principles of how our genes and our environment interact to form us as unique individuals, let's go back to the moment of your conception. At that point in time, you were a single cell barely 1/175 of an inch in diameter—smaller than the period at the end of this sentence. This new cell, called a *zygote*, then began a process of rapid cell division that resulted in a multimillion-celled infant (you) some 9 months later.

The vast changes that occur during the 9 months of a full-term pregnancy are usually divided into three stages: the **germinal period**, **embryonic period**, and **fetal period** (**Process Diagram 9.1**). Prenatal growth and growth during the first few years after birth are both *proximodistal* (near to far), which means that the innermost parts of the body develop before the outermost parts. Thus, a fetus's arms develop before its hands and fingers. Development at this stage also proceeds *cephalocaudally* (head to tail)—a fetus's head is disproportionately large compared with the lower part of its body. Can you see how these two terms—"proximodistal" and "cephalocaudal"—help explain why infants can lift their head before they can lift their arms and lift their arms before lifting their legs?

Hazards to Prenatal Development
As you recall, human development begins with the genes we inherit from our biological parents, and epigenetic factors like age, lifestyle, and diseases can dramatically affect how (and if) these inherited genes are expressed. For example, during pregnancy the *placenta* connects the fetus to the mother's uterus and serves as the link for delivery of food and elimination of wastes. Moreover, it screens out some, but not all, harmful substances. As you can see in **Table 9.2**, environmental hazards such as X-rays, toxic waste, drugs, and diseases can still cross the placental barrier and have an *epigenetic effect*—meaning

Germinal period The first stage of prenatal development, beginning with ovulation and followed by conception and implantation in the uterus; the first 2 weeks of pregnancy.

Embryonic period The second stage of prenatal development, which begins after uterine implantation and lasts through the eighth week.

Fetal period The third, and final, stage of prenatal development (8 weeks to birth).

> **STOP!** This Process Diagram contains essential information NOT found elsewhere in the text, which is likely to appear on quizzes and exams. Be sure to study it CAREFULLY.

PROCESS DIAGRAM 9.1 **Prenatal Development**

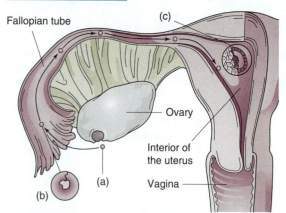

Fallopian tube

(c)

Ovary

Interior of the uterus

(a)

(b)

Vagina

1 **Germinal period: from conception to implantation**
After discharge from either the left or right ovary (a), the ovum travels to the opening of the fallopian tube.

If fertilization occurs (b), it normally takes place in the first third of the fallopian tube. The fertilized ovum is referred to as a zygote.

When the zygote reaches the uterus, it implants itself in the wall of the uterus (c) and begins to grow tendril-like structures that intertwine with the rich supply of blood vessels located there. After implantation, the organism is known as an embryo.

Nestle/Petit Format/Science Source

3 **Fetal period: from eight weeks to birth** After the eighth week, and until the moment of birth, the embryo is called a fetus. At 4 months, all the actual body parts and organs are established. The fetal stage is primarily a time for increased growth and "fine detailing."

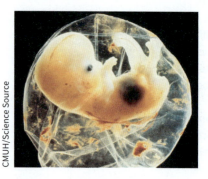

CMUH/Science Source

2 **Embryonic period: from implantation to eight weeks**
At 8 weeks, the major organ systems have become well differentiated. Note that at this stage, the head grows at a faster rate than other parts of the body.

TABLE 9.2 **Sample Prenatal Environmental Conditions That Endanger a Child**

Maternal Factors	Possible Effects on Embryo, Fetus, Newborn, or Young Child	
Malnutrition	Low birth weight, malformations, less developed brain, greater vulnerability to disease	
Exposure to: Environmental toxins, X-rays, excessive stress	Low birth weight, malformations, cancer, hyperactivity, irritability, feeding difficulties	
Legal and illegal drugs: Certain prescription drugs, alcohol, nicotine, cocaine, methamphetamine	Inhibition of bone growth, hearing loss, low birth weight, fetal alcohol spectrum disorders (FASD), intellectual disability, attention deficits in childhood, death	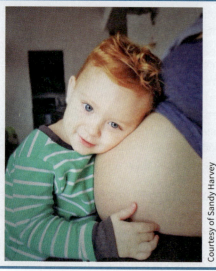
Diseases: Heart and thyroid disease, diabetes, asthma, infectious diseases	Blindness, deafness, intellectual disability, heart and other malformations, brain infection, spontaneous abortion, premature birth, low birth weight, death	

Courtesy of Sandy Harvey

Sources: Centers for Disease Control and Prevention, 2016; Ehrhart et al., 2019; Gupta et al., 2019; Karakochuk et al., 2017; Maisto et al., 2019.

they leave a chemical mark on the DNA that abnormally switches the fetus's genes on or off. These influences generally have the most devastating effects during the first 3 months of pregnancy, making this a *critical period* in development.

Perhaps the most important—and generally avoidable—danger to a fetus comes from drugs, both legal and illegal. Nicotine and alcohol are major **teratogens**, environmental agents that may lead to severe damage and even death during prenatal development. Mothers who smoke tobacco or drink alcohol during pregnancy have significantly higher rates of premature births, low-birth-weight infants, and fetal deaths. Their children also show increased behavior and cognitive problems (Denny et al., 2019; Roozen et al., 2016).

As you can see in **Figure 9.7**, heavy maternal drinking may lead to a cluster of serious abnormalities called *fetal alcohol spectrum disorders (FASD)*. The most severe form of this disorder is known as *fetal alcohol syndrome (FAS)*. Recent research suggests that alcohol may leave chemical marks on DNA that abnormally turn off or on specific genes (Ehrhart et al., 2019; Mason & Zhou, 2015). Tobacco might have a similar epigenetic effect.

For example, children whose mothers smoked during pregnancy are more likely to be obese as adolescents, perhaps because *in utero* exposure to nicotine changes a part of the brain that increases a preference for fatty foods (Gupta et al., 2019; Haghighi et al., 2013, 2014). In addition, mothers who are stressed during their pregnancy are more likely to have daughters who exhibit more anxious behaviors as toddlers (Graham et al., 2019). However, the sons of stressed moms did not show the same anxious behaviors, which researchers suggest might help explain why women are more likely to develop mood disorders. On a more positive note, research has also shown that pregnancy leads to long-lasting alterations in the mother's brain structure, which is believed to improve her ability to protect and interact with her child (Hoekzema et al., 2016).

The pregnant mother obviously plays a primary role in prenatal development given that her nutrition, her health, and almost everything she ingests can cross the placental barrier (a better term might be placental sieve). However, the father also plays a role. Both the father's and mother's tobacco smoking can pollute the air the mother breathes—making pollution an epigenetic environmental factor (e.g., Sharma, 2017; Wu et al., 2019).

[AQ2]   Sadly, through epigenetic factors, parents may even pass on to their offspring (see photo) the effects of their personal early life emotional trauma (A. Curry, 2019; DeAngelis, 2019; Lehrner & Yehuda, 2018). For example, after collecting and analyzing sperm samples from 28 men, the researchers found that men who had been abused as children had substantially lower concentrations of microRNAs, which regulate gene activity (Dickson et al., 2018). A follow-up study found that male mice that were experimentally stressed by being repeatedly moved to different cages had similar lower concentrations of microRNAs, and they passed along these lower concentrations to their offspring.

Epigenetic factors for the father also include possibly transmitting heritable diseases, as well as his exposure to other factors, such as his diet, alcohol, opiates, cocaine, various gases, lead, pesticides, and industrial chemicals, which can all damage sperm (Finegersh et al., 2015; Weyrich et al., 2018; Xavier et al., 2019). Likewise, children of older fathers may be at higher risk of a range of psychological disorders, including attention deficits, bipolar disorder, autism, and schizophrenia (D'Onofrio et al., 2014; McGrath et al., 2014; Wang et al., 2019).

Finally, you've undoubtedly heard that the risks of prenatal complications and birth defects rise for women over the age of 35. But did you know that men may also have a similarly ticking "biological clock"? A review of more than 40 years of research found that men over age 45 may expose their partners to increased pregnancy complications and their unborn children to increased risks of birth defects (Phillips et al., 2019). See the following **STH** **Scientific Thinking Highlight** for more information on prenatal development, and the special issue of herd immunity.

FIGURE 9.7   **Fetal alcohol spectrum disorders (FASD)**   Prenatal exposure to alcohol can result in FASD. Its most severe form is called *fetal alcohol syndrome (FAS)* and includes facial abnormalities and stunted growth. But the most disabling features of FAS are brain damage and neurobehavioral problems, ranging from hyperactivity and learning disabilities to intellectual disability, depression, and psychoses (Brown & Harr, 2018; Popova et al., 2019; Roozen et al., 2016).

Teratogen   Any factor that leads to damage or fetal death during prenatal development.

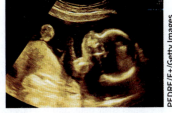

Early Childhood Development

Like the prenatal period, early childhood is a time of rapid physical development. Let's explore three key areas of change in early childhood: *brain, motor,* and *sensory/perceptual development.*

STH **Scientific Thinking Highlight**

Vaccination and Herd Immunity

(APA Goal 2.1) Use scientific reasoning to interpret psychological phenomena

Did you know that Elvis Presley, one of the most popular American celebrities in 1956, once posed for cameras as he was being vaccinated against polio? Why? He was using his fame and popularity as a testimonial to reassure the public that the vaccine was safe (see photo). Thanks in part to Presley's support, by August 1957 90 percent of Americans under 20 had received at least one polio shot (White, 2018).

In sharp contrast to Elvis Presley's advocacy, several modern-day celebrities and politicians have taken a hard stand against vaccinations. Actors like Jim Carrey, Jenny McCarthy, Charlie Sheen, Esai Morales, and Selma Blair, along with politicians like Robert F. Kennedy Jr., all say that it's a question of vaccine safety (a belief that vaccination causes autism), a matter of personal freedom, or a general mistrust of the government and/or large pharmaceutical companies (Roberts, 2018; White, 2018; Zhang et al., 2019).

However well-meaning, these celebrities and politicians are wrong. There is overwhelming scientific consensus supporting the safety of vaccinations, and multiple studies have rejected any link between vaccinations and **autism spectrum disorder (ASD)** or other developmental disorders. For example, one recent study of over 650,000 children born in Denmark from 1999 through 2010, which was published in the highly respected *Annals of Internal Medicine,* found no link between the measles, mumps, rubella (MMR) vaccine and autism (Hviid et al., 2019). In addition, a meta-analysis of five large cohorts also found no relationship between MMR vaccination and autism (Jain et al., 2015).

Where did this distrust in vaccination and the supposed link to autism begin? Most experts trace the problem to Andrew Wakefield and his colleagues' publication of a study in 1998 in *The Lancet,* a top-tier medical journal, claiming that the MMR vaccine caused autism in 12 children (Wakefield et al., 1998). However, scientists and journalists later provided clear evidence that Wakefield and his colleagues falsified their data, and the original study was later officially retracted (e.g., Eggertson, 2010; Taylor et al., 1999). In addition, Wakefield was stripped of his medical license for the falsification of data and his failure to disclose that his research had been funded by lawyers engaged in lawsuits against vaccine-producing companies—a clear conflict of interest (Belluz, 2019; Quick & Larson, 2018).

Sadly, despite this clear evidence disputing the vaccine-autism myth, experts have documented a continuing sharp drop in the rates of vaccination, which in turn has led to serious consequences (e.g., Omer & Yildirim, 2019). Measles, for instance, is an extremely contagious disease and the leading factor in vaccine-preventable illness and death worldwide. Sadly, it was declared to be eliminated in the U.S in 2000, but we're now going backwards and seeing a global resurgence of the disease (Paules et al., 2019).

Thankfully, according to the PEW Research Center, 91 percent of surveyed American adults with high science knowledge believe that vaccines provide high preventive health benefits, whereas only 55 percent of those with low science knowledge agree (Villa, 2019). As expected, survey respondents who did not recognize the definition of "herd immunity" were less likely to rate the benefits of vaccination as high, and were more likely to see a higher risk of side effects.

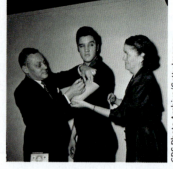
CBS Photo Archive/Getty Images

What is **herd immunity**? This term refers to the indirect protection from infectious diseases that results when most people in a given population become immune, particularly as a result of vaccination (see **Figure 9.8**). In other words, when enough people (approximately 90–95 percent) are immune, no chain of transmission can be established and the entire group can be protected.

Can you see how herd immunity is particularly important for those who are too young or too sick to be vaccinated, and how people might use this information to justify NOT getting vaccinated? Do you recall our original point about celebrities and members of the anti-vaccination movement who persist in their beliefs despite the contrary evidence? As mentioned earlier, they claim it's a matter of personal freedom or a general mistrust of the government, and they apparently rationalize that if not everyone needs to get vaccinated to get immunity, they can safely opt out. As you can see, individuals and families picking and choosing whether to vaccinate, or which vaccinations to get, will quickly limit or eliminate herd immunity. Requiring vaccination is a commonsense measure to protect public health. It's how Elvis Presley and the medical community eradicated polio. It's also the rational and right thing to do.

Q Test Your Scientific Thinking

Imagine you are talking to someone who is a strong opponent of vaccinations. Using the three key principles of scientific thinking—*skepticism, objectivity,* and *rationalism:*

1. Describe how you could have a meaningful conversation on the importance of vaccination. How might this type of dialogue be helpful to both of you?

2. Considering the fact that Wakefield's original, debunked research was conducted on only 12 children, can you see how this type of case study research is among the weakest form of evidence, given its subjective nature (Belluz, 2019). Scientific thinking relies on objective, unbiased research.

3. At risk of leaving you with the impression that there are significant differences in opinion about vaccination, a recent poll of Americans found that 87 percent say vaccines have helped them personally, and nearly 90 percent believe

---

Autism spectrum disorder (ASD) A developmental disorder that typically begins in early childhood and involves problems with social communication and social interaction, as well as restricted, repetitive patterns of behavior, interests, or activities.

Herd immunity A type of indirect protection from infectious diseases that results when most people in a given population become immune, particularly as a result of vaccination.

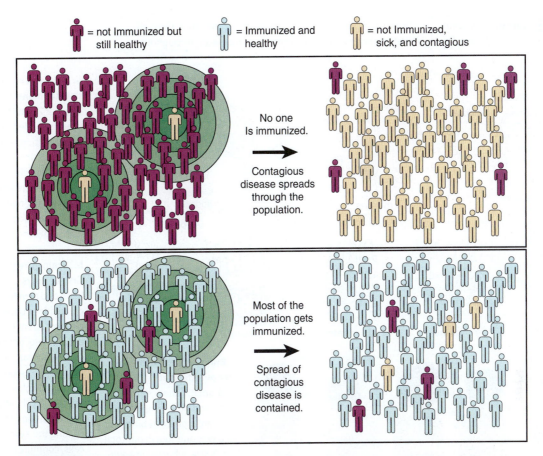

FIGURE 9.8 **The power of herd immunity** The basic idea is that a population or group (the "herd") will gain immunity to a specific disease over time when a significant majority of all its members become immune, particularly through vaccination. As shown in the top diagram, when no one is immunized, contagious diseases can spread throughout the entire population. When most of the population is immunized (bottom diagram), the spread of the disease is minimized.

Source: National Institute of Allergy and Infectious Diseases https://wayback.archive-it. org/7761/20160820104944/https://www.niaid.nih.gov/topics/Pages/communityImmunity.aspx.

parents put their communities at risk by failing to vaccinate their children (Research America, 2018). How might media attention on celebrities and to the anti-vaccination movement mislead the public into believing that a large number of people oppose vaccinations? What about other media stories that suggest strong public differences on topics like the climate crisis? What could you do to check out factual public opinion on these and other media publications?

(Compare your answers with those of your fellow students, family, and friends. Doing so will improve your scientific thinking and your media savvy.)

Brain and Motor Development

Our brains and other parts of the nervous system grow faster than any other part of the body during both prenatal development and the first 2 years of life, as illustrated in **Figure 9.9**. This brain development and learning occur primarily because neurons grow in size and number of dendrites, as well as in the extent of their connections.

Compared to the hidden, internal changes in brain development, the orderly emergence of active movement skills, known as *motor development*, is easily observed and measured. A newborn's first motor abilities are limited to *reflexes*, or involuntary responses to stimulation (Chapter 2). The rooting reflex occurs when something touches a baby's cheek: The infant will automatically turn his or her head, open his or her mouth, and root for a nipple.

In addition to simple reflexes, the infant soon begins to show voluntary control over the movement of various body parts (**Figure 9.10**). Thus, helpless newborns, who cannot even lift their heads, are soon transformed into active toddlers capable of crawling, walking, and

FIGURE 9.9 **Brain development** The brain undergoes dramatic changes from conception through the first few years of life. Notice, however, that our brains continue to change and develop throughout our life span.

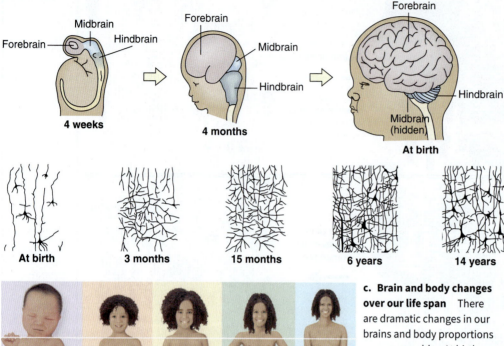

a. Prenatal brain development Recall from Chapter 2 that the human brain is divided into three major sections—the forebrain, midbrain, and hindbrain. Note how at 3 weeks after conception these three brain sections are one long neural tube, which later becomes the brain and spinal cord.

b. Brain growth during the first 14 years As infants learn and develop, synaptic connections between active neurons strengthen, and dendritic connections become more elaborate. Synaptic pruning (reduction of unused synapses) helps support this process. Myelination, the accumulation of fatty tissue coating the axons of nerve cells, continues until early adulthood.

c. Brain and body changes over our life span There are dramatic changes in our brains and body proportions as we grow older. At birth, our head was one-fourth our total body's size, whereas in adulthood, our head is one-eighth.

FIGURE 9.10 **Milestones in motor development** The acquisition and progression of motor skills, from chin up to walking alone, is generally the same for all children, but the environment and personal experiences also play a role. In short, each child will follow his or her own personal timetable (Adolph & Berger, 2012; Berger, 2015).

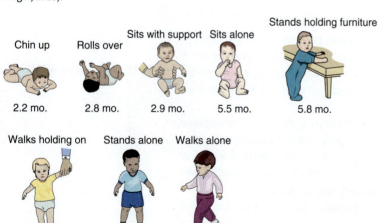

climbing. In fact, babies are highly motivated to begin walking given they can move faster than when crawling, and they get better with practice (Adolph & Berger, 2012; Berger, 2019). Keep in mind that motor development is largely due to natural maturation, but, like brain development, can be affected by environmental influences, such as disease and neglect.

Cultural differences in childrearing can also explain some accelerated or delayed onset ages of major physical milestones, such as walking and crawling. In some regions of Africa, the Caribbean, and India, caregivers vigorously massage and exercise infants as part of daily bathing routines, stretching infants' limbs, tossing them into the air, and propping them into sitting and walking positions (Karasik et al., 2018; Super & Harkness, 2015). Infants who receive this type of massage and exercise typically begin sitting and walking at earlier ages than infants who do not. Interestingly, some research has found that the relatively recent (and medically advised) practice in the United States of putting infants to sleep on their backs rather than their stomachs has resulted in delayed onset of some motor skills (e.g., Gupta, 2019; Safe to Sleep, 2019).

S&P Scientific Thinking and Practical Application

Are you wondering how psychologists conduct research with infants—especially before they can even talk? One of the earliest experimenters, Robert Fantz (1956, 1963), designed a "looking chamber" to find out what infants can see and what holds their attention. Babies are placed on their backs inside the chamber facing a lighted "testing" area above them. Using this apparatus, Fantz and his colleagues measured how long infants stared at various stimuli. They found that infants prefer complex rather than simple patterns and pictures of faces rather than pictures of non-faces (**Figure 9.11**).

Other researchers use newborns' heart rates and certain innate abilities, such as the sucking reflex, to study learning and perceptual development. To study the sense of smell, researchers measure changes in newborns' heart rates when odors are presented. Presumably, if they can smell one odor but not another, their heart rates will change in the presence of the first but not the second. As you may recall from Chapter 4, what all of these researchers are measuring is *habituation*—decreased responsiveness after repeated stimulation. Brain scans, such as fMRI, MRI, and CT, also help developmental scientists detect changes in infants' brains. Using brain scans, scientists have found that the organization of infant brains is remarkably similar to that of adults (Trafton, 2017).

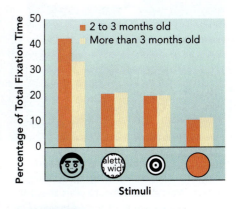

FIGURE 9.11 **Infant visual preferences**

Sensory and Perceptual Development

At birth, and during the final trimester of pregnancy, the developing child's senses are quite advanced. Research shows that a newborn infant prefers his or her mother's voice, providing evidence that the developing fetus can hear sounds outside the mother's body (Minai et al., 2017; Von Hofsten, 2013). This raises the interesting possibility of fetal learning, and some have advocated special stimulation for the fetus as a way of increasing intelligence, creativity, and general alertness (Jarvis, 2014; Van de Carr & Lehrer, 1997).

In addition, a newborn can smell most odors and distinguish between sweet, salty, and bitter tastes. Breast-fed newborns also recognize the odor of their mother's milk compared to other mothers' milk, formula, and other substances (Delaunay-El Allam et al., 2010; Nishitani et al., 2009). Similarly, the newborn's sense of touch and pain is highly developed, as evidenced by reactions to circumcision and to heel pricks for blood testing, and by the fact that their pain reactions are lessened by the smell of their own mother's milk (Nishitani et al., 2009; Rodkey & Riddell, 2013; Vinall & Grunau, 2014).

The newborn's sense of vision, however, is poorly developed. At birth, an infant is estimated to have vision between 20/200 and 20/600 (Haith & Benson, 1998). Imagine what the infant's visual life is like: The level of detail you see at 200 or 600 feet (if you have 20/20 vision) is what an infant sees at 20 feet. Within the first few months, vision quickly improves, and by 6 months it is 20/100 or better. At 2 years, visual acuity is nearly at the adult level of 20/20 (Courage & Adams, 1990).

Puberty The biological changes during adolescence that lead to sexual maturation and the ability to reproduce.

Adolescence

Adolescence is the loosely defined transition period of development between childhood and adulthood, which is considered to be a *critical period* of human development due to all the sweeping changes that occur during this time (Quas, 2014). In the United States, it roughly corresponds to the teenage years. However, the concept of adolescence and its meaning vary greatly across cultures (**Figure 9.12**).

Adolescence officially begins with **puberty**, the period of time when we mature sexually and become capable of reproduction. One of the clearest and most dramatic physical signs of puberty is the *growth spurt*, which is characterized by rapid increases in height, weight, and skeletal

FIGURE 9.12 **Ready for responsibility?** Adolescence is not a universal concept. Unlike the United States and other Western nations, some non-industrialized countries have no need for a slow transition from childhood to adulthood; children simply assume adult responsibilities as soon as possible.

John Miles/The Image Bank/Getty Images

FIGURE 9.13 **Adolescent growth spurt** Note the gender differences in height gain during puberty. Most girls are about 2 years ahead of boys in their growth spurt and are therefore taller than most boys between the ages of 10 and 14.

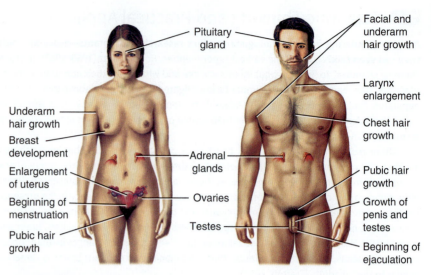

FIGURE 9.14 **Secondary sex characteristics** Complex physical changes in puberty primarily result from hormones secreted from the ovaries and testes, the pituitary gland in the brain, and the adrenal glands near the kidneys.

growth (**Figure 9.13**), and by significant changes in reproductive structures and sexual characteristics. In addition, maturation and hormone secretion lead to rapid development of the ovaries, uterus, and vagina, and the onset of menstruation (*menarche*) in the adolescent female. In the adolescent male, the testes, scrotum, and penis develop, and he experiences his first ejaculation (*spermarche*). The testes and ovaries produce hormones that lead to the development of secondary sex characteristics, such as the growth of pubic hair, deepening of the voice and growth of facial hair in men, and growth of breasts in women (**Figure 9.14**). Do you recall how changes in height and weight, breast development and menstruation for girls, and a deepening voice and beard growth for boys, were such important milestones for you and your adolescent peers?

PAN **Practical Application of Neuroscience**

Have you ever wondered why teenagers seem to sleep so much? Researchers have found that puberty is triggered by changes in the brain, including the release of certain hormones, which occur only during periods of *deep sleep* (D'Ambrosio & Redline, 2014; Shaw et al., 2012). This finding suggests that getting adequate, deep (slow-wave) sleep (see Chapter 5) during adolescence is an essential part of activating the reproductive system. Can you see why the increasing number of sleep problems in adolescents might be a cause for concern, and why parents should actually be encouraging "oversleeping" in their teenagers?

"Young man, go to your room and stay there until your cerebral cortex matures."

The Teenage Brain As you recall, our brains and other parts of the nervous system grow faster than any other part of our bodies during both prenatal development and the first 2 years of life. In contrast to the rapid synaptic growth experienced in the earlier years, the adolescent's brain actively destroys (prunes) unneeded connections. Although it may seem counterintuitive, this pruning actually improves brain functioning by making the remaining connections between neurons more efficient.

[AQ3] Thanks to this pruning and other changes during adolescence, full maturity of the frontal lobes is not accomplished until the mid-20s (**Figure 9.15**). Do you recall your teenage years as a time of exaggerated self-consciousness, feelings of special uniqueness, and risky behaviors (see photo)? Psychologists now believe these effects may be largely due to less-than-fully-developed frontal lobes (see cartoon) (Nyongesa et al., 2019; Tamnes et al., 2017).

FIGURE 9.15 **Changes in the brain**

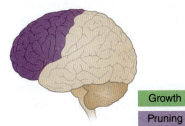

Growth
Pruning

a. Neural growth in the frontal lobes During early childhood (ages 3–6), the frontal lobes experience a significant increase in the connections between neurons, which helps explain a child's rapid cognitive growth.

b. Neural growth in the temporal and parietal lobes This rapid synaptic growth shifts to the temporal and parietal lobes during the ages of 7–15, which corresponds to their significant increases in language and motor skills.

c. Neural pruning in the frontal lobes During ages 16–20, synaptic pruning of unused connections in the frontal lobes leads to increased brain efficiency, but full frontal lobe maturity occurs only in the mid-20s.

Adulthood

When does adulthood begin? In Western cultures, many define it as beginning after high school or college graduation, whereas others mark it as when we get our first stable job and become self-sufficient. Adulthood is typically divided into at least three periods: emerging/young adulthood (ages 20–45), middle adulthood (ages 45–60), and late adulthood (ages 60 to death).

Emerging/Young Adulthood Although young adulthood is generally considered to begin at age 20, many developmental psychologists have added a new term, **emerging adulthood**, to refer to the time from the end of adolescence to the young adult stage, approximately ages 18–25. This stage, which is found primarily in modern cultures, is characterized by the search for a stable job, self-sufficiency, or marriage and parenthood, along with five distinguishing features (Arnett, 2000, 2015; Pusch et al., 2019):

Emerging adulthood The age period from approximately 18–25 in which individuals in modern cultures have left the dependency of childhood, but not yet assumed adult responsibilities.

1. **Identity exploration** Young people decide who they are and what they want out of life.

2. **Instability** A time marked by multiple changes in residences and relationships.

3. **Self-focus** Freed from social obligations and commitments to others, young people at this stage are focused on what they want and need before the constraints of marriage, children, and career.

4. **Feeling in-between** Although taking responsibility for themselves, they still feel in the middle between adolescence and adulthood.

5. **Age of possibilities** A time of optimism and belief that their lives will be better than their parents' (**Figure 9.16**).

During this time period, some individuals experience modest physical increases in height and muscular development, and most of us find this to be a time of maximum strength, sharp senses, and overall stamina. However, a decline in strength and speed becomes noticeable in the 30s, and our hearing starts to decline as early as our late teens.

Middle Adulthood Many physical changes during young adulthood happen so slowly that most people don't notice them until they enter their late 30s or early 40s. Around the age of 40, many people first experience difficulty in seeing things close up and after dark, hair thinning and graying, skin wrinkling, and a gradual loss in height coupled with weight gain.

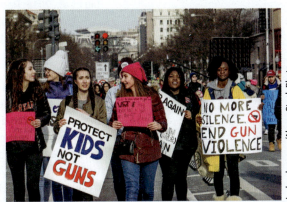

jacky chapman/Alamy Stock Photo

FIGURE 9.16 **Emerging adulthood—the age of possibilities** Around the ages of 18–25, young adults develop new cognitive skills and become more aware of societal issues like gun control and the climate crisis. These newfound abilities allow them to question authority and to stand up against perceived injustices.

For women ages 45–55, *menopause*, the cessation of the menstrual cycle, is the second most important life milestone in physical development. The decreased production of estrogen (the dominant female hormone) produces certain physical changes, including decreases in some types of cognitive and memory skills (Edwards et al., 2019; Kuther & Burnell, 2019). However, the popular belief that menopause (or "the change of life") causes serious psychological mood swings is not supported by current research. In fact, younger women are more likely to report irritability and mood swings, whereas women at midlife generally report positive reactions to aging and the end of the menstrual cycle. They're also less likely to have negative experiences such as headaches (Sievert et al., 2007; Sugar et al., 2014).

In contrast to women, men experience a more gradual decline in hormone levels. Physical changes such as unexpected weight gain, decline in sexual responsiveness, loss of muscle strength, and graying or loss of hair may lead some men (and women as well) to feel depressed, and to see these alterations as a biological signal of aging and mortality. Such physical and psychological changes in men are generally referred to as the *male climacteric* (or *andropause*). However, the popular belief that almost all men (and some women) go through a deeply disruptive midlife crisis, experiencing serious dissatisfaction with their work and personal relationships, is largely a myth.

Late Adulthood

After middle age, most physical changes in development are gradual and occur in the heart and arteries, and in the sensory receptors. Cardiac output (the volume of blood pumped by the heart each minute) decreases, whereas blood pressure increases, due to the thickening and stiffening of arterial walls. Visual acuity and depth perception decline, hearing acuity lessens (especially for high-frequency sounds), smell sensitivity decreases, and some decline in cognitive and memory skills occurs (Dupuis et al., 2015; Fletcher & Rapp, 2013; Newman & Newman, 2015).

Why do we go through so many physical changes? Why do we age and die? Setting aside aging and deaths resulting from disease, abuse, or neglect, known as *secondary aging*, let's focus on *primary aging* (gradual, inevitable age-related changes in physical and mental processes).

According to *cellular-clock theory*, primary aging is genetically controlled. Once the ovum is fertilized, the program for aging and death is set and begins to run. Researcher Leonard Hayflick (1965, 1996) found that human cells seem to have a built-in life span. After about 100 doublings of laboratory-cultured cells, they cease to divide. Based on this limited number of cell divisions, Hayflick suggests that we humans have a maximum life span of about 120 years—we reach the *Hayflick limit*. Why? One answer may be that small structures on the tips of our chromosomes, called *telomeres*, shorten each time a cell divides. After about 100 replications, the telomeres are too short and the cells can no longer divide (Hayashi et al., 2015; Liu et al., 2019; Rode et al., 2015).

The second major explanation of primary aging is *wear-and-tear theory*. Like any machine, repeated use and abuse of our organs and cell tissues may cause our human bodies to simply wear out over time.

Late Adulthood Brain

What about changes in the brain in later years? The public and most researchers long believed aging was inevitably accompanied by major losses in cognitive abilities and widespread death of neurons in the brain. Although this decline does happen with degenerative disorders like Alzheimer disease (AD), it is no longer believed to be an inevitable part of normal aging (Hörder et al., 2018; Solomon et al., 2018). In addition, some research shows that having a strong social network can help stave off cognitive decline (e.g., Cook Maher et al., 2017). Furthermore, age-related cognitive problems are not on a continuum with AD. That is, normal forgetfulness does not mean that serious dementia is around the corner.

Aging does seem to take its toll on the *speed* of information processing (Chapter 7). Decreased speed of processing may reflect problems with *encoding* (putting information into long-term storage) and *retrieval* (getting information out of storage). If memory is like a filing system, older people may just have more filing cabinets, and it may take them longer to initially file and later retrieve information. Although mental speed declines with age, general information processing and much of memory ability are largely unaffected by the aging process (Berger, 2019; Kuther & Burnell, 2019).

For example, despite their concerns about "keeping up with 18-year-olds," older returning students often do as well as or better than their younger counterparts in college classes. This superior performance by older adult students may be due, in part, to their generally greater academic motivation, but it also reflects the importance of prior knowledge. Cognitive psychologists have clearly demonstrated that the more people know, the easier it is for them to lay down new memories. Older students, for instance, generally find this chapter on development easier to master than younger students do. Their interactions with children and greater accumulated knowledge about life changes create a framework upon which to hang new information.

Take-Home Message   In short, the more you know, the more you can learn. Furthermore, gaining more education and having an intellectually challenging life may help you stay mentally sharp in your later years—another reason for going to college and engaging in life-long learning (De Silva et al., 2019; Staff et al., 2018). For more positive news on aging, see the following **PAH** **Practical Application Highlight**.

PAH Practical Application Highlight

Aging—It's Mostly Good News.

(APA Goal 1.3) Describe applications of psychology

How can we use this information to improve our lives regardless of age? In addition to staying intellectually and socially engaged throughout our lives (see photo), research shows that practicing *gratitude exercises* can increase our well-being, happiness, generosity, and life satisfaction (Alkozei et al., 2018; Chaplin et al., 2018; Yoshimura & Berzins, 2017). As you'll see in Chapter 11, simple examples of these exercises include creating a list of things we're grateful for, keeping a daily gratitude list of the top three things that we're grateful for, and writing letters to and visiting people who have had a positive impact on our lives.

Unfortunately, television, magazines, movies, and advertisements generally portray aging as a time of balding and graying hair, sagging body parts, poor vision, hearing loss, and, of course, no sex life. Can you see how these negative media portrayals, combined with our personal fears of aging and death, contribute to our society's widespread **ageism**—prejudice and discrimination based on physical age?

Ageism is also a big factor in job discrimination. According to the latest data from the U.S. Bureau of Labor Statistics, almost 20 percent of Americans over the age of 65 are now working and delaying retirement—some out of desire but most because they need the money (Steverman, 2016). Although age discrimination in employment is illegal in the United States, two-thirds of older job seekers report experiencing it, and those who face such discrimination have significantly lower physical and emotional health, as well as greater declines in health, than those who do not (Applewhite, 2016; Sutin et al., 2015). In addition to the negative effects on the workers' health, did you know that many potential employers assume that older applicants are more likely to be burned out, absent due to illness, and reluctant to travel, as well as less creative and productive? If you're a young adult, you

Blend Images/Peathegee Inc/Media Bakery

may not realize that many people, including potential employers, similarly criticize your group for "needing to have your hands held," "acting entitled," and having no "work ethic" (Applewhite, 2016; Reade, 2015).

Now for some good news: These and other stereotypes about older workers and millennials are seldom based on facts. A large-scale analysis of scientific careers revealed that age is truly just a number. In this study, the researchers found that scientific success comes from a combination of elements, including intelligence, luck, personality, and a new element they called "Q" (Sinatra et al., 2016). This Q factor includes personal skills and strengths, as well as high levels of drive, motivation, openness to new ideas, and ability to work well with others (Carey, 2016).

Further good news comes from recent changes in those previously mentioned negative media and advertising portrayals of older people. Marketing experts have noted the large number of aging baby boomers and are now producing a few ads with a more positive and accurate portrayal of aging as a time of vigor,

Ageism   A form of prejudice or discrimination based on physical age; similar to racism and sexism in its negative stereotypes.

interest, and productivity. Also, as noted in this chapter and in Chapter 2, our brains are constantly changing—thus our cognitive abilities and overall achievements can grow and improve throughout our life span (see **Figure 9.17**).

As we've just seen, widespread misconceptions about an inevitable cognitive decline as we age are largely unfounded. Furthermore, as discussed earlier in the chapter, researchers have found an increase in happiness and overall well-being as we grow older. Why? As we discussed in Chapter 7, one interesting possibility comes from research showing that older adults tend to prefer and pay more sustained attention to positive over negative information (Carstensen, 1993, 2006; Livingstone & Isaacowitz, 2016; Reed et al., 2014). Further research finds that this so-called *age-related positivity effect* may even increase immune functioning and memory, along with improved overall healthy aging and life satisfaction (Carstensen, 2019; Ford et al., 2018; Mikels & Shuster, 2016).

Interestingly, younger people tend to show an opposite approach—preferring negative over positive information and events. Can you see how this might help explain why the college years can feel so painful and troublesome in your 20s, while in later years they might be remembered as "the best years of your life"? It appears that older adults have developed greater emotional regulation, and that they deliberately focus their attention and memory in a positive direction.

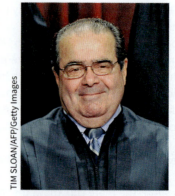

FIGURE 9.17 **Two positive models of aging** As we've emphasized throughout this text, we can all grow and improve from birth to death. Consider the achievements of Justices Ruth Bader Ginsburg and Antonin Scalia of the U.S. Supreme Court. Justice Scalia served from 1986 until his death in 2016, just shy of his 80th birthday. For decades Justice Scalia was the leading conservative voice on the Court. In her younger years, Justice Ginsburg worked tirelessly as a staunch courtroom advocate. Now in her 80s, she serves as a leading liberal voice on the Supreme Court. Fun fact: Despite their diametrically opposed political and legal philosophies, Justice Scalia and Justice Ginsburg had a great deal of mutual respect for one another and were known to be very close friends.

Retrieval Practice 9.2 | Physical Development

Self-Test Completing this self-test, and then checking your answers by clicking on the answer button or by looking in Appendix B, will provide immediate feedback and helpful practice for exams.

1. Behavioral genetics is the study of the relative effects of _____ on behavior and mental processes.

   a. DNA and genetics

   b. natural selection and adaptation

   c. genetics and natural selection

   d. heredity and environment

2. Teratogens are _____.

   a. maternal defects that lead to damage during neonatal development

   b. factors that contribute to damage during prenatal development

   c. popular children's toys that studies have shown lead to damage during early childhood development

   d. environmental diseases that contribute to damage during early childhood development

3. The _____ is the first stage of prenatal development, which begins with conception and ends with implantation in the uterus (the first 2 weeks).

   a. embryonic period   c. critical period

   b. germinal period   d. none of these options

4. The clearest and most physical sign of puberty is the _____, characterized by rapid increases in height, weight, and skeletal growth.

   a. menses   c. growth spurt

   b. spermarche   d. age of fertility

5. Some employers are reluctant to hire older workers (50 years of age and older) because of a generalized belief that they are sickly and will take too much time off. This is an example of _____.

   a. discrimination   c. ageism

   b. prejudice   d. all of these options

Q Test Your Critical Thinking

1. If a mother knowingly ingests a quantity of alcohol, which may have caused her child to develop fetal alcohol syndrome (FAS), is she guilty of child abuse? Why or why not?

2. Based on what you have learned about development during late adulthood, do you think this period is inevitably a time of physical and mental decline? Why or why not?

Real World Application Questions

[AQ2] Can parents' early emotional trauma be passed on to their unborn children?

[AQ3] How is the teenage brain different from that of an adult?

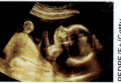

Hint: Look in the text for **[AQ2]** and **[AQ3]**

9.3 Cognitive Development

LEARNING OBJECTIVES

Retrieval Practice   While reading the upcoming sections, respond to each learning objective in your own words.

Summarize the major theories of cognitive development and how cognition changes over the life span.

- **Explain** the roles of schemas, assimilation, and accommodation in cognitive development.
- **Describe** the major characteristics of Piaget's four stages of cognitive development.

- **Compare** Piaget's theory of cognitive development to other theories and later research.

Real World Application Questions

[AQ4] Do babies learn faster when they're sitting up versus lying down?

[AQ5] Does the taking and posting of self-portraits ("selfies") increase narcissism?

What is learned in the cradle, lasts to the grave.   —French proverb

Just as a child's body and physical abilities change, his or her way of knowing and perceiving the world also grows and changes. Jean Piaget [pee-ah-ZHAY] provided some of the first great demonstrations of how children develop thinking and reasoning abilities (Piaget, 1952). He showed that an infant begins at a cognitively "primitive" level, and that intellectual growth progresses in distinct stages, motivated by an innate need to know.

To appreciate Piaget's contributions, we need to consider his three major concepts: schemas, assimilation, and accommodation. **Schemas** are the most basic units of intellect. They act as patterns that organize our interactions with the environment, like an architect's drawings or a builder's blueprints. For most of us, a common, shared schema for a car would likely be "a moving object with wheels and seats for passengers." However, we also develop unique schemas based on differing life experiences (see the **Test Yourself** feature).

Schema   A Piagetian term for a cognitive framework, or "blueprint," formed through interaction with an object or event.

Assimilation   In Piaget's theory, the incorporation (assimilation) of new information into existing schemas.

Accommodation   According to Piaget, the process of adjusting (accommodating) existing schemas to incorporate new information.

PA Practical Application

Test Yourself: Do You Have an Artistic Schema?

Study the "impossible figure" of an elephant, and then try drawing this same figure without tracing it. Students with artistic training generally find it relatively easy to reproduce because they've developed unique

visual skills, whereas the rest of us find it very hard or "impossible." This is because we lack the necessary artistic schema, but with training and practice we could learn to easily draw the figure.

In the first few weeks of life, the infant apparently has several *schemas* based on the innate reflexes of sucking, grasping, and so on. These schemas are primarily motor and may be little more than stimulus-and-response mechanisms (e.g., the nipple is presented, and the baby sucks). Soon, other schemas emerge. The infant develops a more detailed schema for eating solid food, a different schema for the concepts of "mother" and "father," and so on.

Assimilation and *accommodation* are the two major processes by which schemas grow and change over time. **Assimilation** is the process of absorbing new information into existing schemas. For instance, infants use their sucking schema not only in sucking nipples, but also in sucking blankets and fingers. In **accommodation**, existing ideas are modified to fit new information. Accommodation generally occurs when new information or stimuli cannot be assimilated. New schemas are developed or old schemas are changed to better fit with the new information. An infant's first attempt to eat solid food with a spoon is a good example of both assimilation and accommodation (**Figure 9.18**).

Courtesy of Teresa Jacob

FIGURE 9.18   **Assimilation plus accommodation**   When feeding from a spoon, infants initially try to suck on the spoon—an example of assimilation. Later, they learn to shape their lips around the spoon, and to use their lips and tongue to pull the food into their mouths—an example of accommodation.

iStock.com/jfairone

[AQ4] Surprisingly, researchers in one study found that babies who sat upright (see photo) while they explored different objects were much better at distinguishing between those objects than babies who were lying down while they explored (Woods & Wilcox, 2013). Although the researchers weren't exactly sure why sitting up helped babies learn more about different objects, it may be that a sitting position allows babies to better reach for, hold, and manipulate objects.

Stages of Cognitive Development

According to Piaget, all children go through approximately the same four stages of cognitive development, regardless of the culture in which they live (**Process Diagram 9.2**). Piaget also believed that these stages cannot be skipped given that skills acquired at earlier stages are essential to mastery of later stages (Berger, 2019; Lightfoot et al., 2018).

> **STOP!** This Process Diagram contains essential information NOT found elsewhere in the text, which is likely to appear on quizzes and exams. Be sure to study it CAREFULLY.

PROCESS DIAGRAM 9.2 **Piaget's Four Stages of Cognitive Development**

Step ① Sensorimotor stage (birth to age 2)	**Limits** • Lacks "significant" language and object permanence (understanding that things continue to exist even when not seen, heard, or felt) **Abilities** • Uses senses and motor skills to explore and develop cognitively **Example** • Children at this stage like to explore and play with their food.	Mcimage/Shutterstock.com
Step ② Preoperational stage (ages 2–7)	**Limits** • Cannot perform mental "operations" (lacks reversibility and conservation) • Egocentric thinking (inability to consider another's point of view) • Animistic thinking (believing all things are living) **Abilities** • Has significant language and thinks symbolically **Example** • Children at this stage often believe the moon follows them.	evgenyatamanenko/iStock/Getty Images
Step ③ Concrete operational stage (ages 7–11)	**Limits** • Cannot think abstractly and hypothetically • Thinking tied to concrete, tangible objects and events **Abilities** • Can perform "operations" on concrete objects • Understands conservation (realizing that changes in shape or appearance can be reversed) • Less egocentric **Example** • Children at this stage begin to question the existence of Santa.	Hill Street Studios/DigitalVision/Getty Images
Step ④ Formal operational stage (ages 11 and over)	**Limits** • Adolescent egocentrism at the beginning of this stage, with related problems (imaginary audience and personal fable) **Abilities** • Can think abstractly and hypothetically **Example** • Children at this stage generally show great concern for physical appearance.	Adrian Burke/Corbis/Getty Images

FIGURE 9.19 **Testing for object permanence** Prior to about 8 months of age, Piaget believed that infants tend to lack object permanence, as shown by the child in the two photos with the stuffed dog. Note when the toy dog is in plain sight, the infant reaches for it. However, when the view of the dog is blocked from sight, the infant appears to believe that the toy no longer exists. In contrast, the older child, searching beneath the sofa for the hidden toy in the third photo, apparently knows that the object still exists even if it is hidden. According to Piagetian theory, the child searching for the toy is demonstrating that she has formed a mental representation (a schema) of the object and has acquired a recognition of object permanence. Note, however, that modern researchers believe that object permanence appears much earlier than 8 months. Infants may fail to look for hidden objects given they don't know how to look for them, not because they believe the objects no longer exist (Baillargeon & DeVos, 1991; Berger, 2019; Gerson & Woodward, 2014). In other words, Piaget may have mistaken infants' motor incompetence for conceptual incompetence.

Sensorimotor Stage

The **sensorimotor stage** lasts from birth until "significant" language acquisition (about age 2). During this time, children explore the world and develop their schemas primarily through their senses and motor activities—hence the term "sensorimotor." One important concept that infants lack at the beginning of the sensorimotor stage is **object permanence**—an understanding that objects continue to exist even when they cannot be seen, heard, or touched (**Figure 9.19**).

Preoperational Stage

During the **preoperational stage** (roughly ages 2–7), language advances significantly, and the child begins to think symbolically—using symbols, such as words, to represent concepts. Three other qualities characterize this stage: *inability to perform mental operations*, *egocentrism*, and *animism*.

1. **Inability to perform mental operations** Piaget labeled this period "preoperational" given that the child lacks *operations*, meaning the ability to imagine an action and mentally reverse it. For instance, preoperational children do not understand that milk poured into a tall, thin glass is not "more" than the same amount poured into a short, wide glass. This is because they lack the concept of *reversibility*—understanding that some things that have been changed can be returned to their original state. They also lack the concept of **conservation**—the principle that certain characteristics (such as volume) stay the same, even though appearances may change. If you'd like to perform your own informal tests of conservation, see the **Test Yourself** feature on the next page.

2. **Egocentrism** Children at this stage are typically **egocentric**, which refers to the preoperational child's limited ability to distinguish between his or her own perspective and someone else's. Egocentrism is not the same as "selfishness." Preschoolers who move in front of you to get a better view of the TV, or repeatedly ask questions while you are talking on the telephone, are not being selfish. They are demonstrating their natural limits and egocentric thought processes. Children in this stage naively assume that others see, hear, feel, and think exactly as they do. Consider the following telephone conversation between a 3-year-old, who is at home, and her mother, who is at work:

> MOTHER: Emma, is that you?
>
> EMMA: (Nods silently.)
>
> MOTHER: Emma, is Daddy there? May I speak to him?
>
> EMMA: (Twice nods silently.)

Egocentric preoperational children fail to understand that the phone caller cannot see their nodding head. Charming as this is, preoperational children's egocentrism also sometimes

Sensorimotor stage Piaget's first stage of cognitive development (birth to approximately age 2), in which schemas are developed through sensory and motor activities.

Object permanence According to Piaget, an understanding that objects continue to exist even when they cannot be seen, heard, or touched directly; a hallmark of Piaget's preoperational stage.

Preoperational stage Piaget's second stage of cognitive development (roughly ages 2–7); it is characterized by significant language, but the child lacks operations (reversible mental processes), and thinking is egocentric and animistic.

Conservation According to Piaget, the understanding that certain physical characteristics (such as volume) remain unchanged, even though appearances may change; a hallmark of Piaget's concrete operational stage.

Egocentrism In cognitive development, the inability to take the perspective of another person; a hallmark of Piaget's preoperational stage.

leads them to believe their "bad thoughts" caused their sibling or parent to get sick or that their misbehavior caused their parents' marital problems. Given that they think the world centers on them, they often cannot separate reality from what goes on inside their own head.

3. **Animism** During this stage, children generally believe objects, such as the moon, trees, clouds, and bars of soap, have motives, feelings, and intentions (e.g., "The moon follows me when I walk," "Dark clouds are angry," and, "Soap sinks to the bottom of the bathtub because it is tired"). *Animism* refers to the belief that all things are living (or animated).

PA Practical Application

Test Yourself: Putting Piaget to the Test

If you have access to children in the preoperational or concrete operational stages, try some of the following experiments, pictured below,

which researchers often use to test Piaget's various forms of conservation. The equipment is easily obtained, and you will find their responses fascinating. Keep in mind that this should be done as a game. The child should not feel that he or she is failing a test or making a mistake.

Type of conservation task (average age at which concept is fully grasped)	Your task as experimenter . . .	Child is asked . . .
Length (ages 6–7)	**Step 1** Center two sticks of equal length. Child agrees that they are of equal length. **Step 2** In full view of the child, move one stick sideways.	**Step 3** "Which stick is longer?" Preoperational child will say that one of the sticks is longer. Child in concrete stage will say that they are both the same length.
Substance amount (ages 6–7)	**Step 1** Center two identical clay balls. Child acknowledges that the two have equal amounts of clay. **Step 2** While the child is watching, flatten one of the balls.	**Step 3** "Do the two pieces have the same amount of clay?" Preoperational child will say that the flat piece has more clay. Child in concrete stage will say that the two pieces have the same amount of clay.
Liquid volume (ages 7–8)	**Step 1** Present two short/wide-glasses with liquid at the same level. Child agrees that liquid is at the same height in both glasses. **Step 2** In full view of the child, pour the liquid from one of the short/wide glasses into the tall, thin one.	**Step 3** "Do the two glasses have the same amount of liquid?" Preoperational child will say that the tall, thin glass has more liquid. Child in concrete stage will say that the two glasses have the same amount of liquid.
Area (ages 8–10)	**Step 1** Center two identical pieces of cardboard with wooden blocks placed on them in identical positions. Child acknowledges that the same amount of space is left open on each piece of cardboard. **Step 2** While the child is watching, scatter the blocks on one piece of the cardboard.	**Step 3** "Do the two pieces of cardboard have the same amount of open space?" Preoperational child will say that the cardboard with scattered blocks has less open space. Child in concrete stage will say that both pieces have the same amount of open space.

Q Test Your Critical Thinking

1. Based on their responses, are the children you tested in the preoperational or concrete stage?

2. If you repeat the same tests with each child, do their answers change? Why or why not?

Concrete Operational Stage

At approximately age 7, children enter the **concrete operational stage**. During this time, many important thinking skills emerge. However, as the name implies, thinking tends to be limited to *concrete*, tangible objects and events. Unlike preoperational children, youngsters in this stage are less egocentric in their thinking and become capable of true logical thought. As most parents know, many children now stop believing in Santa Claus because they logically conclude that one man can't deliver presents to everyone in one night.

Now that they understand the concept of *reversibility*, concrete operational children can successfully perform "operations." They recognize that certain physical attributes (such as volume) remain unchanged, although the outward appearance may be altered. This understanding of conservation is a hallmark of children in the concrete stage.

Concrete operational stage Piaget's third stage of cognitive development (roughly ages 7–11), in which the child can think logically about concrete, tangible objects and events.

Formal Operational Stage

The final period in Piaget's theory, the **formal operational stage**, typically begins around age 11. In this stage, children begin to apply their operations to abstract concepts in addition to concrete objects. They become capable of hypothetical thinking ("What if?"), which allows systematic formulation and testing of concepts. For example, before filling out applications for part-time jobs, adolescents may think about possible conflicts with school and friends, the number of hours they want to work, and the kind of work for which they are qualified.

Formal operational thinking also allows the adolescent to construct a well-reasoned argument based on hypothetical concepts and logical processes. Consider the following argument:

Formal operational stage Piaget's fourth stage of cognitive development (around age 11 and beyond), characterized by abstract and hypothetical thinking.

1. If you hit a glass with a feather, the glass will break.
2. You hit a glass with a feather.

What is the logical conclusion? The correct answer, "The glass will break," is contrary to fact and direct experience. Therefore, the child in the concrete operational stage would have difficulty with this task, whereas the formal operational thinker understands that this problem is about abstractions that need not correspond to the real world.

Along with the benefits of this cognitive style come several problems. Adolescents in the early stages of the formal operational period generally demonstrate a type of egocentrism different from that of the preoperational child (see photo and the following **Test Yourself** feature). Adolescents certainly recognize that others have unique thoughts and perspectives. However, they may fail to differentiate between what they are thinking and what others are thinking. If they get a new haircut or fail to make the sports team, they may be overly concerned about how others will react. Instead of considering that everyone is equally wrapped up in his or her own appearance, concerns, and plans, they tend to believe that they are the center of others' thoughts and attentions. David Elkind (1967, 2007) referred to this as the *imaginary audience*.

Although adolescents often believe that others are always watching and evaluating them (the imaginary audience), they also, ironically, think they are special and unique. They tend to believe that they alone are having insights or difficulties that no one else understands or experiences. Sadly, these feelings of special uniqueness, known as the *personal fable,* are associated with several forms of risk taking, such as engaging in sexual intercourse without protection, driving dangerously, indoor tanning, and experimenting with drugs (Banerjee et al., 2015; Popovac & Hadlington, 2019). Adolescents apparently recognize the dangers of risky activities, but they believe the rules and statistics just don't apply to them. Recall from the discussion earlier that psychologists now believe these effects may be largely due to the teen's less-than-fully-developed frontal lobes. In sum, the imaginary audience apparently results from an inability to differentiate the self from others, whereas the personal fable may be a product of differentiating too much. Thankfully, these two forms of adolescent egocentrism tend to decrease during later stages of the formal operational period.

Tony Garcia/Image Source/Getty Images

[AQ5] Adolescent egocentrism or narcissism? Piaget describes most children and adolescents as being egocentric, which is a major characteristic of narcissism. Given the growing popularity of taking and posting self-portraits ("selfies") on social media (see photo), have you wondered if this practice might increase narcissism? Research on this topic does find that narcissistic individuals do in fact take and post more selfies, and that these actions have a self-reinforcing effect that maintains the narcissist's positive self-views (Halpern et al., 2016).

PA Practical Application

Test Yourself: Did You Experience Adolescent Egocentrism?

Do these descriptions of the imaginary audience and personal fable ring true for you? If so, do you now understand how these beliefs might help explain some of the problems and challenges you faced in adolescence? As implied in this photo, many teens have difficulty accepting comfort and support from parents due to their belief that no one has ever felt or experienced what they have. One young woman remembered being very upset in middle school when her mother tried to comfort her over the loss of an important relationship. "I felt like she couldn't possibly know how it felt—no one could. I couldn't believe that anyone had ever suffered like this or that things would ever get better." Best advice for parents? Have patience and be comforting and reassuring. Teenagers whose parents use harsh verbal discipline (yelling or making serious threats) show more symptoms of depression and more behavior problems (lying, trouble in school, fighting with peers) (Wang & Kenny, 2014).

Steve Debenport/E+/Getty Images

Evaluating Piaget

As influential as Piaget's account of cognitive development has been, there are other important theories and criticisms of Piaget to consider. First, research shows that Piaget may have underestimated young children's cognitive development. As we discussed earlier, infants seem to develop concepts like object permanence much earlier than Piaget suggested. Piaget also believed that infancy and early childhood were a time of extreme egocentrism in which children have little or no understanding of the perspective of others. However, research finds that empathy develops at a relatively young age (**Figure 9.20**). Even juvenile chimpanzees will soothe a frightened or injured peer (Freidin et al., 2017; Goodall, 1990). Furthermore, Piaget's theory of children's limited perception of volume, see again the previous Test Yourself and **Figure 9.21**, may be more the result of everyday experiences with mental simulation than childhood stages of cognitive development.

Second, Piaget's model, like other stage theories, has been criticized for not sufficiently taking into account genetic and cultural differences (Newman & Newman, 2015; Shweder, 2011). During Piaget's time, genetic influences on cognitive abilities were poorly understood, but as in the case of epigenetics, there has been a rapid explosion of information in this field in the past few years. In addition, formal education and specific cultural experiences can significantly

Liz Banfield/Photolibrary/Getty Images

FIGURE 9.20 **Are preoperational children always egocentric?** Some toddlers and preschoolers clearly demonstrate empathy for other people. How does this ability to take another's perspective contradict Piaget's beliefs about egocentrism in very young children?

Asergieiev/iStock/Getty Images

FIGURE 9.21 **Which jar is larger?** Research shows that most adults believe the jar that is right side up is larger because they have learned to judge volume by estimating the container's size by imagining filling it up (Perfecto et al., 2019). Can you see how children in Piaget's test may have "failed" the volume conservation test due to their relative lack of experience in pouring liquid into various vessels?

affect cognitive development. Consider the following example from a researcher attempting to test the formal operational skills of a farmer in Liberia (Scribner, 1977):

> RESEARCHER: All Kpelle men are rice farmers. Mr. Smith is not a rice farmer. Is he a Kpelle man?
>
> KPELLE FARMER: I don't know the man. I have not laid eyes on the man myself.

Instead of reasoning in the "logical" way of Piaget's formal operational stage, the Kpelle farmer reasoned according to his specific cultural and educational training, which apparently emphasized personal knowledge. Not knowing Mr. Smith, the Kpelle farmer did not feel qualified to comment on him. Thus, Piaget's theory may have underestimated the effect of culture on a person's cognitive functioning.

Vgotsky and ToM

Before going on, let's consider two prominent alternative views on cognitive development. In contrast to Piaget's focus on internal schemas, Russian psychologist Lev Vygotsky emphasized the sociocultural influences on a child's cognitive development (Vygotsky, 1962). According to Vygotsky, children construct knowledge through their culture, language, and collaborative social interactions with more experienced thinkers (Scott, 2015; Vasileva & Balyasnikova, 2019; Yasnitsky, 2015). Unlike Piaget, Vygotsky also believed that adults play an essential instructor role in development and that this instruction is particularly helpful when it falls within a child's **zone of proximal development (ZPD)**, described in **Figure 9.22**.

In addition to Vygotsky's emphasis on the sociocultural influences, researchers have questioned why children in the preoperational stage cannot take another's point of view and how they eventually learn to do so. In response to these inquiries, an entire area of research has emerged regarding how young children think about their own minds, and the minds of others. According to this research, children become less egocentric when they begin to understand that other people don't have the same thoughts and feelings that they do—an achievement called **theory of mind (ToM)** (Conway et al., 2019; Poulin-Dubois et al., 2018; Weimer et al., 2017).

One of the first experiments on ToM was conducted with children between the ages of three and nine (Wimmer & Perner, 1983). The children first listened to a story about Maxi and how his mother moved some chocolate from a blue cupboard to a green one (**Figure 9.23**). When asked

Upper limit
(tasks beyond reach at present)

Zone of proximal development (ZPD)
(tasks achievable with guidance)

Lower limit
(tasks achieved without help)

FIGURE 9.22 Vygotsky's zone of proximal development (ZPD)   Have you heard of "instructional scaffolding"? This term refers to providing support during the learning process that is tailored to the needs of the student. Vygotsky was one of the first to apply the general idea of scaffolding to early cognitive development. He proposed that the most effective teaching focuses on tasks between those a learner can do without help (the lower limit) and those he or she cannot do even with help (the upper limit). In this middle *zone of proximal development (ZPD)*, tasks and skills can be "stretched" to higher levels with the guidance and encouragement of a more knowledgeable person.

Zone of proximal development (ZPD)   Vygotsky's concept of the difference between what children can accomplish on their own and what they can accomplish with the help of others who are more competent.

Theory of mind (ToM)   The understanding that other people don't have the same thoughts and feelings that we do, which generally develops during early childhood.

a.   b.   c.   d.

FIGURE 9.23 Theory of mind (ToM)   Each child research participant is told a story about a boy named Maxi who watches while his mother places some chocolate she plans to use to make a cake in a blue cupboard (a). Maxi then goes out to play (b), and while he is outside his mother makes the cake and puts the leftover chocolate in a green cupboard (c). Then Maxi comes back in, wanting some chocolate (d). At this point, the researcher asks the child listening to the story not where the chocolate is, but which cupboard Maxi will look in.

where Maxi will look for the chocolate, the children not only had to remember that the chocolate was moved, but also, more importantly, had to recognize that Maxi had no way of knowing that his mom moved the chocolate, since he was playing outside during the move. Therefore, Maxi will assume the chocolate is still in the blue cupboard. Interestingly, 3- and 4-year-olds often fail such tests, pointing to the actual position of the chocolate versus where Maxi will think it is. They apparently are unable to understand that although they know where the chocolate is, Maxi doesn't. On the other hand, most 6-year-olds succeed.

This type of experimentation supports Piaget's notion that young preoperational children are highly egocentric. It also goes on to explain that most children eventually do develop the understanding that their thoughts and feelings differ from those of others through a combination of maturation and social experiences. Can you see how the apparently simple task in Figure 9.23 actually requires a high level of thought? And why children who have difficulty in developing their ToM will find it difficult to engage in pretend play or understand why people do and say the things they do? Some researchers believe the lack of ToM also helps explain the problems with communication and social interactions typical of children with autism spectrum disorder (ASD) and attention-deficit/hyperactivity disorder (ADHD) (Cantio et al., 2016; Kuijper et al., 2017; Smit et al., 2019).

Despite criticisms, however, Piaget's contributions to psychology are enormous. As one scholar put it, "assessing the impact of Piaget on developmental psychology is like assessing the impact of Shakespeare on English literature or Aristotle on philosophy—impossible" (Beilin, 1992, p. 191).

Retrieval Practice 9.3 | Cognitive Development

Self-Test   Completing this self-test, and then checking your answers by clicking on the answer button or by looking in Appendix B, will provide immediate feedback and helpful practice for exams.

1. _____ was one of the first scientists to demonstrate that a child's intellect is fundamentally different from that of an adult's.

   a. Baumrind   **c.** Piaget

   b. Beck   **d.** Elkind

2. _____ occurs when existing schemas are used to absorb new information, whereas _____ makes changes and modifications to the schemas.

   a. Adaptation; accommodation

   b. Adaptation; reversibility

   c. Egocentrism; postschematization

   d. Assimilation; accommodation

3. A child who believes that trees have feelings is probably in the _____ stage of development.

   a. sensorimotor   **c.** egocentric

   b. preoperational   **d.** concrete operational

4. The ability to think abstractly and hypothetically occurs in Piaget's _____ stage.

   a. egocentric

   b. postoperational

   c. formal operational

   d. concrete operational

5. In Vygotsky's theory of cognitive development, the area between what children can accomplish on their own and what they can accomplish with the help of others who are more competent is called the _____.

   a. concrete operational area

   b. postoperational zone

   c. formal operational limits

   d. zone of proximal development

Q Test Your Critical Thinking

1. Piaget's theory states that all children progress through all the discrete stages of cognitive development in order and without skipping any. Do you agree with this theory? Do you know any children who seem to contradict this theory?

2. Based on what you've learned about schemas, what are some new schemas you've developed as part of your transition from high school to college?

Real World Application Questions

[AQ4] Do babies learn faster when they're sitting up versus lying down?

[AQ5] Does the taking and posting of self-portraits ("selfies") increase narcissism?

iStock.com/jfairone

Tony Garcia/ Image Source/ Getty Images

Hint: look in the text for **[AQ4]** and **[AQ5]**

9.4 | Social-Emotional Development

LEARNING OBJECTIVES

Retrieval Practice   While reading the upcoming sections, respond to each Learning Objective in your own words.

Summarize how social-emotional factors affect development across the life span.

- **Review** attachment and the four key parenting styles.
- **Describe** Kohlberg's theory of moral development.

- **Review** Thomas and Chess's temperament theory.
- **Summarize** Erikson's eight psychosocial stages of development.

Real World Application Question

[AQ6] Can foreign travel lead to moral flexibility and immoral behaviors?

In addition to physical and cognitive development, developmental psychologists study the way social and emotional factors affect development over the life span. In this section, we focus on *attachment*, *parenting styles*, *moral reasoning*, and *personality*.

Attachment

An infant arrives in the world with a multitude of behaviors that encourage a strong bond of **attachment** with primary caregivers. Do you recall the discussion at the start of the chapter on the nature-nurture controversy? Researchers who advocate the nativist, or innate, position suggest that newborn infants are biologically equipped with verbal and non-verbal behaviors (such as crying, clinging, and smiling) and imprinting ("following") behaviors (such as crawling and walking after the caregiver) that elicit instinctive nurturing responses from the caregiver (Bowlby, 1969, 1989, 2000).

Studies have found numerous benefits of attachment. For children, a good attachment is associated with lower levels of aggressive behavior, fewer sleep problems, and less social withdrawal (Ding et al., 2014; Lightfoot et al., 2018). A recent large-scale survey of middle-aged and older adults also found that those who had memories of higher parental affection in early childhood were more likely to have better self-rated health and lower depressive symptoms (Chopik & Edelstein, 2019).

But as in the sad case of Genie, discussed at the start of this chapter, some children never form appropriate, loving attachments. What happens to these children? Researchers have investigated this question in two ways: They have looked at children and adults who spent their early years in institutions without the stimulation and love of a regular caregiver. They've also studied children who lived at home but were physically isolated under abusive conditions.

Tragically, infants raised in impersonal or abusive surroundings suffer from a number of problems. They seldom cry, coo, or babble; they become rigid when picked up; and they have few language skills. As for their social-emotional development, they tend to form shallow or anxious relationships. Some appear forlorn, withdrawn, and uninterested in their caretakers, whereas others seem insatiable in their need for affection. They also tend to show intellectual, physical, and perceptual deficiencies, along with increased susceptibility to infection, and neurotic "rocking" and isolation behaviors. There are even cases where healthy babies who were well-fed and kept in clean diapers—but seldom held or stimulated—actually died from lack of attachment (Bowlby, 2000; Duniec & Raz, 2011; Spitz & Wolf, 1946). Some research suggests that childhood emotional abuse and neglect may be as harmful, in terms of long-term mental problems, as physical and sexual abuse (Spinazzola et al., 2014).

Attachment   A strong emotional bond with special others that endures over time.

FIGURE 9.24   **Harlow's study and contact comfort**   Although Harlow's studies of attachment in infant monkeys would be considered unethical today, they did clearly demonstrate that *touch*, and not *feeding*, is crucial to attachment.

Contact Comfort   Harry Harlow and his colleagues (1950, 1971) also investigated the variables that might affect attachment. They created two types of wire-framed surrogate (substitute) "mother" monkeys: one covered by soft terry cloth and one left uncovered (**Figure 9.24**). The infant monkeys were fed by either the cloth or the wire mother, but they otherwise had access to both mothers. The researchers found that the infant monkeys overwhelmingly preferred the soft cloth surrogate—even when the wire surrogate was the one providing the food—as shown in

JGI/Jamie Grill/Getty Images

FIGURE 9.25 **The power of touch** Parents around the world tend to kiss, nuzzle, comfort, and respond to their children with lots of physical contact, which points out its vital role in infant development. It also provides support for the biological, nature argument for attachment.

Figure 9.24. In addition, monkeys "reared" by a cloth mother clung frequently to the soft material of their surrogate mother and developed greater emotional security and curiosity than did monkeys assigned only to the wire mother.

Thanks in part to Harlow's "monkey research," psychologists discovered that *contact comfort*, the pleasurable, tactile sensations provided by a soft and cuddly "parent," is one of the most important variables in attachment (**Figure 9.25**). Further support comes from a study described in Chapter 4, which explains why hospitals now advise that all newborns, particularly those who are born premature, should receive "kangaroo care," in which babies have skin-to-skin contact with a parent (Boundy et al., 2016; Gayen et al., 2019; Mekonnen et al., 2019). For more information on how touch affects us—even as adults—see the following **PP** **PositivePsych**.

Ainsworth's Levels of Attachment
Although physical contact between caregiver and child appears to be an innate, biological part of attachment, Mary Ainsworth and her colleagues discovered several interesting differences in the type and level of human attachment (**Figure 9.26**) (Ainsworth, 1967; Ainsworth et al., 1978; Zeanah & Gleason, 2015). For example, infants with a secure attachment style generally had caregivers who were sensitive and responsive to their signals of distress, happiness, and fatigue. In contrast, anxious/avoidant infants had caregivers who were aloof and distant, and anxious/ambivalent infants had inconsistent caregivers, who alternated between strong affection and indifference. Caregivers of disorganized/disoriented infants tended to be abusive or neglectful.

As a scientific and critical thinker, can you offer additional explanations for attachment, other than differences in caregivers? What about differences in the infants themselves? Researchers have found that the *temperament* (a personality dimension discussed later in the chapter) of the child does play an important role. An infant who is highly anxious and avoidant might not accept or respond to a caregiver's attempts to comfort and soothe. In addition, children and their parents share genetic tendencies, and attachment patterns may reflect these shared genes. Finally, critics

---

PP Practical Application: PositivePsych

Adults Need Hugs Too

(APA Goal 1.3) Describe applications of psychology

As we've just seen, contact comfort is critical for the physical and mental well-being of both monkey and human infants. But did you know that the touch of others is an invaluable and important asset throughout our life span (see photo)? Human touch has been repeatedly shown to be an effective way to solicit and provide social support (e.g., Robinson et al., 2015). It can also reduce pain, heart rate, and blood pressure, and increase levels of oxytocin. Even something as simple as a hand massage can reduce disruptive behaviors in patients with dementia (Fu et al., 2013).

Interestingly, hugs appear to be a particularly effective way of touching. In fact, people who get more frequent hugs are less susceptible to infection and experience less severe illness symptoms (Cohen et al., 2015). The researchers in this study suggest that a hug by a trusted person may act as an effective means of conveying support, and increasing the frequency of hugs might help reduce the deleterious effects of stress.

Take-Home Message Although hugs and other forms of loving touch can reduce stress and promote emotional well-being, uninvited touch generally makes us uncomfortable (Harjunen et al., 2017). Even a friendly pat on the back or "high five" may be too personal. When contemplating hugging or touching other people, it's wise to carefully monitor their physical reactions. Ask yourself questions such as, "Do they relax and lean in when I try to hug them, or do they stiffen and move backward?" and, "Do they

Roberto Westbrook/Tetra images/Getty Images

initiate similar touching, or is it only one-sided?" It's always safer to ask, "Would you like (or mind) a hug?"

Moreover, touch of any kind is a particularly "touchy" situation in the workplace and with young children. The most loving and best-intentioned touch can be seen as a power play, as intimidating or aggressive, or as sexual harassment. The general rule is "Hands off." And parents and caregivers are advised to teach children about "good touch" versus "bad touch." For more details on the power and problems with touch, see the **PAH** Practical Application Highlight in Chapter 10.

FIGURE 9.26 **Research on infant attachment**   For most children, parents are the earliest and most important factor in social development, and the attachment between parent and child is of particular interest to developmental psychologists.

1. After mother and baby spend some time in the experimental room, a stranger enters.

2. The mother then leaves the baby alone with the stranger.

3. The mother returns, and the stranger leaves.

4. The mother leaves, and the baby is alone until the stranger returns.

5. Once again, the mother returns, and the stranger leaves.

a. Strange situation procedure   Mary Ainsworth and her colleagues (1967, 2010) found significant differences in the typical levels of attachment between infants and their mothers using a technique called the strange situation procedure, in which they observed how infants responded to the presence or absence of their mother and a stranger.

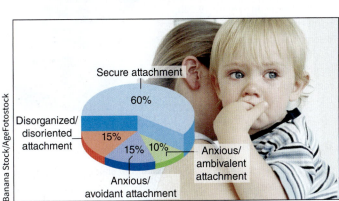

Secure
Infant seeks closeness with mother when stranger enters. Uses her as a safe base from which to explore, shows moderate distress on separation from her, and is happy when she returns.
Anxious/ambivalent
Infant becomes very upset when mother leaves the room and shows mixed emotions when she returns.
Anxious/avoidant
Infant does not seek closeness or contact with the mother and shows little emotion when the mother departs or returns.
Disorganized/disoriented
Infant exhibits avoidant or ambivalent attachment, often seeming either confused or apprehensive in the presence of the mother.

b. Degrees of attachment   Using the strange situation procedure, Ainsworth found that children could be divided into three groups: *secure, anxious/avoidant,* and *anxious/ambivalent*. Later, psychologist Mary Main added a fourth category, *disorganized/disoriented* (Main & Solomon, 1986, 1990).

have suggested that Ainsworth's research does not account for cultural variations, such as cultures that encourage infants to develop attachments to multiple caregivers (Rothbaum et al., 2007; van IJzendoorn & Bakermans-Kranenburg, 2010).

Attachment Styles in Adulthood   Researchers have also examined how varying types of attachment as infants might shape our later adult life. For example, a recent study found that an early secure attachment appears to serve as a protective factor against cognitive decline and dementia in older adulthood (Walsh et al., 2019). Surprisingly, insecurely attached adults tend to be more (not less) risk taking in their consumer purchases compared to those who are securely attached (Li et al., 2019). Why? The researchers suggested that the insecurely attached focus on short-term benefits versus long-term ones, which leads to distorted perceptions of risk and safety.

Researchers have also found that a secure attachment pattern is associated with higher subjective well-being, whereas adolescents and young adults with avoidant and anxious attachment patterns show more depressive symptoms (Desrosiers et al., 2014; Galinha et al.,

2014). Another study found an association between pathological jealousy and the anxious/ambivalent style of attachment (Costa et al., 2015).

Interestingly, research shows that the style of attachment we develop as infants also tends to carry over into our adult approaches to intimacy and affection within romantic relationships. As might be expected, men who grow up in nurturing families are more likely to have secure attachments to their romantic partners as adults (Waldinger & Schulz, 2016). In contrast, both men and women who experienced either unresponsive or overly intrusive parenting during childhood are more likely to avoid committed romantic relationships as adults (Dekel & Farber, 2012). Finally, research finds that when talking about their romantic relationships, those with an avoidant attachment style tend to use fewer "we" words (like "us" and "ours") compared to those with other attachment patterns, which may reveal their avoidant tendencies in relationships (Dunlop et al., 2019). You can check your own romantic attachment style in the following **Test Yourself** feature. However, keep in mind that it's always risky to infer causation from correlation (see Chapter 1). Even if early attachment experiences are correlated with our later relationships, they do not determine them. Throughout life, we can learn new social skills and different approaches to all our relationships.

PA Practical Application

Test Yourself: What's Your Romantic Attachment Style?

Thinking of your current and past romantic relationships, place a check next to the statement that best describes your personal feelings and reactions:

_____ **1.** I find it relatively easy to get close to others and am comfortable depending on them and having them depend on me. I don't often worry about being abandoned or about someone getting too close.

_____ **2.** I am somewhat uncomfortable being close. I find it difficult to trust partners completely or to allow myself to depend on them. I am nervous when anyone gets close, and love partners often want me to be more intimate than is comfortable for me.

_____ **3.** I find that others are reluctant to get as close as I would like. I often worry that my partner doesn't really love me or won't stay with me. I want to merge completely with another person, and this desire sometimes scares people away.

According to research, 55 percent of adults agree with item 1 (secure attachment), 25 percent choose number 2 (anxious/avoidant attachment), and 20 percent choose item 3 (anxious/ambivalent attachment) (adapted from Fraley & Shaver, 1997; Hazan & Shaver, 1987). Note that the percentages for these adult attachment styles do not perfectly match those in Figure 9.26b, partly due to the fact that the disorganized/disoriented attachment pattern was not included in this measurement of adult romantic attachments.

Beatriz Vera/Shutterstock.com

Q Test Your Critical Thinking

1. Do your responses as an adult match your childhood attachment experiences?

2. Does your romantic attachment style negatively affect your present relationship? If so, how might you use this new information to make positive changes?

Parenting Styles

How much of our personality comes from the way our parents treat us as we're growing up? Researchers since the 1920s have studied the effects of different methods of childrearing on children's behavior, development, and mental health. Classic studies by Diana Baumrind (1980, 2013) found that parenting styles could be reliably divided into four broad patterns—*permissive-neglectful*, *permissive-indulgent*, *authoritarian*, and *authoritative*—which can be differentiated by their degree of *control/demandingness* (C) and *warmth/responsiveness* (W) (**Table 9.3**).

As you might expect, authoritative parenting, which encourages independence but still places controls and limits on behavior, is generally the most beneficial for both parents and children (Gherasim et al., 2017; Kuppens & Ceulemans, 2019). Sadly, research has found a link between permissive parenting and college students' sense of "academic entitlement," which in turn is associated with more perceived stress and poorer mental health (Barton & Hirsh, 2016).

TABLE 9.3   **Parenting Styles**

Parenting Style	Description	Example	Potential Effects on Children
Permissive-Neglectful (low C, low W)	Parents make few demands, with little structure or monitoring (low C). They also show little interest or emotional support; may be actively rejecting (low W).	"I don't care about you—or what you do."	Children tend to have poor social skills, and little self-control (being overly demanding and disobedient).
Permissive-Indulgent (low C, high W)	Parents set few limits or demands (low C), but are highly involved and emotionally connected (high W).	"I care about you—and you're free to do what you like."	Children often fail to learn respect for others, and tend to be impulsive, immature, and out of control.
Authoritarian (high C, low W)	Parents are rigid and punitive (high C), but low on warmth and responsiveness (low W).	"I don't care what you want. Just do it my way, or else."	Children tend to be easily upset, moody, and aggressive, and often fail to learn good communication skills.
Authoritative (high C, high W)	Parents generally set and enforce firm limits (high C), while being highly involved, tender, and emotionally supportive high W).	"I really care about you, but there are rules, and you need to be responsible."	Children generally become self-reliant, self-controlled, high achieving, and emotionally well adjusted; also seem more content, goal oriented, friendly, and socially competent.

> **TIP** Are you having trouble understanding the difference between authoritarian and authoritative parenting styles?   An easy way to remember the difference is to notice the two Rs in authoRitaRian, and imagine a Rigid Ruler. Then note the last two Ts in authoriTaTive, and picture a Tender Teacher.

Sources: Baumrind, 2013; Berger, 2019; Hosokawa & Katsura, 2019; Lightfoot et al., 2018.

In contrast, authoritarian parenting by mothers and fathers is linked with increased behavior problems (Hosokawa & Katsura, 2019; Tavassolie et al., 2016). For example, one interesting study found that teenagers whose parents used a controlling style—such as withholding love or creating feelings of guilt—later have more difficulty working out conflicts with friends and romantic partners (Oudekerk et al., 2015).

Regarding the general quality of parental warmth, cross-cultural and longitudinal studies suggest that a lack of parental warmth and/or parental rejection may have long-lasting negative effects (Friesen et al., 2017; Suizzo et al., 2016; Wu & Chao, 2011). The neglect and indifference shown by rejecting parents tend to be correlated with hostile, aggressive children who have a difficult time establishing and maintaining close relationships. As might be expected, these children are more likely to develop psychological problems that require professional intervention.

Evaluating Baumrind's Research   Before concluding that the authoritative pattern is the only way to raise successful children, you should know that many children raised in the other styles also become caring, cooperative adults. Criticism of Baumrind's findings generally falls into three areas:

1. **Child temperament**   Research shows that a child's unique temperament (a personality dimension discussed later in the chapter) may affect the parents' chosen parenting style, just as the parenting style may shape a child's temperament (Bradley & Corwyn, 2008; Miller et al., 2011; Pitzer et al., 2017). In other words, the parents of mature and competent children may have developed the authoritative style as a result of the children's behavior, rather than vice versa.

2. **Parent and child expectations**   Cultural research suggests that a parent's expectations of a child's temperament and a child's expectations of how parents should behave also play important roles in parenting (Laungani, 2007; Manczak et al., 2016; Zhang et al., 2011). As you read earlier in this chapter, adolescents in Korea expect strong parental control and interpret it as a sign of love and deep concern. Adolescents in North America, however, might interpret the same behavior as a sign of parental hostility and rejection.

3. **Limited attention to father's role in parenting**   Until recently, the father's role in discipline and child care was largely ignored by most developmental researchers. But fathers have begun to take a more active role in childrearing, and there has been a corresponding

increase in research. From these studies, we now know that children do best with authoritative dads who are absorbed with, excited about, and responsive to their children.

Children also do best when parents share the same, consistent parenting style. However, mothers and fathers often differ in their approaches, and research shows that such differences may increase marital conflict and child behavior problems (Tavassolie et al., 2016).

Moral Development

> Morality is the basis of things and truth is the substance of all morality.
> —Mahatma Gandhi (Leader of Indian Independence, Philosopher)

Morality The ability to take the perspective of, or empathize with, others and to distinguish right from wrong.

Earlier, we noted that juvenile chimpanzees will soothe a frightened or injured peer. How can we explain such early emergence and cross-species evidence of **morality**—the ability to take the perspective of, or empathize with, others and to distinguish between right and wrong? From a biological and cultural perspective, some researchers suggest that morality may be prewired, evolutionarily based, and culturally universal (Curry et al., 2019; Keltner et al., 2014; Workman & Reader, 2014).

Behaviors like the juvenile chimpanzees' attempt to soothe and help other animals promote the survival of the species. Therefore, evolution may have provided us with a biological basis for moral acts. Surprisingly, biological research also shows that our morality might be linked with actual changes in the brain. While in an fMRI machine that measured their brain activity, participants were asked to play computer games in which they benefitted from lying to an unseen partner (Garret et al., 2016). When these participants told their first small lie, their amygdala showed a strong emotional response. However, as the games continued—and their lies escalated—the amygdala responses grew weaker. The researchers suggested that this reduced amygdala response may be associated with an overall reduced response to dishonesty, and that this type of "slippery slope" might apply to other behaviors. What do you think?

Noting that biology is only one part of the *biopsychosocial model,* in this section we will focus our attention on the psychological and social factors that explain how moral thoughts, feelings, and actions change over the life span.

Kohlberg's Research   Consider the following situation:

> In Europe, a cancer-ridden woman was near death, but an expensive drug existed that might save her. The woman's husband, Heinz, begged the druggist to sell the drug cheaper or to let him pay later. But he refused. Heinz became desperate and broke into the druggist's store and stole it. (Adapted from Kohlberg, 1964, pp. 18–19)

Was Heinz right to steal the drug? What do you consider moral behavior? Is morality "in the eye of the beholder," or are there universal moral truths and principles? Whatever your answer, your ability to think, reason, and respond to Heinz's dilemma may demonstrate your current level of moral development.

One of the most influential researchers in moral development was Lawrence Kohlberg (1927–1987). He presented what he called "moral stories" like the Heinz dilemma to people of all ages, not to see whether they judged Heinz right or wrong but to examine the reasons they gave for their decisions. On the basis of his findings, Kohlberg (1964, 1984) developed a model of moral development, with three broad levels each composed of two distinct stages (**Process Diagram 9.3**). Individuals at each stage and level may or may not support Heinz's stealing of the drug, but their reasoning changes from level to level. At the first *preconventional level*, morality is self-centered and based on rewards, punishments, and exchange of favors. In contrast, during the second *conventional level* moral judgments are based on compliance with the rules and values of society. Individuals at the third *postconventional level* develop personal standards for right and wrong. They define morality in terms of abstract principles and values that apply to all situations and societies.

Assessing Kohlberg's Theory   Kohlberg's ideas have led to considerable research on how we think about moral issues. For example, are people who achieve higher stages on

STOP! This Process Diagram contains essential information NOT found elsewhere in the text, which is likely to appear on quizzes and exams. Be sure to study it CAREFULLY.

PROCESS DIAGRAM 9.3   **Kohlberg's Stages of Moral Development**

Step ❶
Preconventional level
Morality is based on rewards, punishment, and exchange of favors.

Step ❷
Conventional level Moral judgments are based on compliance with the rules and values of society.

Step ❸
Postconventional level   Individuals develop personal standards for right and wrong, and define morality in terms of abstract principles and values that apply to all situations and societies.

PRECONVENTIONAL LEVEL

(Stages 1 and 2—birth to adolescence)
Moral judgment is *self-centered*. What is right is what one can get away with, or what is personally satisfying.

❶ Punishment-obedience orientation

Focus is on self-interest—obedience to authority and avoidance of punishment. Because children at this stage have difficulty considering another's point of view, they ignore people's intentions.

❷ Instrumental-exchange orientation

Children become aware of others' perspectives, but their morality is based on reciprocity—an equal exchange of favors.

CONVENTIONAL LEVEL

(Stages 3 and 4—adolescence to young adulthood)
Moral reasoning is *other-centered*. Conventional societal rules are accepted because they help ensure the social order.

❸ Good-child orientation

Primary moral concern is being nice and gaining approval; judges others by their intentions—"His heart was in the right place."

❹ Law-and-order orientation

Morality based on a larger perspective—societal laws. Understanding that if everyone violated laws, even with good intentions, there would be chaos.

POSTCONVENTIONAL LEVEL

(Stages 5 and 6—adulthood)
Moral judgments based on *personal standards for right and wrong*. Morality is defined in terms of abstract principles and values that apply to all situations and societies.

❺ Social-contract orientation

Appreciation for the underlying purposes served by laws. Societal laws are obeyed because of the "social contract," but they can be morally disobeyed if they fail to express the will of the majority or fail to maximize social welfare.

❻ Universal-ethics orientation

"Right" is determined by universal ethical principles (e.g., non-violence, human dignity, freedom) that moral authorities might view as compelling or fair. These principles apply whether or not they conform to existing laws.

Sources: Based on Kohlberg, L. (1969). Stage and sequence: The cognitive developmental approach to socialization. In D. A. Goslin (Ed.), *The handbook of socialization theory and research* (p. 376, Table 6.2). Chicago, IL: Rand McNally.

Kohlberg's scale really more moral than others? Or do they just "talk a good game"? Some researchers have shown that a person's sense of moral identity, meaning the use of moral principles to define oneself, is often a good predictor of his or her behavior in real-world situations (Johnston et al., 2013; Stets & Carter, 2012). But others have found that situational factors are better predictors of moral behavior (Antonaccio et al., 2017; Bandura, 1989, 2008; Noval & Stahl, 2015). Employees, for instance, are more likely to voluntarily participate in environmentally "green" behaviors at work if their supervisors model such behaviors themselves (Kim et al., 2017a).

Furthermore, research based on hypothetical situations, like Kohlberg's, may not reflect true moral behaviors in actual situations. In one study in which participants had to make real-life moral decisions to administer an electrical shock to a single mouse or allow five other mice to receive the shock, they were twice as likely to NOT shock the single mouse when confronted with a hypothetical versus a real version of the dilemma (Bostyn et al., 2018). Note that the participants did not know that the shock they supposedly delivered to the mice was bogus. People may also behave more "morally" in some situations than others. For example, both men and women tell more sexual lies during casual relationships than during close relationships (Williams, 2001). For more on possible gender and cultural issues related to moral development, see the following **GCD** **Gender and Cultural Diversity**.

GCD **Gender** and **Cultural Diversity**

Can Diversity Affect Moral Development?

(APA Goal 2.5) Incorporate sociocultural factors in scientific inquiry

Are there gender differences in moral development? In Kohlberg's studies, women tended to be classified at a lower level of moral reasoning than men. As noted in **Figure 9.27**, researcher Carol Gilligan suggested that this was true because Kohlberg's theory emphasizes values more often held by men, such as rationality and independence, while deemphasizing common female values, such as concern for others and belonging (Gilligan, 1977, 1990, 1993). Gilligan later expanded on this "care versus justice" difference between women and men by saying that these two positions are not mutually exclusive (Gilligan, 2011).

Although some research has supported a gender difference in moral reasoning based on differences in values (e.g., Armstrong et al., 2019), other studies in this area have not found consistent support (Giammarco, 2016; Gibbs, 2014; Mercadillo et al., 2011). Interestingly, a study of over 6,000 participants did clarify that women are more likely than men to have a stronger emotional aversion to causing harm to others (Friesdorf et al., 2015). However, both sexes engage in similar levels of rational evaluations of the outcomes of harmful action.

Can culture also affect moral development? Several cross-cultural studies do support Kohlberg's model, whereas other studies find significant differences as a function of culture (Csordas, 2014; Endicott & Endicott, 2014; Rest et al., 1999). For instance, cross-cultural comparisons of responses to Heinz's moral dilemma show that Europeans and Americans tend to consider whether they like or identify with the victim in questions of morality (Miller & Bersoff, 1998). In contrast, Hindu Indians consider social responsibility and personal concerns two separate issues. Researchers suggest that the difference may reflect the Indians' broader sense of social responsibility. Furthermore, in India, Papua New Guinea, and China, as well as in Israeli kibbutzim, people don't choose between the rights of the individual and the rights of society (as the top levels of Kohlberg's model require). Instead, most people seek a compromise solution that accommodates both interests (Killen & Hart, 1999; Miller & Bersoff, 1998). Thus, Kohlberg's standard for judging the highest level of

Ted Foxx/Alamy Stock Photo

FIGURE 9.27 **Gilligan versus Kohlberg** According to Carol Gilligan, women score "lower" on Lawrence Kohlberg's stages of moral development given they are socialized to assume more responsibility for the care of others. What do you think?

morality (the postconventional level) may be more applicable to cultures that value individualism over community and interpersonal relationships.

Looking beyond cultural differences in Kohlberg's specific stages of moral development, modern researchers (e.g., Graham et al., 2016) emphasize the need to examine a broader range of factors *within* a given culture, such as religion, social ecology (weather, crop conditions, residential mobility), and social institutions (kinship structures, economic markets), rather than the differences *between* cultures mentioned above.

[AQ6] Before going on, we'd like to share a particularly intriguing study related to cultural differences and morality. Given the common belief that foreign travel experiences enhance one's education and reduce intergroup bias, many will be disturbed by a study that reveals a darker side to travel (Lu et al., 2017). These researchers found that experiences abroad encouraged not only cognitive flexibility but also a type of moral flexibility or relativism that may lead to immoral behaviors. Fortunately, this effect seemed to apply only to broad, brief travel to many countries, which exposes the traveler to a wide variety of differing moral codes over a short time.

Recognizing that travel time is limited for most people and that tourists often want to visit several countries in one trip, the authors of this study suggest that travelers review their own moral values and standards before leaving home. Can you see how the popular study abroad programs offered at many universities and colleges, in which students typically spend several weeks, a semester, or even an entire year in one country, might be ideal? They provide more time and experiences that should lead to a deeper understanding of the differing moral codes and values of the host country (see photo).

Courtesy of Lee Decker

Personality Development

As an infant, did you lie quietly and seem oblivious to loud noises? Or did you tend to kick and scream and respond immediately to every sound? Did you respond warmly to people, or did you fuss, fret, and withdraw? Your answers to these questions help determine what developmental psychologists call your **temperament**, an individual's innate disposition or behavioral style and typical emotional response.

Temperament   An individual's innate disposition or behavioral style and typical emotional response.

Thomas and Chess's Temperament Theory   One of the earliest and most influential theories regarding temperament came from the work of psychiatrists Alexander Thomas and Stella Chess (Thomas & Chess, 1977, 1987, 1991). These researchers found that approximately 65 percent of the babies they observed could be reliably separated into three categories:

1. **Easy children**   These infants were happy most of the time, were relaxed and agreeable, and adjusted easily to new situations (approximately 40 percent).
2. **Difficult children**   Infants in this group were moody, easily frustrated, tense, and overreactive in most situations (approximately 10 percent).
3. **Slow-to-warm-up children**   These infants showed mild responses, were somewhat shy and withdrawn, and needed time to adjust to new experiences and people (approximately 15 percent).

Follow-up studies have found that certain aspects of these temperament styles tend to be consistent and enduring throughout childhood and even adulthood (Kopala-Sibley et al., 2018; Sayal et al., 2014). But that is not to say every shy, cautious infant ends up a shy adult. Many events take place between infancy and adulthood that shape an individual's development. Moreover, culture can also influence infant temperament. One study found that Dutch babies tend to be happier and easier to soothe, whereas babies born in the United States are typically more active and vocal (Sung et al., 2015). These temperament differences are thought to reflect cultural differences in parenting styles and values.

One of the most influential factors in early personality development is *goodness of fit* between a child's nature, parental behaviors, and the social and environmental setting (Newland & Crnic, 2017; Smiley et al., 2016). For example, a slow-to-warm-up child does best if allowed time to adjust to new situations. Similarly, a difficult child thrives in a structured, understanding environment, but not in an inconsistent, intolerant home. Alexander Thomas, one of the pioneers of temperament research, thinks parents should work with their child's temperament rather than try to change it. Can you see how this idea of goodness of fit is yet another example of how nature and nurture interact?

Erikson's Psychosocial Theory   Like Piaget and Kohlberg, Erik Erikson developed a stage theory of development. He identified eight **psychosocial stages** of social development, with each stage marked by a "psychosocial" crisis or conflict that must be successfully resolved for proper future development (**Process Diagram 9.4**).

Psychosocial stages   Erikson's theory that identifies eight developmental stages, each involving a crisis that must be successfully resolved for proper future development.

> **STOP!** This Process Diagram contains essential information NOT found elsewhere in the text, which is likely to appear on quizzes and exams. Be sure to study it CAREFULLY.

PROCESS DIAGRAM 9.4 **Erikson's Eight Stages of Psychosocial Development** Erikson identified eight stages of development, each of which is associated with its own unique psychosocial crisis.

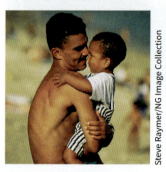
Steve Raymer/NG Image Collection

1 Trust versus mistrust (birth–age 1)

Infants learn to *trust* or *mistrust* their caregivers and the world based on whether or not their needs—such as food, affection, safety—are met.

Courtesy of Karen Huffman

2 Autonomy versus shame and doubt (ages 1–3)

Toddlers start to assert their sense of independence (*autonomy*). If caregivers encourage this self-sufficiency, the toddler will learn to be independent versus feeling *shame* and *doubt.*

Courtesy of Sandy Harvey

3 Initiative versus guilt (ages 3–6)

Preschoolers learn to *initiate* activities and develop self-confidence and a sense of social responsibility. If not, they feel irresponsible, anxious, and *guilty*.

Courtesy of Linda Locklear

4 Industry versus inferiority (ages 6–12)

Elementary school-aged children who succeed in learning new, productive life skills develop a sense of pride and competence (industry). Those who fail to develop these skills feel inadequate and unproductive (*inferior*).

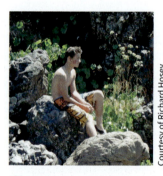
Courtesy of Richard Hosey

5 Identity versus role confusion (ages 12–20)

Adolescents develop a coherent and stable self-definition (*identity*) by exploring many roles and deciding who or what they want to be in terms of career, attitudes, and so on. Failure to resolve this *identity crisis* may lead to apathy, withdrawal, and/or *role confusion*.

Courtesy of Richard Hosey

6 Intimacy versus isolation (early adulthood)

Young adults form lasting, meaningful relationships that help them develop a sense of connectedness and *intimacy* with others. If not, they become psychologically *isolated*.

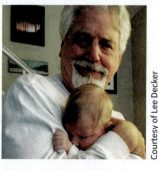
Wavebreakmedia/Shutterstock.com

7 Generativity versus stagnation (middle adulthood)

The challenge for middle-aged adults is in nurturing the young, and making contributions to society through their work, family, or community activities. Failing to meet this challenge leads to self-indulgence and a sense of *stagnation*.

Courtesy of Lee Decker

8 Ego integrity versus despair (late adulthood)

During this stage, older adults reflect on their past. If this reflection reveals a life well-spent, the person experiences self-acceptance and satisfaction (*ego integrity*). If not, he or she experiences regret and deep dissatisfaction (*despair*).

The name for each psychosocial stage reflects the specific crisis encountered at that stage and two possible outcomes. For example, the crisis or task of most young adults is *intimacy versus isolation*. This age group's developmental challenge is establishing deep, meaningful relations with others. Those who don't meet this challenge risk social isolation. Erikson believed that the more successfully we overcome each psychosocial crisis, the better chance we have to develop in a healthy manner (Erikson, 1950).

Many psychologists agree with Erikson's general idea that psychosocial crises, which are based on interpersonal and environmental interactions, do contribute to personality and social development (Kuiper et al., 2016; Lightfoot et al., 2018; Major et al., 2016). As an example, researchers have found that adolescence is a critical time for consolidating one's identity and developing sexual and non-sexual intimacy—thus supporting Erikson's stage six (Brandell & Brown, 2015). These researchers also found that successful resolution of this stage may be harder in modern times due to adolescents' increased exposure to social media, pornography, casual "hook-ups," and recreational drugs and alcohol.

Erikson's conclusions have been criticized in three major areas (Kroger, 2015; Robinson, 2016; Schwartz et al., 2016). First, his narrow focus on only one challenge for each developmental stage ignores other critical tasks in the same period. Second, Erikson's psychosocial stages are difficult to test scientifically. Third, the labels Erikson used to describe the eight stages may not be entirely appropriate cross-culturally. In individualistic cultures, *autonomy* is highly preferable to *shame and doubt*. But in collectivist cultures, the preferred resolution might be *dependence* or *merging relations* (Berry et al., 2011).

Despite their limits, Erikson's stages have greatly contributed to the study of North American and European psychosocial development. By suggesting that development continues past adolescence, Erikson's theory has encouraged ongoing research and theory development.

Take-Home Message   As you've discovered in this chapter, our physical, cognitive, and social-emotional development continue throughout our lives. Given the information in this chapter, we firmly believe you'll be better equipped to deal with life's inevitable changes, challenges, and difficulties. You have our best wishes for a happy, successful, and satisfying life throughout all your stages of development.

Before going on, be sure to complete the final Retrieval Practice, and then answer the critical thinking questions in the **Test Your Critical Thinking**.

Retrieval Practice 9.4 | Social-Emotional Development

Self-Test   Completing this self-test, and then checking your answers by clicking on the answer button or by looking in Appendix B, will provide immediate feedback and helpful practice for exams.

1. According to Harlow's research with cloth and wire surrogate mother monkeys, _____ is one of the most important variables in attachment.

   a. contact comfort
   b. comfort food
   c. neonatal breast feeding
   d. age group peer contact ("free play" periods)

2. Five-year-old Tyler believes "bad things are what you get punished for." Tyler is at Kohlberg's _____ stage of morality.

   a. law-and-order orientation
   b. punishment-obedience orientation
   c. good-child orientation
   d. social-contract orientation

3. You have a child who is a month old and seems to be shy and withdrawn, and who needs time to adjust to new experiences. According to Thomas and Chess's temperament theory, your child might be classified as a(n) _____ child.

   a. insecurely attached
   b. introverted
   c. slow-to-warm-up
   d. difficult

4. According to Erikson, industry is the result of the successful completion of the _____ stage of development.

   a. infancy and toddlerhood
   b. ages 6 through 12
   c. young adulthood
   d. middle adulthood

5. Erikson suggested that problems in adulthood are sometimes related to unsuccessful resolution of one of his eight stages. For each of the following individuals, identify the most likely "problem" stage:

   a. _____ Marcos has trouble keeping friends and jobs because he feels unsafe, and he continually asks for guarantees and reassurance of his worth.

   b. _____ Ann has attended several colleges without picking a major, has taken several vocational training programs, and has had numerous jobs over the past 10 years.

   c. _____ Teresa is reluctant to apply for a promotion even though her coworkers have encouraged her to do so. She lacks self-confidence and feels guilty that she will be taking a job from someone else.

   d. _____ George continually obsesses over the value of his life. He regrets that he left his wife and children for a job in another country and failed to maintain contact.

Q Test Your Critical Thinking

1. Describe how attachment has influenced your social development. Which of Ainsworth's attachment styles best describes you?

2. What stage of moral development do you think you would qualify for, according to Kohlberg? Do you agree or disagree with this categorization?

3. How have your sex and gender affected your social development?

Real World Application Question

[AQ6] Can foreign travel lead to moral flexibility and immoral behaviors?

Hint: Look in the text for **[AQ6]**

Courtesy of Lee Decker

Q Test Your Critical Thinking

Did you notice or wonder why we provided six Real World Application Questions [AQ1–AQ6] throughout this chapter? We've found that they not only help you to engage with and master the material, they also have an important and lasting impact on your critical thinking skills. For additional mastery and enrichment, consider the following questions:

1. People are often surprised, amused, and sometimes even critical of infants, like the one in this photo, who messily play with their food. Using Piaget's stage of sensorimotor development, explain why this type of "messiness" is a healthy, normal example of cognitive development.

2. What schemas might the child build by "exploring" her food in this way?

3. How might the various attachment styles correlate with Baumrind's parenting styles? Which parenting style do you believe is the best? Why?

4. Do you believe that men and women reason differently about morality? If so, what might be the pros and cons of these differences?

5. Which Eriksonian stage do you think best explains your current personality and life choices?

6. Upon completion of your study of this chapter, which side of the nature–nurture debate do you most support? Why?

Amy Whitt/Radius Images/Getty Images

Summary

9.1 Studying Development 274

- **Developmental psychology** is the study of age-related changes in behavior and mental processes, including stages of growth, from conception to death. Development is an ongoing, lifelong process.

- The three most important debates or questions in human development are about *nature versus nurture* (including studies of maturation and **critical periods**), *stages versus continuity*, and *stability versus change*.

- Developmental psychologists use two special techniques in their research: **cross-sectional design** and **longitudinal design**. Although both have valuable attributes, each has disadvantages. Cross-sectional studies can confuse genuine age differences with *cohort effects*. On the other hand, longitudinal studies are expensive and time consuming. Both research techniques also suffer from restricted generalizability.

- Cultural psychologists suggest that: (1) culture may be the major determinant of development, (2) human development cannot be studied outside its sociocultural context, (3) each culture's ethnotheories are key determinants of behavior, and (4) culture is largely invisible to its participants.

9.2 Physical Development 279

- Prenatal development begins at conception, and is divided into three stages: the **germinal period** (ovulation to implantation), **the embryonic period** (implantation to 8 weeks), **and the fetal period** (8 weeks to birth).

- Throughout our life span, environmental, **epigenetic** factors affect how our inherited genes are expressed. During pregnancy, the *placenta* serves as the link for food and the elimination of wastes, and it screens out some harmful substances—but not **teratogens**, such as alcohol and nicotine.

- Early childhood is a time of rapid physical development, including brain, motor, and sensory/perceptual development. During *adolescence*, both boys and girls undergo dramatic changes in appearance and physical capacity. **Puberty** is the period of adolescence when a person becomes capable of reproduction.

- During the period of **emerging adulthood**, approximately ages 18–25, individuals in Western nations have left the dependency of childhood, but not yet assumed adult responsibilities.

- During adulthood, most individuals experience only minor physical changes until middle age. Around age 45–55, women experience *menopause*, the cessation of the menstrual cycle. At the same time, men experience a gradual decline in the production of sperm and testosterone, as well as other physical changes, known as the *male climacteric*.

- After middle age, most physical changes in development are gradual and occur in the heart and arteries as well as in the sensory receptors.

9.3 Cognitive Development   293

- Piaget believed an infant's intellectual growth progresses in distinct stages, motivated by an innate need to know. He also proposed three major concepts: **schemas**, patterns that organize our interactions with the environment; **assimilation**, absorbing new information "as is" into existing schemas; and **accommodation**, adjusting old schemas or developing new ones to fit with new information.

- According to Piaget, all children progress through four stages of cognitive development: the **sensorimotor stage**, the **preoperational stage**, the **concrete operational stage**, and the **formal operational stage**.

- In the sensorimotor stage, children acquire **object permanence**. During the preoperational stage, children are better equipped to use symbols. But their language and thinking are limited by their lack of operations, **egocentrism**, and animism. In the concrete operational stage, children learn to perform operations (to think about concrete things while not actually doing them). They understand the principles of **conservation** and reversibility. During the formal operational stage, the adolescent is able to think abstractly and deal with hypothetical situations, but is prone to a type of adolescent egocentrism.

- Aging was once believed to involve widespread death of neurons in the brain. Although mental speed declines with age, general information processing and much of memory ability are largely unaffected by the aging process. Despite research on the **age-related positivity effect**, one of the greatest problems for the elderly is the various negative stereotypes that contribute to our society's widespread **ageism**.

- Piaget's account of cognitive development has been enormously influential, but it has received significant criticisms. Vygotsky emphasized the sociocultural influences on a child's cognitive development, rather than Piaget's internal schemas. In addition, Vygotsky believed that adults play an important instructor role in development and that this instruction is particularly helpful when it falls within a child's **zone of proximal development (ZPD)**. Piaget has also been criticized for underestimating children's abilities, as well as the genetic and cultural influences on cognitive development. The **theory of mind (ToM)** presents another alternative to Piaget. It proposes that children become less egocentric when they recognize that other people don't have the same thoughts and feelings that they do.

9.4 Social-Emotional Development   301

- Harlow and his colleagues' research with monkeys raised by cloth or wire "mothers" found that *contact comfort* might be the most important factor in **attachment**.

- Using the strange situation procedure, Ainsworth found that children could be divided into three groups: secure, anxious/avoidant, and anxious/ambivalent. Mary Main later added a fourth category, disorganized/disoriented.

- In addition to attachment patterns, Baumrind's four parenting styles—*permissive-neglectful, permissive-indulgent, authoritarian*, and *authoritative*—also affect a child's social development.

- Kohlberg proposed three levels in the evolution of moral reasoning: the **preconventional level** (stages 1 and 2), the **conventional level** (stages 3 and 4), and the **postconventional level** (stages 5 and 6).

- Thomas and Chess studied differences among infants in their **temperament**, and found that most could be classified into three categories: *easy, difficult*, and *slow to warm up*.

- Erikson identified eight **psychosocial stages** of development, each marked by a crisis (such as the adolescent *identity crisis*) related to a specific developmental task.

Key Terms

Retrieval Practice   Write your own definition for each term before turning back to the referenced page to check your answer.

Kuttelvaserova Stuchelova/Shutterstock.com

Sex, Gender, and Sexuality

Dayna More/123RF

Real World Application Questions

Things you'll learn in Chapter 10

[AQ1] Do some cultures find romantic kissing repulsive?

[AQ2] Do AI voice assistants, like Apple's Siri, reinforce gender stereotypes?

[AQ3] Is gender identity a choice?

[AQ4] Is "hooking up" more common today than dating?

[AQ5] Is "stranger = danger" largely a myth?

[AQ6] What are the two key ingredients for an effective apology?

Throughout the chapter, look for the [AQ1]–[AQ6] icons. They indicate where the text addresses these questions.

CHAPTER OUTLINE

LEARNING OBJECTIVES

Retrieval Practice   While reading the upcoming sections, respond to each Learning Objective in your own words.

Summarize the early studies and modern research in human sexuality.

- **Describe** the limits and contributions of the early studies of sexuality.

- **Discuss** the advances in modern sexuality research and the major findings and value of cross-cultural studies of sexuality.

Real World Application Question

[AQ1] Do some cultures find romantic kissing repulsive?

This chapter begins with a brief look at how we study sexuality, followed by a section that discusses sexual identity and behavior. Then we explore sex problems and disorders. We close with a look at sex in modern life, including sexual victimization, communication, and conflict. Before we start our examination of the early studies of sexuality, check out some of the myths and misconceptions about this field in the **Test Yourself**.

PA Practical Application

Test Yourself: Common Myths About Sexuality

True or False?

1. The breakfast cereal Kellogg's Corn Flakes was originally developed to discourage masturbation.
2. Nocturnal emissions and masturbation are signs of abnormal sexual adjustment.
3. Sex and gender are essentially the same.
4. Androgyny is a type of homosexuality.
5. "Transsexual" is just another word for a transvestite.
6. Men and women are more alike than different in their sexual responses.
7. Sexual skill and satisfaction are learned behaviors that can be increased through education and training.
8. The American Psychiatric Association and the American Psychological Association (APA) consider homosexuality a type of mental illness.
9. Sex education should begin as early as possible.

ammentorp/123RF

10. Rape is a crime of passion.
11. Men can't be raped.
12. "Assertiveness" is just another word for aggressiveness.

Answers: 1. T 2. F 3. F 4. F 5. F 6. T 7. T 8. F 9. T 10. F 11. F 12. F

Early Studies

People have probably always been interested in understanding their **sexuality**. But cultural and religious forces have often led them to suppress and control this interest.

During the 19th century, people in polite society avoided mentioning any part of the body covered by clothing, so the breast of chickens became known as "white meat," and male doctors examined female patients in totally dark rooms (Carroll, 2019; Orrells, 2015; Pettit & Hegarty, 2014).

Medical experts during this Victorian period warned that masturbation led to blindness, impotence, acne, and insanity. Believing a bland diet helped suppress sexual desire, Dr. John Harvey Kellogg and Sylvester Graham developed the original Kellogg's Corn Flakes and graham crackers and marketed them as foods that would discourage masturbation

Sexuality   The ways in which we experience and express ourselves as sexual beings; includes sexual arousal, orientation, and behaviors.

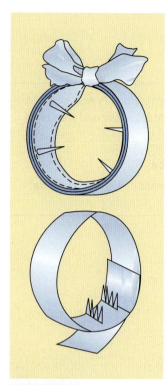

FIGURE 10.1 **Victorian sexual practice** During the 19th century, men were encouraged to wear spiked rings around their penises at night. Can you explain why?

Answer: The Victorians believed nighttime erections and emissions ("wet dreams") were dangerous. If the man had an erection, the spikes would cause great pain and quickly awaken him.

(Maunder, 2016; Money et al., 1991; Wills, 2019). One of the most serious concerns of many doctors was nocturnal emissions, which were believed to lead to brain damage and death. Special devices were even marketed for men to wear at night to prevent sexual arousal (**Figure 10.1**).

As a modern-day college student, it's most likely challenging for you to understand these early practices and myths. One of the first physicians to question them was Havelock Ellis (1858–1939). When he first heard of the dangers of nocturnal emissions, Ellis was frightened; he had had personal experience with the problem. His fear led him to frantically search the medical literature, where instead of a cure he found only predictions of gruesome illness and eventual death. He was so upset he contemplated suicide.

Ellis eventually decided he could give meaning to his life by keeping a detailed diary of his deterioration. He planned to dedicate the book to science when he died. However, after several months of careful observation, Ellis realized that the experts were wrong. He wasn't dying. He wasn't even sick. Angry that he had been so misinformed, he spent the rest of his life developing reliable and accurate sex information. Today, thanks in part to his informal case study of his own sexuality, Havelock Ellis is acknowledged as one of the most influential pioneers in the field of sex research.

Modern Research

Alfred Kinsey and his colleagues (1948, 1953) were among the first modern sex researchers. They personally surveyed and interviewed more than 18,000 participants, asking detailed questions about their sexual activities and preferences. The results shocked the nation. Kinsey reported that 37 percent of men and 13 percent of women had engaged in adult same-sex behavior to the point of orgasm. Although Kinsey's interviewing techniques were excellent, his data have been heavily criticized for violating certain ethical and research standards.

Since Kinsey's time, literally thousands of similar surveys and interviews have been conducted on such topics as contraception, abortion, premarital sex, sexual orientation, and sexual behavior. By comparing Kinsey's data to the responses found in later surveys, we can see how sexual practices have changed over the years. Given the value of empirical, scientifically based surveys and interviews, particularly for the lesbian, gay, bisexual, transgender, queer, or questioning (LGBTQ+) community, the American Psychological Association adopted an official resolution recommending that research studies include sexual orientation and gender identity in their data collection (American Psychological Association, 2016).

In addition to surveys, interviews, and case studies, some researchers have employed biological research methods, as well as direct laboratory experimentation and observational methods. For instance, direct laboratory experimentation and observation were first conducted by William Masters and Virginia Johnson (1961, 1966, 1970) and their research colleagues. To experimentally document the physiological changes that occur in sexual arousal and response, they first enlisted several hundred male and female volunteers. Then, using intricate physiological measuring devices, the researchers carefully monitored participants' bodily responses as they masturbated or engaged in sexual intercourse. Masters and Johnson's research findings have been hailed as a major contribution to our knowledge of sexual physiology. A brief summary of their results is presented later in this chapter.

Researchers have also found several cultural differences in sexuality. For example, a cross-cultural study asked both U.S. and Dutch parents whether they would allow their teenage child to spend the night with a dating partner in their own home. Interestingly, only 9 percent of U.S. parents said they would allow such a sleepover, compared to a whopping 93 percent of the Dutch parents (Schalet, 2011). In the Netherlands, and many Scandinavian countries, comprehensive sex education, including information about birth control and sexual pleasuring, is required. In contrast, such programs continue to be controversial in the United States. For more information on modern research in sexuality, see the **RC** **Research Challenge** and the **GCD** **Gender & Cultural Diversity**.

RC Scientific Thinking: **Research Challenge**

Why Do Men and Women Lie About Sex?

(APA Goal 2.4) Interpret, design, and conduct basic psychological research

Do you recall from Chapter 1 our discussion of how research results may be contaminated when participants are asked questions about sensitive topics, like sexuality (see cartoon)? Or how they might distort their responses in an attempt to present themselves in a positive light? This type of *social desirability bias* is of particular concern when we study sexual behaviors. A fascinating example comes from a study that asked randomly assigned college students to complete a questionnaire regarding how often they engaged in 124 different gender-typical behaviors (Fisher, 2013). Some of these behaviors were considered more typical of men (such as wearing dirty clothes and telling obscene jokes), whereas other behaviors were more common among women (such as writing poetry and lying about their weight). Half of the participants completed these questionnaires while attached to what they were told was a polygraph machine (or lie detector), although in reality this machine was not working. The other half completed the questionnaires without being attached to such a machine.

Can you predict how students responded? Among the participants who believed they were attached to the supposed lie detector, and that it could reliably detect their lies, men were more likely to admit that they sometimes engaged in behaviors seen as more appropriate for women, such as writing poetry. In contrast, women were more likely to admit that they sometimes engaged in behaviors judged more appropriate for men, such as telling obscene jokes. Even more intriguing, men reported having had more sexual partners when they weren't hooked up to the lie detector than when they were. The reverse was true for women. They reported fewer partners when they were not hooked up to the lie detector than when they were.

How does the *social desirability response* help explain these differences? We're all socialized from birth to conform to norms (unwritten rules) for our culturally approved male and female behaviors. Therefore, participants who were NOT attached to the supposed lie detector provided more "gender appropriate" responses. Men admitted telling obscene jokes and reported having more sexual partners, whereas women admitted lying about their weight and reported having fewer sexual partners.

These findings were virtually reversed when participants believed they were connected to a machine that could detect their lies. This fact provides a strong example of the dangers of the social desirability response. It also reminds us, as either researchers or

Would you have a moment to take a short survey about your experience?

Chatfield, Jason/Cartoon Stock

consumers, to be very careful when interpreting findings regarding sexual attitudes and behaviors. Gender roles may lead to inaccurate reporting and exaggerated gender differences.

Identify the Research Method

1. Based on the information provided, did this study (Fisher, 2013) use descriptive, correlational, and/or experimental research?

2. If you chose:

   o *descriptive research*, is this a naturalistic or laboratory observation, survey/interview, case study, and/or archival research?

   o *correlational research*, is this a positive, negative, or zero correlation?

   o *experimental research*, label the IV, DV, experimental group(s), and control group. (Note: If participants were not randomly assigned to groups, list it as a *quasi-experimental design*.)

   o both *descriptive* and *correlational* research, answer the corresponding questions for both.

Check your answers by clicking on the answer button or by looking in Appendix B.

Note: The information provided in this study is admittedly limited, but the level of detail is similar to what is presented in most textbooks and public reports of research findings. Answering these questions, and then comparing your answers to those provided, will help you become a better scientific and critical thinker and consumer of scientific research.

GCD **Gender** and **Cultural Diversity**

Sexuality Across Cultures

(APA Goal 2.5) Incorporate sociocultural factors in scientific inquiry

Sex researchers interested in both similarities and variations in human sexual behavior conduct cross-cultural studies of sexual practices, techniques, and attitudes (e.g., Beach, 1977; Buss, 2011; Espinosa-Hernández et al., 2016). Their studies of different societies put sex in a broader perspective. One cross-cultural study found similarities and differences in the perceptions of interpersonal touching,

such as handshakes and hugs. Researchers who compared one Western country (the United Kingdom) with one East Asian country (Japan) found that participants in both countries allowed women to touch their bodies more than men (Suvilehto et al., 2019). Furthermore, all participants touch and are touched more by their mothers than their fathers. As expected, in both countries, the body locations where social touch is allowed were closely related to the strength of the emotional bond between the person touched and the toucher—meaning that more touching was allowed by romantic partners, followed by close family members and relatives.

Mangaia (Polynesian Island)	Yolngu (Island near Australia)	Inis Beag (Irish Island)
Childhood sexuality: • Children readily exposed to sex. • Adolescents are given direct instruction in techniques for pleasuring their sexual partners. • Both boys and girls are encouraged to have many partners.	**Childhood sexuality:** • Permissive attitude toward childhood sexuality. • Parents soothe infants by stroking their genitals. • Nudity accepted from infancy through old age.	**Childhood sexuality:** • Sexual expression is strongly discouraged. • Children learn to abhor nudity and are given no information about sex. • Young girls are often shocked by their first menstruation.
Adult sexuality: • After marriage, three orgasms per night are not uncommon for men. • Men are encouraged to "give" three orgasms to their female partner for every one of their own. • Adults practice a wide range of sexual behaviors.	**Adult sexuality:** • Men can have many wives and are generally happy with their sex life. • Women are given no choice in marital partner and little power in the home. • Women are apathetic about sex, seldom orgasmic, and generally unhappy.	**Adult sexuality:** • Little sex play before intercourse. • Female orgasm is unknown or considered deviant. • Numerous misconceptions about sex (e.g., intercourse can be debilitating, menopause causes insanity).

FIGURE 10.2 Cross-cultural differences in sexual behavior
Note: "Inis Beag" is a pseudonym used to protect the privacy of residents of this Irish island, which is another interesting cultural difference. The other communities cited apparently don't require pseudonyms.

Sources: Burns, 2019; Gregersen, 1996; Marshall, 1971; Money et al., 1991; Orrells, 2015.

Can you see how cross-cultural studies of sex not only expose cultural similarities and differences, they also help counteract *ethnocentrism*, the tendency to judge our own cultural practices as "normal" and preferable to those of other groups? Did you know that fewer than half of the 168 cultures studied around the world engage in romantic/sexual kissing (Jankowiak et al., 2015)? **[AQ1]** Perhaps even more surprising is the fact that many people in sub-Saharan Africa, New Guinea, the Amazon, and many native cultures in Central America find this type of kissing uncomfortable or even repulsive (see photo).

astarot/Shutterstock.com

Furthermore, some members of Tiwi society, off the northern coast of Australia, believe young girls will not develop breasts or menstruate unless they first experience intercourse. Research in Samoa and Mexico has also found that both cultures recognize a third gender—more specifically, males who are feminine and sexually attracted to adult males (Willis, 2018). This third gender is well integrated into the community and men who have sex with both the third gender and other men are more common than men who have sex exclusively with women. See **Figure 10.2** for more examples of cultural variations in sexuality.

Although other cultures' practices may seem unnatural and strange to us, we forget that our own sexual rituals may appear equally curious to others. As an example of possible ethnocentrism, carefully consider how you feel about the common American practice of routine circumcision of infant boys.

S&P Scientific Thinking and Practical Application

What do modern physicians recommend about infant circumcision? Despite the fact that one in three males is currently circumcised around the world (see photo), there is considerable controversy over its practice (Piontek & Albani, 2019). At one point, the American Academy of Pediatrics (AAP) decided that the reported medical benefits of circumcision were so statistically small that the procedure should *NOT* be routinely performed (American Academy of Pediatrics, 1999, 2005).

This position was later revised. In 2012, the AAP concluded that the health benefits of newborn male circumcision outweigh the risks, but the benefits are not great enough to recommend universal newborn circumcision ... the final choice should still be left to parents (American Academy of Pediatrics, 2012). In contrast to this AAP position, most physicians and health experts in other parts of the Western world, including Europe, Canada, and Australia, still contend that there is no compelling medical benefit to newborn circumcision, and that the

PhotoStock-Israel/Alamy Stock Photo

AAP reversal may reflect a cultural or religious rationale (Earp, 2015; Frisch et al., 2013; Myers, 2015). Others have argued that, at a minimum, we should wait until the boys are old enough to decide for themselves (Erlings, 2016). What do you think?

Retrieval Practice 10.1 | Studying Human Sexuality

Self-Test   Completing this self-test, and then checking your answers by clicking on the answer button or by looking in Appendix B, will provide immediate feedback and helpful practice for exams.

1. During the Victorian period, it was believed that _____ led to blindness, impotence, acne, and insanity, whereas _____ led to brain damage and death.

   a. female orgasms; male orgasms

   b. masturbation; nocturnal emissions

   c. menstruation; menopause

   d. oral sex; sodomy

2. _____ was a major pioneer in sex research who used an informal case study method to record his own sexuality.

   a. B. F. Skinner

   b. Sigmund Freud

   c. Alfred Kinsey

   d. Havelock Ellis

3. Some of the earliest and most extensive surveys and interviews of human sexual behavior in the United States were conducted by _____.

   a. Havelock Ellis

   b. William Masters and Virginia Johnson

   c. Emily and John Roper

   d. Alfred Kinsey and his colleagues

4. Direct laboratory experimentation and observation of human sexuality were first conducted by _____.

   a. Alfred Kinsey

   b. William Masters and Virginia Johnson

   c. Havelock Ellis

   d. all of these individuals

5. Cross-cultural studies of human sexuality help counteract _____, the tendency to view our culture's sexual practices as normal and preferable to those of other groups.

   a. sexual prejudice   **c.** ethnocentrism

   b. ethnic typing   **d.** sexual predation

Q Test Your Critical Thinking

1. Which of the major sex researchers (Ellis, Kinsey, or Masters and Johnson) do you think contributed the most valuable information to the field of human sexuality? Why?

2. Which of the cross-cultural sexual practices do you find most interesting? Why?

Real World Application Question

[AQ1]   Do some cultures find romantic kissing repulsive?

astarot/Shutterstock.com

Hint: Look in the text for **[AQ1]**

10.2 Sexual Identity and Behavior

LEARNING OBJECTIVES

Retrieval Practice   While reading the upcoming sections, respond to each Learning Objective in your own words.

Review the key terms and concepts underlying sex versus gender.

- **Contrast** sex, gender, and intersex.
- **Review** the normal variations in biological sex and gender.
- **Discuss** the theories of gender-role development and potential problems with gender roles.
- **Describe** how we form our gender identity and its variations.

- **Discuss** the various theories, myths, and complexity of sexual orientation, and the myths and dangers of sexual prejudice.
- **Review** the major factors involved in sexual arousal and response.

Real World Application Questions

[AQ2] Do AI voice assistants, like Apple's Siri, reinforce gender stereotypes?

[AQ3] Is gender identity a choice?

Have you noticed that the first question most people ask after a baby is born is "Is it a girl or a boy?" What would life be like if there were no divisions according to maleness or femaleness? Would your career plans or friendship patterns change? These questions reflect the role of *sex* and *gender* in our lives—the two major topics in this section.

Describing Sex and Gender

Sex The state of being biologically male or female; also, sexual activities.

Gender The psychological and sociocultural traits typically associated with a person's biological sex, such as masculinity or femininity.

Intersex A person with reproductive or sexual anatomy that doesn't clearly fall into either category of biologically male or female.

The term **sex** is defined as the state of being biologically male or female, such as having a penis or vagina. The term also includes sexual activities, like masturbation and sexual intercourse. **Gender**, on the other hand, encompasses the psychological and sociocultural traits typically associated with a person's biological sex, such as "masculinity" and "femininity." In other words, *sex* is biological and *gender* is psychological and sociocultural.

It's important to recognize that sex and gender are not separate entities. Instead, they're interrelated and continually interacting throughout our life span. As you may recall from Chapter 9, the field of *epigenetics* studies how non-genetic factors can dramatically affect how (and if) certain genes are expressed. Although it's easy to see how genes affect our biological sex, what's surprising is that environmental factors (such as how the world responds to our perceived gender) may lead to permanent brain changes in males and females (e.g., Cortes et al., 2019).

How do we know this? Given the ethical and logistical impossibilities of controlled experiments with developing humans, epigenetic studies with rodents are common. From these studies, it's well known that mother rats lick their newborn male rats more than their females, and that the amount of maternal care (licking) directly affects sex-related hormone receptors in the brain (e.g., Kurian et al., 2010; Moore & Morelli, 1979). Using a paintbrush to simulate maternal licking, one experimental study gave extra attention (paintbrush strokes) to randomly assigned newborn female rats, and the treatment did, in fact, masculinize the newborn female rats' brains (Edelmann & Auger, 2011).

Obviously, it's a leap from rats to humans, but throughout history parents and society have treated people differently based on their perceived gender. Interestingly, a modern study found that fathers of sons engaged in more rough-and-tumble play and used more achievement-related words, like "proud" and "win," with their sons (Mascaro et al., 2017). In contrast, fathers with daughters were more attentive and responsive to their daughters' needs and spoke more openly about emotions, including sadness.

What's the take-away message? If we now know that this type of gender-based treatment may have permanent effects on brain development, what are the implications of our current fascination with gender, and "gender reveal" parties that celebrate and focus such great attention on the sex of the child—even before its birth?

FIGURE 10.3 Questioning biological sex? Multiple award–winning South African track star, Caster Semenya (pictured here), is a female—as documented by her official birth certificate (Gregory, 2019). Her competitors, however, have argued that she has an unfair advantage over other women because they believe she is in fact a man. Despite some newspaper reports suggesting Semenya has internal testes that produce higher levels of testosterone, she was officially cleared to continue competing as a female, and she went on to win gold in both the 2012 and 2016 Olympics. (For privacy reasons, the official results of Semenya's tests were not made public.)

Normal Variations in Biological Sex
As you can see in **Table 10.1**, there are at least five different dimensions of biological sex and three dimensions of gender. Also, keep in mind that, like personality traits of conscientiousness and extraversion, sex and gender should be seen as being composed of two long continuums. Like colors in a rainbow, the dimensions of sex and gender fall into various positions along the line between two sets of endpoints—male and female/masculine and feminine.

When there is consistency among the five dimensions of biological sex, we typically say the person is either male or female. However, when one or more of these dimensions is inconsistent or ambiguous, it's harder to categorize any one individual as "simply" male or female (see **Figure 10.3**).

For instance, some people have a combination or variation of male and female biological characteristics, such as chromosomes, hormones, or genitals. Some individuals are born with a variation of chromosomes, such as XXY, that is different from the typical XX (female) and XY (male). When a person has reproductive or sexual anatomy that doesn't clearly fall into either category of biologically male or female, they are often classified as being **intersex**.

Normal Variations in Gender
Just as there are multiple dimensions of sex, we also have at least three dimensions of gender—*gender identity*, *gender role*, and *gender expression*.

TABLE 10.1 Dimensions of Sex and Gender*

	Typically Male	Typically Female
Sex (Biological) Dimensions		
1. Chromosomes	XY	XX
2. Gonads	Testes	Ovaries
3. Hormones	Mainly androgens	Mainly estrogens
4. Primary sex characteristics (see figure on the right) (external genitals)	Penis, scrotum	Labia minor, clitoris, vaginal opening
(internal accessory structures)	Prostate gland, seminal vesicles, vas deferens, ejaculatory duct, Cowper's gland	Vagina, uterus, fallopian tubes, cervix
5. Secondary sex characteristics (see Chapter 9)	Beard, lower voice, wider shoulders, body hair (arm pits, chest, and pubic area), sperm emission	Breasts, wider hips, body hair (arm pits and pubic area), menstruation
Gender (Psychological/Sociocultural) Dimensions		
1. Gender identity (self-definition)	Perceives self as male	Perceives self as female
2. Gender expression	Masculine (male hairstyles, clothing, pronouns—he, him, his)	Feminine (female hairstyles, clothing, pronouns—she, her, her)
3. Gender role (societal expectations)	Masculinity ("Boys like trucks and sports")	Femininity ("Girls like dolls and clothes")

***Key Take-Home Message** Both sex and gender are NOT either/or categories. Instead, they exist on a continuum and involve several, overlapping dimensions.

Let's look first at **gender identity**—our multifaceted sense of self-identification as being a man or a woman or some position between the two. Many people think in *gender binary* terms—believing there are only these two genders, which are distinct and unchanging. As you can see in **Figure 10.4**, however, there are numerous options for gender identity.

Gender expression is how we outwardly display our choice in gender identities. Under most circumstances, we choose our hairstyles, clothing, and social expressions (such as names and pronouns) to match our chosen gender identities. Have you noticed how often people choose the "other sex" costumes when outfitting themselves for Halloween? Or how many women tend to wear dresses and high heels when they want to appear more feminine, whereas many men will choose suits and ties when desiring to appear more masculine?

In contrast to how we present our gender to the world (*gender expression*), there's another, more hidden, dimension of gender, called **gender roles**, which are defined as the psychological and sociocultural defined prescriptions and beliefs about the "appropriate" thoughts, feelings, and actions of men and women. These gender roles and gender expressions vary substantially across cultures and even within the same culture. Interestingly, individual gender identity is typically formed largely in our first few years of life, whereas *gender roles* are developed covertly long before we are consciously aware of them (Brannon, 2016; Keatley et al., 2017; Tosh, 2016).

Gender identity The self-identification as being a man or a woman or some position between the two.

Gender expression The outward display of one's gender identity, including choice of hairstyles, clothing, and pronouns.

Gender roles The psychological and sociocultural prescriptions and beliefs about the "appropriate" thoughts, feelings, and actions of men and women, also known as sex roles.

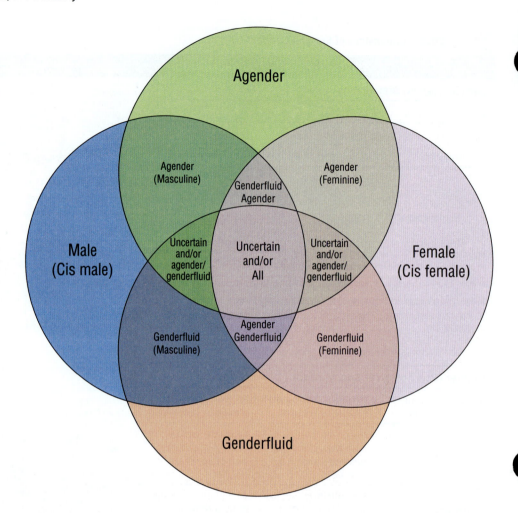

FIGURE 10.4 **Variations in gender identity are normal** Like the dimensions of biological sex, there are numerous overlapping categories for gender identity. Some individuals do not identify as having a particular gender—*agendered* (the top green circle). Others do not identify as having a fixed gender—*genderfluid* (the bottom orange circle). In addition, some identify as uncertain and/or as all genders (the overlapping center circles). Note that when someone's gender identification matches the biological sex they were assigned at birth, today's generally accepted term is "cisgender"—*cis male* or *cis female* (the two edges of the outer blue and purple circles in this diagram).

Theories of Gender-Role Development

By age 2, virtually all children are well aware of gender roles. From parents and other social forces, they quickly learn that boys "should" be strong, independent, aggressive, dominant, and achieving, whereas girls "should" be soft, dependent, passive, emotional, and "naturally" interested in other children. The existence of similar gender roles in many cultures suggests that evolution and biology may play a role in their formation. However, most research emphasizes two major psychosocial theories of gender-role development: social-learning theory and cognitive-developmental theory (**Figure 10.5**).

Social-learning theory emphasizes the power of the immediate situation and observable behaviors on gender-role development. Girls learn how to be "feminine," and boys learn how to be "masculine" in two major ways: (1) They receive rewards or punishments for specific gender-role behaviors, and (2) they watch and imitate the behavior of others, particularly their same-sex parent (Bandura, 1989, 2008; Risman & Davis, 2013). A boy who puts on his father's tie or baseball cap wins big, indulgent smiles from his parents. But what would happen if he put on his mother's nightgown or lipstick? Parents, teachers, and friends generally reward or punish behaviors according to traditional gender-role expectations. Thus, a child "socially learns" what it means to be male or female.

According to *cognitive-developmental theory*, social learning is part of gender-role development, but it's much more than a passive process of receiving rewards or punishments and modeling others. Instead, cognitive developmentalists suggest that children actively observe, interpret, and judge the world around them (Bem, 1981, 1993; Leaper, 2013; Starr & Zurbriggen, 2017). As children process information about the world, they also create internal rules governing correct behaviors for boys and for girls. On the basis of these rules, they form *gender schemas* (mental images) of how they should act.

Potential Problems with Gender Roles

Unfortunately, these gender schemas and gender-role prescriptions and beliefs are sometimes so oversimplified or unfair when

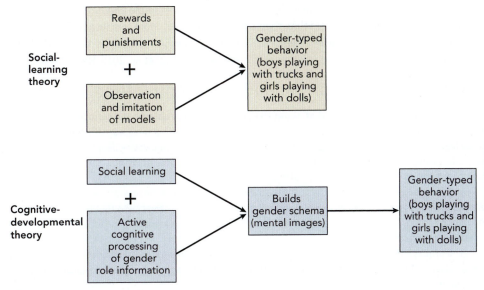

FIGURE 10.5 **Gender-role development**   Social-learning theory focuses on a child's passive process of learning about gender through observation, rewards, and punishments, whereas cognitive-developmental theory emphasizes a child's active role in building a gender schema. Which theory do you think best explains how the children in this photo learn what type of clothes are "appropriate" for their respective genders?

applied to all men and women that they're known as **gender-role stereotypes**. Beliefs such as "women are good at cleaning and cooking, whereas men are good at fixing things and managing the money" are good examples of gender-role stereotypes. For example, did you know that researchers have found that male attorneys who show anger may be more likely to be hired than female attorneys who exhibit the same behavior (Salerno et al., 2018)? When nearly 700 participants watched videos of male or female attorneys presenting the same closing argument in either a neutral or an angry tone, the male attorneys who expressed anger were seen as powerful and full of conviction, whereas female attorneys expressing the same emotion were seen as shrill and obnoxious. The participants also were more likely to say they would hire the angry male attorney versus the angry female attorneys.

[AQ2]   Another intriguing example of potential bias comes from voice assistants, like Apple's Siri and Amazon's Alexa (see photo), which have been found to reinforce existing gender stereotypes (Gajanan, 2019). According to a United Nations report, these voices project an image of women as docile, eager-to-please helpers, who are available at any time and will respond immediately regardless of the commander's tone or hostility (UNESCO, 2019). What do you think? Many people have played games with these assistants just to see how far they can go and how the "women" are programmed to respond. Do you think subtle influences, like female voice assistants, make a difference in our perceptions of female gender roles? Think about how the games and reactions might change if these assistants' voices were male.

What about career options? Can you predict some of the inherent problems with traditional gender roles and gender-role stereotypes? One example comes from a meta-analysis which combined 78 studies spanning five decades of "Draw-a-Scientist" activities (Miller et al., 2018). This meta-analysis showed that children still more often associate science with men—not women. Surprisingly, this pattern is less pronounced in younger children, perhaps because older children have seen more male than female scientists in their daily lives. Hopefully, modern movies, like the hit film *Black Panther* featuring a tech-savvy female scientist (see photo), may help counteract these pervasive gender stereotypes.

Perhaps the biggest problem with gender-role stereotypes is how these sociocultural expectations for how women and men should think, feel, or act can seriously limit both sexes not only in their career options, but also in their choice

Gender-role stereotypes
Oversimplified or unfair beliefs and expectations about typical thoughts, feelings, and actions that are applied to all men and women.

of friendships, activities, and even their lifetime earnings. As an example and further discussed in Chapter 15, women still earn far less than their male counterparts. More specifically, for every dollar earned by White men: Asian women earn $0.85, White women $0.77, Black women $0.61, Native American women $0.58, and Latina women $0.53 (AAUW, 2019; Graf et al., 2019; Hegewisch, 2019).

S&P Scientific Thinking and Practical Application

In addition to income inequality, what about the other inherent problems and serious consequences of gender roles? Researchers within the *Global Early Adolescent Study*, interested in the period of adolescence (ages 10–19) and the power of gender-role expectations, interviewed young people and their parents across five continents and 15 different countries about their experiences of growing up as a boy or girl in their communities (Chandra-Mouli et al., 2018).

Unfortunately, but as expected, the scientists found that around the world boys are viewed as trouble and predators, whereas girls are seen as victims. In addition, adolescents themselves (ages 10–19) generally begin to internalize and fully embrace a universally accepted central theme—boys are strong and independent whereas girls are weak and vulnerable.

The problems for girls are obvious and somewhat well-known—limited mobility and career options, sexual assault, child marriage, early school dropouts, unplanned pregnancy, and an increased risk of serious depression.

Boys also pay a heavy price. According to this study's findings, they're more likely to engage in violence and dangerous behaviors like smoking, drinking, and using drugs at an earlier age. In addition to also being victims of sexual assaults and sex-related problems, their expected role as trouble-makers and predators places them at increased risk of being injured in traffic accidents and death by homicide and suicide. Further confirmation of the damage from male gender roles comes from a meta-analysis of almost 20,000 participants. These researchers found that conforming to masculine norms is linked with poorer social functioning and mental health for men, as well as with being less willing to seek psychological help (Wong et al., 2017).

Robert Blum, one of the lead authors of the *Global Early Adolescent Study*, says, "To believe that some are beneficiaries and some are victims is absolutely wrong—everyone is a victim of these gender norms" (cited in Singh, 2017).

Gender Expression—Androgyny How can we decrease gender bias and these dangerous gender-role stereotypes. First, it's important to note that studies do show that gender roles are becoming less rigidly defined (Brannon, 2016; Gartzia et al., 2018; Levant & Wong, 2017). Second, we can encourage children and adults to more freely express both their "masculine" and "feminine" characteristics and traits. For instance, both men and women could learn to be assertive (and aggressive when necessary), but also gentle and nurturing. Combining characteristics in this way is known as **androgyny [an-DRAH-juh-nee]** (see the following **Test Yourself**).

Androgyny [an-DRAH-juh-nee]
A combination of both masculine and feminine characteristics and traits; from the Greek *andro* for "male" and *gyn* for "female."

PA Practical Application

Test Yourself: Are You Androgynous?

Social psychologist Sandra Bem (1974, 1993) developed a personality measure for androgyny that has been widely used in research. You can take this version of Bem's test by rating yourself on the following items. Give yourself a number between 1 (never or almost never true) and 7 (always or almost always true).

1. _____ Analytical
2. _____ Affectionate
3. _____ Competitive
4. _____ Compassionate
5. _____ Aggressive

6. _____ Cheerful
7. _____ Independent
8. _____ Gentle
9. _____ Athletic
10. _____ Sensitive

Now add up your points for all the odd-numbered items; then add up your points for the even-numbered items. If you have a higher total

Mark Bowden/123RF

AzmanJaka/E+/Getty Images

Androgynous individuals are freer to enjoy all the benefits of traditionally "feminine" and/or "masculine" situations.

on the odd-numbered items, you are more "masculine." If you scored higher on the even-numbered items, you are more "feminine" in your adherence to traditional gender roles. If your score is fairly even, you are more androgynous.

While many individuals are satisfied with traditional views of gender, research finds that this type of androgynous blending of traits leads to higher self-esteem and more success and adjustment in today's complex society given that it allows us to display whatever behaviors and traits are most appropriate in a given situation (Bem, 1981, 1993; Brannon, 2016; Wood & Fixmer-Oraiz, 2019).

Explaining Sex and Gender

In the previous section, we *described* sex and gender. Now we need to *explain* some of the core issues. How do we develop our gender identity? This is one of the most controversial questions in the ongoing nature versus nurture debate. Scientists on the nature side suggest that inborn genetic and biological factors not only determine our physical sex but also help program our gender identity and specific differences between men and women. In contrast, those on the nurture side believe that most aspects of gender and human sexuality are determined largely by social influences. As you've seen throughout this text, the answer to the debate is almost always provided by the *biopsychosocial model*, which proposes an interaction among biology, psychology, and social forces.

Why is Gender Identity Important?
One of the best ways to illustrate the significance of gender identity, and the fine nuances of gender and sex differences, is through the famous case study of "John/Joan." In 1963, two identical twin boys were taken to their family doctor to be circumcised. Tragically, the first twin's penis was damaged beyond repair. Following the medical experts' advice, the child's testes were removed, his genitalia modified, and estrogen administered so he could be raised as a girl.

During their childhood, the twins were brought to Johns Hopkins Hospital each year for physical and psychological evaluation, and the story of "John/Joan" (the name used by Johns Hopkins) was heralded as proof that gender is made—not born. Unfortunately, follow-up studies indicate that despite being raised from infancy as a girl, "Joan" did not feel like a girl and avoided most female activities and interests. As she entered adolescence, her appearance and masculine way of walking led classmates to tease her and call her "cave woman." By age 14, she was so unhappy that she contemplated suicide. Her father tearfully explained what had happened earlier, and for Joan, "All of a sudden everything clicked. For the first time, things made sense, and I understood who and what I was" (Thompson, 1997, p. 83).

After the truth came out, "John/Joan" reclaimed his male gender identity and renamed himself David (**Figure 10.6**). Following a double mastectomy (removal of both breasts) and construction of an artificial penis, he married a woman and adopted her children. David, his parents, and his twin brother all suffered enormously from the original accident and its long aftermath. Sadly, in 2004, David died by suicide. No one knows what went through David's mind when he decided to end his life. However, he had just separated from his wife, lost his job, and experienced the failure of a big investment. His twin brother had also died by suicide shortly before. Most suicidal individuals, experts say, "have multiple motives, which come together in a perfect storm of misery" (Colapinto, 2004).

Looking again at the dimensions of sex and gender (Table 10.1), can you see why this case study of "John/Joan" is so important? Although he was born a chromosomal male, the child's genital sex was altered first by the doctor who accidentally damaged his penis, and later by surgeons who removed his testes and created a "preliminary" vagina. Experts at the time believed this surgery, along with female hormones and "appropriate" gender-role expectations of the parents, would be enough to create a stable female gender identity. But David ultimately rejected this female gender assignment.

Variations in Gender Identity Are Normal
In contrast to this rare, tragic accident that created serious problems with gender identity for David, there is a much larger group of people who experience normal variations in their gender identity. Some individuals, for example, are born with the biological characteristics of one sex, but identify with the other gender. This is known as being **transgender** (having a gender identity that does not match one's biological sex).

Transgender   The state of having a gender identity that does not match one's biological sex; being born with the biological characteristics of one sex but feeling psychologically as if one belongs to the other gender.

Reuters Pictures

FIGURE 10.6 David, previously known as "John/Joan"

Thomas Niedermueller/Getty Images Entertainment/Getty Images

FIGURE 10.7 **The struggle for gender identity** In 2015, the public was fascinated by the story of Bruce Jenner's famous journey from being a male Olympic decathlon icon, referred to as the "world's greatest athlete," to a woman, Caitlyn Jenner (pictured here). Caitlyn gave extensive interviews about this journey and her painful gender identity struggles, which were best summarized with her simple statement that "nature made a mistake" (Bissinger, 2015).

[AQ3] Is gender identity a choice? Some individuals who are transgender report feeling as if they are victims of a "birth defect," and may have a deep and lasting discomfort with their sexual anatomy. In fact, there is evidence (e.g., Grady, 2018; Saraswat et al., 2015) showing that gender identity is, in large part, biologically driven, so it does not appear to be a personal choice and definitely NOT something that can be changed through therapy. Further evidence comes from a study with 32 transgender children, ages 5–12, indicating that their gender identity is deeply held and is not the result of confusion about gender identity or pretense (Olson et al., 2015). The study used implicit measures that operate outside conscious awareness and are, therefore, less susceptible to modification than self-report measures. These and other studies of transgender children suggests that gender identity is really deeply held and not just a phase that could be "outgrown."

Sadly, transgender children and adults are more likely to experience ostracism, harassment, bullying, and psychological problems, including self-mutilation, suicide attempts, and drug abuse (Ghabrial, 2017; Rinehart & Espelage, 2016; Tosh, 2016). In some cases, they undergo medical procedures and/or drug therapies to change their bodies physically to be more like the other sex (**Figure 10.7**). The good news is that transgender kids (ages 3–12) who have transitioned, and are treated like the gender they identify with, do not differ from other kids on rates of depression and are only slightly higher on anxiety (Olson et al., 2016). So, this study suggests that living as the "wrong gender," not being transgender, leads to depression.

Being transgender is frequently confused with *gender-bending* or *cross-dressing*. In these cases, individuals adopt the dress (cross-dress) and often the gender-role behaviors typical of the other sex. Some people occasionally or routinely dress up as the other sex for personal or erotic pleasure, and some entertainers cross-dress as part of their job. However, transgender people often dress in clothing opposite to their biological sex, but they're not considered to be cross-dressing. Their motivation is to look like the "right" sex—the one that matches their gender identity (Buehler, 2014; Colizzi et al., 2014; Tosh, 2016).

PA Practical Application

What should you do if you meet someone who has an unusual or ambiguous set of gendered characteristics and you're not sure what to say or do or how to interact with them? Although it's somewhat normal to be a bit uncomfortable when you encounter someone who's not conforming to traditional gender expectations, it's probably not a good idea to pepper them with specific questions about their gender. However, if you're in a relaxed situation and the person seems open to conversation, many trans people may welcome respectfully asked questions, such as, "What pronouns do you prefer to use?" and then just go on interacting with them as you would with anyone else. (Trans people often prefer "they" or "them" rather than the traditional "he," "him," "his" or "she," "her," and "hers.") If the person prefers not to be identified as either male or female, respect their wishes. If you feel you can't ask, then use the pronoun consistent with the way the person presents himself or herself publicly (e.g., by style of clothing). Or better yet, just avoid using pronouns. In short, the goal is to create an environment that's safe and welcoming for people of all genders and gender expressions.

Sexual orientation An enduring emotional, romantic, and/or erotic attraction.

Heterosexual A sexual orientation in which a person is attracted (sexually, emotionally, and/or romantically) to people of another biological sex.

Lesbian/Gay A sexual orientation in which a person is attracted (sexually, emotionally, and/or romantically) to people of the same biological sex.

Bisexual A sexual orientation in which a person is attracted (sexually, emotionally, and/or romantically) to both men and women.

Sexual Orientation

As we've just seen, there is continuing confusion over gender identity terms, such as cross-dressing, gender-bending, and transgender. We also have numerous misunderstandings and overlapping terms regarding **sexual orientation**, our emotional, romantic, and/or erotic attraction to others. Here's a brief list of the important terms:

- The most common orientation is **heterosexual**, meaning the person is attracted (sexually, emotionally, and/or romantically) to people of another biological sex. (The Greek word *hetero* means "other.")

- When people are attracted to people of the same sex, the traditional (but outdated) term is *homosexual*. (The Greek word *homo* means "same.") The preferred terms are **lesbian** and/or **gay**.

- The term **bisexual** *generally refers to being attracted to people of both biological sexes.* However, there is considerable controversy within the gay community as to what it means to be bisexual, and some believe the term *pansexual* was created to provide a more inclusive label (Doyle, 2019; Hinsliff, 2019).

- **Pansexual** generally refers to being attracted to members of all genders, as well as to those who do not feel that they have a gender (**Figure 10.8**).

- When people do not experience erotic, sexual attraction, but may experience emotional or romantic attraction, the term **asexual** is generally used.

- Also note that a new acronym, LGBTQ+, is sometimes used to refer to people who identify themselves as *lesbian, gay, bisexual, transgender, queer/questioning,* or *genderqueer.* (To better reflect the diversity within the group, some prefer the acronym QUILTBAG, which includes queer and questioning, intersex, lesbian, transgender and two-spirit, bisexual, asexual and ally, and gay and genderqueer.)

PAN Practical Application of Neuroscience

What leads people to be sexually interested in members of their own sex, the opposite sex, or all sexes? The roots of human sexual orientation are poorly understood. However, most studies suggest that genetics and biology play a major role (Balthazart, 2018; Fausto-Sterling, 2019; LeVay, 2003, 2012). Interestingly, a genetic study of almost 500,000 participants from the U.S., U.K., and Sweden found multiple loci (meaning fixed positions on chromosomes) that were associated with same-sex sexual behaviors (Ganna et al., 2019). This recent research provides clear biological, polygenic evidence for nonheterosexual behaviors. In addition, a comprehensive review of the scientific literature suggests that, along with biological factors, certain environmental forces (particularly in the prenatal environment) may play some role in influencing sexual orientation (Bailey et al., 2016). However, these environmental forces do not involve the social environment, and these studies do not support the notion that sexual orientation can be taught or learned. Most importantly, the origins of sexual orientation, biological or otherwise, have no bearing on any individual's right to equality (Soh, 2017).

Do you recognize how a biological foundation for sexual orientation challenges some of the most enduring myths and misconceptions about sexual orientation (see **Table 10.2**)? Or how these misconceptions often contribute to **sexual prejudice**, which is a negative attitude directed toward individuals based on their sexual orientation? Many gay, lesbian, bisexual, and transgender people experience serious discrimination, as well as dangerous verbal and physical attacks, disrupted family and peer relationships, and high rates of anxiety, depression, and suicide (Elder, 2016; Ghabrial, 2017; Gorsuch, 2019). Sadly, the risk of suicide may be particularly high among youths in the earliest stages of "coming out"—publicly revealing their sexual orientation (Dirkes et al., 2016).

buzzfuss/123RF

FIGURE 10.8 **Bisexual versus pansexual** For many years, bisexuality was "simply" defined as being sexually attracted to both biological sexes—male and female. Celebrities like Miley Cyrus (pictured here) and Janelle Monae self-identify as "pansexual," meaning they are attracted to members of all genders, as well as to those who do not feel that they have a gender. In other words, pansexuality is about being all-inclusive (gender, gender identity, gender expression, and sexual orientation), whereas bisexuality tends to be primarily associated with sexual orientation.

Pansexual A sexual orientation in which a person is attracted to members of all genders, as well as to those who do not feel that they have a gender.

Asexual A sexual orientation in which a person does not experience erotic, sexual attraction to others, but may experience emotional or romantic attraction.

Sexual prejudice A negative attitude directed toward individuals based on their sexual orientation.

TABLE 10.2 **Sexual Orientation Myths**

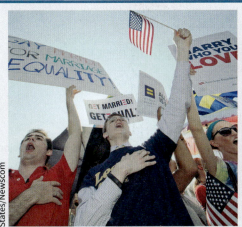

Patsy Lynch/Polaris Images/Washington/DC/United States/Newscom

Myth #1: Seduction theory Gays and lesbians were seduced as children by adults of their own sex.

Myth #2: "By default" theory Gays and lesbians were unable to attract partners of the other sex or have had unhappy heterosexual experiences.

Myth #3: Poor parenting theory Sons become gay due to domineering mothers and weak fathers. Daughters become lesbians because their mothers were weak or absent or their fathers were their primary role model.

Myth #4: Modeling theory Children raised by gay and lesbian parents usually end up adopting their parents' sexual orientation.

Marriage equality In 2013, the U.S. Supreme Court ruled the federal Defense of Marriage Act (DOMA), which defined marriage as a union between one man and one woman, unconstitutional. In 2015, in the case of *Obergefell v. Hodges*, the court went further and held that all states are required to issue marriage licenses to same-sex couples, and to recognize same-sex marriages validly performed in other jurisdictions. These decisions, along with other judicial and legislative action and changing societal views surrounding gay marriage, have lessened the misunderstandings and myths surrounding sexual orientation.

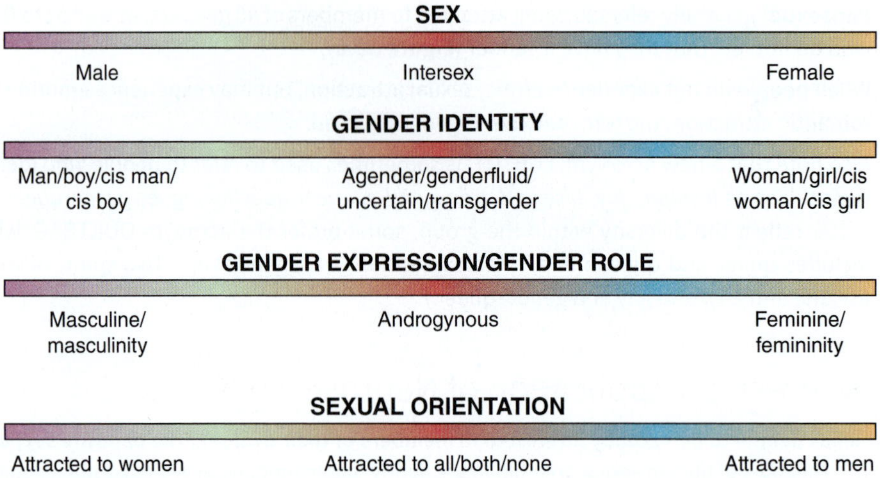

SEX

| Male | Intersex | Female |

GENDER IDENTITY

| Man/boy/cis man/ cis boy | Agender/genderfluid/ uncertain/transgender | Woman/girl/cis woman/cis girl |

GENDER EXPRESSION/GENDER ROLE

| Masculine/ masculinity | Androgynous | Feminine/ femininity |

SEXUAL ORIENTATION

| Attracted to women | Attracted to all/both/none | Attracted to men |

FIGURE 10.9 **The continuum of sexual characteristics and behaviors** Like personality traits of conscientiousness and extraversion, sexual traits are not binary (either/or) options. They vary on a continuum.

Take-Home Message Just as the meaning of the term "intelligence"(Chapter 8) and the diagnostic labels for psychological disorders (Chapter 13) have evolved and changed over the years, so too have sexuality labels. The term "sexual prejudice" is now preferred over the older, outdated "homophobia," which implies an individual pathology. In contrast, the term *sexual prejudice* reflects the fact that, like all forms of prejudice, it is socially constructed. If you're feeling confused and overwhelmed with all the new termi-nology and concepts in this section, keep in mind that almost all aspects of our sexuality fall into four general categories that all exist on a continuum: *sex*, *gender identity*, *gender expression/gender role*, and *sexual orientation* (**Figure 10.9**). Also note that these existing categories, terms, and definitions are likely to continue to evolve over time. Welcome to the rainbow.

Keep in mind that some people may technically fit within one or more of these categories but not identify themselves as such. It is each individual's right to accept or reject any term, definition, or label imposed by others. The general rule when referring to any person or group of people is to be respectful and to use the term that the group or individual prefers. For more information, visit www.genderspectrum.org.

> I learned compassion from being discriminated against. Everything bad that's ever happened to me has taught me compassion.
>
> —Ellen DeGeneres

Sexual Arousal and Response

As we've seen in the previous sections, there is strong motivation to engage in sexual behavior. It's essential for the survival of our species, and for most humans (and some other animals), a sexual relationship fulfills many needs, including the desire for connection, intimacy, pleasure, and the release of sexual tension.

Pair bonding The formation of enduring relationships between adult mates.

Sex may also play a critical role in **pair bonding**—the formation of enduring relation-ships between adult mates. A longitudinal study found that sexual satisfaction remained elevated approximately 48 hours after sex and that spouses who experienced stronger, lin-gering "afterglows" reported significantly higher marital satisfaction over time (Meltzer et al., 2017). However, another study revealed that engaging in more frequent sex is associated with greater overall well-being—but only up to a point (Muise et al., 2016). Past the frequency of once a week, satisfaction and well-being level off. It isn't that having sex more than once a week lessens satisfaction, it's just that you don't get more satisfaction past the "break-even point" of once a week.

Sexual relationships are important to both men and women. But are there differences in their arousal and response? Sitcoms and cartoons often portray men and women in stereotypical fashion with men always aroused and hunting for sex, while the woman is typically using sex to manipulate the man. However, research has shown that men and women are far more alike than different in their sexual arousal and response. Like waffles and pancakes, the two supposedly "opposite" genders have very similar body parts and ingredients when it comes to sex. How do we know this? How do researchers scientifically test what happens to the human body when an individual or a couple engages in sexual activities?

As mentioned at the start of this chapter, William Masters and Virginia Johnson (1966) were the first to conduct laboratory studies on what happens to the human body during sexual activity. They attached recording devices to male and female volunteers and monitored or filmed their physical responses as they moved from non-arousal, to orgasm, and back to non-arousal. They labeled the bodily changes during this series of events a **sexual response cycle** (**Process Diagram 10.1**). Later researchers expanded on their work, documenting differences between the male and female sexual response pattern (**Figure 10.10**).

> **STOP!** This Step-by-Step Diagram contains essential information NOT found elsewhere in the text, which is likely to appear on quizzes and exams. Be sure to study it CAREFULLY.

Masters and Johnson identified a typical four-stage pattern of sexual response. Note that this simplified description does not account for individual variation, and should not be used to judge what's "normal."

Sexual response cycle
Masters and Johnson's model of the typical human sexual response, consisting of four stages—excitement, plateau, orgasm, and resolution.

Excitement phase The first stage of the sexual response cycle, characterized by increasing levels of arousal and engorgement of the genitals.

Plateau phase The second stage of the sexual response cycle; period of sexual excitement prior to orgasm.

Orgasm phase The third stage of the sexual response cycle, when pleasurable sensations peak and orgasm occurs.

Refractory period A period of time following orgasm, during which further orgasm is considered physiologically rare for men.

Resolution phase The fourth, and final, stage of the sexual response cycle, when the body returns to its unaroused state.

PROCESS DIAGRAM 10.1   **Masters and Johnson's View of the Sexual Response Cycle**

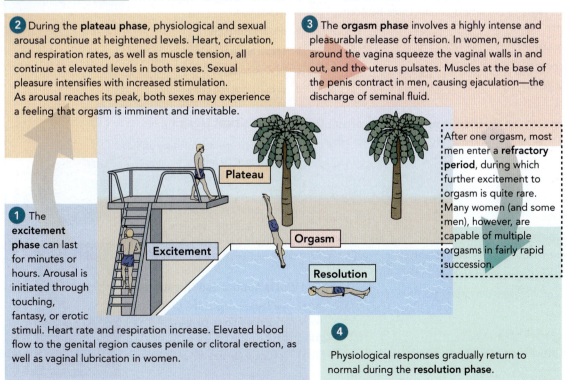

2 During the **plateau phase**, physiological and sexual arousal continue at heightened levels. Heart, circulation, and respiration rates, as well as muscle tension, all continue at elevated levels in both sexes. Sexual pleasure intensifies with increased stimulation. As arousal reaches its peak, both sexes may experience a feeling that orgasm is imminent and inevitable.

3 The **orgasm phase** involves a highly intense and pleasurable release of tension. In women, muscles around the vagina squeeze the vaginal walls in and out, and the uterus pulsates. Muscles at the base of the penis contract in men, causing ejaculation—the discharge of seminal fluid.

1 The **excitement phase** can last for minutes or hours. Arousal is initiated through touching, fantasy, or erotic stimuli. Heart rate and respiration increase. Elevated blood flow to the genital region causes penile or clitoral erection, as well as vaginal lubrication in women.

After one orgasm, most men enter a **refractory period**, during which further excitement to orgasm is quite rare. Many women (and some men), however, are capable of multiple orgasms in fairly rapid succession.

4 Physiological responses gradually return to normal during the **resolution phase**.

Plateau

Excitement

Orgasm

Resolution

FIGURE 10.10 **Comparing male and female sexual response patterns** Although the overall pattern of sexual response is similar in the two sexes, there is more variation in specific patterns among women.

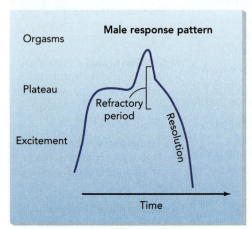

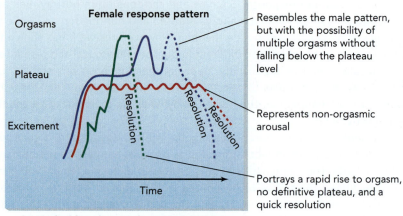

a. Typical male sexual response pattern
Immediately after orgasm, men generally enter a refractory period, which lasts from several minutes to up to a day.

b. Typical female sexual response pattern
Note the greater variety in sexual response among women versus men.

Retrieval Practice 10.2 | Sexual Identity and Behavior

Self-Test Completing this self-test, and then checking your answers by clicking on the answer button or by looking in Appendix B, will provide immediate feedback and helpful practice for exams.

1. The term _____ refers to the constructed psychological and sociocultural supposed differences between men and women, whereas _____ refers to the biological differences between men and women.

   a. sex; gender identity

   b. gender; gender role

   c. androgyny; gender role

   d. gender; sex

2. _____ refers to one's self-identification as either a man or a woman.

   a. Sex role

   b. Assigned sex

   c. Gender dysphoria

   d. Gender identity

3. Androgyny is another word for a(n) _____.

   a. transgender person, gay, or lesbian individual

   b. combination of both male and female traits

   c. oversupply of androgens during prenatal development

   d. cross-dresser

4. A transgender person has a _____.

   a. mismatch between his or her gender identity and biological sex

   b. mismatch between his or her gender role and biological sex

   c. heterosexual preference for sexual gratification

   d. need to wear clothing of the other sex for sexual gratification

5. Masters and Johnson describe _____, the bodily response to sexual arousal, which consists of excitement, plateau, orgasm, and resolution.

   a. sex-orgasm cycle

   b. sexual arousal cycle

   c. E.P.O.R. sex cycle

   d. sexual response cycle

Q Test Your Critical Thinking

1. Do you believe gender roles are primarily determined by innate, biological factors or are they learned from society?

2. Why do you think attitudes in Western society have become more accepting of gay marriage and the LGBT community in recent years?

Real World Application Questions

[AQ2] Do AI voice assistants, like Apple's Siri, reinforce gender stereotypes?

[AQ3] Is gender identity a choice?

Hint: Look in the text for **[AQ2]** and **[AQ3]**

10.3 | Sexual Disorders and Problems

LEARNING OBJECTIVES

Retrieval Practice While reading the upcoming sections, respond to each Learning Objective in your own words.

Summarize the major disorders and problems in sexuality.

• **Describe** the paraphilic disorders, including fetishism and exhibitionism, and their treatment.

• **Explain** how biological, psychological, and social factors influence sexual dysfunction.

• **Discuss** the major treatments for sexual dysfunction.

• **Identify** the key issues related to STIs and the special problem of AIDS.

Real World Application Question

[AQ4] Is "hooking up" more common today than dating?

When we are functioning well sexually, we tend to take this part of our lives for granted. But what happens when things don't go smoothly? Why are some people sexually aroused by exposure to objects or situations that are potentially self-destructive or that victimize others? Why does normal sexual functioning stop for some people and never begin for others? What are the major diseases that can be spread through sexual behavior? We will explore these questions in the following section.

Paraphilic Disorders

People obviously have differing preferences for particular types of sexual activities. Some may even engage in "kinky" or unusual sexual behavior, such as sex in socially unacceptable situations or with unusual stimuli (Balon, 2016; Merrick, 2016). Unusual sexual practices between two consenting adults are generally not a problem, unless the sexual interest or activity is potentially harmful to self or others, or creates personal distress. In such cases, they may be classified as a **paraphilic disorder**—a group of psychosexual disorders involving disturbing and repetitive sexual fantasies, urges, or behaviors that cause distress or impairment to the person or harm or risk of harm to others (American Psychiatric Association, 2013). Let's examine two of the most common paraphilias—*fetishistic disorder* and *exhibitionistic disorder*.

Paraphilic disorder Any of a group of psychosexual disorders involving disturbing and repetitive sexual fantasies, urges, or behaviors that lead to distress or impairment to the person or harm or risk of harm to others.

Fetishistic Disorder In *fetishistic disorder*, the individual uses inanimate objects or parts of the human body to achieve sexual arousal and satisfaction (American Psychiatric Association, 2013; Trail, 2015). Someone might have a fetish and become aroused by seeing and touching silky material, or by touching or smelling someone's shoe or foot. Or someone may simply find a particular object or body part appealing and arousing. In contrast to this type of *fetishism,* individuals with a clinical *fetishistic disorder* experience significant distress or impairment of their sexual, social, or other important areas of functioning. For example, someone may find it impossible to become aroused or achieve orgasm when the preferred fetish object or body part is unavailable.

Exhibitionistic Disorder *Exhibitionistic disorder*, often called indecent exposure, involves recurrent and intense sexual arousal from fantasies, urges, or behaviors associated with exposing one's genitals to unsuspecting and non-consenting observers (American Psychiatric Association, 2013). This exhibitionistic ("flashing") behavior sometimes includes masturbating or performing sexual acts in a public location. An important aspect of the arousal is the surprise experienced by the victim. The exhibitionist generally does not desire any sexual contact with that person. People who have this paraphilia may engage in exhibitionism or may have recurring, obsessive sexual fantasies about doing so.

Explaining and Treating Paraphilic Disorders   As discussed in Chapter 13, psychological disorders are often difficult to identify and treat, in part because numerous biological, psychological, and sociocultural factors may interact and contribute to such disorders (Berlin, 2019; Kingston, 2016; Saadat, 2015). Biological factors such as traumatic brain injury (TBI), hormones, and alcohol abuse are suspected factors in paraphilias. In comparison, the psychoanalytic perspective believes that paraphilias represent a return to a sexual habit or behavior from childhood.

On the other hand, the learning, or behaviorist, perspective describes paraphilias as a result of conditioning. Particular sexual habits and paraphilias are apparently learned from observing other people, or from receiving reinforcement or reward for engaging in them. A person who engages in exhibitionistic behavior, for example, may experience increased arousal from anxiety about being caught engaging in such behavior, which for some can be quite rewarding. Surprisingly, from a sociocultural perspective, exhibitionism may somewhat reflect varying social norms. Women wearing clothing that exposes their breasts or buttocks and men showing their buttocks ("mooning") others for shock value have both been described as socially sanctioned exhibitionism. However, keep in mind that true exhibitionistic disorder is much more complex and serious, primarily because it involves genital exposure to unsuspecting and non-consenting victims.

Regardless of the actual origins, treatments are clearly needed to help people with such disorders find healthier and more positive outlets for their sexual pleasures. Some individuals have difficulty forming relationships with others, and group therapy can help build their social skills. Therapy also encourages victim empathy and taking responsibility for one's own actions.

In addition, paraphilias can be treated using cognitive-behavior therapy, which focuses on replacing the positive associations between sexual pleasure and a particular object or behavior with negative ones. This is the first step toward eliminating the unhealthy patterns of arousal. In aversive conditioning, the person might be told to imagine a particularly arousing scene (such as the fetish object itself or exhibitionism). Then she would be asked to immediately visualize a negative outcome, such as getting arrested or seriously injured. After creating new negative associations with the fetish object or behavior to replace the previously positive ones, the therapist can work on creating healthier associations.

Sexual Dysfunctions

In contrast to paraphilic disorders, many sexual problems involve common, everyday difficulties. These problems come under the official label of **sexual dysfunction**, or difficulty in sexual functioning (**Table 10.3**). In this section, we discuss how biology, psychology, and social forces, as represented in the *biopsychosocial model*, all contribute to sexual difficulties.

Sexual dysfunction A difficulty in sexual functioning; a significant disturbance in a person's ability to respond sexually, or to experience sexual pleasure.

Biological Factors   Although many people consider it unromantic, a large part of sexual arousal and behavior is clearly the result of biological processes (Carroll, 2019; Segarra-Echebarría et al., 2015; Shackelford & Hansen, 2015). *Erectile dysfunction*, the inability to get or maintain an erection firm enough for intercourse, and *orgasmic dysfunction*, the inability to respond to sexual stimulation to the point of orgasm, often reflect lifestyle factors like cigarette smoking. They are also related to medical conditions such as diabetes, alcoholism, circulatory problems, and reactions to certain prescription and non-prescription drugs. Furthermore, many people fail to recognize that drinking alcohol, even in moderate doses, can interfere with sexual functioning. Sexual responsiveness is also affected by stress, illness, and simple fatigue. Interestingly, hormones (especially testosterone) have a clear effect on sexual desire in both men and women, though their precise role is not well understood.

In addition, recall from Chapter 2 that sexual functioning is largely controlled by the spinal cord and the autonomic nervous system (ANS). An orgasm is a "simple" spinal cord reflex, whereas the ANS is composed of two subsystems: the sympathetic, which prepares the body for "fight-flight-freeze," and the parasympathetic, which maintains bodily processes at a steady, even balance. In other words, all individuals must be in parasympathetic dominance for arousal to occur, and sympathetic dominance to experience orgasm.

TABLE 10.3   **Major Male and Female Sexual Dysfunctions**

Male		Female		Both Male and Female	
Disorder	**Source**	**Disorder**	**Source**	**Disorder**	**Source**
Erectile disorder*		**Female orgasmic disorder**		**Female sexual interest/arousal disorder, male hypoactive sexual desire disorder**	
Marked difficulty in obtaining or maintaining an erection during sexual activity or until its completion; marked decrease in erectile rigidity • Lifelong (present since beginning of sexual activity) or acquired (began after a period of relatively normal sexual functioning) *Must be experienced on almost all or all occasions of sexual activity (approximately 75 percent to 100 percent)	**Physical:** chronic illness, diabetes, circulatory conditions, heart disease, drugs, fatigue, alcohol, hormones, inappropriate or inadequate stimulation **Psychological:** performance anxiety, difficulty expressing desires, not wanting to have sex, peer pressure, antisexual education or upbringing	*Marked delay, infrequency, or absence of orgasm; markedly reduced intensity of orgasmic sensations* • Generalized (not limited to certain types of stimulation, situations, or partners), or situational (only occurs with certain types of stimulation, situations or partners)	**Physical:** chronic illness, diabetes, drugs, fatigue, alcohol, hormones, pelvic disorders, inappropriate or inadequate stimulation **Psychological:** guilt, fear of discovery, hurried experiences, difficulty expressing desires, severe relationship distress, antisexual education or upbringing	*Avoids sexual relations due to disinterest*	**Physical:** hormones, drugs, alcohol, chronic illness **Psychological:** antisexual education or upbringing, depression, anxiety, sexual trauma, relationship problems, gender identity confusion
Premature (early) ejaculation		**Vaginismus**		**Substance/ medication-induced sexual dysfunction**	
Persistent or recurrent pattern of ejaculation during partnered sexual activity within approximately 1 minute following vaginal penetration and before the individual wishes it • Generalized (not limited to certain types of stimulation, situations, or partners) or situational (only occurs with certain types of stimulation, situations, or partners)	**Primarily psychological:** guilt, fear of discovery, hurried experiences, learning to ejaculate as quickly as possible	*Involuntary vaginal spasms making penile insertion impossible, or difficult and painful*	**Primarily psychological:** inadequate lubrication, learned association of pain or fear with intercourse, antisexual education or upbringing	*Insufficient sexual desire or arousal, and/or delayed or lack of orgasm*	**Physical:** substance intoxication or withdrawal from drugs (e.g., alcohol, cocaine) or after exposure to medication (e.g., antidepressants)

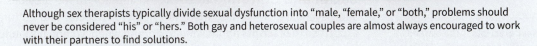

Although sex therapists typically divide sexual dysfunction into "male, "female," or "both," problems should never be considered "his" or "hers." Both gay and heterosexual couples are almost always encouraged to work with their partners to find solutions.

For more information, check out www.goaskalice.columbia.edu/Cat6.html.

Sources: Adapted from American Psychiatric Association, 2013; Carroll, 2019; Chen et al., 2019; Strassberg et al., 2015.

Surprisingly, some patients in comas still experience orgasms, and certain key sexual behaviors do not require the cerebral cortex to operate. How is this possible? Human reflexes such as blinking, sneezing, and blushing are unlearned and automatic. They occur without conscious effort or motivation. Sexual arousal for both men and women is partially reflexive and somewhat analogous to simple reflexes. For example, a puff of air produces an automatic closing of the eyes. Similarly, certain stimuli such as stroking of the genitals can lead to automatic arousal in both men and women. In both situations, nerve impulses from the receptor site travel to the spinal cord. The spinal cord then responds by sending messages to target organs or glands. Normally, the blood flow into organs and tissues through the arteries is balanced by an equal outflow through the veins. During sexual arousal, however, the arteries dilate beyond the capacity of the veins to carry the blood away. This normally results in erection of the penis in men and an engorged clitoris and surrounding tissue in women.

As we've just seen, the human body is biologically prepared to become aroused and respond to erotic stimulation. Generally, if a man or woman stays in arousal and parasympathetic dominance long enough, orgasms will occur. If this is so automatic, why do some people have difficulty getting aroused? Unlike the case in simple reflexes such as the eye blink, psychological factors, such as negative thoughts or high emotional states, may block sexual arousal.

Snapshots

Jason Love/CartoonStock

Another form of performance anxiety?

Performance anxiety The fear of being judged in connection with sexual activities.

Sexual scripts The learned, socially constructed guidelines for our sexual interactions.

Psychological Influences

Do you see why the parasympathetic branch must be in control during arousal, or even for normal biological functions (see cartoon)? The person needs to be relaxed enough to allow blood to flow to the genital area. Anxieties associated with certain sexual experiences, such as fear of pregnancy or sexually transmitted infections, may cause sympathetic dominance, which in turn blocks sexual arousal. Many individuals discover that they need locked doors, committed relationships, and reliable birth control to fully enjoy sexual relations.

One of the least recognized psychological blocks to sexual arousal is **performance anxiety**, the fear of being judged in connection with sexual activity. Men commonly experience problems with erections or sufficient arousal (especially after drinking alcohol), and both men and women wonder whether their "performance" will satisfy their partner. Both partners also frequently worry about their attractiveness and their ability to reach orgasm. Do you see how these performance fears can lead to sexual problems? Once again, increased anxiety leads to sympathetic nervous system dominance, which blocks blood flow to the genitals.

Stress and anxiety may also affect couples who are having difficulty becoming pregnant or are using fertility treatments, such *as in vitro* fertilization. Such treatments often lead to lower levels of sexual desire and pleasure (Daniluk et al., 2014; Omani-Samani et al., 2019; Smith et al., 2015). On a related note, research has confirmed what was long suspected—women who are highly stressed are less likely to conceive (Akhter et al., 2016).

Social and Cultural Factors

In addition to the previously mentioned biological and psychological factors, there are numerous social and cultural factors that provide explicit **sexual scripts** about what to do, and when, where, how, and with whom we should have sex (Gagnon, 1990; Järvinen & Henriksen, 2018; Leiting & Yeater, 2017). During the 1950s, societal messages said the "best" sex was at night, in a darkened room, only between a man and a woman, with the man on top and the woman on bottom. Today, the messages are bolder and more varied, partly due to media portrayals. Compare the sexual scripts portrayed in **Figure 10.11**.

FIGURE 10.11 **Changing sexual scripts** Television and movies in the 1950s and 1960s allowed only married couples to be shown in a bedroom setting (and only in long pajamas and separate twin-size beds). Contrast this with modern times, where very young, unmarried couples are commonly portrayed in one bed, scantily dressed or nude, and sometimes even engaging in various stages of intercourse.

Sexual scripts may be less rigid today than they once were, but a major difficulty remains. Many sexual behaviors do not fit society's scripts and expectations, and we all unconsciously internalize societal messages without recognizing that they affect our values and behaviors. One study of seventh grade students found that those who believed that their peers were having sex were 2.5 times more likely themselves to have sex by ninth grade—see photo (Johnson-Baker et al., 2016). Can you see how this increase in sexual behavior demonstrates the power of perceived peer norms and sexual scripts in influencing behavior?

Another important change among high school and college students involves their casual forms of sexual activities. Not so recently, dating was the major route to sexual interactions. Following predictable scripts, the man was expected to initiate the first date, organize it, and initiate sexual activity, whereas the woman waited to be asked out and then accepted or rejected the man's sexual overtures.

[AQ4] Today, more casual, no-strings-attached, "hooking-up" relationships (see photo) have at least partially replaced the more traditional romantic dating relationships. Some research, however, suggests the hook-up culture on college campuses has been overstated. A study of first-year college women found that 56 percent of the women reported having sex with a romantic partner, whereas only 40 percent reported having sex in the context of a hook-up (Fielder et al., 2013). Research also finds that using smartphone apps to connect with potential partners is becoming one of the most common forms of dating, with Tinder being the most popular app among young adults (Sumter & Vandenbosch, 2019). In addition, these researchers found that compared to users, non-users of this so-called "mobile dating" were more likely to be heterosexual, low in sexual permissiveness, and high in dating anxiety. Several motivations were cited by users, including ease of communication, casual sex, thrill of excitement, and love.

Gender Roles and Sex Problems

Modern sexual behaviors also still reflect a **double standard**, which tends to support and advocate male sexuality while discouraging and even shaming female sexuality. Despite many changes in recent years, men are more likely to be encouraged to explore their sexuality and to bring a certain level of sexual knowledge into relationships. In contrast, women are generally expected to permit or stop male advances and to refrain from sexual activity until married—or at least "in love." One study found that when male adolescents reported "having sex," they gained in peer acceptance, whereas female adolescents reporting the same behavior experienced decreases in peer acceptance (Kreager et al., 2016). However, these gender differences reversed when it came to "making out." In this case, male adolescents' peer acceptance declined, while the female adolescents' acceptance increased. Studies like these demonstrate how traditional gender-role expectations, sexual scripts, and the double standard might affect our sexual behaviors and attitudes. But what about our political beliefs? See the following **STH** **Scientific Thinking Highlight**.

Double standard The beliefs, values, and norms that subtly encourage male sexuality and discourage female sexuality.

STH Scientific Thinking Highlight

Can Political Affiliation Predict Sexual Behavior?

(APA Goal 2.1) Use scientific reasoning to interpret psychological phenomena

Historically, the general American view has been that liberals typically believe the government's major function is to ensure equal opportunity and equality for all, whereas conservatives believe that government should focus on national defense and the freedom to pursue individual goals. But little was known about how each group's political values aligned with their sexual behaviors and attitudes—until now.

Using a web-based sampling technique, researchers directly asked American participants about their individual sexual practices and their political preferences (Hatemi et al., 2017). As might be expected, those with more conservative attitudes, ideologies, and partisan leanings tended to report engaging in more traditional sexual behaviors, such as kissing and missionary position (man on top) sex. In contrast, those who are more liberal politically reported more masturbation and more adventurous sex, such as using sex toys. They also engage in "liberal sex," such as having sex with someone they met on the same day and have more sexual partners in their lifetime. Those with more conservative orientations, however, reported they were more satisfied with their sex life.

Q Test Your Scientific Thinking

As you recall from Chapter 1, scientific thinking is an approach to information that combines a high degree of *skepticism* (questioning what "everybody knows") with *objectivity* (using empirical data to separate fantasy from reality) and *rationalism* (practicing logical reasoning). Using these three principles, consider the following questions:

1. **Skepticism** What do you think? Does this fit with what you know about liberals and conservatives? Why do you think conservatives are supposedly more satisfied with their sex life? Scientific thinkers approach ideas and proposals like these with skepticism.

2. **Objectivity** Are the authors' assumptions supported by the data? Although the one cited research study found positive correlations between political affiliation and sexual practices (Hatemi et al., 2017), what more do we need to do before accepting their conclusions? Scientific thinkers also carefully analyze data for value and content. Could this be an example of participant bias, with the conservative respondents being less likely to report their true sexual behaviors? What about lack of replication, the third-variable problem, sample bias, and so on? Scientific thinkers gather information and delay judgment until adequate data is available.

3. **Rationalism** Setting aside the limited data from other research, can we logically infer that liberals are more liberal in their sexual practices and that the reverse is true for conservatives? Could it be that sexual practices are more likely to be linked with parental beliefs, religious training, socioeconomic status, and other factors? Assuming the link is true between political affiliation and sexual practices, can you predict the logical consequences and potential problems that might arise in a sexual union between two people who hold strong and opposite political views?

(Compare your answers with those of fellow students, family, and friends. Doing so will improve your scientific thinking and your media savvy.)

Sex Therapy

Mangostar/Shutterstock.com

How do therapists work with sex problems (see photo)? Clinicians usually begin with interviews and examinations to determine whether the problem is biological, psychological, or, more likely, a combination of both.

Organic contributors to sexual dysfunction include medical conditions such as diabetes and heart disease, medications such as antidepressants, and drugs such as alcohol and tobacco—see **Table 10.4**. In fact, many who are addicted to drugs or alcohol experience sexual problems even after they stop using these substances (Carroll, 2019; Del Río et al., 2015;

TABLE 10.4	**Sexual Effects of Legal and Illegal Drugs**
Drug	**Effects**
Alcohol	Moderate to high doses inhibit arousal; chronic abuse leads to damage to testes, ovaries, and the circulatory and nervous systems
Tobacco	Decreases blood flow to the genitals, thereby reducing the frequency and duration of erections and vaginal lubrication
Cocaine and amphetamines	Moderate to high doses and chronic use result in inhibition of orgasm and decrease in erection and lubrication
Barbiturates	Moderate to high doses lead to decreased desire, erectile disorders, and delayed orgasm

Vallejo-Medina & Sierra, 2013). Erectile disorders are the problems most likely to have an organic component, and numerous drugs and other medical procedures have been developed to treat them.

Sex therapists also emphasize psychological and social factors. Years ago, the major psychological treatment for sexual dysfunction was long-term psychoanalysis. This treatment was based on the assumption that sexual problems resulted from *deep-seated conflicts* that originated in childhood. During the 1950s and 1960s, behavior therapists proposed that sexual dysfunction was *learned*. (See Chapter 14 for a more complete description of both psychoanalysis and behavior therapy.) It wasn't until the early 1970s and the publication of Masters and Johnson's *Human Sexual Inadequacy* that sex therapy gained national recognition. Given that the model that Masters and Johnson developed is still a popular choice of many sex therapists, we will use it as our example of how psychological sex therapy is conducted.

Masters and Johnson's Sex Therapy Program

Masters and Johnson's approach is founded on four major principles:

1. **Relationship focus**   Unlike forms of therapy that focus on the individual, Masters and Johnson's (see photo) sex therapy focuses on the relationship between two people. To counteract any blaming tendencies, each partner is considered fully involved and affected by sexual problems. Both partners are taught positive communication and conflict resolution skills.

2. **Investigation of both biological and psychosocial factors**   Medication and many physical disorders can lead to or aggravate sexual dysfunctions. Therefore, Masters and Johnson emphasize the importance of medical histories and exams. They also explore psychosocial factors, such as how the couple first learned about sex and their current attitudes, gender-role training, and sexual scripts.

3. **Emphasis on cognitive factors**   Recognizing that many problems result from performance anxiety and *spectatoring*—mentally watching and evaluating responses during sexual activities—therapists discourage couples from setting goals and judging sex in terms of success or failure.

4. **Specific behavioral techniques**   Couples are seen in an intensive 2-week counseling program. They explore their sexual values and misconceptions and practice specific behavioral exercises. "Homework assignments" usually begin with a *sensate focus* exercise in which the partners take turns gently caressing each other and communicating what is pleasurable. There are no goals or performance demands. Later exercises and assignments are tailored to the couple's particular sex problem. For more suggestions for healthy sexuality, see the following **Test Yourself**.

Experiments in sex?   William Masters and Virginia Johnson were the first researchers to use direct laboratory experimentation and observation to study human sexuality.

Diana Walker/The LIFE Images Collection/Getty Images

PA # Practical Application

Test Yourself: Tips for Healthy Sexuality

Which of the following general recommendations for healthy sexuality do you think would be most helpful? Least helpful? Which would you be most likely to try in your own life? Sex therapists generally recommend:

- Beginning sex education as early as possible. Children should be given an opportunity to discuss sexuality in an open, honest fashion.
- Avoiding goal- or performance-oriented approaches. Therapists often remind clients that there really is no "right" way to have sex.

When couples or individuals attempt to judge or evaluate their sexual lives or to live up to others' expectations, they risk making sex a job rather than a pleasure.

- Communicating openly with your partner. Mind reading belongs onstage, not in the bedroom. Partners need to tell each other what feels good and what doesn't. Sexual problems should be openly discussed without blame, anger, or defensiveness. If the problem does not improve within a reasonable time, consider getting professional help.

Before going on, it's important to emphasize that not all sexual problems are serious enough to require sex therapy. For example, did you know that during the early stages of dating and romantic relationships, most couples find their sexual passion for one another is often intense, but that over time this passion tends to "naturally" decline? Given that sexual desire has important implications for relationship satisfaction and maintenance, it's reassuring to know that researchers using various research methods have found that engaging in novel activities with a long-term romantic partner definitely helps reignite that early stage of sexual desire (Muise et al., 2019).

Sexually Transmitted Infections (STIs)

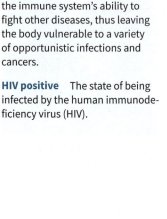

Sexually transmitted infection (STI) An infection generally transmitted by vaginal, oral, or anal sex.

As we've just seen, early sex education and open communication between partners are essential for full sexual functioning. In addition, they're key to avoiding and controlling **sexually transmitted infections (STIs)**, formerly called sexually transmitted diseases (STDs), venereal disease (VD), or social diseases. "STI" is the term used to describe the disorders associated with more than 25 infectious organisms transmitted through sexual activity.

Each year, of the millions of North Americans who contract one or more STIs, a substantial majority are under age 35. Also, as **Figure 10.12** shows, women are at much greater risk than men of contracting major STIs. It is extremely important for sexually active people to get a medical diagnosis and treatment for any suspicious symptoms and to inform their partners. If left untreated, many STIs can lead to severe problems, including infertility, ectopic pregnancy, cancer, and even death.

AIDS (acquired immunodeficiency syndrome) A disease in which the human immunodeficiency virus (HIV) destroys the immune system's ability to fight other diseases, thus leaving the body vulnerable to a variety of opportunistic infections and cancers.

STIs such as genital warts and chlamydial infections have reached epidemic proportions, and even though the rate of **AIDS (acquired immunodeficiency syndrome)** has declined, it still needs our attention. As you may know, AIDS results from infection with the *human immunodeficiency virus* (*HIV*). A standard blood test can determine whether someone is **HIV positive**, which means he or she has been infected by the HIV virus. Keep in mind that being infected is not the same as having AIDS. Some HIV infected individuals may go on to develop AIDS, which is the final stage of the HIV infection process.

HIV positive The state of being infected by the human immunodeficiency virus (HIV).

It's important to know that with the right medications, people can have a normal, or near-normal, life span with HIV or AIDS. The key is early treatment with antiretroviral drugs. Nonetheless, there is no known cure for HIV in most cases, and AIDS remains a serious, potentially fatal health risk.

Sadly, some people still believe AIDS can be transmitted through casual contact, such as sneezing, shaking hands, sharing drinking glasses or towels, social kissing, or contact with sweat or tears. Tragically, some even mistakenly believe that you can contract HIV while donating blood. Others are mistrustful of gay people, given that gay men were the first highly visible victims. All of these are *false* beliefs.

HIV spreads only by direct contact with bodily fluids—primarily blood, semen, and vaginal secretions, but also occasionally through breast milk and non-sterile needles. As you probably

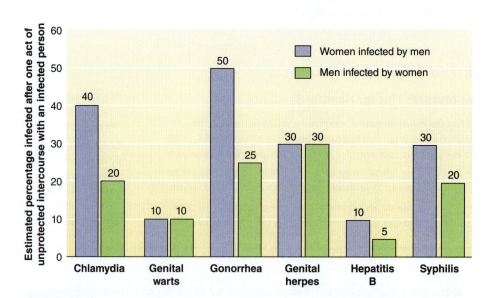

FIGURE 10.12 **Male–female differences in susceptibility to sexually transmitted infections (STIs)** These percentages represent the chances of infection for men and women after a single act of intercourse with an infected partner.

PP **Practical Application: PositivePsych**

Can Good Moods Lead to Safer Sex?

(APA Goal 1.3) Describe applications of psychology

Given the fact that some STIs are incurable and some can be fatal, have you ever wondered why so many individuals fail to use condoms in all their sexual encounters (e.g., Ritchwood et al., 2016)? One set of researchers hypothesized that someone's level of depression and well-being might provide some answers, so they examined a very unique sample of 106 sexually active, HIV-positive gay men living in New York (Wilson et al., 2014). The participants completed weekly surveys that asked about their sexual behavior, depression, and well-being during the prior week. The results showed that men who reported an increase in their well-being in a given week were more likely to have safe sex (66 percent), compared to a normal week (46 percent). The inverse also held true: Those who reported higher-than-usual levels of depression were more likely to engage in risky sexual behaviors (69 percent). As the lead author noted, "We all have bad days and good days, and bad weeks and good weeks. That's life. But it turns out that how moods change can be a big factor in influencing condom use."

Why? One possibility is that those who are feeling bad may give up on using condoms (perhaps because their feelings of

Prostock-studio/Shutterstock.com

sadness make practicing safer sex seem less important). Second, people who feel bad about themselves are probably less likely to stand up for themselves and thereby insist on condom use. Can you see how this research in positive psychology may help improve safer sex behavior for all couples? "Simply" learning new strategies for regulating our moods and feeling better about ourselves could lead to safer sex.

know, anyone can get HIV and AIDS, including men, women, children, and people who are gay or straight (Cohen et al., 2019; Fauci et al., 2019; Malavé et al., 2014).

At this point, it's important to offset all these depressing facts about STIs with some good news; see the **PP** **PositivePsych** feature. You'll be further reassured to know that most STIs are readily cured in their early stages. See **Figure 10.13** for an overview of the signs and symptoms of the most common STIs. As you study this figure, remember that

---

Male Symptoms ♂
- Unusual discharge from penis
- Soreness inside penis

→

Possible STIs
- Chlamydia
- Gonorrhea
- Nongonococcal urethritis (NGU)

Female Symptoms ♀
- Unusual vaginal discharge
- Out-of-cycle abdominal pain
- Unusual vaginal bleeding

→

Possible STIs
- Chlamydia
- Gonorrhea
- Monilia (yeast)
- Trichomoniasis
- Vaginitis

Symptoms for Both Men and Women ♂♀
- Painful intercourse or urination
- Diarrhea
- Painful sore or blisters on or around genital area
- Rash on hands and feet or entire body
- Small, pink, cauliflower-shaped growths on or around sex organs
- Intense itching
- Flulike feeling, sore throat
- Swollen glands in groin

→

Possible STIs
- Acquired immunodeficiency syndrome (AIDS)
- Crabs
- Genital warts
- Hepatitis
- Herpes
- Scabies
- Syphilis

FIGURE 10.13 **Common sexually transmitted infections (STIs)** Keep in mind that you may have an STI without having any of the danger signs listed here. If you have symptoms or concerns, see your doctor and follow all medical recommendations. This generally includes returning for a checkup to make sure you are no longer infected. If you would like more information, check out www.niaid.nih.gov/factsheets/stdinfo.htm. For further detailed information about STIs, visit www.safesex.org

Sources: Adapted from Burns, 2019; King & Regan, 2015.

many infected people are *asymptomatic*, meaning they lack obvious symptoms. You can have one or more of the diseases without knowing it. Furthermore, it's often impossible to tell whether a sexual partner is infectious. That's why the best strategy is prevention (see the following **Test Yourself**).

PA Practical Application

Test Yourself: Protecting Yourself and Others from STIs

The following safer sex suggestions are not intended to be moralistic but to help reduce your chances of contracting HIV/AIDS and other STIs:

1. **Remain abstinent or have sex with one mutually faithful, uninfected partner.** Be selective about sexual partners and postpone physical intimacy until laboratory tests verify that you are both free of STIs.

2. **Don't share needles, syringes, or other drug equipment—and don't have sex with someone who does.** If you must share, use bleach to clean and sterilize your needles and syringes. Also, if you're engaging in tattooing or body piercing, be sure the needles are sterilized.

3. **Don't have sex if you or your partner is impaired by alcohol or other drugs.** The same is true for your friends: "Friends don't let friends drive (or have sex) when drunk (or drug impaired)."

4. **Use condoms.** Although condoms do not provide 100 percent protection, when used consistently and correctly, using them is still one of the very best ways to decrease your chances of contracting STIs, while simultaneously helping to prevent unwanted pregnancies.

5. **Educate yourself.** Learn the signs and symptoms of STIs. If you have more than one sexual partner, experts recommend having regular medical exams (every 3 to 6 months), and if you think you might be infected, get help right away.

Retrieval Practice 10.3 | Sexual Disorders and Problems

Self-Test Completing this self-test, and then checking your answers by clicking on the answer button or by looking in Appendix B, will provide immediate feedback and helpful practice for exams.

1. The only thing that sexually arouses Jim is the sight of women's high heels. His type of paraphilic disorder is called _____.

    a. pornophilia

    b. frotteurism

    c. exhibitionism

    d. fetishism

2. _____ teach us "what to do, when, where, how, and with whom."

    a. Sex surrogates

    b. Sexual scripts

    c. Sex manuals

    d. Sex therapists

3. The fear of being judged in connection with sexual activity is known as _____.

    a. decreased sexual desire

    b. sexual dysfunctions

    c. inhibited orgasm

    d. performance anxiety

4. All of the following are principles of Masters and Johnson's approach to sex therapy except _____.

    a. setting goals to improve sexual performance

    b. examining the relationship between the two people

    c. using medical histories and physical examinations

    d. exploring individual attitudes and sex education

5. Someone with AIDS is infected with a virus that attacks the _____.

    a. central nervous system

    c. immune system

    b. peripheral nervous system

    d. mucous membranes

Q Test Your Critical Thinking

1. Do you believe biological, psychological, or social factors best explain sexual problems?

2. If you had a sexual problem, would you go to a sex therapist? Why or why not?

Real World Application Question

[AQ4] Is "hooking up" more common today than dating?

Dean Mitchell/Getty Images

Hint: Look in the text for **[AQ4]**

10.4 Real World Sexuality

LEARNING OBJECTIVES

Retrieval Practice   While reading the upcoming sections, respond to each Learning Objective in your own words.

Summarize the major issues of sex and modern life.

- **Discuss** the risks and methods of prevention for sexual victimization, including child sexual abuse and rape.

- **Describe** the important elements of sexual communication.
- **Differentiate** the various forms of conflict and suggestions for their resolution.

Real World Application Questions

[AQ5] Is "stranger = danger" largely a myth?

[AQ6] What are the two key ingredients for an effective apology?

Sexuality can be a source of vitality and tender bonding. But when sexual activity becomes a forcible act against the wishes of another person, it can be very traumatizing. In this section, we look at the dark side of human sexuality—*sexual victimization*. Then we conclude with perhaps the most important topics of all—*sexual communication and conflict resolution*.

Sexual Victimization

Any sexual activity that includes lack of consent or the coercion, exploitation, or assault of another is a serious problem and both men and women can experience sexual victimization. As you can see in **Figure 10.14**, sexual behaviors and assault, like sexual identity and sexual orientation, exist on a continuum. In this section we examine three types of sexual violence: *child sexual abuse, sexual assault*, and *sexual harassment*.

Child Sexual Abuse (CSA)   A substantial number of children and adolescents are *sexually abused* by adults or other adolescents. According to the World Health Organization (WHO), **child sexual abuse (CSA)**, also known as *child molestation* or *pedophilia*, refers to *the involvement of a child in sexual activity that he or she does not fully comprehend, is unable to give informed*

Child sexual abuse (CSA)
Involving a child in sexual activity that he or she does not fully comprehend, is unable to give informed consent to, or for which the child is not developmentally prepared and cannot give consent, or that violates the laws or social taboos of society.

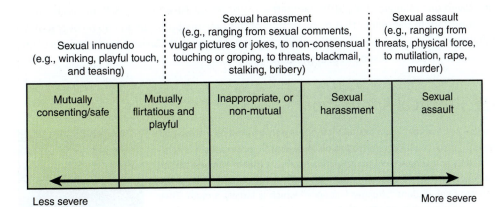

Sexual innuendo (e.g., winking, playful touch, and teasing)	Sexual harassment (e.g., ranging from sexual comments, vulgar pictures or jokes, to non-consensual touching or groping, to threats, blackmail, stalking, bribery)		Sexual assault (e.g., ranging from threats, physical force, to mutilation, rape, murder)	
Mutually consenting/safe	Mutually flirtatious and playful	Inappropriate, or non-mutual	Sexual harassment	Sexual assault

Less severe   More severe

FIGURE 10.14 **Sexual behavior and assault continuum**   When considering the behaviors and information portrayed in this figure, keep in mind that it's impossible to include all variations and categories. Also, as mentioned at the start of the chapter, many different sexual behaviors between two consenting adults can be an enriching and important part of our lives. Sadly, they can also be dangerous and destructive. Hopefully, this diagram helps clarify the two extremes. Like the earlier Figure 10.9, which included four similar continuums for sex, gender identity, gender expression, and sexual orientation, it's important to remember that sexual behaviors are not binary, good/bad, options.

consent to, or for which the child is not developmentally prepared and cannot give consent, or that violates the laws or social taboos of society (cited in Choudhry et al., 2018). It can refer to a number of different behaviors, including touching a child's genitals, masturbating in front of a child, or engaging in digital penetration, oral–genital stimulation, or vaginal or anal intercourse. It can also occur in the absence of any physical contact, such as when an abuser watches a child undress or exposes genitals to a child. Soliciting a child to engage in acts for the sexual gratification of others or viewing or disseminating child pornography is also considered child sex abuse (American Psychiatric Association, 2013; Crosson-Tower, 2015; Vrolijk-Bosschaart et al., 2018).

As sadly expected, children who are sexually abused may experience long-term psychological, physical, and behavioral problems. Common reactions include depression, anxiety, guilt, fear, sexual dysfunction, withdrawal, acting out, and problems with sleeping, eating, or school performance. In addition, sexually abused children may show inappropriate knowledge of, or interest in, sexual activity. As adults, they're also at increased risk of sexual revictimization, as well as depression, anxiety, insomnia, posttraumatic stress disorder (PTSD), problems with alcohol and drugs, aggressive and criminal behaviors, and difficulty in adult sexual relationships (Nguyen et al., 2017; Teicher & Samson, 2016; Waldron et al., 2015).

The effects of CSA vary according to a number of factors, but in general, the longer the abuse occurred, the closer the relationship between the perpetrator and the victim, and the more violent the assault, the greater the negative effects (Carroll, 2019; Karakurt & Silver, 2014; Seshadri & Ramaswamy, 2019). The consequences also vary in part depending on whether and how quickly a child reports the abuse. Children who confide shortly after the abuse, and in an adult who believes them, generally experience less trauma than children who do not disclose the offense. Sadly, many children wait years to tell someone about what occurred. In fact, one study found that half of all victims wait as long as 5 years before telling someone, and 25 percent never disclose the abuse (Hébert et al., 2009). The good news is that a cross-cultural meta-analysis (which combined results from 24 studies) found that school-based programs teaching children about sexual abuse leads to more children disclosing such abuse (Walsh et al., 2015).

Why would a child not reveal this type of abuse immediately? Adult sexual predators typically lie and distort their abusive sexual behaviors as a way of manipulating and confusing the intended child victim. Even before the abuse begins, most abusers engage in a "seduction stage" in which they typically "groom" their victims by gradually and methodically building trust with the child and the adults who surround him or her. During the abuse, the predator then uses power, fear, isolation, and verbal threats ("No one will believe you") or physical threats ("I'll kill you and/or your family") to discourage the child from revealing the abuse. Thus, the child may stay silent, deny the abuse, misremember, or even forcibly forget in order to protect themselves or a loved one (Alaggia et al., 2019; Bennett & O'Donohue, 2016; McNally & Robinaugh, 2015). It's important to remember that many victims of this type of abuse can and do recover to have fulfilling romantic and sexual relationships. This is not to say that CSA isn't a very serious crime, and our top priority must be to prevent it.

PA Practical Application

Do you believe that most sexual violence is perpetrated by a stranger? [AQ5] If so, you'll be surprised to discover that in most cases it is committed by someone known to the victim, such as a friend, family member, neighbor, or trusted acquaintance. Ironically, most parents believe the conventional wisdom *"stranger = danger,"* which is largely a myth. They frequently warn their children to be wary of all unknown persons, when, in fact, up to 90 percent of child sexual abuse is committed by someone known to the victim and who the family trusts—not a stranger (Liedle, 2019; Masilo, 2018; Whealin & Barnett, 2014). Tragically, this "stranger danger" myth leaves parents and the public less alert to the real dangers from relatives, coaches, and even trusted religious leaders. As you may recall, the systemic child abuse committed by numerous Roman Catholic priests was highlighted in the Academy Award–winning 2015 film *Spotlight* (see photo).

Photo 12/Alamy Stock Photo

Given that children are far more likely to be abused (and kidnapped) by someone they know, experts are now suggesting a new phrase—"tricky people"—which refers to people who appear friendly and harmless, and then trick the child into trusting them (Liedle, 2019). Children should be warned about about both these tricky people and strangers (see photo), while also reminding them that not all strangers are bad. They can, in fact, help in an emergency. In addition, keep in mind that the "stranger = danger" myth applies to all ages—the majority of teen and adult sexual assault victims also knew their perpetrator (Merken & James, 2019). More information on preventing both CSA and rape is provided later in this section.

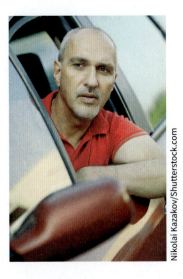

Nikolai Kazakov/Shutterstock.com

Sexual Assault and Harassment

Have you noticed how often these two terms have appeared in the news lately? Thanks in part to the large number of women and men sharing their stories as part of the #MeToo movement, many celebrities, businessmen, and high-ranking politicians have lost their positions due to repeated accusations of sexual assault and harassment. This increasing attention and public discourse is a vital step toward addressing this serious social issue (e.g., Dzau & Johnson, 2018; Herbenick et al., 2019).

What exactly is sexual assault and sexual harassment? According to the most recent and official definition, **sexual assault** is any non-consensual sexual act proscribed by federal, tribal, or state law, including when the victim lacks the capacity to consent (U.S. Department of Justice, 2019). Examples include child sexual assault (CSA), fondling, groping, and rape.

A similar official (but abbreviated) definition of **sexual harassment** is unwelcome sexual advances, requests for sexual favors, and other verbal or physical conduct of a sexual nature, particularly within a workplace environment (U.S. Equal Employment Opportunity Commission, 2019). Examples include creating a hostile environment, repeated sexual jokes and comments, and body language that makes an individual feel uncomfortable.

Note that both sexual assault and harassment definitions can vary by state and country, and that both are "umbrella" terms that include a wide range of behaviors. Also, as mentioned at the start of this section, child sexual abuse (CSA), sexual assault, and harassment also happen to men and boys. Keep in mind that these forms of sexual violence also exist on a continuum (see again Figure 10.14).

Given that rape is perhaps the most serious forms of sexual assault, let's focus on it. Like sexual assault and harassment, the legal definition of **rape** varies from state to state, but it is generally defined as unlawfully coercing oral, anal, or vaginal penetration upon a person through force, or threat of force, or without consent or upon someone who is incapable of giving consent (due to age or physical or mental incapacity). As clear-cut as this definition seems, many people misunderstand what constitutes rape. To test your own knowledge, try the following **Test Yourself**.

Sexual assault Any non-consensual sexual act proscribed by federal, tribal, or state law, including when the victim lacks the capacity to consent.

Sexual harassment Any unwelcome sexual advances, requests for sexual favors, and other verbal or physical conduct of a sexual nature.

Rape The unlawful act of coercing oral, anal, or vaginal penetration upon a person through force or threat of force or without consent, or upon someone incapable of giving consent (due to age or physical or mental incapacity).

PA Practical Application

Test Yourself: Myths About Rape

True or False?

_____ 1. Rape doesn't happen that often.

_____ 2. A man cannot be raped by a woman.

_____ 3. Rape is a crime of passion.

_____ 4. Women secretly want to be raped.

_____ 5. Male sexuality is biologically overpowering and beyond control.

_____ 6. Rape is usually violent and involves a stranger.

_____ 7. There are many false reports of rape.

_____ 8. Most people report rape or sexual assault to the police.

_____ 9. If a person didn't fight back, he or she wasn't really raped.

_____ 10. Women and girls often play hard to get and say "no" when they really mean "yes."

All these statements are false. But popular culture and media often support these myths, and a large number of men and women believe rape myths like these (Garland et al., 2016; Gravelin et al., 2019; O'Neal & Hayes, 2019). Using your scientific and critical thinking skills, can you explain how gender-role conditioning, media portrayals, and lack of general information help perpetuate these myths?

Without consent, it's rape
In March 2013, Trent Mays, age 17, and Ma'lik Richmond, age 16 (pictured here), were found guilty of sexually assaulting a 16-year-old female classmate who was intoxicated and thus unable to give legal consent. Sadly, this type of sexual assault occurs far too often in both high schools and colleges.

AP Images/Keith Srakocic

Like CSA, only around 10 percent of rapes are committed by strangers, and it directly or indirectly affects many people. In the United States alone, sexual violence affects millions of people each year. More than 1 in 5 women and 1 in 38 men have experienced completed or attempted rape in their lifetimes (Centers for Disease Control and Prevention, 2019; Mental Health America, 2019).

Unfortunately, these official numbers most likely underestimate the true prevalence of such violence. Survivors are often reluctant to report the assault or to seek help due to fears of retaliation (against themselves or others), power disparities (adult versus child, employer versus employee, etc.), and/or intimidation (perceived loss of the love of adults, career setbacks). To make matters worse, many women are blamed or criticized for not fully resisting or fighting back despite the presence of a gun or other life-threatening factors and/or incapacitation due to alcohol and other drugs, mental illness, intellectual disability, or other influences that prevent full resistance or conscious consent.

Another serious impediment to reducing sexual violence is the pervasive myths and stigma associated with rape, CSA, and other forms of sexual assault. Sadly, far too many people still believe that being a survivor of sexual violence brings disgrace or dishonor on themselves or their families. Also, the belief that false reports of sexual violence are common is a widely held misconception. In fact, the percentage of these reports is very low—between 2 percent and 10 percent—and less than 6 percent of rapes result in arrest, with only 0.006 percent of rapists ever being incarcerated (National Sexual Violence Resource Center, 2019; Villines, 2018).

Unfortunately, many assaults are never reported out of fear of the "he said/she said" dilemma, in which the survivor recognizes it would likely be his or her word against the perpetrator's. It is an unfortunate truth that sexual assault crimes are some of the most difficult cases to prove. Given that there is often little or no physical evidence—and that the main element, consent or lack thereof, is inherently subjective—it is difficult to establish guilt beyond a reasonable doubt. However, in the vast majority of cases an individual who reports a sexual crime actually suffered a violent physical assault, which forcefully robbed him or her of a personal sense of security and body integrity—an act that will possibly haunt him or her for the rest of their life.

What are some of the psychological and physical consequences of sexual violence? There are numerous short- and long-term physical and mental health problems related to sexual violence (Centers for Disease Control and Prevention, 2019). Survivors may experience chronic pain, headaches and migraines, back pain, and gynecological and gastrointestinal problems. In addition to the physical consequences of rape, equally serious psychological and social consequences include lasting fear, anxiety, depression, guilt, distrust of others, and strained relationships with family members, friends, and romantic partners. Some victims develop PTSD and experience painful flashbacks, in which they mentally re-experience the trauma of the attack. Some respond by engaging in unhealthy behaviors, including taking drugs, smoking cigarettes, vomiting, overeating, and even attempting suicide (Burns, 2019; Çelikel et al., 2015; Zinik & Padilla, 2016). When assessing the physical and psychological consequences of rape, we need to recognize the suffering of the victim's family, friends, and sexual partners as well. They also need support, education, and counseling to deal with their own feelings, as well as guidance in their reactions and support for the victim. For more tips on preventing and dealing with sexual violence, see the **PAH** **Practical Application Highlight**.

Sexual Communication

Communication about the facts versus myths surrounding sexual violence is critical. It's also particularly important in finding and maintaining a healthy sexual relationship. We need to learn how to clearly communicate with words, as well as non-verbally, through facial expressions, eye contact, and body language (e.g., Adams & Nelson, 2016; Hwang & Matsumoto, 2016). In this section, we focus on a major problem in sexual communication—male/female differences.

PAH **Practical Application Highlight**

Preventing Sexual Violence

(APA Goal 1.3) Describe applications of psychology

What can we do to help prevent and reduce child sexual abuse (CSA), sexual harassment, and sexual assault (see photo)? Recovering from sexual violence takes time. Survivors often go through an initial period of coping with the immediate physical and emotional trauma, followed by a lengthy "reorganization" phase in which they try to get back to their normal life. Survivors often benefit from individual and group therapy with other survivors. When PTSD has developed, cognitive therapy or treatment with antidepressants may also be useful.

Preventing sexual violence is obviously a crucial goal, and experts generally recommend the following research-based suggestions:

Tinnakorn jorruang/Shutterstock.com

1. **Education**   Parents, schools, religious organizations, and other groups can provide basic education about healthy sexuality, safe dating, and intimate relationship skills. During these prevention discussions, be sure to include the positive aspects of loving touch and sexuality, which the child will discover as an adult—and sexual assault survivors will rediscover in future healthy relationships. Parents should offer both their male and female children age-appropriate sexual information in concrete terms.

2. **Personal boundaries**   Remind children, adults, and ourselves that each person has the right to their own body. No one has permission to touch another unless it's okay with them (see photo of book cover). Don't force children to hug someone (even a loving family member) if they don't want to. Educate children and adults about the difference between "good" and "bad" touches (see **Figure 10.15**). Furthermore, no one has a right to sex. Being in a relationship and having given prior consent does not omit the need for ongoing, current consent.

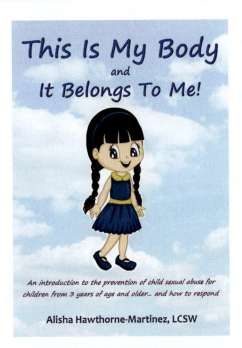

This Is My Body *and* It Belongs To Me!

An introduction to the prevention of child sexual abuse for children from 3 years of age and older... and how to respond

Alisha Hawthorne-Martinez, LCSW

3. **Personal empowerment**   Remind children (and adults) that they have rights. As we discuss in *Conflict Resolution,* a later section of this chapter, being assertive is the act of confidently and directly standing up for your rights. When it comes to sexuality, it means that you have the right to say "no" to any person who asks you to participate in any activity or bodily contact that makes you feel uncomfortable. Encourage children to trust their own feelings when they think something is wrong—and to speak up. *Consent* is not the absence of a "no." It's an informed and freely given "yes."

4. **Risk reduction**   To prevent CSA and sexual assault, we also need to increase public awareness of the risks and facts. How do we do this?

   o Develop mass media messages—on television and the Internet, and in newspapers and magazines—that promote violence-free relationships and social norms that protect against violence.

   o Emphasize the importance of bystanders stepping in to report, stop, and prevent an assault.

   o Help parents identify signs and symptoms of CSA and violent attitudes and behaviors in their children.

   o Create protective environments and enforce policies at school, at work, and in other social environments that address sexual violence.

   o Increase public awareness of the fact that men and boys are also frequently assaulted.

   o Recognizing that CSA perpetrators are most often family members, friends, or trusted people in positions of authority, create and lobby for open-door policies and the reduction or elimination of private, one-adult/one-child situations. Similar awareness and other precautions are important for adults, given that they are also most likely to be sexually assaulted by people they know. "Stranger = danger" is also largely a myth for sexual violence.

   o Regarding CSA, instruct children that no matter what anyone tells them, "body secrets" are not okay, and reassure them that they will NOT get in trouble for reporting the secret.

FIGURE 10.15 **Continuum of "good/bad" touch** When considering the behaviors described in this continuum, note that it's not meant to discourage all touching of children and adults. As we know from Chapter 9, people, like Harlow's monkeys, can be greatly harmed when deprived of touch. However, it can be very helpful to teach children (and adults) the difference between caring, comforting touch and when it may become confusing, inappropriate, or even harmful and dangerous.

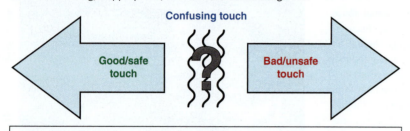

Confusing touch

Good/safe touch

Bad/unsafe touch

Good/Safe Touch = Physical expression of affection, caring, and/or warmth (e.g., hugs, pats on the head or back, kisses on the cheek, "high-five hand claps")

Confusing Touch = Physical expression that creates confusion and uneasy feelings and/or is age or power differentially inappropriate (e.g., between adult and child or employer and employee)

Bad/Unsafe Touch = Physical contact that is age-inappropriate (e.g., between adult and child), forced, non-consenting, and/or manipulative (e.g., touching, fondling, groping, rubbing against)

○ For both children and adults, if you suspect abuse, or if a child or adult reports it, stay calm, protect the child or adult from further contact with the abuser, and report it to the police.

For more information on CSA, contact the National Children's Alliance (www.nca-on-line.org) or the National Child Abuse hotline (1-800-4-A-Child).

For more information on sexual violence, contact the Rape, Abuse & Incest National Network (www.rainn.org) or the Centers for Disease Control and Prevention (https://www.cdc.gov/features/sexualviolence/index.html).

Male/Female Differences in Communication Have you heard that men and women communicate so differently that they seem to be from two separate cultures or planets—as in the title of the popular book *Men Are from Mars, Women Are from Venus?* This idea is appealing due to popular stereotypes and our own occasional difficulties communicating "across genders" (see cartoon). However, research shows that these differences are small and not characteristic of all men and women or of all mixed-gender conversations (Carothers & Reis, 2013; Hyde, 2014; Wood & Fixmer-Oraiz, 2019). On the other hand, they may help explain and prevent some communication misunderstandings (see **Table 10.5**).

Researcher Deborah Tannen (1990, 2007, 2011) believes that boys and girls learn different styles of communication from early childhood and that these styles sometimes carry over into

Roz Chast/Cartoon Stock

TABLE 10.5   Communication Differences Between the Genders

In General, Men Tend To...	In General, Women Tend To...	
Use speech to convey information, exert control, preserve independence, and enhance their status	Use speech to achieve and share intimacy, promote closeness, and maintain relationships	**What's wrong with this communication?** Can you use information from this table to identify possible problems in this photo?
Talk more than women, interrupt women more than women interrupt men, and interrupt women more often than they interrupt other men	Talk more than men when they have more power in a relationship	
Be more directive and assertive ("I want to get there by noon")	Be more indirect and tentative, using hedges ("kind of") and disclaimers ("I'm not sure what time we should get there")	
Talk more about politics, sports, and careers when they're in same-gender pairs	Talk more about feelings and relationships when they're in same-gender pairs	
Remain calm and problem oriented during conflict and seek compromise solutions to problems	Become more sensitive to the feelings of others during conflict, more easily express both positive and negative emotions, and send double messages (such as smiling while making a critical comment)	
Prefer spoken communication	Prefer written communication	
Prefer to work out their problems by themselves	Prefer to talk out solutions with another person	
Make critical comments on the work of a colleague	Compliment the work of a colleague	
Be less sensitive to reading and sending non-verbal messages	Be better at reading and sending non-verbal messages	

Sources: Leaper, 2019; LeMaster & Johnson, 2019; Levant & Wong, 2017; Tannen, 1990, 2007, 2011; Wood & Fixmer-Oralz, 2019

most of their adult social interactions. In her book *You Just Don't Understand*, Tannen (1990) says that the first steps in improving communication between men and women are accepting that there are some differences in gender communication styles, realizing it is not a matter of one style being right or wrong, and then working to understand the other gender's occasionally differing styles.

Following the publication of Tannen's research, a large number of investigations have looked at gender differences in communication. These studies have verified that some differences do exist, but they may reflect differences in status and power more than gender. This is good news. Given that communication is essential for healthy sexuality, as well as in our professional and personal lives, men and women can use this information to better understand one another and work around their small, but sometimes meaningful differences.

Conflict Resolution

One of the most important, and most difficult, areas of communication is conflict management, and the way we handle it is a major predictor of relationship satisfaction and longevity. Carol Rusbult and her colleagues describe four major types of responses—*voice, loyalty, neglect*, and *exit*—that people typically use in handling conflict (Drigotas et al., 1995; Rusbult & Zembrodt, 1983; Rusbult et al., 1982).

The first, and generally seen as the most constructive, strategy is *voice*, which means talking things over to try to resolve the conflict. When done properly, it helps maintain and affirm the relationship given that it involves direct problem solving and creative "win-win" solutions. If your partner seems to be avoiding your sexual advances, you could discuss how his or her resistance makes you feel and possible solutions. (Perhaps he or she is exhausted from work, and you could renegotiate the workload at home.)

Loyalty is defined as quiet forgiveness, acceptance, and accommodation, while remaining committed to a relationship and simply waiting patiently for things to get better. Loyalty sounds as if it could be a good strategy, but it's less often associated with favorable consequences for conflict management, possibly because it is a less visible and more indirect strategy (Cahn, 2013; Kammrath & Dweck, 2006).

The other two conflict strategies (neglect and exit) are clearly destructive. *Neglect*, giving up on the relationship and withdrawing from it emotionally, and *exit*, active moves to threaten or leave the relationship, are far too common and should be avoided if you want to build or maintain a healthy sexual relationship. Fortunately, people who have high relationship investment and satisfaction are more likely to use a constructive strategy for resolving conflicts (see the following **Test Yourself**).

PA Practical Application

Test Yourself: How Do You Handle Conflict?

Rate how likely you would be to use each strategy for handling conflict in a romantic relationship on a scale of 1 to 5 (1 meaning "I would definitely not do this" and 5 meaning "I would definitely do this").

_____ **1.** I would end the relationship.

_____ **2.** I would tell my partner to leave.

_____ **3.** I would talk to my partner about what was bothering me.

_____ **4.** I would suggest things that I thought would help us.

_____ **5.** I would hope that if I just hung in there, things would get better.

_____ **6.** I would wait patiently.

_____ **7.** I guess I would just sort of let things fall apart.

_____ **8.** I would get angry and wouldn't talk at all.

What were your highest and lowest scores? Items 1 and 2 measure exit, items 3 and 4 measure voice, items 5 and 6 measure loyalty, and items 7 and 8 measure neglect (Rusbult et al., 1982).

Another researcher, John Gottman, has conducted extensive research on relationship conflict (Gottman, 2015; Gottman & Silver, 2012). Using a variety of measures (physiological, non-verbal, verbal, and questionnaire) to assess and follow large samples of couples over long periods of time, his research has revealed four styles of conflict that are particularly destructive:

- **Criticism**—complaining about some features of the relationship
- **Contempt**—acting as if sickened or repulsed by the partner
- **Defensiveness**—protection of the self
- **Stonewalling**—emotionally withdrawing and refusing to participate in conversation

All these strategies can lead to increased isolation and withdrawal. In fact, Gottman calls these styles of conflict the "Four Horsemen of the Apocalypse," meaning that the end of a relationship, the *apocalypse*, will be brought on by four horsemen—the four negative styles of conflict.

The *stonewalling* approach is part of another conflict style called the *demand/withdraw interaction pattern*, in which one partner attempts to start a discussion by criticizing, complaining, or suggesting change (Baucom et al., 2015; King & DeLongis, 2013; Knobloch-Fedders et al., 2014). The other partner then attempts to end this discussion—or avoid the issue—by maintaining silence or withdrawing from the situation. In a heterosexual relationship, the man is more likely to withdraw from conflict and the woman is more likely to take a leading role in initiating and discussing it.

In contrast to the demand/*withdraw* pattern of interaction, some couples just avoid and deny the presence of any conflict in a relationship. Unfortunately, denial prevents couples from solving their problems at early stages, which can lead to even greater problems later on. On the other hand, expressing anger and disagreement also leads to lower marital satisfaction (Bloch et al., 2014; Gottman, 2015; MacKenzie et al., 2014). In fact, couples who show high levels of negative communication in their first few years of marriage are more likely than others to get divorced (Lavner & Bradbury, 2012; Worthington et al., 2015).

As we've just seen, demanding, withdrawing, avoiding, denying, and expressing anger and disagreement all seem to lead to relationship problems. So, what's the answer? Given that conflict is an inevitable and even healthy part of all our relationships, we need to learn better strategies for working through conflicts in a positive and productive way. See the following **Test Yourself**.

PA Practical Application

Test Yourself: Conflict Resolution Skills

What can we do to successfully manage conflict in our own relationships? Understanding the other person's point of view and putting ourselves in their place is a good first step. People who can adopt their partner's perspective show more constructive responses to conflict.

Second, given that conflict and disagreements are an inevitable part of close relationships, people need to be able to forgive personal wrongdoings and apologize (Enright & Fitzgibbons, 2015; Flora & Segrin, 2015). Those who remember relationship transgressions their partner committed in a more positive and less severe light are more likely to have lasting and satisfying relationships (Gottman, 2015). Similarly, apologies minimize conflict, lead to forgiveness, and help you maintain relationship closeness.

[AQ6] What makes for an effective apology? Research has identified six components (Lewicki et al., 2016):

- Acknowledgment of responsibility
- Offer of repair
- Declaration of repentance
- Expression of regret
- Explanation of what went wrong
- Request for forgiveness

JGI/Jamie Grill/Getty Images

Research also shows that the first two, acknowledgment of responsibility and an offer of repair, are the most important. Keep these tips in mind after your next conflict. A good apology will save or strengthen all your relationships—romantic and otherwise (see photo).

Saying "No"   Now that we've discussed how to admit and to properly apologize when we're wrong, how do we handle situations when we're NOT wrong and we really just need to say "NO"? How do you handle conflict in your everyday life? Do you stick up for your rights, or do you allow others to walk all over you? Do you say what you feel, or do you say what you think other people want you to say? Do you initiate relationships with people, or do you shy away from them? Beginning in childhood, most of us were socialized to be "nice," to say "yes," and to please others. Regrettably, being overly nice often means sacrificing our own needs, which in turn allows hostility and frustration to accumulate and weaken our relationships.

What do we need to do to offset these problems? First, let's consider **assertiveness**, which is defined as confidently and directly standing up for your rights without infringing on those of others. It often involves striking a balance between passive and aggressive behavior. It means you directly and honestly request things you want and say "no" to things you don't want. When we are assertive, we are much more likely to achieve our goals and to be liked and respected by others. Assertive people also tend to have higher levels of self-esteem, self-worth, and self-satisfaction given they have more control over their life choices and direction (Parray, 2018; Speed et al., 2019). Most importantly, they are more likely to avoid serious conflicts and to resolve them more effectively.

As mentioned in the previous definition, assertiveness also strikes a balance between passive and aggressive behavior. What's the difference? *Passive behavior* involves failing to stand up for your rights even when you are fully justified in doing so. Although passive individuals often "get along" with everyone, they are less respected and less likely to achieve their personal goals. They also are self-denying and self-inhibiting, experience low self-esteem, and feel hurt and anxious (Alberti & Emmons, 2008; Brassard et al., 2015; Hays, 2014). In addition, passive sex partners may be seen as lackluster and as contributing little to the relationship.

Unfortunately, some people even resort to aggressive behaviors when faced with sexual and other forms of conflict. As you'll discover in Chapter 15, *aggression* is any behavior intended to harm another. During conflict, an aggressive person will stand up for his or her rights, disregarding potential harm to others and possibly using insults, threats, and even physical intimidation and attacks. Aggressive behavior is more likely than passive behavior to get you what you want in the short term. But like passiveness, it too has negative long-term consequences. Others may initially give in to aggressive people and feel intimidated by them, yet they rarely like or respect them. Think about how much you liked or respected classroom or playground bullies when you were growing up. In addition, aggressive behavior far too often provokes aggressive responses from others that can easily escalate into serious violence.

Assertiveness   The act of confidently and directly standing up for your rights, or putting forward your views, without infringing on the rights and views of others; striking a balance between passivity and aggression.

For more tips on assertiveness and how to effectively say "no," see the following **Test Yourself**.

PA Practical Application

Test Yourself: How to Say "No"

One of the most important steps in becoming assertive is learning how to say "no." When faced with a sexual or other situation in which you want to refuse the requests of another or to protect your own rights, try the following:

- **Be assertive non-verbally** Look the person in the eye, keep your head up, and keep your body firm but relaxed. Stand at an appropriate distance—not too close or too far away. Don't be a "shrinking violet."

- **Use strong verbal signals** Speak clearly, firmly, and at a volume that can be easily heard.

- **Be strong** People are often persistent in their requests. Be prepared to repeat your refusal. Stick to your guns.

- **Just say "no"** You don't have to explain why you're refusing. You have the right to say "no" without an explanation. But if you feel that you must explain why you're declining, try saying, "Thanks, but no. I really can't..." "I really appreciate the offer, but no. I'm not interested/too busy/don't want any..." "Please don't take this personally. I like you, but no, I don't..." or "I enjoy your company, and I'd like to do something together, but no..."

Can you see how studying and accepting our right to be assertive may strengthen our resolve to speak up and defend ourselves in sexual situations and in all other parts of life? Keep in mind that assertive behavior doesn't guarantee that we'll achieve our goals or force others to respect our rights. But it can definitely increase our chances of doing so.

Before going on, be sure to complete the final Retrieval Practice, and then answer the critical thinking questions in the **Test Your Critical Thinking**.

Retrieval Practice 10.4 | Real World Sexuality

Self-Test Completing this self-test, and then checking your answers by clicking on the answer button or by looking in Appendix B, will provide immediate feedback and helpful practice for exams.

1. Good suggestions for counseling parents and other caregivers about avoiding child sexual abuse include _____.
   a. presenting sexual information to both male and female children in concrete terms and using age-appropriate language
   b. teaching a child the difference between "okay" and "not okay" touches
   c. recognizing that abusers are most often family members, friends, or trusted people in positions of authority
   d. all these options

2. Which of the following is a myth about rape?
   a. A man cannot be raped by a woman.
   b. All women secretly want to be raped.
   c. Women cannot be raped against their will.
   d. All these options.

3. Research has shown that _____ are more likely to use speech to convey information, exert control, preserve independence, and enhance their status, whereas _____ tend to use speech to achieve and share intimacy, promote closeness, and maintain relationships.
   a. older men; younger men
   b. older women; younger women

   c. men; women
   d. heterosexuals; women and men

4. According to John Gottman's research, _____ means emotionally withdrawing and refusing to participate in conversation.
   a. defensiveness   c. stonewalling
   b. contempt   d. neglect

5. _____ is defined as confidently and directly standing up for your rights without infringing on those of others.
   a. Androgyny   c. Ambitiousness
   b. Assertiveness   d. All of these options

Q Test Your Critical Thinking

1. Do you think male/female differences in communication are a significant contributor to sexual and relationship problems between the sexes? Why or why not?

2. How can you use the tips on managing conflict and learning to say "no" to improve your own relationships?

Real World Application Questions

[AQ5] Is "stranger = danger" largely a myth?

[AQ6] What are the two key ingredients for an effective apology?

Nikolai Kazakov/Shutterstock.com

JGI/Jamie Grill/Getty Images

Hint: Look in the text for **[AQ5]** and **[AQ6]**

Q Test Your Critical Thinking

Did you notice or wonder why we provided six Real World Application Questions [AQ1–AQ6] throughout this chapter? We've found that they not only help you to engage with and master the material, they also have an important and lasting impact on your critical thinking skills. For additional mastery and enrichment, consider the following questions:

1. The couple kissing in this photo is considered immoral and disgusting in some cultures. Is that response an example of ethnocentrism? Why or why not?

2. Do you think male infants should be circumcised? Why or why not?

3. If you had your life to live over, what would you see as advantages and disadvantages of coming back as the other sex?

4. Modern music, TV, and movies generally portray sex as glamorous and immediately satisfying for both partners. How might this popular portrayal contribute to sexual problems?

5. Were you surprised to learn that child sexual abuse (CSA) is far more likely to be committed by a friend or family member than a stranger? Can you explain why this is not a highly publicized fact?

iStock.com/piranka

6. Which of the three topics—gender differences, conflict, or lack of assertiveness—do you think is the biggest contributor to sexual communication problems

Summary

10.1 Studying Human Sexuality   315

- Although sex has always been an important part of human interest, motivation, and behavior, it received little scientific attention before the 20th century. Havelock Ellis was among the first to study human sexuality despite the repression and secrecy of 19th-century Victorian times. Alfred Kinsey and his colleagues were the first to conduct large-scale, systematic surveys and interviews of the sexual practices and preferences of U.S. adults during the 1940s and 1950s. In the 1960s, the research team of William Masters and Virginia Johnson pioneered the use of actual laboratory measurement and observation of human physiological response during sexual activity.

- Cross-cultural studies provide important information about the similarities and variations in human sexuality. They also help counteract *ethnocentrism*—the tendency to judge our culture as "normal" and preferable to others.

10.2 Sexual Identity and Behavior   319

- **Sex** refers to biological differences between men and women, such as having a penis or vagina, or to physical activities such as masturbation and intercourse. **Gender** encompasses the socially constructed differences between men and women, such as "masculinity" and "femininity."

- Our **gender identity** (self-identification as a man or woman) and our gender expression (outward displays of gender identity) are not binary, either/or options. Our **gender roles** (the defined psychological and sociocultural traits associated with biological sex) are largely formed in the first few years of life.

- The *social-learning theory* of gender-role development emphasizes rewards, punishments, observation, and imitation, whereas the *gender-schema theory* combines social-learning theory with active cognitive processing. When gender-role prescriptions and beliefs are overly general, and applied to all men and women, they're known as **gender-role stereotypes**.

- Variations in gender identity and sexual orientation are normal. People who are **transgender** experience a mismatch between their biological sex and their gender identity. **Sexual orientation** (being heterosexual, gay, lesbian, bisexual, LGBTQ+) refers to our primary emotional and erotic attraction.

- The human motivation for sex is extremely strong. Masters and Johnson first studied and described the **sexual response cycle**, the series of physiological and sexual responses that occur during sexual activity.

10.3 Sexual Disorders and Problems   331

- People who experience personal distress over their sexual interests or whose sexual arousal or response depends entirely on these interests may be classified as having a **paraphilic disorder**, such as *fetishistic disorder* or *exhibitionistic disorder*.

- Biology plays a key role in both sexual arousal and response. Ejaculation and orgasm are partly reflexive, and the parasympathetic nervous system must be dominant for sexual arousal to occur. The sympathetic nervous system must be dominant for orgasm to occur. Psychological factors like negative early sexual experiences, fears of negative consequences from sex, and **performance anxiety** contribute to **sexual dysfunction**. Sexual arousal and response are also related to social forces, such as early gender-role training and **sexual scripts**, which teach us what to consider as the "best" sex.

- During sex therapy, tests and interviews are often used to determine the origin(s) of the sexual dysfunction. William Masters and Virginia Johnson emphasize a couple's relationship, biological and psychosocial factors, cognitions, and specific behavioral techniques.

- The dangers and rate of sexually transmitted infections (STIs) are high, and they are higher for women than for men. However, most STIs can be cured in their early stages. **AIDS (acquired immunodeficiency syndrome)** is transmitted only through sexual contact or exposure to infected bodily fluids, though many people have irrational fears of contagion. Many North Americans are **HIV positive** and therefore carriers.

10.4   Real World Sexuality   341

- **Child sexual abuse (CSA)** and **rape** are two of the most common forms of sexual victimization. The effects vary according to a number of factors, but they often lead to long-term psychological, physical, and behavioral problems. There are several ways to prevent or reduce the risks of sexual victimization.

- Effective sexual communication and conflict resolution may reduce the risks of sexual victimization, and they're also essential in healthy sexual relationships. Understanding gender and individual differences in communication and conflict is also critical.

Key Terms

Retrieval Practice   Write a definition for each term before turning back to the referenced page to check your answer.

- AIDS (acquired immunodeficiency syndrome)   338
- androgyny [an-DRAH-juh-nee]   324
- asexual   327
- assertiveness   349
- bisexual   326
- child sexual abuse (CSA)   341
- double standard   335
- excitement phase   329
- gender   320
- gender expression   321
- gender identity   321
- gender roles   321
- gender-role stereotypes   323

- heterosexual   326
- HIV positive   338
- intersex   320
- Lesbian/gay   326
- orgasm phase   329
- pair bonding   328
- pansexual   327
- paraphilic disorder   331
- performance anxiety   334
- plateau phase   329
- rape   343
- refractory period   329
- resolution phase   329
- sex   320

- sexual assault   343
- sexual dysfunction   332
- sexual harassment   343
- sexual prejudice   327
- sexuality   315
- sexually transmitted infection (STI)   338
- sexual orientation   326
- sexual response cycle   329
- sexual scripts   334
- transgender   325

CHAPTER 11

Kuttelvaserova Stuchelova/Shutterstock.com

Motivation and Emotion

AlpamayoPhoto/iStock/Getty Images

Real World Application Questions

Things you'll learn in Chapter 11

[AQ1] How does arousal interfere with performance?

[AQ2] Can cognitive expectancies lead to problem drinking?

[AQ3] How does heavy use of social media increase the risk of eating disorders?

[AQ4] Can airport security agents increase their effectiveness by simply talking to passengers?

[AQ5] Is America one of the top 10 happiest nations in the world?

[AQ6] Smartphones make communicating easier—but is it better?

Throughout the chapter, look for the [AQ1]–[AQ6] icons. They indicate where the text addresses these questions.

CHAPTER OUTLINE

11.1 Theories of Motivation

LEARNING OBJECTIVES

Retrieval Practice While reading the upcoming sections, respond to each Learning Objective in your own words.

Summarize the major theories of motivation.

- **Define** motivation.
- **Discuss** the three key biological theories of motivation.

- **Describe** two psychological theories of motivation.
- **Explain** how biopsychosocial theories apply to motivation.

Real World Application Questions

[AQ1] How does arousal interfere with performance?

[AQ2] Can cognitive expectancies lead to problem drinking?

Research in *motivation* and *emotion* attempts to answer "what," "why," and "how" questions. In other words, motivation energizes and directs behavior, whereas emotion is the "feeling" response. (Both *motivation* and *emotion* come from the Latin *movere*, meaning "to move.") In this chapter, we start with the major theories and concepts of motivation, followed by two important sources of motivation—hunger and achievement. Then we turn to the basic components and theories related to emotion, concluding with a look at how we experience emotions.

Motivation A set of factors that activate, direct, and maintain behavior, usually toward some goal.

This first section begins with a look at **motivation**, factors that activate, direct, and maintain behavior, usually toward some goal. What motivates you? Why are you in college and working to achieve your lifetime dreams? How do you feel about some of the chronic anxieties and frustrations that generally come with being in college? Years of research on motivation has created six major theories, which fall into three general categories—*biological*, *psychological*, and *biopsychosocial* (**Table 11.1**).

While studying these six theories, try to identify which one best explains your personal behaviors, such as going to college or choosing a lifetime partner. This type of personal focus will not only improve your exam performance but also may lead to increased self-knowledge and personal motivation.

Biological Theories

Many theories of motivation focus on inborn biological processes that control behavior. Among these biologically oriented theories are *instinct*, *drive-reduction*, and *arousal* theories.

TABLE 11.1 Six Major Theories of Motivation

	Theory	Description
	Biological	
	1. Instinct	Motivation results from innate, biological instincts, which are unlearned responses found in almost all members of a species.
	2. Drive reduction	Motivation begins with a biological need (a lack or deficiency) that elicits a *drive* toward behavior that will satisfy the original need and restore homeostasis.
	3. Optimal arousal	Organisms are motivated to achieve and maintain an optimal level of arousal.
	Psychological	
	4. Incentive	Motivation results from external stimuli that "pull" the organism in certain directions.
	5. Cognitive	Motivation is affected by expectations and attributions, or how we interpret or think about our own or others' actions.
	Biopsychosocial	
	6. Maslow's hierarchy of needs	Lower needs like hunger and safety must be satisfied before advancing to higher needs (such as belonging and self-actualization).

Mattias Klum/National Geographic Image Collection

Name That Theory Curiosity is an important aspect of both human and non-human experience. Which of the six theories of motivation best explains this behavior?

FIGURE 11.1   **Instincts**

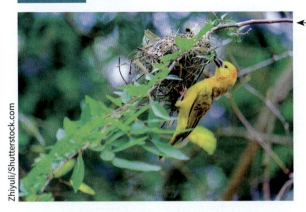

Zhiyuli/Shutterstock.com

a. Instinctual behaviors are obvious in many animals. Birds build nests, bears hibernate, and salmon swim upstream to spawn.

b. Sociobiologists such as Edward O. Wilson (1975, 1978) believe that humans also have instincts, like competition or aggression, which are genetically transmitted from one generation to another.

SDI Productions/iStock/Getty Iamges

One of the earliest researchers, William McDougall (1908), proposed that humans had numerous **instincts**, which was strictly defined as *fixed, unlearned response patterns found in almost all members of a species* (**Figure 11.1**). Examples of these instincts included repulsion, curiosity, and self-assertiveness. Other researchers later added their favorite instincts, and by the 1920s, the list of recognized instincts had become impossibly long. One researcher found listings for more than 10,000 human instincts (Bernard, 1924). In addition, the label *instinct* led to unscientific, circular explanations—"men are aggressive because they are instinctively aggressive" or "women are maternal because they have a natural maternal instinct."

In the 1930s, the concepts of drive and reduction began to replace the theory of instincts. According to **drive-reduction theory** (Hull, 1952), when biological needs such as food, water, and oxygen are unmet, a state of tension known as a *drive* is created. The organism is then motivated to reduce that drive. The overall goal of drive reduction is to restore **homeostasis**— our body's tendency to maintain equilibrium, or a steady state of internal balance (**Process Diagram 11.1**). To keep our bodies functioning at an appropriate level, numerous biological

Instinct   The fixed, unlearned response patterns found in almost all members of a species.

Drive-reduction theory   The theory that motivation begins with a physiological need (a lack or deficiency) that elicits a drive toward behavior that will satisfy the original need; once the need is met, a state of balance (homeostasis) is restored, and motivation decreases.

Homeostasis   Our body's tendency to maintain equilibrium, or a steady state of internal balance.

STOP!   This Process Diagram contains essential information NOT found elsewhere in the text, which is likely to appear on quizzes and exams. Be sure to study it CAREFULLY.

PROCESS DIAGRAM 11.1   **Drive-Reduction Theory**   When we are hungry or thirsty, the disruption of our normal state of equilibrium creates a drive that motivates us to search for food or water. Once action is taken and the need is satisfied, homeostasis is restored, and our motivation decreases.

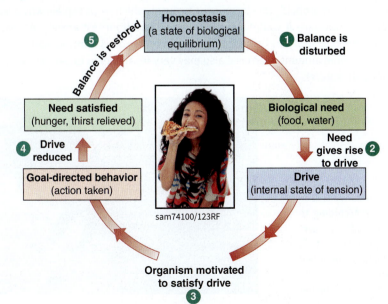

5 Balance is restored

Homeostasis (a state of biological equilibrium)

1 **Balance is disturbed**

Need satisfied (hunger, thirst relieved)

Biological need (food, water)

4 **Drive reduced**

Need gives rise to drive 2

Goal-directed behavior (action taken)

Drive (internal state of tension)

sam74100/123RF

Organism motivated to satisfy drive 3

FIGURE 11.2 Optimal level of arousal

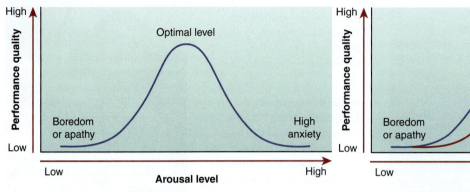

a. Normal everyday optimal arousal Our need for stimulation (the arousal motive) suggests that behavior efficiency increases as we move from boredom or apathy to increased alertness. However, once we pass the optimal level of arousal, our performance declines. When taking an exam, for example, you don't want to be too anxious or overly relaxed. When studying for an exam, you may be too relaxed and bored, so try to artificially increase your anxiety by drinking coffee and reminding yourself of the importance of the exam. In contrast, most students are overly anxious during the actual exam, so try to relax and take deep breaths before and during the exam—and maybe skip the coffee.

b. Optimal arousal for difficult versus easy tasks As you can see, the optimal level of arousal also depends on the task—difficult tasks require lower arousal, whereas easier tasks need higher arousal for maximum performance. When taking a difficult and very important exam, practice mindfulness meditation and the other stress relievers we discussed in Chapter 3. However, when listening to a basic lecture, try to increase your arousal by reminding yourself that the lecture is important and taking copious notes—review the tips for student success at the end of Chapter 1.

Optimal-arousal theory
The theory that organisms are motivated to achieve and maintain an optimal level of arousal, which maximizes their performance.

Yerkes-Dodson law The law stating that maximum performance is related to levels of arousal; complex tasks require a relatively low level of arousal, whereas simple tasks require a relatively high arousal level.

states must be balanced within a certain range, including hunger, blood glucose, temperature, and oxygenation.

In addition to having obvious biological needs, humans and other animals are innately curious and require a certain amount of novelty and complexity from the environment. According to **optimal-arousal theory**, organisms are motivated to achieve and maintain an optimal level of arousal that maximizes their performance. To gain this optimal arousal, the **Yerkes-Dodson law** states that performance increases with physiological and mental arousal—but only up to a certain level.

[AQ1] Both too much and too little arousal diminish performance (**Figure 11.2**). Maximum performance on complex, unfamiliar tasks requires a moderately low level of arousal, whereas simple, well-learned tasks require a moderately high arousal level. Can you see how this information could be helpful in your everyday life? Have you ever "blanked out" during a very important exam and couldn't answer questions that you thought you knew the answers to? This is probably due to your overarousal, which helps explain why overlearning is so important—especially if you're someone who suffers from test anxiety. As discussed in Chapter 1, you need to study and practice until the information is firmly locked in place (overlearning). The desired amount of arousal also may vary from person to person (see photo and the **Test Yourself** feature).

PA Practical Application

Test Yourself: Sensation Seeking

What motivates people to bungee jump over deep canyons (see photo) or white-water raft down dangerous rivers? According to research, these "high-sensation seekers" may be biologically "prewired" to need a higher-than-usual level of stimulation (Haas et al., 2019; Zuckerman, 1979, 2014). Researchers have also identified several factors that characterize sensation seeking, including the finding that light and binge-drinkers of alcohol tend to be higher

in sensation seeking (Breivik et al., 2019; Chomsri et al., 2018; Zuckerman & Aluja, 2015):

- Thrill and adventure seeking (skydiving, driving fast, or traveling to an unusual, "off the beaten path" location)
- Experience seeking (unusual friends, exotic foods or restaurants, drug experimentation)
- Disinhibition ("letting loose")
- Susceptibility to boredom (lower tolerance for repetition and sameness)

To sample the questions asked on tests for sensation seeking, circle the choice (a or b) that best describes you:

1. **a.** I would like a job that requires a lot of traveling.
   b. I would prefer a job in one location.
2. **a.** I get bored seeing the same old faces.
   b. I like the comfortable familiarity of everyday friends.
3. **a.** The most important goal of life is to live it to the fullest and experience as much as possible.
   b. The most important goal of life is to find peace and happiness.

4. **a.** I would like to try parachute jumping.
   b. I would never want to try jumping out of a plane, with or without a parachute.
5. **a.** I prefer people who are emotionally expressive even if they are a bit unstable.
   b. I prefer people who are calm and even-tempered.

Source: Zuckerman, M. (1978, February). The search for high sensation, *Psychology Today*, pp. 38–46.

Q Test Your Critical Thinking

1. If you answered mostly "a" to these five questions, you're probably a high-sensation seeker. If so, what do you do to satisfy that urge, and what can you do to make sure it doesn't get out of control?
2. If you are low in sensation seeking, has this trait interfered with some aspect of your life? If so, what could you do to improve your functioning in this area?
3. How might having either a very high or very low score on these questions cause trouble in relationships, or in your choice of a career?

Psychological Theories

Instinct, drive reduction, and optimal arousal are biological theories that explain some motivations, but why do we continue to eat after our biological needs have been met? Why do some of us work overtime when our salary is sufficient to meet all basic biological needs? These questions are best answered by psychosocial theories that emphasize incentives and cognition.

Unlike drive-reduction theory, which states that internal factors *push* people in certain directions, **incentive theory** maintains that external stimuli *pull* people toward desirable goals or away from undesirable ones. Most of us initially eat because our hunger "pushes" us (drive-reduction theory). But the sight of apple pie or ice cream too often "pulls" us toward continued eating (incentive theory).

What about using rewards to increase motivation? Researchers interested in increasing good grades, adherence to school rules, and regular school attendance found that paying middle-school students $2.00 daily for each goal met was enough incentive to produce higher reading test scores, especially for boys and those with disciplinary problems in the past (Fryer, 2010). But as you'll discover later in this chapter, this type of *extrinsic reward* (paying students for achieved goals) may create problems and unintended consequences.

In addition to incentives, psychological theories also include cognitions, which means that motivation is directly affected by *attributions*, or the ways in which we interpret or think about our own and others' actions (see the **Test Yourself**).

Incentive theory   The theory that motivation results from external stimuli that "pull" an organism in certain directions.

S&P Scientific Thinking and Practical Application

Test Yourself: Using Attributions to Explain Grades

Imagine that you received a high grade on a test in your psychology course (see photo). You can interpret that grade in several ways: You earned it because you really studied, you "lucked out," the test was easy, or the textbook was exceptionally interesting and helpful (our preferred attribution). As you might expect, people who attribute their

successes to personal control and effort tend to work harder toward their goals than people who attribute their successes to luck (Aruguete & Hardy, 2016; Karaman et al., 2019; Weiner, 1972, 2015).

Maridav/iStock/Getty Images

Expectancies, or what we believe or assume will happen, are also important to motivation (Best et al., 2016; Tamir et al., 2015; Sanderson, 2019). If you anticipate that you will receive a promotion at work, you're more likely to work overtime for no pay than if you do not expect a promotion.

Prostock-studio/Shutterstock.com

FIGURE 11.3 **Expectancies as psychological motivators** What expectations might these people have about the champagne that will motivate them to drink it? Think about all the advertisements for alcohol and the pressure from others to "join in." Can you see how these expectancies and pressures might contribute to problem drinking?

Hierarchy of needs Maslow's view that basic human motives form a hierarchy; the lower motives (such as physiological and safety needs) must be met before advancing to higher needs (such as belonging and self-actualization).

Self-actualization The humanistic term for the inborn drive to realize our full potential and to develop all our talents and capabilities.

Interestingly, people generally expect low/light versions of alcohol, tobacco, and foods to be less harmful. However, a recent study found that when alcoholic drinks were labeled as lower in strength, research participants actually increased the amount they consumed (Vasiljevic et al., 2018). **[AQ2]** Similarly, expectancies that alcohol will increase sociability and decrease anxiety and negative emotions lead many people to increase their alcohol consumption, particularly in unfamiliar social settings (Anthenien et al., 2017; Baines et al., 2016; Fairbairn & Bresin, 2017). See **Figure 11.3**.

Biopsychosocial Theories

Research in psychology generally emphasizes either biological or psychosocial factors (nature or nurture). However, approaches that combine biological, psychological and social/cultural factors (the biopsychosocial model) almost always provide the best explanation, and the theories of motivation are no exception. One researcher who believed in biopsychosocial factors as predictors of motivation was Abraham Maslow (1954, 1999). He believed we all have numerous needs that compete for fulfillment but that some needs are more important than others. For example, your need for food and shelter is generally more important than your need for good grades.

As you can see in **Figure 11.4**, Maslow proposed a **hierarchy of needs**, starting with survival needs at the bottom (which must be met before others) and self-actualization needs at the top. This seems intuitively correct: A starving person would first look for food, then love and friendship, and then self-esteem.

This *hierarchy of needs,* as well as general humanistic concepts, such as **self-actualization**, the inborn drive to develop all our talents and capabilities, have played major roles in psychology, economics, and other related fields (D'Souza & Gurin, 2016; Hsu, 2016; van Lenthe et al., 2015). As an example, standard marketing texts often use this hierarchy of needs to imply that brand consumption is a natural, driving force in shopping behaviors. Ironically, Maslow's work and humanistic ideals would emphasize less, not more, consumption (Hackley, 2007).

Maslow's critics argue that parts of his theory are poorly researched and biased toward Western preferences for individualism. Furthermore, some have misinterpreted his theory to suggest that the lower needs must be satisfied before someone can achieve self-actualization. However, Maslow believed we move back and forth between the needs based on the situation (Compton & Hoffman, 2019; Logue, 2019). People obviously seek to satisfy higher-level needs even when their lower-level needs have not been met. Protestors all over the world have used starvation as a way to protest unfair laws and political situations.

FIGURE 11.4 **Maslow's hierarchy of needs** Maslow's theory of motivation suggests that we all share a compelling need to "move up"—to grow, improve ourselves, and ultimately become "self-actualized."

Self-actualization needs: to find self-fulfillment and realize one's potential

Esteem needs: to achieve, be competent, gain approval, and excel

Belonging and love needs: to affiliate with others, be accepted, and give and receive affection

Safety needs: to feel secure and safe, to seek pleasure and avoid pain

Physiological needs: hunger, thirst, and maintenance of internal state of the body

Jessica Rinaldi/Boston Globe/Getty Images

Retrieval Practice 11.1 | Theories of Motivation

Self-Test   Completing this self-test, and then checking your answers by clicking on the answer button or by looking in Appendix B, will provide immediate feedback and helpful practice for exams.

1. Motivation is best defined as _____.

    a. a set of factors that activate, direct, and maintain behavior, usually toward a goal

    b. the physiological and psychological arousal that occurs when a person really wants to achieve a goal

    c. what makes you do what you do

    d. goal-directed unconscious thoughts

2. _____ says people are "pulled" by external stimuli to act a certain way.

    a. Cognitive theory

    b. Incentive theory

    c. Maslow's hierarchy of needs

    d. Drive reduction theory

3. According to Maslow's _____, some motives have to be satisfied before a person can advance to fulfilling higher motives.

    a. psychosexual stages of development

    b. moral stages of development

    c. psychosocial stages of development

    d. hierarchy of needs

4. The humanistic term for the inborn drive to develop all one's talents and capabilities is known as _____.

    a. a cognitive "peak"

    b. self-actualization

    c. a hierarchy of needs

    d. drive-perfection theory

Q Test Your Critical Thinking

1. Why are modern biological theories of instincts more scientifically useful than older instinct theories?

2. At what level would you rank yourself on Maslow's hierarchy of needs? What can you do to advance to a higher level?

Real World Application Questions

[AQ1]   How does arousal interfere with performance?

fizkes/Shutterstock.com

[AQ2]   Can cognitive expectancies lead to problem drinking?

Prostock-studio/Shutterstock.com

Hint: Look in the text for **[AQ1]** and **[AQ2]**

11.2 | Motivation and Behavior

LEARNING OBJECTIVES

Retrieval Practice   While reading the upcoming sections, respond to each Learning Objective in your own words.

Review how the key factors of motivation affect behavior.

- **Discuss** the major factors that influence hunger and eating.
- **Describe** the major eating problems and disorders.

- **Define** achievement motivation and list the characteristics of high achievers.
- **Compare** extrinsic and intrinsic motivation.

Real World Application Question

[AQ3]   How does heavy use of social media increase the risk of eating disorders?

Why do people put themselves in dangerous situations? Why do salmon swim upstream to spawn? Behavior results from many motives. As an example, we discuss the need for sleep in Chapter 5, and we look at aggression, altruism, and interpersonal attraction in Chapter 15. Here, we focus on two basic motives: hunger and achievement. Then we turn to a discussion of how different kinds of motivation affect our intrinsic interests and performance.

Hunger and Eating

What motivates hunger? Is it your growling stomach? Or is it the sight of a juicy hamburger or the smell of a freshly baked cinnamon roll?

The Stomach   Early hunger researchers believed that the stomach controlled hunger, by contracting to send hunger signals when it was empty. Today, we know it's more complicated. As dieters who drink lots of water to keep their stomachs feeling full have been disappointed to discover, sensory input from an empty stomach is not essential for feeling hungry. In fact, humans and non-human animals without stomachs continue to experience hunger.

However, there is a connection between the stomach and feeling hungry. Receptors in the stomach and intestines detect levels of nutrients, and specialized pressure receptors in the stomach walls signal feelings of either emptiness or *satiety* (fullness). The stomach and other parts of the gastrointestinal tract also release chemical signals that play a role in hunger. Interestingly, as you'll see in Chapter 13, the stomach and other parts of the gastrointestinal system may also play a role in depression and other psychological disorders (Weir, 2018).

Biochemistry   Like the stomach, the brain and other parts of the body produce numerous neurotransmitters, hormones, enzymes, and other chemicals that affect hunger and satiety. Research in this area is complex due to the large number of known (and unknown) bodily chemicals and the interactions among them. It's unlikely that any one chemical controls our hunger and eating. Other internal factors, such as *thermogenesis*— the heat generated in response to food ingestion—also play a role (Hudson et al., 2015; Williams, 2014).

The Brain   In addition to its chemical signals, particular brain structures influence hunger and eating. Let's look at the *hypothalamus*, which helps regulate eating, drinking, and body temperature.

Early research suggested that one area of the hypothalamus, the lateral hypothalamus (LH), stimulates eating, while another area, the ventromedial hypothalamus (VMH), creates feelings of satiation, signaling the animal to stop eating (Teitelbaum & Stellar, 1954). When the VMH area was destroyed in rats, researchers found that the rats overate to the point of extreme obesity (**Figure 11.5**). In contrast, when the LH area was destroyed, the animals starved to death if they were not force-fed.

Later research, however, showed that the LH and VMH areas are not simple on–off switches for eating. Lesions (damage) to the VMH not only lead ultimately to severe weight gain but also make animals picky eaters that reject a wide variety of foods. Can you see how this picky eating doesn't match the idea that VMH-lesioned rats overeat because they aren't satiated and just can't stop eating? Furthermore, normal rats force-fed to become overweight also become picky eaters. Today, researchers know that the hypothalamus plays an important role in hunger and eating, but it is not the brain's "eating center." In fact, hunger and eating, like virtually all other behaviors, are influenced by numerous neural circuits that run throughout the brain.

Psychosocial Factors   The internal motivations for hunger we've discussed (the stomach, biochemistry, and the brain) are powerful. But *psychosocial factors*—

FIGURE 11.5   **How the brain affects eating**   Several areas of the brain are active in the regulation of hunger.

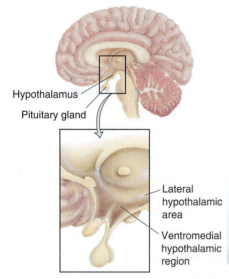

Hypothalamus
Pituitary gland

Lateral hypothalamic area
Ventromedial hypothalamic region

Voisin/Phanie/Science Source

a. Parts of the brain involved in hunger   This diagram shows a section of the human brain, including the ventromedial hypothalamus (VMH) and the lateral hypothalamus (LH), which are involved in the regulation of hunger.

b. How destruction of select brain areas affects hunger   After the ventromedial area of the hypothalamus of the rat on the left was destroyed, its body weight tripled. A rat of normal weight is shown on the right for comparison.

for example, spying a luscious dessert or smelling a pizza, or even simply noticing that it's almost lunchtime—can be equally important stimulus cues for hunger and eating. In fact, researchers have found that simply looking at pictures of high-fat foods, such as hamburgers, cookies, and cheesecake, can stimulate parts of the brain in charge of appetite, thereby increasing feelings of hunger and cravings for sweet and salty foods (Luo et al., 2015; Schüz et al., 2015).

Another important psychosocial influence on when, what, where, and why we eat is cultural conditioning. People in the United States tend to eat dinner at around 6 p.m., whereas people in Spain and South America tend to eat around 10 p.m. When it comes to *what* we eat, have you ever eaten guinea pig, dog, horse meat, or fried insects (see photo)? This might sound repulsive to you, yet most Hindus in India would feel a similar revulsion at the thought of eating meat from cows.

In sum, numerous biological and psychosocial factors operate in the regulation of hunger and eating (**Figure 11.6**), and researchers are still struggling to discover and explain how all these processes work together.

VCG/Visual China Group/Getty Images

FIGURE 11.6 **Key mechanisms in hunger regulation**   Different parts of your body communicate with your brain to trigger feelings of hunger.

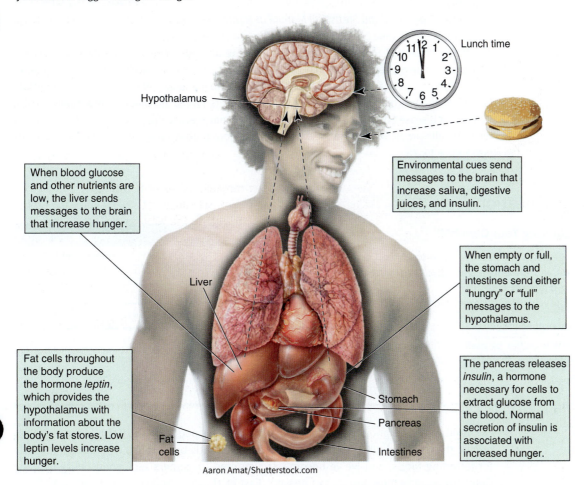

Hypothalamus

Lunch time

When blood glucose and other nutrients are low, the liver sends messages to the brain that increase hunger.

Environmental cues send messages to the brain that increase saliva, digestive juices, and insulin.

Liver

When empty or full, the stomach and intestines send either "hungry" or "full" messages to the hypothalamus.

Fat cells throughout the body produce the hormone *leptin*, which provides the hypothalamus with information about the body's fat stores. Low leptin levels increase hunger.

The pancreas releases *insulin*, a hormone necessary for cells to extract glucose from the blood. Normal secretion of insulin is associated with increased hunger.

Stomach

Pancreas

Fat cells

Intestines

Aaron Amat/Shutterstock.com

FIGURE 11.7 **Obesity and the NFL** Did you know that the weight of offensive linemen in the NFL has increased 27 percent from the 1970s to the 2000s—from an average of 249 pounds to 315 pounds? Or that every 10 pounds football players gain from high school to college, or from college to the professional level, increases their risk of heart disease by 14 percent? Although these players, particularly linemen, were encouraged to increase their weight while playing in the NFL, in retirement they not only have trouble losing the weight, but they're also at high risk for numerous health problems, including diabetes, hypertension, and cardiac problems. The fact that damage to their back, knees, and feet from playing football hinders or prevents exercise in retirement further exacerbates the players' health problems (Belson, 2019; Churchill et al., 2018).

ZUMA Press/Alamy Stock Photo

Obesity An eating problem involving a body mass index of 30 or above, based on height and weight.

Eating Problems and Disorders

The same biopsychosocial forces that explain hunger and eating also play a role in four serious eating problems and disorders: *obesity*, *anorexia nervosa*, *bulimia nervosa*, and *binge-eating disorder*.

Obesity

Each year billions of dollars are spent treating serious and life-threatening medical problems related to obesity, with consumers spending billions more on largely ineffective weight-loss products and services. Imagine yourself being born and living your life on another planet, but you could receive all the Earth's normal television channels. Given that almost all the television stars, newscasters, and commercial spokespeople you've ever seen are very thin, would you wonder why there are so many ads promoting weight loss? How would you explain the recent news that obesity has reached epidemic proportions in the United States and other developed nations?

Obviously, there is a large gap between the select few appearing on television and the real world. In fact, almost one-fourth of all adults in the United States are considered to be overweight or medically obese (Centers for Disease Control and Prevention, 2018; Hales et al., 2018). In 2013, obesity was officially classified as a disease in the latest version of the *Diagnostic and Statistical Manual of Mental Disorders (DSM-5)* (American Psychiatric Association, 2013). (See Chapter 13 for a discussion of the DSM-5.)

What is **obesity**? The most widely used measure of weight status is *body mass index (BMI)*, which is a single numerical value that calculates height in relation to weight (see **Test Yourself**). Sadly, obesity is one of our greatest health threats due to its significant link with serious illnesses like heart disease, diabetes, stroke, and certain cancers (American Diabetes Association, 2019; Centers for Disease Control and Prevention, 2017a; Samaras et al., 2019). Surprisingly, obesity and related health problems like heart disease are also serious problems for some professional athletes (see **Figure 11.7**).

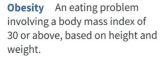 **Practical Application**

Test Yourself: Calculating Your Own BMI

To determine your BMI, use the *Adult BMI Calculator* at the Centers for Disease Control and Prevention site: http://www.cdc.gov/healthyweight/assessing/bmi/adult_bmi/

You can also compute your BMI by following these three steps:

1. Multiply your weight in pounds by 703.
2. Multiply your height in inches by itself (e.g., if your height is 63 inches, you would multiply 63 × 63).
3. Divide step 1 by step 2.

If Your BMI Is:	You Are:
18.5 and below	Underweight
18.5 to 24.9	Normal weight
25.0 to 29.9	Overweight
30.0 and above	Obese

Note: If your BMI is overly affected by muscle or bone mass, rather than fat, it's possible to have a high BMI and still be healthy.

Source: Centers for Disease Control and Prevention, 2017b

Controlling weight is a particularly difficult task for people in the United States. We are among the most sedentary people of all, we're constantly bombarded with advertisements for fattening foods, and we've become accustomed to "supersized" cheeseburgers, "Big Gulp" drinks, and huge servings of dessert (Fast et al., 2015; Folkvord et al., 2016; McCrory et al., 2019). Moreover, we've been taught that we should eat three meals a day, whether we're hungry or not; that "tasty" food requires lots of salt, sugar, and fat; and that food is an essential part of the workplace and almost all social gatherings. Researchers have even found that the widespread use of microwaves may help explain the rise in obesity (Kanazawa & von Buttlar, 2019). Why? It appears that warm food leads to more total calories consumed than cold food.

PAN   Practical Application of Neuroscience

What about those people who can seemingly eat anything they want and still not add pounds?   This may be a result of their ability to burn more calories in the process of thermogenesis, a higher metabolic rate, or other possible individual and environmental factors (A. W. Fischer et al., 2019; Katzmarzyk et al., 2019; Trayhurn, 2018). In addition, researchers have isolated a large number of genes that contribute to normal and abnormal weight (Dallner et al., 2019; Lotta et al., 2019; van Dijk et al., 2015). However, researchers also cautioned that more research is needed, and that human appetite and obesity are undoubtedly more complex than a single gene or hormone. In addition, this focus on genes should not encourage people to feel helpless against obesity.

Eating Disorders   The three major eating disorders—*anorexia nervosa*, *bulimia nervosa*, and *binge-eating disorder*—are found in all ethnicities, socioeconomic classes, and both sexes, however, they are more common in women (American Psychiatric Association, 2013; Bohon, 2015; Eddy et al., 2016). **Anorexia nervosa** is characterized by an overwhelming fear of becoming obese, a need for control, the use of dangerous weight-loss measures, and a body image that is so distorted that even a skeletal, emaciated body is seen as fat. The resulting extreme malnutrition often leads to osteoporosis, bone fractures, interruption of menstruation in women, and loss of brain tissue. Research has also shown that anorexia may be linked with particular brain activation patterns—such as the part of the brain linked with automatic responding (Foerde et al., 2015). This means that people with anorexia may make food decisions based on habit (e.g., I only eat low-fat foods), and not on reward centers, as do healthy people. Do you see how this might help explain why people with anorexia have such difficulty changing their behavior?

Occasionally, a person suffering from anorexia nervosa succumbs to the desire to eat and gorges on food, then vomits or takes laxatives. However, this type of bingeing and purging is more characteristic of **bulimia nervosa**. Individuals with bulimia go on recurrent eating binges and then purge by self-induced vomiting, use of laxatives, and/or excessive exercise. They often show impulsivity in other areas, sometimes engaging in excessive shopping, alcohol abuse, or petty shoplifting (Bénard et al., 2019; Miller et al., 2019; Pearson et al., 2015). The vomiting associated with bulimia nervosa may lead to severe damage to the teeth, throat, and stomach. It also leads to cardiac arrhythmia, metabolic deficiencies, and serious digestive disorders.

Note that bulimia is similar to but not the same as **binge-eating disorder**. This disorder involves recurrent episodes of consuming large amounts of food in a discrete period of time, while feeling a lack of control over eating. However, the individual does not try to purge (American Psychiatric Association, 2013; Burton & Abbott, 2019). Individuals with binge-eating disorder generally eat until they are uncomfortable and eat more rapidly due to embarrassment at the large quantities they are consuming. They also tend to feel disgusted, depressed, or very guilty after bingeing.

There are many suspected factors that contribute to anorexia nervosa, bulimia nervosa, and binge-eating disorder. Some theories focus on physical origins, such as hypothalamic disorders, low levels of various neurotransmitters, and genetic or hormonal disorders (e.g., Himmerich et al., 2019). Other theories emphasize psychosocial factors, such as a need for perfection, a perceived loss of control, teasing about body weight, destructive thought patterns, depression, dysfunctional families, distorted body image, and emotional or sexual abuse (e.g., American Psychiatric Association, 2013; Burton & Abbott, 2019; Schneider, 2015). **[AQ3]** Unfortunately, studies have found that women who frequently use social media are at greater risk of showing disordered eating. Apparently, browsing sites like Facebook is associated with more body dissatisfaction. Women who compare their own photos with those of their friends, and women who overvalue receiving comments and "likes" on their status updates (see photo), are at particular risk of eating disorders (Mabe et al., 2014).

Anorexia nervosa   An eating disorder characterized by an obsessive fear of obesity, a need for control, self-imposed starvation, and a severe loss of weight.

Bulimia nervosa   An eating disorder characterized by recurrent episodes of consuming large quantities of food (bingeing), followed by self-induced vomiting, use of laxatives, and/or excessive exercise (purging).

Binge-eating disorder   An eating disorder characterized by recurrent episodes of consuming large amounts of food (bingeing), but not followed by purge behaviors.

Dean Drobot/123RF

TABLE 11.2 **Symptoms of Anorexia Nervosa, Bulimia Nervosa, and Binge-Eating Disorder**

Anorexia Nervosa	Bulimia Nervosa	Binge-Eating Disorder	
• Weight less than 85 percent of normal for age and height • Intense fear of gaining weight, even when underweight • Persistent behavior to avoid weight gain • Distorted body image, denial of seriousness of weight loss	• Repeated episodes of binge eating, consuming unusually large amounts of food in a short period of time • Feeling out of control during the binge episode • Purging behaviors after eating, including vomiting, use of laxatives, or other medications, and/or excessive exercise • Alternating between overeating and fasting	• Repeated episodes of binge eating, consuming unusually large amounts of food in a short period of time • Feeling out of control during the binge episode • Eating much more rapidly than normal, eating large amounts when not feeling physically hungry • Feelings ashamed and guilty after bingeing • No compensatory purging behaviors, such as vomiting, laxatives, and/or excessive exercise	Many celebrities, like Lady Gaga (pictured here), have publicly shared their battles with eating disorders. But does this type of publicity increase or decrease the chance that their fans will suffer similar problems?  Chris Wolf/FilmMagic/Getty Images

Regardless of the origins of these eating disorders, it's important to recognize the symptoms of anorexia, bulimia, and binge-eating disorder (**Table 11.2**) and to seek therapy if the symptoms apply to you. The key point to remember is that all eating disorders are serious chronic conditions that require treatment.

Achievement Motivation

> You have brains in your head. You have feet in your shoes. You can steer yourself in any direction you choose. You're on your own, and you know what you know. And you are the guy who'll decide where to go.
>
> —Theodor Seuss Geisel, "Dr. Seuss" (American writer, poet, cartoonist)

Achievement motivation The desire to excel, especially in competition with others.

Do you wonder what motivates Olympic athletes to work so hard for a gold medal? Or what drives someone like Oprah Winfrey, famous television star, thriving businesswoman, and generous philanthropist? The key to understanding what motivates high-achieving individuals lies in what psychologist Henry Murray (1938) identified as a high need for achievement (nAch), or **achievement motivation**. See the following **Test Yourself**.

PA Practical Application

Test Yourself: Need for Achievement (nAch)

Researchers have identified at least six traits that distinguish people with a high nAch (Harwood et al., 2015; McClelland, 1958, 1993; Mokrova et al., 2013; Schunk & Zimmerman, 2013; Stadler et al., 2016). Place a check mark next to each trait that applies to you or to ones that you may want to work to develop:

• _____ **Preference for moderately difficult tasks** People high in nAch avoid tasks that are too easy since they offer little challenge or satisfaction. They also avoid extremely difficult tasks given that the probability of success is too low.

• _____ **Competitiveness** High-achievement-oriented people are more attracted to careers and tasks that involve competition and an opportunity to excel.

• _____ **Preference for clear goals with competent feedback** High-achievement-oriented people tend to prefer tasks with clear outcomes and situations in which they can receive feedback on their performance. Likewise, they prefer criticism from a harsh but competent evaluator to criticism from one who is friendlier but less competent.

- _____ **Self-regulation and personal responsibility** High-achievement-oriented people purposefully control their thoughts and behaviors to attain their goals. In addition, they prefer being personally responsible for a project so that they can feel satisfied when the task is well done.

- _____ **Mental toughness and persistence** High-achievement-oriented people have a mindset that allows them to persevere through difficult circumstances. It includes attributes like sacrifice and self-denial, which helps them maintain concentration and motivation when things aren't going well.

- _____ **More accomplished** People who have high nAch scores generally do better than others on exams, earn better grades in school, and excel in their chosen professions.

In addition to these six individual personality traits associated with nAch, researchers have found that highly motivated children tend to have parents who encourage independence and frequently reward successes (Aunola et al., 2013; Feng et al., 2019; Pomerantz & Kempner, 2013). In fact, children's motivation for academic success—along with their study skills—are better predictors of long-term math achievement than IQ (Murayama et al., 2012).

Our cultural values also affect achievement needs. In fact, a study of 13,000 identical and fraternal twins from six different countries found that academic motivation (enjoyment of reading, math, science, etc.) is about half determined by these types of environmental experiences, with the other half being governed by genetics (Kovas et al., 2015).

Before leaving you with the impression that having a high need for achievement (nAch) is always desirable, consider what happens when we encounter life's inevitable failures. Some have suggested that striving for impossible goals can lead to dangerous perfectionism, depression, and drug abuse (e.g., Luthar & Kumar, 2018; Simmons, 2019; Sisk et al., 2018). The following **STH Scientific Thinking Highlight** even discusses potential benefits to losing.

Extrinsic motivation A type of motivation for a task or activity based on external incentives, such as rewards and punishments.

Intrinsic motivation A type of motivation for a task or activity based on internal incentives, such as enjoyment and personal satisfaction.

Extrinsic versus Intrinsic Motivation

Have you ever noticed that for all the money and glory they receive, professional athletes often don't look like they're enjoying themselves very much? What's the problem? Why don't they appreciate how lucky they are to be able to make a living by playing games?

One way psychologists attempt to answer questions about motivation is by distinguishing between **extrinsic motivation**, based on external rewards or punishments, and **intrinsic motivation**, based on internal, personal satisfaction from a task or activity (Deci & Moller, 2005; C. Fischer et al., 2019; Ryan & Deci, 2013). When we perform a task for no ulterior purpose, we use internal, personal reasons—"I like it"; "It's fun"—(see photo). But when extrinsic rewards are added, the explanation shifts to external, impersonal reasons ("I did it for the money"; "I did it to please my parents"). This shift often decreases enjoyment and hampers performance. This is as true for professional athletes as it is for anyone else.

A classic experiment demonstrating this effect was conducted with preschool children who liked to draw (Lepper et al., 1973). These researchers found that children who were given paper and markers, and promised a reward for their drawings, were subsequently less interested in drawing than children who were not given a reward, or who were given an unexpected reward for their pictures when they were done. Likewise, a decade-long study of over 10,000 West Point cadets found that those who were motivated to pursue a military career for internal reasons, such as personal ambition, were more likely to receive early career promotions than those who attended a military academy for external reasons, such as family expectations (Wrzesniewski et al., 2014).

As it turns out, however, there is considerable controversy over individual differences in what motivates someone, and under what conditions giving external, extrinsic rewards increases or decreases motivation (Deci & Ryan, 1985, 2012; Koo et al., 2015; Pope & Harvey, 2015). Furthermore, research shows that not all extrinsic motivation is bad. A study of elementary school

Courtesy of Sandy Harvey

Intrinsic motivation Judging by the expression on this child's face, he is jumping in the pool for the sheer joy and pleasure of swimming—intrinsic motivation.

STH Scientific Thinking Highlight

Do Losers Sometimes Actually Win?

(APA Goal 2.1) Use scientific reasoning to interpret psychological phenomena

Can being a high achiever and having a high-pressure job actually take years off your life? To test this question, researchers in one study examined life expectancy of candidates for head-of-country elections—meaning president or prime minister—in a number of different countries (Olenski et al., 2015). Specifically, the researchers gathered data on the number of years candidates lived after their final campaign for office. They then compared whether candidates who won the election—and thus served as head of country—had fewer years of life than those who lost the election—and thus didn't serve in this capacity. The researchers gathered data from 17 countries (including the United States, Australia, the United Kingdom, and Canada) over nearly 300 years (from 1722 to 2015).

As predicted, winning an election was actually bad for candidates' longevity. Candidates who lost the election lived an average of an additional 17.8 years, whereas those who won lived only an average of an additional 13.4 years. In this case, it actually hurts to win—the winning candidate lost an additional 4.4 years of life. Although these numbers don't explain exactly how winning an election led to a shorter life expectancy, researchers believe that the greater stress experienced by heads of country likely helps explain this difference.

Q Test Your Scientific Thinking

As you recall from Chapter 1, scientific thinking is an approach to information that combines a high degree of *skepticism* (questioning what "everybody knows") with *objectivity* (using empirical data to separate fantasy from reality) and with *rationalism* (practicing logical reasoning). Using these three principles, consider the following questions:

1. **Skepticism** What do you think? "Everybody knows" that being president or prime minister is an incredibly stressful job. You often hear people asking, "Who would even want that job?" But is that true? Maybe people in that position have so many helpers and advisers that they actually experience less stress? Scientific thinkers approach ideas and research conclusions with skepticism.

2. **Objectivity** Are the authors' assumptions supported by the data? What more information do we need to have before accepting their conclusions? Scientific thinkers carefully analyze data for value and content. Is this a possible illusory correlation and there is in fact NO real connection between the variables? Or could this be an example of the third-variable problem? Maybe the winners shared one or more specific personality traits, like having a very high nAch, which helped them win, and then the variable of personality traits better explains why the winners didn't live as long as their losing competitors. In Chapter 1, we emphasized the dangers of confusing correlation with causation, and here the researchers are suggesting that the link between winning an election and having a lower life expectancy was *caused* by the stress of serving in these high-pressure jobs. Another problem might be potential sample bias. Are people in all high-pressure jobs at risk of dying earlier or is it just winners of head-of-country elections? Scientific thinkers gather information and delay judgment until adequate data is available.

3. **Rationalism** Setting aside the limited data from other research, can we logically conclude that losing an election actually leads to a longer life? Could it be that the lavish lifestyle (and not the daily stressors) of being a president or prime minister was a better explanation for the decreased life expectancy of the winners? Maybe having servants who do all your chores and feed you whatever you want 24/7 isn't what many of us consider a "dream situation" after all. What do you think? Has reading this section affected your thoughts about winning and losing—or even your career choices?

---

students who were simply mailed books weekly during the summer or were mailed books along with a reading incentive or were assigned to a control group with no books or incentives found that students who were initially more motivated to read were also more responsive to incentives (Guryan et al., 2015). As you can see in **Figure 11.8**, extrinsic rewards with "no strings attached" can actually increase motivation.

How does this apply to you and your everyday life? As a college student facing many high-stakes exams, have you noticed how often professors try to motivate their students with "scare tactics," such as frequently reminding you of how your overall GPA and scores on certain exams may be critical for entry into desirable jobs or for admittance to graduate programs? Does this type of extrinsic motivation help or hurt your motivation? One study found that when instructors use extrinsic consequences, such as fear tactics, as motivational tools, their students' intrinsic motivation and exam scores decrease (Putwain & Remedios, 2014). In fact, fear of failure may be one of the greatest detriments to intrinsic motivation (Covington & Müeller, 2001; Ma et al., 2014; Moreno-Murcia et al., 2019).

FIGURE 11.8 **How extrinsic rewards can sometimes be motivating**

Controlling reward
(manipulates and controls behavior)

School gives
every student
a small reward
for attendance

Student is
extrinsically
motivated:
"I'll attend school
if I get the reward."

Approval reward
(praise and approval for
desired behavior)

Parents:
"We'll be very happy
if you get A's like our
neighbor's boy."

Student is
extrinsically
motivated:
"I'll get good grades
to get their approval."

Informing reward
(feedback or information on
level of performance)

School gives
small reward for
students with
outstanding attendance

Student is
intrinsically
motivated:
"I enjoy going
to school
every day."

"No strings" treat
(unexpected reward with no
contingencies attached)

Parents:
"You've been studying pretty
hard tonight. Let's take a break
and go out for ice cream."

Student is
intrinsically
motivated:
"It's nice that Dad
noticed me studying
and an ice cream
sounds great."

a. Controlling or approval rewards
If extrinsic rewards are used to control, or gain approval, they generally decrease motivation. When schools pay all students for simple attendance, or when parents give children approval or privileges for achieving good grades, they may unintentionally decrease the children's motivation to attend school or get good grades.

b. Informing or "no strings" rewards
Extrinsic rewards can be motivating if they are used to inform, and if there are "no strings" attached. When a small reward is provided for outstanding attendance, or a surprise treat is offered for good grades, it may increase both motivation and enjoyment.

What should teachers and students do instead? Rather than emphasizing high exam scores or overall GPA, researchers recommend focusing on specific behaviors required to avoid failure and attain success. As a student you can focus on improving your overall study techniques and test taking skills. See again the *Secrets of Student Success* at the end of Chapter 1. For additional help, check with your professors or your college counseling center. For help with increasing your overall motivation, see the following **Test Yourself**.

PA Practical Application

Test Yourself: Tips for Increasing Motivation

Both intrinsic and extrinsic motivation have important implications for raising children, running a business, or even studying this text. If you want to improve your effectiveness in any of these areas, consider the following guidelines:

1. **Emphasize intrinsic reasons for behaviors** Rather than thinking about all the people you'll impress with good grades or all the great jobs you'll get when you finish college, focus instead on personally satisfying, intrinsic reasons. Think about how exciting it is to learn new things, or the value of becoming a scientific and critical thinker.

2. **Limit extrinsic rewards** In general, it is almost always better to use the least possible extrinsic reward and for the shortest possible time period. When children are first learning to play a musical instrument, it may help to provide small rewards until they gain a certain level of mastery. But once a child is working happily or practicing for the sheer joy of it, it is best to leave him or her alone. Similarly, if you're trying to increase your study time, begin by rewarding yourself for every significant improvement.

But don't reward yourself when you're handling a difficult assignment easily. Save rewards for when you need them. Keep in mind that we're speaking primarily of concrete extrinsic rewards. Praise and positive feedback are generally safe to use and often increase intrinsic motivation.

3. **Provide appropriate rewards** Use extrinsic rewards to provide feedback for competency or outstanding performance—not for simply engaging in the behavior. Schools can enhance intrinsic motivation by giving medals or privileges to students with no absences, rather than giving money for simple attendance. Similarly, you should reward yourself with a movie or a call to a friend *after* you've studied hard for your scheduled time period or done particularly well on an exam. Don't reward yourself for halfhearted attempts.

4. **Just do it** We've mentioned many times the value of distributed practice. You really can't "cram" when it comes to workouts, brushing your teeth, losing and maintaining weight, or keeping up with employer demands. You "simply" have to get up and get started. Don't think. Just do. The first few minutes of exercise are always the hardest, and the same is true for almost every aspect of life. Get up, get started, power through. You'll thank yourself later.

Retrieval Practice 11.2 | Motivation and Behavior

Self-Test Completing this self-test, and then checking your answers by clicking on the answer button or by looking in Appendix B, will provide immediate feedback and helpful practice for exams.

1. Motivation for eating is found _____.

   a. in the stomach

   b. in the ventromedial section of the hypothalamus

   c. throughout the brain

   d. throughout the body

2. Maria appears to be starving herself and has obviously lost a lot of weight in just a few months. You suspect she might be suffering from _____.

   a. anorexia nervosa   c. obesity phobia

   b. bulimia nervosa   d. none of these options

3. _____ is NOT listed as a trait of a high nAch person?

   a. Competitiveness   c. Self-regulation

   b. Mental toughness   d. Emotional intelligence

4. The desire to excel, especially in competition with others, is known as _____.

   a. drive-reduction theory   c. achievement motivation

   b. intrinsic motivation   d. all these options

5. Alexandria spends hours working in her garden. Which type of motivation is most likely driving her behavior?

   a. extrinsic motivation   c. external incentives

   b. a high need for   d. intrinsic motivation
      achievement

Q Test Your Critical Thinking

1. Most adults (and many children) find it difficult to control their weight. Using information from this chapter, can you identify the factors or motives that best explain their experience?

2. How can you restructure elements of your personal, work, or school life to increase your intrinsic versus extrinsic motivation?

Real World Application Question

[AQ3] How does heavy use of social media increase the risk of eating disorders?

Dean Drobot/123RF

Hint: Look in the text for **[AQ3]**

11.3 | Components and Theories of Emotion

LEARNING OBJECTIVES

Retrieval Practice While reading the upcoming sections, respond to each Learning Objective in your own words.

Summarize the major components and theories of emotion.

- **Define** emotion.

- **Discuss** emotion's biological, cognitive, and behavioral components.

- **Compare** the three major theories of emotion and the facial-feedback hypothesis.

Real World Application Question

[AQ4] Can airport security agents increase their effectiveness by simply talking to passengers?

Emotion A complex pattern of feelings that includes arousal (heart pounding), cognitions (thoughts, values, and expectations), and expressive behaviors (smiles, frowns, and gestures).

Emotions play an important role in our lives. They color our dreams, memories, and perceptions. When they are disordered, they contribute significantly to psychological problems. High levels of anger and anxiety have even been associated with an increased risk of a heart attack (Buckley et al., 2015). But what do we really mean by the term **emotion**? In everyday usage, we use it to describe feeling states; we feel "thrilled" when our political candidate wins an election, "dejected" when our candidate loses, and "miserable" when our loved ones reject us. Obviously, what is specifically meant by these terms, or what we personally experience with different emotions, can vary greatly among individuals. In this section, we will focus on the three basic components of emotions, along with its three major theories.

Three Components of Emotion

Psychologists define and study emotion according to three basic components—*biological*, *cognitive*, and *behavioral* (see **Figure 11.9**).

Biological (Arousal) Component

Internal physical changes occur in our bodies whenever we experience an emotion. Imagine walking alone on a dark street and having someone jump from behind a stack of boxes and start running toward you. How would you respond? Like most people, you would probably interpret the situation as threatening and would run. Your predominant emotion, fear, would inspire several physiological reactions, such as increased heart rate and blood pressure, perspiration, and goose bumps (piloerection). Such biological reactions are controlled by certain brain structures and by the autonomic branch of the nervous system (ANS).

Our emotional experiences appear to result from important interactions between several areas of the brain, particularly the *cerebral cortex* and *limbic system* (Grimm et al., 2014; Kemp et al., 2015; Schulze et al., 2016). As we discuss in Chapter 2, the cerebral cortex, the outermost layer of the brain, serves as our body's ultimate control and information-processing center that enables us to recognize and regulate our emotions.

Studies of the limbic system, located in the innermost part of the brain, have shown that one area, the **amygdala**, plays a key role in emotion—especially fear (**Figure 11.10**). It sends signals to the other areas of the brain, causing increased heart rate and other physiological reactions related to fear. Sadly, children with high levels of anxiety tend to have larger amygdalae, as well as stronger connections between the amygdala and other parts of the brain (Qin et al., 2014).

Emotional arousal sometimes occurs without our conscious awareness. According to psychologist Joseph LeDoux (1996, 2014), when the *thalamus* (the brain's sensory switchboard) receives sensory inputs, it sends separate messages up to the cortex, which "thinks" about the stimulus, and to the amygdala, which immediately activates the body's alarm system (**Figure 11.11**). Although this dual pathway occasionally leads to "false alarms," such as when we mistake a stick for a snake, LeDoux believes it is a highly adaptive warning system essential to our survival. He states that "the time saved by the amygdala in acting on the thalamic interpretation, rather than waiting for the cortical input, may be the difference between life and death" (LeDoux, 1996, p. 166).

As important as the brain is to emotion, it is the *autonomic nervous system* (Chapter 2) that produces the obvious signs of arousal. These largely automatic responses result from interconnections between the ANS and various glands and muscles (**Figure 11.12**).

Cognitive (Thinking) Component

Emotional reactions are very individual: What you experience as intensely pleasurable may be boring or aversive to another. To study the cognitive (thought) component of emotions, psychologists typically use self-report techniques, such as surveys and interviews. However, people are sometimes unable or unwilling to accurately remember or describe their emotional states. For these reasons, our cognitions about our own and others' emotions are difficult to measure scientifically. This is why many researchers supplement participants' reports on their emotional experiences with methods that assess emotional experience indirectly (e.g., measuring physiological responses such as heart rate, pupil dilation, blood flow).

People who undergo trauma often find it difficult to identify and manage their overwhelming emotions. Fortunately, a new imaging method that measures activity within the amygdala may provide help (Keynan et al., 2016). Can you see how providing individuals with specific cognitive feedback on their particular level of arousal could help people manage not only the arousal itself (the emotional component) but also the behavioral expression component—the topic of our next section?

Behavioral (Expressive) Component

Emotional expression is a powerful form of communication, and facial expressions may be our most important form of emotional communication. Researchers have developed sensitive techniques to measure subtleties

FIGURE 11.9 **The three components of emotion—in action** This politician shows his anger in various ways, including his red face (biological component), his obvious appraisal that the reporter's question is unfair (cognitive component), and his yelling at the reporter, and gesturing with his hands and arms (behavioral components).

VIKTORIYA KRASOVSKAYA/123RF

Amygdala A part of the limbic system linked to the production and regulation of emotions—especially aggression and fear.

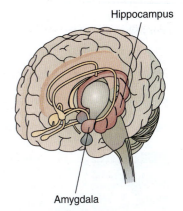

Hippocampus

Amygdala

FIGURE 11.10 **The limbic system's role in emotion** In addition to being involved in drive regulation, memory, and other functions, the limbic system is very important in emotions. It consists of several subcortical structures that form a border (or limbus) around the brain stem.

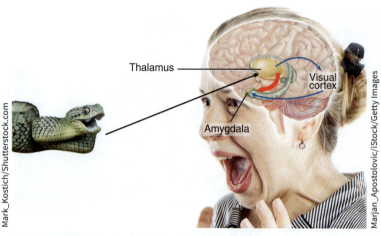

Mark_Kostich/Shutterstock.com

Marjan_Apostolovic/iStock/Getty Images

Thalamus — Visual cortex

Amygdala

	Sympathetic		Parasympathetic
Pupils dilated	**Eyes**	Pupils constricted
Decreased saliva	**Mouth**	Increased saliva
Vessels constricted (skin cold and clammy)	**Skin**	Vessels dilated (normal blood flow)
Respiration increased	**Lungs**	Respiration normal
Increased heart rate	**Heart**	Decreased heart rate
Increased epinephrine and norepinephrine	**Adrenal glands**	Decreased epinephrine and norepinephrine
Decreased motility	**Digestion**	Increased motility

FIGURE 11.11 **Fast and slow pathways for fear** When visual sensory input arrives at the thalamus, the thalamus sends it along a fast route directly to the amygdala (the red arrow), as well as along a slower, more indirect route to the visual cortex (the blue arrow). This speedy, direct route allows us to quickly respond to a feared stimulus (like the snake) even before we're consciously aware of our emotions or behaviors. In contrast, the indirect route, engaging the visual cortex, provides more detailed information that allows us to consciously evaluate the danger of this particular snake and our most appropriate response.

FIGURE 11.12 **Emotion and the autonomic nervous system (ANS)** During emotional arousal, the sympathetic branch of the autonomic nervous system (ANS) prepares the body for fight-flight-freeze. (The hormones epinephrine and norepinephrine keep the system under sympathetic control until the emergency is over.) The parasympathetic branch returns the body to a more relaxed state (homeostasis).

Courtesy Karen Huffman

Courtesy Karen Huffman

a.   b.

FIGURE 11.13 **Duchenne smile** People who show a Duchenne, or real, smile **(a)** and laughter elicit more positive responses from strangers. They also enjoy better interpersonal relationships and personal adjustment than those who use a social smile **(b)** (Bujisic et al., 2014; Krumhuber et al., 2014; Prkachin & Silverman, 2002).

of feeling and to differentiate honest expressions from fake ones. Perhaps most interesting is the difference between the *social smile* and the *Duchenne smile* (named after French anatomist Duchenne de Boulogne, who first described it in 1862). See **Figure 11.13**. In a false social smile, our voluntary cheek muscles are pulled back, but our eyes are unsmiling. Smiles of real pleasure, on the other hand, use the muscles not only around the cheeks but also around the eyes.

The Duchenne smile illustrates the importance of non-verbal means of communicating emotion. We all know that people communicate in ways other than speaking or writing. However, few people recognize the full importance of non-verbal signals (see **Test Yourself**).

PA Practical Application

Test Yourself: The Power of Non-verbal Cues

Imagine yourself as a job interviewer. Your first applicant greets you with a big smile, full eye contact, a firm handshake, and an erect, open posture (see photo). The second applicant doesn't smile, looks down, offers a weak handshake, and slouches. Whom do you think you will hire?

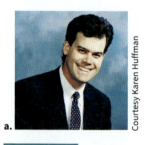

Dinis Tolipov/123RF

Psychologist Albert Mehrabian would say that you're much less likely to hire the second applicant due to his or her "mixed messages." Mehrabian's research suggests that when we're communicating feelings or attitudes and our verbal and non-verbal dimensions don't match, the receiver trusts the predominant form of communication, which is about 93 percent non-verbal and consists of the way the words are said and the facial expression rather than the literal meaning of the words (Mehrabian, 1968, 1971, 2007).

Unfortunately, Mehrabian's research is often overgeneralized, and many people misquote him as saying that "over 90 percent of communication is non-verbal." Clearly, if a police officer says, "Put your hands up," his or her verbal words might carry 100 percent of the meaning. However, when we're confronted with a mismatch between verbal and non-verbal communication, we tend to give far more attention to the non-verbal because we believe it more often tells us what someone is really thinking or feeling. The importance of non-verbal communication, particularly facial expressions, is further illustrated by the popularity of smileys and other emoticons in our everyday email and text messages.

Before going on, it's important to note that there are obvious limits to the power of non-verbal cues. **[AQ4]** A study examining airport security found that agents who were trained to not only observe (see photo), but also to talk with passengers, were more accurate at detecting dishonesty than those who only examined body language, such as lack of eye contact, nervousness, and fidgeting (Ormerod & Dando, 2015).

Jim West/Alamy Stock Photo

Three Theories of Emotion

Researchers generally agree that emotion has biological, cognitive, and behavioral components, but there is less agreement about *how* we experience emotions (Christenfeld & Mandler, 2013). The major competing theories are the *James-Lange theory*, the *Cannon-Bard theory*, and *Schachter and Singer's two-factor theory* (**Process Diagram 11.2**).

Imagine that you're walking in the forest and suddenly see a coiled snake on the path next to you. What emotion would you experience? Most people would say they would be very afraid. But why? Common sense tells us that our hearts pound and we tremble when we're afraid and that we cry when we're sad. But according to the **James-Lange theory**, felt emotions begin with bodily arousal of the ANS (Chapter 2). This arousal (a pounding heart, breathlessness, trembling all over) then leads us to experience the emotion we call "fear." Contrary to popular opinion, James wrote: "We feel sorry because we cry, angry because we strike, afraid because we tremble" (James, 1890, pp. 449–450).

In contrast, the **Cannon-Bard theory** proposes that arousal and emotion occur separately but simultaneously. Following perception of an emotion-provoking stimulus, the thalamus (a subcortical brain structure) sends two simultaneous messages: one to the ANS, which leads to bodily arousal, and one to the brain's cortex, which is responsible for awareness of the felt emotion.

Finally, Schachter and Singer's **two-factor theory** suggests that our emotions start with bodily arousal followed by a conscious, cognitive appraisal. We then look to external cues from the environment and from others around us to find a label and explanation for the arousal.

James-Lange theory A theory of emotion suggesting that the subjective experience of emotion results from bodily arousal, rather than being its cause ("I feel sad because I'm crying"); bodily arousal is the basis for feeling emotions.

Cannon-Bard theory A theory proposing that emotions and bodily changes occur simultaneously ("I'm crying and feeling sad at the same time"); bodily arousal plus brain processing occurring simultaneously is the basis for feeling emotions.

Two-factor theory Schachter and Singer's theory that emotion depends upon two factors—bodily arousal and cognitive labeling of that arousal; bodily arousal leads to labels which are the basis for feeling emotions.

> **STOP!** This Process Diagram contains essential information NOT found elsewhere in the text, which is likely to appear on quizzes and exams. Be sure to study it CAREFULLY.

PROCESS DIAGRAM 11.2   **Comparing Three Major Theories of Emotion**

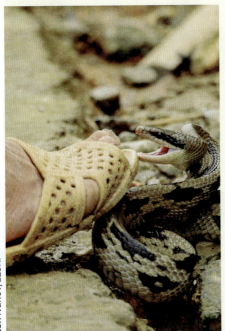

Anton Ivanov/123RF

Stimulus

James-Lange theory (bodily arousal is the basis for feeling emotions)
Perception of an environmental stimulus (snake) triggers bodily arousal, which we experience as a felt emotion (fear).

⇒ Bodily arousal ⇒ Emotion: **FEAR**

Cannon-Bard theory (bodily arousal and brain processing occur simultaneously is the basis for feeling emotions)
Perception of an environmental stimulus (snake) triggers the thalamus to send a simultaneous message that activates a bodily arousal at the same time as the felt emotion (fear).

⇒ Thalamus relays information ⇒ Bodily arousal
⇒ Emotion: **FEAR**

Schachter and Singer's two-factor theory (bodily arousal leads to labels which are the basis for feeling emotions)
Perception of an environmental stimulus (snake) triggers bodily arousal, which we cognitively appraise and label ("I'm afraid"). Then, the appraisal (label) is felt as the emotion (fear).

⇒ Bodily arousal ⇒ Label ("I'm scared") ⇒ Emotion: **FEAR**

Therefore, if we cry at a wedding, we label our emotion as joy or happiness. If we cry at a funeral, we label the emotion as sadness.

In their classic study demonstrating this effect, Schachter and Singer (1962) gave research participants injections of epinephrine (adrenaline), a hormone/neurotransmitter that produces feelings of arousal, or saline shots (a placebo), and then exposed the participants to either a happy or angry confederate (**Figure 11.14**). The way participants responded suggested that arousal could be labeled happiness or anger, depending on the context. Thus, Schachter and Singer's research demonstrated that emotion is determined by two factors: bodily arousal and cognitive appraisal (labeling).

FIGURE 11.14 **Schachter and Singer's classic study**

Experimenter	Informed group	Ignorant group	Misinformed group	Placebo group

Got epinephrine; told about effects — Got epinephrine; told nothing about effects — Got epinephrine; deceived about effects — Got saline instead of epinephrine; told nothing about effects

a. Step 1—participants given injection Participants in this study were first told that this was a study of how certain vitamins affect visual skills, and then they were asked for permission to be injected with a small shot of the vitamin "Suproxin." (This injection actually was a shot of the hormone/neurotransmitter epinephrine [or adrenaline], which triggers feelings of arousal such as racing heart, flushed skin, and trembling hands.) Those participants who gave permission were then divided into four groups and given injections. Those in the three groups who received the shot of epinephrine were correctly informed about the drug's effects, ignorant of the effects, or misinformed about the effects. Those in the fourth placebo group received a neutral saline solution.

Happy confederate

I feel strange, it must be the injection — I feel strange, sort of "happy" like that fella — I feel strange. I guess I feel very happy like that guy over there. — I feel strange, sort of happy like that fella

b. Step 2—participants placed in room with happy or angry confederate Each participant was then placed in a room with either a "happy" or an "angry" trained confederate (who was actually an accomplice of the experimenter). Both the participants and confederate were told that before they could take the supposed vision test, they needed to complete a questionnaire and allow time for the drug to take effect. Confederates in each condition were instructed to behave in line with the supposed emotion: acting joyously in the happy condition—flying paper airplanes, bouncing a ball, etc.—or pretending to be irate in the angry condition—complaining about the experiment, refusing to answer some items on the questionnaire, etc. As predicted, when participants were placed in a room with the happy confederate, they rated themselves as happy. They also behaved in a more joyous way, engaging in more "happy" acts, just like the confederate had modeled. When placed with the angry, irritated confederate, they reported feeling angry and behaved more irately. Although the participants were feeling similar effects of the epinephrine, they labeled those effects differently (happy or angry), depending on the external cues in their environment, and acted accordingly.

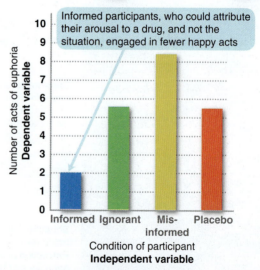

Informed participants, who could attribute their arousal to a drug, and not the situation, engaged in fewer happy acts

c. Step 3—participants' self-reported their emotions This effect on emotions was most apparent in the groups that were misinformed about the true effects of the injections. Why? Those in the informed group correctly attributed their arousal to the drug rather than to the environment.

Schachter and Singer's two-factor theory may have important practical implications. Depending on the cues present in our environment, we apparently can interpret exactly the same feelings of arousal in very different ways. If you're shy or afraid of public speaking, try interpreting your feelings of nervousness as the result of too much coffee or the heating in the room. Some research on this type of *misattribution of arousal* has had positive outcomes (Greenaway et al., 2015; Jouffre, 2015; Webber et al., 2015).

A common negative example might be when we're frustrated by a heavy traffic jam, yet we yell at our friends or family. We've misattributed the actual cause of arousal from the traffic jam to other people.

Before going on, we need to add one more approach regarding our emotional reactions. According to the facial-feedback hypothesis, movements of our facial muscles produce, and may even intensify, our subjective experience of emotion (see the **Test Yourself**).

PA Practical Application

Test Yourself: Testing the Facial-Feedback Hypothesis

Hold a pen or pencil between your teeth with your lips somewhat closed and then with your mouth open and teeth showing (see photos). Spend about 30 seconds in each position. How do you feel? According to research, pleasant feelings are more likely when teeth are showing than when they are not. Note that when you hold the pen with your teeth showing, your cheek muscles are forced to draw up into a smile. Does this support the idea that facial expressions affect your emotions? If true, can you also see how this would support the James-Lange theory that bodily arousal is the basis for feeling emotions—not the other way around as suggested by the two-factor theory?

Source: Adapted from Strack et al., 1988.

Mark Owens/John Wiley & Sons, Inc.

In other words, the process of moving our muscles to create facial expressions reportedly creates our emotional experience, which may in turn support the James-Lange theory. Further evidence supporting this hypothesis comes from the cosmetic treatment known as Botox (see **Figure 11.15**).

As demonstrated in the Test Yourself, one group of researchers tested the facial-feedback hypothesis by asking people to watch cartoons while holding a pen between their teeth. When they were then asked to rate the cartoons, those with their teeth showing found the cartoons significantly funnier than those who watched the cartoons with their lips somewhat closed (Strack et al., 1988).

You may have noticed that throughout this text we emphasize the importance of replicating research findings, and in the case of the facial-feedback hypothesis researchers have suggested that the results of the original study may have been overstated (e.g., Noah et al., 2018; Wagenmakers et al., 2016). The original research (Stack et al., 1988) reported a difference of 0.82 in the funniness ratings of the cartoons, whereas this meta-analysis conducted on several previous studies revealed a rating difference ranging from –0.11 to +0.16.

What's the take-home message? Although the results of the original facial-feedback hypothesis have been overblown, the basic idea that changing facial expressions alters our emotions has been generally supported (e.g., Strack, 2016). For example, researchers have found that just watching another's facial expressions is linked with an automatic, *reciprocal* change in our own facial muscles (Dimberg & Thunberg, 1998; Pawling et al., 2017; Wood et al., 2016). When people are exposed to pictures of angry faces, for example, the eyebrow muscles involved in frowning are activated. In contrast, the smile muscles show a significant increase in activity when participants are shown photos of a happy face. In follow-up research using the *subliminal perception* techniques discussed in Chapter 4, scientists have shown that this automatic, matching response occurs even *without* the participant's attention or conscious awareness (e.g., Dimberg et al., 2000).

For more on the notion that changing facial expressions alters emotions, see the following **RC** **Research Challenge**.

Prostock-studio/Shutterstock.com

FIGURE 11.15 **Botox and the facial-feedback hypothesis** Injections of the botulinum toxin (Botox) into the forehead muscles work well to relax frown lines for cosmetic purposes, but they also appear to reduce chronic migraines and depression (Blumenfeld et al., 2019; Maasumi et al., 2015). One study found that depression scores dropped 42 percent in Botox patients versus 15 percent for patients who received placebo injections (Magid et al., 2014). Unfortunately, given that Botox injections also inhibit our unconscious imitation of others' facial expressions, they may similarly inhibit our sensitive understanding and empathy for others (Baumeister et al., 2016; Sifferlin, 2017).

RC Scientific Thinking: **Research Challenge**

Can Fake Smiling Lead to Heavy Drinking?

(APA Goal 2.4) Interpret, design, and conduct basic psychological research

What's your take-home message from the *facial-feedback hypothesis*? If it's true that making certain facial expressions, like smiling, triggers an emotion like happiness, shouldn't we all just "fake" smile all the time—and suppress our negative emotions? Surprisingly, researchers have found that employees who are forced to smile and act happy with customers (see photo), while also needing to hide any feelings of annoyance, may be at greater risk of heavier drinking after work (Grandey et al., 2019).

Based on phone interviews of 1,592 U.S. workers, the researchers also discovered that the link between forced smiles and acting happy (surface acting) was stronger for those who are impulsive or who lack autonomy over their work. As the lead author, Grandey, said, "If you're impulsive or constantly told how to do your job, it may be harder to rein in your emotions all day, and when you get home, you don't have that self-control to stop after one drink" (Science News, 2019).

As might be expected, the association between surface acting and heavier drinking was larger for employees in service positions with one-time encounters with customers versus those who those who work in relationship situations, such as health care or education. What do you think? Can you use this information in your own life to reduce your stress or to create a healthier work environment?

Identify the Research Method

1. Based on the information provided, did this study (Grandey et al., 2019) use descriptive, correlational, and/or experimental research?

David Noví/123RF

2. If you chose:
   - *descriptive research*, is this a naturalistic or laboratory observation, survey/interview, case study, and/or archival research?
   - *correlational research*, is this a positive, negative, or zero correlation?
   - *experimental research*, label the IV, DV, experimental group(s), and control group. (**Note:** If participants were not randomly assigned to groups, list it as a *quasi-experimental design*.)
   - *both descriptive and correlational*, answer the corresponding questions for both.

Check your answers by clicking on the answer button or by looking in Appendix B.

Note: The information provided in this study is admittedly limited, but the level of detail is similar to what is presented in most textbooks and public reports of research findings. Answering these questions, and then comparing your answers to those provided, will help you become a better scientific and critical thinker and consumer of scientific research

Evaluating Theories of Emotion

Which theory is correct? As you may imagine, each theory has its limits. The *James–Lange theory* fails to acknowledge that physiological arousal can occur without emotional experience (e.g., when we exercise). Furthermore, this theory requires a distinctly different pattern of arousal for each emotion. Otherwise, how do we know whether we are sad, happy, or mad? Positron emission tomography (PET) scans, and other forms of brain imaging, do show subtle differences in the overall physical arousal with basic emotions, such as happiness, fear, and anger (Gu et al., 2019; Levenson, 1992, 2007; Werner et al., 2007). But most people are not aware of these slight variations. Thus, there must be other explanations for how we experience emotion.

The *Cannon–Bard theory* (that arousal and emotions occur simultaneously and that all emotions are physiologically similar) has received some experimental support. Recall from our earlier discussion that victims of spinal cord damage still experience emotions—often more intensely than before their injuries. Other research shows that instead of the thalamus, however, it is the limbic system, hypothalamus, and prefrontal cortex that are activated in emotional experience (Junque, 2015; LeDoux, 2007; Templin et al., 2019).

As mentioned earlier, research on the *facial-feedback hypothesis* has found a distinctive physiological response for basic emotions such as fear, sadness, and anger—thus partially confirming James–Lange's initial position. Facial feedback does seem to contribute to the intensity of our subjective emotional experience and our overall moods. So, if you want to change a bad mood or intensify a particularly good emotion, adopt the appropriate facial expression. Try smiling when you're sad and expanding your smiles when you're happy.

Finally, Schachter and Singer's *two-factor theory* emphasizes the importance of cognitive labels in emotions. But research shows that some neural pathways involved in emotion bypass the cortex and go directly to the limbic system. Recall our earlier example of jumping at the sight of a supposed snake and then a second later using the cortex to interpret what it was. This and other evidence suggest that emotions can take place without conscious cognitive processes. Thus, emotion is not simply the labeling of arousal.

In sum, certain basic emotions are associated with subtle differences in arousal. These differences can be produced by changes in facial expressions or by organs controlling the autonomic nervous system. In addition, "simple" emotions (fear and anger) do not initially require conscious cognitive processes. This allows a quick, automatic emotional response that can later be modified by cortical processes. On the other hand, "complex" emotions (jealousy, grief, depression, embarrassment, love) seem to require more extensive cognitive processes. If you'd like a simple, fun experiment with your own emotional arousal, try the following **Test Yourself**.

PA Practical Application

Test Yourself: **Recapturing "First-Time" Experience**

Have you ever felt a little sad that you don't enjoy the small things in life that once brought you great joy or small moments of happiness? If so, research shows that experiencing familiar things in novel, new ways can help revitalize your levels of enjoyment (O'Brien & Smith, 2019). As you can see in this photo, just eating popcorn with chopsticks, versus your hands, could boost the fun. Why? It helps you re-experience familiar things in an unfamiliar way—as they were in your "first experience." Can you think of how you could use this research in other ways to boost your enjoyment in your relationships and everyday life?

Source: De Passe Entertainment

Retrieval Practice 11.3 | Components and Theories of Emotion

Self-Test   Completing this self-test, and then checking your answers by clicking on the answer button or by looking in Appendix B, will provide immediate feedback and helpful practice for exams.

1. The three components of emotion are _____.
   a. cognitive, biological, and behavioral
   b. perceiving, thinking, and acting
   c. positive, negative, and neutral
   d. active/passive, positive/negative, and direct/ indirect

2. You feel anxious because you are sweating and your heart is beating rapidly. This statement illustrates the _____ theory of emotion.
   a. two-factor
   c. Cannon-Bard
   b. James-Lange
   d. physiological feedback

3. According to the _____, arousal and emotions occur separately but simultaneously.
   a. Cannon-Bard theory
   b. James-Lange theory
   c. facial-feedback hypothesis
   d. two-factor theory

4. Schacter and Singer's two factor theory emphasizes the _____ component of emotion.
   a. stimulus-response
   c. behavioral-imitation
   b. physiological
   d. cognitive

5. You grin broadly while your best friend tells you she was just accepted to medical school. The facial-feedback hypothesis predicts that you will feel _____.
   a. happy
   b. envious
   c. angry
   d. all of these emotions

Q Test Your Critical Thinking

1. If you were going on a date with someone or applying for an important job, how might you use the three key theories of emotion to increase the chances that things will go well?

2. Why do you think people around the world experience and express the same basic emotions, and what evolutionary advantages might help explain these similarities?

Real World Application Question

[AQ4]   Can airport security agents increase their effectiveness by simply talking to passengers?

Jim West/Alamy Stock Photo

Hint: Look in the text for **[AQ4]**

11.4 | Experiencing Emotions

LEARNING OBJECTIVES

Retrieval Practice While reading the upcoming sections, respond to each Learning Objective in your own words.

Review how emotions affect behavior.

- **Describe** the role of culture and evolution on emotion.
- **Summarize** the problems with using polygraph testing as a lie detector.

- **Discuss** the major components of happiness.

Real World Application Questions

[AQ5] Is America one of the top 10 happiest nations in the world?

[AQ6] Smartphones make communicating easier—but is it better?

How do culture and evolution affect our emotions? Is the polygraph an effective way to detect lies? Why are some people happier than others? Can romantic love survive long-distance relationships? These are just a few of the questions, topics, and emotional experiences we'll explore in this section.

Culture and Evolution

Are emotions the same across all cultures? Given the seemingly vast array of emotions within our own culture, it may surprise you to learn that some researchers believe that all our feelings can be condensed into six to 12 culturally universal emotions (**Table 11.3**). These researchers hold that other emotions, such as love, are simply combinations of primary emotions with variations in intensity. Also as you can see in the bottom of Table 11.3, most of these emotions are present in early infancy.

However, other research suggests that this previous list of basic emotions could be combined and reduced to just four: happiness, sadness, surprise/fear, and disgust/anger (Jack et al., 2016). Regardless of the exact number, researchers tend to agree that across cultures, a facial expression of emotion such as a smile is recognized by all as a sign of pleasure, whereas a frown is recognized as a sign of displeasure.

From an evolutionary perspective, the idea of universal facial expressions makes adaptive sense given that such expressions signal others about our current emotional state (Awasthi & Mandal, 2015; Ekman & Keltner, 1997; Hwang & Matsumoto, 2015). Charles Darwin first advanced the evolutionary theory of emotion in 1872. He proposed that expression of emotions evolved in different species as a part of survival and natural selection. Expressions of fear help other human and non-human animals avoid danger, whereas expressions of anger and aggression are useful when fighting for mates or resources. Modern evolutionary theory suggests that basic emotions originate in the *limbic system*. Given that higher brain areas like the cortex developed later than the subcortical limbic system, evolutionary theory proposes that basic emotions evolved before thought.

Studies with infants provide further support for an evolutionary basis for emotions. For example, infants who are born deaf and blind show similar facial expressions in similar situations (Denmark et al., 2014; Field et al., 1982; Gelder et al., 2006). In addition, a study showed that families may have characteristic facial expressions, shared even by family members who have been blind from birth (Peleg et al., 2006). This collective evidence points to a biological, evolutionary basis for emotional expression and decoding.

Psychosocial Factors and Emotion

In addition to culture and evolution, psychosocial factors also clearly affect our emotions and their expression. As an example, research shows that college football victories in the 2 weeks

TABLE 11.3 **Sample Basic Emotions**

Note the strong similarities among the five lists.

Carroll Izard	Paul Ekman and Wallace Friesen	Silvan Tomkins	Robert Plutchik	Rachael Jack et al.
Fear	Fear	Fear	Fear	Surprise/fear
Anger	Anger	Anger	Anger	Disgust/anger
Disgust	Disgust	Disgust	Disgust	Disgust/anger
Surprise	Surprise	Surprise	Surprise	Surprise/fear
Sadness	Sadness	—	Sadness	Sadness
Joy	Happiness	Enjoyment	Joy	Happiness
Shame	—	Shame	—	
Contempt	Contempt	Contempt	—	
Interest	—	Interest	Anticipation	
Guilt	—	—	—	
—	—	—	Acceptance	
—	—	Distress	—	

Q Test Yourself

Using this list of emotions, try to identify the specific emotion reflected in each of the six infant faces.

Vladimir Godnik/Getty Images

ICHIRO/DigitalVision/Getty Images

Blend Images/Getty Images

arnoaltix/iStock/Getty Images

Flashon Studio/Shutterstock.com

Rubberball/Nicole Hill/Getty Images

Answer: From left to right (top row) = fear, sadness, surprise (bottom row) = anger, joy/happiness, disgust.

before gubernatorial elections can add three to four percentage points to the incumbent party vote (Lee et al., 2017). These researchers concluded that the football victories increased voters' happiness and well-being, which apparently spread to their current governor and thereby affected their voting behaviors.

Research has even shown that our emotions are sometimes contagious. To test the hypothesis that certain emotions might spread through social media, researchers first evaluated both positive and negative emotions conveyed in Facebook posts (Coviello et al., 2014). Then they compared the frequency of these emotional expressions with the amount of rainfall in each poster's city. As you might expect, people tend to post more negative emotions and fewer positive emotions on rainy days. The researchers then examined how one person's Facebook post could impact the mood expressions posted by his or her friends living in other cities. They found that having a friend post something negative on Facebook increases the probability of writing a negative post and decreases the likelihood of a positive post.

In short, emotions are much more complex than originally thought. For example, even though we may all share similar facial expressions for some emotions, how we communicate our emotions still varies across cultures, situations, and even among people within a single situation (Barrett et al., 2019). Furthermore, each culture has its own **display rules** that govern how, when, and where to express them (Dzokoto et al., 2018; Ekman, 1993, 2004; Hess & Hareli, 2015).

Display rules A set of informal cultural norms that control when, where, and how emotions should be expressed.

S&P Scientific Thinking and Practical Application

How do we learn our culture's display rules? Parents and other adults pass along their culture's specific emotional *display rules* to children by responding negatively or ignoring some emotions and being supportive and sympathetic to others. Public physical contact is also governed by display rules. Did you know that Americans, Europeans, and Asians are less likely than people in other cultures to touch one another, and that only the closest family members and friends might hug in greeting or farewell? In contrast, Latin Americans and Middle Easterners often kiss, embrace, and hold hands as a sign of casual friendship (Axtell, 2007). In fact, some Middle Eastern men commonly greet one another with a kiss (as shown in the photo). Can you imagine this same behavior among men in the United States, who generally just shake hands, or pat one another's shoulders? Keep these cultural differences in mind when you're traveling. The "thumbs up" gesture is widely used in America to mean everything is okay, or the desire to hitch a ride. However, in many Middle Eastern countries, the same gesture is similar to an American's raised middle finger.

Behrouz Mehri/AFP/Getty Images

Polygraph An instrument that measures sympathetic arousal (heart rate, respiration rate, blood pressure, and skin conductivity) to detect emotional arousal, which in turn supposedly reflects lying versus truthfulness.

In addition to culture, gender, family background, norms, and individual differences affect our emotions and their expression (**Figure 11.16**). As you'll see in the following **GCD Gender and Cultural Diversity**, even a nation's historical pattern of migration may have an effect on our emotional displays.

Image Source/DigitalVision/Getty Images

SOCHI 2014
ODD ANDERSEN/AFP/Getty Images

FIGURE 11.16 **Can you identify these emotions?** Most people easily recognize the emotional expression of happiness, such as the two women in the photo. However, on occasion, our facial expressions don't seem to match our presumed emotions, as is the case in the photo of the male skier. In this case, the obviously happy skier is wiping away tears after winning gold in the 2014 Olympics, and he looks sad rather than happy.

The Polygraph as a Lie Detector

We've discussed the way emotions are affected by culture and evolution. Now we turn our attention to one of the hottest, and most controversial, topics in emotion research—the **polygraph**.

The polygraph is a machine that measures physiological indicators (such as heart rate and blood pressure) to detect emotional arousal, which supposedly reflects whether or not you are lying. Traditional polygraph tests are based on the assumption that when people lie, they feel stressed, and that this stress can be measured. As you can see in **Figure 11.17**, during a polygraph test multiple (*poly*) signals from special sensors assess four major indicators of stress and autonomic arousal: heart rate (pulse), blood pressure, respiration (breathing) rate, and perspiration (or

FIGURE 11.17 **Polygraph testing**   Polygraph testing is based on the assumption that when we lie, we feel guilty, fearful, or anxious.

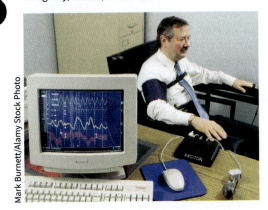

a. Standard polygraph test   To measure overall physiological arousal, a band around the person's chest measures breathing rate, a cuff monitors heart rate and blood pressure, while finger electrodes measure sweating, or galvanic skin response (GSR).

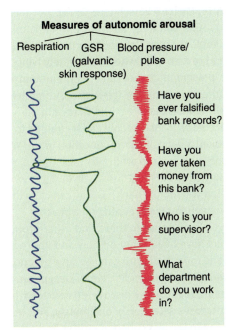

Measures of autonomic arousal

Respiration   GSR   Blood pressure/
              (galvanic   pulse
              skin response)

Have you ever falsified bank records?

Have you ever taken money from this bank?

Who is your supervisor?

What department do you work in?

b. Sample print-out of the subject's level of arousal   Note how the GSR rises sharply in response to the question "Have you ever taken money from this bank?"

GCD **Gender** and **Cultural Diversity**

Does Your Smile Tell Others Where You're From?

(APA Goal 2.5) Incorporate sociocultural factors in scientific inquiry

As we've just seen, a small number of emotions and facial expressions may be universal, but certain aspects of emotionally expressive behaviors vary widely across culture. What explains this cultural variance in expressiveness? One group of researchers have suggested that some differences may be the result of *historical heterogeneity*—meaning the degree to which a country's present-day population descended through migration from numerous versus few source countries over a period of 500 years (Rychlowska et al., 2015).

To test this hypothesis, the researchers carefully analyzed existing data on cultural rules for displaying emotions from 32 countries (Matsumoto et al., 2008). As predicted, countries with less migration tended to be less expressive. Why? The researchers suggest that over time homogeneous countries, those with less diversity, develop stronger display rules for how emotions should be openly expressed. In Japan, for instance, when subordinates are upset around their bosses they're more likely to conceal these feelings with smiles. For countries with a more diverse past, though, people need to beef up their facial expressions, perhaps to overcome cultural and language barriers.

In their follow-up research, the team zeroed in on a particular kind of facial expression: the smile (Rychlowska et al., 2015). They conducted a new study of 726 people in nine countries, including the United States, Japan, and France. Here again, participants were asked to complete a questionnaire regarding cultural rules for emotional expression. But in this case, they were asked to consider what constituted a good reason for someone else to smile, such the person in this photo—he or she "is a happy person," "wants to sell you something," and/or "feels inferior to you." The participants rated each reason to smile on a scale from strongly disagree to strongly agree.

The researchers then compared the results for each country with their migration numbers. In further support of their initial hypothesis, countries with less migration and less diversity thought smiles were related to the social hierarchy—people smile supposedly because they "feel inferior to you." In contrast, countries with greater and more diverse immigration over the past 500 years were more likely to interpret smiles as friendly gestures.

Can you now see how your smile may tell others where you're from? If you smile more to strangers, you're more likely to be from countries with a history of numerous immigrants from various areas—such as the United States—compared to others who come from nations with fewer immigrants.

skin conductivity). If the participant's bodily responses significantly increase when responding to key questions, the examiner will infer that the participant is lying (Ginton, 2017; Grubin, 2016; Meijer & Verschuere, 2015).

Can you imagine what problems might be associated with the polygraph? First, many people become stressed even when telling the truth, whereas others can conceal their stress, and remain calm when deliberately lying. Second, emotions cause physiological arousal, and a polygraph cannot tell which emotion is being felt (anxiety, irritation, excitement, or any other emotion). For this reason, some have suggested the polygraph should be relabeled as an "arousal detector." The third, and perhaps most important, problem is one of questionable accuracy. In fact, people can be trained to beat a lie detector (Kaste, 2015; Wollan, 2015). When asked a general control question (e.g., "Where do you live?"), participants wishing to mislead the examiner can artificially raise their arousal levels by imagining their worst fears (e.g., being burned to death or buried alive). Then when asked relevant/guilty knowledge questions (e.g., "Did you rob the bank?"), they can calm themselves by practicing meditation tricks (e.g., imagining themselves relaxing on a beach).

In response to these and other problems, countless research hours and millions of dollars have been spent on new and improved lie-detection techniques. Although most people (and many police officers) believe that non-verbal cues—such as gaze aversion and increased movement—are indicative of deception, there is limited support for these beliefs (Bogaard et al., 2016). As we discovered earlier with the airport security research, talking to passengers increases detection of dishonesty, and certain verbal cues can detect lying. For example, liars tend to tell less coherent stories and are less likely to make spontaneous corrections to their stories (Vrij et al., 2010).

Perhaps the most promising method for lie detection is the use of brain scans, such as *functional magnetic resonance imaging (fMRI)* (Cook & Mitschow, 2019; Jiang et al., 2015). Unfortunately, each of these new lie-detection techniques has potential problems. Furthermore, researchers have questioned their reliability and validity, and civil libertarians and judicial scholars raise doubts about their ethics and legality (Kaste, 2015; Lilienfeld et al., 2015; Roskey, 2013). While research on improved methods for lie detection continues, note that you are never under personal obligation (legal or otherwise) to take a polygraph test, the admissibility of these tests is not universal, laws have been passed to restrict their use, and we should remain skeptical of their ability to detect guilt or innocence (Cino, 2018; Granhag et al., 2015; Tomash & Reed, 2013).

The Psychology of Happiness

> You can only become truly accomplished at something you love. Don't make money your goal. Instead, pursue the things you love doing, and then do them so well that people can't take their eyes off you. —Maya Angelou (American Poet, Author, Dancer)

Bikeriderlondon/Shutterstock.com

What emotion is most important for your overall life satisfaction? If you said "happiness," you're on the right track. Although some people do report wanting to be wealthy, research around the world repeatedly finds that once we have enough money to meet our basic needs for comfort and security, additional funds fail to significantly increase our level of happiness (Diener & Biswas-Diener, 2002, 2008; Sanderson, 2019; Whillans et al., 2016). In short, more is not always better. **[AQ5]** As a case in point, the United States, the wealthiest nation in the world (see photo), ranked 10th per capita out of 157 nations on happiness (Helliwell et al., 2016). This report measures things like per capita gross domestic product (GDP), social support, and healthy years of life expectancy. For more tips on happiness, see the following **PAH** **Practical Application Highlight**.

PAH Practical Application Highlight

Five Tips for Increased Happiness

(APA Goal 1.3) Describe applications of psychology

Have you heard the old saying that "money (beyond our basic needs) can't buy happiness" (see cartoon)? If that's the case, what can we do instead? Here are five research-based suggestions:

1. **Express gratitude** Consider the striking effects of the following experiment (Emmons & McCullough, 2003). Participants were first randomly assigned to one of three groups, and then simply asked to write down:

   o "Five things you're grateful for in your life over the last week." The participants' lists included such things as God, kindness from friends, and the Rolling Stones. (Group 1: Gratitude condition.)

   o "Five daily hassles from the last week." Participants in this second group listed items like too many bills to pay, trouble finding parking, and a messy kitchen. (Group 2: Hassles condition.)

   o "Five events that occurred in the last week." This group's list included events such as attending a music festival, learning CPR, and cleaning out a closet. (Group 3: Events condition.)

   Before the experiment started, all participants kept daily journals recording their moods, physical health, and general attitudes, which the researchers later used to compare how people in these three groups changed over time.

   As you might have expected, participants in the gratitude condition reported feeling happier. In fact, they were 25 percent happier after completing this very simple assignment. Likewise, they were more optimistic about the future and felt better about their lives. What was unexpected was that this group did almost 1.5 hours more exercise a week than those in the hassles or events condition, and had fewer symptoms of illness.

   Further evidence of a positive link between gratitude and happiness comes from studies showing that developing and expressing gratitude are linked to reduced cardiac risk, fewer symptoms of anxiety and depression, improved relationships with others, and a less critical and more compassionate relationship with yourself (Mills et al., 2015; Petrocchi & Couyoumdjian, 2016). Keep in mind that your everyday expressions of gratitude can be very small. Simply thanking people who have helped us or given us good service at a restaurant, or writing down three things we are grateful for each night before going to bed, can have a substantial positive impact on our well-being, happiness, and life satisfaction.

2. **Change your behavior** As you discovered in Chapters 3 and 5, getting enough exercise, getting enough sleep, and spending time in nature all help make us feel better—both physically and mentally (Panza et al., 2017; Seresinhe et al., 2019; Zhang & Chen, 2019). Surprisingly, research finds that simply reading a book you love increases happiness (Berns et al., 2013). Reading apparently helps us feel connected to characters in a book, which in turn helps us feel connected with other people. Reading can also increase positive feelings, especially if the book inspires you to think about your own life in a new way, or to take action toward reaching your own goals. So, grab a book you find personally enjoyable (not necessarily one you

"All I want is a chance to prove money can't make me happy."

Patrick Hardin/Cartoon Stock

"should read"). Then make a point of reading every day—a few minutes before bed, on a lunch break, or during your daily commute on public transportation.

Another easy behavioral change that will increase your happiness is to act happy. Research shows that just changing your voice to a happier tone actually increases happiness (Aucouturier et al., 2016).

3. **Spend your money and time wisely** People who spend money on life experiences—*doing things*—show greater enduring happiness than those who spend money buying material possessions—*having things*. Spending money on tickets to the "big game," a Broadway show, or a fabulous trip is a great way to increase happiness. On the other hand, the pleasure we get from spending money on an expensive car, watch, or shoes is limited and momentary.

   Why? One factor is anticipation. It's more enjoyable to anticipate experiences than to anticipate acquiring possessions. For most, the pleasure we get from looking forward to a 2-week trip is substantially greater than the pleasure we get from anticipating buying a new car. Another explanation is that we're far more likely to share experiences with others, whereas we generally acquire material possessions for solo use.

   A second way to spend your money wisely is to share it with others. Research shows that giving to others and performing acts of kindness and service are powerful ways to increase happiness (Aknin et al., 2019; Nelson et al., 2016).

   Just as it's important to spend and give your money wisely, the same is true about your time. Given that the two are often interrelated, it's important to note that "money is simply something you trade your life energy for" (Robin et al., 2009). If you're currently making $10 an hour and you're considering buying a new iPhone for $650, you need to calculate the real time/money cost. Are you willing to work 65 hours for that new phone? Really? In short, spending your money and time wisely, and giving them to others, leads to more happiness because it has a longer shelf-life—meaning the joy and satisfaction last much longer than when we spend them on ourselves (e.g., O'Brien & Kassirer, 2019).

4. **Build and maintain close relationships** As mentioned in Chapter 1, people who are happy tend to invest money, time, and energy into having high-quality, close relationships (Amati et al., 2018; Lee & Kawachi, 2019).

Fortunately, even non-human animals appear to benefit from forming and maintaining relationships with humans. As you might expect, the stress levels of dogs admitted to animal shelters is high. However, just 15 minutes of human interaction and petting can significantly reduce the dogs' cortisol levels, which as you recall from Chapter 3 is a common and reliable measure of stress (Willen et al., 2017). Keep in mind, however, that the benefits of a rich social life are primarily based on face-

Twinsterphoto/
Shutterstock.com

to-face interactions, not smartphones, Facebook, and so on. **[AQ6]** Although smartphones make communicating easier (see photo), research finds that it's not necessarily better. In fact, when young adults rated social interactions that combined computer-mediated communication devices, like phones, with their face to face (ftf) meetings, they felt worse and less connected than when the interactions were solely ftf (Kushlev & Heintzelman, 2018).

5. **Choose and pursue worthy goals** This final tip for increasing happiness involves making a list of your most personally valuable and worthy goals, and the specific things you want to accomplish—daily and long-term. Note, however, that pursuing happiness (or money) for its own sake can backfire. Have you heard about people who win the lottery and later become less happy and satisfied? This type of **adaptation-level phenomenon** reflects the fact that we tend to judge a new situation or stimuli relative to a neutral level defined by our previous experiences with them. We win the lottery or get a new job with a higher income and naturally experience an initial surge of pleasure. We then adjust our neutral level higher, which, in turn, requires ever-increasing improvements to gain a meaningful increase in happiness.

In other words, happiness, like all emotions, is fleeting, and it's incredibly difficult to go backward. This so-called *hedonic treadmill* shows us that the pleasures we acquire in all parts of our lives—money, material possessions, status, and even our relationships—can quickly become part of our everyday baseline and taken for granted, until they're taken away.

Can you see how the previous tips in this list—expressing gratitude, changing your behavior, spending your time and money wisely, and building and maintaining close relationships—can help offset the dangers of this adaptation-level phenomenon? For further insights on happiness, see the following **PP PositivePsych**.

Adaptation-level phenomenon A tendency to judge a new situation or stimuli relative to a neutral, "normal" level based on our previous experiences; we then adapt to this new level and it becomes the new "normal."

PP Practical Application: PositivePsych

Can Long-Distance Relationships Survive?

(APA Goal 1.3) Describe applications of psychology

One of the key ingredients to health and happiness is frequent physical contact within a satisfying romantic relationship. Yet up to 75 percent of college students report having been in a long-distance romantic relationship (LDR), and over three million American spouses successfully live apart for a variety of reasons (cited in Borelli et al., 2015). How do these couples manage to survive (and even flour-

asiseeit/E+/Getty Images

ish) despite the relative lack of physical contact, reduced communication, and financial burdens associated with being separated by large geographical distances (see photo)? The answer may be that they practice what's called *relational savoring* (Borelli et al., 2014). "Savoring" has been defined as the process of attending to, intensifying, and prolonging the positive emotions attached to experiences (Bryant & Veroff, 2007), meaning paying close attention to and relishing and delighting in experiences shared with our significant other.

Interested in the possibility that relational savoring in LDR couples might result in better emotional states and protection against relationship threats, researchers studied wives of

military service members before and during their spouses' military deployment (Borelli et al., 2015). Participants were assigned to one of three groups. Wives in the neutral (control) condition were asked to think about and mentally replay their normal morning routine from the time they woke up until they left for work/school. In the *personal savoring* (experimental) condition, the wives were asked to focus and reflect on a personal positive experience. In the *relational savoring* (second experimental) condition, the wives were prompted to think about a positive experience with their partner when they felt especially "cherished, protected, or accepted."

In all conditions, participating wives reported on not only the details surrounding the experience but also their thoughts and feelings. They were then asked to spend 2 minutes mentally reliving the event. Perhaps surprisingly, only the LDR participants who engaged in *relational savoring* showed increases in their positive emotions, decreases in their negative emotions, and increases in relationship satisfaction following a simulated relationship stressor task.

What's the important takeaway? If a brief laboratory experiment prompting LDR participants to engage in relational savoring can have such positive personal and relationship effects, think about how it could be applied to your own life. While practicing the gratitude exercises mentioned earlier, remind yourself to stop and "savor" those moments and memories of times you felt particularly cherished, protected, and/or accepted by your romantic partner.

Before going on, be sure to complete the final Retrieval Practice, and then answer the critical thinking questions in the **Test Your Critical Thinking**.

Retrieval Practice 11.4 | Experiencing Emotions

Self-Test   Completing this self-test, and then checking your answers by clicking on the answer button or by looking in Appendix B, will provide immediate feedback and helpful practice for exams.

1. According to evolutionary theory, basic emotions, like fear and anger, seem to originate in _____.
   a. higher cortical areas of the brain
   b. subtle changes in facial expressions
   c. the limbic system
   d. the interpretation of environmental stimuli

2. Cultural norms governing emotional expressions are called _____.
   a. extrinsic guidelines
   b. emotion regulators
   c. display rules
   d. none of these options

3. Which of the following is/are recommended for increasing happiness?
   a. express gratitude
   b. spend your money and time wisely
   c. choose worthy goals
   d. all of these options

4. The polygraph, or lie detector, measures primarily the _____ component of emotions.
   a. physiological   c. cognitive
   b. articulatory   d. subjective

5. What is TRUE about the polygraph?
   a. It does, in fact, measure autonomic arousal.
   b. It cannot tell which emotion is being felt.
   c. People can be trained to beat a polygraph.
   d. All of these options are true.

Q Test Your Critical Thinking

1. How might differing cultural display rules explain why American tourists are often criticized by local residents for being "too loud and aggressive"?

2. After reading the section on polygraph tests, would you be willing to take a "lie detector" test if you were accused of a crime? Why or why not?

Real World Application Questions

[AQ5]   Is America one of the top 10 happiest nations in the world?

Bikeriderlondon/Shutterstock.com

[AQ6]   Smartphones make communicating easier—but is it better?

Twinsterphoto/Shutterstock.com

Hint: Look in the text for **[AQ5]** and **[AQ6]**

Q Test Your Critical Thinking

Did you notice or wonder why we provided six Real World Application Questions [AQ1–AQ6] throughout this chapter? We've found that they not only help you to engage with and master the material, they also have an important and lasting impact on your critical thinking skills. For additional mastery and enrichment, consider the following questions:

1. Non-human animals, like the kitten in this photo, sometimes display what we humans would label "curiosity." How might this trait be important for the survival and achievement of both human and non-human animals?

2. How do you think non-human animal motivation, like this kitten's, might differ from that of humans?

Tetra Images/Superstock

3. Think about your favorite hobbies or recreational activities (e.g., riding your bike, watching TV, playing video games). How would you explain these activities using the six theories of motivation (see Table 11.1, p. 356)?

4. Imagine yourself in a career as a health psychologist (Chapter 3). What type of public health efforts would you recommend to treat eating disorders?

5. Think back to a time when you felt very angry and upset over a misunderstanding with a special friend. Which of the three key components of emotion (biological, cognitive, or behavioral) best accounted for the intensity of your feelings? Which of the three major theories (the James-Lange, Cannon-Bard, or two-factor theory) best explains your overall emotional experience?

6. Do you believe people can (and should) control their emotions? Why or why not?

Summary

11.1 Theories of Motivation   354

- Biological theories of **motivation** emphasize **instincts**, drives (produced by the body's need for **homeostasis**), and arousal (the need for novelty, complexity, and stimulation).

- Psychological theories focus on the role of incentives, attributions, and expectancies in cognition.

- Maslow's **hierarchy of needs** theory takes a biopsychosocial approach. It prioritizes needs, with survival needs at the bottom and higher needs at the top.

11.2 Motivation and Behavior   359

- Both biological factors (the stomach, biochemistry, the brain) and psychosocial factors (stimulus cues and cultural conditioning) affect hunger and eating. These factors play a similar role in **obesity, anorexia nervosa, bulimia nervosa,** and **binge-eating disorder**.

- A high need for achievement (nAch), or **achievement motivation**, is generally learned in early childhood primarily through interactions with parents.

- Providing **extrinsic motivation** like money or praise for an intrinsically satisfying activity can undermine people's enjoyment and interest—their **intrinsic motivation**—for the activity. However, under the right conditions, extrinsic rewards can sometimes be motivational.

11.3 Components and Theories of Emotion   368

- All **emotions** have three basic components: *biological arousal* (e.g., heart pounding), *cognitive* (thoughts, values, and expectations), and *behavioral expressions* (e.g., smiling and

frowning). Studies of the biological component find that emotions involve a general, non-specific arousal of the autonomic nervous system.

- According to the **James-Lange theory**, emotions follow from physiological changes. The **Cannon-Bard theory** suggests that emotions and physiological changes occur simultaneously. The **two-factor theory** suggests that emotions depend on two factors—physiological arousal and a cognitive labeling of that arousal. Each theory emphasizes different sequences or aspects of the three elements. Other research emphasizes how different pathways in the brain trigger faster and slower emotional responses.

11.4 Experiencing Emotions   376

- Some researchers believe across all cultures people experience several basic, universal emotions, and that we express and recognize these emotions in essentially the same way. These findings and studies with infants support this evolutionary theory of emotion.

- Psychosocial factors also affect our emotions, and researchers note that *display rules* for emotional expression vary across cultures.

- **Polygraph** tests attempt to detect lying by measuring physiological signs of guilt, fear, and/or anxiety. Due to several problems with its underlying assumptions and accuracy, most courts do not accept polygraph test results, laws have been passed to restrict its use, and we should remain skeptical.

- Happiness is a popular topic in positive psychology. Tips for increasing happiness include expressing gratitude, changing your behavior, spending your money and time wisely, building and maintaining close relationships, and choosing worthy goals.

Key Terms

Retrieval Practice   Write a definition for each term before turning back to the referenced page to check your answer.

- achievement motivation 364
- adaptation-level phenomenon 382
- amygdala 369
- anorexia nervosa 363
- binge-eating disorder 363
- bulimia nervosa 363
- Cannon-Bard theory 371
- display rules 378

- drive-reduction theory 355
- emotion 368
- extrinsic motivation 365
- hierarchy of needs 358
- homeostasis 355
- incentive theory 357
- instinct 355
- intrinsic motivation 365

- James-Lange theory 371
- motivation 354
- obesity 362
- optimal-arousal theory 356
- polygraph 378
- self-actualization 358
- two-factor theory 371
- Yerkes-Dodson law 356

Personality

Tom Wang/Shutterstock.com

12.1 Understanding Personality

LEARNING OBJECTIVES

Retrieval Practice While reading the upcoming sections, respond to each Learning Objective in your own words.

Summarize personality's major characteristics and how they are measured.

- **Define** personality.
- **Describe** the possible situational and cultural effects on personality.
- **Discuss** the role of biology in personality.

- **Review** the methods and limits of personality assessment.

Real World Application Questions

[AQ1] Will eating from a shared plate increase cooperation?

[AQ2] Can social media posting be used to measure personality?

Personality Our unique and relatively stable pattern of thoughts, feelings, and actions.

Character Value judgments about an individual's morals, values, and ethical behaviors.

Temperament An individual's innate disposition or behavioral style and typical emotional response.

Collection Christophel/Alamy Stock Photo

FIGURE 12.1 **Personality versus character and temperament** If you're one of the millions of fans of the TV sitcom *The Big Bang Theory*, you're familiar with the Sheldon Cooper character, the zany physicist. But how would you describe his personality, character, and temperament? Attempting to answer these questions will help you understand the differences between these terms.

What Is Personality?

In the first section of this chapter, we begin by defining personality followed by a discussion of the biological contributors to personality. Then we examine the tools and techniques psychologists have developed to measure, compare, and evaluate our individual personalities. The remainder of the chapter examines the four leading theories of personality—psychoanalytic/psychodynamic, trait, humanistic, and social-cognitive.

What exactly is "**personality**"? Most psychologists define it as our *unique and relatively stable pattern of thoughts, feelings, and actions*. In other words, it describes how we are different from other people and what patterns of behavior are typical of us. You might qualify as an "extravert," for example, if you're talkative and outgoing most of the time. Or you may be described as "conscientious" if you're responsible and self-disciplined on most occasions.

Keep in mind that personality is not the same as **character**, which refers to value judgments about a person's ethics, morals, values, and integrity. Similarly, personality should not be confused with temperament. As discussed in Chapter 9, **temperament** is defined as the individual's innate disposition or behavioral style and characteristic emotional response (e.g., easy, difficult, or slow-to-warm-up children). See **Figure 12.1**.

Now that we've defined personality and how it differs from character and temperament, how would you describe your personality to others? Would you say, "I am funny and the life of the party" and/or, "I am kind and generous"? We all have a sense of our own personality—it's what we mean when we say "myself."

But what is this so-called "self"? It's generally the image we have of ourselves that develops over time and in a variety of ways—especially by our interactions with important people throughout our lives. As you'll see in the upcoming sections of this chapter, there are at least five main personality theories that help explain how we develop our sense of self. However, before going on, it's important to look at how the culture we belong to also affects our sense of self—and therefore our personalities. See the following **GCD** **Gender and Cultural Diversity**.

Situational Effects on Personality
In addition to the continuum of personalities within any culture, the situation we're in also influences us. You may reveal an entirely different personality or "self" when you're with friends than when you're with your family or in a college classroom.

GCD **Gender** and **Cultural Diversity**

Can Culture Affect Your Personality?

(APA Goal 2.5) Incorporate sociocultural factors in scientific inquiry

Are you someone who likes being the center of attention? If so, you may have noticeable body art and you probably choose clothing and hair styles that help you stand out in a crowd. On the other hand, if you're someone who prefers to blend in and not to be noticed, you're less likely to have body art and you're more likely to select conservative clothing and hair styles.

This choice between standing out versus blending in is a core component and basic difference between the personalities of people in individualist versus collectivist cultures (Fang et al., 2016; Moleiro et al., 2017; Smith & Robinson, 2019). As you can see in **Table 12.1**, *individualist cultures* emphasize individual rights and freedom, and the needs and goals of the individual are prioritized over the needs and goals of the group. When asked to complete the statement "I am…," people from individualist cultures tend to respond with personality traits ("I am shy"; "I am outgoing") or their occupation ("I am a teacher"; "I am a student").

Collectivist cultures, however, emphasize connections to others and conformity to social norms. The person is defined and understood primarily by looking at his or her place in the social unit. Relatedness, connectedness, and interdependence are valued, as opposed to separateness, independence, and individualism. When asked to complete the statement "I am…," people from collectivist cultures tend to mention their families or nationality ("I am a daughter"; "I am a Chinese"). Would you like a simple test of your own personality and the possible effects from your culture? See the following **Test Yourself**.

TABLE 12.1	A Comparison Between Individualist and Collectivist Cultures
Sample Individualist Countries	**Sample Collectivist Cultures**
United States	Korea
Australia	China
Great Britain	India
Canada	Japan
The Netherlands	West Africa region
Germany	Thailand
New Zealand	Taiwan
Sample Individualist Values	**Sample Collectivist Values**
Independence	Interdependence
Individual rights	Obligations to others
Self-sufficiency	Reliance on group
Individual achievement	Group achievement
Independent living	Living with kin
Personal failure leads to shame and guilt	Failing the group leads to shame and guilt

PA Practical Application

Test Yourself: Are you an Individualist or a Collectivist?

If asked to draw a circle with yourself in the center, and the people in your life as separate circles surrounding you, which of the two diagrams comes closest to your personal view?

If you chose (a), you probably have an *individualistic* orientation, seeing yourself as an independent, separate self. However, if you chose (b), you're more closely aligned with a *collectivist* culture, seeing yourself as interdependent and interconnected with others.

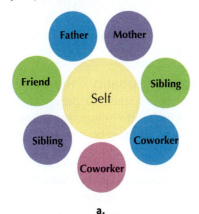

a.   b.

Now, consider the children depicted in **Figure 12.2**. Can you see how learning more about the possible cultural effects on personality may provide increased understanding of ourselves, our friends, and our families, while also improving our understanding and sensitivity to other cultures? Americans generally define *sincerity* as behaving in accordance with our inner feelings, whereas people from collectivist cultures tend to see their equivalent word for sincerity as behavior that conforms to a person's role expectations and duties (Yamada, 1997). This explains why collectivistic behaviors might appear insincere to Americans.

Keep in mind, however, that these sample countries and their selected values exist on a continuum. Within each country there is a wide range of individual differences. Some people in collectivist cultures are very independent and committed to individual rights and freedom. Likewise, some in individualist countries are interdependent and focused on obligations to others.

FIGURE 12.2 **Individualist and collectivist cultures**

a. When we consider people as individuals, we don't always get a complete picture of their personalities.

b. Stepping back to see the same individuals in a broader context can provide new insights. With this "bigger picture" (the child's immediate surroundings and his or her group's behavior) in mind, can you better understand why each child might be feeling and acting as he or she is?

[AQ1] Your personality may also be revealed (or affected) by small situational factors, such as how you eat your meals. For example, when North American families go out to restaurants, most members tend to order individual dishes that reflect what each person prefers. But did you know that when a family in China goes out to dinner, they typically order multiple dishes that everyone shares? Surprisingly, a recent experiment found that strangers who shared food from a single plate (e.g., a Chinese-style meal—see photo) actually increased cooperation and decreased competition in later testing compared to those who ate from separate plates (Wooley & Fishbach, 2019).

Can you see how this research-based example demonstrates how a simple change in a situation might directly affect your behavior? Using your scientific thinking, would you conclude that sharing food actually "causes" more cooperation and less competition? Or did the experiment only test how that specific testing situation temporarily affected the participants' personalities? As you recall from Chapter 1, there are limits (and benefits) to all forms of research. Hopefully, your take-home message is that understanding personality and all that contributes to it is a complex and fascinating business.

Biological Contributors to Personality

Now that we've defined personality and examined its possible cultural effects, let's explore how biological factors may influence it.

Three Major Contributors to Personality

Hans Eysenck, the trait theorist mentioned later in the chapter, was one of the first to propose that personality traits are biologically based—at least in part. Modern researchers also support a biological basis for personality, and they've divided the major contributors into three basic categories: *brain structures*, *neurochemistry*, and *genetics*.

Brain Structures

How do we decide in the real world which risks are worth taking and which are not (see photo)? Research using functional magnetic resonance imaging (fMRI) and other brain-mapping techniques have revealed specific areas of the brain that correlate with trait impulsiveness and areas that differ between people with risk-averse versus risk-seeking personalities (Rass et al., 2016; Shi et al., 2019). Research has also found that increased electroencephalographic (EEG) activity in the left frontal lobe of the brain is associated with sociability or extraversion, whereas greater EEG activity in the right frontal lobes is associated with shyness and introversion (Fishman & Ng, 2013; Tellegen, 1985).

FIGURE 12.3   **Identical versus fraternal twins**

Identical twins   Same sex only   Fraternal twins   Same or opposite sex

a. Identical (*monozygotic*—one egg) twins   These two individuals share 100 percent of the same genes given that they develop from a single egg fertilized by a single sperm. They also share the same placenta, and are always the same sex.

b. Fraternal (*dizygotic*—two eggs) twins   These two individuals share, on average, 50 percent of their genes given that they are formed when two separate sperm fertilize two separate eggs. Although they share the same general environment within the womb, they are no more genetically similar than non-twin siblings. They're simply 9-month "womb mates."

Neurochemistry   A major limitation of research on brain structures and personality is the difficulty of identifying which structures are uniquely connected with particular personality traits. Neurochemistry seems to offer more precise data on how biology influences personality. For example, sensation seeking (Chapter 11) has consistently been linked with high levels of monoamine oxidase (MAO), an enzyme that regulates levels of neurotransmitters such as dopamine (Trofimova & Robbins, 2016; Zuckerman, 1994, 2004, 2014). Likewise, dopamine seems to be correlated with personality traits such as, feeling in control of one's actions, novelty seeking, and extraversion (e.g., Fischer et al., 2019; Harris et al., 2015; Render & Jansen, 2019).

PAN   Practical Application of Neuroscience

How can neurochemistry have such effects?   Studies suggest that high-sensation seekers (see photo) and extraverts generally experience less physical arousal than introverts from the same stimulus (Fishman & Ng, 2013; Munoz & Anastassiou-Hadjicharalambous, 2011). Extraverts' low arousal apparently motivates them to seek out situations that will elevate their arousal.

FurmanAnna/iStock/Getty Images

Genetics   Personality traits like sensation seeking and extraversion may also be inherited. In addition, our genes may predict how we parent or even possible criminal behaviors, as measured by arrest records (Armstrong et al., 2014; van den Berg et al., 2016; Wertz et al., 2018). As might be expected, another study found that individuals with a "niceness gene" were more likely to report engaging in various types of prosocial behaviors, such as giving blood, volunteering, and donating to charitable organizations (Poulin et al., 2012).

This recognition that genetic factors have a significant influence on personality has contributed to the relatively new field called *behavioral genetics*, which attempts to determine the extent to which behavioral differences among people are due to genetics as opposed to the environment (see Chapter 9).

One way to measure genetic influences is to compare similarities in personality between identical twins and fraternal twins (see **Figure 12.3**). Twin studies of certain personality traits, for example, suggest that genetic factors account for about 40 to 50 percent of personality traits (Bouchard, 1997, 2013; McCrae et al., 2010; Plomin et al., 2016).

In addition to conducting twin studies, researchers compare the personalities of parents with those of their biological children and their adopted children (see **Figure 12.4**). Studies of extraversion and

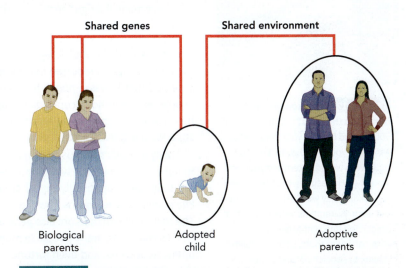

Shared genes   Shared environment

Biological parents   Adopted child   Adoptive parents

FIGURE 12.4   **Adoption studies**   If adopted children are more like their biological family in some trait, then genetic factors probably had the greater influence. Conversely, if adopted children resemble their adopted family, even though they do not share similar genes, then environmental factors may predominate.

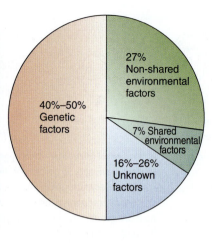

FIGURE 12.5 **Biopsychosocial, multiple influences on personality** Can you see how psychological and social factors (as part of the shared and non-shared environment), combined with genetic factors—the biopsychosocial model—might contribute to this child's apparent shyness?

Source: Bouchard, 1997, 2013; McCrae et al., 2004, 2010; Plomin et al., 2016.

neuroticism have found that parents' traits correlate moderately with those of their biological children and hardly at all with those of their adopted children (Bouchard, 1997; McCrae et al., 2000).

Evaluating Biological Theories Modern research in biological theories has provided exciting insights and established clear links between some personality traits and various brain areas, neurotransmitters, and genes. However, researchers are careful to emphasize that personality traits are never the result of a single biological process (Cicchetti, 2016; Latzman et al., 2015; Turkheimer et al., 2014). Some believe the importance of the unshared environment—aspects of the environment that differ from one individual to another, even within a family—has been overlooked. Others fear that research on "genetic determinism" could be misused to "prove" that an ethnic or a racial group is inferior, that male dominance is natural, or that social progress is impossible.

Take-Home Message There is no doubt that biological studies have produced valuable results. However, as is true for all the theories discussed in this chapter, no single theory explains everything we need to know about personality. Each theory offers different insights into how a person develops the distinctive set of characteristics we call "personality." That's why, instead of adhering to any one theory, many psychologists believe in the *biopsychosocial approach*, or the idea that several factors—biological, psychological, and social—overlap in their contributions to personality (**Figure 12.5**).

Measuring Personality

You have a strong need for other people to like and admire you. You tend to be critical of yourself. Although you have some personality weaknesses, you are generally able to compensate for them. At times, you have serious doubts about whether you have made the right decision or done the right thing.

—Adapted from Ulrich et al., 1963

Does this sound like you? A high percentage of research participants who read a similar personality description reported that the description was "very accurate"—even after they were informed that it was a *phony* horoscope (Hyman, 1981). Other research shows that many people read their horoscopes daily, some just for entertainment while others firmly believe their particular astrological horoscopes were written especially for them (Sugarman et al., 2011; Wyman & Vyse, 2008).

Why are such spurious personality assessments so popular? One reason is that they seem to tap into our unique selves. Supporters of these horoscopes, however, ignore the fact that the traits they supposedly reveal are characteristics that almost everyone shares. Do you know anyone who doesn't "have a strong need for other people to like and admire" them? The traits in horoscopes are also generally flattering, or at least neutral.

As you know, many people in modern times still consult fortune-tellers, horoscope columns, tarot cards, and even fortune cookies in Chinese restaurants to assess their personalities. Surprisingly, people in the past actually consulted *phrenologists*, who believed our unique personalities are reflected in various bumps on our heads (**Figure 12.6**).

Unlike these *unscientific* pseudopsychologies, scientific research has provided much more reliable and valid methods for measuring personality (Berger, 2015; Dana, 2014). Clinical and

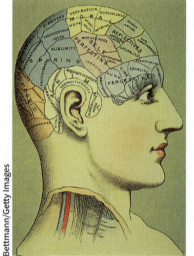

FIGURE 12.6 **Personality and bumps on the head?** In the 1800s, if you wanted to have your personality assessed, you would go to a phrenologist, who would determine your personality by measuring the bumps on your skull. They would then compare those measurements with a chart that associated different areas of the skull with particular traits, such as *sublimity* (ability to squelch natural impulses, especially sexual) and *ideality* (ability to live by high ideals). What traits might be measured if we still believed in phrenology today?

counseling psychologists, psychiatrists, and other helping professionals use these modern methods to help with the diagnosis of patients and to assess their progress in therapy. Personality assessments can be grouped into a few broad categories: *interviews*, *observations*, *objective tests*, and *projective tests*.

Interviews and Observations

We all use informal "interviews" to get to know other people. When first meeting someone, we usually ask about his or her job, academic interests, family, or hobbies. Psychologists also use interviews. In an unstructured format, interviewers get impressions and pursue hunches or let the interviewee expand on information that promises to disclose personality characteristics. In structured interviews, the interviewer asks specific questions in order to evaluate the interviewee's responses more objectively and compare them with others' responses.

In addition to conducting interviews, psychologists also assess personality by directly and methodically observing behavior. They look for examples of specific behaviors and follow a careful set of evaluation guidelines. For instance, a psychologist might arrange to observe a troubled client's interactions with his or her family. Does the client become agitated by the presence of certain family members and not others? Does he or she become passive and withdrawn when asked a direct question? Through careful observation, the psychologist gains valuable insights into the client's personality as well as family dynamics (**Figure 12.7**).

As a further complement to face-to-face observations, psychologists have used social media outlets—such as Facebook and Instagram—to observe personality. For instance, an examination of Facebook likes and photographs can accurately predict a number of traits and attributes, including sexual orientation, ethnicity, religious and political views, personality, intelligence, happiness, use of addictive substances, parental separation, age, and gender (e.g., Choi & Shin, 2017; Hong et al., 2017; Yang, 2019). **[AQ2]** Similarly, researchers have examined how individuals' social media posts (see photo) correlated with their personalities (see **Figure 12.8**). As might be expected, researchers have found that narcissists more frequently post updates about their achievements, whereas extraverts more frequently post updates on their social activities

FIGURE 12.7 Behavioral observation How might careful observation help a psychologist better understand a troubled client's personality and family dynamics?

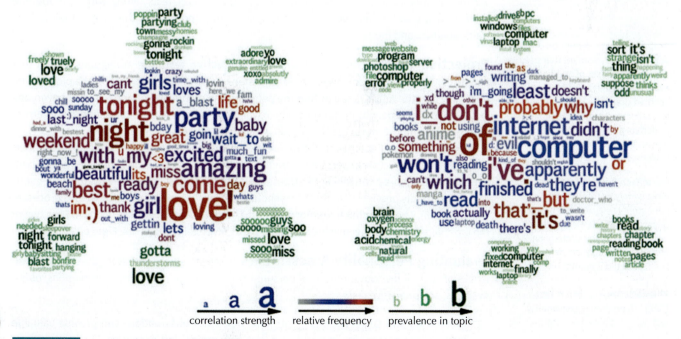

FIGURE 12.8 Facebook test of your personality To discover more about the types of words associated with different personality traits, check out this website demonstration: http://wwbp.org/personality_wc.html

Source: Park et al. JPSP Automatic personality assessment through social media language. Jun 1, 2015;© 2015 by the American Psychological Association. Reproduced with permission.

(Marshall et al., 2015). Surprisingly, an analysis of Instagram users revealed that users with more visually appealing, colorful layouts on their account are seen as having more socially desirable traits (Harris & Bardey, 2019), In addition, selfies taken alone appear to indicate narcissism whereas selfies taken with others are seen as reflecting a "down-to-earth" persona.

Objective Tests

Objective personality tests, or inventories, are the most widely used method of assessing personality, for two reasons: They can be administered to a large number of people relatively quickly, and they can be evaluated in a standardized fashion. Some objective tests measure one specific personality trait, such as sensation seeking (Chapter 11) or locus of control. However, psychologists in clinical, counseling, and industrial settings often wish to assess a range of personality traits. To do so, they generally use multitrait, *multiphasic* inventories.

The most widely researched and clinically used self-report method of personality assessment is the **Minnesota Multiphasic Personality Inventory (MMPI)**—or its revisions, the MMPI-2 and the MMPI-2-RF (Butcher, 2000, 2011; Chmielewski et al., 2017; Williams & Lally, 2017). The latest version, the MMPI-2-RF, consists of 338 statements. Participants respond with True, False, or Cannot Say. The following are examples of the kinds of statements found on the MMPI:

> My stomach frequently bothers me.
>
> I have enemies who really wish to harm me.
>
> I sometimes hear things that other people can't hear.
>
> I would like to be a mechanic.
>
> I have never indulged in any unusual sex practices.

Did you notice that some of these questions are about very unusual, abnormal behavior? Although there are many "normal" questions on the full MMPI, the test was originally designed to reveal abnormal personality traits and behaviors, and it's currently also used to help clinical and counseling psychologists diagnose psychological disorders. In addition, it's sometimes employed for various screening purposes, such as in hiring decisions and forensic settings.

Other objective personality measures are less focused on abnormal personality traits. A good example is the NEO Personality Inventory–Revised, which assesses the dimensions of the five-factor model.

Note that personality tests like the MMPI are often confused with *career inventories*, or vocational interest tests. Career counselors use these latter tests (along with aptitude and achievement tests) to help people identify occupations and careers that match their unique traits, abilities, and interests.

Projective Tests

Unlike objective tests, **projective tests** use ambiguous stimuli that people can perceive in many ways. When you listen to a piece of music or look at a picture, you might say that the music is sad or that the people in the picture look happy—but not everyone would have the same interpretation. Some psychologists believe that these different interpretations reveal important things about each individual's personality.

As the name implies, projective tests are meant to allow test takers to "project" their underlying motives, conflicts and personality traits onto the test materials. Recognizing that respondents may be unable or unwilling to express their true feelings if asked directly, the ambiguous stimuli reportedly provide an indirect "psychological X-ray" of important unconscious processes (Hogan, 2018). The **Rorschach Inkblot Test** and **Thematic Apperception Test (TAT)** are two of the most widely used projective tests (Cashel, 2016; Silverstein, 2013). See **Figure 12.9**.

Evaluating Personality Assessments

Let's evaluate the strengths and the challenges of each of the four methods of personality assessment: *interviews, observations, objective tests*, and *projective tests*.

1. **Interviews and Observations**   Both interviews and observations can provide valuable insights into personality, but they are time-consuming and expensive. Furthermore, raters of personality tests frequently disagree in their evaluations of the same individuals. Interviews and observations also take place in unnatural settings, and, in fact, the very presence of an observer can alter a person's behavior. For example, can you recall a time

---

Minnesota Multiphasic Personality Inventory (MMPI)   The most widely researched and clinically used self-report method of personality assessment; originally designed to reveal abnormal personality traits and behaviors, it's also used for various screening purposes.

Projective test   A method of personality assessment that uses a standardized set of ambiguous stimuli, such as inkblots or abstract drawings, which allow test takers to "project" their underlying motives, conflicts, and personality traits onto the test materials.

Rorschach Inkblot Test   The most widely used projective personality test, which is based on interpretations of test takers' projections of their underlying motives, conflicts, and personality traits onto ten inkblots.

Thematic Apperception Test (TAT)   A projective personality test, which is based on interpretations of test takers' projections of their underlying motives, conflicts, and personality traits revealed through the stories they make up about ambiguous scenes.

FIGURE 12.9 **Sample projective tests**   The verbal or written responses participants make to projective tests reportedly reflect unconscious, hidden parts of their personalities that they unintentionally "project" onto the stimuli.

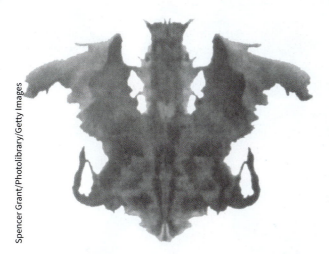

a. Rorschach Inkblot test   Introduced in 1921 by Swiss psychiatrist Hermann Rorschach, this test involves 10 inkblots, like the one pictured here, which are shown one at a time. Test takers are then asked to report what figures or objects they see in each of them.

b. Thematic Apperception Test (TAT)   Created by personality researcher Henry Murray in 1938, this projective test consists of a series of ambiguous black-and-white pictures, like the one displayed here, that are shown to the test taker, who is asked to create a story related to each one.

in which you were nervous in a job interview, and maybe didn't act quite the same as you would in a more relaxed setting?

2. **Objective Tests**   Tests like the MMPI-2 provide specific, objective information about a broad range of personality traits in a relatively short period. However, they are subject to at least three major criticisms:

- **Deliberate deception and social desirability bias**   Some items on personality inventories are easy to see through, so respondents may fake particular personality traits. In addition, some respondents want to look good and will answer questions in ways that they perceive are socially desirable. For instance, people might try to come across as less hostile and more kind to others in their responses to some test items. Also, self-report data among some groups may be misleading because the respondents do not see themselves accurately. As an example, narcissists typically have an excessive form of self-love and overevaluate their performance (Guedes, 2017).

    To avoid these problems, the MMPI-2 has built-in validity scales. In addition, personality researchers and some businesses avoid self-reports. Instead, they rely on other people, such as friends or coworkers, to rate an individual's personality, as well as how their personality influences their work performance (Connelly & Hülsheger, 2012). In fact, three meta-analyses, involving over 44,000 participants, found that ratings from others were better predictors of actual behavior, academic achievement, and job performance than those based on self-reports (Connelly & Ones, 2010).

- **Diagnostic difficulties**   In addition to the problems with all self-report inventories, when they are used for diagnosis, overlapping items sometimes make it difficult to pinpoint a disorder (Ben-Porath, 2013; Hogan, 2018; Hunsley et al., 2015). Clients with severe disorders sometimes score within the normal range, and normal clients sometimes score within the elevated range (Borghans et al., 2011; Morey, 2013). In addition, well-known sex and temperament differences have also been linked with psychological disorders, such as drug addiction and depression, and these overlapping factors again makes it difficult to make a precise diagnosis (Stam et al., 2019).

- **Cultural bias and inappropriate use**   Some critics think the standards for "normalcy" on objective tests fail to recognize the impact of culture (Dana, 2014; Geisinger & McCormick, 2013; Malgady et al., 2014). For example, research examining personality traits in members

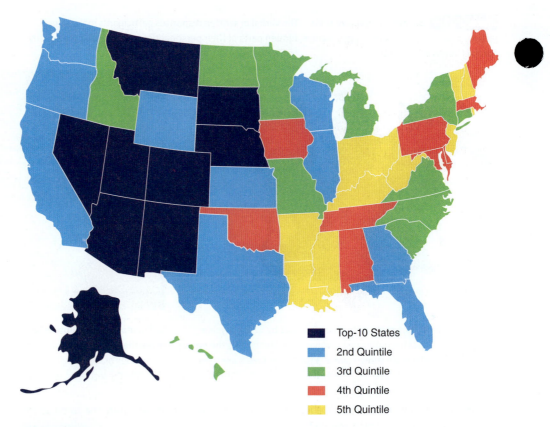

Top-10 States
2nd Quintile
3rd Quintile
4th Quintile
5th Quintile

FIGURE 12.10 **Entrepreneurship in the United States** Note the state you currently live in. Does the degree of entrepreneurship shown on this map match with that of the people you know in your area? Do you agree with the researchers' conclusions that migration patterns might explain the types of personality differences that you may have observed? If not, can you think of other "third-variable" (Chapter 1) explanations?

Copyright ©2013 by the American Psychological Association. Reproduced with permission. Obschonka, et al. The regional distribution and correlates of an entrepreneurship-prone personality profile in the United States, Germany, and the United Kingdom: A socioecological perspective. Journal of Personality and Social Psychology, Vol 105(1), Jul 2013, 104–122. The use of APA information does not imply endorsement by APA.

of the Tsimané culture, a community of foragers and farmers in Bolivia with relatively little contact with the outside world, reveals two distinct dimensions of personality—prosociality and industriousness—instead of the more widely accepted five personality traits (Gurven et al., 2013).

Differences in personality may also be seen in different parts of a single country. One study of over half a million people in the United States revealed regional differences in personality traits linked with entrepreneurial activity, defined as business-creation and self-employment rates (Obschonka et al., 2013). As you can see in **Figure 12.10**, certain regions are much more entrepreneurial than others. Why? The authors of the study suggested that the higher scores in the West, for example, might be a reflection of America's historical migration patterns of people moving from the East into the West (or from outside of America). They cite other research (e.g., Rentfrow et al., 2008) that suggests this selective migration may have had a lasting effect on personality due to the heritability of personality traits and the passing on of norms and values within the regions.

What do you think? How would you explain the differences? Can you see the overall value of expanding our study of personality from just looking at differences between individuals to examining regional differences, and how this expansion might increase our understanding of how personality is formed and its potential applications?

3. **Projective Tests** A major disadvantage of projective tests is that they're extremely time-consuming to administer and interpret. However, given the ambiguous stimuli and the fact that the method is unstructured, proponents suggest test-takers may be more willing to talk honestly about sensitive topics. Critics point out, however, that the *reliability* and *validity*

(Chapter 8) of projective tests is among the lowest of all tests of personality (Hartmann & Hartmann, 2014; Hunsley et al., 2015; Koocher et al., 2014). (Recall from Chapter 8 that reliability—the consistency of test results—and validity—whether the test actually measures what it was designed to measure—are the two most important criteria for a good test.)

As you can see, each of these methods has limits, which is why psychologists typically combine the results from various scientific methods to create a fuller picture of any individual's personality. However, you're unlikely to have access to this type of professional analysis, so what's the most important take-home message? Beware of pop-psych books and pop-culture personality quizzes in magazines and on websites. They may be entertaining, but they're rarely based on standardized testing or scientific research of any kind, and you should never base decisions on their input.

Finally, throughout this text, we have emphasized the value of critical thinking, which is useful in evaluating personality tests (see the following **Test Yourself**).

S&P Scientific Thinking and Practical Application

Test Yourself: What's Wrong with Pseudopersonality Quizzes?

The personality horoscope presented at the start of this section contains several logical fallacies. Using your critical thinking skills, can you see how the following three factors help explain why so many people believe in phony personality descriptions and predictions?

Barnum Effect

We often accept pseudopersonality descriptions and horoscope predictions because we believe they are accurate. We assume these tests have somehow tapped into our unique selves. In fact, they are ambiguous, broad statements that fit just about anyone (e.g., "You have a strong need for other people to like and admire you"). The existence of such generalities led to the term *the Barnum effect*, named for the legendary circus promoter P. T. Barnum, who said, "Always have a little something for everyone" (Wyman & Vyse, 2008).

Confirmation Bias

Look again at the "bogus" personality profile that was provided at the start of this section on measuring personality. Now count the number of times you agree with the statements. According to the *confirmation bias* (Chapter 8), we tend to notice and remember events that confirm our expectations and ignore those that are non-confirming (Dibbets

& Meesters, 2017; Digdon, 2017). If we see ourselves as independent thinkers, for example, we ignore the "needing to be liked by others" part and vice versa.

Self-Serving Biases

Now check the overall tone of the same bogus personality profile. Do you see how the traits are generally positive and flattering—or at least neutral? According to several *self-serving biases*, we tend to maximize the positivity of our self-views by preferring information that maintains our positive self-image (Sanjuán & Magallares, 2014; Sedkides & Alicke, 2012). In fact, research shows that the more favorable a personality description is, the more people believe it, and the more likely they are to believe it is personally unique (Guastello et al., 1989).

Taken together, these three logical fallacies help explain the common support for pop-psych personality tests and newspaper horoscopes. They offer something for everyone (*Barnum effect*). We pay attention only to what confirms our expectations (*confirmation bias*). And we like flattering descriptions (*self-serving biases*). You can test your understanding of these three biases in the following:

Q Test Your Critical Thinking

Using the information in this section, can you identify the two major fallacies in this cartoon?

Answer: self-serving biases and the Barnum effect.

Retrieval Practice 12.1 | Understanding Personality

Self-Test Completing this self-test, and then checking your answers by clicking on the answer button or by looking in Appendix B, will provide immediate feedback and helpful practice for exams.

1. _____ theories emphasize the importance of genetics in the development of personality.
   a. Behavioral genetics
   c. Social/personal genetics
   b. Behavioral metrics
   d. Biometrical engineering

2. Some research indicates that genetic factors account for about _____ of personality.
   a. 10–12 percent
   c. 25–38 percent
   b. 12–25 percent
   d. 40–50 percent

3. In the 1800s, if you wanted to have your personality assessed, you would go to a phrenologist, who would determine your personality by studying/measuring _____.
   a. projective tests
   b. ambiguous stimuli results
   c. inkblot stain responses
   d. bumps on your head

4. The Rorschach Inkblot Test is an example of a(n) _____ test.
   a. projective
   c. inkblot
   b. ambiguous stimuli
   d. all of these options

5. Two important criteria for evaluating the usefulness of tests used to assess personality are _____.
   a. concurrence and prediction
   c. consistency and correlation
   b. reliability and validity
   d. diagnosis and prognosis

Q Test Your Critical Thinking

1. If biological factors explain certain personality traits, what advice would you give to someone who is painfully shy and wants to become more outgoing?

2. Which method of personality assessment (interviews, behavioral observations, objective testing, or projective-testing) do you think is likely to be most informative? Can you think of circumstances in which one kind of assessment might be more effective than the others?

Carlina Teteris/Moment/Getty Images

Real World Application Questions

[AQ1] Will eating from a shared plate increase cooperation?

[AQ2] Can social media posting be used to measure your personality?

pixdeluxe/iStock/Getty Images

Hint: Look in the text for **[AQ1]** and **[AQ2]**

12.2 | Psychoanalytic/Psychodynamic Theories

LEARNING OBJECTIVES

Retrieval Practice While reading the upcoming sections, respond to each Learning Objective in your own words.

Summarize the major concepts of psychoanalytic/psychodynamic theories of personality.

- **Review** the major concepts of Freud's psychoanalytic theory.

- **Compare** psychoanalytic and psychodynamic theories of personality.

- **Discuss** the major criticisms of psychoanalytic theories.

Real World Application Question

[AQ3] Are people with negative attitudes toward gay people repressing their own sexual desires?

Freud's Psychoanalytic Theory

Conscious In Freudian terms, thoughts or motives that a person is currently aware of or is remembering.

Preconscious Freud's term for thoughts, motives, or memories that exist just beneath the surface of awareness and can be called to consciousness when necessary.

One of the earliest theories of personality was Sigmund Freud's psychoanalytic perspective, which emphasized unconscious processes and unresolved past conflicts. Working from about 1890 until he died in 1939, Freud developed a theory of personality that has been one of the most influential—and controversial—theories in all of science (Bornstein & Huprich, 2015; Carducci, 2015; Cordón, 2012). Let's examine some of Freud's most basic and debatable concepts.

Levels of Consciousness Freud called the mind the "psyche" and asserted that it contains three *levels of consciousness*, or awareness: the **conscious**, the **preconscious**, and the unconscious (**Figure 12.11**). For Freud, the unconscious is all-important since it serves as a reservoir that stores our largely unacceptable thoughts, feelings, memories, and other information. It lies beneath our conscious awareness. However, it supposedly still has an enormous impact on our behavior—like the hidden part of the iceberg that sank the ocean liner *Titanic*.

Given that many of our unconscious thoughts and motives are unacceptable and threatening, Freud believed that they are normally *repressed* (held out of awareness). However, they are sometimes unintentionally revealed by dreams or slips of the tongue (**Figure 12.12**).

Personality Structure

In addition to proposing that the mind functions at three levels of consciousness, Freud also believed personality was composed of three mental structures: the *id*, *ego*, and *superego* (**Figure 12.13**).

According to Freud, the **id** is the first personality structure that is present at birth, completely unconscious, and striving to meet basic drives, such as hunger, thirst, sex, and aggression. It is immature, impulsive, and irrational. When its primitive drives build up, the id seeks immediate gratification—a concept known as the *pleasure principle*. In other words, the id is like a newborn baby: It wants what it wants when it wants it.

Freud further believed that the second personality structure, the **ego**, is the largely conscious "executive" that deals with the demands of reality. It is responsible for planning, problem solving, reasoning, and controlling the potentially destructive energy of the id in ways that are compatible with the external world. Thus, the ego is responsible for delaying gratification when necessary. Contrary to the id's pleasure principle, the ego operates on the *reality principle.* It understands and deals with objects and events in the real world. Be careful not to confuse this Freudian personality structure with the more common usage of the term "ego"—meaning a person's sense of self-esteem or self-importance.

FIGURE 12.11   Freud's three levels of consciousness

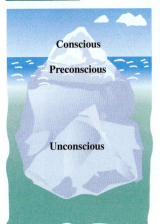

Conscious

Preconscious

Unconscious

Although Freud never used the analogy himself, his levels of awareness are often compared to an iceberg:

- The tip of the iceberg would be analogous to the *conscious* mind, which is above the water and open to easy inspection.
- The *preconscious* mind (the area only shallowly submerged) contains information that can be viewed with a little extra effort.
- The large base of the iceberg is somewhat like the *unconscious*, completely hidden from personal inspection.

Unconscious   Freud's term for the reservoir of largely unacceptable thoughts, feelings, memories, and other information that lies beneath conscious awareness; in modern terms, subliminal processing that lies beneath the absolute threshold.

Id   According to Freud, the first personality structure that is present at birth, completely unconscious, and striving to meet basic drives, such as hunger, thirst, sex, and aggression; it operates on the pleasure principle.

Ego   In Freud's theory, the second personality structure that is largely conscious, and the "executive," which deals with the demands of reality; it operates on the reality principle.

"Good morning, beheaded—uh, I mean beloved."

FIGURE 12.12   Freudian slips   Freud believed that a small slip of the tongue (now known as a *Freudian slip*) can reflect unconscious feelings that we normally keep hidden.

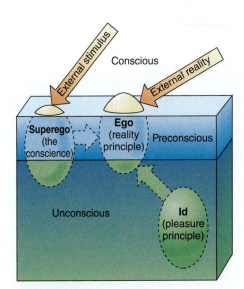

FIGURE 12.13   Freud's personality structure   According to Freud, personality is composed of three structures—the id, ego, and superego. Note how the ego is primarily conscious and preconscious, whereas the id is entirely unconscious.

FIGURE 12.14 Why do we use defense mechanisms?

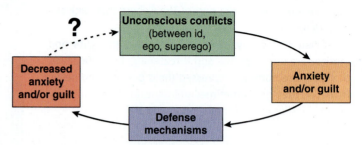

a. Intellectualization at work? Freud believed defense mechanisms help us deal with unconscious conflicts, which explains why these physicians may *intellectualize* and distance themselves from the gruesome aspects of their work to avoid personal anxieties. Defense mechanisms can be healthy and helpful if we use them in moderation or on a temporary basis.

b. Defense mechanisms as a vicious cycle Unfortunately, defense mechanisms generally distort reality, and they create some of our most dangerous habits through a vicious self-reinforcing cycle. An alcoholic who uses his paycheck to buy drinks may feel very guilty, but he can easily reduce this conflict by *rationalizing* that he deserves to relax and unwind with alcohol because he works so hard.

Superego In Freud's theory, is the third personality structure that serves as the center of morality, providing internalized ideals and standards for judgment; often referred to as the "conscience."

The final part of the psyche to develop is the **superego**, the third personality structure that serves as the center of morality. It provides internalized ideals and standards for judgment, and is often referred to as the "conscience." When thinking about having sex, the superego might warn, "only when you're married," whereas the id would demand it "right now." Trying to meet the demands of both the id and superego, the ego might say, "Let's practice safe sex in a committed relationship."

Defense Mechanisms   As you might expect, the "morality" demands of the superego often conflict with the "infantile" needs and drives of the id. When the ego fails to satisfy both the id and the superego, anxiety slips into conscious awareness. Because anxiety is uncomfortable, Freud believed we avoid it through **defense mechanisms**, strategies the ego uses to reduce anxiety. Although defense mechanisms do help relieve the conflict-created anxiety, they distort reality and may increase self-deception (**Figure 12.14**). In addition to intellectualization and rationalization (shown in Figure 12.14), Freud identified several other defense mechanisms (**Table 12.2**).

Defense mechanisms Freud's term for the strategies the ego uses to reduce anxiety, which distort reality and may increase self-deception.

TABLE 12.2   Sample Psychological Defense Mechanisms

Defense Mechanism	Description	Example
Repression	Preventing painful or unacceptable thoughts from entering consciousness	Forgetting the details of a tragic accident
Sublimation	Redirecting socially unacceptable impulses into acceptable activities	Redirecting aggressive impulses by becoming a professional fighter
Denial	Refusing to accept an unpleasant reality	Alcoholics refusing to admit their addiction
Rationalization	Creating a socially acceptable excuse to justify unacceptable behavior	Justifying cheating on an exam by saying "everyone else does it"
Intellectualization	Ignoring the emotional aspects of a painful experience by focusing on abstract thoughts, words, or ideas	Discussing your divorce without emotion while ignoring the hidden, underlying pain
Projection	Transferring unacceptable thoughts, motives, or impulses to others	Becoming unreasonably jealous of your mate while denying your own attraction to others
Reaction formation	Not acknowledging unacceptable impulses and overemphasizing their opposite	Promoting a petition against adult bookstores even though you are secretly fascinated by pornography
Regression	Reverting to immature ways of responding	Throwing a temper tantrum when a friend doesn't want to do what you'd like
Displacement	Redirecting impulses from the original source toward a less threatening person or object	Yelling at a coworker after being criticized by your boss

Psychosexual Stages

Psychosexual Stages Although defense mechanisms are now an accepted part of modern psychology, other Freudian ideas are more controversial (Breger, 2014). For example, according to Freud, strong biological urges residing within the id push all children through five universal **psychosexual stages** (**Process Diagram 12.1**). The term "psychosexual" reflects Freud's belief that children experience sexual feelings from birth (in different forms from those experienced by adolescents and adults). Each of the five psychosexual stages is named for the type of sexual pleasure that supposedly characterizes the stage—for instance, the oral phase is named for the mouth, the key erogenous zone during infancy.

According to Freud, at each psychosexual stage the id's impulses and social demands come into conflict. Therefore, if a child's needs are not met, or are overindulged, at one particular

Psychosexual stages In Freudian theory, five developmental periods (oral, anal, phallic, latency, and genital) during which particular kinds of pleasures must be gratified if personality development is to proceed normally.

> **STOP!** This Process Diagram contains essential information NOT found elsewhere in the text, which is likely to appear on quizzes and exams. Be sure to study it CAREFULLY.

PROCESS DIAGRAM 12.1 Freud's Five Psychosexual Stages of Development

Psychosexual development

Name of stage (Approximate age)	Erogenous zone (Key conflict or developmental task)	
1 **Oral** (0–18 months)	**Mouth** (Weaning from breast or bottle)	
2 **Anal** (18 months–3 years)	**Anus** (Toilet training)	
3 **Phallic** (3–6 years)	**Genitals** (Overcoming the Oedipus complex by identifying with same-sex parent)	
4 **Latency** (6 years–puberty)	**None** (Interacting with same-sex peers)	
5 **Genital** (puberty–adult)	**Genitals** (Establishing intimate relationships with others)	

Courtesy of Sandy Harvey

TIP What do you think Freud would say about this child's stage of development? Is this some form of fixation or just normal play? It's important to note that many of Freud's terms and concepts have been heavily criticized and are not widely accepted in modern, scientific psychology—particularly these psychosexual stages of development. However, we discuss them here because words like *id, ego, superego, anal-retentive,* and *Oedipus complex* remain in common, everyday usage and are a large and persistent part of Western culture. Therefore, you need to be aware of their origin and their limited scientific credibility, which will be further discussed in the later evaluation section.

stage, the child supposedly may *fixate,* and a part of his or her personality will remain stuck at that stage. Freud believed most individuals successfully pass through each of the five stages. But during stressful times, they may return (or *regress*) to an earlier stage in which prior needs were badly frustrated or overgratified.

1. **Oral stage** (birth to 18 months)   During this period, an infant receives satisfaction through sucking, eating, biting, and so on. Given that the infant is highly dependent on parents and other caregivers to provide opportunities for oral gratification, fixation at this stage can easily occur. If caregivers overindulge an infant's oral needs, the child may fixate and as an adult become gullible ("swallowing" anything), dependent, and passive. The underindulged child, however, will develop into an aggressive, sadistic person who exploits others. According to Freud, orally fixated adults often orient their life around their mouth—overeating, becoming an alcoholic, smoking, or talking a great deal.

WILBUR

Wilbur Dawbarn/CartoonStock

2. **Anal stage** (18 to 36 months)   Once the child becomes a toddler, his or her erogenous zone shifts to the anus. The child supposedly receives satisfaction by having and retaining bowel movements. Given this is the time when most parents begin toilet training, the child's desire to control his or her own bowel movements often leads to strong conflict. Adults who are fixated at this stage, in Freud's view, may develop an *anal-retentive* (see cartoon) personality and be highly controlled and compulsively neat. Or they may be very messy, disorderly, rebellious, and destructive—the so-called *anal-expulsive* personality.

3. **Phallic stage** (3 to 6 years)   During the *phallic stage*, the major center of pleasure is the genitals. Masturbation and "playing doctor" with other children are common during this time. According to Freud, a 3- to 6-year-old boy also develops an unconscious sexual longing for his mother and jealousy and hatred for the rival father. This attraction creates a conflict Freud called the **Oedipus complex**, named after Oedipus, the legendary Greek king who unwittingly killed his father and married his mother. The young boy reportedly experiences guilt and fear of punishment from the rival father, perhaps by castration. The anxiety this produces is supposedly repressed into the unconscious, which leads to the development of the superego. The boy then identifies with his father and adopts the male gender role. If this stage is not resolved completely or positively, or the child fixates at this stage, Freud believed the boy grows up resenting his father and generalizes this feeling to all authority figures.

Oedipus complex   According to Freud, during the phallic stage (ages 3 to 6 years), a young boy develops a sexual attraction to his mother and rivalry with his father.

What happens with little girls? Because a girl does not have a penis, she logically does not fear castration and fails to fully complete this stage and move on to successful identification with her mother. According to Freud, she develops *penis envy* and fails to develop an adequate superego, which Freud believed resulted in women being morally inferior to men. (You are undoubtedly surprised or outraged by this statement, but remember that Freud was a product of his times. Sexism was common at this point in history. However, most modern psychodynamic theorists reject this sexism and Freud's notion of penis envy, as we will see in the next section.)

4. **Latency period** (6 years to puberty)   Following the phallic stage, children supposedly repress sexual thoughts and engage in non-sexual activities, such as developing social and intellectual skills. The task of this stage is to develop successful interactions with same-sex peers and refine appropriate gender roles.

5. **Genital stage** (puberty to adulthood)   With the beginning of adolescence, the genitals are again erogenous zones. Adolescents seek to fulfill their sexual desires through emotional attachment to others. Unsuccessful outcomes at this stage lead to participation in sexual relationships based only on lustful desires, not on respect and commitment.

Psychodynamic/Neo-Freudian Theories

Some initial followers of Freud later extended his theories, often in social and cultural directions. They became known as neo-Freudians, or "new" Freudians. These theorists accepted most of Freud's basic ideas, such as the id, ego, superego, and defense mechanisms, but broke away for various reasons.

Alfred Adler (1870–1937) was the first to leave Freud's inner circle. Instead of seeing behavior as motivated by unconscious forces, Adler believed it is purposeful and goal directed. According to his *individual psychology*, we are motivated by our goals in life—especially our goals of obtaining security and overcoming feelings of inferiority (Carlson & Englar-Carlson, 2013).

Adler believed that almost everyone suffers from an **inferiority complex**, or deep feelings of inadequacy and incompetence that arise from our feelings of helplessness as infants (Adler, 1927/1954). According to Adler, these early feelings result in a "will-to-power" that can take one of two paths. It can lead children to strive to develop superiority over others through dominance, aggression, or expressions of envy. Or, on a more positive note, it can encourage them to develop their full potential and creativity and to gain mastery and control of their lives (**Figure 12.15**).

Another early Freud follower turned dissenter, Carl Jung [pronounced as *Yoong*], developed *analytical psychology*. Like Freud, Jung (1875–1961) emphasized unconscious processes, but he believed that the unconscious contains positive and spiritual motives as well as sexual and aggressive forces.

Jung also thought that we have two forms of the unconscious mind: the personal unconscious and the collective unconscious. The *personal unconscious* is created from our individual experiences, whereas the **collective unconscious** is identical in each person and is inherited (Jung, 1933, 1936/1969). The collective unconscious consists of primitive images and patterns of thought, feeling, and behavior that Jung called **archetypes** (**Figure 12.16**).

Given the archetypal patterns in the collective unconscious, we supposedly perceive and react in certain predictable ways. One set of archetypes refers to gender roles (Chapter 10). Jung claimed that both males and females have patterns for feminine aspects of personality—*anima*—and masculine aspects of personality—*animus*—which allow us to express both masculine and feminine personality traits and to understand the opposite sex.

Like Adler and Jung, psychoanalyst Karen Horney [HORN-eye] (1885–1952) was an influential follower of Freud who later came to reject major aspects of Freudian theory. She is credited

Inferiority complex Adler's idea that feelings of inferiority develop from early childhood experiences of helplessness and incompetence.

Collective unconscious Jung's name for the deepest layer of the unconscious, which contains universal memories and archetypes shared by all people due to our common ancestral past.

Archetypes Jung's term for the collective, universal images and patterns, residing in the unconscious, that have symbolic meaning for all people.

Hero Images/Getty Images

FIGURE 12.15 **An upside to feelings of inferiority?** Adler suggested that the will-to-power could be positively expressed through social interest—by identifying with others and cooperating with them for the social good. Can you explain how these volunteers might be fulfilling their will-to-power interest?

World History Archive/Alamy Stock Photo

FIGURE 12.16 **Archetypes and American film** Jung believed that archetypal patterns can be found throughout history and in popular novels, myths, and films. Assuming you're familiar with the classic film *The Wizard of Oz*, can you see how the main characters might fit some of the possible archetypes or universal behaviors we all share? The Scarecrow is seeking wisdom, the Cowardly Lion is looking for courage, and the Tin Man is searching for love. The main star, Dorothy, is looking for self-knowledge and to integrate all the parts of her traveling companions into one primary self, which some believe explains the universal appeal of this particular film (e.g., Boyd, 2011).

FIGURE 12.17 **Oral fixation or simple self-soothing?** Is this an example of Freud's earliest stage of psychosexual development, or just a part of all infants' normal attempts to self-soothe, or their evolutionarily adaptive sucking behaviors?

Basic anxiety According to Horney, adults experience feelings of helplessness and insecurity because as children they felt alone and isolated in a hostile environment.

with having developed a creative blend of Freudian, Adlerian, and Jungian theory, along with the first feminist critique of Freud's theory (Horney, 1939, 1945). Horney emphasized women's positive traits and suggested that most of Freud's ideas about female personality reflected male bias and misunderstanding. For example, women's everyday experience with social inferiority led to power envy, not to Freud's idea of biological *penis envy*.

In addition, Horney believed personality development depends largely on social relationships—particularly on the relationship between parent and child. She believed that when a child's needs are not met by nurturing parents, the child may develop lasting feelings of helplessness and insecurity. The way people respond to this so-called **basic anxiety**, in Horney's view, sets the stage for later adult psychological health. She believed that everyone copes with this basic anxiety in one of three ways—we move toward, away from, or against other people—and that psychological health requires a balance among these three styles.

In sum, Horney proposed that our adult personalities are shaped by our childhood relationship with our parents—not by fixation or regression at some stage of psychosexual development, as Freud argued. Keep in mind that most of the major ideas of Adler, Jung, and Horney, along with concepts from other key figures such as Erik Erikson (Chapter 9), have evolved into the modern *psychodynamic perspective* described in Chapter 14. In contrast to the traditional Freudian focus on the id, ego, superego, and psychosexual stages, psychodynamic theorists emphasize the *dynamic* relations between conscious and unconscious processes and current problems (Barber & Solomonov, 2016; Beail, 2016).

Evaluating Psychoanalytic Theories

Before going on, let's consider the major criticisms of Freud's psychoanalytic theories (Carducci, 2015; Gagnepain et al., 2014; Koocher et al., 2014):

- **Inadequate empirical support** Many psychoanalytic concepts—such as the psychosexual stages—cannot be empirically tested.
- **Overemphasis on sexuality, biology, and unconscious forces** Modern psychologists believe Freud underestimated the role of learning and culture in shaping personality (**Figure 12.17**).
- **Sexism** Many psychologists, beginning with Karen Horney, reject Freud's theories as derogatory toward women.

In contrast to the claim of inadequate empirical support, numerous modern studies have supported certain Freudian concepts like defense mechanisms and the belief that a lot of our information processing occurs outside our conscious awareness (*automatic processing*, Chapter 5, and *implicit memories*, Chapter 7). **[AQ3]** In addition, one study combining four experiments found that people who identify as having a heterosexual orientation, but show a strong sexual attraction to same-sex people in psychological tests, tend to have more homophobic attitudes (sexual prejudice) and higher levels of hostility toward gay people (Weinstein et al., 2012). Can you see how Freud's theory might suggest that these negative attitudes and beliefs spring from unconscious repression of same-sex desires? Moreover, many contemporary clinicians still value Freud's insights about childhood experiences and unconscious influences on personality development (e.g., Barratt, 2019; de Tychey et al., 2016; Schimmel, 2014).

Take-Home Message Freud was clearly wrong on many counts. However, he still ranks as one of the giants of psychology. Furthermore, it's easy to criticize Freud if you don't remember that he began his work at the start of the 20th century. We can only imagine how our current theories will look 100 years from now. Although Freud and his theories were wrong on many accounts, he has earned a lasting place among the pioneers in psychology. Today there are few Freudian purists. Instead, modern psychodynamic theorists and psychoanalysts tend to place less emphasis on sexual instincts and more on sociocultural influences on personality development.

> Many aspects of Freudian theory are indeed out of date, and they should be:
> Freud died in 1939, and he has been slow to undertake further revisions.
>
> —Psychologist Drew Westen (1998)

Retrieval Practice 12.2 | Psychoanalytic/Psychodynamic Theories

Self-Test Completing this self-test, and then checking your answers by clicking on the answer button or by looking in Appendix B, will provide immediate feedback and helpful practice for exams.

1. According to Freud, thoughts, motives, or memories that lie just beneath the surface of awareness are stored in the _____.

   a. preoperational stage **c.** subconscious

   b. unconscious **d.** preconscious

2. In Freudian terms, the _____ seeks immediate gratification. The _____ is the "executive" that deals with the demands of reality, and the _____ is the center of morality that provides standards for judgment; often referred to as the "conscience."

   a. psyche; ego; id

   b. id; ego; superego

   c. conscious; preconscious; unconscious

   d. oral stage; anal stage; phallic stage

3. According to Freud, when anxiety slips into our conscious awareness, we tend to avoid it through the use of _____.

   a. latency overcompensation

   b. the Oedipus complex

   c. regression to the oral stage

   d. defense mechanisms

4. During the _____ phase, the Oedipus complex is reportedly the major conflict in psychosexual development for boys.

   a. oral **c.** phallic

   b. latent **d.** genital

5. Three of the most influential neo-Freudians were _____.

   a. Plato, Aristotle, and Descartes

   b. Dr. Laura, Dr. Phil, and Dr. Ruth

   c. Adler, Jung, and Horney

   d. none of these options

Q Test Your Critical Thinking

1. If scientists have so many problems with Freud, why do you think his theories are still popular with the public? Should psychologists continue to discuss his theories (and include them in textbooks)?

2. What is a possible example of sexism in Freud's psychoanalytic theory?

Real World Application Question

[AQ3] Are people with negative attitudes toward gay people repressing their own sexual desires?

Hint: Look in the text for **[AQ3]**

jonathandowney/E+/Getty Images

12.3 | Trait Theories

LEARNING OBJECTIVES

Retrieval Practice While reading the upcoming sections, respond to each Learning Objective in your own words.

Review the major concepts of the various trait theories.

- **Explain** how early trait theorists approached the study of personality.

- **Describe** the Big Five personality traits.

- **Summarize** the major contributions and criticisms of trait theory.

Real World Application Question

[AQ4] Do introverts really not like people and always want to be alone?

Think for a moment about the key personality characteristics of your best friend. You might say: "He's a great guy who's a lot of fun to be with. But I sometimes get tired of his constant jokes and pranks. On the other hand, he does listen well and will be serious when I need him to be."

When describing another's personality, we generally use terms that refer to that person's most frequent and typical characteristics ("fun," "constant jokes and pranks," "listens well"). These unique and defining characteristics are the foundation for the *trait approach*, which seeks to discover what characteristics form the core of human personality.

Early Trait Theorists

An early study of dictionary terms found almost 4,500 words that described personality **traits** (Allport & Odbert, 1936). Faced with this enormous list, Gordon Allport (1937) believed that the

Trait A relatively stable personality characteristic that describes a pattern of thinking, feeling, and acting.

best way to understand personality was to arrange a person's unique personality traits into a hierarchy, with the most pervasive or important traits at the top.

Later psychologists reduced the list of possible personality traits using a statistical technique called *factor analysis*, in which large arrays of data are grouped into more basic units (factors). Raymond Cattell (1950, 1990) condensed the list of traits to 16 source traits (see **Test Yourself**). Hans Eysenck (1967, 1990) reduced the list even further. He described personality as a relationship among three basic types of traits: *extraversion–introversion, neuroticism* (the tendency toward insecurity, anxiety, guilt, and moodiness), and *psychoticism* (being out of touch with reality).

PA Practical Application

Test Yourself: **Constructing Your Own Personality Profile**

Note how Cattell's 16 source traits exist on a continuum, from low to high. There are extremes at either end, such as reserved and less intelligent at the far left and outgoing and more intelligent at the far right. Average falls somewhere in the middle. To construct your own profile, add a dot on each line that represents your own degree of each personality trait and then connect the dots with a line.

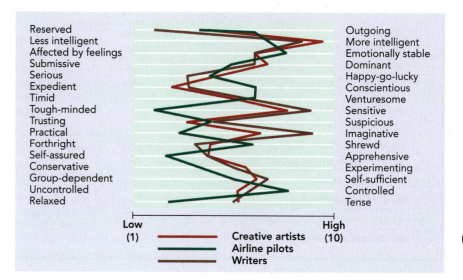

Low (1)		High (10)
Creative artists		
Airline pilots		
Writers		

Modern Trait Theory

Five-factor model (FFM)
A model of personality traits that includes five basic dimensions: openness, conscientiousness, extraversion, agreeableness, and neuroticism; informally called the Big Five.

Factor analysis was also used to develop the **five-factor model (FFM)**, which is the most promising modern trait theory (Costa & McCrae, 2011; McCrae & Costa, 2013). A handy way to remember this model is to note that the first letters of the five words spell *ocean* (**Figure 12.18**).

Combining previous research findings and the long list of possible personality traits, researchers discovered that these five traits came up repeatedly, even when different tests were used:

O Openness People who rate high on this factor are original, imaginative, curious, open to new ideas, artistic, and interested in cultural pursuits. For instance, if you score high on this dimension, you probably enjoy talking with people with sharply different opinions because you realize that what the other person is saying may have value. People low on this trait generally like routine and prefer to maintain the status quo. Surprisingly, researchers have found that openness and extraversion were two of the five factors most strongly associated with particular musical preferences (Nave et al., 2018). Can you imagine why?

C Conscientiousness This factor ranges from responsible, self-disciplined, organized, and achieving at the high end, to irresponsible, careless, impulsive, lazy, and undependable at the other. If you are often late to class or social events, and commonly misplace things, you may be low on conscientiousness. As you might expect, research shows that those who show more effort in their homework during early adolescence will later show increases in conscientiousness (Göllner et al., 2017). Also as expected, those who are conscientious are

Big Five traits

	Low scorers	High scorers
1 **O**penness	Down-to-earth Uncreative Conventional Not curious	Imaginative Creative Original Curious
2 **C**onscientiousness	Negligent Lazy Disorganized Late	Conscientious Hard-working Well-organized Punctual
3 **E**xtraversion	Loner Quiet Passive Reserved	Joiner Talkative Active Affectionate
4 **A**greeableness	Suspicious Critical Ruthless Irritable	Trusting Lenient Soft-hearted Good-natured
5 **N**euroticism	Calm Even-tempered Comfortable Unemotional	Worried Temperamental Self-conscious Emotional

FIGURE 12.18 **The five-factor model (FFM)** Different adjectives may describe your personality, depending on whether you score high or low in each of the "Big Five" traits. Note that the lines on the right, below each factor's "low" and "high scorers," indicate that each factor exists on a continuum. If you'd like more details, take the five-factor self-test at www.personalitytest.org.uk

Q Test Your Critical Thinking

1. Do you think these five factors accurately reflect your key personality traits? Why or why not?

2. Some have said that scoring high on the first four factors shows an individual is strong in the "nice" traits. Under what conditions could scoring low on extraversion (being introverted) be advantageous?

more likely to succeed in their goal pursuits, such as healthy eating and frequent physical exercise (Ludwig et al., 2019).

E Extraversion   This factor contrasts people who are outgoing, talkative, and assertive with those high in introversion, which describes individuals who tend to be retiring, quiet, and mild mannered. If you dislike being the center of attention and enjoy your time alone, you're probably more introverted. The reverse is true for someone who is extraverted. There are many myths and misconceptions about introversion and extraversion. To clarify these misunderstandings, try the following **Test Yourself**.

S&P Scientific Thinking and Practical Application

Overcoming Misconceptions About Introversion and Extraversion

Test Yourself: True or False?

_____ **1.** Introverts don't like people and always want to be alone.

_____ **2.** Introverts don't like to talk.

_____ **3.** Introverts are shy.

_____ **4.** Extraverts are bad listeners.

_____ **5.** Extraverts are shallow.

_____ **6.** Extraverts don't like quiet time or being alone.

_____ **7.** You're either an introvert or an extravert.

Each of these statements is false. After reading the previous section on introversion versus extraversion and our fast-paced, highly competitive society, you may think that it's better to be extraverted. But introverted people aren't necessarily "wallflower" social rejects. They have their own strengths and typically prefer being alone and quiet given they desire less stimulation. Most people agree that Abraham Lincoln was one of the greatest U.S. presidents of all time (see photo), and some may consider Lady Gaga or Jay-Z to be among the greatest musical talents. But did you know that all of these individuals are self-described as shy and introverted?

Gary Morrow/EyeEm/Getty Images

In short, introverts and extraverts just have differing ways of interacting with others and processing information. **[AQ4]** Introverts value people—particularly close friends—and while they're very comfortable being alone, introverts also crave authentic and sincere connections with a few others (see photo). Similarly, many believe introverts don't like to talk and are shy. In reality, they just avoid "small talk" and prefer to think about what they want to say before speaking. Furthermore,

Iakov Filimonov/123RF

keep in mind that shyness and introversion are not the same. Unlike shy people, introverts are not necessarily afraid of others or of being judged by them. They just prefer less stimulating environments with fewer people.

There are also several myths about extraversion. For instance, extraverts are sometimes mistakenly considered to be bad listeners or shallow due to their talkativeness and high sociability. Although extraverts do like a certain amount of quiet time and being alone, they also enjoy socializing in large groups because they tend to process thoughts and information as they're speaking and interacting with others. In contrast, introverts process their thoughts and information through self-reflection.

Regarding the myth that you're either an introvert or an extravert, you've discovered throughout this text that most aspects of human nature fall on a continuum and that most people fall somewhere in the middle. Personality is like creativity, intelligence, and physical height. We all have relative amounts of different traits. No one is either totally introverted or totally extraverted.

> I am rather inclined to silence, and whether that be wise or not, it is at least more unusual nowadays to find a man who can hold his tongue than to find one who cannot.
>
> —Abraham Lincoln

A Agreeableness   This trait describes a person's basic emotional style. Individuals who score high in this factor are typically easygoing and pleasant to be around, whereas low scorers are often irritable and difficult. Given that almost everyone likes to think of themselves as agreeable, it's difficult to accurately assess ourselves on this dimension. You may want to take the five-factor self-test mentioned in Figure 12.18.

N Neuroticism (*or emotional stability*)   People who score high in neuroticism are emotionally unstable and prone to insecurity, anxiety, guilt, worry, and moodiness. People at the other end are emotionally stable, calm, even-tempered, easygoing, and relaxed. Again, most of us like to believe we're emotionally stable, so it may be helpful to take the self-grading online quiz featured in Figure 12.18.

This five-factor model (FFM) has led to numerous research follow-ups and intriguing insights about personality (Barceló, 2017; Choi & Shin, 2017; Wilmot et al., 2019). One large-scale study of profile photos on social media found several interesting correlations with the FFM, with users high in agreeableness or extraversion being more likely to post colorful pictures of people that convey emotion (Liu et al., 2016). On the other hand, people who are high in openness or neuroticism posted fewer photos of people.

Other studies indicate that these five personality traits (particularly openness, conscientiousness, and agreeableness) are linked with real-world outcomes, such as job performance. For example, a large meta-analysis comparing results from 25 studies found that teacher effectiveness was positively correlated with all FFM factors—except for agreeableness (Kim et al., 2019). Why isn't agreeableness associated with teacher effectiveness? The authors explained that it may be a statistical artifact, meaning that they only examined one profession—teaching.

Does the FFM also correlate with student success? As expected, conscientiousness was particularly linked with academic grade point average (GPA), especially in subjects that students generally find less interesting (Brandt et al., 2019; Steinmayr & Kessels, 2017; Vecchione et al., 2017). Based on your own college experience, can you see why this makes intuitive sense? How would you explain why extraversion does not positively correlate with GPA?

What about non-human animals? Do you think they have distinct personalities? If so, do they also have specific personality traits that might be associated with a longer life span? (See the **RC Research Challenge**.)

Evaluating Trait Theories

The five-factor model (FFM) is the first model to achieve the major goal of trait theory—to describe and organize personality characteristics using the smallest number of traits. Psychologist David Buss and his colleagues (1989, 2008) surveyed more than 10,000 men and women from 37 countries and found a surprising level of agreement in the characteristics

RC Scientific Thinking: **Research Challenge**

Do Non-Human Animals Have Unique Personalities?

(APA Goal 2.4) Interpret, design, and conduct basic psychological research

Pet owners have long believed that their dogs and cats have unique personalities, and a growing body of research tends to support these beliefs. When 78 dogs of all shapes and sizes were rated by both owners and strangers, a strong correlation was found on traits such as affection versus aggression, anxiety versus calmness, and intelligence versus stupidity. In addition, these researchers found that personalities vary widely within a breed, which means that not all pit bulls are aggressive and not all Labrador retrievers are affectionate (Gosling et al., 2004).

A separate study found that dog personalities change over time, and compared to other age groups, six- to eight-year-old dogs were most responsive to training but also more aggressive toward people and other animals (Chopik & Weaver, 2019). Research also shows that several species have distinct personalities, including gorillas (see photo), macaques, bonobos, marmosets, orangutans, and chimpanzees (Adams et al., 2015; Weiss et al., 2015; Wergård et al., 2016). Furthermore, chimpanzee personality traits are quite similar to those described by the five-factor model (FFM) of human personality (Latzman et al., 2015). Research has even found evidence of personality traits in cockroaches (Planas-Sitjà et al., 2015).

To discover whether particular personality traits were associated with a longer life expectancy in non-human animals, researchers studied 298 gorillas in zoos and sanctuaries across North America (Weiss et al., 2013). Using standardized measures similar to the FFM, they asked zookeepers, volunteers, researchers, and caretakers who knew the gorillas well to score each gorilla's personality. With these scorings, they reliably identified four distinct personality traits: *dominance, extraversion, neuroticism,* and *agreeableness.*

Next, the researchers examined the association between levels of each of these personality traits and life expectancy. They found that gorillas scoring high on extraversion, which included behaviors such as sociability, activity, play, and curiosity, lived longer lives. This link was found in both male and female gorillas and across all the different types of environments in which this research was conducted.

What might explain this link? One possibility is that extraverted apes—just like extraverted people—develop stronger social networks, which helps increase survival and reduce stress. Can you think of other possible explanations? Also, do

Eric Gevaert/Shutterstock.com

you recognize how identifying personality traits in non-human animals might be very beneficial for our human and non-human animal relationships—as well as for our collective overall well-being (e.g., Wilson et al., 2019)?

Identify the Research Method

1. Based on the information provided, did this study (Weiss et al., 2013) use descriptive, correlational, and/or experimental research?

2. If you chose:
   o *descriptive research*, is this a naturalistic or laboratory observation, survey/interview, case study, and/or archival research?
   o *correlational research*, is this a positive, negative, or zero correlation?
   o *experimental research*, label the IV, DV, experimental group(s), and control group. (**Note:** If participants were not randomly assigned to groups, list it as a *quasi-experimental design*.)
   o both *descriptive* and *correlational*, answer the corresponding questions for both.

Check your answers by clicking on the answer button or by looking in Appendix B.

Note: The information provided in this study is admittedly limited, but the level of detail is similar to what is presented in most textbooks and public reports of research findings. Answering these questions, and then comparing your answers to those provided, will help you become a better scientific and critical thinker and consumer of scientific research.

---

that men and women value in a mate (**Table 12.3**). Note that both sexes tend to prefer mates with traits that closely match the FFM—dependability (conscientiousness), emotional stability (low neuroticism), pleasing disposition (agreeableness), and sociability (extraversion).

Why is there such a high degree of shared preferences for certain personality traits? Scientists suggest that these traits may provide an evolutionary advantage, which is

TABLE 12.3 Mate Preferences and the Five-Factor Model (FFM)

What Men Most Want in a Mate	What Women Most Want in a Mate
1. Mutual attraction—love	1. Mutual attraction—love
2. Dependable character	2. Dependable character
3. Emotional stability and maturity	3. Emotional stability and maturity
4. Pleasing disposition	4. Pleasing disposition
5. Good health	5. Education and intelligence
6. Education and intelligence	6. Sociability
7. Sociability	7. Good health
8. Desire for home and children	8. Desire for home and children
9. Refinement, neatness	9. Ambition and industriousness
10. Good looks	10. Refinement, neatness

Volodymyr Vaksman/123RF

Source: Based on Buss et al., 1990.

confirmed by cross-cultural studies and the comparative studies mentioned earlier. Research is particularly clear about the advantages of being conscientious, extraverted, and agreeable—and less neurotic. For instance, people who are conscientious have better health, which is clearly advantageous (Israel et al., 2014). Surprisingly, agreeableness is actually associated with more financial hardship (Matz & Gladstone, 2019). The researchers suggest that agreeable people may simply care less about money. In this case, nice guys may actually finish last!

In addition to having strong support from cross-cultural and comparative studies, trait theories, like the FFM, allow us to predict real-life preferences and behaviors, such as our political attitudes, beliefs, and voting preferences, and even how much time we spend on social media (Bakker et al., 2016; Hart et al., 2015; Kircaburun & Griffiths, 2018). Furthermore, people who are extraverted prefer upbeat, energetic, and rhythmic types of music, such as rap and hip-hop (Langmeyer et al., 2012). In contrast, people who are open to experience prefer complex, intense, and rebellious music, such as classical and rock. As you might expect, personality may even affect your career choice and job satisfaction (see the following **Test Yourself**).

PA Practical Application

Test Yourself: Matching Your Personality with Your Career

As mentioned earlier, the FFM traits of conscientiousness, agreeableness, and openness are clearly linked with success. Personality traits are also clearly linked with overall life satisfaction (e.g., Steel et al., 2019). An interesting longitudinal study measured young adults on their Big Five personality traits and their vocational interest orientations and then repeated the same measures 6 years later (Golle et al., 2019). Interestingly, the researchers found that those who chose the vocational versus the academic pathway were later found to be higher in conscientiousness and less interested in investigative, social, and enterprising activities. Can you see how this study suggests that your environment—college or vocational school—can shape your personality?

What about other factors, such as the worker's job satisfaction? Do some personality characteristics make you better suited for certain jobs than others? According to psychologist John Holland's *personality–job fit theory*, a match (or "good fit") between our individual personality and our career choice is a major factor in determining job satisfaction (Holland, 1985, 1994). Research shows that a good fit between personality and occupation helps increase subjective well-being, job success, and job satisfaction. In other words, people tend to be happier and like their work when they're well matched to their jobs (Joeng et al., 2013; Perkmen & Sahin, 2013; Williamson et al., 2013). Check this table to see what job would be a good match for your personality.

Personality Characteristics	Holland Personality Type	Matching/Congruent Occupations
Shy, genuine, persistent, stable, conforming, practical	**1. Realistic:** Prefers physical activities that require skill, strength, and coordination	Mechanic, drill press operator, assembly-line worker, farmer
Analytical, original, curious, independent	**2. Investigative:** Prefers activities that involve thinking, organizing, and understanding	Biologist, economist, mathematician, news reporter
Sociable, friendly, cooperative, understanding	**3. Social:** Prefers activities that involve helping and developing others	Social worker, counselor, teacher, clinical psychologist
Conforming, efficient, practical, unimaginative, inflexible	**4. Conventional:** Prefers rule-regulated, orderly, and unambiguous activities	Accountant, bank teller, file clerk, manager
Imaginative, disorderly, idealistic, emotional, impractical	**5. Artistic:** Prefers ambiguous and unsystematic activities that allow creative expression	Painter, musician, writer, interior decorator
Self-confident, ambitious, energetic, domineering	**6. Enterprising:** Prefers verbal activities with opportunities to influence others and attain power	Lawyer, real estate agent, public relations specialist, small business manager

Source: Adapted and reproduced with special permission of the publisher, Psychological Assessment Resources, Inc., 16204 North Florida Avenue, Lutz, Florida 33549, from the *Dictionary of Holland Occupational Codes*, 3rd edition, by Gary D. Gottfredson, Ph.D., and John L. Holland, Ph.D., Copyright 1982, 1989, 1996. Further reproduction is prohibited without permission from PAR, Inc.

Situation vs. Interaction

As you've just seen, trait theories have had a fair share of success. However, others have argued that the situation is a better predictor of personality than individual personalities. Imagine having a professor who is a stickler for being on time to his or her class, and one day when you're rushing to class you notice a new, large sign saying "Please stay off the grass." Even if you scored high on the personality trait of conscientiousness, you might ignore the sign and take the shortcut across the grass.

Walter Mischel in 1968 was one of the first psychologists to suggest that behaviors are determined more by situations than by the personality traits a person possesses—a position now called **situationism**. As you can imagine, this theory sparked considerable attention within the scientific community, which later became known as the *person/situation debate*. Today, most personality psychologists agree that both the person and situation are important. The current dominant theory is **interactionism**, meaning that behaviors are determined by an interaction between situations and the personality traits a person possesses.

Situationism The theory that behaviors are determined more by situations rather than by the personality traits a person possesses.

Interactionism The theory that behaviors are determined by an interaction between situations and the personality traits a person possesses.

Stability vs. Change

Now that we've agreed on interactionism, other questions arise—are our personalities stable or can they change? The answers are complex. Some research shows considerable stability in personality traits, whereas others have shown that under some circumstances personality does change. One study of newlyweds' personalities found that over the first 18 months of marriage, husbands showed significant declines in extraversion and agreeableness and a significant increase in conscientiousness (Lavner et al., 2018). In contrast, the wives showed significant declines in agreeableness, neuroticism, and openness.

Can you see how this study illustrates not only that personality can change, but also that it does so naturally over time and in new situations (e.g., marriage)? Considering the natural changes over time, researchers studied data from participants who took personality tests in high school and then took the same test 50 years later (Damian et al., 2019). They found that on average participants became more conscientious, more emotionally stable, and more agreeable over time. However, those who were most conscientious as teenagers remained more conscientious than their peers 50 years later. This study illustrates how personality does change somewhat, but differences also remain over time.

Finally, research also shows that certain stressful life events, such as being unemployed or experiencing natural disasters, can change our personalities (Boyce et al., 2015; Kandler et al., 2015; Lyons et al., 2019). Moreover, we can sometimes deliberately change our personalities if we have specific goals in mind (Hudson & Fraley, 2015). Would you like to be a more positive person and maybe change some parts of your own personality? See the **PAH** **Practical Application Highlight**.

PAH Practical Application Highlight

Can (and Should) We Improve Our Personality Traits?

(APA Goal 1.3) Describe applications of psychology

Have you ever admired the personalities of others and wished you could be more like them? The good news is that many different types of positive traits can increase through training. In one study, researchers randomly divided 178 adults into three groups for a period of 10 weeks (Proyer et al., 2013). One group focused on increasing the traits of "curiosity," "gratitude," "optimism," "humor," and "enthusiasm," while another group focused on increasing the traits of "appreciation of beauty," "creativity," "kindness," "love of learning," and "foresight." The third group served as a control and did not complete any type of training. People in the two treatment groups completed brief exercises at some point each day, such as writing a thank you letter (to practice gratitude) or paying attention to things they found beautiful in the world (to train their appreciation of beauty).

Can you predict what happened? Findings revealed that people who focused on increasing positive traits, such as optimism and enthusiasm, indeed experienced greater life satisfaction at the end of the training sessions compared to those in the other two groups. Interestingly, a recent large longitudinal research study found that optimistic individuals are also less likely to suffer from chronic diseases and more likely to live longer (Lee et al., 2019).

Frederick M. Brown/Stringer/Getty Images Entertainment/Getty Images

As you can see, there are numerous and valid reasons for wanting to improve our personalities. On the other hand, it's important to note that psychologists only *describe* personality traits. We don't advise on what traits *should be changed*. That's for you as an individual to decide. Moreover, personality traits (like "beauty") are largely in the "eye of the beholder." What traits some people decide are preferable over others depend on the group, culture, and history.

Keep in mind that almost all personality traits have both positive and negative characteristics. Furthermore, as mentioned earlier, personality traits exist on a continuum and they often vary depending on the situation. No one is entirely extraverted nor always introverted. Some shy people can be very extraverted in small groups but introverted around people they don't know in large groups or parties. Stephen Colbert (see photo) is much admired for his apparently extraverted personality while hosting *The Late Show*. But he has admitted that while being on stage is very enjoyable and even exhilarating, he'd rather be home in bed with a good book than in a nightclub as a customer (Pearson, 2018).

Retrieval Practice 12.3 | Trait Theories

Self-Test Completing this self-test, and then checking your answers by clicking on the answer button or by looking in Appendix B, will provide immediate feedback and helpful practice for exams.

1. ______ is a statistical technique that groups large arrays of data into more basic units.
   - **a.** MMPI
   - **b.** FFM
   - **c.** Factor analysis
   - **d.** Regression analysis
2. What are the Big Five personality traits in the five-factor model?
   - **a.** conscientiousness, openness, extraversion, agreeableness, and neuroticism
   - **b.** shyness, conscientiousness, extraversion, agreeableness, and neuroticism
   - **c.** shyness, conscientiousness, introversion, agreeableness, and neuroticism
   - **d.** none of these options
3. People who score high in ______ are emotionally unstable and prone to insecurity, anxiety, guilt, worry, and moodiness.
   - **a.** openness
   - **b.** conscientiousness
   - **c.** extraversion
   - **d.** neuroticism
4. Trait theories of personality have been criticized for ______.
   - **a.** failing to explain why people develop specific traits
   - **b.** not including a large number of central traits
   - **c.** failing to identify which traits last and which are transient
   - **d.** not considering situational determinants of personality
   - **e.** all but one of these options
5. Which of the following is NOT associated with the trait theories of personality?
   - **a.** Cattell
   - **b.** Allport
   - **c.** Rorschach
   - **d.** Eysenck

Q Test Your Critical Thinking

1. After reading the descriptions for each of the Big Five personality dimensions, how well do you think they describe someone you know very well? Can you predict how he or she might score on each of these traits?
2. Do you believe someone can change his or her core personality traits? Why or why not?

Real World Application Question

[AQ4] Do introverts really not like people and always want to be alone?

Iakov Filimonov/123RF

Hint: Look in the text for **[AQ4]**

12.4 # Humanistic Theories

LEARNING OBJECTIVES

Retrieval Practice   While reading the upcoming sections, respond to each learning objective in your own words.

Summarize the major concepts of humanistic theories of personality.

- **Discuss** the importance of self-actualization in humanistic theories.
- **Explain** why self-concept and unconditional positive regard are key aspects of Rogers's theory of personality.

- **Describe** how Maslow's hierarchy of needs affects personality.
- **Evaluate** the strengths and weaknesses of humanistic theories of personality.

Real World Application Question

[AQ5] What parenting skills are also associated with increased marital satisfaction?

Humanistic theories of personality emphasize each person's internal feelings, thoughts, and sense of basic worth. In contrast to Freud's generally negative view of human nature, humanists believe that people are naturally good (or, at worst, neutral) and that they possess a natural tendency toward **self-actualization**, an inborn drive to develop all their talents and capabilities.

According to this view, our personality and behavior depend on how we perceive and interpret the world, not on traits, unconscious impulses, or rewards and punishments. Humanistic psychology was developed largely by Carl Rogers and Abraham Maslow.

Self-actualization   The humanistic term for the inborn drive to realize our full potential and to develop all our talents and capabilities.

Rogers's Theory

To psychologist Carl Rogers (1902–1987), the most important component of personality is our **self-concept**, the way we see and feel about ourselves. Rogers emphasized that mental health and adjustment reflect the degree of overlap (congruence) between our perceived real and ideal selves (see the following **Test Yourself**). This self-perception is relatively stable over time and develops from our life experiences, particularly the feedback and perception of others.

Self-concept   The image of oneself that develops from interactions with others and life experiences.

🔴 PA Practical Application

Test Yourself: Measuring Your Personal Self-Concept

Stop for a moment and briefly describe yourself as you'd *ideally* like to be and as how you *actually* are. Now draw two circles, labeled "real self" and "ideal self," depicting how much your two perceived selves overlap.

(a) According to Carl Rogers, if your real self and ideal self are nearly the same, with considerable overlap in the two circles, you have *congruence* between your two "selves" and a positive self-concept.

(b) Unfortunately, many people have experienced negative life events and feedback from others that have led to negative self-concepts. In Rogers's view, poor mental health and personality

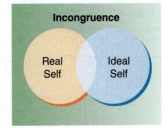

a. Well-adjusted individual
Considerable overlap between the ideal and real selves.

b. Poorly adjusted individual
Little overlap between the ideal and real selves.

maladjustment develop from a mismatch, or *incongruence*, between our ideal and real selves.

Why do some people develop negative self-concepts and poor mental health (see cartoon)? Rogers believed that such outcomes generally result from early childhood experiences with parents and other adults who make their love and acceptance *conditional* and contingent on behaving in certain ways and expressing only certain feelings. Imagine being a child who is repeatedly told that your naturally occurring negative feelings and behaviors (which we all have) are totally unacceptable and unlovable. Can you see how your self-concept may become distorted? And why as an adult you might develop a shy, avoidant personality, always doubting the love and approval of others because they don't know "the real person hiding inside"?

LOW SELF-ESTEEM

Unconditional positive regard
Rogers's term for love and acceptance with no "strings" (contingencies) attached.

To help children develop their fullest personality and life potential, Rogers cautioned that adults need to create an atmosphere of **unconditional positive regard**—love and acceptance with no "strings" (contingencies) attached (Ray & Jayne, 2016; Schneider et al., 2015). **[AQ5]** Interestingly, parents who engage in responsive caregiving, a form of unconditional positive regard (see photo), also tend to show this same pattern of behavior toward their spouses, which in turn leads to higher levels of relationship satisfaction (Millings et al., 2013). This suggests that unconditional positive regard is important in all types of relationships.

This is NOT to say that adults must approve of everything a child does. Rogers emphasizes that we must separate the value of the person from his or her behaviors—encouraging the person's innate positive nature, while discouraging destructive or hostile behaviors. Humanistic psychologists in general suggest that both children and adults must control their behavior so they can develop a healthy self-concept and satisfying relationships with others (**Figure 12.19**).

Maslow's Theory

FIGURE 12.19 Unconditional positive regard In response to a child who is angry and hits his or her younger sibling, the parent acknowledges that it is the behavior that is unacceptable, and not the child: "I know you're angry with your sister, but we don't hit. And you won't be able to play with her for a while unless you control your anger."

Like Rogers, Abraham Maslow believed there is a basic goodness to human nature and a natural tendency toward *self-actualization*. Maslow saw personality development as a natural progression from lower to higher levels—a basic *hierarchy of needs* (Chapter 11). As newborns, we focus on physiological needs like hunger and thirst, and then as we grow and develop, we move on through four higher levels (**Figure 12.20**). Surveys from 123 countries found that people from around the world do share a focus on the same basic needs, and when those needs are met, they report higher levels of happiness (Tay & Diener, 2011).

According to Maslow, self-actualization is our inborn drive to develop all our talents and capacities. It requires understanding our own potential, accepting ourselves and others as unique individuals, and taking a problem-centered approach to life (Maslow, 1970). Self-actualization is an ongoing process of growth rather than an end product or accomplishment.

Maslow believed that only a few, rare individuals, such as Albert Einstein, Mohandas Gandhi, and Eleanor Roosevelt, become fully self-actualized. However, he saw self-actualization as part of every person's basic hierarchy of needs, and as an ongoing process of growth rather than an end product or accomplishment. (See Chapter 11 for more information about Maslow's theory.)

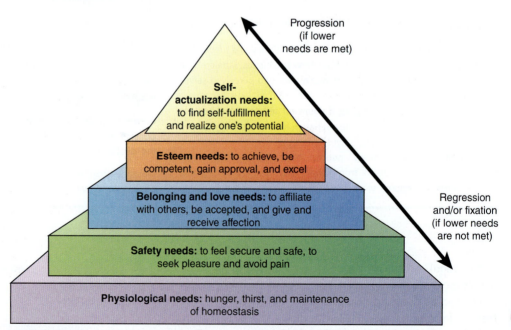

FIGURE 12.20 Maslow's hierarchy of needs Although our natural movement is upward from physical needs toward the highest level, *self-actualization*, Maslow believed we sometimes "regress" toward a lower level—especially under stressful conditions. During national disasters, people first rush to stockpile food and water (physiological needs) and then often clamor for a strong leader to take over, enforce the rules, and make things right (safety needs).

Evaluating Humanistic Theories

Humanistic psychology was extremely popular during the 1960s and 1970s. It was seen as a refreshing new perspective on personality after the negative determinism of the psychoanalytic approach and the mechanical nature of learning theories (Chapter 6). Although this early popularity has declined, humanistic theories have provided valuable insights that are useful for personal growth and self-understanding. They likewise play a major role in contemporary counseling and psychotherapy, as well as in modern childrearing, education, and managerial practices (D'Souza & Gurin, 2016; Hopper, 2019; Proctor et al., 2016).

However, humanistic theories have been criticized (Berger, 2015; Henwood et al., 2014; Nolan, 2012) for several reasons, including:

1. **Naïve assumptions**   Some critics suggest that humanistic theories are unduly optimistic and overlook the negative aspects of human nature. Hitler was "self-actualized," was goal-driven, and believed he was fulfilling his potential. Furthermore, how would humanists explain deliberate mass genocide of large groups of people, horrific racist and terrorist attacks, and humankind's ongoing history of war and murder?

2. **Poor testability and inadequate evidence**   Like many psychoanalytic terms and concepts, humanistic concepts such as unconditional positive regard and self-actualization are difficult to define operationally and to test scientifically. Others suggest that humanistic theories don't account for the change in personality. For example, data from a meta-analysis of 191 studies reveals that our levels of self-esteem tend to increase from ages 4 to 11, remain stable from 11 to 15, increase strongly until age 60, remain stable until 70, and then slightly decline until age 90 (Orth et al., 2018).

3. **Narrowness**   Like trait theories, humanistic theories have been criticized for merely describing personality rather than explaining it. For example, where does the motivation for self-actualization come from? To say that it is an "inborn drive" doesn't satisfy those who favor using experimental research and scientific standards to study personality.

Retrieval Practice 12.4 | Humanistic Theories

Self-Test   Completing this self-test, and then checking your answers by clicking on the answer button or by looking in Appendix B, will provide immediate feedback and helpful practice for exams.

1. The _____ approach emphasizes internal experiences, like feelings, thoughts, and the basic worth of the individual.

   a. humanistic
   b. psychodynamic
   c. personalistic
   d. motivational

2. Rogers suggested that _____ is necessary for a child to develop his or her fullest personality and life potential.

   a. authoritative parenting
   b. a challenging environment
   c. unconditional positive regard
   d. a friendly neighborhood

3. _____ believed in the basic goodness of individuals and their natural tendency toward self-actualization.

   a. Karen Horney
   b. Alfred Adler
   c. Abraham Maslow
   d. Carl Jung

4. To become self-actualized, we need to _____.

   a. understand our own potential
   b. accept ourselves and others as unique individuals
   c. take a problem-centered approach to life
   d. all of these options

5. A major criticism of humanistic psychology is that most of its concepts and assumptions _____.

   a. are invalid
   b. are unreliable
   c. are naive
   d. lack a theoretical foundation

Q Test Your Critical Thinking

1. Do you agree with Rogers that unconditional positive regard from parents is key to healthy personality development? Why or why not?

2. Thinking of the traits of a fully self-actualized person, can you identify someone who exhibits all or most of these qualities? Do you consider self-actualization a worthy goal? Why or why not?

Real World Application Question

[AQ5] What parenting skills are also associated with increased marital satisfaction?

MAD_Production/Shutterstock.com

Hint: Look in the text for **[AQ5]**

12.5 Social-Cognitive Theories

Retrieval Practice While reading the upcoming sections, respond to each Learning Objective in your own words.

Review the major concepts of social-cognitive theories of personality.

- **Explain** Bandura's approach to personality.
- **Describe** Rotter's theory of personality.

- **Summarize** the strengths and weaknesses of the social-cognitive perspective on personality.

Real World Application Question

[AQ6] Can spending time in a foreign country change your personality?

As you've just seen, psychoanalytic/psychodynamic, trait, and humanistic theories all tend to focus on internal, personal factors in personality development. In contrast, *social-cognitive* theories emphasize the influence of our *social* interpersonal interactions with the environment, along with our *cognitions*—our thoughts, feelings, expectations, and values.

Bandura's Theory

Self-efficacy Bandura's term for a person's learned expectation of success in a given situation; another term for self-confidence.

Albert Bandura (see Chapter 6) has played a major role in reintroducing thought processes into personality theory. Cognition, or thought, is central to his concept of **self-efficacy**, which is very similar to our everyday notion of self-confidence (Bandura, 1997, 2011; Herrero-Hahn et al., 2017; Raeder et al., 2019).

According to Bandura, if you have a strong sense of self-efficacy, you believe you can generally succeed and reach your goals, regardless of past failures and current obstacles. Your degree of self-efficacy will in turn affect which challenges you choose to accept and the effort you expend in reaching your goals (Bruning & Kauffman, 2016; Phan & Ngu, 2016). See the **PP** **PositivePsych** feature on the next page.

Reciprocal determinism Bandura's belief that internal personal factors, the environment, and the individual's behavior all work as interacting (reciprocal) determinants of each other.

How does self-efficacy affect personality? Bandura sees personality as being shaped by **reciprocal determinism**, which means that internal factors within the *person* (his or her personality, thoughts, expectations, etc.), the external *environment*, and his or her *behavior* all work as interacting (reciprocal) determinants of each other (**Figure 12.21**).

Interestingly, one study found that the research participants' self-efficacy could be negatively affected by reading information about how their behavior made no meaningful impact on climate change (e.g., using less water, turning down the heat) (Salomon et al., 2017). After reading the information, they not only reported less intention toward conservation but even increased their energy consumption 1 week later. On a more positive note, perceived self-efficacy in older adults is associated with better cognitive functions, and it may even help reduce stress and prevent cognitive decline (Korten et al., 2017).

FIGURE 12.21 **Bandura's theory of reciprocal determinism** According to Albert Bandura, personality is determined by a three-way, reciprocal interaction of the internal characteristics of the person, the external environment, and the person's behavior.

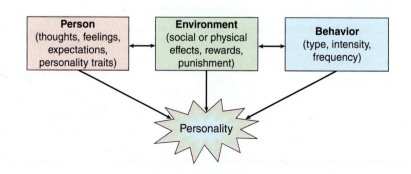

PP **Practical Application: PositivePsych**

Self-Efficacy in Daily Life

(APA Goal 1.3) Describe applications of psychology

The classic children's story *The Little Engine That Could* illustrates how we learn self-efficacy as a result of our personal experiences with success (see photo). The little engine starts up a steep hill, saying, "I think I can, I think I can." After lots of hard work and perseverance, she ends up at the top of the hill and says, "I thought I could, I thought I could."

Bandura emphasized that self-efficacy is a *learned* expectation of success, but only in a given situation. It doesn't necessarily transfer to other circumstances. Bandura would suggest that the little engine's newfound self-efficacy will help her climb future hills. However, it wouldn't necessarily improve her overall speed or ability to turn sharp corners. Similarly, self-defense training significantly affects a woman's belief that she can improve her odds of escaping from or disabling a potential assailant or rapist (Weitlauf et al., 2001). But it does not lead her to feel more capable in all areas of her life.

How then can we transfer self-efficacy to other parts of our everyday life? If you've experienced success as an athlete, a parent, or even a video game player, consider how the skills you've demonstrated in these areas can be transferred to your academic life. Instead of saying, "I just can't find time to study" or, "I never do well on tests," remind yourself of how your ongoing

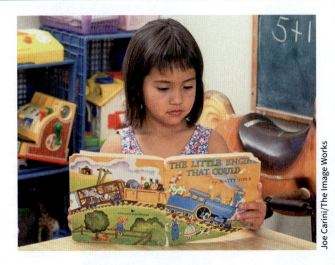

Joe Carini/The Image Works

success in athletics, parenting, or video games has resulted from good time management, hours of practice, patience, hard work, and perseverance. Applying skills that are the same as or similar to skills you've successfully used before will help move you from, "I can't" to "I think I can." And then when you get your first high grade in a difficult course, you can move on to, "I know I can, I know I can."

Using Bandura's concept of self-efficacy, do you see how your own beliefs will affect how others respond to you and thereby influence your chance for success? Your belief ("I can succeed") will affect behaviors ("I'll work hard and ask for a promotion"), which in turn will affect the environment ("My employer recognized my efforts and promoted me").

Rotter's Theory

Julian Rotter's theory is similar to Bandura's in that it suggests that learning experiences create *cognitive expectancies* that guide behavior and influence the environment (Rotter, 1954, 1990). According to Rotter, your behavior or personality is determined by: (1) what you expect to happen following a specific action, and (2) the reinforcement value attached to specific outcomes.

To understand your personality and behavior, Rotter used personality tests that measure your internal versus external *locus of control* (Chapter 3). Rotter's tests ask participants to respond to statements such as, "People get ahead in this world primarily by luck and connections rather than by hard work and perseverance" and, "When someone doesn't like you, there is little you can do about it."

As you may suspect, people with an *external locus of control* think the environment and external forces have primary control over their lives, whereas people with an *internal locus of control* think they can personally control events in their lives through their own efforts. Despite the satirical humor in the cartoon (**Figure 12.22**), research

Mike Twohy/Conde Nast/The Cartoon Bank

"We're encouraging people to become involved in their own rescue."

FIGURE 12.22   **Locus of control and achievement**
Despite this cartoon's humorous message, research does link a perception of control with higher achievement, greater life satisfaction, better emotional stability, and overall mental health (e.g., Albert & Dahling, 2016; Chiang et al., 2019; Nowicki, 2016).

finds that people with an internal locus of control are generally healthier and more productive. However, recall from Chapter 3 that under certain stressful situations, such as being the victim of bullying, it may be better to temporarily adopt an external locus of control. This means that when we face truly uncontrollable external events, it's sometimes more advantageous to place the cause of the event on external forces and the cause of others' behavior upon individuals—in this case the person doing the bullying (Reknes et al., 2019).

Evaluating Social-Cognitive Theories

primagefactory/123RF

The social-cognitive perspective holds several advantages. First, it offers testable, objective hypotheses and operationally defined terms, and it relies on empirical data. Second, social-cognitive theories emphasize the role of cognitive processes in personality, and that both personality and situations predict behavior in real-world situations (Sherman et al., 2015). **[AQ6]** Relatedly, high school students who study abroad (thereby experiencing a change in environment) show greater changes in personality than those who do not (Hutteman et al., 2015). For instance, exchange students showed substantial increases in their self-esteem compared to those who stayed home (see photo).

As we discussed earlier, there's a wealth of modern research connecting the Big Five personality traits to success in both work and academic settings, and these traits are closely related to the social-cognitive traits of self-efficacy and an internal locus of control. However, critics argue that social-cognitive theories focus too much on situational influences, and fail to adequately acknowledge the stability of personality, as well as sociocultural, emotional, and biological influences (Ahmetoglu & Chamorro-Premuzic, 2013; Cea & Barnes, 2015; Middleton et al., 2018). One of the most influential studies on the potential stability of personality traits is the now classic "marshmallow test"—the lead researcher, Walter Mischel, was even a guest on the *Stephen Colbert* show. For more information, see the following **STH** **Scientific Thinking Highlight**.

STH Scientific Thinking Highlight

Could You Pass the Stanford Marshmallow Test?

(APA Goal 2.1) Use scientific reasoning to interpret psychological phenomena

Beginning in the early 1960s and 1970s, psychologist Walter Mischel and his colleagues conducted numerous experiments on *delayed gratification*, which is defined as "putting off a pleasurable experience in exchange for a larger but later reward." In their most famous study, they recruited over 600 children between the ages of 4 and 6 who attended a preschool at Stanford University (Mischel & Ebbesen, 1970). Each child was led into a room and seated alone at a table with a very tempting marshmallow within easy reach. They were then told they could eat the marshmallow at any time, but if they waited for 15 minutes, they would get two marshmallows. The child was then left alone, while the researchers watched and recorded how long each child would wait before giving into temptation.

Can you predict what happened? See **Figure 12. 23**.

What makes this very simple research important is that the researchers continued to study these children for more than 40 years. The amount of time the children were able to delay eating the first marshmallow, and wait for the second one (delayed gratification), was supposedly a significant predictor of who ended up with higher SAT scores, lower levels of substance

Courtesy of Lee Decker

FIGURE 12.23 **Psychology and marshmallows?** Some children in this study quietly stared at the marshmallow while waiting for the experimenter to return. Others wiggled in their chairs, kicked at the table, smelled or petted the marshmallow, sang songs, or simply looked away—all in an attempt to resist temptation. And, as expected of preschoolers, a large number of children immediately ate the marshmallow as soon as the researcher left the room. Only a third of the preschoolers delayed gratification long enough to get the second marshmallow.

abuse, a lower likelihood of obesity, better responses to stress, greater academic performance and social skills as reported by their parents, and generally better scores in a range of other life measures (Caleza et al., 2016; Mischel, 1966, 2014; Mischel et al., 2011).

Why do we say "supposedly" about the research findings? At least one attempt to replicate the original study found that the results were significantly less than initially reported (Watts et al., 2018). Despite the weak results, however, there are still two key things to remember about this marshmallow study. First, it's a good example of longitudinal research (**Figure 12.24**). Second, the ability to delay gratification is a valuable personality trait. As you know, in every stage of our lives there are always numerous "marshmallows"—a fun party versus studying, an attractive new sexual partner versus our committed relationship, a fancy new sports car versus saving for retirement—that will potentially distract us from our long-term goals and personal best interests. The "simple" answer appears to be that when faced with critical decisions we need to continually make mindful choices. If you'd like more information on the importance of self-control and delay of gratification with numerous practical applications, see Mischel's book *The Marshmallow Test* (Mischel, 2014).

Q   Test Your Scientific Thinking

As you recall from Chapter 1, scientific thinking is an approach to information that combines a high degree of *skepticism* (questioning what "everybody knows") with *objectivity* (using empirical data to separate fantasy from reality) and with *rationalism* (practicing logical reasoning). Using these three principles, consider the following questions:

1. **Skepticism**   What do you think? What would you have done as a preschool child in this same situation? Would you have eaten the marshmallow right away or delayed your gratification? Do you think this test would accurately predict your current level of achievement and personality? Scientific thinkers approach ideas and research conclusions with skepticism.

2. **Objectivity**   Are the author's assumptions supported by the data? As we discussed here, and in the Scientific Thinking Highlight for Chapter 1, later attempts to replicate this so-called marshmallow study found that their results were much weaker than those found by Mischel and his colleagues. Scientific thinkers carefully analyze data for value and content. Could this be an example of participant bias, with the children trying to please the adults? Or could the findings reflect possible demand characteristics and experimenter bias, with the researchers inadvertently signaling to at least some of the children the desired responses? What about the third-variable problem, sample bias, and so on? As discussed in Chapter 1, the longitudinal follow-up research found that children tested in 2000 waited 1 minute longer than those in the 1980s and 2 minutes longer than those tested in the 1960s. The researchers suggested that the generational differences may be explained by the fact that more children are attending preschool, where they

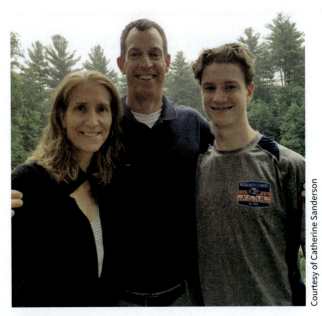

Courtesy of Catherine Sanderson

FIGURE 12.24   **A personal example of longitudinal research**   The spouse of one of the authors of this book (CAS) was one of the original participants in the marshmallow study. The fact that the researchers have continued to follow up with him—and his wife and children—provides a good example of the decades-long commitment and diligence required in longitudinal research. Also, as evidence of psychology's strict ethical guidelines for research, even now, over 40 years later, the researchers will not disclose whether or not the author's husband ate the marshmallow.

learn skills like self-control (Carlson et al., 2018). Do you see why scientific thinkers gather information and delay judgment until adequate data is available?

3. **Rationalism**   Setting aside the limited data from other research, can we logically conclude that the children who ate (or did not eat) the marshmallow right away will be less (or more) likely to succeed in later life? Could it be that the ability to delay gratification is better linked with parental beliefs, religious training, socioeconomic status, or other factors? What about the research premise that delay of gratification is a valuable trait? Logic dictates that to achieve our long-term goals, we must control our desire for immediate pleasure. Smokers give up the pleasure of cigarettes in order to live a healthier and longer life.

Does this mean we can accept the basic premise even though the data is questionable? This is where rationalism is a bit tricky but still useful. Throughout our lives, there will be many instances where we won't have empirical data to guide our decisions. Can you see that good scientific thinking sometimes allows us to accept certain ideas that make logical and rational sense even though they're not "research backed"?

Before going on, be sure to complete the final Retrieval Practice, and then answer the critical thinking questions in the **Test Your Critical Thinking**.

Retrieval Practice 12.5 | Social-Cognitive Theories

Self-Test Completing this self-test, and then checking your answers by clicking on the answer button or by looking in Appendix B, will provide immediate feedback and helpful practice for exams.

1. According to Bandura, _____ relies on a person's belief about whether he or she can successfully engage in behaviors related to personal goals.

   a. self-actualization   **c.** self-efficacy

   b. self-esteem   **d.** self-congruence

2. Bandura's theory of _____ suggests that the person, behavior, and environment all interact to produce personality.

   a. self-actualization   **c.** self-efficacy

   b. self-esteem maximization   **d.** reciprocal determinism

3. _____ suggests that learning experiences create cognitive expectancies that guide behavior and influence the environment.

   a. Walter Mischel   **c.** Abraham Maslow

   b. Julian Rotter   **d.** Carl Sagan

4. According to Rotter, people with a(n) _____ believe the environment and external forces control events, whereas those with a(n) _____ believe in personal control.

   a. self-actualized personality; efficacy personality

   b. external locus of control; internal locus of control

   c. fatalistic view; humanistic opinion

   d. global locus of control; selfish locus of control

5. A criticism of the social-cognitive approach is that it focuses too much on _____ in understanding personality.

   a. scientific research   **c.** situational influences

   b. unconscious forces   **d.** expectancies

Q Test Your Critical Thinking

1. How would Bandura's social-cognitive concept of self-efficacy explain why bright students sometimes don't do well in college?

2. Do you have an internal or external locus of control? How might this affect your academic and lifetime achievement?

Real World Application Question

[AQ6] Can spending time in a foreign country change your personality?

primagefactory/123RF

Hint: Look in the text for **[AQ6]**

Q Test Your Critical Thinking

Did you notice or wonder why we provided six Real World Application Questions [AQ1–AQ6] throughout this chapter? We've found that they not only help you to engage with and master the material, they also have an important and lasting impact on your critical thinking skills. For additional mastery and enrichment, consider the following questions:

1. As first discussed in Chapter 9 and throughout this chapter, early childhood relationships, particularly between parent and child, are very important to our personality development and overall psychological health. According to the five psychosexual stages of development, how might Freud interpret the photo of this mother and son's obvious attachment to one another? Can you think of an alternative, more logical, explanation for their attachment?

2. Can you identify one or more defense mechanisms that you use in your life? If you find them to be unhealthy, what can you do to change them?

3. How would Rogers's emphasis on unconditional positive regard and Bandura's social-cognitive concept of self-efficacy relate to this mother's display of pleasure at her son's attempt to dry her hair?

4. If you agree that self-actualization is a worthy goal, what are you doing to move in that direction?

5. Which theory of personality discussed in this chapter do you find most useful in understanding yourself and others? Why?

Cameron/Corbis/Getty Images

Summary

12.1 Understanding Personality   386

- **Personality** is defined as unique and relatively stable patterns of thoughts, feelings, and actions.
- Certain brain areas may contribute to personality. However, neurochemistry seems to offer more precise data on how biology influences personality. Research in *behavioral genetics* indicates that genetic factors also strongly influence personality.
- Psychologists use four basic methods to measure or assess personality: interviews, observations, objective tests, and projective techniques.

12.2 Psychoanalytic/Psychodynamic Theories   396

- Freud believed that the mind contained three *levels of consciousness*: conscious, preconscious, and **unconscious**. He proposed that most psychological disorders originate from unconscious memories and instincts.
- Freud also asserted that personality was composed of the **id**, **ego**, and **superego**. When the ego fails to satisfy both the id and the superego, anxiety reportedly slips into conscious awareness, which triggers **defense mechanisms**.
- Freud proposed that all children go through five **psychosexual stages**: oral, anal, phallic, latency, and genital. How specific conflicts at each of these stages are resolved is supposedly important to personality development.
- *Neo-Freudians* such as Adler, Jung, and Horney were influential followers of Freud who later rejected major aspects of Freudian theory. Adler emphasized the inferiority complex and the compensating will-to-power. Jung introduced the **collective unconscious** and **archetypes**. Horney stressed the importance of basic anxiety and refuted Freud's idea of penis envy, replacing it with power envy.

12.3 Trait Theories   403

- Early trait theorists, like Allport, believed that the best way to understand personality was to arrange a person's unique personality **traits** into a hierarchy. Cattell and Eysenck later reduced the list of possible personality traits using *factor analysis*.
- The **five-factor model (FFM)** is the most promising modern personality theory. It identified five major dimensions or traits: *openness*, *conscientiousness*, *extraversion*, *agreeableness*, and *neuroticism*.

12.4 Humanistic Theories   411

- Humanistic theories focus on internal feelings, thoughts, and sense of basic worth.
- According to Rogers, mental health and adjustment are related to the degree of congruence between our **self-concept** and life experiences. Rogers argued that poor mental health results when young children do not receive **unconditional positive regard** from caregivers.
- Maslow saw personality as the quest to fulfill basic physiological needs and to move toward the highest level of **self-actualization**.

12.5 Social-Cognitive Theories   414

- Social-cognitive theorists emphasize the importance of our interactions with the environment, along with our cognitions.
- According to Bandura, **self-efficacy** affects which challenges we choose to accept and the effort we expend in reaching goals. His concept of **reciprocal determinism** states that our self-efficacy beliefs also affect others' responses to us.
- Rotter's theory says that learning experiences create *cognitive expectancies* that guide behavior and influence the environment. Rotter believed that having an internal versus external *locus of control* affects personality and achievement.

Key Terms

Retrieval Practice   Write a definition for each term before turning back to the referenced page to check your answer.

Kuttelvaserova Stuchelova/Shutterstock.com

CHAPTER **13**

Psychological Disorders

Real World Application Questions

Things you'll learn in Chapter 13

[AQ1] How often is the insanity defense successful in criminal trials?

[AQ2] Can so-called "trigger warnings" actually provoke and prolong anxiety disorders?

[AQ3] How do electronic devices and social media affect our mental health?

[AQ4] Are children who experience trauma at increased risk of developing schizophrenia later in life?

[AQ5] Are most people with antisocial personality disorder above average in intelligence?

[AQ6] Do certain psychological disorders exist in some cultures but not in others?

Throughout the chapter, look for the [AQ1]–[AQ6] icons. They indicate where the text addresses these questions.

Iakov Filimonov/Shutterstock.com

CHAPTER OUTLINE

13.1 # Understanding Psychological Disorders

LEARNING OBJECTIVES

Retrieval Practice   While reading the upcoming sections, respond to each Learning Objective in your own words.

Summarize the study of psychological disorders.

- **Define** psychological disorders and the three criteria for identifying them.
- **Review** the myths, stigma, and discrimination surrounding mental illness.

- **Explain** the seven perspectives regarding psychological disorders.
- **Discuss** the pros and cons of classifying disorders and the use of the *Diagnostic and Statistical Manual of Mental Disorders (DSM)*.

Real World Application Question

[AQ1] How often is the insanity defense successful in criminal trials?

This chapter begins with a discussion of how psychological disorders are described, explained, and classified. Then we explore three major categories of psychological disorders: anxiety disorders, depressive and bipolar disorders, and schizophrenia. Next we cover the other disorders, including neurodevelopmental, obsessive-compulsive, dissociative, and personality disorders. We close with important key factors related to psychological disorders.

Describing and Explaining Psychological Disorders

Most people agree that neither the artist who stays awake for 72 hours finishing a painting nor the shooter who kills school children is behaving normally. But what exactly is "normal"? How do we distinguish between eccentricity in the first case and abnormal behavior in the second? It's obviously difficult to distinguish normal from abnormal behavior. Who gets to decide? What are the criteria and cut-off points?

Understanding Psychological Disorders   Most mental health professionals agree that the term "abnormal behavior" is misleading and confusing. The preferred term is **psychological disorder**, which can be defined as patterns of behaviors, thoughts, or emotions considered pathological (diseased or disordered) for one or more of three reasons: *deviance, dysfunction,* or *distress* (**Table 13.1**). The study of abnormal behavior

Psychological disorder
Patterns of behaviors, thoughts, or emotions considered pathological (diseased or disordered) for one or more of three reasons: deviance, dysfunction, and distress.

TABLE 13.1   Three Common Criteria for Identifying Psychological Disorders

Criteria	DSM-5 Possible Examples	Limitations/Problems
1. Deviance Behaviors, thoughts, or emotions that deviate from a society or culture's norms, values, or laws	*Paraphilia* Sexual attraction to unusual sexual activities or objects, which leads to social difficulties or distress.	People and societies often disagree about what is deviant (e.g., in some cultures, kissing is considered repulsive, whereas the clothing and behavior of Lady Gaga is deviant in the U.S., but generally tolerated in celebrities).
2. Dysfunction Behaviors, thoughts, or emotions that interfere with daily functioning	*Major Depressive Disorder* Recurrent depressive symptoms, such as sadness, lethargy, or loss of pleasure, which have elevated to the point that they markedly interfere with the individual's occupational or social life.	It may be difficult to determine when behavior, thoughts, or emotions begin to interfere with daily functioning (e.g., individuals suffering from depression may fail to recognize that their moods and behaviors are causing serious relationship and/or occupational problems).
3. Distress Behaviors, thoughts, or emotions that lead to significant personal distress	*Anxiety disorders* Problems characterized by disabling (uncontrollable and disruptive) fear or anxiety, which markedly interfere with the individual's occupational or social life.	What's distressing to some people is not to others (e.g., an individual's unrealistic and uncontrollable fear of spiders might be distressing to that person but not to others, whereas someone with an antisocial personality disorder will hurt others, while experiencing little or no personal distress or remorse).

Karwai Tang/Getty Images Entertainment/Getty Images

Psychological disorder
Pop star Lady Gaga (pictured here) has been voted the world's best-loved eccentric celebrity. She is considered by most to be entertaining—and certainly not abnormal or mentally ill.

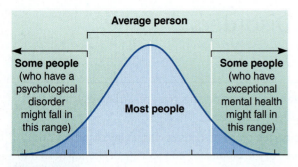

FIGURE 13.1 The normal curve and general mental health
Note how most individuals fall in the middle range of overall mental health. However, some who have a psychological disorder might fall to the far left of the curve, whereas others who have exceptional mental health might fall to the far right.

and psychological disorders is called *psychopathology.* As you read this chapter, keep in mind that abnormal behavior and psychological disorders, like intelligence and creativity, are not composed of two discrete categories—"normal" and "abnormal." Instead, mental health lies along a somewhat normal curve (see **Figure 13.1**).

When considering these three criteria for psychological disorders, also remember that no single criterion is adequate by itself. Furthermore, judgments of what is personally distressing and what is deviant or dysfunctional vary historically and cross-culturally. Perhaps the most serious concern in modern times is the common misperception of the actual danger posed by those with psychological disorders. See the **PAH Practical Application Highlight** for more coverage of this and other myths about mental illness.

PAH Practical Application Highlight

Myths, Stigma, and Discrimination in Mental Illness

(APA Goal 1.3) Describe applications of psychology

As shown in **Table 13.2**, there are numerous myths and misconceptions about mental illness. These false beliefs can lead to significant problems, including the following:

- Bullying, harassment, and physical violence
- Reluctance to seek help or treatment
- Limited public understanding of or support for funding mental health treatment
- Fewer opportunities for housing, education, employment, health care, and social activities
- Lack of support and understanding from friends and family

These reactions can in turn lead to devastating, even life-threatening, consequences. In this section, we'll explore two additional and very serious issues—stigma and discrimination.

Describing Myths, Stigma, and Discrimination   In 2010, the U.S. Surgeon General published a landmark mental health report identifying myths and *stigma* as a public health concern. What exactly is stigma? Mental health officials have often used "stigma" when referring to the publics' generally negative attitude toward mental illness and related negative stereotypes in which mental illness is viewed as a mark of disgrace. More recently, others have suggested that *discrimination* is a better term because the problem is actually a civil and human rights issue (Abderholden, 2019).

TABLE 13.2   **Common Myths About Psychological Disorders**

• **Myth: Mentally ill people are often dangerous and unpredictable.** **Fact:** Most people with psychological disorders, even those out of touch with reality, pose no immediate danger to themselves or others. In fact, they are far more likely to be the *victims* of violence than the perpetrators. The stereotype that connects mental illness and violence persists because of prejudice, selective media attention, and negative portrayals in movies and on television.	• **Myth: Psychological disorders are a sign of personal weakness.** **Fact:** Just as individuals with cancer or other diseases are normally not held responsible for their illness, people shouldn't be blamed for their psychological disorders. Like all other illnesses, psychological disorders are a function of many factors, such as exposure to stress, genetic predispositions, a host of personal and sociocultural experiences, and family background.
• **Myth: People with psychological disorders act in bizarre ways and are very different from normal people.** **Fact:** This is true for only a small minority of individuals and during a relatively brief portion of their lives. In fact, sometimes even mental health professionals find it difficult to distinguish normal from abnormal behaviors without formal screening.	• **Myth: A mentally ill person is only suited for low-level jobs and will never fully recover.** **Fact:** With therapy, the vast majority of those diagnosed with psychological disorders eventually improve and go on to lead normal, productive lives. Moreover, the extreme symptoms of some psychological disorders are generally only temporary. U.S. President Abraham Lincoln, British Prime Minister Winston Churchill, scientist Isaac Newton, and other high-achieving people all suffered from serious psychological disorders at various times throughout their careers.

Sources: Arkowitz & Lilienfeld, 2017; Kring & Johnson, 2018; National Alliance on Mental Health, 2015; Survey: Americans Becoming More Open, 2019.

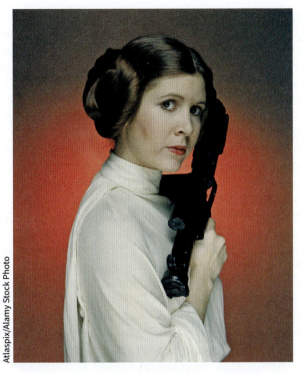

Atlaspix/Alamy Stock Photo

Carrie Frances Fisher (1956–2016)—a mental health hero The original Princess Leia of the famous *Star Wars* film series, Carrie Fisher, is remembered today as a famous and beloved Hollywood star. She's also celebrated as a mental health hero for her groundbreaking stance against the stigma of mental illness. Fisher told the *Huffington Post*, "At times, being bipolar can be an all-consuming challenge, requiring a lot of stamina and even more courage, so if you're living with this illness and functioning at all, it's something to be proud of, not ashamed of" (Holmes, 2016).

The good news is that simply educating others about mental health can reduce stigma and discrimination (see photo). For instance, when researchers provided fact-based literacy programs on mental health to children with a parent or family member suffering from a psychological disorder, they found that the youths' general understanding of mental health increased, as well as their use of positive coping strategies (Riebschleger et al., 2019). A recent survey of Americans also found that most adults have positive views about psychological disorders (Survey: Americans Becoming More Open, 2019). In fact, 87 percent of American adults agreed that having a mental health disorder is nothing to be ashamed of, and 86 percent said they believe that people with psychological disorders can get better.

Unfortunately, in this same survey, 39 percent of the respondents said they would view someone differently if they knew the person had a mental health disorder, and 33 percent agreed that "people with mental health disorders scare me." Sadly, young adults (18–34 years of age) reported the most shame and the poorest mental health of all those surveyed.

Dangers of Myths, Stigma, and Discrimination There's obviously a need for continuing education to combat the remaining myths, stigma, and discrimination surrounding mental illness—particularly given the media's intensive coverings of mass shootings

Joe Raedle/Getty Images News/Getty Images

Media coverage and mass shootings Following the murders of 17 people at Marjory Stoneman Douglas High School in Parkland, Florida, many people once again blamed mental health problems for the shootings (Qiu & Bank, 2018; Riggio, 2018). This occurred despite the fact that mass shootings involving serious mental illness represent only one percent of all gun homicides each year (Gold & Simon, 2016).

and the tendency to always focus blame on the mentally ill (see photo) (Baker, 2015; Mannarini & Rossi, 2019; Survey: Americans Becoming More Open, 2019).

To make matters worse, the media seldom, if ever, mentions the fact that people with mental illness are less often perpetrators of violence than they are victims of violence or a casualty of their own self-destructive behaviors (Arkowitz & Lilienfeld, 2017; Metzl & MacLeish, 2015).

What can you do as an individual?

- Carefully study the disorders described in this chapter and then explore the vast array of reliable resources available on the Internet (e.g., apa.org/; psychologicalscience.org/; aha. org; and ourworldindata.org/mental-health).

- Try not to think of psychological disorders as "problems" and the people who suffer from them as simply "victims limited by those problems." Focus instead on their achievements.

- Recognize that psychological disorders are largely invisible. It's easier to understand and support those who are blind, on crutches, or in a wheelchair. Because of the myths, stigma, and discrimination associated with mental illness, many famous and successful individuals are also reluctant to "come out," and therefore their accomplishments remain hidden from public awareness. Throughout this chapter, note how we include many photos of and stories about famous people with disorders to highlight their accomplishments and to provide positive role models.

The mentally ill frighten and embarrass us. And so we marginalize the people who most need our acceptance. What mental health needs is more sunlight, more candor, more unashamed conversation.

—Glenn Close (actress, mental health advocate)

FIGURE 13.2 **Witchcraft or mental illness?** During the European Renaissance, some people who may have been suffering from mental disorders were accused of witchcraft and tortured or hung.

Psychiatry The branch of medicine that deals with the diagnosis, treatment, and prevention of mental disorders.

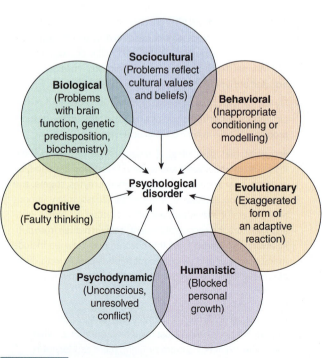

FIGURE 13.3 **Seven psychological perspectives** As you can see in this diagram, the seven major perspectives differ in their various explanations for psychological disorders, but there is considerable overlap.

Explaining Psychological Disorders

What causes abnormal behavior? Evidence suggests people in ancient times bore holes in the skulls of "patients" who, surprisingly, often survived the ordeal. Many believe this "surgery" was designed to treat head trauma, intracranial diseases, and to relieve pressure from mental disorders (e.g., Caruso & Sheehan, 2017; Kushner et al., 2018). In one form or another, this practice continued into fairly recent history, a process known as *trephining* or *trepanation* (see photo).

During the European Middle Ages, evil spirits and witchcraft were often blamed for causing psychological disorders. Patients were sometimes treated with an exorcism, which was a religious or spiritual practice designed to evict the so-called "demons" by making the troubled person's body inhospitable through lengthy prayers, fasting, and beatings (Campbell et al., 2017; Iheanacho et al., 2016; Stefanovics et al., 2016). Later, during the Renaissance period (14th to the 17th century), many believed that some individuals chose to consort with the Devil. These so-called "witches" were often tortured, imprisoned for life, or executed—often by drowning or hanging (**Figure 13.2**).

As the Renaissance ended, special mental hospitals called *asylums* began to appear in Europe. Initially designed to provide quiet retreats from the world and to protect society, the asylums unfortunately became overcrowded, inhumane prisons. Improvement came in 1792, when Philippe Pinel, a French physician, was placed in charge of a Parisian asylum. Believing that inmates' behavior was caused by underlying physical illness, he insisted that they be unshackled and removed from their dark, unheated cells. Fortunately, many inmates improved so dramatically that they could be released.

Today, Pinel's actions reflect the ideals of the modern *medical model*, which assumes that diseases (including mental illness) have physical causes that can be diagnosed, treated, and possibly cured and prevented. This medical model is the foundation of the branch of medicine known as **psychiatry**, which deals with the diagnosis, treatment, and prevention of mental disorders.

In contrast to this medical model, psychologists believe that focusing on "mental illness" overlooks important social and cultural factors, as well as our own personal thoughts, feelings, and actions that contribute to psychological disorders. Therefore, we take a multifaceted approach to explaining psychological disorders, as shown in **Figure 13.3**. For example, imagine yourself with an intense fear (or phobia) of rats. In your case, behavioral psychologists might look at your unique learning history and experiences with rats, whereas a biological psychologist might consider genetic factors, such as your parental history of high anxiety. In contrast, a psychologist from a sociocultural perspective might look at your sociocultural background. Some people live in conditions where rats present a clear and present danger; other people might have a phobia of owls given they come from a culture that fears owls, believing they are harbingers of death.

In addition to these seven psychological perspectives, psychologists generally agree that most aspects of human thoughts, feelings, and actions are influenced or controlled by an interaction between nature and nurture. For instance, a family history (one or more relatives with the disorder) increases the possibility that someone may inherit a biological vulnerability. Social, cultural, and environmental factors also affect whether or not this inherited predisposition will go on to become a psychological disorder (see photo).

Classifying Psychological Disorders

Having described and explained psychological disorders, we now need to classify those disorders into specific categories. Why? As you may have noticed in your basic biology courses, classification of animals into mammals, primates, and homo sapiens helps us organize a wide variety of animals into discrete and more coherent categories. Similar forms of classification are used in psychology. Can you see that without a clear, reliable system for classifying the wide range of psychological disorders, scientific research on them would be almost impossible, and communication among mental health professionals would be seriously impaired?

Sociocultural factors at work   Researchers have found that college students of Mexican heritage with migrant farming backgrounds have more symptoms of anxiety and depression than those without this type of background (Mejía & McCarthy, 2010). What environmental stressors might best explain such differences?

WHO Classification System   To create order and to encourage scientific research, the World Health Organization (WHO) has created and published several versions of their classification system. The most recent edition, the *International Classification of Diseases* (ICD-10), presents categories and statistics for the psychological disorders most prevalent around the world—see the sample in **Figure 13.4** (Ritchie & Roser, 2018).

DSM Classification System   Within the United States, mental health specialists generally use a different classification system, known as the ***Diagnostic and Statistical Manual of Mental Disorders (DSM)***. This manual has been updated and revised several times, and the latest version, the fifth edition, was published in 2013 (American Psychiatric Association, 2013). The current *DSM-5* identifies and describes the symptoms of approximately 400 disorders, which are grouped into 22 categories. Note that we list only 18 categories in **Table 13.3**. The first eight are discussed in this chapter, categories 9–15 are discussed in other chapters of this text, and categories 16–18 are beyond the scope of this book. Also, keep in mind that people may be diagnosed with more than one disorder at a time, a condition referred to as **comorbidity**. For instance, depression and substance abuse—or depression and anxiety—are often experienced together.

Why have there been so many revisions to the *DSM*? Each edition has expanded the list of disorders and changed the descriptions and categories to reflect the latest in scientific research. Consider the terms *neurosis* and *psychosis*. In previous editions of the *DSM*, the term "neurosis" reflected the belief that all neurotic conditions arise from unconscious conflicts (Chapter 12). Today, conditions that were previously grouped under the heading *neurosis* have been formally studied and redistributed as separate categories.

Unlike neurosis, the term *psychosis* is still listed in the current edition of the *DSM* because it remains useful for distinguishing the most severe psychological disorders, such as schizophrenia. **Psychosis** is generally defined as a serious psychological condition in which thoughts and perceptions are so impaired that the individual loses contact with external reality.

This loss of contact with reality is most evident in the two key features of psychosis—delusions and hallucinations. **Delusions** are false, imaginary beliefs that persist despite clear evidence to the contrary, such as delusions of grandeur or persecution. In comparison, **hallucinations** are false, imaginary

Diagnostic and Statistical Manual of Mental Disorders (DSM)   A manual developed by the American Psychiatric Association that is used primarily to classify psychological disorders.

Comorbidity   The co-occurrence of two or more disorders in the same person at the same time, as when a person suffers from both depression and alcoholism.

Psychosis   A serious psychological condition in which thoughts and perceptions are so impaired that the individual loses contact with external reality.

Delusion   A false, imaginary belief that persists despite clear evidence to the contrary, such as delusions of grandeur or persecution; a symptom associated with psychosis.

Hallucination   A false, imaginary sensory perception that occurs without an external, objective source, such as hearing voices that others cannot hear; a symptom associated with psychosis.

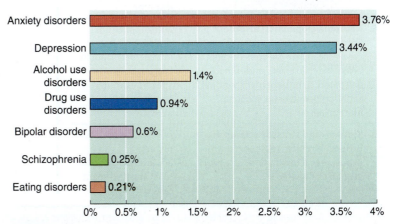

FIGURE 13.4   **Proportion of major psychological disorders worldwide, 2017**

Source: https://ourworldindata.org/mental-health

TABLE 13.3   DSM Sample Subcategories of Psychological Disorders*

Name and Description	Example	Name and Description	Example
1. **Anxiety disorders** Problems resulting from disabling (uncontrollable and disruptive) fear or anxiety.	• specific phobia • social anxiety disorder • generalized anxiety disorder • panic disorder	10. **Sleep–wake disorders** Dissatisfaction regarding the quality, timing, and amount of sleep (see Chapter 5).	• insomnia disorder • hypersomnolence disorder • narcolepsy • central sleep apnea
2. **Depressive disorders** Problems characterized by depressive symptoms, such as sadness, lethargy, or loss of pleasure.	• major depressive disorder • disruptive mood dysregulation disorder	11. **Substance-related and addictive disorders** A cluster of cognitive, behavioral, and physiological symptoms related to alcohol, tobacco, other drugs, and gambling (see Chapter 5).	• alcohol use disorder • caffeine intoxication • opioid use disorder • stimulant use disorder
3. **Bipolar and related disorders** Problems associated with alternating episodes of depression and mania.	• bipolar I disorder • bipolar II disorder • cyclothymic disorder	12. **Sexual dysfunctions** Disorders involving problems with sexual arousal, desire, orgasm, or pain (see Chapter 10).	• erectile disorder • female sexual interest/arousal disorder • male hypoactive sexual desire disorder
4. **Schizophrenia spectrum and other psychotic disorders** Group of disorders characterized by delusions, hallucinations, disorganized thinking or motor behavior, and negative symptoms, such as diminished emotional expression.	• schizophrenia • schizoaffective disorder • delusional disorder	13. **Paraphilic disorders** Sexual attraction to unusual sexual activities or objects that leads to social difficulties or distress (see Chapter 10).	• voyeuristic disorder • frotteuristic disorder • sexual sadism disorder
5. **Obsessive-compulsive and related disorders** Group of disorders characterized by the presence of obsessions, compulsions, preoccupations, and repetitive behaviors or mental acts.	• obsessive-compulsive disorder • body dysmorphic disorder • hoarding disorder	14. **Gender dysphoria** Distress that may accompany the incongruence between a person's experienced or expressed gender and assigned gender (see optional Chapter 10).	• gender dysphoria
6. **Dissociative disorders** Group of disorders characterized by the disruption and discontinuity in the normal integration of consciousness, memory, identity, emotion, perception, body representation, motor control, and behavior.	• dissociative amnesia • depersonalization/derealization disorder • dissociative identity disorder	15. **Feeding and eating disorders** Problems related to persistent disturbance of eating or eating related behavior (see Chapter 11).	• anorexia nervosa • bulimia nervosa • binge-eating disorder • avoidant/restrictive food intake disorder
7. **Personality disorders** Problems related to an enduring pattern of experience and behavior that deviates markedly from the expectations of an individual's culture and leads to distress or impairment.	• borderline personality disorder • narc tic personality disorder • paranoid personality disorder • antisocial personality disorder	16. **Somatic symptom and related disorders** Problems related to an unusual preoccupation with physical health or physical symptoms producing significant distress and impairment.	• somatic symptom disorder • conversion disorder • factitious disorder
8. **Neurodevelopmental disorders** Developmental deficits that typically manifest early in development, often before the child enters grade school, and produce impairments of personal, social, academic, or occupational functioning.	• autism spectrum disorder • intellectual disability • language disorder • specific learning disorder	17. **Disruptive, impulse-control, and conduct disorders** Problems related to kleptomania (impulsive stealing), pyromania (setting of fires), and other disorders characterized by inability to resist impulses, drives, or temptations to perform certain acts harmful to self or others.	• intermittent explosive disorder • conduct disorder • kleptomania
9. **Trauma- and stressor-related disorders** Problems associated with exposure to a traumatic or stressful event (see Chapter 3).	• posttraumatic stress disorder • acute stress disorder • reactive attachment disorder	18. **Neurocognitive disorders** A group of disorders involving cognitive function, including Alzheimer's disease, Huntington's disease, and physical trauma to the brain.	• major and mild neurocognitive disorders due to traumatic brain injury or other factors • delirium

*Categories 1–8 are covered in this chapter, and 9–15 are discussed in Chapters 3, 5, 10, and 11.
Sources: Barlow et al., 2017; Kring & Johnson, 2018; Ritchie & Roser, 2018.

sensory perceptions that occur without an external objective source, such as hearing voices that others do not hear (see photo).

What about the term *insanity*? **Insanity** is a legal term indicating that a person cannot be held responsible for his or her actions, or is incompetent to manage his or her own affairs, because of mental illness. In the law, the definition of mental illness rests primarily on a person's inability to tell right from wrong. Unfortunately, many people still believe that most criminals who use the "insanity defense" are generally successful in avoiding punishment. **[AQ1]** However, as mentioned earlier, this defense is used in fewer than one percent of all cases that reach trial, and it's successful in only a fraction of those (see photo). Furthermore, according to the American Psychiatric Association, the "not guilty by reason of insanity" defendants generally spend just as much—or more—time confined in a psychiatric institution as they would have served if they'd been found guilty and sentenced to prison (Butera, 2018; McKinley & Ransom, 2018; Phillip, 2015.)

Take-Home Message   Although the term "insanity" is often used in the media and in casual conversations, it's seldom used by psychologists. People experience specific psychological disorders—they're not "insane."

Evaluating the *DSM* Classification System

Why do we need a *DSM*? It creates order and the classification of psychological disorders is essential to scientific study. Unfortunately, the *DSM* also has several limitations and potential problems (Clark et al., 2017; Ghaemi, 2018; Vandeleur et al., 2015). For example, critics suggest that it may be casting too wide a net and *overdiagnosing*. Given that insurance companies compensate physicians and psychologists only if each client is assigned a specific *DSM* code number, can you see how compilers of the *DSM* may be encouraged to add more diagnoses?

In addition, the *DSM-5* has been criticized for a potential *cultural bias*. It does provide two sections on cultural issues and cultural formulation, along with a glossary of cultural concepts of distress. However, critics suggest that the overall classification still reflects a Western European and U.S. perspective (Bredström, 2017; Hsu, 2016; Jacob, 2014).

Perhaps the most troubling criticism of the *DSM* is its possible overreliance on the medical model and the way it may unfairly label people. Consider the classic (and controversial) study conducted by David Rosenhan (1973) in which he and seven colleagues presented themselves at several hospital admissions offices complaining of hearing voices (a classic symptom of schizophrenia). Aside from making this single false complaint and providing false names and occupations, the researchers answered all questions truthfully. Not surprisingly, given their reported symptom, they were all diagnosed with differing psychological disorders and admitted to the hospital. Once there, the "patients" stopped reporting any symptoms and behaved as they normally would, yet none were ever recognized by hospital staff as phony. Although all eight of these pseudo-patients were eventually released, after an average stay of 19 days, seven out of the eight were assigned a label on their permanent medical record of "schizophrenia in remission."

What do you think about this Rosenhan study? It has been criticized on several accounts, but do you see how it demonstrates some of the inherent dangers and "stickiness" of labels? As mentioned earlier, the myths, stigma, and discrimination surrounding mental illness create numerous problems, including lifetime career and social barriers for those struggling with the disorder itself. We encourage you to keep this in mind as you study the upcoming disorders.

PK6289/iStock/Getty Images

Delusions and hallucinations versus illusions   As you may recall from Chapter 4, delusions and hallucinations are not the same as *illusions*, which are misleading perceptions of reality that are similarly experienced by others. As demonstrated in this photo, virtually everyone shares the same "moon illusion," in which the moon appears larger near the horizon, or with structures like this bridge in the foreground, compared to when it's higher up in the sky. In contrast, someone suffering from psychosis might hear voices from someone on the bridge (an auditory hallucination) or believe the bridge was built simply to honor their greatness (a delusion of grandeur).

Jefferson Siegel/New York Daily News/Getty Images

The insanity plea—guilty of a crime or mentally ill?   On June 25, 2019, the case of Thomas Gilbert Jr., accused of shooting and killing his father in 2015, finally went to trial. Gilbert (pictured here in the orange suit with his defense attorney) is a Princeton graduate who worked at a surf shop, but enjoyed a lavish lifestyle supported by his wealthy father. His defense team noted that Gilbert had been diagnosed and treated for years for severe compulsive disorder, depressive disorder, paranoid disorder, and psychosis. Therefore, they claimed he was too mentally ill to know right from wrong. In rebuttal, the prosecutors pointed out that Gilbert's web browsing history showed that he had searched for "Hitman Services" and that the murder occurred shortly after the father greatly reduced his monthly allowance. This evidence was used to show premeditation, and the jury found him guilty of murder—despite the plea of insanity. Gilbert currently faces up to life in prison (Jacobs, 2019; Sandoval, 2019).

Insanity   The legal (not clinical) designation for a situation in which an individual cannot be held responsible for his or her actions or is incompetent to manage his or her own affairs because of mental illness; inability to tell right from wrong.

Retrieval Practice 13.1 | Understanding Psychological Disorders

Self-Test Completing this self-test, and then checking your answers by clicking on the answer button or by looking in Appendix B, will provide immediate feedback and helpful practice for exams.

1. In the early treatment of psychological disorders, _____ was used to relieve pressure from mental disorders, whereas _____ was designed to drive the Devil out through prayer, fasting, and so on.

   a. trephining; exorcism

   b. demonology; hydrotherapy

   c. the medical model; the dunking test

   d. none of these options

2. _____ is the branch of medicine that deals with the diagnosis, treatment, and prevention of psychological disorders.

   a. Psychology

   b. Psychiatry

   c. Psychobiology

   d. Psychodiagnostics

3. The *DSM* provides _____ for mental disorders.

   a. categorical descriptions

   b. a global perspective

   c. a classification system

   d. all but one of these options

Q Test Your Critical Thinking

1. Can you think of cases in which someone might have a psychological disorder not described by the three criteria deviance, dysfunction, and distress?

2. Do you think the insanity plea, as it is currently structured, should be abolished? Why or why not?

Jefferson Siegel/New York Daily News/Getty Images

Real World Application Question

[AQ1] How often is the insanity defense successful in criminal trials?

Hint: Look in the text for **[AQ1]**

13.2 Anxiety Disorders

LEARNING OBJECTIVES

Retrieval Practice   While reading the upcoming sections, respond to each Learning Objective in your own words.

Summarize the major types of anxiety disorders.

- **Describe** the characteristics of generalized anxiety disorder (GAD), panic disorder, and phobias.

- **Explain** how biopsychosocial factors contribute to anxiety disorders.

Real World Application Question

[AQ2] Can so-called "trigger warnings" actually provoke and prolong anxiety disorders?

Anxiety disorder One of a group of psychological disorders characterized by disabling (uncontrollable and disruptive) fear or anxiety, which interfere with daily functioning.

When facing a very important exam, job interview, or first date, have you ever broken out in a cold sweat, felt your heart pounding, and had trouble breathing? Everyone feels nervous on occasion. But when the experiences and symptoms of fear and anxiety become disabling (uncontrollable and disrupting) or start to get in the way of daily living, mental health professionals may diagnose an **anxiety disorder**, which are among the most frequently occurring psychological disorders in the U.S. and around the world (National Institute of Mental Health, 2016; Newman, 2018; Ritchie & Roser, 2018). Fortunately, they're also among the easiest disorders to treat and offer some of the best chances for recovery (see Chapter 14).

Describing Anxiety Disorders

In this section, we discuss *generalized anxiety disorder* (GAD), *panic disorder*, and *phobias* (**Figure 13.5**). Although we cover these three specific disorders separately, they often occur together and their symptoms typically overlap.

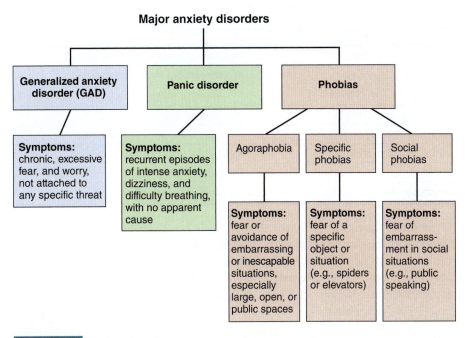

Major anxiety disorders

Generalized anxiety disorder (GAD)

Symptoms: chronic, excessive fear, and worry, not attached to any specific threat

Panic disorder

Symptoms: recurrent episodes of intense anxiety, dizziness, and difficulty breathing, with no apparent cause

Phobias

Agoraphobia

Specific phobias

Social phobias

Symptoms: fear or avoidance of embarrassing or inescapable situations, especially large, open, or public spaces

Symptoms: fear of a specific object or situation (e.g., spiders or elevators)

Symptoms: fear of embarrassment in social situations (e.g., public speaking)

FIGURE 13.5 Anxiety disorders

Generalized Anxiety Disorder
Sufferers of **generalized anxiety disorder (GAD)** experience persistent, uncontrollable, and free-floating, non-specified anxiety. The fears and anxiety are described as "free-floating" because they're unrelated to any specific threat—thus the term "generalized" anxiety disorder. Sadly, the fears and anxieties of GAD are generally chronic and uncontrollable. Because of persistent muscle tension and autonomic fear reactions, people with this disorder may develop headaches, heart palpitations, dizziness, and insomnia, making it even harder to cope with normal daily activities. The disorder affects twice as many women as men (American Psychiatric Association, 2013; Watson & Greenberg, 2017).

Generalized anxiety disorder (GAD) An anxiety disorder characterized by persistent, uncontrollable, and free-floating nonspecified anxiety.

Panic Disorder
Most of us have experienced feelings of intense panic, such as after narrowly avoiding a potentially fatal traffic collision. However, people with **panic disorder** endure repeated sudden onsets of extreme terror and inexplicable *panic attacks*. Symptoms include severe heart palpitations, trembling, dizziness, difficulty breathing, and feelings of impending doom. The reactions are so intense that many sufferers believe they are having a heart attack. Panic disorder is diagnosed when several apparently spontaneous panic attacks lead to a persistent concern about future attacks. A common complication of panic disorder is agoraphobia, discussed in the next section.

Panic disorder An anxiety disorder in which sufferers experience repeated sudden onsets of intense terror and inexplicable panic attacks; symptoms include severe heart palpitations, dizziness, trembling, difficulty breathing, and feelings of impending doom.

Phobias
Just as most of us have experienced feelings of panic, we may also share a common fear of spiders, sharks, or snakes. However, people who suffer from true **phobias** experience a persistent, intense, irrational fear and avoidance of a *specific* object, activity, or situation. These fears are so disabling that they significantly interfere with their daily life. Although the person recognizes that the level of fear is irrational, the experience is still one of overwhelming anxiety, and a full-blown panic attack may follow. The fifth edition of the *DSM* divides phobias into separate categories: agoraphobia, specific phobias, and social anxiety disorder (social phobia).

Phobia A persistent, intense, irrational fear and avoidance of a specific object, activity, or situation.

People with *agoraphobia* fear being in embarrassing or difficult situations, especially large, open, or public spaces, in which their panic symptoms might occur and it would be hard to escape, and where help may not be available. In severe cases, people with agoraphobia may eventually refuse to leave the perceived safety of their homes.

A *specific phobia* is a fear of a specific object or situation. Claustrophobia (fear of closed spaces) and acrophobia (fear of heights) are the specific phobias most often treated by therapists (see **Table 13.4** for a list of other specific phobias). People with specific phobias generally recognize that their fears are excessive and unreasonable, but they are unable to control their anxiety and will go to great lengths to avoid the feared stimulus.

TABLE 13.4	Sixteen Common and Uncommon Specific Phobias
Aerophobia—fear of flying	Glossophobia—fear of public speaking
Anemophobia—fear of wind	Katsaridaphobia—fear of cockroaches
Arachnophobia—fear of spiders	Nomophobia—fear of losing mobile phone coverage
Atychiphobia—fear of failure	Panophobia—fear of everything
Barophobia—fear of gravity	Phonophobia—fear of your own voice
Coulrophobia—fear of clowns	Somniphobia—fear of sleep
Ergophobia—fear of work or responsibility	Triskaidekaphobia—fear of the number 13
Gamophobia—fear of marriage	Zoophobia—fear of animals

People with *social anxiety disorder* (formerly called *social phobia*) are irrationally afraid of embarrassing themselves in social situations. Fears of public speaking and of eating in public are the two most common social phobias. The fear of public scrutiny and potential humiliation may become so pervasive that normal life is disrupted. People with this disorder are also four times more likely than the average person to abuse alcohol (Buckner & Terlecki, 2016).

Explaining Anxiety Disorders

Why do people develop anxiety disorders? Research has focused on several interacting, biopsychosocial perspectives (**Figure 13.6**).

Cognitive/Learning Factors   Researchers generally agree on the two major cognitive/learning contributions to anxiety disorders:

1. **Faulty cognitive processes**   People with anxiety disorders generally have habits of thinking, or cognitive processes, that make them prone to fear. These faulty cognitions, in turn, make them hypervigilant—meaning they constantly scan their environment for signs of danger and ignore signs of safety. In addition, they tend to magnify uncertain information and ordinary threats and failures and to be hypersensitive to others' opinions of them.

2. **Maladaptive learning**   In contrast to the cognitive explanation, learning theorists suggest anxiety disorders result from inadvertent and improper conditioning. As discussed in Chapter 6, during classical conditioning, if a neutral stimulus (NS), such as a rat, becomes paired with an unconditioned stimulus (US), such as a sudden, frightening noise, it becomes a conditioned stimulus (CS) that elicits a conditioned emotional response (CER)—in this case, fear. To make matters worse, the person generally begins to avoid all rats (or even their photos) in order to reduce anxiety (an operant conditioning process known as negative reinforcement), which may lead to a phobia. See **Process Diagram 13.1**.

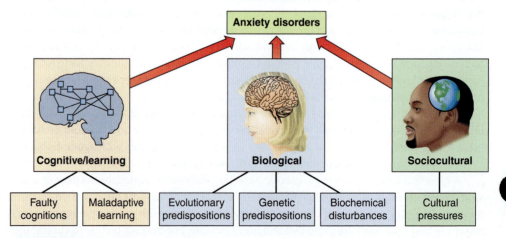

FIGURE 13.6 **Anxiety disorders**   The biopsychosocial model takes into account the wide variety of factors that contribute to anxiety disorders.

STOP! This Process Diagram contains essential information NOT found elsewhere in the text, which is likely to appear on quizzes and exams. Be sure to study it CAREFULLY.

PROCESS DIAGRAM 13.1 **How Do We Learn Phobias?**   One dated, but still useful, explanation may be Mowrer's *two-factor theory of avoidance learning* (Mowrer, 1951, 1960), which suggests that the fears associated with phobias are learned through classical conditioning, and then the avoidance behaviors are reinforced through operant conditioning. Consider the example of Little Albert's classically conditioned fear of rats, previously discussed in Chapter 6.

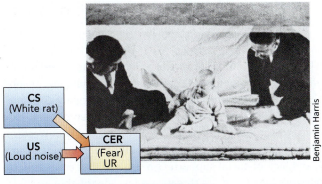

Step 1 Classical conditioning   John Watson and his assistant, Rosalie Rayner, paired a white rat with a loud noise (a hammer hitting a steel bar) to condition an infant (named Little Albert) to fear rats.

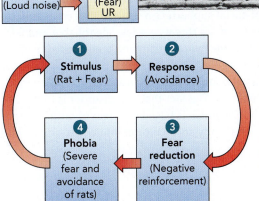

Step 2 Operant conditioning   Later Albert might have learned to avoid rats through operant conditioning. Avoiding rats would reduce Albert's fear, giving unintended reinforcement to his fearful behavior.

Step 3 Phobia   Note how the reduction in fear in Step 2 produced by avoiding the rat leads to negative reinforcement of Albert's fears. Given that reinforcement increases behavior, can you see how the little girl in this photo may experience an initial fearful event with a rat, and then how she might later get "stuck" in a vicious cycle that perpetuates the intense, irrational fears known as a phobia?

[AQ2]   The process diagram demonstrates how the vicious cycle of classical conditioning paired with operant conditioning may lead to phobias, but what about the recent demand for so-called "trigger warnings," which are designed to flag material that might actually provoke and prolong anxiety disorders (see photo)? Surprisingly, research shows that these warnings have only a minimal effect on participants' distress—even for those with a history of trauma (Sanson et al., 2019). They also may unintentionally reinforce anxieties by encouraging people to avoid negative material, and thereby perpetuate psychological disorders such as phobias and PTSD. However, the warnings do allow time for people to prepare themselves (mentally and physically)—rather than being blindsided by potentially challenging or traumatizing material.

Along with maladaptive learning through classical and operant conditioning, anxiety disorders may develop from modeling and imitation. In fact, research suggests that this type of social learning makes anxiety disorders the most "contagious" of all psychological disorders (Dean, 2015). By comparing 385 sets of identical twins and 486 sets of fraternal twins, researchers found a direct environmental (versus genetic) transmission from parents to offspring (Eley et al., 2015). Note that in this case the word "contagious" does not mean that we can catch an anxiety disorder from a sneeze or cough, but rather that children "catch it" primarily by watching and modeling their anxious parent's behaviors. The role of environmental, social learning in the transmission of anxiety is well established. But the good news for parents with anxiety disorders is that certain behaviors, such as monitoring your own anxiety (see photo) and

Possible evolution of a phobia? People suffering from trypophobia have a fear of holes, and researchers have found a surprising similarity between the pattern of holes that sparks strong phobic reactions and the natural markings on dangerous animals, like certain snakes and the poison dart frog (see photo) (Cole & Wilkins, 2013). A somewhat similar pattern of holes is found on certain poisonous mushrooms (see photo). Can you see how being able to quickly recognize (and avoid) poisonous animals and plants might have served as an evolutionary advantage that later evolved into a phobia?

encouraging your children to take small age-appropriate risks, can minimize the chances of passing it on to your children (Dean, 2015).

Biological Factors Some researchers believe phobias reflect an evolutionary predisposition to fear things that were dangerous to our ancestors (see photo). Unfortunately, many who suffer from panic disorder seem genetically predisposed toward an overreaction of the autonomic nervous system. Stress and arousal also seem to play a role in panic attacks, and drugs such as caffeine or nicotine and even hyperventilation can provoke an attack, all suggesting a biochemical disturbance.

Biological support also comes from the fact that women greatly outnumber men in diagnoses of anxiety disorders, suggesting that sex hormones, such as estrogen and progesterone, may be involved (Li & Graham, 2017). In addition, research shows that disturbed sleep is linked to both anxiety disorders and chronic depression (Wassing et al., 2016).

Sociocultural Factors There are numerous sociocultural factors that contribute to anxiety. For example, children who suffer psychological abuse—including bullying, severe insults, overwhelming demands, and isolation—are at greater risk for developing GAD and social anxiety disorder (Flett et al., 2016; Spinazzola et al., 2014). Research on cultural factors suggests the sharp rise in anxiety disorders in the past 50 years, particularly in Western industrialized countries, may be due in part to our fast-paced lives—along with our increased mobility, decreased job security, and lack of social support. Can you see that compared to the dangers our early human ancestors faced, today's threats are less identifiable and less immediate, which may lead some people to become hypervigilant and predisposed to anxiety disorders?

Some Japanese experience a type of social phobia called *taijin kyofusho* (*TKS*), a morbid dread of doing something to embarrass *others*. The fact that this disorder is quite different from the Western version of social phobia, which is based on a fear of criticism and self-embarrassment, is another example of the many sociocultural influences on anxiety disorders.

S&P Scientific Thinking and Practical Application

Knowing that people with anxiety disorders experience significant distress and disruption in their lives, what can we do to help? One encouraging note is that people who are more active are less likely to develop anxiety disorders, and exercise training can reduce symptoms of anxiety, depression, and stress-related disorders (Anderson & Shivakumar, 2013; Kandola et al., 2018). In other words, you can, in fact, run away from your fears! Former NFL running back and Heisman Trophy winner Ricky Williams (see photo) was diagnosed with a social anxiety disorder so severe that he could barely look people in the eye and dreaded meeting fans on the street (Chittenden, 2018; Huston, 2018).

Similarly, Emma Stone (see photo), Academy Award–winning movie star, experienced such severe panic attacks that she developed agoraphobia and seldom left her home (Gonzalez, 2018; Svetkey, 2017). Thanks to therapy, however, both Williams and Stone now have healthy coping styles. They often speak publicly about their psychological disorders and personal experiences, hoping to boost public awareness and support of those with mental illness.

Retrieval Practice 13.2 | Anxiety Disorders

Self-Test Completing this self-test, and then checking your answers by clicking on the answer button or by looking in Appendix B, will provide immediate feedback and helpful practice for exams.

1. Persistent, uncontrollable, and free-floating, non-specified anxiety might be diagnosed as a _____.
   a. generalized anxiety disorder
   b. panic disorder
   c. phobia
   d. all these options

2. In _____ disorder, the individual suffers brief attacks of intense apprehension.
   a. phobic
   b. posttraumatic stress
   c. panic
   d. dissociative fugue

3. A persistent, intense, irrational fear and avoidance of a specific object or situation is known as _____.
   a. a panic disorder
   b. a phobia
   c. the "scared-cat" syndrome
   d. paranoia

4. In the Japanese social phobia called TKS, people fear that they will _____.
   a. evaluate others negatively
   b. embarrass themselves
   c. embarrass others
   d. be embarrassed by others

Q Test Your Critical Thinking

1. Why do you suppose anxiety disorders are among the easiest disorders to both "catch" and treat?

2. How would you explain the high number of anxiety disorders in the United States?

Real World Application Question

[AQ2] Can so-called "trigger warnings" actually provoke and prolong anxiety disorders?

Westend61/Getty Images

Hint: Look in the text for **[AQ2]**

13.3 | Depressive and Bipolar Disorders

LEARNING OBJECTIVES

Retrieval Practice While reading the upcoming sections, respond to each Learning Objective in your own words.

Review the symptoms, causal factors, and dangers of depressive and bipolar disorders.

- **Describe** depressive disorders and bipolar disorders and how they differ.

- **Summarize** research on the biological and other psychological factors that contribute to depressive and bipolar disorders.

Real World Application Question

[AQ3] How do electronic devices and social media affect our mental health?

Both depressive disorders and bipolar disorders are characterized by extreme disturbances in emotional states. Thus, both are sometimes referred to as *mood disorders* or *affective disorders*—the word "affective" is synonymous with feelings or emotions.

Describing Depressive and Bipolar Disorders

Let's face it. We all experience shifts in our emotions on a somewhat regular basis—you may experience intense sadness when you fail a critical exam and high elation when you receive an A in another course. Such emotional shifts are generally linked to life experiences and they are temporary. When the shifts occur for no apparent reason and the extreme emotions are prolonged, the condition may qualify as a *depressive* or *bipolar disorder*.

S&P Scientific Thinking and Practical Application

Did you know that J. K. Rowling suffers from serious depression? Joanne Rowling, better known as J. K. Rowling, is a British novelist, screenwriter, and film producer famous for her authorship of the *Harry Potter* series of fantasy novels (see photo), along with several other books that have earned her great wealth and fame. Despite Rowling's repeated and generous donations of large sums to charity, she was second on the list of the world's richest authors in 2018, and was confirmed as the highest paid novelist in the world (Reed, 2019).

Given Rowling's apparently wildly successful life, most people are surprised to learn of her depression and the hardships she's encountered throughout her lifetime. She reports that her teenage years and early adulthood were very unhappy due to her mother's protracted illness, a strained relationship with her father, and a painful divorce. Following her divorce, she saw herself as such a dismal failure that she even contemplated suicide.

Fortunately, therapy helped her climb out of her diagnosed clinical depression, and she later reported that it was her experiences with such deep despair that led her to create the *Dementors*—the soul-sucking monsters found in the *Harry Potter* series (Mazza, 2016; Rana, 2017).

> I think you have a moral responsibility when you've been given far more than you need to do wise things with it and give intelligently.
>
> —J. K. Rowling

Major depressive disorder (MDD) A psychological disorder characterized by significant depressive symptoms, such as sadness, lethargy, or loss of pleasure, lasting for two weeks or more.

Bipolar disorder A psychological disorder characterized by repeated episodes of mania (unreasonable elation, often with hyperactivity) alternating with depression.

Mania A state of abnormally elevated mood (either euphoric or irritable); also characterized by mental and physical hyperactivity, insomnia, and poor judgment.

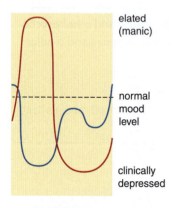

— Bipolar disorder
— Major depressive disorder

FIGURE 13.7 **Depressive versus bipolar disorders** If depressive disorder and bipolar disorder were depicted on a graph, they might look something like this. Remember that only in bipolar disorder do people experience manic episodes.

Major Depressive Disorder Along with experiencing normal mood changes, almost everyone also feels depressed at some point in his or her life, especially following the loss of a job, end of a relationship, or the death of a loved one. But people with **major depressive disorder (MDD)** suffer with recurring and extreme bouts of depressive symptoms, such as sadness, lethargy, or loss of pleasure, that last for two weeks or more, and occur without an obvious link to external causes. Those who suffer from MDD may become so deeply sad and discouraged that they have trouble sleeping, lose (or gain) significant weight, and feel so fatigued that they cannot go to work or school or even comb their hair and brush their teeth.

Individuals with MDD also have trouble concentrating, making decisions, and being social. In addition, they often have difficulty recognizing their common "thinking errors," such as *tunnel vision,* which involves focusing on only certain aspects of a situation (usually the negative parts) and ignoring other interpretations or alternatives. Do you see how this type of depressed thinking would deepen depression and possibly even lead to suicide?

Bipolar Disorder When depression is *unipolar* and the depressive episode ends, the person generally returns to a normal emotional level. People with **bipolar disorder**, however, rebound to the opposite state, known as **mania**, which is characterized by unreasonable elation and hyperactivity (**Figure 13.7**). You can remember the term "bipolar disorder" (previously called manic depression) by noting that the person's moods alternate between two "poles"—mania (highs) and depression (lows). Keep in mind that these mood swings can be mild or severe, and can last for hours, days, or even months.

During a manic episode, individuals often feel unusually "high" and optimistic and experience unrealistically high self-esteem and grandiose beliefs about their abilities and powers. Although mania feels good at first, it has serious and often dangerous side effects, such as becoming aggressive and engaging in reckless behaviors, including inappropriate sexual activity, gambling away savings, giving away valuable possessions, or going on wild spending sprees.

In addition, individuals with bipolar disorder are often hyperactive and may not sleep for days at a time without becoming apparently fatigued. Thinking is faster than normal and can change abruptly to new topics, showing "rapid flight of ideas." Speech is also rapid ("pressured speech"), making it difficult for others to get a word in edgewise. A manic episode may last a few days or a few months, and it generally ends abruptly. The ensuing depressive episode generally lasts three times as long as the mania (Leigh, 2015; Ray, 2015).

The lifetime risk for bipolar disorder is low—between 0.5 percent and 1.6 percent—but it can be one of the most debilitating and lethal disorders. Due in part to the impulsivity associated with this disorder, the suicide rate is between 10 percent and 20 percent among sufferers (Depp et al., 2016; Ketter & Miller, 2015).

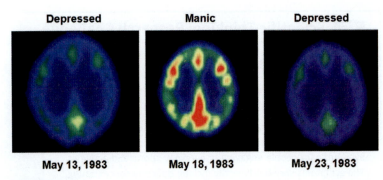

Depressed	Manic	Depressed
May 13, 1983	May 18, 1983	May 23, 1983

FIGURE 13.8 **PET scans and bipolar disorder** These three front-facing PET scans were taken during three extreme states of bipolar disorder: a beginning depressed state (May 13 photo), a manic phase (May 18 photo), and a depressed state after the manic phase (May 23 photo). Given that the red and yellow colors reflect increased brain activity, and that brain energy consumption rises and falls with the emotional ups and downs of bipolar disorder, you can easily see in the center photo how brain activity is heightended during the manic phase.

Courtesy of Prof. Lewis R Baxter and Prof. Michael E Phelps/UCLA School of Medicine

Explaining Depressive and Bipolar Disorders

What are the major biological and other psychological factors that contribute to depressive and bipolar disorders?

Biological Factors Several biological factors, including genes, appear to contribute to depression and other mood disorders (Bernaras et al., 2019; Lei et al., 2019; Strachan et al., 2017). Similarly, imbalances in neurotransmitters, including GABA, serotonin, norepinephrine, and dopamine, have been linked with mood disorders (Bernaras et al., 2019; Morgan, 2017; Peacock et al., 2017). Brain structures and functions also play a critical role. As you can see in **Figure 13.8**, studies have found both diminished and heightened brain activity during the extreme states of bipolar disorder (Brady et al., 2017; Cantisani et al., 2016; Carlson et al., 2017).

PAN Practical Application of Neuroscience

Given the strong biological basis of these disorders, how can scientists and the public use this information in everyday life? Through the use of fMRI brain scans, researchers believe they can better detect the brain's neural signals associated with suicidal thoughts—and possibly help predict and prevent suicide (Just et al., 2017). Surprisingly, *psilocybin*, a hallucinogen from "magic" mushrooms, and *ketamine*, a dangerous date rape/party drug, may help reduce the symptoms of depression and bipolar disorder (Kishimoto et al., 2016; Mithoefer et al., 2016; Silberner, 2019). However, these drugs remain controversial due to the relative lack of empirical evidence on their effectiveness, some serious side effects, and the potential for abuse. Can you see how the chemicals in these drugs and in the foods we eat might lead to physiological changes in the brain and body (**Figure 13.9**)?

Before leaving this section on the biological factors, we need to point out the strong scientific evidence that professional athletes who experience serious brain injuries are at significant risk of developing depressive and bipolar disorders and other problems as they age. See the **RC** **Research Challenge**.

Other Psychological Factors Now that we've covered some of the major biological factors in depression and bipolar disorder, let's consider the key psychological perspectives. The psychoanalytic approach sees depression as the result of anger turned inward or as the aftermath of experiencing a real or imagined loss, which is internalized as guilt, shame, self-hatred, and ultimately self-blame.

FIGURE 13.9 **Junk food and depression?** Some studies have found that people who regularly eat junk food (such as croissants, chips, candy, and doughnuts) are at increased risk of developing depression (Gangwisch et al., 2015; Sánchez-Villegas et al., 2011).

LightField Studios/Shutterstock.com

RC Scientific Thinking: **Research Challenge**

Head Injuries and Depression

(APA Goal 2.4) Interpret, design, and conduct basic psychological research

Concussions, or mild traumatic brain injuries (mTBIs), are common occurrences for athletes, military personnel, accident victims, and even ordinary people engaging in everyday sports and activities. The symptoms vary but typically include difficulty concentrating, sleep disturbances, fatigue, depression, and anxiety (Broshek et al., 2015). Less common but more serious reactions occur after repeated concussions and brain trauma.

Unfortunately, professional athletes often experience numerous concussions and may develop *chronic traumatic encephalopathy (CTE),* a progressive degenerative brain disease. In turn, individuals with CTE are more likely to develop depressive and bipolar disorders, as well as Parkinson's disease, PTSD, schizophrenia, stroke, and other serious problems (Falcon et al., 2019; Lim et al., 2019; Tharmaratnam et al., 2018). CTE can even lead to suicide (see photo).

There is some good news, however. Researchers have identified for the first time how head injuries can alter genes, leading to serious brain diseases (Meng et al., 2017). This group of researchers first trained 20 rats to escape from a maze, a small tunnel-like structure commonly used to study spatial learning and memory in rodents. Next, they produced brain injuries by randomly choosing 10 of the 20 rats and injecting them with a special fluid. The other 10 rats did not receive the injections. When they later tested all the rats in the same maze, the brain-injured rats took about 25 percent longer to solve the maze than the non-injured rats. The researchers then examined the genes from five animals in each group and found that these types of concussive brain injuries actually reprogram genes. This reprogramming can then lead to a predisposition to neurological and psychiatric disorders.

How is this good news? Many of the rats' altered genes have counterparts in humans, and the study identified specific genes that are affected by traumatic brain injuries (TBIs). Knowing which genes are responsible helps identify them as the best targets for better diagnosis and possible future treatments for several neurological and psychological disorders.

Identify the Research Method

1. Based on the information provided, did this study (Meng et al., 2017) use descriptive, correlational, and/or experimental research?

Kent Horner/Getty Images Sport/Getty Images

Brain damage and professional sports   As discussed in Chapter 7, Junior Seau, who played in the NFL for 20 years, died by suicide from a gunshot wound to his chest in 2012 at the age of 43. Later studies concluded that he suffered from *chronic traumatic encephalopathy (CTE),* a form of concussion-related brain damage that has been found in numerous NFL players.

2. If you chose
   - *descriptive research*, is this a naturalistic or laboratory observation, survey/interview, case study, and/or archival research?
   - *correlational research*, is this a positive, negative, or zero correlation?
   - *experimental research*, label the IV, DV, experimental group(s), and control group. (Note: If participants were not randomly assigned to groups, list the design as *quasi-experimental.*)
   - both *descriptive* and *correlational* research, answer the corresponding questions for both.

Check your answers by clicking on the answer button or by looking in Appendix B.

Note: The information provided in this study is admittedly limited, but the level of detail is similar to what is presented in most textbooks and public reports of research findings. Answering these questions, and then comparing your answers to those provided, will help you become a better scientific and critical thinker and consumer of scientific research.

In contrast, the cognitive perspective suggests that depression is explained, at least in part, by negative thinking patterns, including a tendency to ruminate or obsess about problems (Arora et al., 2015; Izadpanah et al., 2017; Topper et al., 2017). As you can see in **Figure 13.10**, this pattern of depressive thinking may lead to a vicious, self-perpetuating cycle.

The humanistic school generally suggests that depression results when a person demands perfection of himself or herself, or when positive growth is blocked (McCormack & Joseph, 2014; Short & Thomas, 2015).

Learned helplessness Seligman's term for a state of helplessness, or resignation, in which human or non-human animals fail to act to escape from a situation due to a history of repeated failures in the past.

From the behavioral perspective, learning experiences play a critical role. According to **learned helplessness** theory (Seligman, 1975, 2007), depression occurs when people (and other animals) become resigned to the idea that they are helpless to escape from a painful situation due to a history of repeated failures. Among humans, learned helplessness may lead to depression if the person routinely attributes failure to factors that are internal ("my own weakness"), stable ("this weakness is longstanding and unchanging"), and global ("this weakness is

FIGURE 13.10   Depression as a vicious cycle   Have you heard that *depression is a snake that bites its own tail*? This expression reflects cognitive theories that depression results from a vicious cycle of destructive thoughts, emotions, and behaviors. Following one or more stressful, negative events (Step 1), people may ruminate and obsessively think about their personal failures and problems, while also worrying about events that are generally outside their control (Step 2). As a result of these persistent, negative thoughts, individuals tend to develop feelings of hopelessness, helplessness, sadness, and low self-esteem (Step 3). These emotional problems then generally lead to behavior problems, including decreased activities, social withdrawal, and decreased productivity (Step 4). Do you recognize how these cognitive, emotional, and behavioral problems (Steps 2-4) can lead to failures at work and in relationships, which then leads to or exacerbates depression (Step 5), and how other future stressors will inevitably add to and perpetuate this cycle? (See Chapter 14 for tips on how to break this cycle.)

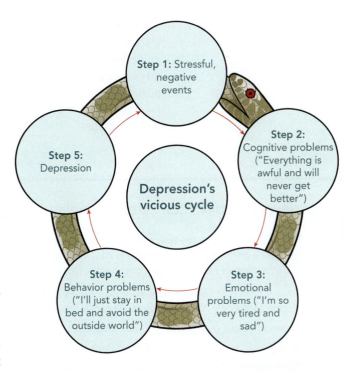

a problem in lots of settings") (Bernaras et al., 2019; Smalheiser et al., 2014; Travers et al., 2015).

Sociocultural and Evolutionary Factors   In contrast to the biological and psychological perspectives we've just discussed, the sociocultural explanation of depression and bipolar disorder focuses on environmental stressors (such as poverty and unemployment), disturbances in interpersonal relationships, and histories of abuse or assault (Bernaras et al., 2019; Frodl et al., 2017; Opel et al., 2019).

   [AQ3]   An unexpected additional finding is that high social media, Internet, and phone use are linked with mental health problems, including depression, suicidal thoughts, and anxiety, for both teens and adults—see photo (Keles et al., 2019; Panova & Lleras, 2016; Twenge et al., 2018). This is particularly true when the technologies are used to avoid negative experiences or feelings. However, no link with mental health was found when they're used merely to escape boredom.

   On a related note, recent polls from the Pew Research Center found that more than half of adults in most emerging economies say that mobile phones and the Internet have had a *bad* impact on children, whereas 70 percent of adults in these countries say that mobile phones and social media have mostly been *good* for them personally (Anderson & Silver, 2019). What do you think? As a scientific and critical thinker, how would you explain the difference?

   Research from an evolutionary perspective suggests that moderate depression may be a normal and healthy adaptive response to a very real loss, such as the death of a loved one. Therefore, severe clinical depression may just be an extreme version of this generally adaptive response, which helps us conserve energy and allows us to step back and reassess our goals (Beck & Bredemeier, 2016; Neumann & Walter, 2015).

Take-Home Message   Keep in mind that clinical depression and bipolar disorders almost always require professional help (see Chapter 14). The good news is that treatment for both disorders can significantly reduce their symptoms and greatly improve overall functioning (Black et al., 2017; Data-Franco et al., 2017). However, suicide is a particular danger in these and other psychological disorders. If you or someone you know seems to be at risk, please study and review the myths, danger signs, and tips for what to do and what not to do, which are all discussed near the end of this chapter.

   Another point to remember is that depression is more than a mental disorder. It affects the entire body, which might help explain why people suffering from depression often feel extremely tired, as well as why depression may be linked with cancer, cardiovascular disease, and premature death (Kenner, 2018; Péquignot et al., 2019; Vaccarino et al., 2019). One of the major culprits appears to be inflammation or oxidative stress—a bodily imbalance that inhibits the ability to destroy toxic substances (Khandaker et al., 2019; Lindqvist et al., 2017). Fortunately, physical activity can be helpful in improving both mental and physical health. Specifically, exercise can reduce the symptoms and severity of anxiety and depression (Kandola et al., 2018; Knapen et al., 2015; Tasci et al., 2018).

Finally, to end on an even more positive note, if you're suffering from a depressive or bipolar disorder, note that you are not alone. Many successful writers, singers, scientists, and musicians, including Mariah Carey, Bebe Rexha, Russell Brand, and Carrie Fisher have been diagnosed with depression and/or bipolar disorder. Thanks to their courage and willingness to publicly discuss their lives, these famous figures have increased support, understanding, and funding for both depressive and bipolar disorders, as well as decreasing the associated stigma and stereotypes.

Retrieval Practice 13.3 | Depressive and Bipolar Disorders

Self-Test Completing this self-test, and then checking your answers by clicking on the answer button or by looking in Appendix B, will provide immediate feedback and helpful practice for exams.

1. A major difference between depressive disorder and bipolar disorder is that only in bipolar disorder do people have _____.

   a. hallucinations or delusions   c. manic episodes

   b. depression   d. a biochemical imbalance

2. When experiencing _____, the individual is typically highly excited and impulsive and has unrealistically high self-esteem.

   a. hyperarousal   c. elation-excess syndrome (EES)

   b. mania   d. pituitary overload

3. According to the theory known as _____, when faced with a painful situation from which there is no escape, animals and people enter a state of helplessness and resignation.

   a. autonomic resignation   c. resigned helplessness

   b. helpless resignation   d. learned helplessness

4. Internal, stable, and global attributions of failure or unpleasant circumstances are associated with _____ disorders.

   a. anxiety   c. depressive

   b. delusional   d. bipolar

Q Test Your Critical Thinking

1. Have you ever felt seriously depressed? How would you distinguish between "normal" depression and a serious depressive disorder?

2. Can you think of a personal example of how major depression served as a possible evolutionary advantage?

Real World Application Question

[AQ3]   How do electronic devices and social media affect our mental health?

Singkham/Shutterstock.com

Hint: Look in the text for [AQ3]

13.4 Schizophrenia

LEARNING OBJECTIVES

Retrieval Practice   While reading the upcoming sections, respond to each Learning Objective in your own words.

Review how psychologists define, classify, and explain schizophrenia.

- **Identify** schizophrenia and its five common symptoms.
- **Compare** the positive and negative symptoms of schizophrenia.

- **Summarize** the biological and other psychological factors that contribute to schizophrenia.

Real World Application Question

[AQ4] Are children who experience trauma at increased risk of developing schizophrenia later in life?

Imagine that your 17-year-old son's behavior has changed dramatically over the past few months. He has gone from being actively involved in sports and clubs to suddenly quitting all activities and refusing to go to school. He now talks to himself—mumbling and yelling out at times—and no longer regularly showers or washes his hair. Recently he announced, "The voices are telling me to jump out the window" (Kotowski, 2012).

This description is taken from the true case history of a patient who suffers from **schizophrenia**. We offer it as an example of the five major symptoms of schizophrenia: disturbances in *perception* (seeing or hearing things that others don't), *language* (bizarre words and meanings), *thought* (impaired logic), *emotion* (exaggerated or blunted), and *behavior* (peculiar movements and social withdrawal). In addition, some have serious problems caring for themselves, relating to others, and holding a job.

Schizophrenia is one of the most widespread and devastating psychological disorders. Approximately one percent of people in any given adult population will develop it in their lifetime, and approximately half of all people who are admitted to mental hospitals are diagnosed with this disorder. Schizophrenia usually emerges between the late teens and the mid-30s and only rarely prior to adolescence or after age 45. Interestingly, it appears to be equally prevalent in men and women, but it's generally more severe and strikes earlier in men (Brown & Lau, 2016; Castle & Buckley, 2015; World Health Organization, 2018a).

Schizophrenia A group of severe psychological disorders involving major disturbances in perception, language, thought, emotion, and behavior.

S&P Scientific Thinking and Practical Application

Is schizophrenia the same as multiple personalities?
Schizophrenia is often confused with dissociative identity disorder, which is commonly referred to as *split* or *multiple personality disorder* (see cartoon). Literally translated, *schizophrenia* means "split mind," but when Eugen Bleuler coined the term in 1911, he was referring to the fragmenting of thought processes and emotions, not of personalities (Neale et al., 1983). As we discuss later in this chapter, dissociative identity disorder is popularly referred to as having a "split personality"—the rare and controversial condition of having more than one distinct personality.

Mike Flanagan/Cartoon Stock

Why does this matter? Confusing schizophrenia with multiple personalities is not only technically incorrect, it also trivializes the devastating effects of both disorders, which may include severe anxiety, social isolation, unemployment, homelessness, substance abuse, clinical depression, and even suicide (Arkowitz & Lilienfeld, 2017; Joseph et al., 2015; Lasalvia et al., 2015).

Symptoms of Schizophrenia

Schizophrenia is a group of disorders characterized by a disturbance in one or more of the following areas: *perception*, *language*, *thought*, *emotions,* and *behavior*.

Perception   The senses of people with schizophrenia may be either enhanced or blunted. The filtering and selection processes that allow most people to concentrate on whatever they choose are impaired, and sensory stimulation is jumbled and distorted. People with schizophrenia may experience *hallucinations* (false, imaginary sensory perceptions that occur without external stimuli). Auditory hallucinations (hearing voices and sounds) are one of the most common symptoms of schizophrenia. On rare occasions, people with schizophrenia hurt others in response to their distorted perceptions. But a person with schizophrenia is more likely to be self-destructive and suicidal than violent toward others.

Language   For people with schizophrenia, words lose their usual meanings and associations, logic is impaired, and thoughts are disorganized and bizarre. When language disturbances are mild, the individual jumps from topic to topic. With more severe disturbances, the person jumbles phrases and words together (into a "word salad") or creates artificial words.

Thought   The most common—and frightening—thought disturbance experienced by people with schizophrenia is lack of contact with reality (psychosis). Recall that psychosis refers to

"That's the doctor who is treating me for paranoia. I don't trust him."

Bob Zahn/Conde Nast/The Cartoon Bank

a serious loss of contact with reality. In extreme cases, the illness is so severe that it's considered a psychosis and treatment may require institutional or custodial care. The *DSM-5* places schizophrenia within the category of "schizo-phrenic spectrum and other psychotic disorders."

Delusions, false or irrational beliefs that are maintained despite clear evidence to the contrary, are also common thought disturbances in people with schizophrenia (see cartoon). We all experience exaggerated thoughts from time to time, such as thinking a friend is trying to avoid us, but the delu-sions of schizophrenia are much more extreme. As an example, if someone falsely believed that the postal worker who routinely delivered mail to his house every afternoon was a co-conspirator in a plot to kill him, this would likely qualify as a *delusion of persecution* or paranoia. In *delusions of gran-deur*, people believe that they are someone very important, such as Jesus Christ or the Queen of England. In *delusions of control,* the person believes his or her thoughts or actions are being controlled by outside and alien forc-es—"the CIA is controlling my thoughts."

Emotion   For some individuals with schizophrenia, their emotions are exaggerated and fluctuate rapidly. At other times, they may experience *flattened affect*—almost no emotional response of any kind.

Behavior   Disturbances in behavior may take the form of unusual actions that have spe-cial meaning to the person with schizophrenia. One patient massaged his head repeatedly to "clear it" of unwanted thoughts. People with schizophrenia also may become *cataleptic* and assume a nearly immobile stance for an extended period.

Classifying Schizophrenia

Schizophrenia was once classified into several subtypes, including *paranoid, catatonic, dis-organized, undifferentiated*, and *residual*. However, the latest version of the *DSM-5* focuses on the symptoms discussed earlier, such as hallucinations, disorganized speech, delusions, and disorganized behavior. It also differentiates between negative and positive symptoms. *Negative symptoms* include the loss or absence of normal functions. Impaired attention, limited or toneless speech, flat or blunted emotions, and social withdrawal are all clas-sic negative symptoms of schizophrenia. In contrast, *positive symptoms* are additions to or exaggerations of normal functions. Delusions and hallucinations are examples of posi-tive symptoms. Interestingly, negative symptoms are more often found in slow-developing schizophrenia, whereas positive symptoms are more common when schizophrenia devel-ops rapidly.

TIP   Do you recall the distinction made in Chapter 6—negative and positive are not bad or good?   Instead, "negative symptoms" means that something is taken away. In this case when someone engages in limited speech or social withdrawal, daily functioning is "taken away" because it's so far below normal levels. Similarly, "positive symptoms" means that abnormal behaviors, such as hallucinations and delusions, have been "added" above and beyond normal levels.

Explaining Schizophrenia

Just as schizophrenia has various symptoms and comes in many different forms, it also comes with a wide variety of suspected contributing factors. We begin with the biological.

Biological Factors   Most biological explanations of schizophrenia focus on genetics, neurotransmitters, and brain abnormalities:

- **Genetics**   Current research indicates that the risk for schizophrenia increases with genetic similarity (Arnedo et al., 2015; Gottesman, 1991; Reble et al., 2017). This means that people who share more genes with a person who has schizophrenia are more likely to develop the disorder (**Figure 13.11**). Genetic influences on schizophrenia are a well-established fact, and research has also found a similar pattern of gene expression in patients with autism, bipolar disorder, and major depression (Gandal et al., 2018).

- **Biochemistry** According to the *dopamine hypothesis*, overactivity of certain dopamine neurons in the brain contributes to some forms of schizophrenia (Howes et al., 2017; Jauhar et al., 2019). This hypothesis is based on two observations. First, administering amphetamines increases the amount of dopamine and can produce (or worsen) some symptoms of schizophrenia, especially in people with a genetic predisposition to the disorder. Second, drugs that reduce dopamine activity in the brain also reduce or eliminate some symptoms of schizophrenia. Disruptions in gonadal and other hormones may play an additional role in schizophrenia (Riecher-Rössler, 2017).

- **Brain abnormalities** A third area of research in schizophrenia explores links to abnormalities in brain function and structure (e.g., Steullet, 2019; Wolff & Vann, 2019). Researchers have found larger cerebral ventricles (fluid-filled spaces in the brain) and right hemisphere dysfunction in some people with schizophrenia (Berger et al., 2017; Gurin & Blum, 2017; Young & Wimmer, 2017). Also, some people with chronic schizophrenia have a lower level of activity in specific areas of the brain (**Figure 13.12**).

Prenatal and Other Environmental Factors
Clearly, biological factors contribute to schizophrenia. But the fact that the heritability of schizophrenia is only 48 percent even in identical twins—who share identical genes—tells us that nongenetic factors must contribute the remaining percentage. Furthermore, as we've seen throughout this text, *epigenetic* (meaning "in addition to genetic") factors often influence whether or not specific genes will be expressed.

If you're concerned about your personal chances of developing schizophrenia, remember that with environmental factors even identical twins are not destined to develop the same diseases. In addition, most psychologists believe there are several possible environmental and psychosocial contributors. For example, prenatal stress and viral infections, birth complications, low birth weight, immune responses, maternal malnutrition, and advanced age of either parent are all suspected factors in the development of schizophrenia (Kneeland & Fatemi, 2013; Meyer, 2016; Webb, 2016).

[AQ4] Sadly, children who experience severe trauma before age 16 are three times more likely than other people to develop schizophrenia—see photo (Bentall et al., 2012; DeRosse et al., 2014). People who experience stressful living environments, including poverty, unemployment, and crowding, are also at increased risk (Brown & Lau, 2016; Hastings et al., 2019; Sweeney et al., 2015).

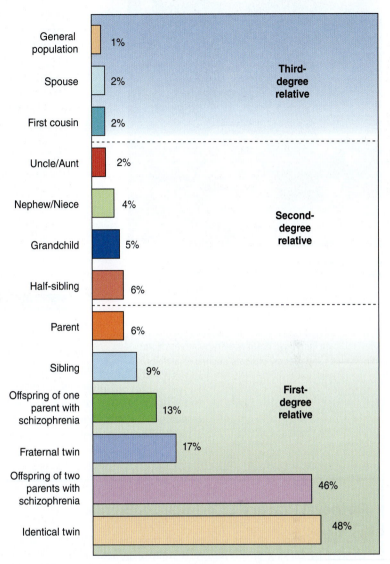

Relationship to person with schizophrenia

Relationship	Percentage of risk
General population	1%
Spouse	2%
First cousin	2%
Uncle/Aunt	2%
Nephew/Niece	4%
Grandchild	5%
Half-sibling	6%
Parent	6%
Sibling	9%
Offspring of one parent with schizophrenia	13%
Fraternal twin	17%
Offspring of two parents with schizophrenia	46%
Identical twin	48%

Third-degree relative: General population, Spouse, First cousin
Second-degree relative: Uncle/Aunt, Nephew/Niece, Grandchild, Half-sibling
First-degree relative: Parent, Sibling, Offspring of one parent with schizophrenia, Fraternal twin, Offspring of two parents with schizophrenia, Identical twin

Percentage of risk

FIGURE 13.11 **Genetics and schizophrenia** As dramatically shown by this figure, the lifetime risk of developing schizophrenia is strongly linked with genetic inheritance. Is this a positive or negative correlation?

Answer: A positive correlation—the risk of developing schizophrenia increases as the genetic relatedness to an individual with schizophrenia increases.

Daniel Jędzura/123RF

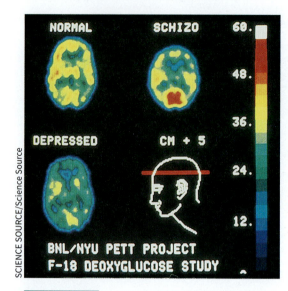

FIGURE 13.12 **Brain activity in schizophrenia**
Using these positron emission tomography (PET) scans, compare the normal levels of brain activity with those of a person with schizophrenia, and then with those of a person with depression. Warmer colors (reds and yellows) indicate increased brain activity, whereas cooler colors (blues and greens) indicate decreased activity.

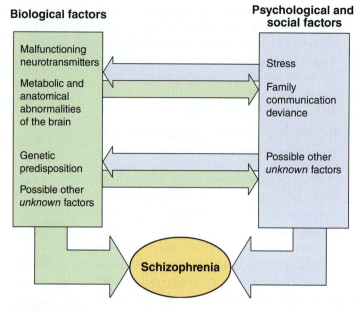

FIGURE 13.13 **The biopsychosocial model and schizophrenia**

How should we evaluate these differing theories and findings about schizophrenia? Like virtually all psychological disorders, schizophrenia is probably the result of a combination of known and unknown interacting factors (**Figure 13.13**). The good news is that a similar combination of psychological and medical research will someday lead to a better understanding of the precise factors that contribute to schizophrenia and, ideally, to its cure and prevention.

Retrieval Practice 13.4 | Schizophrenia

Self-Test Completing this self-test, and then checking your answers by clicking on the answer button or by looking in Appendix B, will provide immediate feedback and helpful practice for exams.

1. Major disturbances in perception, language, thought, emotion, and behavior may be diagnosed as _____.

   a. schizophrenia   **c.** borderline psychosis

   b. multiple dissociative disorder   **d.** neurotic psychosis

2. In extreme cases, schizophrenia is a form of _____, a term describing general lack of contact with reality.

   a. multiple personality disorder   **c.** borderline polar psychosis

   b. psychosis   **d.** all of these options

3. _____ refers to "split mind," whereas _____ refers to "split personality."

   a. Psychosis; neurosis

   b. Insanity; multiple personalities

   c. Schizophrenia; dissociative identity disorder (DID)

   d. Paranoia; borderline

4. Perceptions for which there are no appropriate external stimuli are called _____, and the most common type among people suffering from schizophrenia is _____.

   a. hallucinations; auditory   **c.** delusions; auditory

   b. hallucinations; visual   **d.** delusions; visual

Q Test Your Critical Thinking

1. Most of the disorders discussed in this chapter have some evidence for a genetic predisposition. What would you tell a friend who has a family member with one of these disorders and fears that he or she might develop the same disorder?

2. What do you think are the most important factors that contribute to schizophrenia?

Real World Application Question

[AQ4] Are children who experience trauma at increased risk of developing schizophrenia later in life?

Hint: Look in the text for **[AQ4]**

13.5 | Other Disorders

LEARNING OBJECTIVES

Retrieval Practice While reading the upcoming sections, respond to each Learning Objective in your own words.

Review the main features of neurodevelopmental, obsessive-compulsive, dissociative, and personality disorders.

- **Summarize** the distinguishing features of ADHD and autism.

- **Identify** obsessive-compulsive disorder and its major symptoms.

- **Describe** dissociative disorders.

- **Discuss** personality disorders, including antisocial personality disorder (ASPD) and borderline personality disorder (BPD).

Real World Application Question

[AQ5] Are most people with antisocial personality disorder above average in intelligence?

Now that we've discussed anxiety disorders, depressive and bipolar disorders, and schizophrenia, we can explore four additional disorders: neurodevelopmental, obsessive-compulsive, dissociative, and personality.

Neurodevelopmental Disorders

Our study of psychological disorders so far has focused on adults, but some children and teenagers also are challenged by physical, cognitive, or socioemotional symptoms that can make learning or social relationships difficult. These **neurodevelopmental disorders** usually begin during childhood but tend to persist into adulthood (World Health Organization, 2018b). They often arise from abnormal brain development and can result in a wide range of disorders, including intellectual disability (discussed in Chapter 8) as well as difficulties in communication and learning. We will focus on two of the most common neurodevelopmental disorders: *attention-deficit/hyperactivity disorder* and *autism spectrum disorder.*

Neurodevelopmental disorders
A group of disorders that usually begin in early life, causing problems with communication, cognitive abilities, social relationships, and behavior.

Attention-Deficit/Hyperactivity Disorder (ADHD)

Do you find it difficult to sit through a typical class lecture or to focus on studying? Or do you often fail to meet deadlines or forget to pay your bills? Although most of us find these tasks challenging at times, we can generally force ourselves to power through and do what needs to be done. Someone with ADHD, though, often finds such tasks nearly impossible.

Attention-deficit/hyperactivity disorder (ADHD), previously known as attention deficit disorder (ADD), is a developmental disorder characterized by a pattern of inattention and hyperactivity-impulsivity that is present in multiple settings and interferes with social, educational, or work functioning. According to the American Psychiatric Association's *Diagnostic and Statistical Manual of Mental Disorders (DSM-5)* (2013), about five percent of children have ADHD, with about twice as many boys as girls meeting the official diagnostic criteria. Symptoms typically begin prior to the age of 12 and in many cases last into adulthood.

Attention-deficit/hyperactivity disorder (ADHD) A common developmental disorder characterized by a pattern of inattention and hyperactivity-impulsivity.

Explaining ADHD Like most psychological processes, ADHD has many contributing and interacting factors, with the greatest contributors being neurological and genetic (Faraone & Larsson, 2019; Kim et al., 2017). The symptoms of ADHD, such as inattention and hyperactivity-impulsivity, contribute to various problems. An *inattentive* child may often forget to turn in assignments, daydream in class instead of listening to the teacher, and lose track of his or her books, pencils, and other items. In comparison, children with *hyperactivity* and *impulsivity* may have significant difficulty in school due to the inability to remain seated during class or to carefully read through instructions or test questions.

Experts once believed most children would "grow out" of ADHD. However, evidence suggests that some aspects of the disorder tend to persist into adolescence and adulthood (Guelzow et al., 2017). Specifically, symptoms of hyperactivity generally decline with age,

Olympic swimming star, Michael Phelps At the age of 10, Phelps became so upset at coming in second at a swim meet that he angrily threw his goggles onto the pool deck. His mother quickly reminded him that sportsmanship counted as much as winning, and together they designed a C-shaped hand signal, which she could give him from the stands, that stood for "compose yourself" (Dutton, 2014). Like many others with ADHD, Michael found that competitive sports helped him focus and successfully deal with his disorder. In fact, Michael Phelps currently holds the world record for the most medals won by any Olympic athlete at 28 (23 Gold).

whereas inattention and impulsivity persist. Women with ADHD are more likely than men to experience the *inattentive* symptoms of ADHD, such as being easily sidetracked at work, missing appointments or important details in a meeting, and misplacing significant items like car keys or a wallet. Men with ADHD more often exhibit *impulsivity* symptoms, such as having difficulty waiting their turn while standing in line, butting into others' conversations, or blurting out the answer to a question before it has been completed.

Do you see how these symptoms of ADHD might logically impede success at school or work (Weyandt et al., 2017)? They can also have a deep impact on self-esteem and interpersonal relationships. In addition, people with ADHD are more likely to suffer from serious anxiety, depression, and substance abuse disorders and to self-injure or even make a suicide attempt (Barkley, 2017; Chen et al., 2014; Rucklidge et al., 2016). These findings have prompted researchers and clinicians to closely examine and evaluate the various treatments for ADHD.

What are the treatments for ADHD? Currently, there are three major options: medications, behavior therapy, and school accommodations and interventions. In most cases, a combination of all three works best, but the most common treatment for ADHD is stimulant medication (such as Ritalin or Adderall).

PAN Practical Application of Neuroscience

Why has the use of ADHD medication markedly increased in the last 20 years? Contrary to what you might expect, the areas of the brain that help us to focus, pay attention, and control behavior are actually under aroused in someone with ADHD. Therefore, for many people with ADHD, stimulant medications help to reduce hyperactivity and improve their ability to pay attention. For others, though, the medication's side effects may be unacceptable, and finding the correct medication and dosage can be challenging. An additional concern is the increased use of ADHD drugs recreationally, to improve academic and job performance and as weight-loss aids (Martinez-Raga et al., 2016; McCarthy et al., 2018; Moran et al., 2019). Although the effectiveness of ADHD medications is well documented, there is little information regarding how they affect non-ADHD users. One worrisome study noted changes in brain chemistry resulting in increased risk-taking behaviors and disruptions in the sleep-wake cycle (Robison et al., 2017).

Fortunately, many with ADHD may benefit from behavioral interventions at home and at school. These behavioral strategies include giving clear step-by-step instructions, immediate feedback on tasks, and ample warning before transitioning between activities (e.g., Monastra, 2014). An example of a behavioral intervention comes from renowned Olympic athlete Michael Phelps, who was diagnosed with ADHD in childhood (see photo).

One of the most puzzling and controversial aspects of this disorder is determining how many children (and adults) actually have ADHD. See the STH **Scientific Thinking Highlight**.

STH Scientific Thinking Highlight

Do We All Have ADHD?

(APA Goal 2.1) Use scientific reasoning to interpret psychological phenomena

Have you heard people say things like, "These days everyone has ADHD" or, "The Internet and phones are so distracting that we're all becoming ADHD"? Why do so many people believe there's a sudden epidemic of ADHD sufferers? In this age of high stress, 24/7 news coverage, and everyone multitasking just to keep pace with constant global change, it may feel as if we do in fact all have ADHD.

What are the actual statistics? According to some of the latest data, an estimated 6.1 million (9.4 percent) U.S. children 2–17 years of age have received a diagnosis of ADHD (Danielson et al., 2018). ADHD is also prevalent among adults (Geffen & Forster, 2018), and

the number of children and adults being diagnosed with ADHD appears to be on the rise.

So what's going on? Does everyone really have ADHD, or are parents, teachers, and therapists just mislabeling normal high-energy behavior as pathological? It's certainly possible that ADHD is being over diagnosed. In fact, one study found that the rates of diagnosis and treatment for ADHD are significantly higher among children born close to the cutoff dates for initial school entry than among their older peers (Layton et al., 2018). This suggests that their comparatively fidgety behavior may be due to their relative immaturity.

One factor that could be exacerbating the symptoms of ADHD is that almost all children today spend more time indoors, with less opportunity for exercise than children had in the past. Children today are also more likely to be in institutional settings, such as day care and preschool, at very young ages. These environments may require more attention and behavioral control than some children can handle—particularly those truly suffering from ADHD. Among older kids, teens, and young adults, the increased pressure for high standardized test scores and academic and career success is particularly troublesome.

Can you see how this might prompt teachers, caregivers, and parents to seek a medical solution? Another possible factor, along with parents, teachers, and medical practitioners who label normal behavior as pathological, is aggressive campaigning by pharmaceutical companies (Molina & Pelham, 2014; Monastra, 2014).

Countering suggestions that the rise in ADHD is due to misdiagnosis, over diagnosis, and confusion with other disorders are experts who point to the strong genetic link to ADHD and the possibility that ADHD may in fact be underdiagnosed (e.g., Faraone & Larsson, 2019; Kooij et al., 2019).

Take-Home Message If you have ADHD and struggle with extreme impulsivity, restlessness, and other often-debilitating symptoms, it must be infuriating and demoralizing to have people minimizing and doubting the serious challenges you face in your everyday life. If you don't have ADHD, can you see how this controversy might lead those with the disorder to question their own strength and character—and to hesitate to seek help?

The overly simplistic claim that "everyone has ADHD" is one more example of the dangers of the numerous and damaging myths, stigma, and discrimination discussed at the start of this chapter. ADHD is a serious and potentially life-threatening illness that deserves our support and understanding.

Q Test Your Scientific Thinking

What do you think?

1. Try applying the three key principles of scientific thinking—*skepticism*, *objectivity*, and *rationalism*—to your personal beliefs and positions on whether or not ADHD is being over- or underdiagnosed. Did this type of scientific thinking help clarify or modify your own beliefs and positions? Why or why not?

2. Describe how you could use these same principles to have a meaningful conversation with someone who may have ADHD. How might this type of dialogue be helpful?

3. Finally, do you believe ADHD would be as controversial if drugs were not the major form of treatment? Where could you find the most reliable facts on ADHD medications?

(Compare your answers with those of fellow students, family, and friends. Doing so will improve your scientific thinking and your media savvy.)

Autism Spectrum Disorder (ASD)

Autism spectrum disorder (ASD) is a developmental disorder that typically begins in early childhood and involves problems with social communication and social interaction, as well as restricted, repetitive patterns of behavior, interests, or activities.

Autism may be one of the most familiar yet least understood of the developmental disorders. As with ADHD, the reported cases of ASD have risen sharply over the years and experts disagree about the explanations for this increase (e.g., Arkowitz & Lilienfeld, 2017; Graf et al., 2017). Sadly, film and television portrayals of the disorder far too often create a distorted view of a person with extraordinary talents (such as a mathematical or musical prodigy) and a complete lack of emotional or social skills. The truth is somewhere in between (see photo).

AF archive/Alamy Stock Photo

Does Sheldon Cooper have ASD? The creators of the award-winning TV sitcom, *The Big Bang Theory*, insist the Sheldon character is not designed to portray someone with autism. However, his lack of empathy, poor social skills, and excessive interests in special topics, like trains, are some of the signs of high-functioning ASD. Some have criticized the show for presenting a version of "cute autism" that creates unrealistic expectations. On the other hand, others suggest it offers good modeling and hope for people with ASD—Sheldon and his group of nerdy friends all have successful careers and active social lives. What do you think? Does Sheldon's character help or hurt in the fight against stereotypes and discrimination against people with ASD?

The most recent *Diagnostic and Statistical Manual of Mental Disorders (DSM-5)* made a significant change in the way autism-related disorders are categorized. The previously separate diagnoses (autistic, Asperger's, childhood disintegrative, and pervasive developmental disorders) are now combined into a single category, *autism spectrum disorder (ASD)*. The use of the term "spectrum" refers to a *range* of symptoms, problems, and challenges associated with the disorder. Professionals (and the public) often refer to individuals with autism as being "on the spectrum"—meaning they fall somewhere along a continuum ranging from mild to more serious degrees of the disorder. Although many people think of ASD as only a childhood disorder, it occurs in all ages, and among all racial, ethnic, and socioeconomic groups.

What are the Primary Symptoms of ASD? They generally fall into two main types: social/communicative and behavioral. People with ASD often have difficulty with both verbal and non-verbal communication. They may respond inappropriately in conversations, misinterpret abstract or emotional content, or fail to interpret non-verbal cues (such as looking pointedly at one's watch or rolling one's eyes). In conversations, people with ASD may seem to be talking *at* rather than *with* you, because they focus entirely on their own interests and ideas. Some individuals with

Autism spectrum disorder (ASD) A developmental disorder that typically begins in early childhood and involves problems with social communication and social interaction, as well as restricted, repetitive patterns of behavior, interests, or activities.

ASD may lack the ability to speak at all or may have cognitive impairments (such as low IQ). In such cases, communication may be made easier through the use of handheld touchscreen technologies that allow for messaging or emailing. Even those who are non-verbal and cannot read or write may be able to communicate by choosing pictures on a touch screen—a picture of a food they want to eat or a symbol that indicates they need to use the bathroom.

The behavioral symptoms vary, but most people with ASD show a strong preference for routine and are upset by—and resistant to—any efforts to change things. People with ASD tend to have intense, restricted interests, often focused on inappropriate objects (such as train schedules or light switches). In more severe cases, the behavioral symptoms may take the form of self-injury, such as head-banging or self-biting.

What Contributes to ASD?   As you might expect, ASD is a complex neurodevelopmental condition, but most research suggests that biological factors are the greatest contributors (Butler, 2017; Geschwind & State, 2015; Kim et al., 2017). For instance, its heritability is high and brain development in infants with autism is typically abnormal. Researchers have found that infants later diagnosed with autism had smaller-than-average head size at birth but had heads and brains much larger than normal by 6 to 14 months (Libero et al., 2016; Martinez-Murcia et al., 2016; Sacco et al., 2015). Brain-imaging studies suggest that the areas of the cortex most affected by these abnormal growth patterns, the frontal lobes, are those areas essential to complex functions such as attention, social behavior, and language.

Interestingly, research suggests that ASD's established link with a lack of theory of mind (ToM) is also probably biologically based (Cheng et al., 2015; Frith, 2016; Hutchins & Prelock, 2015). As discussed in Chapter 9, ToM is the ability to understand that others don't share the same thoughts and feelings that we do. Experts believe that this impediment helps explain the communication and social interaction problems typical of people with ASD, as well as those with ADHD.

What are the Best Treatments for ASD?   Although symptoms and severity may vary widely, ASD treatment should begin as early as possible. Treatment options usually focus on increasing effective communication, learning social skills, and decreasing problematic behaviors. Many treatment programs use *operant conditioning*, a form of therapy that you learned about in Chapter 6. This approach attempts to shape and reward desired behaviors (such as making eye contact) through the use of reinforcement. Children with ASD may also need speech and occupational therapy to directly address language or motor difficulties. Although there is no medication that specifically targets autism, children who also have other symptoms, such as hyperactivity or anxiety, may benefit from medication.

Take-Home Message   It's important to dispel the persistent myth that ASD is caused by vaccines or by the preservatives used in vaccines. As discussed in the *Scientific Thinking Highlight* for Chapter 9, numerous studies have failed to find any causal link between vaccinations and autism. The one well-publicized study reporting such a link was clearly fraudulent and later retracted (e.g., Eggertson, 2010; Hviid et al., 2019). There is a similar lack of strong evidence for dietary or environmental factors. It's easy to understand, though, how well-meaning parents would grasp at any potential solution to prevent or treat this devastating disorder. However, again as we discussed in Chapter 9, parents who refuse to vaccinate needlessly expose their children and others to dangerous consequences.

Obsessive-compulsive disorder (OCD)   A psychological disorder characterized by persistent, unwanted, fearful thoughts (obsessions) and irresistible urges to perform repetitive and ritualized behaviors (compulsions).

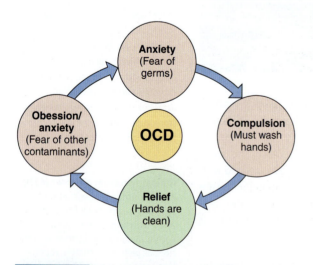

FIGURE 13.14 **The vicious cycle of obsession and compulsion**   Note how the anxiety connected to obsessions about germs leads to compulsive behaviors that relieve the anxiety. However, the relief, which only temporarily reduces the anxiety, ultimately reinforces and increases the original obsessions—thus creating a vicious cycle.

Obsessive-Compulsive Disorder (OCD)

Do you sometimes worry about whether or not you locked your doors and feel compelled to run back and check? Most people do. However, people with **obsessive compulsive disorder (OCD)** experience persistent, unwanted, fearful thoughts (obsessions) and irresistible urges to perform repetitive and ritualized behaviors (compulsions) to help relieve the anxiety created by the obsession (see **Figure 13.14**).

In adulthood, women experience OCD at a slightly higher rate than men, whereas men are more commonly affected in childhood (American Psychiatric Association, 2013).

Common examples of obsessions are fear of germs, being hurt, or of hurting others, and troubling religious or sexual thoughts. Examples of compulsions are repeatedly checking, counting, cleaning, washing all or specific body parts, or putting things in a certain order. As mentioned before, everyone worries and sometimes double-checks, but people with OCD have these thoughts and do these rituals for an hour or more each day.

Imagine what it would be like to worry so obsessively about germs that you compulsively wash your hands hundreds of times a day, until they are raw and bleeding. Most sufferers of OCD realize that their actions are senseless. But when they try to stop the behavior, they experience mounting anxiety, which is relieved only by giving in to the compulsions.

Given that numerous biopsychosocial factors contribute to OCD, it is most often treated with a combination of psychotherapeutic drugs, cognitive behavior therapy (CBT), and exposure and response prevention (ERP) therapy (Fontenelle & Yücel, 2019; Hirschtritt et al., 2017; Lee et al., 2019). A key component of ERP therapies is controlled exposure to the anxiety-producing stimulus or situation, while preventing negative consequences, which leads to extinction. See Chapters 6 and 14 and **Figure 13.15** for examples of how to cope with OCD.

Dissociative Disorders

If you've ever been daydreaming while driving home from your college campus, and then could not remember making one single turn, you may have experienced a normal form of *dissociation*, meaning a mild disconnection from your immediate surroundings. The most dramatic extremes of this type of detachment are the **dissociative disorders**, characterized by a sudden break (*dissociation*) in conscious awareness, self-identity, and memory. Note that this is a disconnection or detachment from immediate surroundings or from physical or emotional experience. It is very different from the loss of contact with reality seen in *psychosis*.

There are several forms of dissociative disorders, including dissociative amnesia and dissociative identity disorder (DID). However, all are characterized by a splitting apart (a *dissociation*) of significant aspects of experience from memory or consciousness.

The most controversial, and least common, dissociative disorder is **dissociative identity disorder (DID)**—previously known as multiple personality disorder. An individual with this disorder has at least two separate and distinct personalities (or *identities*) (**Figure 13.16**). Each personality has unique memories, behaviors, and social relationships. Transition from one personality to another occurs suddenly and is often prompted by psychological stress (Brand et al., 2016; Huntjens et al., 2016). Typically, there is a "core" personality, who has no knowledge or awareness of the alternate personalities, but is often aware of lost memories and lost periods of time. The disorder is diagnosed evenly among men and women (American Psychiatric Association, 2013).

Why is DID a controversial diagnosis? Some experts suggest that many cases are faked or result from false memories or an unconscious need to please a therapist (Arkowitz & Lilienfeld, 2017; Lynn et al., 2016; Merckelbach et al., 2016). In contrast, a study comparing women with genuine diagnoses of DID, female actors asked to simulate DID, women with PTSD, and healthy controls supported previous findings that DID is rooted in traumatic experiences, such as neglect or abuse in childhood (Vissia et al., 2016).

Personality Disorders

Imagine if the characteristics of someone's personality were so inflexible and maladaptive that they significantly impaired the person's ability to function. This is what occurs with **personality disorders**. Several types of personality disorders are included in this category in the *DSM*, but here we will focus on antisocial personality disorder (ASPD) and borderline personality disorder (BPD).

FIGURE 13.15 Managing OCD Many celebrities suffer from OCD, including actors Megan Fox (pictured here) and Leonardo DiCaprio, and singer/actor Justin Timberlake. Fortunately, people can learn to manage the symptoms of OCD, through therapy and medication, and lead highly productive and fulfilling lives.

Dissociative disorder One of a group of psychological disorders characterized by a sudden break (*dissociation*) in conscious awareness, self-identity, and memory.

Dissociative identity disorder (DID) A psychological disorder characterized by the presence of two or more distinct personality systems (or identities) in the same individual; previously known as multiple personality disorder (MPD).

Personality disorder A psychological disorder characterized by chronic, inflexible, maladaptive personality traits, which contribute to significant impairment of social and occupational functioning.

FIGURE 13.16 A personal account of DID Herschel Walker, Pro Bowl NFL football player, Olympic bobsledder, business and family man, now suggests that each of the people who played these roles were actually his "alters," or alternate personalities. He has been officially diagnosed as having *dissociative identity disorder (DID)*. Although some have suggested that the disorder helped him succeed as a professional athlete, it played havoc with his personal life. He's now in treatment and has written a book, *Breaking Free*, hoping to change the public's image of DID.

Antisocial personality disorder (ASPD) A personality disorder characterized by egocentrism and a lack of conscience, remorse, or empathy for others.

Antisocial Personality Disorder (ASPD)

Have you ever met, or worked for someone, who was unusually self-centered, manipulative, deceitful, and willing to use others for personal gain? People with **antisocial personality disorder (ASPD)**—sometimes called *psychopaths* or *sociopaths*—are typically egocentric and exhibit a lack of conscience, remorse, or empathy for others. Individuals with ASPD also typically act impulsively, without giving thought to the consequences. They are usually poised when confronted with their destructive behavior and feel contempt for anyone they are able to manipulate. Moreover, they typically change jobs and relationships suddenly and often have a history of truancy from school or of being expelled for destructive behavior.

Tragically, those with ASPD feel little personal distress, they're seldom motivated to change, and their maladaptive behaviors may lead to considerable harm to others (e.g., Baskin-Sommers et al., 2016; Brem et al., 2018; Newcorn et al., 2016). These behaviors typically begin in childhood or early adolescence and continue through adulthood. They also lie so far outside the ethical and legal standards of society that many consider ASPD the most serious of all psychological disorders.

Surprisingly, people with antisocial personalities can be charming and persuasive, and they often have remarkably good insight into the needs and weaknesses of other people. [AQ5] However, despite the myths, movie portrayals, and popular opinion, high intelligence is NOT one of the characteristics of ASPD identified in the *DSM* (see photo). In fact, one study found that most people with ASPD actually score *lower* than average on intelligence tests (American Psychiatric Association, 2013; de Ribera et al., 2019). Why are they so often portrayed as "evil genius masterminds"? It may be that their charm, persuasiveness, and self-confidence just make them appear more intelligent than they are.

What contributes to ASPD? Twin and adoption studies suggest a possible genetic predisposition (Dhamija et al., 2016; Rosenström et al., 2017). Researchers also have found abnormally low autonomic activity during stress, right-hemisphere abnormalities, reduced gray matter in the frontal lobes, and biochemical disturbances in people with ASPD (Jiang et al., 2015; Kumari et al., 2014; Smith et al., 2016). In addition, MRI brain scans of incarcerated people who show little empathy and remorse for their violent crimes (rape, murder, or attempted murder) reveal reduced gray matter volume in the prefrontal cortex (Gregory et al., 2012).

Evidence also exists for environmental or psychological factors. People with ASPD often come from homes characterized by severely abusive parenting styles, emotional deprivation, harsh and inconsistent disciplinary practices, residential instability, and antisocial parental behavior (Crego & Widiger, 2016; Dargis et al., 2016; Mok et al., 2016). Still other studies show a strong interaction with both heredity and the environment (Dhamija et al., 2016; Rosenström et al., 2017).

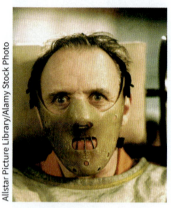

Allstar Picture Library/Alamy Stock Photo

Famous characters with ASPD
In the movie, *Silence of the Lambs*, Anthony Hopkins (pictured here) portrayed a vicious, highly intelligent, serial killer with ASPD. However, most people who have this disorder are not vicious killers nor necessarily intelligent. But they may still harm others in less dramatic ways—as crooked politicians or ruthless leaders, such as King Joffrey from the television program *Game of Thrones*.

Borderline Personality Disorder (BPD)

Mary's troubles first began in adolescence. She began to miss curfew, was frequently truant, and her grades declined sharply. Mary later became promiscuous and prostituted herself several times to get drug money . . . . She also quickly fell in love and overly idealized new friends. But when they quickly (and inevitably) disappointed her, she would angrily cast them aside. . . . Mary's problems, coupled with a preoccupation with inflicting pain on herself (by cutting and burning) and persistent thoughts of suicide, eventually led to her admittance to a psychiatric hospital at age 26 (Kring et al., 2010, pp. 354–355).

Borderline personality disorder (BPD) A psychological disorder characterized by severe instability in emotions, relationships, and self-image, along with impulsive and self-destructive behaviors.

Mary's experiences are all classic symptoms of **borderline personality disorder (BPD)**. The core features of this disorder include a pervasive pattern of instability in emotions, relationships, and self-image, along with impulsive and self-destructive behaviors, such as truancy, promiscuity, drinking, gambling, and eating sprees. In addition, people with BPD may attempt suicide and sometimes engage in self-mutilating ("cutting") behaviors (Calati & Courtet, 2016; Khan et al., 2017; Sher et al., 2016).

Those with BPD often see themselves and everyone else in absolute terms—as either perfect or worthless. Constantly seeking reassurance from others, they also may quickly erupt in anger at the slightest sign of disapproval. As you might expect, this disorder is typically marked by a long history of broken friendships, divorces, and lost jobs.

Unfortunately, people with this disorder appear to have a deep well of intense loneliness and a chronic fear of abandonment. Given their troublesome personality traits, friends, lovers, and even family members and therapists often do in fact "abandon" them—thus creating a self-fulfilling prophecy. Sadly, this disorder is among the most commonly diagnosed and functionally disabling of all psychological disorders (Arntz, 2015; Gunderson & Links, 2014; Rizvi & Salters-Pedneault, 2013). Although the term *borderline personality disorder* originally implied that the person was on the borderline between neurosis and psychosis, BPD has little relation to most psychotic disorders. The good news is that BPD can be reliably diagnosed and it often does respond to professional intervention—particularly in young people (Bateman & Fonagy, 2016; Edel et al., 2017; Rizvi et al., 2017).

What contributes to BPD? Some research points to environmental factors, such as a childhood history of neglect, emotional deprivation, and physical, sexual, or emotional abuse (Bichescu-Burian et al., 2017; Chesin et al., 2015; Hunt et al., 2015). From a biological perspective, BPD tends to run in families, and some data suggest that it is a result of impaired functioning of the brain's frontal lobes and limbic system, areas that control impulsive behaviors (Denny et al., 2016; Soloff et al., 2017; Visintin et al., 2016). As an example, research using neuroimaging reveals that people with BPD show more activity in parts of the brain associated with the experience of negative emotions, coupled with less activity in parts of the brain that help suppress negative emotion (Ruocco et al., 2013). As in almost all other psychological disorders, most researchers agree that BPD results from an interaction of biopsychosocial factors (Crego & Widiger, 2016; Skoglund et al., 2019; Stone, 2014).

Retrieval Practice 13.5 | Other Disorders

Self-Test Completing this self-test, and then checking your answers by clicking on the answer button or by looking in Appendix B, will provide immediate feedback and helpful practice for exams.

1. Women with ADHD are more likely than men to experience the _____ symptoms of ADHD, whereas men more often exhibit _____ symptoms.

   a. inattentive; impulsivity

   b. behavioral; cognitive

   c. depressive; anxiety

   d. hyperactivity; inattentive

2. Repetitive, ritualistic behaviors, such as hand washing, counting, or putting things in order, are called a(n) _____.

   a. obsessions   c. ruminations

   b. compulsions   d. phobias

3. A disorder characterized by disturbances in conscious awareness, self-identity, and memory is known as a(n) _____.

   a. dissociative disorder

   b. disoriented disorder

   c. displacement disorder

   d. identity disorder

4. _____ is characterized by the presence of two or more separate and distinct personality systems in the same individual.

   a. Multiple-personality dysfunction (MPD)

   b. Disassociation disorder (DD)

   c. Fictional-actor delusion (FAD)

   d. Dissociative identity disorder (DID)

Q Test Your Critical Thinking

1. How would you explain to others that schizophrenia is not the same as dissociative identity disorder (DID) (formerly called multiple personality disorder [MPD])?

2. Does the fact that research shows a genetic component to antisocial personality disorder change your opinion regarding the degree of guilt and responsibility of a mass-murdering terrorist after a vicious shooting spree?

Real World Application Question

[AQ5] Are most people with antisocial personality disorder above average in intelligence?

Hint: Look in the text for **[AQ5]**

13.6 | Key Issues in Psychological Disorders

LEARNING OBJECTIVES

Retrieval Practice   While reading the upcoming sections, respond to each Learning Objective in your own words.

Summarize the role of gender and cultural differences, suicide, and ACEs on psychological disorders.

- **Discuss** the possible gender differences in depression.

- **Explain** why it is difficult to directly compare psychological disorders, such as schizophrenia, across cultures.

- **Describe** the dangers and myths of suicide and how to prevent it.

- **Discuss** how adverse childhood experiences (ACEs) and resilience are related to psychological disorders.

Real World Application Question

[AQ6]   Do certain psychological disorders exist in some cultures but not in others?

We began this chapter by discussing the complexities and problems with defining, identifying, and classifying psychological disorders. In this final section, we explore a few of the many ways in which men and women differ in their experience with psychological disorders. We then look at cultural variations in psychological disorders and how to avoid ethnocentrism. We close with two issues that are far too often a part of psychological disorders—suicide and adverse childhood experiences (ACEs).

Gender and Cultural Effects

When you picture someone suffering from depression, anxiety, alcoholism, or antisocial personality disorder, what is the gender of each person? Most people tend to visualize a woman for the first two of these examples, and a man for the last two. Interestingly, research does support several gender differences among the various psychological disorders.

Let's start with the well-established fact that around the world, the rate of severe depression for women is about double that for men (Kuehner, 2017; World Health Organization, 2017). Why is there such a striking gender difference? Certain risk factors for depression (such as genetic predisposition, marital problems, pain, and medical illness) are common to both men and women. However, poverty is a well-known contributor to many psychological disorders, and women are far more likely than men to fall into the lowest socioeconomic groups. Women also experience more wage disparity and discrimination in the work force, sexual trauma, partner abuse, and chronic stress in their daily lives, which are all well-known contributing factors to depression and other disorders (Kelly et al., 2016; Oram et al., 2017; Salk et al., 2017).

Research also suggests that some gender differences in depression may relate to the way women and men regulate their emotions. One study found that women tend to use more flexible and different emotion regulation strategies than men (Goubet & Chrysikou, 2019). For instance, women more often engage in problem-solving, self-blame, social support, and emotional expression, whereas men more often use avoidant, withdrawal, and suppression strategies to deal with their emotions.

Another possible explanation for gender differences in the diagnosis of depression may be that most common symptoms of stereotypical depression, such as crying, low energy, dejected facial expressions, and withdrawal from social activities, are more socially acceptable for women than for men in most Western cultures. In contrast, men in these same societies are typically socialized to suppress their emotions and to show their distress by acting out (being aggressive), acting impulsively (driving recklessly and committing petty crimes), or engaging in substance abuse. Given these differences in socialization and behaviors, combined with the fact that gender differences in depression are more pronounced in cultures with traditional gender roles, male depression may "simply" be expressed in less stereotypical ways, and therefore be underdiagnosed (Fields & Cochran, 2011; Pérez & Gaviña, 2015; Seedat et al., 2009).

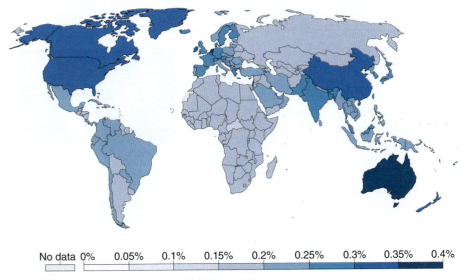

No data 0%   0.05%   0.1%   0.15%   0.2%   0.25%   0.3%   0.35%   0.4%

Source: IHME, Global Burden of Disease–Richie & Roser, 2018.

FIGURE 13.17   **Share of the population with schizophrenia**   Note how the prevalence of schizophrenia varies between countries, typically ranging from 0.2 to 0.45 (Ritchie & Roser, 2018). How might cultural differences contribute to these wide variations?

Understanding the importance of gender differences, genetic predispositions, external environmental factors (like poverty), and social and cultural factors, such as gender expectations about how depression is expressed, may help mental health professionals better understand individual and gender-related differences in depression.

Culture and Psychological Disorders

Among the Chippewa, Cree, and Montagnais-Naskapi Indians in Canada, there is a disorder called *windigo*—or *wiitiko*—*psychosis*, characterized by delusions and cannibalistic impulses. Believing they have been possessed by the spirit of a windigo, a cannibal giant with a heart and entrails of ice, victims become severely depressed (Faddiman, 1997). As the malady begins, the individual typically experiences loss of appetite, diarrhea, vomiting, and insomnia, and he or she may see people turning into beavers and other edible animals. In later stages, the victim becomes obsessed with cannibalistic thoughts and may even attack and kill loved ones in order to devour their flesh (Berreman, 1971; Thomason, 2014). If you were a therapist, how would you treat this disorder? Does it fit neatly into any category of psychological disorders that we've discussed in this chapter?

Keep in mind that individuals from different cultures experience psychological disorders in a variety of ways. To simplify things, let's focus on schizophrenia. As you can see in **Figure 13.17**, the share of the global population suffering from schizophrenia is different around the world— yet the rate for men and women is approximately the same (around 10.5 million each) (Ritchie & Roser, 2018). It is unclear whether these numerical differences result from actual differences in prevalence of the disorder or from differences in definition, diagnosis, or reporting (Hsu, 2016; Luhrmann et al., 2015; McLean et al., 2014). The symptoms of schizophrenia also vary across cultures (Campbell et al., 2017; López & Guarnaccia, 2016), as do the particular stressors that may provoke its onset (**Figure 13.18**).

Surprisingly, despite the advanced treatment facilities and methods in industrialized nations, the prognosis for people with schizophrenia is sometimes better in non-industrialized societies. The reason may be that the core symptoms of schizophrenia (poor rapport with others, incoherent speech, and so on) make it more difficult to survive in highly industrialized countries. In addition, in most industrialized nations families and other support groups are less likely to feel responsible for relatives and friends who have schizophrenia (Akyeampong et al., 2015; Burns et al., 2014; Eaton et al., 2012). On the other hand, some less developed countries, such as Indonesia, still shackle and confine their mentally ill in filthy cells without basic human rights (Quiano, 2016). For more information on cultural similarities and differences in psychological disorders, see the following **GCD** **Gender and Cultural Diversity** feature.

David Alan Harvey/National Geographic Image Collection

a. Some stressors are culturally specific, such as feeling possessed by evil forces or being the victim of witchcraft.

RubberBall Productions/Brand X Pictures/Getty Images

b. Other stressors are shared by many cultures, such as the unexpected death of a loved one or loss of a job.

FIGURE 13.18   **What is stressful?**

GCD Gender and Cultural Diversity

Avoiding Ethnocentrism

(APA Goal 2.5) Incorporate sociocultural factors in scientific inquiry

Most research on psychological disorders originates and is conducted primarily in Western cultures. Do you see how such a restricted sampling can limit our understanding of these disorders? Or how this limited view could lead to *ethnocentrism*—a view that one's own culture is "correct?"

Fortunately, cross-cultural researchers have devised ways to overcome these difficulties (Bernal et al., 2014; Hsu, 2016; Sue et al., 2016). For example, Robert Nishimoto (1988) has found several *culture-general symptoms* that are useful in diagnosing disorders across cultures (**Table 13.5**)

[AQ6] In addition, Nishimoto found several *culture-bound symptoms*, which are unique to different groups and generally appear

CRIS BOURONCLE/AFP/ Getty Images

only in one population (see photo). Vietnamese and Chinese respondents report "fullness in head," Mexican respondents note "problems with [their] memory," and Anglo-American respondents report "shortness of breath" and "headaches." Apparently, people learn to express their problems in ways that are acceptable to others in the same culture (Brislin, 2000; Hsu, 2016; Shannon et al., 2015).

This division between culture-general and culture-bound symptoms also helps us better understand depression. Certain symptoms of depression (such as intense sadness, poor concentration, and low energy) seem to exist across all cultures (Walsh & Cross, 2013; World Health Organization, 2011). As evidence of some culture-bound symptoms, feelings of guilt are found more often in North America and Europe than in other parts of the world. Furthermore, in China, *somatization* (the conversion of depression into bodily complaints) occurs more frequently than it does in other parts of the world (Grover & Ghosh, 2014; Lim et al., 2011).

Just as there are culture-bound symptoms, researchers also have found culture-bound disorders (**Figure 13.19**). The earlier example of windigo psychosis, a disorder limited to a few groups of Canadian Indians, illustrates just such a case. Interestingly, the distinctions between many of the previously culture-bound and cultural-general symptoms and disorders may be disappearing as a result of globalization (Kato & Kanba, 2016; Ventriglio et al., 2016).

TABLE 13.5	Culture-General Symptoms of Mental Health Difficulties	
Nervous	Trouble sleeping	Low spirits
Weak all over	Personal worries	Restless
Feel apart, alone	Can't get along	Hot all over
Worry all the time	Can't do anything worthwhile	Nothing turns out right

Source: Brislin, 2000.

Puerto Rican and other Latin cultures *Ataque de nervios* ("attack of nerves")	Southeast Asian, Malaysian, Indonesian, Thai Running amok	West African Brain fog	Ethiopian Possession by the *Zar*	South Chinese and Vietnamese *Koro*	Westerners *Anorexia nervosa* (as other countries become Westernized they're showing some rare cases of anorexia)
Symptoms: Trembling, heart palpitations, and seizure-like episodes often associated with the death of a loved one, accidents, or family conflict	**Symptoms:** Wild, out-of-control, aggressive behaviors and attempts to injure or kill others	**Symptoms:** "Brain tiredness," a mental and physical response to the challenges of schooling	**Symptoms:** Involuntary movements, mutism, or incomprehensible language	**Symptoms:** Belief that the penis is retracting into the abdomen and that when it is fully retracted, death will result; attempts to prevent the supposed retraction may lead to severe physical damage	**Symptoms:** Occurs primarily among young women; preoccupied with thinness, they exercise excessively and refuse to eat; death can result

FIGURE 13.19 Culture-bound disorders Some disorders are fading as remote areas become more Westernized, whereas other disorders (such as anorexia nervosa) are spreading as other countries adopt Western values.

Suicide

Did you know that up to 90 percent of people who have died by suicide were previously diagnosed with mental disorders, such as depression, substance-related and addictive disorders, psychosis, and anxiety (Brådvik, 2018)? Or that around the world, suicide is the second-leading cause of death among young adults—ages 15 to 20—and that within the U.S. suicide increased by

35 percent among adults (ages 18 to 34) between 2007 and 2017 (Trust for America's Health, 2019; World Health Organization, 2018c). Fortunately, the suicide rate *deceased* in other countries, like Japan, China, Russia, and most of Western Europe during that same time period (Weir, 2019).

PA Practical Application—Understanding and Preventing Suicide

What leads to death by suicide? Like many of the problems associated with psychological disorders, suicide is an extremely complex issue with multiple contributing factors. Even people who enjoy enormous fame and financial success may be at risk (see photos). The one constant and tragic fact is that many of these deaths were permanent solutions to what might have been temporary problems. Suicide is a lifelong catastrophe for families and entire communities. What can we do? The first step is to clarify the myths and misunderstandings (**Table 13.6**), along with recognizing the danger signs and when to seek help for ourselves and others.

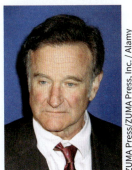

Celebrity deaths by suicide You may know the famous people pictured here: comedian Robin Williams and TV personalities Simone Battle and Anthony Bourdain. These three individuals all died by suicide, along with fashion designer Kate Spade, musician Kurt Cobain, Olympic medalist Jeret Peterson, football player Junior Seau, writers Virginia Woolf and Ernest Hemingway, and artist Vincent van Gogh.

TABLE 13.6	**Common Myths About Suicide**

Can you identify which of the following are true and which are false?

1. Suicides can trigger "copycat" attempts.
2. People who talk about suicide are less likely to actually complete it.
3. Suicide usually takes place with little or no warning.
4. Suicidal people are fully intent on dying.
5. Children of parents who attempt suicide are at greater risk of dying by suicide.
6. Suicidal people remain so forever.
7. Men are more likely than women to kill themselves by suicide.
8. When a suicidal person has been severely depressed and seems to be "snapping out of it," the danger of suicide decreases substantially.
9. Only depressed people die by suicide.
10. Thinking about suicide is rare.
11. Asking a depressed person about suicide will push him or her over the edge and cause a suicidal act that might not otherwise have occurred.
12. Self-injury, such as cutting, burning, and hitting oneself, inevitably escalates to suicide.

Now, compare your responses to the experts' answers and explanations:

1. **True** There is substantial evidence that media reports of deaths by suicide are linked with an increase in the number of copycat suicides—particularly the deaths of celebrities (e.g., Bridge et al., 2019; Çelik et al., 2016; Fahey et al., 2018). Although the term "copycat" has been criticized for possibly trivializing the deep suffering that leads to suicide (Owens, 2016), intense media coverage does increase a type of mimicry among some individuals. As we'll discuss later in this chapter, the fictional and somewhat glamourous portrayal of suicide in the Netflix series *13 Reasons Why* (see photo) was associated with a significant increase in teen suicides (Sanson et al., 2019).

Actor Katherine Langford portrayed Hannah, the lead character in the controversial Netflix series, *13 Reasons Why*, about suicide.

2. and 3. **False** Up to three-quarters of those who die by suicide do talk about suicide and give warnings about their intentions beforehand. They may say, "If something happens to me, I want you to . . . ", or "Life just isn't worth living." They also provide behavioral

(Continued)

TABLE 13.6	Common Myths About Suicide (*Continued*)

clues, such as giving away valued possessions, withdrawing from family and friends, and losing interest in favorite activities.

4. False   Only about 3 percent to 5 percent of suicidal people truly intend to die. Most are just unsure about how to go on living. Unfortunately, they can't see their problems objectively enough to recognize alternative courses of action. They often gamble with death, arranging it so that fate or others will save them. However, once the suicidal crisis passes, they're generally grateful to be alive.

5. True   Children of parents who have attempted or died by suicide are at much greater risk of following in their footsteps. It has been said that "The person who dies by suicide puts his psychological skeleton in the survivor's emotional closet" (cited in Schneidman, 1969, p. 225).

6. False   People who want to kill themselves are usually suicidal only for a limited period.

7. True   Although women are much more likely to attempt suicide, men are far more likely to actually complete it (see **Figure 13.20**).

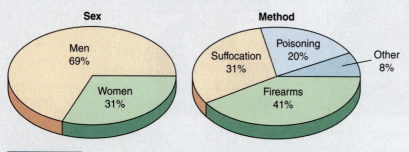

FIGURE 13.20   **Suicides, by sex and method of death, among those with known mental health conditions**   As you can see, a far higher proportion of suicides are committed by men. However, psychological disorders could have been present in other suicides and not diagnosed, known, or reported (Centers for Disease Control and Prevention, 2018).

8. False   When people are first coming out of a depression, they are at greater risk because they now have the energy to actually attempt suicide.

9. False   Suicide rates are highest among people with major depressive disorders. In addition, suicide is the leading contributor to premature death in people who suffer from schizophrenia, anxiety disorders, and alcohol and other substance-related disorders. Poor physical health, serious illness, loneliness, unemployment, and even natural disasters also may push some people over the edge.

10. False   Estimates from various studies are that 40 percent to 80 percent of the general public have thought about attempting suicide at least once in their lives.

11. False   Because society often considers suicide a terrible, shameful act, asking directly about it can give the person permission to talk. In fact, not asking is more likely to lead to further isolation and depression.

12. False   Although people who engage in self-injuring behaviors are at significantly greater risk of suicide (e.g., Chesin et al., 2017), their intention is not to kill themselves, and the behaviors don't inevitably lead to suicide. This problem is officially known as **nonsuicidal self-injury (NSSI)**. Most common among adolescents and young adults, NSSI usually results from attempts to punish oneself for perceived faults, to provide distraction from painful emotions through physical pain, and to express internal feelings in an external way (Bresin et al., 2018; Mayo Clinic, 2017; Scherr et al., 2019). This is particularly true for individuals who are unaware of and less able to cope with feelings of anger (Thomassin et al., 2017).

General Sources: American Association of Suicidology, 2019; Arkowitz & Lilienfeld, 2017; Birmaher & Brent, 2016; Rebok et al., 2015; World Health Organization, 2019.

Nonsuicidal self-injury (NSSI)
A serious behavior problem in which people deliberately harm themselves without lethal intent.

What Can You Do If You Think Someone Is Suicidal?   If you have friends or loved ones who you think might be planning to injure themselves, it may feel as if you're walking through a minefield when you're attempting to comfort and help them. What do the experts suggest?

What NOT to Do:

- **Don't ignore the warning signs.**   Depression, like cancer or heart disease, is a life-threatening disease. Knowing the symptoms, risk factors, and emergency signs of suicide (see **Table 13.7**), can increase your confidence in how and when to intervene (Ramchand et al., 2016).

- **Don't equate suicide with "selfishness."**   Just as we wouldn't say that someone suffering from cancer or heart disease died because he or she lacked courage and was being selfish, we need to recognize the courage and strength of the chronically and deeply depressed who struggle each day NOT to die.

- **Don't be afraid to discuss suicide.**   In a calm voice, ask the person a direct question, such as "Are you thinking of hurting yourself?" Many people fear the topic of suicide because they think they might put that idea into the other person's head. As mentioned before, the reality is that virtually every adult knows what suicide is, and many have even considered

TABLE 13.7   Danger Signs for Suicide

General symptoms:

- the three H's—feeling Helpless, Hopeless, and Hapless
- alcohol and other drug abuse
- irritability
- loss of interest in daily activities
- persistent fatigue and lack of energy and strength
- insomnia or excessive sleeping
- difficulty concentrating or feeling very restless
- noticeably reduced or increased appetite

Risk factors:

- previous history of substance abuse or suicide attempt
- family history of substance abuse, suicide attempt, suicide, or mental illness

- firearms, medications, or other methods for suicide readily available
- recent emotional trauma, such as incarceration, loss of a loved one, or loss of an important job

Emergency signs:

- increasing use of alcohol and other drugs
- acting anxious or agitated or displaying extreme mood swings
- talking about unbearable pain, feeling trapped, or being a burden to others
- talking about wanting to die or having no reason to live
- talking about wanting to kill oneself or seeking revenge
- social withdrawal and sleeping too little or too much
- seeking methods for suicide, such as buying a gun

Sources: American Association of Suicidology, 2019; Arkowitz & Lilienfeld, 2017; Birmaher & Brent, 2016; Brådvik, 2018; Handley et al., 2018; National Institute of Mental Health, 2016; World Health Organization, 2019.

it for themselves. Furthermore, people who are told "you can't be seriously considering suicide" often feel even more alone, become less likely to share their true feelings, and become more likely to actually attempt suicide.

- **Don't abandon the person after the suicidal crisis has seemingly passed.**   Depression and suicidal thoughts don't magically disappear. For many, the fight against depression is a painful lifelong struggle, and your friend or loved one needs your ongoing support.

What to Do:

- **Stay with the person.**   Encourage him or her to talk to you rather than to withdraw. Show the person that you care, but do not give false reassurances that "everything will be okay." If you feel personally unsafe with the person or that you can't handle the crisis by yourself, share your suspicions with parents, friends, or others who can help in a suicidal crisis. To save a life, you may have to betray a secret when someone confides in you.

- **Be Rogerian.**   As mentioned in Chapters 12 and 14, Carl Rogers's four essential qualities of communication (*empathy, unconditional positive regard, genuineness,* and *active listening*) are probably the best, and safest, approach for any situation—including talking with a depressed, suicidal person.

- **Reduce access to lethal means.**   Given that more than half of all suicides in the U.S. are the result of firearms, reducing their access is one of the most effective methods of suicide prevention (Centers for Disease Control and Prevention, 2018b; Weir, 2019).

- **Find help fast.**   If a friend or loved one mentions suicide or if you believe he or she is considering it, remove any weapons, medications, or other means the person might use to harm himself or herself. Discourage the person from using alcohol or illegal drugs, and get professional help fast. Most cities have walk-in centers that provide emergency counseling. Also, consider talking to the person's family, a therapist, or the toll-free 7/24 hotline 1-800-SUICIDE or 1-800-273-TALK. If you think the situation calls for emergency intervention, call 911 or go to the emergency room without delay.

Adverse Childhood Experiences (ACEs)

We all intuitively "know" that a troubled childhood creates significantly higher risks of serious psychological disorders, as well as physical, emotional, and behavioral problems. But what do we really know? What does the scientific research show?

One of the largest research studies of later-life health and its connection to *adverse childhood experiences (ACEs)* was conducted by Kaiser Permanente, a large American medical insurance company, and the Centers for Disease Control and Prevention (CDC). The original study involved two waves of data collection from 1995 to 1997, with over 17,000 participants who were recruited to complete confidential surveys regarding their childhood experiences and current health status and behaviors. Researchers from this study and others have documented a significant link between ACEs and health and social problems across the lifespan (e.g., Felitti et al., 1998; Merrick et al., 2018; Ranjbar & Erb, 2019).

Adverse childhood experiences (ACEs) Abuse, neglect, and other potentially traumatic events, occurring before the age of 18, which may have negative lasting effects on physical and mental well-being.

What exactly are **adverse childhood experiences (ACEs)**? This term is used to describe all types of abuse, neglect, and other potentially traumatic events that occur before the age of 18, and may have negative lasting effects on physical and mental well-being.

The adverse events included in this study were divided into ten categories—three related to child abuse (emotional, physical, and sexual), two connected with child neglect (emotional and physical), and five involving household challenges (mother treated violently, mental illness, divorce or separation, substance abuse, and an incarcerated family member). Each category had a value of one point and participants could receive a score from 0 to 10.

Tragically, almost two-thirds of study participants reported at least one ACE, and as the number of ACEs increased the participants' risk for negative outcomes also increased. Why? The toxic levels of stress created by ACEs are believed to disrupt healthy physical, cognitive, and socioemotional development. Victims of ACEs often experience significant lifelong problems related to *chronic pain* (Chapter 3), which currently affects millions of people around the world (Ortiz, 2019; Ranjbar & Erb, 2019). Experiencing these traumatic events is also linked to compulsive eating leading to obesity, as well as smoking, alcohol and drug abuse, and other lifelong unhealthy behaviors. Researchers suggest that such behaviors are often attempts to cope with the emotional pain, anger, anxiety, and depression related to the earlier ACEs.

Keep in mind that the presence of ACEs does not mean that any one individual will inevitably experience poor life outcomes. Even when childhood trauma has occurred, several protective factors, including certain personality traits, such as *optimism* (Chapter 12) and *resilience* (discussed in the following **PP** **PositivePsych** feature), can help to offset many of the potential negative health and life outcomes. If you or someone you know has experienced several ACEs, it is particularly important to seek therapy, which can substantially reduce the risk of these negative outcomes. You'll learn more about methods of therapy in Chapter 14.

In addition, it's also very important to address the larger societal conditions, like homelessness, poverty, mass incarceration, and so on, which put children and families at risk. The following link from the CDC offers specific strategies designed to create safe, stable, nurturing relationships and environments, which hopefully may prevent ACEs before they happen: https://www.cdc.gov/violenceprevention/childabuseandneglect/essentials.html

Resilience The ability to recover from or adapt effectively in the face of adversity.

PP Practical Application: **PositivePsych**

Promoting Resilience in Children and Adults

(APA Goal 1.3) Describe applications of psychology

The bamboo that bends is stronger than the oak that resists.
— Japanese proverb

Children fortunate enough to grow up with days filled with play and discovery, nights that provide rest and security, and dedicated, loving parents usually turn out fine. But what about those who are raised in violent, impoverished, or neglectful situations? We all know that a troubled childhood creates significantly higher risks of serious psychological disorders, as well as physical, emotional, and behavioral problems. What is it about some children

living in harsh circumstances that helps them survive and prosper, despite the odds?

The answer apparently is **resilience**—the ability to recover and adapt effectively in the face of adversity. Like bamboo that bends in strong winds, a resilient person flexes in response to hard times. Resilience has been studied throughout the world in a variety of situations, including homelessness, natural disasters, war, and family violence (e.g., Laird et al., 2019; Miller et al., 2018; Ortiz, 2019). This topic is of particular interest to positive psychologists because it can teach us better ways to reduce risk, promote competence, and shift the course of development in more positive directions.

What characterizes a resilient child? Two pioneering researchers—Ann Masten and Douglas Coatsworth (1998)—identified several traits and the environmental circumstances that might account for the resilient child's success: (1) good intellectual functioning; (2) relationships with caring adults; and, as they grow older, (3) the ability to regulate their attention, emotions, and behavior. These traits obviously

dpa/dpa picture alliance/Alamy Stock Photo

overlap. Good intellectual functioning, for example, may help resilient children solve problems or protect themselves from adverse conditions, as well as attract the interest of teachers who serve as nurturing adults. Their greater intellectual skills also may help them learn from their experiences and from the caring adults, so in later life they have better self-regulation skills.

Resiliency is not just a trait developed in childhood that helps us cope and compensate during difficult times. Adversity can sometimes even promote healthy development in certain adults (Konnikova, 2016). Recall from Chapter 3 that researchers interested in the psychological adjustment, including anxiety and depression, of female students before the 2007 mass school shooting at Virginia Tech compared data collected as part of an already ongoing study and then again after the event (Mancini et al., 2016). As you would expect, some students experienced continued distress, whereas others showed psychological improvement and resilience following these attacks. This phenomenon, known as *posttraumatic growth*, suggests that trauma can, at least at times, lead to positive outcomes (Tedeschi & Blevins, 2015; Zhou & Wu, 2016).

What are the characteristics of adult resilience? One study found that practicing *compassion* and *meditation* (see Chapters 3 and 5) are valuable components of resilience (Newman, 2016). According to psychologist George Bonanno (2012), another component is *perception*. Do you perceive adversity as filled with meaning and an opportunity to grow and change? Or do you see it as devastating and uncontrollable?

The good news is that we can develop a more resilient perception of adversity by cultivating the trait of *self-efficacy* and an *internal locus of control* (Chapter 12), as well as a more o*ptimistic, attributional style* (Chapter 15). Research also suggests that individuals who have an anxiety growth mindset—that is, who believe that anxiety, like intelligence, is not a fixed trait—show more resilience and positive coping than those without this mindset (Schroder et al., 2017).

Finally, it's also important to recognize the potential dangers associated with this focus on a growth mindset and resilience. Although a growth mindset does encourage everyone to persevere and to believe that hard work always pays off, it may backfire when we all eventually fail in the face of impossible odds (Luthar & Kumar, 2018; Simmons, 2019; Sisk et al., 2018). In addition, the emphasis on resilience, when taken to extremes, may lead to a dangerous form of "blaming the victim." People who are homeless or mentally ill, as well as student activists protesting racism and sexism, have been blamed for lacking resilience, when critics should instead be questioning the larger social policies that create and maintain these situations. While resilience is a useful concept and its skills can be developed, we must consider all the factors leading to adversity and avoid placing all the responsibility for survival on an individual (Sehgal, 2015).

Thinking back to the resilient child, Masten and Coatsworth remind us, "If we allow the prevalence of known risk factors for development to rise while resources for children fall, we can expect the competence of individual children and the human capital of the nation to suffer" (Masten & Coatsworth, 1998, p. 216).

Before going on, be sure to complete the final Retrieval Practice, and then answer the critical thinking questions in the **Test Your Critical Thinking** feature.

Retrieval Practice 13.6 | Key Issues in Psychological Disorders

Self-Test Completing this self-test, and then checking your answers by clicking on the answer button or by looking in Appendix B, will provide immediate feedback and helpful practice for exams.

1. Which of the following are examples of culture-general symptoms of mental health difficulties that are useful in diagnosing disorders across cultures?

   a. trouble sleeping   **c.** can't get along

   b. worry all the time   **d.** all of these options

2. Symptoms of mental illness that generally only appear in one population group are known as _____.

   a. culture-bound symptoms

   b. group specific disorders

   c. group-think syndrome

   d. culture-specific maladies

3. Which of the following is a myth about suicide?

   a. People who talk about it are less likely to actually do it

   b. Suicide usually occurs with little or no warning

   c. People who are suicidal are always fully intent on dying

   d. All of these options

4. _____ is NOT a contributor to ACEs.

   a. Physical abuse

   b. Parental separation or divorce

   c. Resilience

   d. An incarcerated household member

Q Test Your Critical Thinking

1. Culture clearly has strong effects on psychological disorders. How does this influence what you think about what is normal or abnormal?

2. As you've seen, some research suggests that depression in men is often overlooked because men are socialized to suppress their emotions and encouraged to express their distress by acting out, being impulsive, or engaging in substance abuse. Does this ring true with your own experiences and observations of others? If so, how might we change this situation?

Real World Application Question

[AQ6] Do certain psychological disorders exist in some cultures but not in others?

CRIS BOURONCLE/AFP/Getty Images

Hint: Look in the text for **[AQ6]**

Q Test Your Critical Thinking

Did you notice and wonder why we provided six Real World Application Questions [AQ1–AQ6] throughout this chapter? We've found that they not only help you to engage with and master the material, but also have an important and lasting impact on your critical thinking skills. For additional mastery and enrichment, consider the following questions:

1. Is this man's behavior abnormal? Which criteria for psychological disorders do his piercings and tattoos meet? Which do they not?

2. Can you think of any behavior *you* exhibit that might be considered abnormal if your own cultural norms were not taken into account?

3. We've all experienced anxiety. Which of the explanations described in this section do you feel best describes your personal experiences with it? Why?

4. Recall an experience you've had with depression. How was it similar to or different from what was discussed in the section on major depressive disorders?

5. In the section on schizophrenia, we pointed out that if one identical twin develops schizophrenia, there is a 48 percent chance that the other twin will do so as well. How does this high correlation support the biological predisposition model?

vgajic/E+/Getty Images

6. Think about someone you know—a friend, a family member, or yourself—who suffers from one of the disorders described in this chapter. How does the information we've provided differ from or match what you've discovered from your own or others' experiences?

Summary

13.1 Understanding Psychological Disorders 421

- **Psychological disorder** is defined as patterns of behavior, thoughts, or emotions considered pathological for one or more of these three reasons: *deviance*, *dysfunction*, and *distress*. Mental health exists on a continuum—not discrete categories of "normal" and "abnormal."

- The stigma and discrimination surrounding mental illness are serious public health concerns.

- Historically psychological disorders were blamed on evil spirits and witchcraft. These beliefs were eventually replaced by the medical model, which in turn gave rise to the modern specialty of **psychiatry**. In contrast to the medical model, psychology offers a multifaceted approach.

- The *Diagnostic and Statistical Manual of Mental Disorders (DSM)* provides detailed descriptions and classifications of psychological disorders. It also allows standardized diagnosis and improved communication among professionals and between professionals and patients.

13.2 Anxiety Disorders 428

- **Anxiety disorders** include **generalized anxiety disorder (GAD)**, **panic disorder**, and **phobias** (including agoraphobia, specific phobias, and social anxiety disorder).

- Psychological (faulty cognitions and maladaptive learning), biological (evolutionary and genetic predispositions, biochemical disturbances), and sociocultural (cultural pressures in industrialized nations) factors likely all contribute to anxiety. Classical and operant conditioning may also contribute to phobias.

13.3 Depressive and Bipolar Disorders 433

- Both depressive and bipolar disorders are characterized by extreme disturbances in emotional states. People suffering from **depressive disorders** may experience a lasting depressed mood without a clear provocation. In contrast, people with **bipolar disorder** alternate between periods of depression and mania (characterized by hyperactivity and poor judgment).

- Biological factors play a significant role in mood disorders. Psychosocial theories of depression focus on environmental stressors and disturbances in interpersonal relationships, thought processes, self-concept, and learning history, including **learned helplessness**.

13.4 Schizophrenia 438

- **Schizophrenia** is a group of disorders, each characterized by a disturbance in perception (including **hallucinations**), language, thought (including **delusions**), emotions, and behavior.

- In the past, researchers divided schizophrenia into multiple subtypes. More recently, researchers have proposed focusing instead on **positive schizophrenia symptoms** versus **negative schizophrenia symptoms**.

- Most biological theories of schizophrenia focus on genetics, neurotransmitters, and brain abnormalities. Psychologists believe that there are also at least two possible psychosocial contributors: stress and communication disorders in families.

13.5 Other Disorders   443

- **Attention-deficit/hyperactivity disorder (ADHD)** and **autism spectrum disorder (ASD) are two** of the most common **neurodevelopmental disorders.** ADHD is characterized by a pattern of inattention and hyperactivity/impulsivity. ASD involves problems with social communication and social interaction, as well as restricted, repetitive patterns of behavior, interests, or activities.

- **Obsessive-compulsive disorder (OCD)** involves persistent, unwanted, fearful thoughts (obsessions) and irresistible urges to perform an act or repeated rituals (compulsions), which help relieve the anxiety created by the obsession. Given that numerous biopsychosocial factors contribute to OCD, it is most often treated with a combination of drugs and cognitive behavior therapy (CBT).

- **Dissociative disorders** are characterized by a major loss of memory without a clear physical explanation. A controversial, subtype of these disorders, **dissociative identity disorder (DID)**, involves the presence of two or more distinct personality systems in the same individual. Environmental variables appear to play a primary role in dissociative disorders. Dissociation can be a form of escape from a past trauma.

- **Personality disorders** occur when inflexible, maladaptive personality traits lead to significant impairment of social and occupational functioning. **Antisocial personality disorder** is characterized by egocentrism and a lack of conscience, remorse, or empathy for others. The most common personality disorder is **borderline personality disorder (BPD)**. Its core features are impulsivity and instability in mood, relationships, and self-image.

13.6 Key Issues in Psychological Disorders   450

- Men and women differ in their rates and experiences of psychological disorders. Some symptoms, as well as some disorders, are *culture general*, whereas others are *culture bound*.

- Death by suicide is an increased risk for people with psychological disorders, but there are ways to detect and prevent it.

- Adverse childhood experiences (ACEs) are common and closely related to psychological disorders.

- Mental health can be improved and protected by developing **resilience**—the ability to recover or adapt effectively in the face of adversity.

Key Terms

Retrieval Practice   Write a definition for each term before turning back to the referenced page to check your answer.

CHAPTER 14

Kuttelvaserova Stuchelova/Shutterstock.com

Therapy

fizkes/Shutterstock.com

Real World Application Questions

Things you'll learn in Chapter 14

[AQ1] Can accepting fears and worries, rather than trying to eliminate them, help decrease PTSD?

[AQ2] Does simply watching other children play with dogs reduce dog phobias in young children?

[AQ3] Can media portrayals of suicide, like *13 Reasons Why*, unintentionally encourage it?

[AQ4] Can the dangerous party drug ketamine relieve depression and suicidal thoughts?

[AQ5] Is electroconvulsive therapy (ECT) painful, dangerous, and possibly causing permanent brain damage?

[AQ6] Is therapy delivered over your phone effective?

Throughout the chapter, look for the [AQ1]–[AQ6] icons. They indicate where the text addresses these questions.

CHAPTER OUTLINE

14.1 | Talk Therapies

LEARNING OBJECTIVES

Retrieval Practice   While reading the upcoming sections, respond to each Learning Objective in your own words.

Review the three main forms of talk therapies.

- **Define** psychotherapy.
- **Describe** psychoanalysis and psychodynamic therapies, along with their core techniques and criticisms.

- **Discuss** humanistic therapies and their key techniques and evaluation.
- **Discuss** cognitive therapies and their core principles and evaluation.

Real World Application Question

[AQ1] Can accepting fears and worries, rather than trying to eliminate them, help decrease PTSD?

Throughout this text, we have emphasized the *science* of psychology, and this chapter is no exception. Here we explore how psychological science is applied during **psychotherapy** to treat psychological disorders and improve overall psychological functioning and adjustment to life.

Can you see how this definition is contrary to the common stereotype and stigma that therapy is only for seriously disturbed individuals? Therapy provides all of us with an opportunity to address our own specific problems, while also learning better thinking, feeling, and behavioral skills that will improve our everyday lives.

In this chapter, we'll discuss the three major approaches to psychotherapy (**Figure 14.1**). Along the way we'll work to demystify and destigmatize its practice, and dispel some of the most common myths (**Table 14.1**). We begin with the so-called talk therapies—psychoanalysis/psychodynamic, humanistic, and cognitive. Next we look at behavior therapies and the roles of classical and operant conditioning, and observational learning. Then we examine biomedical (or biological) therapies, including psychopharmacology, electroconvulsive therapy (ECT), and psychosurgery. Our final section looks at psychotherapy in perspective—its goals, effectiveness, and formats, along with cultural and gender issues.

We begin our discussion of professional psychotherapy with traditional psychoanalysis and its modern counterpart, psychodynamic therapies. Then we explore humanistic and cognitive

Psychotherapy   Any of a group of therapies used to treat psychological disorders and/or to improve psychological functioning and adjustment to life.

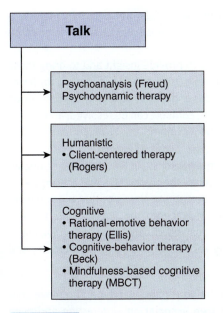
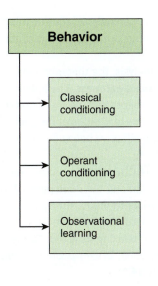
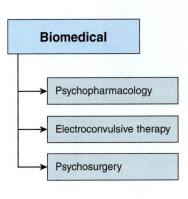

FIGURE 14.1   **An overview of the three major approaches to therapy**

TABLE 14.1	Therapy Myths

- *Myth: There is one best therapy.*
  Fact: Many problems can be treated equally well with many different forms of therapy.

- *Myth: Therapists can read your mind.*
  Fact: Good therapists often seem to have an uncanny ability to understand how their clients are feeling and to know when someone is trying to avoid certain topics. This is not due to any special mind-reading ability; it simply reflects their specialized training and daily experience working with troubled people.

- *Myth: People who go to therapists are crazy or weak.*
  Fact: Most people seek counseling due to stress in their lives or because they realize that therapy can improve their level of functioning. It is difficult to be objective about our own problems. Seeking therapy is a sign of wisdom and personal strength.

- *Myth: Only the rich can afford therapy.*
  Fact: Therapy can be expensive. But many clinics and therapists charge on a sliding scale, based on the client's income. Some insurance plans also cover psychological services.

- *Myth: If I am taking meds, I don't need therapy.*
  Fact: Medications, such as antidepressants, are only one form of therapy. They can change brain chemistry, but they can't teach us to think, feel, or behave differently. Research suggests that a combination of drugs and psychotherapy may be best for some situations, whereas in other cases, psychotherapy or drug therapy alone may be most effective.

Rapping about therapy? Counter to the myth that people who seek therapy are "crazy or weak," Jay-Z (pictured here) is an American rapper and songwriter, winner of 22 Grammys and the 2019 NAACP Image Award, while also being married to the iconic Beyoncé. He proudly admits (and raps) about how therapy gave him a "huge advantage in everyday life" (Lebowitz, 2017).

Kevin Mazur/Getty Images Entertainment/Getty Images

Sources: Arkowitz & Lilienfeld, 2017; Magnavita & Anchin, 2014; Seay & Sun, 2016.

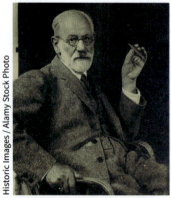

Sigmund Freud (1856–1939)
Freud believed that during psychoanalysis, the therapist's (or psychoanalyst's) major goal was to bring unconscious conflicts into consciousness.

Historic Images / Alamy Stock Photo

Psychoanalysis A type of talk therapy, originated by Sigmund Freud, that emphasizes analysis and bringing unconscious thoughts and conflicts into conscious awareness.

Free association In psychoanalysis, reporting whatever comes to mind without monitoring its contents.

therapies. Although these therapies differ significantly, they're often grouped together as "talk therapies" because they emphasize communication between the therapist and client, as opposed to the behavioral and biomedical therapies we discuss later.

Psychoanalysis/Psychodynamic Therapies

In **psychoanalysis**, a person's *psyche* (or mind) is *analyzed*. Traditional psychoanalysis is based on Sigmund Freud's central belief that abnormal behavior is based in unconscious conflicts (see photo).

During psychoanalysis, the therapist's major goal is to provide insight and to bring these conflicts into conscious awareness. The individual comes to understand the reasons for his or her dysfunction and realizes that the childhood conditions under which the conflicts developed no longer exist. Once this realization or insight occurs, the conflicts can be resolved, and the client can develop more adaptive behavior patterns (Barber & Solomonov, 2016; Bonomi, 2015).

Major Therapy Techniques As you recall from Chapter 12, in Freudian theory, unconscious conflicts occur among the three parts of the psyche—the id, the ego, and the superego. Unfortunately, according to Freud, the ego has strong *defense mechanisms* that block unconscious thoughts from coming to light. Thus, to gain insight into the unconscious, the ego must be "tricked" into relaxing its guard. To meet that goal, psychoanalysts employ five major methods: *free association, dream analysis, analyzing resistance, analyzing transference*, and *interpretation* (**Figure 14.2**).

Free Association According to Freud, when you let your mind wander and remove conscious censorship over thoughts—a process called **free association**—interesting and even bizarre connections seem to spring into awareness. Freud believed that the first thing to come to a patient's mind is often an important clue to what the person's unconscious wants to conceal.

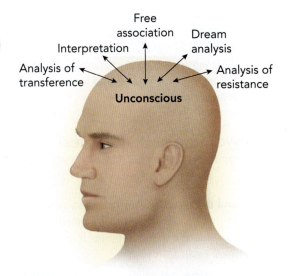

FIGURE 14.2 **The five key techniques for psychoanalysis**

"... AND WHAT DO YOU THINK THE CRACKER MIGHT REPRESENT?"

Leo Cullum/Cartoon Stock

FIGURE 14.3 **Freud's dream analysis** As shown in this popular cartoon, psychoanalysis is often portrayed as a client lying on a couch engaging in dream analysis. Freud believed that this arrangement—with the client relaxed and the therapist out of his or her view—helps the client let down his or her defenses, making the unconscious more accessible.

Dream Analysis Recall from Chapter 5 that, according to Freud, our psychological defenses are supposedly lowered during sleep. Therefore, our forbidden desires and unconscious conflicts are supposedly more freely expressed during dreams. Even while dreaming, however, we recognize these feelings and conflicts as unacceptable and must disguise them as images that have deeper symbolic meaning (**Figure 14.3**). Thus, using Freudian **dream analysis**, a dream of riding a horse or driving a car might be analyzed as just the surface description, or *manifest content*. In contrast, the hidden, underlying meaning, or *latent content*, might be analyzed as a desire for, or concern about, sexual intercourse.

Analysis of Resistance During free association or dream analysis, Freud found that clients often show an inability or unwillingness to discuss or reveal certain memories, thoughts, motives, or experiences. If the client suddenly "forgets" what he or she was saying or completely changes the subject, the therapist will work to identify these possible cases of **resistance**, and then help the client face his or her problems and learn to deal with them more realistically.

Analysis of Transference Freud believed that during psychoanalysis, clients disclose intimate feelings and memories, and the relationship between the therapist and client may become complex and emotionally charged. As a result, clients often apply, or *transfer*, some of their unresolved emotions and attitudes from past relationships onto the therapist. A client might interact with the therapist as if the therapist were a lover or parent. The therapist uses this process of **transference** to help the client "relive" painful past relationships in a safe, therapeutic setting so that he or she can move on to healthier relationships.

Interpretation The core of all psychoanalytic therapy is **interpretation**. During free association, dream analysis, resistance, and transference, the analyst listens closely and tries to find patterns and hidden conflicts. At the right time, the therapist explains or interprets the underlying meanings to the client.

Psychodynamic Therapies A modern derivative of Freudian psychoanalysis, **psychodynamic therapies**, includes both Freud's theories and those of his major followers—Carl Jung, Alfred Adler, Karen Horney, and Erik Erikson. In contrast to psychoanalysis, psychodynamic therapies are shorter and less intensive (once or twice a week versus several times a week and only for a few weeks or months versus years). Also, the client is treated face-to-face rather than reclining on a couch, and the therapist takes a more directive approach rather than waiting for unconscious memories and desires to slowly be uncovered.

Dream analysis In psychoanalysis, interpretation of the underlying true meaning of dreams to reveal unconscious processes.

Resistance In psychoanalysis, the client's inability or unwillingness to discuss or reveal certain memories, thoughts, motives, or experiences.

Transference In psychoanalysis, the process by which a client attaches (transfers) to the therapist emotional reactions related to someone else in the client's life.

Interpretation A psychoanalyst's explanation of a client's free associations, dreams, resistance, and transference; more generally, any statement by a therapist that presents a problem in a new way.

Psychodynamic therapies A newer group of talk therapies that focuses on conscious processes and current problems; briefer, more directive, and more modern forms of psychoanalysis.

wavebreakmedia/Shutterstock.com

FIGURE 14.4 **Interpersonal therapy (IPT)** IPT, a variation of psychodynamic therapy, focuses on current relationships, with the goal of relieving immediate symptoms and teaching better ways to solve interpersonal problems. Research shows that it's effective for a variety of disorders, including depression, relationship conflict, eating disorders, and drug addiction (Johnson et al., 2019; Miniati et al., 2018; Normandin et al., 2015).

Humanistic therapies A group of talk therapies that emphasizes maximizing a client's inherent capacity for self-actualization by providing a non-judgmental, accepting atmosphere.

In addition, contemporary psychodynamic therapists focus less on unconscious, early-childhood roots of problems and more on conscious processes and current problems (Barber & Solomonov, 2016; Göttken et al., 2014; Short & Thomas, 2015). Such refinements have helped make treatments shorter, more available, and more effective for an increasing number of people. See **Figure 14.4** for one of the most popular modern forms of psychodynamic therapies.

Evaluating Psychoanalysis/Psychodynamic Therapies There are three major criticisms of these therapies (Ackerman, 2019; Grünbaum, 2015; Paris, 2017):

- **Question of repressed memories and unconscious conflict** As you've just seen, psychoanalysis is largely rooted in the assumption that repressed memories and unconscious conflicts actually exist, and this assumption is the subject of heated, ongoing debate (see Chapters 7 and 12).

- **Limited applicability** Psychoanalysis is time-consuming (often lasting several years with four to five sessions a week) and expensive. Furthermore, critics suggest that it applies only to a select group of highly motivated, articulate clients with less severe disorders, and not to complex disorders like schizophrenia.

- **Lack of scientific credibility** Modern therapy and medicine expect all treatments to be supported by evidence—the *evidence-based practice (EBP) movement*. Therefore, it's difficult, if not impossible, to scientifically document the major tenets of psychoanalysis. How do we prove or disprove the existence of an unconscious mind, or the meaning of unconscious conflicts and symbolic dream images?

On the other hand, research does show that traditional psychoanalysis can be effective for those who have the time and money. Psychodynamic therapies are similarly effective but less expensive than psychoanalysis mainly because they take place over a shorter period of time (Muir & Hibberd, 2019; Steinert et al., 2017).

Humanistic Therapies

As you've just seen, the psychoanalytic and psychodynamic focus on the unconscious. In contrast, the humanistic approach emphasizes conscious processes and present versus past experiences. The name **humanistic therapies** reflects this focus on the human characteristics of a person's potential for self-actualization, free will, and self-awareness. Humanistic therapists assume that people with problems are suffering from a disruption of their normal growth potential and, hence, their self-concept. When obstacles are removed, the individual is free to become the self-accepting, self-actualized person everyone is capable of being (D'Souza & Gurin, 2016; Ray, 2019; Winston et al., 2017).

Michael Rougier/The LIFE Picture Collection/Getty Images

Carl Rogers (1902–1987)

Client-centered therapy A form of talk therapy, developed by Carl Rogers, that provides a warm, supportive atmosphere that encourages self-actualization and improves the client's self-concept; techniques include empathy, unconditional positive regard, genuineness, and active listening.

> In my early professional years, I was asking the question: How can I treat, or cure, or change this person? Now I would phrase the question in this way: How can I provide a relationship which this person may use for his own personal growth?
> —Carl Rogers (founder of client-centered therapy)

Carl Rogers (see photo) is one of the best-known humanistic therapists. He developed an approach, referred to as **client-centered therapy** (**Figure 14.5**), which encourages clients to actualize their potential and to relate to others in genuine ways. (Rogers used the term "client" based on his belief that the label "patient" implied that someone was sick or mentally ill rather than responsible and competent.)

Client-centered therapy, like psychoanalysis and psychodynamic therapies, explores thoughts and feelings as a way to obtain insight into the contributors to unhealthy behaviors. For Rogerian therapists, however, the focus is on providing an accepting atmosphere and encouraging healthy emotional experiences. Clients are responsible for discovering their own maladaptive patterns.

FIGURE 14.5 **Client-centered therapy** Recall how you've felt when you've been with someone who considers you to be a worthy and good person with unlimited potential, a person who believes that your "real self" is unique and valuable. These are the feelings that are nurtured in humanistic therapy.

"Just remember, son, it doesn't matter whether you win or lose—unless you want Daddy's love."

FIGURE 14.6 **Unconditional versus conditional positive regard** According to Rogers, clients need to feel unconditionally accepted by their therapists in order to recognize and value their own emotions, thoughts, and behaviors. As this cartoon sarcastically implies, some parents withhold their love and acceptance unless the child lives up to their expectations.

Major Therapy Techniques Rogerian therapists create a therapeutic relationship by focusing on four important qualities of communication: *empathy, unconditional positive regard, genuineness*, and *active listening*.

Empathy Using the technique of **empathy**, a sensitive understanding and sharing of another person's inner experience, therapists pay attention to body language and listen for subtle cues to help them understand the emotional experiences of clients. To further help clients explore their feelings, the therapist uses open-ended statements such as "You found that upsetting" or "You haven't been able to decide what to do about this" rather than asking questions or offering explanations.

Unconditional Positive Regard Regardless of the clients' problems or behaviors, humanistic therapists offer them **unconditional positive regard**, Rogers's term for love and acceptance with no "strings" (contingencies) attached. In therapy, it's a type of genuine caring and nonjudgmental attitude toward people based on their innate value as individuals. They avoid evaluative statements such as "That's good" and "You did the right thing" given that such comments imply that the therapist is judging the client. Rogers believed that most of us receive conditional acceptance from our parents, teachers, and others, which leads to poor self-concepts and psychological disorders (**Figure 14.6**).

Genuineness Humanists believe that when therapists use **genuineness** and honestly share their thoughts and feelings with their clients, the clients will in turn develop self-trust and honest self-expression.

Active Listening Using **active listening**, which includes reflecting, paraphrasing, and clarifying what the client is saying, the clinician communicates that he or she is genuinely interested and paying close attention (see the **Test Yourself**).

Empathy In Rogerian terms, a sensitive understanding and sharing of another's inner experience.

Unconditional positive regard Rogers's term for love and acceptance with no "strings" (contingencies) attached.

Genuineness In Rogerian terms, being personally authentic and sincere; the awareness of one's true inner thoughts and feelings and the ability to share them honestly with others.

Active listening A communication technique that requires listening with total attention to what another is saying; techniques include reflecting, paraphrasing, and clarifying what the person says and means.

PA **Practical Application**

Test Yourself: Using Active Listening

Would you like to try active listening in your personal life? If so, keep in mind that to *reflect* is to show the person that you have "heard" both the words they are saying, as well as the emotions they are experiencing. This shows the speaker that you are trying your best to understand their messages. To *paraphrase* is to summarize in different words what the other person is saying. To *clarify* is to check that both the speaker and listener understand what the other is saying and feeling.

When a professional uses active listening (as shown in the photo), he or she might notice a client's furrowed brow and downcast eyes while he is discussing his military

experiences and then might respond, "It sounds like you're angry with your situation and feeling pretty miserable right now." Can you see how this statement reflects the client's anger, paraphrases his complaint, and gives feedback to clarify the communication? This type of attentive, active listening is a relatively simple and well-documented technique that you can use to improve your communication with virtually anyone—professors, employers, friends, family, and especially your romantic partner.

Evaluating Humanistic Therapies   Supporters say that there is empirical evidence for the efficacy of client-centered therapy, whereas critics argue that outcomes such as self-actualization and self-awareness are difficult to test scientifically. Furthermore, research on specific humanistic techniques has had mixed results (Cain et al., 2016; Raffagnino, 2019; Ray, 2019).

Cognitive Therapies

Cognitive therapies   A group of talk therapies that focuses on changing faulty thought processes (cognitions); based on the assumption that thoughts intervene between events and reactions.

Cognitive therapies assume that faulty thoughts (cognitions) are the primary source of problems, and that our thoughts intervene between events and our reactions to them. Like psychoanalysts and humanists, cognitive therapists believe that exploring unexamined beliefs can produce insight into the reasons for disturbed thoughts, feelings, and behaviors. However, instead of believing that a change occurs as a result of insight, cognitive therapists suggest that *negative self-talk*, the unrealistic things a person tells himself or herself, is most important. One study of people with eating disorders found that changing a client's irrational thoughts and self-talk, such as, "If I eat that cake, I will become fat instantly" or "I'll never have a dating relationship if I don't lose 20 pounds," resulted in their having fewer negative thoughts about their bodies (Bhatnagar et al., 2013).

Cognitive restructuring   A therapeutic process of learning to identify and dispute irrational or maladaptive thought patterns.

Through a process called **cognitive restructuring**, clients learn to identify and dispute their irrational or maladaptive thought patterns. Do you see how identifying our irrational thoughts, and then challenging them, might in turn help us to become more psychologically healthy (**Figure 14.7**)?

Ellis's Rational-Emotive Behavior Therapy (REBT)   One of the best-known cognitive therapists, Albert Ellis, suggested that irrational beliefs are the primary culprit in problem emotions and behaviors. He proposed that most people mistakenly believe they are unhappy or upset due to external, outside events, such as receiving a bad grade on an exam. Ellis suggested that, in reality, these negative emotions result from faulty interpretations and

FIGURE 14.7   **Using cognitive restructuring to improve sales**

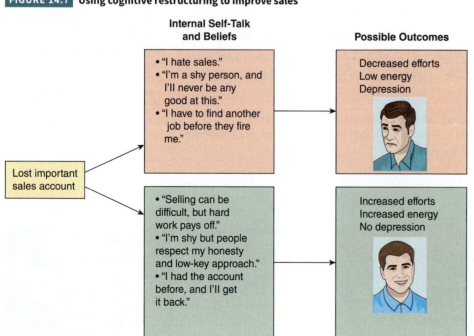

Internal Self-Talk and Beliefs

• "I hate sales."
• "I'm a shy person, and I'll never be any good at this."
• "I have to find another job before they fire me."

Lost important sales account

• "Selling can be difficult, but hard work pays off."
• "I'm shy but people respect my honesty and low-key approach."
• "I had the account before, and I'll get it back."

Possible Outcomes

Decreased efforts
Low energy
Depression

Increased efforts
Increased energy
No depression

a. Note how the negative interpretation and destructive self-talk lead to destructive and self-defeating outcomes.

b. Cognitive therapy teaches clients to challenge and change their negative beliefs and negative self-talk into positive ones, which, in turn, leads to more positive outcomes. Can you think of other situations in which such reinterpretation could be helpful?

> **STOP!** This Process Diagram contains essential information NOT found elsewhere in the text, which is likely to appear on quizzes and exams. Be sure to study it CAREFULLY.

PROCESS DIAGRAM 14.1 **Ellis's Rational-Emotive Behavior Therapy (REBT)** If you receive a poor performance evaluation at work, you might directly attribute your bad mood to the negative feedback. Psychologist Albert Ellis (see photo) would argue that your self-talk ("I always mess up") between the event and the feeling is what actually upsets you. Furthermore, ruminating on all the other times you've "messed up" in your life maintains your negative emotional state and may even lead to anxiety, depression, and other psychological disorders.

To treat these problems, Ellis developed an A–B–C–D approach: **A** stands for *activating event*, **B** the person's *belief system*, **C** the emotional *consequences*, and **D** the act of *disputing* erroneous beliefs. During therapy, Ellis helped his clients identify the A, B, C's underlying their irrational beliefs by actively arguing with, cajoling, and teasing them—sometimes in very blunt, confrontational language. Once clients recognized their self-defeating thoughts, he worked with them on how to *dispute* those beliefs and create and test out new, rational ones. These new beliefs then changed the maladaptive emotions—thus breaking the vicious cycle. (Note the arrow under D that goes backward to B.)

Albert Ellis (1913–2007)
The best years of your life are the ones in which [you] decide your problems are your own. You do not blame them on your mother, the ecology, or the president. You realize that you control your own destiny.
—Albert Ellis

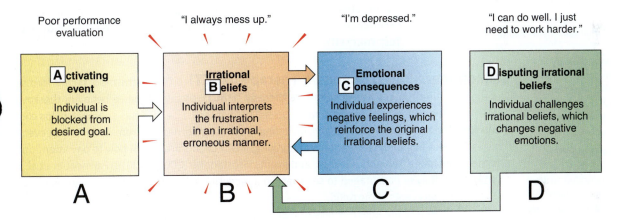

irrational beliefs (such as interpreting the bad grade as a sign of your incompetence and an indication that you'll never qualify for graduate school or a good job).

To deal with these irrational beliefs, Ellis developed **rational-emotive behavior therapy (REBT)** (Ellis & Ellis, 2011, 2014; Stephenson et al., 2017; Turner, 2018). (See **Process Diagram 14.1**—shown above—and the following **Test Yourself**.)

Rational-emotive behavior therapy (REBT) A form of talk therapy, developed by Albert Ellis, that focuses on eliminating negative emotional reactions through logic, confrontation, and examination of irrational beliefs.

PA Practical Application

Test Yourself: Overcoming Irrational Misconceptions

Are you bothered by irrational misconceptions? Albert Ellis believed that people often require the help of a therapist to see through their defenses, and to challenge their self-defeating thoughts. For mild, everyday problems, our students have found that they can improve their own irrational beliefs and responses with the following suggestions:

1. **Identify and confront your belief system** Identify your irrational beliefs by asking yourself why you feel the particular emotions you do. Then, by confronting your thoughts and feelings,

you can discover the irrational assumptions creating the problematic consequences.

2. **Evaluate consequences** Rather than perpetuating negative emotions by assuming they must be experienced, focus on whether your reactions make you more effective and enable you to solve your problems. It's gratifying when people you cherish love you in return. But if they don't, continuing to pursue them, or insisting that they must love you, will only be self-defeating.

3. **Practice effective ways of thinking and behaving** Imagine and rehearse thoughts and behaviors that are more effective, and outcomes that are more successful.

Negative thoughts about oneself:
"I'm a social failure."

Depression

Negative thoughts about one's experiences:
"Every encounter I have with people is a total disaster."

Negative thoughts about the future:
"Things will never improve. I'll never get along with people."

FIGURE 14.8 **The cognitive triad of depression**
According to Beck, some individuals typically think about themselves and their futures, along with their personal life experiences, in destructive, illogical ways. This so-called cognitive triad of negative thinking leads people to see themselves as inadequate, to view the future as bleak, and to exaggerate everyday negative experiences. Do you recognize how this triad of negativity feeds into and maintains depression?

Cognitive-behavior therapy (CBT) A type of therapy, developed by Aaron Beck, that combines cognitive therapy (changing faulty thinking) with behavior therapy (changing maladaptive behaviors).

Mindfulness-based cognitive therapy (MBCT) A therapy based on non-judgmental awareness of current events; a blend of cognitive therapy and meditation.

Kayana Szymczak for The Boston Globe/Getty Images

Beck's Cognitive-Behavior Therapy (CBT) Another well-known cognitive therapist, Aaron Beck, also believes psychological problems result from illogical thinking and destructive self-talk (Beck, 1976, 2000; Cristea et al., 2017; Moore et al., 2019). But Beck seeks to directly confront and change the behaviors associated with destructive cognitions. Beck's **cognitive-behavior therapy (CBT)** is designed to reduce *both* self-destructive thoughts *and* self-destructive behaviors.

Imagine for a moment that you are seeking therapy for serious depression. Using CBT, your therapist might begin by talking with you about the famous *cognitive triad of depression.* As shown in **Figure 14.8**, depression is often linked with three forms of negative and illogical thinking—about oneself, one's experiences, and the future. With this triad in mind, your therapist might first provide you with tips and homework to help you recognize and keep track of your thoughts. Next, the therapist could help you develop ways to test these automatic thoughts against reality.

Once you and other CBT clients recognize that negative attitudes are largely a product of faulty thought processes, you would move on to CBT's second phase of therapy—persuading the client to actively pursue pleasurable activities. Depressed individuals often lose motivation, even for experiences they used to find enjoyable. Simultaneously taking an active rather than a passive role and reconnecting with enjoyable experiences can help in recovering from depression (see the following **Test Yourself**).

Mindfulness-Based Cognitive Therapy (MBCT) One of the more recent forms of therapy, **mindfulness-based cognitive therapy (MBCT)**, blends cognitive-behavior therapy (CBT) with the mindfulness meditation discussed in Chapter 3. Like CBT, this approach helps clients focus on their stream of thoughts, including their fears, worries, and ruminations. However, instead of recalling their past patterns of thinking, MBCT clients are taught how to pay attention to their immediate thoughts, feelings, and events (Frostadottir & Dorjee, 2019; Parmentier et al., 2019). Next, they're encouraged to see them in a receptive and non-judgmental way—as mere *passing* events of the mind.

To test the effectiveness of MBCT, 62 military veterans suffering from PTSD were divided into two groups (Possemato et al., 2016). One group received the standard primary care, whereas the other received training in MBCT (see photo). While both groups improved, those in the mindfulness group had significantly larger reductions in PTSD and depression, and maintained their gains at the 8-week follow-up. **[AQ1]** Can you see how by accepting their fears and worries rather than trying to eliminate them, the veterans were less upset and affected by them? Mindfulness-based cognitive therapy has been successfully applied to other psychological problems such as depression, personality disorders, and substance abuse (Dimidjian et al., 2016; Ottavi et al., 2016; Zemestani & Fazeli, 2019).

PA Practical Application

Test Yourself: A Cognitive Approach to Lifting Depression

Psychologist Aaron Beck (pictured here) believed that faulty thought processes are the core issue in many psychological disorders. One of the most successful applications of his cognitive-behavior therapy (CBT) is in the treatment of depression (Beck et al., 2012, 2015; Dobson, 2016; Sun et al., 2019). Beck identified several thinking patterns believed to be common among depression-prone people. Recognizing these patterns in our own thought processes may help prevent or improve the occasional bad moods we all experience. Clients are first taught the three C's—to catch (identify), challenge, and change their irrational or maladaptive thought patterns. Here we provide an example of how to label the three C's for the first problem of *selective perception.* Then try to do the same for the other four maladaptive patterns.

Aaron Beck (1921–)

Clem Murray/Tribune News Service/PA/USA/Newscom

- **Selective perception**   Focusing selectively on negative events while ignoring positive events. (*Catch the thought* = "Why am I the only person alone at this party?"; *Challenge it* = "I notice four other single people at this party"; *Change it* = "Being single has several advantages. I'll bet some of the couples are actually envying my freedom.")

- **Overgeneralization**   Drawing sweeping, global, negative conclusions based on one incident, and then assuming that conclusion applies to unrelated areas of life. "My girlfriend yelled at me for not picking her up on time. I'm so forgetful. I'll never succeed in a professional career."

- **Magnification and minimization**   Exaggerating the importance of small, undesirable events and grossly underestimating larger, positive ones. Despite having earned high grades in all her classes, an A student concludes: "This B on my last organic chemistry quiz means that I can't go on to med school, so I should just drop out of college right now."

- **Personalization**   Taking responsibility and blame for events that are actually unrelated to the individual. "My adult child is unmarried and doesn't want to have children. I must have been a bad parent."

- **All-or-nothing thinking**   Seeing things as black-or-white categories—where everything is either totally good or bad, right or wrong, a success or a failure. ("If I don't get straight A's, I'll never get a good job.")

Evaluating Cognitive Therapies   Cognitive therapies are highly effective treatments for depression, as well as anxiety disorders, bulimia nervosa, anger management, addiction, and even some symptoms of schizophrenia and insomnia (Hundt et al., 2016; Mennin et al., 2018; Palermo et al., 2016). However, both Beck and Ellis have been criticized for ignoring or denying the client's unconscious dynamics, overemphasizing rationality, and minimizing the importance of the client's past (Granillo et al., 2013; Hammack, 2003).

Other critics suggest that many cognitive therapies are successful because they employ behavior techniques, not because they change the underlying cognitive structure (Bandura, 1969, 2008; Granillo et al., 2013; Walker & Lampropoulos, 2014). Imagine that you sought treatment for depression and learned to curb your all-or-nothing thinking, along with identifying activities and behaviors that lessened your depression. You can see why it's difficult to identify whether changing your cognitions or changing your behavior was the most significant therapeutic factor. But to clients who have benefited, it doesn't matter. CBT combines both, and it has a proven track record for lifting depression.

Retrieval Practice 14.1 | Talk Therapies

Self-Test   Completing this self-test, and then checking your answers by clicking on the answer button or by looking in Appendix B, will provide immediate feedback and helpful practice for exams.

1. Psychoanalysis/psychodynamic, humanistic, and cognitive therapies are often grouped together as _____.

   a. talk therapies
   b. behavior therapies
   c. analytic therapies
   d. cognitive restructuring

2. The system of psychotherapy developed by Freud that seeks to bring unconscious conflicts into conscious awareness is known as _____.

   a. transference
   b. cognitive restructuring
   c. psychoanalysis
   d. the "hot seat" technique

3. A _____ therapist emphasizes the importance of empathy, unconditional positive regard, genuineness, and active listening.

   a. psychodynamic
   b. phenomenological behavior
   c. cognitive-behavior
   d. client-centered

4. According to rational-emotive behavior therapy (REBT), _____ often lead to depression and/or anxiety.

   a. unmet expectations
   b. stimulus events
   c. conditioning experiences
   d. irrational beliefs

5. Aaron Beck practices _____ therapy, which attempts to change not only destructive thoughts but the associated behaviors as well.

   a. psycho-behavior
   b. cognitive-behavior
   c. thinking-acting
   d. belief-behavior

Q Test Your Critical Thinking

1. Would you rather go to a therapist who uses modern psychodynamic therapy or one who practices traditional psychoanalysis? Why?

2. What is the significance of the term "*client-centered therapy*"?

Real World Application Question

[AQ1]   Can accepting fears and worries, rather than trying to eliminate them, help decrease PTSD?

Kayana Szymczak for The Boston Globe/ Getty Images

Hint: Look in the text for **[AQ1]**

14.2 | Behavior Therapies

LEARNING OBJECTIVES

Retrieval Practice While reading the upcoming sections, respond to each Learning Objective in your own words.

Summarize the treatment techniques and criticisms of behavior therapies.

- **Describe** how classical conditioning is used in therapy.
- **Explore** how operant conditioning is used in therapy.
- **Explain** how observational learning is used in therapy.

- **Describe** two major criticisms of behavior therapies.

Real World Application Questions

[AQ2] Does simply watching other children play with dogs reduce dog phobias in young children?

[AQ3] Can media portrayals of suicide, like *13 Reasons Why*, unintentionally encourage it?

Behavior therapies A group of therapies that uses learning principles to reduce or eliminate maladaptive behaviors; techniques are based on classical and operant conditioning, along with observational learning.

The previously discussed talk therapies are often called insight therapies since they focus on self-awareness, but often having insight is not enough. In **behavior therapies**, the focus is on the problem behavior itself rather than on insight and other underlying factors. The client's feelings and interpretations are not disregarded, they're just not emphasized. Instead, the therapist identifies the maladaptive behaviors that occur and adaptive behaviors that are absent, and then attempts to shift the balance of the two, drawing on the learning principles of *classical conditioning, operant conditioning,* and *observational learning* (Chapter 6).

Classical Conditioning

Behavior therapists use the principles of classical conditioning to decrease maladaptive behaviors by creating new associations to replace the faulty ones (see cartoon). We will explore two techniques based on these principles: *systematic desensitization* and *aversion therapy*.

Sidney Harris/ScienceCartoonsPlus.com

Systematic Desensitization Recall from Chapter 6 that classical conditioning occurs when a neutral stimulus (NS) becomes associated with an unconditioned stimulus (US) to elicit a conditioned response (CR). Sometimes a classically conditioned fear response becomes so extreme that we call it a phobia. To treat phobias, behavior therapists often use **systematic desensitization**, which begins with relaxation training, followed by exposure to increasingly anxiety-producing stimuli or situations, while the client remains relaxed (Hezel & Simpson, 2019; Tyner et al., 2016; Wolpe & Plaud, 1997). See **Figure 14.9** for a graphic illustration and description of systematic desensitization useful for overcoming a fear of elevators.

Systematic desensitization A behavior therapy technique that begins with relaxation training, followed by exposure to increasingly anxiety-producing stimuli or situations, while the client remains relaxed.

Thankfully, if you or someone you know suffers from phobias, such as a fear of spiders, you'll be glad to know that after just 2 or 3 hours of therapy, starting with simply looking at photos of spiders (see photo), and then moving next to a tarantula in a glass aquarium, clients are able to eventually pet and hold the spider with their bare hands (Hauner et al., 2012).

How does relaxation training desensitize someone? Recall from Chapter 2 that the parasympathetic nerves control autonomic functions when we are relaxed. Given that the opposing sympathetic nerves are dominant when we are anxious, it is physiologically impossible to be both relaxed and anxious at the same time. The key to success is teaching the client how to replace his or her fear response with relaxation when *exposed* to the fearful stimulus, which explains why these and related approaches are often referred to as *exposure therapies*. Modern virtual reality technology

iStock.com/Okea

FIGURE 14.9 **Systematic desensitization** The therapist and client work together to construct a fear hierarchy, a ranked listing of 10 or so related anxiety-arousing images—from the least fearful to the most. Then, while in a state of relaxation, the client mentally visualizes, or physically experiences, anxiety-producing items at the lowest level of the hierarchy, and then works his or her way up to the most anxiety-producing items at the top. In sum, each progressive step on the fear hierarchy is repeatedly paired with relaxation, until the fear response or phobia is extinguished.

also uses systematic desensitization to expose clients to feared situations while physically remaining in the therapist's office (**Figure 14.10**).

Aversion Therapy

As we've just seen, to reduce phobias systematic desensitization substitutes a pleasant (relaxed) response to an unpleasant, fearful stimulus (like a spider). In sharp contrast to this approach, **aversion therapy** uses classical conditioning techniques to create unpleasant (*aversive*) associations and responses rather than to extinguish them (e.g., Abramowitz et al., 2019). People who engage in excessive drinking, for instance, build up a number of pleasurable associations with alcohol. These pleasurable associations cannot always be prevented. Therefore, aversion therapy provides *negative associations* to compete with the pleasurable ones (**Figure 14.11**).

FIGURE 14.10 **Virtual reality therapy** Rather than just using mental imaging or actual physical experiences of a fearful situation, virtual reality headsets allow a client with a fear of heights, for example, to have virtual experiences ranging from riding in an elevator to being at the edge of a tall building.

Katarzyna Białasiewicz/123RF

Anna Lurye/123RF

1.
| Unconditioned Stimulus (US): Nauseating Drug | → | Unconditioned Response (UR): Nausea |

2.
| Targeted Stimulus: Alcohol | + | Unconditioned Stimulus (US): Nauseating Drug |

3.
| Conditioned Stimulus (CS): Alcohol | → | Conditioned Response (CR): Nausea |

FIGURE 14.11 **Aversion therapy** The goal of aversion therapy is to create an undesirable, or *aversive*, response to a stimulus a person would like to avoid, such as alcohol. Here, a man savors his drink just before the nauseating effects of the drug Antabuse begin. After repeated pairings of alcohol with nausea, the person learns a new, undesirable association—alcohol leads to vomiting.

Aversion therapy A type of behavior therapy that pairs an aversive (unpleasant) stimulus with a maladaptive behavior in order to elicit a negative reaction to the target stimulus.

Most

In a crowded elevator as doors close

Stepping onto elevator with a few other people

Doors open to empty elevator

Amount of anxiety

Pressing the elevator call button

Approaching a bank of elevator doors

Least Looking at a building with outside elevators

Operant Conditioning

As we discovered in Chapter 6, consequences are the heart of operant conditioning. Using a form of therapy called *behavior modification*, therapists provide reinforcement as a consequence for appropriate behaviors, and they withhold reinforcement for inappropriate behaviors. In this section, we'll focus on two major behavior modification techniques—*shaping* and *token economies*.

Token economy A form of behavior therapy involving awarding "tokens" for desired behavior that can be exchanged later for rewards.

Modeling therapy A type of therapy characterized by watching and imitating models that demonstrate desirable behaviors.

Shaping   Imagine that you're a therapist and your client is a young child suffering from *autism*, a serious neurodevelopmental disorder discussed in Chapter 13. One of the most difficult challenges for these children is acquiring appropriate language and communication. To develop these and other complex skills, behavior modification therapists typically use *shaping*, a process of applying immediate rewards for successive approximations of the target behaviors (see Chapter 6).

Again, if you were a therapist working to build language skills with a child suffering with autism, you might first reward the child for connecting pictures or other devices with words. As the child progresses with appropriate rewards for increasing levels of language, you would eventually limit rewards to times when the child uses his or her words to communicate with others.

Obviously, this is a simplistic example. However, the process of shaping is an invaluable technique in therapy situations, and it can also be very helpful on an informal basis if you or someone you know suffers from the common problem of excessive shyness (see the following **Test Yourself**).

drbimages/E+/Getty Images

PA Practical Application

Test Yourself: Overcoming Shyness

Shaping can help people acquire social skills and greater assertiveness. If you are painfully shy (see photo), a clinician might first ask you to role-play simply saying hello to someone you find attractive. Then you might practice behaviors that gradually lead you to suggest a meeting or date. During such role-playing, or behavior rehearsal, the clinician gives you feedback and reinforcement for each successive step you take toward the end goal.

FIGURE 14.12 **A familiar token economy?** Do you remember checking off items on a list to show you'd finished your chores? Or receiving stars or other stickers in elementary school for the number of books you read? A similar system is used in various mental health settings to reward clients for behaviors designed to improve their psychological functioning.

John D. Buffington/Getty Images

Token Economies   For clients in an inpatient treatment facility, adaptive behaviors can be taught or increased with techniques that provide immediate reinforcement in the form of tokens, which are objects or symbols that can be later exchanged for primary rewards, such as food, TV time, a private room, or outings. In a program like this, which is called a **token economy** (**Figure 14.12**), clients might at first be given tokens for merely attending group therapy sessions. Later they will be rewarded only for actually participating in the sessions. Eventually, the tokens can be discontinued when the client receives the reinforcement of being helped by participation in the therapy sessions (Jowett Hirst et al., 2016; Mullen et al., 2015).

Observational Learning

tobkatrina/Shutterstock.com

We all learn many things by observing others. Therapists use this principle in **modeling therapy**, in which clients are asked to observe and imitate appropriate models as they perform desired behaviors. **[AQ2]** For example, researchers successfully treated 4- and 5-year-old children with severe dog phobias by asking them first to watch other children play with dogs (see photo), and then to gradually approach and get physically closer to the dogs themselves

(May et al., 2013). When this type of therapy combines live modeling with direct and gradual practice, it is called *participant modeling*. This type of modeling is also effective in social skills training and assertiveness training (**Figure 14.13**).

MASH/Photodisc/Getty Images

FIGURE 14.13 **Observational learning** During modeling therapy, a client might learn how to interview for a job by first watching the therapist role-play the part of the interviewee. The client then imitates the therapist's behavior and plays the same role. Over the course of several sessions, the client becomes gradually desensitized to the anxiety of interviews.

S&P Scientific Thinking and Practical Application

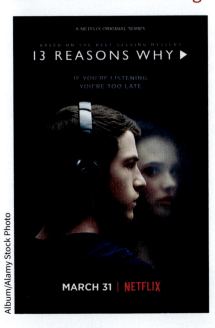

Album/Alamy Stock Photo

Did you see (or hear about) the Netflix television series *13 Reasons Why* (see photo)? The program depicts the life of a suburban teen who dies by suicide after leaving 13 recordings explaining her reasons. Even before the show premiered, experts warned that it could lead to an increase in teen suicides. **[AQ3]** Tragically, following the release of this series, a study did find a significant increase in monthly suicide rates among U.S. youth ages 10 to 17 (Bridge et al., 2019). Is this a horrific consequence of inappropriate modeling?

As you recall from Chapter 1, and as a scientific and critical thinker, you recognize that this type of correlation can never prove causation. However, the association is troubling and even the researchers suggested that caution is warranted regarding the exposure of children and adolescents to the series. Critics argue that the program glamorizes suicide and suggests it's an effective way to get even with others or to end emotional suffering (Welch, 2019).

What do you think? Given what we've just discussed regarding observational learning and modeling therapy, along with the previous discussion of "copycat suicides" in Chapter 13, how can we prevent the potential devastating consequences of this type of "inappropriate modeling"? Some have suggested (and tried) public service warnings that appear before such programs. However, as we also discussed in Chapter 13, these so-called trigger warnings (Sanson et al., 2019) had little effect—at least for anxiety disorders. In fact, they may even unintentionally reinforce anxiety and fears due to avoidance learning.

Until we have more research and better answers, perhaps the best public approach is to remind media producers that suicide should never be glamorized or depicted as a reasonable coping strategy to end suffering. In addition, the media can include information encouraging troubled people to seek help, while also highlighting the successful careers of people who have suffered but found therapy that helps them successfully cope with their depression.

On a personal level, if you are depressed or know someone who is, you can review the tips we offered in Chapter 13 regarding suicide, as well as the techniques for what to do and what NOT to do if you think someone is suicidal. In addition, keep in mind that the empirically based therapies discussed in this chapter are available and directly applicable for suicide prevention.

Take-Home Message: Depression is treatable. With greater public awareness and more open discussion of the realities versus the glamorization of suicide, we can hopefully prevent more deaths by suicide—and the needless guilt and horrific suffering of those who are left behind.

Evaluating Behavior Therapies   Research clearly shows that behavior therapy can benefit adults as well as children. The various forms of treatment make it effective for a large number of people, and for treating a large array of specific psychological disorders (e.g., Geschwind et al., 2019; Michie et al., 2018; Scott & Cogburn, 2018). Criticisms of behavior therapy fall into three major categories:

- **Generalizability** According to critics, in the real world clients are not consistently reinforced or punished, and therefore therapy-acquired behaviors may disappear. For instance, one study found that drivers who were involved in a severe collision initially reduced their risky driving, but only for the first month after the collision (O'Brien et al., 2017). To deal with this possible lack of generalizability, behavior therapists encourage clients to recognize external, real-world rewards and to generate their own internal reinforcements. They can then apply these rewards after their newly acquired behaviors.

- **Neglect of other approaches**   Some opponents contend that behavior therapies ignore or diminish the importance of unconscious, cognitive, and biological factors, which also contribute to psychological disorders.

- **Ethics**   Critics maintain that it is unethical for one person to control another's behavior. Behaviorists reply that rewards and punishments already control our behaviors. By making these controls overt, and by teaching people how to change their own behaviors, behavior therapy actually increases individual freedom.

Despite these criticisms, behavior therapy is generally recognized as one of the most effective treatments for numerous problems, including phobias, obsessive-compulsive disorder, eating disorders, sexual dysfunctions, autism, intellectual disabilities, and delinquency (Cusack et al., 2016; Munsch et al., 2019; Spiegler, 2016). For an immediate practical application of behavior therapy to your college life, see the following **Test Yourself**.

PA   Practical Application

Test Yourself: Do You Have Test Anxiety?

Nearly everyone is somewhat anxious when handed an important exam (see photo). If you find this anxiety helpful and invigorating, skip this activity. On the other hand, if the days and evenings before a major exam are ruined by your anxiety and you sometimes "freeze up" while taking a test, try these tips, based on the three major forms of behavior therapy.

1. Classical Conditioning

This informal type of systematic desensitization will help decrease your feelings of anxiety:

Step 1   Review and practice the relaxation technique taught in Chapter 3.

Step 2   Create a 10-step "test-taking" hierarchy—starting with the least anxiety-arousing image (perhaps the day your instructor first mentions an upcoming exam) and ending with actually taking the exam.

Step 3   Beginning with the least-arousing image—say, hearing about the exam—picture yourself at each stage. While maintaining a calm, relaxed state, mentally work your way through all ten steps. If you become anxious at any stage, stay there, repeating your relaxation technique until the anxiety diminishes.

Step 4   If you start to feel anxious the night before the exam, or even during the exam itself, remind yourself to relax. Take a few moments to shut your eyes and review how you worked through your hierarchy.

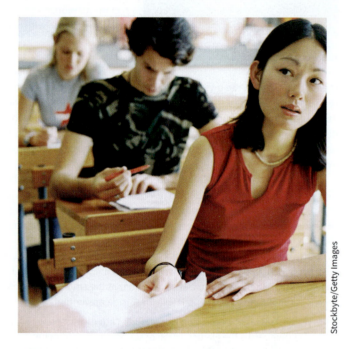

Stockbyte/Getty Images

by clicking on the answer button or by looking in Appendix B. Then move on to the longer self-grading quizzes that are available on our website, www.wiley.com/college/huffman. Following each of these "successive approximations," be sure to reward yourself in some way—call a friend, play with your children or pets, watch a video, or maybe check your social media page.

2. Operant Conditioning

One of the best ways to avoid "freezing up" or "blanking out" on a test is to be fully prepared. To maximize your preparation, "shape" your behavior. Start small by answering the multiple-choice questions at the end of each major section of each chapter then check your answers

3. Observational Learning

Talk with your classmates who are getting good grades. Ask them for suggestions on how they prepare for exams and how they handle their own test anxieties. This type of modeling and observational learning can be very helpful—and it's a nice way to make friends.

Retrieval Practice 14.2 | Behavior Therapies

Self-Test Completing this self-test, and then checking your answers by clicking on the answer button or by looking in Appendix B, will provide immediate feedback and helpful practice for exams.

1. The main focus in behavior therapy is to increase _____ and decrease _____.

   a. positive thoughts and feelings; negative thoughts and feelings

   b. adaptive behaviors; maladaptive behaviors

   c. coping resources; coping deficits

   d. all these options

2. _____ pairs relaxation with a graduated hierarchy of anxiety-producing situations to extinguish the anxiety.

   a. Modeling

   b. Shaping

   c. Systematic desensitization

   d. Maslow's pyramid training

3. In behavior therapy, _____ techniques use shaping and tokens to increase adaptive behaviors.

   a. classical conditioning   c. social learning

   b. modeling   d. operant conditioning

4. In contrast to systematic desensitization, _____ uses classical conditioning techniques to create anxiety rather than prevent its arousal.

   a. anxiety-modeling therapy   c. anxiety therapy

   b. aversion therapy   d. subversion therapy

5. Asking clients with snake phobias to watch other (non-phobic) people handle snakes is an example of _____ therapy.

   a. time out   c. virtual reality

   b. aversion   d. participant modeling

Q Test Your Critical Thinking

1. Imagine that you were going to use the principles of cognitive-behavioral therapy to change some aspect of your own thinking and behavior. If you'd like to quit smoking, or be more organized, how would you identify the faulty thinking perpetuating these behaviors and fears?

2. Once you've identified your faulty thinking patterns, what could you do to change your behavior?

3. Under what circumstances might behavior therapy be unethical?

tobkatrina/Shutterstock.com

Real World Application Questions

[AQ2] Does simply watching other children play with dogs reduce dog phobias in young children?

[AQ3] Can media portrayals of suicide, like *13 Reasons Why*, unintentionally encourage it?

Album/Alamy Stock Photo

Hint: Look in the text for **[AQ2]** and **[AQ3]**

14.3 | Biomedical Therapies

LEARNING OBJECTIVES

Retrieval Practice While reading the upcoming sections, respond to each Learning Objective in your own words.

Review the types of biomedical therapies, and their risks and benefits.

- **Describe** biomedical therapies.
- **Identify** the major types of drugs used to treat psychological disorders.
- **Explain** what happens in electroconvulsive therapy and psychosurgery.

- **Summarize** the risks and benefits associated with biomedical therapies.

Real World Application Questions

[AQ4] Can the dangerous party drug ketamine relieve depression and suicidal thoughts?

[AQ5] Is electroconvulsive therapy (ECT) painful, dangerous, and possibly causing permanent brain damage?

Certain problem behaviors seem to be caused, at least in part, by chemical imbalances or disturbed nervous system functioning, and, as such, they can be treated with **biomedical therapies**. Psychiatrists or other medical personnel are generally the only ones who use biomedical (biological) therapies. However, in some states, licensed psychologists can prescribe certain medications, and they often work with clients receiving biomedical therapies. In this section,

Biomedical therapies A group of therapies designed to alter brain functioning with biological or physical techniques, such as drugs, electroconvulsive therapy, and psychosurgery.

we will discuss three types of biomedical therapies: *psychopharmacology, electroconvulsive therapy (ECT)*, and *psychosurgery*.

Psychopharmacology

Beginning in the 1950s, the field of **psychopharmacology** has effectively used drugs to relieve or control the major symptoms of psychological disorders (see cartoon). In some instances, using a psychotherapeutic drug is similar to administering insulin to people with diabetes, whose own bodies fail to manufacture enough. In other cases, drugs have been used to relieve or suppress the symptoms of psychological disturbances even when the underlying factors were not thought to be biological. As shown in **Table 14.2**, psychotherapeutic drugs are classified into four major categories: *antianxiety, antipsychotic, mood stabilizer*, and *antidepressant*.

"The drug has, however, proved more effective than traditional psychoanalysis."

Psychopharmacology The use of drugs to relieve or control the major symptoms of psychological disorders.

TABLE 14.2   Psychotherapeutic Drug Treatments for Psychological Disorders

	Description	Examples (Trade Names)
Antianxiety Drugs Medications used to reduce anxiety and decrease overarousal in the brain; also known as anxiolytics or minor tranquilizers	**Antianxiety drugs** lower the sympathetic activity of the brain—the crisis mode of operation—so that anxiety is diminished, and the person is calmer and less tense. Unfortunately, they're also potentially dangerous since they can reduce alertness, coordination, and reaction time. Moreover, they can have a synergistic (intensifying) effect with other drugs, which may lead to severe drug reaction—and even death.	Ativan Halcion Klonopin Librium Restoril Tranxene Valium Xanax
Antipsychotic Drugs Medications used to diminish or eliminate symptoms of psychosis; also known as neuroleptics or major tranquilizers	**Antipsychotic drugs** reduce the agitated behaviors, hallucinations, delusions, and other symptoms associated with psychotic disorders, such as schizophrenia. Traditional antipsychotics work by decreasing activity at the dopamine receptors in the brain. A large number of clients markedly improve when treated with antipsychotic drugs.	Abilify Clozaril Geodon Haldol Invega Latuda Risperdal Seroquel Thorazine Zyprexa
Mood-Stabilizer Drugs Medications used to treat the combination of manic episodes and depression characteristics of bipolar disorders	**Mood-stabilizer drugs** help steady mood swings, particularly for those suffering from bipolar disorder, a condition marked by extremes of both mania and depression. Given that these drugs generally require up to 3 or 4 weeks to take effect, their primary use is in preventing future episodes, and helping to break the manic-depressive cycle.	Depakote Eskalith CR Lamictal Lithium Neurontin Tegretol Topamax Trileptal
Antidepressant Drugs Medications used to treat depression, some anxiety disorders, obsessive-compulsive disorder, posttraumatic stress disorder, and certain eating disorders (such as bulimia)	**Antidepressant drugs** are used primarily to reduce depression. There are several types of antidepressant drugs, including *selective serotonin reuptake inhibitors (SSRIs)*, *serotonin and norepinephrine reuptake inhibitors (SNRIs)*, norepinephrine and dopamine reuptake inhibitors (NDRIs), and *atypical antidepressants*. Each class of drugs affects neurochemical pathways in the brain in a slightly different way, increasing or decreasing the availability of certain chemicals. SSRIs (such as *Paxil* and *Prozac*) are by far the most commonly prescribed antidepressants. The atypical antidepressants are prescribed for those who fail to respond to, or experience undesirable side effects from, other antidepressants. It's important to note that it can take weeks or months for antidepressants to achieve their full effect.	Anafranil Celexa Cymbalta Effexor Elavil Lexapro Nardil Norpramin Parnate Paxil Pristiq Prozac Sarafem Tofranil Wellbutrin Zoloft

TIP Do you find these four drug categories confusing? If so, just remember that anti-anxiety drugs generally create feelings of tranquility and relaxation, while also decreasing overarousal in the brain. In contrast, antipsychotic drugs are designed to diminish or eliminate symptoms of psychosis, such as hallucinations. On the other hand, mood-stabilizer drugs attempt to level off the emotional highs and lows of bipolar disorder. Interestingly, antidepressants were originally designed to lift depression—hence their name. However, they're now being successfully used in the treatment of some anxiety disorders, obsessive-compulsive disorder, posttraumatic stress disorder, and certain eating disorders.

How Do Drug Treatments Actually Work? For most psychotherapeutic medications, including antidepressants, the best understood action of the drugs is to correct an imbalance in the levels of neurotransmitters in the brain (**Figure 14.14**). **[AQ4]** Surprisingly, recent research has found that the drug *ketamine*, a dangerous date rape/party drug (see photo) known as Special K, also works to manage the symptoms of major depression, suicidal behaviors, and bipolar disorders. Widely known in the medical field for its anesthetic properties, ketamine changes the levels of brain neurotransmitters and appears to decrease thoughts of suicide by targeting parts of the brain responsible for executive and emotional processing (Lee et al., 2016).

Syda Productions/
Shutterstock.com

FIGURE 14.14 **How antidepressants affect the brain** Antidepressants are believed to work by increasing the availability of serotonin or norepinephrine, neurotransmitters that normally elevate mood and arousal. Shown here is the action of some of the most popular antidepressants—Prozac, Paxil, and other selective serotonin reuptake inhibitors (SSRIs).

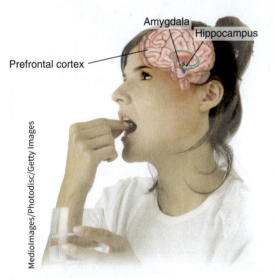

Medioimages/Photodisc/Getty Images

a. Serotonin's effect on the brain Some people with depression are believed to have lower levels of serotonin. Serotonin works in the prefrontal cortex, the hippocampus, and other parts of the brain to regulate mood, sleep, and appetite, among other things.

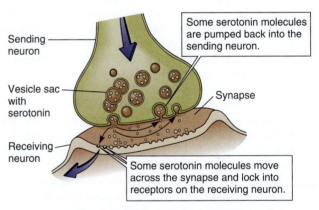

b. Normal neural transmission Sending neurons normally release an excess of neurotransmitters, including serotonin. Some of the serotonin locks into receptors on the receiving neuron, but excess serotonin is pumped back into the sending neuron (called *reuptake*) for storage and reuse. If serotonin is reabsorbed too quickly, there is less available to the brain, which may result in depression.

c. Partial blockage of reuptake by SSRIs SSRIs, like Prozac, partially block the normal reuptake of excess serotonin, which leaves more serotonin molecules free to stimulate receptors on the receiving neuron. This increased neural transmission restores the normal balance of serotonin in the brain.

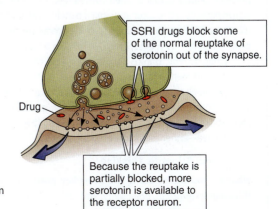

Due to its antisuicide effects, rapid onset, high efficacy, and good tolerability, ketamine shows promise as a potential treatment for depression and bipolar disorders (Hirota & Lambert, 2018; Li et al., 2016; Reardon, 2015). In fact, Food and Drug Administration (FDA) regulators in the United States have recently approved a prescription-only nasal spray of esketamine, a form of ketamine, which is currently under careful supervision and tight restrictions (Paddock, 2019; Traynor, 2019). For now, ketamine remains controversial due to the relative lack of empirical evidence, some serious side effects, and the potential for abuse (Zhang et al., 2016). For additional intriguing (and controversial) psychotherapeutic drug research, see the following **STH** **Scientific Thinking Highlight**.

In addition to correcting imbalances in the brain's neurotransmitters, other studies suggest that psychotherapeutic drugs, primarily antidepressants, may relieve depression and thoughts of suicide in three additional ways. They increase *neurogenesis*, the production of new neurons; or *synaptogenesis*, the production of new synapses; or they stimulate or depress activity in various areas of the brain (Lei et al., 2019; Samuels et al., 2016; Walker et al., 2015).

STH Scientific Thinking Highlight

Do Psychedelic Drugs Lead to psychosis?

(APA Goal 2.1) Use scientific reasoning to interpret psychological phenomena

Beginning in the 1960s, reports of "acid casualities" among drug users, especially during famous music festivals like "Woodstock" (see photo), led to several myths and rumors about psychedelic drugs. For example, many believed that even one "trip" with a psychedelic drug, such as LSD, psilocybin (the active ingredient in "magic mushrooms"), or mescaline (found in the peyote cactus) could trigger the onset of actual psychosis. As you may know, these drugs have been illegal in the United States since 1970 and are classified as schedule one drugs—"the most dangerous drugs" with no medicinal use.

Surprisingly, two recent studies contradict these earlier fears and assumptions. In the first study, researchers analyzed data from more than 135,000 people who took part in the annual U.S. National Survey on Drug Use and Health (NSDUH) conducted from 2008 to 2011 (Johansen & Krebs, 2015). Of the 14 percent who reported use of psychedelics, the researchers found no increased risk of mental disorders, including schizophrenia, anxiety disorders, psychosis, depression, or suicide attempts. The second study, which analyzed 190,000 NSDUH respondents from 2008 to 2012, also found no link between psychedelic use and adverse mental health outcomes (Hendricks et al., 2015). In fact, both studies suggested that psychedelic drug use may have produced lasting positive improvements in mental health. Other researchers have reviewed clinical trials, many that were double-blind and placebo-controlled, that showed positive relief of anxiety and depression in patients with cancer and similar benefits with both alcohol and nicotine addiction, along with improving overall psychological well-being (Cameron et al., 2019; Elsey, 2017; Polito & Stevenson, 2019).

What do you think? Should psychedelics be used to treat physical and mental illnesses? Is this recent interest in psychedelics a flashback or a flash-in-the-pan? Only further research can fully answer these questions. (In the meantime, please note that our inclusion of this research on psychedelics is not a recommendation for their use—either medically or recreationally.)

Q Test Your Scientific Thinking

What do you think? Using the three key principles of scientific thinking—*skepticism, objectivity,* and *rationalism*:

Archives du 7eme Art/Photos 12/Alamy Stock Photo

1. **Skepticism** Given the title and topic of this report, "Do Psychedelic Drugs Lead to Psychosis?" were you predisposed to believe or discount the information? Scientific thinkers approach claims like these with mild to deep skepticism.

2. **Objectivity** Knowing that correlation does not mean causation, could this be an example of the third-variable problem or an illusory correlation? How could you objectively test the hypothesis that psychedelic drugs contribute to psychosis? Where could you find the most reliable facts on psychedelic drugs? Scientific thinkers gather information and delay judgment until adequate data is available.

3. **Rationalism** How can we logically explain why so many people believe psychedelic drugs lead to psychosis? Would these drugs be as controversial if they weren't associated with the "hippies" and the 1960s? Describe how you could use these three principles of scientific thinking to have a logical conversation with someone who may be currently using psychedelic drugs, or has used them in the past. How might this type of dialogue be helpful?

(Compare your answers with those of your fellow students, family, and friends. Doing so will improve your scientific thinking and your media savvy.)

Electroconvulsive Therapy and Psychosurgery

As you may know from classic films, like *One Flew Over the Cuckoo's Nest*, there is a long, and generally distorted, history of using electrical stimulation to treat psychological disorders. **[AQ5]** In modern times, however, research has failed to confirm the widespread myth that ECT "shock therapy" is painful, is dangerous, and leads to permanent brain damage. In fact, it may even generate new neurons (Arkowitz & Lilienfeld, 2017; Singh & Kar, 2017; Srienc et al., 2018). In today's **electroconvulsive therapy (ECT)**, also known as electroshock therapy (EST), a moderate, painless electrical current is passed through the brain (**Figure 14.15**). This can be done by placing electrodes on the outside of both sides of the head (bilateral ECT), or on only one side of the head (unilateral ECT). The current triggers a widespread firing of neurons, or brief seizures.

Despite not knowing exactly how ECT works, and the possibility that it may result in some short-term and long-term memory problems, the risks of untreated, severe depression are generally considered greater than the risks of ECT (Andrade et al., 2016; Berman & Prudic, 2013). Today it's used almost exclusively to treat serious depression when drugs and psychotherapy have failed, or in cases where rapid response is needed—as is the case with suicidal clients (Fligelman et al., 2016; Kellner et al., 2015; Vallejo-Torres et al., 2015). In sum, ECT can quickly reverse symptoms of certain mental illnesses and often works when other treatments have been unsuccessful.

The most extreme, and least used, biomedical therapy is **psychosurgery**—brain surgery performed to reduce serious debilitating psychological problems. Attempts to change disturbed thoughts, feelings, and behavior by altering the brain have a long history. In Roman times, it was believed that a sword wound to the head could relieve insanity. In 1936, Portuguese neurologist Egaz Moniz first treated uncontrollable psychoses with a form of psychosurgery called a **lobotomy**, in which he cut the nerve fibers between the frontal lobes (where association areas for monitoring and planning behavior are found) and the thalamus and hypothalamus.

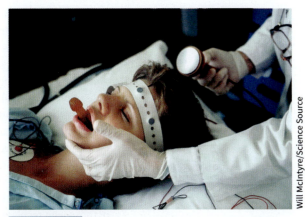

FIGURE 14.15 **Electroconvulsive therapy (ECT)** Modern ECT treatments are conducted with considerable safety precautions, including muscle-relaxant drugs that dramatically reduce muscle contractions, and medication to help clients sleep through the procedure. Note, however, that ECT is rarely used today, and generally only when other treatments have failed.

Will McIntyre/Science Source

Electroconvulsive therapy (ECT) A biomedical therapy based on passing electrical current through the brain; it is used almost exclusively to treat serious depression when drugs and psychotherapy have failed.

Psychosurgery A form of biomedical therapy that involves alteration of the brain to bring about desirable behavioral, cognitive, or emotional changes; generally used when clients have not responded to other forms of treatment.

Lobotomy An outmoded neurosurgical procedure for mental disorders, which involved cutting nerve pathways between the frontal lobes and the thalamus and hypothalamus.

PAN Practical Application of Neuroscience

Why did lobotomies develop such a bad reputation? Although early lobotomy surgeries did reduce emotional outbursts and aggressiveness, some clients were left with debilitating brain damage. Two of the most notable examples were Rosemary Kennedy, the sister of President John F. Kennedy (see photo), and Rose Williams, sister of American playwright Tennessee Williams. Both women were permanently incapacitated from lobotomies performed in the early 1940s. Thankfully, these types of lobotomies and related psychosurgery virtually stopped in the mid-1950s, when antipsychotic drugs came into use.

New York Times Co./Archive Photos/Getty Images

Evaluating Biomedical Therapies

Like all other forms of therapy, biomedical therapies have both proponents and critics. In this section, we'll consider the pros and cons of each of the biomedical therapies—*psychopharmacology, ECT,* and *psychosurgery*.

Psychopharmacology In modern times, psychotherapeutic drugs, like the antipsychotics that we just mentioned, have led to revolutionary changes in mental health. Before these drugs were introduced, many patients were destined to spend a lifetime in psychiatric institutions. Today, most improve enough to return to their homes and lead successful lives—if they continue to take their medications to prevent relapse.

On the other hand, drug therapy has been criticized on several grounds. First, although psychotherapeutic drugs may relieve symptoms for some people, they seldom provide cures, and some individuals become physically dependent. Furthermore, psychiatric medications can result in a variety of side effects, ranging from mild fatigue to severe impairments in memory and movement, along with the risk of unexpected deaths (Lawrence et al., 2017; Mentzel et al., 2017; Ray et al., 2019).

On a more positive note, drug therapy is often very effective when combined with talk therapy. For example, researchers have tested whether children and teenagers experiencing clinical depression would benefit from receiving cognitive-behavioral therapy (CBT) along with medication. In one study, 75 youths (ages 8 to 17) received either an antidepressant alone, or an antidepressant along with CBT for 6 months (Kennard et al., 2014). Of those who received only the drug, 26.5 percent experienced continued depression, compared to only nine percent of those who received the drug combined with CBT.

ECT and Alternative Neurostimulation Therapies

As mentioned earlier, ECT is a controversial form of treatment, yet it still serves as a valuable last resort for severe depression that has not responded to other forms of treatment. In addition to ECT, many therapists in recent years have been using various alternative treatments (see **Figure 14.16**). Unlike ECT, which uses electricity, **repetitive transcranial magnetic stimulation (rTMS)** uses magnetic pulses to stimulate or suppress parts of the brain. To treat depression, an electromagnetic coil is usually placed over the scalp and the prefrontal cortex, a region linked to deeper parts of the brain that regulate mood. Currently, rTMS's advantages over ECT are still unclear, but studies have shown marked improvement in depression, and clients experience fewer side effects (Blumberger et al., 2019; Papadopoulou et al., 2018; Yadollahpour et al., 2016).

In comparison, during **transcranial direct current stimulation (tDCS)**, a relatively weak direct current is delivered to specific, targeted areas of the brain using electrodes attached to the scalp. Originally developed to help patients with brain injuries, it's currently being used to investigate brain–behavior relationships, as a treatment for depression and other disorders, and to increase cognitive performance on a variety of tasks in healthy adults (Bennabi & Haffen, 2018; Huang et al., 2019; Thair et al., 2017; Wang et al., 2018).

Psychosurgery

Given that all forms of psychosurgery are generally irreversible and potentially dangerous with serious or even fatal side effects, psychosurgery is considered experimental and remains a highly controversial treatment. Some critics say that it should be banned

Repetitive transcranial magnetic stimulation (rTMS) A biomedical treatment that uses repeated magnetic field pulses targeted at specific areas of the brain.

Transcranial direct current stimulation (tDCS) A biomedical treatment that uses direct electrical currents to stimulate specific parts of the brain.

FIGURE 14.16 Alternative neurostimulation treatments

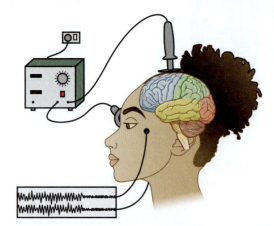

a. Electroconvulsive therapy (ECT) An electric current strong enough to trigger a seizure is applied to the skull outside of the brain.

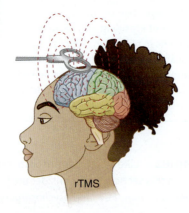

b. Repetitive transcranial magnetic stimulation (rTMS) A coil is placed on the outside of the skull, and magnetic pulses from the coil stimulate or suppress activity in the brain.

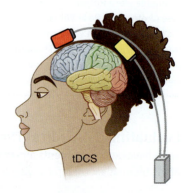

c. Transcranial direct current stimulation (tDCS) A weak electrical current is applied to the skull to stimulate specific, targeted areas of the brain.

altogether. Recently, psychiatrists have been experimenting with a much more limited and precise neurosurgical procedure called *deep brain stimulation* (*DBS*). The surgeon drills two tiny holes into the skull and implants electrodes in the area of the brain believed to be associated with a specific disorder (**Figure 14.17**). These electrodes are then connected to a "pacemaker" implanted in the chest or stomach that sends low-voltage electricity to the problem areas in the brain. Over time, this repeated stimulation can bring about significant improvement in Parkinson's disease, epilepsy, major depression, and other disorders (Fields, 2015; Kim et al., 2016; Lipsman et al., 2015). Research has also shown that clients who receive DBS along with antidepressants show lower rates of depression than those who receive either treatment alone (Brunoni et al., 2013).

Before going on, be sure to study **Table 14.3** carefully. It provides a side-by-side comparison of all the major forms of therapy we've discussed so far, which makes it a valuable and convenient way to review and compare all the key terms and concepts.

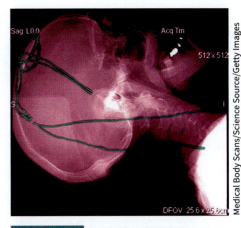

FIGURE 14.17 **Deep brain stimulation (DBS)** Stimulation from the implanted electrodes in the client's brain may bring relief to those suffering from Parkinson's disease, epilepsy, major depression, and other disorders.

Medical Body Scans/Science Source/Getty Images

TABLE 14.3 **Side-by-Side Comparison of Treatments for Psychological Disorders**

Type of Treatment	Key Assumptions and Goals	Major Techniques	Strengths	Weaknesses
Psychoanalysis/ Psychodynamic	**Key assumption about origins of disorder** Unconscious, unresolved conflicts **Key goal of therapy** Provide insight by bringing unconscious thoughts and conflicts into conscious awareness	**Psychoanalysis** (Freud) • Free association • Dream analysis • Analysis of resistance • Analysis of transference • Interpretation **Psychodynamic therapies** • Face-to-face • Techniques similar to psychoanalysis but more likely to offer advice and support	**Psychoanalysis** • Can be effective for those who have the time and money **Psychodynamic therapies** • Benefits similar to those of psychoanalysis with shorter duration of treatment	• Question of repressed memories and unconscious conflicts • Limited applicability • Lacks scientific support
Humanistic	**Key assumption about origins of disorder** Blocked personal growth **Key goal of therapy** Maximize clients' inherent capacity for self-actualization, free will, and self-awareness	**Client-centered therapy** (Rogers) • Empathy • Unconditional positive regard • Genuineness • Active listening **General humanistic therapy** • Emphasis on providing an accepting atmosphere and encouraging healthy emotional experiences • Focus on conscious processes and present versus past experiences • Clients responsible for discovering their own maladaptive patterns	• Recognizes positives of human nature • Some empirical evidence of efficacy	• Self-actualization and self-awareness difficult to test scientifically • Mixed research results on specific humanistic techniques
Cognitive	**Key assumption about origins of disorder** Faulty, distorted thinking **Key goal of therapy** Help clients identify and correct faulty, distorted thinking	• Cognitive restructuring • Rational-emotive behavior therapy (REBT) (Ellis) • Cognitive-behavior therapy (CBT) (Beck) • Mindfulness-based cognitive therapy (MBCT)	Highly effective treatments for depression, as well as anxiety disorders, bulimia nervosa, anger management, addiction, and even some symptoms of schizophrenia and insomnia	• Dysfunctional thinking may result from, not necessarily cause, abnormal functioning • May neglect unconscious dynamics and importance of client's past • Success may be due to behavior techniques, not to changes in faulty thinking

(Continued)

TABLE 14.3 Side-by-Side Comparison of Treatments for Psychological Disorders (*continued*)

Type of Treatment	Key Assumptions and Goals	Major Techniques	Strengths	Weaknesses
Behavior	**Key assumption about origins of disorder** Inappropriate conditioning and learning **Key goal of therapy** Reduce or eliminate maladaptive behaviors and increase adaptive ones	• Classical conditioning (desensitization, aversion therapy) • Operant conditioning (behavior modification, shaping, token economies) • Observational learning (modeling, social-skills and assertiveness training)	Most widely researched and scientifically documented treatments; highly effective for phobias, obsessive-compulsive disorder, and other psychological disorders	• Effects of treatment may not generalize to the real world • May neglect unconscious, cognitive, and biological processes • May be unethical to control another's behavior
Biomedical	**Key assumption about origins of disorder** Problems with brain structure or functioning, genetics, biochemistry **Key goal of therapy** Improve structural or biochemical brain functioning and relieve symptoms	• Psychopharmacology • Electroconvulsive therapy • Psychosurgery	Often effective when problems don't respond to other treatments	• Psychopharmacology may relieve symptoms but seldom provides cures; also, problems with side effects and possible physical drug dependence • ECT and psychosurgery may have dangerous and permanent side effects

Retrieval Practice 14.3 | Biomedical Therapies

Self-Test Completing this self-test, and then checking your answers by clicking on the answer button or by looking in Appendix B, will provide immediate feedback and helpful practice for exams.

1. The study of the effects of drugs on behavior and mental processes is known as _____.

   a. psychiatry
   b. psychoanalysis
   c. psychosurgery
   d. psychopharmacology

2. The effectiveness of antipsychotic drugs is thought to result primarily from decreasing activity at the _____ receptors.

   a. serotonin
   b. dopamine
   c. epinephrine
   d. all these options

3. In electroconvulsive therapy (ECT), _____.

   a. current is never applied to the left hemisphere
   b. a moderate, painless electrical current is passed through the brain to treat serious depression when drugs and psychotherapy have failed
   c. convulsions are extremely painful and long lasting
   d. most clients receive hundreds of treatments because it is safer than in the past

4. ECT is used primarily to treat _____.

   a. phobias
   b. conduct disorders
   c. severe depression
   d. schizophrenia

5. The original form of psychosurgery developed by Egaz Moniz disconnected the _____ lobes from the thalamus and hypothalamus.

   a. occipital
   b. parietal
   c. temporal
   d. frontal

Q Test Your Critical Thinking

1. Are the potential benefits of psychopharmacology worth the risks? Is it ever ethical to force someone to take drugs to treat his or her mental illness?

2. If you, or someone you loved, were seriously depressed, would you be in favor of ECT? Why or why not?

Real World Application Questions

[AQ4] Can the dangerous party drug ketamine relieve depression and suicidal thoughts?

[AQ5] Is electroconvulsive therapy (ECT) painful, dangerous, and possibly causing permanent brain damage?

Syda Productions/ Shutterstock.com

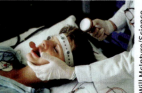

Will McIntyre/Science Source

Hint: Look in the text for **[AQ4]** and **[AQ5]**

14.4 | Psychotherapy in Perspective

LEARNING OBJECTIVES

Retrieval Practice   While reading the upcoming sections, respond to each Learning Objective in your own words.

Review the key issues in psychotherapy.

- **Summarize** the goals and overall effectiveness of psychotherapy.
- **Describe** group, couples, family, and telehealth/electronic therapies.

- **Identify** the key cultural and gender issues important in therapy.
- **Summarize** the major options for someone interested in becoming a therapist or seeking therapy.

Real World Application Question

[AQ6] Is therapy delivered over your phone effective?

It's currently estimated that there are more than 1,000 approaches to psychotherapy, and the number is continuing to rise (Gaudiano et al., 2015; Magnavita & Anchin, 2014). So how would you choose the appropriate one for yourself or for someone you know? In the first part of this section, we discuss five goals common to all psychotherapies. Then we explore specific formats for therapy as well as considerations of culture and gender. Our aim is to help you synthesize the material in this chapter and put what you have learned about each of the major forms of therapy into a broader context.

Therapy Goals and Effectiveness

All major forms of therapy are designed to help the client in five specific areas (**Figure 14.18**). Although most therapists work with clients in several of these areas, the emphasis varies according to the therapist's training and whether it is psychodynamic, cognitive, humanistic, behaviorist, or biomedical. Clinicians who regularly borrow freely from various theories are said to take an **eclectic approach**.

Does therapy work? After years of controlled studies and *meta-analyses*—a method of statistically combining and analyzing data from many studies—researchers have fairly clear

Eclectic approach   A perspective that combines elements of various therapies to find the most appropriate treatment; also known as integrative therapy.

FIGURE 14.18 **The five most common goals of therapy**   Most therapies focus on one or more of these five goals. Can you identify which would be of most interest to psychodynamic, humanistic, cognitive, and behavioristic therapists?

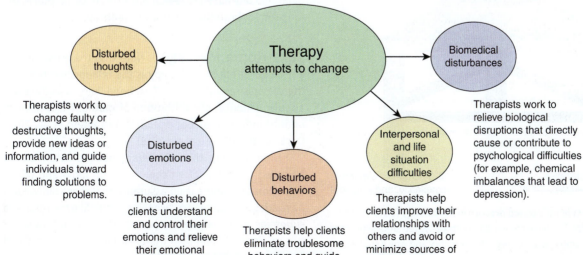

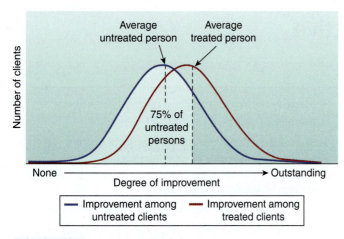

FIGURE 14.19 **Is therapy generally effective?** The average person who receives therapy is better off after it than a similar person who does not get treatment (Lilliengren et al., 2016; Smith et al., 1980; Smith & Glass, 1977). An analysis of more than 435 studies on the effectiveness of therapy for treating psychological disorders in children and adolescents revealed that therapy can lead to improvements in many different types of psychological disorders, including anxiety, autism, depression, disruptive behavior, eating problems, substance use, and traumatic stress (Chorpita et al., 2011).

Evidence-based practice in psychology (EBPP) A therapy approach that integrates the best available evidence with clinicians' expertise, along with the clients' characteristics, culture, and preferences.

Therapeutic alliance A bond between the therapist and client based on mutual trust, respect, understanding, and cooperation; an essential factor in successful therapy.

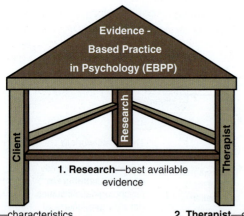

FIGURE 14.20 **Evidence-based practice in psychology (EBPP)** The ideal treatment plan has been compared to a three-legged stool supported by: (1) the best available research regarding whether and why a specific treatment works; (2) the therapist's expertise, experience, and judgment; and (3) the client's personal characteristics, culture, and preferences.

evidence that it does. As shown in **Figure 14.19**, early meta-analytic reviews combined studies of almost 25,000 people and found that the average person who received treatment was better off than 75 percent of the untreated control clients (Smith et al., 1980; Smith & Glass, 1977).

Studies also show that short-term treatments can sometimes be as effective as long-term treatments and that multiple forms of therapies are equally effective for various disorders (Hansen et al., 2019; Lilliengren et al., 2016; Öst & Ollendick, 2017). As you'll see in the following **RC** **Research Challenge**, even informal therapy techniques, such as exercises in self-compassion, can produce significant improvements in well-being and overall mental health (e.g., Frostadottir & Dorjee, 2019).

As we've just seen, some studies find that several forms of therapy are equally effective for various disorders. However, other studies suggest that certain disorders are better treated with specific approaches. For example, anxiety disorders seem to respond best to exposure-based CBT, whereas symptoms of schizophrenia can be significantly relieved with medication (Bullis & Hofmann, 2016; Gillihan & Foa, 2016; Yoshinaga et al., 2019).

Finally, in recent years, *empirically supported* practice, or **evidence-based practice in psychology (EBPP)**, has been gaining momentum because it uses empirical methods and seeks to identify which therapies have received the clearest research support for particular disorders (Ashmore et al., 2019; Gray et al., 2015; Hamilton et al., 2016). As you might expect, when it comes to therapy and treatment decisions for particular clients, relying solely on research can be difficult. Evidence for some disorders is conflicting or non-existent. Furthermore, each client has his or her own specific characteristics, culture, and preferences, and those needs must be respected when designing the optimal treatment plan.

A special task force of the American Psychological Association (APA) endorsed the goals of EBPP, while also recognizing the competing needs and positions of research, therapist, and client—see **Figure 14.20** (APA Presidential Task Force, 2006). Note how this three-prong model provides flexibility for the clinician, while also incorporating the needs of the client and the best scientific evidence (Hamilton et al., 2016; Jordan et al., 2017; Norcross & Wampold, 2018). Like all other movements, EBPP has been criticized. But this type of empirically based research promises to be helpful in the long run for both therapists and clients alike.

Take-Home Message Note that the most important factor in effective therapy is the relationship between the therapist and the client. This bond, known as the **therapeutic alliance**, should be one of mutual trust, respect, understanding, and cooperation (Constantino et al., 2017; Doran et al., 2017; Xu et al., 2019).

Unfortunately, this is generally not the case with the so-called therapists often showcased on radio and television. Moreover, there is no assurance that these individuals have adequate training or licensing—titles like *therapist* and *counselor* are generally not protected, licensed terms. For tips on finding a qualified therapist for yourself or a loved one, see the **PAH** *Practical Application Highlight* at the end of this chapter.

RC Scientific Thinking: **Research Challenge**

Can Simple Self-Compassion Improve Your Mental and Physical Health?

(APA Goal 2.4) Interpret, design, and conduct basic psychological research

What do you do when you've made a mistake or are having a really bad day? For far too many of us, the tendency is to berate ourselves for all our failures and shortcomings. In comparison, people who are naturally good at *self-compassion*, which refers to a kind and nurturing attitude toward one's self, can easily differentiate between making a bad mistake or having bad day and being a bad person. Unfortunately, the concept of self-compassion is almost a foreign concept for many people—particularly for those who were raised in abusive or harsh, unloving environments.

The good news is that self-reflection and other skills (see cartoon) associated with self-compassion can be taught and measured. In a recent study, researchers recruited 135 university students and randomly placed them in one of five groups, each of which listened to an 11-minute audio recording (Kirschner et al., 2019). Two of the five groups then performed short-term self-compassion exercises, compared to three different exercises in the other conditions—negative thinking (rumination), positive thinking (excitement), or a neutral assignment. During the exercises, each participant's physiological arousal (heart rate and sweat response) was also measured.

As you might expect, participants in the two self-compassion groups and the positive thinking condition all reported greater self-compassion, connection with others, and decreased self-criticism compared to the negative thinking (rumination) and neutral groups. In addition, the two self-compassion groups showed a significantly lower physiological arousal level.

What's the take-home message? The researchers suggested that being kind to oneself allows our bodies to relax and to feel safe—which is important for stress reduction, regeneration, and healing.

Identify the Research Method

1. Based on the information provided, did this study (Kirschner et al., 2019) use descriptive, correlational, and/or experimental research?

2. If you chose:
   - *descriptive research*, is this a naturalistic or laboratory observation, survey/interview, case study, and/or archival research?

Paul Noth/The New Yorker Collection/The Cartoon Bank

"Have you tried turning off your conscious mind and then turning it back on again?"

   - *correlational research*, is this a positive, negative, or zero correlation?
   - *experimental research*, label the IV, DV, experimental group(s), and control group. (Note: If participants were not randomly assigned to groups, list it as a *quasi-experimental design*.)
   - both *descriptive* and *correlational*, answer the corresponding questions for both.

Check your answers by clicking on the answer button or by looking in Appendix B.

Note: The information provided in this study is admittedly limited, but the level of detail is similar to what is presented in most textbooks and public reports of research findings. Answering these questions, and then comparing your answers to those provided, will help you become a better scientific and critical thinker and consumer of scientific research.

Therapy Formats

The therapies described earlier in this chapter are conducted primarily in a face-to-face, therapist-to-client format. In this section, we focus on several major alternatives: *group, family,* and *couples therapies,* which treat several individuals simultaneously, and *telehealth/electronic therapy,* which treats individuals via the Internet, email, and smartphones.

Group Therapies
In **group therapies**, multiple people meet together to work toward therapeutic goals. Typically, a group of 8 to 10 people meet with a therapist on a regular basis to talk about problems in their lives (**Figure 14.21**).

A variation on group therapy is the **self-help group**. Unlike other group approaches, self-help groups are not guided by a professional. They are simply circles of people who share a common problem, such as alcoholism, obesity, or breast cancer, and who meet to give and receive support.

Group therapies A form of therapy in which a number of people with similar concerns meet together with a professional to work toward therapeutic goals.

Self-help group A leaderless or non–professionally guided group in which members assist each other with a specific problem, as in Alcoholics Anonymous.

FIGURE 14.21 **A satirical look at group therapy** We're using this cartoon to lighten the mood of this chapter, but rest assured that group therapy can be very effective in real life.

FIGURE 14.22 **Family therapy** Many families initially come into therapy believing that one member is the cause of all their problems. However, family therapists often find that this "identified client" is a scapegoat for deeper disturbances. How could changing ways of interacting within the family system promote the health of individual family members and the family as a whole?

Programs such as Alcoholics Anonymous, Narcotics Anonymous, and Spenders Anonymous are examples of self-help groups. Although group members don't get the same level of individual attention found in one-on-one therapies, group and self-help therapies provide their own unique advantages (Bateganya et al., 2015; Castillo et al., 2016; Friedman et al., 2017). They are far less expensive than one-on-one therapies and provide a broader base of social support. Group members can also learn from each other's experiences, share insights and coping strategies, and role-play social interactions together.

For instance, researchers who have studied group sessions in 12-step programs, like Alcoholics Anonymous, have found that people suffering from a combination of social anxiety disorders and substance abuse disorders show lower rates of relapse than those who don't participate in these self-help groups. This is particularly true if they also provide help to others as a sponsor or mentor (Pagano et al., 2013, 2015). Therapists often recommend these alternative formats of therapy to their clients, and research suggests that they can be very effective, either alone or in addition to individual psychotherapy (McGillicuddy et al., 2015; O'Farrell et al., 2016; Wagener, 2019).

Couples and Family Therapies

Given that a family or marriage is a system of interdependent parts, the problem of any one individual inevitably affects everyone. Therefore, all members are potential beneficiaries of therapy (Ahluwalia et al., 2018; Bartle-Haring et al., 2018; Smith, 2016). The line between family and couples therapy is often blurred. Here, our discussion will focus on *family therapy*, in which the primary aim is to change maladaptive family interaction patterns (**Figure 14.22**). All members of the family attend therapy sessions, though at times the therapist may see family members individually or in twos or threes.

Family therapy is useful in treating a number of disorders and clinical problems. As an example, the therapist can help families improve their communication styles and reframe their problems as a family issue versus an individual one. It can also be the most favorable setting for the treatment of adolescent substance abuse and eating disorders (Dodge, 2016; Kanbur & Harrison, 2016; Wufong et al., 2019). For an unusual approach to couples therapy, see the following **RC** **Research Challenge**.

Telehealth/Electronic Therapy

Today, millions of people are receiving advice and professional therapy in newer electronic formats such as the Internet, email, virtual reality (VR), and interactive web-based conference systems such as Skype (e.g., O'Hara, 2019). This latest form of electronic therapy, often referred to as *telehealth*, allows clinicians to reach more clients and provide them with greater access to information regarding their specific concerns.

S&P Scientific Thinking and Practical Application

Therapy—Is there an app for that? **[AQ6]** Studies have long shown that therapy outcomes improve with increased client contact. To increase this contact, research finds that the electronic/telehealth format may be the easiest and most cost-effective method (Adams et al., 2018; Gannon et al., 2019; Lawes-Wickwar et al., 2018). For example, a nationwide study of cognitive behavior therapy in an evidence-based behavioral health program, delivered via phone (see photo) or video, found high patient satisfaction and significant reductions in symptoms of depression, anxiety, and stress (Dent et al., 2018).

RC Scientific Thinking: **Research Challenge**

Can Watching Movies Prevent Divorce?

(APA Goal 2.4) Interpret, design, and conduct basic psychological research

As we all know, roughly half of all U.S. marriages end in divorce. Numerous secular and religious institutions have attempted to reduce this rate with various early marriage intervention programs. To examine whether simple self-help strategies, such as watching and discussing movies about relationships (see photo), might offer some of the same benefits as these professionally led intervention programs, researchers randomly assigned 174 couples to one of four groups (Rogge et al., 2013):

- Group 1 (control) received no training or instructions.
- Group 2 (conflict management) learned active listening strategies to help discuss heated issues.
- Group 3 (compassion and acceptance training) learned strategies for finding common ground and showing empathy.
- Group 4 (minimal intervention—movie and talk) attended a 10-minute lecture on relationship awareness and how watching couples in movies could help increase awareness of their own behaviors.

MAD_Production/Shutterstock.com

Following this initial assignment to groups, Group 1 received no training at all, but members of this group were similar to those in the three other groups in terms of age, education, ethnicity, relationship satisfaction, and other dimensions. Groups 2 and 3 attended weekly lectures, completed homework assignments, and met with a trained therapist periodically. In contrast, Group 4 only attended a 10-minute lecture, watched a romantic comedy, and then discussed 12 questions about the screen couple's interactions (e.g., "Did they try using humor to keep things from getting nasty?"). They were then sent home with a list of 47 relationship-oriented movies and allowed to choose their favorite one to watch and discuss once a week for the next month.

The researchers then followed up with all couples three years later to see which of these approaches was most effective in preventing divorce. Much to their surprise, couples in all three of the intervention groups were far less likely to get divorced compared to those in the control group. Specifically, 24 percent of couples in the control group were divorced, compared to only 11 percent of those in each of the other three groups. Even more surprising, this study shows that a simple self-help strategy of watching and discussing five relationship movies over one month's time can be just as effective at reducing the divorce or separation rate as more intensive early marriage counseling programs led by trained psychologists.

Do you see how this study has exciting wide-scale, national applications? If "movie date night" can double as therapy, many U.S. couples might be saved from the very high emotional and financial costs of divorce. What about your own current or future relationships? If simply sharing and discussing a relationship movie now and then with your romantic partner might strengthen that relationship, why not try it? You can learn more about this study (and see a list of recommended movies with guided discussion questions) at http://www.courses.rochester.edu/surveys/funk/

Identify the Research Method

1. Based on the information provided, did this study (Rogge et al., 2013) use descriptive, correlational, and/or experimental research?

2. If you chose:
   - *descriptive research*, is this a naturalistic or laboratory observation, survey/interview, case study, and/or archival research?
   - *correlational research*, is this a positive, negative, or zero correlation?
   - *experimental research*, label the IV, DV, experimental group(s), and control group. (**Note:** If participants were not randomly assigned to groups, list it as a *quasi-experimental design*.)
   - both *descriptive* and *correlational*, answer the corresponding questions for both.

Check your answers by clicking on the answer button or by looking in Appendix B.

Note: The information provided in this study is admittedly limited, but the level of detail is similar to what is presented in most textbooks and public reports of research findings. Answering these questions, and then comparing your answers to those provided, will help you become a better scientific and critical thinker and consumer of scientific research.

Using electronic options such as the Internet and smartphones does provide alternatives to traditional one-on-one therapies, but, as you might expect, these unique approaches also raise concerns (e.g., O'Hara, 2019). Professional therapists fear, among other things, that without interstate and international licensing, or a governing body to regulate this type of therapy, there are no means to protect clients from unethical practices or incompetent therapists. What do you think? Would you be more likely to participate in therapy if it were offered via your smartphone, email, or a website? Or is this too impersonal for you?

Institutionalization

We all want our right to freedom. But what about people who threaten suicide or are potentially violent? Should some people be involuntarily committed to protect them from their own mental disorders? Despite Hollywood film portrayals, forced institutionalization of people with mental illness is generally reserved for only the most serious and life-threatening situations. Even so, it poses serious ethical problems.

Involuntary Commitment

The legal grounds for involuntary commitment vary from nation to nation (e.g., Holder et al., 2018; Ryan & Callagan, 2017). In the United States, while the specific language for involuntary commitment may vary from state to state, the U.S. Supreme Court has ruled there is no constitutional basis for "confining persons involuntarily if they are dangerous to no one and can live safely in freedom" (cited in Mental Policy.Org, n.d.).

Generally, people can be sent to psychiatric hospitals against their will in the following circumstances:

- They are believed to pose a danger to themselves (usually suicidal) or to others (potentially violent).
- They are in serious need of treatment (indicated by bizarre behavior and loss of contact with reality).
- There is no reasonable, less restrictive alternative.

In emergencies, psychologists and other professionals can also authorize temporary commitment for 24 to 72 hours. During this observation period, laboratory tests can be performed to rule out medical illnesses that could be contributing to the symptoms. Furthermore, clients generally receive psychological testing, medication, and short-term therapy during this period.

Deinstitutionalization

Although the courts have established stringent requirements for involuntary commitment, abuses and problems with long-term, chronic institutionalization do occur. In addition, properly housing and caring for people with mental illness is very expensive.

To address these problems, many states have a policy of *deinstitutionalization*, which involves discharging clients from mental hospitals as soon as possible and discouraging admissions. Deinstitutionalization has been a humane and positive step for many. Unfortunately, some clients are discharged without continuing provision for their protection. Many of these people ultimately end up living in rundown hotels or understaffed nursing homes, in jails, or on the street with no shelter or means of support. Keep in mind that a sizable percentage of homeless people also suffer from some form of serious mental illness, along with economic factors such as increased unemployment, underemployment, and a shortage of low-income housing (Allday, 2016; Gentil et al., 2019; National Alliance on Mental Illness, n.d.).

What else can be done? Rather than returning clients to state hospitals, most clinicians suggest expanding and improving community care (**Figure 14.23**). They also recommend that general hospitals be equipped with special psychiatric units where those who are acutely ill can receive inpatient care. For less disturbed individuals and chronically ill clients, they often recommend walk-in clinics, crisis intervention services, improved residential treatment facilities, and psychosocial and vocational rehabilitation. State hospitals can then be reserved for the most unmanageable cases.

Before going on, be sure to carefully consider the important therapy issues in the following **GCD** **Gender and Cultural Diversity**.

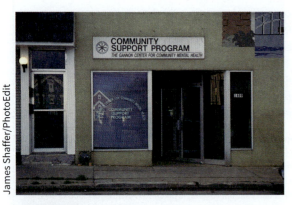

FIGURE 14.23 **Outpatient support** Community mental health (CMH) centers are a prime example of alternatives to institutionalization. CMH centers provide outpatient services such as individual and group therapy and prevention programs. They also coordinate short-term inpatient care and programs for discharged clients, such as halfway houses and aftercare services. The major downside of CMH centers and their support programs is that they are expensive. Investing in primary prevention programs (such as more intervention programs for people at high risk for mental illness) could substantially reduce these costs.

James Shaffer/PhotoEdit

GCD Gender and Cultural Diversity

How Do Culture and Gender Affect Psychotherapy?

(APA Goal 2.5) Incorporate sociocultural factors in scientific inquiry

Cultural Issues in Therapy   The therapies described in this chapter are based on Western European and North American culture. Does this mean they are unique? Or do these psychotherapists accomplish some of the same things that, say, a native healer or shaman does? When we look at therapies in all cultures, we find that they have certain key features in common (Barnow & Balkir, 2013; Gopalkrishnan, 2018; Hall & Ibaraki, 2016):

- **Naming the problem**   People often feel better just knowing that others experience the same problem and that the therapist has had experience with it.
- **Demonstrating the right qualities**   Clients must feel that the therapist is caring, competent, approachable, and concerned with finding solutions to their problems.
- **Establishing credibility and trust**   Word-of-mouth testimonials and status symbols, such as diplomas on the wall, establish a therapist's credibility and trust, which a native healer may earn by serving as an apprentice to a revered healer.
- **Placing the problem in a familiar framework**   Some cultures believe evil spirits are the major source of psychological disorders, so therapy is directed toward eliminating these spirits. Similarly, in cultures that emphasize the importance of early childhood experiences and the unconscious mind as the major factor in mental disorders, therapy will be framed around these familiar issues.
- **Applying techniques to bring relief**   In all cultures, therapy includes action. Either the client or the therapist must do something, and what the therapist does must fit the client's expectations—whether it is performing a ceremony to expel demons or talking with the client about his or her thoughts and feelings.
- **Meeting at a special time and place**   The fact that therapy occurs outside the client's everyday experiences seems to be an important feature of all therapies.

Although there are basic similarities in therapies across cultures, there are also important differences. In the traditional Western European and North American model, the emphasis is on the client's self and on his or her having independence and control over his or her life—qualities that are highly valued in individualistic cultures. In collectivist cultures, however, the focus of therapy is on interdependence and the acceptance of life realities (Hornsey et al., 2019; Lee et al., 2015; Seay & Sun, 2016). See **Figure 14.24**.

Not only does culture affect the types of therapy that are developed, it also influences the therapist's perceptions. What one culture considers abnormal behavior may be quite common—and even healthy—in others. For this reason, recognizing cultural differences is very important for building trust between therapists and clients and for effecting behavior change.

Gender and Therapy   In our individualistic Western culture, men and women present different needs and problems to therapists. Research has identified four unique concerns related to

FIGURE 14.24 **Emphasizing interdependence**   In Japanese Naikan therapy, clients sit quietly from 5:30 a.m. to 9:00 p.m. for 7 days and are visited by an interviewer every 90 minutes. During this time, they reflect on their relationships with others in order to discover personal guilt for having been ungrateful and troublesome and to develop gratitude toward those who have helped them (Itoh & Hikasa, 2014; Zhang et al., 2014).

gender and psychotherapy (Moulding, 2016; Sambrook Smith et al., 2019; World Health Organization, 2019):

1. **Rates of diagnosis and treatment of mental disorders**   Women are diagnosed and treated for mental illness at a much higher rate than men. Is that due to historical biases against women and mental illness? Are women more in need, as a group, then men? Or is it that women are more likely to discuss their problems and to seek help? Are there cultural factors discouraging men from asking for attention in this area? More research is needed to answer these questions.

2. **Stresses of poverty**   Women are disproportionately likely to be poor. Poverty contributes to stress, which is directly related to many psychological disorders.

3. **Violence against women**   Rape, incest, and sexual harassment—which are much more likely to happen to women than to men—may lead to depression, insomnia, posttraumatic stress disorder, eating disorders, and other problems.

4. **Stresses of multiple roles and gender-role conflict**   Despite the many changes in gender roles in modern times, restrictive definitions of femininity and masculinity still limit both genders' well-being and human potential. Furthermore, most men and women today serve in many roles, as family members, students, wage earners, and so forth. The conflicting demands of their numerous roles often create special stresses unique to each gender.

Therapists must be sensitive to possible connections between clients' problems and their gender, as well as to issues of cultural diversity (De Bord et al., 2017; Levant & Powell, 2017; Sambrook Smith et al., 2019). For example, rather than emphasizing talk therapy and drugs to relieve depression, therapists could also explore ways to relieve the stresses of multiple roles or poverty for both women and men. In your case as a college student, can you see how discussing ways to reduce stressors and financial costs associated with a college education might help improve your own mental health?

Well-being therapy (WBT) A newer form of psychotherapy aimed at enhancing psychological well-being by focusing on personal growth and noticing and savoring the positive aspects of life.

Before going on, we'd like to leave this chapter on a practical and positive note. The psychotherapy techniques we've discussed are generally directed toward improving psychological disorders. However, psychologists are also committed to enhancing overall well-being and daily psychological functioning. In line with that, we offer the following **PP** **PositivePsych**, along with a **PAH** **Practical Application Highlight**.

PP Practical Application: **PositivePsych**

Using Psychology to Promote Mental Health

(APA Goal 1.3) Describe applications of psychology

As you've seen throughout this text, psychology focuses on three major areas—*thoughts*, *feelings*, and *actions*. In this section, we'll focus on psychological tips for promoting not only your own personal mental health, but also the world's.

Promoting Your Personal Mental Health   To increase your everyday well-being and protect your mental health, consider the following research-based positive psychology suggestions for each area:

1. **Recognize and control your thoughts.**   Would you like to be happier and more often in a great mood? You might start by reviewing and implementing the suggestions in the **PositivePsych** happiness section in Chapter 11. In addition, as discussed earlier, the three C's of Beck's cognitive therapy (catching, challenging, and changing our faulty thought processes) are key to successful therapy—as well as in everyday life.

   Research also finds that having a positive view of the future and an optimistic, attributional style are important to mental health (Kleiman et al., 2017; Roepke & Seligman, 2016; Sachsenweger et al., 2015). Depressed people often suffer from a *depressive attribution style* of thinking, which means that they typically attribute negative events to internal, stable, and global factors. For example, they might think, "I failed because I'm unlucky, I have been throughout my life, and it affects all parts of my life." The good news is that social connections with others, which we discuss later in this list, can reduce this type of thinking (Bourassa et al., 2017; Cruwys et al., 2015).

   In addition, there is a wealth of research on the power of meditation in recognizing and gaining control of your thought processes. As discussed in Chapter 3, *mindfulness-based stress reduction (MBSR)* is linked with numerous health benefits, from better concentration and physical health to improved mental well-being (Creswell et al., 2019; Farb et al., 2018; Shapiro & Carlson, 2017).

2. **Acknowledge and express your feelings.**   Although we all have negative emotions and conflicts that often need to be acknowledged and resolved, as a general rule recognizing and expressing your *positive* emotions, particularly feelings of *gratitude*, is an important avenue to mental health (see again Chapter 11's **PositivePsych** happiness feature).

Mark Bowden/123RF

Noting what you're thankful for—from appreciating your significant other to catching the bus or subway before the doors close—will definitely improve your ability to cope with life's challenges. Being grateful also tends to increase your personal self-esteem and overall well-being (Chowdhury, 2019; Sztachańska et al., 2019).

Interestingly, **well-being therapy (WBT)**, which focuses on personal growth and noticing and savoring the positive aspects of our lives (see photo), has been successful in promoting overall mental health, as well as in increasing resilience and sustained recovery from several psychological disorders (Nierenberg et al., 2016; Ruini & Fava, 2014).

Empathy is equally important. As you recall from our earlier discussion of Rogers's client-centered therapy, empathy involves being a sensitive listener who understands and shares another's inner experience. The good news is that when you're being empathic, you're not only improving another person's self-acceptance and mental health, but also your own. In fact, providing emotional support (empathy) to another may be more important than practical, instrumental support in increasing the provider's well-being (Morelli et al., 2015). In short, compassionate sharing of feelings and experiences benefits both parties, perhaps because it helps all of us feel more accepted and less alone during life's inevitable ups and downs.

Finally, *love for yourself* may be the most important emotional key to protecting your mental health. Self-care and self-compassion are not "selfish." As mentioned earlier, self-compassion refers to a kind and nurturing attitude toward yourself, and research shows that it is positively linked with improved mental and physical health (Kirschner et al., 2019;

Stephenson et al., 2018). In other words, prioritize your well-being. When you're feeling frustrated and overwhelmed, allow yourself to say "no." Along with all the resources for coping mentioned in Chapter 3, keep in mind that "no" is a complete sentence. You don't have to explain your reasons for taking care of and loving yourself.

3. **Recognize and change your behaviors.** As discussed in several chapters of this text, "simply" eating the right food, getting enough exercise and sleep, and spending time in nature are all important to our well-being and may help protect our mental health (Engemann et al., 2019; Tillmann et al., 2018; Triantafillou et al., 2019). For example, research finds that even moderate exercise—20 to 30 minutes of walking a day—can prevent episodes of depression in the long term (Mammen & Faulkerner, 2013). Other research suggests that moderate exercise may be as helpful as psychotherapy or antidepressants (Ku et al., 2017; Kvam et al., 2016). One study found that weight training reduced depression (Gordon et al., 2018), and a survey of over 1.2 million people in the United States revealed that those who exercise report having 1.5 fewer days of poor mental health a month, compared to those who do not exercise (Chekroud et al., 2018).

A second behavioral change that increases psychological health is to make someone else feel good. Studies show that volunteering and expressing kindness to others has a cyclical effect—doing a good deed for others makes them happier, which in turns makes you happier (Anik et al., 2011; Xi et al., 2016). As previously mentioned, spending time in nature is important to mental health, but it also unexpectedly increases our willingness to help. In a very simple field experiment, confederates (people who were part of the experiment) "accidentally" dropped a glove while walking on a path into an urban green park filled with large trees, lawns, and flowers (Guéguen & Stefan, 2016). Researchers found that passersby who saw the dropping of the glove while leaving the park were far more likely to help by picking up the glove than those who were heading into the park.

Perhaps the most important action you can take to protect your mental health is to enjoy and maintain your social connections. Research shows that people who feel more connected to others have lower rates of anxiety and depression (Laird et al., 2019; McLeigh, 2015; Nguyen et al., 2019). For this and many other reasons, we need to remind ourselves to spend as much time as possible with our friends and loved ones, whether it's going on vacation or just watching a movie together.

Promoting the World's Mental Health   The World Health Organization (WHO) has researched and organized the key worldwide contributors to mental health into three major categories—*individual attributes, social and economic circumstances,* and *environmental factors* (see **Table 14.4**). Each category also includes adverse and protective factors. Note that these issues interact and may even negate one another, so the occurrence of one factor or category obviously does not necessarily result in a psychological disorder.

As expected, the contributors to and severity of psychological disorders around the world are complex. But we included this table to remind all of us that mental health is a global issue. As a global citizen and scientific thinker, can you imagine what we could do both locally and internationally to improve the lives and mental health of our fellow citizens around the world?

TABLE 14.4   Potential Contributors to Mental Health Around the World

Individual Attributes		Social Circumstances		Environmental Factors	
Adverse Factors	**Protective Factors**	**Adverse Factors**	**Protective Factors**	**Adverse Factors**	**Protective Factors**
Low self-esteem	Self-esteem, confidence	Loneliness, bereavement	Social support of family and friends	Poor access to basic services	Equality of access to basic services
Cognitive and emotional maturity	Ability to solve problems and manage stress	Neglect, family conflict	Good parenting and family interaction	Injustice and discrimination	Social justice, tolerance, integration
Medical illness, substance use	Physical health, fitness	Exposure to violence/abuse	Physical security and safety	Social and gender inequalities	Social and gender equality
		Low income and poverty	Economic security	Exposure to war or disaster	Physical security and safety
		Difficulties or failure at school	Scholastic achievement		
		Work stress, unemployment	Satisfaction and success at work		

Source: World Health Organization (n.d.).

PAH **Practical Application Highlight**

Tips for Finding a Therapist

(APA Goal 1.3) Describe applications of psychology

Each of us struggles to balance our personal lives and unique vulnerabilities with the stresses of our environment. We all need help at different times in our lives, and when these stresses and vulnerabilities overwhelm our natural coping mechanisms, professional therapy can provide invaluable relief (see photo). But how do we find a good therapist for our specific needs?

If you have time (and the money) to explore options, be sure to "shop around" for a therapist best suited to your specific goals. Consulting your college counseling system for referrals can be an important first step, and they typically offer some free services. If you're confused about all the numerous types of therapists and their training, **Table 14.5** provides a handy and quick overview of the major types of mental health professionals. For general help in locating a skilled therapist, identifying what types of initial questions to ask, learning how to gain the most benefits during therapy, and so on, consult the American Psychological Association (APA) website.

Wavebreakmedia Ltd/ Getty Images

TABLE 14.5	**Searching for a Mental Health Professional?**

Most colleges have counseling or career centers with numerous resources and trained staff to help you with your search for a therapist. To give you an overview of the general field of psychotherapy, we've included a brief summary of the major types of mental health professionals, their degrees, required education beyond the bachelor's degree, job description, and type of training.

Major Types of Mental Health Professionals

Occupational Title	Degree	Nature of Training
Clinical Psychologists	PhD (doctor of philosophy) PsyD (doctor of psychology)	Most clinical psychologists have a doctoral degree with training in research and clinical practice, and a supervised 1-year internship in a psychiatric hospital or mental health facility. As clinicians, they work with clients suffering from mental disorders, but many also work in colleges and universities as teachers and researchers, in addition to having their own private practice.
Counseling Psychologists	MA (master of arts) PhD (doctor of philosophy) PsyD (doctor of psychology) EdD (doctor of education)	Counseling psychologists typically have a doctoral degree with training that focuses on less severe mental disorders, such as emotional, social, vocational, educational, and health-related concerns. In addition to providing psychotherapy, other career paths are open, such as teaching, research, and vocational counseling.
Pastoral Counselor	None MA (master of arts) PhD (doctor of philosophy) DD (doctor of divinity)	Pastoral counselors combine spiritual advice and psychotherapy, and generally must hold a license and at least a master's or doctoral degree in their field of study. They typically work for counseling centers, churches, community programs, and hospitals.
Psychiatrists	MD (doctor of medicine)	After 4 years of medical school, an internship and residency in psychiatry are required, which includes supervised practice in psychotherapy techniques and biomedical therapies. Given that psychiatrists are MDs, in most U.S. states, psychiatrists are generally the only mental health specialists who can regularly prescribe drugs.
Psychiatric Nurses	RN (registered nurse) MSN (master of science in nursing) DNP (doctor of nursing philosophy) PhD (doctor of philosophy)	Psychiatric nurses must be registered nurses (RNS), and a bachelor of science in nursing is preferred (BSN), followed by advanced training in psychological therapies and the care of patients in hospital settings, and/or clients in mental health facilities.
Psychiatric Social Workers	BSW) (bachelor of social work) MSW (master's in social work) DSW (doctor of social work) PhD (doctor of philosophy)	Psychiatric social workers usually begin with a bachelor's degree in social work, and most go on to earn a master's degree in social work, followed by advanced training and experience in hospitals or outpatient settings working with people who have psychological problems.
School Psychologists	MA (master of arts) PhD (doctor of philosophy) PsyD (doctor of psychology) EdD (doctor of education)	School psychologists generally begin with a bachelor's degree in psychology, followed by graduate training in psychological assessment and counseling for school-related issues and problems.

Sources: Jaekel & Kortegast, 2016; Metz, 2016; Silvia et al., 2017; Social Work Guide, 2019; Sternberg, 2017; U.S. Bureau of Labor Statistics, 2019.

Once you've decided on two or three potential therapists, you may want to arrange a preliminary consultation. At that initial meeting, feel free to ask about your therapist's fees, credentials, and experience dealing with your particular issues. In addition, pay close attention to your feelings of connection with the different therapists you are interviewing. As you discovered earlier in this chapter, the *therapeutic alliance* is very important in psychotherapy.

Like romantic dating, therapy is a close relationship and not every therapist will be a good fit for you. Also, like dating, the therapeutic relationship is complex and challenging. It is critical to find someone who is trustworthy and caring. The emotional bond you form with your therapist may be the most important part of successful treatment. As you may recall from Chapter 2, the hormone (and neurotransmitter) *oxytocin* is believed by some to promote love, attachment, and social bonding. In situations of trust and caring, some research has found that it may increase the willingness to go along with and conform to the opinions of others (Geng et al., 2018; Luo et al., 2017; Xu et al., 2019).

If you don't have time to shop around or if you are in a crisis—having suicidal thoughts, failing grades, or being the victim of abuse—*get help fast* (see Chapter 13). Most communities have telephone hotlines that provide counseling on a 24-hour basis, and most colleges and universities have counseling centers that provide immediate, short-term therapy to students free of charge.

Finally, if you are encouraging others to seek therapy, you might offer to help locate a therapist—and to go with them for the first visit. If they refuse help and the problem affects you, it's often a good idea to seek therapy yourself. You will gain insights and skills that will help you deal with the situation more effectively.

Q Test Your Critical Thinking

1. If you were looking for a therapist, would you want the therapist's gender and culture to be the same as yours? Why or why not?

2. Do you think all insurance companies should be required to offer mental health coverage? Why or why not?

Before going on, be sure to complete the final Retrieval Practice, and then answer the critical thinking questions in the **Test Your Critical Thinking**.

Retrieval Practice 14.4 | Psychotherapy in Perspective

Self-Test Completing this self-test, and then checking your answers by clicking on the answer button or by looking in Appendix B, will provide immediate feedback and helpful practice for exams.

1. When therapists combine techniques from various therapies, they are said to be using _____.

   a. psychosynthetic therapy

   b. biomedical therapy

   c. managed care

   d. an eclectic approach

2. A(n) _____ group does not have a professional leader, and members assist each other in coping with a specific problem.

   a. self-help

   b. encounter

   c. peer

   d. behavior

3. _____ treats the family as a unit, and members work together to solve problems.

   a. Aversion therapy   **c.** A self-help group

   b. An encounter group   **d.** Family therapy

4. Which of the following is *not* a culturally universal feature of therapy?

   a. naming the problem

   b. demonstrating the right qualities

   c. establishing rapport among family members

   d. placing the problem in a familiar framework

5. A Japanese therapy designed to help clients discover personal guilt for having been ungrateful and troublesome to others and to develop gratitude toward those who have helped them is known as _____ therapy.

   a. Kyoto

   b. Okado

   c. Naikan

   d. Nissan

Q Test Your Critical Thinking

1. Which of the universal characteristics of therapists do you believe is the most important? Why?

2. If a friend were having relationship problems, how would you convince him or her to go to a couples or family therapist, using information you've gained in this chapter?

Real World Application Question

[AQ6] Is therapy delivered over your phone effective?

mikered/iStock/ Getty Imageso

Hint: Look in the text for **[AQ6]**

Q Test Your Critical Thinking

Did you notice or wonder why we provided six Real World Application Questions **[AQ1–AQ6]** throughout this chapter? We've found that they not only help you to engage with and master the material, they also have an important and lasting impact on your critical thinking skills. For additional mastery and enrichment, consider the following questions:

1. In the 2013 movie *Side Effects* (see photo), Rooney Mara and Channing Tatum portray a successful young couple, Emily and Martin, whose entire world falls apart when Emily's psychiatrist prescribes a new (fictional) psychoactive drug called Ablixa to treat her anxiety. The true *side effects* of the drug, as well as the underlying motivations and mental health of the main characters, are revealed only during the film's final scenes. How might this film contribute to negative stereotypes of psychotherapy and psychopharmacology?

2. Given that advertising for the fictional drug in this *Side Effects* movie closely matches the ads for actual psychoactive drugs, what special dangers and applications does widespread advertising for psychotherapeutic drugs pose for the real world?

3. Can you think of a Hollywood film that offers a positive portrayal of psychotherapy or psychopharmacology?

4. You undoubtedly had certain beliefs and ideas about therapy before reading this chapter. Has studying this chapter changed any of those beliefs and ideas?

5. Which form of therapy described in this chapter do you personally find most appealing? Why?

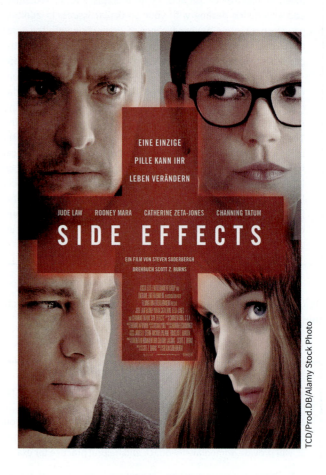

TCD/Prod.DB/Alamy Stock Photo

Summary

14.1 Talk Therapies 461

- **Psychotherapy** refers to techniques employed to improve psychological functioning and promote adjustment to life. There are three general approaches to therapy—*talk, behavior,* and *biomedical.*

- In **psychoanalysis**, the therapist seeks to identify the patient's unconscious conflicts and to help the patient resolve them. The five major techniques of psychoanalysis are **free association, dream analysis, analysis of resistance, analysis of transference,** and **interpretation.**

- In modern **psychodynamic therapy**, treatment is briefer, and the therapist takes a more directive approach (and puts less emphasis on unconscious childhood memories) than in traditional psychoanalysis.

- **Humanistic therapy** seeks to maximize personal growth, encouraging people to actualize their potential and relate to others in genuine ways.

- Rogers's client-centered therapy emphasizes **empathy, unconditional positive regard, genuineness**, and **active listening**.

- **Cognitive therapy** focuses on faulty thought processes and beliefs to treat problem behaviors. Through insight into negative **self-talk** (the unrealistic things people say to themselves), the therapist can use **cognitive restructuring** to challenge and change destructive thoughts or inappropriate behaviors.

- Ellis's **rational-emotive behavior therapy (REBT)** focuses on eliminating negative emotional reactions through logic, confrontation, and examination of irrational beliefs. In comparison, Beck's **cognitive-behavior therapy (CBT)** combines cognitive therapy (including changing faulty thinking) with behavior therapy (changing maladaptive behaviors).

- In **mindfulness-based cognitive therapy (MBCT)**, therapists help clients attain a state of consciousness that attends to ongoing events in a receptive and non-judgmental way.

14.2 Behavior Therapies 470

- In **behavior therapy**, the focus is on the problem behavior itself rather than on any underlying factors. The therapist uses learning principles to change behavior.

- Classical conditioning techniques include **systematic desensitization** and **aversion therapy**.

- Operant conditioning techniques used to increase adaptive behaviors include *shaping* and *reinforcement*.

- In **modeling therapy**, clients observe and imitate others who are performing the desired behaviors.

14.3 Biomedical Therapies   475

- **Biomedical therapies** are based on the premise that it is chemical imbalances or disturbed nervous system functioning that contribute to problem behaviors.

- **Psychopharmacology** is the most common form of biomedical therapy. Major classes of drugs used to treat psychological disorders are **antianxiety drugs, antipsychotic drugs, mood stabilizer drugs,** and **antidepressant drugs**.

- In **electroconvulsive therapy (ECT)**, an electrical current is passed through the brain, stimulating seizures that produce changes in the central and peripheral nervous systems. ECT is used primarily in cases of severe depression that do not respond to other treatments.

- In **repetitive transcranial magnetic stimulation (rTMS)**, powerful electromagnets generate pulsed magnetic fields that are targeted at specific areas of the brain to treat depression.

- The most extreme biomedical therapy is **psychosurgery**. *Lobotomy*, an older form of psychosurgery, is now outmoded and often replaced with a more limited and precise surgical procedure called *deep brain stimulation* (*DBS*).

14.4 Psychotherapy in Perspective   483

- All major forms of therapy are designed to address disturbed thoughts, disturbed emotions, disturbed behaviors,

interpersonal and life situation difficulties, and biomedical disturbances.

- Many therapists take an **eclectic approach** and combine techniques from various theories. Research indicates that, overall, therapy does work.

- In **group therapy**, multiple people meet together to work toward therapeutic goals. A variation is the self-help group, which is not guided by a professional. Therapists often refer their clients to group therapy and **self-help groups** in order to supplement individual therapy.

- In couples and family therapy, the aim is to change maladaptive patterns of interaction. Given that a marriage or family is a system of interdependent parts, all members are encouraged to attend all therapy sessions; however, the therapist may see members individually or in twos or threes.

- Telehealth/electronic therapy allows clinicians to reach more clients and provide greater access to information. But there are concerns about licensing, regulations, and abuses.

- Under specific circumstances, people can be involuntarily committed to mental hospitals for diagnosis and treatment. Problems with involuntary commitment led to deinstitutionalization—discharging as many patients as possible and discouraging admissions. Community services such as community mental health (CMH) centers help offset problems with deinstitutionalization.

- Therapies in all cultures share some common features, as well as important differences. Therapists must be sensitive and responsive to possible gender issues and cultural differences in order to build trust with clients and effect behavioral change.

Key Terms

Retrieval Practice   Write a definition for each term before turning back to the referenced page to check your answer.

- active listening   465
- aversion therapy   471
- behavior therapies   470
- biomedical therapies   475
- client-centered therapy   464
- cognitive-behavior therapy (CBT)   468
- cognitive restructuring   466
- cognitive therapies   466
- dream analysis   463
- eclectic approach   483
- electroconvulsive therapy (ECT)   479
- empathy   465
- evidence-based practice in psychology (EBPP)   484

- free association   462
- genuineness   465
- group therapies   485
- humanistic therapies   464
- interpretation   463
- lobotomy   479
- mindfulness-based cognitive therapy (MBCT)   468
- modeling therapy   473
- psychoanalysis   462
- psychodynamic therapies   463
- psychopharmacology   476
- psychosurgery   479
- psychotherapy   461

- rational-emotive behavior therapy (REBT)   467
- repetitive transcranial magnetic stimulation (rTMS)   480
- resistance   463
- self-help group   485
- systematic desensitization   470
- therapeutic alliance   484
- token economy   472
- transcranial direct current stimulation (tDCS)   480
- transference   463
- unconditional positive regard   465
- well-being therapy (WBT)   490

Kuttelvaserova Stuchelova/Shutterstock.com

CHAPTER **15**

Social Psychology

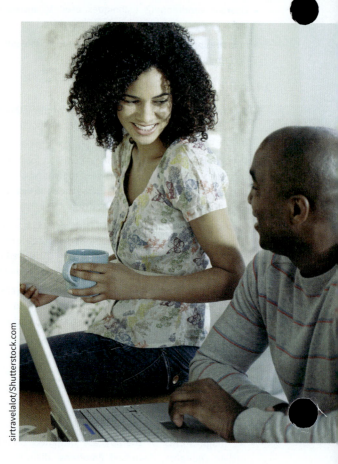

sirtravelalot/Shutterstock.com

15.1 | Social Cognition

LEARNING OBJECTIVES

Retrieval Practice   While reading the upcoming sections, respond to each Learning Objective in your own words.

Review the field of social psychology and its largest subfield—social cognition.

- **Define** social psychology and social cognition.
- **Describe** person perception and the importance of first impressions.
- **Discuss** the attributional process and its errors, biases, and cultural factors; along with how to reduce the errors and biases.

- **Identify** attitudes, their three components, and how they're formed and changed.
- **Discuss** prejudice, its three components, and the factors that increase or decrease it.

Real World Application Questions

[AQ1] Why do athletes often blame their losses on bad officiating?

[AQ2] Can reading *Harry Potter* books increase positivity towards gay people?

Social psychology, one of the largest branches in the field of psychology, focuses on the scientific study of how other people influence our thoughts, feelings, and actions. For many students and psychologists, your authors included, this field of psychology is the most important and exciting of all since it's about all of us and real world issues. It's also because almost everything we do is *social*. Unlike earlier chapters that focused on individual processes, like sensation and perception, memory, or personality, this chapter studies how large social forces, such as groups and social norms, bring out the best and worst in all of us. This chapter is organized around three central themes: *social cognition*, *social influence*, and *social relations*. Before reading on, check the misconceptions you may have about these topics in the following **Test Yourself**.

Social psychology   The scientific study of how others influence our thoughts, feelings, and actions.

PA Practical Application

Test Yourself: How Much Do You Know About the Social World?

True or False?

_____ 1. People from individualistic cultures are more likely to "blame the victim" than those from collectivist cultures.

_____ 2. Persuasion is the most effective way to change attitudes.

_____ 3. Prejudice can operate even without a person's conscious awareness.

_____ 4. People wearing masks are more likely than unmasked individuals to engage in aggressive acts.

_____ 5. Emphasizing gender differences may create and perpetuate prejudice.

_____ 6. Violent video games are a clear cause of increased aggression.

_____ 7. You're more likely to get help from one person than from a large number of people.

_____ 8. Opposites attract.

_____ 10. Romantic love generally starts to fade after 6 to 30 months.

_____ 11. Punching a pillow when you're angry can make you feel even more upset.

_____ 12. Flirting is a powerful way to increase your attractiveness to a potential mate.

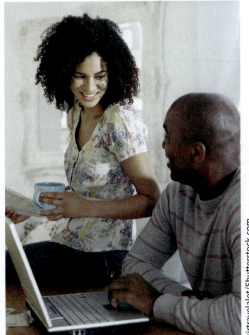

sirtravelalot/Shutterstock.com

Answers: Two of these statements are false. You'll find the answers within this chapter.

We begin this chapter with *social cognition*. As you recall from earlier chapters, *cognition* is just another word for "thinking," and social cognition is simply the cognitive processes we use to think about ourselves and others. In this section we'll look at four of the major topics in social cognition—*person perception, attributions, attitudes,* and *prejudice.*

Person Perception

Person perception   The mental processes we use to form impressions of others.

Think back to when you first met someone who's currently very important in your life or when you first became a fan of your favorite musician. Can you remember what first attracted you to that person? **Person perception** refers to the processes we use to form impressions of others. A recent study asked listeners to evaluate personality traits of someone simply speaking the Spanish word "Hola" and the English word "Hello" (Baus et al., 2019). Regardless of the language used and whether or not it was the native or foreign language of the listener, ratings of the personality traits of the speaker were highly consistent among the listeners. This and other research suggests that our perceptions of others are formed very quickly and based on very little information, such as a person's face and facial expressions, general appearance, and even the sound of a single word.

Why is this important? Researchers in this latest study suggested that this type of quick evaluation may provide an evolutionary advantage. Obtaining quick information about the intent of others helps us evaluate whether to approach or to avoid a stranger.

As you might expect, person perception and *first impressions* also play a major role in online communication (e.g., Dibb, 2019; White et al., 2017). Social media users know that their initial profile photo can have a lasting impact, which helps explain why women tend to take and display photographs of themselves from a low relative physical position. Research finds that this posture is designed to emphasize their smaller size and youthful features (Makhanova et al., 2017). In contrast, men more often post photos from a high relative physical position to emphasize their size and dominance. Your profile picture may also affect your job search. One study found that during recruiters' first hiring decisions, those who have the best (most attractive) photo obtained 38 percent more job interviews (Baert, 2018).

What's the take-home message? First impressions DO matter. If you'd like specific tips on managing your first impressions in a job interview, see the following **Test Yourself**.

Attributions

Attribution   The explanations we make about the causes of behaviors or events.

Have you ever been in a serious argument with a loved one—perhaps a parent, close friend, or romantic partner? If so, how did you react? Were you overwhelmed with feelings of anger? Did you attribute the fight to the other person's ugly, mean temper and consider ending the relationship? Or did you calm yourself with thoughts of how he or she is normally a rational person and therefore must be unusually upset by something that happened at work or elsewhere?

Can you see how these two alternative explanations, or **attributions**, for behavior or events can either destroy or maintain relationships? The study of attributions is a major topic in social cognition and social psychology. Everyone wants to understand and explain why people behave as they do and why events occur as they do. But social psychologists have discovered another explanation: Developing logical attributions for people's behavior makes us feel safer and more in control (Heider, 1958; Lindsay et al., 2015). Unfortunately, our attributions are frequently marred by several attributional biases and errors.

Fundamental attribution error (FAE)   The tendency of observers to overestimate the influence of internal, dispositional factors on a person's behavior, while underestimating the impact of external, situational factors.

Attributional Errors and Biases   Considering the previous example of how we often attribute disagreements to the bad character of the other person, can you now see that the failure to consider possible situational factors, like pressures at work, may be the result of our own misguided biases in thinking? Let's look at some of the major errors and biases in the attributional process.

Fundamental Attribution Error (FAE)   As we've just discussed, the focus on personal, dispositional factors, rather than situational factors, in our explanations for others' behavior is so common that it's called the **fundamental attribution error (FAE)** (Hopthrow et al.,

PA Practical Application

Test Yourself: Tips for a Great Interview

Most interviews involve a face-to-face meeting with one or more interviewers who are using the meeting as an alternative to, or in addition to, the application form. Their questions are typically designed to measure your:

Attitudes—"Did you like your last job?" "Do you prefer working in groups or alone?"

Job experiences—"What did you do in your last job?"

Personal background —"What was your college major?"

Interviewers also use this face-to-face meeting to assess your communication and interpersonal skills. Successful applicants are typically friendly (but not overly so), eager (but not desperate), and **assertive** (but not aggressive).

Here are additional, specific tips. Just put a check by those you want to work on or try in your next interview.

_____ 1. **Research**   Before your interview, research the company, manager, and supervisors, as well as the knowledge, skills, abilities, and other personal characteristics required for the advertised position. The information you gather can be invaluable in helping you respond to interview questions, and in deciding how much you want to work for this particular company. Also, knowing things like the history and size of the company will show the interviewer that you are serious about your job search.

_____ 2. **Role playing**   Ask someone to help you practice playing both interviewer and interviewee, which provides perspective on both roles. Encourage honest feedback about your verbal and non-verbal habits that may affect your interview, such as do you nervously jiggle your feet or avoid eye contact? Finally, brainstorm ahead of time about potential interview questions and then practice giving your best responses.

_____ 3. **Personality**   Interviewers generally like friendly, eager, and assertive applicants. These are basic personality traits you've undoubtedly displayed before—when meeting new friends, for example. Recognizing that you've used these skills in the past may help you relax in the interview and be yourself.

_____ 4. **Body language**   Your non-verbal behavior during the interview is also significant. When others are speaking, give non-verbal cues that they have your undivided attention, including head nods, laughing or smiling when appropriate, and maintaining eye contact. Also, while listening or talking, try the following "head, shoulders, knees, and toes" technique:

Head

- Keep your eyes focused on the interviewer without staring. Averting your gaze makes you seem less certain, less trustworthy, and less truthful.
- Occasionally smile during both questions and answers.

Shoulders

- Keep your back straight, head up, arms at your side, and hands clasped below your waist.
- Minimize hand movements and keep them below shoulder level.
- When making an emphatic point, lean forward slightly.

Knees and Toes

- Sit with your feet flat on the floor. If legs are crossed, it should be at the ankles and underneath the chair.
- If the interview is conducted while you are walking or standing, try not to shift your weight or rock back and forth.

2017; Ross, 1977; Wang & Hall, 2018). Another example of the FAE and its possible unforeseen negative consequences comes from a study of math and science instructors at one public university (Wieman & Welsh, 2016). The instructors who believed that the greatest barrier to student learning was the internal deficiencies of the students were also the ones who used fewer effective teaching methods. Can you see how the instructors' beliefs that their students are responsible for their own difficulties may have led them to overlook possible situational factors, such as teaching methods, to explain poor student performance?

Why do we commit the FAE? One popular explanation is that human personalities and behaviors are more _salient_, or noticeable, than situational factors. Note in **Figure 15.1** how this so-called **saliency bias** helps us understand why some people complain that homeless people begging for money "should just go out and get a job"—a phenomenon also called blaming the victim.

Self-Serving Bias   Unlike the FAE, which commonly occurs when we're explaining others' behaviors, the **self-serving bias** refers to attributions (explanations) we make for our own behavior. In this case, we tend to favor internal (personality) attributions for our successes and external (situational) attributions for our failures. This bias is motivated by our desire to maintain positive self-esteem and a good public image (Lilly & Wipawayangkool, 2018; Putnam et al., 2018; Wiggin & Yalch, 2015). Students often take personal credit for

Assertiveness   The behavior of confidently and directly standing up for your rights or putting forward your views without infringing on the rights or views of others; striking a balance between passivity and aggression.

Saliency bias   A type of attributional bias in which people tend to focus on the most noticeable (salient) factors when explaining behavior.

Self-serving bias   The tendency to credit success to internal, personality factors, while blaming failure on external, situational factors.

FIGURE 15.1 **Attribution in action** One explanation for the FAE is that human personalities and behaviors are more salient or noticeable than situational factors. Do you see how studying this text and taking your college psychology course enriches your study of the "real world"? Now you also have a label to explain the satire within this cartoon.

Actor–observer effect The tendency to attribute other people's behavior to personality factors, while attributing our own behavior to situational factors.

doing well on an exam. If they fail a test, however, they tend to blame the instructor, the textbook, or the "tricky" questions. **[AQ1]** Similarly, elite Olympic athletes more often attribute their wins to internal (personal) factors, such as their skill and effort, while attributing their losses to external (situational) factors, such as bad equipment or poor officiating—see photo (Aldridge & Islam, 2012; Mackinnon et al., 2015).

How do we explain the discrepancy between the attributions we make for ourselves and those we make for others? According to the **actor–observer effect** (Jones & Nisbett, 1971), when examining our own behaviors, we are the *actors* in the situation and know more about our own intentions and behaviors and naturally look to the environment for explanations: "I didn't tip the waiter due to the poor service." In contrast, when explaining the behavior of others, we are *observing* the actors and therefore tend to blame the person, using a personality attribution: "She didn't tip the waiter because she's cheap" (**Figure 15.2**).

Culture and Attributional Biases
Both the fundamental attribution error and the self-serving bias may depend in part on cultural factors (Hu et al., 2017; Mason & Morris, 2010; Miller, 1984). In highly individualistic cultures, like the United States, people are defined and understood as individual selves, largely responsible for their own successes and failures.

In contrast, people in collectivistic cultures, like China and Japan, are primarily defined as members of their social network, responsible for doing as others expect. Accordingly, they tend to be more aware of situational constraints on behavior, making the FAE less common (Bond, 2015; Iselin et al., 2015; Tang et al., 2014).

Likewise, the self-serving bias is also much less common in collectivistic cultures where self-esteem is related not to doing better than others but to fitting in with the group (Anedo, 2014; Berry et al., 2011; Morris, 2015). In Japan, for instance, the ideal person is aware of his or her shortcomings and continually works to overcome them—rather than thinking highly of himself or herself (Heine & Renshaw, 2002; Shand, 2013).

Before going on, consider our current global interconnections, and what might happen if a collectivistic country decided to increase its supply of nuclear arms. According to the FAE and self-serving bias, nations that share an individualistic focus would likely attribute this buildup to the aggressive nature of the nation's leaders. In contrast, nations with a collectivistic focus would be more likely to interpret the same behaviors as a natural form of self-protection. Do you see how this might lead to escalating tensions, serious misunderstandings, and even potentially devastating consequences like wars between nations? Would you like to reduce your own attributional biases? See the following **Test Yourself**.

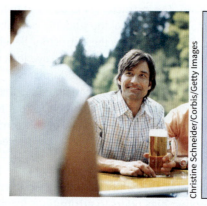

Actor		Observer
Situational attribution		**Dispositional attribution**
Focuses attention on external factors		Focuses on the personality of the actor
"I don't even like drinking beer, but it's the best way to meet women."		"He seems to always have a beer in his hand; he must have a drinking problem."

FIGURE 15.2 **The actor–observer effect** We tend to explain our own behavior in terms of external factors (situational attributions) and others' behavior in terms of their internal characteristics (dispositional attributions).

PA Practical Application

Test Yourself: How to Reduce Attributional Errors and Biases

The key to making more accurate attributions begins with determining whether a given action stems mainly from personality factors, or from the external situation. Unfortunately, we too often focus on internal, dispositional (personality) factors. Why? We all naturally take cognitive shortcuts (Chapter 8), and we each tend to have unique and enduring personality traits (Chapter 12). To offset this often misguided preference for internal attributions, we can ask ourselves these four questions:

1. **Is the behavior unique or shared by others?** If a large, or increasing, number of people are engaging in the same behavior, such as rioting or homelessness, it's most likely the result of external, situational factors.

2. **Is the behavior stable or unstable?** If someone's behavior is relatively enduring and permanent, it may be correct to make a stable, personality attribution. However, before giving up on a friend who is often quick-tempered and volatile, we may want to consider his or her entire body of personality traits. If he or she is also generous, kind, and incredibly devoted, we could overlook these imperfections.

3. **Was the cause of the behavior controllable or uncontrollable?** Victims of crime, like rape or robbery, are too often blamed for their misfortune—they shouldn't have "been in that part of town," "walking alone," or "dressed in expensive clothes." Obviously, these are inaccurate and unfair personality attributions, as well as examples of "blaming the victim."

4. **What would I do in the same situation?** Given our natural tendency toward the *self-serving* bias and the *actor-observer effect*, if we conclude that we would behave in the same way, the behavior is most likely the result of external, situational factors.

If you're concerned that these four questions may be too time-consuming, save them for significant situations, such as when you're considering starting or ending a relationship, serving on a jury, and so on. In ordinary daily life, you can follow a much simpler set of rules: Given our natural tendency to make internal, personality attributions, try erring in the opposite direction. In other words, look first for possible external explanations of others' behaviors. Then train yourself to "give others the benefit of the doubt." This two-step plan will not only reduce attributional errors and biases, it may even save, or at least improve, your relationships.

Attitudes

When we observe and respond to the world around us, we are seldom completely neutral. Rather, our responses toward subjects as diverse as pizza, gun control, and music reflect our **attitudes**, which are *learned* evaluations of a particular idea, object, person, or event. Social psychologists generally agree that most attitudes have three ABC components: *Affective* (feelings), *Behavioral* (actions), and *Cognitive* (thoughts/beliefs) (**Figure 15.3**). These three elements also interact. For example, the stronger our feelings and thoughts are the more likely they are to affect and predict our behavior. The reverse is also true—our behavior can affect and predict our thoughts, beliefs, and feelings.

Attitude A set of learned evaluations of a particular idea, object, person, or event.

Attitude Formation   As mentioned earlier, we learn our attitudes, and this learning can happen very quickly—and often without our conscious awareness. For example, children who

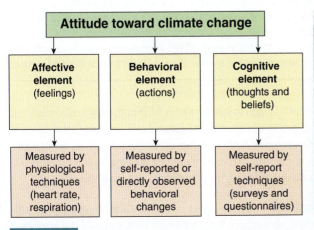

FIGURE 15.3 **Attitude components**   When social psychologists study attitudes, they measure each of the three ABC components: Affective, Behavioral, and Cognitive.

grow up in a strongly Democratic or Republican household are more likely to later register and vote with the party they were exposed to as children.

Perhaps the best way to understand this and other forms of attitude formation is to recall from Chapter 6 that virtually all learning occurs in three major ways—*associative*, *cognitive-social*, and *biological*. In the case of associative learning, we form our attitudes from association—either implicitly through classical conditioning or explicitly through operant conditioning. Children who were raised in either a strongly Democratic or strongly Republican household undoubtedly overheard negative comments about the other political party, and thereby developed *implicit*, classically conditioned attitudes, which they're largely unaware of, toward the two political parties.

dpa picture alliance/Alamy Stock Photo

Ernesto Ruscio/Getty Images Entertainment/Getty Images

S&P Scientific Thinking and Practical Application

Are we classically conditioned toward a preference for certain body types? Given the high percentage of very thin women and lean, "ripped" men displayed in magazines, on TV, and at the movies, it's easy to see why many people in our Western culture develop an implicit, classically-conditioned attitude and shared preference for a certain, limited body type. Fortunately, research finds that simply showing 100 women photographs of plus-size models led them to change their initial attitudes, which had been to prefer the thin ideal (Boothroyd et al., 2012). Can you see how ads that offer more realistic images (such as the photo of the woman in the leather jacket), might improve the overall self-image of both men and women? Sadly, the devastating effects of anorexia are seldom shown by the media (like this photo of model Isabel Caro who died of anorexia at age 28).

In contrast to our implicit attitudes resulting from classical conditioning, we also develop *explicit* attitudes that we're consciously aware of through operant conditioning. For example, we may change our political preferences in adulthood to match those of our close friends or romantic partners as a result of their rewarding smiles and affirmations when we agree with their political choices, along with their punishing comments and frowns when we disagree.

According to the *cognitive-social* process of learning, we also learn and develop our attitudes as a result of thinking about and observing the world around us. We learn to like or dislike certain candidates and political ideas due to what we perceive as logical arguments and persuasive ads, and from observations of the behaviors and policies of political leaders.

PAN Practical Application of Neuroscience

Can biology play a role in our attitudes? Research shows that several biological factors, such as genetics, also influence our learning and attitude formation. One large study of over 12,000 twin pairs sampled over the course of four decades, and from five different countries including the United States, suggested that our political attitudes, on average, are about 60 percent environmental and about 40 percent genetic (Hatemi et al., 2014). Although some disagree and/or question the exact percentages, the biological argument may offer good news for our current state of highly divisive politics. Why? Recognizing that our political attitudes result, at least in part, from biology, may lead us to have more empathy for and understanding of those with whom we disagree (e.g., Vedantam et al., 2018). Furthermore, even if our attitudes are due in part to genetics, the largest percentage is still subject to change, as we'll see in the next section.

Attitude Change
Although attitudes begin to form in early childhood, they're obviously not permanent, a fact that advertisers and politicians know and exploit. As we've seen in the classical conditioning study on preference for body types described above, we can sometimes change attitudes through experiments. However, a much more common method is to make direct, persuasive appeals, such as in ads against drunk driving that say, "Friends Don't Let Friends Drive Drunk."

The Power of Cognitive Dissonance
Psychologists have identified an even more efficient strategy for attitude change than persuasion. We now know that some of the strongest personal attitudinal change comes when we notice contradictions between our thoughts, feelings, and/or actions—the three components of all attitudes. Such contradictions typically lead to a state of unpleasant psychological tension, known as **cognitive dissonance**.

Cognitive dissonance The unpleasant psychological tension we experience after noticing contradictions between our thoughts, feelings, and/or actions.

According to Leon Festinger's (1957) *cognitive dissonance theory*, we all share a strong need for consistency among our thoughts, feelings, and actions, and when we notice inconsistencies we experience unpleasant dissonance. To relieve this discomfort, we are highly motivated to change one or more of the three ABC components of our attitudes. Someone who is engaged to be married might notice a feeling of attraction to someone other than his intended spouse, and then might experience unpleasant tension from the contradiction (cognitive dissonance between his feelings of attraction and his belief that you should only feel that way about your spouse). To relieve the discomfort, he could break off the engagement, or, more appropriately, change his belief based on an understanding that feelings of attraction to others are normal and to be expected both before and after getting married.

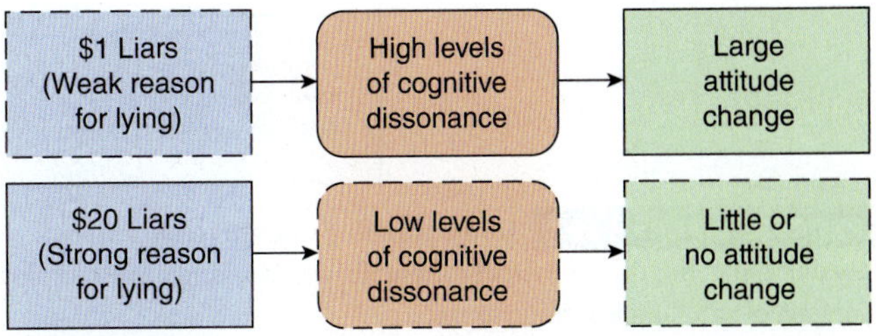

FIGURE 15.4 **Why cheap lies hurt more** Note how lying for $20 creates less cognitive dissonance and less attitude change than lying for $1.

Recognizing that cognitive dissonance is often an effective approach to attitude change in all our lives, it's important to fully understand it. Let's closely examine the classic study by Leon Festinger and J. Merrill Carlsmith (1959). These experimenters asked college students to perform several very boring tasks, such as turning wooden pegs or sorting spools into trays. They were then paid either $1 or $20 to lie to NEW research participants by telling them that the boring tasks were actually very enjoyable and fun. Surprisingly, those who were paid just $1 to lie subsequently changed their minds about the task, and actually reported more positive attitudes toward it, than those who were paid $20.

Why was there more attitude change among those who were paid only $1? All participants who lied to other participants presumably recognized the discrepancy between their initial beliefs and feelings (the task was boring) and their behavior (telling others it was enjoyable and fun). However, as you can see in **Figure 15.4**, the participants who were given insufficient monetary justification for lying (the $1 liars) apparently experienced greater *cognitive dissonance*. Therefore, to reduce their discomfort, they expressed more liking for the dull task compared to those who received sufficient monetary justification (the $20 liars). This second group had little or no motivation to change their attitude—they lied for the money. (Note that in 1959, when the experiment was conducted, $20 would have been the economic equivalent of about $175 today.)

Do you see the potential danger in how easily some participants in this classic study changed their thoughts and feelings about the boring task in order to match their behavior? Have you ever met someone whom you initially didn't like but you had to spend time with him or her and over time you actually began to like that person? Do you recognize how the initial discrepancy between your thoughts and feelings ("I'm an honest person but I'm pretending to like this person") might have led to cognitive dissonance, which in turn led to a change in your feelings?

A clever experiment found that taking a simple pain killer (versus a placebo) can significantly reduce the amount of attitude change (DeWall et al., 2015). The acetaminophen apparently reduced the individual's overall pain, including the discomfort created from *cognitive dissonance*, so the person was less motivated to change his or her attitude. One of our clever college students suggested that this experiment and cognitive dissonance theory might explain why many people like parties with lots of alcohol—it removes their sexual inhibitions. What do you think? Do you agree?

On a larger, national and international, scale consider how cognitive dissonance might help explain why military leaders keep sending troops to a seemingly endless war zone. They obviously can't change the actions that led to the initial loss of lives, so they may reduce their cognitive dissonance by replacing their previous cognitions (thoughts) that the loss of military lives is untenable, with a new cognition that the loss of military lives is justifiable given we're ultimately saving lives at home and/or in war-torn areas. Given the importance of this theory to your everyday life, be sure to carefully study **Process Diagram 15.1**.

Culture and Cognitive Dissonance The experience of cognitive dissonance may depend on a distinctly Western way of thinking about and evaluating the self. As we mentioned earlier, people in Eastern cultures tend not to define themselves in terms of their individual accomplishments. For this reason, making a bad decision may not pose the same threat to self-esteem that it would in more individualistic cultures, such as the United States (Carpenter, 2019; Frazer et al., 2017; Na & Chan, 2015).

> **STOP!** This Process Diagram contains essential information NOT found elsewhere in the text, which is likely to appear on quizzes and exams. Be sure to study it CAREFULLY.

PROCESS DIAGRAM 15.1 **Understanding Cognitive Dissonance** We've all noticed that people often say one thing, but do another. For example, why do some health professionals, who obviously know the dangers of smoking, continue to smoke?

1 When inconsistencies or conflicts exist between our thoughts, feelings, and actions, they can lead to strong feelings of psychological discomfort (*cognitive dissonance*).

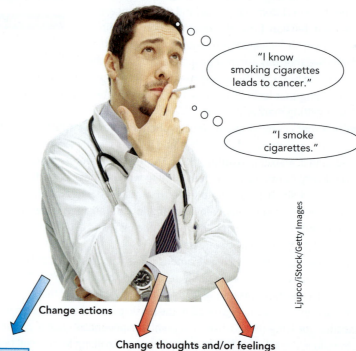

"I know smoking cigarettes leads to cancer."

"I smoke cigarettes."

Ljupco/iStock/Getty Images

2 To reduce this cognitive dissonance, we are motivated to change our thoughts, feelings, and/or actions.

Change actions

Change thoughts and/or feelings

3a Changing actions, such as quitting smoking, can be hard to do.

"I don't smoke cigarettes any more."

3b If unable or unwilling to change their actions, individuals can use one or more of the four methods shown here to change their thoughts and/or feelings.

Change perceived importance of one of the conflicting cognitions: "Experiments showing that smoking causes cancer have only been done on animals."

Modify one or both of the conflicting cognitions or feelings: "I don't smoke that much." "I don't care if I die earlier. I love smoking!"

Add additional cognitions: "I only eat healthy foods, so I'm better protected from cancer."

Deny conflicting cognitions are related: "There's no real evidence linking cigarettes and cancer."

Overall Summary

Step 1	Step 2	Step 3	Step 4
People are motivated to maintain consistency in their thoughts, feelings, and actions.	When inconsistencies or conflicts exist between our thoughts, feelings, or actions, they can lead to ...	Unpleasant psychological tension (cognitive dissonance).	To reduce this cognitive dissonance, we are motivated to change our thoughts, feelings, and/or actions.

Prejudice A learned, unjustified negative attitude toward members of a particular group; it includes thoughts (stereotypes), feelings, and behavioral tendencies (discrimination).

Discrimination An unjustifiable, negative action directed toward members of a group; also the behavioral component of prejudice.

Prejudice

I'm going to assume I'm a racist when I'm talking about a race that isn't mine because I don't know what that experience is like.

—Stephen Colbert

Prejudice, which literally means "prejudgment," is a learned, unjustified negative attitude toward members of a particular group. Like all other attitudes, it's composed of three ABC elements: *Affective* (emotions about the group), *Behavioral* (**discrimination**—*an unjustifiable,* *negative action directed toward* members of a group), and *Cognitive* (**stereotypes**—overgeneralized beliefs about members of a group).

> **TIP** What is the difference between prejudice and discrimination? When we use the term "prejudice" here, we are referring to all three of these components. Note, though, that a prejudiced individual may not act on his or her attitudes, which means that someone could be prejudiced against a specific group but not discriminate against them. In short, prejudice involves all three ABC components, whereas discrimination only involves behavior.

Stereotypes The overgeneralized beliefs about members of a group; also the cognitive component of prejudice.

The Self-Fulfilling Prophecy

Obviously prejudice and discrimination are serious problems in the United States and around the world. However, another unforeseen, and potentially dangerous, problem with *stereotypes* is the **self-fulfilling prophecy**—the process by which expectations about a person, group, or situation lead to the fulfillment of those expectations.

Why is this dangerous? Experiments on self-fulfilling prophecy show us that people can play a determining role in shaping (or even creating) social reality. If we hold negative opinions about an individual or members of a group, a vicious cycle can occur (**Figure 15.5**). In other words, expectations that were initially untrue become true.

Self-fulfilling prophecy The process by which expectations about a person, group, or situation lead to the fulfillment of those expectations.

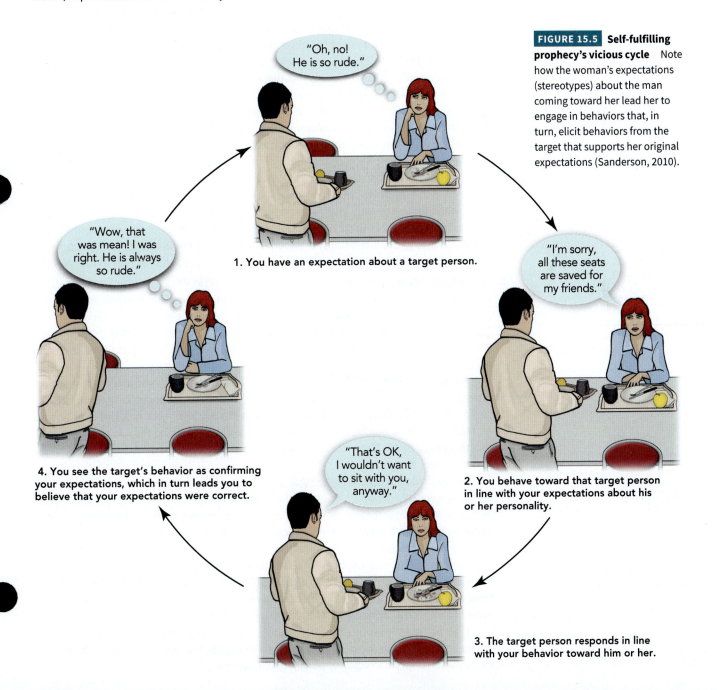

FIGURE 15.5 **Self-fulfilling prophecy's vicious cycle** Note how the woman's expectations (stereotypes) about the man coming toward her lead her to engage in behaviors that, in turn, elicit behaviors from the target that supports her original expectations (Sanderson, 2010).

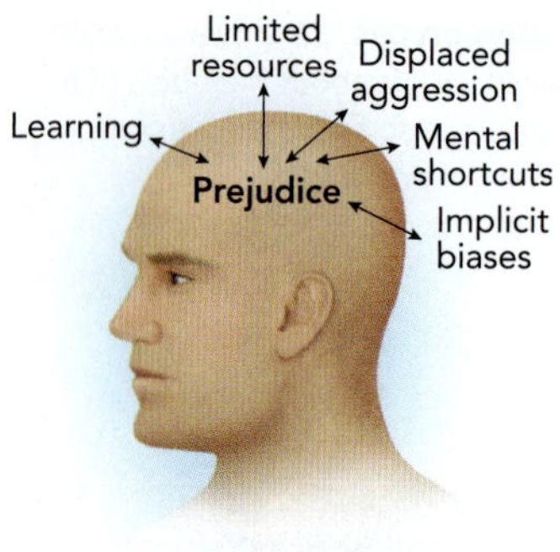

FIGURE 15.6 **Which source do you think best explains prejudice?**

Perhaps one of the best historical examples of the *self-fulfilling prophecy* and its dangerous consequences took place in 1930. At that time, the United States appeared to be on the road to recovery after the stock market crash in 1929. Unfortunately, people's confidence in financial institutions was still shaky, and many depositors withdrew their bank funds, which, in turn, forced those banks to liquidate their loans and ultimately close their doors. Rumors about these bank closures soon led to widespread panic and similar withdrawal of funds by depositors, which spread from town to town, thus leading to massive failures of hundreds of banks. Note how once again the original unfounded fears and expectations (of bank closures) actually became true. Tragically, this so-called bank run turned the potential recovery into the beginning of what became one of the worst economic disasters in American history—the *Great Depression* (Banking Panics of 1930–31, 2013).

Common Sources of Prejudice

How does prejudice originate? Five commonly cited sources are *learning*, *limited resources*, *displaced aggression*, *mental shortcuts*, and *implicit biases* (**Figure 15.6**).

1. **Learning** People learn prejudice the same way they learn other attitudes—primarily through *classical conditioning* and *observational learning* (Chapter 6). For example, a form of classical conditioning and observational learning occurs after repeated exposure to negative stereotypical portrayals of people of color and women in movies, magazines, TV, and the Internet. This type of repeated pairing of negative images with particular groups of people builds viewers' prejudice against those groups (Brown et al., 2017; Gattino & Tartaglia, 2015; Killen et al., 2015). Similarly, hearing parents, friends, and public figures express their prejudices creates and reinforces prejudice (Koike et al., 2017; Miklikowska, 2017). *Ethnocentrism*, believing our own culture represents the norm or is superior to others, is another form of a classically conditioned or observationally learned prejudice.

   We also develop prejudice through operant conditioning. When people make prejudicial remarks or "jokes," they often gain attention and even approval from others. Sadly, denigrating others is also reinforcing given that it boosts group cohesion among the initiators, while simultaneously fostering a negative disposition toward the targeted outgroup (Fein & Spencer, 1997; Ford, 2015; Ho & O'Donohoe, 2014). Furthermore, once someone has one or more negative interactions or experiences with members of a specific group, he or she may generalize the resulting bad feelings and prejudice to all members of that group.

2. **Limited resources** A second source of prejudice is that in situations of limited resources, prejudice pays off. Most of us understand that prejudice and discrimination exact a high price on their victims, but few appreciate the significant economic and political advantages they offer to the dominant group (Bonilla-Silva, 2016; Dreu et al., 2015; Wilkins et al., 2015). The stereotype that people of color are inferior to Whites helps justify and perpetuate a social order in which White Americans hold disproportionate power and resources.

   To make matters worse, during economic downturns, prejudice and discrimination intensify. For instance, during the U.S. economic recession that began in December 2007, surveys found that Whites felt less warmly about Blacks, held more negative explicit and implicit attitudes about Blacks, and were more likely to condone the use of stereotypes (Bianchi et al., 2018). They also were more willing to perceive inequality between groups as natural and acceptable.

   Although most people recognize that prejudice and discrimination unfairly disadvantage certain groups, *affirmative action*, one of the methods designed to offset this type of inequality, has always been controversial—particularly when it comes to college admissions. A recent study found that while 61 percent of Americans favor affirmative action programs for people of color, nearly 75 percent believe race or ethnicity should NOT be considered for college admissions (Hoover, 2019). How can both things be true? As discussed in Chapter 6, most Americans appear to be in favor of more diversity in a college's student body. However, the idea of considering race or ethnicity as part of the decision-making process for college admission seems to some like an "unfair" advantage (Baker, 2019; Goodkind, 2019).

   Like many of the problems with prejudice, the problems and solutions for our limited resources are complex. However, most Americans agree that our entire society benefits if every person is given an equal opportunity to succeed.

3. **Displaced aggression** As a child, did you ever feel like hitting a sibling who was tormenting you? Frustration sometimes leads people to attack the perceived cause of that frustration. But, as history has shown, when the source is ambiguous, or too powerful and capable of retaliation, people often redirect their aggression toward an alternate, innocent target, known as a *scapegoat* (Gangloff et al., 2016; Ralph et al., 2016; Shigemura & Chhem, 2016). Blacks, Jews, Native Americans, and other less empowered groups have a long and tragic history of being scapegoated. Examples include blaming gay men in the 1980s for the AIDS epidemic and attributing the housing and banking collapse of 2008 to people of color and members of the working class for buying houses they could not afford. Similarly, some politicians use immigrant, ethnic, and religious groups as scapegoats for numerous problems (**Figure 15.7**).

FIGURE 15.7 **Prejudice and immigration** Can you explain how all five of the listed sources of prejudice help explain this situation?

4. **Mental shortcuts** The fourth source of prejudice comes from everyday *mental shortcuts* that we create to simplify our complex social world (McFarlane, 2014; Prati et al., 2015). As discussed in Chapter 8, mental shortcuts, including stereotypes, allow quick judgments about others, thereby freeing up mental resources for other activities. However, keep in mind that although some stereotypes are partially true, when they're overgeneralized and applied to all members of entire groups they can lead to unforeseen, negative outcomes.

For example, people use stereotypes as mental shortcuts when they create ingroups and outgroups. An *ingroup* is any category to which people see themselves as belonging; an *outgroup* is all other categories. Research finds that ingroup members judge themselves more positively (as being more attractive, having better personalities, and more deserving of resources) compared with outgroup members—a phenomenon known as **ingroup favoritism** (Hughes et al., 2017; Wilkins et al., 2018; Yu et al., 2016). Members of the ingroup also tend to judge members of the outgroup as more alike and less diverse than members of their own group, a phenomenon aptly known as the **outgroup homogeneity effect** (**Figure 15.8**) (Brewer, 2015; Kang & Lau, 2013; Ratner & Amodio, 2013).

A sad example of the outgroup homogeneity effect occurs during wars and international conflicts. Viewing people on the other side as simply faceless enemies makes it easier to kill large numbers of soldiers and civilians. This type of dehumanization and facelessness also perpetuates our current high levels of fear and anxiety associated with terrorism (Greenwald & Pettigrew, 2014; Haslam, 2015; Lee et al., 2014).

Ingroup favoritism The tendency to judge members of the ingroup more positively than members of an outgroup.

Outgroup homogeneity effect The tendency to judge members of an outgroup as more alike and less diverse than members of the ingroup.

Implicit bias A hidden, automatic attitude that may guide behaviors independent of a person's awareness or control.

5. **Implicit biases** Like all attitudes, prejudice can operate even without a person's conscious awareness or control—a process known as automatic or **implicit bias** (Axt, 2018; Eberhardt, 2019; Petersen, 2018). As you may recall from Chapter 8, we naturally put things into groups or categories to help us make sense of the world around us. Unfortunately, the prototypes and hierarchies we develop are sometimes based on negative, incorrect stereotypes of various groups that later lead to implicit biases.

In one experimental study, teachers who read about an act of student misbehavior recommended a more severe punishment for students with a Black-sounding name, such as DeShawn or Darnell, compared to students with a White-sounding name, like Greg or Jake (Okonofua & Eberhardt, 2015). Another study found that teachers grade boys higher than girls (when names are known) on math tests, although the girls outscore the boys on math tests when the tests are graded anonymously (Lavy & Sand, 2015). On the other hand, comparable gender differences aren't seen for tests in other subjects, such as English and foreign language ability. Finally, a study of actual National Football League games found that Black quarterbacks are more likely than White quarterbacks to be benched after making a mistake (Volz, 2017).

Is there a good way to identify our hidden, implicit biases? A common method is the *Implicit Association Test (IAT)*. However, critics have questioned the validity of these implicit bias tests—are they measuring what they were designed to measure?—and have made suggestions for improvement (e.g., Brownstein et al, 2019; DeAngelis, 2019). If you'd like to take the test, go to: https://implicit.harvard.edu/implicit.

To examine another form of prejudice that affects more than half the world's population, see the following **STH** **Scientific Thinking Highlight**.

FIGURE 15.8 **The outgroup homogeneity effect?** Although this cartoon is satirical and humorous, the danger of this erroneous belief is real. When members of specific groups are not recognized as varied and complex individuals, it's easier to treat them in discriminatory ways.

STH Scientific Thinking Highlight

Have Women Really "Come a Long Way, Baby"?

(APA Goal 2.1) Use scientific reasoning to interpret psychological phenomena

In the 1960s, when the feminist movement was gaining in strength and popularity, and attitudes toward women's rights were shifting, the Virginia Slims tobacco company attempted to capitalize on that change. Using their own form of cognitive retraining and classical conditioning (Chapter 6), they created clever ads that paired smoking their brand of cigarettes with being independent, stylish, confident, and liberated. Their campaign line, "You've come a long way, baby," remains one of the most famous in U.S. history (see photo).

But is this true? Women have definitely made considerable gains, including laws protecting them from domestic violence and laws providing family medical leave. There are also more women in the halls of political power than ever before. Yet they still have a long way to go before reaching equality with men. Consider the following examples based on recent research.

Within the United States:

- Given that men and women have different work histories, experiences, and career opportunities, it's difficult to pinpoint the exact pay gap between the sexes, but one common estimate is that for full-time, year-round workers, women still earn far less that their White male counterparts. Specifically, for every dollar earned by White men: Asian women earn $0.85, White women $0.77, Black women $0.61, Native American women $0.58, and Latina women $0.53 (AAUW, 2019; Graf et al., 2019; Hegewisch, 2019).

- Women who speak up in meetings, or during participation in the "wild," are much less likely to be considered leaders, even when the ideas they share are the same as a man's in the same setting (McClean et al., 2018).

- As discussed in Chapter 10, female attorneys who express anger in the courtroom are seen as shrill and obnoxious, whereas male attorneys who express similar anger are seen as powerful and full of conviction (Salerno et al., 2018).

- When asked to draw a scientist, a meta-analysis of 78 studies found that children are still far more likely to draw a man versus a woman, and the difference is the greatest among older children (Miller et al., 2018).

Around the world:

- The economic participation and opportunity gap between men and women is currently 41.9 percent among the 149 countries studied, and experts predict it will take more than a hundred years for this gap to close (The Global Gender Gap, 2018).

- Among these same 149 countries, only 17 currently have women as heads of state, and women hold only 34 percent of all managerial positions (The Global Gender Gap, 2018).

- Out of 15 countries, including the United States, women are at far greater risk of gender-based violence than men (Blum et al., 2017).

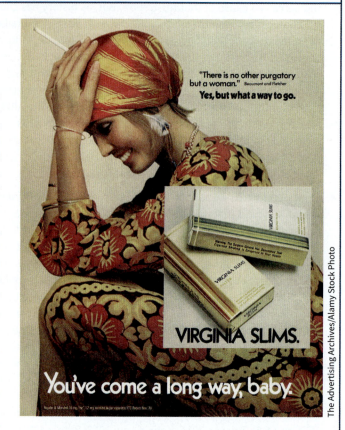

"There is no other purgatory but a woman." *Beaumont and Fletcher*
Yes, but what a way to go.

VIRGINIA SLIMS.

You've come a long way, baby.

The Advertising Archives/Alamy Stock Photo

Q Test Your Scientific Thinking

As you recall from Chapter 1, scientific thinking is an approach to information that combines a high degree of *skepticism* (questioning what "everybody knows") with *objectivity* (using empirical data to separate fantasy from reality) and with *rationalism* (practicing logical reasoning).

1. **Skepticism** Given the title and topic of the report cited at the beginning of this highlight "Have Women Really 'Come a Long Way, Baby'?" were you predisposed to believe or discount the information? Did the cited research change your attitudes? Why or why not?

2. **Objectivity** Imagine you are talking to someone who is a strong believer or denier of sexism within the United States and around the world. Using the objective research and statistics cited above, how could you use the information to have a meaningful conversation on these topics with these two individuals? How might this type of dialogue be helpful to both of you?

3. **Rationalism** Given the serious national and international challenges that we all face, solving these problems logically demands innovative engineering solutions (Roscoe et al., 2019), as well as the input of all people—regardless of gender, ethnicity, age, and so on. What can (and should) we do to correct this persistent sexism?

(Compare your answers with those of your fellow students, family, and friends. Doing so will improve your scientific thinking and your media savvy.)

a.

b.

c.

FIGURE 15.9 **The high price of prejudice** If pictures truly are "worth a thousand words," these photos speak volumes about the atrocities associated with prejudice: **(a)** the Holocaust, when millions of Jews, and other groups, were exterminated by the Nazis; **(b)** slavery in the United States, where millions of Africans were bought and sold as slaves; and **(c)** the 2016 nightclub shooting in Orlando, Florida, which left 49 people dead and 53 wounded, was a painful reminder of the ongoing dangers members of the lesbian, gay, bisexual, transgender, and others in the LGBT+ community still face in modern America.

How Can We Reduce Prejudice?

As you can see in **Figure 15.9**, prejudice has a long, sad global history. The atrocities committed against the Jews and other groups during the Holocaust, as well as the current crises in the Middle East, offer stark reminders of the cost of human hatred. Within the United States, we also have a long history of personal atrocities, including the enslavement of Blacks, Native Americans, and others, along with persistent racial and gender disparities in employment, wealth, education, and healthcare, as well as ongoing stigma about mental illness (Chapters 13 and 14). Examples like these provide troubling evidence of the ongoing costs of prejudice (Glaser, 2015; Koike et al., 2017; Saridi et al., 2017).

At this point you may need some encouraging news. If so, you'll be relieved to know that longitudinal studies from 2007 to 2016 of explicit and implicit attitudes toward sexual orientation, race, skin tone, age, and disability have all found positive changes toward more neutral attitudes (Charlesworth & Banaji, 2019). Also, recent surveys have shown that America's youth are generally less prejudiced and far more accepting of racial and ethnic diversity, including sexual orientation, than older generations (Parker et al., 2019).

Other than waiting for time to pass, what can we do right now? See the following list of five major approaches: *cooperation with common goals*, *intergroup contact*, *cognitive retraining*, *cognitive dissonance*, and *empathy induction* (**Figure 15.10**).

1. **Cooperation with common goals** Research shows that one of the best ways to combat prejudice and discrimination is to encourage *cooperation* rather than *competition* (Kuchenbrandt et al., 2013; Price et al., 2013). Muzafer Sherif and his colleagues (1966, 1998) conducted an ingenious study to show the role of competition in promoting prejudice. The researchers artificially created strong feelings of ingroup and outgroup identification in a group of 11- and 12-year-old boys at a summer camp. They did this by physically separating the boys into different cabins and assigning different projects to each group, such as building a diving board or cooking out in the woods.

After each group developed strong feelings of group identity and allegiance, the researchers set up a series of competitive games, including tug-of-war and touch football. They awarded desirable prizes to the winning teams. As a result of this treatment, the groups began to pick fights, call each other names, and raid each other's camps. Researchers pointed to these behaviors as evidence of the experimentally produced prejudice.

The good news is that after using competition to create prejudice between the two groups, the researchers created

FIGURE 15.10 **How can we reduce prejudice?** The nonprofit organization, *Habitat for Humanity*, works in local communities in over 70 countries to bring people together to build homes, communities and hope for families in need of decent and affordable housing. Do you recognize how the five approaches to combating prejudice are at work in this situation? Similarly, how might large changes in social policy, such as criminal justice reform, integrated housing, and increased civil rights legislation, gradually change attitudes and eventually lead to decreased prejudice and discrimination?

Kevin Winter/Getty Images

FIGURE 15.11 **Breaking the "gay barrier"** Michael Sam (pictured here accepting the Arthur Ashe Courage Award) became the first openly gay National Football League draftee in 2014. In 2015, Sam signed a 2-year contract with the Montreal Alouettes of the Canadian Football League, thus becoming the first openly gay player in the CFL's history.

Godong/Alamy Stock Photo

FIGURE 15.12 **[AQ2]** *Harry Potter* **reduces prejudice?** A clever study found that high school students who had read more books in the *Harry Potter* series had more positive feelings toward gay people, and showed lower levels of prejudice toward immigrants (Vezzali et al., 2015). On the other hand, as a scientific and critical thinker, can you see how this study might reflect a potential sample and/or participant bias? Maybe adolescents with a more conservative background are less likely to read *Harry Potter*?

"mini-crises" and tasks that required expertise, labor, and cooperation from both groups. Prizes were awarded to all and prejudice between the groups slowly began to dissipate. By the end of the camp, the earlier hostilities and *ingroup favoritism* had vanished. Sherif's study showed not only the importance of cooperation as opposed to competition but also the importance of *superordinate goals* (the mini-crises) in reducing prejudice. Modern research agrees with Sherif's findings regarding the value of cooperation and common goals (Rutland & Killen, 2015; Sierksma et al., 2015; Zhang, 2015).

2. **Intergroup contact** A second approach to reducing prejudice is to increase contact and positive experiences between groups. One longitudinal study of German, Dutch, and Swedish students found that even indirect contact with other groups served to promote later direct contact (Wölfer et al., 2019). However, as you just discovered with Sherif's study of the boys at the summer camp, contact can sometimes increase prejudice. Increasing contact may only work under certain conditions, such as *close interaction*, *interdependence* (superordinate goals that require cooperation), and *equal status*. In support of this finding, studies show that when Whites live in more ethnically diverse neighborhoods, there is a decrease in racism, as well as an increase in cognitive flexibility and the willingness to help others (Nai et al., 2018; Pauker et al., 2018). Can you see how this might be a reflection of their close interaction, interdependence, and equal status?

3. **Cognitive retraining** One unusual study of cognitive retraining found that when Chinese children were trained to individuate other-race Black faces, there was a long-term reduction in pro-Asian/anti-Black bias (Qian et al., 2019). Another unique cognitive retraining approach, known as *racial colorblindness*, suggests that all people are fundamentally the same and that we should ignore racial and ethnic differences. In other words, just treat everyone as an individual. But others believe avoiding or ignoring racial/ethnic categories discounts serious racial/ethnic inequalities and thereby preserves the status quo (Babbitt et al., 2016; Bonilla-Silva, 2016). What do you think? Which approach do you think would lead to more equality and less prejudice and discrimination?

Finally, we can use cognitive retraining to reduce prejudice by encouraging people to selectively pay attention to *similarities* rather than *differences* between individuals and groups (Gaertner & Dovidio, 2014; Phillips & Ziller, 1997; West et al., 2014). Can you imagine what might happen if we didn't divide people into groups, such as people of color versus White (colorless?), Christian versus Muslim, or men versus women? Interestingly, the U.K. recently banned all advertisements that promote gender stereotypes, like women being bad at driving, or only boys aspiring to be engineers and only girls dreaming of being dancers (Perrigo, 2019). It will affect ads on TV, public places, and social media. Do you think it will reduce gender inequalities? Why or why not?

4. **Cognitive dissonance** As you may recall from the previous section on attitudes, one of the most efficient methods to change an attitude is with *cognitive dissonance*, and prejudice is an attitude.

Each time we meet someone who does not conform to our prejudiced views, we experience dissonance—"I thought all gay men were effeminate. This guy is a deep-voiced professional athlete. I'm confused." To resolve the dissonance, we can maintain our stereotypes by saying, "This gay man is an exception to the rule." However, if we continue our contact with a large variety of gay men, or when the media includes numerous instances of gay individuals, this "exception to the rule" defense eventually breaks down, the need for cognitive consistency rises, and attitude change (prejudice reduction) is likely to happen (Armstrong et al., 2017; Papageorgiou, 2013). See **Figure 15.11**.

5. **Empathy induction** We've saved the best for last. Very surprising—and very encouraging—research has shown that we can successfully reduce prejudice by "simply" taking another's perspective—as demonstrated in the **RC** **Research Challenge** (Boag & Carnelley, 2016; Broockman & Kalla, 2016; Miklikowska, 2017). This type of *empathy induction* is further promoted by televised specials and Hollywood movies, such as *The Green Book, The Hate U Give,* and *Smoke Signals,* that help us understand and sympathize with the pressures and heroic struggles of marginalized people to gain respect and equal rights. Surprisingly, even just reading *Harry Potter* books appears to make people more tolerant (**Figure 15.12**).

RC Scientific Thinking: **Research Challenge**

Can a 10-Minute Conversation Reduce Prejudice?

(APA Goal 2.4) Interpret, design, and conduct basic psychological research

As we all know, advertising campaigns or even talking directly to people rarely, if ever, persuades people to change their attitudes—especially on sensitive topics like politics or prejudice. However, a study sent letters to 35,550 homes in the Miami area asking individuals to participate in a study for a small reward, which resulted in 1,825 volunteer participants (Broockman & Kalla, 2016). The researchers then randomly assigned 56 canvassers—some transgender, others not—to knock on the doors of 501 of these participants to have a 10-minute conversation. Half of the canvassers talked about being transgender (meaning a person whose self-identity does not conform to the sex they were assigned at birth). The other canvassers talked about recycling. In both cases, participants completed a survey before and after the conversation to measure their attitudes regarding transgender people. The effects were really remarkable. A 10-minute conversation with a random stranger led to decreases in *transphobia* greater than American's average decrease in homophobia from 1998 to 2012. More importantly, these effects lasted at least 3 months. Interestingly, it didn't matter whether the interviewer was transgender or not.

What did matter, and why these researchers succeeded where most others have failed, is that they trained the canvassers in a new technique called deep canvassing. Rather than just presenting facts and talking "to" someone, the canvassers asked participants to recall and discuss personal experiences they had had with judgment or prejudice. Afterward, they were encouraged to think about how their story related to those of transgender people. In short, this deep-canvassing technique is another form of *empathy induction*—encouraging active perspective taking leads to reduced prejudice.

Why has this research been so widely cited in scientific journals and the mass media as being "groundbreaking" and "monumentally important" (Bohannon, 2016; Resnick, 2016)? It's because deeply held attitudes, like prejudice, are notoriously difficult to change and this approach offers a promising method for prejudice reduction. For example, if it can work on something like transphobia, it might also be used to change public opinion about gay marriage, climate change, immigration, and other important topics. How can you use this in your own life if you want to change your own or others' attitudes? The first step would be recalling a similar personal experience and the accompanying painful emotions and reactions. Then encourage yourself and others to try to imagine the suffering of

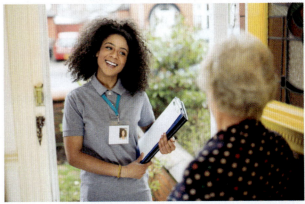

sturti/E+/Getty Images

another group—such as that of gay or transgender people. As we've noted throughout this text, *empathy*, placing ourselves in the shoes of another, is key to better social relations in almost all parts of life.

Identify the Research Method

1. Based on the information provided, did this study (Broockman & Kalla, 2016) use descriptive, correlational, and/or experimental research?

2. If you chose:
   - *descriptive research*, is this a naturalistic or laboratory observation, survey/interview, case study, and/or archival research?
   - *correlational research*, is this a positive, negative, or zero correlation?
   - *experimental research*, label the IV, DV, experimental group(s), and control group.

     (**Note:** If participants were not randomly assigned to groups, list it as a *quasi-experimental design*.)
   - both *descriptive* and *correlational*, answer the corresponding questions for both.

Check your answers by clicking on the answer button or by looking in Appendix B.

Note: The information provided in this study is admittedly limited, but the level of detail is similar to what is presented in most textbooks and public reports of research findings. Answering these questions, and then comparing your answers to those provided, will help you become a better scientific and critical thinker and a more informed consumer of scientific research.

Retrieval Practice 15.1 | Social Cognition

Self-Test   Completing this self-test, and then checking your answers by clicking on the answer button or by looking in Appendix B, will provide immediate feedback and helpful practice for exams.

1. The explanations we make about behaviors or events are called _____.
   a. impression management
   b. stereotaxic determination
   c. attributions
   d. person perception

2. The two major attribution mistakes we make are _____ and _____.
   a. the fundamental attribution error; self-serving bias
   b. situational attributions; dispositional attributions

c. actor bias; observer bias

d. stereotypes; biases

3. _____ is the cognitive component of prejudice.

a. Harassment

b. A stereotype

c. Discrimination

d. All of these options

4. Which of the following is an example of the outgroup homogeneity effect?

a. "You don't belong here."

b. "We are all alike."

c. "You can't tell those people apart."

d. All of these options.

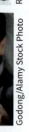
RTimages/iStock/Getty Images

Godong/Alamy Stock Photo

Q Test Your Critical Thinking

1. Why do we tend to blame others for their misfortunes but deny responsibility for our own failures?

2. Have you ever changed a strongly held attitude? What led you to do so?

3. Do you believe you are free of prejudice? After reading this chapter, which of the many factors that result in prejudice do you think is most important to change?

Real World Application Questions

[AQ1] Why do athletes often blame their losses on bad officiating?

[AQ2] Can reading *Harry Potter* books increase positivity towards gay people?

Hint: Look in the text for **[AQ1]** and **[AQ2]**

15.2 | Social Influence

LEARNING OBJECTIVES

Retrieval Practice While reading the upcoming sections, respond to each Learning Objective in your own words.

Review the main types of social influence.

- **Discuss** conformity and the factors that contribute to it.
- **Review** compliance and the three strategies for inducing it.
- **Describe** obedience and the factors that increase it.

- **Explain** how group membership, performance, and decision making influence us.

Real World Application Question

[AQ3] Does believing your neighbors value energy conservation make it more likely that you'll do the same?

[AQ4] Why are we so surprised when our preferred presidential candidate loses?

In the previous section, we explored the way we think about and interpret ourselves and others through *social cognition*. We now focus on *social influence*: how situational factors and other people affect us. In this section, we explore four key topics—*conformity*, *compliance*, *obedience*, and *group processes*.

Conformity

Imagine that you have volunteered for a psychology experiment on visual perception. All participants are shown two cards. The first card has only a single vertical line on it, while the second card has three vertical lines of varying lengths. Your task is to determine which of the three lines on the second card (marked A, B, or C) is the same length as the single line on the first card (marked X)—see **Figure 15.13**.

During this experiment, you are seated around a table with six other people and everyone is called on in order. Given that you are seated to the left of the seventh participant, you are always next to last to provide your answers. On the first two trials, everyone agrees on the correct line. However, on the third trial, your group is shown two cards like those in Figure 15.13. The first participant chooses line A as the closest in length to line X, an obvious wrong answer. When the second, third, fourth, and fifth participants also say line A, you really start to wonder: "What's going on here? Are they wrong, or am I?"

What do you think you would do at this point in the experiment? Would you stick with your convictions and say line B, regardless of what the others have answered? Or would you go along

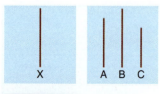

FIGURE 15.13 **Solomon Asch's study of conformity** Which line (A, B, or C) is most like line X? How would you answer? Could anyone convince you otherwise?

with the group? What you don't know is that the other six participants are actually *confederates* of the experimenter (i.e., they're working with the experimenter and purposely giving wrong answers). Their incorrect responses were designed to test your own and the other true participants' degree of **conformity**, which is defined as a change in thoughts, feelings, or actions due to real or imagined group pressure (see cartoon).

In the original version of this experiment, conducted by Solomon Asch, more than one-third of the participants conformed and agreed with the group's obviously incorrect choice (Asch, 1951). (Participants in a control group experienced no group pressure and almost always chose correctly.) Asch's study has been conducted in at least 17 countries, and the amount of conformity has varied depending upon factors such as age and personality (Mori et al., 2014; Tennen et al., 2013; Trautmann-Lengsfeld & Hermann, 2014). Using a similar Asch research setup, researchers found that some participants were even willing to adjust their moral decisions when faced with social pressure (Kundu & Cummins, 2013).

It's important to note that two-thirds of the participants did NOT conform on at least one trial, and 25 percent consistently defied the majority opinion on all trials (Griggs, 2015a). However, outside experimental labs, conformity in the real world is still a widespread and generally beneficial part of our daily lives. Just think of what might happen if most people refused to conform to our basic societal rules and norms while driving, shopping, or even in your college classroom. Still, to the onlooker, conformity is often difficult to understand. Even the conformer sometimes has a hard time explaining his or her behavior. Let's look at three factors that drive conformity:

- **Normative social influence**   Have you ever asked what others are wearing to a party, or copied your neighbor at a dinner party to make sure you picked up the right fork? One of the first reasons we conform is that we want to go along with group *norms*, which are expected behaviors generally adhered to by members of a group. A study of Twitter, for instance, found that tweeters are more likely to share a tweet if it already has a high number of retweets (Lee & Oh, 2017).

    We generally submit to this type of **normative social influence** out of our need for approval and acceptance by the group. Furthermore, conforming to group norms makes us feel good and it's often more adaptive to conform (Feeney et al., 2017; Shang et al., 2017). On some occasions, however, conformity can be harmful (see **Figure 15.14**). (For another real-world example of cultural norms, see the following **GCD** **Gender and Cultural Diversity**.)

- **Informational social influence**   Have you ever bought a specific product simply because of a friend's recommendation? In this case, you probably conformed not to gain your friend's approval, an example of *normative social influence*, but due to your assumption that he or she had more information than you did. This is an example of **informational social influence**. Given that participants in Asch's experiment observed all the other participants giving unanimous decisions on the length of the lines, can you see how they may have conformed given that they believed the others had more information than they did?

- **Reference groups**   The third major factor in conformity is the power of **reference groups**—people we most admire, like, and want to resemble. Attractive actors and popular sports stars are paid millions of dollars to endorse products because advertisers know that we want to be as cool as LeBron James or as beautiful as Emma Stone (Arsena et al., 2014; Schulz, 2015). Of course, we also have more important reference groups in our lives—parents, friends, family members, teachers, religious leaders, and classmates—all of whom affect our willingness to conform.

    Research shows that these people (called social referents) affect overall "simple" conformity, like the participants in the Asch study. But, more importantly, they can also have an outsized influence over others' attitudes and behaviors. One study found that by encouraging a small set of popular high school students to take a public stance against typical forms of conflict, such as bullying, overall levels of conflict were reduced by an estimated 30 percent (Paluck et al., 2016). Similarly, popular high school students' attitudes about alcohol use have been shown to have a substantial influence on alcohol consumption by other students in their school (Teunissen et al., 2012). Ironically, popular peers who had *negative* attitudes toward alcohol use were even more influential in determining rates of teenage drinking than those with positive attitudes.

"Jerry always did sip from the cup of a different brewer."

Chris Wildt/Cartoon Stock

Conformity   A change in thoughts, feelings, or actions due to real or imagined group pressure.

Normative social influence   A type of conforming based on the need to be liked, accepted, and approved of by others.

Informational social influence   A type of conforming based on the need for information and direction.

Reference groups   Any group that individuals use as a standard for evaluating themselves.

Lucky Business/Shutterstock.com

FIGURE 15.14   **The clear and present dangers of conformity**   Regardless of ads from tanning salons and the high number of users, studies have found clear evidence that tanning beds are associated with an increased risk of skin cancer and premature skin aging. *Normative social influence* is a strong predictor of the intention to use the beds despite the risks (Carcioppolo et al., 2017; McWhirter & Hoffman-Goetz, 2015; Torborg, 2019).

GCD Gender and Cultural Diversity

How Does Culture Affect Our Personal Space?

(APA Goal 2.5) Incorporate sociocultural factors in scientific inquiry

Culture and socialization have a lot to do with shaping norms for personal space. How close we stand to our close friends, acquaintances, and strangers varies widely between countries. If someone invades the culturally defined invisible "personal bubble" around our bodies, we generally feel very uncomfortable (Axtell, 2007; Fadel & Garcia-Navarro, 2013; Welsch et al., 2019).

Can you see how this may help explain why some people from the United States feel awkward when traveling to countries where people maintain smaller or even larger interpersonal distances? One study of over 9,000 people in 42 countries found that people from "contact cultures" (Southern European, Latin American, and Middle Eastern) tend to stand closer to others and to touch more compared to "non-contact cultures" (Northern Europe, North America, parts of Asia) (Sorokowska et al., 2017). The researchers concluded that the higher a country's average temperature, the closer people will stand to a stranger. As you can see in this photo, these Middle-Eastern men are apparently comfortable with a smaller personal space and with showing male-to-male affection.

As you may have noticed, children in Western cultures tend to stand very close to others until they are socialized to recognize and maintain greater personal distance. Also, friends stand closer than strangers, women (compared to men) tend to prefer more distance with strangers, and violent prisoners prefer approximately three times as much personal space as nonviolent prisoners (Andersen, 2014; Axtell, 2007; Iachini et al., 2016).

If you'd like to test your own culture's norm for personal space, try this informal *norm violation* exercise. Approach a

JAAFAR ASHTIYEH/AFP/Getty Images

fellow student on campus and ask for directions to the bookstore, library, or some other landmark. As you are talking, move toward the person until you invade his or her personal space. You should be close enough to almost touch toes. How does the person respond? How do you feel? Now repeat the process with another student. This time try standing 5 to 6 feet away while asking directions. Which procedure was most difficult for you? Most people think this will be a fun assignment. However, they often find it extremely difficult to willingly break unwritten cultural norms for personal space.

Q Test Your Critical Thinking

1. How might cultural differences in personal space help explain why U.S. travelers abroad are sometimes seen as being "too loud and brassy"?

2. Given that people have different norms for personal space, what effect might this have on their relationships?

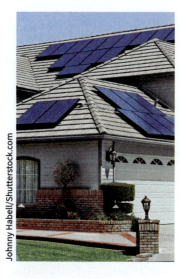

Johnny Habell/Shutterstock.com

Compliance The act of either actively or passively agreeing to the requests of others.

Reference groups may also depend on chemical factors. As you may recall from Chapter 2, the hormone (and neurotransmitter) *oxytocin* promotes love, attachment, empathy, and social bonding (Geng et al., 2018; Marsh et al., 2017). It also increases conformity to the opinions of others, which is very important during psychotherapy (De Dreu & Kret, 2016; Luo et al., 2017; Xu et al., 2019). **[AQ3]** Research shows that even our neighbors can have reference group influence. In this case, simply believing that our neighbors value energy conservation (see photo) can increase our own willingness to conform and to take similar energy-saving measures (Jachimowicz et al., 2018). Considering our current climate change crisis, can you see how this "simple act of conformity" could have lasting positive effects?

Compliance

As we've seen, conformity involves going along with the group. The norms and pressures to conform and "fit in" are usually indirect and we passively respond. But what happens if someone makes a direct request for us to do something? If we do what they request—either actively or passively—it's called **compliance**. We're *actively* complying if someone asks us to do them a favor or to "friend them" on Facebook. In comparison, we're *passively* complying if we don't object when someone crowds ahead of us in line or when someone is smoking in a "No Smoking" area.

What Factors Increase Compliance?
There are three major strategies that increase the odds that we will comply with others (see **Table 15.1**). Let's start with the *foot-in-the-door*

TABLE 15.1   Three Major Strategies for Inducing Compliance

Technique	Description	Example
Foot-in-the-door	After agreeing to an initial small request, we're more likely to later comply with a second, larger, request.	A neighbor asks you to bring in her trashcans while she's away on vacation. Once she's gone, she calls and asks you to water her garden. You comply given your former commitment.
Door-in-the-face	If we refuse an initial large request, we're more likely to later comply to a second, smaller, request.	You ask your parents for an expensive Lexus car for graduation, and when they refuse, you ask for a Toyota Camry. They agree because the second request seems reasonable compared to the first.
Lowballing	If we agree and commit to a behavior, we're likely to continue to act even when "hidden costs" are added on.	You agree to buy an automobile at a given price. However, even when they add on unanticipated costs for the floor mats, air conditioning, etc., you still feel compelled to pay the higher price because of your initial agreement.

technique. In a classic study (Freedman & Fraser, 1966), people were first asked to place a small sign near their front door that said, "Be a Safe Driver." Two weeks later, these same residents were asked to put a large, billboard-sized sign on their front lawn saying, "Drive Carefully." Can you guess what happened? Only a few of the residents who were in a second group, which was only asked to place the large billboard sign on their lawn, agreed. In contrast, 76 percent of those who first agreed to the smaller request went on and later agreed to the larger sign. Apparently, once we agree to an initial request, we feel obligated to continue on that same course.

The opposite strategy, the *door-in-the-face technique*, involves first refusing an initially large request and then feeling obligated to agree to a second, more modest, one. Interestingly, one of your authors (CAS) once had a research assistant ask her if she could drive him to and from the airport (about an hour away to pick up his girlfriend) because he didn't have a car. She initially refused due to the time and effort involved—and her very busy schedule. However, when he followed up with a request to "just borrow her car," she agreed. Upon later reflection, she recognized that her assistant had clearly mastered the door-in-the-face technique.

The third major compliance technique, *lowballing*, is a familiar one to all of us. We initially agree to purchase a bargain ticket with a discount airline and then find out there are extra fees for checking bags, choosing a seat, or even having a carry on bag. We then continue with the booking despite the added costs due to the initial agreement. Here's another experimental study example: When researchers asked students to participate in a psychology study that would begin at 7:00 A.M., only 31 percent agreed (Cialdini et al., 1978). However, when a second group was asked simply to participate in a psychology study with no time specified, 56 percent agreed. After the agreement from students in the second group, the *low ball* was introduced—students were informed that the study would begin at 7:00 A.M. Even though they were told they could opt out if they so wished, none of them did so, and on the day of the experiment, 95 percent of those who had initially agreed showed up. We recognize that this does sound a lot like the foot-in-the-door, but in this lowballing situation, the "hidden costs" were revealed only after the initial agreement.

Take-Home Message   Most of the time when we comply, the consequences are generally inconsequential. However, sometimes compliance resulting in false confessions or false identifications can lead to tragic results for innocent people (Alvarez-Toro & Lopez-Morales, 2018). One of the best examples comes from *The Innocence Project*, a leading organization in the United States dedicated to exonerating the wrongly convicted and innocents who plead guilty. This organization found that between 1989 and 2016, false confessions were present in 31 percent of DNA-exonerated cases, and in 63 percent of homicide DNA exonerations. In addition, 11 percent of the nation's 362 DNA-based exonerations since 1989 involved people who plead guilty to serious crimes they didn't commit (DNA Exonerations in the U.S., 2018).

If you're wondering why an innocent person would ever confess to a crime they didn't commit, consider this very simple study (Redlich & Goodman, 2003). After a group of 12- to 13-year-olds was stationed at a computer, they were told to type the letters that the researcher read to them. They were also warned NOT to touch the ALT key because doing so would crash the computer and all data would be lost. After researchers read a section of letters, the computer

David McNew/Getty Images

FIGURE 15.15 **Good reasons for conforming, complying, and obeying** These people willingly obey the firefighters who order them to evacuate a building, and many lives are saved. What would happen to our everyday functioning if most people did not go along with the crowd, did not comply with requests, or generally did not obey orders?

Obedience The act of following direct commands, usually from an authority figure.

screen automatically turned black and stopped working, and the researchers (acting distressed) asked the children, "Did you hit the ALT key?" Although no participant actually touched the ALT key, about 69 percent confessed to hitting the key, and 39 percent came to believe they actually pressed the button but couldn't remember doing so.

Obviously, the young age of these children makes them more vulnerable, and confessing to crashing a computer is very different than confessing to a crime. However, the researchers suggest that the psychological processes are the same. Sadly, research finds that not only children, but also those with intellectual disabilities or psychological disorders are more likely to misunderstand the implications and to make false confessions during police interviews (Alvarez-Toro & Lopez-Morales, 2018; Janzen, 2019; Volbert et al., 2019). Keep these studies in mind if you ever serve on a jury, and when you hear of false confessions and false identifications.

Obedience

As we've seen, conformity means going along with the group, whereas compliance is going along with a direct request from others. A third form of social influence, **obedience**, involves going along with direct commands, usually from someone in a position of authority. From very early childhood, we're socialized to respect and obey our parents, teachers, and other authority figures.

Conformity, compliance, and obedience aren't always bad (**Figure 15.15**). In fact, we generally conform, comply, and obey most of the time given that it's in our own best interests (and everyone else's) to do so. We stand in line at a movie theater instead of pushing ahead of others, which allows an orderly purchasing of tickets and social life to proceed with safety, order, and predictability.

Sometimes, however, it's important not to conform, comply, or obey. We don't want people engaging in risky sex or drug use just to be part of the crowd. Recognizing and resisting destructive forms of obedience are particularly important to our society—and to social psychology. Let's start with an examination of a classic series of studies on obedience by Stanley Milgram (1963, 1974).

Imagine that you have responded to a newspaper ad seeking volunteers for a study on memory. At the Yale University laboratory, an experimenter explains to you and another participant that he is studying the effects of punishment on learning and memory. You are selected to play the role of the "teacher." The experimenter leads you into a room where he straps the other participant—the "learner"—into a chair. He applies electrode paste to the learner's wrist "to avoid blisters and burns" and attaches an electrode that is connected to a shock generator.

Next, you're led into an adjacent room and told to sit in front of this same shock generator, which is wired through the wall to the chair of the learner. (The setup for the experiment is illustrated in **Figure 15.16.**) The shock machine consists of 30 switches representing successively higher levels of shock, from 15 volts to 450 volts. Written labels appear below each group of switches, ranging from "Slight Shock" to "Danger: Severe Shock," all the way to "XXX." The experimenter explains that it is your job to teach the learner a list of word pairs and to punish any errors by administering a shock. With each wrong answer, you are to increase the shock by one level.

You begin teaching the word pairs, but the learner's responses are often wrong. Before long, you are inflicting shocks that you can only assume must be extremely painful. After you administer 150 volts, the learner begins to protest: "Get me out of here...I refuse to go on."

You hesitate, and the experimenter tells you to continue. He insists that even if the learner refuses to answer, you must keep increasing the shock levels. But the other person is obviously in pain. What will you do?

The psychologist who designed this study, Stanley Milgram, was actually investigating not punishment and learning but obedience to authority: Would participants obey the

FIGURE 15.16 **Milgram's study on obedience** Under orders from an experimenter, would you, as "teacher," use this shock generator to shock a man (the "learner") who is screaming and begging to be released? Few people believe they would, but research shows otherwise.

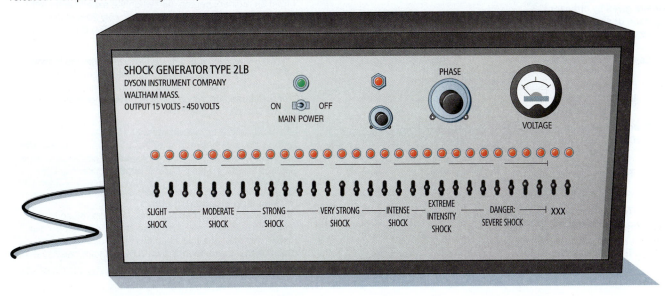

Milgram's Shock Generator

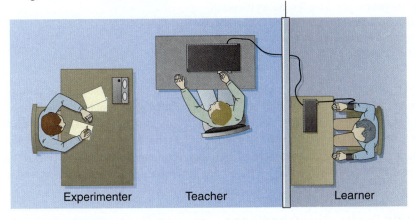

Experimental Set Up

experimenter's prompts and commands to shock another human being? In Milgram's public survey, fewer than 25 percent thought they would go beyond 150 volts, and no respondents predicted that they would go past the 300-volt level. Yet 65 percent of the teacher-participants in this series of studies obeyed completely—going all the way to the end of the scale (450 volts), even beyond the point when the "learner" (Milgram's confederate) stopped responding altogether.

Even Milgram was surprised by his results. Before the study began, he polled a group of psychiatrists, and they predicted that most people would refuse to go beyond 150 volts and that fewer than 1 percent of those tested would "go all the way." But, as Milgram discovered, 65 percent of his participants—men and women of all ages and from all walks of life—administered the highest voltage. The study has been partially replicated many times and in many other countries (Corti & Gillespie, 2015; Haslam et al., 2015). For example, a study in Poland found that 90 percent of the participants were willing to administer the highest level of "shock" (Doliński et al., 2017).

Note, however, that Milgram's research has been heavily criticized and his full original setup could never be undertaken today due to serious ethical and moral considerations (Baumrind, 2015; Gibson, 2019; Griggs, 2017). Deception is a necessary part of some research, but the degree of it in Milgram's research and the discomfort of the participants would never be allowed under today's research standards. In addition, recent reviews have revealed that Milgram failed to adequately debrief some participants, and to use a standard procedure for all

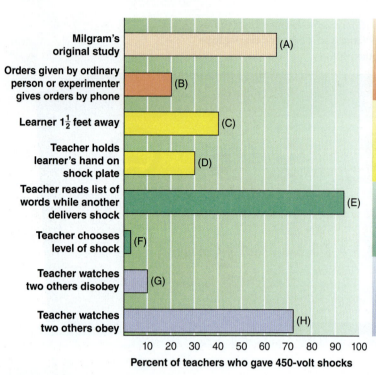

1. Legitimacy and closeness of the authority figure
In the original study, orders came from an experimenter assumed to have authority. However, when orders came from an ordinary person, and when the experimenter left the room and gave orders by phone, only 20% of the teachers gave the full 450-volt shocks. (Bar B on graph.)

2. Remoteness of the victim
When the learner was only 1½ feet away from the teacher, 40% of the teachers gave the highest level of shocks. Surprisingly, when the teacher had to actually hold the learner's hand on the shock plate, obedience was still 30%. (Bars C and D on graph.)

3. Assignment of responsibility
When the teacher simply read the list of words, while another delivered the shock, obedience jumped to almost 94%. However, when the teacher was responsible for choosing the level of shock, only 3% obeyed. (Bars E and F on graph.)

4. Modeling or imitating others
When teachers watched two other teachers refuse to shock the learner, only 10% gave the full 450-volt shocks. However, when they watched two other teachers obey, their obedience jumped to over 70% (Milgram, 1963, 1974). (Bars G and H on graph.)

FIGURE 15.17 **Four factors that affect why we obey** As you can see in the first bar on the graph, 65 percent of the participants in Milgram's early studies gave the learner the full 450-volt level of shocks. Note also how the color coding on the other bars on the graph (dark pink, yellow, green, and blue) corresponds to the four major conditions that either increased or decreased obedience to authority.

participants—two research requirements discussed in Chapter 1. These findings raise serious concerns about the validity of Milgram's findings and the ethical treatment of his participants.

One final, important reminder: The *"learner" was an accomplice of the experimenter and only pretended to be shocked.* Milgram provided specific scripts that he or she followed at every step of the experiment. In contrast, the "teachers" were true volunteers who believed they were administering real shocks. Although many suffered and protested, in the final analysis, most still obeyed.

Understanding Destructive Obedience

Why did the teachers in Milgram's study obey the orders to shock a fellow participant, despite their moral objections? Are there specific circumstances that increase or decrease obedience? In a series of follow-up studies, Milgram found several important factors that influenced obedience: *legitimacy and closeness of the authority figure, remoteness of the victim, assignment of responsibility,* and *modeling or imitation of others* (Auzoult, 2015; Greenberg et al., 2015; Reicher, 2014). See **Figure 15.17**.

In addition to these four factors that Milgram identified, researchers have discovered other important factors in obedience, including the following:

- **Socialization** Can you see how socialization might help explain many instances of mindless and sometimes destructive obedience? From an early age, we're all taught to listen to and respect people in positions of authority. In this case, participants in Milgram's study came into the research lab with a lifetime of socialization toward the value of scientific research and respect for the experimenter's authority. They couldn't suddenly step outside themselves and question the morality of this particular experimenter and his orders. Do you also see how the failure to appreciate the power of the experimenter's orders is another example of the fundamental attribution error (FAE), which we discussed at the beginning of this chapter?

- **Conformity and compliance techniques** Can you recognize how almost all the techniques that increase conformity and compliance, such as normative and informational influence and the foot-in-the door, also played a role in the participants' behaviors in the Milgram study? For example, the initial mild level of shocks may have worked as a *foot-in-the-door technique,* in which a first small request is used as a setup for later larger requests. Once Milgram's participants complied with the initial request, they might have felt obligated to continue.

- **Adherence to ideologies**   Some film critics and political commentators have suggested that popular movies like *American Sniper*, with their heavy emphasis on unwavering obedience to authority, might be encouraging a military ideology that justifies the wartime killing of others (e.g., Frangicetto, 2015). In support of this position, archival research on Milgram's original study found that the "teachers" were actually happy to participate—in spite of the emotional stress (Haslam et al., 2015). Why? The participants believed they were contributing to a valuable enterprise with virtuous goals. Do you agree with archival researchers who suggest that the major ethical problem with Milgram's study lies not with the stress generated for the teachers, but with the ideology used to justify harming others?

- **Relaxed moral guard**   One common intellectual illusion that hinders scientific and critical thinking about obedience is the belief that only evil people do evil things, or that evil announces itself. The experimenter in Milgram's study looked and acted like a reasonable person who was simply carrying out a research project. Since he was not seen as personally corrupt and evil, the participants' normal moral guard was down, which can maximize obedience. As philosopher Hannah Arendt has suggested, the horrifying thing about the Nazis was not that they were so deviant but that they were so "terrifyingly normal."

S&P Scientific Thinking and Practical Application

Why is the Milgram experiment so important?   Although this study was highly unethical and controversial, it does highlight the dangers of mindless obedience. We obviously don't want soldiers (or anyone else) mindlessly following orders just because they were told to do so by an authority figure. His research also reminds us of the power of modeling and imitation. As you recall from Figure 15.17, after watching two other teachers refuse to shock the learner, only 10 percent went all the way to 450-volt shocks. Although the forces underlying obedience can be loud and powerful, even one quiet, courageous, dissenting voice can make a difference. For examples of how a lone voice can free others to disobey, consider the following:

Bettmann/Getty Images

Rosa Parks   One of the most beautiful and historically important examples of civil disobedience occurred in Alabama in 1955. Rosa Parks boarded a bus (see photo) and, as expected in those times, obediently sat in the back section marked "Negroes." When the bus became crowded, the driver told her to give up her seat to a White man. Surprisingly for those days, Parks quietly but firmly refused and was eventually forced off the bus by police and arrested.

This single act of disobedience was a major catalyst for the civil rights movement and the later repeal of Jim Crow laws in the South. Today, Rosa Parks's courageous stand also inspires the rest of us to carefully consider when it is appropriate and good to obey authorities and when we must resist unethical or immoral demands.

picture alliance/Getty Images

Greta Thunberg   Noting that climate threat may be one of the most important factors in war and conflict, the Swedish environmental activist teenager Greta Thunberg (photo of Ms. Thunberg with microphones) was nominated for a Nobel Peace Prize in 2019 in recognition of her work leading a youth campaign to stop climate change.

Ms. Thunberg has also spoken before the UN Climate Change Conference in Poland; the World Economic Forum in Davos, Switzerland; and the UK Houses of Parliament. Just 9 months before the Nobel Prize nomination and all these speaking engagements, she was a lone figure outside the Swedish Parliament carrying a simple sign advocating for a "School Strike for Climate" (photo of Ms. Thunberg in yellow jacket).

Today Ms. Thunberg has more than 2.8 million followers on Twitter and has inspired hundreds of thousands of students at schools around the world to hold similar climate strikes. She's also continuing to bravely chastise world leaders for their inaction, and calling for immediate action from all of us—"Behave like our house is on fire, because it is" (Haynes, 2019; Leung, 2019).

Michael Campanella/Getty Images News/Getty Images

Q Test Your Critical Thinking

1. What do you think are the major social psychological factors contributing to Rosa Parks's and Greta Thunberg's acts of civil disobedience?

2. Do these two models of disobedience encourage you to follow their examples? Why or why not?

Deindividuation The reduced self-consciousness, inhibition, and personal responsibility that sometimes occurs in a group, particularly when the members feel anonymous.

Group Processes

We've just discussed conformity, compliance, and obedience, so now we can explore how our behaviors are influenced by group processes, including membership, performance, and decision making.

Group Membership
How do the roles that we play within groups affect our behavior? This question fascinated social psychologist Philip Zimbardo. In his famous study at Stanford University, 24 young college men were paid $15 a day for participating in a two-week simulation of prison life (Haney et al., 1973; Zimbardo, 2007). Zimbardo's *Stanford Prison Experiment (SPE)* has been the subject of numerous movies, books, and even previous editions of introductory psychology texts, including this one. In recent times, however, it has been the subject of serious criticisms, including biased and incomplete collection of data, *demand characteristics*, and the *lack of replication*—see Chapter 1. Due to the strength of these criticisms and our commitment to mythbusting, we chose to no longer cover the SPE in this text (Bartels, 2019; Le Texier, 2019; Resnick, 2018).

In contrast to the lack of support for the SPE, research does find that when we become part of a crowd or group we tend to lose our individual identities. Have you ever wondered why mobs sometimes riot—setting fires, looting businesses, and basically doing things most individuals would never do in their everyday lives? Mob riots are universal and have a long recorded history dating back to 203 B.C. Social psychology has explained this type of behavior as examples of **deindividuation**. To be deindividuated means that we feel less self-conscious, less inhibited, and less personally responsible. This is particularly true when we feel anonymous (see photo).

Deindividuation—good or bad?
Deindividuation can be healthy and positive when we're part of a happy, celebratory crowd. But research also finds that it can be unhealthy and very destructive, as is the case with mob riots and online cyberbullying (Peled, 2019; Silver, 2019).

Group Performance
How does being in a group and in the presence of others affect our performance? It depends. Sometimes having others around actually improves our performance—a phenomenon known as **social facilitation**. However, at other times, when people are observing us, or when we're working in a group, our performance may be diminished, which is sometimes called *social impairment* (Belletier et al., 2019; Panagopoulos, 2018; Zajonc, 1965).

How can both things be true? Think of times when you were assigned to work as a group for a class project and then to give an individual presentation in class. If your group's task was simple, or if you had practiced your individual presentation many times, the presence of others probably increased your arousal and improved your performance—*social facilitation*. In contrast, if your group's task was difficult, or you were not well prepared for your talk, the presence of others would likely lead to overarousal and impaired performance—*social impairment* (see **Figure 15.18**).

Another factor, which is closely related to social impairment, is the degree to which our performance is monitored—and we're held personally responsible for the outcome.

As you may have experienced when working in a group, it's easier for some people to slack off and do less than others. This phenomenon is called **social loafing** (Amichai-Hamburger, 2016; Kim et al., 2016; Latané et al., 1979). These same "loafers" will work harder when working alone once they realize they will be solely accountable for the outcome.

Given that social loafing is one of the major complaints about group assignments, how can we reduce this type of free riding off the efforts of others? Each individual's contributions can be made more identifiable, and all group members can be given the opportunity to anonymously assign points or grades to other group members. Teachers and supervisors should also work to increase team identification. When members of a group closely identify with other members and the team, they're more motivated to increase their efforts (e.g., Baumeister et al., 2016; De Cuyper et al., 2016).

Social facilitation The tendency for an individual's performance on an easy task to improve due to the presence of others.

Social loafing The tendency for individuals to exert less effort in a group due to reduced accountability and risk of detection.

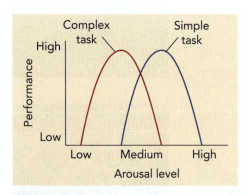

FIGURE 15.18 Social facilitation versus social impairment; Social facilitation in action. According to social facilitation theory (and the *Yerkes-Dodson law*, Chapter 11), we perform best at simple, well-learned tasks when our arousal is moderately high. But this same arousal leads to worse performance when the task is difficult and new.

Take-Home Message   Although group membership can have both positive and negative effects, let's end this discussion on just the positive aspects. As discussed in Chapter 3, social relations are critical to our overall well-being. In addition, despite widespread concern about social media, research shows that those fears may be overblown, and that social media in fact can be beneficial when it's used to make meaningful social connections (Clark et al., 2018; Mahase, 2019). Research even finds that as the number of our social roles increases there is less age-related loss of lung function (Crittenden et al., 2018). Why is this noteworthy? Lung function is an important marker of overall health and longevity. In short, group membership is generally a very good thing.

Group Decision Making

We've just seen how group membership affects the way we think about ourselves, but how do groups affect our decisions? Are two (or more) heads truly better than one? Most people assume that group decisions are more conservative, cautious, and middle-of-the-road than individual decisions. But is this true? Initial investigations indicated that after discussing an issue, people in groups actually supported riskier decisions than decisions they made as individuals before the discussion (Stoner, 1961). Subsequent research on this *risky-shift phenomenon*, however, shows that some groups support riskier decisions while others support more conservative decisions (Atanasov & Kunreuther, 2016; Liu & Latané, 1998; McGloin & Thomas, 2016).

Group Polarization

How can we tell whether a given group's decision will be risky or conservative? A group's final decision depends primarily on its dominant *preexisting* tendencies. If the dominant initial position is risky, the final decision will be even riskier, and the reverse is true if the initial position is conservative—a process called **group polarization** (Davis & Mason, 2016; Keating et al., 2016; Mikulincer et al., 2015).

What leads to group polarization? It appears that as individuals interact and share their opinions, they pick up new and more persuasive information that supports their original opinions, which may help explain why American politics has become so polarized in recent years (Gruzd & Roy, 2014; Suhay, 2015; Westfall et al., 2015). In addition, group polarization may explain how if we only interact and work with like-minded people, or only read newspapers and watch news programs that support our preexisting opinions, and talk politics only with those who agree with us, we're likely to become even more polarized. One study in Washington, DC found that interns who worked in a partisan workplace became more polarized in their opinions than those who worked in less partisan environments (Jones, 2013).

Group polarization is also important within the legal system. Imagine yourself as a member of a jury (**Figure 15.19**). In an ideal world, attorneys from both sides would present the essential facts of the case. Then, after careful deliberation, each individual juror would move from his or her initially neutral position toward the defendant to a more extreme position— either conviction or acquittal. In a not-so-ideal world, the quality of legal arguments from opposing sides may not be equal, you and the other members of the jury may not be neutral at the start, and group polarization may lead most jurors to make riskier or more conservative judgments than they would have on their own.

Groupthink

A related phenomenon is **groupthink**, which occurs when maintaining harmony among group members becomes more important than making a good decision (Brodbeck & Guillaume, 2015; Janis, 1972;

Group polarization   The tendency for the decisions and opinions of group members to become more extreme (either riskier or more conservative), depending on the members' initial dominant tendency.

Groupthink   The faulty decision making that occurs when maintaining group harmony becomes more important than making a good decision.

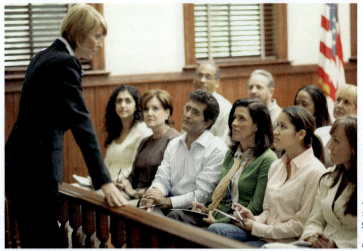

FIGURE 15.19   **Juries and group polarization**   When might group polarization be both a desirable and an undesirable part of jury deliberation?

Fuse/Getty Images

FIGURE 15.20 **How groupthink occurs**

a. The process of groupthink begins when group members feel a strong sense of cohesiveness and isolation from the judgments of qualified outsiders. Add a directive leader and little chance for debate, and we have the recipe for a potentially dangerous decision.

Michelle Marsan/Shutterstock.com

b. Few people realize that the decision to marry can be a form of groupthink. (Remember that a "group" can have as few as two members.) When planning a marriage, a couple may show symptoms of groupthink such as an illusion of invulnerability ("We're different—we won't ever get divorced"), collective rationalizations ("Two can live more cheaply than one"), shared stereotypes of the outgroup ("Couples with problems just don't know how to communicate"), and pressure on dissenters ("If you don't support our decision to marry, we don't want you at the wedding").

Groupthink

Antecedent Conditions

1 A highly cohesive group of decision makers
2 Insulation of the group from outside influences
3 A directive leader
4 Lack of procedures to ensure careful consideration of the pros and cons of alternative actions
5 High stress from external threats with little hope of finding a better solution than that favored by the leader

Strong desire for group consensus—the groupthink tendency

Symptoms of Groupthink

1 Illusion of invulnerability
2 Belief in the morality of the group
3 Collective rationalizations
4 Stereotypes of outgroups
5 Self-censorship of doubts and dissenting opinions
6 Illusion of unanimity
7 Direct pressure on dissenters

Symptoms of Poor Decision Making

1 An incomplete survey of alternative courses of action
2 An incomplete survey of group objectives
3 Failure to examine risks of the preferred choice
4 Failure to reappraise rejected alternatives
5 Poor search for relevant information
6 Selective bias in processing information
7 Failure to develop contingency plans

Low probability of successful outcome

Simone Biles honors her fellow survivors After winning her fifth U.S. all-around title at the Gymnastics Championships in 2019, Simone Biles wore a teal leotard to honor her fellow survivors of sexual abuse, which was committed by their former USA Gymnastics and Michigan State University doctor Larry Nassar (Cohen, 2018). Teal is the symbolic color for sexual assault awareness and prevention. Thanks in large part to Biles and other victims' courageous public accusations, Nassar was eventually convicted and sentenced to 100 to 175 years in prison (Cacciola & Mather, 2018; Schilken, 2019).

ZUMA Press/Alamy Stock Photo

Jones et al., 2016). As you can see in **Figure 15.20**, there are many factors that explain groupthink, but the two most important might be the pressure for uniformity and the unwillingness to hear dissenting information. Many highly publicized tragedies—from our failure to anticipate the attack on Pearl Harbor in 1941 to the terrorist attacks of September 11 and the subsequent war in Iraq—have been blamed on groupthink. Groupthink might also help explain why so many coaches or other members of the gymnastics community failed to respond to approximately 500 allegations of sexual abuse by Larry Nassar, who served for many years as the Team USA Gymnastics doctor—see photo (Barajas, 2018; Domonoske & Romo, 2018).

Preventing Groupthink How can we prevent, or at least minimize, groupthink? As a scientific and critical thinker, first study the list of the antecedent conditions and symptoms of groupthink provided in Figure 15.20, and then try generating your own ideas for possible solutions. For example, you might suggest that group leaders either absent themselves from discussions or remain impartial and silent. Second, you might suggest that group members avoid isolation, be encouraged to voice their dissenting opinions, and seek advice and input from outside experts. A third option is to suggest that members generate as many alternatives as possible and that they vote by secret ballot versus a show of hands. Finally, you might suggest that group members be reminded that they will be held responsible for their decisions, which will help offset the illusion of invulnerability, collective rationalizations, stereotypes, and so on.

Some of these recommendations for avoiding groupthink were carefully implemented in the decisions that led to the 2011 assassination raid on Osama bin Laden's compound. Before the final call, each member of President Obama's decision-making team was polled, and Vice President Joe Biden felt free to disagree (Landler, 2012). For an in-depth, fascinating look at groupthink, watch the classic 1957 film *Twelve Angry Men*.

On a final, more personal level, can you see how spending time on social media, like Snapchat or Instagram, might increase both group polarization and groupthink? It's because we generally "friend" or "follow" people on social media who share our values and attitudes. Research has found that this limited information pool creates a type of "political bubble," in which we're more likely to post and read one-sided news stories and comments that we and our friends favor (Bakshy et al., 2015). Furthermore, researchers have found that people tend to "unfriend" those with different political views, which can become particularly common during heated political times, such as the recent U.S. elections (John & Dvir-Gvirsman, 2015). **[AQ4]** Does this research also help explain why people become so upset when their preferred presidential candidate loses (see photo)? Our restricted political bubble has created a misperception that virtually "everyone I know voted for him or her."

Ann E Parry/Alamy Stock Photo

Retrieval Practice 15.2 | Social Influence

Self-Test   Completing this self-test, and then checking your answers by clicking on the answer button or by looking in Appendix B, will provide immediate feedback and helpful practice for exams.

1. The act of changing thoughts, feelings, or actions as a result of real or imagined group pressure is called _____.

   a. norm compliance   **c.** conformity

   b. obedience   **d.** mob rule

2. What percentage of people in Milgram's original study were willing to give the highest level of shock (450 volts)?

   a. 45 percent

   b. 90 percent

   c. 65 percent

   d. 10 percent

3. Which of the following factors may contribute to destructive obedience?

   a. remoteness of the victim

   b. foot-in-the-door

   c. socialization

   d. all these options.

4. One of the most critical factors in deindividuation is _____.

   a. loss of self-esteem

   b. anonymity

   c. identity diffusion

   d. group cohesiveness

5. Faulty decision making that occurs when maintaining group harmony becomes more important than making a good decision is known as _____.

   a. the risky-shift   **c.** groupthink

   b. group polarization   **d.** destructive conformity

Q Test Your Critical Thinking

1. Explain how group membership has affected your own behavior and decision making.

2. How might Milgram's results relate to some aspects of modern warfare?

3. Have you ever done something wrong in a group that you would not have done if you were alone? What have you learned from this chapter that might help you avoid this behavior in the future?

Real World Application Questions

[AQ3]   Does believing your neighbors value energy conservation make it more likely that you'll do the same?

[AQ4]   Why are we so surprised when our preferred presidential candidate loses?

Johnny Habell/Shutterstock.com

Ann E Parry/Alamy Stock Photo

Hint: Look in the text for **[AQ3]** and **[AQ4]**

15.3 Social Relations

LEARNING OBJECTIVES

Retrieval Practice While reading the upcoming sections, respond to each Learning Objective in your own words.

Summarize the influence of interpersonal relations.

- **Discuss** aggression and the factors that increase and decrease it.

- **Describe** altruism, why we do and don't help, and how to promote it.

- **Identify** interpersonal attraction and love, along with the factors that affect them.

Real World Application Questions

[AQ5] Can engagement in the arts increase cooperation and prosocial behavior?

[AQ6] How does simple nearness (proximity) influence attraction?

Aggression Any behavior intended to inflict psychological or physical harm on another individual.

Donald Reilly/Conde Nast/The Cartoon Bank

"It's a guy thing."

Bruce Leighty - Sports Images/Alamy Stock Photo

FIGURE 15.21 **Aggression in sports** Researchers who examined over 57,000 Major League Baseball games from 1952 through 2009 found that on hot days, baseball pitchers were more likely to deliberately throw at and hit a batter in retaliation after a batter on their own team had been hit by the opposing pitcher (Larrick et al., 2011).

Kurt Lewin (1890–1947), often considered the "father of social psychology," was among the first to suggest that all behavior results from interactions between the individual and the environment. In this final section, on *social relations*, we explore how we develop and are affected by interpersonal relations, including aggression, altruism, and interpersonal attraction.

Aggression

Why do people act aggressively? What exactly is aggression? When we intentionally try to inflict psychological or physical harm on another, psychologists define it as **aggression**. Although many people confuse aggression with being assertive, remember from the start of this chapter that *assertiveness* is just standing up for your personal rights, whereas aggression's deliberate harm to others is often a form of trampling on others' rights. Let's explore the various factors that increase aggression and possible ways to reduce it.

Biological Explanations Given aggression's long and cross-cultural history, many believe that humans are instinctively aggressive (Giacolini & Sabatello, 2019; Holekamp & Strauss, 2016). Although most social psychologists reject this "instinct" argument, many do accept the fact that biology plays a role. Twin studies have found that some individuals are genetically predisposed to have hostile, irritable temperaments and to engage in aggressive acts (Eisner et al., 2017; Pappa et al., 2016). Aggression has also been linked with brain injuries, the hormone testosterone (see cartoon), and lowered levels of some neurotransmitters (Angus et al., 2016; Ellis, 2019; Klasen et al., 2019).

Psychosocial Explanations Substance abuse (particularly alcohol abuse) is a major factor in many forms of aggression (Banks et al., 2017; Crane et al., 2017; Kose et al., 2015). Similarly, aversive stimuli, such as loud noise, heat, pain, bullying, insults, and foul odors, may also increase aggression (Anderson, 2001; DeWall et al., 2013; LaMotte et al., 2017)—see **Figure 15.21**.

In addition, social-learning theory suggests that people raised in a culture with aggressive models will develop more aggressive responses (Farrell et al., 2014; Kirk & Hardy, 2014; Suzuki & Lucas, 2015). Consider the fact that the United States has a high rate of violent crime, and there are widespread portrayals of violence on TV, the Internet, movies, and video games, which may contribute to aggression in both children and adults (Breuer et al., 2015; Gentile et al., 2017; Prescott et al., 2018). Psychologist Bryan Gibson and his colleagues were among the first to demonstrate experimentally that watching documentary-type reality TV shows in which verbal and relational (e.g., bullying) aggression are prevalent increases viewer aggression more than watching violent crime drama (Gibson et al., 2016).

S&P Scientific Thinking and Practical Application

What about violent video games?   Interestingly, the research linking violent media and video games with increased aggression is controversial and hotly debated within the psychological community (and the general public). Several meta-analyses suggest that media violence can increase aggressive behavior, as well as aggressive thoughts, angry feelings, desensitization, and overall physiological arousal (e.g., Bushman, 2016; Calvert et al., 2017; Shao & Wang, 2019). On the other hand, other researchers have found little or no detrimental effects of violent video gameplay (e.g., Ferguson, 2010, 2015; Hoffman, 2014; Kühn et al., 2019).

Mario Tama/Getty Images News/Getty Images

Do you recall the tragic August weekend in 2019 when 31 people were killed and dozens injured in two unrelated mass shootings in El Paso, Texas and Dayton, Ohio (see photo)? Did you also notice how many politicians and media pundits attempted to blame the massacre on violent video games, the media, and/or mental illness (e.g., Ferguson, 2019; Ranney & Gold, 2019; Sullivan, 2019)?

Using the three steps of scientific thinking (skepticism, objectivity, and rationalism), can you first note why we should all remain skeptical of these claims, particularly given the unresolved nature of the actual scholarly research on video games cited above? Second, consider the potential lack of objectivity and bias of those who promote violent video games as the cause for mass shootings. Is their desire to protect their right to gun ownership influencing their opinions? Finally, using the third step of scientific thinking, is it rational to shift the blame for violence onto issues like video games, the media, or mental illness? As discussed in Chapter 13, the majority of those with mental illness are not violent. In fact, they are far more likely to be victims of violent crime than the perpetrators. Furthermore, mental illness is shared cross-culturally, yet the United States far exceeds all other nations in the number of mass shootings. Can you see how shifting the blame of gun violence on to these other targets is not only illogical, but can also lead to misunderstandings and misdirection? In addition, will it hinder efforts to address mental illness, further stigmatize the mentally ill, and minimize other issues, such as the need for better laws related to who should have access to the type of weapons that facilitate mass shootings? What do you think?

Reducing Aggression   Did you know that in many countries attitudes toward those who ride bicycles on public highways are mostly negative, and that a significant number of cyclists have been victims of serious harassment and aggression (e.g., Delbosc et al., 2019)? Why? These researchers and others suggest that hostile attitudes and aggressive acts toward cyclists (and others) are due, at least in part, to **dehumanization**, which occurs when we see or treat others as less than fully human. Throughout history, dehumanization typically has been directed against marginalized individuals due to their political, racial, ethnic, religious, and sexual identities. However, in recent times cyclists who compete for space on the highways have been conceptualized as an inferior group and as a target of negative attitudes and behaviors, such as using a car to deliberately cut off a cyclist or throwing an object at a cyclist.

Dehumanization   The process of depriving a person or group of positive human qualities.

To change these attitudes and reduce the aggression, researchers suggest that we should "humanize" the individuals or groups. In the case of cyclists, we can promote public service campaigns designed to help people see cyclists as friends, family members, and neighbors (see **Figure 15.22**).

What are some other ways to reduce aggression? Some people believe we should release aggressive impulses by engaging in harmless outlets, such as exercising vigorously, punching a pillow, or watching competitive sports. But studies suggest that this type of *catharsis* often doesn't really help and may even intensify the feeling (Bushman, 2002, 2019; Konecni, 2015; Tonnaer et al., 2019).

A more effective approach is to introduce *incompatible responses*. Because certain emotional responses, such as empathy and humor, are incompatible with aggression, purposely making a joke or showing some sympathy for an opposing person's point of view can reduce anger and frustration (Baumeister & Bushman, 2014; Ellis, 2019; Gottman, 2015).

Before going on, it's also important to talk about how to reduce the numerous sociocultural factors that contribute to aggression, including gender, developmental issues, and socioeconomic factors. In addition, the presence and easy access to guns greatly increases the damage one

Used with permission of Bike BloNo and Artezen LLC

FIGURE 15.22 **Reducing prejudice and aggression toward cyclists**   Despite the many benefits that cyclists provide for all of us, such as less traffic on the highways and reduced carbon emissions from cars, they're often the target of prejudice, harassment, and deliberate acts of aggression. Can you see how ads like these might help humanize the cyclists and thereby reduce these negative acts?

AP Images/Mark Pardew

FIGURE 15.23 **An example of true altruism?** A firefighter gives water to a koala during the devastating Black Saturday bushfires in Victoria, Australia, in 2009.

individual can do, particularly to those targeted by hate and prejudice (Bauer-Wolf, 2019; Frattaroli & Buggs, 2016; Mitchell & Bromfield, 2019). Given that the rate of gun homicides in the United States remains substantially higher than in almost every other nation in the world, the American Psychological Association (APA) commissioned a panel of experts to investigate the best methods for preventing gun violence. Consider their three key recommendations:

1. **Primary (or universal) prevention** Involves healthy development in the general population, such as teaching better social and communication skills to all ages.

2. **Secondary (or selective) prevention** Consists of providing assistance for at-risk individuals, including mentoring programs and conflict-mediation services.

3. **Tertiary (or indicated) prevention** Involves intensive services for individuals with a history of aggressive behavior to prevent a recurrence or escalation of aggression, such as programs that rehabilitate juvenile offenders (American Psychological Association, 2013).

Altruism Prosocial behaviors designed to help or benefit others.

Evolutionary theory of helping A theory suggesting that altruism is an instinctual behavior, which has evolved because it favors survival of the helper's genes.

Anek Suwannaphoom/123RF

Altruism

After reading about all the problems with aggression, you will no doubt be relieved to discover that human beings also behave in positive ways. People help and support one another by donating blood, giving time and money to charities, aiding stranded motorists, and so on. **Altruism**, a form of *prosocial behavior*, consists of behaviors designed to help or benefit others (**Figure 15.23**).

Researchers have revealed several interesting activities and factors that contribute to altruism. For example, exercises such as journaling about who and what we're grateful for can decrease materialism and increase contributions to charity (Chaplin et al., 2019). **[AQ5]** An interesting study has shown that "simply" engaging in the arts increases cooperation and prosocial behavior—see photo (de Vyver & Abrams, 2018). Considering the current U.S. problems with economic inequality and political division, can you see how this is an important finding and a practical application of social psychology?

Why Do We Help? There are three key approaches that predict when and why we help (**Figure 15.24**). The **evolutionary theory of helping** suggests that altruism is an instinctual

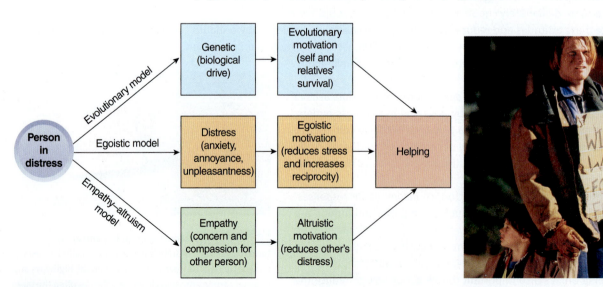

Bruce Ayres/The Image Bank/Getty Images

FIGURE 15.24 **Three models for helping altruism** Which of the three models for helping shown in this figure do you think provides the best explanation for why someone might give food or money to the man in this photo?

behavior that has evolved given that it favors survival of the helper's genes (Kurzban et al., 2015; Richardson, 2015; Wilson, 2015). By helping our own biological child, or another relative, we increase the odds of our own genes' survival.

Interestingly, we do know that several areas of the prefrontal cortex are most active when we're thinking and behaving socially. Furthermore, these areas are much larger in the human brain than in other animals (**Figure 15.25**). This may mean that we're prewired to be more generous and altruistic to our fellow humans.

Other research suggests that altruism may actually be self-interest in disguise. According to this **egoistic model of helping**, we help others due to anticipated gain, such as later reciprocation, increased self-esteem, and/or avoidance of distress or guilt (Dickert et al., 2015; Schroeder & Graziano, 2015). Interestingly, one study found that even babies and young children favor those who have been kind to them in the past (Wynn et al., 2018).

In addition to the evolutionary and egoistic models, we have the **empathy–altruism hypothesis** (Humphrey & Adams, 2017; Lebowitz & Dovidio, 2015; Patil et al., 2018). This perspective holds that simply seeing or hearing of another person's suffering can create *empathy*—a subjective grasp of that person's feelings or experiences. When we feel empathic toward another, we are motivated to help that person for his or her own sake. For example, middle school students who had been bullied are more likely to say that they would help another student who was being bullied (Batanova et al., 2014). Similarly, many educators believe that storybook reading is an important way to nurture children's empathy skills—as shown by the slogan "books build empathy" and the annual Empathy Day celebrated in U.K. schools. An interesting study found that this type of book reading is best when it fosters identification with characters who are dissimilar from the readers, and when they minimize ingroup bias (Kucirkova, 2019).

On the other hand, it was once believed altruism may be innate given that newborn infants show empathy by crying at the sound of another infant's cries. However, a study, with improved controls, found that newborns cry only to the cries of another newborn—and NOT to the cries of older infants (Ruffman et al., 2019). This suggests that a newborn's cries are distinct AND particularly aversive, leading the other child to cry out of pain or annoyance. This suggests that empathy may not be innate.

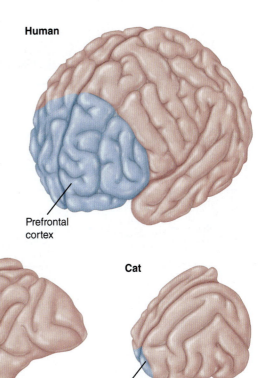

FIGURE 15.25 **Across the species** The prefrontal cortex of human beings is proportionately larger than that of other animals. In addition, it is very active during social behavior, suggesting that it plays an important role in human social functioning.

Egoistic model of helping A proposed explanation for helping that suggests we help because of anticipated gain—later reciprocation, increased self-esteem, and/or avoidance of distress and guilt.

Empathy–altruism hypothesis A proposed explanation for helping that suggests we help due to empathy for someone in need.

Why Don't We Help?

In 1964, a young woman, Kitty Genovese, was brutally stabbed to death near her apartment building in New York City. The attack occurred at about 3:00 a.m. and lasted for over half an hour. According to news reports at the time, 38 of her neighbors supposedly watched the repeated attacks, and heard her screams for help—yet no one came to her aid. Finally, one neighbor called the police, but it was too late. Kitty Genovese had died. The story of Kitty Genovese's murder gained national attention, however, later investigations found the early news reports to be filled with errors (Griggs, 2015b; Seedman & Hellman, 2014).

Despite the inaccuracies, this case inspired psychologists John Darley and Bibb Latané (1968) to conduct a large number of studies investigating exactly when, where, and why we do or don't help our fellow human beings. They found that whether or not someone helps depends on a series of interconnected events and decisions: The potential helper must notice what is happening, interpret the event as an emergency, accept personal responsibility for helping, decide how to help, and then actually initiate the helping behavior (**Process Diagram 15.2**).

STOP! This Process Diagram contains essential information NOT found elsewhere in the text, which is likely to appear on quizzes and exams. Be sure to study it CAREFULLY.

PROCESS DIAGRAM 15.2 **When and Why Don't We Help?** According to Latané and Darley's five-step decision process (1968), if our answer at each step is "yes," we will help others. If our answer is "no" at any point, the helping process ends.

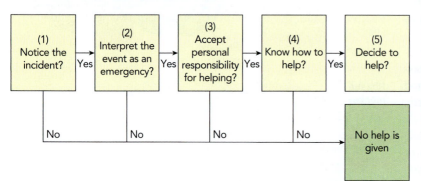

Sami Sarkis/Photodisc/Getty Images

How does this sequence explain television news reports and "caught on tape" situations, such as the recent stabbing and killing of teenager Khaseem Morris outside a strip mall on Long Island, New York (Polisi, 2019)? Why did as many as 70 of his peers do nothing to help while some even videotaped the incident with their phones? Potential helpers must first notice the incident and interpret it as an emergency (steps 1 and 2). However, the breakdown in the decision to help generally comes at the third step—*accepting personal responsibility for helping*. In follow-up interviews, onlookers often report that they failed to intervene and accept responsibility because they were certain that someone must already have called for "official" help, such as the police or an ambulance. This so-called **bystander effect** is a well-known problem that affects our helping behavior (Bennett et al., 2017; Brewster & Tucker, 2016; Casey et al., 2017).

Why are we less likely to help when others are around? According to the principle of **diffusion of responsibility**, we assume the responsibility for acting is shared, or diffused, among all onlookers. In contrast, when we're the lone observer, we recognize that we have the sole responsibility for acting. As a scientific and critical thinker, can you see how *informational social influence*, which we discussed earlier, may also play a role? Given that people in a group monitor the behavior of others to determine how to behave, we often fail to act, assuming others have more information than we do. For a practical application of all these terms, see the following **Test Yourself**.

Bystander effect A phenomenon in which the greater the number of bystanders, the less likely it is that any one individual will feel responsible for seeking help or giving aid to someone who is in need of help.

Diffusion of responsibility The dilution (diffusion) of personal responsibility for acting when others are present.

PA Practical Application

Test Yourself: Saving Your Own Life

In one of the earliest studies of the failure to interpret a situation as an emergency, participants were asked to complete a questionnaire, either alone or with others (Latané & Darley, 1968). While they were working, a large amount of smoke was pumped into the room through a vent to simulate an emergency (see photo). As you might expect, most of the participants working alone, about 75 percent, quickly reported the smoke. In contrast, fewer than 40 percent reported smelling smoke when three other participants were in the room, and only 10 percent reported the smoke when they were with passive participants who ignored the smoke. Keep this study in mind when you're in a true emergency situation. Do not simply rely on others for information. Make your own quick decisions to act. It may save your life.

AndrewJohnson/E+/Getty Images

How Can We Promote Helping?   Considering what we've just learned about the *bystander effect, diffusion of responsibility*, and *informational social influence*, what are the best ways to ensure getting help from others? Imagine that you're being viciously attacked in a public place. What should you do?

1. You first need to have them *notice the event*. You can do this by yelling and making a lot of noise to call attention to your situation.

2. Second, observers must *interpret the situation as an emergenc*y, so you'll need to clarify what's happening by screaming something like, "Help me! I'm being attacked."

3. Third, to encourage others to *take personal responsibility*, try looking any bystander in the eye and say something like, "You in the blue coat, call 911."

Given these three steps, do you see why the traditional advice most parents give to their children to prevent their abductions is problematic? Most parents only teach their children to yell and scream, but they forget that screaming children are often ignored. Bystanders most often assume the child is just misbehaving. Instead, children should be taught to make eye contact with an adult who may be watching, and then to shout something like: "This isn't my parent. Help me."

In reverse situations in which you are the bystander—and not the victim—the first step is to notice the incident and clarify if it's an emergency. If it seems unclear whether someone needs help or not, simply ask, "Do you need help?" Note, however, that there are occasions when someone in desperate need of help can't verbally respond to questions. As an example, during the final stages of drowning (versus just distressed swimming), victims are trying so hard to inhale and stay afloat that they're unable to call or signal for help. (For more information on the *instinctive drowning response*, see http://mariovittone.com/2010/05/154/).

In addition to these personal suggestions for increasing altruism, there are things we can do at the societal level. For instance, highly publicized television programs, like ABC's *What Would You Do?* and *CNN Heroes*, that honor and reward altruism also increase helping. Enacting laws that protect helpers from legal liability, so-called good Samaritan laws, further encourages helping behavior. If you'd like more information on acts of true altruism, such as kidney donation, see the following **PP** **PositivePsych** feature.

PP **Practical Application: PositivePsych**

Would You Donate a Kidney to a Stranger?

(APA Goal 1.3) Describe applications of psychology

In what is a particularly remarkable act of altruism, each year people donate one of their kidneys to strangers—the recipients are unknown and unrelated to the donors (see photo). These altruistic individuals receive nothing in return, and generally experience serious pain and discomfort, along with a somewhat lengthy period of recovery. What prompts this type of generosity? Under what conditions would you donate a kidney to a stranger? Some research suggests that people who feel good about themselves overall are more likely to engage in other types of prosocial behavior, such as volunteering and giving money to charity, which might explain organ donation.

To examine this idea, researchers in the United States compared rates of kidney donations in different states with each state's overall level of well-being (Brethel-Haurwitz & Marsh, 2014). As predicted, states with higher rates of kidney donation tended to have higher rates of well-being. This finding held true even after

the researchers took into account other factors that could explain this relationship, such as household income, age, education, religion, and mental and physical health.

What do you think? Beyond giving a kidney while you're alive, are

PA images/Alamy Stock Photo

you registered as an organ donor upon your death? Given the thousands of people who die each year who are on waiting lists for donor organs, should we adopt policies like considering everyone to be a donor unless they officially opt out? If you'd like more information on the facts and myths about organ donation, visit: http://www.americantransplantfoundation.org/about-transplant/facts-and-myths/.

Nancy Brown/Photographer's Choice/Getty Images

Philippe Bourseiller/The Image Bank/Getty Images

FIGURE 15.26 **Culture and attraction** Which of these two women do you find most attractive? Both women appear healthy, but can you see how your cultural background might train you to prefer one look over the other?

Pictorial Press Ltd/Alamy Stock Photo

FIGURE 15.27 **Ideal body dimensions?** Research in 2016 found that the average Playboy Playmate had a waist size of 23.5 inches, whereas Jessica Rabbit—the cartoon character pictured here—was estimated to have a waist size of 10 inches (Lassek & Gaulin, 2016). Research of comic books and action figures marketed to boys and young men show similar exaggerated proportions, with many dolls having tiny waists and biceps much larger than virtually any human.

Interpersonal Attraction

Why do we feel admiration, liking, friendship, intimacy, lust, or love for others? Psychologists have found three compelling factors that explain these feelings of interpersonal attraction: *physical attractiveness*, *proximity*, and *similarity*. Each influences attraction in different ways.

Physical Attractiveness The way we look—including facial characteristics, body size and shape, and manner of dress—is one of the most important factors in our initial attraction, liking, or loving of others (Buss, 2003, 2011; Buss & Schmitt, 2019; Olderbak et al., 2017). Interestingly, a cross-cultural study of over 4,000 women from 34 countries found that in societies where offspring survival is higher and economic conditions are favorable, heterosexual women show a stronger preference for men with more masculine looking faces (Marcinkowska et al., 2019). Likewise, the heterosexual male's tendency to prefer women with more feminine looking faces was found to be similarly correlated with the health of the nation (Marcinkowska et al., 2014). In contrast, heterosexual women with a greater fear of crime and violence showed a stronger preference for men with lower facial signs of masculinity (Borras-Guevara et al., 2017).

Evolutionary psychologists have long argued that heterosexual men supposedly prefer young and attractive women because these traits are believed to indicate better health, sound genes, and high fertility. Likewise, heterosexual women supposedly prefer attractive, healthy-looking men, whose traits also demonstrate good genes. Researchers have found that these traits are particularly important to women who are in long-term relationships, but interested in possibly "mate switching," meaning they're looking for a better alternative to their current mate (Buss & Schmitt, 2019). According to evolutionary theorists, women also prefer men with maturity and resources, reportedly because such partners tend to be better providers, and the responsibility of rearing and nurturing children has historically fallen primarily on women's shoulders (Buss, 1989, 2011; Souza et al., 2016; Valentine et al., 2014). However, a study of online dating found that perceptions of wealth did not affect men's or women's partner selections (Tskhay et al., 2017).

On the other hand, beauty is also in "the eye of the beholder." What we judge as beautiful varies somewhat from era to era and culture to culture (**Figure 15.26**). The Chinese once practiced foot binding because small feet were considered beautiful in women. All the toes except the big one were bent under a young girl's foot and into the sole. Tragically, the incredible pain and physical distortion made it almost impossible for her to walk. She also suffered chronic bleeding and frequent infections throughout her life (Dworkin, 1974).

Even in modern times, cultural demands for attractiveness encourage an increasing number of men and women to undergo expensive, and often painful, surgery to *increase* the size of their eyes, breasts, lips, chest, penis, and buttocks. Ironically, they also use surgery to *decrease* the size of their nose, ears, chin, stomach, hips, and thighs (Azzarito et al., 2016; Jackson & Vares, 2015; Jeffreys, 2015). Sadly, but not surprisingly, when photos of actual college women were compared to a sample of Playboy Playmates and to imaginary women (e.g., cartoon and video-game characters), the college women were seen as the least attractive, and for both male and female raters, waist size was the most important determinant of female attractiveness (Lassek & Gaulin, 2016). Even more disturbing was the fact that the ideal, imaginary woman's measurements were nothing close to reality (see **Figure 15.27**).

S&P   Scientific Thinking and Practical Application

How can psychology increase your dating appeal?   So how do those of us who are not "superstar beautiful" manage to find mates? Researchers have found that past the initial meeting, a host of other factors such as charisma, humor, personality, intelligence, and compassion become more important (Dillon et al., 2016; Talamas et al., 2016; Tornquist & Chiappe, 2015). Furthermore, research (and experience) shows that both sexes generally don't hold out for partners who are ideally attractive. Instead, according to *matching hypothesis* and *mating intelligence* studies, we tend to select partners whose physical attractiveness approximately matches our own (Dillon et al., 2016; McClintock, 2014; Regan, 1998, 2011).

Among the least recognized but most effective ways to increase attractiveness is through flirting (see **Figure 15.28**). Why is flirting so effective? It signals availability and romantic interest. Specifically, given that almost everyone fears rejection, flirting provides positive cues of your interest (Hall & Xing, 2015; Kurzban, 2014; Sprecher et al., 2015). Note, however, that if you're not truly interested or available for dating, flirting can be unfair and misleading. If you'd like more tips and information on flirting, try these semi-scientific websites:

- http://www.sirc.org/publik/flirt.pdf
- http://theweek.com/articles/448643/how-flirt-according-science

In addition, studies on body language conducted in the United States found that both men and women with "bigger postures"—outstretched arms and spread-apart legs—were judged more romantically appealing than those with limbs held tight (e.g., Vacharkulksemsuk et al., 2016) (**Figure 15.29**).

Aleksandr Davydov/123RF
Olena Yakobchuk/123RF

FIGURE 15.28   Expert flirting tips   Although there are many ways to flirt, the two most universally successful ones for both sexes are *smiling* and *eye contact*.

Courtesy of Lee Decker

FIGURE 15.29   Body language and romantic attraction   Why are "bigger postures" more appealing? According to research, an expansive posture signals dominance, which is socially and culturally desirable in the United States, and thereby increases an individual's chance of being selected as a potential mate (Vacharkulksemsuk et al., 2016). Note that this research was conducted via speed-dating and smartphone-based dating applications. The results may not hold up past a second date.

Proximity   [AQ6] Attraction also depends on the two people being in the same place at the same time. Thus, *proximity*, or geographic nearness, is another major factor in attraction—see photo (Finkel et al., 2015; Greenberg et al., 2015; Sprecher et al., 2015). One examination of over 300,000 Facebook users found that even though people can have relationships with people throughout the world, the likelihood of a friendship decreases as distance between people increases (Nguyen & Szymanski, 2012). If you're wondering if this is a case of correlation being confused with causation, that's great. You're becoming an educated consumer of research and a good scientific and critical thinker.

In fact, there is experimental evidence supporting a potentially causative link between proximity and attraction. As mentioned earlier, the hormone (and neurotransmitter) *oxytocin* promotes love, attachment, and social bonding, while also increasing conformity to the opinions of others (De Dreu & Kret, 2016; Luo et al., 2017; Xu et al., 2019). It is also connected with proximity. In one intriguing experiment, the intranasal administration of oxytocin stimulated heterosexual men in monogamous relationships, but not single ones, to keep a much greater distance between themselves and an attractive woman during a first encounter (Scheele et al.,

Gelpi/Shutterstock.com

mentatdgt/Shutterstock.com

FIGURE 15.30 **Repeated exposure—why we generally dislike photos of ourselves** Like all of us, the model in these photos is likely to prefer the photo with her hair draped over her left shoulder rather than the photo with it draped over her right shoulder, because it is a reversed image, similar to the one she sees every day in the mirror. Given we're accustomed to seeing our own faces in a mirror (repeated exposures), most of us prefer this familiar mirror image, and we're surprised when our close friends typically say our photos looks just like us (Mita et al., 1977). Can you see how this is a good example of the power of repeated exposure?

2012). The researchers concluded that oxytocin may help maintain monogamous relationships by making men avoid close personal proximity to other women.

Why is proximity so important in interpersonal attraction? It is due, in large part, to *repeated exposure.* Just as familiar people become more physically attractive over time, repeated exposure also increases overall liking (**Figure 15.30**). Do you now understand how exposure explains why modern advertisers tend to run highly redundant ad campaigns with familiar faces and jingles? In short, repeated exposure generally increases liking.

Can you see how this makes sense from an evolutionary point of view? Familiar things that we've seen before are less likely to pose a threat than novel stimuli (Kongthong et al., 2014; Monin, 2003; Yoshimoto et al., 2014). Interestingly, unusual, unfamiliar things are more likely to be threatening, so we're generally more alert to them. For example, research finds that false news stories spread faster on social media than real news stories—particularly political stories (Vosoughi et al., 2018). The researchers suggest that false news spreads more rapidly since it tends to be more novel than true news.

Similarity The major cementing factor for long-term relationships, whether liking or loving, is *similarity.* We tend to prefer, and stay with, people who are most like us—those who share our ethnic background, social class, interests, and attitudes (Brooks & Neville, 2017; Brown & Brown, 2015). One study found that people even judge others as less attractive if they hold a dissimilar political candidate preference (Nicholson et al., 2016). In other words, "birds of a feather flock together."

What about the old saying "opposites attract"? Although many people believe that couples need differences to "keep the spark alive," a large-scale study of over 47,000 participants found clear evidence that personality *similarity* between romantic partners and friends was most important (Youyou et al., 2017). An attraction to a seemingly opposite person is most often based on the recognition that in one or two core personality traits, that person offers something we lack.

In short, lovers can enjoy some differences, but similarity is a far better predictor of long-term relationships. The following **Test Yourself** feature offers a fun test of your understanding of the three factors in interpersonal attraction.

PA **Practical Application**

Test Yourself: Understanding Interpersonal Attraction

Based on your reading of this section, can you explain Kvack's love for the wooden dummy (see cartoon)?

Answers: Research shows that similarity is the best predictor of long-term relationships. As shown here, however, many people ignore dissimilarities and hope that their chosen partner will change over time.

Loving Others

It's easy to see how physical attractiveness, proximity, and similarity affect our attraction toward others. But how do we make sense of love? Why do we love some people and not others? Many people find the subject to be alternately mysterious, exhilarating, comforting—and even maddening. In this section, we explore *Sternberg's triangular theory of love*, along with research on *consummate love*, *romantic love*, and *companionate love*.

Robert Sternberg, a well-known researcher on creativity and intelligence (Chapter 8), also produced a **triangular theory of love** (Sternberg, 1986, 1988, 2006). As you can see in **Figure 15.31**, his theory suggests that different types and stages of love result from three basic components:

- **Intimacy** Emotional closeness and connectedness, mutual trust, friendship, warmth, self-disclosure, and forming of "love maps"

- **Passion—sexual** Attraction and desirability, physical excitement, a state of intense longing to be with the other

- **Commitment** Permanence and stability, the decision to stay in the relationship for the long haul, and the feelings of security that go with this intention

For Sternberg, a healthy degree of all three components in both partners characterizes the fullest form of love, **consummate love**. Trouble occurs when one of the partners has a higher or lower need for one or more of the components. If one partner has a much higher need for intimacy, for instance, and the other partner has a stronger interest in passion, this lack of compatibility can be fatal to the relationship—unless the partners are willing to compromise and strike a mutually satisfying balance (Sternberg, 2014).

When you think of romantic love, do you imagine falling in love, a magical experience that puts you on cloud nine? **Romantic love**, which Sternberg suggests is a combination of passion and intimacy, has intrigued people throughout history (Acevedo & Aron, 2014; Fehr, 2015; Gottman, 2015). Its intense joys and sorrows have also inspired countless poems, novels, movies, and songs around the world. A cross-cultural study by anthropologists William Jankowiak and Edward Fischer found romantic love in 147 of the 166 societies they studied. They concluded that "romantic love constitutes a human universal or, at the least, a near universal" (1992, p. 154).

Romantic love may be almost universal and historical in nature (see **Figure 15.32**). However, even in the most devoted couples, the intense attraction and excitement of romantic love generally begin to fade 6 to 30 months after the relationship begins. In comparison, **companionate love**, which Sternberg defines as a combination of commitment and intimacy, tends to grow and evolve over time (Fehr et al., 2014; Hatfield & Rapson, 1996; Livingston, 1999). Why? Further research explains that companionate love is based on a combination of deep and lasting trust, caring,

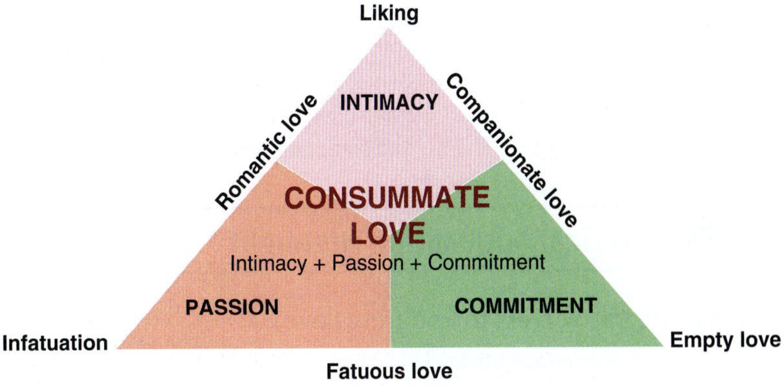

FIGURE 15.31 **Sternberg's triangular theory of love** According to Sternberg, we all experience various forms and stages of love, six of which are seen as being on the outside of the triangle. He proposes that only true *consummate love* is inside the triangle because it includes a healthy balance of intimacy, passion, and commitment. Note that the balance among these three components naturally shifts and changes over the course of a relationship, but relationships based on only one or two of these elements are generally less fulfilling and less likely to survive.

Triangular theory of love Sternberg's theory that different stages and types of love result from three basic components—*intimacy*, *passion*, and *commitment*; Sternberg's consummate love is a combination of all three components.

Consummate love Sternberg's strongest and most enduring type of love, based on a balanced combination of intimacy, passion, and commitment.

Romantic love According to Sternberg, feelings of attraction based on a combination of passion and intimacy.

Companionate love According to Sternberg, feelings of attraction based on a combination of commitment and intimacy.

FIGURE 15.32 **History's oldest case of romantic love?** Archaeologists have found what they labeled as evidence of prehistoric love—"Romeo and Juliet" skeletons engaged in a 6,000-year-old face-to-face hug in Mantua, Italy. The prehistoric pair is believed to have been a man and a woman buried between 5,000 and 6,000 years ago. The fact that they were probably buried at the same time indicates a possible sudden and tragic death.

tolerance, and friendship, which slowly develop as couples grow and spend more time together. In contrast, romantic love is largely based on mystery and fantasy. People often fall in love with what they want another person to be—and these illusions usually fade with the realities of everyday living (Fletcher & Simpson, 2000; Levine, 2001). For more helpful information about both romantic and companionate love, see the following **PAH** **Practical Application Highlight**.

PAH Practical Application Highlight

What Are the Secrets to Enduring Love?

By Thomas Frangicetto, Northampton Community College, Bethlehem, PA

(APA Goal 1.3) Describe applications of psychology

How can we keep *romantic love* alive (see photo)? One of the most constructive ways is to recognize its fragile nature and nurture it with carefully planned surprises, flirting, flattery, and special dinners and celebrations. In the long run, however, romantic love's most important function might be to keep us attached long enough to move on to the deeper and more enduring companionate love.

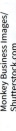

As you can see in the figure, romantic love is high in the beginning of a relationship, but it tends to diminish over time, with periodic resurgences, or "spikes."

In contrast, *companionate love* usually steadily increases over time. One reason may be that satisfaction grows as we come to recognize the lasting value of commitment and intimacy (Gottman, 2011, 2015; Jacobs Bao & Lyubomirsky, 2013; Regan, 2011).

One suggestion for maximizing companionate love is to overlook each other's faults. People are more satisfied with relationships when they have a somewhat idealized perception of their partner (Barelds & Dijkstra, 2011; Morry et al., 2014; Regan,

— Romantic love
— Companionate love

Years of relationship

2011). This makes sense in light of research on cognitive dissonance (discussed earlier). Idealizing our mates allows us to believe we have a good deal—and thereby avoid any cognitive dissonance that might arise when we see an attractive alternative. As Benjamin Franklin wisely said, "Keep your eyes wide open before marriage, and half shut afterwards".

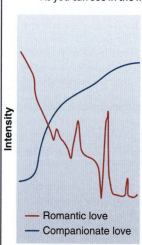

Would you like even more tips regarding the secrets of happy marriages and committed romantic relationships—as shown in the photo? Renowned psychologist and marriage researcher John Gottman believes he knows what works and doesn't work

in happy relationships, and there's nothing secret about it. Based on over four decades of rigorous scientific observation, Gottman and his colleagues have identified seven basic principles they believ explain why some relationships grow and flourish, whereas others deteriorate and die (Gottman, 2011; Gottman & Gottman, 2015; Navarra et al., 2016).

To evaluate your own relationship, take the following quiz based on these same seven principles. (**Note:** Although written primarily for marital spouses, the principles apply to all long-term relationships—friends, lovers, and even parents and children. In addition, please be aware that Gottman's research has thus far focused on heterosexual couples, so it isn't clear how the gendered patterns discussed in this section influence satisfaction in same-sex relationships.)

Principle 1: Enhance your "love maps."

Does your partner know about the major events in your life and your goals, worries, and dreams for the future? Do you know the same about him or her?   Yes ___ No ___

Emotionally intelligent (Chapter 8) couples are "intimately familiar" with each other's lives given that both partners pay attention to one another and are willing to share their innermost thoughts and feelings. Gottman says this type of attention and sharing leads to the creation of richly detailed love maps. Our partner should be the one person in the world who knows us almost as well as we know ourselves—and vice versa.

Principle 2: Nurture your fondness and admiration.

Do you basically like and respect your partner?   Yes ___ No ___

Although happily married couples may, at times, feel annoyed by their partner's personality quirks, they still consider their spouse worthy of honor and respect. Nurturing fondness and expressing admiration are essential factors in a mutually rewarding and durable romance. How important is this principle? Gottman answers: "When this sense is completely missing from a marriage, the relationship cannot be revived."

Principle 3: Turn toward each other instead of away.

Do you and your partner believe it's okay to tune each other out when your conversations become boring or mundane? Yes ___ No ___

Think again. According to Gottman: "When couples stay tuned to one another, even when their talking seems trivial, and when they engage in lots of chitchat, I can be pretty sure that they will stay happily married." While these exchanges may seem inconsequential, they represent moments of bonding—the couple is *turning toward each other*. Couples headed for divorce rarely have these small, but crucial, moments of connection. Turning toward one another is the basis of emotional connection, romance, passion, and a good sex life.

Principle 4: Let your partner influence you.

Do you believe that "welcoming divergent views" doesn't necessarily include your partner's views?   Yes ___ No ___

It may take two to "make or break a marriage," but on this principle, women tend to have the positive edge. Gottman's research reveals that women more often "let their husbands influence their decision making by taking their opinions and feelings into account." What about men? "They often do not return the favor." Gottman advises men to adopt the female approach given that most successful and stable marriages are those in which power and influence are shared.

Principle 5: Solve your solvable problems.

Do you believe that "love conquers all" or that good communication can solve all your problems?   Yes ___ No ___

Gottman suggests that what makes a good marriage is not communication, but how partners perceive one another and how they handle inevitable conflicts. He puts it simply: "When a husband and wife respect each other and are open to each other's point of view, they have a good basis for resolving any differences that arise." In addition to focusing on our partner's positive traits and accepting that he or she has our best interests at heart, Gottman suggests five steps for successful problem solving: (1) Soften your startup. (It's not what you say as much as how you say it.) (2) Learn to make and receive "repair attempts." (3) Soothe yourself and each other. ("Turn toward" one another with words or behaviors that help soften the conflict.) (4) Compromise. (5) Be tolerant of one another's faults.

Unfortunately, when we're really angry with our partner and emotionally threatened, we may not be able to remember these five steps. We become overwhelmed by "emotional flooding," and our physiological "fight-flight-freeze" response kicks in—we want to attack, tune out (freeze), or run away. To make matters worse, during this time of high arousal, our higher, logical cognitive processes are limited (Chapter 3). In this heightened state, we may fail to recognize or accept repair attempts, as well as the need to soothe ourselves and our partner. Can you see why this lethal combination so often leads to an inevitable increase in tension and anger? The good news is that you can successfully cope with experiences of "flooding" by saying things like "Let's stop for now. I need to calm down." Then agree when and where you'll resume your discussion.

Principle 6: Overcome gridlock.

Do you believe that major differences of opinion will destroy a marriage?   Yes ___ No ___

Gottman finds that about 70 percent of marital conflicts are unsolvable. Do you find this surprising? It actually should be reassuring. Knowing that we all have "irreconcilable differences" with those we love means that we don't need to assume that they will automatically lead to divorce or the loss of valuable relationships. Instead of wasting huge amounts of time and energy arguing our case in the hopes of changing our partner's opinions, we need to recognize that serious and perpetual problems are generally about core values and personal views of the world—which seldom change. The goal in ending "gridlock"—those situations that seemingly won't yield to agreement—is *not* to solve the problem as much as it is to progress from gridlock to engage in dialogue. Gottman's unhappy couples are often stuck in "loss-loss loops," whereas his successful couples learn to engage in dialogue and then "live with the problem."

Keep in mind that gridlock is often rooted in oppositional hopes or dreams. Gottman's happy couples recognize this and understand that helping each other realize their competing desires is one of the goals of marriage. They try to establish some level of "initial compromise," and then continue working on bridging or ending the gridlock with mutual respect and compromise.

Principle 7: Create shared meaning.

Do you and your partner work to create an intentional, shared purpose for your relationship?   Yes ___ No ___

While similar to establishing "love maps," this principle encourages partners to work at developing a *deeper sense of shared meaning*. Successful couples go out of their way to create traditions and rituals that help them stay connected. They routinely schedule and honor holiday and birthday get-togethers, they have a designated date night or family home evening, or they always hug or kiss before bed or leaving one another in the morning. This results in the sort of shared history that becomes an almost "spiritual dimension that has to do with creating an inner life together—a culture rich with symbols and rituals."

In sum, if we want our love and relationships to not only last, but also flourish, we need to be willing to work at nurturing, repairing, and protecting them. For additional information on John Gottman's extensive research and available book titles, go to: www.gottman.com

Final Note to Our Readers   As the authors of this text, and your tour guides through the fascinating world of psychology, we hope you've enjoyed the journey. For us, the key take-home message, which we hope you'll always remember, is that every human on this planet is an exclusive combination of a physical body, a complex system of mental processes, and large sociocultural factors. Our deepest wish is that you'll make the most out of your own unique combination, and will apply what you've learned about yourself and others to improve your own life and the world around you.

Warmest regards,

Catherine A. Sanderson   Karen R. Huffman

Before going on, be sure to complete the final Retrieval Practice, and then answer the critical thinking questions in the **Test Your Critical Thinking**.

Retrieval Practice 15.3 | Social Relations

Self-Test   Completing this self-test, and then checking your answers by clicking on the answer button or by looking in Appendix B, will provide immediate feedback and helpful practice for exams.

1. One of the most effective ways to reduce aggression is to
   _____.
   a. release aggressive impulses with catharsis
   b. introduce incompatible responses
   c. encourage competition
   d. none of these options

2. Altruism refers to actions designed to help others when _____.
   a. there is no obvious benefit to oneself
   b. there is a benefit to the altruistic person
   c. he or she has previously helped you
   d. he or she is in a position to help you in the future

3. Onlookers to crimes sometimes fail to respond to cries for help due to the _____ phenomenon.
   a. empathy–altruism
   b. egoistic model
   c. inhumanity of large cities
   d. diffusion of responsibility

4. The positive feelings we have toward others are called _____.
   a. affective relations
   b. interpersonal attraction
   c. interpersonal attitudes
   d. affective connections

5. Feelings of attraction based on a combination of commitment and intimacy are called _____.
   a. companionate love
   b. intimate love
   c. passionate love
   d. all these options

Q Test Your Critical Thinking

1. Which of the major theories of aggression do you believe explains most acts of violence? Explain.

2. Which of the three major theories of helping do you find best explains why you tend to help others?

Real World Application Questions

[AQ5]   Can engagement in the arts increase cooperation and prosocial behavior?

Anek Suwannaphoom/123RF

[AQ6]   How does simple nearness (proximity) influence attraction?

Gelpi/Shutterstock.com

Hint: Look in the text for **[AQ5]** and **[AQ6]**

Q Test Your Critical Thinking

Did you notice or wonder why we provided six Real World Application Questions [AQ1–AQ6] throughout this chapter? We've found that they not only help you to engage with, and master the material, they also have an important and lasting impact on your critical thinking skills. For additional mastery and enrichment, consider the following questions:

1. What did you think of the ad (pictured here) and the idea that "humanizing" cyclists might reduce hostile attitudes and aggressive acts against them? Can you think of other, and perhaps better, ways to change these responses?

2. In both Asch's conformity experiment and Milgram's study of obedience, the presence of another person greatly affected the behaviors of the research participants. How would you explain this?

3. Thinking about the most important romantic relationship in your life, explain how each of the major factors in interpersonal attraction—physical attractiveness, proximity, and similarity—affect this relationship.

Used with permission of Bike BloNo and Artezen LLC

4. Imagine yourself with a career as a social psychologist. Which of the key factors discussed in this chapter would you be most and least interested in studying? Why?

Summary

15.1 Social Cognition   497

- **Social psychology** is the study of how other people influence our thoughts, feelings, and actions. **Social cognition**, the way we think about and interpret ourselves and others, relies on **person perception**, the processes we use to form impressions of others, and **attributions**, which help us explain behaviors and events. However, these attributions are frequently marred by the **fundamental attribution error (FAE)**, the **self-serving bias**, and the **actor observer effect**, some of which may depend in part on cultural factors.

- **Attitudes** have three ABC components: *Affective, Behavioral,* and *Cognitive.* An efficient strategy for changing attitudes is to create **cognitive dissonance**.

- Like all other attitudes, **prejudice** also includes three ABC components. In addition, five commonly cited sources of prejudice are *learning, limited resources, displaced aggression, mental shortcuts,* and *implicit biases.*

- How can we overcome prejudice? There are five general approaches: *cooperation with common goals, intergroup contact, cognitive retraining, cognitive dissonance,* and *empathy induction.*

15.2 Social Influence   512

- **Conformity** involves changes in thoughts, feelings, or actions in response to real or imagined group pressure. People conform out of a desire for liking, acceptance, or approval (**normative social influence**), out of a need for more information and direction (**informational social influence**), and to match the behavior of those they like, admire, and want to be like (**reference group**).

The act of **compliance** refers to either actively or passively agreeing to the requests of others. There are three major strategies used in compliance: *foot-in-the-door, door-in-the face,* and *lowballing.*

- **Obedience** refers to following direct commands, usually from an authority figure. Milgram's study showed that a surprisingly large number of people obey orders even when they believe another human being is physically harmed as a result.

- Milgram's research demonstrated the startling power of social situations to create obedience. Legitimacy and closeness of the authority figure, remoteness of the victim, assignment of responsibility, and modeling or imitation of others are the four major factors in obedience.

- The degree of deception and discomfort to which Milgram's participants were subjected raises serious ethical questions, and the same study would never be done today.

- To decrease destructive obedience, we need to reexamine *socialization, conformity and compliance techniques, adherence to ideologies,* and a *relaxed moral guard.*

- Group membership is affected by several factors, including **deindividuation**, **social facilitation**, and **social loafing**. In addition, as we interact with others, **group polarization** and **groupthink** tend to occur. Both processes may hinder effective decision making.

15.3 Social Relations   524

- **Aggression** is any behavior intended to inflict psychological or physical harm to another. Several biological factors may help explain aggression, including genetic predisposition, aggression circuits in the brain, hormones, and neurotransmitters. Psychosocial explanations for aggression include substance abuse, aversive stimuli, media violence, and social learning.

- How can we reduce aggression? Releasing aggressive feelings through violent acts or watching violence (catharsis) is not an effective way to reduce aggression. Introducing incompatible responses (such as humor) and teaching social and communication skills are more efficient. Overcoming **dehumanization** is another possible way to reduce aggression.

- **Altruism** refers to actions designed to help others with no obvious benefit to the helper. Evolutionary theory suggests that **altruism** is an evolved, instinctual behavior. Other research suggests that helping may actually be self-interest in disguise—the **egoistic model**. The **empathy–altruism hypothesis** proposes that although altruism is occasionally based on selfish motivations, it is sometimes truly selfless and motivated by empathy or concern for others.

- Latané and Darley found that in order for helping to occur, the potential helper must notice what is happening, interpret the event as an emergency, take personal responsibility for helping, know how to help, and then actually initiate the helping behavior.

- Psychologists have found at least three compelling factors in **interpersonal attraction:** physical attractiveness, proximity, and similarity. Sternberg suggests that **consummate love** depends on a healthy degree of intimacy, passion, and commitment.

Key Terms

Retrieval Practice   Write a definition for each term before turning back to the referenced page to check your answer.

- actor–observer effect   500
- aggression   524
- altruism   526
- assertiveness   499
- attitude   501
- attribution   498
- bystander effect   528
- cognitive dissonance   502
- companionate love   533
- compliance   514
- conformity   513
- consummate love   533
- dehumanization   525
- deindividuation   520

- diffusion of responsibility   528
- discrimination   504
- egoistic model of helping   527
- empathy–altruism hypothesis   527
- evolutionary theory of helping   526
- fundamental attribution error (FAE)   498
- group polarization   521
- groupthink   521
- implicit bias   507
- informational social influence   513
- ingroup favoritism   507
- normative social influence   513
- obedience   516
- outgroup homogeneity effect   507

- person perception   498
- prejudice   504
- reference groups   513
- romantic love   533
- saliency bias   499
- self-fulfilling prophecy   505
- self-serving bias   499
- social facilitation   520
- social loafing   520
- social psychology   497
- stereotype   505
- triangular theory of love   533

Statistics and Psychology

Have you noticed how often you're bombarded by numbers: "On sale for 30 percent off," "70 percent chance of rain," "9 out of 10 doctors recommend," "Your scores on the SAT were in the 75th percentile"? Businesses and advertisers use numbers to convince you to buy their products. College admission officers use SAT percentile scores to help them decide whom to admit to their programs. Also, as you've seen throughout this text, psychologists use numbers to support or refute psychological hypotheses and to meet our four main goals—to describe, explain, predict, and change behavior and mental processes.

When we use numbers in these ways, we're using statistics. **Statistics** is a branch of applied mathematics that uses numbers to describe and analyze information on a subject. If you're considering a major in psychology, you may be surprised to learn that a full course in statistics is generally required for this major. Why? Statistics make it possible for psychologists to quantify the information we obtain in our studies. We can then critically analyze and evaluate this information. Statistical analysis is imperative for researchers to describe, predict, or explain behavior. As you'll recall from the so-called "Bobo doll" study in Chapter 15. Albert Bandura and his colleagues (1973) proposed that watching live or recorded violence causes aggressive behavior in children. In carefully controlled experiments, he gathered numerical information and analyzed it according to specific statistical methods. The statistical analysis helped him substantiate that the aggression of his participants and the aggressive acts they had seen modeled live or played back from previous filming were related, and that the relationship was not mere coincidence.

Although statistics is a branch of applied mathematics, you don't have to be a math genius to understand it. Simple arithmetic is all we need for most of the calculations. For more complex statistics involving more complicated mathematics, computer programs are readily available. What is more important than learning the mathematical computations, however, is developing an understanding of when and why each type of statistic is used. The purpose of this appendix is to help you develop this understanding and to become a better consumer of the statistics that bombard us each day. In addition, we hope to increase your appreciation for the important role this form of math plays in the science of psychology.

Statistics The branch of applied mathematics that deals with the collection, calculation, analysis, interpretation, and presentation of numerical facts or data.

Gathering and Organizing Data

Psychologists design their studies to facilitate gathering information about the factors they want to study. The information they obtain is known as *data* (data is plural; its singular is datum). When the data are gathered, they are generally in the form of numbers; if they aren't, they are converted to numbers. After they are gathered, the data must be organized in such a way that statistical analysis is possible. In the following section, we will examine the methods used to gather and organize information.

Variables

When studying a behavior, psychologists normally focus on one particular factor to determine whether it has an effect on the behavior. This factor is known as a *variable*, which is, in effect, anything that can assume more than one value (see Chapter 1). Height, weight, sex, eye color, and scores on an IQ test or a video game are all factors that can assume more than one value and are therefore variables. Some will vary between people, such as eye color, or may even vary within one person, such as scores on a video game (the same person might get 10,000 points on one try and only 800 on another). In contrast to a variable, anything that remains the same and does not vary is called a *constant*. If researchers use only women in their research, then sex is a constant, not a variable.

In non-experimental studies, variables can be factors that are merely observed through naturalistic observation or case studies, or they can be factors about which people are questioned in a test or survey. In experimental studies, the two major types of variables are independent and dependent variables.

Independent variables are those that are manipulated by the experimenter. For example, suppose we were to conduct a study to determine whether the sex of the debater influences the outcome of a debate. In this study, one group of participants watches a videotape of a debate between a man arguing the "pro" side and a woman arguing the "con"; another group watches the same debate, but with the pro and con roles reversed. Note that in both cases, the debaters follow a prepared "pro" or "con" script. Also note that the form of the presentation viewed by each group (whether "pro" is argued by a man or a woman) is the independent variable because the experimenter manipulates the form of presentation seen by each group.

Another example might be a study to determine whether a particular drug has any effect on a manual dexterity task. To study this question, we would administer the drug to one group and no drug to another. The independent variable would be the amount of drug given (some or none).

The *dependent variable* is a factor that results from, or depends on, the independent variable. It is a measure of some outcome or, most commonly, a measure of the participants' behavior. In the debate example, each participant's choice of the winner of the debate would be the dependent variable. In the drug experiment, the dependent variable would be each participant's score on the manual dexterity task.

Frequency Distributions

After conducting a study and obtaining measures of the variable(s) being studied, psychologists need to organize the data in a meaningful way. **Table A.1** presents test scores from a Math Aptitude Test collected from 50 college students. This information is called *raw data* because there is no order to the numbers. They are presented as they were collected and are therefore "raw."

The lack of order in raw data makes them difficult to study. Thus, the first step in understanding the results of an experiment is to impose some order on the raw data. There are several ways to do this. One of the simplest is to create a *frequency distribution*, which shows the number of times a score or event occurs. Although frequency distributions are helpful in several ways, the major advantages are that they allow us to see the data in an organized manner and they make it easier to represent the data on a graph.

The simplest way to make a frequency distribution is to list all the possible test scores, then tally the number of people *(N)* who received those scores. **Table A.2** presents a frequency distribution using the raw data from Table A.1. As you can see, the data are now easier to read.

TABLE A.1	Math Aptitude Test Scores for 50 College Students			
73	57	63	59	50
72	66	50	67	51
63	59	65	62	65
62	72	64	73	66
61	68	62	68	63
59	61	72	63	52
59	58	57	68	57
64	56	65	59	60
50	62	68	54	63
52	62	70	60	68

TABLE A.2   **Frequency Distribution of 50 Students on Math Aptitude Test**

Score	Frequency	Score	Frequency
73	2	61	2
72	3	60	2
71	0	59	5
70	1	58	1
69	0	57	3
68	5	56	1
67	1	55	0
66	2	54	1
65	3	53	0
64	2	52	2
63	5	51	1
62	5	50	3
			Total 50

This type of frequency distribution is practical when the number of possible scores is 50 or fewer. However, when there are more than 10 possible scores it can be even harder to make sense out of the frequency distribution than the raw data. This can be seen in **Table A.3**, which presents the hypothetical Psychology Aptitude Test scores for 50 students. Even though there are only 50 actual scores in this table, the number of possible scores ranges from a high of 1390 to a low of 400. If we included zero frequencies there would be 100 entries in a frequency distribution of this data, making the frequency distribution much more difficult to understand than the raw data. If there are more than 20 possible scores, therefore, a *group frequency distribution* is normally used.

In a *group frequency distribution,* individual scores are represented as members of a group of scores or as a range of scores (see **Table A.4**). These groups are called *class intervals*. Grouping these scores makes it much easier to make sense out of the distribution, as you can see from the relative ease in understanding Table A.4 as compared to Table A.3. Group frequency distributions are also easier to represent on a graph.

When graphing data from frequency distributions, the class intervals are typically represented along the *abscissa* (the horizontal or *x* axis). The frequency is represented along the *ordinate* (the vertical or *y* axis). Information can be graphed in the form of a bar graph, called a *histogram*, or in the form of a point or line graph, called a *polygon*. **Figure A.1** shows a

TABLE A.3   **Psychology Aptitude Test Scores for 50 College Students**

1350	750	530	540	750
1120	410	780	1020	430
720	1080	1110	770	610
1130	620	510	1160	630
640	1220	920	650	870
930	660	480	940	670
1070	950	680	450	990
690	1010	800	660	500
860	520	540	880	1090
580	730	570	560	740

TABLE A.4	Group Frequency Distribution of Psychology Aptitude Test Scores for 50 College Students	
Class Interval		**Frequency**
1300–1390		1
1200–1290		1
1100–1190		4
1000–1090		5
900–990		5
800–890		4
700–790		7
600–690		10
500–590		9
400–490		4
Total		50

histogram presenting the data from Table A.4. Note that the class intervals are represented along the bottom line of the graph (the *x* axis) and the height of the bars indicates the frequency in each class interval. Now look at **Figure A.2**. The information presented here is exactly the same as that in Figure A.1 but is represented in the form of a polygon rather than a histogram. Can you see how both graphs illustrate the same information? Even though graphs like these are quite common today, we have found that many students have never been formally taught how to read graphs, which is the topic of our next section.

How to Read a Graph

Every graph has several major parts. The most important are the labels, the axes (the vertical and horizontal lines), and the points, lines, or bars. Find these parts in Figure A.1.

The first thing we should all notice when reading a graph is the labels because they tell what data are portrayed. Usually the data consist of the descriptive statistics, or the numbers used to measure the dependent variables. For example, in Figure A.1 the horizontal axis is labeled "Psychology Aptitude Test Scores," which is the dependent variable measure; the vertical axis is labeled "Frequency," which means the number of occurrences. If a graph is not labeled, as we sometimes see in TV commercials or magazine ads, it is useless and should be ignored. Even when a graph *is* labeled, the labels can be misleading. For example, if graph designers want to distort the information, they can elongate one of the axes. If you'd like more information on how information can be distorted when you "elongate the axes," see the following **Test Yourself**.

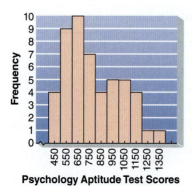

FIGURE A.1 A histogram illustrating the information found in Table A.4

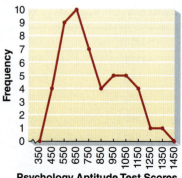

FIGURE A.2 A polygon illustrating the information found in Table A.4

S&P Scientific Thinking and Practical Application

Test Yourself: Do You Know How Graphs are Used to "Lie With Statistics"?

Imagine yourself as part of a group of very wealthy, unethical politicians who want to decrease their personal income taxes. If the current annual tax rate increase for the imaginary people in their personal tax bracket was actually less than one percent over the last 20 years, how could they create a graph that would help justify a tax reduction for their group?

Potential Solution: As you know, we normally don't provide "answers" to these scientific thinking exercises because this type of thinking generally has multiple alternatives. Furthermore, in this particular case it might feel somewhat unethical to give you tips on "how to lie with statistics." However, unless you've taken a full course in statistics, you probably can't answer this question and we believe that a fully educated public is better able to protect itself. In addition, we're including one possible solution here to increase your scientific thinking skills and to demonstrate a useful, practical example of the dangers associated with the misuse of statistics.

Returning to our hypothetical group of wealthy politicians, imagine how they could first create a horizontal axis for the 20-year tax increase, like the one in Figure A.2—labeled "Psychology Aptitude Test Scores." But instead of showing the full 20 years, they could create fewer data points by only including the even numbered years. Do you see how this would result in making the line on the graph appear much steeper—thereby implying that their group's tax increase was much larger (and higher) than it actually was.

To make matters worse, they could also stretch the vertical axis (the "Frequency" on Figure A.2), so that the line represents 20 increments (one for each of the 20 years). The overall result would depict a very steep upward slope for taxes paid by the wealthy, even though their actual tax increase was less than one percent. Does this help you see why it's so important to pay careful attention to the information presented in graphs? For more examples of misleading and unethical uses of statistics see the following links:

https://www.buzzfeednews.com/article/katienotopoulos/graphs-that-lied-to-us

https://www.statisticshowto.datasciencecentral.com/misleading-graphs/

https://www.forbes.com/sites/naomirobbins/2012/02/16/misleading-graphs-figures-not-drawn-to-scale/#75f31c4715ef

---

Next, we need to focus on the bars, points, or lines on the graph. In the case of histograms like the one in Figure A.1, each bar represents the class interval. The width of the bar stands for the width of the class interval, whereas the height of the bar stands for the frequency in that interval. Look at the third bar from the left in Figure A.1. This bar represents the interval "600 to 690 Psychology Aptitude Scores," which has a frequency of 10. Can you see how this directly corresponds to the same class interval in Table A.4? Graphs and tables are both merely alternate ways of illustrating information.

Reading point or line graphs is the same as reading a histogram. In a point graph, each point represents two numbers, one found along the horizontal axis and the other found along the vertical axis. A polygon is identical to a point graph except that it has lines connecting the points. Figure A.2 is an example of a polygon, where each point represents a class interval and is placed at the center of the interval and at the height corresponding to the frequency of that interval. To make the graph easier to read, the points are connected by straight lines.

Displaying the data in a frequency distribution or in a graph is much more useful than merely presenting raw data and can be especially helpful when researchers are trying to find relations between certain factors. However, as we explained earlier, if psychologists want to make precise predictions or explanations, we need to perform specific mathematical computations on the data. How we use these computations, or statistics, is the topic of our next section.

Uses of the Various Statistics

The statistics psychologists use in a study depend on whether they are trying to describe and predict behavior or explain it. When they use statistics to describe behavior, as in reporting the average score on the hypothetical Psychology Aptitude Test, they are using **descriptive statistics**. When they use them to explain behavior, as Bandura did in his study of children modeling aggressive behavior seen on film, they are using **inferential statistics**.

Descriptive Statistics

Descriptive statistics are the numbers used to describe the dependent variable. They can be used to describe characteristics of a *population* (an entire group, such as all people living in the United

Descriptive statistics Mathematical methods used to describe and summarize sets of data in a meaningful way.

Inferential statistics Mathematical procedures that provide a measure of confidence about how likely it is that a certain result appeared by chance.

States) or a *sample* (a part of a group, such as a randomly selected group of 25 students from a given college or university). The major descriptive statistics include measures of central tendency (mean, median, and mode), measures of variation (variance and standard deviation), and correlation.

Measures of Central Tendency

Statistics indicating the center of the distribution are called *measures of central tendency,* which include the mean, median, and mode. They are all scores that are typical of the center of the distribution. The **mean** is the arithmetic average, and it is what most of us think of when we hear the word "average." The **median** is the middle score in a distribution—half the scores fall above it and half fall below it. The **mode** is the score that occurs most often.

Mean   The arithmetic average of a distribution, which is obtained by adding the values of all the scores and dividing by the number of scores (N).

Median   The halfway point in a set of data; half the scores fall above the median, and half fall below it.

Mode   The score that occurs most frequently in a data set.

Mean

What is your average exam score in your psychology class? What is the average yearly rainfall in your part of the country? What is the average reading test score in your city? When these types of questions ask for the average, they're generally asking for the "mean." The arithmetic *mean* is the weighted average of all the raw scores, which is computed by totaling all the raw scores and then dividing that total by the number of scores added together. In statistical computation, the mean is represented by an "X" with a bar above it ($\bar{X}$, pronounced "X bar"), each individual raw score by an "X," and the total number of scores by an "N." For example, if we wanted to compute the $\bar{X}$ of the raw statistics test scores from our first example, Table A.1, we would sum all the X's (Σ, with Σ meaning sum) and divide by N (number of scores). In Table A.1, the sum of all the scores is equal to 3100 and there are 50 scores. Therefore, the mean of these scores is

$$\bar{X} = \frac{3100}{50} = 62$$

Table A.5 illustrates how to calculate the mean for 10 IQ scores.

Median

The *median* is the middle score in the distribution once all the scores have been arranged in rank order. If N (the number of scores) is odd, then there actually is a middle score and that middle score is the median. When N is even, there are two middle scores and the median is the mean of those two scores. **Table A.6** shows the computation of the median for two different sets of scores, one set with 15 scores and one with 10.

TABLE A.5	Computation of the Mean for 10 IQ Scores
IQ Scores X	
143	
127	
116	
98	
85	
107	
106	
98	
104	
116	
$\Sigma X = 1100$	

$$\text{Mean} = \bar{X} = \frac{\Sigma X}{N} = \frac{1,100}{10} = 110$$

TABLE A.6	Computation of the Median for Odd and Even Numbers of IQ Scores
IQ	**IQ**
139	137
130	135
121	121
116	116
107	108 ← middle score
101	106 ← middle score
98	105
96 ← middle score	101
84	98
83	97
82	N = 10
75	N is even
75	
68	
65	
N = 15	$\text{Median} = \frac{106 + 108}{2} = 107$
N is odd	

TABLE A.7	Finding the Mode for Two Different Distributions
IQ	**IQ**
139	139
138	138
125	125
116 ←	116 ←
116 ←	116 ←
116 ←	116 ←
107	107
100	98 ←
98	98 ←
98	98 ←
Mode = most frequent score	Mode = 116 and 98
Mode = 116	

Mode   Of all the measures of central tendency, the easiest to compute is the *mode*, which is merely the most frequent score. It is computed by finding the score that occurs most often. Whereas there is always only one mean and only one median for each distribution, there can be more than one mode. **Table A.7** shows how to find the mode in a distribution with one mode (unimodal) and in a distribution with two modes (bimodal).

There are several advantages to each of these measures of central tendency, but in psychological research the mean is used most often.

Measures of Variation   When describing a distribution, it is not sufficient merely to give the central tendency; it is also necessary to give a *measure of variation*, which is a measure of the spread of the scores. By examining this **range**, or spread of scores, we can determine whether the scores are bunched around the middle or tend to extend away from the middle. **Figure A.3** shows three different distributions, all with the same mean but with different spreads of scores. You can see from this figure that, in order to describe these different distributions accurately, there must be some measures of the variation in their spread. The most widely used measure of variation is the **standard deviation**, which is represented by a lowercase s. The standard deviation is a measurement of how much the scores in a distribution deviate from the mean. The formula for the standard deviation is

$$s = \sqrt{\frac{\Sigma(X - \bar{X})^2}{N}}$$

Table A.8 illustrates how to compute the standard deviation.

Most distributions of psychological data are bell-shaped. That is, most of the scores are grouped around the mean, and the farther the scores are from the mean in either direction, the fewer the scores. Notice the bell shape of the distribution in **Figure A.4**. Distributions such as this are called **normal distributions**. In normal distributions, as shown in Figure A.4, approximately two-thirds of the scores fall within a range that is one standard deviation below the mean to one standard deviation above the mean. For example, the Wechsler IQ tests (see Chapter 8) have a mean of 100 and a standard deviation of 15. This means that approximately two-thirds of the people taking these tests will have scores between 85 and 115.

Correlation   Suppose for a moment that you are sitting in the student union with a friend. To pass the time, you and your friend decide to play a game in which you try to guess the height of the next man who enters the union. The winner, the one whose guess is closest to the person's actual height, gets a piece of pie paid for by the loser. When it is your turn, what do you guess? If you're like most people, you'll probably try to estimate the mean of all the men in the union and use that as your guess. The mean is almost always our best guess when we have no other information.

Now let's change the game a little and add a friend who stands outside the union and weighs the next man who enters the union. If your friend texts you with the information that this

Range   A measure of the dispersion of scores between the highest and lowest scores.

Standard deviation   A computed measure of how much scores in a sample differ from the mean of the sample.

Normal distribution   A symmetrical, bell-shaped curve that represents a set of data in which most scores occur in the middle of the possible range, with fewer and fewer scores near the extremes.

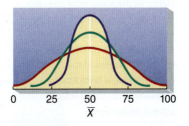

FIGURE A.3   **Three distributions having the same mean but a different variability**

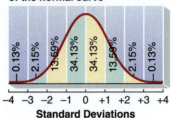

Percent of cases under portions of the normal curve

0.13% 2.15% 13.59% 34.13% 34.13% 13.59% 2.15% 0.13%

−4 −3 −2 −1 0 +1 +2 +3 +4
Standard Deviations

FIGURE A.4 **A normal distribution forms a bell-shaped curve** In a normal distribution, two-thirds of the scores lie between one standard deviation above and one standard deviation below the mean.

TABLE A.8	Computation of the Standard Deviation for 10 IQ Scores	
IQ Scores X	$X - \overline{X}$	$(X - \overline{X})^2$
143	33	1089
127	17	289
116	6	36
98	−12	144
85	−25	625
107	−3	9
106	−4	16
98	−12	144
104	−6	36
116	6	36
$\Sigma X = 1100$		$\Sigma (X - \overline{X})^2 = 2424$

Standard Deviation = s

$$= \sqrt{\frac{\Sigma(X - \overline{X})^2}{N}} = \sqrt{\frac{2424}{10}}$$

$$= \sqrt{242.4} = 15.569$$

man weighs 125 pounds, without seeing him would you still predict that he's of average height? Probably not. You'd most likely guess that he's below the mean. Why? Because you intuitively understand that there is a *correlation* (Chapter 1), a relationship, between height and weight, with tall people usually weighing more than short people. Given that 125 pounds is less than the average weight for men, you'll probably guess a less-than-average height. The statistic used to measure this type of relationship between two variables is called a correlation coefficient.

Correlation Coefficient   A *correlation coefficient* (Chapter 1) measures the relationship between two variables, such as height and weight or IQ and annual income. Given any two variables, there are three possible relationships between them: *positive, negative*, and *zero* (no relationship). A *positive relationship* exists when the two variables vary in the same direction (e.g., as height increases, weight normally also increases). A *negative relationship* occurs when the two variables vary in opposite directions (e.g., as temperatures go up, hot chocolate sales go down). There is a *zero* (no) *relationship* when the two variables vary totally independently of one another (e.g., there is no relationship between your height and the number of times you brush your teeth). **Figure A.5** illustrates these three types of correlations.

FIGURE A.5   **Three types of correlation**   Positive correlation (top left): as the number of days of class attendance increases, so does the number of correct exam items. Negative correlation (top right): as the number of days of class attendance increases, the number of incorrect exam items decreases. Zero correlation (bottom): the day of the month on which one is born has no relationship to the number of correct exam items.

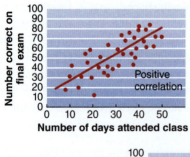

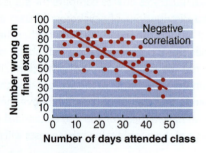

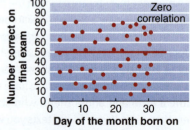

TABLE A.9	Computation of Correlation Coefficient Between Height and Weight for 10 Men			
Height (inches)		Weight (pounds)		
X	X^2	Y	Y^2	XY
73	5,329	210	44,100	15,330
64	4,096	133	17,689	8,512
65	4,225	128	16,384	8,320
70	4,900	156	24,336	10,920
74	5,476	189	35,721	13,986
68	4,624	145	21,025	9,860
67	4,489	145	21,025	9,715
72	5,184	166	27,556	11,952
76	5,776	199	37,601	15,124
71	5,041	159	25,281	11,289
Total = 700	49,140	1,630	272,718	115,008

$$r = \frac{N \cdot \Sigma XY - \Sigma X \cdot \Sigma Y}{\sqrt{[N \cdot \Sigma X^2 - (\Sigma X)^2]} \ \sqrt{[N \cdot \Sigma Y^2 - (\Sigma Y)^2]}}$$

$$r = \frac{10 \cdot 115,008 - 700 \cdot 1,630}{\sqrt{[10 \cdot 49,140 - 700^2]} \ \sqrt{[10 \cdot 272,718 - 1,630^2]}}$$

$$r = 0.92$$

The computation and the formula for a correlation coefficient (correlation coefficient is delineated by the letter "*r*") are shown in **Table A.9**. The correlation coefficient *(r)* always has a value between +1 and −1 (it is never greater than +1 and it is never smaller than −1). When *r* is close to +1, it signifies a high positive relationship between the two variables (as one variable goes up, the other variable also goes up). When *r* is close to −1, it signifies a high negative relationship between the two variables (as one variable goes up, the other variable goes down). When *r* is 0, there is no linear relationship between the two variables being measured.

Correlation coefficients can be quite helpful in making predictions. Bear in mind, however, that predictions are just that: *predictions.* They will have some error as long as the correlation coefficients on which they are based are not perfect (+1 or −1). Also, correlations cannot reveal any information regarding causation. Merely because two factors are correlated, it does not mean that one factor causes the other. Consider, for example, ice cream consumption and swimming pool use. These two variables are positively correlated with one another, in that as ice cream consumption increases, so does swimming pool use. However, no one would seriously suggest that eating ice cream *causes* swimming, or vice versa. Keep this ice cream and swimming correlation in mind when you see star athletes promoting various products. Despite what advertisers for cereals want you to believe, the fact that LeBron James eats Wheaties and can do a slam dunk does not mean that you will be able to do one if you eat the same breakfast. The only way to determine the *cause* of behavior is to conduct an experiment and analyze the results by using inferential statistics.

Inferential Statistics

Knowing the descriptive statistics associated with different distributions, such as the mean and standard deviation, can enable us to make comparisons between various distributions. By making these comparisons, we may be able to observe whether one variable is related to another or whether one variable has a causal effect on another. When we design an experiment specifically to measure causal effects between two or more variables, we use *inferential statistics* to analyze the data collected. Although there are many inferential statistics, the one we will discuss is the t-test, since it is the simplest.

TABLE A.10	Reaction Times in Milliseconds (MSEC) for Participants in Alcohol and No Alcohol Conditions and Computation of t	
RT (msec) Alcohol X_1	**RT (msec) No Alcohol X_2**	
200	143	
210	137	
140	179	
160	184	
180	156	
187	132	
196	176	
198	148	
140	125	
159	120	
$SX_1 = 1{,}770$	$SX_2 = 1{,}500$	
$N_1 = 10$	$N_2 = 10$	
$\overline{X}_1 = 177$	$\overline{X}_2 = 150$	
$s_1 = 24.25$	$s_2 = 21.86$	
$\Sigma_{\overline{x}1} = \dfrac{S}{\sqrt{N_1 - 1}} = 8.08$	$\Sigma_{\overline{x}2} = \dfrac{S}{\sqrt{N_2 - 1}} = 7.29$	

$$S_{\overline{X}1 - \overline{X}2} = \sqrt{S_{\overline{x}_1}^2 + S_{\overline{x}_2}^2} = \sqrt{8.08^2 + 7.29^2} = 10.88$$

$$t = \frac{\overline{X}_1 - \overline{X}_2}{S_{\overline{x}1 - \overline{x}2}} = \frac{177 - 150}{10.88} = 2.48$$

$$t = 2.48, p < .05$$

Understanding a T-Test Suppose we believe that drinking alcohol causes a person's reaction time to slow down. To test this hypothesis, we recruit 20 participants and separate them into two groups. We ask the participants in one group to drink a large glass of orange juice with one ounce of alcohol for every 100 pounds of body weight (e.g., a person weighing 150 pounds would get 1.5 ounces of alcohol). We ask the control group to drink an equivalent amount of orange juice with no alcohol added. Fifteen minutes after the drinks, we have each participant perform a reaction time test that consists of pushing a button as soon as a light is flashed. (The reaction time is the time between the onset of the light and the pressing of the button.) **Table A.10** shows the data from this hypothetical experiment. It is clear from the data that there is definitely a difference in the reaction times of the two groups: There is an obvious difference between the means. However, it is possible that this difference is due merely to chance. To determine whether the difference is real or due to chance, we can conduct a t-test. We have run a sample t-test in Table A.10.

The logic behind a t-test is relatively simple. In our experiment we have two samples. If each of these samples is from the *same* population (e.g., the population of all people, whether drunk or sober), then any difference between the samples will be due to chance. On the other hand, if the two samples are from *different* populations (e.g., the population of drunk individuals *and* the population of sober individuals), then the difference is a significant difference and not due to chance.

If there is a significant difference between the two samples, then the independent variable must have caused that difference. In our example, there is a significant difference between the alcohol and the no alcohol groups. We can tell this because p (the probability that this t value will occur by chance) is less than .05. To obtain the p, we need only look up the t value in a statistical table, which is found in any statistics book. In our example, because there is a significant difference between the groups, we can reasonably conclude that the alcohol did cause a slower reaction time.

Take-Home Message In this brief Appendix A, we've discussed the major topics of how to gather and organize your data and the common uses of various statistics. For more information, consult a statistics textbook, such as the https://www.mathsisfun.com/data/index.html

On the other hand, you may be feeling overwhelmed and may not want more information. You might also be overly anxious and very concerned knowing that psychology majors need to take one or more full courses in statistics. If so, don't panic! Learning statistics is much like learning another language. You begin with the basic rules of "grammar," which in the case of statistics involves the use of symbols and notation. Later, you'll advance on to practice with conversation, which in statistics means hours of homework.

We recognize that doing homework and learning another language may not sound appealing to you at this time. However, it's important to know that a basic understanding of statistics is essential to conducting or interpreting research—and to becoming an informed, everyday consumer. Furthermore, "fluency" in the language of statistics will make you much more employable and could even earn you a higher salary.

Note that if you truly panic at the thought of studying statistics, or suffer from serious "math anxiety," your psychology instructor or college counselor can provide specific guidance and advice. In addition, the following website offers immediate options and self-help techniques: https://www.wikihow.com/Understand-and-Use-Basic-Statistics

Answers to Self-Test Retrieval Practice Questions and Research Challenges

Chapter 1   The Science of Psychology

Self-Test 1.1 What is Psychology? (p. 12) 1. d. 2. a. 3. c. 4. a. **Self-Test 1.2 Scientific Research (p. 19)** 1. b. 2. b. 3. d. 4. d. **Self-Test 1.3 Psychology's Research Methods (p. 31)** 1. b. 2. a. 3. c. 4. b. **Research Challenge (p. 30)** Question 1: Descriptive. Question 2: Survey. **Self-Test 1.4 Secrets of Student Success (p. 37)** 1. c. 2. a. 3. a. 4. d.

Chapter 2   Neuroscience and Biological Foundations

Self-Test 2.1 Neural and Hormonal Processes (pp. 49–50) 1. c. 2. d. 3. c. 4. b. 5. c. **Self-Test 2.2 Nervous System Organization (pp. 56–57)** 1. d. 2. a. 3. d. 4. c. 5. d. **Self-Test 2.3 A Tour Through the Brain (p. 63)** 1. b. 2. d. 3. c. 4. c. **Self-Test 2.4 The Cerebral Cortex (p. 71)** 1. b. 2. d. 3. c. 4. c. **Research Challenge (p. 66)** Question 1: Descriptive. Question 2: Case study.

Chapter 3   Stress, Coping, and Health Psychology

Self-Test 3.1 Understanding Stress (p. 84) 1. d. 2. c. 3. c. 4. b. 5. c. **Self-Test 3.2 Stress and Illness (p. 90)** 1. b. 2. d. 3. d. 4. b. 5. d. **Research Challenge (p. 95)** Question 1: Descriptive and correlational. Question 2: Survey/interview; positive correlation (increased exercise is associated with improved mental health). **Self-Test 3.3 Stress Management (p. 97)** 1. a. 2. d. 3. b. 4. d. 5. d. **Self-Test 3.4 Health Psychology (p. 101)** 1. d. 2. a. 3. a. 4. d. 5. c.

Chapter 4   Sensation and Perception

Self-Test 4.1 Understanding Sensation (p. 111) 1. b. 2. a. 3. c. 4. a. 5. b. **Self-Test 4.2 How We See and Hear (p. 118)** 1. c. 2. b. 3. b. 4. c. **Self-Test 4.3 Our Other Important Senses (p. 123)** 1. c. 2. c. 3. d. 4. d. 5. b. **Self-Test 4.4 Understanding Perception (pp. 134–135)** 1. c. 2. a. 3. b. 4. b. **Research Challenge (p. 132)** Question 1: Experimental. Question 2: IV = doctor's notes about hypothetical male patient with race as either

Black or White. DV = clinician's perceptions of the patient. Experimental group = participants who rated the hypothetical male patient. Control group = no control group was mentioned.

Chapter 5   States of Consciousness

Self-Test 5.1 Understanding Consciousness (p. 141) 1. b. 2. a. 3. d. 4. b. 5. d. **Self-Test 5.2 Understanding Sleep and Dreams (p. 152)** 1. d. 2. c. 3. a. 4. a. 5. c. **Self-Test 5.3 Psychoactive Drugs (p. 163)** 1. a. 2. d. 3. a. 4. a. 5. c. **Research Challenge (p. 159)** Question 1: Experimental. Question 2: IV = low or no alcohol consumption. DV = ratings of Dutch language skills. Experimental group(s) = chatting in Dutch with low alcohol consumption. Control group = chatting in Dutch with no alcohol consumption. **Self-Test 5.4 Meditation and Hypnosis (p. 167)** 1. d. 2. d. 3. b. 4. c. 5. b.

Chapter 6   Learning

Self-Test 6.1 Classical Conditioning (p. 179) 1. c. 2. c. 3. d. 4. d. 5. b. **Self-Test 6.2 Operant Conditioning (p. 192)** 1. b. 2. a. 3. c. 4. d. 5. c. **Research Challenge (p. 186)** Question 1: Experimental. Question 2: IV = presence of owner or bowl of treats. DV = dog's choice of owner or treats. (Note that there was no mention of random assignment or of a control group, so this might qualify as a quasi-experimental design.) **Self-Test 6.3 Cognitive-Social Learning (pp. 196–197)** 1. d. 2. c. 3. c. 4. a. 5. b. **Self-Test 6.4 Biology of Learning (p. 201)** 1. c. 2. d. 3. b. 4. d. 5. c.

Chapter 7   Memory

Self-Test 7.1 The Nature of Memory (p. 215) 1. d. 2. d. 3. a. 4. b. 5. c. **Research Challenge (p. 207)** Question 1: Experimental. Question 2: IVs = taking a general photo, taking a zoomed-in photo, merely observing a museum object. DV = accuracy of memory for the object viewed or photographed. Experimental groups = participants taking a general photo, participants taking a zoomed-in photo. Control groups = participants who

simply observed the museum object. **Self-Test 7.2 Forgetting (p. 221)** 1. a. 2. b. 3. c. 4. b. 5. c. **Self-Test 7.3 Biological Bases of Memory (p. 228)** 1. c. 2. d. 3. d. 4. c. 5. c. **Self-Test 7.4 Memory Distortions and Improvement (p. 235)** 1. c. 2. a. 3. c. 4. d. 5. d.

Chapter 8   Thinking, Language, and Intelligence

Self-Test 8.1 Thinking (pp. 248–249) 1. c. 2. a. 3. b. 4. c. **Research Challenge (p. 248)** Question 1: Descriptive and correlational. Question 2: Archival research; zero correlation between creativity and most psychological disorders, but creativity was positively correlated with bipolar disorder. **Self-Test 8.2 Language (p. 256)** 1. d. 2. d. 3. c. 4. b. 5. d. **Self-Test 8.3 Intelligence (p. 260)** 1. d. 2. a. 3. a. 4. b. **Self-Test 8.4 Intelligence Controversies (pp. 269–270)** 1. d. 2. b. 3. a. 4. d. 5. d.

Chapter 9   Life Span Development

Self-Test 9.1 Studying Development (p. 279) 1. d. 2. d. 3. b. 4. a. 5. c. **Research Challenge (p. 275)** 1. Descriptive. 2. Case study. **Self-Test 9.2 Physical Development (p. 292)** 1. d. 2. b. 3. b. 4. c. 5. d. **Self-Test 9.3 Cognitive Development (p. 300)** 1. c. 2. d 3. b. 4. c. 5. d. **Self-Test 9.4 Social-Emotional Development (pp. 311–312)** 1. a. 2. b. 3. c. 4. b. 5. (a) Marcos = trust versus mistrust, (b) Ann = identity versus role confusion, (c) Teresa = initiative versus guilt, (d) George = ego integrity versus despair.

Chapter 10   Sex, Gender, and Sexuality

Self-Test 10.1 Studying Human Sexuality (p. 319) 1. b. 2. d. 3. d. 4. b. 5. c. **Research Challenge (p. 317)** Question 1.: Experimental. Question 2.: IV = whether or not hooked up to "lie detector," DV = participants' reporting of particular behaviors. Experimental Group group = participants supposedly hooked up to "lie detector." Control Group group = participants not hooked up to "lie detector." **Self-Test

10.2 Sexual Identity and Behavior (p. 330) 1. d. 2. d. 3. b. 4. a. 5. d. **Self-Test 10.3 Sexual Disorders and Problems (p. 340)** 1. d. 2. b. 3. d. 4. a. 5. c. **Self-Test 10.4 Real World Sexuality (p. 350)** 1. d. 2. d. 3. c. 4. c. 5. b.

Chapter 11   Motivation and Emotion

Self-Test 11.1 Theories of Motivation (p. 359) 1. a. 2. b. 3. d. 4. b. **Self-Test 11.2 Motivation and Behavior (p. 368)** 1. d. 2. a. 3. d. 4. c. 5. d. **Self-Test 11.3 Components and Theories of Emotion (p. 375)** 1. a. 2. b. 3. a. 4. d. 5. a. **Research Challenge (p. 374)** 1. Descriptive and correlational. 2. Survey/ interview; positive correlation (increased fake smiling was associated with increased drinking). **Self-Test 11.4 Experiencing Emotions (p. 383)** 1. c. 2. c. 3. d. 4. a. 5. d.

Chapter 12   Personality

Self-Test 12.1 Understanding Personality (p. 396) 1. a. 2. d. 3. d. 4. d. 5. b. **Self-Test 12.2 Psychoanalytic/Psychodynamic Theories (p. 403)** 1. d. 2. b. 3. d. 4. c. 5. c. **Self-Test 12.3 Trait Theories (p. 410)** 1. c. 2. a. 3. d. 4. e. 5. c. **Research Challenge (p. 407)** 1. Descriptive and correlational. 2. Descriptive = naturalistic observation. Correlational = positive correlation (increased gorilla life expectancy was associated with personality trait of extroversion). **Self-Test 12.4 Humanistic**

Theories (p. 413) 1. a. 2. c. 3. c. 4. d. 5. c. **Self-Test 12.5 Social-Cognitive Theories (p. 418)** 1. c. 2. d. 3. b. 4. b. 5. c.

Chapter 13   Psychological Disorders

Self-Test 13.1 Understanding Psychological Disorders (p. 428) 1. a. 2. b. 3. d. **Self-Test 13.2 Anxiety Disorders (p. 433)** 1. a. 2. c. 3. b. 4. c. **Self-Test 13.3 Depressive and Bipolar Disorders (p. 438)** 1. c. 2. b. 3. d. 4. c. **Research Challenge (p. 436)** Question 1: Experimental. Question 2: IV = fluid injections in the brain. DV1 = time to solve maze. DV2 = changes in the genes of the IV group. Experimental group = rats that received fluid injections in their brains. Control group = rats that did not receive fluid injections in their brains. **Self-Test 13.4 Schizophrenia (p. 442)** 1. a. 2. b. 3. c. 4. a. **Self-Test 13.5 Other Disorders (p. 449)** 1. a. 2. b. 3. a. 4. d. **Self-Test 13.6 Key Issues in Psychological Disorders (p. 457)** 1. d. 2. a. 3. d. 4. c.

Chapter 14   Therapy

Self-Test 14.1 Talk Therapies (p. 469) 1. a. 2. c. 3. d. 4. d. 5. b. **Self-Test 14.2 Behavior Therapies (p. 475)** 1. b. 2. c. 3. d. 4. b. 5. d. **Self-Test 14.3 Biomedical Therapies (p. 482)** 1. d. 2. b. 3. b. 4. c. 5. d. **Self-Test 14.4 Psychotherapy in Perspective (p. 493)** 1. d. 2. a. 3. d. 4. c. 5. c. **Research Challenge (p. 485)** Question 1:

Experimental. Question 2: IV (part 1) = listening to varying types of audio recordings. IV (part 2) = varying exercises. Two self-compassion groups and three different exercise groups— negative thinking, positive thinking, or neutral assignment. DV1 = degree of self-compassion, connection with others, self-criticism, rumination. DV2 = assessment of all participants' physiological arousal. Experimental Group(s) = the four "intervention" groups. Control Group = group with neutral assignment. **Research Challenge (p. 487)** Question 1: Experimental. Question 2: IV = varying amounts of training or instructions, including how to watch movies. DV = divorce rate after 3 years. Experimental Group(s) = the three "intervention" groups. Control Group = couples who received no training or instructions.

Chapter 15   Social Psychology

Self-Test 15.1 Social Cognition (pp. 511–512) 1. c. 2. a. 3. b. 4. c. **Research Challenge (p. 511)** Question 1: Experimental. Question 2: IV = topic discussed (being transgendered or recycling). DV = degree of transphobia. Experimental Group = those that discussed transgender issues. Control Group = those that discussed recycling. **Self-Test 15.2 Social Influence (p. 523)** 1. c. 2. c. 3. d. 4. b. 5. c. **Self-Test 15.3 Social Relations (p. 536)** 1. b. 2. a. 3. d. 4. b. 5. a.

Absolute threshold The minimum amount of stimulation necessary to consciously detect a stimulus 50 percent of the time.

Accommodation According to Piaget, the process of adjusting (accommodating) existing schemas to incorporate new information.

Achievement motivation The desire to excel, especially in competition with others.

Acquisition (in classical conditioning) Learning occurs (is acquired) when an organism involuntarily links a neutral stimulus (NS) with an unconditioned stimulus (US), which in turn elicits the conditioned response (CR).

Acquisition (in operant conditioning) Learning occurs (is acquired) when an organism voluntarily links a response with a consequence, such as a reward.

Action potential A neural impulse, or brief electrical charge, that carries information along the axon of a neuron; movement is generated when positively charged ions move in and out through channels in the axon's membrane.

Activation–synthesis theory of dreams The theory that dreams are a by-product of random, spontaneous stimulation of brain cells during sleep, which the brain combines (synthesizes) into coherent patterns, known as dreams.

Active listening A communication technique that requires listening with total attention to what another is saying; techniques include reflecting, paraphrasing, and clarifying what the person says and means.

Actor–observer effect The tendency to attribute other people's behavior to personality factors, while attributing our own behavior to situational factors.

Acute stress A short-term state of arousal, in response to a perceived threat or challenge that has a definite endpoint.

Adaptation/protection theory of sleep The theory that sleep evolved to conserve energy and provide protection from predators.

Adaptation-level phenomenon A tendency to judge a new situation or stimuli relative to a neutral, "normal" level based on our previous experiences; we then adapt to this new level and it becomes the new "normal."

Addiction A broad term that describes a condition in which the body requires a drug (or specific activity) in order to function without physical and psychological reactions to its absence; it is often the outcome of tolerance and dependence.

Adverse childhood experiences (ACEs) Abuse, neglect, and other potentially traumatic events, occurring before the age of 18, which may have negative lasting effects on physical and mental well-being.

Ageism A form of prejudice or discrimination based on physical age; similar to racism and sexism in its negative stereotypes.

Age-related positivity effect The relative preference in older adults for positive over negative information in attention and memory.

Aggression Any behavior intended to inflict psychological or physical harm on another individual.

Agonist drug A substance that binds to a receptor and mimics or enhances a neurotransmitter's effect.

AIDS (acquired immunodeficiency syndrome) A disease in which the human immunodeficiency virus (HIV) destroys the immune system's ability to fight other diseases, thus leaving the body vulnerable to a variety of opportunistic infections and cancers.

Algorithm A logical, step-by-step procedure that, if followed correctly, will always eventually solve the problem.

All-or-nothing principle The principle that a neuron's response to a stimulus is either to fire with a full-strength response or not to fire at all; also known as the all-or-none law.

Altered state of consciousness (ASC) A temporary mental state, other than ordinary waking consciousness, that includes sleep, dreaming, psychoactive drug use, meditation, and hypnosis.

Altruism Prosocial behaviors designed to help or benefit others.

Amygdala A part of the limbic system linked to the production and regulation of emotions—especially aggression and fear.

Androgyny [an-DRAH-juh-nee] A combination of both masculine and feminine characteristics and traits; from the Greek *andro* for "male" and *gyn* for "female."

Anorexia nervosa An eating disorder characterized by an obsessive fear of obesity, a need for control, self-imposed starvation, and a severe loss of weight.

Antagonist drug A substance that binds to a receptor and blocks a neurotransmitter's effect.

Anterograde amnesia The inability to form new memories; forward-acting amnesia.

Antisocial personality disorder (ASPD) A personality disorder characterized by egocentrism and a lack of conscience, remorse, or empathy for others.

Anxiety disorder One of a group of psychological disorders characterized by disabling (uncontrollable and disruptive) fear or anxiety, which interfere with daily functioning.

Applied research A type of research primarily conducted to solve practical, real-world problems; generally conducted outside the laboratory.

Approach–approach conflict A forced choice between two options, both of which have equally desirable characteristics.

Approach–avoidance conflict A forced choice involving one option with equally desirable and undesirable characteristics.

Archetypes Jung's term for the collective, universal images and patterns, residing in the unconscious, that have symbolic meaning for all people.

Archival research A descriptive research technique that studies existing data to find answers to research questions.

Artificial intelligence (AI) The scientific field concerned with creating machines that can simulate human thought processes and performance.

Asexual A sexual orientation in which a person does not experience erotic, sexual attraction to others, but may experience emotional or romantic attraction.

Assertiveness The behavior of confidently and directly standing up for your rights or putting forward your views without infringing on the rights or views of others; striking a balance between passivity and aggression.

Assimilation In Piaget's theory, the incorporation (assimilation) of new information into existing schemas.

Association areas The "quiet" areas in the cerebral cortex involved in interpreting, integrating, and acting on information processed by other parts of the brain.

Associative learning Learning that two stimuli or events occur or happen together.

Attachment A strong emotional bond with special others that endures over time.

Attention-deficit/hyperactivity disorder (ADHD) A common developmental disorder characterized by a pattern of inattention and hyperactivity-impulsivity.

Attitude A set of learned evaluations of a particular idea, object, person, or event.

Attribution The explanations we make about the causes of behaviors or events.

Audition The sense or act of hearing.

Autism spectrum disorder (ASD) A developmental disorder that typically begins in early childhood and involves problems with social communication and social interaction, as well as restricted, repetitive patterns of behavior, interests, or activities.

Automatic processes The mental activities that require minimal attention and generally have little impact on other activities.

Autonomic nervous system (ANS) The subdivision of the peripheral nervous system (PNS) that controls the body's involuntary motor responses by connecting the central nervous system (CNS) and the smooth muscles, cardiac muscle, and glands.

Availability heuristic A cognitive strategy (or shortcut) that involves estimating the frequency or likelihood of an event based on information that is readily available in our memory.

Aversion therapy A type of behavior therapy that pairs an aversive (unpleasant) stimulus with a maladaptive behavior in order to elicit a negative reaction to the target stimulus.

Avoidance–avoidance conflict A forced choice between two options, both of which have equally undesirable

Axon A long, tube-like structure that conveys impulses away from a neuron's cell body toward other neurons or to muscles or glands.

Basic anxiety According to Horney, adults experience feelings of helplessness and insecurity because as children they felt alone and isolated in a hostile environment.

Basic research A type of research primarily conducted to advance core scientific knowledge; most often conducted in universities and research laboratories.

Behavior therapies A group of therapies that uses learning principles to reduce or eliminate maladaptive behaviors; techniques are based on classical and operant conditioning, along with observational learning.

Behavioral genetics The study of the relative effects of heredity and the environment on behavior and mental processes.

Behavioral perspective A modern approach to psychology that emphasizes objective, observable environmental influences on overt behavior.

Binge-eating disorder An eating disorder characterized by recurrent episodes of consuming large amounts of food (bingeing), but not followed by purge behaviors.

Binocular cues Visual input from two eyes, which allows perception of depth or distance.

Biological perspective A modern approach to psychology that focuses on genetics and biological processes.

Biological preparedness The built-in (innate) readiness to form associations between certain stimuli and responses.

Biomedical therapies A group of therapies designed to alter brain functioning with biological or physical techniques, such as drugs, electroconvulsive therapy, and psychosurgery.

Biopsychosocial model Modern psychology's theme that sees biological, psychological, and social processes as interrelated and interacting influences.

Bipolar disorder A psychological disorder characterized by repeated episodes of mania (unreasonable elation, often with hyperactivity) alternating with depression.

Bisexual A sexual orientation in which a person is attracted (sexually, emotionally, and/or romantically) to both men and women.

Blind spot The point at which the optic nerve leaves the eye, which contains no receptor cells for vision—thus creating a "blind spot."

Borderline personality disorder (BPD) A psychological disorder characterized by severe instability in emotions, relationships, and self-image, along with impulsive and self-destructive behaviors.

Bottom-up processing Information processing that starts at the "bottom" with an analysis of smaller features and then builds on them to create complete perceptions; data-driven processing that moves from the parts to the whole.

Brainstem An area of the brain that includes much of the midbrain, pons, and medulla; responsible for automatic survival functions, such as respiration and heartbeat.

Bulimia nervosa An eating disorder characterized by recurrent episodes of consuming large quantities of food (bingeing), followed by self-induced vomiting, use of laxatives, and/or excessive exercise (purging).

Burnout A state of physical, mental, and emotional exhaustion resulting from chronic exposure to high levels of stress, with little personal control.

Bystander effect A phenomenon in which the greater the number of bystanders, the less likely it is that any one individual will feel responsible for seeking help or giving aid to someone who is in need of help.

Cannon-Bard theory A theory proposing that emotions and bodily changes occur simultaneously ("I'm crying and feeling sad at the same time"); bodily arousal plus brain processing occurring simultaneously is the basis for feeling emotions.

Case study A descriptive research technique involving an in-depth study of a single research participant or a small group of individuals.

Cataclysmic event A stressful occurrence that happens suddenly and generally affects many people simultaneously.

Cell body The part of a neuron that contains the cell nucleus and other structures that help the neuron carry out its functions; also known as the soma.

Central nervous system (CNS) The part of the nervous system consisting of the brain and spinal cord.

Cerebellum The hindbrain structure responsible for coordinating fine muscle movement, balance, and some perception and cognition.

Cerebral cortex The thin surface layer on the cerebral hemispheres that regulates most complex behavior, including sensations, motor control, and higher mental processes.

Character Value judgments about an individual's morals, values, and ethical behaviors, characteristics.

Child sexual abuse (CSA) Involving a child in sexual activity that he or she does not fully comprehend, is unable to give informed consent to, or for which the child is not developmentally prepared and cannot give consent,

Chromosome A thread-like molecule of DNA (deoxyribonucleic acid) that carries genetic information.

Chronic pain A continuous or recurrent pain experienced over a period of 6 months or longer.

Chronic stress A continuous state of arousal in which demands are perceived as greater than the inner and outer resources available for dealing with them.

Chunking A memory technique involving grouping separate pieces of information into larger, more manageable units (or chunks).

Circadian rhythm The internal, biological clock governing bodily activities, such as the sleep/wake cycle, and temperature, that occur on a 24- to 25-hour cycle. (*Circa* means "about," and *dies* means "day.")

Classical conditioning Learning that develops through involuntarily paired associations; a previously neutral stimulus (NS) is paired (associated) with an unconditioned stimulus (US) to elicit a conditioned response (CR).

Client-centered therapy A form of talk therapy, developed by Carl Rogers, that provides a warm, supportive atmosphere that encourages self-actualization and improves the client's self-concept; techniques include empathy, unconditional positive regard, genuineness, and active listening.

Cochlea [KOK-lee-uh] The fluid-filled, coiled tube in the inner ear that contains the receptors for hearing.

Coding The process in which neural impulses travel by different routes to different parts of the brain; it allows the brain to detect various physical stimuli as distinct sensations.

Cognition The mental activities involved in acquiring, storing, retrieving, and using knowledge

Cognitive dissonance The unpleasant psychological tension we experience after noticing contradictions between our thoughts, feelings, and/or actions.

Cognitive map A mental image of a three-dimensional space that an organism has navigated.

Cognitive offloading The use of external resources to decrease the information processing requirements of a task in order to reduce the cognitive demand.

Cognitive perspective A modern approach to psychology that focuses on the mental processes used in thinking, knowing, remembering, and communicating.

Cognitive restructuring A therapeutic process of learning to identify and dispute irrational or maladaptive thought patterns.

Cognitive therapies A group of talk therapies that focuses on changing faulty thought processes (cognitions); based on the assumption that thoughts intervene between events and reactions.

Cognitive view of dreams The perspective that dreaming is a type of information processing that helps us organize and interpret our everyday experiences.

Cognitive-behavior therapy (CBT) A type of therapy, developed by Aaron Beck, that combines cognitive therapy (changing faulty thinking) with behavior therapy (changing maladaptive behaviors).

Cognitive-social learning theory A theory that emphasizes the roles of thinking and social learning.

Collective unconscious Jung's name for the deepest layer of the unconscious, which contains universal memories and archetypes shared by all people due to our common ancestral past.

Comorbidity The co-occurrence of two or more disorders in the same person at the same time, as when a person suffers from both depression and alcoholism.

Companionate love According to Sternberg, feelings of attraction based on a combination of commitment and intimacy.

Compliance The act of either actively or passively agreeing to the requests of others.

Concrete operational stage Piaget's third stage of cognitive development (roughly ages 7–11), in which the child can think logically about concrete, tangible objects and events.

Conditioned emotional response (CER) An emotion, such as fear, that becomes a learned, conditioned response to a previously neutral stimulus (NS), such as a loud noise.

Conditioned response (CR) A learned reaction to a conditioned stimulus (CS) that occurs after previous repeated pairings with an unconditioned stimulus (US).

Conditioned stimulus (CS) A previously neutral stimulus (NS) that, after repeated pairings with an unconditioned stimulus (US), comes to elicit a conditioned response (CR).

Conditioning The process of learning associations between stimuli and behavioral responses.

Conduction hearing loss A type of hearing loss that results from damage to the mechanical system that conducts sound waves to the cochlea; also called conduction deafness.

Cones Retinal receptor cells with high sensitivity to color and detail, but low sensitivity in dim light.

Confirmation bias The tendency to prefer information that confirms our preexisting positions or beliefs and to ignore or discount contradictory evidence; also known as remembering the "hits" and ignoring the "misses."

Conformity A change in thoughts, feelings, or actions due to real or imagined group pressure.

Confounding variable An extraneous factor that, if not held constant, may contaminate, or confound, the experimental results; also known as the third-variable problem in correlational research.

Conscious In Freudian terms, thoughts or motives that a person is currently aware of or is remembering.

Consciousness Our awareness of ourselves and our environment.

Conservation According to Piaget, the understanding that certain physical characteristics (such as volume) remain unchanged, even though appearances may change; a hallmark of Piaget's concrete operational stage.

Consolidation The process by which LTM memories become stable in the brain; neural changes that take place when a memory is formed.

Constructive process The process of organizing and shaping information during encoding, storage, and retrieval of memories.

Consummate love Sternberg's strongest and most enduring type of love, based on a balanced combination of intimacy, passion, and commitment.

Continuous reinforcement A pattern in which every correct response is reinforced.

Control group The group that is not manipulated (i.e., receives no treatment) during an experiment; participants who are NOT exposed to the independent variable (IV).

Controlled processes The mental activities that require focused attention and generally interfere with other ongoing activities.

Convergent thinking A type of thinking that seeks the single best solution to a problem.

Corpus callosum A bundle of neural fibers that connects the brain's two hemispheres.

Correlation coefficient A number from −1.00 to +1.00 that indicates the direction and strength of the relationship between two variables.

Correlational research A type of research that examines possible relations between variables; designed to meet the goal of *prediction*.

Creativity The ability to produce original, appropriate, and valued outcomes in a novel way; it has three characteristics originality, fluency, and flexibility.

Critical period A specific time during which an organism must experience certain stimuli in order to develop properly in the future.

Critical thinking The process of objectively evaluating, comparing, analyzing, and synthesizing information.

Cross-sectional design In developmental psychology, a research technique that measures individuals of various ages at one point in time and provides information about age differences.

Crystallized intelligence (gc) The store of knowledge and skills gained through experience and education; it tends to increase over the life span.

Debriefing A discussion procedure conducted at the end of an experiment or study; participants are informed of the study's design and purpose, possible misconceptions are clarified, questions are answered, and explanations are provided for any possible deception.

Defense mechanisms Freud's term for the strategies the ego uses to reduce anxiety, which distort reality and may increase self-deception.

Dehumanization The process of depriving a person or group of positive human qualities.

Deindividuation The reduced self-consciousness, inhibition, and personal responsibility that sometimes occurs in a group, particularly when the members feel anonymous.

Delusion A false, imaginary belief that persists despite clear evidence to the contrary, such as delusions of grandeur or persecution; a symptom associated with psychosis.

Demand characteristics Any aspect of a study that unknowingly communicates to participants how the experimenter wants them to behave; either the researcher or subtle cues or signals within the study, create an implicit *demand* for how participants should behave.

Dendrites The branching fibers of a neuron that receive information (signals) from other neurons and convey impulses toward the cell body.

Dependent variable (DV) The variable that is observed and measured for change; the factor that is affected by (or dependent on) the independent variable.

Depressant A drug that decreases bodily processes and overall responsiveness.

Depth perception The ability to perceive three-dimensional space and to accurately judge distance.

Descriptive research A type of research that systematically observes and records behavior and mental processes without manipulating variables; designed to meet the goal of *description*.

Descriptive statistics Mathematical methods used to describe and summarize sets of data in a meaningful way.

Developmental psychology The study of age-related behavior and mental processes from conception to death.

Diagnostic and Statistical Manual of Mental Disorders (DSM) A manual developed by the American Psychiatric Association that is used primarily to classify psychological disorders.

Difference threshold The smallest physical difference between two stimuli that is consciously detectable 50 percent of the time; also called the *just noticeable difference (JND)*.

Diffusion of responsibility The dilution (diffusion) of personal responsibility for acting when others are present.

Discrimination An unjustifiable, negative action directed toward members of a group; also the behavioral component of prejudice.

Discrimination (in classical conditioning) A learned ability to distinguish (discriminate) between similar stimuli so as NOT to involuntarily respond to a new stimulus as if it were the previously conditioned stimulus (CS); the opposite of generalization.

Discrimination (in operant conditioning) A learned ability to distinguish (discriminate) between similar stimuli based on whether the response to the stimuli is reinforced or punished, and then to voluntarily respond accordingly; the opposite of generalization.

Display rules A set of informal cultural norms that control when, where, and how emotions should be expressed.

Dissociative disorder One of a group of psychological disorders characterized by a sudden break (*dissociation*) in conscious awareness, self-identity, and memory.

Dissociative identity disorder (DID) A psychological disorder characterized by the presence of two or more distinct personality systems (or identities) in the same individual; previously known as multiple personality disorder (MPD).

Distress The unpleasant, undesirable stress caused by aversive conditions.

Distributed practice A learning strategy in which studying or practice is broken up into a number of short sessions over a period of time; also known as spaced repetition.

Divergent thinking A type of thinking that produces many solutions to the same problem.

DNA The main constituent of chromosomes found in all living organisms, which transmits hereditary characteristics from parents to children; short for *deoxyribonucleic acid*.

Double standard The beliefs, values, and norms that subtly encourage male sexuality and discourage female sexuality.

Double-blind study An experimental technique in which both the participants and the researcher(s) are unaware of (blind to) who is in the experimental and control groups.

Dream analysis In psychoanalysis, interpretation of the underlying true meaning of dreams to reveal unconscious processes.

Drive-reduction theory The theory that motivation begins with a physiological need (a lack or deficiency) that elicits a drive toward behavior that will satisfy the original need; once the need is met, a state of balance (homeostasis) is restored, and motivation decreases.

Drug abuse A type of drug taking that leads to emotional or physical harm to the drug user or others.

Eclectic approach A perspective that combines elements of various therapies to find the most appropriate treatment; also known as integrative therapy.

Ego In Freud's theory, the second personality structure that is largely conscious, and the "executive," which deals with the demands of reality; it operates on the reality principle.

Egocentrism In cognitive development, the inability to take the perspective of another person; a hallmark of Piaget's preoperational stage.

Egoistic model of helping A proposed explanation for helping that suggests we help because of anticipated gain—later reciprocation, increased self-esteem, and/or avoidance of distress and guilt.

Elaborative rehearsal A process of forming numerous connections of new information to material already stored in long-term memory (LTM); a memory improvement technique that makes information more meaningful and the memory more durable and lasting.

Electroconvulsive therapy (ECT) A biomedical therapy based on passing electrical current through the brain; it is used almost exclusively to treat serious depression when drugs and psychotherapy have failed.

Embryonic period The second stage of prenatal development, which begins after uterine implantation and lasts through the eighth week.

Emerging adulthood The age period from approximately 18–25 in which individuals in modern cultures have left the dependency of childhood, but not yet assumed adult responsibilities.

Emotion A complex pattern of feelings that includes arousal (heart pounding), cognitions (thoughts, values, and expectations), and expressive behaviors (smiles, frowns, and gestures).

Emotional Intelligence (EI) The ability to perceive, understand, manage, and utilize emotions accurately and appropriately.

Emotion-focused coping The strategies we use to relieve or regulate our emotional reactions to a stressful situation.

Empathy In Rogerian terms, a sensitive understanding and sharing of another's inner experience.

Empathy–altruism hypothesis A proposed explanation for helping that suggests we help due to empathy for someone in need.

Encoding The first step of the ESR memory model; the process of moving sensory information into memory storage.

Encoding, storage, and retrieval (ESR) model A memory model that involves three processes: *encoding* (getting information in), *storage* (retaining information for future use), and *retrieval* (recovering information).

Encoding-specificity principle The principle that retrieval of information is improved if cues received at the time of recall are consistent with those present at the time of encoding.

Endocrine system A network of glands located throughout the body that manufacture and secrete hormones into the bloodstream.

Endorphin A chemical substance in the nervous system similar in structure and action to opiates; involved in pain control, pleasure, and memory.

Epigenetics The study of how non-genetic factors, such as age, environment, lifestyle, or disease, affect how (and if) genes are expressed; "epi" means "above" or "outside of."

Episodic memory A subsystem of long-term memory (LTM) that stores autobiographical events and the contexts in which they occurred; a mental diary of a person's life.

Ethnocentrism The belief that one's culture is typical of all cultures; also, viewing one's own ethnic group (or culture) as central and "correct" and judging others according to this standard.

Eustress The pleasant, desirable stress that arouses us to persevere and accomplish challenging goals.

Evidence-based practice in psychology (EBPP) A therapy approach that integrates the best available evidence with clinicians' expertise, along with the clients' characteristics, culture, and preferences.

Evolutionary perspective A modern approach to psychology that stresses natural selection, adaptation, and reproduction.

Evolutionary theory of helping A theory suggesting that altruism is an instinctual behavior, which has evolved because it favors survival of the helper's genes.

Excitement phase The first stage of the sexual response cycle, characterized by increasing levels of arousal and engorgement of the genitals.

Executive functions (EFs) A set of higher-order cognitive processes controlled by the brain's frontal lobes.

Experiment A careful manipulation of one or more independent variables to measure their effect on other dependent variables; allows the determination of cause and- effect relationships.

Experimental group The group that is manipulated (i.e., receives treatment) in an experiment; participants who are exposed to the independent variable (IV).

Experimental research A type of research that involves the manipulation and control of variables to determine cause and effect; designed to meet the goal of *explanation*.

Experimenter bias A problem that occurs when the experimenter's behavior and/or expectations inadvertently influence (bias) the outcome of the research.

Explicit/declarative memory A subsystem within long-term memory (LTM) that involves conscious, easily described (declared) memories; it consists of semantic memories (facts) and episodic memories (personal experiences).

External locus of control The belief that chance or outside forces beyond our control determine our fate.

Extinction (in classical conditioning) The gradual diminishing of a conditioned response (CR) when the unconditioned stimulus (US) is withheld or removed.

Extinction (in operant conditioning) The gradual diminishing of a conditioned response when it is no longer reinforced.

Extrasensory perception (ESP) The perceptual, so-called "psychic," abilities that supposedly go beyond the known senses (e.g., telepathy, clairvoyance, and precognition).

Extrinsic motivation A type of motivation for a task or activity based on external incentives, such as rewards and punishments.

Feature detectors Neurons in the brain's visual system that respond to specific characteristics of stimuli, such as shape, angle, or movement.

Fetal period The third, and final, stage of prenatal development (8 weeks to birth).

Five-factor model (FFM) A model of personality traits that includes five basic dimensions: openness, conscientiousness, extraversion, agreeableness, and neuroticism; informally called the Big Five.

Fixed interval (FI) schedule A pattern in which a reinforcer is delivered for the first response made after a fixed period of time.

Fixed ratio (FR) schedule A pattern in which a reinforcer is delivered for the first response made after a fixed number of responses.

Flashbulb memory (FBM) A vivid, detailed, and near-permanent memory of an emotionally significant moment or event; memory resulting from a form of automatic encoding, storage, and later retrieval.

Fluid intelligence (*gf*) The ability to think speedily and abstractly and to solve novel problems; it tends to decrease over the life span.

Forebrain The collection of upper-level brain structures including the cerebral cortex, limbic system, thalamus, and hypothalamus.

Formal operational stage Piaget's fourth stage of cognitive development (around age 11 and beyond), characterized by abstract and hypothetical thinking.

Fovea A tiny pit in the center of the retina that is densely filled with cones; it is responsible for sharp vision.

Free association In psychoanalysis, reporting whatever comes to mind without monitoring its contents.

Frequency theory for hearing The theory that pitch perception depends on how often the auditory nerve fires.

Frontal lobes The two lobes at the front of the brain that govern motor control, speech production, and higher cognitive processes, such as executive functions, intelligence, and personality.

Frustration A negative emotional state resulting from a blocked goal.

Functional fixedness A barrier to problem solving that comes from thinking about objects as functioning only in their usual or customary way.

Functionalism James's approach that explored how mental and behavioral processes function to enable organisms to adapt to the environment.

Fundamental attribution error (FAE) The tendency of observers to overestimate the influence of internal, dispositional factors on a person's behavior, while underestimating the impact of external, situational factors.

Gate control theory of pain The theory that pain sensations are processed and altered by certain cells in the spinal cord, which act as gates to interrupt and block some pain signals while sending others on to the brain.

Gender The psychological and sociocultural traits typically associated with a person's biological sex, such as masculinity or femininity.

Gender expression The outward display of one's gender identity, including choice of hairstyles, clothing, and pronouns.

Gender identity The self-identification as being a man or a woman or some position between the two.

Gender roles The psychological and sociocultural prescriptions and beliefs about the "appropriate" thoughts, feelings, and actions of men and women, also known as sex roles.

Gender-role stereotypes Oversimplified or unfair beliefs and expectations about typical thoughts, feelings, and actions

Gene A segment of DNA (deoxyribonucleic acid) that occupies a specific place on a particular chromosome, and carries the code for hereditary transmission.

General adaptation syndrome (GAS) Selye's three-stage (alarm, resistance, exhaustion) reaction to chronic stress; a pattern of non-specific, adaptational responses to a continuing stressor.

General intelligence (*g*) Spearman's term for a common skill set that underlies all intellectual behavior.

Generalization (in classical conditioning) A conditioned response (CR) spreads (generalizes) and comes to be involuntarily elicited not only by the conditioned stimulus (CS) but also by stimuli similar to the CS; the opposite of discrimination.

Generalization (in operant conditioning) Voluntarily responding to a new stimulus as if it were the original, previously conditioned stimulus (CS); the opposite of discrimination.

Generalized anxiety disorder (GAD) An anxiety disorder characterized by persistent, uncontrollable, and free-floating non-specified anxiety.

Genuineness In Rogerian terms, being personally authentic and sincere; the awareness of one's true inner thoughts and feelings and the ability to share them honestly with others.

Germinal period The first stage of prenatal development, beginning with ovulation and followed by conception and implantation in the uterus; the first 2 weeks of pregnancy.

Glial cells The cells that provide structural, nutritional, and other functions for neurons; also called glia or neuroglia.

Grammar The set of rules (syntax and semantics) governing the use and structure of language.

Group polarization The tendency for the decisions and opinions of group members to become more extreme (either riskier or more conservative), depending on the members' initial dominant tendency.

Group therapies A form of therapy in which a number of people with similar concerns meet together with a professional to work toward therapeutic goals.

Groupthink The faulty decision making that occurs when maintaining group harmony becomes more important than making a good decision.

Growth/development theory of sleep The theory that sleep is correlated with changes in the structure and organization of the brain due to growth and development.

Gustation The sense or act of tasting; receptors are located in the tongue's taste buds.

Habituation The brain's learned tendency to ignore or stop responding to unchanging information; an example of top-down processing.

Hallucination A false, imaginary sensory perception that occurs without an external, objective source, such as hearing voices that others cannot hear; a symptom associated with psychosis.

Hallucinogen A drug that produces sensory or perceptual distortions.

Hassles The small problems of daily living that may accumulate and become a major source of stress.

Health psychology A subfield of psychology that studies how biological, psychological, and social factors influence health, illness, and health-related behaviors.

Herd immunity A type of indirect protection from infectious diseases that results when most people in a given population become immune, particularly as a result of vaccination.

Heterosexual A sexual orientation in which a person is attracted (sexually, emotionally, and/or romantically) to people of another biological sex.

Heuristic An educated guess, or "rule of thumb," often used as a shortcut for problem solving; it does not guarantee a solution to a problem but does narrow the alternatives.

Hierarchy of needs Maslow's view that basic human motives form a hierarchy; the lower motives (such as physiological and safety needs) must be met before advancing to higher needs (such as belonging and self-actualization).

Higher-order conditioning A new conditioned stimulus (CS) is created through pairing with a previously conditioned stimulus (CS); also known as second-order conditioning.

Hindbrain The lower or hind region of the brain; a collection of structures including the medulla, pons, and cerebellum.

Hippocampus The seahorseshaped part of the limbic system involved in forming and retrieving memories.

HIV positive The state of being infected by the human immunodeficiency virus (HIV).

Homeostasis Our body's tendency to maintain equilibrium, or a steady state of internal balance.

Hormone Chemical messengers manufactured and secreted by the endocrine glands, which circulate in the bloodstream to produce bodily changes or maintain normal bodily functions.

HPA axis Our body's delayed stress response, involving the hypothalamus, pituitary, and adrenal cortex; also called the hypothalamic–pituitary–adrenocortical (HPA) axis.

Humanistic perspective A modern approach to psychology that perceives human nature as naturally positive and growth seeking; it emphasizes free will and self-actualization.

Humanistic therapies A group of talk therapies that emphasizes maximizing a client's inherent capacity for self-actualization by providing a non-judgmental, accepting atmosphere.

Hypnosis An altered state of consciousness (ASC) characterized by deep relaxation and a trance-like state of heightened suggestibility and intense focus.

Hypothalamus The small forebrain structure beneath the thalamus that helps govern the endocrine system (e.g., temperature), motives or drives (e.g., hunger, thirst, sex), and is linked to emotions and the reward system.

Hypothesis A tentative and testable statement and possible explanation about the relationship between two or more variables; an educated guess about the outcome of a scientific study.

Id According to Freud, the first personality structure that is present at birth, completely unconscious, and striving to meet basic drives, such as hunger, thirst, sex, and aggression; it operates on the pleasure principle.

Illusion A false or misleading perception shared by others in the same perceptual environment.

Illusory correlation A mistaken perception that a relationship exists between variables when no such relationship actually exists.

Implicit bias A hidden, automatic attitude that may guide behaviors independent of a person's awareness or control.

Implicit/nondeclarative memory A subsystem within long-term memory (LTM) that contains memories independent of conscious recall; it consists of procedural motor skills, priming, and simple classically conditioned responses.

Imprinting The process by which attachments are formed during critical periods in early life.

Inattentional blindness The failure to notice a fully visible, but unexpected, stimulus when our attention is directed elsewhere; also known as perceptual blindness.

Incentive theory The theory that motivation results from external stimuli that "pull" an organism in certain directions.

Independent variable (IV) The variable that is manipulated and controlled by the experimenter to determine its causal effect on the dependent variable; also called the treatment variable.

Inferential statistics Mathematical procedures that provide a measure of confidence about how likely it is that a certain result appeared by chance.

Inferiority complex Adler's idea that feelings of inferiority develop from early childhood experiences of helplessness and incompetence.

Informational social influence A type of conforming based on the need for information and direction.

Informed consent A participant's agreement to take part in a study after being told what to expect.

Ingroup favoritism The tendency to judge members of the ingroup more positively than members of an outgroup.

Inner ear The semicircular canals, vestibular sacs, and cochlea, which generate neural signals that are sent to the brain.

Insanity The legal (not clinical) designation for a situation in which an individual cannot be held responsible for his or her actions or is incompetent to manage his or her own affairs because of mental illness; inability to tell right from wrong.

Insight A sudden understanding or realization of how a problem can be solved.

Insomnia A sleep disorder characterized by persistent problems in falling asleep, staying asleep, or awakening too early.

Instinct The fixed, unlearned response patterns found in almost all members of a species.

Instinctive drift The tendency for conditioned responses to revert (drift back) to innate response patterns.

Intelligence The global capacity to think rationally, act purposefully, profit from experience, and deal effectively with the environment.

Intelligence quotient (IQ) An index of intelligence initially derived from standardized tests, computed by dividing mental age (MA) by chronological age (CA) and then multiplying by

100; it is now derived by comparing individual scores with the scores of others of the same age.

Interactionism The theory that behaviors are determined by an interaction between situations and the personality traits a person possesses.

Internal locus of control The belief that we control our own fate.

Interpretation A psychoanalyst's explanation of a client's free associations, dreams, resistance, and transference; more generally, any statement by a therapist that presents a problem in a new way.

Intersex A person with reproductive or sexual anatomy that doesn't clearly fall into either category of biologically male or female.

Intrinsic motivation A type of motivation for a task or activity based on internal incentives, such as enjoyment and personal satisfaction.

James-Lange theory A theory of emotion suggesting that the subjective experience of emotion results from bodily arousal, rather than being its cause ("I feel sad because I'm crying"); bodily arousal is the basis for feeling emotions.

Kinesthesis The sense that provides information about the location, orientation, and movement of individual body parts relative to each other; receptors are located in muscles, joints, and tendons.

Language A form of communication using sounds or symbols combined according to specified rules.

Language acquisition device (LAD) According to Chomsky, an innate mechanism within the brain that enables a child to analyze language and extract the basic rule of grammar.

Latent content of dreams According to Freud, a dream's unconscious, hidden meaning is disguised in symbols within the dream's manifest content (story line).

Latent learning Hidden learning that exists without behavioral signs.

Law of effect Thorndike's rule that any behavior followed by pleasant consequences is likely to be repeated, whereas any behavior followed by unpleasant consequences is likely to be reduced.

Learned helplessness Seligman's term for a state of helplessness, or resignation, in which human or non-human animals fail to act to escape from a situation due to a history of repeated failures in the past.

Learning A relatively permanent change in behavior or mental processes resulting from experience.

Learning/memory theory of sleep The theory that sleep is important for learning and for the consolidation, storage, and maintenance of memories.

Lesbian/Gay A sexual orientation in which a person is attracted (sexually, emotionally, and/or romantically) to people of the same biological sex.

Levels of processing model A model of memory based on a continuum of memory processing ranging from shallow to intermediate to deep, with deeper processing leading to improved encoding, storage, and retrieval.

Limbic system The interconnected group of forebrain structures involved with emotions, drives, and memory; its two most important structures are the hippocampus and amygdala.

Lobotomy An outmoded neurosurgical procedure for mental disorders, which involved cutting nerve pathways between the frontal lobes and the thalamus and hypothalamus.

Longitudinal design In developmental psychology, a research design that measures individuals over an extended period and gives information about age changes.

Long-term memory (LTM) The third stage of memory, which stores information for long periods of time; the capacity is virtually limitless, and the duration is relatively permanent.

Long-term potentiation (LTP) A long-lasting increase in neural sensitivity; a biological mechanism for learning and memory.

Maintenance rehearsal The act of repeating information over and over to maintain it in short-term memory (STM).

Major depressive disorder (MDD) A psychological disorder characterized by significant depressive symptoms, such as sadness, lethargy, or loss of pleasure, lasting for two weeks or more.

Mania A state of abnormally elevated mood (either euphoric or irritable); also characterized by mental and physical hyperactivity, insomnia, and poor judgment.

Manifest content of dreams In Freudian dream analysis, the "surface," or remembered, story line, which contains symbols that mask the dream's latent content (the true meaning).

Massed practice A study technique in which time spent learning is grouped (or massed) into long unbroken intervals; also called "cramming."

Mean The arithmetic average of a distribution, which is obtained by adding the values of all the scores and dividing by the number of scores (N).

Median The halfway point in a set of data; half the scores fall above the median, and half fall below it.

Meditation A group of techniques generally designed to focus attention, block out distractions, and produce an altered state of consciousness (ASC); it's believed to enhance self-knowledge and well-being through reduced self-awareness.

Medulla The hindbrain structure responsible for vital automatic functions, such as respiration and heartbeat.

Memory The persistence of learning over time; the process by which information is encoded, stored, and retrieved.

Mental age (MA) An individual's level of mental development relative to that of others; it was initially compared to chronological age (CA) to calculate IQ.

Mental set A fixed-thinking approach to problem solving that sees only solutions that have worked in the past.

Meta-analysis A statistical technique for combining and analyzing data from many studies in order to determine overall trends.

Midbrain The collection of structures in the middle of the brain responsible for coordinating movement patterns, sleep, and arousal.

Middle ear The hammer, anvil, and stirrup structures of the ear, which concentrate eardrum vibrations onto the cochlea's oval window.

Mindfulness-based cognitive therapy (MBCT) A therapy based on non-judgmental awareness of current events; a blend of cognitive therapy and meditation.

Mindfulness-based stress reduction (MBSR) A stress reduction strategy based on developing a state of consciousness that attends to ongoing events in a receptive and non-judgmental way.

Minnesota Multiphasic Personality Inventory (MMPI) The most widely researched and clinically used self-report method of personality assessment; originally designed to reveal abnormal personality traits and behaviors, it's also used for various screening purposes.

Mirror neurons Neurons that fire (or are activated) when an action is performed, as well as when the actions or emotions of another are observed; believed to be responsible for empathy, imitation, language, and the deficits of some mental disorders.

Misinformation effect A memory error resulting from misleading information being presented after an event, which alters memories of the event itself.

Mnemonic A strategic device that makes use of familiar information during the encoding of new information to enhance later recall.

Mode The score that occurs most frequently in a data set.

Modeling therapy A type of therapy characterized by watching and imitating models that demonstrate desirable behaviors.

Monocular cues Visual input from a single eye alone that contributes to perception of depth or distance.

Morality The ability to take the perspective of, or empathize with, others and to distinguish right from wrong.

Morpheme The smallest meaningful unit of language, formed from a combination of phonemes.

Motivation A set of factors that activate, direct, and maintain behavior, usually toward some goal.

Myelin sheath The layer of fatty insulation wrapped around the axon of some neurons that increases the rate at which neural impulses travel.

Narcolepsy A sleep disorder characterized by uncontrollable sleep attacks. (*Narco* means "numbness," and *lepsy* means "seizure.")

Natural selection Darwin's principle of an evolutionary process in which heritable traits that increase an organism's chances of survival or reproduction are more likely to be passed on to succeeding generations.

Nature–nurture controversy An ongoing dispute about the relative contributions of nature (biological and genetic factors) and nurture (environment and learning) in behavior and mental processes.

Negative punishment A process by which taking away (or removing) a stimulus following a response decreases the likelihood that the response will be repeated.

Negative reinforcement A process by which taking away (or removing) a stimulus following a response increases the likelihood that the response will be repeated.

Neurodevelopmental disorders A group of disorders that usually begin in early life, causing problems with communication, cognitive abilities, social relationships, and behavior.

Neurogenesis The formation (generation) of new neurons.

Neuron The basic building block (nerve cell) of the nervous system; responsible for receiving, integrating, and transmitting electrochemical information.

Neuroplasticity The brain's lifelong ability to reorganize and change its structure and function by forming new neural connections.

Neurotransmitter A chemical messenger released by neurons that travels across the synapse allowing neurons to communicate with one another.

Neutral stimulus (NS) A stimulus that, before conditioning, does not naturally bring about the response of interest.

Nightmares The anxiety-arousing dreams that generally occur near the end of the sleep cycle, during REM sleep.

Non-rapid-eye-movement (NREM) sleep The sleep stages (1 through 3) during which a sleeper does not show rapid eye movements.

Nonsuicidal self-injury (NSSI) A serious behavior problem in which people deliberately harm themselves without lethal intent.

Normal distribution A statistical term used to describe how traits are distributed within a population; IQ scores usually form a symmetrical, bell-shaped curve, with most scores falling near the average, and fewer scores near the extremes.

Normal distribution A symmetrical, bell-shaped curve that represents a set of data in which most scores occur in the middle of the possible range, with fewer and fewer scores near the extremes.

Normative social influence A type of conforming based on the need to be liked, accepted, and approved of by others.

Obedience The act of following direct commands, usually from an authority figure.

Obesity An eating problem involving a body mass index of 30 or above, based on height and weight.

Object permanence According to Piaget, an understanding that objects continue to exist even when they cannot be seen, heard, or touched directly; a hallmark of Piaget's preoperational stage.

Observation A descriptive research technique that assesses and records behavior and mental processes in natural, real-world and/or laboratory settings.

Observational learning The learning of new behaviors or information by watching and imitating others (also known as social learning or modeling).

Obsessive-compulsive disorder (OCD) A psychological disorder characterized by persistent, unwanted, fearful thoughts (obsessions) and irresistible urges to perform repetitive and ritualized behaviors (compulsions).

Occipital lobes The two lobes at the back of the brain that are primarily responsible for vision and visual perception.

Oedipus complex According to Freud, during the phallic stage (ages 3 to 6 years), a young boy develops a sexual attraction to his mother and rivalry with his father.

Olfaction The sense or act of smelling; receptors are located in the nose's nasal cavity.

Operant conditioning Learning through voluntary behavior and its subsequent consequences; consequences that are reinforcing increase behavioral tendencies, whereas consequences that are punishing decrease them.

Operational definition A precise description of how the variables in a study will be observed, manipulated, and measured.

Opiate/opioid A drug derived from opium that numbs the senses and relieves pain.

Opponent-process theory of color The theory that all color perception is based on three systems, each of which contains two color opposites (red versus green, blue versus yellow, and black versus white).

Optimal-arousal theory The theory that organisms are motivated to achieve and maintain an optimal level of arousal, which maximizes their performance.

Optimism A tendency to expect the best and to see the best in all things.

Orgasm phase The third stage of the sexual response cycle, when pleasurable sensations peak and orgasm occurs.

Outer ear The pinna, auditory canal, and eardrum structures, which funnel sound waves to the middle ear.

Outgroup homogeneity effect The tendency to judge members of an outgroup as more alike and less diverse than members of the ingroup.

Pair bonding The formation of enduring relationships between adult mates.

Panic disorder An anxiety disorder in which sufferers experience repeated sudden onsets of intense terror and inexplicable panic attacks; symptoms include severe heart palpitations, dizziness, trembling, difficulty breathing, and feelings of impending doom.

Pansexual A sexual orientation in which a person is attracted to members of all genders, as well as to those who do not feel that they have a gender.

Parallel distributed processing (PDP) model The theory that memory is stored throughout the brain in web-like connections among interacting processing units operating simultaneously, rather than sequentially; also known as connectionism.

Paraphilic disorder Any of a group of psychosexual disorders involving disturbing and repetitive sexual fantasies, urges, or behaviors that lead to distress or impairment to the person or harm or risk of harm to others.

Parasympathetic nervous system The subdivision of the autonomic nervous system (ANS) that is responsible for calming the body and conserving energy.

Parietal lobes The two lobes located at the top of the brain in which bodily sensations are received and interpreted.

Partial (intermittent) reinforcement A pattern in which some, but not all, correct responses are reinforced.

Participant bias A problem that occurs when a research participant's behavior and/or expectations inadvertently influence (bias) the outcome of the research.

Perception The process of selecting, organizing, and interpreting sensory information into meaningful objects and events.

Perceptual constancy The tendency to perceive the environment as stable, despite changes in the sensory input.

Perceptual set The readiness to perceive in a particular manner, based on expectations.

Performance anxiety The fear of being judged in connection with sexual activities.

Peripheral nervous system (PNS) The part of the nervous system composed of the nerves connecting the central nervous system (CNS) to the rest of the body.

Person perception The mental processes we use to form impressions of others.

Personality Our unique and relatively stable pattern of thoughts, feelings, and actions.

Personality disorder A psychological disorder characterized by chronic, inflexible, maladaptive personality traits, which contribute to significant impairment of social and occupational functioning.

Pheromones [FARE-oh-mones] Chemical signals released by organisms that trigger certain responses, such as aggression or sexual mating, in other members of the same species.

Phobia A persistent, intense, irrational fear and avoidance of a specific object, activity, or situation.

Phoneme The smallest basic unit of speech or sound in any given language.

Physical dependence The changes in bodily processes that make a drug necessary for minimal functioning.

Place theory for hearing The theory that pitch perception is linked to the particular spot on the cochlea's basilar membrane that is most stimulated.

Placebo An inactive substance or fake treatment used as a control technique in experiments; often used in drug research.

Placebo effect A change that occurs when a participant's expectations or beliefs, rather than the actual drug or treatment, influences the experimental outcome.

Plateau phase The second stage of the sexual response cycle; period of sexual excitement prior to orgasm.

Polygraph An instrument that measures sympathetic arousal (heart rate, respiration rate, blood pressure, and skin conductivity) to detect emotional arousal, which in turn supposedly reflects lying versus truthfulness.

Pons The hindbrain structure involved in respiration, movement, waking, sleep, and dreaming.

Positive affect The experience or expression of positive feelings (affect), including happiness, joy, enthusiasm, and contentment.

Positive psychology The study of optimal human functioning; emphasizes positive emotions, traits, and institutions.

Positive punishment A process by which adding (or presenting) a stimulus following a response decreases the likelihood that the response will be repeated.

Positive reinforcement A process by which adding (or presenting) a stimulus following a response increases the likelihood that the response will be repeated.

Posttraumatic stress disorder (PTSD) A long-lasting, trauma and stressor-related disorder that overwhelms an individual's ability to cope.

Preconscious Freud's term for thoughts, motives, or memories that exist just beneath the surface of awareness and can be called to consciousness when necessary.

Prejudice A learned, unjustified negative attitude toward members of a particular group; it includes thoughts (stereotypes), feelings, and behavioral tendencies (discrimination).

Preoperational stage Piaget's second stage of cognitive development (roughly ages 2–7); it is characterized by significant language, but the child lacks operations (reversible mental processes), and thinking is egocentric and animistic.

Primary punisher Any unlearned, innate stimulus, such as hunger or thirst, that punishes a response and thus decreases the probability that it will recur.

Primary reinforcer Any unlearned, innate stimulus (like food, water, or sex) that reinforces a response and thus increases the probability that it will recur.

Priming A form of memory activation that supposedly occurs when exposure (often unconscious) to previously stored information predisposes (or *primes*) our response to related stimuli.

Proactive interference A memory problem that occurs when old information disrupts (*interferes* with) the recall of new information; forward-acting interference.

Problem-focused coping The strategies we use to deal directly with a stressor to eventually decrease or eliminate it.

Projective test A method of personality assessment that uses a standardized set of ambiguous stimuli, such as inkblots or abstract drawings, which allow test takers to "project" their underlying motives, conflicts, and personality traits onto the test materials.

Prototype A mental image or best example that embodies the most typical features of a concept or category.

Psychiatry The branch of medicine that deals with the diagnosis, treatment, and prevention of mental disorders.

Psychoactive drug A chemical that changes mental processes, such as conscious awareness, mood, and perception.

Psychoanalysis A type of talk therapy, originated by Sigmund Freud, that emphasizes analysis and bringing unconscious thoughts and conflicts into conscious awareness.

Psychodynamic perspective A modern approach to psychology that emphasizes unconscious dynamics—motives, conflicts, and past experiences; based on the psychoanalytic approach.

Psychodynamic therapies A newer group of talk therapies that focuses on conscious processes and current problems; briefer, more directive, and more modern forms of psychoanalysis.

Psychological dependence The psychological desire or craving to achieve a drug's effect.

Psychological disorder Patterns of behaviors, thoughts, or emotions considered pathological (diseased or disordered) for one or more of three reasons: deviance, dysfunction, and distress.

Psychology The scientific study of behavior and mental processes.

Psychoneuroimmunology The interdisciplinary field that studies the effects of psychological and other factors on the immune system.

Psychopharmacology The use of drugs to relieve or control the major symptoms of psychological disorders.

Psychophysics The study of the link between the physical characteristics of stimuli and the psychological experience of them.

Psychosexual stages In Freudian theory, five developmental periods (oral, anal, phallic, latency, and genital) during which particular kinds of pleasures must be gratified if personality development is to proceed normally.

Psychosis A serious psychological condition in which thoughts and perceptions are so impaired that the individual loses contact with external reality.

Psychosocial stages Erikson's theory that identifies eight developmental stages, each involving a crisis that must be successfully resolved for proper future development.

Psychosurgery A form of biomedical therapy that involves alteration of the brain to bring about desirable behavioral, cognitive, or emotional changes; generally used when clients have not responded to other forms of treatment.

Psychotherapy Any of a group of therapies used to treat psychological disorders and to improve psychological functioning and adjustment to life.

Puberty The biological changes during adolescence that lead to sexual maturation and the ability to reproduce.

Punishment   Adding or removing a stimulus following a response and thereby decreasing the likelihood that the response will be repeated.

Random assignment   A research technique for assigning participants to experimental or control conditions so that each participant has an equal chance of being in either group; minimizes the possibility of biases or preexisting differences within or between the groups.

Random sample   A sample that allows each member of the population of interest an equal chance of being selected.

Range   A measure of the dispersion of scores between the highest and lowest scores.

Rape   The unlawful act of coercing oral, anal, or vaginal penetration upon a person through force or threat of force or without consent, or upon someone incapable of giving consent (due to age or physical or mental incapacity).

Rapid-eye-movement (REM) sleep   The fourth stage of sleep, marked by rapid eye movements, irregular breathing, high-frequency brain waves, paralysis of large muscles, and often dreaming.

Rational-emotive behavior therapy (REBT)   A form of talk therapy, developed by Albert Ellis, that focuses on eliminating negative emotional reactions through logic, confrontation, and examination of irrational beliefs.

Reciprocal determinism   Bandura's belief that internal personal factors, the environment, and the individual's behavior all work as interacting (reciprocal) determinants of each other.

Reference groups   Any group that individuals use as a standard for evaluating themselves.

Reflex   An innate, automatic response to a stimulus that has a biological relevance for an organism (e.g., the knee-jerk reflex).

Refractory period   A period of time following orgasm, during which further orgasm is considered physiologically rare for men.

Reinforcement   Adding or removing a stimulus following a response and thereby increasing the likelihood that the response will be repeated.

Reliability   The degree to which a test produces similar scores each time it is used; stability or consistency of the scores produced by an instrument.

Repair/restoration theory of sleep   The theory that sleep allows organisms to repair their bodies or recuperate from depleting daily waking activities.

Repetitive transcranial magnetic stimulation (rTMS)   A biomedical treatment that uses repeated magnetic field pulses targeted at specific areas of the brain.

Replicate   To repeat or duplicate the essence of a research study using different situations or

participants to determine if the basic findings can be reproduced; replication helps demonstrate reliability of research findings.

Representativeness heuristic   A cognitive strategy (or shortcut) that involves making judgments based on how well something matches (represents) an existing prototype or stereotype.

Repression   According to Freud's psychoanalytic theory, a basic coping or defense mechanism that prevents anxiety-provoking thoughts, feelings, and memories from reaching consciousness.

Resilience   The ability to recover from or adapt effectively in the face of adversity.

Resistance   In psychoanalysis, the client's inability or unwillingness to discuss or reveal certain memories, thoughts, motives, or experiences.

Resolution phase   The fourth, and final, stage of the sexual response cycle, when the body returns to its unaroused state.

Reticular formation (RF)   The set of neurons that helps screen incoming information and helps control arousal.

Retina   The light-sensitive inner surface of the back of the eye, which contains the receptor cells for vision (rods and cones).

Retrieval   The third step of the ESR memory model; recovery of information from memory storage.

Retrieval cues   A prompt or stimulus that aids recall or retrieval of a stored piece of information from long-term memory (LTM).

Retroactive interference   A memory problem that occurs when new information disrupts (*interferes* with) the recall of old "retro" information; backward-acting interference.

Retrograde amnesia   The inability to retrieve information from the past; backward-acting amnesia.

Rods   Retinal receptor cells with high sensitivity in dim light, but low sensitivity to details and color.

Romantic love   According to Sternberg, feelings of attraction based on a combination of passion and intimacy.

Rorschach Inkblot Test   The most widely used projective personality test, which is based on interpretations of test takers' projections of their underlying motives, conflicts, and personality traits onto ten inkblots.

Saliency bias   A type of attributional bias in which people tend to focus on the most noticeable (salient) factors when explaining behavior.

SAM system   Our body's initial, rapid-acting stress response, involving the sympathetic nervous system and the adrenal medulla; also called the sympatho–adreno–medullary (SAM) system.

Sample bias   A bias that may occur when research participants are unrepresentative of the larger population or population of interest.

Schedules of reinforcement   Specific patterns of reinforcement (either fixed or variable) that determine when a behavior will be reinforced.

Schema   A Piagetian term for a cognitive framework, or "blueprint," formed through interaction with an object or event.

Schizophrenia   A group of severe psychological disorders involving major disturbances in perception, language, thought, emotion, and behavior.

Scientific method   The cyclical and cumulative research process used for gathering and interpreting objective information in a way that minimizes error and yields dependable results.

Scientific thinking   An approach to information that combines a high degree of skepticism with objectivity and rationalism.

Secondary punisher   Any learned stimulus, such as poor grades or a parking ticket, that punishes a response and thus decreases the probability that it will recur.

Secondary reinforcer   Any learned stimulus (like money, praise, or attention) that reinforces a response and thus increases the probability that it will recur.

Selective attention   The process of focusing conscious awareness on a specific stimulus, while filtering out a range of other stimuli occurring simultaneously.

Self-actualization   The humanistic term for the inborn drive to realize our full potential and to develop all our talents and capabilities.

Self-concept   The image of oneself that develops from interactions with others and life experiences.

Self-efficacy   Bandura's term for a person's learned expectation of success in a given situation; another term for self-confidence.

Self-fulfilling prophecy   The process by which expectations about a person, group, or situation lead to the fulfillment of those expectations.

Self-help group   A leaderless or non–professionally guided group in which members assist each other with a specific problem, as in Alcoholics Anonymous.

Self-serving bias   The tendency to credit success to internal, personality factors, while blaming failure on external, situational factors.

Semantic memory   A subsystem of long-term memory (LTM) that stores general knowledge; a mental encyclopedia or dictionary.

Sensation   The process of detecting, and converting, raw sensory information from the external and internal environments and transmitting it to the brain.

Sensorimotor stage Piaget's first stage of cognitive development (birth to approximately age 2), in which schemas are developed through sensory and motor activities.

Sensorineural hearing loss A type of hearing loss resulting from damage to the cochlea's receptor (hair) hearing cells or to the auditory nerve; also called nerve deafness.

Sensory adaptation The sensory receptors' innate tendency to fatigue and stop responding to ongoing and unchanging stimuli; an example of bottom-up processing.

Sensory memory The initial memory stage, which holds sensory information; it has relatively large capacity, but the duration is only a few seconds.

Serial-position effect A characteristic of memory retrieval in which information at the beginning and end of a series is remembered better than material in the middle.

Sex The state of being biologically male or female; also, sexual activities.

Sexual assault Any non-consensual sexual act proscribed by federal, tribal, or state law, including when the victim lacks the capacity to consent.

Sexual dysfunction A difficulty in sexual functioning; a significant disturbance in a person's ability to respond sexually, or to experience sexual pleasure.

Sexual harassment Any unwelcome sexual advances, requests for sexual favors, and other verbal or physical conduct of a sexual nature.

Sexual orientation An enduring emotional, romantic, and/or erotic attraction.

Sexual prejudice A negative attitude directed toward individuals based on their sexual orientation.

Sexual response cycle Masters and Johnson's model of the typical human sexual response, consisting of four stages—excitement, plateau, orgasm, and resolution.

Sexual scripts The learned, socially constructed guidelines for our sexual interactions.

Sexuality The ways in which we experience and express ourselves as sexual beings; includes sexual arousal, orientation, and behaviors.

Sexually transmitted infection (STI) An infection generally transmitted by vaginal, oral, or anal sex.

Shaping Reinforcement is delivered for successive approximations of the desired response.

Short-term memory (STM) The second memory stage, which temporarily stores sensory information and sends information to and receives information from long-term memory (LTM); its capacity is limited to five to nine items, and it has a duration of about 30 seconds.

Single-blind study An experimental technique in which only the participants are unaware of (blind to) who is in the experimental and control groups.

Situationism The theory that behaviors are determined more by situations rather than by the personality traits a person possesses.

Sleep apnea A sleep disorder of the upper respiratory system resulting from a repeated interruption of breathing during sleep; it also leads to loud snoring, poor-quality sleep, and excessive daytime sleepiness.

Sleep terrors The abrupt awakenings from NREM (non-rapid-eye-movement) sleep accompanied by intense physiological arousal and feelings of panic.

Social facilitation The tendency for an individual's performance on an easy task to improve due to the presence of others.

Social loafing The tendency for individuals to exert less effort in a group due to reduced accountability and risk of detection.

Social psychology The scientific study of how others influence our thoughts, feelings, and actions.

Sociocultural perspective A modern approach to psychology that emphasizes social interaction and the cultural determinants of behavior and mental processes.

Somatic nervous system (SNS) A subdivision of the peripheral nervous system (PNS) that connects the central nervous system (CNS) to sensory receptors and controls skeletal muscles.

Source amnesia A memory error that occurs when we forget the origin of a previously stored memory; also called source confusion or source misattribution.

Split-brain surgery The cutting of some fibers within the corpus callosum to separate the brain's two hemispheres; used medically to treat severe epilepsy; provides information on the functions of the two hemispheres.

Spontaneous recovery The reappearance of a previously extinguished conditioned response (CR).

SQ4R method A study technique based on six steps: Survey, Question, Read, Recite, Review, and wRite.

Standard deviation A computed measure of how much scores in a sample differ from the mean of the sample.

Standardization Establishing a set of uniform procedures for administering and scoring a test; also, establishing norms based on the scores of a pretested group.

Statistics The branch of applied mathematics that deals with the collection, calculation, analysis, interpretation, and presentation of numerical facts or data.

Stem cells Immature (uncommitted) cells that have the potential to develop into almost any type of cell, depending on the chemical signals they receive.

Stereotype threat The awareness of a negative stereotype directed toward a group, which leads members of that group to respond in a self-fulfilling way that impairs their performance.

Stereotypes The over-generalized beliefs about members of a group; also the cognitive component of prejudice.

Stimulant A drug that increases overall activity and general responsiveness.

Storage The second step of the ESR memory model; retention of encoded information over time.

Structuralism Wundt's and Titchener's approach that used introspection to study the basic elements (or structures) of the mind.

Subliminal perception The detection of stimuli below the absolute threshold for conscious awareness.

Superego In Freud's theory, is the third personality structure that serves as the center of morality, providing internalized ideals and standards for judgment; often referred to as the "conscience."

Survey/interview A descriptive research technique that questions a large sample of people to assess their behaviors and mental processes.

Sympathetic nervous system The subdivision of the autonomic nervous system (ANS) that is responsible for arousing the body and mobilizing its energy during times of stress; also called the "fight-flight-freeze" system.

Synapse The space between the axon tip of the sending neuron and the dendrite and cell body of the receiving neuron; during an action potential, neurotransmitters are released and flow across the synapse.

Systematic desensitization A behavior therapy technique that begins with relaxation training, followed by exposure to increasingly anxiety-producing stimuli or situations, while the client remains relaxed.

Taste aversion A classically conditioned dislike for, and avoidance of, a specific food whose ingestion is followed by illness.

Technostress A feeling of anxiety or mental pressure from overexposure to or involvement with technology; stress caused by an inability to cope with modern technology.

Temperament An individual's innate disposition or behavioral style and typical emotional response.

Temporal lobes The two lobes above the ears, one on each side of the brain, that are involved in audition (hearing), language comprehension, memory, and some emotional control.

Teratogen Any factor that leads to damage or fetal death during prenatal development.

Thalamus The forebrain structure at the top of the brainstem that relays sensory messages to and from the cerebral cortex.

Thematic Apperception Test (TAT) A projective personality test, which is based on interpretations of test takers' projections of their underlying motives, conflicts, and personality traits revealed through the stories they make up about ambiguous scenes.

Theory A broad explanation for a set of observations or facts that have been substantiated through repeated testing.

Theory of mind (ToM) The understanding that other people don't have the same thoughts and feelings that we do, which generally develops during early childhood.

Therapeutic alliance A bond between the therapist and client based on mutual trust, respect, understanding, and cooperation; an essential factor in successful therapy.

Third-variable problem A situation in which a variable that has not been measured affects (confounds) a relationship between two or more other variables; also known as a problem of confounding.

Three-stage memory model A memory model based on the passage of information through three stages (sensory, short term, and long-term memory).

Tip-of-the-tongue (TOT) phenomenon A strong, confident feeling of knowing something, while not being able to retrieve it at the moment.

Token economy A form of behavior therapy involving awarding "tokens" for desired behavior that can be exchanged later for rewards.

Tolerance The bodily adjustment to continued use of a drug in which the drug user requires greater dosages to achieve the same effect.

Top-down processing Information processing that starts at the "top" with higher-level analysis (prior knowledge and expectations) and then works "down" to recognize individual features as a unified whole; conceptually driven processing that moves from the whole to the parts.

Trait A relatively stable personality characteristic that describes a pattern of thinking, feeling, and acting.

Transcranial direct current stimulation (tDCS) A biomedical treatment that uses direct electrical currents to stimulate specific parts of the brain.

Transduction The process of converting sensory stimuli into neural impulses that are sent along to the brain (e.g., transforming light waves into neural impulses).

Transference In psychoanalysis, the process by which a client attaches (transfers) to the therapist emotional reactions related to someone else in the client's life.

Transgender The state of having a gender identity that does not match one's biological sex; being born with the biological characteristics of one sex but feeling psychologically as if one belongs to the other gender.

Triangular theory of love Sternberg's theory that different stages and types of love result from three basic components—*intimacy, passion,* and *commitment*; Sternberg's consummate love is a combination of all three components.

Triarchic theory of intelligence Sternberg's theory that intelligence involves three forms: analytical, creative, and practical.

Trichromatic theory of color The theory that color perception results from three types of cones in the retina, each of which is most sensitive to either red, green, or blue; other colors result from a mixture of these three.

Two-factor theory Schachter and Singer's theory that emotion depends upon two factors—bodily arousal and cognitive labeling of that arousal; bodily arousal leads to labels which are the basis for feeling emotions.

Unconditional positive regard Rogers's term for love and acceptance with no "strings" (contingencies) attached.

Unconditioned response (UR) An unlearned reaction to an unconditioned stimulus (US) that occurs without previous conditioning.

Unconditioned stimulus (US) A stimulus that elicits an unconditioned response (UR) without previous conditioning.

Unconscious Freud's term for the reservoir of largely unacceptable thoughts, feelings, memories, and other information that lies beneath conscious awareness; in modern terms, subliminal processing that lies beneath the absolute threshold.

Validity The degree to which a test measures what it is intended to measure.

Variable Any factor that can vary or change and can be observed, measured, and verified.

Variable interval (VI) schedule A pattern in which a reinforcer is delivered for the first response made after a variable period of time whose average is predetermined.

Variable ratio (VR) schedule A pattern in which a reinforcer is delivered for the first response made after a variable number of responses whose average is predetermined.

Vestibular sense The sense that provides information about balance and movement; receptors are located in the inner ear.

Volley principle for hearing An explanation for pitch perception suggesting that clusters of neurons take turns firing in a sequence of rhythmic volleys, and that pitch depends on the frequency of these volleys.

Well-being therapy (WBT) A newer form of psychotherapy aimed at enhancing psychological well-being by focusing on personal growth and noticing and savoring the positive aspects of life.

Wish-fulfillment view of dreams The Freudian belief that dreams provide an outlet for unacceptable desires.

Withdrawal The discomfort and distress, including physical pain and intense cravings, experienced after stopping the use of an addictive drug.

Working memory A newer term for short-term memory (STM) that emphasizes the active processing of information.

Yerkes-Dodson law The law stating that maximum performance is related to levels of arousal; complex tasks require a relatively low level of arousal, whereas simple tasks require a relatively high arousal level.

Zone of proximal development (ZPD) Vygotsky's concept of the difference between what children can accomplish on their own and what they can accomplish with the help of others who are more competent.

Aagaard, J. (2019). Multitasking as distraction: A conceptual analysis of media multitasking research. *Theory & Psychology, 29*(1), 87–99. https://doi.org/10.1177/0959354318815766

AAUW. (2019). Economic security: The simple truth about the gender pay gap. *American Association of University Women* (AAUW). Retrieved from https://www.aauw.org/research/the-simple-truth-about-the-gender-pay-gap/

Abderholden, S. (2019, March 7). It's not stigma, it's discrimination. *NAMI.* Retrieved April 23, 2019 from https://www.nami.org/Blogs/NAMI-Blog/March-2019/It-s-Not-Stigma-It-s-Discrimination

Abeywardena, S., Yuan, Q., Tzemanaki, A., Psomopoulou, E., Droukas, L., Melhuish, C., & Dogramadzi, S. (2019). Estimation of tool-tissue forces in robot-assisted minimally invasive surgery using neural networks. *Frontiers in Robotic and AI, 6:*56. doi:10.3389/frobt.2019.00056

Abramowitz, J. S., Deacon, B. J., & Whiteside, S. P. H. (2019). *Exposure therapy for anxiety: Principles and practice (*2nd ed.). New York, NY: Guilford.

Acevedo, B. P., & Aron, A. P. (2014). Romantic love, pair-bonding, and the dopaminergic reward system. In M. Mikulincer & P. R. Shaver (Eds.), *Mechanisms of social connection: From brain to group* (pp. 55–69). Washington, DC: American Psychological Association. doi:10.1037/14250-004

Ackerman, C. (2019, June 4). Psychoanalysis: A brief history of Freud's psychoanalytic theory. *Positive Psychology Program.* Retrieved from https://positivepsychologyprogram.com/psychoanalysis/

Adams, M. J., Majolo, B., Ostner, J., Schülke, O., De Marco, A., Thierry, B., . . . Weiss, A. (2015). Personality structure and social style in macaques. *Journal of Personality and Social Psychology, 109,* 338–353. http://dx.doi.org/10.1037/pspp0000041

Adams, R. B., Jr., & Nelson, A., J. (2016). Eye behavior and gaze. In D. Matsumoto, H. C. Hwang, & M. G. Frank (Eds.), *APA handbook of nonverbal communication* (pp. 335–362). Washington, DC: American Psychological Association. http://dx.doi.org/:10.1037/14669-013

Adams, S. M., Rice, M. J., Jones, S. L., Herzog, E., Mackenzie, L. J., & Oleck, L. G. (2018). TeleMental health: Standards, reimbursement, and interstate practice. *Journal of the American Psychiatric Nurses Association, 24*(4), 295–305. https://doi.org/10.1177/1078390318763963

Adams, Z. W., Sieverdes, J. C., Brunner-Jackson, B., Mueller, M., Chandler, J., Diaz, V., . . . Treiber, F. A. (2018). Meditation smartphone application effects on prehypertensive adults' blood pressure: Dose-response feasibility trial. *Health Psychology, 37*(9), 850–860. http://dx.doi.org/10.1037/hea0000584

Addis, D. R., Leclerc, C. M., Muscatell, K., & Kensinger, E. A. (2010). There are age-related changes in neural connectivity during the encoding of positive, but not negative, information. *Cortex, 46,* 425–433. http://doi.org/10.1016/j.cortex.2009.04.011

Adi, A., & Mathbout, M. (2018). The duty to protect: Four decades after Tarasoff. *American Journal of Psychiatry, 13*(4), 6–8. https://psychiatryonline.org/doi/full/10.1176/appi.ajp-rj.2018.130402

Adi-Japha, E., & Karni, A. (2016). Time for considering constraints on procedural memory consolidation processes: Comment on Pan and Rickard (2015) with specific reference to developmental changes. *Psychological Bulletin, 142,* 568–571. http://dx.doi.org/10.1037/bul0000048

Adler, A. (1927/1954). *Understanding human nature.* New York, NY: Greenburg.

Adolph, K. E., & Berger, S. E. (2012). Physical and motor development. In M. H. Bornstein & M. E. Lamb (Eds.), *Cognitive development: An advanced textbook* (pp. 257–318). New York, NY: Psychology Press.

Adolph, K. E., Dretch, K. S., & LoBue, V. (2014). Fear of heights in infants? *Current Directions in Psychological Science, 23*(1), 60–66. doi:10.1177/0963721413498895

Adulterants in Drugs. (2019). *American Addiction Centers.* Retrieved July 13, 2019 from https://americanaddictioncenters.org/ecstasy-abuse/adulterants-in-drugs-mdma

A Guide to Worldwide Pet Ownership. (2017, January 3). *Pet Secure.* Retrieved from: http://www.petsecure.com.au/pet-care/a-guide-toworldwide-pet-ownership/

Ahluwalia, H., Anand, T., & Suman, L. N. (2018). Marital and family therapy. *Indian Journal of Psychiatry, 60*(Suppl 4), S501–S505. doi:10.4103/psychiatry.IndianJPsychiatry_19_18

Ahmetoglu, G., & Chamorro-Premuzic, T. (2013). *Psych 101. Personality 101.* New York, NY: Springer.

Ainsworth, M. D. S. (1967). *Infancy in Uganda: Infant care and the growth of love.* Baltimore, MD: Johns Hopkins University Press.

Ainsworth, M. D. S. (2010). Security and attachment. In R. Volpe (Ed.), *The secure child: Timeless lessons in parenting and childhood education* (pp. 43–53). Charlotte, NC: Information Age.

Ainsworth, M. D. S., Blehar, M., Waters, E., & Wall, S. (1978). *Patterns of attachment: Observations in the strange situation and at home.* Hillsdale, NJ: Erlbaum.

Akhter, S., Marcus, M., Kerber, R. A., Kong, M., & Taylor, K. C. (2016). The impact of periconceptional maternal stress on fecundability. *Annals of Epidemiology, 26,* 710–716. http://dx.doi.org/10.1016/j.annepidem.2016.07.015

Aknin, L. B., Whillans, A. V., Norton, M. I., & Dunn, E. W. (2019, March 20). Happiness and prosocial behavior: An evaluation of the evidence. *World Happiness Report.* Retrieved June 5, 2019 from https://worldhappiness.report/ed/2019/happiness-and-prosocial-behavior-an-evaluation-of-the-evidence/

Akyeampong, E., Hill, A. G., & Kleinman, A. (Eds.). (2015). *The culture of mental illness and psychiatric practice in Africa.* Bloomington, IN: Indiana University Press.

Alaggia, R., Collin-Vézina, D., & Lateef, R. (2019). Facilitators and barriers to child sexual abuse (CSA) disclosures: A research update (2000–2016). *Trauma, Violence, & Abuse, 20*(2), 260–283. https://doi.org/10.1177/1524838017697312

Albalooshi, S., Moeini-Jazani, M., Fennis, B. M., & Warlop, L. (2019). Reinstating the resourceful self: When and how self-affirmations improve executive performance of the powerless. *Personality and Social Psychology Bulletin.* https://doi.org/10.1177/0146167219853840

Alberti, R. E., & Emmons, M. L. (2008). *Your perfect right: Assertiveness and equality in your life and relationships.* Waupaca, WI: Impact Publications.

Albert, M. A., & Dahling, J. J. (2016). Learning goal orientation and locus of control interact to predict academic self-concept and academic performance in college students. *Personality and Individual Differences, 97,* 245–248. http://dx.doi.org/10.1016/j.paid.2016.03.074

Albright, T. D. (2015). Perceiving. *Daedalus, 144,* 22–41. doi:10.1162/DAED_a_00315

Aldrich, D. P., & Meyer, M. A. (2015). Social capital and community resilience. *American Behavioral Scientist, 59,* 254–269. http://dx.doi.org/10.1177/0002764214550299

Aldridge, L. J., & Islam, M. R. (2012). Cultural differences in athlete attributions for success and failure: The sports pages revisited. *International Journal of Psychology, 47,* 67–75. doi:10.1080/00207594.2011.585160

Alkhars, M., Evangelopoulos, N., Pavur, R., & Kulkarni, S. (2019). Cognitive biases resulting from the representativeness heuristic in operations management: An experimental investigation. *Psychology Research and Behavior Management, 12,* 263–276. doi:10.2147/PRBM.S193092

Alkozei, A., Smith, R., & Killgore, W. D. S. (2018). Gratitude and subjective wellbeing: A proposal of two causal frameworks. *Journal of Happiness Studies, 19*(5), 1519–1542. http://dx.doi.org/10.1007/s10902-017-9870-1

Allan, J. L., McMinn, D., & Daly, M. (2016). A bidirectional relationship between executive function and health behavior: Evidence, implications, and future directions. *Frontiers in Neuroscience, 10*(386). http://dx.doi:10.3389/fnhum.2014.01044:

Allday, E. (2016, June 29). The streets' sickest, costliest: The mentally ill. *San Francisco Chronicle.* Retrieved from http://projects.sfchronicle.com/sf-homeless/mental-health/

Allen, P., Moore, H., Corcoran, C. M., Gilleen, J., Kozhuharova, P., Reichenberg, A., & Malaspina, D. (2019). Emerging temporal lobe dysfunction in people at clinical high risk for psychosis. *Frontiers in Psychiatry, 10*(298). doi:10.3389/fpsyt.2019.00298

Allen, R. J. (2018). Classic and recent advances in understanding amnesia. *F1000Research, 7,* 331. doi:10.12688/f1000research.13737.1

Allport, G. W. (1937). *Personality: A psychological interpretation.* New York, NY: Holt, Rinehart and Winston.

Allport, G. W., & Odbert, H. S. (1936). Trait names: A psycho-lexical study. *Psychological Monographs: General and Applied, 47,* 1–21.

Alvarez-Toro, A., & Lopez-Morales, C. A. (2018). Revisiting the false confession problem. *Journal of the American Academy of Psychiatry and the Law, 46*(1), 34–44. http://www.jaapl.org/content/46/1/34

Alvear, S. A. (2019). The additive advantage and bilingual programs in a large urban school district. *American Educational Research Journal, 56*(2), 477–513. doi:https://doi.org/10.3102/0002831218800986

Amati, V., Meggiolaro, S., Rivellini, G., & Zaccarin, S. (2018). Social relations and life satisfaction: The role of friends. *Genus, 74*(1), 7. doi:10.1186/s41118-018-0032-z

Amazing Meeting, The. (2011). The amazing one: James Randi. Retrieved from http://www.amazingmeeting.com/speakers#randi

American Academy of Pediatrics. (1999). Circumcision policy statement. *Pediatrics, 103,* 686–693. https://pediatrics.aappublications.org/content/pediatrics/103/3/686.full.pdf

American Academy of Pediatrics. (2005). Policy statement: AAP publications retired and reaffirmed. *Pediatrics, 116,* 796.

American Academy of Pediatrics. (2012). Circumcision policy statement. *Pediatrics, 30,* 585–586. http://dx.doi.org/10.1542/peds.2012-1989

American Association of Suicidology. (2019). *Facts and statistics.* AAS. Retrieved from https://suicidology.org/facts-and-statistics/

American College of Cardiology. (2019, March 7). E-cigarettes linked to heart attacks, coronary artery disease, and depression. *ACC.* Retrieved from https://www.acc.org/about-acc/press-releases/2019/03/07/10/03/ecigarettes-linked-to-heart-attacks-coronary-artery-disease-and-depression

American Diabetes Association. (2019). Cardiovascular disease and risk management: Standards of medical care in diabetes. *Diabetes Care, 42*(Suppl. 1):S103–S123. https://hyp.is/JHhz_lCrEembFJ9LIVBZIw/care.diabetesjournals.org/content/42/Supplement_1/S103

American Heart Association. (2013). *Statistical fact sheet: 2013 update.* Retrieved from: http://www.heart.org/idc/groups/heartpublic/@ wcm/@sop/@smd/documents/downloadable/ucm_319588.pdf

American Heart Association. (2018). Is vaping better than smoking? AHA. Retrieved from https://www.heart.org/en/healthy-living/healthy-lifestyle/quit-smoking-tobacco/is-vaping-safer-than-smoking

American Psychiatric Association. (2013). *DSM: Diagnostic and statistical manual of mental disorders* (5th ed.). Washington, DC: American Psychiatric Association.

American Psychological Association. (2013). Gun violence: Prediction, prevention, and policy. *Public and Member Communications, Public Affairs Office.* Washington, DC: American Psychological Association. http://dx.doi.org/10.1-37/e647302013-001

American Psychological Association. (2016). *Resolution on data about sexual orientation and gender identity.* Retrieved from: http://www.apa.org/about/policy/data-sexualorientation.aspx

American Psychological Association (APA). (2009). Committee on Animal Research and Ethics (CARE) Annual Report 2009. *APA.* http://www.apa.org/science/leadership/care/2009-report.aspx

American Psychological Association (APA). (2014). *Graduate study in psychology: 2014.* Washington, DC: American Psychological Association.

American Psychological Association (APA). (2016). *2015 APA survey of psychology health service providers.* Retrieved March 8, 2019 from https://www.apa.org/workforce/publications/15-health-service-providers

American Time Use Survey—2017 Results. (2018, June 28). *News Release Bureau of Labor Statistics.* Retrieved from https://www.bls.gov/news.release/pdf/atus.pdf

Amichai-Hamburger, Y., Gazit, T., Bar-Ilan, J., Perez, O., Aharony, N., Bronstein, J., & Sarah Dyne, T. (2016). Psychological factors behind the lack of participation in online discussions. *Computers in Human Behavior, 55*(Part A), 268–277. http://dx.doi.org/10.1016/j.chb.2015.09.009

Amlien, I. K., Sneve, M. H., Vidal-Piñeiro, D., Walhovd, K. B., & Fjell, A. M. (2019). Elaboration benefits source memory encoding through centrality change. *Scientific Reports, 9.* https://www.nature.com/articles/s41598-019-39999-1

Andersen, P. A. (2014). Nonverbal immediacy in interpersonal communication. In A. W. Siegman & S. Feldman (Eds.), *Multichannel integrations of nonverbal behavior* (pp. 1–36). New York, NY: Psychology Press.

Anderson, C. A. (2001). Heat and violence. *Current Directions in Psychological Science, 10,* 33–38. doi:10.1111/1467-8721.00109

Anderson, E. M., Gomez, D., Caccamise, A., McPhail, D., & Hearing, M. (2019). Chronic unpredictable stress promotes cell-specific plasticity in prefrontal cortex D1 and D2 pyramidal neurons. *Neurobiology of Stress, 10,* 100152. doi:10.1016/j.ynstr.2019.100152

Anderson, E., & Shivakumar, G. (2013). Effects of exercise and physical activity on anxiety. *Frontiers in Psychiatry, 4*(27). doi:10.3389/fpsyt.2013.00027

Anderson, M. C., Ochsner, K. N., Kuhl, B., Cooper, J., Robertson, E., Gabrieli, S. W., . . . Gabrieli, J. D. E. (2004). Neural systems underlying the suppression of unwanted memories. *Science, 303,* 232–235. http://dx.doi.org/10.1126/science.1089504

Anderson, M., & Silver, L. (2019, March 7). 7 key findings about mobile phone and social media use in emerging economies. *Pew Research Center.* Retrieved April 24, 2019 from https://www.pewresearch.org/fact-tank/2019/03/07/7-key-findings-about-mobile-phone-and-social-media-use-in-emerging-economies/

Andics, A., Gábor, A., Gácsi, M., Faragó, T., Szabó, D., & Miklósi, Á. (2016). Neural mechanisms for lexical processing in dogs. *Science, 353*(6303), 1030–1032. http://dx.doi.org/10.1126/science.aaf3777

Andrade, C., Arumugham, S. S., & Thirthalli, J. (2016). Adverse effects of electroconvulsive therapy. *Psychiatric Clinics of North America, 39,* 513–530. http://dx.doi.org/10.1016/j.psc.2016.04.004

Anedo, A. O. (2014). Culture as a vehicle for studying individual differences. *Unizik Journal of Arts and Humanities, 12,* 104–125.

Angus, D. J., Schutter, D. J. L. G., Terburg, D., van Honk, J., & Harmon-Jones, E. (2016). A review of social neuroscience research on anger and aggression. In E. Harmon-Jones & M. Inzlicht (Eds.), *Social neuroscience: Biological approaches to social psychology* (pp. 223–246). New York, NY: Routledge/Taylor & Francis Group.

Anicich, E. M., Swaab, R. I., & Galinsky, A. D. (2015). Hierarchical cultural values predict success and mortality in high-stakes teams. *Proceedings of the National Academy of Sciences of the United States of America, 112,* 1338–1343. http://dx.doi.org/10.1073/pnas.1408800112

Anik, L., Aknin, L. B., Norton, M. I., & Dunn, E. W. (2011). Feeling good about giving: The benefits (and costs) of self-interested charitable behavior. In D. M. Oppenheimer & C. Y. Olivola (Eds.), *The science of giving: Experimental approaches to the study of charity* (pp. 3–13). New York, NY: Psychology Press.

Anisman, H. (2016). *Health psychology.* Thousand Oaks, CA: Sage.

Anker, J. J., Kushner, M. G., Thuras, P., Menk, J., & Unruh, A. S. (2016). Drinking to cope with negative emotions moderates alcohol use disorder treatment response in patients with co-occurring anxiety disorder. *Drug and Alcohol Dependence, 159,* 93–100. doi:10.1016/j.drugalcdep.2015.11.031

Antes, A. L. (2016). Navigating the gray areas of scientific work: Questionable research practices and training in the responsible conduct of research. In A. Dade, L. Olafson, & S. M. DiBella (Eds.), *Implementing a comprehensive research compliance program: A handbook for research officers* (pp. 145–180). New York, NY: Springer.

Anthenien, A. M., Lembo, J., & Neighbors, C. (2017). Drinking motives and alcohol outcome expectancies as mediators of the association between negative urgency and alcohol consumption. *Addictive Behaviors, 66,* 101–107. http://dx.doi.org/10.1016/j.addbeh.2016.11.009

Anthony, A. (2019, May 22). New York might make it illegal to text while walking. *CNN.* Retrieved from https://www.cnn.com/2019/05/20/us/new-york-walking-while-texting-trnd/index.html

Antonaccio, O., Botchkovar, E. V., & Hughes, L. A. (2017). Ecological determinants of situated choice in situational action theory: Does neighborhood matter? *Journal of Research in Crime and Delinquency, 54*(2), 208–243. http://dx.doi.org/10.1177/0022427816678908

Antón, E., Carreiras, M., & Duñabeitia, J. A. (2019.) The impact of bilingualism on executive functions and working memory in young adults. *PLoS ONE, 14*(2): e0206770. https://doi.org/10.1371/journal.pone.0206770

Antunes, H. K., Leite, G. S., Lee, K. S., Barreto, A. T., Santos, R. V., Souza, H. S., . . . de Mello, M. T. (2016). Exercise deprivation increases negative mood in exercise-addicted subjects and modifies their biochemical markers. *Physiology & Behavior, 156,* 182–190. http://dx.doi.org/10.1016/j.physbeh.2016.01.028

APA Congressional Briefing. (2015). APA congressional briefing highlights role of animal research in understanding human development. *Psychological Science Agenda, 29.* http://dx.doi.org/10.1037/e525222015-003

APA Presidential Task Force on Evidence-Based Practice. (2006). Evidence-based practice in psychology. *American Psychologist, 61*(4), 271–285. http://dx.doi.org/10.1037/0003-066X.61.4.271

APA Press Release. (2017, February 22). APA's survey finds constantly checking electronic devices linked to significant stress for most Americans. *American Psychological Association.* Retrieved from http://dx.doi.org/10.1037/e501052017-001

Applewhite, A. (2016, September 3). You're how old? We'll be in touch. *The New York Times.* Retrieved from https://www.nytimes.com/2016/09/04/opinion/sunday/youre-how-oldwell-be-in-touch.html

Arkowitz, H., & Lilienfeld, S. O. (2017). *Facts and fictions in mental health.* Hoboken, NJ: Wiley-Blackwell.

Armstrong, J., Friesdorf, R., & Conway, P. (2019). Clarifying gender differences in moral dilemma judgments: The complementary roles of harm aversion and action aversion. *Social Psychological and Personality Science, 10*(3), 353–363. https://doi.org/10.1177/1948550618755873

Armstrong, M., Morris, C., Abraham, C., & Tarrant, M. (2017). Interventions utilizing contact with people with disabilities to improve children's attitudes toward disability: A systematic review and meta-analysis. *Disability and Health Journal, 10*(1), 11–22. http://dx.doi.org/10.1016/j.dhjo.2016.10.003

Armstrong, T. A., Boutwell, B. B., Flores, S., Symonds, M., Keller, S., & Gangitano, D. A. (2014). Monoamine oxidase A genotype, childhood adversity, and criminal behavior in an incarcerated sample. *Psychiatric Genetics, 24,* 164–171. http://dx.doi.org/10.1097/YPG.0000000000000033

Arnal, P. J., Drogou, C., Sauvet, F., Regnauld, J., Dispersyn, G., Faraut, B., . . . Chennaoui, M. (2016). Effect of sleep extension on the subsequent testosterone, cortisol and prolactin responses to total sleep deprivation and recovery. *Journal of Neuroendocrinology, 28,* 1–9. http://dx.doi.org/10.1111/jne.12346

Arnedo, J., Svrakic, D. M., del Val, C., Romero-Zaliz, R., Hernández-Cuervo, H., Fanous, A. H., . . . Molecular Genetics of Schizophrenia Consortium. (2015). Uncovering the hidden risk architecture of the schizophrenias: Confirmation in three independent genomewide association studies. *The American Journal of Psychiatry, 172,* 139–153. http://dx.doi.org/10.1176/appi.ajp2014.14040435

Arnett, J. J. (2000). Emerging adulthood: A theory of development from the late teens through the twenties. *American Psychologist, 55,* 469–480. https://doi.org/10.1037/0003-066X.55.5.469

Arnett, J. J. (2015). Identity development from adolescence to emerging adulthood: What we know and (especially) don't know. In K. C. McLean & M. Sved (Eds.), *The Oxford handbook of identity development* (pp. 53–64). New York, NY: Oxford University Press.

Arntz, A. (2015). Borderline personality disorder. In A. T. Beck, D. D. Davis, & A. Freeman (Eds.), *Cognitive therapy of personality disorders* (3rd ed., pp. 366–390). New York, NY: Guilford.

Aronson, J., Jannone, S., McGlone, M., & Johnson-Campbell, T. (2009). The Obama effect: An experimental test. *Journal of Experimental Social Psychology, 45,* 957–960. http://dx.doi.org/10.1016/j.jesp.2009.05.006

Arora, P., Pössel, P., Barnard, A. D., Terjesen, M., Lai, B. S., Ehrlich, C. J., . . . Gogos, A. K. (2015). Cognitive interventions. In R. Flanagan, K. Allen, & E. Levine (Eds.), *Cognitive and behavioral interventions in the schools: Integrating theory and research into practice* (pp. 221–248). New York, NY: Springer.http://dx.doi.org/10.1007/978-1-4939-1972-7

Arsena, A., Silvera, D. H., & Pandelaere, M. (2014). Brand trait transference: When celebrity endorsers acquire brand personality traits. *Journal of Business Research, 67,* 1537–1543. http://dx.doi.org/10.1016/j.jbusres.2014.01.011

Aruguete, M. S., & Hardy, P. M. (2016). Performance attributions of African American and White college students. *North American Journal of Psychology, 18,* 257–268.

Asch, S. E. (1951). Effects of group pressure upon the modification and distortion of judgment. In H. Guetzkow (Ed.), *Groups, leadership, and men: Research in human relations* (pp. 170–190). Pittsburgh, PA: Carnegie Press.

Ashmore, J. A., Ditterich, K. W., Conley, C. C., Wright, M. R., Howland, P. S., Huggins, K. L., . . . Andersen, B. L. (2019). Evaluating the effectiveness and implementation of evidence-based treatment: A multisite hybrid design. *American Psychologist, 74*(4), 459–473. http://dx.doi.org/10.1037/amp0000309

Ashrafioun, L., Pigeon, W. R., Conner, K. R., Leong, S. H., & Oslin, D. W. (2016). Prevalence and correlates of suicidal ideation and suicide attempts among veterans in primary care referred for a mental health evaluation. *Journal of Affective Disorders, 189,* 344–350. http://dx.doi.org/10.1016/j.jad.2015.09.014

Ashton, J. (2013, January 29). 10 cures for technostress. *Remodelista.* Retrieved from https://www.remodelista.com/posts/10-cures-for-technostress/

Ashworth, D. K., Sletten, T. L., Junge, M., Simpson, K., Clarke, D., Cunnington, D., & Rajaratnam, S. M. W. (2015). A randomized controlled trial of cognitive behavioral therapy for insomnia: An effective treatment for comorbid insomnia and depression. *Journal of Counseling Psychology, 62,* 115–123. doi:10.1037/cou0000059

Askenasy, J. J. (2016). Low facing dreams. *Abnormal and Behavioral Psychology, 2,* 109. http://dx.doi.org/10.4172/abp.1000109

Atanasov, P. D., & Kunreuther, H. (2016). Cautious defection: Group representatives cooperate and risk less than individuals. *Journal of Behavioral Decision Making, 29,* 372–380. http://dx.doi.org/10.1002/bdm.1880

Atkinson, R. C., & Shiffrin, R. M. (1968). Human memory: A proposed system and its control processes. In K. W. Spence & J. T. Spence (Eds.), *The psychology of learning and motivation* (Vol. 2, pp. 90–91). New York, NY: Academic Press.

Aucouturier, J. -J., Johansson, P., Hall, L., Segnini, R., Mercadié, L., & Watanabe, K. (2016). Covert digital manipulation of vocal emotion alter speakers' emotional states in a congruent direction. *Proceedings of the National Academy of Sciences of the United States of America, 113,* 948–953. http://dx.doi.org/10.1073/pnas.1506552113

Au, E. W. M. (2015). Locus of control, self efficacy, and the mediating effect of outcome control: Predicting course-level and global outcomes in an academic context. *Anxiety, Stress & Coping: An International Journal, 28,* 425–444. http://dx.doi.org/10.1080/10615806.2014.976761

Augustinack, J. C., van der Kouwe, A. J. W., Salat, D. H., Benner, T., Stevens, A. A., Annese, J., . . . Corkin, S. (2014). H.M.'s contributions to neuroscience: A review and autopsy studies. *Hippocampus, 24,* 1267–1286. http://dx.doi.org/10.1002/hipo.22354

Aunola, K., Viljaranta, J., Lehtinen, E., & Nurmi, J. E. (2013). The role of maternal support of competence, autonomy and relatedness in children's interests and mastery orientation. *Learning and Individual Differences, 25,* 171–177. doi:10.1016/j.lindif.2013.02.002

Auzoult, L. (2015). Autonomy and resistance to authority. *Swiss Journal of Psychology, 74,* 49–53. doi:10.1024/1421-0185/a000149

Avieli, H., Ben-David, S., & Levy, I. (2016). Predicting professional quality of life among professional and volunteer caregivers. *Psychological Trauma: Theory, Research, Practice, and Policy, 8,* 80–87. http://dx.doi.org/10.1037/tra0000066

Awasthi, A., & Mandal, M. K. (2015). Facial expressions of emotions: Research perspectives. In M. K. Mandal & A. Awasthi (Eds.), *Understanding facial expressions in communication: Cross-cultural and multidisciplinary perspectives* (pp. 1–18). New York, NY: Springer. http://dx.doi.org/10.1007/978-81-322-1934-7_1

Axtell, R. E. (2007). *Essential do's and taboos: The complete guide to international business and leisure travel.* Hoboken, NJ: Wiley.

Axt, J. R. (2018). The best way to measure explicit racial attitudes is to ask about them. *Social Psychological and Personality Science, 9*(8), 896–906. https://doi.org/10.1177/1948550617728995

Aziz, W., Wang, W., Kesaf, S., Mohamed, A. A., Fukazawa, Y., & Shigemoto, R. (2014). Distinct kinetics of synaptic structural plasticity, memory formation, and memory decay in massed and spaced learning. *Proceedings of the National Academy of Sciences of the United States of America, 11,* E194–E202. doi:10.1073/pnas.1303317110

Azzarito, L., Simon, M., & Marttinen, R. (2016). "Stop photoshopping!": A visual participatory inquiry into students' responses to a body curriculum. *Journal of Teaching in Physical Education, 35*(1), 54–69. http://dx.doi.org/10.1123/jtpe.2014-0166

Babbitt, L. G., Toosi, N. R., & Sommers, S. R. (2016). A broad and insidious appeal: Unpacking the reasons for endorsing racial color blindness. In H. A. Neville, M. E. Gallardo, & D. W. Sue (Eds.), *The myth of racial color blindness: Manifestations, dynamics, and impact* (pp. 53–68). Washington, DC: American Psychological Association. http://dx.doi.org/10.1037/14754-004

Babel, P. (2016). Memory of pain induced by physical exercise. *Memory, 24,* 548–559. http://dx.doi.org/10.1080/09658211.2015.1023809.

Bachhuber, B., Arnsten, J. H., & Wurm, G. (2019). Use of cannabis to relieve pain and promote sleep by customers at an adult use dispensary. *Journal of Psychoactive Drugs.* doi:10.1080/02791072.2019.1626953

Bachmann, C. H., Wijlaars, L. P., Kalverdijk, L. J., Burcu, M., Glaeske, G., Schuiling-Veninga, C. C. M., . . . Zito, J. M. (2017). Trends in ADHD medication use in children and adolescents in five western countries, 2005–2012. *European Neuropsychopharmacology, 27*(5), 484–493. http://dx.doi.org/10.1016/j.euroneuro.2017.03.002

Baddeley, A. D. (1992). Working memory. *Science, 255,* 556–559. http://dx.doi.org/10.1126/science.1736359

Baddeley, A. D. (2007). *Working memory, thought, and action. Oxford psychology series.* New York, NY: Oxford University Press.

Baddeley, A. D., Eysenck, M. W., & Anderson, M. C. (2015). *Memory.* New York, NY: Psychology Press.

Baert, S. (2018). Facebook profile picture appearance affects recruiters' first hiring decisions. *New Media & Society, 20*(3), 1220–1239. https://doi.org/10.1177/1461444816687294

Bagheri, B., Meshkini, F., Dinarvand, K., Alikhani, Z., Haysom, M., & Rasouli, M. (2016). Life psychosocial stresses and coronary artery disease. *International Journal of Preventive Medicine, 7, 106.* http://dx.doi.org/10.4103/2008-7802.190598

Bailey, G. (2018). Myopia (nearsightedness): Causes and treatments. *All About Vision.* Retrieved from https://www.allaboutvision.com/conditions/myopia.htm

Bailey, J. M., Vasey, P. L., Diamond, L M., Breedlove, S. M., Vilain, E., & Epprecht, M. (2016). Sexual orientation, controversy, and science. *Psychological Science in the Public Interest, 17,* 45–101. http://dx.doi.org/10.1177/1529100616637616

Baillargeon, R., & DeVos, J. (1991). Object permanence in young infants: Further evidence. *Child Development, 62,* 1227–1246. http://dx.doi.org/10.2307/1130803

Baines, L., Jones, A., & Christiansen, P. (2016). Hopelessness and alcohol use: The mediating role of drinking motives and outcome expectancies. *Addictive Behaviors Reports, 4,* 65–69. http://dx.doi.org/10.1016/j.abrep.2016.11.001

Baker, D. J. (2019, April 12). Why might states ban affirmative action? *Brookings.* https://www.brookings.edu/blog/brown-center-chalkboard/2019/04/12/why-might-states-ban-affirmative-action/

Baker, S. (2015, January 3). Breaking the taboo: It's time to talk about mental health. *CNN Vital Signs.* http://www.cnn.com/search/?text=breaking+the+taboo+it%27s+time+to +talk+about+mental+health+baker

Bakker, B. N., Klemmensen, R., Nørgaard, A. A., & Schumacher, G. (2016). Stay loyal or exit the party? How openness to experience and extroversion explain vote switching. *Political Psychology, 37,* 419–429. http://dx.doi.org/10.1111/pops.12257

Bakou, A., Margiotoudi, K., Kouroupa, A., & Vatakis, A. (2014). Temporal and sensory experiences in the dreams of sighted and congenital blind individuals. *Procedia-Social and Behavioral Sciences, 126,* 188–189. http://dx.doi.org/10.1016/j.sbspro.2014.02.364

Bakshy, E., Messing, S., & Adamic, L. A. (2015). Exposure to ideologically diverse news and opinion on Facebook. *Science, 348,* 1130–1132. http://dx.doi.org/10.1126/science.aaa1160

Bak, T. H., Long, M. R., Vega-Mendoza, M., & Sorace, A. (2016). Novelty, challenge, and practice: The impact of intensive language learning on attentional functions. *PLoS ONE, 11,* e0153485. http://dx.doi.org/10.1371/journal.pone.0153485.

Balon, R. (Ed.) (2016). *Practical guide to paraphilia and paraphilic disorders.* Cham, CH: Springer International Publishing. http://dx.doi.org/10.1007/978-3-319-42650-1

Balthazart, J. (2018). Fraternal birth order and sexual orientation. *Proceedings of the National Academy of Sciences of the United States of America, 115*(2), 234–236. doi:10.1073/pnas.1719534115

Bandura, A. (1969). *Principles of behavior modification.* New York, NY: Holt, Rinehart & Winston.

Bandura, A. (1989). Self-regulation of motivation and action through internal standards and goal systems. In L. A. Pervin (Ed.), *Goals concepts in personality and social psychology* (pp. 19–85). Hillsdale, NJ: Erlbaum.

Bandura, A. (1989). Social cognitive theory. In R. Vasta (Ed.), *Annals of child development Vol. 6. Six theories of child development* (pp. 1–60). Greenwich, CT: JAI Press.

Bandura, A. (1997). *Self-efficacy: The exercise of control.* New York, NY: Freeman.

Bandura, A. (2008). Reconstrual of "free will" from the agentic perspective of social cognitive theory. In J. Baer, J. C. Kaufman, & R. F. Baumeister (Eds.), *Are we free? Psychology and free will* (pp. 86–127). New York, NY: Oxford University Press.

Bandura, A. (2011). But what about that gigantic elephant in the room? In R. M. Arkin (Ed.), *Most underappreciated: 50 prominent social psychologists describe their most unloved work* (pp. 51–59). New York, NY: Oxford University Press.

Bandura, A. (2011). Social cognitive theory. In P. A. M. Van Lange, A. W. Kruglanski, & E. T. Higgins (Eds.), *Handbook of theories of social psychology* (Vol. 1, pp. 349–373). Thousand Oaks, CA: Sage.

Bandura, A., Ross, D., & Ross, S. (1961). Transmission of aggression through imitation of aggressive models. *Journal of Abnormal & Social Psychology, 63,* 575–582. http://dx.doi.org/10.1037/h0045925

Bandura, A., & Walters, R. H. (1963). *Social learning and personality development.* New York, NY: Holt, Rinehart and Winston.

Banerjee, S. C., Greene, K., Yanovitzky, I., Bagdasarov, Z., Choi, S. Y., & Magsamen-Conrad, K. (2015). Adolescent egocentrism and indoor tanning: Is the relationship direct or mediated? *Journal of Youth Studies, 18,* 357–375. http://dx.doi.org/10.1080/13676261.2014.963536

Banking Panics of 1930-31. (2013, November 22). *Federal Reserve History.* Retrieved May 13, 2019 from https://www.federalreservehistory.org/essays/banking_panics_1930-31

Bankó, É. M., & Vidnyánszky, Z. (2010). Retention interval affects visual short-term memory encoding. *Journal of Neurophysiology, 103,* 1425–1430. http://dx.doi.org/10.1152/jn.00868.2009

Banks, G., Hadenfeldt, K., Janoch, M., Manning, C., Ramos, K., & Patterson Silver Wolf, D. A. (2017). Gun violence and substance abuse. *Aggression and Violent Behavior, 34,* 113–116. http://dx.doi.org/10.1016/j.avb.2017.02.002

Banks, J. B., Tartar, J. L., & Tamayo, B. A. (2015). Examining factors involved in stressrelated working memory impairments: Independent or conditional effects? *Emotion, 15,* 827–836. http://dx.doi.org/10.1037/emo0000096

Barajas, J. (2018, December 10). How the fallout from Larry Nassar's sex abuse has grown. *PBS News Hour.* Retrieved from https://www.pbs.org/newshour/nation/how-the-fallout-from-larry-nassars-sex-abuse-has-grown

Barber, J. P., & Solomonov, N. (2016). Psychodynamic theories. In J. C. Norcross, G. R. VandenBos, D. K. Freedheim, & B. O. Olatunji (Eds.), *APA handbook of clinical psychology: Theory and research, Vol. 2* (pp. 53–77). Washington, DC: American Psychological Association. http://dx.doi.org/10.1037/14773-003

Barceló, J. (2017). The association between agreeableness, extraversion, and support for secessionist movements: Evidence from a large survey of more than 33,000 respondents in Catalonia. *Personality and Individual Differences, 107,* 102–107. http://dx.doi.org/10.1016/j.paid.2016.11.029

Barelds, D. P. H., & Dijkstra, P. (2011). Positive illusions about a partner's personality and relationship quality. *Journal of Research in Personality, 45,* 37–43.

Barker, L. A. (2016). *Obama on our minds: The impact of Obama on the psyche of America.* New York, NY: Oxford University Press.

Barkley, R. A. (2017). *When an adult you love has ADHD: Professional advice for parents, partners, and siblings.* Washington, DC: American Psychological Association. http://dx.doi.org/10.1037/15963-004

Barling, J., Barnes, C. M., Carleton, E., & Wagner, D. T. (2016). *Work and sleep research insights for the workplace.* New York, NY: Oxford University Press.

Barlow, D. H., Durand, V. M., & Hofmann, S. G. (2017). *Abnormal psychology: An integrative approach* (8e). Boston, MA: Cengage.

Barlow, F. K. (2019). Nature vs. nurture is nonsense: On the necessity of an integrated genetic, social, developmental, and personality psychology. *Australian Journal of Psychology, 71,* 68–79. doi:10.1111/ajpy.12240

Barnes, J. C., Boutwell, B. B., & Beaver, K. M. (2014). Genetic and nonshared environmental factors predict handgun ownership in early adulthood. *Death Studies, 38,* 156–164. http://dx.doi.org/10.1080/07481187.2012.738769

Barnow, S., & Balkir, N. (Eds.). (2013). *Cultural variations in psychopathology: From research to practice.* Cambridge, MA: Hogrefe.

Barratt, B. B. (2019). Oedipality and oedipal complexes reconsidered: On the incest taboo as key to the universality of the human condition. *The International Journal of Psychoanalysis, 100*(1), 7–31. doi:10.1080/00207578.2018.1489704

Barrett, D., Sogolow, Z., Oh, A., Panton, J., Grayson, M., & Justiniano, M. (2014). Content of dreams from WWII POWs. *Imagination, Cognition and Personality, 33,* 193–204. http://dx.doi.org/10.2190/IC.33.1–2.

Barrett, L. F., Adolphs, R., Marsella, S., Martinez, A. M., & Pollack, S. D. (2019). Emotional expressions reconsidered: Challenges to inferring emotion from human facial movements. *Psychological Science in the Public Interest, 20*(1), 1–68. https://doi.org/10.1177/1529100619832930

Bartels, J. (2019). Revisiting the Stanford prison experiment, again: Examining demand characteristics in the guard orientation. *Journal of Social Psychology, 159*(6), 780–790. doi:10.1080/00224545.2019.1596058

Bartle-Haring, S., Slesnick, N., & Murnan, A. (2018). Benefits to children who participate in family therapy with their substance-using mother. *Journal of Marital and Family Therapy, 44*(4), 671–686. doi:10.1111/jmft.12280

Barton, A. L., & Hirsch, J. K. (2016). Permissive parenting and mental health in college students: Mediating effects of academic entitlement. *Journal of American College Health, 64,* 1–8. http://dx.doi.org/10.1080/07448481.2015.1060597

Baskin-Sommers, A., Stuppy-Sullivan, A. M., & Buckholtz, J. W. (2016). Psychopathic individuals exhibit but do not avoid regret during counterfactual decision making. *Proceedings of the National Academy of Sciences of the United States of America, 113*(50), 14438–14443. http://dx.doi.org/10.1073/pnas.1609985113

Batanova, M., Espelage, D. L., & Rao, M. A. (2014). Early adolescents' willingness to intervene: What roles do attributions, affect, coping, and self-reported victimization play? *Journal of School Psychology, 52,* 279–293. http://dx.doi.org/10.1016/j.jsp.2014.02.001

Bateganya, M. H., Amanyeiwe, U., Roxo, U., & Dong, M. (2015). Impact of support groups for people living with HIV on clinical outcomes: A systematic review of the literature. *Journal of Acquired Immune Deficiency Syndromes, 68,* S368–S374. http://dx.doi.org/10.1097/QAI.0000000000000519

Bateman, A. W., & Fonagy, P. (2016). The role of mentalization in treatments for personality disorder. In W. J. Livesley, G. Dimaggio, & J. F. Clarkin (Eds.), *Integrated treatment for personality disorder: A modular approach* (pp. 148–172). New York, NY: Guilford.

Baucom, B. R., Dickenson, J. A., Atkins, D. C., Baucom, D. H., Fischer, M. S., Weusthoff, S., . . . Zimmermann, T. (2015). The interpersonal process model of demand/withdraw behavior. *Journal of Family Psychology, 29,* 80–90. http://dx.doi.org/10.1037/fam0000044.

Bauer, G., & Hämmig, O. (Eds.). (2014). *Bridging occupational, organizational, and public health: A transdisciplinary approach.* New York, NY: Springer.

Bauer, P. J., & Larkina, M. (2014). Childhood amnesia in the making: Different distributions of autobiographical memories in children and adults. *Journal of Experimental Psychology: General, 143,* 597–611. http://dx.doi.org/10.1037/a0033307

Bauer-Wolf, J. (2019, February 19). Still taking a knee against racism. *Inside Higher Ed.* Retrieved June 12, 2019 from https://www.insidehighered.com/news/2019/02/19/college-students-are-still-taking-knee-against-racism

Baugh, C. M., Kiernan, P. T., Kroshus, E., Daneshvar, D. H., Montenigro, P. H., Mc-Kee, A. C., & Stern, R. A. (2015). Frequency of head-impact-related outcomes by position in NCAA Division 1 collegiate football players. *Journal of Neurotrauma, 32,* 314–326. http://dx.doi.org/10.1089/neu.2014.3582

Baumeister, J. C., Papa, G., & Foroni, F. (2016). Deeper than skin deep – The effect of botulinum toxin-A on emotion processing. *Toxicon, 118,* 86. http://dx.doi.org/10.1016/j.toxicon.2016.04.044

Baumeister, R. F., Ainsworth, S. E., & Vohs, K. D. (2016). Are groups more or less than the sum of their members? The moderating role of individual identification. *Behavioral and Brain Sciences, 39:* e137. http://dx.doi.org/10.1017/S0140525X15000618

Baumeister, R. F., & Bushman, B. (2014). *Social psychology and human nature* (3rd ed.). Boston, MA: Cengage.

Bäuml, K.-H. T. (2019). Context retrieval as a critical component in selective memory retrieval. *Current Directions in Psychological Science, 28*(2), 177–182. https://doi.org/10.1177/0963721419827520

Baumrind, D. (1980). New directions in socialization research. *American Psychologist, 35,* 639–652.

Baumrind, D. (2013). Authoritative parenting revisited: History and current status. In R. E. Larzelere, A. S. Morris, & A. W. Harrist (Eds.), *Authoritative parenting: Synthesizing nurturance and discipline for optimal child development* (pp. 11–34). Washington, DC: American Psychological Association.

Baumrind, D. (2015). When subjects become objects: The lies behind the Milgram legend. *Theory & Psychology, 25*(5), 690–696. http://dx.doi.org/10.1177/0959354315592062

Baus, C., McAleer, P., Marcoux, K., Belin, P., & Costa, A. (2019). Forming social impressions from voices in native and foreign languages. *Scientific Reports, 9*(1), 414. https://www.nature.com/articles/s41598-018-36518-6

Beach, F. A. (1977). *Human sexuality in four perspectives.* Baltimore, MD: The Johns Hopkins University Press.

Beail, N. (2016). Psychodynamic psychotherapy. In C. Hemmings & N. Bouras (Eds.), *Psychiatric and behavioral disorders in intellectual and developmental disabilities* (3rd ed., pp. 151–160). New York, NY: Cambridge University Press.

Beck, A. T. (1976). *Cognitive therapy and the emotional disorders.* New York, NY: International Universities Press.

Beck, A. T. (2000). *Prisoners of hate.* New York, NY: Harper Perennial.

Beck, A. T., & Bredemeier, K. (2016). A unified model of depression: Integrating clinical, cognitive, biological, and evolutionary perspectives. *Clinical Psychological Science, 4,* 596–619. http://dx.doi.org/10.1177/2167702616628523

Beck, A. T., Freeman, A., & Davis, D. D. (2015). General principles and specialized techniques in cognitive therapy of personality disorders. In A. T. Beck, D. D. Davis, & A. Freeman (Eds.), *Cognitive therapy of personality disorders* (3rd ed., pp. 97–124). New York, NY: Guilford.

Beck, A. T., Haigh, E. A. P., & Baber, K. F. (2012). Biological underpinnings of the cognitive model of depression: A prototype for psychoanalytic research. *Psychoanalytic Review, 99,* 515–537.

Becker, L., & Rohleder, N. (2019). Time course of the physiological stress response to an acute stressor and its associations with the primacy and recency effect of the serial position curve. *PLoS ONE*. Retrieved from doi:https://doi.org/10.1101/568352

Begley, S. (2017, August 23). What are the chances of winning the Powerball? *Money*. Retrieved from http://money.com/money/4912123/powerball-chances-2017/

Behen, M. E., & Chugani, H. T. (2015). Functional and structural correlates of early severe social deprivation. In R. K. Schutt, L. J. Seidman, & M. Keshavan (Eds.), *Social neuroscience: Brain, mind, and society* (pp. 280–319). Boston, MA: Harvard University Press. https://doi.org/10.4159/9780674286719-012

Beilin, H. (1992). Piaget's enduring contribution to developmental psychology. *Developmental Psychology, 28,* 191–204.

Belkind-Gerson, J., Hotta, R., Whalen, M., Nayyar, N., Nagy, N., Cheng, L., . . . Dietrich, J. (2016). Engraftment of enteric neural pro-genitor cells into the injured adult brain. *BMC Neuroscience, 17,* Article 5. http://dx.doi. org/10.1186/s12868-016-0238-y

Belletier, C., Normand, A., & Huguet, P. (2019). Social-facilitation-and-impairment Effects: From motivation to cognition and the social brain. *Current Directions in Psychological Science, 28*(3), 260–265. https://doi.org/10.1177/0963721419829699

Belluz, J. (2019, March 5). Research fraud catalyzed the anti-vaccination movement. Let's not repeat history. *Vox*. Retrieved from https://www.vox.com/2018/2/27/17057990/andrew-wakefield-vaccines-autism-study

Belson, K. (2019, January 17). The N.F.L.'s obesity scourge. *The New York Times*. Retrieved from https://www.nytimes.com/2019/01/17/sports/football/the-nfls-obesity-scourge.html?emc=edit_nn_p_20190117&nl=morning-briefing&nlid=72977952section%3-DlongRead&section=longRead&te=1

Bem, S. L. (1974). The measurement of psychological androgyny. *Journal of Consulting and Clinical Psychology, 42,* 155–162. http://dx.doi.org/10.1037/h0036215

Bem, S. L. (1981). Gender schema theory: A cognitive account of sex typing. *Psychological Review, 88,* 354–364. http://dx.doi.org/10.1037/0033-295X.88.4.354

Bem, S. L. (1993). *The lenses of gender: Transforming the debate on sexual inequality*. New Haven, CT: Yale University Press.

Bénard, M., Bellisle, F., Kesse-Guyot, E., Julia, C., Andreeva, V. A., Etilé, F., . . . Péneau, S. (2019). Impulsivity is associated with food intake, snacking, and eating disorders in a general population. *The American Journal of Clinical Nutrition, 109*(1), 117–126. https://doi.org/10.1093/ajcn/nqy255

Bender, A. D., Filmer, H. L., Naughtin, C. K., & Dux, P. E. (2017). Dynamic, continuous multitasking training leads to task-specific improvements but does not transfer across action selection tasks. *NPJ Science of Learning, 2,* 14. doi:10.1038/s41539-017-0015-4

Benjamin, L. T., Cavell, T. A., & Shallen-Berger, W. R. (1984). Staying with initial answers on objective tests: Is it a myth? *Teaching of Psychology, 11,* 133–141. https://doi.org/10.1177/009862838401100303

Bennabi, D., & Haffen, E. (2018). Transcranial direct current stimulation (tDCS): A promising treatment for major depressive disorder? *Brain Sciences, 8*(5), 81. doi:10.3390/brainsci8050081

Benner, A. D., Wang, Y., Shen, Y., Boyle, A. E., Polk, R., & Cheng, Y.-P. (2018). Racial/ethnic discrimination and well-being during adolescence: A meta-analytic review. *American Psychologist, 73*(7), 855–883. http://dx.doi.org/10.1037/amp0000204

Bennett, N., & O'Donohue, W. T. (2016). Child abuser's threats and grooming techniques. In W. T. O'Donohue & M. Fanetti (Eds.), *Forensic interviews regarding child sexual abuse: A guide to evidence-based practice* (pp. 307–316). Cham, CH: Springer International Publishing. http://dx.doi.org/10.1007/978-3-319-21097-1_1

Bennett, S., Banyard, V. L., & Edwards, K. M. (2017). The impact of the bystander's relationship with the victim and the perpetrator on intent to help in situations involving sexual violence. *Journal of Interpersonal Violence, 32*(5), 682–702. http://dx.doi.org/10.1177/0886260515586373

Bennion, K. A., Steinmetz, K. R. M., Kensinger, E. A., & Payne, J. D. (2015). Sleep and cortisol interact to support memory consolidation. *Cerebral Cortex, 25,* 646–657. http://dx.doi.org/10.1093/cercor/bht255

Ben-Porath, Y. S. (2013). Self-report inventories: Assessing personality and psychopathology. In J. R. Graham, J. A. Naglieri, & I. B. Weiner (Eds.), *Handbook of psychology, Vol. 10. Assessment psychology* (2nd ed., pp. 622–644). Hoboken, NJ: Wiley.

Benson, H. (2000). *The relaxation response*. New York, NY: HarperTorch.

Bentall, R. P., Wickham, S., Shevlin, M., & Varese, F. (2012). Do specific early-life adversities lead to specific symptoms of psychosis? A study from the 2007 The Adult Psychiatric Morbidity Survey. *Schizophrenia Bulletin, 38,* 734–740. doi:10.1093/schbul/sbs049

Beny, Y., & Kimchi, T. (2016). Conditioned odor aversion induces social anxiety towards females in wild-type and TrpC2 knockout male mice. *Genes, Brain and Behavior, 15,* 722–732. http://dx.doi.org/10.1111/gbb.12320

Beran, M. J., Parrish, A. E., Perdue, B. M., & Washburn, D. A. (2014). Comparative cognition: Past, present, and future. *International Journal of Comparative Psychology, 27,* 3–30.

Bergendahl, I. A., Salvanes, A. G. V., & Braithwaite, V. A. (2016). Determining the effects of duration and recency of exposure to environmental enrichment. *Applied Animal Behaviour Science, 176,* 163–169. http://dx.doi.org/10.1016/j.applanim.2015.11.002

Berger, G. E., Bartholomeusz, C. F., Wood, S. J., Ang, A., Phillips, L. J., Proffitt, T., . . . Pantelis, C. (2017). Ventricular volumes across stages of schizophrenia and other psychoses. *Australian & New Zealand Journal of Psychiatry, 51*(10), 1041–1051. https://doi.org/10.1177/0004867417715914

Berger, J. (2015). *Personality* (9th ed.). Stamford, CT: Cengage.

Berger, K. S. (2015). *Developing person through childhood and adolescence* (10th ed.). New York, NY: Worth.

Berger, K. S. (2019). *Invitation to the life span (10th ed.)*. New York, NY: Macmillan.

Berlin, F. S. (2019). Paraphilic disorders: A better understanding. *Current Psychiatry, 18*(4), 22–18. Retrieved from https://mdedge-files-live.s3.us-east-2.amazonaws.com/files/s3fs-public/CP01804022.PDF

Berman, J., & Prudic, J. (2013). Electroconvulsive therapy. In J. J. Mann, P. J. McGrath, & S. P. Roose (Eds.), *Clinical handbook for the management of mood disorders* (pp. 311–324). New York, NY: Cambridge University Press. http://dx.doi.org/10.1017/CBO9781139175869.024

Bernal, G., Cumba-Avilés, E., & Rodriguez-Quintana, N. (2014). Methodological challenges in research with ethnic, racial, and ethnocultural groups. In F. T. L. Leong, L. Comas-Díaz, G. C. Nagayama Hall, V. C. McLoyd, & J. E. Trimble (Eds.), *APA handbook of multicultural psychology: Vol. 1. Theory and research* (pp. 105–123). Washington, DC: American Psychological Association. doi:10.1037/14189-006

Bernaras, E., Jaureguizar, J., & Garaigordobil, M. (2019). Child and adolescent depression: A review of theories, evaluation instruments, prevention programs, and treatments. *Frontiers in Psychology, 10,* 1664–1078. doi:10.3389/fpsyg.2019.00543

Bernard, L. L. (1924). *Instinct.* New York, NY: Holt.

Berns, G. S., Blaine, K., Prietula, M. J., & Pye, B. E. (2013). Short- and long-term effects of a novel on connectivity in the brain. *Brain Connectivity, 3,* 590–600. http://dx.doi.org/10.1089/brain.2013.0166

Berns, G. S., Brooks, A. M., & Spivak, M. (2015). Scent of the familiar: An fMRI study of canine brain responses to familiar and unfamiliar human and dog odors. *Behavioural Processes, 110,* 37–46. doi:10.1016/j.beproc.2014.02.011

Berreman, G. (1971). *Anthropology today.* Del Mar, CA: CRM.

Berry, J., Poortinga, Y., Breugelmans, S., Chasiotis, A., & Sam, D. (2011). *Cross-cultural psychology: Research and applications* (3rd ed.). Cambridge, UK: Cambridge University Press.

Berry, J. W., & Ataca, B. (2010). Cultural factors in stress. In G. Fink (Ed.), *Stress consequences: Mental, neuropsychological and socioeconomic* (pp. 640–645). San Diego, CA: Elsevier Academic Press.

Berry, J. W., Kim, U., Minde, T., & Mok, D. (1987). Comparative studies of acculturative stress. *International Migration Review, 21,* 491–511. http://dx.doi.org/10.2307/2546607

Best, M., Lawrence, N. S., Logan, G. D., McLaren, I. P. L., & Verbruggen, F. (2016). Should I stop or should I go? The role of associations and expectancies. *Journal of Experimental Psychology: Human Perception and Performance, 42,* 115–137. http://dx.doi.org/10.1037/xhp0000116

Bevan, J. L., Gomez, R., & Sparks, L. (2014). Disclosures about important life events on Facebook: Relationships with stress and quality of life. *Computers in Human Behavior, 39,* 246–253. http://dx.doi.org/10.1016/j.chb.2014.07.021

Beyens, I., Frison, E., & Eggermont, S. (2016). "I don't want to miss a thing": Adolescents' fear of missing out and its relationship to adolescents' social needs, Facebook use, and Facebook related stress. *Computers in Human Behavior, 64,* 1–8. http://dx.doi.org/10.1016/j.chb.2016.05.083

Bhatnagar, K. A. C., Wisniewski, L., Solomon, M., & Heinberg, L. (2013). Effectiveness and feasibility of a cognitive-behavioral group intervention for body image disturbance in women with eating disorders. *Journal of Clinical Psychology, 69,* 1–13.

Bianchi, E. C. (2014). Entering adulthood in a recession tempers later narcissism. *Psychological Science, 25,* 1429–1437. http://dx.doi.org/10.1177/0956797614532818

Bianchi, E. C. (2015). Assessing the robustness of the relationship between entering adulthood in a recession and narcissism. *Psychological Science, 26,* 537–538. http://dx.doi.org/10.1177/0956797614568157

Bianchi, E. C., Hall, E. V., & Lee, S. (2018). Reexamining the link between economic downturns and racial antipathy: Evidence that prejudice against Blacks rises during recessions. *Psychological Science, 29*(10), 1584–1597. https://doi.org/10.1177/0956797618777214

Bianchi, M. (Ed.). (2014). *Sleep deprivation and disease: Effects on the body, brain and behavior.* New York, NY: Springer.

Bichescu-Burian, D., Steyer, J., Steinert, T., Grieb, B., & Tschöke, S. (2017). Trauma-related dissociation: Psychological features and psychophysiological responses to script-driven imagery in borderline personality disorder. *Psychophysiology, 54*(3), 452–461. http://dx.doi.org/10.1111/psyp.12795

Bin-Hasan, S., Rakesh, K., Kapur, K., & Owens, J. (2019). School start time change, sleep duration, and driving accidents in high school students. *Chest, 155*(4), 303a. Retrieved from doi:10.1016/j.chest.2019.02.294

Birditt, K. S., & Newton, N. J. (2016). Theories of social support and aging. In N. A. Pachana (Ed.), *Encyclopedia of gerontology* (pp. 1–7). New York, NY: Springer.

Birmaher, B., & Brent, D. A. (2016). Depressive and disruptive mood dysregulation disorders. In M. K. Dulcan (Ed.), *Dulcan's textbook of child and adolescent psychiatry* (pp. 245–276). Arlington, VA: American Psychiatric Publishing.

Bissinger, B. (2015). Caitlyn Jenner: The full story. *Vanity Fair.* Retrieved from http://www.vanityfair.com/hollywood/2015/06/caitlynjenner-bruce-cover-annie-leibovitz

Blacha, C., Schmid, M. M., Gahr, M., Freudenmann, R. W., Plener, P. L., Finter, F., . . . Schönfeldt-Lecuona, C. (2013). Self-inflicted testicular amputation in first lysergic acid diethylamide use. *Journal of Addiction Medicine, 7,* 83–84.

Black, C. N., Bot, M., Scheffer, P. G., & Penninx, B. W. J. H. (2017). Oxidative stress in major depressive and anxiety disorders, and the association with antidepressant use; results from a large adult cohort. *Psychological Medicine, 47*(5), 936–948. http://dx.doi.org/10.1017/S0033291716002828 17l

Black, J., & Barnes, J. L. (2015). Fiction and social cognition: The effect of viewing award-winning television dramas on theory of mind. *Psychology of Aesthetics, Creativity, and the Arts, 9,* 423–429. http://dx.doi.org/10.1037/aca0000031

Blake, A. B., Nazarian, M., & Castel, A. D. (2015). The Apple of the mind's eye: Everyday attention, metamemory, and reconstructive memory for the Apple logo. *The Quarterly Journal of Experimental Psychology, 68,* 858–865. doi:10.1080/17470218.2014.1002798

Bleske-Rechek, A., Morrison, K. M., & Heidtke, L. D. (2015). Causal inference from descriptions of experimental and non-experimental research: Public understanding of correlation-versus-causation. *The Journal of General Psychology, 142,* 48–70. doi:10.1080/00221309.2014.977216

Bliss, T., & Collingridge, G. (2019). Persistent memories of long-term potentiation and the N-methyl-d-aspartate receptor. *Brain and Neuroscience Advances.* https://doi.org/10.1177/23982128 1984821

Bloch, L., Haase, C. M., & Levenson, R. W. (2014). Emotion regulation predicts marital satisfaction: More than a wives' tale. *Emotion, 14,* 130–144. http://dx.doi.org/10.1037/a0034272

Blumberger, D. M., Vila-Rodriguez, F., Thorpe, K. E., Daskalakis, Z. J., & Downar, J. (2019). Repetitive transcranial magnetic stimulation for depression – Authors' reply. *The Lancet, 393* (10170), 403–404. https://www.thelancet.com/journals/lancet/article/PIIS0140-6736(18)32837-X/fulltext

Blumberg, M. S. (2015). Developing sensorimotor systems in our sleep. *Current Directions in Psychological Science, 24,* 32–37. http://dx.doi.org/10.1177/0963721414551362

Blumenfeld, A. M., Tepper, S. J., Robbins, L. D., Adams, A. M., Buse, D. C., Orejudos, A., & Silberstein, S. D. (2019). Effects of onabotulinumtoxinA treatment for chronic migraine on common comorbidities including depression and anxiety. *Journal of Neurology, Neurosurgery & Psychiatry, 90,* 353–360. https://jnnp.bmj.com/content/90/3/353.citation-tools

Blum, R. W., Mmari, K., & Moreau, C. (2017). It begins at 10: How gender expectations shape early adolescence around the world. *Journal of Adolescent Health, 61*(4), Pages S3–S4.

Boag, E. M., & Carnelley, K. B. (2016). Attachment and prejudice: The mediating role of empathy. *British Journal of Social Psychology, 55,* 337–356. http://dx.doi.org/10.1111/bjso.12132

Boag, S. (2012). *Freudian repression, the unconscious, and the dynamics of inhibition.* London, UK: Karnac.

Boccara, C. N., Nardin, M., Stella, F., O'Neill, J., & Csicsvari, J. (2019). The entorhinal cognitive map is attracted to goals. *Science, 363*(6434), 1443–1447. doi:10.1126/science.aav4837

Bogaard, G., Meijer, E. H., Vrij, A., & Merckelbach, H. (2016). Strong, but wrong: Lay people's and police officers' beliefs about verbal and nonverbal cues to deception. *PLoS ONE, 11*(6): e0156615. http://dx.doi.org/10.1371/journal.pone.0156615

Bohannon, J. (2016, April 7). For real this time: Talking to people about gay and transgender issues can change their prejudices. *Science.* http://dx.doi.org/10.1126/science.aaf9890

Bohon, C. (2015). Feeding and eating disorders. In L. W. Roberts & A. K. Louie (Eds.), *Study guide to DSM-5®* (pp. 233–250). Arlington, VA: American Psychiatric Publishing.

Bolton, S., & Robinson, O. J. (2017). The impact of threat of shock-induced anxiety on memory encoding and retrieval. *Learning & Memory (Cold Spring Harbor, N.Y.), 24*(10), 532–542. doi:10.1101/lm.045187.117

Bonanno, G. A. (2012). Uses and abuses of the resilience construct: Loss, trauma, and health-related adversities. *Social Science & Medicine, 74,* 753–756. http://dx.doi.org/10.1016/j.socscimed.2011.11.022

Bond, M. H. (Ed.). (2015). *Oxford handbook of Chinese psychology.* New York, NY: Oxford University Press.

Bongers, P., & Jansen, A. (2017). Emotional eating and Pavlovian learning: Evidence for conditioned appetitive responding to negative emotional states. *Cognition and Emotion, 31*(2), 284–297. http://dx.doi.org/10.1080/02699931.2015.1108903

Bonilla-Silva, E. (2016). Down the rabbit hole: Color-blind racism in Obamerica. In H. A. Neville, M. E. Gallardo, & D. W. Sue (Eds.), *The myth of racial color blindness: Manifestations, dynamics, and impact* (pp. 25–38). Washington, DC: American Psychological Association. http://dx.doi.org/10.1037/14754-002

Bonomi, C. (2015). *The cut and the building of psychoanalysis, Volume 1: Sigmund Freud and Emma Eckstein.* London, UK, New York, NY: Routledge.

Bönstrup, M., Iturrate, I., Thompson, R., Cruciani, G., Censor, N., & Cohen, L. G. (2019). A rapid form of offline consolidation in skill learning. *Current Biology, 29*(8), 1346–1351.e4. doi:10.1016/j.cub.2019.02.049

Boothroyd, L. G., Tovee, M. T., & Pollett, T. (2012). Mechanisms of change in body size preferences. *PLoS ONE, 7:* e48691.

Borelli, J. L., Rasmussen, H. F., Burkhart, M. L., & Sbarra, D. A. (2015). Relational savoring in long-distance romantic relationships. *Journal of Social and Personal Relationships, 32,* 1083–1108. doi:10.1177/0265407514558960

Borelli, J. L., Sbarra, D. A., Snavely, J. E., McMakin, D. L., Coffey, J. K., Ruiz, S. K., . . . Chung, S. Y. (2014). With or without you: Attachment avoidance predicts non-deployed spouses' reactions to relationship challenges during deployment. *Professional Psychology: Research and Practice, 45,* 478–487. http://dx.doi.org/10.1037/a0037780

Borghans, L., Golsteyn, B. H. H., Heckman, J., & Humphries, J. E. (2011). Identification problems in personality psychology. *Personality and Individual Differences, 51*(3), 315–320. http://doi.org/10.1016/j.paid.2011.03.029

Bornstein, M. H., Arterberry, M. E., & Lamb, M. E. (2014). *Development in infancy: A contemporary introduction* (5th ed.). New York, NY: Psychology Press.

Bornstein, R. F., & Huprich, S. K. (2015). Prologue: Toward an empirically informed 21st-century psychoanalysis: Challenges and opportunities. *Psychoanalytic Inquiry, 35*(Supp1), 2–4. http://dx.doi.org/10.1080/07351690.2014.987589

Borras-Guevara, M. L., Batres, C., & Perrett, D. I. (2017). Aggressor or protector? Experiences and perceptions of violence predict preferences for masculinity. *Evolution and Human Behavior, 38*(4), 481–489. https://doi.org/10.1016/j.evolhumbehav.2017.03.004

Bostyn, D. H., Sevenhant, S., & Roets, A. (2018). Of mice, men, and trolleys: Hypothetical judgment versus real-life behavior in trolley-style moral dilemmas. *Psychological Science, 29*(7), 1084–1093. https://doi.org/10.1177/0956797617752640

Botella, C., Bretón-López, J., Serrano, B., García-Palacios, A., Quero, S., & Baños, R. (2014). Treatment of flying phobia using virtual reality exposure with or without cognitive restructuring: Participants' preferences. *Revista de Psicopatología y Psicología Clínica, 19,* 157–169. doi:10.5944/rppc.vol.19.num.3.2014.13898

Bouchard Jr., T. J. (2016). Genes and behavior: Nature via nurture. In R. J. Sternberg, S. T. Fiske, & D. J. Foss (Eds.), *Scientists making a difference: One hundred eminent behavioral and brain scientists talk about their most important contributions* (pp. 73–76). New York, NY: Cambridge University Press.

Bouchard, T. J., Jr. (1997). The genetics of personality. In K. Blum & E. P. Noble (Eds.), *Handbook of psychiatric genetics* (pp. 273–296). Boca Raton, FL: CRC Press.

Bouchard, T. J., Jr. (2013). Genetic influence on human psychological traits. In S. M. Downes & E. Machery (Eds.), *Arguing about human nature: Contemporary debates. Arguing about philosophy* (pp. 139–144). New York, NY: Routledge/Taylor & Francis Group.

Bouchard, T. J., Jr., & McGue, M. (1981). Familial studies of intelligence: A review. *Science, 212,* 1055–1059. http://dx.doi.org/10.1126/science.7195071

Boucher, K. L., Rydell, R. J., & Murphy, M. C. (2015). Forecasting the experience of stereotype threat for others. *Journal of Experimental Social Psychology, 58,* 56–62. http://dx.doi.org/10.1016/j.jesp.2015.01.002

Bougard, C., Davenne, D., Espie, S., Moussay, S., & Léger, D. (2016). Sleepiness, attention and risk of accidents in powered two-wheelers. *Sleep Medicine Reviews, 25,* 40–51. http://dx.doi.org/10.1016/j.smrv.2015.01.006

Boukhris, O., Abdessalem, R., Ammar, A., Hsouna, H., Trabelsi, K., Engel, F. A., . . . Chtourou, H. (2019). Nap opportunity during the daytime affects performance and perceived exertion in 5-m shuttle run test. *Frontiers in Physiology, 10:*779. doi:10.3389/fphys.2019.00779

Boundy, E. O., Dastjerdi, R., Spiegelman, D., Fawzi, W. W., Missmer, S. A., Lieberman, E., . . . Chan, G. J. (2016). Kangaroo mother care and neonatal outcomes: A meta-analysis. *Pediatrics, 137,* 1–16. doi:10.1542/peds.2015-2238

Bourassa, K. J., Memel, M., Woolverton, C., & Sbarra, D. A. (2017). Social participation predicts cognitive functioning in aging adults over time: Comparisons with physical health, depression, and physical activity. *Aging & Mental Health, 21*(2), 133–146. http://dx.doi.org/10.1080/13607863.2015.1081152

Bourne, L. E., Dominowski, R. L., & Loftus, E. F. (1979). *Cognitive processes.* Englewood Cliffs, NJ: Prentice Hall.

Bouton, M. E., & Todd, T. P. (2014). A fundamental role for context in instrumental learning and extinction. *Behavioural Processes, 104,* 13–19. http://dx.doi.org/10.1016/j.beproc.2014.02.012

Bowlby, J. (1969). *Attachment and loss: Vol. 1. Attachment.* New York, NY: Basic Books.

Bowlby, J. (1989). *Secure attachment.* New York, NY: Basic Books.

Bowlby, J. (2000). *Attachment.* New York, NY: Basic Books.

Boyce, C. J., Wood, A. M., Daly, M., & Sedikides, C. (2015). Personality change following unemployment. *Journal of Applied Psychology, 100*, 991–1011. http://dx.doi.org/10.1037/a0038647

Boyd, R. (2011). The Wizard of Oz—a myth for our age. *Energetics.* Retrieved from https://energeticsinstitute.com.au/articles/wizard-of-oz/

Bradley, R. H., & Corwyn, R. F. (2008). Infant temperament, parenting, and externalizing behavior in first grade: A test of the differential susceptibility hypothesis. *Journal of Child Psychology and Psychiatry, 49*, 124–131.

Brådvik, L. (2018). Suicide risk and mental disorders. *International Journal of Environmental Research and Public Health, 15*(9), 2028. doi:10.3390/ijerph15092028

Brady, R. O., Jr., Tandon, N., Masters, G. A., Margolis, A., Cohen, B. M., Keshavan, M., & Öngür, D. (2017). Differential brain network activity across mood states in bipolar disorder. *Journal of Affective Disorders, 207*, 367–376. http://dx.doi.org/10.1016/j.jad.2016.09.041

Brand, B. L., Vissia, E. M., Chalavi, S., Nijenhuis, E. R. S., Webermann, A. R., Draijer, N., & Reinders, A. A. T. S. (2016). DID is trauma based: Further evidence supporting the trauma model of DID. *Acta Psychiatrica Scandinavica, 134*(6), 560–563. http://dx.doi.org/10.1111/acps.12653

Brandell, J. R., & Brown, S. (2015). The new "bridge to adulthood": Searching for meaning and cohesion in the nexus of "hook-ups," Internet porn, and instant messages. *Smith College Studies in Social Work, 85*, 387–408. http://dx.doi.org/10.1080/00377317.2015.1089676

Brandt, N. D., Lechner, C. M., Tetzner, J., & Rammstedt, B. (2019). Personality, cognitive ability, and academic performance: Differential associations across school subjects and school tracks. *Journal of Personality.* https://doi.org/10.1111/jopy.12482

Branković, M. (2019). Who believes in ESP: Cognitive and motivational determinants of the belief in extra-sensory perception. *Europe's Journal of Psychology, 15*(1), 120–139. doi:10.5964/ejop.v15i1.1689

Brannon, L. (2016). *Gender: Psychological perspectives* (6th ed.). New York, NY: Psychology Press.

Brannon, L., Feist, J., & Updegraff, J. A. (2018). *Health psychology: An introduction to behavior and health* (9th ed.). Boston, MA: Cengage.

Brannon, T. N., Markus, H. R., & Taylor, V. J. (2015). "Two souls, two thoughts," two self-schemas: Double consciousness can have positive academic consequences for African Americans. *Journal of Personality and Social Psychology, 108*, 586–609. http://dx.doi.org/10.1037/a0038992

Brassard, A., Dupuy, E., Bergeron, S., & Shaver, P. R. (2015). Attachment insecurities and women's sexual function and satisfaction: The mediating roles of sexual self-esteem, sexual anxiety, and sexual assertiveness. *Journal of Sex Research, 52*, 110–119. http://dx.doi.org/10.1080/00224499.2013.838744.

Bratsberg, B., & Rogeberg, O. (2018). Flynn effect and its reversal are both environmentally caused. *Proceedings of the National Academy of Sciences of the United States of America, 115*(26), 6674–6678. doi:10.1073/pnas.1718793115

Bredström, A. J. (2017). Culture and context in mental health diagnosing: Scrutinizing the DSM-5 revision. *Journal of Medical Humanities,* 1–17. https://doi.org/10.1007/s10912-017-9501

Breger, L. (2014). Psychopathia sexualis: Sexuality in old and new psychoanalysis. *Journal of Clinical Psychology, 70*, 147–159. http://dx.doi.org/10.1002/jclp.22066

Breivik, G., Sand, T. S., & Sookermany, A. M. (2019). Risk-taking and sensation seeking in military contexts: A literature review. *SAGE Open.* https://doi.org/10.1177/2158244018824498

Breland, K., & Breland, M. (1961). The misbehavior of organisms. *American Psychologist, 16*, 681–684. http://dx.doi.org/10.1037/h0040090

Brem, M. J., Florimbio, A. R., Elmquist, J., Shorey, R. C., & Stuart, G. L. (2018). Antisocial traits, distress tolerance, and alcohol problems as predictors of intimate partner violence in men arrested for domestic violence. *Psychology of Violence, 8*(1), 132–139. doi:10.1037/vio0000088

Bresin, K., Kling, L., & Verona, E. (2018). The effect of acute physical pain on subsequent negative emotional affect: A meta-analysis. *Personality Disorders, 9*(3), 273–283. doi:10.1037/per0000248

Brethel-Haurwitz, K. M., & Marsh, A. A. (2014). Geographical differences in subjective well-being predict extraordinary altruism. *Psychological Science, 25*, 762–771. doi:10.1177/0956797613516148

Breuer, J., Scharkow, M., & Quandt, T. (2015). Sore losers? A reexamination of the frustration-aggression hypothesis for colocated video game play. *Psychology of Popular Media Culture, 4*, 126–137. http://dx.doi.org/10.1016/j.iheduc.2015.01.001

Brewer, L. C., Redmond, N., Slusser, J. P., Scott, C. G., Chamberlain, A. M., Djousse, L., . . . Sims, M. (2018). Stress and achievement of cardiovascular health metrics: The American Heart Association Life's Simple 7 in Blacks of the Jackson Heart Study. *Journal of the American Heart Association, 7*(11), e008855. doi:10.1161/JAHA.118.008855

Brewer, M. B. (2015). Motivated entitativity: When we'd rather see the forest than the trees. In S. J. Stroessner & J. W. Sherman (Eds.), *Social perception from individuals to groups* (pp. 161–176). New York, NY: Psychology Press.

Brewer, N., Weber, N., Wootton, D., & Lindsay, D. D. (2012). Identifying the bad guy in a lineup using confidence judgments under deadline pressure. *Psychological Science, 23*, 1208–1214. http://dx.doi.org/10.1177/0956797612441217

Brewster, M., & Tucker, J. M. (2016). Understanding bystander behavior: The influence of and interaction between bystander characteristics and situational factors. *Victims & Offenders, 11*(3), 455–481. http://dx.doi.org/10.1080/15564886.2015.1009593

Bridge, J. A., Greenhouse, J. B., Ruch, D., Stevens, J., Ackerman, J., Sheftall, A. H., . . . Campo, J. V. (2019). Association between the release of Netflix's *13 Reasons Why* and suicide rates in the United States: An interrupted times series analysis. *Journal of the American Academy of Child & Adolescent Psychiatry.* https://doi.org/10.1016/j.jaac.2019.04.020

Bright, P., & Filippi, R. (2019). Editorial: Perspectives on the "Bilingual advantage": Challenges and opportunities. *Frontiers in Psychology, 10*, 1346. doi:10.3389/fpsyg.2019.01346

Brislin, R. W. (2000). *Understanding culture's influence on behavior* (3rd ed.). Ft.Worth, TX: Harcourt.

Brivio, E., Gaudioso, F., Vergine, I., Mirizzi, C. R., Reina, C., Stellari, A., & Galimberti, C. (2018). Preventing technostress through positive technology. *Frontiers in Psychology, 9*:2569. doi:10.3389/fpsyg.2018.02569

Brodbeck, F. C., & Guillaume, Y. R. (2015). Effective decision making and problem solving in projects. In E. Bendoly, W. Van Wezel, & D. Bachrach (Eds.), *Applied psychology for project managers* (pp. 37–52). Berlin, DE: Springer.

Brodsky, S. L. & Gutheil, T. G. (Eds.). (2016). *The expert witness: More maxims and guidelines for testifying in court* (2nd ed., pp. 156–159). Washington, DC: American Psychological Association. http://dx.doi.org/10.1037/14732-038

Brody, G. H., Yu, T., Chen, E., Beach, S. R. H., & Miller, G. E. (2016). Family-centered prevention ameliorates the longitudinal association between risky family processes and epigenetic aging. *Journal of Child Psychology and Psychiatry, 57*, 566–574. http://dx.doi.org/10.1111/jcpp.12495

Broockman, D., & Kalla, J. (2016). Durably reducing transphobia: A field experiment on door-to-door canvassing. *Science, 353*, 220–224. http://dx.doi.org/10.1126/science.aad9713

Brooks, J. E., & Neville, H. A. (2017). Interracial attraction among college men: The influence of ideologies, familiarity, and similarity. *Journal of Social and Personal Relationships, 34*(2), 166–183. http://dx.doi.org/10.1177/0265407515627508

Broshek, D. K., DeMarco, A. P., & Freeman, J. R. (2015). A review of post-concussion syndrome and psychological factors associated with concussion. *Brain Injury, 29*(2), 228–237. http://dx.doi.org/10.3109/02699052.2014.974 674.

Brown, A. S., & Lau, F. S. (2016). A review of the epidemiology of schizophrenia. In M. V. Pletnikov & J. Waddington (Eds.), *Modeling the psychopathological dimensions of schizophrenia: From molecules to behavior* (pp. 17–30). San Diego, CA: Elsevier Academic Press. http://dx.doi.org/10.1016/B978-0-12-800981-9. 00002-X

Brown, C. S., Ali, H., Stone, E. A., & Jewell, J. A. (2017). U.S. children's stereotypes and prejudicial attitudes toward Arab Muslims. *Analyses of Social Issues and Public Policy, 17*(1), 60–83. http://dx.doi.org/10.1111/asap.12129

Brown, E., Gonzalez-Liencres, C., Tas, C., & Brüne, M. (2016). Reward modulates the mirror neuron system in schizophrenia: A study into the mu rhythm suppression, empathy, and mental state attribution. *Social Neuroscience, 11*, 175–186. http://dx.doi.org/10.1080/17470919.2015.1053982

Brown, J., & Harr, D. (2018). Perceptions of fetal alcohol spectrum disorder (FASD) at a mental health outpatient treatment provider in Minnesota. *International Journal of Environmental Research and Public Health, 16*(1), 16. doi:10.3390/ijerph16010016

Brown, L. M., Frahm, K. A., & Bongar, B. (2013). Crisis intervention. In G. Stricker, T. A. Widiger, & I. B. Weiner (Eds.), *Handbook of psychology, Vol. 8. Clinical psychology* (2nd ed., pp. 408–430). Hoboken, NJ: Wiley.

Brown, M. A., & Brown, J. D. (2015). Self-enhancement biases, self-esteem, and ideal mate preferences. *Personality and Individual Differences, 74*, 61–65. http://dx.doi.org/10.1016/j.paid.2014.09.039

Brown, R., & Kulik, J. (1977). Flashbulb memories. *Cognition, 5*, 73–99. http://dx.doi.org/10.1016/0010-0277(77)90018-X

Brownstein, M., Madva, A., & Gawronski, B. (2019). What do implicit measures measure? *WIREs Cognitive Science*, e1501. https://doi.org/10.1002/wcs.1501

Brown, W. A. (2013). *The placebo effect in clinical practice.* New York, NY: Oxford University Press.

Bruning, R. H., & Kauffman, D. F. (2016). Self-efficacy beliefs and motivation in writing development. In C. A. MacArthur, S. Graham, & J. Fitzgerald (Eds.), *Handbook of writing research* (2nd ed., pp. 160–173). New York, NY: Guilford.

Bruni, S., Gerbella, M., Bonini, L., Borra, E., Coude, G., Ferrari, P. F., . . . Rozzi, S. (2018). Cortical and subcortical connections of parietal and premotor nodes of the monkey hand mirror neuron network. *Brain Structure and Function, 223*(4), 1713–1729. Retrieved from https://doi.org/10.1007/s00429-017-1582-0

Brunoni, A. R., Valiengo, L., Baccaro, A., Zanao, T. A., de Oliveira, J. F., Goulart, A., . . . Fregni, F. (2013). The sertraline vs electrical current therapy for treating depression clinical study: Results from a factorial, randomized, controlled trial. *JAMA Psychiatry, 70*, 383–391.

Brussoni, M., Gibbons, R., Gray, C., Ishikawa, T., Sandseter, E. B. H., Bienenstock, A., . . . Tremblay, M. S. (2015). What is the relationship between risky outdoor play and health in children? A systematic review. *International Journal of Environmental Research and Public Health, 12*, 6423–6454. http://dx.doi.org/10.3390/ijerph120606423

Bryant, F. B., & Veroff J. (2007). *Savoring: A new model of positive experience.* Mahwah, NJ: Lawrence Erlbaum.

Bryant, N. B., & Gómez, R. L. (2015). The teen sleep loss epidemic: What can be done? *Translational Issues in Psychological Science, 1*, 116–125. http://dx.doi.org/10.1037/tps0000020

Buchy, L., Cannon, T. D., Anticevic, A., Lyngberg, K., Cadenhead, K. S., Cornblatt, B. A., . . . Addington, J. (2015). Evaluating the impact of cannabis use on thalamic connectivity in youth at clinical high risk of psychosis. *BMC Psychiatry, 15*, Article 276. doi:10.1186/s12888-015-0656-x

Buckley, T., Soo Hoo, S. Y., Fethney, J., Shaw, E., Hanson, P. S., & Tofler, G. H. (2015). Triggering of acute coronary occlusion by episodes of anger. *European Heart Journal: Acute Cardiovascular Care, 4*, 493–498. http://doi.org/10.1177/2048872615568969

Buckner, J. D., & Terlecki, M. A. (2016). Social anxiety and alcohol-related impairment: The mediational impact of solitary drinking. *Addictive Behaviors, 58*, 7–11. http://dx.doi.org/10.1016/j.addbeh.2016.02.006

Buehler, S. (2014). *What every mental health professional needs to know about sex.* New York, NY: Springer.

Bugental, D. B., & Johnston, C. (2000). Parental and child cognitions in the context of the family. *Annual Review of Psychology, 51*, 315–344. https://doi.org/10.1146/annurev.psych.51.1.315

Buglass, S. L., Binder, J. F., Betts, L. R., & Underwood, J. D. (2017). Motivators of online vulnerability: The impact of social network site use and FOMO. *Computers in Human Behavior, 66*, 248–255. http://dx.doi.org/10.1016/j.chb.2016.09.055

Bui, D. C., & McDaniel, M. A. (2015). Enhancing learning during lecture note-taking using outlines and illustrative diagrams. *Journal of Applied Research in Memory and Cognition, 4*, 129–135. http://dx.doi.org/10.1016/j.jarmac.2015.03.002

Bujisic, M., Wu, L. L., Mattila, A., & Bilgihan, A. (2014). Not all smiles are created equal: Investigating the effects of display authenticity and service relationship on customer tipping behavior. *International Journal of Contemporary Hospitality Management, 26*, 293–306. doi:10.1108/IJCHM10-2012-0181

Bullis, J. R., & Hofmann, S. G. (2016). Adult anxiety and related disorders. In C. M. Nezu & A. M. Nezu (Eds.), *The Oxford handbook of cognitive and behavioral therapies* (pp. 291–311). New York, NY: Oxford University Press.

Burns, J. K., Tomita, A., & Kapadia, S. (2014). Income inequality and schizophrenia: Increased schizophrenia incidence in countries with high levels of income inequality. *International Journal of Social Psychiatry, 60*, 185–196. http://dx.doi.org/10.1177/0020764013481426

Burns, S. (2019). *Psychology of sex and gender.* New York, NY: Macmillan.

Burston, J. J., Valdes, A. M., Woodhams, S. G., Mapp, P. I., Stocks, J., Watson, D., . . . Chapman, V. (2019). The impact of anxiety on chronic musculoskeletal pain and the role of astrocyte activation. *Pain, 160*(3), 658–669. doi:10.1097/j.pain.0000000000001445

Burton, A. L., & Abbott, M. J. (2019). Processes and pathways to binge eating: Development of an integrated cognitive and behavioural model of binge eating. *Journal of Eating Disorders, 7*:18. https://doi.org/10.1186/s40337-019-0248-0

Burton, N. (2018, August 08). How the language you speak influences the way you think. *Psychology Today.* Retrieved from https://www.psychologytoday.com/us/blog/hide-and-seek/201808/how-the-language-you-speak-influences-the-way-you-think

Bushman, B. J. (2002). Does venting anger feed or extinguish the flame? Catharsis, rumination, distraction, anger and aggressive responding. *Personality & Social Psychology Bulletin, 28,* 724–731.

Bushman, B. J. (2016). *Aggression and violence: A social psychological perspective.* New York, NY: Psychology Press.

Bushman, B. J. (2016). Violent media and hostile appraisals: A meta-analytic review. *Aggressive Behavior, 42*(6), 605–613. http://dx.doi.org/10.1002/ab.21655

Bushman, B. J. (2019). Aggression and violence. In R. Biswas-Diener & E. Diener (Eds.), *Noba textbook series: Psychology.* Champaign, IL: DEF publishers. http://noba.to/63vj7ykn

Buss, D. M. (1989). Sex differences in human mate preferences: Evolutionary hypotheses tested in 37 cultures. *Behavioral and Brain Sciences, 12,* 1–49.

Buss, D. M. (2003). *The evolution of desire: Strategies of human mating.* New York, NY: Basic.

Buss, D. M. (2008). *The evolution of desire: Strategies of human mating* (4th ed.). New York, NY: Basic Books.

Buss, D. M. (2011). *Evolutionary psychology: The new science of the mind* (4th ed.). Upper Saddle River, NJ: Prentice-Hall.

Buss, D. M. (2015). *The handbook of evolutionary psychology* (2nd ed.). Hoboken, NJ: Wiley.

Buss, D. M., Abbott, M., Angleitner, A., Asherian, A., Biaggio, A., Blanco-Villasenor, A., . . . Yang, K.-S. (1990). International preferences in selecting mates: A study of 37 cultures. *Journal of Cross-Cultural Psychology, 21,* 5–47. http://dx.doi.org/10.1177/0022022190211001

Buss, D. M., & Schmitt, D. P. (2019). Mate preferences and their behavioral manifestations. *Annual Review of Psychology, 70,* 77–110. doi:10.1146/annurev-psych-010418-103408

Butcher, J. N. (2000). Revising psychological tests: Lessons learned from the revision of the MMPI. *Psychological Assessment, 12,* 263–271.

Butcher, J. N. (2011). *A beginner's guide to the MMPI-2* (3rd ed.). Washington, DC: American Psychological Association.

Butera, C. (2018, March 8). We asked three experts to discuss the role of criminal intent and insanity in our legal system. *Pacific Standard.* Retrieved from https://psmag.com/news/insanity-legal-system

Butler, M. G. (2017). Clinical and genetic aspects of the 15q11.2 BP1–BP2 microdeletion disorder. *Journal of Intellectual Disability Research, 61*(6), 568–579. http://dx.doi.org/10.1111/jir.12382

Buxton, O. M., Cain, S. W., O'Connor, S. P., Porter, J. H., Duffy, J. F., Wang, W., . . . Shea, S. A. (2012). Adverse metabolic consequences in humans of prolonged sleep restriction combined with circadian disruption. *Science Translational Medicine, 4,* 129ra43. doi:10.1126/scitranslmed.3003200

Cacciola, S., & Mather, V. (2018, January 24). Larry Nassar sentencing: "I just signed your death warrant." *The New York Times.* Retrieved from https://www.nytimes.com/2018/01/24/sports/larry-nassar-sentencing.html

Cadle, C. E., & Zoladz, P. R. (2015). Stress time-dependently influences the acquisition and retrieval of unrelated information by producing a memory of its own. *Frontiers in Psychology, 6:*910. doi:10.3389/fpsyg.2015.00910

Cahn, D. D. (2013). *Intimates in conflict: A communication perspective.* Hillsdale, NJ: Erlbaum.

Cain, D. J., Keenan, K., & Rubin, S. (Eds.). (2016). *Humanistic psychotherapies: Handbook of research and practice* (2nd ed.). Washington, DC: American Psychological Association.

Caine, R. N., Caine, G., McClintic, C., & Klimek, K. J. (2016). *12 brain/mind learning principles in action: Teach for the development of higher-order thinking and executive function* (3rd ed.). Thousand Oaks, CA: Corwin Press.

Cain, M. S., Leonard, J. A., Gabrieli, J. D., & Finn, A. S. (2016). Media multitasking in adolescence. *Psychonomic Bulletin & Review, 23*(6), 1932–1941. http://dx.doi.org/10.3758/s13423-016-1036-3

Calati, R., & Courtet, P. (2016). Is psychotherapy effective for reducing suicide attempt and non-suicidal self-injury rates? Meta-analysis and meta-regression of literature data. *Journal of Psychiatric Research, 79,* 8–20. http://dx.doi.org/10.1016/j.jpsychires.2016.04.003

Calderwood, C., & Ackerman, P. L. (2016). The relative salience of daily and enduring influences on off-job reactions to work stress. *Stress and Health, 32*(5), 587–596. http://dx.doi.org/10.1002/smi.2665

Caldwell-Harris, C. L. (2019, January 15). Our language affects what we see. *Scientific American.* Retrieved from https://www.scientificamerican.com/article/our-language-affects-what-we-see/

Caleza, C., Yãnez-Vico, R. M., Mendoza, A., & Iglesias-Linares, A. (2016). Childhood obesity and delayed gratification behavior: A systematic review of experimental studies. *The Journal of Pediatrics, 169,* 201–207. http://dx.doi.org/10.1016/j.jpeds.2015.10.008

Calvert, S. L., Appelbaum, M., Dodge, K. A., Graham, S., Nagayama Hall, G. C., Hamby, S., & Hedges, L. V. (2017). The American Psychological Association Task Force assessment of violent video games: Science in the service of public interest. *American Psychologist, 72*(2), 126–143. http://dx.doi.org/10.1037/a0040413

Camera, D., Coleman, H. A., Parkington, H. C., Jenkins, T. A., Pow, D. V., Boase, N., . . . Poronnik, P. (2016). Learning, memory and long-term potentiation are altered in Nedd4 heterozygous mice. *Behavioural Brain Research, 303,* 176–181. http://dx.doi.org/10.1016/j.bbr.2016.01.054

Camerer, C., Dreber, A., Holzmeister, F., Ho, T. H., Huber, J., Johannesson, M., . . . Wu, H. (2018). Evaluating the replicability of social science experiments in Nature and Science between 2010 and 2015. *Nature Human Behaviour, 2,* 637–644. https://doi.org/10.1038/s41562-018-0399

Cameron, L. P., Benson, C. J., DeFelice, B. C., Fiehn, O., & Olson, D. E. (2019). Chronic, intermittent microdoses of the psychedelic N, N-Dimethyltryptamine (DMT)produce positive effects on mood and anxiety in rodents. *ACS Chemical Neuroscience, 10*(7), 3261–3270. doi:10.1021/acschemneuro.8b00692

Campbell, J. R., & Feng, A. X. (2011). Comparing adult productivity of American mathematics, physics, and chemistry Olympians with Terman's longitudinal study. *Roeper Review: A Journal on Gifted Education, 33,* 18–25. http://dx.doi.org/10.1080/02783193.2011.530203

Campbell, M. M., Sibeko, G., Mall, S., Baldinger, A., Nagdee, M., Susser, E., & Stein, D. J. (2017). The content of delusions in a sample of South African Xhosa people with schizophrenia. *BMC Psychiatry, 17,* Article 41. doi:10.1186/s12888-017-1196-3

Campbell, S. N., Zhang, C., Monte, L., Roe, A. D., Rice, K. C., Tach., Y., . . . Rissman, R. A. (2015). Increased tau phosphorylation and aggregation in the hippocampus of mice overexpressing corticotropin-releasing factor. *Journal of Alzheimer's Disease, 43,* 967–976. http://dx.doi.org/10.3233/JAD-141281.

Cantio, C., Jepsen, J. R. M., Madsen, G. F., Bilenberg, N., & White, S. J. (2016). Exploring 'the autisms' at a cognitive level. *Autism Research, 9*(12), 1328–1339. http://dx.doi.org/10.1002/aur.1630

Cantisani, A., Koenig, T., Stegmayer, K., Federspiel, A., Horn, H., Müller, T. J., . . . Walther, S. (2016). EEG marker of inhibitory brain activity correlates with resting-state cerebral blood flow in the reward system in major depression. *European Archives of Psychiatry and Clinical Neuroscience, 266*(8), 755–764. http://dx.doi.org/10.1007/s00406-015-0652-7

Cao, Y., Trillo-Tinoco, J., Sierra, R. A., Anadon, C., Dai, W., Mohamed, E., . . . Rodriguez, P. C. (2019). ER stress-induced mediator C/EBP homologous protein thwarts effector T cell activity in tumors through T-bet repression. *Nature Communications, 10*(1), article number 1280. doi:10.1038/s41467-019-09263-1

Cappelli, P. (2019). Your approach to hiring is all wrong. *Harvard Business Review.* Retrieved from https://hbr.org/2019/05/recruiting

Caputo, I. (2019, January 10). Japan's shrinking labor force is finding new ways to fight karoshi—"death by overwork." *PRI's The World.* Retrieved from https://www.pri.org/stories/2019-01-10/japan-s-shrinking-labor-force-finding-new-ways-fight-kar-shi-death-overwork

Carbone, S., Canada, J. M., Billingsley, H. E., Siddiqui, M. S., Elagizi, A., & Lavie, C. J. (2019). Obesity paradox in cardiovascular disease: Where do we stand? *Vascular Health Risk Management, 15*, 89–100. doi:10.2147/VHRM.S168946

Carcea, I., & Froemke, R. C. (2019). Biological mechanisms for observational learning. *Current Opinion in Neurobiology, 54*, 178–185. http://froemkelab.med.nyu.edu/sites/default/files/1-s2.0-S0959438818300874-main.pdf

Carcioppolo, N., Dunleavy, V. O., & Yang, Q. (2017). How do perceived descriptive norms influence indoor tanning intentions? An application of the theory of normative social behavior. *Health Communication, 32*(2), 230–239. http://dx.doi.org/10.1080/10410236.2015.1120697

Carducci, B. J. (2015). *Psychology of personality: Viewpoints, research, and applications* (3rd ed.). Hoboken, NJ: Wiley.

Carey, B. (2016, November 3). When it comes to success, age really is just a number. *The New York Times.* Retrieved from https://www.nytimes.com/2016/11/04/science/stemcareers-success-achievement.html?_r=0

Carlson, J. D., & Englar-Carlson, M. (2013). Adlerian therapy. In J. Frew & M. D. Spiegler (Eds.), *Contemporary psychotherapies for a diverse world* (1st rev. ed., pp. 87–129). New York, NY: Routledge.

Carlson, J. M., Rubin, D., & Mujica-Parodi, L. R. (2017). Lost emotion: Disrupted brain-based tracking of dynamic affective episodes in anxiety and depression. *Psychiatry Research: Neuroimaging, 260*, 37–48. http://dx.doi.org/10.1016/j.pscychresns.2016.12.002

Carlson, S. M., Shoda, Y., Ayduk, O., Aber, L., Schaefer, C., Sethi, A., . . . Mischel, W. (2018). Cohort effects in children's delay of gratification. *Developmental Psychology, 54*(8), 1395–1407. http://dx.doi.org/10.1037/dev0000533

Carney, C., Harland, K. K., & McGehee, D.V. (2016). Using event-triggered naturalistic data to examine the prevalence of teen driver distractions in rear-end crashes. *Journal of Safety Research, 57*, 47–52. http://dx.doi.org/10.1016/j.jsr.2016.03.010

Carothers, B. J., & Reis, H. T. (2013). Men and women are from Earth: Examining the latent structure of gender. *Journal of Personality and Social Psychology, 104*, 385–407. http://dx.doi.org/10.1037/a0030437

Carpenter, C. J. (2019). Cognitive dissonance, ego-involvement, and motivated reasoning. *Annals of the International Communication Association, 43*(1), 1–23. doi:10.1080/23808985.2018.1564881

Carpenter, S. K., & Yeung, K. L. (2017). The role of mediator strength in learning from retrieval. *Journal of Memory and Language, 92*, 128–141. http://dx.doi.org/10.1016/j.jml.2016.06.008

Carrillo, M., Han, Y., Migliorati, F., Liu, M., Gazzola, V., & Keysers, C. (2019). Emotional mirror neurons in the rat's anterior cingulate cortex. *Current Biology, 29*(8), 1301–1312.e6. https://doi.org/10.1016/j.cub.2019.03.024.

Carroll, J. L. (2019). *Sexuality now: Embracing diversity* (6th ed.). Boston, MA: Cengage.

Carskadon, M. A., Wolfson, A. R., Acebo, C., Tzischinsky, O., & Seifer, R. (1998). Adolescent sleep patterns, circadian timing, and sleepiness at a transition to early school days. *Sleep, 21*, 871–881.

Carstensen, L. L. (1993). Motivation for social contact across the life span: A theory of socioemotional selectivity. In J. E. Jacobs (Ed.), *Nebraska symposium on motivation, 1992: Developmental perspectives on motivation* (pp. 209–254). Lincoln, NE: University of Nebraska Press.

Carstensen, L. L. (2006). The influence of a sense of time on human development. *Science, 312*, 1913–1915. doi:10.1126/science.1127488

Carstensen, L. L. (2019). Integrating cognitive and emotion paradigms to address the paradox of aging. *Cognition and Emotion, 33*(1), 119–125. doi:10.1080/02699931.2018.1543181

Carta, I., Chen, C. H., Schott, A., Dorizan, S., & Khodakhah, K. (2019). Cerebellar modulation of the reward circuitry and social behavior. *Science, 363*(6424), eaav0581. http://dx.doi:10.1126/science.aav0581

Carter, K. A., Hathaway, N. E., & Lettieri, C. F. (2014). Common sleep disorders in children. *American Family Physician, 89*, 368–377.

Caruso, J. P., & Sheehan, J. P. (2017). Psychosurgery, ethics, and media: A history of Walter Freeman and the lobotomy. *Neurosurgical Focus FOC, 43*(3), E6. Retrieved from https://thejns.org/focus/view/journals/neurosurg-focus/43/3/article-pE6.xml

Casey, E. A., Lindhorst, T., & Storer, H. L. (2017). The situational-cognitive model of adolescent bystander behavior: Modeling bystander decision-making in the context of bullying and teen dating violence. *Psychology of Violence, 7*(1), 33–44. http://dx.doi.org/10.1037/vio0000033

Cashel, M. L. (2016). What counselors should know about personality assessments. In I. Marini & M. A. Stebnicki (Eds.), *The professional counselor's desk reference* (2nd ed., pp. 299–303). New York, NY: Springer.

Castaldelli-Maia, J. M., Ventriglio, A., & Bhugra, D. (2016). Tobacco smoking: From 'glamour' to 'stigma.' A comprehensive review. *Psychiatry and Clinical Neurosciences, 70*, 24–33. doi.org/10.1111/pcn.12365

Castillo, D. T., Chee, C. L., Nason, E., Keller, J., C'de Baca, J., Qualls, C., Fallon, S. K., . . . Keane, T. M. (2016). Group-delivered cognitive/exposure therapy for PTSD in women veterans: A randomized controlled trial. *Psychological Trauma: Theory, Research, Practice, and Policy, 8*, 404–412. http://dx.doi.org/10.1037/tra0000111

Castillo, D. T., Chee, C. L., Nason, E., Keller, J., C'de Baca, J., Qualls, C., . . . Keane, T. M. (2016). Group-delivered cognitive/exposure therapy for PTSD in women veterans: A randomized controlled trial. *Psychological Trauma: Theory, Research, Practice, and Policy, 8*, 404–412. http://dx.doi.org/10.1037/tra0000111

Castle, D. J., & Buckley, P. F. (2015). *Oxford psychiatry library. Schizophrenia* (2nd ed., rev. and updated). New York, NY: Oxford University Press.

Cattell, R. B. (1950). *Personality: A systematic, theoretical, and factual study.* New York, NY: McGraw-Hill.

Cattell, R. B. (1963). Theory of fluid and crystallized intelligence: A critical experiment. *Journal of Educational Psychology, 54*, 1–22.

Cattell, R. B. (1971). *Abilities: Their structure, growth, and action.* Boston, MA: Houghton Mifflin.

Cattell, R. B. (1990). Advances in Cattellian personality theory. In L. A. Pervin (Ed.), *Handbook of personality: Theory and research* (pp. 101–110). New York, NY: Guilford.

CDC. (2016, February 18). 1 in 3 adults don't get enough sleep. *CDC Newsroom*. Retrieved from http://www.cdc.gov/media/releases/2016/p0215-enough-sleep.html

Cea, N. F., & Barnes, G. E. (2015). The development of addiction-prone personality traits in biological and adoptive families. *Personality and Individual Differences, 82,* 107–113. http://dx.doi.org/10.1016/j.paid.2015.02.035

Cehajic, S., Brown, R., & Castano, E. (2008). Forgive and forget? Antecedents and consequences of intergroup forgiveness in Bosnia and Herzegovina. *Political Psychology, 29*(3), 351–367. doi:10.1111/j.1467-9221.2008.00634.x.

Çelikel, A., Demirkiran, D. S., Özsoy, S., Zeren, C., & Arslan, M. M. (2015). Factors associated with PTSD in cases of sexual assault. *Journal of Psychiatry, 18*:1. doi:10.4172/2378-5756.1000181

Çelik, M., Kalenderoğlu, A., Almiş, H., & Turgut, M. (2016). TV programı sonrası gelişen Ölüm Kastı Olmayan Taklit İntiharlar: Beş Yaşında İki Olgu. / Copycat suicides without an intention to die after watching TV programs: Two cases at five years of age. *Nöropsikiyatri Arşivi/Archives of Neuropsychiatry, 53*(1), 83–84. doi:10.5152/npa.2015.9988

Centers for Disease Control and Prevention. (2017a). Adult obesity causes and consequences. *CDC.* Retrieved from https://www.cdc.gov/obesity/adult/causes.html

Centers for Disease Control and Prevention. (2017b). Healthy weight—it's not a diet, it's a lifestyle! *CDC* Retrieved from: http://www.cdc.gov/healthyweight/assessing/bmi/adult_bmi/english_bmi_calculator/bmi_calculator.html.

Centers for Disease Control and Prevention. (2018, August 13). Adult obesity facts. *CDC.* Retrieved from https://www.cdc.gov/obesity/data/adult.html

Centers for Disease Control and Prevention (2018, June 7). Suicide rates rising across the U.S. *CDC Newsroom.* https://www.cdc.gov/media/releases/2018/p0607-suicide-prevention.html

Centers for Disease Control and Prevention. (2019). Preventing sexual violence. *CDC.* Retrieved April 19, 2019 from https://www.cdc.gov/features/sexualviolence/index.html

Centers for Disease Control and Prevention (CDC). (2016). Smoking and tobacco use. *CDC.* Retrieved from http://www.cdc.gov/tobacco/data_statistics/fact_sheets/fast_facts/

Centers for Disease Control and Prevention (CDC). (2019). Tips impact and results. *CDC.* Retrieved from https://www.cdc.gov/tobacco/campaign/tips/about/impact/campaign-impact-results.html

Centers for Disease Control (CDC). (2016). A to Z: Before and during pregnancy. *Centers for Disease Control.* Retrieved from http://www.cdc.gov/ncbddd/index.html

Centers for Disease Control (CDC). (2016). TBI: Get the facts. *Centers for Disease Control and Prevention.* Retrieved from http://www.cdc.gov/traumaticbraininjury/get_the_facts.html

Cesario, J. (2014). Priming, replication, and the hardest science. *Perspectives on Psychological Science, 9,* 40–48. http://dx.doi.org/10.1177/1745691613513470

Chambers, A. M., & Payne, J. D. (2015). The memory function of sleep. In D. R. Addis, M. Barense, & A. Duarte (Eds.), *The Wiley handbook on the cognitive neuroscience of memory* (pp. 218–243). Hoboken, NJ: Wiley. http://dx.doi.org/10.1002/9781118332634.ch11

Chamine, I., Atchley, R., & Oken, B. S. (2018). Hypnosis intervention effects on sleep outcomes: Systematic review. *Journal of Clinical Sleep Medicine, 14*(2), 271–283. Retrieved from https://www.ncbi.nlm.nih.gov/pmc/articles/PMC5786848/

Chandra-Mouli, V., Amin, A., & Plesons, M. (2018). Global early adolescent study: Implications of the findings of phase 1 for policies and programmes. *GFMER.* Retrieved from https://www.gfmer.ch/SRH-Course-2018/adolescent-health/pdf/GEAS-Chandra-Mouli-2018.pdf

Chang, A.-M., Aeschbach, D., Duffy, J. F., & Czeisler, C. A. (2015). Evening use of light-emitting eReaders negatively affects sleep, circadian timing, and next-morning alertness. *Proceedings of the National Academy of Sciences of the United States of America, 112,* 1232–1237. http://dx.doi.org/10.1073/pnas.1418490112

Chang, H. Y., Keyes, K. M., Mok, Y., Jung, K. J., Shin, Y.-J., & Jee, S. H. (2015). Depression as a risk factor for overall and hormone-related cancer: The Korean cancer prevention study. *Journal of Affective Disorders, 173,* 1–8. http://dx.doi.org/10.1016/j.jad.2014.10.064

Chan, N. W., Burkhardt, J., & Flyr, M. (2019). The effects of recreational marijuana legalization and dispensing on opioid mortality. *Economic Inquiry.* Retrieved from doi:10.1111/ecin.12819

Chaplin, L. N., John, D. R., Rindfleisch, A., & Froh, J. J. (2018). The impact of gratitude on adolescent materialism and generosity. *The Journal of Positive Psychology, 14*(4), 502–511. doi:10.1080/17439760.2018.1497688

Chapman, B., Fiscella, K., Duberstein, P., Kawachi, I., & Muennig, P. (2014). Measurement confounding affects the extent to which verbal IQ explains social gradients in mortality. *Journal of Epidemiology and Community Health, 68,* 728–733. http://dx.doi.org/10.1136/jech-2013-203741

Charlesworth, T. E. S., & Banaji, M. R. (2019). Patterns of implicit and explicit attitudes: I. Long-term change and stability from 2007 to 2016. *Psychological Science, 30*(2), 174–192. https://doi.org/10.1177/0956797618813087

Chekroud, S., Gueorguieva, R., Zheutlin, A., Paulus, M., Krumholz, H., Krystal, J., & Chekroud, A. (2018). Association between physical exercise and mental health in 1-2 million individuals in the USA between 2011 and 2015: A cross-sectional study. *Lancet Psychiatry, 5*(9), 739–746. doi:10.1016/S2215-0366(18)30227-X

Chekroud, S. R., Gueorguieva, R., Zheutlin, A. B., Paulus, M., Krumholz, H. M., Krystal, J. H., & Chekroud, A. M. (2018). Association between physical exercise and mental health in 1·2 million individuals in the USA between 2011 and 2015: A cross-sectional study. *The Lancet Psychiatry, 5*(9), 739–746. doi:10.1016/S2215-0366(18)30227-X

Cheng, J., Niles, A. N., & Craske, M. G. (2017). Exposure reduces negative bias in self-rated performance in public speaking fearful participants. *Journal of Behavior Therapy and Experimental Psychiatry, 54,* 101–107. http://dx.doi.org/10.1016/j.jbtep.2016.07.006.

Cheng, J. T., Tracy, J. L., Ho, S., & Henrich, J. (2016). Listen, follow me: Dynamic vocal signals of dominance predict emergent social rank in humans. *Journal of Experimental Psychology: General, 145,* 536–547. doi:10.1037/xge0000166

Cheng, W., Rolls, E. T., Gu, H., Zhang, J., & Feng, J. (2015). Autism: Reduced connectivity between cortical areas involved in face expression, theory of mind, and the sense of self. *Brain: A Journal of Neurology, 138*(5), 1382–1393. http://dx.doi.org/10.1093/brain/awv051

Chen, L., Shi, G.R., Huang, D.D., Li, Y., Ma, C. C., Shi, M., . . . Shi, G. J. (2019). Male sexual dysfunction: A review of literature on its pathological mechanisms, potential risk factors, and herbal drug intervention. *Biomedicine & Pharmacotherapy, 112,* 108585. https://doi.org/10.1016/j.biopha.2019.01.046

Chen, M.-H., Su, T.-P., Chen, Y.-S., Hsu, J.-W., Huang, K.-L., Chang, W.-H., . . . Bai, Y.-M. (2014). Higher risk of mood disorders among adolescents with ADHD and asthma: A nationwide prospective study. *Journal of Affective Disorders, 156,* 232–235. http://dx.doi.org/10.1016/j.jad.2013.10.053

Chen, P., Chavez, O., Ong, D. C., & Gunderson, B. (2017). Strategic resource for learning: A self-administered intervention that guides self-reflection on effective resource use enhances academic performance. *Psychological Science, 28*(6), 774–785. http://dx.doi.org/10.1177/0956797617696456

Chen, S., Yao, N., Qian, M., & Lin, M. (2016). Attentional biases in high social anxiety using a flanker task. *Journal of Behavior Therapy and Experimental Psychiatry, 51,* 27–34. Doi:10.1016/j.jbtep.2015.12.002

Chesin, M., Fertuck, E., Goodman, J., Lichenstein, S., & Stanley, B. (2015). The interaction between rejection sensitivity and emotional maltreatment in borderline personality disorder. *Psychopathology, 48,* 31–35. doi:10.1159/00036519

Chesin, M. S., Galfavy, H., Sonmez, C. C., Wong, A., Oquendo, M. A., Mann, J. J., & Stanley, B. (2017). Nonsuicidal self-injury is predictive of suicide attempts among individuals with mood disorders. *Suicide & Life-threatening Behavior, 47*(5), 567–579. doi:10.1111/sltb.12331

Chiang, Y. T., Fang, W. T., Kaplan, U., & Ng, E. (2019). Locus of control: The mediation effect between emotional stability and pro-environmental behavior. *Sustainability, 11*(3), 820. https://doi.org/10.3390/su11030820

Chittenden, B. (2018, January 4). What happened to Ricky Williams? Where is he now? *Earn the Necklace.* Retrieved April 28, 2019 from https://www.earnthenecklace.com/what-happened-to-ricky-williams-where-is-he-now/

Chmielewski, M., Zhu, J., Burchett, D., Bury, A. S., & Bagby, R. M. (2017). The comparative capacity of the Minnesota Multiphasic Personality Inventory–2 (MMPI–2) and MMPI–2 Restructured Form (MMPI-2-RF) validity scales to detect suspected malingering in a disability claimant sample. *Psychological Assessment, 29,* 199–208. http://dx.doi.org/10.1037/pas0000328

Choi, D.-H., & Shin, D.-H. (2017). Exploring political compromise in the new media environment: The interaction effects of social media use and the Big Five personality traits. *Personality and Individual Differences, 106,* 163–171. http://dx.doi.org/10.1016/j.paid. 2016.11.022

Choi, H. Y., & Lee, C.-H. (2019). Can beta-endorphin be used as a biomarker for chronic low back pain? A meta-analysis of randomized controlled trials. *Pain Medicine, 20*(1), 28–36. https://dx.doi.org/10.1093/pm/pny186

Chomsky, N. (1968). *Language and mind.* New York, NY: Harcourt, Brace, World.

Chomsky, N. (1980). *Rules and representations.* New York, NY: Columbia University Press.

Chomsri, P., Likhitsathian, S., Aramrattana, A., & Siviroj, P. (2018). Self-efficacy, sensation seeking, right attitude, and readiness to change among alcohol drinkers in a Thai vocational school. *Addictive Behaviors Reports, 8,* 107–112. doi:10.1016/j.abrep.2018.08.006

Chopik, W. J., & Edelstein, R. S. (2019). Retrospective memories of parental care and health from mid- to late life. *Health Psychology, 38*(1), 84–93. http://dx.doi.org/10.1037/hea0000694

Chopik, W. J., & Weaver, J. R. (2019). Old dog, new tricks: Age differences in dog personality traits, associations with human personality traits, and links to important outcomes. *Journal of Research in Personality, 79,* 94–108. https://doi.org/10.1016/j.jrp.2019.01.005

Chorpita, B. F., Daleiden, E. L., Ebesutani, C., Young, J., Becker, K. D., Nakamura, B. J., . . . Starace, N. (2011). Evidence-based treatments for children and adolescents: An updated review of indicators of efficacy and effectiveness. *Clinical Psychology: Science and Practice, 18,* 154–172.

Choudhry, V., Dayal, R., Pillai, D., Kalokhe, A. S., Beier, K., & Patel, V. (2018). Child sexual abuse in India: A systematic review. *PLoS ONE* (10):e0205086. doi:10.1371/journal.pone.0205086

Chou, E. Y. (2018). Naysaying and negativity promote initial power establishment and leadership endorsement. *Journal of Personality and Social Psychology, 115*(4), 638–656. http://dx.doi.org/10.1037/pspi0000135

Chowdhury, M. R. (2019). The neuroscience of gratitude and how it affects anxiety and grief. *Positive Psychology Program.* Retrieved from https://positivepsychologyprogram.com/neuroscience-of-gratitude/

Christenfeld, N. J. S., & Mandler, G. (2013). Emotion. In D. K. Freedheim & I. B. Weiner (Eds.), *Handbook of psychology, Vol. 1. History of psychology* (2nd ed., pp. 177–197). Hoboken, NJ: Wiley.

Christian, J. B., Bourgeois, N. E., & Lowe, K. A. (2015). Cholesterol screening in US adults and awareness of high cholesterol among individuals with severe hypertriglyceridemia: National Health and Nutrition Examination Surveys 2001–2008. *Journal of Cardiovascular Nursing, 30,* 26–34. http://dx.doi.org/10.1097/JCN.0000000000000101

Christie, A. (2018, November 28). Deciphering the language of dolphins. *BioWeb.* Retrieved from http://bioweb.ie/language-dolphins/

Chrysikou, E. G., Motyka, K., Nigro, C., Yang, S.-I., & Thompson-Schill, S. L. (2016). Functional fixedness in creative thinking tasks depends on stimulus modality. *Psychology of Aesthetics, Creativity, and the Arts, 10*(4), 425–435. http://dx.doi.org/10.1037/aca000005

Chucair-Elliott, A. J., Elliott, M. H., Cohen, A., & Carr, D. J. (2015). Corneal stem cells: A source of cell renewal with therapeutic potential. In M. Babizhayev, D., Wan-Cheng Li, A. Kasus-Jacobi, L. Žorić, & J. Alió (Eds.), *Studies on the cornea and lens* (pp. 99–113). New York, NY: Springer.

Churchill, T. W., Krishnan, S., Weisskopf, M., Yates, B. S., Speizer, F. E., Kim, J. H., . . . Baggish, A. L. (2018). Weight gain and health affliction among former National Football League players. *The American Journal of Medicine, 131*(12), 1491–1498. https://doi.org/10.1016/j.amjmed.2018.07.042

Cialdini, R. B., Cacioppo, J. T., Bassett, R., & Miller, J. A. (1978). Low-ball procedure for producing compliance: Commitment then cost. *Journal of Personality and Social Psychology, 36*(5), 463–476. http://dx.doi.org/10.1037/0022-3514.36.5.463

Cicchetti, D. (2016). Socioemotional, personality, and biological development: Illustrations from a multilevel developmental psychopathology perspective on child maltreatment. *Annual Review of Psychology, 67,* 187–211. http://dx.doi.org/10.1146/annurevpsych-122414-033259

Cino, J. G. (2018, Ocober 1). Is a polygraph a reliable lie detector? *PhysOrg.* Retrieved from https://phys.org/news/2018-10-polygraph-reliable-detector.html

Cirelli, L. K., Einarson, K. M., & Trainor, L. J. (2014). Interpersonal synchrony increases prosocial behavior in infants. *Developmental Science, 17,* 1003–1011. doi:10.1111/desc.12193

Ciria, A., López, F., & Lara, B. (2019). Perceived duration: The interplay of top-down attention and task-relevant information. *Frontiers in Psychology.* 10:490. doi:10.3389/fpsyg.2019.00490

Clark, J. L., Algoe, S. B., & Green, M. C. (2018). Social network sites and well-being: The role of social connection. *Current Directions in Psychological Science, 27*(1), 32–37. https://doi.org/10.1177/0963721417730833

Clark, L. A., Cuthbert, B., Lewis-Fernández, R., Narrow, W. E., & Reed, G. M. (2017). Three approaches to understanding and classifying mental disorder: ICD-11, DSM-5, and the National Institute of Mental Health's Research Domain Criteria (RDoC). *Psychological Science in the Public Interest, 18*(2), 72–145. https://doi.org/10.1177/1529100617727266

Clifford, K. (2015). Understanding a silent killer. UTMB Health. Retrieved from http://www.utmb.edu/impact-archive/article.aspx?IAID=1744

Coates, J. M., Gullo, M. J., Feeney, G. F. X., Young, R. M., & Donnor, J. P. (2018). A randomized trial of personalized cognitive-behavior therapy for alcohol use disorder in a public health clinic. *Frontiers in Psychiatry, 9*:297. doi:10.3389/fpsyt.2018.00297

Cohen, A. B. (Ed.). (2014). *Culture reexamined: Broadening our understanding of social and evolutionary influences.* Washington, DC: American Psychological Association. http://dx.doi.org/10.1037/14274-000

Cohen, C., Janicki-Deverts, D., Doyle, W. J., Miller, G. E., Frank, E., Rabin, B. S., & Turner, R. B. (2012). Chronic stress, glucocorticoid receptor resistance, inflammation, and disease risk. *Proceedings of the National Academy of Sciences of the United States of America, 109,* 5995–5999. http://dx.doi.org/10.1073/pnas.1118355109

Cohen, J. (2018, August 20). Simone Biles wears teal leotard in honor of Larry Nassar abuse survivors. *ENews.* Retrieved from https://www.eonline.com/news/961507/simone-biles-wears-teal-leotard-in-honor-of-larry-nassar-abuse-survivors

Cohen, J. A., Scheid, J., & Gerson, R. (2014). Transforming trajectories for traumatized children. *Journal of the American Academy of Child and Adolescent Psychiatry, 53,* 9–13. doi:10.1016/j.jaac.2013.10.004

Cohen, M., Makurumidze, G., Pereira, L. F., Bourgeois, J. A., & Cozza, K. L. (2019). HIV/AIDS psychiatry - a paradigm for HIV prevention and integrated compassionate care. *World Psychiatry, 18*(2), 240–241. Retrieved from doi:10.1002/wps.20643

Cohen, N., Margulies, D. S., Ashkenazi, S., Schaefer, A., Taubert, M., Henik, A., . . . Okon-Singer, H. (2016). Using executive control training to suppress amygdala reactivity to aversive information. *NeuroImage, 125,* 1022–1031. http://dx.doi.org/10.1016/j.neuroimage.2015.10.069

Cohen, R. A. (2014). Mutual constraint of memory and attention. In R. A. Cohen (Ed.), *The neuropsychology of attention* (pp. 763–777). New York, NY: Springer. http://dx.doi.org/10.1007/978-0-38772639-7_24

Cohen, S., Doyle, W. J., Turner, R. B., Alper, C. M., & Skoner, D. P. (2003). Sociability and susceptibility to the common cold. *Psychological Science, 14,* 389–395. http://dx.doi.org/10.1111/1467-9280.01452

Cohen, S., Janicki-Deverts, D., Turner, R. B., & Doyle, W. J. (2015). Does hugging provide stress-buffering social support? A study of susceptibility to upper respiratory infection and illness. *Psychological Science, 26,* 135–147. http://doi.org/10.1177/0956797614559284

Cohn, M. A., Pietrucha, M. E., Saslow, L. R., Hult, J. R., & Moskowitz, J. T. (2014). An online positive affect skills intervention reduces depression in adults with type 2 diabetes. *The Journal of Positive Psychology, 9,* 523–534. doi:10.1080/17439760.2014.920410

Colapinto, J. (2004, June 3). Gender gap: What were the real reasons behind David Reimer's suicide? *Slate.* Retrieved from http://www.slate.com/articles/health_and_science/medical_examiner/2004/06/gender_gap.html

Cole, D. L. (1982). Psychology as a liberating art. *Teaching of Psychology, 9,* 23–26.

Cole, G. G., & Wilkins, A. J. (2013). Fear of holes. *Psychological Science, 24*(10), 1980–1985. https://doi.org/10.1177/0956797613484937

Cole, M., Gray, J., Glick, J. A., & Sharp, D. W. (1971). *The cultural context of learning and thinking.* New York, NY: Basic Books.

Colizzi, M., Costa, R., & Todarello, O. (2014). Transsexual patients' psychiatric comorbidity and positive effect of cross-sex hormonal treatment on mental health: Results from a longitudinal study. *Psychoneuroendocrinology, 39,* 65–73. http://dx.doi.org/10.1016/j.psyneuen.2013.09.029

Collins, E. K., Mccabe, J. A., Hauptman, A. J., Meyers-Orr, B. M., & Stern, B. Z. (2014, August). Does picture generation enhance keyword mnemonic learning? Presented at American Psychological Association (APA) Annual Convention, Washington, DC. http://dx.doi.org/10.1037/e544392014-001

Colman, I., Jones, P. B., Kuh, D., Weeks, M., Naicker, K., Richards, M., & Croudace, T. J. (2014). Early development, stress and depression across the life course: Pathways to depression in a national British birth cohort. *Psychological Medicine, 44,* 2845–2854. http://dx.doi.org/10.1017/S0033291714000385

Compton, W. C., & Hoffman, E. (2019). *Positive psychology: The science of happiness and flourishing.* Thousand Oaks, CA: Sage.

Cona, F., Lacanna, M., & Ursino, M. (2014). A thalamo-cortical neural mass model for the simulation of brain rhythms during sleep. *Journal of Computational Neuroscience, 37,* 125–148. http://dx.doi.org/10.1007/s10827-013-0493-1

Concha, A. R., Guest, C. M., Harris, R., Pike, T. W., Feugier, A., Zulch, H., & Mills, D. S. (2019). Canine olfactory thresholds to amyl acetate in a biomedical detection scenario. *Frontiers in Veterinary Science, 5,* 345. doi:10.3389/fvets.2018.00345

Connelly, B. S., & Hülsheger, U. R. (2012). A narrower scope or a clearer lens of personality? Examining sources of observers' advantages over self-reports for predicting performance. *Journal of Personality, 80,* 603–631. http://dx.doi.org/10.1111/j.14676494.2011.00744.x

Connelly, B. S., & Ones, D. S. (2010). Another perspective on personality: Meta-analytic integration of observers' accuracy and predictive validity. *Psychological Bulletin, 136,* 1092–1122. http://dx.doi.org/10.1037/a0021212

Considering a Career. (2011). Becoming a health psychologist. *APA Division 38.* Retrieved from http://www.health-psych.org/AboutHowtoBecome.cfm

Constantino, M. J., Morrison, N, R., Coyne, A. E., & Howard, T. (2017). Exploring therapeutic alliance training in clinical and counseling psychology graduate programs. *Training and Education in Professional Psychology, 11*(4), 219–226. http://dx.doi.org/10.1037/tep0000157

Contreras, J. B., Richardson, J., & Kotagal, S. (2019). Sexsomnia in an adolescent. *Journal of Clinical Sleep Medicine, 15*(3), 505–507. doi:10.5664/jcsm.7686.

Conway, J.R., Catmur, C. & Bird, G. (2019). Understanding individual differences in theory of mind via representation of minds, not mental states. *Psychonomic Bulletin Review, 26*(3), 798–812. https://doi.org/10.3758/s13423-018-1559-x

Cook, G., & Mitschow, C. (2019). Beyond the polygraph: Deception detection and the autonomic nervous system. *Federal Practitioner, 36*(7), 316–321. https://www.ncbi.nlm.nih.gov/pmc/articles/PMC6654171/

Cook Maher, A., Kielb, S., Loyer, E., Connelley, M., Rademaker, A., Mesulam, M. M., . . . Rogalski, E. (2017). Psychological well-being in elderly adults with extraordinary episodic memory. *PloS ONE, 12*(10), e0186413. doi:10.1371/journal.pone.0186413

Cook, P. F., Brooks, A., Spivak, M., & Berns, G. S. (2015). Regional brain activity in awake unrestrained dogs. *Journal of Veterinary Behavior: Clinical Applications and Research, 16,* 104–112. http://dx.doi.org/10.1016/j.jveb.2015.12.003

Cook, P. F., Prichard, A., Spivak, M., & Berns, G. S. (2016). Awake canine fMRI predicts dogs' preference for praise versus food. *Social Cognitive and Affective Neuroscience, 11*(12), 1853–1862. http://dx.doi.org/10.1101/062703

Cooper, J. O., Heron, T. E., & Heward, W. L. (2019). *Applied behavior analysis* (3rd ed.). Upper Saddle River, NJ: Pearson.

Cordón, L. (2012). *All things Freud: An encyclopedia of Freud's world* (Vols. 1–2). Santa Barbara, CA: Greenwood.

Corkin, S. (2013). *Permanent present tense: The unforgettable life of the amnesic patient, H. M.* New York, NY: Basic Books.

Corona, R., Rodríguez, V. M., McDonald, S. E., Velazquez, E., Rodríguez, A., & Fuentes, V. E. (2017). Associations between cultural stressors, cultural values, and Latina/o college students' mental health. *Journal of Youth and Adolescence, 46,* 63–77. http://dx.doi.org/10.1007/s10964-016-0600-5

Correia, S. S., & Goosens, K. A. (2016). Input specific contributions to valence processing in the amygdala. *Learning & Memory, 23*(10), 534–543. http://dx.doi.org/10.1101/lm.037887.114

Corr, P. J., & Cooper, A. J. (2016). The Reinforcement Sensitivity Theory of Personality Questionnaire (RST-PQ): Development and validation. *Psychological Assessment, 28*(11), 1427–1440. http://dx.doi.org/10.1037/pas0000273

Cortes, L. R., Cisternas, C. D., & Forger, N. G. (2019). Does gender leave an epigenetic imprint on the brain? *Frontiers in Neuroscience, 13,* 173. doi:10.3389/fnins.2019.00173

Corti, K., & Gillespie, A. (2015). Revisiting Milgram's cyranoid method: Experimenting with hybrid human agents. *The Journal of Social Psychology, 155,* 30–56. doi:10.1080/00224545.2014.959885

Costa, A. L., Sophia, E. C., Sanches, C., Tavares, H., & Zilberman, M. L. (2015). Pathological jealousy: Romantic relationship characteristics, emotional and personality aspects, and social adjustment. *Journal of Affective Disorders, 174,* 38–44. http://dx.doi.org/10.1016/j.jad.2014.11.017

Costa, P. T., Jr., & McCrae, R. R. (2011). The five-factor model, five-factor theory, and interpersonal psychology. In L. M. Horowitz & S. Strack (Eds.), *Handbook of interpersonal psychology: Theory, research, assessment, and therapeutic interventions* (pp. 91–104). Hoboken, NJ: Wiley.

Courage, M. L., & Adams, R. J. (1990). Visual acuity assessment from birth to three years using the acuity card procedures: Cross-sectional and longitudinal samples. *Optometry and Vision Science, 67,* 713–718.

Courtemanche, F., Labonté-LeMoyne, E., Léger, P.-M., Fredette, M., Senecal, S., Cameron, A.-F., . . . Bellavance, F. (2019). Texting while walking: An expensive switch cost. *Accident Analysis & Prevention, 127,* 1–8. https://doi.org/10.1016/j.aap.2019.02.022

Coviello, L., Sohn, Y., Kramer, A. D. I., Marlow, C., Franceschetti, M., Christakis, N. A., & Fowler, J. H. (2014). Detecting emotional contagion in massive social networks. *PLoS ONE, 9*(3):e90315. http://dx.doi.org/10.1371/journal.pone.0090315

Covington, M. V., & Müeller, K. J. (2001). Intrinsic versus extrinsic motivation: An approach/avoidance reformulation. *Educational Psychology Review, 132,* 157–176.

Coyne, J. C., & Tennen, H. (2010). Positive psychology in cancer care: Bad science, exaggerated claims, and unproven medicine. *Annals of Behavioral Medicine, 39,* 16–26. http://dx.doi.org/10.1007/s12160-009-9154-z

Craik, F. I., & Lockhart, R. S. (1972). Levels of processing: A framework for memory research. *Journal of Verbal Learning and Verbal Behavior, 11,* 671–684. http://dx.doi.org/10.1016/S0022-5371(72)80001-X

Craik, F. I., & Tulving, E. (1975). Depth of processing and the retention of words in episodic memory. *Journal of Experimental Psychology: General, 104,* 268–294. http://dx.doi.org/10.1037/0096-3445.104.3.268

Crane, C. A., Licata, M. L., Schlauch, R. C., Testa, M., & Easton, C. J. (2017). The proximal effects of acute alcohol use on female aggression: A meta-analytic review of the experimental literature. *Psychology of Addictive Behaviors, 31*(1), 21–26. http://dx.doi.org/10.1037/adb0000244

Crego, C., & Widiger, T. A. (2016). Personality disorders. In J. E. Maddux & B. A. Winstead (Eds.), *Psychopathology: Foundations for a contemporary understanding* (4th ed., pp. 218– 236). New York, NY: Routledge/Taylor & Francis Group.

Creswell, J. D., Lindsay, E. K., Villalba, D. K., & Chin, B. (2019). Mindfulness training and physical health: Mechanisms and outcomes. *Psychosomatic Medicine, 81*(3), 224–232. doi:10.1097/PSY.0000000000000675

Creswell, J. D., Taren, A. A., Lindsay, E. K., Greco, C. M., Gianaros, P. J., Fairgrieve, A., . . . Gerris, J. L. (2016). Alterations in resting-state functional connectivity link mindfulness meditation with reduced Interleukin-6: A randomized controlled trial. *Biological Psychiatry, 80*(1), 53–61. https://doi.org/10.1016/j.biopsych.2016.01.008

Cristea, I. A., Stefan, S., Karyotaki, E., David, D., Hollon, S. D., & Cuijpers, P. (2017). The effects of cognitive behavioral therapy are not systematically falling: A revision of Johnsen and Friborg (2015). *Psychological Bulletin, 143*(3), 326–340. http://dx.doi.org/10.1037/bul0000062

Crittenden, C. N., Murphy, M. L. M., & Cohen, S. (2018). Social integration and age-related decline in lung function. *Health Psychology, 37*(5), 472–480. http://dx.doi.org/10.1037/hea0000592

Crosson-Tower, C. (2015). *Confronting child and adolescent sexual abuse.* Thousand Oaks, CA: Sage Publications.

Cruwys, T., South, E. I., Greenaway, K. H., & Haslam, S. A. (2015). Social identity reduces depression by fostering positive attributions. *Social Psychological and Personality Science, 6,* 65–74. http://dx.doi.org/10.1177/1948550614543309

Csordas, T. J. (2014). Afterword: Moral experience in anthropology. *Ethos, 42,* 139–152. doi:10.1111/etho.12043

Cuartero, M. I., de la Parra, J., Pérez-Ruiz, A., Bravo-Ferrer, I., Durán-Laforet, V., García-Culebras, A., . . . Lizasoain, I. (2019). Abolition of aberrant neurogenesis ameliorates cognitive impairment after stroke in mice. *Journal of Clinical Investigation, 129*(4), 1536–1550. https://dx.doi.org/10.1172/JCI120412

Cubillo, A., Makwana, A. B., & Hare, T. A. (2019). Differential modulation of cognitive control networks by monetary reward and punishment. *Social Cognitive and Affective Neuroscience, 14*(3), 305–317. doi:10.1093/scan/nsz006

Cundiff, J. M., & Matthews, K. A. (2018). Friends with health benefits: The long-term benefits of early peer social integration for blood pressure and obesity in midlife. *Psychological Science, 29*(5), 814–823. doi:10.1177/0956797617746510

Curry, A. (2019, July 18). Parent's emotional trauma may change their children's biology. Studies in mice show how. *Science.* Retrieved from https://www.sciencemag.org/news/2019/07/parents-emotional-trauma-may-change-their-children-s-biology-studies-mice-show-how

Curry, O. S., Mullins, D. A., & Whitehouse, H. (2019). Is it good to cooperate? Testing the theory of morality-as-cooperation in 60 societies. *Current Anthropology, 60*(1), 47–69. doi:10.1086/701478

Curtiss, S. (1977). *Genie: A psycholinguistic study of a modern-day "wild child."* New York, NY: Academic Press.

Cusack, K., Jonas, D. E., Forneris, C. A., Wines, C., Sonis, J., Middleton, J. C., . . . Gaynes, B. N. (2016). Psychological treatments for adults with posttraumatic stress disorder: A systematic review and meta-analysis. *Clinical Psychology Review, 43,* 128–141. http://dx.doi.org/10.1016/j.cpr.2015.10.003

Cutler, D. M., & Lleras-Muney, A. (2006). Education and health: Evaluating theories and evidence. *National Bureau of Economic Research.* Retrieved from http://www.nber.org/papers/w12352

Cyr, M., Tau, G. Z., Fontaine, M., Levin, F. R., & Marsh, R. (2019). Deficient functioning of frontostriatal circuits during the resolution of cognitive conflict in cannabis-using youth. *Journal of the American Academy of Child & Adolescent Psychiatry, 58*(7), 702–711. doi:10.1016/j.jaac.2018.09.436

Dahlhamer, J., Lucas, J., Zelaya, C., Nahin, R., Mackey, S., DeBar, L., . . . Helmick, C. (2018). Prevalence of chronic pain and high-impact chronic pain among adults - United States, 2016. *Morbidity and Mortality Weekly Report, 67*(36), 1001–1006. doi:10.15585/mmwr.mm6736a2

Dale, A., Lortie-Lussier, M., Wong, C., & De Koninck, J. (2016). Dreams of Canadian students: Norms, gender differences, and comparison with American norms. *Journal of Cross-Cultural Psychology, 47*(7), 941–955. http://dx.doi.org/10.1177/0022022116655788

Dallner, O. S., Marinis, J. M., Lu, Y.-H., Birsoy, K., Werner, E., Fayzikhodjaeva, G., . . . Friedman, J. M. (2019). Dysregulation of a long noncoding RNA reduces leptin leading to a leptin-responsive form of obesity. *Nature Medicine, 25,* 507–516. doi:10.1038/s41591-019-0370-1

Damasio, H. (2018). Phineas Gage: The brain and the behavior. *Revue Neurologique, 174*(10), 738–739. doi:10.1016/j.neurol.2018.09.005

D'Ambrosio, C., & Redline, S. (2014). Sleep across the lifespan. In S. Redline & N. Berger (Eds.), *Impact of sleep and sleep disturbances on obesity and cancer* (pp. 1–23). New York, NY: Springer.

Damian, R. I., Spengler, M., Sutu, A., & Roberts, B. W. (2019). Sixteen going on sixty-six: A longitudinal study of personality stability and change across 50 years. *Journal of Personality and Social Psychology, 117*(3), 674–695. http://dx.doi.org/10.1037/pspp0000210

Dana, R. H. (2014). Personality tests and psychological science: Instruments, populations, practice. In F. T. L. Leong, L. Comas-Díaz, G. C. Nagayama Hall, V. C. McLoyd, & J. E. Trimble (Eds.), *APA handbooks in psychology. APA handbook of multicultural psychology, Vol. 2. Applications and training* (pp. 181–196). Washington, DC: American Psychological Association. http://dx.doi.org/10.1037/14187-011

Danielson, M. L., Bitsko, R. H., Ghandour, R. M., Holbrook, J. R., Kogan, M. D., & Blumberg, S. J. (2018). Prevalence of parent-reported ADHD diagnosis and associated treatment among U.S. children and adolescents, 2016. *Journal of Clinical Child and Adolescent Psychology, 47*(2), 199–212. doi:10.1080/15374416.2017.1417860

Daniluk, J. C., Koert, E., & Breckon, E. (2014). Sexuality and infertility. In Y. Binik & K. Hall (Eds.), *Principles and practice of sex therapy* (pp. 419–435). New York, NY: Guilford.

Dargis, M., Newman, J., & Koenigs, M. (2016). Clarifying the link between childhood abuse history and psychopathic traits in adult criminal off enders. *Personality Disorders: Theory, Research, and Treatment, 7,* 221–228. http://dx.doi.org/10.1037/per0000147

Darley, J. M., & Latané, B. (1968). Bystander intervention in emergencies: Diffusion of responsibility. *Journal of Personality and Social Psychology, 8,* 377–383.

Darwin, C. (1859). The origin of species by means of natural selection; or the preservation of favoured races in the struggle for life. *Nature, 5,* 318–319. http://dx.doi.org/10.1038/005318a0

Darwin, C. (1872). *The expression of emotions in animals and man.* London, UK: Murray. http://dx.doi.org/10.1037/10001-000

Data-Franco, J., Singh, A., Popovic, D., Ashton, M., Berk, M., Vieta, E., . . . Dean, O. M. (2017). Beyond the therapeutic shackles of the monoamines: New mechanisms in bipolar disorder biology. *Progress in Neuro-Psychopharmacology & Biological Psychiatry, 72,* 73–86. http://dx.doi.org/10.1016/j.pnpbp. 2016.09.004

Davies, M. S., Strickland, T. L., & Cao, M. (2014). Neuropsychological evaluation of culturally diverse populations. In F. T. L. Leong, L. Comas-Díaz, G. C. Nagayama Hall, V. C. McLoyd, & J. E. Trimble (Eds.), *APA handbook of multicultural psychology, Vol. 2: Applications and training* (pp. 231–251). Washington, DC: American Psychological Association. http://dx.doi.org/10.1037/14187-014

Davis, N. T., & Mason, L. (2016). Sorting and the split-ticket: Evidence from presidential and subpresidential elections. *Political Behavior, 38,* 337–354. http://dx.doi.org/10.1007/s11109-015-9315-7

Dawkins, R. (2016). *The selfish gene: 40th anniversary edition.* New York, NY: Oxford University Press.

Dawson, K. M., O'Brien, K. E., & Beehr, T. A. (2016). The role of hindrance stressors in the job demand–control–support model of occupational stress: A proposed theory revision. *Journal of Organizational Behavior, 37,* 397–415. http://dx.doi.org/10.1002/job.2049

Day, M. A. (2016). The application of mindfulness-based cognitive therapy for chronic pain. In S. J. Eisendrath (Ed.), *Mindfulness-based cognitive therapy: Innovative applications* (pp. 65–74). Cham, CH: Springer International Publishing. http://dx.doi.org/10.1007/978-3-319-29866-5_6

Day, M. V., & Ross, M. (2014). Predicting confidence in flashbulb memories. *Memory, 22,* 232–242. http://dx.doi.org/10.1080/09658211.2013.778290

DeAngelis, T. (2019, March). Continuing education: How does implicit bias by physicians affect patients' health care? *Monitor on Psychology.* Retrieved from http://www.apamonitor-digital.org/apamonitor/201903/MobilePagedArticle.action?articleId=1466313&app=false#articleId1466313

DeAngelis, T. (2019). The legacy of trauma. *Monitor on Psychology.* Retrieved from https://www.apa.org/monitor/2019/02/legacy-trauma

Dean, J. (2015). The most common mental health problem is "contagious." *PsyBlog.* Retrieved from http://www.spring.org.uk/2015/05/the-most-common-mental-health-problem-is-contagious.php

DeBord, K. A., Fischer, A. R., Bieschke, K. J., & Perez, R. M. (Eds.). (2017). *Handbook of sexual orientation and gender diversity in counseling and psychotherapy.* Washington, DC: American Psychological Association.

de Bruijn, D. M., & de Graaf, I. M. (2016). The role of substance use in same-day intimate partner violence: A review of the literature. *Aggression and Violent Behavior, 27,* 142–151. doi:10.1016/j.avb.2016.02.010

Deci, E. L., & Moller, A. C. (2005). The concept of competence: A starting place for understanding intrinsic motivation and self-determined extrinsic motivation. In A. J. Elliot & C. S. Dweck (Eds.), *Handbook of competence and motivation* (pp. 579–597). New York, NY: Guilford.

Deci, E. L., & Ryan, R. M. (1985). *Intrinsic motivation and self-determination in human behavior.* New York, NY: Plenum.

Deci, E. L., & Ryan, R. M. (2012). Self determination theory. In P. A. M. Van Lange, A. W. Kruglanski, & E. T. Higgins (Eds.), *Handbook of theories of social psychology* (Vol. 1, pp. 416–436). Thousand Oaks, CA: Sage.

De Cuyper, B., Boen, F., Van Beirendonck, C., Vanbeselaere, N., & Fransen, K. (2016). When do elite cyclists go the extra mile? Team identification mediates the relationship between perceived leadership qualities of the captain and social laboring. *International Journal of Sport Psychology, 47*(4), 355–372.

De Dreu, C. K. W., & Kret, M. E. (2016). Oxytocin conditions intergroup relations through upregulated in-group empathy, cooperation, conformity, and defense. *Biological Psychiatry, 79,* 165–173. doi:10.1016/j.biopsych.2015.03.020

Deeb, R., Judge, P., Peterson, E., Lin, J. C., & Yaremchuk, K. (2014). Snoring and carotid artery intima-media thickness. *The Laryngoscope, 124,* 1486–1491. http://dx.doi.org/10.1002/lary.24527

Deer, T. R., Jain, S., Hunter, C., & Chakravarthy, K. (2019). Neurostimulation for intractable chronic pain. *Brain Sciences, 9*(2), 23. doi:10.3390/brainsci9020023

Dekel, S., & Farber, B. A. (2012). Models of intimacy of securely and avoidantly attached young adults. *The Journal of Nervous and Mental Disease, 200,* 156–162. http://dx.doi.org/10.1097/NMD.0b013e3182439702

Delahaij, R., & van Dam, K. (2016). Coping style development: The role of learning goal orientation and metacognitive awareness. *Personality and Individual Differences, 92,* 57–62. http://dx.doi.org/10.1016/j.paid.2015.12.012

Delaunay-El Allam, M., Soussignan, R., Patris, B., Marlier, L., & Schaal, B. (2010). Long-lasting memory for an odor acquired at the mother's breast. *Developmental Science, 13,* 849–863. doi:10.1111/j.1467-7687.2009.00941.x.

Delbosc, A., Naznin, F., Haslam, N., & Hawarth, N. (2019). Dehumanization of cyclists predicts self-reported aggressive behaviour toward them: A pilot study. *Transportation Research Part F: Traffic Psychology and Behaviour, 62,* 681–689. https://doi.org/10.1016/j.trf.2019.03.005.

Delgado-Gaitan, C. (1994). Socializing young children in Mexican-American families: An intergenerational perspective. In P.M. Greenfield & R.R. Cocking (Eds.), *Cross-cultural roots of minority child development* (pp. 55–86). Hillsdale, NJ: Erlbaum.

Del Río, F. J., Cabello, F., & Fernández, I. (2015). Influence of substance use on the erectile response in a sample of drug users. *International Journal of Clinical and Health Psychology, 15,* 37–43. doi:10.1016/j.ijchp.2014.10.002

Dement, W. C., & Wolpert, E. (1958). The relation of eye movements, bodily motility, and external stimuli to dream content. *Journal of Experimental Psychology, 53,* 543–553. http://dx.doi.org/10.1037/h0040031

de Meuse, K. (1985). The relationship between life events and indices of class room performance. *Teaching of Psychology, 12,* 146–149. Retrieved from https://doi.org/10.1207/s15328023top1203_8

Denmark, T., Atkinson, J., Campbell, R., & Swettenham, J. (2014). How do typically developing deaf children and deaf children with autism spectrum disorder use the face when comprehending emotional facial expressions in British sign language? *Journal of Autism and Developmental Disorders, 44,* 2584–2592. http://dx.doi.org/10.1007/s10803-014-2130-x

Denny, B. T., Fan, J., Liu, X., Guerreri, S., Mayson, S. J., Rimsky, L., . . . Koenigsberg, H. W. (2016). Brain structural anomalies in borderline and avoidant personality disorder patients and their associations with disorder-specific symptoms. *Journal of Affective Disorders, 200,* 266–274. http://dx.doi.org/10.1016/j.jad.2016.04.053

Denny, C. H., Acero, C. S., Naimi, T. S., & Kim, S. Y. (2019). Consumption of alcohol beverages and binge drinking among pregnant women aged 18-44 years - United States, 2015-2017. *Morbidity and Mortality Weekly Report, 68*(16), 365–368. doi:10.15585/mmwr.mm6816a1

Denovan, A., & Macaskill, A. (2017). Stress and subjective well-being among first year UK undergraduate students. *Journal of Happiness Studies, 18*(2), 505–525. http://dx.doi.org/10.1007/s10902-016-9736-y

Denson, T. F., Blundell, K. A., Schofield, T. P., Schira, M., M., & Kramer, U. M. (2018). The neural correlates of alcohol-related aggression. *Cognitive, Affective & Behavioral Neuroscience, 18*: 203. https://doi.org/10.3758/s13415-017-0558-0

Dent, L., Peters, A., Kerr, P. L., Mochari-Greenberger, H., & Pande, R. L. (2018). Promoting high-value mental health care: Using telehealth to implement cognitive-behavioral therapy. *Psychiatric Services, 69*(4), 370–373. doi:10.1176/appi.ps.201700477

Depner, C. M., Melanson, E. L., Eckel, R. H., Snell-Bergeon, J. K., Perreault, L., Bergman, B. C., . . . Wright, K. P. (2019). Ad libitum weekend recovery sleep fails to prevent metabolic dysregulation during a repeating pattern of insufficient sleep and weekend recovery sleep. *Current Biology, 29*(6), 957–967.e4. doi:10.1016/j.cub.2019.01.069.

Depp, C. A., Moore, R. C., Dev, S. I., Mausbach, B. T., Eyler, L. T., & Granholm, E. L. (2016). The temporal course and clinical correlates of subjective impulsivity in bipolar disorder as revealed through ecological momentary assessment. *Journal of Affective Disorders, 193,* 145–150. http://dx.doi.org/10.1016/j.jad.2015.12.016

de Ribera, O., Kavish, N., Katz, I. M., & Boutwell, B. B. (2019). Untangling intelligence, psychopathy, antisocial personality disorder, & conduct problems. A meta-analytic review. *BioRxiv.* Retrieved from https://doi.org/10.1101/100693

DeRosse, P., Nitzburg, G. C., Kompancaril, B., & Malhotra, A. K. (2014). The relation between childhood maltreatment and psychosis in patients with schizophrenia and non-psychiatric controls. *Schizophrenia Research, 155,* 66–71. http://dx.doi.org/10.1016/j.schres.2014.03.009

deShazo, R. D., Parker, S. B., Williams, D., Ingram, J. B., Elsohly, M., Rodenmeyer, K., & McCullouch, K. (2019). Marijuana's effects on brain structure and function: what do we know and what should we do? A brief review and commentary. *The American Journal of Medicine, 132*(3), 281–285. https://www.amjmed.com/article/S0002-9343(18)30872-6/fulltext

De Silva, N. A., Gregory, M. A., Venkateshan, S. S., Verschoor, C. P., & Kuspinar, A. (2019). Examining the association between life-space mobility and cognitive function in older adults: A systematic review. *Journal of Aging Research*, Article ID 3923574. https://doi.org/10.1155/2019/3923574.

DeSoto, K. A., & Roediger, H. L. (2019). Remembering the presidents. *Current Directions in Psychological Science, 28*, 138–144. https://doi.org/10.1177/0963721418815685

Desrosiers, A., Sipsma, H., Callands, T., Hansen, N., Divney, A., Magriples, U., & Kershaw, T. (2014). "Love hurts": Romantic attachment and depressive symptoms in pregnant adolescent and young adult couples. *Journal of Clinical Psychology, 70,* 95–106. http://dx.doi.org/10.1002/jclp.21979

de Tychey, C., Vandelet, E., Laurent, M., Lighezzolo-Alnot, J., Prudent, C., & Evrard, R. (2016). Child sexual abuse, baby gender, and intergenerational psychic transmission: An exploratory, projective psychoanalytic approach. *Psychoanalytic Review, 103,* 221–250. http://dx.doi.org/10.1521/prev.2016.103.2.221

de Vivo, L., Bellesi, M., Marshall, W., Bushong, E. A., Ellisman, M. H., Tononi, G., & Cirelli, C. (2017). Ultrastructural evidence for synaptic scaling across the wake/sleep cycle. *Science (New York, N.Y.), 355*(6324), 507–510. doi:10.1126/science.aah5982

de Vyver, J. V., & Abrams, D. (2018). The arts as a catalyst for human prosociality and cooperation. *Social Psychological and Personality Science, 9*(6), 664–674. https://doi.org/10.1177/1948550617720275

DeWall, C. N., Anderson, C. A., & Bushman, B. J. (2013). Aggression. In H. Tennen, J. Suls, & I. B. Weiner (Eds.), *Handbook of psychology, Vol. 5. Personality and social psychology* (2nd ed., pp. 449–466). Hoboken, NJ: Wiley.

DeWall, C. N., Chester, D. S., & White, D. S. (2015). Can acetaminophen reduce the pain of decision-making? *Journal of Experimental Social Psychology, 56,* 117–120. http://dx.doi.org/10.1016/j.jesp.2014.09.006

Dewar, M., Alber, J., Butler, C., Cowan, N., & Della Sala, S. (2012). Brief wakeful resting boosts new memories over the long term. *Psychological Science, 23*, 955–960. http://dx.doi.org/10.1177/0956797612441220

Deweese, M. M., Robinson, J. D., Cinciripini, P. M., & Versace, F. (2016). Conditioned cortical reactivity to cues predicting cigarette related or pleasant images. *International Journal of Psychophysiology, 101*, 59–68. http://dx.doi.org/10.1016/j.ijpsycho.2016.01.007

Dhamija, D., Tuvblad, C., & Baker, L. A. (2016). Behavioral genetics of the externalizing spectrum. In T. P. Beauchaine & S. P. Hinshaw (Eds.), *The Oxford handbook of externalizing spectrum disorders* (pp. 105–124). New York, NY: Oxford University Press.

Diamond, A. (2013). Executive functions. *Annual Review of Psychology, 64*, 135–168. http://dx.doi.org/10.1146/annurevpsych-113011-143750

Diamond, A. (2016). Why improving and assessing executive functions early in life is critical. In J. A. Griffin, P. McCardle, & L. S. Freund (Eds.), *Executive function in preschool-age children: Integrating measurement, neurodevelopment, and translational research* (pp. 11–43). Washington, DC: American Psychological Association. http://dx.doi.org/10.1037/14797-002

Diaz, K. M., Boothill, J. N., Seals, S. R., Hooker, S. P., Sims, M., Dubbert, P. M., . . . Shimbo, D. (2016). Sedentary behavior and subclinical atherosclerosis in African Americans: Cross-sectional analysis of the Jackson heart study. *International Journal of Behavioral Nutrition and Physical Activity, 13*, 31. http://dx.doi.org/10.1186/s12966-016-0349-y

Dibb, B. (2019). Social media use and perceptions of physical health. *Heliyon, 5*(1), e00989. Retrieved from doi:10.1016/j.heliyon.2018.e00989

Dibbets, P., & Meesters, C. (2017). The influence of stimulus valence on confirmation bias in children. *Journal of Behavior Therapy and Experimental Psychiatry, 54*, 88–92. http://dx.doi.org/10.1016/j.jbtep.2016.07.007

Dickert, S., Västfjäll, D., & Slovic, P. (2015). Neuroeconomics and dual information processes underlying charitable giving. In E. A. Wilhelms & V. F. Reyna (Eds.), *Neuroeconomics, judgment, and decision making* (pp. 181–199). New York, NY: Psychology Press.

Dickie, A. C., Bell, A. M., Iwagaki, N., Polgár, E., Gutierrez-Mecinas, M., Kelly, R., . . . Todd, A. J. (2019). Morphological and functional properties distinguish the substance P and gastrin-releasing peptide subsets of excitatory interneuron in the spinal cord dorsal horn. *Pain, 160*(2), 442–462. doi:10.1097/j.pain.0000000000001406

Dickson, D. A., Paulus, J. K., Mensah, V., Lem, J., Saavedra-Rodriquez, L., Gentry, A., & Feig, L. A. (2018). Reduced levels of miRNAs 449 and 34 in sperm of mice and men exposed to early life stress. *Translational Psychiatry, 8*:101. https://doi.org/10.1038/s41398-018-0146-2

Diefenbach, S., Hassenzahl, M., Eckoldt, K., Hartung, L., Lenz, E., & Laschke, M. (2017). Designing for well-being: A case study of keeping small secrets. *The Journal of Positive Psychology, 12*(2), 151–158. http://dx.doi.org/10.1080/17439760.2016.1163405

Dieleman, G. C., Huizink, A. C., Tulen, J. H. M., Utens, E. M. W. J., & Tiemeier, H. (2016). Stress reactivity predicts symptom improvement in children with anxiety disorders. *Journal of Affective Disorders, 196*, 190–199. http://dx.doi.org/10.1016/j.jad.2016.02.022

Diener, E., & Biswas-Diener, R. (2002). Will money increase subjective well-being? A literature review and guide to needed research. *Social Indicators Research, 57*, 119–169.

Diener, E., & Biswas-Diener, R. (2008). *Happiness: Unlocking the mysteries of psychological wealth.* Hoboken, NJ: Blackwell. http://dx.doi.org/10.1002/9781444305159

Diener, E. & Biswas-Diener, R. (2019). The replication crisis in psychology. In R. Biswas-Diener & E. Diener (Eds), *Noba textbook series: Psychology.* Champaign, IL: DEF publishers. DOI:nobaproject.com

Diener, E., & Tay, L. (2015). Subjective well-being and human welfare around the world as reflected in the Gallup World Poll. *International Journal of Psychology, 50*, 135–149. doi:10.1002/ijop.12136

DiFeliceantonio, A. G., Mabrouk, O. S., Kennedy, R. T., & Berridge, K. C. (2012). Enkephalin surges in dorsal neostriatum as a signal to eat. *Current Biology, 22*, 1918–1924. http://dx.doi.org/10.1016/j.cub.2012.08.014

Digdon, N. (2017). The Little Albert controversy: Intuition, confirmation bias, and logic. *History of Psychology.* http://dx.doi.org/10.1037/hop0000055

Dijksterhuis, A. (2014). Welcome back theory! *Perspectives on Psychological Science, 9*(1), 72–75. https://doi.org/10.1177/1745691613513472

Dillon, H. M., Adair, L. E., Geher, G., Wang, Z., & Strouts, P. H. (2016). Playing smart: The mating game and mating intelligence. *Current Psychology: A Journal for Diverse Perspectives on Diverse Psychological Issues, 35*(3), 414–420. http://dx.doi.org/10.1007/s12144-015-9309-y

Dillon, S. (2009, January 22). Study sees an Obama effect as lifting Black test-takers. *The New York Times.* Retrieved from http://www.nytimes.com/2009/01/23/education/23gap.html

Dimberg, U., & Thunberg, M. (1998). Rapid facial reactions to emotion facial expressions. *Scandinavian Journal of Psychology, 39*(1), 39–46.

Dimberg, U., Thunberg, M., & Elmehed, K. (2000). Unconscious facial reactions to emotional facial expressions. *Psychological Science, 11*(1), 86–89.

Dimidjian, S., Goodman, S. H., Felder, J. N., Gallop, R., Brown, A. P., & Beck, A. (2016). Staying well during pregnancy and the postpartum: A pilot randomized trial of mindfulness based cognitive therapy for the prevention of depressive relapse/recurrence. *Journal of Consulting and Clinical Psychology, 84*, 134–145. http://dx.doi.org/10.1037/ccp0000068

Dimitrov, S., Lange, T., Gouttefangeas, C., Jensen, A. T.R., Szczepanski, M., Lehnnolz, J., . . . Besedovsky, L. (2019). Gαs-coupled receptor signaling and sleep regulate integrin activation of human antigen-specific T cells. *The Journal of Experimental Medicine, 216*(3), 517–526. doi:10.1084/jem.20181169

Ding, Y. H., Xu, X., Wang, Z. Y., Li, H. R., & Wang, W. P. (2014). The relation of infant attachment to attachment and cognitive and behavioural outcomes in early childhood. *Early Human Development, 90*, 459–464. http://dx.doi.org/10.1016/j.earlhumdev.2014.06.004.

Dinsmore, D. L., & Alexander, P. A. (2016). A multi dimensional investigation of deep-level and surface-level processing. *Journal of Experimental Education, 84*, 213–244. http://dx.doi.org/10.1080/00220973.2014.979126

Din, S.-U., Ishfaq, M., Khan, M.I., & Khan, M.A. (2019). A study of role stressors and job satisfaction: The case of MNCs in collectivist context. *Behavioral Sciences, 9*(5), 49. https://doi.org/10.3390/bs9050049

Dirkes, J., Hughes, T., Ramirez-Valles, J., Johnson, T., & Bostwick, W. (2016). Sexual identity development: Relationship with lifetime suicidal ideation in sexual minority women. *Journal of Clinical Nursing, 25*, 3545–3556. http://dx.doi.org/10.1111/jocn.13313

Divecha, D. (2019, February 15). How neuroscience can help your kid make good choices. *Greater Good Magazine.* Retrieved from https://greatergood.berkeley.edu/article/item/how_neuroscience_can_help_your_kid_make_good_choices

Dixon, R. W., Youssef, G. J., Hasking, P., Yücel, M., Jackson, A. C., & Dowling, N. A. (2016). The relationship between gambling attitudes, involvement, and problems in adolescence: Examining the moderating role of coping strategies and parenting styles. *Addictive Behaviors, 58*, 42–46. http://dx.doi.org/10.1016/j.addbeh.2016.02.011

Djordjevic, N. (2019, May 28). 35 alarming chronic pain statistics: America vs. Europe. *Medalerthelp.org.* Retrieved from https://medalerthelp.org/chronic-pain-statistics/

DNA Exonerations in the United States. (2018). *Innocence Project.* Retrieved from https://www.innocenceproject.org/dna-exonerations-in-the-united-states/

Dobrow Riza, S., Ganzach, Y., & Liu, Y. (2018). Time and job satisfaction: A longitudinal study of the differential roles of age and tenure. *Journal of Management, 44*(7), 2558–2579. http://dx.doi.org/10.1177/0149206315624962

Dobson, K. S. (2016). The efficacy of cognitive behavioral therapy for depression: Reflections on a critical discussion. *Clinical Psychology: Science and Practice, 23*, 123–125. http://dx.doi.org/10.1111/cpsp.12151

Dodge, E. (2016). Forty years of eating disorder–focused family therapy—The legacy of 'psychosomatic families'. *Advances in Eating Disorders, 4*, 219–227. http://dx.doi.org/10.1080/21662630.2015.1099452

Dolev-Cohen, M., & Barak, A. (2013). Adolescents' use of instant messaging as a means of emotional relief. *Computers in Human Behavior, 29*, 58–63. http://dx.doi.org/10.1016/j.chb.2012.07.016

Doliński, D., Grzyb, T., Folwarczny, M., Grzybała, P., Krzyszycha, K., Martynowska, K., & Trojanowski, J. (2017). Would you deliver an electric shock in 2015? Obedience in the experimental paradigm developed by Stanley Milgram in the 50 years following the original studies. *Social Psychological and Personality Science, 8*(8), 927–933. https://doi.org/10.1177/1948550617693060

Dombrowski, S. C. (2015). *Psychoeducational assessment and report writing.* New York, NY: Springer. http://dx.doi.org/10.1007/978-1-4939-1911-6

Domhoff, G. W. (2003). *The scientific study of dreams: Neural networks, cognitive development, and content analysis.* Washington, DC: American Psychological Association.

Domhoff, G. W. (2010). Dream content is continuous with waking thought, based on preoccupations, concerns, and interests. *Sleep Medicine Clinics, 5*, 203–215.

Domonoske, C. A., & Romo, V. (2018, January 31). Nassar returns to court for 3ed sentencing; USA Gymnastics board resigns. *NPR.* Retrieved from https://www.npr.org/sections/thetwo-way/2018/01/31/582120231/nassar-returns-to-court-for-third-sentencing-as-usa-gymnastics-board-resigns

D'Onofrio, B. M., Rickert, M. E., Frans, E., Kuja-Halkola, R., Almqvist, C., Sjolander, A., . . . Lichtenstein, P. (2014). Paternal age at childbearing and offspring psychiatric and academic morbidity. *JAMA Psychiatry, 71*, 432–438. http://dx.doi.org/10.1001/jamapsychiatry.2013.4525

Doran, J. M., Safran, J. D., & Muran J. C. (2017). An investigation of the relationship between the alliance negotiation scale and psychotherapy process and outcome. *Journal of Clinical Psychology, 73*(4), 449–465. http://dx.doi.org/10.1002/jclp.22340

Doré, B. P., Tompson, S. H., O'Donnell, M. B., An, L. C., Strecher, V., & Falk, E. B. (2019). Neural mechanisms of emotion regulation moderate the predictive value of affective and value-related brain responses to persuasive messages. *Journal of Neuroscience, 39*(7), 1293–1300. http://dx.doi:10.1523/JNEUROSCI.1651-18.2018

Dovey, T. M., Boyland, E. J., Trayner, P., Miller, J., Rarmoul-Bouhadjar, A., Cole, J., & Halford, J. C. (2016). Alterations in taste perception due to recreational drug use are due to smoking a substance rather than ingesting it. *Appetite, 107*, 1–8. http://dx.doi.org/10.1016/j.appet.2016.07.016

Doyle, M. (2019, February 18). The difference between bisexual and pansexual matters less than solidarity among LGBTQ folks, advocates say. *Bustle.* Retrieved from https://www.bustle.com/p/the-difference-between-bisexual-pansexual-matters-less-than-solidarity-among-lgbtq-folks-advocates-say-15959039

Draganich, C., & Erdal, K. (2014). Placebo sleep affects cognitive functioning. *Journal of Experimental Psychology: Learning, Memory, and Cognition, 40*, 857–864. http://dx.doi.org/10.1037/a0035546

Drake, E. C., Sladek, M. R., & Doane, L. D. (2016). Daily cortisol activity, loneliness, and coping efficacy in late adolescence: A longitudinal study of the transition to college. *International Journal of Behavioral Development, 40*, 334–345. http://dx.doi.org/10.1177/0165025415581914

Dresler, M., Shirer, W. R., Konrad, B. N., Müller, N., Wagner, I. C., Fernández, G., . . . Greicius, M. D. (2017). Mnemonic training reshapes brain networks to support superior memory. *Neuron, 93*(5), 1227–1235.e6. doi:10.1016/j.neuron.2017.02.003

Dreu, C. K. W. D., Aaldering, H., & Saygi, Ö. (2015). Conflict and negotiation within and between groups. In M. Mikulincer, P. R. Shaver, J. F. Dovidio, & J. A. Simpson (Eds.), *APA handbook of personality and social psychology, Vol. 2. Group processes* (pp. 151–176). Washington, DC: American Psychological Association. http://dx.doi.org/10.1037/14342-006

Drew, L. (2013). What is the point of sleep? *New Scientist, 217,* 38–39.

Drexler, S. M., Merz, C. J., Hamacher-Dang, T. C., Tegenthoff, M., & Wolf, O. T. (2015). Effects of cortisol on reconsolidation of reactivated fear memories. *Neuropsychopharmacology, 40,* 3036–3043. http://dx.doi.org/10.1038/npp.2015.160.

Drigotas, S. M., Whitney, G. A., & Rusbult, C. E. (1995). On the peculiarities of loyalty: A diary study of responses to dissatisfaction in everyday life. *Personality and Social Psychology Bulletin, 21*(6), 596–609. http://dx.doi.org/10.1177/0146167295216006

Driscoll, I., Shumaker, S. A., Snively, B. M., Margolis, K. L., Manson, J. E., Vitolins, M. Z., . . . Espeland, M. A. (2016). Relationships between caffeine intake and risk for probable dementia or global cognitive impairment: The Women's Health Initiative Memory Study. *The Journals of Gerontology: Series A, 71*(12), 1596–1602. https://doi.org/10.1093/gerona/glw078

D'Souza, J., & Gurin, M. (2016). The universal significance of Maslow's concept of self-actualization. *The Humanistic Psychologist, 44,* 210–214. http://dx.doi.org/10.1037/hum0000027

Dubessy, A.-L., Leu-Semenescu, S., Attali, V., Maranci, J.-B., & Arnulf, I. (2017). Sexsomnia: A specialized non-REM parasomnia? *Sleep, 40*(2), zsw043. https://doi.org/10.1093/sleep/zsw043

Duniec, E., & Raz, M. (2011). Vitamins for the soul: John Bowlby's thesis of maternal deprivation, biomedical metaphors and the deficiency model of disease. *History of Psychiatry, 22,* 93–107.

Dunlop, B. W., Rajendra, J. K., Craighead, W. E., Kelley, M. E., McGrath, C. L., Choi, K. S., . . . Mayberg, H. S. (2017). Functional connectivity of the subcallosal cingulate cortex and differential outcomes to treatment with cognitive-behavioral therapy or antidepressant medication for major depressive disorder. *The American Journal of Psychiatry, 174*(6), 533–545. doi:10.1176/appi.ajp.2016.16050518

Dunlop, W. L., Karan, A., Wildinson, D., & Harake, N. (2019). Love in the first degree: Individual differences in first-person pronoun use and adult romantic attachment styles. *Social Psychological and Personality Science,* 194855061984745. doi:10.1177/1948550619847455

Dunlosky, J., Rawson, K. A., Marsh, E. J., Nathan, M. J., & Willingham, D. T. (2013). Improving students' learning with effective learning techniques: Promising directions from cognitive and educational psychology. *Psychological Science in the Public Interest, 14,* 4–58. http://dx.doi.org/10.1177/1529100612453266

Dunn, E. W., Aknin, L. B., & Norton, M. I. (2008). Spending money on others promotes happiness. *Science, 319,* 1687–1688. doi:10.1126/science.1150952

Dunsmoor, J. F., Kroes, M. C.W., Li, J., Daw, N. D., Simpson, H. B., & Phelps, E. A. (2019). Role of human ventromedial prefrontal cortex in learning and recall of enhanced extinction. *The Journal of Neuroscience, 39*(17), 3264–3276. doi:10.1523/JNEUROSCI.2713-18.2019

Dunster, G. P., de la Iglesia, L., Ben-Hamo, M., Nave, C., Fleischer, J. G., Panda, S., & de la Iglesia, H. O. (2018). Sleepmore in Seattle: Later school start times are associated with more sleep and better performance in high school students. *Science Advances,* Dec:eaau6200

Dupuis, K., Pichora-Fuller, M. K., Chasteen, A. L., Marchuk, V., Singh, G., & Smith, S. L. (2015). Effects of hearing and vision impairments on the Montreal Cognitive Assessment. *Aging, Neuropsychology, and Cognition, 22,* 413–437. http://dx.doi.org/10.1016/j.neurobiolaging.2015.02.028

Dutton, J. (2014). ADHD parenting advice from Michael Phelps' Mom. ADDitude. Retrieved from http://www.additudemag.com/adhd/article/1998.html

Dweck, C. S. (2012). Mindsets and human nature: Promoting change in the Middle East, the schoolyard, the racial divide, and willpower. *American Psychologist, 67,* 614–622. http://dx.doi.org/10.1037/a0029783

Dweck, C. S., & Yeager, D. S. (2019). Mindsets: A view from two eras. *Perspectives on Psychological Science, 14*(3), 481–496. https://doi.org/10.1177/1745691618804166

Dworkin, A. (1974). *Woman hating.* New York, NY: Dutton.

Dye, C. D., & Foley, C. A. (2017). Interpreting the data: Scientific inference. In M. Blume & B. C. Lust (Eds.), *Research methods in language acquisition: Principles, procedures, and practices* (pp. 211–225). Washington, DC: American Psychological Association. http://dx.doi.org/10.1037/15968-012

Dzau, V. J., & Johnson, P. A. (2018). Ending sexual harassment in academic medicine. *New England Journal of Medicine, 379,* 1589–1591. https://doi.org/10.1056/NEJMp1809846

Dzokoto,V.A.,Osei-Tutu,A.,Kyei,J.J.,Twum-Asante,M.,Attah,D.A.,& Ahorsu, D. K. (2018). Emotion norms, display rules, and regulation in the Akan society of Ghana: An exploration using proverbs. *Frontiers in Psychology, 9*:1916. doi:10.3389/fpsyg.2018.01916

Earp, B. D. (2015). Do the benefits of male circumcision outweigh the risks? A critique of the proposed CDC guidelines. *Frontiers in Pediatrics, 3,* 18. http://dx.doi.org/10.3389/fped.2015.00018

Eaton, N. R., Keyes, K. M., Krueger, R. F., Balsis, S., Skodol, A. E., Markon, K. E., . . . Hasin, D. S. (2012). An invariant dimensional liability model of gender differences in mental disorder prevalence: Evidence from a national sample. *Journal of Abnormal Psychology, 121,* 282–288. doi:10.1037/a0024780

Ebbinghaus, H. (1885). *Memory: A contribution to experimental psychology.* New York, NY: Dover Publications.

Eberhardt, J. L. (2019). *Biased: Uncovering the hidden prejudice that shapes what we see, think, and do.* New York, NY: Viking.

Eddy, K. T., Murray, H. B., & Le Grange, D. (2016). Eating and feeding disorders. In M. K. Dulcan (Ed.), *Dulcan's textbook of child and adolescent psychiatry* (2nd ed., pp. 435–460). Arlington, VA: American Psychiatric Publishing, Inc.

Edelmann, M. N., & Auger, A. P. (2011). Epigenetic impact of simulated maternal grooming on estrogen receptor alpha within the developing amygdala. *Brain, Behavior, and Immunity, 25*(7), 1299–1304. doi:10.1016/j.bbi.2011.02.009

Edel, M.-A., Raaff, V., Dimaggio, G., Buchheim, A., & Brüne, M. (2017). Exploring the effectiveness of combined mentalization based group therapy and dialectical behavior therapy for inpatients with borderline personality disorder—A pilot study. *British Journal of Clinical Psychology, 56*(1), 1–15. http://dx.doi.org/10.1111/bjc.12123

Edelson, L. R., Mokdad, C., & Martin, N. (2016). Prompts to eat novel and familiar fruits and vegetables in families with 1-3 year-old children: Relationships with food acceptance and intake. *Appetite, 99,* 138–148. http://dx.doi.org/10.1016/j.appet.2016.01.015

Edwards, H., Duchesne, A., Au, A. S., & Einstein, G. (2019). The many menopauses: Searching the cognitive research literature for menopause types. *Menopause, 26*(1), 45–65. doi:10.1097/GME.0000000000001171

Eggertson, L. (2010). Lancet retracts 12-year-old article linking autism to MMR vaccines. *Canadian Medical Association Journal, 182*(4), E199–E200. doi:10.1503/cmaj.109-3179

Ehrhart, F., Roozen, S., Verbeek, J., Koek, G., Kok, G., van Kranen, H., . . . Curfs, L. M. G. (2019). Review and gap analysis: Molecular pathways leading to fetal alcohol spectrum disorders. *Molecular Psychiatry, 24*, 10–17. https://doi.org/10.1038/s41380-018-0095-4

Ehrlich, K. B., Miller, G. E., Rohleder, N., & Adam, E. K. (2016). Trajectories of relationship stress and inflammatory processes in adolescence. *Development and Psychopathology, 28*, 127–138. http://dx.doi.org/10.1017/S0954579415000334

Eichenbaum, H. (2013). Memory systems. In R. J. Nelson, S. J. Y. Mizumori, & I. B. Weiner (Eds.), *Handbook of psychology, Vol. 3. Behavioral neuroscience* (2nd ed., pp. 551–573). Hoboken, NJ: Wiley.

Eisner, P., Klasen, M., Wolf, D., Zerres, K., Eggermann, T., Eisert, A., & Mathiak, K. (2017). Cortico-limbic connectivity in MAOA-L carriers is vulnerable to acute tryptophan depletion. *Human Brain Mapping, 38*(3), 1622–1635. http://dx.doi.org/10.1002/hbm.23475

Ekman, P. (1993). Facial expression and emotion. *American Psychologist, 48*, 384–392.

Ekman, P. (2004). *Emotions revealed: Recognizing faces and feelings to improve communication and emotional life.* Thousand Oaks, CA: Owl.

Ekman, P., & Keltner, D. (1997). Universal facial expressions of emotion: An old controversy and new findings. In U. C. Segerstrale & P. Molnar (Eds.), *Nonverbal communication: Where nature meets culture* (pp. 27–46). Mahwah, NJ: Erlbaum.

El-Bar, N., Laufer, O., Yoran-Hegesh, R., & Paz, R. (2017). Over-generalization in youth with anxiety disorders. *Social Neuroscience, 12*(1), 76–85. http://dx.doi.org/10.1080/17470919.2016.1167123

Elder, A. B. (2016). Experiences of older transgender and gender nonconforming adults in psychotherapy: A qualitative study. *Psychology of Sexual Orientation and Gender Diversity, 3*, 180–186. http://dx.doi.org/10.1037/sgd0000154

Eldred, S. M., & Eligon, J. (2016, May 10). Prince's doctor arrived with test results only him dead. *The New York Times.* Retrieved from http://www.nytimes.com/2016/05/11/arts/music/princes-doctor-arrived-with-test-results-only-to-find-him-dead.html

Eley, T. C., McAdams, T. A., Rijsdijk, F. V., Lichtenstein, P., Narustye, J., Reiss, D., . . . Neiderhiser, J. M. (2015). The intergenerational transmission of anxiety: A children of twins study. *The American Journal of Psychiatry, 172*, 630–637. http://dx.doi.org/10.1176/appi.ajp.2015.14070818

Elgendi, M., Kumar, P., Barbic, S., Howard, N., Abbott, D., & Cichocki, A. (2018). Subliminal priming-State of the art and future perspectives. *Behavioral Sciences (Basel, Switzerland), 8*(6), 54. doi:10.3390/bs8060054

El Haj, M., Gandolphe, M. C., Wawrziczny, E., & Antoine, P. (2016). Flashbulb memories of Paris attacks: Recall of these events and subjective reliving of these memories in a case with Alzheimer disease. *Medicine, 95*(46), e5448. doi:10.1097/MD.0000000000005448

Eligon, J., Kovaleski, S. F., & Coscarelli, J. (2016, May 4). Prince's addiction and an intervention too late. *The New York Times.* Retrieved from http://www.nytimes.com/2016/05/05/arts/music/friends-sought-help-for-princesaddiction-lawyer-says.html?_r=0

Elkind, D. (1967). Egocentrism in adolescence. *Child Development, 38*, 1025–1034.

Elkind, D. (2007). *The hurried child: Growing up too fast too soon* (25th anniversary ed.). Cambridge, MA: Da Capo.

Ellis, A., & Ellis, D. J. (2011). *Rational emotive behavior therapy.* Washington, DC: American Psychological Association.

Ellis, A., & Ellis, D. J. (2014). Rational emotive behavior therapy. In G. R. VandenBos, E. Meidenbauer, & J. Frank-McNeil (Eds.), *Psychotherapy theories and techniques: A reader* (pp. 289–298). Washington, DC: American Psychological Association. http://dx.doi.org/10.1037/14295-031

Ellis, A. R. (2019). A conceptual framework for preventing aggression in elementary schools. *Conflict Resolution Quarterly, 36*, 183–206. https://doi.org/10.1002/crq.21231

Ellis, N. (2019). Essentials of a theory of language cognition. *Modern Language Journal, 103*(Supplement 2019), 39–60. https://onlinelibrary.wiley.com/doi/full/10.1111/modl.12532

Elsey, J. W. B. (2017). Psychedelic drug use in healthy individuals: A review of benefits, costs, and implications for drug policy. *Drug Science, Policy and Law.* https://doi.org/10.1177/2050324517723232

Emmons, R. A., & McCullough, M. E. (2003). Counting blessings versus burdens: An experimental investigation of gratitude and subjective well-being in daily life. *Journal of Personality and Social Psychology, 84*, 377–389. http://dx.doi.org/10.1037/0022-3514.84.2.377

Endicott, K. L., & Endicott, K. M. (2014). Batek childrearing and morality. In D. Narvaez, K. Valentino, A. Fuentes, J. J. McKenna, & P. Gray (Eds.), *Ancestral landscapes in human evolution: Culture, childrearing and social wellbeing* (pp. 108–125). New York, NY: Oxford University Press.

Engemann, K., Pedersen, C. B., Arge, L., Tsirogiannis, C., Mortensen, P. B., & Svenning, J-C. (2019). Residential green space in childhood is associated with lower risk of psychiatric disorders from adolescence into adulthood. *Proceedings of the National Academy of Sciences of the United States of America, 116*(11), 5188–5193. doi:10.1073/pnas.1807504116

English, T., & Carstensen, L. L. (2015). Does positivity operate when the stakes are high? Health status and decision making among older adults. *Psychology and Aging, 30*, 348–355. http://dx.doi.org/10.1037/a0039121

Enright, R. D., & Fitzgibbons, R. P. (2015). *Forgiveness therapy: An empirical guide for resolving anger and restoring hope.* Washington, DC: American Psychological Association. http://dx.doi.org/10.1037/14526-000

Epley, N., & Schroeder, J. (2014). Mistakenly seeking solitude. *Journal of Experimental Psychology: General, 143*, 1980–1999. doi:10.1037/a0037323

Erikson, E. (1950). *Childhood and society.* New York, NY: Norton.

Erlings, E. I. J. (2016). The law and practices of ritual male circumcision: Time for review. In S. Deb (Ed.), *Child safety, welfare and well-being: Issues and challenges* (pp. 95–113). New York, NY: Springer Science + Business Media. http://dx.doi.org/10.1007/978-81-322-2425-9_8

Ernst, H. M., Kuhlmann, B. G., & Vogel, T. (2019). The origin of illusory correlations: Biased judgments converge with inferences, not with biased memory. *Experimental Psychology, 66*(3), 195–206. http://dx.doi.org/10.1027/1618-3169/a000444

Erviti, M., Semal, C., Wright, B. A., Amestoy, A., Bouvard, M. P., & Demany, L. (2015). A late emerging auditory deficit in autism. *Neuropsychology, 29*, 454–462. http://dx.doi.org/10.1037/neu0000162

Esch, T. (2014). The neurobiology of meditation and mindfulness. In S. Schmidt & H. Walach (Eds.), *Meditation—neuroscientific approaches and philosophical implications* (pp. 153–173). New York, NY: Springer. http://dx.doi.org/10.1007/978-3-319-01634-4_9

Esmaeilikia, M., Radun, I., Grzebieta, R., & Olivier, J. (2019). Bicycle helmets and risky behavior: A systematic review. *Transportation*

Research Part F. Traffic Psychology and Behavior, 60, 299–310. https://doi.org/10.1016/j.trf.2018.10.026

Espinosa-Hernández, G., Vasilenko, S. A., & Bámaca-Colbert, M. Y. (2016). Sexual behaviors in Mexico: The role of values and gender across adolescence. *Journal of Research on Adolescence, 26,* 603–609. http://dx.doi.org/10.1111/jora.12209

Esposito, G., Manian, N., Truzzi, A., & Bornstein, M. H. (2017). Response to infant cry in clinically depressed and non-depressed mothers. *PLoS ONE, 12*(1): e0169066. http://dx.doi.org/10.1371/journal.pone.0169066

Ethical Principles of Psychologists and Code of Conduct. (2016). In A.E. Kazdin (Ed.), *Methodological issues and strategies in clinical research* (4th ed., pp. 495–512). Washington, DC: American Psychological Association. http://dx.doi.org/10.1037/14805-030

Evans, G. W., Otto, S., & Kaiser, F. G. (2018). Childhood origins of young adult environmental behavior. *Psychological Science, 29*(5), 679–687. https://doi.org/10.1177/0956797617741894

Eysenck, H. J. (1967). *The biological basis of personality.* Springfield, IL: Thomas.

Eysenck, H. J. (1990). Biological dimensions of personality. In L. A. Pervin (Ed.), *Handbook of personality: Theory and research* (pp. 244–276). New York, NY: Guilford.

Fabre, B., Grosman, H., Mazza, O., Nolazco, C., Machulsky, N. F., Mesch, V., . . . Berg, G. (2013). Relationship between cortisol, life events and metabolic syndrome in men. *Stress, 16,* 16–23. doi:10.3109/10253890.2012.676112.

Faddiman, A. (1997). *The spirit catches you and you fall down.* New York, NY: Straus & Giroux.

Fadel, L., & Garcia-Navarro, L. (2013). How different cultures handle personal space. *NPR.* Retrieved from http://www.npr.org/sections/codeswitch/2013/05/05/181126380/how-differentcultures-handle-personal-space

Fagelson, M., & Baguley, D. M. (2016). Influences of amplified music. D. M. Baguley & M. Fagelson (Eds.), *Tinnitus: Clinical and research perspectives* (pp. 129–143). San Diego, CA: Plural Publishing.

Fahey, R. A., Matsubayashi, T., & Ueda, M. (2018). Tracking the Werther Effect on social media: Emotional responses to prominent suicide deaths on twitter and subsequent increases in suicide. *Social Science & Medicine, 219,* 19–29. https://doi.org/10.1016/j.socscimed.2018.10.004

Fahnehjelm, K. T., Törnquist, A. L., Olsson, M., Bäckström, I., Grönlund, M. A., & Winiarski, J. (2016). Cataract after allogeneic hematopoietic stem cell transplantation in childhood. *Acta Paediatrica, 105,* 82–89. http://dx.doi.org/10.1111/apa.13173

Fairbairn, C. E., & Bresin, K. (2017). The effects of contextual familiarity on alcohol expectancies. *Experimental and Clinical Psychopharmacology, 25,* 13–23. http://dx.doi.org/10.1037/pha0000103

Falcon, B., Zivanov, J., Zhang, W., Murzin, A.G., Garringer, H. J., Vidal, R., . . . Scheres, S. H. W. (2019). Novel tau filament fold in chronic traumatic encephalopathy encloses hydrophobic molecules. *Nature, 568,* 420–423. doi:10.1038/s41586-019-1026-5

Fall, T., Kuja-Halkola, R., Dobney, K., Westgarth, C., & Magnusson, P. K. E. (2019). Evidence of large genetic influences on dog ownership in the Swedish Twin Registry has implications for understanding domestication and health associations. *Scientific Reports, 9*(1). doi:10.1038/s41598-019-44083-9

Fang, J., Prybutok, V., & Wen, C. (2016). Shirking behavior and socially desirable responding in online surveys: A cross-cultural study comparing Chinese and American samples. *Computers in Human Behavior, 54,* 310–317. doi:10.1016/j.chb.2015.08.019

Fan, H., Li, T.-F., Gong, N., & Wang, Y.-X. (2016). Shanzhiside methylester, the principle effective iridoid glycoside from the analgesic herb Lamiophlomis rotata, reduces neuropathic pain by stimulating spinal microglial β-endorphin expression. *Neuropharmacology, 101,* 98–109. doi:10.1016/j.neuropharm.2015.09.010

Fantz, R. L. (1956). A method for studying early visual development. *Perceptual and Motor Skills, 6,* 13–15.

Fantz, R. L. (1963). Pattern vision in newborn infants. *Science, 140,* 296–297.

Faraone, S. V., & Larsson, H. (2019). Genetics of attention deficit hyperactivity disorder. *Molecular Psychiatry, 24,* 562–575. https://doi.org/10.1038/s41380-018-0070-0

Farb, N., Anderson, A., Ravindran, A., Hawley, L., Irving, J., Mancuso, E., . . . Segal, Z. V. (2018). Prevention of relapse/recurrence in major depressive disorder with either mindfulness-based cognitive therapy or cognitive therapy. *Journal of Consulting and Clinical Psychology, 86*(2), 200–204. http://dx.doi.org/10.1037/ccp0000266

Farmer, T. A., & Matlin, M. W. (2019). *Cognition* (10th ed.). Hoboken, NJ: Wiley.

Farrell, A. D., Mehari, K. R., Kramer-Kuhn, A., & Goncy, E. A. (2014). The impact of victimization and witnessing violence on physical aggression among high-risk adolescents. *Child Development, 85,* 1694–1710. doi:10.1111/cdev.12215

Fast Facts. (2019). *Centers for Disease Control and Prevention (CDC).* Retrieved July 13, 2019 from https://www.cdc.gov/tobacco/data_statistics/fact_sheets/fast_facts/index.htm

Fast, L. C., Harman, J. J., Maertens, J. A., Burnette, J. L., & Dreith, F. (2015). Creating a measure of portion control self efficacy. *Eating Behaviors, 16,* 23–30. http://dx.doi.org/10.1016/j.eatbeh.2014.10.009

Fauci, A. S., Redfield, R. R., Sigounas, G., Weahkee, M. D., & Giroir, B. P. (2019). Ending the HIV epidemic: A plan for the United States. *Journal of the American Medical Association, 321*(9), 844–845. doi:10.1001/jama.2019.1343

Fausto-Sterling, A. (2019). Gender/sex, sexual orientation, and identity are in the body: How did they get there? *The Journal of Sex Research, 56*(4–5), 529–555. doi:10.1080/00224499.2019.1581883

Federal Communications Commission (FCC). (2019, April 8). The dangers of distracted driving. *Federal Communications Commission.* Retrieved from https://www.fcc.gov/consumers/guides/dangers-texting-while-driving

Feeney, E. L., Leacy, L., O'Kelly, M., Leacy, N., Phelan, A., Crowley, L., . . . Horner, K. (2019). Sweet and umami taste perception differs with habitual exercise in males. *Nutrients, 11*(1), 155. doi:10.3390/nu11010155

Feeney, J. R., Pliner, P., Polivy, J., & Herman, C. P. (2017). The persistence of and resistance to social norms regarding the appropriate amount to eat: A preliminary investigation. *Appetite, 109,* 93–99. http://dx.doi.org/10.1016/j.appet.2016.11.031

Fehr, B. (2015). Love: Conceptualization and experience. In M. Mikulincer, P. R. Shaver, J. A. Simpson, & J. F. Dovidio (Eds.), *APA handbook of personality and social psychology, Vol. 3. Interpersonal relations* (pp. 495–522). Washington, DC: American Psychological Association. http://dx.doi.org/10.1037/14344-018

Fehr, B., Harasymchuk, C., & Sprecher, S. (2014). Compassionate love in romantic relationships: A review and some new findings. *Journal of Social and Personal Relationships, 31,* 575–600. doi:10.1177/0265407514533768.

Fein, S., & Spencer, S. J. (1997). Prejudice as self-image maintenance: Affirming the self through derogating others. *Journal of Personality and Social Psychology, 73,* 31–44.

Feldman, S. (2014). *Development across a lifetime* (7th ed.). Essex, UK: Pearson.

Felitti, V. J., Anda, R. F., Nordenberg, D., Williamson, D. F., Spitz, A. M., Edwards, V., . . . Marks, J. S. (1998). Adverse childhood experiences. *American Journal of Preventive Medicine, 14*(4), 245–258. doi:10.1016/S0749-3797(98)00017-8

Felson, J. (2014). What can we learn from twin studies? A comprehensive evaluation of the equal environments assumption. *Social Science Research, 43,* 184–199. http://dx.doi.org/10.1016/j.ssresearch.2013.10.004

Feng, K., Zhao, X., Liu, J., Cai, Y., Ye, Z., Chen, C., & Xue, G. (2019). Spaced learning enhances episodic memory by increasing neural pattern similarity across repetitions. *Journal of Neuroscience, 39*(27), 5351–5360. doi:10.1523/JNEUROSCI.2741-18.2019

Feng, X., Xie, K., Gong, S., Gao, L., & Cao, Y. (2019). Effects of parental autonomy support and teacher support on middle school students' homework effort: Homework autonomous motivation as mediator. *Frontiers in Psychology, 10,* 612. doi:10.3389/fpsyg.2019.00612

Ferguson, C. J. (2010). Violent crime research: An introduction. In C. J. Ferguson (Ed.), *Violent crime: Clinical and social implications* (pp. 3–18). Thousand Oaks, CA: Sage.

Ferguson, C. J. (2015). Does movie or video game violence predict societal violence? It depends on what you look at and when—Revised. *Journal of Communication, 65,* 193–212. http://dx.doi.org/10.1111/jcom.12142

Ferguson, C. J. (2019, August 5). Analysis: Why it's time to stop blaming video games for real-world violence. *PBS News Hour.* Retrieved from https://www.pbs.org/newshour/science/analysis-why-its-time-to-stop-blaming-video-games-for-real-world-violence

Fernald, A., Marchman, V. A., & Weisleder, A. (2013). SES differences in language processing skill and vocabulary are evident at 18 months. *Developmental Science, 16,* 234–248. doi:10.1111/desc.12019

Fernandes, M. A., Wammes, J. D., & Meade, M. E. (2018). The surprisingly powerful influence of drawing on memory. *Current Directions in Psychological Science, 27*(5), 302–308. https://doi.org/10.1177/0963721418755385

Ferrie, A. (2015, April 4). Source amnesia and advertising. *The Consumer Psychologist.* Retrieved from http://www.theconsumerpsychologist.com/2015/04/04/sourceamnesia-and-advertising/

Festinger, L. (1957). *A theory of cognitive dissonance.* Stanford, CA: Stanford University Press.

Festinger, L. A., & Carlsmith, J. M. (1959). Cognitive consequences of forced compliance. *Journal of Abnormal and Social Psychology, 58,* 203–210.

Fielder, R. L., Carey, K. B., & Carey, M. P. (2013). Are hookups replacing romantic relationships? A longitudinal study of first-year female college students. *The Journal of Adolescent Health, 52,* 657–659. http://dx.doi.org/10.1016/j.jadohealth.2012.09.001

Field, K. M., Woodson, R., Greenberg, R., & Cohen, D. (1982). Discrimination and imitation of facial expressions by neonates. *Science, 218,* 179–181. http://dx.doi.org/10.1016/S0163-6383(83)90316-8

Fields, A., & Cochran, S. (2011). Men and depression: Current perspectives for health care professionals. *American Journal of Lifestyle Medicine, 5,* 92–100. https://doi.org/10.1177/1559827610378347

Fields, J. A. (2015). Effects of deep brain stimulation in movement disorders on cognition and behavior. In A. I. Tröster (Ed.), *Clinical neuropsychology and cognitive neurology of Parkinson's disease and other movement disorders* (pp. 332–375). New York, NY: Oxford University Press.

Finegersh, A., Rompala, G. R., Martin, D. I. K., & Homanics, G. E. (2015). Drinking beyond a lifetime: New and emerging insights into paternal alcohol exposure on subsequent generations. *Alcohol, 49,* 461–470. http://dx.doi.org/10.1016/j.alcohol.2015.02.008

Finkel, E. J., Norton, M. I., Reis, H. T., Ariely, D., Caprariello, P. A., Eastwick, P. W., . . . Maniaci, M. R. (2015). When does familiarity promote versus undermine interpersonal attraction? A proposed integrative model from erstwhile adversaries. *Perspectives on Psychological Science, 10,* 3–19. http://dx.doi.org/10.1177/1745691614561682

Finley, E. P., Bollinger, M., Noël, P. H., Amuan, M. E., Copeland, L. A., Pugh, J., . . . Pugh, M. J. V. (2015). A national cohort study of the association between the Polytrauma Clinical Triad and suicide related behavior among US veterans who served in Iraq and Afghanistan. *American Journal of Public Health, 105,* 380–387. http://dx.doi.org/10.2105/AJPH.2014.301957

Fischer, A. W., Schlein, C., Cannon, B., Heeren, J., & Nedergaard, J. (2019). Intact innervation is essential for diet-induced recruitment of brown adipose tissue. *American Journal of Physiology-Endocrinology and Metabolism, 316*:3, E487–E503.

Fischer, C., Malycha, C. P., & Schafmann, E. (2019). The influence of intrinsic motivation and synergistic extrinsic motivators on creativity and innovation. *Frontiers in Psychology, 10*:137. doi:10.3389/fpsyg.2019.00137

Fischer, R., Lee, A., & Verzijden, M. N. (2019). Dopamine genes are linked to extraversion and neuroticism personality traits, but only in demanding climates. *Nature Scientific Reports, 8*:1733. https://www.nature.com/articles/s41598-017-18784-y

Fisher, T. D. (2013). Gender roles and pressure to be truthful: The bogus pipeline modifies gender differences in sexual but not non-sexual behavior. *Sex Roles, 68,* 401–414. doi:10.1007/s11199-013-0266-3

Fishman, I., & Ng, R. (2013). Error related brain activity in extraverts: Evidence for altered response monitoring in social context. *Biological Psychology, 93,* 225–230. http://dx.doi.org/10.1016/j.biopsycho.2013.02.010

Fitch, W. T. (2018). What animals can teach us about human language: The phonological continuity hypothesis. *Current Opinion in Behavioral Sciences, 21,* 68–75. https://www.sciencedirect.com/science/article/pii/S2352154617301262

Flannery, J. E., Beauchamp, K. G., & Fisher, P. A. (2017). The role of social buffering on chronic disruptions in quality of care: Evidence from caregiver-based interventions in foster children. *Social Neuroscience, 12*(1), 86–91. http://dx.doi.org/10.1080/17470919.2016.1170725

Fleming, R. W. (2014). Visual perception of materials and their properties. *Vision Research, 94,* 62–75. doi:10.1016/j.visres.2013.11.004

Fletcher, B. R., & Rapp, P. R. (2013). Normal neurocognitive aging. In R. J. Nelson, S. J. Y. Mizumori, & I. B. Weiner (Eds.), *Handbook of psychology, Vol. 3. Behavioral neuroscience* (2nd ed., pp. 643–663). Hoboken, NJ: Wiley.

Fletcher, G. J. O., & Simpson, J. A. (2000). Ideal standards in close relationships: Their structure and functions. *Current Directions in Psychological Science, 9,* 102–105.

Flett, G. L., Goldstein, A. L., Pechenkov, I. G., Nepon, T., & Wekerle, C. (2016). Antecedents, correlates, and consequences of feeling like you don't matter: Associations with maltreatment, loneliness, social anxiety, and the five-factor model. *Personality and Individual Differences, 92,* 52–56. http://dx.doi.org/10.1016/j.paid.2015.12.014

Fligelman, B., Pham, T., Bryson, E. O., Majeske, M., & Kellner, C. H. (2016). Resolution of acute suicidality after a single right unilateral electroconvulsive therapy. *The Journal of ECT, 32,* 71–72. http://dx.doi.org/10.1097/YCT.0000000000000258

Flora, J., & Segrin, C. (2015). Family conflict and communication. In L. Turner & R. West (Eds.), *The SAGE handbook of family communication* (pp. 91–106). Thousand Oaks, CA: Sage Publishing.

Flynn, J. R. (1987). Massive IQ gains in 14 nations: What IQ tests really measure. *Psychological Bulletin, 101,* 171–191. http://dx.doi.org/10.1037/0033-2909.101.2.171

Flynn, J. R. (2019). Reservations about Rushton. *Psych 1*(1), 35–43. https://doi.org/10.3390/psych1010003

Flynn, J., te Nijenhuis, J., & Metzen, D. (2014). The *g* beyond Spearman's *g*: Flynn's paradoxes resolved using four exploratory meta-analyses. *Intelligence, 44,* 1–10. http://dx.doi.org/10.1016/j.intell.2014.01.009

Foerde, K., Steinglass, J., Shohamy, D., & Walsh, B. T. (2015). Neural mechanisms supporting maladaptive food choices in anorexia nervosa. *Nature Neuroscience, 18,* 1571–1573.http://dx.doi.org/10.1038/nn.4136

Foley, H. J., & Bates, M. (2019). *Sensation and perception* (6th ed.). New York, NY: Routledge.

Folkvord, F., Anschütz, D. J., & Buijzen, M. (2016). The association between BMI development among young children and (un)healthy food choices in response to food advertisements: A longitudinal study. *The International Journal of Behavioral Nutrition and Physical Activity, 13,* Article 16. http://dx.doi.org/10.1186/s12966-016-0340-7

Fonger, A. M., & Malott, R. W. (2018). Using shaping to teach eye contact to children with autism spectrum disorder. *Behavior Analysis in Practice, 12*(1), 216–221. doi:10.1007/s40617-018-0245-9

Fontenelle, L. R., & Yücel, M. (2019). A clinical staging model for obsessive-compulsive disorder: Is it ready for prime time? *EClinicalMedicine, 7,* 65–72. doi:10.1016/j.eclinm.2019.01.014

Ford, J. H., DiBiase, H. D., Ryu, E., & Kensinger, E. A. (2018). It gets better with time: Enhancement of age-related positivity effect in the six months following a highly negative public event. *Psychology and Aging, 33*(3), 419–424. doi:10.1037/pag0000250

Ford, T. E. (2015). The social consequences of disparagement humor: Introduction and over-view. *Humor, 28,* 163–169. http://dx.doi.org/10.1515/humor-2015-0016

Forthmannm, B., Bürkner, P.-C., Szardenings, C., Benedek, M., & Holling, H. (2019). A new perspective on the multidimensionality of divergent thinking tasks. *Frontiers in Psychology, 10:*985. doi:10.3389/fpsyg.2019.00985

Foulkes, D. (1993). Children's dreaming. In D. Foulkes & C. Cavallero (Eds.), *Dreaming as cognition* (pp. 114–132). New York, NY: Harvester Wheatsheaf.

Foulkes, D. (1999). *Children's dreaming and the development of consciousness.* Cambridge, MA: Harvard University Press.

Frakt, A. (2019, June 3). Does your education level affect your health? *New York Times.* Retrieved from https://www.nytimes.com/2019/06/03/upshot/education-impact-health-longevity.html

Fraley, R. C., & Shaver, P. R. (1997). Adult attachment and the suppression of unwanted thoughts. *Journal of Personality and Social Psychology, 73,* 1080–1091.

Fralick, M., Sy, E., Hassan, A., Burke, M. J., Mostofsky, E., & Karsies, T. (2019). Association of concussion with the risk of suicide: A systematic review and meta-analysis. *JAMA Neurology. 76*(2), 144–151. doi:10.1001/jamaneurol.2018.3487

Francis, G. (2012). Too good to be true: Publication bias in two prominent studies from experimental psychology. *Psychonomic Bulletin & Review, 19,* 151–156. doi:10.3758/s13423-012-0227-9

Franconeri, S. L., Alvarez, G. A., & Cavanagh, P. (2013). Flexible cognitive resources: Competitive content maps for attention and memory. *Trends in Cognitive Sciences, 17,* 134–141. http://dx.doi.org/10.1016/j.tics.2013.01.010

Frangicetto, T. (2015, May 22). American Sniper and the warrior cult. *Buck County Courier Times,* p. A9. Retrieved from http://www.buckscountycouriertimes.com/opinion/op-ed/american-sniper-and-the-warrior-cult/article_c9ec7de8-5f18-59dd-9300-c8f78603052f.html

Frattaroli, S., & Buggs, S. A. L. (2016). Decreasing gun violence: Social and public health interventions. In L. H. Gold & R. I. Simon (Eds.), *Gun violence and mental illness* (pp. 381–406). Arlington, VA: American Psychiatric Association.

Frazer, A. L., Rubens, S., Johnson-Motoyama, M., DiPierro, M., & Fite, P. J. (2017). Acculturation dissonance, acculturation strategy, depressive symptoms, and delinquency in Latina/o adolescents. *Child & Youth Care Forum, 46*(1), 19–33. http://dx.doi.org/10.1007/s10566-016-9367-9

Freedheim, D. K., & Weiner, I. B. (Eds.). (2013). *Handbook of psychology, Volume 1, History of psychology* (2nd ed.). Hoboken, NJ: Wiley.

Freedman, J. L., & Fraser, S. C. (1966). Compliance without pressure: The foot-in-the-door technique. *Journal of Personality and Social Psychology, 4*(2), 195–202. http://dx.doi.org/10.1037/h0023552

Freeman, T. P., Hindocha, C., Green, S. F., & Bloomfield, M. A. P. (2019). Medicinal use of cannabis based products and cannabinoids. *The BMJ, 365.* doi:10.1136/bmj.l1141

Freidin, E., Carballo, F., & Bentosela, M. (2017). Direct reciprocity in animals: The roles of bonding and affective processes. *International Journal of Psychology, 52*(2), 163–170. http://dx.doi.org/10.1002/ijop.12215

French, A. S., Sellier, M.-J., Moutaz, A. A., Guigue, A., Chabaud, M.-A., Reeb, P. D., . . . Marion-Poll, F. (2015). Dual mechanism for bitter avoidance in Drosophila. *The Journal of Neuroscience, 35,* 3990–4004. doi:10.1523/JNEUROSCI.1312-14.2015

Frenda, S. J., Patihis, L., Loftus, E. F., Lewis, H. C., & Fenn, K. M. (2014). Sleep deprivation and false memories. *Psychological Science, 25,* 1674–1681. http://dx.doi.org/10.1177/0956797614534694.

Friedman, E. M., Ruini, C., Foy, R., Jaros, L., Sampson, H., & Ryff, C. D. (2017). Lighten UP! A community-based group intervention to promote psychological well-being in older adults. *Aging & Mental Health, 21*(2), 199–205. http://dx.doi.org/10.1080/13607863.2015.109 3605

Friedman, M. J. (2015). The human stress response. In N. C. Bernardy & M. J. Friedman (Eds.), *A practical guide to PTSD treatment: Pharmacological and psychotherapeutic approaches* (pp. 9–19). Washington, DC: American Psychological Association. http://dx.doi.org/10.1037/14522-002

Friesdorf, R., Conway, P., & Gawronski, B. (2015). Gender differences in responses to moral dilemmas: A process dissociation analysis. *Personality and Social Psychology Bulletin, 41,* 696–713. doi:10.1177/0146167215575731

Friesen, M. D., Horwood, L. J., Fergusson, D. M., & Woodward, L. J. (2017). Exposure to parental separation in childhood and later parenting quality as an adult: Evidence from a 30-year longitudinal study. *Journal of Child Psychology and Psychiatry, 58,* 30–37. http://dx.doi.org/10.1111/jcpp.12610

Frisch, M., Aigrain, Y., Barauskas, V., Bjarnason, R., Boddy, S.-A., Czauderna, P., . . . Wijnen, R. (2013). Cultural bias in the AAP's 2012 technical report and policy statement on male circumcision. *Pediatrics, 131*(4), 796–800. https://doi.org/10.1542/peds.2012-2896

Frith, U. (2016, December 30). Theory of mind. Serious Science. Retrieved from http://seriousscience.org/theory-of-mind-7939

Frodl, T., Janowitz, D., Schmaal, L., Tozzi, L., Dobrowolny, H., Stein, D. J., . . . Grabe, H. J. (2017). Childhood adversity impacts on brain subcortical structures relevant to depression. *Journal of Psychiatric Research, 86*, 58–65. http://dx.doi.org/10.1016/j.jpsychires.2016.11.010

Frostadottir, A. D., & Dorjee, D. (2019). Effects of mindfulness based cognitive therapy (MBCT) and compassion focused therapy (CFT) on symptom change, mindfulness, self-compassion, and rumination in clients with depression, anxiety, and stress. *Frontiers in Psychology, 10*:1099. doi:10.3389/fpsyg.2019.01099

Fryer, R. G. (2010). Financial incentives and student achievement: Evidence from randomized trials. *The National Bureau of Economic Research.* Retrieved from https://www.nber.org/papers/w15898

Fu, C. Y., Moyle, W., & Cooke, M. (2013). A randomised controlled trial of the use of aromatherapy and hand massage to reduce disruptive behaviour in people with dementia. *BMC Complementary and Alternative Medicine, 13*, Article 165. http://dx.doi.org/10.1155/2013/790792

Fyhri, A., & Phillips, R.O. (2013). Emotional reactions to cycle helmet use. *Accident Analysis and Prevention, 50*, 59–63. doi:10.1016/j.aap.2012.03.027.

Gable, S. L., Hopper, E. A., & Schooler, J. W. (2019). When the muses strike: Creative ideas of physicists and writers routinely occur during mind wandering. *Psychological Science, 30*(3), 396–404. doi.org/10.1177/0956797618820626

Gaertner, S. L., & Dovidio, J. F. (2014). *Reducing intergroup bias: The common ingroup identity model.* New York, NY: Routledge.

Gagnepain, P., Henson, R. N., & Anderson, M. C. (2014). Suppressing unwanted memories reduces their unconscious influence via targeted cortical inhibition. *Proceedings of the National Academy of Sciences of the United States of America, 111,* E1310–E1319. http://dx.doi.org/10.1073/pnas.1311468111

Gagnon, J. H. (1990). The explicit and implicit use of the scripting perspective in sex research. *Annual Review of Sex Research, 1*(1), 1–43. doi:10.1080/10532528.1990.10559854

Gagnon, M., & Cormier, S. (2019). Retrieval practice and distributed practice: The case of French Canadian students. *Canadian Journal of School Psychology, 34*(2), 83–97. https://doi.org/10.1177/0829573518773225

Gajanan, M. (2019, May 22). AI voice assistants reinforce gender biases, U.N. report says. *Time.* Retrieved from https://time.com/5593436/ai-voice-assistants-gender-bias/?utm_source=time.com&utm_medium=email&utm_campaign=the-brief-pm&utm_content=2019052220pm&xid=newsletter-brief

Galinha, I. C., Garcia-Martín, M. A., Gomes, C., & Oishi, S. (2016). Criteria for happiness among people living in extreme poverty in Maputo, Mozambique. *International Perspectives in Psychology: Research, Practice, Consultation, 5,* 67–90. doi:10.1037/ipp0000053

Galinha, I. C., Oishi, S., Pereira, C. R., Wirtz, D., & Esteves, F. (2014). Adult attachment, love styles, relationship experiences and subjective well-being: Cross-cultural and gender comparison between Americans, Portuguese, and Mozambicans. *Social Indicators Research, 119,* 823–852. http://dx.doi.org/10.1007/s11205-013-0512-7

Gallagher, B. J. III, & Jones, B. J. (2016). Neglect and hereditary risk: Their relative contribution to schizophrenia with negative symptomatology. *International Journal of Social Psychiatry, 62,* 235–242. http://dx.doi.org/10.1177/0020764015623974

Gamble, T., & Walker, I. (2016). Wearing a bicycle helmet can increase risk taking and sensation seeking in adults. *Psychological Science, 27,* 289–294. doi:10.1177/0956797615620784

Gandal, M. J., Haney, J. R., Parikshak, N. N., Leppa, V., Ramaswami, G., Hartl, C., . . . Geschwind, D. H. (2018). Shared molecular neuropathology across major psychiatric disorders parallels polygenic overlap. *Science, 359*(6376), 693–697. doi:10.1126/science.aad6469)

Ganesan, S., Magee, M., Stone, J. E., Mulhall, M. D., Collins, A., Howard, M. E., . . . Sletten, T. L. (2019). The impact of shift work on sleep, alertness and performance in healthcare workers. *Scientific Reports, 9*(1), 4635. doi:10.1038/s41598-019-40914-x

Gangloff, K. A., Connelly, B. L., & Shook, C. L. (2016). Of scapegoats and signals: Investor reactions to CEO succession in the aftermath of wrongdoing. *Journal of Management, 42*(6), 1614–1634. http://dx.doi.org/10.1177/0149206313515521

Gangwisch, J. E., Hale, L., Garcia, L., Malaspina, D., Opler, M. G., Payne, M. E., . . . Lane, D. (2015). High glycemic index diet as a risk factor for depression: Analyses from the Women's Health Initiative. *American Journal of Clinical Nutrition, 102,* 454–463. http://dx.doi.org/10.3945/ajcn.114.103846

Ganna, A., Verweij, K. J. H., Nivard, M. G., Maier, R., Wedow, R., Busch, A. S., . . . Zietxch, B. P. (2019). A genome-wide association study of same-sex sexual behavior identifies loci associated with human sexual orientation. *Science, 365*:6456. https://science.sciencemag.org/content/365/6456/eaat7693

Gannon, J., Atkinson, J. H., Chircop-Rollick, T., D'Andrea, J., Garfin, S., Patel, S., . . . Rutledge, T. (2019). Telehealth therapy effects of nurses and mental health professionals from 2 randomized controlled trials for chronic back pain. *The Clinical Journal of Pain, 35*(4), 295–303. doi:10.1097/AJP.0000000000000678

Gao, Z., Davis, C., Thomas, A. M., Economo, M. N., Abrego, A. M., Svoboda, K., . . . Li, N. (2018). A cortico-cerebellar loop for motor planning. *Nature, 563*(7729), 113–116. https://doi.org/10.1038/s41586-018-0633-x

Gao, Z., Gao, Q., Tang, N., Shui, R., & Shen, M. (2016). Organization principles in visual working memory: Evidence from sequential stimulus display. *Cognition, 146,* 277–288. http://dx.doi.org/10.1016/j.cognition.2015.10.005

Garcia, J., & Koelling, R. A. (1966). Relation of cue to consequence in avoidance learning. *Psychonomic Science, 4,* 123–124. http://dx.doi.org/10.3758/BF03342209

Gardner, B., Phillips, L. A., & Judah, G. (2016). Habitual instigation and habitual execution: Definition, measurement, and effects on behaviour frequency. *British Journal of Health Psychology, 21,* 613–630. http://dx.doi.org/10.1111/bjhp.12189

Gardner, H. (1983). *Frames of mind.* New York, NY: Basic.

Gardner, H. (2008). Who owns intelligence? *The Jossey-Bass reader on the brain and learning* (pp. 120–132). San Francisco, CA: Jossey-Bass.

Gardner, R. A., & Gardner, B. T. (1969). Teaching sign language to a chimpanzee. *Science, 165,* 664–672.

Gardstrom, S., & Sorel, S. (2015). Music therapy methods. In B. Wheeler (Ed.), *Music therapy handbook* (pp. 116–128). New York, NY: Guilford.

Garg, R., Levin, E., & Tremblay, L. (2016). Emotional intelligence: Impact on post-secondary academic achievement. *Social Psychology of Education, 19*(3), 627–642. http://dx.doi.org/10.1007/s11218-016-9338-x

Garland, T. S., Branch, K. A., & Grimes, M. (2016). Blurring the lines: Reinforcing rape myths in comic books. *Feminist Criminology, 11,* 48–68. http://dx.doi.org/10.1177/1557085115576386

Garrett, B. (2015). *Brain and behavior: An introduction to biological psychology* (4th ed.). Thousand Oaks, CA: Sage.

Garrett, N., Lazzaro, S. C., Ariely, D., & Sharot, T. (2016). The brain adapts to dishonesty. *Nature Neuroscience, 19*(12), 1727–1732. doi:10.1038/nn.4426

Gartzia, L., Pizarro, J., & Baniandres, J. (2018). Emotional androgyny: A preventive factor of psychosocial risks at work? *Frontiers in Psychology, 9,* 2144. doi:10.3389/fpsyg.2018.02144

Gattino, S., & Tartaglia, S. (2015). The effect of television viewing on ethnic prejudice against immigrants: A study in the Italian context. *International Journal of Intercultural Relations, 44,* 46–52. doi:10.1016/j.ijintrel.2014.11.004

Gaudiano, B. A., Dalrymple, K. L., Weinstock, L. M., & Lohr, J. M. (2015). The science of psychotherapy: Developing, testing, and promoting evidence-based treatments. In S. O. Lilienfeld, S. J. Lynn, & J. M. Lohr (Eds.), *Science and pseudoscience in clinical psychology* (2nd ed., pp. 155–190). New York, NY: Guilford.

Gayen, G., Bhowmik, A., & Nandy, M. (2019). Study of feeding practice and factors influencing it among preterm babies getting kangaroo mother care in a tertiary care hospital. *Journal of Clinical Neonatology, 8,* 5–9. http://www.jcnonweb.com/text.asp?2019/8/2/85/257128

Gazes, Y., Bowman, F. D., Razlighi, Q. R., O'Shea, D., Stern, Y., & Habeck, C. (2016). White matter tract covariance patterns predict age-declining cognitive abilities. *NeuroImage, 125,* 53–60. http://dx.doi.org/10.1016/j.neuroimage.2015.10.016

Gazzaniga, M. S. (2009). The fictional self. In D. J. H. Mathews, H. Bok, & P. V. Rabins (Eds.), *Personal identity and fractured selves: Perspectives from philosophy, ethics, and neuroscience* (pp. 174–185). Baltimore, MD: Johns Hopkins University Press.

Geffen, J., & Forster, K. (2018). Treatment of adult ADHD: A clinical perspective. *Therapeutic Advances in Psychopharmacology, 8*(1), 25–32. doi:10.1177/2045125317734977

Geher, G., Betancourt, K., & Jewell, O. (2017). The link between emotional intelligence and creativity. *Imagination, Cognition and Personality, 37*(1), 5–22. https://doi.org/10.1177/0276236617710029

Geher, G., & Kaufman, S. B. (2013). *Mating intelligence unleashed: The role of the mind in sex, dating, and love.* Oxford, UK: Oxford University Press.

Geisinger, K. F., & McCormick, C. (2013). Testing and assessment in cross-cultural psychology. In J. R. Graham, J. A. Naglieri, & I. B. Weiner (Eds.), *Handbook of psychology, Vol. 10: Assessment psychology* (2nd ed., pp. 114–139). Hoboken, NJ: Wiley.

Gelder, B. D., Meeren, H. K., Righart, R., Stock, J. V., van de Riet, W. A., & Tamietto, M. (2006). Beyond the face: Exploring rapid influences of context on face processing. *Progress in Brain Research, 155,* 37–48.

Geng, Y., Zhao, W., Zhou, F., Ma, X., Yao, S., Hurlemann, R., . . . Kendrick, K. M. (2018). Oxytocin enhancement of emotional empathy: Generalization across cultures and effects on amygdala activity. *Frontiers in Neuroscience, 12,* 512. doi:10.3389/fnins.2018.00512

Gentile, D. A., Berch, O. N., Choo, H., Khoo, A., & Walsh, D. A. (2017). Bedroom media: One risk factor for development. *Developmental Psychology, 53*(12), 2340–2355. http://dx.doi.org/10.1037/dev0000399

Gentil, L., Grenier, G., Bamvita, J. M., Dorvil, H., & Fleury, M. J. (2019). Profiles of quality of life in a homeless population. *Frontiers in Psychiatry, 10,* 10. doi:10.3389/fpsyt.2019.00010

Geronazzo, M., Bedin, A., Brayda, L., Campus, C., & Avanzini, F. (2016). Interactive spatial sonification for non-visual exploration of virtual maps. *International Journal of Human-Computer Studies, 85,* 4–15. http://dx.doi.org/10.1016/j.ijhcs.2015.08.004

Gerring, J. P., & Vasa, R. A. (2016). The Oxford handbook of head injury and externalizing behavior. In T. P. Beauchaine & S. P. Hinshaw (Eds), *The Oxford handbook of externalizing spectrum disorders* (pp. 403–415). New York, NY: Oxford University Press.

Gershoff, E. T., Goodman, G. S., Miller-Perrin, C., Holden, G. W., Jackson, Y., & Kazdin, A. E. (2019). There is still no evidence that physical punishment is effective or beneficial: Reply to Larzelere, Gunnoe, Ferguson, and Roberts (2019) and Rohner and Melendez-Rhodes (2019). *American Psychologist, 74*(4), 503–505. http://dx.doi.org/10.1037/amp0000474

Gerson, S. A., & Woodward, A. L. (2014). Learning from their own actions: The unique effect of producing actions on infants' action understanding. *Child Development, 85,* 264–277. http://dx.doi.org/10.1111/cdev.12115

Gerstorf, D., Hülür, G., Drewelies, J., Eibich, P., Duezel, S., Demuth, I., . . . Lindenberger, U. (2015). Secular changes in late-life cognition and well-being: Towards a long bright future with a short brisk ending? *Psychology and Aging, 30,* 301–310. http://dx.doi.org/10.1037/pag0000016

Geschwind, D. H., & State, M. W. (2015). Gene hunting in autism spectrum disorder: On the path to precision medicine. *The Lancet Neurology, 14,* 1109–1120. http://dx.doi.org/10.1016/S1474-4422(15)00044-7

Geschwind, N., Arntz, A., Bannink, F., & Peeters, F. (2019). Positive cognitive behavior therapy in the treatment of depression: A randomized order within-subject comparison with traditional cognitive behavior therapy. *Behaviour Research and Therapy, 116,* 119–130. https://doi.org/10.1016/j.brat.2019.03.005

Geyer, S., Jacobs, M., & Hsu, N.J. (2019). Immunity against bacterial infection of the central nervous system: An astrocyte perspective. *Frontiers in Molecular Neuroscience, 12*(57). http://dx.doi:10.3389/fnmol.2019.00057

Ge, Y., Knittel, C. R., MacKenzie, D., & Zoepf, R. (2016). Racial and gender discrimination in transportation network companies. *National Bureau of Economic Research Working Paper*, No. 22776.

Ghabrial, M. A. (2017). "Trying to figure out where we belong": Narratives of racialized sexual minorities on community, identity, discrimination, and health. *Sexuality Research & Social Policy, 14,* 42–55. http://dx.doi.org/10.1007/s13178-016-0229-x women-technology-inequality-10-yearsfemale

Ghaemi, S. N. (2018). After the failure of DSM: Clinical research on psychiatric diagnosis. *World Psychiatry, 17*(3), 301–302. doi:10.1002/wps.20563

Gherasim, L. R., Brumariu, L. E., & Alim, C. L. (2017). Parenting style and children's life satisfaction and depressive symptoms: Preliminary findings from Romania, France, and Russia. *Journal of Happiness Studies, 18*(4), 1013–1028. http://dx.doi.org/10.1007/s10902-016-9754-9

Ghose, T. (2013). "JUST A THEORY": Misused Science Words. *Scientific American*. Retrieved from https://www.scientificamerican.com/article/just-a-theory-7-misused-science-words/

Giacolini, T., & Sabatello, U. (2019). Psychoanalysis and affective neuroscience. The motivational/emotional system of aggression in human relations. *Frontiers in Psychology, 9,* 2475. doi:10.3389/fpsyg.2018.02475

Giammarco, E. A. (2016). The measurement of individual differences in morality. *Personality and Individual Differences, 88,* 26–34. http://dx.doi.org/10.1016/j.paid.2015.08.039

Gibbons, J. A., Lukowski, A. F., Walsh, K. M., Smeland, J. N., & Smith, C. L. (2018). Evidence of encoding specificity for the effects of synopses on the recognition of believable and unbelievable news headlines. *Psychology & Psychological Research International Journal, 3*(7). https://medwinpublishers.com/PPRIJ/PPRIJ16000178.pdf

Gibbs, J. C. (2014). *Moral development and reality: Beyond the theories of Kohlberg, Hoffman, and Haidt* (3rd ed.). New York, NY: Oxford University Press.

Gibbs, N. (1995, October 2). The EQ factor. *Time,* 60–68.

Gibson, B., Thompson, J., Hou, B., & Bushman, B. J. (2016). Just harmless entertainment? Effects of surveillance reality TV on physical aggression. *Psychology of Popular Media Culture, 5,* 66–73. http://dx.doi.org/10.1037/ppm0000040

Gibson, E. J., & Walk, R. D. (1960). The visual cliff. *Scientific American, 202,* 67–71.

Gibson, S. (2019). Obedience without orders: Expanding social psychology's conception of obedience. *British Journal of Social Psychology, 58*(1), 241–259. https://onlinelibrary.wiley.com/doi/full/10.1111/bjso.12272

Gilbert, S. J. (2015). Strategic off loading of delayed intentions into the external environment. *The Quarterly Journal of Experimental Psychology, 68*(5), 971–992. http://dx.doi.org/10.1080/17470218.2014.972963

Gilkerson, J., Richards, J. A., Warren, S. F., Oller, D. K., Russo, R., & Vohr, B. (2018). Language experience in the second year of life and language outcomes in late childhood. *Pediatrics, 142*(4), e20174276. doi:10.1542/peds.2017-4276

Gilligan, C. (1977). In a different voice: Women's conception of morality. *Harvard Educational Review, 47,* 481–517.

Gilligan, C. (1990). Teaching Shakespeare's sister. In C. Gilligan, N. Lyons, & T. Hanmer (Eds.), *Mapping the moral domain* (pp. 73–86). Cambridge, MA: Harvard University Press.

Gilligan, C. (1993). Adolescent development reconsidered. In A. Garrod (Ed.), *Approaches to moral development: New research and emerging themes* (pp. 264–280). New York, NY: Teachers College Press.

Gilligan, C. (2011). *Joining the resistance.* Oxford, UK: Polity Press.

Gillihan, S. J., & Foa, E. B. (2016). Exposure based interventions for adult anxiety disorders, obsessive-compulsive disorder, and posttraumatic stress disorder. In C. M. Nezu & A. M. Nezu (Eds.), *The Oxford handbook of cognitive and behavioral therapies* (pp. 96–117). New York, NY: Oxford University Press.

Ginton, A. (2017). Examining different types of comparison questions in a field study of CQT polygraph technique: Theoretical and practical implications. *Journal of Investigative Psychology and Offender Profiling, 14*(3), 281–293. http://dx.doi.org/10.1002/jip.1475

Ginzburg, H. M., & Bateman, D. J. (2008). New Orleans medical students post-Katrina—An assessment of psychopathology and anticipatory transference of resilience. *Psychiatric Annals, 38,* 145–156. http://dx.doi.org/10.3928/00485713-20080201-01

Glantz, S. A. (2019). The evidence of electronic cigarette risks is catching up with public perception. *JAMA Network Open, 2*(3):e19109. Retrieved from https://jamanetwork.com/journals/jamanetworkopen/fullarticle/2729460

Glaser, J. (2015). *Suspect race: Causes and consequences of racial profiling.* New York, NY: Oxford University Press.

Godden, D. R., & Baddeley, A. D. (1975). Context-dependent memory in two natural environments: On land and underwater. *British Journal of Psychology, 66*(3), 325–331. http://dx.doi.org/10.1111/j.2044-8295.1975.tb01468.x

Goh, G. H., Mark, P. J., & Maloney, S. K. (2016). Altered energy intake and the amplitude of the body temperature rhythm are associated with changes in phase, but not amplitude, of clock gene expression in the rat suprachiasmatic nucleus in vivo. *Chronobiology International, 33,* 85–97. http://dx.doi.org/10.3109/07420528.2015.1112395

Goldfarb, D., Goodman, G. S., Larson, R. P., Eisen, M. L., & Qin, J. (2019). Long-term memory in adults exposed to childhood violence: Remembering genital contact nearly 20 years later. *Clinical Psychological Science, 7*(2), 381–396. https://doi.org/10.1177/2167702618805742

Goldfinch, A. (2015). *Rethinking evolutionary psychology.* New York, NY: Palgrave Macmillan.

Gold, L. H., & Simon, R. I. (2016). *Gun violence and mental illness.* Arlington, VA: American Psychiatric Association Publishing.

Goldstein, E. B. (2014). *Sensation and perception* (9th ed.). Belmont, CA: Cengage.

Goldstein, E. B. (2015). *Cognitive psychology: Connecting mind, research, and everyday experience* (4th ed.). Stamford, CT: Cengage.

Goldstein, E. B. (2019). *Cognitive psychology: Connecting mind, research, and everyday experience* (5th ed.). Boston, MA: Cengage.

Goldstein, R. B., Smith, S. M., Chou, S. P., Saha, T. D., Jung, J., Zhang, H., . . . Grant, B. F. (2016). The epidemiology of DSM-5 posttraumatic stress disorder in the United States: Results from the national epidemiologic survey on alcohol and related conditions-iii. *Social Psychiatry and Psychiatric Epidemiology, 51*(8), 1137–1148. http://dx.doi.org/10.1007/s00127-016-1208-5

Goleman, D. (1980, February). 1,528 little geniuses and how they grew. *Psychology Today,* 28–53.

Goleman, D. (1995). *Emotional intelligence: Why it can matter more than IQ.* New York, NY: Bantam.

Goleman, D. (2000). *Working with emotional intelligence.* New York, NY: Bantam Doubleday.

Goleman, D. (2008). Leading resonant teams. In F. Hesselbein & A. Shrader (Eds.), *Leader to leader 2: Enduring insights on leadership from the Leader to Leader Institute's award-winning journal* (pp. 186–195). San Francisco, CA: Jossey-Bass.

Golle, J., Rose, N., Göllner, R., Spengler, M., Stoll, G., Hübner, N., . . . Nagengast, B. (2019). School or work? The choice may change your personality. *Psychological Science, 30*(1), 32–42. https://doi.org/10.1177/0956797618806298

Göllner, R., Damian, R. I., Rose, N., Spengler, M., Trautwein, U., Nagengast, B., & Roberts, B. W. (2017). Is doing your homework associated with becoming more conscientious? *Journal of Research in Personality, 71,* 1–12. https://doi.org/10.1016/j.jrp.2017.08.007.

Gonzalez, S. (2018, October 2). Emma Stone opens up about ongoing battle with anxiety. *CNN Entertainment.* Retrieved from https://www.cnn.com/2018/10/02/entertainment/emma-stone-anxiety/index.html

González, V. V., Navarro, V., Miguez, G., Betancourt, R., & Laborda, M. A. (2016). Preventing the recovery of extinguished ethanol tolerance. *Behavioural Processes, 124,* 141–148. http://dx.doi.org/10.1016/j.beproc.2016.01.004

Goodall, J. (1990). *Through a window: My thirty years with the chimpanzees of Gombe.* Boston, MA: Houghton-Mifflin.

Goodchild, M., Nargis, N., & Tursan d'Espaignet, E. (2018). Global economic cost of smoking-attributable diseases. *Tobacco Control, 27*(1), 58–64. doi:10.1136/tobaccocontrol-2016-053305

Goodkind, N. (2019, March 22). An end to affirmative action? Why the college admissions scandal could fulfill critics' wish to scrap race-based programs. *Newsweek.* https://www.newsweek.

com/2019/04/12/affirmative-action-college-admissions-statistics-scandal-1372652.html

Goodman, G. S., Gonzalves, L., & Wolpe, S. (2019). False memories and true memories of childhood trauma: Balancing the risks. *Clinical Psychological Science, 7*(1), 29–31. https://doi.org/10.1177/2167702618797106

Goodmon, L. B., Smith, P. L., Ivancevich, D., & Lundberg, S. (2014). Actions speak louder than personality: Effects of Facebook content on personality perceptions. *North American Journal of Psychology, 16*(1), 105.

Goodwin, J., & Goodwin, K. (2013). *Research in psychology: Methods and design* (7th ed.). Hoboken, NJ: Wiley.

Gopalkrishnan, N. (2018). Cultural diversity and mental health: Considerations for policy and practice. *Frontiers in Public Health, 6*, 179. doi:10.3389/fpubh.2018.00179

Gordin, M. D. (2017). The problem with pseudoscience: Pseudoscience is not the antithesis of professional science but thrives in science's shadow. *EMBO Reports, 18*(9), 1482–1485. doi:10.15252/embr.201744870

Gordon, B. R., McDowell, C. P., Hallgren, M., Meyer, J. D., Lyons, M., & Herring, M. P. (2018). Association of efficacy of resistance exercise training with depressive symptoms: Meta-analysis and meta-regression analysis of randomized clinical trials. *JAMA Psychiatry, 75*(6), 566–576. doi:10.1001/jamapsychiatry.2018.0572

Goriounova, N., & Mansvelder, H. D. (2019). Genes, cells and brain areas of intelligence. *Frontiers in Human Neuroscience, 13*:44. doi:10.3389/fnhum.2019.00044

Gorsuch, M. M. (2019). Gender, sexual orientation, and behavioral norms in the labor market. *ILR Review, 72*(4), 927–954. Retrieved from https://doi.org/10.1177/0019793919832273

Gosling, S. D., Kwan, V. S. Y., & John, O. P. (2004). A dog's got personality: A cross-species comparative approach to personality judgments in dogs and humans. *Journal of Personality and Social Psychology, 85*, 1161–1169. http://dx.doi.org/10.1037/0022-3514.85.6.1161

Gottesman, I. I. (1991). *Schizophrenia genesis: The origins of madness.* New York, NY: Freeman.

Göttken, T., White, L. O., Klein, A. M., & von Klitzing, K. (2014). Short-term psychoanalytic child therapy for anxious children: A pilot study. *Psychotherapy, 51*, 148–158. http://dx.doi.org/10.1037/a0036026

Gottman, J. M. (2011). *The science of trust: Emotional attunement for couples.* New York, NY: Norton.

Gottman, J. M. (2015). *Principia amoris: The new science of love.* New York, NY: Routledge/Taylor & Francis Group.

Gottman, J. M., & Gottman, J. S. (2015). Gottman couple therapy. In A. S. Gurman, J. L. Lebow, & D. K. Snyder (Eds.), *Clinical handbook of couple therapy* (pp. 129–157). New York, NY: Guilford.

Gottman, J. M., & Silver, N. (2012). *What makes love last: How to build trust and avoid betrayal.* New York, NY: Simon & Schuster.

Goubet, K. E., & Chrysikou, E. G. (2019). Emotion regulation flexibility: Gender differences in context sensitivity and repertoire. *Frontiers in Psychology, 10*:935. Retrieved from doi:10.3389/fpsyg.2019.00935

Goyal, M., Singh, S., Sibinga, E. M., Gould, N. F., Rowland-Seymour, A., Sharma, R., . . . Haythornthwaite, J. A. (2014). Meditation programs for psychological stress and wellbeing: A systematic review and meta-analysis. *JAMA Internal Medicine, 174*, 357–368. http://dx.doi.org/10.1001/jamainternmed.2013.13018

Goyer, J. P., Garcia, J., Purdie-Vaughns, V., Binning, K. R., Cook, J. E., Reeves, S. L., . . . Cohen, G. L. (2017). Self-affirmation facilitates minority middle schoolers' progress along college trajectories.

Proceedings of the National Academy of Sciences of the United States of America, 114(29), 7594–7599. doi:10.1073/pnas.1617923114

Graber, R., Turner, R., & Madill, A. (2016). Best friends and better coping: Facilitating psychological resilience through boys' and girls' closest friendships. *British Journal of Psychology, 107*, 338–358. http://dx.doi. org/10.1111/bjop.12135

Grady, D. (2018, October 22). Anatomy does not determine gender, experts say. *The New York Times.* Retrieved March 29, 2019 from https://www.nytimes.com/2018/10/22/health/transgender-trump-biology.html

Graf, N., Brown, A., & Patten, E. (2019, March 22). The narrowing, but persistent, gender gap in pay. *FactTank.* Retrieved from https://www.pewresearch.org/fact-tank/2019/03/22/gender-pay-gap-facts/

Graf, S., Linhartova, P., & Sczesny, S. (2019, April 18). The effects of news report valence and linguistic labels on prejudice against social minorities. *Journal of Media Psychology.* doi:10.1080/15213269.2019.1584571

Graf, W., Miller, G. E., Epstein, L. G., & Rapin, I. (2017). The autism "epidemic": Ethical, legal, and social issues in a developmental spectrum disorder. *Neurology, 88*(14), 1371–1380. http://dx.doi.org/10.1212/WNL.0000000000003791

Graham, A. M., Rasmussen, J. M., Entringer, S., Ben Ward E., Rudolph, M. D., Gilmore, J. H., . . . Buss, C. (2019). Maternal cortisol concentrations during pregnancy and sex-specific associations with neonatal amygdala connectivity and emerging internalizing behaviors. *Biological Psychiatry, 85*(2), 172–181. doi:10.1016/j.biopsych.2018.06.023

Graham, J., Meindl, P., Beall, E., Johnson, K. M., & Zhang, L. (2016). Cultural differences in moral judgment and behavior, across and within societies. *Current Opinion in Psychology, 8*, 125–130. http://dx.doi.org/10.1016/j.copsyc.2015.09.007

Grandey, A. A., Frone, M. R., Melloy, R. C., & Sayre, G. M. (2019). When are fakers also drinkers? A self-control view of emotional labor and alcohol consumption among U.S. service workers. *Journal of Occupational Health Psychology, 24*(4), 482–497. doi:10.1037/ocp0000147

Granhag, P. A., Vrij, A., & Verschuere, B. (Eds.). (2015). *Detecting deception: Current challenges and cognitive approaches.* Malden, MA: Wiley-Blackwell.

Granillo, M. T., Perron, B. E., Jarman, C., & Gutowski, S. M. (2013). Cognitive behavioral therapy with substance use disorders: Theory, evidence, and practice. In M. G. Vaughn & B. E. Perron (Eds.), *Social work practice in the addictions* (pp. 101–118). New York, NY: Springer.

Gravelin, C. R., Biernat, M., & Bucher, C. E. (2019). Blaming the victim of acquaintance rape: Individual, situational, and sociocultural factors. *Frontiers in Psychology, 9*, 2422. doi:10.3389/fpsyg.2018.02422

Gray, M. J., Hassija, C. M., Jaconis, M., Barrett, C., Zheng, P., Steinmetz, S., & James, T. (2015). Provision of evidence-based therapies to rural survivors of domestic violence and sexual assault via telehealth: Treatment outcomes and clinical training benefits. *Training and Education in Professional Psychology, 9*, 235–241. doi:10.1037/tep0000083

Greenaway, K. H., Storrs, K. R., Philipp, M. C., Louis, W. R., Hornsey, M. J., & Vohs, K. D. (2015). Loss of control stimulates approach motivation. *Journal of Experimental Social Psychology, 56*, 235–241. http://dx.doi.org/10.1016/j.jesp.2014.10.009

Greenberg, D. L. (2004). President Bush's false [flashbulb] memory of 9/11/01. *Applied Cognitive Psychology, 18*, 363–370. http://dx.doi.org/10.1002/acp.1016

Greenberg, J. (2018, June 4). Four reasons overworking is overrated and unhealthy—expert column. *Inside Business.* Retrieved from https://pilotonline.com/inside-business/news/columns/article_6c6a4d26-67fa-11e8-9371-07a9ed065f36.html

Greenberg, J., Schmader, T., Arndt, J., & Landau, M. (2015). *Social psychology: The science of everyday life.* New York, NY: Worth.

Greene, J. (2016). *Thinking and language* (5th ed.). New York, NY: Routledge.

Greenfield, P. (1984). A theory of the teacher in the learning activities of everyday life. In B. Rogoff & J. Lave (Eds.), *Everyday cognition* (pp. 117–138). Cambridge, MA: Harvard University Press.

Greenfield, P. (1994). *Cross-cultural roots of minority child development.* Hillsdale, NJ: Erlbaum.

Greenfield, P. M. (2012). Social change and human development: An autobiographical journey. In M. J. Gelfand, C. Y. Ciu, & Y. Y. Hong (Eds.), *Advances in Culture and Psychology, 2,* 90–138. New York, NY: Oxford University Press. doi:10.1093/acprof:oso/9780199840694.001.0001

Greenwald, A. G., & Pettigrew, T. F. (2014). With malice toward none and charity for some: Ingroup favoritism enables discrimination. *American Psychologist, 69,* 669–684. http://dx.doi.org/10.1037/a0036056

Gregersen, E. (1996). *The world of human sexuality: Behaviors, customs, and beliefs.* New York, NY: Irvington.

Gregory, S. (2019, July 18). Caster Semenya won't stop fighting for her right to run, just as she is. *Time.* Retrieved from https://time.com/5629249/caster-semenya-interview/

Gregory, S., Fytche, D., Simmons, A., Kumari, V., Howard, M., Hodgins, S., & Blackwood, N. (2012). The antisocial brain: Psychopathy matters. *Archives of General Psychiatry, 69,* 962–972.

Griggs, R. (2015a). The disappearance of independence in textbook coverage of Asch's social pressure experiments. *Teaching of Psychology, 42*(2), 137–142. doi:10.1177/0098628315569939

Griggs, R. A. (2015b). The Kitty Genovese story in introductory psychology textbooks: Fifty years later. *Teaching of Psychology, 42,* 149–152. http://dx.doi.org/10.1177/0098628315573138

Griggs, R.A. (2015). Coverage of the Phineas Gage story in introductory psychology textbooks: Was Gage no longer Gage? *Teaching of Psychology, 42,* 195–202. http://dx.doi.org/10.1177/0098628315587614

Griggs, R. A. (2017). Milgram's obedience study: A contentious classic reinterpreted. *Teaching of Psychology, 44*(1), 32–37. http://dx.doi.org/10.1177/0098628316677644

Grimm, S., Pestke, K., Feeser, M., Aust, S., Weigand, A., Wang, J., . . . Bajbouj, M. (2014). Early life stress modulates oxytocin effects on limbic system during acute psychosocial stress. *Social Cognitive and Affective Neuroscience, 9,* 1828–1835. doi:10.1093/scan/nsu020

Grover, S., & Ghosh, A. (2014). Somatic symptom and related disorders in Asians and Asian Americans. *Asian Journal of Psychiatry, 7,* 77–79. http://dx.doi.org/10.1016/j.ajp.2013.11.014

Grubin, D. (2016). Polygraph testing of sex offenders. In D. R. Laws & W. O'Donohue (Eds.), *Treatment of sex offenders: Strengths and weaknesses in assessment and intervention* (pp. 133–156). Cham, CH: Springer International Publishing. http://dx.doi.org/10.1007/978-3-319-25868-3_6

Grünbaum, A. (2015). Critique of psychoanalysis. In S. Boag, L. A. W. Brakel, & V. Talvitie (Eds.), *Philosophy, science, and psychoanalysis: A critical meeting* (pp. 1–36). London, UK: Karnac Books.

Gruzd, A., & Roy, J. (2014). Investigating political polarization on Twitter: A Canadian perspective. *Policy & Internet, 6,* 28–45. http://dx.doi.org/10.1002/1944-2866.POI354

Guardino, C. M., Schetter, C. D., Saxbe, D. E., Adam, E. K., Ramey, S. L., Shalowitz, M. U., & Community Child Health Network. (2016). Diurnal salivary cortisol patterns prior to pregnancy predict infant birth weight. *Health Psychology, 35,* 625–633. http://dx.doi.org/10.1037/hea0000313

Guastello, S. J., Guastello, D. D., & Craft, L. L. (1989). Assessment of the Barnum effect in computer-based test interpretations. *Journal of Psychology: Interdisciplinary and Applied, 123,* 477–484. http://dx.doi.org/10.1080/0022 3980.1989.10543001

Guedes, M. J. C. (2017). Mirror, mirror on the wall, am I the greatest performer of all? Narcissism and self-reported and objective performance. *Personality and Individual Differences, 108,* 182–185. http://dx.doi.org/10.1016/j.paid.2016.12.030

Guéguen, N., & Stefan, J. (2016). "Green altruism": Short immersion in natural green environments and helping behavior. *Environment and Behavior, 48,* 324–342. http://dx.doi.org/10.1177/0013916514536576

Guelzow, B. T., Loya, F., & Hinshaw, S. P. (2017). How persistent is ADHD into adulthood? Informant report and diagnostic thresholds in a female sample. *Journal of Abnormal Child Psychology, 45,* 301–312. http://dx.doi.org/10.1007/s10802-016-0174-4

Guilford, J. P. (1967). *The nature of human intelligence.* New York, NY: McGraw-Hill.

Gumz, M. L. (Ed.). (2016). *Circadian clocks: Role in health and disease.* New York, NY: Springer Science + Business Media. http://dx.doi.org/10.1007/978-1-4939-3450-8

Gunderson, J. G., & Links, P. (2014). *Handbook of good psychiatric management for borderline personality disorder.* Arlington, VA: American Psychiatric Publishing.

Guo, F., Xu, Q., Salem, H. M. A., Yao, Y., Lou, J., & Huang, X. (2016). The neuronal correlates of mirror therapy: A functional magnetic resonance imaging study on mirror-induced visual illusions of ankle movements. *Brain Research, 1639,* 186–193. http://dx.doi.org/10.1016/j.brainres.2016.03.002

Gupta, R., van Dongen, J., Fu, Y., Abdellaoui, A., Tyndale, R. F., Velagapudi, V., . . . Ollikainen, M. (2019). Epigenome-wide association study of serum cotinine in current smokers reveals novel genetically driven loci. *Clinical Epigenetics, 11*(1), 1. doi:10.1186/s13148-018-0606-9

Gupta, S. (2019, September 10). Culture helps shape when babies learn to walk. *ScienceNews.* Retrieved from https://www.science-news.org/article/culture-helps-shape-when-babies-learn-walk

Gu, R., Huang, W., Camilleri, J., Xu, P., Wei, P., Eickhoff, S. B., & Feng, C. (2019). Love is analogous to money in human brain: Coordinate-based and functional connectivity meta-analyses of social and monetary reward anticipation. *Neuroscience & Biobehavioral Reviews, 100,* 108–128. https://doi.org/10.1016/j.neubiorev.2019.02.017.

Gurin, L., & Blum, S. (2017). Delusions and the right hemisphere: A review of the case for the right hemisphere as a mediator of reality-based belief. *The Journal of Neuropsychiatry, 29,* 225–235. https://doi.org/10.1176/appi.neuropsych.16060118

Gurven, M., von Rueden, C., Massenkoff, M., Kaplan, H., & Lero Vie, M. (2013). How universal is the big five? Testing the five-factor model of personality variation among forager farmers in the Bolivian Amazon. *Journal of Personality and Social Psychology, 104,* 354–370. http://dx.doi.org/10.1037/a0030841

Guryan, J., Kim, J. S., & Park, K. (2015). Motivation and incentives in education: Evidence from a summer reading experiment. *National Bureau of Economic Research,* Working Paper No. 20918.

Gustafsson, P. U., Lindholm, T., & Jönsson, F. U. (2019). Predicting accuracy in eyewitness testimonies with memory retrieval effort and confidence. *Frontiers in Psychology, 10:*703. doi:10.3389/fpsyg. 2019.00703

Gu, S., Wang, F., Cao, C., Wu, E., Tang, Y. Y., & Huang, J. H. (2019). An integrative way for studying neural basis of basic emotions with fMRI. *Frontiers in Neuroscience, 13,* 628. doi:10.3389/fnins.2019.00628

Gutchess, A., & Huff, S. (2016). Cross-cultural differences in memory. In J. Y. Chiao, S.-C. Li, R. Seligman, & R. Turner (Eds.), *The Oxford handbook of cultural neuroscience. Oxford library of psychology* (pp. 155–169). New York, NY: Oxford University Press.

Haaken, J. (2010). *Hard knocks: Domestic violence and the psychology of storytelling.* New York, NY: Routledge/Taylor & Francis Group.

Haas, M., Hiemisch, A., Vogel, M., Wagner, O., Kiess, W., & Poulain, T. (2019). Sensation seeking in 3- to 6-year-old children: Associations with socio-demographic parameters and behavioural difficulties. *BMC Pediatrics, 19*(1), 77. doi:10.1186/s12887-019-1450-6

Hackley, C. (2007). Marketing psychology and the hidden persuaders. *The Psychologist, 20,* 488–490.

Hadden, I. R., Easterbrook, M. J., Nieuwenhuis, M., Fox, K. J. & Dolan, P. (2019). Self-affirmation reduces the socioeconomic attainment gap in schools in England. *British Journal of Educational Psychology.* Retrieved from doi:10.1111/bjep.12291

Haghighi, A., Melka, M. G., Bernard, M., Abrahamowicz, M., Leonard, G. T., Richer, L., . . . Pausova, Z. (2014). Opioid receptor mu 1 gene, fat intake and obesity in adolescence. *Molecular Psychiatry, 19,* 63–68. http://dx.doi.org/10.1038/mp.2012.179

Haghighi, A., Schwartz, D. H., Abrahamowicz, M., Leonard, G. T., Perron, M., Richer, L., . . . Pausova, Z. (2013). Prenatal exposure to maternal cigarette smoking, amygdala volume, and fat intake in adolescence. *JAMA Psychiatry, 70,* 98–105.

Haith, M. M., & Benson, J. B. (1998). Infant cognition. In W. Damon (Series Ed.) & D. Kuhn & R. S. Siegler (Vol. Eds.), *Handbook of child psychology: Vol. 2. Cognition, perception, and language* (5th ed., pp. 199–254). New York, NY: Wiley

Hajak, G., Lemme, K., & Zisapel, N. (2015). Lasting treatment effects in a postmarketing surveillance study of prolonged release melatonin. *International Clinical Psychopharmacology, 30,* 36–42. http://dx.doi.org/10.1097/YIC.0000000000000046

Hales, C. M., Fryar, C. D., Carroll, M. D., Freedman, D. S., & Ogden, C. L. (2018). Trends in obesity and severe obesity prevalence in US youth and adults by sex and age, 2007-2008 to 2015-2016. *Journal of the American Medical Association, 319*(16), 1723–1725. doi:10.1001/jama.2018.3060

Hall, E. V., & Livingston, R. W. (2012). The hubris penalty: Biased responses to "Celebration" displays of black football players. *Journal of Experimental Social Psychology, 48,* 899–904. doi:10.1016/j.jesp.2012.02.004

Hall, G. C. N., & Ibaraki, A. Y. (2016). Multicultural issues in cognitive-behavioral therapy: Cultural adaptations and goodness of fit. In C. M. Nezu & A. M. Nezu (Eds.), *The Oxford handbook of cognitive and behavioral therapies* (pp. 465–481). New York, NY: Oxford University Press.

Hall, J. A., & Xing, C. (2015). The verbal and nonverbal correlates of the five flirting styles. *Journal of Nonverbal Behavior, 39,* 41–68. http://dx.doi.org/10.1007/s10919-014-0199-8

Halpern, D. F. (2014). *Thought and knowledge: An introduction to critical thinking* (5th ed.). New York, NY: Psychology Press.

Halpern, D., Valenzuela, S., & Katz, J. E. (2016). "Selfie-ists" or "Narci-selfiers"?: A cross-lagged panel analysis of selfie taking and narcissism. *Personality and Individual Differences, 97,* 98–101. http://dx.doi.org/10.1016/j. paid.2016.03.019

Halpern, S. D., French, B., Small, D. S., Saulsgiver, K., Harhay, M. O., Audrain-McGovern, J., . . . Volpp, K. G. (2015). Randomized trial of four financial-incentive programs for smoking cessation. *New England Journal of Medicine, 372,* 2108–2117. doi:10.1056/NEJMoa1414293

Hamedani, M. Y. G., & Markus, H. R. (2019). Understanding culture clashes and catalyzing change: A culture cycle approach. *Frontiers in Psychology, 10:*700. doi:10.3389/fpsyg.2019.00700

Hamilton, J., Daleiden, E., & Youngstrom, E. (2016). Evidence-based practice. In M. K. Dulcan (Ed.), *Dulcan's textbook of child and adolescent psychiatry* (2nd ed., pp. 523–537). Arlington, VA: American Psychiatric Publishing.

Hamilton, L. D., & Julian, A. M. (2014). The relationship between daily hassles and sexual function in men and women. *Journal of Sex & Marital Therapy, 40*(5), 379–395. http://dx.doi.org/10.1080/0092623X.2013.864364

Hammack, P. L. (2003). The question of cognitive therapy in a post-modern world. *Ethical Human Sciences and Services, 5,* 209–224.

Handley, T., Rich J., Davies K., Lewin T., & Kelly, B. (2018). The challenges of predicting suicidal thoughts and behaviours in a sample of rural Australians with depression. *International Journal of Environmental Research and Public Health, 15:*928. doi:10.3390/ijerph1505092

Haney, C., Banks, C., & Zimbardo, P. (1973). Interpersonal dynamics in a simulated prison. *International Journal of Criminology and Penology, 1,* 69–97.

Hansen, B., Kvale, G., Hagen, K., Havnen, A., & Öst, L.-G. (2019). The Bergen 4-day treatment for OCD: Four years follow-up of concentrated ERP in a clinical mental health setting. *Cognitive Behaviour Therapy, 48*(2), 89–105. doi:10.1080/16506073.2018.1478447

Harden, B. J., Buhler, A., & Parra, L. J. (2016). Maltreatment in infancy: A developmental perspective on prevention and intervention. *Trauma, Violence, & Abuse, 17*(4), 366–386. http://dx.doi.org/10.1177/1524838016658878

Harjunen, V. J., Spapé, M., Ahmed, I., Jacucci, G., & Ravaja, N. (2017). Individual differences in affective touch: Behavioral inhibition and gender define how an interpersonal touch is perceived. *Personality and Individual Differences, 107,* 8 8–95. http://dx.doi.org/10.1016/j.paid.2016.11.047

Harker, C. M., Ibañez, L. V., Nguyen, T. P., Messinger, D. S., & Stone, W. L. (2016). The effect of parenting style on social smiling in infants at high and low risk for asd. *Journal of Autism and Developmental Disorders, 46,* 2399–2407. http://dx.doi.org/10.1007/s10803-016-2772-y

Harkness, S., Super, C. M., Sutherland, M. A., Blom, M. J. M., Moscardino, U., Mavhdis, C. J., & Axia, G. (2007). Culture and the construction of habits in daily life: Implications for the successful development of children with disabilities. *OTJR: Occupation, Participation and Health, 27,* 33S–40S.

Harley, A., Kumar, D., & Agarwal, A. (2016). The common characteristics between infertility and recurrent pregnancy loss. In A. Bashiri, A. Harlev, & A. Agarwal (Eds.), *Recurrent pregnancy loss: Evidence-based evaluation, diagnosis and treatment* (pp. 143–152). New York, NY: Springer. http://dx.doi.org/10.1007/978-3-319-27452-2_10

Harley, T. A. (2014). *The psychology of language: From data to theory* (4th ed.). New York, NY: Psychology Press.

Harlow, H. F., Harlow, M. K., & Meyer, D. R. (1950). Learning motivated by a manipulation drive. *Journal of Experimental Psychology, 40,* 228–234.

Harlow, H. F., Harlow, M. K., & Suomi, S. J. (1971). From thought to therapy: Lessons from a primate laboratory. *American Scientist, 59,* 538–549.

Harlow, J. (1868). Recovery from the passage of an iron bar through the head. *Publications of the Massachusetts Medical Society, 2,* 237–246.

Harris, E., & Bardey, A. C. (2019). Do Instagram profiles accurately portray personality? An investigation into idealized online self-presentation. *Frontiers in Psychology, 10,* 871. doi:10.3389/fpsyg.2019.00871

Harris, E., McNamara, P., & Durso, R. (2015). Novelty seeking in patients with right- versus left-onset Parkinson disease. *Cognitive and Behavioral Neurology, 28,* 11–16. http://dx.doi.org/10.1097/WNN.0000000000000047.

Hart, J., Nailling, E., Bizer, G. Y., & Collins, C. K. (2015). Attachment theory as a framework for explaining engagement with Facebook. *Personality and Individual Differences, 77,* 33–40. http://dx.doi.org/10.1016/j.paid.2014.12.016

Hartmann, E., & Hartmann, T. (2014). The impact of exposure to Internet-based information about the Rorschach and the MMPI-2 on psychiatric outpatients' ability to simulate mentally healthy test performance. *Journal of Personality Assessment, 99,* 432–444. http://dx.doi.org/10.1080/00223891.2014.882342

Harwood, C. G., Keegan, R. J., Smith, J. M. J., & Raine, A. S. (2015). A systematic review of the intrapersonal correlates of motivational climate perceptions in sport and physical activity. *Psychology of Sport and Exercise, 18,* 9–25. http://dx.doi.org/10.1016/j.psychsport.2014.11.005

Haslam, N. (2015). Dehumanization and intergroup relations. In M. Mikulincer, P. R. Shaver, J. F. Dovidio, & J. A. Simpson (Eds.), *APA handbook of personality and social psychology, Vol. 2. Group processes* (pp. 295–314). Washington, DC: American Psychological Association. http://dx.doi.org/10.1037/14342-011

Haslam, S. A., Reicher, S. D., Millard, K., & McDonald, R. (2015). 'Happy to have been of service': The Yale archive as a window into the engaged followership of participants in Milgram's 'obedience' experiments. *British Journal of Social Psychology, 54,* 55–83. http://dx.doi.org/10.1111/bjso.12074

Hassan, A., Ahmad, J., Ashraf, H., & Ali, A. (2018). Modeling and analysis of the impacts of jet lag on circadian rhythm and its role in tumor growth. *PeerJ, 6:e4877.* Retrieved from https://doi.org/10.7717/peerj.4877

Hastings, P., Serbin, L., Bukowski, W., Helm, J., Stack, D., Dickson, D., . . . Schwartzman, A. (2019). Predicting psychosis-spectrum diagnoses in adulthood from social behaviors and neighborhood contexts in childhood. *Development and Psychopathology.* doi:10.1017/S095457941900021X

Hatemi, P. K., Crabtree, C., & McDermott, R. (2017). The relationship between sexual preferences and political orientations: Do positions in the bedroom affect positions in the ballot box? *Personality and Individual Differences, 105,* 318–325. http://dx.doi.org/10.1016/j.paid.2016.10.008

Hatemi, P. K., Medland, S. E., Klemmensen, R., Oskarsson, S., Littvay, L., Dawes, C. T., . . . Martin, N. G. (2014). Genetic influences on political ideologies: Twin analyses of 19 measures of political ideologies from five democracies and genome-wide findings from three populations. *Behavior Genetics, 44*(3), 282–294. doi:10.1007/s10519-014-9648-8

Hatfield, E., & Rapson, R. L. (1996). *Love and sex: Cross-cultural perspectives.* Needham Heights, MA: Allyn & Bacon.

Hauk, N., Göritz, A. S., & Krumm, S. (2019). The mediating role of coping behavior on the age-technostress relationship: A longitudinal multilevel mediation model. *PLoS ONE, 14*(3): e0213349. Retrieved from https://doi.org/10.1371/journal.pone.0213349

Hauner, K. K., Mineka, S., Voss, J. L., & Paller, K. A. (2012). Exposure therapy triggers lasting reorganization of neural fear processing. *Proceedings of the National Academy of Sciences of the United States of America, 109,* 9203–9208.

Häusler, N., Haba-Rubio, J., Heinzer, R., & Marques-Vidal, P. (2019). Association of napping with incident cardiovascular events in a prospective cohort study. *Heart.* Retrieved from doi:10.1136/heartjnl-2019-314999

Havron, N., Ramus, F., Heude, B., Forhan, A., Cristia, A., & Peyre, H. (2019). The effect of older siblings on language development as a function of age difference and sex. *Psychological Science, 30*(9), 1333–1343. https://doi.org/10.1177/0956797619861436

Hayashi, M. T., Cesare, A. J., Riversa, T., & Karlseder, J. (2015). Cell death during crisis is mediated by mitotic telomere deprotection. *Nature, 522,* 492–496. http://dx.doi.org/10.1038/nature14513

Hayflick, L. (1965). The limited in vitro lifetime of human diploid cell strains. *Experimental Cell Research, 37,* 614–636. http://dx.doi.org/10.1016/0014-4827(65)90211-9

Hayflick, L. (1996). *How and why we age.* New York, NY: Ballantine.

Haynes, H. (2019, May 16). 'Now I am speaking to the whole world.' How teen climate activist Greta Thunberg got everyone to listen. *Time Magazine.* Retrieved from http://time.com/collection-post/5584902/greta-thunberg-next-generation-leaders/

Haynes, T. (2018, May 1). Dopamine, smartphones, & you: A battle for your time. *Science in the News SITN.* Retrieved from http://sitn.hms.harvard.edu/flash/2018/dopamine-smartphones-battle-time/

Hays, P. A. (2014). *Creating well-being: Four steps to a happier, healthier life.* Washington, DC: American Psychological Association.

Hazan, C., & Shaver, P. (1987). Romantic love conceptualized as an attachment process. *Journal of Personality and Social Psychology, 52,* 511–524.

Head, B. F., Dean, E., Flanigan, T., Swicegood, J., & Keating, M. D. (2016). Advertising for cognitive interviews: A comparison of Facebook, Craigslist, and snowball recruiting. *Social Science Computer Review, 34*(3), 360–377. http://dx.doi.org/10.1177/0894439315578240

Hébert, M., Tourigny, M., Cyr, M., McDuff, P., & Joly, J. (2009). Prevalence of childhood sexual abuse and timing of disclosure in a representative sample of adults from Quebec. *The Canadian Journal of Psychiatry/La Revue Canadienne de Psychiatrie, 54*(9), 631–636. doi:10.1177/070674370905400908

Heffner, K. L., Crean, H. F., & Kemp, J. E. (2016). Meditation programs for veterans with posttraumatic stress disorder: Aggregate findings from a multi-site evaluation. *Psychological Trauma: Theory, Research, Practice, and Policy, 8,* 365–374. http://dx.doi.org/10.1037/tra0000106

Hegewisch, A., Phil, M., & Hartmann, H. (2019, March 7). The gender wage gap: 2018 earnings differences by race and ethnicity. Institute for Women's Policy Research. Retrieved from https://iwpr.org/publications/gender-wage-gap-2018/

He, H., Li, J., Xiao, Q., Jiang, S., Yang, Y., & Zhi, S. (2019). Language and color perception: Evidence from Mongolian and Chinese speakers. *Frontiers in Psychology, 10*:551. doi:10.3389/fpsyg.2019.00551

Heider, F. (1958). *The psychology of interpersonal relations.* Hoboken, NJ: Wiley.

Heid, M. (2018, September 4). Is hypnosis real? Here's what science says. *Time.* Retrieved from https://time.com/5380312/is-hypnosis-real-science/

Heimann, M., & Meltzoff, A. N. (1996). Deferred imitation in 9- and 14-month-old infants. *British Journal of Developmental Psychology, 14,* 55–64. http://dx.doi.org/10.1111/j.2044-835X.1996.tb00693.x

Heine, S. J., & Renshaw, K. (2002). Interjudge agreement, self-enhancement, and liking: Cross-cultural divergences. *Personality and Social Psychology Bulletin, 28,* 578–587.

Helliwell, J., Layard, R., & Sachs, J. (2016). *World Happiness Report 2016, Update (Vol. I).* New York, NY: Sustainable Development Solutions Network.

Helm, A. F., & Spencer, R. M. C. (2019). Television use and its effects on sleep in early childhood. *Sleep Health, 5*(3), 241–247. https://doi.org/10.1016/j.sleh.2019.02.009.

Hendricks, P. S., Thorne, C. B., Clark, C. B., Coombs, D. W., & Johnson, M. W. (2015). Classic psychedelic use is associated with reduced psychological distress and suicidality in the United States adult population. *Journal of Psychopharmacology, 29,* 280–288. http://dx.doi.org/10.1177/0269881114565653

Henkel, L. A. (2014). Point and shoot memories: The influence of taking photos on memory for a museum tour. *Psychological Science, 25,* 396–402. https://doi.org/10.1177/0956797613504438

Henwood, B. F., Derejko, K.-S., Couture, J., & Padgett, D. K. (2014). Maslow and mental health recovery: A comparative study of homeless programs for adults with serious mental illness. *Administration and Policy in Mental Health and Mental Health Services Research, 42,* 220–228. http://dx.doi.org/10.1007/s10488-014-0542-8

Herbenick, D., van Anders, S.M., Brotto, L.A. Chivers, M. L., Jawed-Wessel, S., & Galarza, J. (2019). Sexual harassment in the field of sexuality research. *Archives of Sexual Behavior, 48*(4), 997–1006. https://doi.org/10.1007/s10508-019-1405-x

Herculano-Houzel, S. (2017). Numbers of neurons as biological correlates of cognitive capability. *Current Opinion in Behavioral Sciences, 16,* 1–7. https://doi.org/10.1016/j.cobeha.2017.02.004.

Herman, A. I., DeVito, E. E., Jensen, K. P., & Sofuoglu, M. (2014). Pharmacogenetics of nicotine addiction: Role of dopamine. *Pharmacogenomics, 15,* 221–234. http://dx.doi.org/10.2217/pgs.13.246

Herman, L. M., Richards, D. G., & Woltz, J. P. (1984). Comprehension of sentences by bottle nosed dolphins. *Cognition, 16,* 129–139. http://dx.doi.org/10.1016/0010-0277(84)90003-9

Hernandez, R., Kershaw, K. N., Siddique, J., Boehm, J. K., Kubzansky, L. D., Diez-Roux, A., . . . Lloyd-Jones, D. M. (2015). Optimism and cardiovascular health: Multi-ethnic study of atherosclerosis (MESA). *Health Behavior and Policy Review, 2,* 62–73. http://dx.doi.org/10.14485/HBPR.2.1.6

Herrero-Hahn, R., Rojas, J. G., Ospina-Díaz, J. M., Montoya-Juárez, R., Restrepo-Medrano, J. C., & Hueso-Montoro, C. (2017). Cultural adaptation and validation of the cultural self-efficacy scale for Colombian nursing professionals. *Journal of Transcultural Nursing, 28,* 195–202. http://dx.doi.org/10.1177/1043659615613419

Hertel, G., Rauschenbach, C., Thielgen, M. M., & Krumm, S. (2015). Are older workers more active copers? Longitudinal effects of age-contingent coping on strain at work. *Journal of Organizational Behavior, 36,* 514–537. http://dx.doi.org/10.1002/job.1995

Hess, U., & Hareli, S. (2015). The role of social context for the interpretation of emotional facial expressions. In M. Mandal & A. Awasthi (Eds.), *Understanding facial expressions in communication* (pp. 119–141). New Delhi, IN: Springer. doi:10.1007/978-81-322-1934-7_7

Hewlett, B. S., & Roulette, J. W. (2014). Cosleeping beyond infancy: Culture, ecology, and evolutionary biology of bed sharing among Aka foragers and Ngandu farmers of Central Africa. In D. Narvaez, K. Valentino, A. Fuentes, J. J. McKenna, & P. Gray (Eds.), *Ancestral landscapes in human evolution: Culture, childrearing and social wellbeing* (pp. 129–163). New York, NY: Oxford University Press. http://dx.doi.org/10.1093/acprof:oso/9780199964253.003.0010

Hezel, D. M., & Simpson, H. B. (2019). Exposure and response prevention for obsessive-compulsive disorder: A review and new directions. *Indian Journal of Psychiatry, 61*(Suppl 1), S85–S92. doi:10.4103/psychiatry.IndianJPsychiatry_516_18

Hicks, S. D., Jacob, P., Perez, O., Baffuto, M., Gagnon, Z., & Middleton, F. A. (2019). The transcriptional signature of a runner's high. *Medicine & Science in Sports & Exercise, 51*(5), 970–978. doi:10.1249/MSS.0000000000001865

Hilgard, E. R. (1978). Hypnosis and consciousness. *Human Nature, 1,* 42–51.

Hilgard, E. R. (1992). Divided consciousness and dissociation. *Consciousness and Cognition, 1,* 16–31.

Hill, T., Sullman, M. J. M., & Stephens, A. N. (2019). Mobile phone involvement, beliefs, and texting while driving in Ukraine. *Accident Analysis & Prevention, 125,* 124–131. https://doi.org/10.1016/j.aap.2019.01.035

Hillus, J., Moseley, R., Roepke, S., & Mohr, B. (2019). Action semantic deficits and impaired motor skills in autistic adults without intellectual impairment. *Frontiers in Human Neuroscience, 13*:256. doi:10.3389/fnhum.2019.00256

Himmerich, H., Bentley, J., Kan, C., & Treasure, J. (2019). Genetic risk factors for eating disorders: An update and insights into pathophysiology. *Therapeutic Advances in Psychopharmacology, 9,* 2045125318814734. doi:10.1177/2045125318814734

Hinsliff, G. (2019, February, 14). The pansexual revolution: How sexual fluidity became mainstream. *The Guardian.* Retrieved from https://www.theguardian.com/society/2019/feb/14/the-pansexual-revolution-how-sexual-fluidity-became-mainstream

Hirota, K., & Lambert, D. G. (2018). Ketamine and depression. *British Journal of Anaesthesia, 121*(6), 1198–1202. https://doi.org/10.1016/j.bja.2018.08.020

Hirschtritt, M. E., Bloch, M. H., & Mathews, C. A. (2017). Obsessive-compulsive disorder: Advances in diagnosis and treatment. *Journal of the American Medical Association, 317*(13), 1358–1367. doi:10.1001/jama.2017.2200

Hirsh-Pasek, K., Adamson, L., Bakeman, R., Golinkoff, R. M., Pace, A., Yust, P., & Suma, K. (2015). The contribution of early communication to low-income children's language success. *Psychological Science, 26,* 1071–1083. doi:10.1177/0956797615581493

Hirst, W., & Phelps, E. A. (2016). Flashbulb memories. *Current Directions in Psychological Science, 25*(1), 36–41. doi:10.1177/0963721415622487

Hirst, W., Phelps, E. A., Meksin, R., Vaidya, C. J., Johnson, M. K., Mitchell, K. J., . . . Olsson, A. (2015). A ten-year follow-up of a study of memory for the attack of September 11, 2001: Flashbulb memories and memories for flashbulb events. *Journal of Experimental Psychology: General, 144,* 604–623. http://dx.doi.org/10.1037/xge0000055

Hobbs, W. R., Burke, M., Christakis, N. A., & Fowler, J. H. (2016). Online social integration is associated with reduced mortality risk. *Proceedings of the National Academy of Sciences of the United*

States of America, 113(46), 12980–12984. http://dx.doi.org/10.1073/pnas.1605554113

Hobson, J. A. (1999). *Dreaming as delirium: How the brain goes out of its mind.* Cambridge, MA: MIT Press.

Hobson, J. A. (2005). In bed with Mark Solms? What a nightmare! A reply to Domhoff. *Dreaming, 15,* 21–29.

Hobson, J. A., & McCarley, R. W. (1977). The brain as a dream state generator: An activation-synthesis hypothesis of the dream process. *American Journal of Psychiatry, 134,* 1335–1348.

Hobson, J. A., Sangsanguan, S., Arantes, H., & Kahn, D. (2011). Dream logic—The inferential reasoning paradigm. *Dreaming, 21,* 1–15.

Hoekzema, E., Barba-Müller, E., Pozzobon, C., Picado, M., Lucco, F., García-García, D., . . . Vilarroya, O. (2016). Pregnancy leads to long-lasting changes in human brain structure. *Nature Neuroscience, 20*(2), 287–296. doi:10.1038/nn.4458

Hoffman, A. J. (2014). Violent media games and aggression—Is it really time for a mea culpa? *American Psychologist, 69*(3), 305–306. http://dx.doi.org/10.1037/a0035289

Hogan, T. P. (2018). *Psychological testing: A practical introduction* (4th ed.). Hoboken, NJ: Wiley.

Ho, J., & Shu, L. (2019). Need for closure and individual tendency for design fixation and functional fixedness. *Proceedings of the Institution of Mechanical Engineers, Part C: Journal of Mechanical Engineering Science, 233*(2), 476–492. https://doi.org/10.1177/0954406218792583

Holder, S. M., Warren, C., Rogers, K., Griffeth, B., Peterson, E., Blackhurst, D., & Ochonma, C. (2018). Involuntary processes: Knowledge base of health care professionals in a tertiary medical center in upstate South Carolina. *Community Mental Health Journal, 54*(2), 149–157. doi:10.1007/s10597-017-0115-x

Hole, J., Hirsch, M., Ball, E., & Meads, C. (2015). Music as an aid for postoperative recovery in adults: A systematic review and meta-analysis. *The Lancet, 386,* 1659–1671. doi:10.1016/S0140-6736(15)60169-6

Holekamp, K. E., & Strauss, E. D. (2016). Aggression and dominance: An interdisciplinary overview. *Current Opinion in Behavioral Sciences, 12,* 44–51. http://dx.doi.org/10.1016/j.cobeha.2016.08.005

Holland, J. L. (1985). *Making vocational choices: A theory of vocational personalities and work environments* (2nd ed.). Englewood Cliff s, NJ: Prentice Hall.

Holland, J. L. (1994). *Self-directed search form R.* Lutz, FL: Psychological Assessment Resources.

Holman, E. A., Garfin, D. R., & Silver, R. C. (2014). Media's role in broadcasting acute stress following Boston Marathon bombings. *Proceedings of the National Academy of Sciences of the United States of America, 111,* 93–98. http://dx.doi.org/10.1073/pnas.1316265110

Holmes, L. (2016, December 29). A reminder that Carrie Fisher was an O.G. Mental Health Hero. *The Huffington Post.* Retrieved from http://www.huffingtonpost.com/entry/carrie-fisher-mental-health-princess-leia_us_562795dbe4b0bce347031e34

Holmes, R. M., Romeo, L., Ciraola, S., & Grushko, M. (2015). The relationship between creativity, social play, and children's language abilities. *Early Child Development and Care, 185,* 1180–1197. http://dx.doi.org/10.1080/03004430.2014.983916

Holmes, T. H., & Rahe, R. H. (1967). The Social Readjustment Rating Scale. *Journal of Psychosomatic Research, 11,* 213–218. http://dx.doi.org/10.1016/0022-3999(67)90010-4

Ho, M., & O'Donohoe, S. (2014). Volunteer stereotypes, stigma, and relational identity projects. *European Journal of Marketing, 48,* 854–877. http://dx.doi.org/10.1108/EJM-11-2011-0637

Hong, C., Chen, Z., & Li, C. (2017). "Liking" and being "liked": How are personality traits and demographics associated with giving and receiving "likes" on Facebook? *Computers in Human Behavior, 68,* 292–299. http://dx.doi.org/10.1016/j.chb.2016.11.048

Hong, F.-Y., & Chiu, S.-L. (2016). Factors influencing Facebook usage and Facebook addictive tendency in university students: The role of online psychological and Facebook usage motivation. *Stress and Health, 32,* 117–127. doi:10.1002/smi.2585

Hong, S. L., Estrada-Sánchez, A. M., Barton, S. J., & Rebec, G. V. (2016). Early exposure to dynamic environments alters patterns of motor exploration throughout the lifespan. *Behavioural Brain Research, 302,* 81–87. http://dx.doi.org/10.1016/j.bbr.2016.01.007

Hoogwegt, M. T., Versteeg, H., Hansen, T. B., Thygesen, L. C., Pedersen, S. S., & Zwisler, A.-D. (2013). Exercise mediates the association between positive affect and 5-year mortality in patients with ischemic heart disease. *Circulation: Cardiovascular Quality and Outcomes, 6,* 559–566. doi:10.1161/CIRCOUTCOMES.113.000158

Hoover, E. (2019, February 27). What do Americans think about affirmative action? It depends on how you ask. *Chronicle of Higher Education.* Retrieved May 13, 2019 from https://www.chronicle.com/article/What-Do-Americans-Think-About/245779

Hopper, E. (2019, May 25). What is unconditional positive regard in psychology? *Thought Co.* Retrieved from https://www.thoughtco.com/unconditional-positive-regard-4428102

Hopthrow, T., Hooper, N., Mahmood, L., Meier, B. P., & Weger, U. (2017). Mindfulness reduces the correspondence bias. *The Quarterly Journal of Experimental Psychology, 70*(3), 351–360. http://dx.doi.org/10.1080/17470218.2016.1149498

Hörder, H., Johansson, L., Guo, X., Grimby, G., Kern, S., Östling, S., & Skoog, I. (2018). Midlife cardiovascular fitness and dementia: A 44-year longitudinal population study in women. *Neurology, 90*(15), e1298–e1305. doi:10.1212/WNL.0000000000005290

Horney, K. (1939). *New ways in psychoanalysis.* New York, NY: International Universities Press.

Horney, K. (1945). *Our inner conflicts: A constructive theory of neurosis.* New York, NY: Norton.

Hornsey, M. J., Greenaway, K. H., Harris, E. A., & Bain, P. G. (2019). Exploring cultural differences in the extent to which people perceive and desire control. *Personality and Social Psychology Bulletin, 45*(1), 81–92. https://doi.org/10.1177/0146167218780692

Hosokawa, R., & Katsura, T. (2019). Role of parenting style in children's behavioral problems through the transition from preschool to elementary school according to gender in Japan. *International Journal of Environmental Research and Public Health, 16*(1), 21. doi:10.3390/ijerph16010021

Howard, M. E., Jackson, M. L., Berlowitz, D., O'Donoghue, F., Swann, P., Westlake, J., . . . Pierce, R. J. (2014). Specific sleepiness symptoms are indicators of performance impairment during sleep deprivation. *Accident Analysis and Prevention, 62,* 1–8. http://dx.doi.org/10.1016/j.aap.2013.09.003

Howell, J. A., McEvoy, P. M., Grafton, B., Macleod, C., Kane, R. T., Anderson, R. A., & Egan, S. J. (2016). Selective attention in perfectionism: Dissociating valence from perfectionism-relevance. *Journal of Behavior Therapy and Experimental Psychiatry, 51,* 100–108. doi:10.1016/j.jbtep.2016.01.004

Howe, M. L., & Knott, L. M. (2015). The fallibility of memory in judicial processes: Lessons from the past and their modern consequences. *Memory, 23,* 633–656. http://dx.doi.org/10.1080/09658211.2015.1010709

Howes, M. B., & O'Shea, G. (2014). *Human memory: A constructivist view.* San Diego, CA: Elsevier.

Howes, O. D., McCutcheon, R., Owen, M. J., & Murray, R. M. (2017). The role of genes, stress, and dopamine in the development of schizophrenia. *Biological Psychiatry, 81*(1), 9–20. http://dx.doi.org/10.1016/j.biopsych.2016.07.014

Hsiao, S. S., & Gomez-Ramirez, M. (2013). Neural mechanisms of tactile perception. In R. J. Nelson, S. J. Y. Mizumori, & I. B. Weiner (Eds.), *Handbook of psychology, Vol. 3. Behavioral neuroscience* (2nd ed., pp. 206–239). Hoboken, NJ: Wiley.

Hsu, S. (2016). Motivation and emotions: What guides our behavior? In C. Tien-Lun Sun (Ed.), *Psychology in Asia: An introduction* (pp. 211–249). Boston, MA: Cengage.

Hsu, S. (2016). Psychological disorders. In C. Tien-Lun Sun (Ed.), *Psychology in Asia: An introduction* (pp. 349–394). Boston, MA: Cengage.

Huang, L., Deng, Y., Zheng, X., & Liu, Y. (2019). Transcranial direct Current stimulation with halo sport enhances repeated sprint cycling and cognitive performance. *Frontiers in Physiology, 10*(118). doi:10.3389/fphys.2019.00118

Huber, A., Lui, F., Duzzi, D., Pagnoni, G., & Porro, C. A. (2014). Structural and functional cerebral correlates of hypnotic suggestibility. *PLoS ONE, 9,* 1–6. doi:10.1371/journal.pone.0093187

Hu, C. S., Wang, Q., Han, T., Weare, E., & Fu, G. (2017). Differential emotion attribution to neutral faces of own and other races. *Cognition and Emotion, 31*(2), 360–368. http://dx.doi.org/10.1080/02699931.2015.1092419

Hudson, H. M., Gallant-Shean, M. B., & Hirsch, A. R. (2015). Chemesthesis, thermogenesis, and nutrition. In A. Hirsch (Ed.), *Nutrition and sensation* (pp. 175–192). Boca Raton, FL: Taylor & Francis.

Hudson, N. W., & Fraley, R. C. (2015). Volitional personality trait change: Can people choose to change their personality traits? *Journal of Personality and Social Psychology, 109,* 490–507. http://dx.doi.org/10.1037/pspp0000021

Hughes, J. E., Ward, J., Gruffydd, E., Baron-Cohen, S., Smith, P., Allison, C., & Simner, J. (2018). Savant syndrome has a distinct psychological profile in autism. *Molecular Autism, 9*(53). https://doi.org/10.1186/s13229-018-0237-1

Hughes, J. M., Alo, J., Krieger, K., & O'Leary, L. M. (2016). Emergence of internal and external motivations to respond without prejudice in White children. *Group Processes & Intergroup Relations, 19,* 202–216. http://dx.doi.org/10.1177/1368430215603457

Hughes, S., Barnes-Holmes, D., & Smyth, S. (2017). Implicit cross-community biases revisited: Evidence for ingroup favoritism in the absence of outgroup derogation in Northern Ireland. *The Psychological Record, 67*(1), 97–107. http://dx.doi.org/10.1007/s40732-016-0210-3

Hull, C. (1952). *A behavior system.* New Haven, CT: Yale University Press.

Humes, K., & Hogan, H. (2015). Do current race and ethnicity concepts reflect a changing America? In R. Bangs & L. E. Davis (Eds.), *Race and social problems: Restructuring inequality* (pp. 15–38). New York, NY: Springer. http://dx.doi.org/10.1007/978-1-4939-0863-9_2

Humphrey, R. H., & Adams, L. L. (2017). Heroic empathy: The heart of leadership. In S. T. Allison, G. R. Goethals, & R. M. Kramer (Eds.), *Handbook of heroism and heroic leadership* (pp. 459–475). New York, NY: Routledge/Taylor & Francis Group.

Hundt, N. E., Calleo, J. S., Williams, W., & Cully, J. A. (2016). Does using cognitive behavioural therapy skills predict improvements in depression? *Psychology and Psychotherapy: Theory, Research, and Practice, 89,* 235–238. http://dx.doi.org/10.1111/papt.12065

Hunsley, J., Lee, C. M., Wood, J. M., & Taylor, W. (2015). Controversial and questionable assessment techniques. In S. O. Lilienfeld, S. J. Gould, & J. M. Lohr (Eds.), *Science and pseudoscience in clinical psychology* (2nd ed., pp. 42–82). New York, NY: Guilford.

Hunt, E., Bornovalova, M. A., & Patrick, C. J. (2015). Genetic and environmental overlap between borderline personality disorder traits and psychopathy: Evidence for promotive effects of factor 2 and protective effects of factor 1. *Psychological Medicine, 45,* 1471–1481. http://dx.doi.org/10.1017/S003329171400260

Huntjens, R. J. C., Wessel, I., Ostafin, B. D., Boelen, P. A., Behrens, F., & van Minnen, A. (2016). Trauma-related self-defining memories and future goals in Dissociative Identity Disorder. *Behaviour Research and Therapy, 87,* 216–224. http://dx.doi.org/10.1016/j.brat.2016.10.002

Hunt, M. G., Marx, R., Lipson, C., & Young, J. (2018). No more FOMO: Limiting social media decreases loneliness and depression. *Journal of Social and Clinical Psychology, 37*(10), 751–768. doi:10.1521/jscp.2018.37.10.751

Huston, C. (2018, September 28). This week in Heisman history: Ricky honors Doak, rushes for 350. Heisman Trophy. Retrieved April 28, 2019 from https://www.heisman.com/articles/this-week-in-heisman-history-ricky-honors-doak-rushes-for-350/

Hutchins, T. L., & Prelock, P. A. (2015). Beyond the theory of mind hypothesis: Using a causal model to understand the nature and treatment of multiple deficits in autism spectrum disorder. In R. H. Bahr & E. R. Silliman (Eds), *Routledge handbook of communication disorders* (pp. 247–257). New York, NY: Routledge/Taylor & Francis Group.

Hutteman, R., Nestler, S., Wagner, J., Egloff, B., & Back, M. D. (2015). Wherever I may roam: Processes of self-esteem development from adolescence to emerging adulthood in the context of international student exchange. *Journal of Personality and Social Psychology, 108,* 767–783. http://dx.doi.org/10.1037/pspp0000015

Hutton, J. S., Horowitz-Kraus, T., Mendelsohn, A. L., DeWitt, T., Holland, S. K., & the C-MIND Authorship Consortium. (2015). Home reading environment and brain activation in preschool children listening to stories. *Pediatrics, 136,* 466–478. http://dx.doi.org/10.1542/peds.2015-0359

Hu, X., Luo, L., & Fleming, S. M. (2019). A role for metamemory in cognitive offloading. *Cognition, 193,* 104012. https://doi.org/10.1016/j.cognition.2019.104012

Hviid, A., Hansen, J. V., Frisch, M., & Melbye, M. (2019). Measles, mumps, rubella vaccination, and autism: A nationwide cohort study. *Annals of Internal Medicine, 170*(8), 513–520. doi:10.7326/M18-2101

Hwang, H. C., & Matsumoto, D. (2016). Facial expressions. In D. Matsumoto, H. C. Hwang, & M. G. Frank (Eds.), *APA handbook of nonverbal communication* (pp. 257–287). Washington, DC: American Psychological Association. http://dx.doi.org/10.1037/14669-010

Hwang, H., & Matsumoto, D. (2015). Evidence for the universality of facial expressions of emotion. In M. K. Mandal & A. Awasthi (Eds.), *Understanding facial expressions in communication: Cross-cultural and multidisciplinary perspectives* (pp. 41–56). New York, NY:

Hyde, J. S. (2014). Gender similarities and differences. *Annual Review of Psychology, 65,* 373–398. http://dx.doi.org/10.1146/annurevpsych-010213-115057

Hyman, R. (1981). Cold reading: How to convince strangers that you know all about them. In K. Fraizer (Ed.), *Paranormal borderlands of science* (pp. 232–244). Buffalo, NY: Prometheus.

Hyman, R. (1996). The evidence for psychic functioning: Claims vs. reality. *Skeptical Inquirer, 20*, 24–26.

Iachini, T., Coello, Y., Frassinetti, F., Senese, V. P., Galante, F., & Ruggiero, G. (2016). Peripersonal and interpersonal space in virtual and real environments: Effects of gender and age. *Journal of Environmental Psychology, 45*, 154–164. http://dx.doi.org/10.1016/j.jenvp.2016.01.004

Iheanacho, T., Kapadia, D., Ezeanolue, C. O., Osuji, A. A., Ogidi, A. G., Ike, A., . . . Ezeanolue, E. E. (2016). Attitudes and beliefs about mental illness among church-based lay health workers: Experience from a prevention of mother-to-child HIV transmission trial in Nigeria. *International Journal of Culture and Mental Health, 9*(1), 1–13. http://dx.doi.org/10.1080/17542863.2015.1074260

Iliff, J. J., Wang, M., Liao, Y., Plogg, B. A., Peng, W., Gundersen, G. A., . . . Nedergaard, M. (2012). A paravascular pathway facilitates CSF flow through the brain parenchyma and the clearance of interstitial solutes, including amyloid β. *Science Translational Medicine, 4* 147ra111. http://dx.doi.org/10.1126/scitranslmed.3003748

Ingalhalikar, M., Smith, A., Parker, D., Satterthwaite, T. D., Elliott, M. A., Ruparel, K., . . . Verma, R. (2014). Sex differences in the structural connectome of the human brain. *Proceedings of the National Academy of Sciences of the United States of America, 111*, 823–828. doi:10.1073/pnas.1316909110

Ingber, S. (2019, March 11). Olympic cycling medalist Kelly Catlin dead at 23. *NPR.* Retrieved from https://www.npr.org/2019/03/11/702206945/olympic-cycling-medalist-kelly-catlin-dead-at-23

Insel, P., & Roth, W. (1985). *Core concepts in health* (4th ed.). Palo Alto, CA: Mayfield.

Institute for Laboratory Animal Research (ILAR). (2010). Guide for the care and use of laboratory animals. *The National Academies of Sciences Engineering Medicine.* Retrieved from http://dels.nas.edu/ilarn/ilarhome/

Iselin, A. -M. R., Mcvey, A. A., & Ehatt, C. M. (2015). Externalizing behaviors and attribution biases. In T. P. Beauchaine & S. P. Hinshaw (Eds.), *The Oxford handbook of externalizing spectrum disorders* (pp. 347–359). New York, NY: Oxford University Press. http://dx.doi.org/10.1093/oxfordhb/9780199324675.013.12

Israel-Cohen, Y., & Kaplan, O. (2016). Traumatic stress during population-wide exposure to trauma in Israel: Gender as a moderator of the effects of marital status and social support. *Stress and Health, 32*, 636–640. http://dx.doi.org/10.1002/smi.2647

Israel, S., Moffitt, T. E., Belsky, D. W., Hancox, R. J., Poulton, R., Roberts, B., . . . Caspi, A. (2014). Translating personality psychology to help personalize preventive medicine for young adult patients. *Journal of Personality and Social Psychology, 106*, 484–498. http://dx.doi.org/10.1037/a0035687

Ito, H., & Aruga, T. (2018). Japan imposes a legal overtime cap, but mental health issues are complex. *The Lancet Psychiatry, 5*(8), 616–617. Retrieved from https://doi.org/10.1016/S2215-0366(18)30266-9

Itoh, K., & Hikasa, M. (2014). Focusing and Naikan, a uniquely Japanese way of therapy. In G. Madison (Ed.), *Emerging practice in focusing oriented psychotherapy: Innovative theory and applications* (pp. 112–125). London, UK: Jessica Kingsley.

Ivanenko, A., & Johnson, K. P. (2016). Sleep disorders. In M. K. Dulcan (Ed.), *Dulcan's textbook of child and adolescent psychiatry* (2nd ed., pp. 495–519). Arlington, VA: American Psychiatric Publishing. http://dx.doi.org/10.1176/appi.books.9781615370306.md23

Iwakawa, S., Kanmura, Y., & Kuwaki, T. (2019). Orexin receptor blockade-induced sleep preserves the ability to wake in the presence of threat in mice. *Frontiers in Behavioral Neuroscience, 12.* doi:10.3389/fnbeh.2018.00327

Izadpanah, S., Schumacher, M., & Barnow, S. (2017). Anger rumination mediates the relationship between reinforcement sensitivity and psychopathology: Results of a 5-year longitudinal study. *Personality and Individual Differences, 110*, 49–54. http://dx.doi.org/10.1016/j.paid.2017.01.023

Jachimowicz, J. M., Hauser, O. P., O'Brien, J. D., Sherman, E., & Galinsky, A. D. (2018). The critical role of second-order normative beliefs in predicting energy conservation. *Nature Human Behaviour, 2*, 757–764. doi:10.1038/s41562-018-0434-0

Jack, A. I., Boyatzis, R. E., Khawaja, M. S., Passarelli, A. M., & Leckie, R. L. (2013). Visioning in the brain: An fMRI study of inspirational coaching and mentoring. *Social Neuroscience, 8*, 369–384. doi:10.1080/17470919.2013.808259.

Jack, R. E., Sun, W., Delis, I., Garrod, O. G. B., & Schyns, P. G. (2016). Four not six: Revealing culturally common facial expressions of emotion. *Journal of Experimental Psychology: General, 145*, 708–730. http://dx.doi.org/10.1037/xge0000162

Jackson, S. (2016). *Research methods and statistics: A critical thinking approach* (5th ed.). Boston, MA: Cengage.

Jackson, S., & Vares, T. (2015). 'Perfect skin', 'pretty skinny': Girls' embodied identities and post-feminist popular culture. *Journal of Gender Studies, 24*(3), 347–360. http://dx.doi.org/10.1080/09589236.2013.841573

Jacob, K. S. (2014). DSM-5 and culture: The need to move towards a shared model of care within a more equal patient–physician partnership. *Asian Journal of Psychiatry, 7*, 89–91. http://dx.doi.org/10.1016/j.ajp.2013.11.012

Jacobs Bao, K., & Lyubomirsky, S. (2013). Making it last: Combating hedonic adaptation in romantic relationships. *The Journal of Positive Psychology, 8*, 196–206.

Jacobs, S. (2019, June 25). Case of Princeton grad who gunned down father heads to jury after month of testimony. *New York Daily News.* Retrieved June 25, 2019 from https://www.nydailynews.com/new-york/ny-thomas-gilbert-jury-20190625-5pnnknidszbcbgnvttmcko-77ki-story.html

Jaekel, K. S., & Kortegast, C. A. (2016). *Community college students.* In W. K. Killam, S. Degges-White, & R. E. Michel (Eds.), *Career counseling interventions: Practice with diverse clients* (pp. 9–15). New York, NY: Springer.

Jain, A., Marshall, J., Buikema, A., Bancroft, T., Kelly, J. P., & Newschaffer, C. J. (2015). Autism occurrence by MMR vaccine status among US children with older siblings with and without autism. *Journal of the American Medical Association, 313*, 1534–1540. doi:10.1001/jama.2015.3077

James, S. D. (2008, May 7). Wild child speechless after tortured life. *ABC News.* Retrieved from http://abcnews.go.com/Health/story?id54804490&page51

James, W. (1890). *The principles of psychology* (Vol. 2). New York, NY: Holt.

Jandt, F. (2016). *An introduction to intercultural communication: Identities in a global community* (8th ed.). Thousand Oaks, CA: Sage.

Janis, I. L. (1972). *Victims of groupthink: A psychological study of foreign-policy decisions and fiascoes.* Boston, MA: Houghton Mifflin.

Jankowiak, W., & Fischer, E. (1992). Cross-cultural perspective on romantic love. *Ethnology, 31*, 149–155.

Jankowiak, W. R., Volsche, S. L., & Garcia, J. R. (2015). Is the romantic–sexual kiss a near human universal? *American Anthropologist, 117,* 535–539. http://dx.doi.org/10.1111/aman.12286

Janzen, K. (2019). Coerced fate: How negotiation models lead to false confessions. *Journal of Criminal Law and Criminology, 109*(1), 70–102. https://scholarlycommons.law.northwestern.edu/jclc/vol109/iss1/2

Järvinen, M., & Henriksen, T. D. (2018). Controlling intimacy: Sexual scripts among men and women in prostitution. *Current Sociology.* https://doi.org/10.1177/0011392118815945

Jarvis, J. (2014). Auditory and neuronal fetal environment factors impacting early learning development. *International Journal of Childbirth Education, 29,* 27–31.

Jaschik, S. (2018, September 24). The 2018 surveys of admissions leaders: The pressure grows. *Inside Higher Ed.* Retrieved from https://www.insidehighered.com/news/survey/2018-surveys-admissions-leaders-pressure-grows

Jauhar, S., Veronese, M., Nour, M. M., Rogdaki, M., Hathway, P., Natesan, S., . . . Howes, O. D. (2019). The effects of antipsychotic treatment on presynaptic dopamine synthesis capacity in first-episode psychosis: A positron emission tomography study. *Biological Psychiatry, 85*(1), 79–87. doi:10.1016/j.biopsych.2018.07.003

Jaul, E., Meiron, O., & Menczel, J. (2016). The effect of pressure ulcers on the survival in patients with advanced dementia and comorbidities. *Experimental Aging Research, 42*(4), 382–389. http://dx.doi.org/10.1080/0361073X.2016.1191863

Jee, C. (2017, April 11). Six times AI has beaten humans in competitions: AlphaGo, Chinook, IBM Watson, and more: Computers vs humans. *Techworld.* Retrieved from http://www.techworld.com/picture-gallery/big-data/six-times-ai-has-beaten-humans-incompetitions-3636755/

Jeffreys, S. (2015). *Beauty and misogyny: Harmful cultural practices in the West,* (2nd ed.). New York, NY: Routledge/Taylor & Francis Group.

Jensen, M. P., Barber, J., Romano, J. M., Hanley, M. A., Raichle, K. A., Molton, I. R., . . . Patterson, D. R. (2009). Effects of self-hypnosis training and EMG biofeedback relaxation training on chronic pain in persons with spinal-cord injury. *International Journal of Clinical and Experimental Hypnosis, 57*(3), 239–268. http://dx.doi.org/10.1080/00207140902881007

Jensen, M. P., Jamieson, G. A., Lutz, A., Mazzoni, G., McGeown, W. J. Santarcangelo, E. J., . . . Terhune, D. B. (2017). New directions in hypnosis research: Strategies for advancing the cognitive and clinical neuroscience of hypnosis. *Neuroscience of Consciousness, 1,* nix004. Retrieved from https://doi.org/10.1093/nc/nix004

Jeon, H., & Lee, S. H. (2018). From neurons to social beings: Short review of the mirror neuron system research and its socio-psychological and psychiatric implications. *Clinical Psychopharmacology and Neuroscience, 16*(1), 18–31. doi:10.9758/cpn.2018.16.1.18

Jessel, J., & Borrero, J. C. (2014). A laboratory comparison of two variations of differential-reinforcement-of-low-rate procedures. *Journal of Applied Behavior Analysis, 47,* 314–324. doi:10.1002/jaba.114

Jiahui, G., Yang, H., & Duchaine, B. (2018). Developmental prosopagnosics have widespread selectivity reductions across category-selective visual cortex. *Proceedings of the National Academy of Sciences of the United States of America, 115*(28), E6418-E6427. doi:10.1073/pnas.1802246115

Jiang, A., Tran, T. T., Madison, F. N., & Bakker, A. (2019). Acute stress-induced cortisol elevation during memory consolidation enhances pattern separation. *Learning & Memory, 26,* 121–127. doi:10.1101/lm.048546.118

Jiang, W., Liao, J., Liu, H., Huang, R., Li, Y., & Wang, W. (2015). [Brain structure analysis for patients with antisocial personality disorder by MRI]. Zhong nan da xue xue bao yi xue ban=Journal of Central South University. *Medical Sciences, 40,* 123–128. http://dx.doi.org/10.11817/j.issn.1672-7347.2015.02.002

Jiang, W., Liu, H., Zeng, L., Liao, J., Shen, H., Luo, A., . . . Wang, W. (2015). Decoding the processing of lying using functional connectivity MRI. *Behavioral and Brain Functions: BBF, 11*:(1). http://dx.doi.org/10.1186/s12993-014-0046-4

Jiang, W., Zhao, F., Guderley, N., & Manchaiah, V. (2016). Daily music exposure dose and hearing problems using personal listening devices in adolescents and young adults: A systematic review. *International Journal of Audiology, 55,* 197–205. doi:10.3109/14992027.2015.1122237

Jin, M. C., Mesress, Z. A., Azad, T. D., Doulames, V. M., & Veeravagu, A. (2019). Stem cell therapies for acute spinal cord injury in humans: A review. *Journal of Neurosurgery, 46*(3), E10. http://dx.doi:10.3171/2018.12.FOCUS18602.

Jobin, J., Wrosch, C., & Scheier, M. F. (2014). Associations between dispositional optimism and diurnal cortisol in a community sample: When stress is perceived as higher than normal. *Health Psychology, 33,* 382–391. http://dx.doi.org/10.1037/a0032736.

Joeng, J. R., Turner, S. L., & Lee, K. H. (2013). South Korean college students' Holland Types and career compromise processes. *The Career Development Quarterly, 61,* 64–73. http://dx.doi.org/10.1002/j.2161-0045.2013.00036.x

Johansen, P. -O., & Krebs, T. S. (2015). Psychedelics not linked to mental health problems or suicidal behavior: A population study. *Journal of Psychopharmacology, 29,* 270–279. http://dx.doi.org/10.1177/0269881114568039

John, N. A., & Dvir-Gvirsman, S. (2015). "I don't like you any more": Facebook unfriending by Israelis during the Israel–Gaza conflict of 2014. *Journal of Communication, 65,* 953–974. http://dx.doi.org/10.1111/jcom.12188

Johnson-Baker, K. A., Markham, C., Baumler, E., Swain, H., & Emery, S. (2016). Rap music use, perceived peer behavior, and sexual initiation among ethnic minority youth. *Journal of Adolescent Health, 58,* 317–322. http://dx.doi.org/10.1016/j.jadohealth.2015.11.003

Johnson, C. Y. (2019, February 28). Weekend 'catch-up sleep' is a lie. *The Washington Post.* Retrieved from https://www.washingtonpost.com/health/2019/02/28/weekend-catch-up-sleep-is-lie/?utm_term=.620d28fc8caf

Johnson, J. E., Stout, R. L., Miller, T. R., Zlotnick, C., Cerbo, L. A., Andrade, J. T., . . . Wiltsey-Stirman, S. (2019). Randomized cost-effectiveness trial of group interpersonal psychotherapy (IPT) for prisoners with major depression. *Journal of Consulting and Clinical Psychology, 87*(4), 392–406. http://dx.doi.org/10.1037/ccp0000379

Johnson, K.V.-A., & Dunbar, R. I. M. (2016). Pain tolerance predicts human social network size. *Scientific Reports, 6,* Article ID 25267. doi:10.1038/srep25267

Johnston, M. E., Sherman, A., & Grusec, J. E. (2013). Predicting moral outrage and religiosity with an implicit measure of moral identity. *Journal of Research in Personality, 47,* 209–217. doi:10.1016/j.jrp.2013.01.006

Jones, A., Lankshear, A., & Kelly, D. (2016). Giving voice to quality and safety matters at board level: A qualitative study of the experiences of executive nurses working in England and Wales. *International Journal of Nursing Studies, 59,* 169–176. http://dx.doi.org/10.1016/j.ijnurstu.2016.04.007

Jones, D. A. (2013). The polarizing effect of a partisan workplace. *PS: Political Science and Politics, 46,* 67–73. http://dx.doi.org/10.1017/S1049096512001254

Jones, E. E., & Nisbett, R. E. (1971). *The actor and the observer: Divergent perceptions of the causes of behavior.* Morristown, NJ: General Learning.

Jones, S. (2017). Describing the mental health profile of first responders: A systematic review. *Journal of the American Psychiatric Nurses Association, 23*(3), 200–214. https://doi.org/10.1177/1078390317695266

Jones, S. G., & Benca, R. M. (2013). Sleep and biological rhythms. In R. J. Nelson, S. J. Y. Mizumori, & I. B. Weiner (Eds.), *Handbook of psychology, Vol. 3. Behavioral neuroscience* (2nd ed., pp. 365–394). Hoboken, NJ: Wiley.

Joo, Y. J., Lim, K. Y., & Kim, N. H. (2016). The effects of secondary teachers' technostress on the intention to use technology in South Korea. *Computers & Education, 95,* 114–122. http://dx.doi.org/10.1016/j.compedu.2015.12.004

Jordan, C., Reid, A. M., Guzick, A. G., Simmons, J., & Sulkowski, M. L. (2017). When exposures go right: Effective exposure-based treatment for obsessive–compulsive disorder. *Journal of Contemporary Psychotherapy, 47*(1), 31–39. http://dx.doi.org/10.1007/s10879-016-9339-2

Joseph, A. J., Tandon, N., Yang, L. H., Duckworth, K., Torous, J., Seidman, L. J., & Keshavan, M. S. (2015). #Schizophrenia: Use and misuse on Twitter. *Schizophrenia Research, 165,* 111–115. doi:10.1016/j.schres.2015.04.009

Jouffre, S. (2015). Power modulates overreliance on false cardiac arousal when judging target attractiveness: The powerful are more centered on their own false arousal than the powerless. *Personality and Social Psychology Bulletin, 41,* 116–126. http://dx.doi.org/10.1177/0146167214559718

Jowett Hirst, E. S., Dozier, C. L., & Payne, S. W. (2016). Efficacy of and preference for reinforcement and response cost in token economies. *Journal of Applied Behavior Analysis, 49,* 329–345. http://dx.doi.org/10.1002/jaba.294

Jung, C. G. (1933). *Modern man in search of a soul.* New York, NY: Harcourt Brace.

Jung, C. G. (1936/1969). The concept of collective unconscious. In *Collected Works* (Vol. 9, Part 1). Princeton, NJ: Princeton University Press. (Original work published 1936.)

Junger, M., Montoya, L., & Overink, F. -J. (2017). Priming and warnings are not effective to prevent social engineering attacks. *Computers in Human Behavior, 66,* 75–87. http://dx. doi.org/10.1016/j.chb.2016.09.012

Jung, R. E., & Haier, R. J. (2007). The Parieto-Frontal Integration Theory (P-FIT) of intelligence: Converging neuroimaging evidence. *Behavioral and Brain Sciences, 30,* 135–154. http://dx.doi.org/10.1017/S0140525X07001185

Jung, S. H., Wang, Y., Kim, T., Tarr, A., Reader, B., Powell, N., & Sheridan, J. F. (2015). Molecular mechanisms of repeated social defeat-induced glucocorticoid resistance: Role of microrna. *Brain, Behavior, and Immunity, 44,* 195–206. doi:10.1016/j.bbi.2014.09.015

Junque, C. (2015). Structural and functional neuro imaging of cognition and emotion in Parkinson's disease. In A. I. Tröster (Ed.), *Clinical neuropsychology and cognitive neurology of Parkinson's disease and other movement disorders* (pp. 148–178). New York, NY: Oxford.

Juslin, P. N., Barradas, G. T, Ovsiannikow, M., Limmo, J., & Thompson, W. F. (2016). Prevalence of emotions, mechanisms, and motives in music listening: A comparison of individualist and collectivist cultures. *Psychomusicology: Music, Mind, and Brain, 26,* 293–326. http://dx.doi.org/10.1037/pmu0000161

Just, M. A., Pan, L., Cherkassky, V. L., McMakin, D., Cha, C., Nock, M. K., & Brent, D. (2017). Machine learning of neural representations of suicide and emotion concepts identifies suicidal youth. *Nature Human Behavior, 1,* 911–919. doi:10.1038/s41562-017-0234-y

Kaiser, J., Maibach, M., Salpeter, I., Hagenbuch, N., de Souza, V. B. C., Robinson, M. D., & Schwab, M. E. (2019). The spinal transcriptome after cortical stroke: In search of molecular factors regulating spontaneous recovery in the spinal cord. *Journal of Neuroscience, 39*(24), 4714–4726. https://doi.org/10.1523/JNEUROSCI.2571-18.2019

Kaiser, P., Kohen, D. P., Brown, M. L., Kajander, R. L., & Barnes, A. J. (2018). Integrating pediatric hypnosis with complementary modalities: Clinical perspectives on personalized treatment. *Children, 5*(8), 108. doi:10.3390/children5080108

Kamelska-Sadowska, A. M., Wojtkiewicz, J., & Kowalski, I. M. (2019). Review of the current knowledge on the role of stem cell transplantation in neurorehabilitation. *BioMed Research International, 2019,* Article ID 3290894. http://dx.doi:10.1155/2019/3290894

Kammrath, L. K., & Dweck, C. (2006). Voicing conflict: Preferred conflict strategies among incremental and entity theorists. *Personality and Social Psychology Bulletin, 32,* 1497–1508. http://dx.doi.org/10.1177/0146167206291476

Kanazawa, S., & von Buttlar, M.-T. (2019). A potential role of the widespread use of microwave ovens in the obesity epidemic. *Clinical Psychological Science, 7*(2), 340–348. https://doi.org/10.1177/2167702618805077

Kanbur, N., & Harrison, A. (2016). Co-occurrence of substance use and eating disorders: An approach to the adolescent patient in the context of family centered care. A literature review. *Substance Use & Misuse, 51,* 853–860. http://dx.doi.org/10.3109/10826084.2016.1155614

Kandler, C., Kornadt, A. E., Hagemeyer, B., & Neyer, F. J. (2015). Patterns and sources of personality development in old age. *Journal of Personality and Social Psychology, 109,* 175–191. http://dx.doi.org/10.1037/pspp0000028

Kandola, A., Vancampfort, D., Herring, M., Rebar, A., Hallgren, M., Firth, J., & Stubbs, B. (2018). Moving to beat anxiety: Epidemiology and therapeutic issues with physical activity for anxiety. *Current Psychiatry Reports, 20*(8), 63. doi:10.1007/s11920-018-0923-x

Kang, S.-M., & Lau, A. S. (2013). Revisiting the out-group advantage in emotion recognition in a multicultural society: Further evidence for the in-group advantage. *Emotion, 13,* 203–215.

Kaplan, R. L., Van Damme, I., Levine, L. J., & Loftus, E. F. (2016). Emotion and false memory. *Emotion Review, 8,* 8–13. http://dx.doi.org/10.1177/1754073915601228

Kaplan, S., & Richtel, M. (2019, August 31). The mysterious vaping illness that's "becoming an epidemic." *New York Times.* Retrieved from https://www.nytimes.com/2019/08/31/health/vaping-marijuana-ecigarettes-sickness.html?module=inline

Karakochuk, C. D., Whitfield, K. C., Green, T. J., & Kraemer, K. (Eds.). (2017). *The biology of the first 1,000 days.* Milton Park, Abingdon, UK: Taylor & Francis.

Karakurt, G., & Silver, K. E. (2014). Therapy for childhood sexual abuse survivors using attachment and family systems theory orientations. *The American Journal of Family Therapy, 42,* 79–91. http://dx.doi.org/10.1080/01926187.2013.772872

Karaman, M. A., Lerma, E., Vela, J. C., & Watson, J. C. (2019). Predictors of academic stress among college students. *Journal of College Counseling, 22*(1), 41–55. https://doi.org/10.1002/jocc.12113

Karasik, L. B., Tamis-LeMonda, C. S., Ossmy, O., & Adolph, K. E. (2018). The ties that bind: Cradling in Tajikistan. *PLoS ONE, 13*(10): e0204428. https://doi.org/10.1371/journal.pone.0204428

Karpinski, R. I., Kolb, A. M. K., Tetreault, N. A., & Borowski, T. B. (2018). High intelligence: A risk factor for psychological and physiological overexcitabilities. *Intelligence, 66,* 8–23. https://doi.org/10.1016/j.intell.2017.09.001

Kartner, J., Holodynski, M., & Wormann, V. (2013). Parental ethnotheories, social practice and the culture-specific development of social smiling in infants. *Mind, Culture, and Activity, 20,* 79–95. doi:10.1080/10749039.2012.74 2112

Kaste, M. (2015, January 2). Trial of polygraph critic renews debate over tests' accuracy. *NPR.* Retrieved from http://www.npr.org/2015/01/02/371925732/trialof-polygraph-criticrenews-debate-over-tests-accuracy

Katana, M., Röcke, C., Spain, S. M., & Allemand, M. (2019). Emotion regulation, subjective well-being, and perceived stress in daily life of geriatric nurses. *Frontiers in Psychology,* 10:1097. doi:10.3389/fpsyg.2019.01097

Kato, T., & Kanba, S. (2016). Boundless syndromes in modern society: An interconnected world producing novel psychopathology in the 21st century. *Psychiatry and Clinical Neurosciences, 70,* 1–2. http://dx.doi.org/10.1111/pcn.12368

Katzmarzyk, P. T., Chaput, J. P., Fogelholm, M., Hu, G., Maher, C., Maia, J., . . . Tudor-Locke, C. (2019). International study of childhood obesity, lifestyle and the environment (ISCOLE): Contributions to understanding the global obesity epidemic. *Nutrients, 11*(4), 848. doi:10.3390/nu11040848

Kaufman, S. B. (2019, January 4). The neuroscience of creativity: A Q&A with Anna Abraham. *Scientific American.* Retrieved from https://blogs.scientificamerican.com/beautiful-minds/the-neuroscience-of-creativity-a-q-a-with-anna-abraham/

Kaufman, S. B., Kozbelt, A., Silvia, P., Kaufman, J. C., Ramesh, S., & Feist, G. J. (2016). Who finds Bill Gates sexy? Creative mate preferences as a function of cognitive ability, personality, and creative achievement. *The Journal of Creative Behavior, 50,* 294–307. http://dx.doi.org/10.1002/jocb.78

Kaye, L. K., & Pennington, C. R. (2016). "Girls can't play": The effects of stereotype threat on females' gaming performance. *Computers in Human Behavior, 59,* 202–209. http://dx.doi.org/10.1016/j.chb.2016.02.020

Kearney, M. S., & Levine, P. B. (2015). Media influences on social outcomes: The impact of MTV's 16 and Pregnant on teen childbearing. *American Economic Review, 105,* 3597–3632. doi:10.1257/aer.20140012

Keating, J., Van Boven, L., & Judd, C. M. (2016). Partisan underestimation of the polarizing influence of group discussion. *Journal of Experimental Social Psychology, 65,* 52–58. http://dx.doi.org/10.1016/j.jesp.2016.03.002

Keatley, D. A., Allom, V., & Mullan, B. (2017). The effects of implicit and explicit self-control on self-reported aggression. *Personality and Individual Differences, 107,* 154–158. http://dx.doi.org/10.1016/j.paid.2016.11.046

Keats, D. M. (1982). Cultural bases of concepts of intelligence: A Chinese versus Australian comparison. In P. Sukontasarp, N. Yongsiri, P. Intasuwan, N. Jotiban, & C. Suvannathat (Eds.), *Proceedings of the second Asian workshop on child and adolescent development* (pp. 67–75). Bangkok, TH: Burapasilpa Press.

Keith, T. Z., Low, J. A., Reynolds, M. R., Patel, P. G., & Ridley, K. P. (2010). Higher-order factor structure of the Differential Ability Scales-II: Consistency across ages 4 to 17. *Psychology in the Schools, 47*(7), 676–697. https://doi.org/10.1002/pits.20498

Keles, B., McCrae, N., & Grealish, A. (2019). A systematic review: The influence of social media on depression, anxiety and psychological distress in adolescents. *International Journal of Adolescence and Youth.* doi:10.1080/02673843.2019.1590851

Keles, S., Idsøe, T., Friborg, O., Sirin, S., & Oppedal, B. (2017). The longitudinal relation between daily hassles and depressive symptoms among unaccompanied refugees in Norway. *Journal of Abnormal Child Psychology, 45*(7), 1413–1427. http://dx.doi.org/10.1007/s10802-016-0251-8

Keller, S. M., & Tuerk, P. W. (2016). Evidence-based psychotherapy (EBP) non-initiation among veterans offered an EBP for posttraumatic stress disorder. *Psychological Services, 13,* 42–48. http://dx.doi.org/10.1037/ser0000064

Kellner, C. H., Kaicher, D. C., Banerjee, H., Knapp, R. G., Shapiro, R. J., Briggs, M. C., . . . Liebman, L. S. (2015). Depression severity in electroconvulsive therapy (ECT) versus pharmacotherapy trials. *The Journal of ECT, 31,* 31–33. http://dx.doi.org/10.1097/YCT.0000000000000135

Kelly, D. L., Rowland, L. M., Patchan, K. M., Sullivan, K., Earl, A., Raley, H., . . . McMahon, R. P. (2016). Schizophrenia clinical symptom differences in women vs. men with and without a history of childhood physical abuse. *Child and Adolescent Psychiatry and Mental Health, 10,* Article 5. http://dx.doi.org/10.1186/s13034-016-0092-9

Keltner, D., Kogan, A., Piff, P. K., & Saturn, S. R. (2014). The sociocultural appraisals, values, and emotions (SAVE) framework of prosociality: Core processes from gene to meme. *Annual Review of Psychology, 65,* 425–460. http://dx.doi.org/10.1146/annurevpsych-010213-115054

Kemp, A. H., Krygier, J., & Harmon-Jones, E. (2015). Neuroscientific perspectives of emotion. In R. A. Calvo, S. K. D'Mello, J. Gratch, & A. Kappas (Eds.), *The Oxford handbook of affective computing* (pp. 38–53). New York, NY: Oxford. doi:10.1093/oxfordhb/9780199942237.013.016

Kendzerska, T., Mollayeva, T., Gershon, A. S., Leung, R. S., Hawker, G., & Tomlinson, G. (2014). Untreated obstructive sleep apnea and the risk for serious long-term adverse outcomes: A systematic review. *Sleep Medicine Reviews, 18,* 49–59. doi:10.1016/j.smrv.2013.01.003

Keneski, E., Neff, L. A., & Loving, T. J. (2018). The importance of a few good friends: Perceived network support moderates the association between daily marital conflict and diurnal cortisol. *Social Psychological and Personality Science, 9*(8), 962–971. https://doi.org/10.1177/1948550617731499

Kennard, B. D., Emslie, G. J., Mayes, T. L., Nakonezny, P. A., Jones, J. M., Foxwell, A. A., & King, J. (2014). Sequential treatment with fluoxetine and relapse-prevention CBT to improve outcomes in pediatric depression. *The American Journal of Psychiatry, 171,* 1083–1090.

Kenner, B. J. (2018). Early detection of pancreatic cancer: The role of depression and anxiety as a precursor for disease. *Pancreas, 47*(4), 363–367. doi:10.1097/MPA.0000000000001024

Kepner, T. (2016, May 23). Tony Gwynn's family sues tobacco industry, seeking recourse over fatal habit. *The New York Times.* Retrieved from http://www.nytimes.com/2016/05/24/sports/baseball/tony-gwynn-family-sues-tobacco-altria-death.html

Kerns, R. D., Sellinger, J., & Goodin, B. R. (2011). Psychological treatment of chronic pain. *Annual Review of Clinical Psychology, 7,* 411–434. http://dx.doi.org/10.1146/annurev-clinpsy-090310-120430

Kerr, D. C. R., Washburn, I. J., Morris, M. K., Lewis, K. A. G., & Tiberio, S. S. (2015). Event level associations of marijuana and heavy alcohol use with intercourse and condom use. *Journal of Studies on Alcohol and Drugs, 76*, 733–737.

Ketter, T. A., & Miller, S. (2015). Bipolar and related disorders. In L. W. Roberts & A. K. Louie (Eds.), *Study guide to DSM-5®* (pp. 99–111). Arlington, VA: American Psychiatric Publishing.

Keynan, J. N., Meir-Hasson, Y., Gilam, G., Cohen, A., Jackont, G., Kinreich, S., . . . Hendler, T. (2016). Limbic activity modulation guided by functional magnetic resonance imaging–inspired electroencephalography improves implicit emotion regulation. *Biological Psychiatry, 80*(6), 490–496. http://dx.doi.org/10.1016/j.biopsych.2015.12.024

Khalil, R., Godde, B., & Karim, A. A. (2019). The link between creativity, cognition, and creative drives and underlying neural mechanisms. *Frontiers in Neural Circuits, 13*, 18. doi:10.3389/fncir.2019.00018

Khandaker, G. M., Zuber, V., Rees, J. M. B., Carvalho, L., Mason, A. M., Foley, C. N., . . . Burgess, S. (2019). Shared mechanisms between coronary heart disease and depression: Findings from a large UK general population-based cohort. *Molecular Psychiatry.* doi:10.1038/s41380-019-0395-3

Khan, R., Brewer, G., Kim, S., & Centifanti, L. C. M. (2017). Students, sex, and psychopathy: Borderline and psychopathy personality traits are differently related to women and men's use of sexual coercion, partner poaching, and promiscuity. *Personality and Individual Differences, 107*, 72–77. http://dx.doi.org/10.1016/j.paid.2016.11.027

Khosla, N. N., Perry, S. P., Moss-Racusin, C. A., Burke, S. E., & Dovidio, J. F. (2018). A comparison of clinicians' racial biases in the United States and France. *Social Science & Medicine, 206*, 31–37. https://doi.org/10.1016/j.socscimed.2018.03.044.

Killen, M., & Hart, D. (1999). *Morality in everyday life: Developmental perspectives.* New York, NY: Cambridge University Press.

Killen, M., Hitti, A., & Mulvey, K. L. (2015). Social development and intergroup relations. In M. Mikulincer, P. R. Shaver, J. F. Dovidio, & J. A. Simpson (Eds.), *APA handbook of personality and social psychology, Vol. 2. Group processes* (pp. 177–201). Washington, DC: American Psychological Association. http://dx.doi.org/10.1037/14342-007

Kilpatrick, L. A., Suyenobu, B. Y., Smith, S. R., Bueller, J. A., Goodman, T., Creswell, J. D., . . . Naliboff, B. D. (2011). Impact of mindfulness-based stress reduction training on intrinsic brain connectivity. *NeuroImage, 56*, 290–298.

Kim, A., Kim, Y., Han, K., Jackson, S. E., & Ployhart, R. E. (2017a). Multilevel influences on voluntary workplace green behavior: Individual differences, leader behavior, and coworker advocacy. *Journal of Management, 43*(5), 1335–1358. http://dx.doi.org/10.1177/0149206314547386

Kim, D. S., Burt, A. A., Ranchalis, J. E., Wilmot, B., Smith, J. D., Patterson, K. E., . . . Jarvik, G. P. (2017). Sequencing of sporadic Attention-Deficit Hyperactivity Disorder (ADHD) identifies novel and potentially pathogenic de novo variants and excludes overlap with genes associated with autism spectrum disorder. *American Journal of Medical Genetics Part B: Neuropsychiatric Genetics, 174*(4), 381–389. http://dx.doi.org/10.1002/ajmg.b.32527

Kim, K., del Carmen Triana, M., Chung, K., & Oh, N. (2016). When do employees cyberloaf? An interactionist perspective examining personality, justice, and empowerment. *Human Resource Management, 55*(6), 1041–1058. http://dx.doi.org/10.1002/hrm.21699

Kim, K. H. (2011). The creativity crisis: The decrease in creative thinking scores on the Torrance Tests of Creative Thinking. *Creativity Research Journal, 23*(4), 285–295. doi:10.1080/10400419.2011.627805

Kim, L. E., Jörg, V., & Klassen, R. M. (2019). A meta-analysis of the effects of teacher personality on teacher effectiveness and burnout. *Educational Psychology, 31*(1), 163–195. doi:10.1007/s10648-018-9458-2

Kim, S. T., & Park, T. (2019). Acute and chronic effects of cocaine on cardiovascular health. *International Journal of Molecular Sciences, 20*(3), 584. doi:10.3390/ijms20030584

Kim, U., & Choi, S. (1995). Individualism, collectivism, and child development: A Korean perspective. In P. M. Greenfield & R. R. Cocking (Eds.), *Cross-cultural roots of minority child development* (pp. 227–257). Hillsdale, NJ: Erlbaum.

Kim, Y.-K., Na, K.-S., Myint, A.-M., & Leonard, B. E. (2016). The role of pro-inflammatory cytokines in neuroinflammation, neurogenesis and the neuroendocrine system in major depression. *Progress in Neuro-Psychopharmacology & Biological Psychiatry, 64*, 277–284. http://dx.doi.org/10.1016/j.pnpbp.2015.06.008

Kim, Y.-K., Na, K.-S., Myint, A.-M., & Leonard, B. E. (2016). The role of proinflammatory cytokines in neuroinflammation, neurogenesis and the neuroendocrine system in major depression. *Progress in Neuro-Psychopharmacology & Biological Psychiatry, 64*, 277–284. http://dx.doi.org/10.1016/j.pnpbp.2015.06.008

Kim, Y., Morath, B., Hu, C., Byrne, L. K., Sutor, S. L., Frye, M. A., & Tye, S. J. (2016). Antidepressant actions of lateral habenula deep brain stimulation differentially correlate with CaMKII/GSK3/AMPK signaling locally and in the infralimbic cortex. *Behavioural Brain Research, 306*, 170–177. http://dx.doi.org/10.1016/j.bbr.2016.02.039

King, B. M., & Regan, P. (2015). *Human sexuality today* (8th ed.). Upper Saddle River, NJ: Pearson.

King, D. B., & DeLongis, A. (2013). Dyadic coping with stepfamily conflict: Demand and withdraw responses between husbands and wives. *Journal of Social and Personal Relationships, 30,* 198–206. doi:10.1177/0265407512454524

Kingston, D. A. (2016). Hypersexuality disorders and sexual offending. In A. Phenix & H. M. Hoberman (Eds.), *Sexual offending: Predisposing antecedents, assessments and management* (pp. 103–118). New York, NY: Springer Science + Business Media. http://dx.doi.org/10.1007/978-1-4939-2416-5_7

Kinsey, A. C., Pomeroy, W. B., & Martin, C. E. (1948). *Sexual behavior in the human male.* Oxford, UK: Saunders.

Kinsey, A. C., Pomeroy, W. B., Martin, C. E., & Gebhard, P. H. (1953). *Sexual behavior in the human female.* Oxford, UK: Saunders.

Kircaburun, K., & Griffiths, M. D. (2018). Instagram addiction and the Big Five of personality: The mediating role of self-liking. *Journal of Behavioral Addictions, 7*(1), 158–170. doi:10.1556/2006.7.2018.15

Kirk, D. S., & Hardy, M. (2014). The acute and enduring consequences of exposure to violence on youth mental health and aggression. *Justice Quarterly, 31*, 539–567. doi:10.1080/07418825.2012.737471

Kirk, E., Gurney, D., Edwards, R., & Dodimead, C. (2015). Handmade memories: The robustness of the gestural misinformation effect in children's eyewitness interviews. *Journal of Nonverbal Behavior, 39*, 259–273. http://dx.doi.org/10.1007/s10919-015-0210-z

Kirschner, H., Kuyken, W., Wright, K., Roberts, H., Brejcha, & Karl, A. (2019). Soothing your heart and feeling connected: A new experimental paradigm to study the benefits of self-compassion. *Psychological Science, 7*(3), 545–565. https://doi.org/10.1177/2167702618812438

Kishimoto, T., Chawla, J. M., Hagi, K., Zarate, C. A., Kane, J. M., Bauer, M., & Correll, C. U. (2016). Single-dose infusion ketamine and non-ketamine n-methyl-d-aspartate receptor antagonists for unipolar and bipolar depression: A meta-analysis of efficacy, safety and time trajectories. *Psychological Medicine, 46*, 1459–1472. http://dx.doi.org/10.1017/S0033291716000064

Kite, M. E. (2013). Teaching about race and ethnicity. In D. S. Dunn, R. A. R. Gurung, K. Z. Naufel, & J. H. Wilson (Eds.), *Controversy in the psychology classroom: Using hot topics to foster critical thinking* (pp. 169–184). Washington, DC: American Psychological Association.

Kivimäki, M., Nyberg, S. J., Batty, G. D., Fransson, E. I., Heikkila, K., Alfredsson, L., . . . Theorell, T. (2012). Job strain as a risk factor for coronary heart disease: A collaborative metaanalysis of individual participant data. *Lancet, 380*, 1491–1497. http://dx.doi.org/10.1016/S0140-6736(12)60994-5

Klahr, A. M., & Burt, S. A. (2014). Elucidating the etiology of individual differences in parenting: A meta-analysis of behavioral genetic research. *Psychological Bulletin, 140*, 544–586. http://dx.doi.org/10.1037/a0034205

Klasen, M., Wolf, D., Eisner, P. D., Eggermann, T., Zerres, K., Zepf, F. D., . . . Mathiak, K. (2019). Serotonergic contributions to human brain aggression networks. *Frontiers in Neuroscience, 13*, 42. doi:10.3389/fnins.2019.00042

Kleiman, E. M., Chiara, A. M., Liu, R. T., Jager-Hyman, S. G., Choi, J. Y., & Alloy, L. B. (2017). Optimism and well-being: A prospective multi-method and multi-dimensional examination of optimism as a resilience factor following the occurrence of stressful life events. *Cognition and Emotion, 31*(2), 269–283. http://dx.doi.org/10.1080/02699931.2015.110 8284

Klein, R. M., Dilchert, S., Ones, D. S., & Dages, K. D. (2015). Cognitive predictors and age-based adverse impact among business executives. *Journal of Applied Psychology, 100,* 1497–1510. http://dx.doi.org/10.1037/a0038991

Klink, M. (Ed.). (2014). *Interaction of immune and cancer cells*. Vienna, AT: Springer.

Knapen, J., Vancampfort, D., Moriën, Y., & Marchal, Y. (2015). Exercise therapy improves both mental and physical health in patients with major depression. *Disability and Rehabilitation, 37*(16), 1490–1495. doi:10.3109/09638288.2014.972579

Kneeland, R. E., & Fatemi, S. H. (2013). Viral infection, inflammation and schizophrenia. *Progress in Neuro-Psychopharmacology & Biological Psychiatry, 42*, 35–48. http://doi.org/10.1016/j.pnpbp.2012.02.001

Knobloch-Fedders, L. M., Critcheld, K. L., Boisson, T., Woods, N., Bitman, R., & Durbin, C. E. (2014). Depression, relationship quality, and couples' demand/withdraw and demand/submit sequential interactions. *Journal of Counseling Psychology, 61*, 264–279. http://dx.doi.org/10.1037/a0035241

Knutson, J. (2019, May 23). Walking and texting: Should it be illegal while crossing streets? NewsChannel5. Retrieved from https://www.newschannel5.com/news/walking-and-texting-should-it-be-illegal-while-crossing-streets

Koblin, J., & Steel, E. (2015). Brian Williams gts new role at lower salary. *The New York Times*. https://www.nytimes.com/2015/06/19/business/media/brian-williams-nbc-lester-holt.html

Kohlberg, L. (1964). Development of moral character and moral behavior. In L. W. Hoffman & M. L. Hoffman (Eds.), *Review of child development research* (Vol. 1, pp. 381–431). New York, NY: Sage.

Kohlberg, L. (1984). *The psychology of moral development: Essays on moral development* (Vol. 2). San Francisco, CA: Harper & Row.

Köhler, W. (1925). *The mentality of apes.* New York, NY: Harcourt Brace Jovanovich.

Koike, S., Yamaguchi, S., Ohta, K., Ojio, Y., Watanabe, K.-I., & Ando, S. (2017). Mental-health-related stigma among Japanese children and their parents and impact of renaming of schizophrenia. *Psychiatry and Clinical Neurosciences, 71*(3), 170–179. http://dx.doi.org/10.1111/pcn.12423

Kojima, T., Karino, S., Yumoto, M., & Funayama, M. (2014). A stroke patient with impairment of auditory sensory (echoic) memory. *Neurocase, 20,* 133–143. http://dx.doi.org/10.1080/13554794.2012.732091

Kokolus, K., Spangler, H., Povinelli, B., Farren, M., Lee, K., & Repasky, E. (2014). Stressful presentations: Mild chronic cold stress in mice influences baseline properties of dendritic cells. *Frontiers in Immunology, 5*, 23. doi:10.3389/fimmu.2014.00023

Konecni, V. J. (2015). The anger-aggression bidirectional-causation (AABC) model's relevance for dyadic violence, revenge, and catharsis. *Abnormal Behavioral Psychology, 1*:104. doi:10.4172/abp.1000104

Kongthong, N., Minami, T., & Nakauchi, S. (2014). Gamma oscillations distinguish mere exposure from other likability effects. *Neuropsychologia, 54,* 129–138. http://dx.doi.org/10.1016/j.neuropsychologia.2013.12.021

Konnikova, M. (2014, Jan. 14). Goodnight. Sleep clean. *The New York Times.* Retrieved from http://www.nytimes.com/2014/01/12/opinion/sunday/goodnight-sleep-clean.html?nl=todaysheadlines&emc=edit_th_20140112&_r=0

Konnikova, M. (2016, February 11). How people learn to become resilient. *The New Yorker.* Retrieved from http://www.newyorker.com/science/maria-konnikova/the-secret-formulafor-resilience

Konrath, S. H., O'Brien, E. H., & Hsing, C. (2011). Changes in dispositional empathy in American college students over time: A meta-analysis. *Personality and Social Psychology Review, 15*(2), 180–198. doi:10.1177/1088868310377395.

Koo, C., Chung, N., & Nam, K. (2015). Assessing the impact of intrinsic and extrinsic motivators on smart green IT device use: Reference group perspectives. *International Journal of Information Management, 35,* 64–79. http://dx.doi.org/10.1016/j.ijinfomgt.2014.10.001

Koocher, G. P., McMann, M. R., Stout, A. O., & Norcross, J. C. (2014). Discredited assessment and treatment methods used with children and adolescents: A Delphi Poll. *Journal of Clinical Child & Adolescent Psychology, 25*, 1–8. http://dx.doi.org/10.1080/15374416.2014.895941

Kooij, J. J. S., Brjlenga, D., Salerno, L., Jaeschke, R., Bitter, I., Balázs, J., . . . Asherson, P. (2019). Updated European Consensus Statement on diagnosis and treatment of adult ADHD. *European Psychiatry, 56,* 14–34. https://doi.org/10.1016/j.eurpsy.2018.11.001

Kopala-Sibley, D. C., Olino, T., Durbin, E., Dyson, M. W., & Klein, D. N. (2018). The stability of temperament from early childhood to early adolescence: A multi-method, multi-informant examination. *European Journal of Personality, 32*(2), 128–145. doi:10.1002/per.2151

Korten, N. C. M., Comijs, H. C., Penninx, B. W. J. H., & Deeg, D. J. H. (2017). Perceived stress and cognitive function in older adults: Which aspect of perceived stress is important? *International Journal of Geriatric Psychiatry, 32*(4), 439–445. http://dx.doi.org/10.1002/gps.4486

Kose, S., Steinberg, J. L., Moeller, F. G., Gowin, J. L., Zuniga, E., Kamdar, Z. N., . . . Lane, S. D. (2015). Neural correlates of impulsive aggressive behavior in subjects with a history of alcohol dependence. *Behavioral Neuroscience, 129,* 183–196. http://dx.doi.org/10.1037/bne0000038.

Kotagal, S., & Kumar, S. (2013). Childhood onset narcolepsy cataplexy-more than just a sleep disorder. *Sleep, 36,* 161–162.

Kotowski, A. (2012). Case study: A young male with auditory hallucinations in paranoid schizophrenia. *International Journal of Nursing Knowledge, 23,* 41–44. doi:10.1111/j.2047-3095.2011.01197.x

Koutsimani, P., Montgomery, A., & Georganta, K. (2019). The relationship between burnout, depression, and anxiety: A systematic review and meta-analysis. *Frontiers in Psychology, 10,* 284. doi:10.3389/fpsyg.2019.00284

Kovacs, K., & Conway, A. R. A. (2019). What is IQ? Life beyond "general intelligence." *Current Directions in Psychological Science, 28*(2), 189–194. https://doi.org/10.1177/0963721419827275

Kovas, Y., Garon-Carrier, G., Boivin, M., Petrill, S. A., Plomin, R., Malykh, S. B., . . . Vitaro, F. (2015). Why children differ in motivation to learn: Insights from over 13,000 twins from 6 countries. *Personality and Individual Differences, 80,* 51–63. http://dx.doi.org/10.1016/j.paid.2015.02.006

Kovera, M., & Evelo, A. (2017). The case for double-blind lineup administration. *Psychology, Public Policy, and Law, 23.* doi:10.1037/law0000139.

Krahn, L. E., Tovar, M. D., & Miller, B. (2015). Are pets in the bedroom a problem? *Mayo Clinic Proceedings, 90*(12), 1663–1665. doi:10.1016/j.mayocp.2015.08.012

Kraybill, J. H., Kim-Spoon, J., & Bell, M. A. (2019). Infant attention and age 3 executive function. *The Yale Journal of Biology and Medicine, 92*(1), 3–11. https://www.ncbi.nlm.nih.gov/pmc/articles/PMC6430162/

Kreager, D. A., Staff, J., Gauthier, R., Lefkowitz, E. S., & Feinberg, M. E. (2016). The double standard at sexual debut: Gender, sexual behavior and adolescent peer acceptance. *Sex Roles, 75,* 377–392. http://dx.doi.org/10.1007/s11199-016-0618-x

Kreger Silverman, L. (2013). *Psych 101: Giftedness 101.* New York, NY: Springer.

Kreitz, C., Furley, P., Simons, D., & Memmert, D. (2016). Does working memory capacity predict cross-modally induced failures of awareness? *Consciousness and Cognition: An International Journal, 39,* 18–27. http://dx.doi.org/10.1016/j.concog.2015.11.010

Kress, V. E., Hoffman, R. M., Adamson, N., & Eriksen, K. (2013). Informed consent, confidentiality, and diagnosing: Ethical guidelines for counselor practice. *Journal of Mental Health Counseling, 35,* 15–28. http://essential.metapress.com/content/5q82020u18r46007/

Kring, A. M., & Johnson, S. L. (2018). *Abnormal psychology: The science and treatment of psychological disorders* (14th ed.). Hoboken, NJ: Wiley.

Kring, A. M., Johnson, S. L., Davison, G. C., & Neale, J. M. (2010). *Abnormal psychology* (11th ed.). Hoboken, NJ: Wiley.

Krippner, S. (2015). Finding gender differences in dream reports. In M. Kramer & M. Glucksman (Eds.), *Dream research: Contributions to clinical practice* (pp. 56–66). New York, NY: Routledge.

Krishna, G. (1999). *The dawn of a new science.* Los Angeles, CA: Institute for Consciousness Research.

Kroger, J. (2015). Identity development through adulthood: The move toward "wholeness." In K. C. McLean & M. Syed (Eds.), *The Oxford handbook of identity development* (pp. 65–80). New York, NY: Oxford University Press.

Krumhuber, E. G., Likowski, K. U., & Weyers, P. (2014). Facial mimicry of spontaneous and deliberate Duchenne and non-Duchenne smiles. *Journal of Nonverbal Behavior, 38,* 1–11. doi:10.1007/s10919-013-0167-8

Krys, K., Hansen, K., Xing, C., Szarota, P., & Yang, M. M. (2014). Do only fools smile at strangers? Cultural differences in social perception of intelligence of smiling individuals. *Journal of Cross-Cultural Psychology, 45,* 314–321. http://dx.doi.org/10.1177/0022022113513922

Ksiazkiewicz, A., Ludeke, S., & Krueger, R. (2016). The role of cognitive style in the link between genes and political ideology. *Political Psychology, 37*(6), 761–776. http://dx.doi.org/10.1111/pops.12318

Kuchenbrandt, D., Eyssel, F., & Seidel, S. K. (2013). Cooperation makes it happen: Imagined intergroup cooperation enhances the positive effects of imagined contact. *Group Processes & Intergroup Relations, 16,* 636–648. http://dx.doi.org/10.1177/1368430212470172

Kucirkova, N. (2019). How could children's storybooks promote empathy? A conceptual framework based on developmental psychology and literary theory. *Frontiers in Psychology, 10,* 121. doi:10.3389/fpsyg.2019.00121

Kuczaj, S. A. (2017). Animal creativity and innovation. In J. Call, G. M. Burghardt, I. M. Pepperberg, C. T. Snowdon, & T. Zentall (Eds.), *APA handbook of comparative psychology: Perception, learning, and cognition, Vol. 2* (pp. 627–641). Washington, DC: American Psychological Association. http://dx.doi.org/10.1037/0000012-028

Kuehner, C. (2017). Why is depression more common among women than among men? *The Lancet Psychiatry, 4*(2), 146–158. http://dx.doi.org/10.1016/S2215-0366(16)30263-2

Kühn, S., Gleich, T., Lorenz, R. C., Lindenberger, U., & Gallinat, J. (2014). Playing Super Mario induces structural brain plasticity: Gray matter changes resulting from training with a commercial video game. *Molecular Psychiatry, 19,* 265–271. http://dx.doi.org/10.1038/mp.2013.120

Kühn, S., Kugler, D. T., Schmalen, K., Weichenberger, M. Witt, C., & Gallinat, J. (2019). Does playing violent video games cause aggression? A longitudinal intervention study. *Molecular Psychiatry, 24,* 1220–1234. Retrieved from https://doi.org/10.1038/s41380-018-0031-7

Kuijper, S. J. M., Hartman, C. A., Bogaerds-Hazenberg, S. T. M., & Hendriks, P. (2017). Narrative production in children with autism spectrum disorder (ASD) and children with attention-deficit/hyperactivity disorder (ADHD): Similarities and differences. *Journal of Abnormal Psychology, 126,* 63–75. http://dx.doi.org/10.1037/abn0000231

Kuiper, N., Kirsh, G., & Maiolino, N. (2016). Identity and intimacy development, humor styles, and psychological well-being. *Identity: An International Journal of Theory and Research, 16,* 115–125. http://dx.doi.org/10.1080/15283488.2016.1159964

Kuitenbrouwer, P. (2011, December 28). The evil of Aries: Could astrology help point to future jail time? *National Post.* Retrieved from https://nationalpost.com/news/astrology-as-a-sign-of-future-jail-time-experts-remain-skeptical

Kulkarni, S. S., Dewitt, B., Fischhoff, B., Rosengart, M. R., Angus, D. C., Saul, M., . . . Mohan, D. (2019). Defining the representativeness heuristic in trauma triage: A retrospective observational cohort study. *PLoS ONE, 14*(2): e0212201. https://doi.org/10.1371/journal.pone.0212201

Kumari, V., Uddin, S., Premkumar, P., Young, S., Gudjonsson, G. H., Raghuvanshi, S., . . . Das, M. (2014). Lower anterior cingulate volume in seriously violent men with antisocial personality disorder or schizophrenia and a history of childhood abuse. *Australian and New Zealand Journal of Psychiatry, 48,* 153–161. http://dx.doi.org/10.1177/0004867413512690

Kumin, L. (2015). Intellectual disability. In M. R. Kerins (Ed.), *Child and adolescent communication disorders: Organic and neurogenic bases* (pp. 99–151). San Diego, CA: Plural.

Kundu, P., & Cummins, D. D. (2013). Morality and conformity: The Asch paradigm applied to moral decisions. *Social Influence, 8*, 268–279. http://dx.doi.org/10.1080/15534510.2012.727767

Kupferschmidt, K. (2019, April 11). Can atmospheric chemists rescue the stalled quest for a human pheromone? *Science*. doi:10.1126/science.aax6630

Kuppens, S., & Ceulemans, E. J. (2019). Parenting styles: A closer look at a well-known concept. *Journal of Child and Family Studies, 28*(1), 168–181. https://doi.org/10.1007/s10826-018-1242-x

Ku, P.-W., Steptoe, A., & Chen, L.-J. (2017). Prospective associations of exercise and depressive symptoms in older adults: The role of apolipoprotein e4. *Quality of Life Research: An International Journal of Quality of Life Aspects of Treatment, Care & Rehabilitation, 26*(7), 1799–1808. http://dx.doi.org/10.1007/s11136-017-1537-1

Kurian, J. R., Olesen, K. M., & Auger, A. P. (2010). Sex differences in epigenetic regulation of the estrogen receptor-alpha promoter within the developing preoptic area. *Endocrinology, 151*(5), 2297–2305. doi:10.1210/en.2009-0649

Kurth, F., MacKenzie-Graham, A., Toga, A. W., & Luders, E. (2014). Shifting brain asymmetry: The link between meditation and structural lateralization. *Social Cognitive and Affective Neuroscience, 10*, 55–61. http://dx.doi.org/10.1093/scan/nsu029

Kurzban, R. (2014). Covert sexual signaling: Human flirtation and implications for other social species. *Evolutionary Psychology, 12*, 549–569.

Kurzban, R., Burton-Chellew, M. N., & West, S. A. (2015). The evolution of altruism in humans. *Annual Review of Psychology, 66*, 575–599. doi:10.1146/annurev-psych-010814-015355

Kushlev, K., & Dunn, E. W. (2015). Checking email less frequently reduces stress. *Computers in Human Behavior, 43*, 220–228. http://dx.doi.org/10.1016/j.chb.2014.11.005

Kushlev, K., Dunn, E. W., & Lucan, R. E. (2015). Higher income is associated with less daily sadness but not more daily happiness. *Social Psychological and Personality Science, 6*, 483–489. http://dx.doi.org/10.1177/1948550614568161

Kushlev, K., & Heintzelman, S. J. (2018). Put the phone down: Testing a complement–interfere model of computer-mediated communication in the context of face-to-face interactions. *Social Psychological and Personality Science, 9*, 702–710. https://doi.org/10.1177/1948550617722199

Kushner, D. S., Verano, J. W., & Titelbaum, A. R. (2018). Trepanation procedures/outcomes: Comparison of prehistoric Peru with other ancient, medieval, and American Civil War cranial surgery. *World Neurosurgery, 114*, 245–251. https://doi.org/10.1016/j.wneu.2018.03.143

Kuther, T. L., & Burnell, K. (2019). A life span developmental perspective on psychosocial development in midlife. *Adultspan Journal, 18*, 27–39. doi:10.1002/adsp.12067

Kvam, S., Kleppe, C. L., Nordhus, I. H., & Hovland, A. (2016). Exercise as a treatment for depression: A meta-analysis. *Journal of Affective Disorders, 202*, 67–86. http://dx.doi.org/10.1016/j.jad.2016.03.063

Kyaga, S., Landén, M., Boman, M., Hultman, C. M., Långström, N., & Lichtenstein, P. (2012). Mental illness, suicide and creativity: 40-year prospective total population study. *Journal of Psychiatric Research, 47*, 83–90. doi:10.1016/j.jpsychires.2012.09.010

Labouesse, M. A., Lassalle, O., Richetto, J., Iafrati, J., Weber-Stadlbauer, U., Notter, T., . . . Meyer, U. (2017). Hypervulnerability of the adolescent prefrontal cortex to nutritional stress via reelin deficiency. *Molecular Psychiatry, 22*, 961–971. http://dx.doi.org/10.1038/mp.2016.193

Lacagnina, A. F., Brockway, E. T., Crovetti, C. R., Shue, F., McCarty, M. J., Sattler, K. P., . . . Drew, M. R. (2019). Distinct hippocampal engrams control extinction and relapse of fear memory. *Nature Neuroscience, 22*(5), 753–761. doi:10.1038/s41593-019-0361-z

Lafleur, A., & Boucher, V. J. (2015). The ecology of self-monitoring effects on memory of verbal productions: Does speaking to someone make a difference? *Consciousness and Cognition, 36*, 139–146. http://dx.doi.org/10.1016/j.concog.2015.06.015

Laier, C., Schulte, F. P., & Brand, M. (2013). Pornographic picture processing interferes with working memory performance. *Journal of Sex Research, 50*, 642–652. http://dx.doi.org/10.1080/00224499.2012.716873.

Laird, K. T., Krause, B., Funes, C., & Lavretsky, H. (2019). Psychobiological factors of resilience and depression in late life. *Translational Psychiatry, 9*(1), 88. doi:10.1038/s41398-019-0424-7

Lai, V. T., & Narasimhan, B. (2015). Verb representation and thinking-for-speaking effects in Spanish-English bilinguals. In R. G. de Almeida & C. Manouilidou (Eds.), *Cognitive science perspectives on verb representation and processing* (pp. 235–256). Cham, CH: Springer. http://dx.doi.org/10.1007/978-3-319-10112-5_11

Lake, E. M. R., Steffler, E. A., Rowley, C. D., Sehmbi, M., Minuzzi, L., Frey, B. N., & Bock, N. A. (2017). Altered intracortical myelin staining in the dorsolateral prefrontal cortex in severe mental illness. *European Archives of Psychiatry and Clinical Neuroscience, 267*(5), 369–376. https://doi.org/10.1007/s00406-016-0730-5

Lamm, B. (2015). Developmental research across cultures and nations: Challenges, biases, and cautions. In J. D. Wright (Ed.), *International encyclopedia of the social & behavioral sciences* (2nd ed., pp. 326–331). New York, NY: Elsevier. https://doi.org/10.1016/B978-0-08-097086-8.23159-0

LaMotte, A. D., Taft, C. T., Weatherill, R. P., Casement, M. D., Creech, S. K., Milberg, W. P., . . . McGlinchey, R. E. (2017). Sleep problems and physical pain as moderators of the relationship between PTSD symptoms and aggression in returning veterans. *Psychological Trauma: Theory, Research, Practice, and Policy, 9*(1), 113–116. http://dx.doi.org/10.1037/tra0000178

Lampinen, J. M., & Beike, D. R. (2015). *Memory 101. The psych 101 series*. New York, NY: Springer.

Lanciano, T., Curci, A., Matera, G., & Sartori, G. (2018). Measuring the flashbulb-like nature of memories for private events: The flashbulb memory checklist. *Memory, 26*(8), 1053–1064. doi:10.1080/09658211.2018.1428348

Landeira-Fernandez, J. (2015). Participation of NMDA receptors in the lateral hypothalamus in gastric erosion induced by cold-water restraint. *Physiology & Behavior, 140*, 209–214. http://dx.doi.org/10.1016/j.physbeh.2014.12.038

Landers, R. N., & Schmidt, G. B. (2016). *Social media in employee selection and recruitment*. Cham, CH: Springer International Publishing.

Landler, M. (2012). From Biden, a vivid account of Bin Laden decision. *The New York Times*. Retrieved from http://thecaucus.blogs.nytimes.com/2012/01/30/from-biden-avivid-account-of-bin-ladendecision/

Landová, E., Bakhshaliyeva, N., Janovcová, M., Peléšková, Š., Suleymanova, M., Polák, J., . . . Frynta, D. (2018). Association between fear and beauty evaluation of snakes: Cross-cultural findings. *Frontiers in Psychology, 9,* 333. Retrieved from doi:10.3389/fpsyg.2018.00333

Lange, B. P., & Euler, H. A. (2014). Writers have groupies, too: High quality literature production and mating success. *Evolutionary Behavioral Sciences, 8,* 20–30. http://dx.doi.org/10.1037/h0097246

Langmeyer, A., Guglhör-Rudan, A., & Tarnai, C. (2012). What do music preferences reveal about personality? A cross-cultural replication using self-ratings and ratings of music samples. *Journal of Individual Differences, 33,* 119–130. https://doi.org/10.1027/1614-0001/a000082

Lapré, G., & Marsee, M. A. (2016). The role of race in the association between corporal punishment and externalizing problems: Does punishment severity matter? *Journal of Child and Family Studies, 25,* 432–441. http://dx.doi.org/10.1007/s10826-015-0250-3

Lariscy, R. A. W., & Tinkham, S. F. (1999). The sleeper effect and negative political advertising. *Journal of Advertising, 28,* 13–30.

Larrick, R. P., Timmerman, T. A., Carton, A. M., & Abrevaya, J. (2011). Temper, temperature, and temptation: Heat-related retaliation in baseball. *Psychological Science, 22,* 423–428. http://dx.doi.org/10.1177/0956797611399292

Larzelere, M. M., & Campbell, J. S. (2016). Disordered sleep. In M. A. Burg & O. Oyama (Eds.), *The behavioral health specialist in primary care: Skills for integrated practice* (pp. 161–183). New York, NY: Springer.

Lasalvia, A., Penta, E., Sartorius, N., & Henderson, S. (2015). Should the label "schizophrenia" be abandoned? *Schizophrenia Research, 162,* 276–284. http://dx.doi.org/10.1016/j.schres.2015.01.031

Lassek, W. D., & Gaulin, S. J. C. (2016). What makes Jessica rabbit sexy? Contrasting roles of waist and hip size. *Evolutionary Psychology, 14*(2), 1–16. http://dx.doi.org/10.1177/1474704916643459

Latané, B., & Darley, J. M. (1968). Group inhibition of bystander intervention in emergencies. *Journal of Personality and Social Psychology, 10,* 215–221.

Latané, B., Williams, K., & Harkins, S. (1979). Many hands make light the work: The causes and consequences of social loafing. *Journal of Personality and Social Psychology, 37*(6), 822–832. http://dx.doi.org/10.1037/0022-3514.37.6.822

Latham, G. P. (2016). Goal-setting theory: Causal relationships, mediators, and moderators. *Organizational and Institutional Psychology.* doi:10.1093/acrefore/9780190236557.013.12

Latzman, R. D., Freeman, H. D., Schapiro, S. J., & Hopkins, W. D. (2015). The contribution of genetics and early rearing experiences to hierarchical personality dimensions in chimpanzees (Pan troglodytes). *Journal of Personality and Social Psychology, 109,* 889–900. http://dx.doi.org/10.1037/pspp0000040

Laungani, P. D. (2007). *Understanding cross-cultural psychology.* Thousand Oaks, CA: Sage.

Lavner, J. A., & Bradbury, T. N. (2012). Why do even satisfied newlyweds eventually go on to divorce? *Journal of Family Psychology, 26,* 1–10. http://dx.doi.org/10.1037/a0025966

Lavner, J. A., Weiss, B., Miller, J. D., & Karney, B. R. (2018). Personality change among newlyweds: Patterns, predictors, and associations with marital satisfaction over time. *Developmental Psychology, 54*(6), 1172–1185. http://dx.doi.org/10.1037/dev0000491

Lavy, V., & Sand, E. (2015). On the origins of gender human capital gaps: Short and long term consequences of teachers' stereotypical biases. *National Bureau of Economic Research, Working Paper No. 20909.*

Lawes-Wickwar, S., McBain, H., & Mulligan, K. (2018). Application and effectiveness of telehealth to support severe mental illness management: Systematic review. *JMIR Mental Health, 5*(4):e62. doi:10.2196/mental.8816

Lawrence, H. R., Nangle, D. W., Schwartz-Mette, R. A., & Erdley, C. A. (2017). Medication for child and adolescent depression: Questions, answers, clarifications, and caveats. *Practice Innovations, 2*(1), 39–53. http://dx.doi.org/10.1037/pri0000042

Layous, K., Davis, E. M., Garcia, J., Purdie-Vaughns, V., Cook, J. E., & Cohen, G. L. (2017). Feeling left out, but affirmed: Protecting against the negative effects of low belonging in college. *Journal of Experimental Social Psychology, 69,* 227–231. http://dx.doi.org/10.1016/j.jesp.2016.09.008

Layton, T. J., Barnett, M. L., Hicks, T. R., & Jena, A. B. (2018). Attention deficit-hyperactivity disorder and month of school enrollment. *New England Journal of Medicine, 379,* 2122–2130. doi:10.1056/NEJMoa1806828

Lazaridis, I., Tzortzi, O., Weglage, M., Märtin, A., Xuan, Y., Parent, M., . . . Meletis, K. (2019). A hypothalamus-habenula circuit controls aversion. *Molecular Psychiatry, 24*(9), 1351–1368. https://doi.org/10.1038/s41380-019-0369-5

Leaper, C. (2013). Gender development during childhood. In P. D. Zelazo (Ed.), *Oxford handbook of developmental psychology* (pp. 327–377). New York, NY: Oxford University Press.

Leaper, C. (2019). Young adults' conversational strategies during negotiation and self-disclosure in same-gender and mixed gender friendships. *Sex Roles, 81,* 561–575. doi:10.1007/s11199-019-1014-0

Lea, R. G., Davis, S. K., Mahoney, B., & Qualter, P. (2019) Does emotional intelligence buffer the effects of acute stress? A systematic review. *Frontiers in Psychology, 10,* 810. doi:10.3389/fpsyg.2019.00810

Lease, H., Hendrie, G. A., Poelman, A. A. M., Delahunty, C., & Cox, D. N. (2016). A Sensory-Diet database: A tool to characterize the sensory qualities of diets. *Food Quality and Preference, 49,* 20–32. doi:10.1016/j.foodqual.2015.11.010

Leblond, M., Laisney, M., Lamidey, V., Egret, S., de La Sayette, V., Chételat, G., . . . Eustache, F. (2016). Self-reference effect on memory in healthy aging, mild cognitive impairment and Alzheimer's disease: Influence of identity valence. *Cortex, 74,* 177–190. http://dx.doi.org/10.1016/j.cortex.2015.10.017

Lebowitz, M. S., & Dovidio, J. F. (2015). Implications of emotion regulation strategies for empathic concern, social attitudes, and helping behavior. *Emotion, 15,* 187–194. http://dx.doi.org/10.1037/a0038820

Lebowitz, S. (2017, November 30). Jay-Z says "therapy gave him a huge advantage in everyday life." *Business Insider.* Retrieved from https://www.businessinsider.com/jay-z-therapy-gave-him-huge-advantage-everyday-life-2017-11

LeDoux, J. E. (1996). *The emotional brain: The mysterious underpinnings of emotional life.* New York, NY: Simon & Schuster.

LeDoux, J. E. (2007). Emotional memory. *Scholarpedia, 2,* 180.

LeDoux, J. E. (2014). Coming to terms with fear. *Proceedings of the National Academy of Sciences of the United States of America, 111,* 2871–2878. http://dx.doi.org/10.1073/pnas.1400335111

Lee, E., & Chung, W. S. (2019). Glial control of synapse number in healthy and diseased brain. *Frontiers in Cellular Neuroscience, 13,* 42. http://dx.doi:10.3389/fncel.2019.00042

Lee, G. Y., & Kisilevsky, B. S. (2014). Fetuses respond to father's voice but prefer mother's voice after birth. *Developmental Psychobiology, 56,* 1–11. http://dx.doi.org/10.1002/dev.21084

Lee, H., & Oh, H. J. (2017). Normative mechanism of rumor dissemination on Twitter. *Cyberpsychology, Behavior, and Social Networking, 20*(3), 164–171. http://dx.doi.org/10.1089/cyber.2016.0447

Lee, H. S., Jung, H. S., & Sumner, A. (2015). A cross-cultural analysis of perception on ageist attitudes between Korean and American social work students. *Korean Social Science Journal, 42*, 25–37. http://dx.doi.org/10.1007/s10591-015-9337-7

Lee, J. J., Wedow, R., Okbay, A., Kong, E., Maghzian, O., Zacher, M., . . . Cesarini, D. (2018). Gene discovery and polygenic prediction from a genome-wide association study of educational attainment in 1.1 million individuals. *Nature Genetics, 50*(8), 1112–1121. doi:10.1038/s41588-018-0147-3

Lee, K. E., Bryan, S. L., & LaPlant, J. T. (2017). Game day meets election day: Sports records, election results, and the American south*. *Social Science Quarterly, 98*(5), 1422–1434. http://dx.doi.org/10.1111/ssqu.12356

Lee, L. O., James, P., Zevon, E. S., Kim. E. S., Trudel-Fitzgerald, C., Spiro, A., . . . Kubzansky, L. D. (2019). Optimism is associated with exceptional longevity in 2 epidemiologic cohorts of men and women. *Proceedings of the National Academy of Sciences of the United States of America, 116* (37), 18357–18362. doi:10.1073/pnas.1900712116

Lee, M. A., & Kawachi, I. (2019). The keys to happiness: Associations between personal values regarding core life domains and happiness in South Korea. *PloS ONE, 14*(1), e0209821. doi:10.1371/journal.pone.0209821

Lee, M. L., Howard, M. E., Horrey, W. J., Liang, Y., Anderson, C., Shreeve, M. S., . . . Czeisler, C. A. (2016a). High risk of near-crash driving events following night-shift work. *Proceedings of the National Academy of Sciences of the United States of America, 113*, 176–181. http://dx.doi.org/10.1073/pnas.1510383112

Lee, M. T., Mpavaenda, D. N., & Fineberg, N. A. (2019). Habit reversal therapy in obsessive compulsive related disorders: A systematic review of the evidence and CONSORT evaluation of randomized controlled trials. *Frontiers in Behavioral Neuroscience, 13*:79. doi:10.3389/fnbeh.2019.00079

Lee, O. L., James, P., Zevon, E. S., Kim, E. S., Trudel-Fitzgerald, C., Spiro, A., . . . Kubzansky, L. D. (2019). Optimism is associated with exceptional longevity in 2 epidemiologic cohorts of men and women. *Proceedings of the National Academy of Sciences of the United States of America, 116*(37), 18357–18362. doi:10.1073/pnas.1900712116

Lee, T. L., Gelfand, M. J., & Kashima, Y. (2014). The serial reproduction of conflict: Third parties escalate conflict through communication biases. *Journal of Experimental Social Psychology, 54*, 68–72. http://dx.doi.org/10.1016/j.jesp.2014.04.006

Lee, Y., Syeda, K., Maruschak, N. A., Cha, D. S., Mansur, R. B., Wium-Andersen, I. K., . . . McIntyre, R. S. (2016). A new perspective on the anti-suicide effects with ketamine treatment: A procognitive effect. *Journal of Clinical Psychopharmacology, 36*, 50–56. http://dx.doi.org/10.1097/JCP.0000000000000441

Legarreta, M., Graham, J., North, L., Bueler, C. E., McGlade, E., & Yurgelun-Todd, D. (2015). DSM-5 posttraumatic stress disorder symptoms associated with suicide behaviors in veterans. *Psychological Trauma: Theory, Research, Practice, and Policy, 7*, 277–285. http://dx.doi.org/10.1037/tra0000026

Lehr, D. (2009). *The fence: A police cover-up along Boston's racial divide.* New York, NY: HarperCollins.

Lehrner, A., & Yehuda, R. (2018). Cultural trauma and epigenetic inheritance. *Development and Psychopathology, 30*(5), 1763–1777. doi:10.1017/S0954579418001153

Leibowitz, K. A., Hardebeck, E. J., Goyer, J. P., & Crum, A. J. (2019). The role of patient beliefs in open-label placebo effects. *Health Psychology, 38*(7), 613–622. http://dx.doi.org/10.1037/hea0000751

Leichtman, M. D. (2006). Cultural and maturational influences on long-term event memory. In L. Balter & C. S. Tamis-LeMonda (Eds.), *Child psychology: A handbook of contemporary issues* (2nd ed., pp. 565–589). New York, NY: Psychology Press.

Leigh, H. (2015). Affect, mood, emotions: Depressive disorders and bipolar and related disorders. In H. Leigh & J. Strltzer (Eds.), *Hand-book of consultation-liaison psychiatry* (2nd ed., pp. 225–235). New York, NY: Springer. http://dx.doi.org/10.1007/978-3-319-11005-9

Leising, K. J., Wong, J., & Blaisdell, A. P. (2015). Extinction and spontaneous recovery of spatial behavior in pigeons. *Journal of Experimental Psychology: Animal Learning and Cognition, 41*, 371–377. http://dx.doi.org/10.1037/xan0000076

Leiting, K. A., & Yeater, E. A. (2017). A qualitative analysis of the effects of victimization history and sexual attitudes on women's hypothetical sexual assault scripts. *Violence Against Women, 23*, 46–66. http://dx.doi.org/10.1177/1077801216637472

Lei, Y., Wang, J., Wang, D., Li, C., Liu, B., Fang, X., . . . Lu, X.-Y. (2019). SIRT1 in forebrain excitatory neurons produces sexually dimorphic effects on depression-related behaviors and modulates neuronal excitability and synaptic transmission in the medial prefrontal cortex. *Molecular Psychiatry.* doi:10.1038/s41380-019-0352-1.

LeMaster, B., & Johnson, A. L. (2019). Unlearning gender—Toward a critical communication trans pedagogy. *Communication Teacher, 33*:3, 189–198. doi:10.1080/17404622.2018.1467566

Leonard, J. A., Lee, Y., & Schulz, L. E. (2017). Infants make more attempts to achieve a goal when they see adults persist. *Science, 357*(6357), 1290–1294. doi:10.1126/science.aan2317

Leon, M., & Woo, C. (2018). Environmental enrichment and successful aging. *Frontiers in Behavioral Neuroscience, 12*, Article ID 155. doi:10.3389/fnbeh.2018.00155

Lepore, F. (2018). *Finding Einstein's brain.* New Brunswick, NJ: Rutgers University Press.

Lepper, M. R., Greene, D., & Nisbett, R. E. (1973). Undermining children's intrinsic interest with extrinsic rewards: A test of the overjustification hypothesis. *Journal of Personality and Social Psychology, 28*, 129–137.

Leslie, M. (2000, July/August). The vexing legacy of Lewis Terman. *Stanford Magazine.* Retrieved from http://www.stanfordalumni.org/news/magazine/2000/julaug/articles/terman.html

Le Texier, T. (2019). Debunking the Stanford Prison Experiment. *American Psychologist, 74*(7), 823-839. http://dx.doi.org/10.1037/amp0000401

Leung, H. (2019, March 14). Swedish teen climate activist Greta Thunberg has been nominated for the Nobel Peace Prize. *Time Magazine.* Retrieved from http://time.com/5551172/climate-greta-thunberg-nobel-nominated/

Levant, R. F., & Powell, W. A. (2017). The gender role strain paradigm. In R. F. Levant & Y. J. Wong (Eds.), *The psychology of men and masculinities* (pp. 15–43). Washington, DC: American Psychological Association. http://dx.doi.org/10.1037/0000023-002

Levant, R. F., & Wong, Y. J. (2017). *The psychology of men and masculinities.* Washington, DC: American Psychological Association.

LeVay, S. (2003). Queer science: The use and abuse of research into homosexuality. *Archives of Sexual Behavior, 32*, 187–189.

LeVay, S. (2012). *Gay, straight, and the reason why: The science of sexual orientation.* New York, NY: Oxford University Press.

Levenson, R. W. (1992). Autonomic nervous system differences among emotions. *Psychological Science, 3*, 23–27.

Levenson, R. W. (2007). Emotion elicitation with neurological patients. In J. A. Coan & J. B. Allen (Eds.), *Handbook of emotion elicitation and assessment* (pp. 158–168). Oxford, UK: Oxford.

Leventhal, A. M., Cho, J., Andrabi, N., & Barrington-Trimis, J. (2018). Association of reported concern about increasing societal discrimination with adverse behavioral health outcomes in late adolescence. *JAMA Pediatrics, 172*(10), 924–933. doi:10.1001/jamapediatrics.2018.2022

Levey, S. (2014). *Introduction to language development.* San Diego, CA: Plural.

Levine, J. R. (2001). *Why do fools fall in love: Experiencing the magic, mystery, and meaning of successful relationships.* New York, NY: Jossey-Bass.

Levine, P. A. (2015). *Trauma and memory: Brain and body in a search for the living past.* New York, NY: North Atlantic.

Lewicki, R. J., Polin, B., & Lount, R. B. Jr. (2016). An exploration of the structure of effective apologies. *Negotiation and Conflict Management Research, 9,* 177–196. http://dx.doi.org/101111/ncmr.12073

Lewis, S. J., Arseneault, L., Caspi, A., Fisher, H. L., Matthews, T., Moffitt, T. E., . . . Danese, A. (2019). The epidemiology of trauma and post-traumatic stress disorder in a representative cohort of young people in England and Wales. *The Lancet Psychiatry, 6*(3), 247–256. https://doi.org/10.1016/S2215-0366(19)30031-8

Libero, L. E., Burge, W. L., Deshpande, H. D., Pestilli, F., & Kana, R. K. (2016). White matter diffusion of major fiber tracts implicated in autism spectrum disorder. *Brain Connectivity, 6*(9), 691–699. https://doi.org/10.1089/brain.2016.0442

Li, C.-T., Chen, M.-H., Lin, W.-C., Hong, C.-J., Yang, B.-H., Liu, R.-S., . . . Su, T.-P. (2016). The effects of low-dose ketamine on the prefrontal cortex and amygdala in treatment-resistant depression: A randomized controlled study. *Human Brain Mapping, 37,* 1080–1090. http://dx.doi.org/10.1002/hbm.23085

Liedle, C. (2019, June 17). New phrase replacing 'stranger danger' to warn children, parents: 'Tricky people.' *KOMONEWS.* Retrieved from https://komonews.com/news/local/new-phrase-replacing-stranger-danger-to-warn-children-parents-tricky-people

Lightfoot, C., Cole, M., & Cole, S. (2018). *Development of children* (8ᵗʰ ed.). New York, NY: Macmillan.

Li, J., Atasoy, S., Fang, X., Angerer, P., & Ladwig, K. (2019). Combined effect of work stress and impaired sleep on coronary and cardiovascular mortality in hypertensive workers: The MONICA/KORA cohort study. *European Journal of Preventive Cardiology,* doi:10.1177/2047487319839183

Lilienfeld, S. O., Lynn, S. J., & Ammirati, R. J. (2015). Science versus pseudoscience. *The encyclopedia of clinical psychology, 1–7.* Hoboken, NJ: Wiley. doi:10.1002/9781118625392.wbecp572

Lilienfeld, S. O., Lynn, S. J., Ruscio, J., & Beyerstein, B. L. (2010). *50 great myths of popular psychology: Shattering widespread misconceptions about human behavior.* Malden, MA: Wiley-Blackwell.

Lilliengren, P., Johansson, R., Lindqvist, K., Mechler, J., & Andersson, G. (2016). Efficacy of experiential dynamic therapy for psychiatric conditions: A meta-analysis of randomized controlled trials. *Psychotherapy, 53,* 90–104. http://dx.doi.org/10.1037/pst0000024

Lilly, J. D., & Wipawayangkool, K. (2018). When fair procedures don't work: A self-threat model of procedural justice. *Current Psychology, 37*(3), 680–691. http://dx.doi.org/10.1007/s12144-016-9555-7

Lima, A. S., Silva, K., Padovan, C. M., Almeida, S. S., & Hebihara Fukuda, M. T. (2014). Memory, learning, and participation of the cholinergic system in young rats exposed to environmental enrichment. *Behavioural Brain Research, 259,* 247–252. http://dx.doi.org/10.1016/j.bbr.2013.10.046

Limakatso, K., Bedwell, G. J., Madden, V. J., & Parker, R. (2019). The prevalence of phantom limb pain and associated risk factors in people with amputations: A systematic review protocol. *Systematic Reviews, 8*(1), 17. doi:10.1186/s13643-018-0938-8

Lim, A., & Okuno, H. G. (2015). A recipe for empathy: Integrating the mirror system, insula, somatosensory cortex and motherese. *International Journal of Social Robotics, 7,* 35–49. doi:10.1007/s12369-014-0262-y

Lim, D., Condon, P., & DeSteno, D. (2015). Mindfulness and compassion: An examination of mechanism and scalability. *PLoS ONE, 10*(2): e0118221. https://doi.org/10.1371/journal.pone.0118221

Lim, L., Chang, W., Yu, X., Chiu, H., Chong, M., & Kua, E. (2011). Depression in Chinese elderly populations. *Asia-Pacific Psychiatry, 3,* 46–53. https://doi.org/10.1111/j.1758-5872.2011.00119.x

Lim, L., Ho, R., & Ho, C. (2019). Dangers of mixed martial arts in the development of chronic traumatic encephalopathy. *International Journal of Environmental Research and Public Health, 16*(2), 254. doi:10.3390/ijerph16020254

Linden, E. (1993, March 22). Can animals think? *Time,* pp. 54–61.

Lindqvist, D., Dhabhar, F. S., James, S. J., Hough, C. M., Jain, F. A., Bersani, F. S., . . . Mellon, S. H. (2017). Oxidative stress, inflammation and treatment response in major depression. *Psychoneuroendocrinology, 76,* 197–205. http://dx.doi.org/10.1016/j.psyneuen.2016.11.031

Lindsay, D. S., Yonelinas, A. P., & Roediger, H. L., II. (Eds.). (2015). *Remembering: Attributions, processes, and control in human memory: Essays in honor of Larry Jacoby* (C. M. Kelley, Trans.). New York, NY: Psychology Press.

Lindsay, E. K., Chin, B., Greco, C. M., Young, S., Brown, K. W., Wright, A. G. C., . . . Creswell, J. D. (2018). How mindfulness training promotes positive emotions: Dismantling acceptance skills training in two randomized controlled trials. *Journal of Personality and Social Psychology, 115*(6), 944–973. http://dx.doi.org/10.1037/pspa0000134

Lingle, S., & Riede, T. (2014). Deer mothers are sensitive to infant distress vocalizations of diverse mammalian species. *The American Naturalist, 184,* 510–522. http://dx.doi.org/10.1086/677677

Lingle, S., Wyman, M. T., Kotrba, R. Teichroeg, L. J., & Romanow, C. A. (2015). What makes a cry a cry? A review of infant distress vocalizations. *Zoology, 58,* 698–726. https://dx.doi.org/10.1093/czoolo/58.5.698

Lin, H.-C., Manuel, J., McFatter, R., & Cech, C. (2016). Changes in empathy-related cry responding as a function of time: A time course study of adult's responses to infant crying. *Infant Behavior & Development, 42,* 45–59. http://dx.doi.org/10.1016/j.infbeh.2015.10.010

Lin, H., Li, W. P., & Carlson, S. (2019). A privileged working memory state and potential top-down modulation for faces, not scenes. *Frontiers in Human Neuroscience, 13*:2. doi:10.3389/fnhum.2019.00002

Lin, N., Pan, X.-D., Chen, A.-Q., Zhu, Y.-G., Wu, M., Zhang, J., & Chen, X.-C. (2014). Tripchlorolide improves age-associated cognitive deficits by reversing hippocampal synaptic plasticity impairment and NMDA receptor dysfunction in SAMP8 mice. *Behavioural Brain Research, 258,* 8–18. http://dx.doi.org/10.1016/j.bbr.2013.10.010

Lippa, R. A. (2016). Biological influences on masculinity. In Y. J. Wong & S. R. Wester (Eds.), *APA handbook of men and masculinities* (pp. 187–209). Washington, DC: American Psychological Association. http://dx.doi.org/10.1037/14594-009

Lipsman, N., Giacobbe, P., & Lozano, A. M. (2015). Deep brain stimulation for the management of treatment-refractory major depressive disorder. In B. Sun & A. De Salles (Eds.), *Neurosurgical treatments for psychiatric disorders* (pp. 95–104). New York, NY: Springer. http://dx.doi.org/10.1007/978-94-017-9576-0

Li, S. H., & Graham, B. M. (2017). Why are women so vulnerable to anxiety, traumarelated and stress-related disorders? The potential role of sex hormones. *The Lancet Psychiatry, 4*(1), 73–82. http://dx.doi.org/10.1016/S2215-0366(16)30358-3

Littlewood, D. L., Gooding, P. A., Panagioti, M., & Kyle, S. D. (2016). Nightmares and suicide in posttraumatic stress disorder: The mediating role of defeat, entrapment, and hopelessness. *Journal of Clinical Sleep Medicine, 12,* 393–399. http://dx.doi.org/10.5664/jcsm.5592

Liu, J. H., & Latané, B. (1998). Extremitization of attitudes: Does thought-and discussion induced polarization cumulate? *Basic and Applied Social Psychology, 20,* 103–110.

Liu, J., Wang, L., Wang, Z., & Liu, J. P. (2019). Roles of telomere biology in cell senescence, replicative and chronological ageing. *Cells, 8*(1), 54. doi:10.3390/cells8010054

Liu, L., Preotiuc-Pietro, D., Samani, Z. R., Moghaddam, M. E., & Ungar, L. (2016). Analyzing personality through social media profile picture choice. *AAAI Digital Library.* Retrieved from https://sites.sas.upenn.edu/danielpr/publications/analyzingpersonality-through-social-media-profile picture-choice

Livi, A., Lanzilotto, M., Maranesi, M., Fogassi, L., Rizzolatti, G., & Bonini, L. (2019). Agent-based representations of objects and actions in the monkey pre-supplementary motor area. *Proceedings of the National Academy of Sciences of the United States of America, 116*(7), 2691–2700. Retrieved from doi:10.1073/pnas.1810890116

Livingstone, K. M., & Isaacowitz, D. M. (2016). Age differences in use and effectiveness of positivity in emotion regulation: The sample case of attention. In A. D. Ong & C. E. Löckenhoff (Eds.), *Emotion, aging, and health. Bronfenbrenner series on the ecology of human development* (pp. 31–48). Washington, DC: American Psychological Association. http://dx.doi.org/10.1037/14857-003

Livingston, J. A. (1999). Something old and something new: Love, creativity, and the enduring relationship. *Bulletin of the Menninger Clinic, 63,* 40–52.

Li, W. O. (2016). Consciousness: How we perceive and become aware of our world. In C. Tien-Lun Sun (Ed.), *Psychology in Asia: An introduction* (pp. 127–173). Boston, MA: Cengage.

Li, W. O. (2016). Learning and memory: How do we learn and retain new knowledge? In C. Tien-Lun Sun (Ed.), *Psychology in Asia: An introduction* (pp. 175–210). Boston, MA: Cengage.

Li, X., Semenova, S., D'Souza, M. S., Stoker, A. K., & Markou, A. (2014). Involvement of glutamatergic and GABAergic systems in nicotine dependence: Implications for novel pharmacotherapies for smoking cessation. *Neuropharmacology, 76,* 554–565. http://dx.doi.org/10.1016/j.neuropharm.2013.05.042

Li, Y. (2018). Epigenetic mechanisms link maternal diets and gut microbiome to obesity in the offspring. *Frontiers in Genetics, 9,* 342. doi:10.3389/fgene.2018.00342

Li, Y. J., Lu, S., Lan, J., & Jiang, F. (2019). Feel safe to take more risks? Insecure attachment increases consumer risk-taking behavior. *Frontiers in Psychology.* 10:874. doi:10.3389/fpsyg.2019.00874

Lizarbe, B., Soares, A. F., Larsson, S., & Duarte, J. (2019). Neurochemical modifications in the hippocampus, cortex and hypothalamus of mice exposed to long-term high-fat diet. *Frontiers in Neuroscience, 12,* 985. http://dx.doi.org/10.3389/fnins.2018.00985

Lodder, P., Ong, H. H., Grasman, R. P. P. P., & Wicherts, J. M. (2019). A comprehensive meta-analysis of money priming. *Journal of Experimental Psychology: General, 148*(4), 688–712. http://dx.doi.org/10.1037/xge0000570

Loftus, E. F. (1993). Psychologists in the eyewitness world. *American Psychologist, 48,* 550–552. http://dx.doi.org/10.1037/0003-066X.48.5.550

Loftus, E. F. (2002, May/June). My story: Dear Mother. *Psychology Today,* pp. 67–70.

Loftus, E. F. (2010). Afterword: Why parapsychology is not yet ready for prime time. Debating psychic experience: Human potential or human illusion? In S. Krippner & H. L. Friedman (Eds.), *Debating psychic experience: Human potential or human illusion?* (pp. 211–214). Santa Barbara, CA: Praeger/ABC-CLIO.

Loftus, E. F. (2011). How I got started: From semantic memory to expert testimony. *Applied Cognitive Psychology, 25,* 347–348. doi:10.1002/acp.1769

Loftus, E. F., & Cahill, L. (2007). Memory distortion from misattribution to rich false memory. In J. S. Nairne (Ed.), *The foundations of remembering: Essays in honor of Henry L. Roediger, III* (pp. 413–425). New York, NY: Psychology Press.

Logue, G. (2019, January 14). MTSU professor explains psychologist's take on "self-actualized" New Year. *MTSUNews.* Retrieved from https://mtsunews.com/compton-self-actualization-2019/

Lohr, J. B., Palmer, B. W., Eidt, C. A., Aailabovina, S., Mausbach, B. T., Wolkowitz, O. M., . . . Jeste, D. V. (2015). Is post-traumatic stress disorder associated with premature senescence? A review of the literature. *The American Journal of Geriatric Psychiatry, 23,* 709–726. http://dx.doi.org/10.1016/j.jagp.2015.04.001

Lohse, M., Garrido, L., Driver, J., Dolan, R. J., Duchaine, B. C., & Furl, N. (2016). Effective connectivity from early visual cortex to posterior occipitotemporal face areas supports face selectivity and predicts developmental prosopagnosia. *The Journal of Neuroscience, 36,* 3821–3828. doi:10.1523/JNEUROSCI.3621-15.2016

Lombardo, C. (2019, March 23). How admissions really work: If the college admissions scandal shocked you, read this. *NPR.* Retrieved from https://www.npr.org/2019/03/23/705183942/how-admissions-really-work-if-the-college-admissions-scandal-shocked-you-read-th

Lopez, S., Pedrotti, J., & Snyder, C. (2015). *Positive psychology: The scientific and practical explorations of human strengths* (3rd ed.). Thousand Oaks, CA: Sage.

López, S. R., & Guarnaccia, P. J. (2016). Cultural dimensions of psychopathology: The social world's impact on mental disorders. In J. E. Maddux, & B. A. Winstead (Eds.), *Psychopathology: Foundations for a contemporary understanding* (4th ed., pp. 59–75). New York, NY: Routledge/Taylor & Francis Group.

Lotta, L. A., Mokrosiński, J., Mendes de Oliveira, E., Li, C., Sharp, S. J., Luan, J., . . . Farooqi, I. S. (2019). Human gain-of-function MC4R variants show signaling bias and protect against obesity. *Cell, 177*(3), 597–607.e9. doi:10.1016/j.cell.2019.03.044

Loving, T. J., & Sbarra, D. A. (2015). Relationships and health. In M. Mikulincer, P. R. Shaver, J. A. Simpson, & J. F. Dovidio (Eds.), *APA handbooks in psychology. APA handbook of personality and social psychology, Vol. 3. Interpersonal relations* (pp. 151–176). Washington, DC: American Psychological Association. http://dx.doi.org/10.1037/14344-006

Luby, J. L., Barch, D. M., Belden, A., Gaffrey, M. S., Tillman, R., Babb, C., . . . Botteron, K. N. (2012). Maternal support in early childhood predicts larger hippocampal volumes at school age. *Proceedings of the National Academy of Sciences of the United States of America, 109*(8), 2854–2859. doi:10.1073/pnas.1118003109

Lucini, F. A., Del Ferraro, G., Sigman, M. & Makse, H. A. (2019). How the brain transitions from conscious to subliminal perception. *Neuroscience, 411*, 280–290. https://doi.org/10.1016/j.neuroscience.2019.03.047

Lu, C.-Q., Lu, J. J., Du, D.-Y., & Brough, P. (2016). Crossover effects of work-family conflict among Chinese couples. *Journal of Managerial Psychology, 31*, 235–250. http://dx.doi.org/10.1108/JMP-09-2012-0283

Ludwig, R. M., Srivastava, S., & Berkman, E. T. (2019). Predicting exercise with a personality facet: Planfulness and goal achievement. *Psychological Science, 30*(10), 1510–1521. https://doi.org/10.1177/0956797619868812

Luhrmann, T. M., Padmavati, R., Tharoor, H., & Osei, A. (2015). Differences in voice-hearing experiences of people with psychosis in the USA, India and Ghana: Interview-based study. *The British Journal of Psychiatry, 206*, 41–44. http://dx.doi.org/10.1192/bjp.bp.113.139048

Lu, J. G., Quoidbach, J., Gino, F., Chakroff, A., Maddux, W. W., & Galinsky, A. D. (2017). The dark side of going abroad: How broad foreign experiences increase immoral behavior. *Journal of Personality and Social Psychology, 112*, 1–16. http://dx.doi.org/10.1037/pspa0000068

Lukasik, K. M., Waris, O., Soveri, A., Lehtonen, M., & Laine, M. (2019). The relationship of anxiety and stress with working memory performance in a large non-depressed sample. *Frontiers in Psychology, 10*:4. doi:10.3389/fpsyg.2019.00004

Luo, R., Xu, L., Zhao, W., Ma, X., Xu, X., Kou, J., . . . Kendrick, K. M. (2017). Oxytocin facilitation of acceptance of social advice is dependent upon the perceived trustworthiness of individual advisors. *Psychoneuroendocrinology, 83*, 1–8. doi:10.1016/j.psyneuen.2017.05.020

Luo, S., Monterosso, J. R., Sarpelleh, K., & Page, K. A. (2015). Differential effects of fructose versus glucose on brain and appetitive responses to food cues and decisions for food rewards. *Proceedings of the National Academy of Sciences of the United States of America, 112*, 6509–6514. http://dx.doi.org/10.1073/pnas.1503358112

Luria, A. R. (1976). *Cognitive development: Its cultural and social foundations*. Cambridge, MA: Harvard University Press.

Luthar, S. S., & Kumar, N. L. (2018). Youth in high-achieving schools: Challenges to mental health and directions for evidence-based interventions. In A. W. Leschied, D. H. Saklofske, & G. L. Flett (Eds.), *Handbook of school-based mental health promotion: An evidence-informed framework* (pp. 441–458). New York, NY: Springer.

Lynn, C. (2019, April 7). Behind the badge: Suicide's toll on police, other first responders. *Statesman Journal.* Retrieved June 9, 2019 from https://www.statesmanjournal.com/story/news/2019/04/07/police-officers-fire-department-first-responders-depression-suicide-rate/3068917002/

Lynn, S. J., Krackow, E., Loftus, E. F., Locke, T. G., & Lillienfeld, S. O. (2015). Constructing the past: Problematic memory recovery techniques in psychotherapy. In S. O. Lilienfeld, S. J. Lynn, & J. M. Lohr (Eds.), *Science and pseudoscience in clinical psychology* (2nd ed., pp. 210–244). New York, NY: Guilford.

Lynn, S. J., Lilienfeld, S. O., Merckelbach, H., Maxwell, R., Baltman, J., & Giesbrecht, T. (2016). Dissociative disorders. In J. E. Maddux & B. A. Winstead (Eds.), *Psychopathology: Foundations for a contemporary understanding* (4th ed., pp. 298–317). New York, NY: Routledge/Taylor & Francis Group.

Lyons, M., Evans, K., & Helle, S. (2019). Do "dark" personality features buffer against adversity? The associations between cumulative life stress, the dark triad, and mental distress. *SAGE Open.* https://doi.org/10.1177/2158244018822383

Maack, D. J., Buchanan, E., & Young, J. (2015). Development and psychometric investigation of an inventory to assess fight, flight, freeze tendencies: The Fight, Flight, Freeze Questionnaire. *Cognitive Behaviour Therapy, 44*, 117–127. http://dx.doi.org/10.1080/16506073.2014.972443

Maasumi, K., Thompson, N. R., Kriegler, J. S., & Tepper, S. J. (2015). Effect of onabotulinumtoxin A injection on depression in chronic migraine. *Headache: The Journal of Head and Face Pain, 55*(9), 1218–1224.

Mabe, A. G., Forney, K. J., & Keel, P. K. (2014). Do you "like" my photo? Facebook use maintains eating disorder risk. *International Journal of Eating Disorders, 47*, 516–523. http://dx.doi.org/10.1002/eat.22254

MacKenzie, J., Smith, T. W., Uchino, B., White, P. H., Light, K. C., & Grewen, K. M. (2014). Depressive symptoms, anger/hostility, and relationship quality in young couples. *Journal of Social and Clinical Psychology, 33*, 380–396. http://dx.doi.org/10.1521/jscp.2014.33.4.380

Mackinnon, S. P., Smith, S. M., & Carter-Rogers, K. (2015). Multidimensional self-esteem and test derogation after negative feedback. *Canadian Journal of Behavioural Science/Revue Canadienne des Sciences du Comportement, 47*, 123–126. http://dx.doi.org/10.1037/a0038364

MacLean, E. L., & Hare, B. (2018). Enhanced selection of assistance and explosive detection dogs using cognitive measures. *Frontiers in Veterinary Science, 5*:236. doi:10.3389/fvets.2018.00236

Macmillan, M. B. (2000). *An odd kind of fame: Stories of Phineas Gage.* Cambridge, MA: MIT Press.

Macmillan, M., & Lena, M. L. (2010). Rehabilitating Phineas Gage. *Neuropsychological Rehabilitation, 20*, 641–658. http://dx.doi.org/10.1080/09602011003760527

Madden, D. (2019, March 5). The 2018 global shark attack summary is out. *Forbes.* Retrieved from https://www.forbes.com/sites/duncanmadden/2019/03/05/the-2018-global-shark-attack-summary-is-out/#5396b6257400

Maessen, S. E., Ahlsson, F., Lundgren, M., Cutfield, W. S., & Derraik, J. G. B. (2019). Maternal smoking early in pregnancy is associated with increased risk of short stature and obesity in adult daughters. *Scientific Reports, 9:4290.* https://www.nature.com/articles/s41598-019-39006-7

Magid, M., Reichenberg, J. S., Poth, P. E., Robertson, H. T., LaViolette, A. K., Kruger, T. H., & Wollmer, M. A. (2014). Treatment of major depressive disorder using botulinum toxin A: A 24-week randomized, double-blind, placebo-controlled study. *Journal of Clinical Psychiatry, 115*, 71–79. http://dx.doi.org/10. 4088/JCP.13m08845.

Magnavita, J. J., & Anchin, J. C. (2014). *Unifying psychotherapy: Principles, methods, and evidence from clinical science.* New York, NY: Springer.

Mahase, E. (2019). Social media: Concerns over effects on teenagers are overblown and lack evidence. *British Medical Journal, 365.* https://doi.org/10.1136/bmj.l2069

Maier, C., Laumer, S., Weinert, C., & Weitzel, T. (2015). The effects of technostress and switching stress on discontinued use of social networking services: A study of Facebook use. *Information Systems Journal, 25*, 275–308. http://dx.doi.org/10.1111/isj.12068

Maier, S. F., & Seligman, M. E. (2016). Learned helplessness at fifty: Insights from neuroscience. *Psychological Review, 123*(4), 349–367. http://dx.doi.org/10.1037/rev0000033

Main, M., & Solomon, J. (1986). Discovery of an insecure-disorganized attachment pattern. In T. Brazelton & M. W. Yogman (Eds.), *Affective development in infancy* (pp. 95–124). Westport, CT: Ablex.

Main, M., & Solomon, J. (1990). Procedures for identifying infants as disorganized/disoriented during the Ainsworth Strange Situation. In M. T. Greenberg, D. Cicchetti, & E. M. Cummings (Eds.), *Attachment in the preschool years: Theory, research, and intervention, The John D. and Catherine T. MacArthur Foundation series on mental health and development* (pp. 121–160). Chicago, IL: University of Chicago Press.

Maisto, S. A., Galizio, M., & Connors, G. J. (2015). *Drug use and abuse* (7th ed.). Boston, MA: Cengage.

Maisto, S. A., Galizio, M., & Connors, G. J. (2019). *Drug use and abuse* (8th Ed.). Boston, MA: Cengage.

Major, B., Spencer, S., Schmader, T., Wolfe, C., & Crocker, J. (1998). Coping with negative stereotypes about intellectual performance: The role of psychological disengagement. *Personality & Social Psychology Bulletin, 24,* 34–50. https://doi.org/10.1177/0146167298241003

Major, R. J., Whelton, W. J., Schimel, J., & Sharpe, D. (2016). Older adults and the fear of death: The protective function of generativity. *Canadian Journal on Aging, 35,* 261–272. http://dx.doi.org/10.1017/S0714980816000143

Makhanova, A., McNulty, J. K., & Maner, J. (2017). Relative physical position as an impression-management strategy: Sex differences in its use and implications. *Psychological Science, 28*(5), 567–577. https://doi.org/10.1177/0956797616688885

Makinodan, M., Rosen, K. M., Ito, S., & Corfas, G. (2012). A critical period for social experience-dependent oligodendrocyte maturation and myelination. *Science, 337,* 1357–1360. http://dx.doi.org/10.1126/science.1220845.

Malavé, S., Ramakrishna, J., Heylen, E., Bharat, S., & Ekstrand, M. L. (2014). Differences in testing, stigma, and perceived consequences of stigmatization among heterosexual men and women living with HIV in Bengaluru, India. *AIDS Care, 26,* 396–403. http://dx.doi.org/10.1080/09540121.2013.819409

Malgady, R. G., Castagno, R. M., & Cardinale, J. A. (2014). Clinical tests and assessment: Ethno cultural and linguistic bias in mental health evaluation of Latinos. In F. T. L. Leong, L. Comas-Díaz, G. C. Nagayama Hall, V. C. McLoyd, & J. E. Trimble (Eds.), *APA handbooks in psychology. APA handbook of multicultural psychology, Vol. 2. Applications and training* (pp. 165–179). Washington, DC: American Psychological Association. http://dx.doi.org/10.1037/14187-010

Malinowski, J., & Horton, C. L. (2014). Evidence for the preferential incorporation of emotional waking-life experiences into dreams. *Dreaming, 24,* 18–31. doi:10.1037/a0036017

Mallan, K. M., Lipp, O. V., & Cochrane, B. (2013). Slithering snakes, angry men and out-group members: What and whom are we evolved to fear? *Cognition and Emotion, 27,* 1168–1180. http://dx.doi.org/10.1080/02699931.2013.778195

Maloney, E. A., Gunderson, E. A., Levine, S. C., & Beilock, S. L. (2015). Intergenerational effects of parents' math anxiety on children's math achievement and anxiety. *Psychological Science, 26,* 1480–1488. http://dx.doi.org/10.1177/0956797615592630.

Mammen, G., & Faulkner, G. (2013). Physical activity and the prevention of depression: A systematic review of prospective studies. *American Journal of Preventive Medicine, 45,* 649–657. http://dx.doi.org/10.1016/j.amepre.2013.08.001

Manago, A. M., & Greenfield, P. M. (2011). The construction of independent values among Maya women at the forefront of social change: Four case studies. *Ethos, 39*(1), 1–29.

Mancia, M., & Baggott, J. (2008). The early unrepressed unconscious in relation to Matte-Blanco's thought. *International Forum of Psychoanalysis, 17,* 201–212. http://dx.doi.org/10.1080/08037060701676359

Mancini, A. D., Littleton, H. L., & Grills, A. E. (2016). Can people benefit from acute stress? Social support, psychological improvement, and resilience after the Virginia Tech campus shootings. *Clinical Psychological Science, 4,* 401–417. http://dx.doi.org/10.1177/2167702615601001

Mancini, A. D., Littleton, H. L., & Grills, A. E. (2016). Can people benefit from acute stress? Social support, psychological improvement, and resilience after the Virginia Tech campus shootings. *Clinical Psychological Science, 4,* 401–417. http://dx.doi.org/10.1177/2167702615601001

Manczak, E. M., Mangelsdorf, S. C., McAdams, D. P., Wong, M. S., Schoppe-Sullivan, S., & Brown, G. L. (2016). Autobiographical memories of childhood and sources of subjectivity in parents' perceptions of infant temperament. *Infant Behavior & Development, 44,* 77–85. http://dx.doi.org/10.1016/j.infbeh.2016.06.001

Mannarini, S., & Rossi, A. (2019). Assessing mental illness stigma: A complex issue. *Frontiers in Psychology, 9,* 2722. doi:10.3389/fpsyg.2018.02722

Ma, Q., Jin, J., Meng, L., & Shen, Q. (2014). The dark side of monetary incentive: How does extrinsic reward crowd out intrinsic motivation. *Neuro Report: For Rapid Communication of Neuroscience Research, 25,* 194–198. http://dx.doi.org/10.1097/WNR.0000000000000113

Marchant, J. (2016). *Cure: A journey into the science of mind over body.* New York, NY: Crown.

Marcinkowska, U. M., Kozlov, M. V., Cai, H., Contreras-Garduño, J., Dixson, B. J., Oana, G. A., . . . Rantala, M. J. (2014). Cross-cultural variation in men's preference for sexual dimorphism in women's faces. *Biological Letters, 10*(4):20130850. doi:10.1098/rsbl.2013.0850

Marcinkowska, U. M., Rantala, M. J., Lee, A. J., Kozlov, M. V., Aavik, T., Cai, H., . . . Dixson, B. (2019). Women's preferences for men's facial masculinity are strongest under favorable ecological conditions. *Scientific Reports, 9*(1), 3387. doi:10.1038/s41598-019-39350-8

Marczinski, C. A. (2014). *Drug use, misuse, and abuse.* Hoboken, NJ: Wiley.

Market Opinion Research International (MORI). (2005, January). *Use of animals in medical research for coalition for medical progress.* London, UK: Author.

Marsh, A. A., Elfenbein, H. A., & Ambady, N. (2007). Separated by a common language: Nonverbal accents and cultural stereotypes about Americans and Australians. *Journal of Cross-Cultural Psychology, 38,* 284–301. https://doi.org/10.1177/0022022107300275

Marshall, D. S. (1971). Sexual behavior in Mangaia. In D. S. Marshall & R. C. Suggs (Eds.), *Human sexual behavior* (pp. 103–162). Englewood Cliffs, NJ: Prentice Hall.

Marshall, T. C., Lefringhausen, K., & Ferenczi, N. (2015). The Big Five, self-esteem, and narcissism as predictors of the topics people write about in Facebook status updates. *Personality and Individual Differences, 85,* 35–40. http://dx.doi.org/10.1016/j.paid.2015.04.039

Marsh, N., Scheele, D., Feinstein, J. S., Gerhardt, H., Strang, S., Maier, W., & Hurlemann, R. (2017). Oxytocin-enforced norm compliance reduces xenophobic outgroup rejection. *Proceedings of the National Academy of Sciences of the United States of America, 114*(35), 9314–9319. http://dx.doi.org/10.1073/pnas.1705853114

Martínez-Hernáez, A., Carceller-Maicas, N., DiGiacomo, S. M., & Ariste, S. (2016). Social support and gender differences in coping with depression among emerging adults: A mixed-methods study. *Child and Adolescent Psychiatry and Mental Health, 10,* Article 2. http://dx.doi.org/10.1186/s13034-015-0088-x

Martinez-Murcia, F. J., Lai, M.-C., Górriz, J. M., Ramírez, J., Young, A. M. H., Deoni, S. C. L., . . . Suckling, J. (2016). On the brain structure heterogeneity of autism: Parsing out acquisition site effects with significance-weighted principal component analysis. *Human Brain Mapping, 38,* 1208–1223. http://dx.doi.org/10.1002/hbm.23449

Martinez-Raga, J., Ferreros, A., Knecht, C., de Alvaro, R., & Carabal, E. (2016). Attention-deficit hyperactivity disorder medication use: Factors involved in prescribing, safety aspects and outcomes. *Therapeutic Advances in Drug Safety, 8*(3), 87–99. doi:10.1177/2042098616679636

Martin-Storey, A., Serbin, L. A., Stack, D. M., Ledingham, J. E., & Schwartzman, A. E. (2012). Self and peer perceptions of childhood aggression, social withdrawal and likeability predict adult personality factors: A prospective longitudinal study. *Personality and Individual Differences, 53,* 843–848. http://dx.doi.org/10.1016/j.paid.2012.06.018

Marx, D. M., Ko, S. J., & Friedman, R. A. (2009). The "Obama effect": How a salient role model reduces race-based performance differences. *Journal of Experimental Social Psychology, 45,* 953–956. http://dx.doi.org/10.1016/j.jesp.2009.03.012

Mascaro, J. S., Rentscher, K. E., Hackett, P. D., Mehl, M. R., & Rilling, J. K. (2017). Child gender influences paternal behavior, language, and brain function. *Behavioral Neuroscience, 131*(3), 262–273. http://dx.doi.org/10.1037/bne0000199

Masilo, D. T. (2018). Prevention of child sexual abuse within the family system: Guidelines for an educational social group work program. *Journal of Child Sexual Abuse, 27,* 335–346. doi:10.1080/10538712.2018.1430089

Maslow, A. H. (1954). *Motivation and personality.* New York, NY: Harper & Row.

Maslow, A. H. (1970). *Motivation and personality.* New York, NY: Harper & Row.

Maslow, A. H. (1999). *Toward a psychology of being* (3rd ed.). New York, NY: Wiley.

Mason, M. F., & Morris, M. W. (2010). Culture, attribution and automaticity: A social cognitive neuroscience view. *Social Cognitive and Affective Neuroscience, 5*(2–3), 292–306. doi:10.1093/scan/nsq034

Mason, S., & Zhou, F. C. (2015). Editorial: Genetics and epigenetics of fetal alcohol spectrum disorders. *Frontiers in Genetics, 6,* 146. http://dx.doi.org/10.3389/fgene.2015.00146

Masten, A. S., & Coatsworth, J. D. (1998). The development of competence in favorable and unfavorable environments: Lessons from research on successful children. *American Psychologist, 53,* 205–220. http://dx.doi.org/10.1037/0003-066X.53.2.205

Master, A., Cheryan, S., & Meltzoff, A. N. (2016). Computing whether she belongs: Stereotypes undermine girls' interest and sense of belonging in computer science. *Journal of Educational Psychology, 108,* 424–437. http://dx.doi.org/10.1037/edu0000061

Master, S. L., Eisenberger, N. I., Taylor S. E., Naliboff, B. D., Shirinyan, D., & Lieberman, M. D. (2009). A picture's worth: Partner photographs reduce experimentally induced pain. *Psychological Science, 20,* 1316–1318. doi:10.1111/j.1467-9280.2009.02444.x

Masters, W. H., & Johnson, V. E. (1961). Orgasm, anatomy of the female. In A. Ellis & A. Abarbonel (Eds.), *Encyclopedia of sexual behavior* (Vol. 2, pp. 792–805). New York, NY: Hawthorn.

Masters, W. H., & Johnson, V. E. (1966). *Human sexual response.* Boston, MA: Little, Brown.

Masters, W. H., & Johnson, V. E. (1970). *Human sexual inadequacy.* Boston, MA: Little, Brown.

Mateos-Aparicio, P., & Rodríguez-Moreno, A. (2019). The impact of studying brain plasticity. *Frontiers in Cellular Neuroscience, 13*(66). http://dx.doi:10.3389/fncel.2019.00066

Mathes, J., Schredl, M., & Göritz, A. S. (2014). Frequency of typical dream themes in most recent dreams: An online study. *Dreaming, 24,* 57–66. http://dx.doi.org/10.1037/a0035857

Matsumoto, D. (2000). *Culture and psychology: People around the world.* Belmont, CA: Cengage.

Matsumoto, D., Yoo, S. H., & Fontaine, J. (2008). Mapping expressive differences around the world: The relationship between emotional display rules and individualism versus collectivism. *Journal of Cross-Cultural Psychology, 39,* 55–74. doi:10.1177/0022022107311854

Matz, S. C., & Gladstone, J. J. (2019). Nice guys finish last: When and why agreeableness is associated with economic hardship. *Journal of Personality and Social Psychology.* doi:10.1037/pspp0000220

Mauguière, F., & Corkin, S. (2015). H.M. never again! An analysis of H. M. 's epilepsy and treatment. *Revue Neurologique, 171,* 273–281. http://dx.doi.org/10.1016/j.neurol.2015.01.002

Maunder, A. (2016). *Victorian crime, madness, and sensation.* New York, NY: Routledge.

May, A. C., Rudy, B. M., Davis, T. E., & Matson, J. L. (2013). Evidence-based behavioral treatment of dog phobia with young children: Two case examples. *Behavior Modification, 37,* 143–160.

Mayo Clinic. (2017). Self-injury/cutting. *MayoClincic.org.* Retrieved February 22, 2017 from http://www.mayoclinic.org/diseases conditions/self-injury/symptoms-causes/dxc-20165427

Mayordomo-Rodríguez, T., Meléndez-Moral, J. C., Viguer-Segui, P., & Sales-Galán, A. (2015). Coping strategies as predictors of well-being in youth adult. *Social Indicators Research, 122,* 479–489. http://dx.doi.org/10.1007/s11205-014-0689-4

Mazandarani, A., Aguilar-Vafaie, M. E., & Domhoff, G. (2013). Content analysis of Iranian college students' dreams: Comparison with American data. *Dreaming, 23,* 163–174. http://dx.doi.org/10.1037/a0032352

Mazza, E. (2016, February 9). J.K. Rowling has an uplifting message for fan fighting "Dementors" of depression. *Huffington Post.* Retrieved from https://www.huffpost.com/entry/j-k-rowling-depressed-fan-dementors_n_56b99ad3e4b01d80b247a93c

Mazzei, P. (2019, January 14). The odds of dying in the U.S. *New York Times.* Retrieved from https://www.nytimes.com/2019/01/14/us/opioids-car-crash-guns.html

McAlpine, C. S., Kiss, M. G., Rattik, S., He, S., Vassalli, A., Valet, C., . . . Swirski, F. K. (2019). Sleep modulates haematopoiesis and protects against atherosclerosis. *Nature, 566,* 383–387. doi:10.1038/s41586-019-0948-2

McCarthy, S., Neubert, A., Man, K., Banaschewski, T., Buitelaar, J., Carucci, S., . . . Wong, I. (2018). Effects of long-term methylphenidate use on growth and blood pressure: Results of the German Health Interview and Examination Survey for Children and Adolescents (KiGGS). *BMC Psychiatry, 18*(1), 327. doi:10.1186/s12888-018-1884-7

McClean, E. J., Martin, S. R., Emich, K. J., & Woodruff, T. (2018). The social consequences of voice: An examination of voice type and gender on status and subsequent leader emergence. *Academy of Management Journal, 61*(5), 1869–1891.

McClelland, D. C. (1958). Risk-taking in children with high and low need for achievement. In J. W. Atkinson (Ed.), *Motives in fantasy, action, and society* (pp. 306–321). Princeton, NJ: Van Nostrand.

McClelland, D. C. (1993). Intelligence is not the best predictor of job performance. *Current Directions in Psychological Science, 2,* 5–6.

McClelland, J. L. (2011). Memory as a constructive process: The parallel distributed processing approach. In S. Nalbantian, P. M. Matthews, & J. L. McClelland (Eds.), *The memory process: Neuroscientific and humanistic perspectives* (pp. 129–155). Cambridge, MA: MIT Press

McClintock, E. A. (2014). Beauty and status: The illusion of exchange in partner selection? *American Sociological Review, 79,* 575–604. http://dx.doi.org/10.1177/0003122414536391.

McCormack, L., & Joseph, S. (2014). Psychological growth in aging Vietnam veterans: Redefining shame and betrayal. *Journal of Humanistic Psychology, 54,* 336–355. http://dx.doi.org/10.1177/0022167813501393

McCrae, R. R., & Costa, P. T., Jr. (2013). Introduction to the empirical and theoretical status of the five-factor model of personality traits. In T. A. Widiger & P. T. Costa, Jr. (Eds.), *Personality disorders and the five-factor model of personality* (3rd ed., pp. 15–27). Washington, DC: American Psychological Association.

McCrae, R. R., Costa, P. T., Jr., Ostendorf, F., Angleitner, A., Hřebíčková, M., Avia, M. D., . . . Smith, P. B. (2000). Nature over nurture: Temperament, personality, and life span development. *Journal of Personality and Social Psychology, 78,* 173–186. http://dx.doi.org/10.1037/0022-3514.78.1.173

McCrae, R. R., Scally, M., Terracciano, A., Abecasis, G. R., & Costa P. T. Jr. (2010). An alternative to the search for single polymorphisms: Toward molecular personality scales for the five-factor model. *Journal of Personality and Social Psychology, 99,* 1014–1024. http://dx.doi.org/10.1037/a0020964

McCrory, M. A., Harbaugh, A. G., Appeadu, S., & Roberts, S. B. (2019). Fast-food offerings in the United States in 1986, 1991, and 2016 show large increases in food variety, portion size, dietary energy, and selected micronutrients. *Journal of the Academy of Nutrition and Dietetics, 119*(6), 923–933. https://doi.org/10.1016/j.jand.2018.12.004

McDonald, S. (2019, September 13). Mega millions numbers for 09/13/19: Friday jackpot is $172 million. Newsweek. Retrieved from https://www.newsweek.com/mega-millions-drawing-09-13-19-friday-jackpot-172-million-1459259

McDougall, W. (1908). *Social psychology.* New York, NY: Putnam's Sons.

McFall, G. P., McDermott, K. K., & Dixon, R. A. (2019). Modifiable risk factors discriminate memory trajectories in non-demented aging: Precision factors and targets for promoting healthier brain aging and preventing dementia? *Journal of Alzheimer's Disease, 70*(s1), S101–S118. doi:10.3233/JAD-180571

McFarlane, D. A. (2014). A positive theory of stereotyping and stereotypes: Is stereotyping useful? *Journal of Studies in Social Sciences, 8,* 140–163.

McGillicuddy, N. B., Rychtarik, R. G., & Papandonatos, G. D. (2015). Skill training versus 12-step facilitation for parents of substance-abusing teens. *Journal of Substance Abuse Treatment, 50,* 11–17. http://dx.doi.org/10.1016/j.jsat.2014.09.006

McGlinchey, E. L. (2015). Sleep and adolescents. In K. A. Babson & M. T. Feldner (Eds.), *Sleep and affect: Assessment, theory, and clinical implications* (pp. 421–439). San Diego, CA: Elsevier.

McGloin, J. M., & Thomas, K. J. (2016). Incentives for collective deviance: Group size and changes in perceived risk, cost, and reward. *Criminology, 54,* 459–486. http://dx.doi.org/10.1111/1745-9125.12111

McGrath, J. J., Petersen, L., Agerbo, E., Mors, O., Mortensen, P. B., & Pedersen, C. B. (2014). A comprehensive assessment of parental age and psychiatric disorders. *JAMA Psychiatry, 71,* 301–309. http://dx.doi.org/10.1001/jamapsychiatry.2013.4081

McKellar, P. (1972). Imagery from the standpoint of introspection. In P. W. Sheehan (Ed.), *The function and nature of imagery* (pp. 36–61). New York, NY: Academic Press.

McKim, D. B., Niraula, A., Tarr, A. J., Wohleb, E. S., Sheridan, J. F., & Godbout, J. P. (2016). Neuroinflammatory dynamics underlie memory impairments after repeated social defeat. *The Journal of Neuroscience, 36,* 2590–2604. *http://dx.doi.org/10.1523/JNEUROSCI.2394-15.2016*

McKinley, J. C. Jr., & Ransom, J. (2018, March 27). Nanny faces tough insanity test: Did she know killing was wrong? *The New York Times.* Retrieved from https://www.nytimes.com/2018/03/27/nyregion/nanny-murder-trial-insanity-defense.html?emc=edit_th_180328&nl=todaysheadlines&nlid=729779520328

McKinnon, M. C., Palombo, D. J., Nazarov, A., Kumar, N., Khuu, W., & Levine, B. (2015). Threat of death and autobiographical memory: A study of passengers from flight AT236. *Clinical Psychological Science, 3,* 487–502. http://dx.doi.org/10.1177/2167702614542280

McLean, C. P., Su, Y. J., & Foa, E. B. (2015). Mechanisms of symptom reduction in a combined treatment for comorbid posttraumatic stress disorder and alcohol dependence. *Journal of Consulting and Clinical Psychology, 83,* 655–661. http://dx.doi.org/10.1037/ccp0000024

McLean, D., Thara, R., John, S., Barrett, R., Loa, P., McGrath, J., & Mowry, B. (2014). DSM-IV "criterion A" schizophrenia symptoms across ethnically different populations: Evidence for differing psychotic symptom content or structural organization? *Culture, Medicine and Psychiatry, 38,* 406–426. http://dx.doi.org/10.1007/s11013-014-9385-8

McLeigh, J. D. (2015). Creating conditions that promote trust and participation by young people . . . And why it matters. *American Journal of Orthopsychiatry, 85,* S67–S69. http://dx.doi.org/10.1037/ort0000134

McNally, R. J., & Robinaugh, D. J. (2015). Difficulties remembering the past and envisioning the future in people with trauma histories or complicated grief. In L. A. Watson & D. Bersten (Eds.), *Clinical perspectives on autobiographical memory* (pp. 242–264). New York, NY: Cambridge University Press. http://dx.doi.org/10.1017/CBO9781139626767.013

McNulty, J. K., Olson, M. A., Jones, R. E., & Acosta, L. M. (2017). Automatic associations between one's partner and one's affect as the proximal mechanism of change in relationship satisfaction: Evidence from evaluative conditioning. *Psychological Science, 28*(8), 1031–1040. https://doi.org/10.1177/0956797617702014

McSweeney, F. K., & Murphy, E. S. (2017). *The Wiley Blackwell handbook of operant and classical conditioning.* Hoboken, NJ: Wiley.

McWhirter, J. E., & Hoffman-Goetz, L. (2015). North American magazine coverage of skin cancer and recreational tanning before and after the WHO/IARC 2009 classification of indoor tanning devices as carcinogenic. *Journal of Cancer Education, 30*(3), 477–481. http://dx.doi.org/10.1007/s13187-014-0726-7

Medina, J., Benner, K., & Taylor, K. (2019, March 12). Actresses, business leaders and other wealthy parents charged in U.S. college entry fraud. *The New York Times*. Retrieved from https://www.nytimes.com/2019/03/12/us/college-admissions-cheating-scandal.html?action=click&module=inline&pgtype=Homepage

Mehrabian, A. (1968). A relationship of attitude to seated posture orientation and distance. *Journal of Personality and Social Psychology, 10,* 26–30. http://dx.doi.org/10.1037/h0026384

Mehrabian, A. (1971). *Silent messages.* Belmont, CA: Cengage.

Mehrabian, A. (2007). *Nonverbal communication.* New Brunswick, NJ: Aldine Transaction.

Mehra, R., & Strohl, K. P. (2014). Pharmacology of sleep medicine. In K. Strohl (Ed.), *Competencies in sleep medicine* (pp. 27–44). New York, NY: Springer. http://dx.doi.org/10.1007/978-1-4614-9065-4_3

Meijer, E. H., & Verschuere, B. (2015). The polygraph: Current practice and new approaches. In P. A. Granhag, A. Vrij, & B. Verschuere (Eds.), *Detecting deception: Current challenges and cognitive approaches* (pp. 59–80). Hoboken, NJ: Wiley-Blackwell.

Meirick, P. C., & Schartel Dunn, S. (2015). Obama as exemplar: Debate exposure and implicit and explicit racial affect. *Howard Journal of Communications, 26,* 57–73. http://dx.doi.org/10.1080/10646175.2014.986312

Mejía, O. L., & McCarthy, C. J. (2010). Acculturative stress, depression, and anxiety in migrant farmwork college students of Mexican heritage. *International Journal of Stress Management, 17*(1), 1–20. http://dx.doi.org/10.1037/a0018119

Mekonnen, A. G., Yehualashet, S. S., & Bayleyegn, A. D. (2019). The effects of kangaroo mother care on the time to breastfeeding initiation among preterm and LBW infants: A meta-analysis of published studies. *International Breastfeeding Journal, 14*:12. https://doi.org/10.1186/s13006-019-0206-0

Melo-Santos, G., Rodrigues, A. L. F., Tardin, R. H., de Sá Maciel, I., Marmontel, M., Da Silva, M. L., & May-Collado, L. J. (2019). The newly described Araguaian river dolphins, *Inia araguaiaensis* (Cetartiodactyla, Iniidae), produce a diverse repertoire of acoustic signals. *PeerJ, 7*: e6670. doi:10.7717/peerj.6670

Meltzer, A. L., Makhavova, A., Hicks, L. L., French, J. E., McNulty, J. K., & Bradbury, T. N. (2017). Quantifying the sexual afterglow: The lingering benefits of sex and their implications for pair-bonded relationships. *Psychological Science, 28*(5), 587–598. http://dx.doi.org/10.1177/0956797617691361

Meltzoff, A. N., & Moore, M. K. (1977). Imitation of facial and manual gestures by human neonates. *Science, 198,* 75–78. http://dx.doi.org/10.1126/science.198.4312.75

Meltzoff, A. N., & Moore, M. K. (1985). Cognitive foundations and social functions of imitation and intermodal representation in infancy. In J. Mehler & R. Fox (Eds.), *Neonate cognition: Beyond the blooming buzzing confusion* (pp. 139–156). Hillsdale, NJ: Erlbaum.

Meltzoff, A. N., & Moore, M. K. (1994). Imitation, memory, and the representation of persons. *Infant Behavior & Development, 17,* 83–99. http://dx.doi.org/10.1016/0163-6383(94)90024-8

Melzack, R. (1999). Pain and stress: A new perspective. In R. J. Gatchel & D. C. Turk (Eds.), *Psychosocial factors in pain: Critical perspectives* (pp. 89–106). New York, NY: Guilford.

Melzack, R., & Wall, P. D. (1965). Pain mechanisms: A new theory. *Science, 150,* 971–979.

Meng, Q., Zhuang, Y., Ying, Z., Agrawal, R., Yang, X., & Gomez-Pinilla, F. (2017). Traumatic brain injury induces genome-wide transcriptomic, methylomic, and network perturbations in brain and blood predicting neurological disorders. *EBioMedicine, 16,* 184. http://dx.doi.org/10.1016/j.ebiom.2017.01.04

Mennin, D. S., Fresco, D. M., O'Toole, M. S., & Heimberg, R. G. (2018). A randomized controlled trial of emotion regulation therapy for generalized anxiety disorder with and without co-occurring depression. *Journal of Consulting and Clinical Psychology, 86*(3), 268–281. http://dx.doi.org/10.1037/ccp0000289

Mental Health America. (2019). Sexual assault and mental health. *MHA.* Retrieved April 20, 2019 from http://www.mentalhealthamerica.net/conditions/sexual-assault-and-mental-health

Mental Illness Policy Org. (n.d.). Dangerous standard: O'Connor v. Donaldson case summary. Retrieved from https://mentalillnesspolicy.org/legal/survive-safely-oconnor-donaldson.html

Mentzel, T. Q., Lieverse, R., Bloemen, O., Viechtbauer, W., van Harten, P. N., & Genetic Risk and Outcome of Psychosis (GROUP) Investigators. (2017). High incidence and prevalence of drug-related movement disorders in young patients with psychotic disorders. *Journal of Clinical Psychopharmacology, 37*(2), 231–238. http://dx.doi.org/10.1097/JCP.0000000000000666

Meppelink, C. S., Smit, E. G., Fransen, M. L., & Diviani, N. (2019). "I was right about vaccination": Confirmation bias and health literacy in online health information seeking. *Journal of Health Communication, 24*(2), 129–140. doi:10.1080/10810730.2019.1583701

Mercadillo, R. E., Díaz, J. L., Pasaye, E. H., & Barrios, F. A. (2011). Perception of suffering and compassion experience: Brain gender disparities. *Brain and Cognition, 76*(1), 5–14.

Merckelbach, H., Lynn, S. J., & Lilienfeld, S. O. (2016). Vissia and co-workers claim that DID is trauma-based. But how strong is their evidence? *Acta Psychiatrica Scandinavica, 134*(6), 559–560. http://dx.doi.org/10.1111/acps.12642

Merken, S., & James, V. (2019). Perpetrating the myth: Exploring media accounts of rape myths on "women's" networks. *Deviant Behavior.* doi:10.1080/01639625.2019.1603531

Merrick, M. T., Ford, D. C., Ports, K. A., & Guinn, A. S. (2018). Prevalence of adverse childhood experiences from the 2011-2014 Behavioral Risk Factor Surveillance System in 23 states. *JAMA Pediatrics, 172*(11), 1038–1044. doi:10.1001/jamapediatrics.2018.2537

Merrick, W. A. (2016). Changes in DSM-5 diagnostic criteria for paraphilic disorders. *Archives of Sexual Behavior, 45,* 2173–2179. http://dx.doi.org/10.1007/s10508-016-0845-9

Metz, K. (2016). *Careers in mental health: Opportunities in psychology, counseling, and social work.* Hoboken, NJ: Wiley.

Metzl, J., & MacLeish, K. T. (2015). Mental illness, mass shootings, and the politics of American firearms. *American Journal of Public Health, 105,* 240–249. http://dx.doi.org/10.2105/AJPH.2014.302242

Meyer, M. L., Davachi, L., Ochsner, K. N., & Lieberman, M. D. (2019). Evidence that default network connectivity during rest consolidates social information. *Cerebral Cortex, 29*(5), 1910–1920. https://doi.org/10.1093/cercor/bhy071

Meyer, U. (2016). Rodent models of multiple environmental exposures with relevance to schizophrenia. In M. V. Pletnikov & J. Waddington (Eds.), *Modeling the psychopathological dimensions of schizophrenia: From molecules to behavior* (pp. 361–371). San Diego, CA: Elsevier Academic Press.

Michael, R. B., & Garry, M. (2016). Ordered questions bias eyewitnesses and jurors. *Psychonomic Bulletin & Review, 23,* 601–608. http://dx.doi.org/10.3758/s13423-015-0933-1

Michie, S. West, R., Sheals, K., & Godinho, C. A. (2018). Evaluating the effectiveness of behavior change techniques in health-related behavior: A scoping review of methods used. *Translational Behavioral Medicine, 8*(2), 212–224. https://doi.org/10.1093/tbm/ibx019

Middleton, L., Hall, H., & Raeside, R. (2018). Applications and applicability of Social Cognitive Theory in information science research. *Journal of Librarianship and Information Science, 51*(4), 927–937. https://doi.org/10.1177/0961000618769985

Midway, S. R., Wagner, T., & Burgess, G. H. (2019). Trends in global shark attacks. *PLoS ONE, 14*(2), e0211049. doi:10.1371/journal.pone.0211049

Mikels, J. A., & Shuster, M. M. (2016). The interpretative lenses of older adults are not rose-colored—just less dark: Aging and the interpretation of ambiguous scenarios. *Emotion, 16*, 94–100. http://dx.doi.org/10.1037/emo0000104

Miklikowska, M. (2017). Development of anti-immigrant attitudes in adolescence: The role of parents, peers, intergroup friendships, and empathy. *British Journal of Psychology, 108*(3), 626–648. http://dx.doi.org/10.1111/bjop.12236

Mikulincer, M., Shaver, P. R., Dovidio, J. F., & Simpson, J. A. (Eds.). (2015). *APA handbook of personality and social psychology, Vol. 2. Group processes.* Washington, DC: American Psychological Association. http://dx.doi.org/10.1037/14342-000

Milgram, S. (1963). Behavioral study of obedience. *Journal of Abnormal and Social Psychology, 67*, 371–378. http://dx.doi.org/10.1037/h0040525

Milgram, S. (1974). *Obedience to authority: An experimental view.* New York, NY: Harper & Row.

Miller, A. A., & Spencer, S. J. (2014). Obesity and neuroinflammation: A pathway to cognitive impairment. *Brain, Behavior, and Immunity, 42*, 10–21. http://dx.doi.org/10.1016/j.bbi.2014.04.001

Miller, A. E., Racine, S. E., & Klonsky, E. D. (2019). Symptoms of anorexia nervosa and bulimia nervosa have differential relationships to borderline personality disorder symptoms. *Eating Disorders.* doi:10.1080/10640266.2019.1642034

Miller, D. I., & Halpern, D. F. (2014). The new science of cognitive sex differences. *Trends in Cognitive Sciences, 18*, 37–45. doi:10.1016/j.tics.2013.10.011

Miller, D. I., Nolla, K. M., Eagly, A. H., & Uttal, D. H. (2018). The development of children's gender-science stereotypes: A meta-analysis of 5 decades of U.S. draw-a-scientist studies. *Child Development, 89*, 1943–1955. doi:10.1111/cdev.13039

Miller, E. N., & Sherwood, C. C. (2019, February 5). Human intelligence: What single neurons can tell us. *eLIFE.* https://elifesciences.org/articles/44560

Miller, G. A. (1956). The magical number seven, plus or minus two: Some limits on our capacity for processing information. *Psychological Review, 63*, 81–97. http://dx.doi.org/10.1037/h0043158

Miller, G. E., Chen, E., Armstrong, C. C., Carroll, A. L., Ozturk, S., Rydland, K. J., . . . Nusslock, R. (2018). Functional connectivity in central executive network protects youth against cardiometabolic risks linked with neighborhood violence. *Proceedings of the National Academy of Sciences of the United States of America, 115*(47), 12063–12068. doi:10.1073/pnas.1810067115

Miller, J. G. (1984). Culture and the development of everyday social explanation. *Journal of Personality and Social Psychology, 46(5),* 961–978. http://dx.doi.org/10.1037/0022-3514.46.5.961

Miller, J. G., & Bersoff, D. M. (1998). The role of liking in perceptions of the moral responsibility to help: A cultural perspective. *Journal of Experimental Social Psychology, 34,* 443–469. doi:10.1006/jesp.1998.1359

Miller, J. L., Saklofske, D. H., Weiss, L. G., Drozdick, L., Llorente, A. M., Holdnack, J. A., & Prifitera, A. (2016). Issues related to the WISC-V assessment of cognitive functioning in clinical and special groups. In L. G. Weiss, D. H. Saklofske, J. A. Holdnack & A. Prifitera (Eds.), *WISC-V assessment and interpretation: Scientist-practitioner perspectives* (pp. 287–343). San Diego, CA: Elsevier Academic Press. http://dx.doi.org/10.1016/B978-0-12-404697-9.00010-8

Miller, K. B., Lund, E., & Weatherly, J. (2012). Applying operant learning to the stay-leave decision in domestic violence. *Behavior and Social Issues, 21,* 135–151. http://dx.doi.org/10.5210/bsi.v21i0.4015

Miller-Matero, L. R., Chipungu, K., Martinez, S., Eshelman, A., & Eisenstein, D. (2017). How do I cope with pain? Let me count the ways: Awareness of pain coping behaviors and relationships with depression and anxiety. *Psychology, Health & Medicine, 22*(1), 19–27. http://dx.doi.org/10.1080/13548506.2016. 1191659

Miller, S., Daily, L., Leishman, E., Bradshaw, H., & Straiker, A. (2018). Δ9-tetrahydrocannabinol and cannabidiol differentially regulate intraocular pressure. *Investigative Opthalmology & Visual Science, 59*(15), 5904. doi:10.1167/iovs.18-24838

Miller, S. R., Tserakhava, V., & Miller, C. J. (2011). "My child is shy and has no friends: What does parenting have to do with it"? *Journal of Youth and Adolescence, 40*(4), 442–452.

Millings, A., Walsh, J., Hepper, E., & O'Brien, M. (2013). Good partner, good parent: Responsiveness mediates the link between romantic attachment and parenting style. *Personality and Social Psychology Bulletin, 39,* 170–180. http://dx.doi.org/10.1177/0146167212468333

Mills, P. J., Redwine, L., Wilson, K., Pung, M. A., Chinh, K., Greenberg, B. H., . . . Chopra, D. (2015). The role of gratitude in spiritual well-being in asymptomatic heart failure patients. *Spirituality in Clinical Practice, 2*(1), 5–17. http://doi.org/10.1037/scp0000050

Minai, U., Gustafson, K., Fiorentino, R., Jongman, A., & Sereno, J. (2017). Fetal rhythm-based language discrimination. *NeuroReport, 28*(10), 561–564. doi:10.1097/wnr.0000000000000794

Miniati, M., Callari, A., Maglio, A., & Calugi, S. (2018). Interpersonal psychotherapy for eating disorders: Current perspectives. *Psychology Research and Behavior Management, 11*, 353–369. doi:10.2147/PRBM.S120584

Mioč, M., Antelmi, E., Filardi, M., Pizza, F., Ingravallo, F., Nobili, L., . . . Plazzi, G. (2018). Sexsomnia: A diagnostic challenge, a case report. *Sleep Medicine, 43*, 1–3. doi:10.1016/j.sleep.2017.11.1120

Mischel, W. (1966). Theory and research on the antecedents of self-imposed delay of reward. In B. A. Maher (Ed.), *Progress in experimental personality research* (pp. 85–131). New York, NY: Academic Press.

Mischel, W. (2014). *The marshmallow test: Mastering self-control.* New York, NY: Little, Brown, & Company.

Mischel, W., Ayduk, O., Berman, M. G., Casey, B. J., Gotlib, I. H., Jonides, J., . . . Shoda, Y. (2011). 'Willpower' over the life span: Decomposing self-regulation. *Social Cognitive and Affective Neuroscience, 6*, 252–256. doi:10.1093/scan/nsq08

Mischel, W., & Ebbesen, E. B. (1970). Attention in delay of gratification. *Journal of Personality and Social Psychology, 16*, 329–337. doi:10.1037/h0029815.

Mita, T. H., Dermer, M., & Knight, J. (1977). Reversed facial images and the mere exposure hypothesis. *Journal of Personality and Social Psychology, 35*, 597–601.

Mitchell, J. M., O'Neil, J. P., Janabi, M., Marks, S. M., Jagust, W. J., & Fields, H. L. (2012). Alcohol consumption induces endogenous opioid release in the human orbitofrontal cortex and nucleus accumbens. *Science Translational Medicine, 4*(116):116ra6. http://dx.doi.org/10.1126/scitranslmed.3002902

Mitchell, Y. T., & Bromfield, T. L. (2019, January 10). Gun violence and the minority experience. *National Council on Family Relations*. Retrieved June 14, 2019 from https://www.ncfr.org/ncfr-report/winter-2018/gun-violence-and-minority-experience

Mithoefer, M. C., Grob, C. S., & Brewerton, T. D. (2016). Novel psychopharmacological therapies for psychiatric disorders: Psilocybin and MDMA. *The Lancet Psychiatry, 3*, 481–488. doi:10.1016/S2215-0366(15)00576-3

Mok, P. L. H., Webb, R. T., Appleby, L., & Pedersen, C. B. (2016). Full spectrum of mental disorders linked with childhood residential mobility. *Journal of Psychiatric Research, 78*, 57–64. http://dx.doi.org/10.1016/j.jpsychires.2016.03.011

Mokrova, I. L., O'Brien, M., Calkins, S. D., Leerkes, E. M., & Marcovitch, S. (2013). The role of persistence at preschool age in academic skills at kindergarten. *European Journal of Psychology of Education, 28*, 1495–1503. http://dx.doi.org/10.1007/s10212-013-0177-2

Mokrysz, C., Landy, R., Gage, S. H., Munafò, M. R., Roiser, J. P., & Curran, H. V. (2016). Are IQ and educational outcomes in teenagers related to their cannabis use? A prospective cohort study. *Journal of Psychopharmacology, 30*, 159–168. http://dx.doi.org/10.1177/0269881115622241

Moleiro, C., Ratinho, I., & Bernardes, S. (2017). Autonomy-connectedness in collectivistic cultures: An exploratory cross-cultural study among Portuguese natives, Cape-Verdean and Chinese people residing in Portugal. *Personality and Individual Differences, 104*, 23–28. https://doi.org/10.1016/j.paid.2016.07.031

Molina, B. S., & Pelham, W. E., Jr. (2014). Attention-deficit/hyperactivity disorder and risk of substance use disorder: Developmental considerations, potential pathways, and opportunities for research. *Annual Review of Clinical Psychology, 10*, 607–639. doi:10.1146/annurev-clinpsy-032813-153722

Monastra, V. J. (2014). Temperament may be inherited, but emotional control is learned. In V. J. Monastra (Ed.), *Parenting children with ADHD: 10 lessons that medicine cannot teach* (2nd ed., pp. 151–179). Washington, DC: American Psychological Association.

Money, J., Prakasam, K. S., & Joshi, V. N. (1991). Semen-conservation doctrine from ancient Ayurvedic to modern sexological theory. *American Journal of Psychotherapy, 45*(1), 9–13. doi:10.1176/appi.psychotherapy.1991.45.1.9

Monin, B. (2003). The warm glow heuristic: When liking leads to familiarity. *Journal of Personality and Social Psychology, 85*, 1035–1048.

Montag, J. L., Jones, M. N., & Smith, L. B. (2015). The words children hear: Picture books and the statistics for language learning. *Psychological Science, 26*, 1489–1496. doi:10.1177/0956797615594361

Moon, C., Lagercrantz, H., & Kuhl, P. K. (2013). Language experienced in utero affects vowel perception after birth: A two-country study. *Acta Paediatrica, 102*, 156–160. http://dx.doi.org/10.1111/apa.12098

Moore, C. L., & Morelli, G. A. (1979). Mother rats interact differently with male and female offspring. *Journal of Comparative and Physiological Psychology, 93*(4), 677–684. http://dx.doi.org/10.1037/h0077599

Moore, D. A., Nunns, M., Shaw, L., Rogers, M., Walker, E., Ford, T., . . . Coon, J. T. (2019). Interventions to improve the mental health of children and young people with long-term physical conditions: Linked evidence syntheses. *Health Technology Assessment, 23*(22), 1. doi:10.3310/hta23220

Moran, L., V., Ongur, D., Hsu, J., Castro, V. M., Perlis, R. H., & Schneeweiss, S. (2019). Psychosis with methylphenidate or amphetamine in patients with ADHD. *New England Journal of Medicine, 380*(12), 1128–1138. doi:10.1056/NEJMoa1813751

Morelli, S. A., Lee, I. A., Arnn, M. E., & Zaki, J. (2015). Emotional and instrumental support provision interact to predict well-being. *Emotion, 15*, 484–493. http://dx.doi.org/10.1037/emo0000084

Moreno-Murcia, J. A., Huéscar Hernández, E., Conte Marín, L., & Nuñez, J. L. (2019). Coaches' motivational style and athletes' fear of failure. *International Journal of Environmental Research and Public Health, 16*(9), 1563. doi:10.3390/ijerph16091563

Morey, L. C. (2013). Measuring personality and psychopathology. In J. A. Schinka, W. F. Velicer, & I. B. Weiner (Eds.), *Handbook of psychology, Vol. 2. Research methods in psychology* (2nd ed., pp. 395–427). Hoboken, NJ: Wiley.

Morgan, C. A., & Southwick, S. (2014). Perspective: I believe what I remember, but it may not be true. *Neurobiology of Learning and Memory, 112*, 101–103. http://dx.doi.org/10.1016/j.nlm.2013.12.011

Morgan, C. A., Southwick, S., Steffian, G., Hazlett, G. A., & Loftus, E. F. (2013). Misinformation can influence memory for recently experienced, highly stressful events. *International Journal of Law and Psychiatry, 36*, 11–17. http://dx.doi.org/10.1016/j.ijlp.2012.11.002

Morgan, J. (2017). If other ways don't work, try the immune system? *The Lancet Neurology, 16*(2), 109. http://dx.doi.org/10.1016/S1474-4422(16)30307-6

Mori, K., Ito-Koyama, A., Arai, M., & Hanayama, A. (2014). Boys, be independent! Conformity development of Japanese children in the Asch experiment without using confederates. *Psychology, 5*, 617–623. http://dx.doi.org/10.4236/psych.2014.57073.

Morin, C. M., & Edinger, J. D. (2015). Sleepwake disorders. In P. H. Blaney, R. F. Krueger, & T. Millon (Eds.), *Oxford textbook of psychopathology* (3rd ed., pp. 566–588). New York, NY:Oxford University Press.

Morin, C. M., Savard, J., & Ouellet, M.-C. (2013). Nature and treatment of insomnia. In A. M. Nezu, C. M. Nezu, P. A. Geller, & I. B. Weiner (Eds.), *Handbook of psychology, Vol. 9. Health psychology* (2nd ed., pp. 318–339). Hoboken, NJ: Wiley.

Morin-Major, J. K., Marin, M.-F., Durand, N., Wan, N., Juster, R.-P., & Lupien, S. J. (2016). Facebook behaviors associated with diurnal cortisol in adolescents: Is befriending stressful? *Psychoneuroendocrinology, 63*, 238–246. http://dx.doi.org/10.1016/j.psyneuen.2015.10.005

Morling, B. (2015). *Research methods in psychology: Evaluating a world of information* (2nd ed.). New York, NY: Norton.

Morris, B. (2015). *Anthropology of the self: The individual in cultural perspective*. London, UK: Pluto.

Morrison, A. B., Goolsarran, M., Rogers, S. L., & Jha, A. P. (2013). Taming a wandering attention: Short-form mindfulness training in student cohorts. *Frontiers in Human Neuroscience, 7*, 897. http://doi.org/10.3389/fnhum. 2013.00897

Morry, M. M., Kito, M., & Dunphy, L. (2014). How do I see you? Partner enhancement in dating couples. *Canadian Journal of Behavioural Science, 46*, 356–365. http://dx.doi.org/10.1037/a0033167

Moskowitz, J. T., Epel, E. S., & Acree, M. (2008). Positive affect uniquely predicts lower risk of mortality in people with diabetes. *Health Psychology, 27*, S73–S82. doi:10.1037/0278-6133.27.1.S73

Moulding, N. (2016). *Gendered violence, mental health and recovery in everyday lives: Beyond trauma*. London, UK: Taylor & Francis.

Moutsiana, C., Johnstone, T., Murray, L., Fearon, P., Cooper, P. J., Pliatsikas, C., . . . Halligan, S. L. (2015). Insecure attachment during infancy predicts greater amygdala volumes in early adulthood. *Journal of Child Psychology and Psychiatry, 56*, 540–548. http://dx.doi.org/10.1111/jcpp.12317

Mowrer, O. H. (1951). Two-factor learning theory: summary and comment. *Psychological Review, 58*(5), 350–354. http://dx.doi.org/10.1037/h0058956

Mowrer, O. H. (1960). *Learning theory and behavior.* Hoboken, NJ: John Wiley & Sons Inc. http://dx.doi.org/10.1037/10802-000

Mrazek, M. D., Franklin, M. S., Phillips, D. T., Baird, B., & Schooler, J. W. (2013). Mindfulness training improves working memory capacity and GRE performance while reducing mind wandering. *Psychological Science, 24,* 776–781. http://dx.doi.org/10.1177/0956797612459659

Mueller, P. A., & Oppenheimer, D. M. (2014). The pen is mightier than the keyboard: Advantages of longhand over laptop note taking. *Psychological Science, 25,* 1159–1168. http://dx.doi.org/10.1177/0956797614524581

Mueller, P. A., & Oppenheimer, D. M. (2014). The pen is mightier than the keyboard: Advantages of longhand over laptop note taking. *Psychological Science, 25,* 1159–1168. http://dx.doi.org/10.1177/0956797614524581

Muir, D., & Hibberd, F. (2019). Reconceptualising exposure and some implications for cognitive-behavioural and psychodynamic practice. *Behaviour Change, 36*(2), 84–101. doi:10.1017/bec.2019.6

Muise, A., Harasymchuk, C., Day, L. C., Bacev-Giles, C., Gere, J., & Impett, E. A. (2019). Broadening your horizons: Self-expanding activities promote desire and satisfaction in established romantic relationships. *Journal of Personality and Social Psychology, 116*(2), 237–258. http://dx.doi.org/10.1037/pspi0000148

Muise, A., Schimmack, U., & Impett, E. A. (2016). Sexual frequency predicts greater well-being, but more is not always better. *Social Psychological and Personality Science, 7,* 295–302. http://dx.doi.org/10.1177/1948550615616462

Mullen, N. W., Maxwell, H., & Bédard, M. (2015). Decreasing driver speeding with feed-back and a token economy. *Transportation Research Part F: Traffic Psychology and Behaviour, 28,* 77–85. http://dx.doi.org/10.1016/j.trf.2014.11.008

Müller, C. A., Schmitt, K., Barber, A. L., & Huber, L. (2015). Dogs can discriminate emotional expressions of human faces. *Current Biology, 25*(5), 601–605. http://dx.doi.org/10.1016/j.cub.2014.12.055.

Müller, C. P., & Homberg, J. R. (2015). The role of serotonin in drug use and addiction. *Behavioural Brain Research, 277,* 146–192. http://dx.doi.org/10.1016/j.bbr.2014.04.007

Müller, S., Mychajliw, C., Hautzinger, M., Fallgatter, A. J., Saur, R., & Leyhe, T. (2014). Memory for past public events depends on retrieval frequency but not memory age in Alzheimer's disease. *Journal of Alzheimer's Disease, 38,* 379–390. http://dx.doi.org/10.3233/JAD-130923

Munoz, L., & Anastassiou-Hadjicharalambous, X. (2011). Disinhibited behaviors in young children: Relations with impulsivity and autonomic psychophysiology. *Biological Psychology, 86,* 349–359. doi:10.1016/j.biopsycho.2011.01.007

Munsch, S., Wyssen, A., Vanhulst, P., Lalanne, D., Steinemann, S. T., & Tuch, A. (2019). Binge-eating disorder treatment goes online - feasibility, usability, and treatment outcome of an Internet-based treatment for binge-eating disorder: study-protocol for a three-arm randomized controlled trial including an immediate treatment, a waitlist, and a placebo control group. *Trials, 20*(1), 128. doi:10.1186/s13063-019-3192-z

Murayama, K., Perkrun, R., Lichtenfeld, S., & vomHofe, R. (2012). Predicting long-term growth in students' mathematics achievement: The unique contributions of motivation and cognitive strategies. *Child Development, 84,* 1475–1490. doi:10.1111/cdev.12036

Murdock, K. K. (2013). Texting while stressed: Implications for students' burnout, sleep, and well-being. *Psychology of Popular Media Culture, 2,* 207–221. http://dx.doi.org/10.1037/ppm0000012

Murphy, M. (2018, April 15). Neuroscience explains why you need to write down your goals if you actually want to achieve them. *Forbes.* Retrieved from https://www.forbes.com/sites/markmurphy/2018/04/15/neuroscience-explains-why-you-need-to-write-down-your-goals-if-you-actually-want-to-achieve-them/#6f4e9b479059

Murray, H. A. (1938). *Explorations in personality.* Oxford, UK: Oxford.

Myers, A. (2015). Neonatal male circumcision, if not already commonplace, would be plainly unacceptable by modern ethical standards. *The American Journal of Bioethics, 15,* 54–55. http://dx.doi.org/10.1080/15265161.2014.990166

Myers, K. P. (2018). The convergence of psychology and neurobiology in flavor-nutrient learning. *Appetite, 122,* 36–43. https://doi.org/10.1016/j.appet.2017.03.048

Nagasawa, M., Mitsui, S., En, S., Ohtani, N., Ohta, M., Sakuma, Y., . . . Kikusui, T. (2015). Social evolution. Oxytocin-gaze positive loop and the coevolution of human-dog bonds. *Science, 348,* 333–336. http://dx.doi.org/10.1126/science.1261022.

Nai, J., Narayanan, J., Hernandez, I., & Savani, K. (2018). People in more racially diverse neighborhoods are more prosocial. *Journal of Personality and Social Psychology, 114*(4), 497–515. http://dx.doi.org/10.1037/pspa0000103

Nairne, J. S., & Neath, I. (2013). Sensory and working memory. In A. F. Healy, R. W. Proctor, & I. B. Weiner (Eds.), *Handbook of psychology, Vol. 4. Experimental psychology* (2nd ed., pp. 419–445). Hoboken, NJ: Wiley.

Na, J., & Chan, M. Y. (2015). Culture, cognition, and intercultural relations. In J. E. Warnick & D. Landis (Eds.), *Neuroscience in intercultural contexts* (pp. 49–71). New York, NY: Springer Science + Business Media. http://dx.doi.org/10.1007/978-1-4939-2260-4_3

Naneix, F., Darlot, F., Coutureau, E., & Cador, M. (2016). Long-lasting deficits in hedonic and nucleus accumbens reactivity to sweet rewards by sugar overconsumption during adolescence. *European Journal of Neuroscience, 43,* 671–680. http://dx.doi.org/10.1111/ejn.13149

Narvaez, D., Woodbury, R., Cheng, Y., Wang, L., Kurth, A., Gleason, T., . . . Näpflin, C. (2019). Evolved developmental niche provision report: Moral socialization, social thriving, and social maladaptation in three countries. *SAGE Open, 9*(2). https://doi.org/10.1177/2158244019840123

Nash, R. A., Nash, A., Morris, A., & Smith, S. L. (2016). Does rapport-building boost the eyewitness eye closure effect in closed questioning? *Legal and Criminological Psychology, 21*(2), 305–318. http://dx.doi.org/10.1111/lcrp.12073

Nassan, F. L., Arvizu, M., Mínguez-Alarcón, L., Williams, P. L., Attaman, J., Petrozza, J., . . . Keller, M. G. (2019). Marijuana smoking and the markers of testicular function among men from a fertility centre. *Human Reproduction, 34*(4), 715–723. doi:10.1093/humrep/dez002

National Alliance on Mental Health. (2015). People with mental illness enrich our lives. *National Alliance on Mental Illness.* Retrieved May 24, 2015 from http://www2.nami.org/Template.cfm?Section=Helpline1&template=/ContentManagement/ContentDisplay.cfm&-ContentID=4858

National Alliance on Mental Illness (NAMI). (n.d.). Mental health by the numbers. *NAMI.* Retrieved March 16, 2017 from http://www.nami.org/Learn-More/Mental-Health-By-the-Numbers

National Highway Traffic Safety Administration (NHTSA). (2019). Distracted driving. *National Highway Traffic Safety Administration.* Retrieved September 1, 2019 from https://www.nhtsa.gov/risky-driving/distracted-driving

National Institute of Health (NIH). (2019). Opioid overdose crisis. Retrieved March 21, 2018 from https://www.drugabuse.gov/drugs-abuse/opioids/opioid-overdose-crisis

National Institute of Mental Health (NIMH). (2014). Post-traumatic stress disorder. *NIH.gov.* Retrieved from http://www.nimh.nih.gov/health/publications/post-traumatictress-disorder-ptsd/index.shtml

National Institute of Mental Health (NIMH). (2016). Major depression among adults. *NIH. gov.* Retrieved from https://www.nimh.nih.gov/health/statistics/prevalence/majordepression-among-adults.shtml

National Safety Council. (2018). NSC statement on IIHS report on increased pedestrian deaths. Retrieved from https://www.nsc.org/in-the-newsroom/nsc-statement-on-iihs-report-on-increased-pedestrian-deaths

National Safety Council. (2019). Head up, phone down, when headed back to school. Retrieved from https://www.nsc.org/home-safety/safety-topics/distracted-walking/teens

National Sexual Violence Resource Center. (2019). Reporting on sexual violence. *NSVRC.* Retrieved from https://www.nsvrc.org/sexual-violence-reporting-tools

National Sleep Foundation. (2012). *National sleep foundation sleepiness test.* Retrieved from https://sleepfoundation.org/quiz/national-sleep-foundation-sleepiness-test

Navarra, R. J., Gottman, J. M., & Gottman, J. S. (2016). Sound relationship house theory and relationship and marriage education. In J. J. Ponzetti, Jr. (Ed.), *Evidence-based approaches to relationship and marriage education* (pp. 93–107). New York, NY: Routledge/Taylor & Francis Group.

Nave, G., Minxha, J., Greenberg, D. M., Kosinski, M., Stillwell, D., & Rentfrow, J. (2018). Musical preferences predict personality: Evidence from active listening and Facebook likes. *Psychological Science, 29*(7), 1145–1158. https://doi.org/10.1177/0956797618761659

Neale, J. M., Oltmanns, T. F., & Winters, K. C. (1983). Recent developments in the assessment and conceptualization of schizophrenia. *Behavioral Assessment, 5,* 33–54.

Neisser, U. (1967). *Cognitive psychology.* New York, NY: Appleton-Century-Croft s.

Nekitsing, C., Hetherington, M. M., & Blundell-Birtill, P. (2018). Developing healthy food preferences in preschool children through taste exposure, sensory learning, and nutrition education. *Current Obesity Reports, 7*(1), 60–67. doi:10.1007/s13679-018-0297-8

Nelson, C. A., III, Zeanah, C. H., & Fox, N. A. (2019). How early experience shapes human development: The case of psychosocial deprivation. *Neural Plasticity,* Article ID 1676285. https://doi.org/10.1155/2019/1676285

Nelson, S. K., Layous, K., Cole, S. W., & Lyubomirsky, S. (2016). Do unto others or treat yourself? The effects of prosocial and self focused behavior on psychological flourishing. *Emotion, 16,* 850–861. http://dx.doi.org/10.1037/emo0000178

Neubauer, A. C., Grabner, R. H., Freudenthaler, H. H., Beckmann, J. F., & Guthke, J. (2004). Intelligence and individual differences in becoming neurally efficient. *Acta Psychologica, 116,* 55–74. http://dx.doi.org/10.1016/j.actpsy.2003.11.005

Neumann, A., & Walter, S. (2015). Depression as an adaptation: The infection–defense hypothesis and cytokine mechanisms. In T. Breyer (Ed.), *Epistemological dimensions of evolutionary psychology* (pp. 175–196). New York, NY: Springer. http://dx.doi.org/10.1007/978-1-4939-1387-9_9

Newcombe, N. S. (2010). On tending to our scientific knitting: Thinking about gender in the context of evolution. In J. C. Chrisler & D. R. McCreary (Eds.), *Handbook of gender research in psychology, Vol. 1. Gender research in general and experimental psychology* (pp. 259–274). New York, NY: Springer Science 1 Business Media.

Newcorn, J. H., Ivanov, I., Chacko, A., & Javdani, S. (2016). Aggression and violence. In M. K. Dulcan (Ed.), *Dulcan's textbook of child and adolescent psychiatry* (2nd ed., pp. 603–620). Arlington, VA: American Psychiatric Publishing.

Newland, R. P., & Crnic, K. A. (2017). Developmental risk and goodness of fit in the mother-child relationship: Links to parenting stress and children's behaviour problems. *Infant and Child Development, 26*(2), e1980. doi:10.1002/icd.1980

Newman, B. W., & Newman, P. R. (2015). *Theories of human development* (2nd ed.). New York, NY: Psychology Press.

Newman, K. M. (2016). Five science-backed strategies to build resilience. *Greater Good.* Retrieved from http://greatergood.berkeley.edu/article/item/five_science_backed_strategies_to_build_resilience?utm_source=GG+Newsletter+Nov+16%2C+2016&utm_campaign=GG+Newsletter+Nov+16+2016&utm_medium=email

Newman, T. (2018, March 17). Unlocking the personality of a social media addict. *Medical News Today.* Retrieved from https://www.medicalnewstoday.com/articles/321240.php

Newman, T. (2018, September 5). Anxiety in the West: Is it on the rise? *MedicalNewsToday.* Retrieved from https://www.medicalnewstoday.com/articles/322877.php

Ng, H. B., Kao, K. L., Chan, Y. C., Chew, E., Chuang, K. H., & Chen, S. H. (2016). Modality specificity in the cerebro-cerebellar neurocircuitry during working memory. *Behavioural Brain Research, 305,* 164–173. http://dx.doi. org/10.1016/j.bbr.2016.02.027

Ng, T. H., Chung, K.-F., Ho, F. Y.-Y., Yeung, W.-F., Yung, K.-P., & Lam, T.-H. (2015). Sleep wake disturbance in interepisode bipolar disorder and high-risk individuals: A systematic review and meta-analysis. *Sleep Medicine Reviews, 20,* 46–58. http://dx.doi.org/10.1016/j.smrv.2014.06.006

Nguyen, M. H., Le, T. T, & Meirmanov, S. (2019). Depression, acculturative stress, and social connectedness among international university students in Japan: A statistical investigation. *Sustainability, 11*(3), 878. https://doi.org/10.3390/su11030878

Nguyen, T. P., Karney, B. R., & Bradbury, T. N. (2017). Childhood abuse and late marital outcomes: Do partner characteristics moderate the association? *Journal of Family Psychology, 31*(1), 82–92. http://dx.doi.org/10.1037/fam0000208

Nguyen, T., & Szymanski, B. (2012). Using location-based social networks to validate human mobility and relationships models. *Proceedings of the 2012 IEEE/ACM International Conference on Advances in Social Networks Analysis and Mining,* pp. 1247–1253.

Nicholls, H. (2018). *Sleepyhead: The neuroscience of a good night's rest.* Basic Books.

Nicholson, S. P., Coe, C. M., Emory, J., & Song, A. V. (2016). The politics of beauty: The effects of partisan bias on physical attractiveness. *Political Behavior, 38*(4), 883–898. http://dx.doi.org/10.1007/s11109-016-9339-7

Nickerson, R. (1998). Confirmation bias: A ubiquitous phenomenon in many guises. *Review of General Psychology, 2,* 175–220. http://dx.doi.org/10.1037/10892680.2.2.175

Nicklaus, S. (2016). The role of food experiences during early childhood in food pleasure learning. *Appetite, 104,* 3–9. doi:10.1016/j.appet.2015.08.022

NIDA. (2016, May 14). Club drugs. *National Institute of Drug Abuse (NIDA).* Retrieved from https://www.drugabuse.gov/drugs-abuse/club-drugs

NIDA. (2019, January). Opioid overdose crisis. *National Institute on Drug Abuse*. Retrieved from https://www.drugabuse.gov/drugs-abuse/opioids/opioid-overdose-crisis

Nielsen, T., O'Reilly, C., Carr, M., Dumel, G., Godin, L., Solomonova, E., . . . Paquette, T. (2015). Overnight improvements in two REM sleep-sensitive tasks are associated with both REM and NREM sleep changes, sleep spindle features, and awakenings for dream recall. *Neurobiology of Learning and Memory, 122,* 88–97. http://dx.doi.org/10.1016/j.nlm.2014.09.007

Nierenberg, B., Mayersohn, G., Serpa, S., Holovatyk, A., Smith, E., & Cooper, S. (2016). Application of well-being therapy to people with disability and chronic illness. *Rehabilitation Psychology, 61,* 32–43. http://dx.doi.org/10.1037/rep0000060

Nishimoto, R. (1988). A cross-cultural analysis of psychiatric symptom expression using Langer's twenty-two item index. *Journal of Sociology and Social Welfare, 15,* 45–62.

Nishitani, S., Miyamura, T., Tagawa, M., Sumi, M., Takase, R., Doi, H., . . . Shinohara, K. (2009). The calming effect of a maternal breast milk odor on the human newborn infant. *Neuroscience Research, 63,* 66–71. http://dx.doi.org/10.1016/j.neures.2008.10.007

Nishiyama, K., & Johnson, J. V. (1997). Karoshi—Death from overwork: Occupational health consequences of Japanese production management. *International Journal of Health Services, 27,* 625–641. http://dx.doi.org/10.2190/1JPC-679V-DYNT-HJ6G

Noah, T., Schul, Y., & Mayo, R. (2018). When both the original study and its failed replication are correct: Feeling observed eliminates the facial-feedback effect. *Journal of Personality and Social Psychology, 114*(5), 657–664. Retrieved from doi:10.1037/pspa0000121.

Noble, K. G., Houston, S. M., Brito, N. H., Bartsch, H., Kan, E., Kuperman, J. M., . . . Sowell, E. R. (2015). Family income, parental education and brain structure in children and adolescents. *Nature Neuroscience, 18,* 773–778. http://dx.doi.org/10.1038/nn.3983

Nolan, P. (2012). *Therapist and client: A relational approach to psychotherapy.* Malden, MA: Wiley-Blackwell.

Noone, P. A. (2017). The Holmes–Rahe Stress Inventory. *Occupational Medicine, 67*(7), 581–582. https://doi.org/10.1093/occmed/kqx099

Norcross, J., & Wampold, B. (2018). A new therapy for each patient: Evidence-based relationships and responsiveness. *Journal of Clinical Psychology, 74.* doi:10.1002/jclp.22678

Normandin, L., Ensink, K., & Kernberg, O. F. (2015). Transference-focused psychotherapy for borderline adolescents: A neurobiologically informed psychodynamic psychotherapy. *Journal of Infant, Child & Adolescent Psychotherapy, 14,* 98–110. http://dx.doi.org/10.1080/15289168.2015.1006008

Noval, L. J., & Stahl, G. K. (2015). Accounting for proscriptive and prescriptive morality in the workplace: The double-edged sword effect of mood on managerial ethical decision making. *Journal of Business Ethics, 142*(3), 589–602. doi:10.1007/s10551-015-2767-1

Nowicki, S. (2016). *Choice or chance: Understanding your locus of control and why it matters.* New York, NY: Prometheus Books.

Nyarubeli, I. P., Tungu, A. M., Bråtveit, M., & Moen, B. E. (2019). Occupational noise exposure and hearing loss: A study of knowledge, attitude and practice among Tanzanian iron and steel workers. *Archives of Environmental & Occupational Health.* doi:10.1080/19338244.2019.1607816

Nyongesa, M. K., Ssewanyana, D., Mutua, A. M., Chongwo, E., Scerif, G., Newton, C. R. J. C., & Abubakar, A. (2019). Assessing executive function in adolescence: A scoping review of existing measures and their psychometric robustness. *Frontiers in Psychology,* 10:311. doi:10.3389/fpsyg.2019.00311

Oates, K. (2019, April 4). Cyclist Kelly Catlin's death sheds light on the mental health of professional athletes. *Global Sport Matters.* Retrieved from https://globalsportmatters.com/health/2019/04/04/cyclist-kelly-catlins-death-sheds-light-on-the-mental-health-of-professional-athletes/

Obradović, M. M. S., Hamelin, B., Manevski, N., Couto, J. P., Sethi, A., Coissieus, M. M., . . . Bentires-Alj, M. (2019). Glucocorticoids promote breast cancer metastasis. *Nature, 567*(7749), 540–544. doi:10.1038/s41586-019-1019-4

O'Brien, E., & Kassirer, S. (2019). People are slow to adapt to the warm glow of giving. *Psychological Science, 30*(2), 193–204. http://dx.doi.org/10.1177/0956797618814145

O'Brien, E., & Smith, R. W. (2019). Unconventional consumption methods and enjoying things consumed: Recapturing the "first time" experience. *Personality and Social Psychology Bulletin, 45*(1), 67–80. doi:10.1177/0146167218779823

O'Brien, F., Bible, J., Liu, D., & Simons-Morton, B. G. (2017). Do young drivers become safer after being involved in a collision? *Psychological Science, 28*(4), 407–413. http://dx.doi.org/10.1177/0956797616688118

Obschonka, M., Schmitt-Rodermund, E., Silbereisen, R. K., Gosling, S. D., & Potter, J. (2013). The regional distribution and correlates of an entrepreneurship-prone personality profile in the United States, Germany, and the United Kingdom: A socioecological perspective. *Journal of Personality and Social Psychology, 105,* 104–122. http://dx.doi.org/10.1037/a0032275

Ockerman, E. (2016, June 22). 'Infant trackers' help parents keep tables on their babies. *Time.* Retrieved from http://time.com/4376283/quantified-self-parents-apps/

O'Connor, P. J., Hill, A., Kaya, M., & Martin, B. (2019). The measurement of emotional intelligence: A critical review of the literature and recommendations for researchers and practitioners. *Frontiers in Psychology, 10*:1116. doi:10.3389/fpsyg.2019.01116

O'Farrell, K., & Harkin, A. (2017). Stress related regulation of the kynurenine pathway: Relevance to neuropsychiatric and degenerative disorders. *Neuropharmacology, 112,* 307–323. http://dx.doi.org/10.1016/j.neuropharm.2015.12.004

O'Farrell, T. J., Schumm, J. A., Dunlap, L. J., Murphy, M. M., & Muchowski, P. (2016). A randomized clinical trial of group versus standard behavioral couples therapy plus individually based treatment for patients with alcohol dependence. *Journal of Consulting and Clinical Psychology, 84,* 497–510. http://dx.doi.org/10.1037/ccp0000089

O'Hara, D. (2019, June 6). Wearable technology for mental health. *American Psychological Association.* Retrieved from https://www.apa.org/members/content/wearable-technology

Ohayon, M. M., Mahowald, M. W., Dauvilliers, Y., Krystal, A. D., & Leger, D. (2012). Prevalence and comorbidity of nocturnal wandering in the US adult general population. *Neurology, 78,* 1583–1589.

Ohtomo, S. (2017). Exposure to diet priming images as cues to reduce the influence of unhealthy eating habits. *Appetite, 109,* 83–92. http://dx.doi.org/10.1016/j.appet.2016.11.022

Okonofua, J. A., & Eberhardt, J. L. (2015). Two strikes: Race and the disciplining of young students. *Psychological Science, 26*(5), 617–624. http://dx.doi.org/10.1177/0956797615570365

Olderbak, S. G., Malter, F., Wolf, P. S. A., Jones, D. N., & Figueredo, A. J. (2017). Predicting romantic interest at zero acquaintance: Evidence of sex differences in trait perception but not in predictors of interest. *European Journal of Personality, 31,* 42–62. http://dx.doi.org/10.1002/per.2087

Olds, J., & Milner, P. M. (1954). Positive reinforcement produced by electrical stimulation of septal area and other regions of rat brains. *Journal of Comparative and Physiological Psychology, 47,* 419–427. http://dx.doi.org/10.1037/h0058775

Olenski, A. R., Abola, M. V., & Jena, A. B. (2015). Do heads of government age more quickly? Observational study comparing mortality between elected leaders and runners-up in national elections of 17 countries. *British Medical Journal, 351,* h6424. http://dx.doi.org/10.1136/bmj.h6424

Oller, J. W., Jr., Oller, S. D., & Oller, S. N. (2014). *Milestones: Normal speech and language development across the life span* (2nd ed.). San Diego, CA: Plural.

Ollmann, T., Péczely, L., László, K., Kovács, A., Gálosi, R., Berente, E., . . . Zoltán, L. L. (2015). Positive reinforcing effect of neurotensin microinjection into the ventralpallidum in conditioned place preference test. *Behavioural Brain Research, 278,* 470–475. http://dx.doi.org/10.1016/j.bbr.2014.10.021

Ollove, M. (2018, July 13). Police are changing lineups to avoid false IDs. *PEW.* Retrieved from https://www.pewtrusts.org/en/research-and-analysis/blogs/stateline/2018/07/13/police-are-changing-lineups-to-avoid-false-ids

Olson, K. R., Durwood, L., DeMeules, M., & McLaughlin, K. A. (2016). Mental health of transgender children who are supported in their identities. *Pediatrics, 137,* 1–8. http://doi.org/10.1542/peds.2015-3223

Olson, K. R., Key, A. C., & Eaton, N. R. (2015). Gender cognition in transgender children. *Psychological Science, 26,* 467–474. http://dx.doi.org/10.1177/0956797614568156

Omani-Samani, R., Amini, P., Navid, B., Sepidarkish, M., Maroufizadeh, S., & Almasi-Hashiani, A. (2019). Prevalence of sexual dysfunction among infertile women in Iran: A systematic review and meta-analysis. *International Journal of Fertility & Sterility, 12*(4), 278–283. doi:10.22074/ijfs.2019.5395

Omer, S. B., & Yildirim, I. (2019). Further evidence of MMR vaccine safety: Scientific and communications considerations. *Annals of Internal Medicine, 170*(8), 567–568. doi:10.7326/M19-0596

O'Neal, E. N., & Hayes, B. E. (2019). "A rape is a rape, regardless of what the victim was doing at the time": Detective views on how "problematic" victims affect sexual assault case processing. *Criminal Justice Review.* https://doi.org/10.1177/0734016819842639

Oostenbroek, J., Suddendorf, T., Nielsen, M., Redshaw, J., Kennedy-Costantini, S., Davis, J., . . . Slaughter, V. (2016). Comprehensive longitudinal study challenges the existence of neonatal imitation in humans. *Current Biology, 26,* 1334–1338. http://dx.doi.org/10.1016/j.cub.2016.03.047

Opel, N., Redlich, R., Dohm, K., Zaremba, D., Goltermann, J., Repple, J., . . . Dannlowski, U. (2019, April 1). Mediation of the influence of childhood maltreatment on depression relapse by cortical structure: A 2-year longitudinal observational study. *The Lancet, 6*(4), 318–326. https://doi.org/10.1016/S2215-0366(19)30044-6

Open Science Collaboration. (2015). Estimating the reproducibility of psychological science. *Science, 349*(6251), aac4716. doi:10.1126/science.aac4716.

Open Science Collaboration. (2017). Maximizing the reproducibility of your research. In S. O. Lilienfeld & I.D. Waldman (Eds.), *Psychological science under scrutiny: Recent challenges and proposed solutions.* Hoboken, NJ: Wiley.

Ophir, E., Nass, C., & Wagner, A. D. (2009). Cognitive control in media multitaskers. *Proceedings of the National Academy of Sciences of the United States of America, 106*(37), 15583–15587. http://doi.org/10.1073/pnas.0903620106

Oppezzo, M., & Schwartz, D. L. (2014). Give your ideas some legs: The positive effect of walking on creative thinking. *Journal of Experimental Psychology: Learning, Memory, and Cognition, 40,* 1142–1152. http://dx.doi.org/10.1037/a0036577

Oram, S., Khalifeh, H., & Howard, L. M. (2017). Violence against women and mental health. *The Lancet Psychiatry, 4*(2), 158–170. http://dx.doi.org/10.1016/S2215-0366(16)30261-9

Ormerod, T. C., & Dando, C. J. (2015). Finding a needle in a haystack: Toward a psychologically informed method for aviation security screening. *Journal of Experimental Psychology: General, 144,* 76–84. http://dx.doi.org/10.1037/xge0000030

Orrells, D. (2015). *Sex: Antiquity and its legacy.* New York, NY: Oxford University Press.

Orth-Gomér, K., Schneiderman, N., Vaccarino, V., & Deter, H.-C. (Eds.). (2015). *Psychosocial stress and cardiovascular disease in women: Concepts, findings, future perspectives.* Washington, DC: American Psychological Association. http://dx.doi.org/10.1007/978-3-319-09241-6

Orth, U., Erol, R. Y., & Luciano, E. C. (2018). Development of self-esteem from age 4 to 94 years: A meta-analysis of longitudinal studies. *Psychological Bulletin, 144*(10), 1045–1080. http://dx.doi.org/10.1037/bul0000161

Ortiz, R. (2019). Building resilience against the sequelae of adverse childhood experiences: Rise up, change your life, and reform health care. *American Journal of Lifestyle Medicine, 13*(5), 470–479. https://doi.org/10.1177/1559827619839997

Öst, L.-G., & Ollendick, T. H. (2017). Brief, intensive and concentrated cognitive behavioral treatments for anxiety disorders in children: A systematic review and meta-analysis. *Behaviour Research and Therapy, 97,* 134–145. https://doi.org/10.1016/j.brat.2017.07.008

Otgaar, H., Howe, M. L., Merckelbach, H., & Muris, P. (2018). Who is the better eyewitness? Sometimes adults but at other times children. *Current Directions in Psychological Science, 27*(5), 378–385. http://dx.doi.org/10.1177/0963721418770998

Ottavi, P., Passarella, T., Pasinetti, M., Salvatore, G., & Dimaggio, G. (2016). Adapting mindfulness for treating personality disorder. In W. J. Livesley, G. Dimaggio, & J. F. Clarkin (Eds.), *Integrated treatment for personality disorder: A modular approach* (pp. 282–302). New York, NY: Guilford.

Oudekerk, B. A., Allen, J. P., Hessel, E. T., & Molloy, L. E. (2015). The cascading development of autonomy and relatedness from adolescence to adulthood. *Child Development, 86,* 472–485. http://dx.doi.org/10.1111/cdev.12313

Oudiette, D., Dealberto, M.-J., Uguccioni, G., Golmard, J.-L., Merino-Andreu, M., Tafti, M., . . . Arnulf, I. (2012). Dreaming without REM sleep. *Consciousness and Cognition: An International Journal, 21,* 1129–1140. doi:10.1016/j.concog.2012.04.010

Owens, C. (2016). "Hotspots" and "copycats": A plea for more thoughtful language about suicide. *The Lancet Psychiatry, 3*(1), 19–20. http://dx.doi.org/10.1016/S2215-0366(15) 00492-7

Oyarzún, J. P., Càmara, E., Kouider, S., Fuentemilla, L., & de Diego-Balaguer, R. (2019). Implicit but not explicit extinction to threat-conditioned stimulus prevents spontaneous recovery of threat-potentiated startle responses in humans. *Brain and Behavior, 9*(1), e01157. doi:10.1002/brb3.1157

Ozturk, O., Shayan, S., Liszkowski, U., & Majid, A. (2013). Language is not necessary for color categories. *Developmental Science, 16,* 111–115.

Pack, A. A. (2015). Experimental studies of dolphin cognitive abilities. In D. L. Herzing & C. M. Johnson (Eds.), *Dolphin communication and cognition: Past, present, and future* (pp. 175–200). Cambridge, MA: MIT Press.

Paddock, C. (2019, March 12). The FDA approve esketamine nasal spray for severe depression. *Medical News Today*. Retrieved from https://www.medicalnewstoday.com/articles/324656.php

Pagano, M. E., Wang, A. R., Rowles, B. M., Lee, M. T., & Johnson, B. R. (2015). Social anxiety and peer helping in adolescent addiction treatment. *Alcoholism: Clinical and Experimental Research, 39,* 887–895. http://dx.doi.org/10.1111/acer.12691

Pagano, M. E., White, W. L., Kelly, J. F., Stout, R. L., & Tonigan, J. S. (2013). The 10-year course of AA participation and long-term outcomes: A follow-up study of outpatient subjects in Project MATCH. *Substance Abuse, 31,* 51–59. http://doi.org/10.1080/08897077.2012.691450

Paiva, T., Gaspar, T., & Matos, M. G. (2015). Sleep deprivation in adolescents: Correlations with health complaints and health-related quality of life. *Sleep Medicine, 16,* 521–527. http://dx.doi.org/10.1016/j.sleep.2014.10.010

Paivio, A. (1995). *Mental representations: A dual coding approach.* New York, NY: Oxford University Press.

Palermo, T. M., Law, E. F., Fales, J., Bromberg, M. H., Jessen-Fiddick, T., & Tai, G. (2016). Internet delivered cognitive-behavioral treatment for adolescents with chronic pain and their parents: A randomized controlled multicenter trial. *Pain, 157,* 174–185. http://dx.doi.org/10.1097/j.pain.0000000000000348.

Palgi, S., Klein, E., & Shamay-Tsoory, S. G. (2015). Intranasal administration of oxytocin increases compassion toward women. *Social Cognitive and Affective Neuroscience, 10,* 311–317. http://dx.doi.org/10.1093/scan/nsu040

Palmiero, M., Di Giacomo, D., & Passafiume, D. (2016). Can creativity predict cognitive reserve? *The Journal of Creative Behavior, 50,* 7–23. http://dx.doi.org/10.1002/jocb.62

Palombo, D. J., McKinnon, M. C., McIntosh, A. R., Anderson, A. K., Todd, R. M., & Levine, B. (2015). The neural correlates of memory for a life-threatening event: An fMRI study of passengers from flight AT236. *Clinical Psychological Science, 4,* 312–319. doi:10.1177/2167702615589308

Paluck, E. L., Shepherd, H., & Aronow, P. M. (2016). Changing climates of conflict: A social network experiment in 56 schools. *Proceedings of the National Academy of Sciences of the United States of America, 113,* 566–571. http://dx.doi.org/10.1073/pnas.1514483113

Panagopoulos, C. (2018). Evaluation potential and task performance: Evidence from two randomized field experiments in election administration. *Political Psychology, 39*(3), 725-741. http://dx.doi.org/10.1111/pops.12425

Panova, T., & Lleras, A. (2016). Avoidance or boredom: Negative mental health outcomes associated with use of information and communication technologies depend on users' motivations. *Computers in Human Behavior, 58,* 249–258. http://dx.doi.org/10.1016/j.chb.2015.12.062

Panza, G. A., Taylor, B. A., & Thompson, P. D. (2017). Physical activity intensity and subjective well-being in healthy adults. *Journal of Health Psychology, 24*(9), 1257–1267. doi:10.1177/1359105317691589

Papadopoulou, S. L., Ploumis, A., Exarchakos, G., Theodorou, S. J., Beris, A., & Fotopoulos, A. D. (2018). Versatility of repetitive transcranial magnetic stimulation in the treatment of poststroke dysphagia. *Journal of Neurosciences in Rural Practice, 9*(3), 391–396. doi:10.4103/jnrp.jnrp_68_18

Papageorgiou, C. (2013). Mental health promotion and prejudices. *Psychiatriki, 24,* 166–167.

Papathanasiou, I. V., Tsaras, K., Neroliatsiou, A., & Roupa, A. (2015). Stress: Concepts, theoretical models and nursing interventions. *American Journal of Nursing, 4,* 45–50. http://dx.doi.org/10.11648/j.ajns.s.2015040201.19

Pappa, I., St Pourcain, B., Benke, K., Cavadino, A., Hakulinen, C., Nivard, M. G., . . . Tiemeier, H. (2016). A genome-wide approach to children's aggressive behavior: The EAGLE consortium. *American Journal of Medical Genetics Part B: Neuropsychiatric Genetics, 171*(5), 562–572. http://dx.doi.org/10.1002/ajmg.b.32333

Paris, J. (2017). Is psychoanalysis still relevant to psychiatry? *Canadian Journal of Psychiatry. Revue Canadienne de Psychiatrie, 62*(5), 308–312. doi:10.1177/0706743717692306

Park, A. (2016, April 11). 40% of former NFL players had brain injuries. *Time.* Retrieved from http://time.com/4289745/nfl-concussion-symptoms-treatment/

Parker, K., Gra, N., & Igielnik, R. (2019, January 17). Generation Z looks a lot like millennials on key social and political issues. *Pew Research Center.* Retrieved from https://www.pewsocialtrends.org/2019/01/17/generation-z-looks-a-lot-like-millennials-on-key-social-and-political-issues/

Park, G., Schwartz, H. A., Eichstaedt, J. C., Kern, M. L., Kosinski, M., Stillwell, D. J., . . . Seligman, M. E. P. (2015). Automatic personality assessment through social media language. *Journal of Personality and Social Psychology, 108*(6), 934–952. http://dx.doi.org/10.1037/pspp0000020

Parmentier, F., García-Toro, M., García-Campayo, J., Yañez, A. M., Andrés, P., & Gili, M. (2019). Mindfulness and symptoms of depression and anxiety in the general population: The mediating roles of worry, rumination, reappraisal and suppression. *Frontiers in Psychology, 10,* 506. doi:10.3389/fpsyg.2019.00506

Parray, W. M., Ahirwar, G., & Kumar, S. (2018). A study on assertiveness among rural adolescents. *5*(4). *ResearchGate.* Retrieved from doi:10.1729/Journal.18666

Pataka, A., Bonsignore, M. R., Ryan, S., Riha, R. L., Pepin, J.-L., Schiza, S., . . . Grote, L. (2019). Cancer prevalence is increased in females with sleep apnoea–data from the ESADA. *European Respiratory Journal, 53*(6). doi:10.1183/13993003.00091-2019

Pathman, T., & Bauer, P. J. (2013). Beyond initial encoding: Measures of the postencoding status of memory traces predict long-term recall during infancy. *Journal of Experimental Child Psychology, 114,* 321–338. http://dx.doi.org/10.1016/j.jecp.2012.10.004

Patihis, L., & Pendergrast, M. H. (2019). Reports of recovered memories of abuse in therapy in a large age-representative U.S. national sample: Therapy type and decade comparisons. *Clinical Psychological Science, 7*(1), 3–21. https://doi.org/10.1177/2167702618773315

Patil, I., Zanon, M., Novembre, G., Zangrando, N., Chittaro, L., & Silani, G. (2018). Neuroanatomical basis of concern-based altruism in virtual environment. *Neuropsychologia, 116*(Pt A), 34–43. http://dx.doi.org/10.1016/j.neuropsychologia.2017.02.015

Patterson, F., & Linden, E. (1981). *The education of Koko.* New York, NY: Holt, Rinehart and Winston.

Patterson, P. (2002). *Penny's journal: Koko wants to have a baby.* Retrieved from http://www.koko.org/world/journal.phtml?offset58

Pauker, K., Carpinella, C., Meyers, C., Young, D. M., & Sanchez, D. T. (2018). The role of diversity exposure in Whites' reduction in race essentialism over time. *Social Psychological and Personality Science, 9*(8), 944–952. https://doi.org/10.1177/1948550617731496

Paules, C. I., Marston, H. D., & Fauci, A. S. (2019). Measles in 2019—going backward. *New England Journal of Medicine, 380*(23), 2185–2187. https://www.nejm.org/doi/pdf/10.1056/NEJMp1905099

Paul, M. A., Love, R. J., Hawton, A., Brett, K., McCreary, D. R., & Arendt, J. (2015). Sleep deficits in the high Arctic summer in relation to light exposure and behaviour: Use of melatonin as a countermeasure. *Sleep Medicine, 16*, 406–413. http://dx.doi.org/10.1016/j.sleep.2014.12.012

Paul, M., Lech, R. K., Scheil, J., Dierolf, A. M., Suchan, B., & Wolf, O. T. (2016). Acute stress influences the discrimination of complex scenes and complex faces in young healthy men. *Psychoneuroendocrinology, 66*, 125–129. http://dx.doi.org/10.1016/j.psyneuen.2016.01.007

Pawling, R., Kirkham, A. J., Hayes, A. E., & Tipper, S. P. (2017). Incidental retrieval of prior emotion mimicry. *Experimental Brain Research, 235*(4), 1173–1184. http://dx.doi.org/10.1007/s00221-017-4882-y

Payne, B. K., Brown-Iannuzzi, J. L., & Loersch, C. (2016). Replicable effects of primes on human behavior. *Journal of Experimental Psychology: General, 145*(10), 1269–1279. doi:10.1037/xge0000201

Peacock, B. N., Scheiderer, D. J., & Kellermann, G. H. (2017). Biomolecular aspects of depression: A retrospective analysis. *Comprehensive Psychiatry, 73*, 168–180. http://dx.doi.org/10.1016/j.comppsych.2016.11.002

Pear, J. J. (2016). *The science of learning* (2nd ed.). New York, NY: Psychology Press.

Pearson, C. M., Wonderlich, S. A., & Smith, G. T. (2015). A risk and maintenance model for bulimia nervosa: From impulsive action to compulsive behavior. *Psychological Review, 122*, 516–535. http://dx.doi.org/10.1037/a0039268

Pearson, T. (2018, November 4). How do introverts like Stephen Colbert handle their very public fame and their desire to be away from people in general at the same time? *Quora.* Retrieved from https://www.quora.com/How-do-introverts-like-Stephen-Colbert-handle-their-very-public-fame-and-their-desire-to-be-away-from-people-in-general-at-the-same-time

Peled, Y. (2019). Cyberbullying and its influence on academic, social, and emotional development of undergraduate students. *Heliyon, 5*(3), e01393. Retrieved from doi:10.1016/j.heliyon.2019.e01393

Peleg, G., Katzir, G., Peleg, O., Kamara, M., Brodsky, L., Hel-Or, H., . . . Nevo, E. (2006). Hereditary family signature of facial expression. *Proceedings of the National Academy of Sciences of the United States of America, 103*, 15921–15926. http://dx.doi.org/10.1073/pnas.0607551103

Pennington, C. R., Litchfield, D., McLatchie, N., & Heim, D. (2019). Stereotype threat may not impact women's inhibitory control or mathematical performance: Providing support for the null hypothesis. *European Journal of Social Psychology, 49*, 717–734. doi:10.1002/ejsp.2540

Pennycook, G., & Rand, D. G. (2019). Fighting misinformation on social media using crowdsourced judgments of news source quality. *Proceedings of the National Academy of Sciences of the United States of America, 116*(7), 2521–2526. doi:10.1073/pnas.1806781116

Péquignot, R., Dufouil, C., Pérès, K., Artero, S., Tzourio, C., & Empana, J. (2019). Depression increases the risk of death independently from vascular events in elderly individuals: The Three-City Study. *Journal of the American Geriatric Society, 67*, 546–552. doi:10.1111/jgs.15731

Perego, G., Caputi, M., & Ogliari, A. (2016). Neurobiological correlates of psychosocial deprivation in children: A systematic review of neuroscientific contributions. *Child & Youth Care Forum, 45*(3), 329–352. http://dx.doi.org/10.1007/s10566-015-9340-z

Pereira, F. R., McMaster, M. T. B., Polderman, N., de Vries, Y. D. A. T., van den Brink, W., & van Wingen, G. A. (2018). Adverse effects of GHB-induced coma on long-term memory and related brain function. *Drug and Alcohol Dependence, 190*, 29–36. doi:10.1016/j.drugalcdep.2018.05.019

Pérez, P., & Gaviña, J. (2015). Affective disorders. In M. Sáenz-Herrero (Ed.), *Psychopathology in women: Incorporating gender perspective into descriptive psychopathology* (pp. 527–559). Cham, CH: Springer. http://dx.doi.org/10.1007/978-3-319-05870-2

Perfecto, H., Donnelly, K., & Critcher, C. R. (2019). Volume estimation through mental simulation. *Psychological Science, 30*(1), 80–91. https://doi.org/10.1177/0956797618813319

Perkmen, S., & Sahin, S. (2013). Who should study instructional technology? Vocational personality approach. *British Journal of Educational Technology, 44*, 54–65. doi:10.1111/j.1467-8535.2012.01293.x

Perrigo, B. (2019, June 14). The U.K. just banned "harmful gender stereotypes" in advertising. *Time.* Retrieved from https://time.com/5607209/uk-gender-stereotypes-adverts/?utm_source=time.com&utm_medium=email&utm_campaign=the-brief-pm&utm_content=2019061419pm&xid=newsle tter-brief

Peter, C. J., Fischer, L. K., Kundakovic, M., Garg, P., Jakovcevski, M., Dincer, A., . . . Akbarian, S. (2016). DNA methylation signatures of early childhood malnutrition associated with impairments in attention and cognition. *Biological Psychiatry, 80*(10), 765–774. http://dx.doi.org/10.1016/j.biopsych.2016.03.2100

Peteros, R. G., & Maleyeff, J. (2015). Using Lean Six Sigma to improve investment behavior. *International Journal of Lean Six Sigma, 6*, 59–72. http://dx.doi.org/10.1108/IJLSS-03-2014-0007

Petersen, A. M. (2018). Beyond bad apples, toward Black life: A re-reading of the implicit bias research. *Theoretical Criminology. 23*(4), 491–508. https://doi.org/10.1177/1362480618759012

Peters, E., Shoots-Reinhard, B., Evans, A. T., Shoben, A., Klein, E., Tompkins, M. K., . . . Tusler, M. (2019). Pictorial warning labels and memory for cigarette health-risk information over time. *Annals of Behavioral Medicine, 53*(4), 358–371. doi:10.1093/abm/kay050

Petrocchi, N., & Couyoumdjian, A. (2016). The impact of gratitude on depression and anxiety: The mediating role of criticizing, attacking, and reassuring the self. *Self and Identity, 15*, 191–205. http://dx.doi.org/10.1080/15298868.2015.1095794

Pettit, M., & Hegarty, P. (2014). Psychology and sexuality in historical time. In D. L. Tolman, L. M. Diamond, J. A. Bauermeister, W. H. George, J. G. Pfaus, & L. M. Ward (Eds.), *APA handbook of sexuality and psychology: Vol. 1. Person-based approaches* (pp. 63–78). Washington, DC: American Psychological Association. http://dx.doi.org/10.1037/14193-003

Petty, M. (2018, November 13). Dad was told-this is your wheelchair. *Daily Mail.com.* Retrieved from https://www.dailymail.co.uk/health/article-6381883/Christopher-Reeves-son-reveals-family-helped-paralysed-patients-walk-again.html?ito=social-facebook

Pew Research Center. (2016, May 12). Attitudes on same-sex marriage among key demographic groups. *Fact Sheet.* https://www.pewforum.org/fact-sheet/changing-attitudes-on-gay-marriage/

Pew Research Center. (2019, April 10). *Share of U.S. adults using social media, including Facebook, is mostly unchanged since 2018. FactTank.* https://www.pewresearch.org/fact-tank/2019/04/10/share-of-u-s-adults-using-social-media-including-facebook-is-mostly-unchanged-since-2018/

Phan, H. P., & Ngu, B. H. (2016). Sources of self-efficacy in academic contexts: A longitudinal perspective. *School Psychology Quarterly, 31*(4), 548–564. http://dx.doi.org/10.1037/spq0000151

Phillip, A. (2015, February 25). For Chris Kyle's killer, Eddie Ray Routh, life in prison may make jail an asylum. The Washington Post. Retrieved from http://www.washingtonpost.com/news/morning-mix/wp/2015/02/25/for-chris-kyleskillerlife-in-prison-may-make-prison-anasylum/

Phillips, N., Taylor, L., & Bachmann, G. (2019). Maternal, infant and childhood risks associated with advanced paternal age: The need for comprehensive counseling for men. *Maturitas, 125*, 81–84. doi:10.1016/j.maturitas.2019.03.020

Phillips, R. O., Fyhri, A., & Sagberg, F. (2011). Risk compensation and bicycle helmets. *Risk Analysis, 31*, 1187–1195. doi:10.1111/j.1539-6924.2011.01589.x

Phillips, S. T., & Ziller, R. C. (1997). Toward a theory and measure of the nature of nonprejudice. *Journal of Personality and Social Psychology, 72*, 420–434.

Piaget, J. (1952). *The origins of intelligence in children.* New York, NY: Oxford University Press.

Piana, R. (2019, August 10). The opioid overdose crisis: Victims, villains, and the gray area in between. The ASCO Post. Retrieved from https://www.ascopost.com/issues/august-10-2019/the-opioid-overdose-crisis/

Picker, l. (2016). The effects of education on health. *National Bureau of Economic Research.* Retrieved from http://www.nber.org/digest/mar07/w12352.html

Piff, P. K., & Moskowitz, J. P. (2018). Wealth, poverty, and happiness: Social class is differentially associated with positive emotions. *Emotion, 18*(6), 902–905. http://dx.doi.org/10.1037/emo0000387

Piontek, E. A., & Albani, J. M. (2019). Male circumcision: The clinical implications are more than skin deep. *Missouri Medicine, 116*(1), 35–37. https://www.ncbi.nlm.nih.gov/pmc/articles/PMC6390792/

Pitzer, M., Esser, G., Schmidt, M. H., Hohm, E., Banaschewski, T., & Laucht, M. (2017). Child regulative temperament as a mediator of parenting in the development of depressive symptoms: A longitudinal study from early childhood to preadolescence. *Journal of Neural Transmission, 124*(5), 631–641. http://dx.doi.org/10.1007/s00702-017-1682-2

Planas-Sitjà, I., Deneubourg, J.-L., Gibon, C., & Sempo, G. (2015). Group personality during collective decision-making: A multilevel approach. *Proceedings of the Royal Society B, 282.* http://dx.doi.org/10.1098/rspb. 2014.2515.

Plassmann, H., O'Doherty, J., Shiv, B., & Rangel, A. (2008). Marketing actions can modulate neural representations of experienced pleasantness. *Proceedings of the National Academy of Sciences of the United States of America, 105*, 1050–1054. https://doi.org/10.1073/pnas.0706929105

Plattner, F., Hernández, A., Kistler, T. M., Pozo, K., Zhong, P., Yuen, E. Y., . . . Bibb, J. A. (2014). Memory enhancement by targeting Cdk5 regulation of NR2B. *Neuron, 81*, 1070–1083. http://dx.doi.org/10.1016/j.neuron.2014.01.022

Plomin, R., DeFries, J. C., Knopik, V. S., & Neiderhiser, J. M. (2016). Top 10 replicated findings from behavioral genetics. *Perspectives on Psychological Science, 11*, 3–23. http://dx.doi.org/10.1177/1745691615617439

Plomin, R., & von Stumm, S. (2018). The new genetics of intelligence. *Nature Reviews. Genetics, 19*(3), 148–159. doi:10.1038/nrg.2017.104

Plucker, J. A., & Esping, A. (2014). *The psych 101 series: Intelligence 101.* New York, NY: Springer.

Plush, K., Hughes, P., Herde, P., & van Wettere, W. (2016). A synthetic olfactory agonist reduces aggression when sows are mixed into small groups. *Applied Animal Behaviour Science, 185*, 45–51. http://dx.doi.org/10.1016/j.applanim.2016.09.011

Poels, K., & Dewitte, S. (2019). The role of emotions in advertising: A call to action. *Journal of Advertising, 48*(1), 81–90. doi:10.1080/00913367.2019.1579688

Pohl, R. F., Erdfelder, E., Hilbig, B. E., Liebke, L., & Stahlberg, D. (2013). Effort reduction after self-control depletion: The role of cognitive resources in use of simple heuristics. *Journal of Cognitive Psychology, 25*, 267–276. http://dx.doi.org/10.1080/20445911.2012.758101

Polisi, C. (2019, September 19). New York stabbing bystanders show the law's moral limits. *CNN.* Retrieved from https://www.cnn.com/2019/09/19/opinions/new-york-teen-stabbing-bystanders-polisi-index.html?utm_source=CNN+Five+Things&utm_campaign=7ebc313800-EMAIL_CAMPAIGN_2019_09_17_01_11&utm_medium=email&utm_term=0_6da287d761-7ebc313800-107241341

Polito, V., & Stevenson, R. J. (2019). A systematic study of microdosing psychedelics. *PLoS ONE, 14*(2): e0211023. https://doi.org/10.1371/journal.pone.0211023

Pollock, N. C., Noser, A. E., Holden, C. J., & Zeigler-Hill, V. (2016). Do orientations to happiness mediate the associations between personality traits and subjective well-being? *Journal of Happiness Studies, 17*, 713–729. http://dx.doi.org/10.1007/s10902-015-9617-9

Pomerantz, E. M., & Kempner, S. G. (2013). Mothers' daily person and process praise: Implications for children's theory of intelligence and motivation. *Developmental Psychology, 49*, 2040–2046. http://dx.doi.org/10.1037/a0031840

Pomponio, A. T. (2002). *Psychological consequences of terror.* Hoboken, NJ: Wiley.

Pope, K. S., & Vasquez, M. J. T. (2011). *Ethics in psychotherapy and counseling: A practical guide* (4th ed.). Hoboken, NJ: Wiley.

Pope, L., & Harvey, J. (2015). The impact of incentives on intrinsic and extrinsic motives for fitness-center attendance in college first-year students. *American Journal of Health Promotion, 29*, 192–199. doi:10.4278/ajhp.140408-QUAN-135

Popovac, M., & Hadlington, L. (2019). Exploring the role of egocentrism and fear of missing out on online risk behaviours among adolescents in South Africa. *International Journal of Adolescence and Youth.* doi:10.1080/02673843.2019.1617171

Popova, S., Lange, S., Shield, K., Burd, L., & Rehm, J. (2019). Prevalence of fetal alcohol spectrum disorder among special sub-populations: A systematic review and meta-analysis. *Addiction.* doi:10.1111/add.14598

Porritt, F., Shapiro, M., Waggoner, P., Mitchell, E., Thomson, T., Nicklin, S., & Kacelnik, A. (2015). Performance decline by search dogs in repetitive tasks, and mitigation strategies. *Applied Animal Behaviour Science, 166*, 112–122. doi:10.1016/j.applanim.2015.02.013

Portrat, S., Guida, A., Phénix, T., & Lemaire, B. (2016). Promoting the experimental dialogue between working memory and chunking: Behavioral data and simulation. *Memory & Cognition, 44*, 420–434. http://dx.doi.org/10.3758/s13421-015-0572-9

Possemato, K., Bergen-Cico, D., Treatman, S., Allen, C., Wade, M., & Pigeon, W. (2016). A randomized clinical trial of primary care brief mindfulness training for veterans with PTSD. *Journal of Clinical Psychology, 72*, 179–193. http://dx.doi.org/10.1002/jclp.22241

Posthuma, D., de Geus, E. J. C., & Boomsma, D. I. (2001). Perceptual speed and IQ are associated through common genetic factors. *Behavior Genetics, 31,* 593–602. http://dx.doi.org/10.1023/A:1013349512683

Poulin-Dubois, D., Hastings, P. D., Chiarella, S. S., Geangu, E., Hauf, P., Ruel, A., & Johnson, A. (2018). The eyes know it: Toddlers' visual scanning of sad faces is predicted by their theory of mind skills. *PLoS ONE, 13*(12), e0208524. doi:10.1371/journal.pone.0208524

Poulin, M. J., Holman, E. A., & Buffone, A. (2012). The neurogenetics of nice: Receptor genes for oxytocin and vasopressin interact with threat to predict prosocial behavior. *Psychological Science, 23,* 446–452. http://dx.doi.org/10.1177/0956797611428471

Pozzulo, J. (2017). *The young eyewitness: How well do children and adolescents describe and identify perpetrators?* Washington, DC: American Psychological Association. http://dx.doi.org/10.1037/14956-009

Prather, A. A., Janicki-Deverts, D., Hall, M. H., & Cohen, S. (2015). Behaviorally assessed sleep and susceptibility to the common cold. *Sleep, 38,* 1353–1959. doi:10.5665/sleep.4968.

Prati, F., Vasiljevic, M., Crisp, R. J., & Rubini, M. (2015). Some extended psychological benefits of challenging social stereo-types: Decreased dehumanization and a reduced reliance on heuristic thinking. *Group Processes & Intergroup Relations, 18,* 801–816. http://dx.doi.org/10.1177/1368430214567762

Prenderville, J. A., Kennedy, P. J., Dinan, T. G., & Cryan, J. F. (2015). Adding fuel to the fire: The impact of stress on the ageing brain. *Trends in Neurosciences, 38,* 13–25. http://dx.doi.org/10.1016/j.tins.2014.11.001

Prescott, A. T., Sargent, J. D., & Hull, J. G. (2018). Violent video games and aggression metaanalysis. *Proceedings of the National Academy of Sciences of the United States of America, 115*(40), 9882–9888. doi:10.1073/pnas.1611617114

Presti, D. E. (2016). *Foundational concepts in neuroscience: A brain-mind odyssey. The Norton series on interpersonal neurobiology.* New York, NY: W. W. Norton.

Price, J., Lefgren, L., & Tappen, H. (2013). Interracial workplace cooperation: Evidence from the NBA. *Economic Inquiry, 51,* 1026–1034. http://dx.doi.org/10.1111/j.1465-7295.2011.00438.x

Price, T. J., & Prescott, S. A. (2015). Inhibitory regulation of the pain gate and how its failure causes pathological pain. *Pain, 156,* 789–792. doi:10.1097/j.pain.0000000000000139

Primack, B. A., Karim, S. A., Shensa, A., Bowman, N., Knight, J., & Sidani, J. E. (2019). Positive and negative experiences on social media and perceived social isolation. *American Journal of Health Promotion, 33*(6), 859–868. doi:10.1177/0890117118824196

Primeau, M., & O'Hara, R. (2015). Sleep-wake disorders. In L. W. Roberts & A. K. Louie (Eds.), *Study guide to DSM-5®* (pp. 267–290). Arlington, VA: American Psychiatric Publishing.

Prkachin, K. M., & Silverman, B. E. (2002). Hostility and facial expression in young men and women: Is social regulation more important than negative affect? *Health Psychology, 21,* 33–39. doi:10.1037/0278-6133.21.1.33

Proctor, C., Tweed, R., & Morris, D. (2016). The Rogerian fully functioning person: A positive psychology perspective. *Journal of Humanistic Psychology, 56,* 503–529. http://dx.doi.org/10.1177/0022167815605936

Prot, S., Gentile, D. A., Anderson, C. A., Suzuki, K., Swing, E., Lim, K. M., . . . Lam, B. C. (2014). Long-term relations among prosocial-media use, empathy, and prosocial behavior. *Psychological Science, 25,* 358–368. http://dx.doi.org/10.1177/0956797613503854.

Protzko, J., Aronson, J., & Blair, C. (2013). How to make a young child smarter: Evidence from the database of raising intelligence. *Perspectives on Psychological Science, 8,* 25–40. doi:10.1177/1745691612462585

Proyer, R. T., Ruch, W., & Buschor, C. (2013). Testing strengths-based interventions: A preliminary study on the effectiveness of a program targeting curiosity, gratitude, hope, humor, and zest for enhancing life satisfaction. *Journal of Happiness Studies, 14,* 275–292. http://dx.doi.org/10.1007/s10902-012-9331-9

Pullum, G. K. (1991). *The great Eskimo vocabulary hoax and other irreverent essays on the study of language.* Chicago, IL: University of Chicago Press.

Pusch, S., Mund, M., Hagemeyer, B., & Finn, C. (2019). Personality development in emerging and young adulthood: A study of age differences. *European Journal of Personality, 33,* 245–263. https://doi.org/10.1002/per.2181

Putnam, A. L., Ross, M. Q., Soter, L. K., & Roediger, H. L. (2018). Collective narcissism: Americans exaggerate the role of their home state in appraising U.S. history. *Psychological Science, 29*(9), 1414–1422. https://doi.org/10.1177/0956797618772504

Putnam, A. L., Sungkhasettee, V. W., & Roediger, H. L. (2016). Optimizing learning in college: Tips from cognitive psychology. *Perspectives on Psychological Science, 11,* 652–660. http://dx.doi.org/10.1177/1745691616645770

Putwain, D., & Remedios, R. (2014). The scare tactic: Do fear appeals predict motivation and exam scores? *School Psychology Quarterly, 29,* 503–516. http://dx.doi.org/10.1037/spq0000048

Qian, M. K., Quinn, P. C., Heyman, G. D., Pascalis, O., Fu, G., & Lee, K. (2019). A long-term effect of perceptual individuation training on reducing implicit racial bias in preschool children. *Child Development, 90*(3), e290-e305. doi:10.1111/cdev.12971

Qin, S., Young, C. B., Duan, X., Chen, T., Supekar, K., & Menon, V. (2014). Amygdala subregional structure and intrinsic functional connectivity predicts individual differences in anxiety during early childhood. *Biological Psychiatry, 75,* 892–901. http://dx.doi.org/10.1016/j.biopsych.2013.10.006.

Qiu, L., & Bank, F. (2018, February 16). Checking facts and falsehoods about gun violence and mental illness after Parkland shooting. *The New York Times.* Retrieved April 21, 2019 from https://www.nytimes.com/2018/02/16/us/politics/fact-check-parkland-gun-violence-mental-illness.html

Quas, J. A. (2014). Adolescence: A unique period of challenge and opportunity for positive development. *CYF News* (APA). Retrieved from https://www.apa.org/pi/families/resources/newsletter/2014/12/adolescence-development

Quas, J. A., Rush, E. B., Yim, I. S., Edelstein, R. S., Otgaar, H., & Smeets, T. (2016). Stress and emotional valence effects on children's versus adolescents' true and false memory. *Memory, 24,* 696–707. http://dx.doi.org/10.1080/09658211.2015.1045909

Quiano, K. (2016, March 21). Living in chains: In Indonesia, mentally ill kept shackled in filthy cells. *CNN World.* Retrieved from http://www.cnn.com/2016/03/20/asia/indonesiamental-health/

Quick, J. D., & Larson, H. (2018, February 28). The vaccine-autism myth started 20 years ago. Here's why it still endures today. *Time.* Retrieved from https://time.com/5175704/andrew-wakefield-vaccine-autism/

Quintana, D. S., Outhred, T., Westlye, L. T., Malhi, G. S., & Andreassen, O. A. (2016). The impact of oxytocin administration on brain activity: A systematic review and meta-analysis protocol. *Systematic Reviews, 5*, 205. http://dx.doi.org/10.1186/s13643-016-0386-2

Raaska, H., Elovainio, M., Sinkkonen, J., Stolt, S., Jalonen, I., Matomaki, J., . . . Lapinleimu, H. (2013). Adopted children's language difficulties and their relation to symptoms of reactive attachment disorder: FinAdo study. *Journal of Applied Developmental Psychology, 34,* 152–160. http://dx.doi.org/10.1016/j.appdev.2012.12.003

Rabellino, D., Densmore, M., Frewen, P. A., Théberge, J., & Lanius, R. A. (2016). The innate alarm circuit in post-traumatic stress disorder: Conscious and subconscious processing of fear- and trauma-related cues. *Psychiatry Research: Neuroimaging, 248,* 142–150. doi:10.1016/j.pscychresns.2015.12.005

Rabelo, V. C., Holland, K. J., & Cortina, L. M. (2019). From distrust to distress: Associations among military sexual assault, organizational trust, and occupational health. *Psychology of Violence, 9*(1), 78–87. http://dx.doi.org/10.1037/vio0000166

Raeder, F., Karbach, L., Struwe, H., Margraf, J., & Zlomuzica, A. (2019). Low perceived self-efficacy impedes discriminative fear learning. *Frontiers in Psychology, 10,* 1191. doi:10.3389/fpsyg.2019.01191

Raffagnino, R. (2019). Gestalt therapy effectiveness: A systematic review of empirical evidence. *Open Journal of Social Sciences, 7,* 66–83. doi:10.4236/jss.2019.76005

Raine, J. (2016, August 30). Why it's so hard to ignore a baby's cry, according to science. *Time Magazine.* Retrieved from http://theconversation.com/why-its-so-hard-to-ignore-a-babyscry-according-to-science-63245

Rajanahally, S., Raheem, O., Rogers, M., Brisbane, W., Ostrowski, K., Lendvay, T., & Walsh, T. (2019). The relationship between cannabis and male infertility, sexual health, and neoplasm: A systematic review. *Andrology, 7,* 139–147. https://onlinelibrary.wiley.com/doi/full/10.1111/andr.12585

Ralph, B. C. W., Smith, A. C., Seli, P., & Smilek, D. (2019). Yearning for distraction: Evidence for a trade-off between media multitasking and mind wandering. *Canadian Journal of Experimental Psychology/Revue Canadienne de Psychologie Expérimentale.* http://dx.doi.org/10.1037/cep0000186

Ralph, S., Capewell, C., & Bonnett, E. (2016). Disability hate crime: Persecuted for difference. *British Journal of Special Education, 43*(3), 215–232. http://dx.doi.org/10.1111/1467-8578.12139

Ramchand, R., Ayer, L., Geyer, L., & Kofner, A. (2016). Factors that influence chaplains' suicide intervention behavior in the army. *Suicide and Life-Threatening Behavior, 46,* 35–45. http://dx.doi.org/10.1111/sltb.12170

Ramirez, G., McDonough, I. M., & Jin, L. (2017). Classroom stress promotes motivated forgetting of mathematics knowledge. *Journal of Educational Psychology, 109*(6), 812–825. http://dx.doi.org/10.1037/edu0000170

Ramler, T. R., Tennison, L. R., Lynch, J., & Murphy, P. (2016). Mindfulness and the college transition: The efficacy of an adapted mindfulness-based stress reduction intervention in fostering adjustment among first-year students. *Mindfulness, 7,* 179–188. http://dx.doi.org/10.1007/s12671-015-0398-3

Rana, Z. (2017, April 24). How JK Rowling overcame depression and rejection to sell over 400 million books. *Quartz.* Retrieved June 23, 2019 from https://qz.com/961875/how-jk-rowling-overcame-depression-and-rejection-to-end-up-selling-400-million-books/

Randi, J. (2014, January 7). It's not a contest. *James Randi Educational Foundation.* Retrieved from http://www.randi.org/site/index.php/swift-blog/2304-its-not-a-contest.html

Ranjbar, N., & Erb, M. (2019). Adverse childhood experiences and trauma-informed care in rehabilitation clinical practice. *Archives of Rehabilitation Research and Clinical Translation, 1*(12). https://doi.org/10.1016/j.arrct.2019.100003

Ranney, M. L., & Gold, J. (2019, August 7). The dangers of linking gun violence and mental illness. *Time.* Retrieved from https://time.com/5645747/gun-violence-mental-illness/

Rass, O., Ahn, W.-Y., & O'Donnell, B. F. (2016). Resting-state EEG, impulsiveness, and personality in daily and nondaily smokers. *Clinical Neurophysiology, 127,* 409–418. http://dx.doi.org/10.1016/j.clinph.2015.05.007

Ratcliff, R., & Van Dongen, H. P. A. (2018). The effects of sleep deprivation on item and associative recognition memory. *Journal of Experimental Psychology: Learning, Memory, and Cognition, 44*(2), 193–208. http://dx.doi.org/10.1037/xlm0000452

Ratner, C. (2011). *Macro cultural psychology: A political philosophy of mind.* New York, NY: Oxford University Press.

Ratner, K. G., & Amodio, D. M. (2013). Seeing "us vs. them": Minimal group effects on the neural encoding of faces. *Journal of Experimental Social Psychology, 49,* 298–301.

Ravizza, S. M., Uitvlugt, M. G., & Fenn, K. M. (2017). Logged in and zoned out: How laptop Internet use relates to classroom learning. *Psychological Science, 28*(2), 171–180. http://dx.doi.org/10.1177/0956797616677314

Ray, A. L., Ullmann, R., & Francis, M. C. (2015). Pain as a perceptual experience. In T. R. Deer, M. S. Leong, & A. L. Ray (Eds.), *Treatment of chronic pain by integrative approaches: The American Academy of Pain Medicine textbook on patient management* (pp. 1–13). New York, NY: Springer-Verlag. doi:10.1007/978-1-4939-1821-8_1

Ray, D. C. (2019). The child and the counselor: Relational humanism in the playroom and beyond. *The Journal of Humanistic Counseling, 58,* 68–82. doi:10.1002/johc.12090

Ray, D. C., & Jayne, K. M. (2016). Humanistic psychotherapy with children. In D. J. Cain, K. Keenan, & S. Rubin (Eds.), *Humanistic psychotherapies: Handbook of research and practice* (2nd ed., pp. 387–417). Washington, DC: American Psychological Association. http://dx.doi.org/10.1037/14775-013

Raynald, Li, Y., Yu, H., Huang, H., Guo, M., Hua, R., . . . An, Y. (2016). The heterotransplantation of human bone marrow stromal cells carried by hydrogel unexpectedly demonstrates a significant role in the functional recovery in the injured spinal cord of rats. *Brain Research, 1634,* 21–33. http://dx.doi.org/10.1016/j.brainres.2015.10.038

Ray, W. A., Stein, C. M., Murray, K. T., Fuchs, C., Patrick, S. W., Daugherty, J., . . . Cooper, W. O. (2019). Association of antipsychotic treatment with risk of unexpected death among children and youths. *JAMA Psychiatry, 76*(2), 162–171. https://jamanetwork.com/journals/jamapsychiatry/article-abstract/2717966

Ray, W. J. (2015). *Abnormal psychology: Neuroscience perspectives on human behavior and experience.* Thousand Oaks, CA: Sage.

Reade, N. (2015). The surprising truth about older workers. *AARP.* Retrieved from http://www.aarp.org/work/job-hunting/info-07-2013/older-workers-morevaluable.html

Reardon, S. (2015). Rave drug tested against depression: Companies and clinicians turn to ketamine to treat mental-health disorder as pipeline of new drugs dries up. *Nature, 517,* 130–131. http://dx.doi.org/10.1038/517130a

Reble, E., Castellani, C. A., Melka, M. G., O'Reilly, R., & Singh, S. M. (2017). VarScan2 analysis of de novo variants in monozygotic twins discordant for schizophrenia. *Psychiatric Genetics, 27*(2), 62–70. http://dx.doi.org/10.1097/YPG.0000000000000162

Rebok, F., Teti, G. L., Fantini, A. P., Cárdenas-Delgado, C., Rojas, S. M., Derito, M. N. C., & Daray, F. M. (2015). Types of borderline personality disorder (BPD) in patients admitted for suicide-related behavior. *Psychiatric Quarterly, 86,* 49–60. doi:10.1007/s11126-014-9317-3

Redlich, A. D., & Goodman, G. S. (2003). Taking responsibility for an act not committed: The influence of age and suggestibility. *Law and Human Behavior, 27*(2), 141–156. http://dx.doi.org/10.1023/A:1022543012851

Redondo, M. T., Beltrán-Brotóns, J. L., Reales, J. M., & Ballesteros, S. (2015). Word-stem priming and recognition in type 2 diabetes mellitus, Alzheimer's disease patients and healthy older adults. *Experimental Brain Research, 233,* 3163–3174. http://dx.doi.org/10.1007/s00221-015-4385-7

Reed, A. E., Chan, L., & Mikels, J. A. (2014). Meta-analysis of the age-related positivity effect: Age differences in preferences for positive over negative information. *Psychology and Aging, 29,* 1–15. doi:10.1037/a0035194

Reed, J. (2019, April 16). JK Rowling, who denies being a billionaire, made $54 million last year. *Business Insider.* Retrieved from https://www.businessinsider.com/jk-rowling-harry-potter-net-worth-author-millions-fortune-lifestyle-2019-4

Regan, P. (1998). What if you can't get what you want? Willingness to compromise ideal mate selection standards as a function of sex, mate value, and relationship context. *Personality and Social Psychology Bulletin, 24,* 1294–1303.

Regan, P. (2011). *Close relationships.* New York, NY: Routledge/Taylor & Francis Group.

Rehman, I., Mahabadi, N., & Rehman, C. I. (2019). Classical conditioning. *NCBI.* https://www.ncbi.nlm.nih.gov/books/NBK470326/

Reicher, S. (2014). In praise of activism: Rethinking the psychology of obedience and conformity. In C. Antaki & S. Condor (Eds.), *Rhetoric, ideology and social psychology: Essays in honour of Michael Billig* (pp. 94–109). New York, NY: Routledge.

Reilly, D., Neumann, D. L., & Andrews, G. (2019). Gender differences in reading and writing achievement: Evidence from the National Assessment of Educational Progress (NAEP). *American Psychologist, 74*(4), 445–458. http://dx.doi.org/10.1037/amp0000356

Reknes, I., Visockaite, G., Liefooghe, A., Lovakov, A., & Einarsen, S. V. (2019). Locus of control moderates the relationship between exposure to bullying behaviors and psychological strain. *Frontiers in Psychology, 10*:1323. doi:10.3389/fpsyg.2019.01323

Render, A., & Jansen, P. (2019). Dopamine and sense of agency: Determinants in personality and substance use. *PLoS ONE, 14*(3): e0214069. https://doi.org/10.1371/journal.pone.0214069

Renner, F., Kersbergen, I., Field, M., & Werthmann, J. (2018). Dutch courage? Effects of acute alcohol consumption on self-ratings and observer ratings of foreign language skills. *Journal of Psychopharmacology, 32*(1), 116–122. https://doi.org/10.1177/0269881117735687

Rentfrow, P. J. (2014). Geographical differences in personality. In P. J. Rentfrow (Ed.), *Geographical psychology: Exploring the interaction of environment and behavior* (pp. 115–137). Washington, DC: American Psychological Association. http://dx.doi.org/10.1037/14272-007

Rentfrow, P. J., Gosling, S. D., & Potter, J. (2008). A theory of the emergence, persistence, and expression of geographic variation in psychological characteristics. *Perspectives on Psychological Science, 3,* 339–369. http://dx.doi.org/10.1111/j.1745-6924.2008.00084.x

Research America. (2018, May). American's views on vaccines and infectious disease outbreaks. *Zoby Analytics.* Retrieved from https://www.researchamerica.org/sites/default/files/MAY2018_Vaccine-PressRelease_final.pdf

Resnick, B. (2016, April 8). These scientists can prove it's possible to reduce prejudice. *Vox: Science & Health.* Retrieved from http://www.vox.com/2016/4/7/11380974/reduceprejudice-science-transgender

Resnick, B. (2018, June 13). The Stanford Prison Experiment was massively influential. We just learned it was a fraud. *Vox.* Retrieved from https://www.vox.com/2018/6/13/17449118/stanford-prison-experiment-fraud-psychology-replication

Rest, J., Narvaez, D., Bebeau, M., & Thoma, S. (1999). A neo-Kohlbergian approach: The DIT and schema theory. *Educational Psychology Review, 11,* 291–324.

Resuehr, D., Wu, G., Johnson, R. L., Young, M. E., Hogenesch, J. B., & Gamble, K. L. (2019). Shift work disrupts circadian regulation of the transcriptome in hospital nurses. *Journal of Biological Rhythms, 34*(2), 167–177. https://doi.org/10.1177/0748730419826694

Reuter, E.-M., Vieluf, S., Koutsandreou, F., Hübner, L., Budde, H., Godde, B., & Voelcker-Rehage, C. (2019). A non-linear relationship between selective attention and associated ERP markers across the lifespan. *Frontiers in Psychology, 10*:30. doi:10.3389/fpsyg.2019.00030

Rhodes, M., Leslie, S. -J., Yee, K. M., & Saunders, K. (2019). Subtle linguistic cues increase girls' engagement in science. *Psychological Science, 30*(3), 455–466. https://doi.org/10.1177/0956797618823670

Rhudy, J. L. (2016). Emotional modulation of pain. In M. al'Absi & M. A. Flaten (Eds.), *The neuroscience of pain, stress, and emotion: Psychological and clinical implications* (pp. 51–75). San Diego, CA: Elsevier Academic Press. doi:10.1016/B978-0-12-800538-5.00003-0

Richardson, R. C. (2015). Evolutionary psychology, altruism, and kin selection. In T. Breyer (Ed.), *Epistemological dimensions of evolutionary psychology* (pp. 103–115). New York, NY: Springer. doi:10.1007/978-1-4939-1387-9

Riebschleger, J., Costello, S., Cavanaugh, D. L., & Grové, C. (2019). Mental health literacy of youth that have a family member with a mental illness: Outcomes from a new program and scale. *Frontiers in Psychiatry, 10,* 2. doi:10.3389/fpsyt.2019.00002

Riecher-Rössler, A. (2017). Oestrogens, prolactin, hypothalamic-pituitary-gonadal axis, and schizophrenic psychoses. *The Lancet Psychiatry, 4*(1), 63–72. http://dx.doi.org/10.1016/S2215-0366(16)30379-0

Riediger, M., & Luong, G. (2016). Happy to be unhappy? Pro- and contrahedonic motivations from adolescence to old age. In A. D. Ong & C. E. Löckenhoff (Eds.), *Emotion, aging, and health. Bronfenbrenner series on the ecology of human development* (pp. 97–118). Washington, DC: American Psychological Association. http://dx.doi.org/10.1037/14857-006

Riem, M. E., & Karreman, A. (2019). Experimental manipulation of emotion regulation changes mothers' physiological and facial expressive responses to infant crying. *Infant Behavior and Development, 55,* 22–31. https://doi.org/10.1016/j.infbeh.2019.02.003

Riggio, O. (2018, July 11). Mental illness serves as easy scapegoat in mass murder accounts. *Fair.* Retrieved from https://fair.org/home/mental-illness-serves-as-easy-scapegoat-in-mass-murder-accounts/

Rimmele, U., Davachi, L., & Phelps, E. A. (2012). Memory for time and place contributes to enhanced confidence in memories for emotional events. *Emotion, 12,* 834–846. http://dx.doi.org/10.1037/a0028003

Rinehart, S. J., & Espelage, D. L. (2016). A multilevel analysis of school climate, homophobic name-calling, and sexual harassment victimization/perpetration among middle school youth. *Psychology of Violence, 6,* 213–222. http://dx.doi.org/10.1037/a0039095

Risman, B. J., & Davis, G. (2013). From sex roles to gender structure. *Current Sociology, 61,* 733–755. http://dx.doi. org/10.1177/0011392113479315

Ritchie, H., & Roser, M. (2018, April). Mental health. *Our World in Data.* Retrieved from https://ourworldindata.org/mental-health

Ritchwood, T. D., DeCoster, J. Metzger, I. W., Bolland, J. M., & Danielson, C. K. (2016). Does it really matter which drug you choose? An examination of the influence of type of drug on type of risky sexual behavior. *Addictive Behaviors, 60,* 97–102. http://dx.doi. org/10.1016/j. addbeh.2016.03.022

Rivers, S. E., Brackett, M. A., Reyes, M. R., Elbertson, N. A., & Salovey, P. (2013). Improving the social and emotional climate of classrooms: A clustered randomized controlled trial testing the RULER Approach. *Prevention Science, 14,* 77–87. doi:10.1007/s11121-012-0305-2.

Rizvi, S. L., Hughes, C. D., Hittman, A. D., & Vieira Oliveira, P. (2017). Can trainees effectively deliver dialectical behavior therapy for individuals with borderline personality disorder? Outcomes from a training clinic. *Journal of Clinical Psychology, 73,* 1599–1611. doi:10.1002/jclp.22467

Rizvi, S. L., & Salters-Pedneault, K. (2013). Borderline personality disorder. In W. O'Donohue & S. O. Lilienfeld (Eds.), *Case studies in clinical psychological science: Bridging the gap from science to practice* (pp. 301–322). New York, NY: Oxford University Press.

Rizzolatti, G. (2014). Confounding the origin and function of mirror neurons. *Behavioral and Brain Sciences, 37,* 218–219. http://dx.doi. org/10.1017/S0140525X13002471

Rizzolatti, G., Fadiga, L., Fogassi, L., & Gallese, V. (1996). Premotor cortex and the recognition of motor actions. *Cognitive Brain Research, 3,* 131–141. http://dx.doi.org/10.1016/0926-6410(95)00038-0

Rizzolatti, G., Sinigaglia, C., & Anderson, F. (2008). *Mirrors in the brain: How our minds share actions and emotions.* New York, NY: Oxford University Press.

Robbins, L. (2013). Neural stem's stem cells give spinal injury patients hope. Retrieved from http://www.gazette.net/article/20130114/NEWS/130119667/neuralstemx2019-s-stemcells-give-spinal-injury-patients-hope & template=gazette

Robbins, R., Grandner, M. A., Buxton, O. M., Hale, L., Buysse, D. J., Knutson, K. L., . . . Jean-Louis, G. (2019). Sleep myths: An expert-led study to identify false beliefs about sleep that impinge upon population sleep health practices. *Sleep Health, 5*(4), 409–417. doi:10.1016/j.sleh.2019.02.00

Robbins, S. P. (1996). *Organizational behavior: Concepts, controversies, and applications.* Englewood Cliffs, NJ: Prentice Hall.

Roberts, K. (2018, October 28). When it comes to vaccines, celebrities often call the shots. *NBC News.* Retrieved from https://www.nbcnews.com/health/health-care/when-it-comes-vaccines-celebrities-often-call-shots-n925156

Robin, F., Dominguez, J., & Tilford, M. (2009). *Your money or your life: 9 steps to transforming your relationship with money and achieving financial independence.* New York, NY: Penguin Books.

Robinson, F. P. (1970). *Effective study* (4th ed.). New York, NY: Harper & Row.

Robinson, K. J., Hoplock, L. B., & Cameron, J. J. (2015). When in doubt, reach out: Touch is a covert but effective mode of soliciting and providing social support. *Social Psychological and Personality Science, 6,* 831–839. http://dx.doi.org/10.1177/1948550615584197

Robinson, O. (2016). Emerging adulthood, early adulthood, and quarter-life crisis: Updating Erikson for the twenty-first century.

In R. Žukauskienė (Ed.), *Emerging adulthood in a European context* (pp. 17–30). New York, NY: Routledge/Taylor & Francis Group.

Robison, L. S., Ananth, M., Hadjiargyrou, M., Komatsu, D. E., & Panayotis, K. T. (2017). Chronic oral methylphenidate treatment reversibly increases striatal dopamine transporter and dopamine type 1 receptor binding in rats. *Journal of Neural Transmission, 124*(5), 655–667. http://doi.org/10.1007/s00702-017-1680-4

Rode, L., Nordestgaard, B. G., & Bojesen, S. E. (2015). Peripheral blood leukocyte telomere length and mortality among 64,637 individuals from the general population. *Journal of the National Cancer Institute, 107,* djv074. http://dx.doi.org/10.1093/jnci/djv074

Rodkey, E. N., & Riddell, R. P. (2013). The infancy of infant pain research: The experimental origins of infant pain denial. *The Journal of Pain, 14,* 338–350. http://dx.doi.org/10.1016/j. jpain.2012.12.017

Rodríguez-Hidalgo, A. J., Solera, E., & Calmaestra, J. (2018). Psychological predictors of cyberbullying according to ethnic-cultural origin in adolescents: A national study in Spain. *Journal of Cross-Cultural Psychology, 49*(10), 1506–1522. https://doi.org/10.1177/0022022118795283

Roepke, A. M., & Seligman, M. E. P. (2016). Depression and prospection. *British Journal of Clinical Psychology, 55,* 23–48. http://dx.doi.org/10.1111/bjc.12087

Rogge, R. D., Cobb, R. J., Lawrence, E., Johnson, M. D., & Bradbury, T. N. (2013). Is skills training necessary for the primary prevention of marital distress and dissolution? A 3-year experimental study of three interventions. *Journal of Consulting and Clinical Psychology, 81,* 949–961. http://dx.doi.org/10.1037/a0034209

Rohlfs Domínguez, P. (2014). Promoting our understanding of neural plasticity by exploring developmental plasticity in early and adult life. *Brain Research Bulletin, 107,* 31–36. http://dx.doi.org/10.1016/j. brainresbull.2014.05.006

Romeo, R. D. (2017). The impact of stress on the structure of the adolescent brain: Implications for adolescent mental health. *Brain Research, 1654,* 185–191. http://dx.doi.org/10.1016/j. brainres.2016.03.021

Romeo, R. R., Leonard, J. A., Robinson, S. T., West, M. R., Mackey, A. P., Rowe, M. L., & Gabrieli, J. D. E. (2018). Beyond the 30-million-word gap: Children's conversational exposure is associated with language-related brain function. *Psychological Science, 29*(5), 700–710. https://doi.org/10.1177/0956797617742725

Rood, L., Roelofs, J., Bögels, S. M., & Meesters, C. (2012). Stress-reactive rumination, negative cognitive style, and stressors in relationship to depressive symptoms in nonclinical youth. *Journal of Youth and Adolescence, 41,* 414–425. http://dx.doi.org/10.1007/s10964-011-9657-3

Rooney, N. J., Guest, C. M., Swanson, L. C. M., & Morant, S. V. (2019). How effective are trained dogs at alerting their owners to changes in blood glycaemic levels?: Variations in performance of glycaemia alert dogs. *PLoS ONE 14*(1): e0210092. https://doi.org/10.1371/journal.pone.0210092

Roozen, S., Peters, G.-J. Y., Kok, G., Townend, D., Nijhuis, J., & Curfs, L. (2016). Worldwide prevalence of fetal alcohol spectrum disorders: A systematic literature review including meta-analysis. *Alcoholism: Clinical and Experimental Research, 40,* 18–32. http://dx.doi.org/10.1111/acer.12939

Rosch, E. (1978). *Principles of categorization.* In E. Rosch & B. B. Lloyd (Eds.), *Cognition and categorization* (pp. 27–48). Hillsdale, NJ: Erlbaum.

Rosch, E. H. (1973). Natural categories. *Cognitive Psychology, 4,* 328–350. http://dx.doi.org/10.1016/0010-0285(73)90017-0

Roscoe, R. D., Becker, D. V., Branaghan, R. J., Chiou, E. K., Gray, R., Craig, S. D., . . . Cooke, N. J. (2019). Bridging psychology and engineering to make technology work for people. *American Psychologist, 74*(3), 394–406. http://dx.doi.org/10.1037/amp0000444

Rosenhan, D. L. (1973). On being sane in insane places. *Science, 179,* 250–258. http://dx.doi.org/10.1126/science.179.4070.250

Rosenström, T., Ystrom, E., Torvik, F. A., Czajkowski, N. O., Gillespie, N. A., Aggen, S. H., . . . Reichborn-Kjennerud, T. (2017). Genetic and environmental structure of dsm-iv criteria for antisocial personality disorder: A twin study. *Behavior Genetics, 47*(3), 265–277. http://dx.doi.org/10.1007/s10519-016-9833-z

Rosenthal, R. (1965). *Clever Hans: A case study of scientific method, introduction to Clever Hans.* New York, NY: Holt, Rinehart & Winston.

Rosenthal, S. R., Buka, S. L., Marshall, B. D., Carey, K. B., & Clark, M. A. (2016). Negative experiences on Facebook and depressive symptoms among young adults. *Journal of Adolescent Health, 59*(5), 510–516. http://dx.doi.org/10.1016/j.jadohealth.2016.06.023

Rosenzweig, M. R., Bennett, E. L., & Diamond, M. C. (1972). Brain changes in response to experience. *Scientific American, 226,* 22–29. http://dx.doi.org/10.1038/scientificamerican0272-22

Roser, M. (2019). Working Hours. *OurWorldInData.org.* https://ourworldindata.org/working-hours

Roskey, J. W. (2013). The (f)utility of postconviction polygraph testing. *Sexual Abuse: Journal of Research and Treatment, 25,* 259–281. doi:10.1177/1079063212455668

Ross, B. M., & Millson, C. (1970). Repeated memory of oral prose in Ghana and New York. *International Journal of Psychology, 5,* 173–181.

Rossen, J., & Ferguson, C. (2018, March 23). This is your brain on texting—and why you shouldn't walk at the same time. *TODAY.* Retrieved from https://www.today.com/health/textin-while-walking-may-be-more-dangerous-you-think-t125715

Ross, L. (1977). The intuitive psychologist and his shortcomings: Distortions in the attribution process. In L. Berkowitz (Ed.), *Advances in experimental social psychology* (Vol. 10, pp. 173–220). New York, NY: Academic Press.

Rothbaum, F., Kakinuma, M., Nagaoka, R., & Azuma, H. (2007). Attachment and amae: Parent-child closeness in the United States and Japan. *Journal of Cross-Cultural Psychology, 38,* 465–486. http://dx.doi.org/10.1177/0022022107302315

Rothgerber, H., & Wolsiefer, K. (2014). A naturalistic study of stereotype threat in young female chess players. *Group Processes & Intergroup Relations, 17,* 79–90. http://dx.doi.org/10.1177/1368430213490212

Rotter, J. B. (1954). *Social learning and clinical psychology.* Englewood Cliffs, NJ: Prentice Hall.

Rotter, J. B. (1966). Generalized expectancies for internal versus external control of reinforcement. *Psychological Monographs: General & Applied, 80*(1), 1–28. http://dx.doi.org/10.1037/a0032736.

Rotter, J. B. (1990). Internal versus external control of reinforcement: A case history of a variable. *American Psychologist, 45,* 489–493.

Rouder, J. N., Morey, R. D., & Province, J. M. (2013). A Bayes factor meta-analysis of recent extra sensory perception experiments: Comment on Storm, Tressoldi, and Di Risio (2010). *Psychological Bulletin, 139,* 241–247. doi:10.1037/a0029008

Rubin, L. H., Wu, M., Sundermann, E. E., Meyer, V. J., Smith, R., Weber, K. M., . . . Maki, P. M. (2016). Elevated stress is associated with prefrontal cortex dysfunction during a verbal memory task in women with HIV. *Journal of Neurology, 22*(6), 840–851. http://dx.doi.org/10.1007/s13365-016-0446-3

Rubinstein, J. S., Meyer, D. E. & Evans, J. E. (2001). Executive control of cognitive processes in task switching. *Journal of Experimental Psychology: Human Perception and Performance, 27,* 763–797. http://dx.doi.org/10.1037/0096-1523.27.4.763

Rucklidge, J. J., Downs-Woolley, M., Taylor, M., Brown, J. A., & Harrow, S.-E. (2016). Psychiatric comorbidities in a New Zealand sample of adults with ADHD. *Journal of Attention Disorders, 20,* 1030–1038. http://dx-.doi.org/10.1177/1087054714529457

Ruffman, T., O'Brien, K. S., Taumoepeau, M., Latner, J. D., & Hunter, J. A. (2016). Toddlers' bias to look at average versus obese figures relates to maternal anti-fat prejudice. *Journal of Experimental Child Psychology, 142,* 195–202. http://dx.doi.org/10.1016/j.jecp.2015.10.008

Ruffman, T., Then, R., Cheng, C., & Imuta, K. (2019). Lifespan differences in emotional contagion while watching emotion-eliciting videos. *PloS ONE, 14*(1), e0209253. Retrieved doi:10.1371/journal.pone.0209253

Ruini, C., & Fava, G. A. (2014). Increasing happiness by well-being therapy. In K. M. Sheldon & R. E. Lucas (Eds.), *Stability of happiness: Theories and evidence on whether happiness can change* (pp. 147–166). San Diego, CA: Elsevier Academic Press.

Rumbaugh, D. M., von Glasersfeld, E. C., Warner, H., Pisani, P., & Gill, T. V. (1974). Lana (chimpanzee) learning language: A progress report. *Brain and Language, 1,* 205–212. http://dx.doi.org/10.1016/0093-934X(74)90035-2

Ruocco, A. C., Amirthavasagam, S., Choi-Kain, L. W., & McMain, S. F. (2013). Neural correlates of negative emotionality in borderline personality disorder: An activation likelihood-estimation meta-analysis. *Biological Psychiatry, 73,* 153–160. doi:10.1016/j.biopsych.2012.07.014

Rusbult, C. E., & Zembrodt, I. M. (1983). Responses to dissatisfaction in romantic involvements: A multidimensional scaling analysis. *Journal of Experimental Social Psychology, 19*(3), 274–293. http://dx.doi.org/10.1016/0022-1031(83)90042-2

Rusbult, C. E., Zembrodt, I. M., & Gunn, L. K. (1982). Exit, voice, loyalty, and neglect: Responses to dissatisfaction in romantic involvements. *Journal of Personality and Social Psychology, 43,* 1230–1242.

Russell, V. A., Zigmond, M. J., Dimatelis, J. J., Daniels, W. M. U., & Mabandla, M. V. (2014). The interaction between stress and exercise, and its impact on brain function. *Metabolic Brain Disease, 29,* 255–260. http://dx.doi.org/10.1007/s11011-013-9479-y

Russ, S. (2014). Play, culture, and the modern world. In S. W. Russ (Ed.), *Pretend play in childhood: Foundation of adult creativity* (pp. 153–171). Washington, DC: American Psychological Association.

Russ, S., & Wallace, C. E. (2013). Pretend play and creative processes. *American Journal of Play, 6,* 136–148.

Rutland, A., & Killen, M. (2015). A developmental science approach to reducing prejudice and social exclusion: Intergroup processes, social-cognitive development, and moral reasoning. *Social Issues and Policy Review, 9,* 121–154. http://dx.doi.org/10.1111/sipr.12012

Ruzzoli, M., & Soto-Faraco, S. (2014). Alpha stimulation of the human parietal cortex attunes tactile perception to external space. *Current Biology, 24,* 329–332. doi:10.1016/j.cub.2013.12.029

Ryan, C. J., & Callaghan, S. (2017). The impact on clinical practice of the 2015 reforms to the New South Wales Mental Health Act. *Australasian Psychiatry, 25*(1), 43–47. http://dx.doi.org/10.1177/1039856216663738

Ryan, R. M., & Deci, E. L. (2013). Toward a social psychology of assimilation: Self determination theory in cognitive development and education. In B. W. Sokol, F. M. E. Grouzet, & U. Muller (Eds.), *Self-regulation and autonomy: Social and developmental dimensions of human conduct* (pp. 191–207). Cambridge, UK: Cambridge University Press. http://dx.doi.org/10.1017/cbo9781139152198.014

Rychlowska, M., Miyamoto, Y., Matsumoto, D., Hess, U., Gilboa-Schechtman, E., Kamble, S., ... Niedenthal, P. M. (2015). Heterogeneity of long-history migration explains cultural differences in reports of emotional expressivity and the functions of smiles. *Proceedings of the National Academy of Sciences of the United States of America, 112*(19), E2429–E2436. doi:10.1073/pnas.1413661112

Rymer, R. (1993). *Genie: An abused child's first flight from silence.* New York, NY: Harper-Collins.

Saadat, S. (2015). A review on paraphilias. *International Journal of Medical Reviews, 1.* Retrieved from http://journals.bmsu.ac.ir/ijmr/index.php/ijmr/article/view/83

Sacco, R., Gabriele, S., & Persico, A. M. (2015). Head circumference and brain size in autism spectrum disorder: A systematic review and meta-analysis. *Psychiatry Research, 234*(2), 239–251. http://doi.org/10.1016/j.pscychresns.2015.08.016.

Sachsenweger, M. A., Fletcher, R. B., & Clarke, D. (2015). Pessimism and homework in CBT for depression. *Journal of Clinical Psychology, 71*, 1153–1172. http://dx.doi.org/10.1002/jclp.22227

Sacks, O. (2015). *On the move: A life.* New York, NY: Knopf.

Safer, M. A., Murphy, R. P., Wise, R. A., Bussey, L., Millett, C., & Holfeld, B. (2016). Educating jurors about eyewitness testimony in criminal cases with circumstantial and forensic evidence. *International Journal of Law and Psychiatry, 47*, 86–92. http://dx.doi.org/10.1016/j.ijlp.2016.02.041

Safe to Sleep. (2019). Research on back sleeping and SIDS. *Safe to Sleep, National Institutes of Health.* Retrieved from https://safetosleep.nichd.nih.gov/research/science/backsleeping

Salerno, J. M., Phalen, H. J., Reyes, R. N., & Schweitzer, N. J. (2018). Closing with emotion: The differential impact of male versus female attorneys expressing anger in court. *Law and Human Behavior, 42*(4), 385–401. http://dx.doi.org/10.1037/lhb0000292

Salerno, J. M., Phalen, H. J., Reyes, R. N., & Schweitzer, N. J. (2018). Closing with emotion: The differential impact of male versus female attorneys expressing anger in court. *Law and Human Behavior, 42*(4), 385–401. http://dx.doi.org/10.1037/lhb0000292

Salimi, N., Karimi-Shahanjarini, A., Rezapur-Shahkolai, F., Hamzeh, B., Roshanaei, G., & Babamiri, M. (2019). Aggression and its predictors among elementary students. *Journal of Injury and Violence Research, 11*(2), 159–170. doi:10.5249/jivr.v11i2.1102

Salk, R. H., Hyde, J. S., & Abramson, L. Y. (2017). Gender differences in depression in representative national samples: Meta-analyses of diagnoses and symptoms. *Psychological Bulletin, 143*(8), 783–822. doi:10.1037/bul0000102

Salomon, E., Preston, J. L., & Tannenbaum, M. B. (2017). Climate change helplessness and the (de)moralization of individual energy behavior. *Journal of Experimental Psychology: Applied, 23*(1), 15–28. http://dx.doi.org/10.1037/xap0000105

Salovey, P., & Mayer, J. D. (1990). Emotional intelligence. *Imagination, Cognition, and Personality, 9*, 185–211.

Salvi, C., Bricolo, E., Kounios, J., Bowden, E., & Beeman, M. (2016). Insight solutions are correct more often than analytic solutions. *Thinking and Reasoning, 22*(4), 443–460. http://dx.doi.org/10.1080/13546783.2016.1141798

Samaras, K., Tevaearai, H., Goldman, M., le Coutre, J., & Holly, J. (2019). Editorial: With obesity becoming the new normal, what should we do? *Frontiers in Endocrinology, 10*, 250. doi:10.3389/fendo.2019.00250

Sambrook Smith, M., Lawrence, V., Sadler, E., & Easter, A. (2019). Barriers to accessing mental health services for women with perinatal mental illness: Systematic review and meta-synthesis of qualitative studies in the UK. *BMJ Open, 9*, e024803. doi:10.1136/bmjopen-2018-024803

Samuels, B. A., Mendez-David, I., Faye, C., David, S. A., Pierz, K. A., Gardier, A. M., ... David, D. J. (2016). Serotonin 1A and serotonin 4 receptors: Essential mediators of the neurogenic and behavioral actions of anti-depressants. *The Neuroscientist, 22*, 26–45. http://dx.doi.org/10.1177/1073858414561303

Sánchez-Villegas, A., Toledo, E., de Irala, J., Ruiz-Canela, M., Pla-Vidal, J., & Martínez-González, M. A. (2011). Fast-food and commercial baked goods consumption and the risk of depression. *Public Health Nutrition, 15*, 424–432.

Sanderson, C. (2010). *Social psychology.* Hoboken, NJ. Wiley.

Sanderson, C. A. (2013). *Health psychology* (2nd ed.). Hoboken, NJ: Wiley.

Sanderson, C. A. (2019). *The positive shift: Mastering mindset to improve happiness, health, and longevity.* Dallas, TX: BenBella.

Sandner, B., Prang, P., Blesch, A., & Weidner, N. (2015). Stem cell-based therapies for spinal cord regeneration. In H. Kuhn & A. Eisch (Eds.), *Neural stem cells in development, adulthood and disease* (pp. 155–174). New York, NY: Springer.

Sándor, P., Szakadát, S., & Bódizs, R. (2014). Ontogeny of dreaming: A review of empirical studies. *Sleep Medicine Reviews, 18*, 435–449. http://dx.doi.org/10.1016/j.smrv.2014.02.001

Sandoval, E. (2019, June 24). Did a Princeton graduate know killing his father was wrong? *The New York Times.* Retrieved June 23, 2019 from https://www.nytimes.com/2019/06/24/nyregion/murder-trial-thomas-gilbert.html

Sanjuán, P., & Magallares, A. (2014). Coping strategies as mediating variables between self-serving attributional bias and subjective well-being. *Journal of Happiness Studies, 15*, 443–453. http://dx.doi.org/10.1007/s10902-013-9430-2

Sanson, M., Strange, D., & Garry, M. (2019). Trigger warnings are trivially helpful at reducing negative affect, intrusive thoughts, and avoidance. *Clinical Psychological Science, 7*(4), 778–793. https://doi.org/10.1177/2167702619827018

Santos, T. O. (2016). Cognitive changes in aging: Implications for discourse processing. In L. S. Carozza (Ed), *Communication and aging: Creative approaches to improving the quality of life* (pp. 25–65). San Diego, CA: Plural Publishing.

Sarafino, E. P., & Smith, T. W. (2016). *Health psychology: Biopsychosocial interactions* (9th ed.). Hoboken, NJ: Wiley.

Saraswat, A., Weinand, J. D., & Safer, J. D. (2015). Evidence supporting the biologic nature of gender identity. *Endocrine Practice, 21*, 199–204. http://dx.doi.org/10.4158/EP14351.RA

Sargent, J. D., Tanski, S., & Stoolmiller, M. (2012). Influence of motion picture rating on adolescent response to movie smoking. *Pediatrics, 130*, 228–236. http://dx.doi.org/10.1542/peds.2011-1787

Saridi, M., Kordosi, A., Toska, A., Peppou, L. E., Economou, M., & Souliotis, K. (2017). Attitudes of health professionals towards the stigma surrounding depression in times of economic crisis. *International Journal of Social Psychiatry, 63*(2), 115–125. http://dx.doi.org/10.1177/0020764016685348

Sassenberg, K., Moskowitz, G. B., Fetterman, A., & Kessler, T. (2017). Priming creativity as a strategy to increase creative performance by facilitating the activation and use of remote associations. *Journal of Experimental Social Psychology, 68*, 128–138. http://dx.doi.org/10.1016/j.jesp.2016.06.010

Savage-Rumbaugh, E. S. (1990). Language acquisition in a nonhuman species: Implications for the innateness debate. *Developmental Psychobiology, 23*, 599–620. http://dx.doi.org/10.1002/dev.420230706

Saxe, A. M., McClelland, J. L., & Ganguli, S. (2019). A mathematical theory of semantic development in deep neural networks. *Proceedings of the National Academy of Sciences of the United States of America, 116*(23), 11537–11546. https://doi.org/10.1073/pnas. 1820226116

Sayal, K., Heron, J., Maughan, B., Rowe, R., & Ramchandani, P. (2014). Infant temperament and childhood psychiatric disorder: Longitudinal study. *Child: Care, Health and Development, 40*, 292–297. doi:10.1111/cch.12054

Schachter, S., & Singer, J. E. (1962). Cognitive, social, and physiological determinants of emotional state. *Psychological Review, 69*, 379–399.

Schacter, D. L. (2019). Implicit memory, constructive memory, and imagining the future: A career perspective. *Perspectives on Psychological Science, 14*(2), 256–272. https://doi.org/10.1177/1745691618803640

Schaeffer, E. L., Cerulli, F. G., Souza, H. O. X., Catanozi, S., & Gattaz, W. F. (2014). Synergistic and additive effects of enriched environment and lithium on the generation of new cells in adult mouse hippocampus. *Journal of Neural Transmission, 121*, 695–706. http://dx.doi.org/10.1007/s00702-014-1175-5

Schaffert, J., LoBue, C., White, C. L. III, Chiang, H.-S., Didehbani, N., Lacritz, L., . . . Cullum, C. M. (2018). Traumatic brain injury history is associated with an earlier age of dementia onset in autopsy-confirmed Alzheimer's disease. *Neuropsychology, 32*(4), 410–416. http://dx.doi.org/10.1037/neu0000423

Schaie, K. W. (1994). The life course of adult intellectual development. *American Psychologist, 49*, 304–313.

Schalet, A. T. (2011). Not under my roof: Parents, teens, and the culture of sex. Chicago, IL: University of Chicago Press.

Scharrer, E., & Ramasubramanian, S. (2015). Intervening in the media's influence on stereotypes of race and ethnicity: The role of media literacy education. *Journal of Social Issues, 71*, 171–185. http://dx.doi.org/10.1111/josi.12103

Scheele, D., Striepens, N., Güntürkün, O., Deutschländer, S., Maier, W., Kendrick, K. M., & Hurlemann, R. (2012). Oxytocin modulates social distance between males and females. *The Journal of Neuroscience, 32*, 16074–16079.

Scheele, D., Wille, A., Kendrick, K. M., Stoffel-Wagner, B., Becker, B., Güntürkün, O., . . . Hurlemann, R. (2013). Oxytocin enhances brain reward system responses in men viewing the face of their female partner. *Proceedings of the National Academy of Science of the United States of America, 110*, 20308–20313. http://dx.doi.org/10.1073/pnas. 1314190110

Schenk, C. H. (2019). The spectrum of disorders causing violence during sleep. *Sleep Science and Practice, 3*(2). Retrieved from https://doi.org/10.1186/s41606-019-0034-6

Scherr, S., Arendt, F., Frissen,, T., & Oramas, J. (2019). Detecting intentional self-harm on Instagram: Development, testing, and validation of an automatic image-recognition algorithm to discover cutting-related posts. *Social Science Computer Review.* https://doi.org/10.1177/0894439319836389

Schick, T., Jr., & Vaughn, L. (2014). *How to think about weird things: Critical thinking for a new age* (7th ed.). New York, NY: McGraw-Hill.

Schilken, C. (2019, August 8). Simone Biles gets emotional speaking about Larry Nassar scandal. *LA Times.* Retrieved from https://www.latimes.com/sports/story/2019-08-08/simone-biles-larry-nassar-usa-gymnastics

Schimmel, P. (2014). *Sigmund Freud's discovery of psychoanalysis: Conquistador and thinker.* New York, NY: Routledge/Taylor & Francis Group.

Schlichting, M. L., & Preston, A. R. (2014). Memory reactivation during rest supports upcoming learning of related content. *Proceedings of the National Academy of Sciences of the United States of America, 111*, 15845–15850. http://dx.doi.org/10.1073/pnas. 1404396111

Schnall, P. L., Dobson, M., & Landsbergis, P. (2016). Globalization, work, and cardiovascular disease. *International Journal of Health Services, 46*, 656–692. http://dx.doi.org/10.1177/0020731416664687

Schneider, K., Fraser Pierson, J., & Bugental, J. (Eds.). (2015). *The handbook of humanistic psychology.* Thousand Oaks, CA: Sage.

Schneider, M. F. (2015). Eating disorders. In L. Sperry, J. Carlson, J. D. Sauerheber, & J. Sperry (Eds.), *Psychopathology and psychotherapy: DSM-5 diagnosis, case conceptualization, and treatment* (3rd ed., pp. 151–175). New York, NY: Routledge/Taylor & Francis Group.

Schneidman, E. S. (1969). Suicide, lethality and the psychological autopsy. *International Psychiatry Clinics, 6*, 225–250.

Schoenmaker, C., Juffer, F., van IJzendoorn, M. H., van den Dries, L., Linting, M., Vander voort, A., & Bakermans-Kranenburg, M. J. (2015). Cognitive and health-related outcomes after exposure to early malnutrition: The Leiden longitudinal study of international adoptees. *Children and Youth Services Review, 48*, 80–86. http://dx.doi.org/10.1016/j.childyouth.2014.12.010

Schonert-Reichl, K. A., Oberle, E., Lawlor, M. S., Abbott, D., Thomson, K., Oberlander, T. F., & Diamond, A. (2015). Enhancing cognitive and social–emotional development through a simple-to-administer mindfulness based school program for elementary school children: A randomized controlled trial. *Developmental Psychology, 51*, 52–66. http://doi.org/10.1037/a0038454

Schönfeld, L. M., & Wojtecki, L. (2019). Beyond emotions: Oscillations of the amygdala and their implications for electrical neuromodulation. *Frontiers in Neuroscience, 13*, 366. http://dx.doi:10.3389/fnins.2019.00366

Schoon, A., Fjellanger, R., Kjeldsen, M., & Goss, K. U. (2014). Using dogs to detect hidden corrosion. *Applied Animal Behaviour Science, 15*, 43–52. doi:10.1016/j.applanim.2014.01.001.

Schrepf, A., Naliboff, B., Williams, D. A., Stephens-Shields, A. J., Landis, J. R., Gupta, A., . . . MAPP Research Network. (2018). Adverse childhood experiences and symptoms of urologic chronic pelvic pain syndrome: A multidisciplinary approach to the study of chronic pelvic pain research network study. *Annals of Behavioral Medicine, 52*(10), 865–877. https://doi.org/10.1093/abm/kax060

Schroder, H. S., Yalch, M. M., Dawood, S., Callahan, C. P., Brent Donnellan, M., & Moser, J. S. (2017). Growth mindset of anxiety buffers the link between stressful life events and psychological distress and coping strategies. *Personality and Individual Differences, 110*, 23–26. http://dx.doi.org/10.1016/j.paid. 2017.01.016

Schroeder, D. A., & Graziano, W. G. (Eds.). (2015). *The Oxford handbook of prosocial behavior.* Oxford, UK: Oxford University Press.

Schuetze, B. A., Eglington, L. G., & Kang, S. H. K. (2019). Retrieval practice benefits memory precision. *Memory, 27*(8), 1091–1098. doi:10.1080/09658211.2019.1623260

Schulze, L., Schmahl, C., & Niedtfeld, I. (2016). Neural correlates of disturbed emotion processing in borderline personality disorder: A multimodal meta-analysis. *Biological Psychiatry, 79*, 97–106. http://dx.doi.org/10.1016/j.biopsych.2015.03.027

Schulz, H. M. (2015). Reference group influence in consumer role rehearsal narratives. *Qualitative Market Research: An International Journal, 18*, 210–229. http://dx.doi.org/10.1108/QMR-02-2012-0009

Schunk, D. H., & Zimmerman, B. J. (2013). Self regulation and learning. In W. M. Reynolds, G. E. Miller, & I. B. Weiner (Eds.), *Handbook*

of psychology, Vol. 7. Educational psychology (2nd ed., pp. 45–68). Hoboken, NJ: Wiley.

Schüz, B., Bower, J., & Ferguson, S. G. (2015). Stimulus control and affect in dietary behaviours. An intensive longitudinal study. *Appetite, 87,* 310–317. http://dx.doi.org/10.1016/j.appet.2015.01.002

Schwartz, A. J., Boduroglu, A., & Gutchess, A. H. (2014). Cross-cultural differences in categorical memory errors. *Cognitive Science, 38,* 997–1007. doi:10.1111/cogs.12109

Schwartz, B., & Krantz, J. (2016). *Sensation and perception.* Thousand Oaks, CA: Sage.

Schwartz, S. J., Zamboanga, B. L., Luyckx, K., Meca, A., & Ritchie, R. (2016). Identity in emerging adulthood: Reviewing the field and looking forward. In J. J. Arnett (Ed.), *The Oxford handbook of emerging adulthood* (pp. 401–420). New York, NY: Oxford University

Science News. (2019, April 9). Forcing a smile for customers linked with more drinking after work. *Science Daily.* Retrieved from https://www.sciencedaily.com/releases/2019/04/190409135838.htm

Scott, C. (2015). *Learn to teach: Teach to learn.* New York, NY: Cambridge University Press.

Scott, H. K., & Cogburn, M. (2018, October 27). Behavior modification. *StatPearls.* Retrieved from: https://www.ncbi.nlm.nih.gov/books/NBK459285/

Scott-Phillips, T. C. (2015). Nonhuman primate communication, pragmatics, and the origins of language. *Current Anthropology, 56,* 56–80.

Scribner, S. (1977). Modes of thinking and ways of speaking: Culture and logic reconsidered. In P. N. Johnson-Laird & P. C. Wason (Eds.), *Thinking: Readings in cognitive science* (pp. 324–339). New York, NY: Cambridge University Press.

Sdrulla, A. D., Chen, G., & Mauer, K. (2015). Definition and demographics of addiction. In A. Kaye, N. Vadivelu, & R. Urman (Eds.), *Substance abuse* (pp. 1–15). New York, NY: Springer.

Seay, T. A., & Sun, C. T. L. (2016). Psychotherapies: What can be done when the mind is unwell? In C. Tien-Lun Sun (Ed.), *Psychology in Asia: An introduction* (pp. 395–422). Boston, MA: Cengage.

Sebelius, K. (2014). *The health consequences of smoking—50 years of progress: A report of the Surgeon General.* Atlanta, GA: US Department of Health and Human Services, Centers for Disease Control and Prevention, National Center for Chronic Disease Prevention and Health Promotion, Office on Smoking and Health. Retrieved from http://www.surgeongeneral.gov/library/reports/50-years-of-progress/execsummary.Pdf

Sedikides, C., & Alicke, M. D. (2012). Self enhancement and self-protection motives. In R. M. Ryan (Ed.), *The Oxford handbook of human motivation. Oxford library of psychology* (pp. 303–322). New York, NY: Oxford University Press.

Seedat, S., Scott, K. M., Angermeyer, M. C., Berglund, P., Bromet, E. J., Brugha, T. S., . . . Kessler, R. C. (2009). Cross-national associations between gender and mental disorders in the World Health Organization World Mental Health Surveys. *Archives of General Psychiatry, 66,* 785–795. doi:10.1001/archgenpsychiatry.2009.36

Seedman, A. A., & Hellman, P. (2014). *Fifty years after Kitty Genovese: Inside the case that rocked our faith in each other.* New York, NY: The Experiment.

Segaert, K., Lucas, S. J. E., Burley, C. V., Segaert, P., Milner, A. E., Ryan, M., & Wheeldon, L. (2018). Higher physical fitness levels are associated with less language decline in healthy ageing. *Scientific Reports, 8,* Article number: 6715. doi:10.1038/s41598-018-24972-1

Segarra-Echebarría, R., Fernández-Pérez, I., García-Moncho, J. M., & Delarze-Carrillo, L. (2015). Psychosexual development and sexual dysfunctions. In M. Sáenz-Herrero (Ed.), *Psychopathology in women:*

Incorporating gender perspective into descriptive psychopathology (pp. 25–51). Cham, CH: Springer International Publishing. http://dx.doi.org/10.1007/978-3-319-05870-2

Sehgal, P. (2015, December 1). The profound emptiness of "resilience." *The New York Times Magazine.* Retrieved from http://www.nytimes.com/2015/12/06/magazine/the-profoundemptiness-of-resilience.html?_r=1

Sekiguchi, A., Kotozaki, Y., Sugiura, M., Nouchi, R., Takeuchi, H., Hanawa, S., . . . Kawashima, R. (2014). Long-term effects of postearthquake distress on brain microstructural changes. *BioMed Research International, Volume 2014,* Article ID 180468. http://doi.org/10.1155/2014/180468

Seligman, M. E. P. (1975). *Helplessness: On depression, development, and death.* San Francisco, CA: Freeman.

Seligman, M. E. P. (2003). The past and future of positive psychology. In C. L. M. Keyes & J. Daidt (Eds.), *Flourishing: Positive psychology and the life well-lived* (pp. xi–xx). Washington, DC: American Psychological Association.

Seligman, M. E. P. (2007). Coaching and positive psychology. *Australian Psychologist, 42,* 266–267.

Seligman, M. E. P. (2011). *Flourish: A visionary new understanding of happiness and well being.* Riverside, NJ: Atria.

Seligman, M. E. P. (2018). *The hope circuit: A psychologist's journey from helplessness to optimism.* New York, NY: Hatchette.

Seligman, M. E. P., & Maier, S. F. (1967). Failure to escape traumatic shock. *Journal of Experimental Psychology, 74,* 1–9. http://dx.doi.org/10.1037/h0024514

Sella, F., Berteletti, I., Lucangeli, D., & Zorzi, M. (2017). Preschool children use space, rather than counting, to infer the numerical magnitude of digits: Evidence for a spatial mapping principle. *Cognition, 158,* 56–67. http://dx.doi.org/10.1016/j.cognition.2016.10.010

Selvi, F. F., Karakaş, S. A., Boysan, M., & Selvi, Y. (2015). Effects of shift work on attention deficit, hyperactivity, and impulsivity, and their relationship with chronotype. *Biological Rhythm Research, 46,* 53–61. doi:10.1080/09291016.2014.948299

Selye, H. (1936). A syndrome produced by diverse nocuous agents. *Nature, 138,* 32. http://dx.doi.org/10.1038/138032a0

Selye, H. (1974). *Stress without distress.* Philadelphia, PA: Saunders.

Selye, H. (1983). The stress concept: Past, present, and future. In C. L. Cooper (Ed.), *Stress research* (pp. 1–20). New York, NY: Wiley.

Sénécal, V., Deblois, G., Beauseigle, D., Schneider, R., Brandenburg, J., Newcombe, J., . . . Arbour, N. G. (2016). Production of IL-27 in multiple sclerosis lesions by astrocytes and myeloid cells: Modulation of local immune responses. *Glia, 64,* 553–569. http://dx.doi.org/10.1002/glia.22948

Seresinhe, C. I., Preis, T., MacKerron, G., & Moat, H. S. (2019). Happiness is greater in more scenic locations. *Scientific Reports 9,* Article number: 4498. https://www.nature.com/articles/s41598-019-40854-6

Seshadri, S., & Ramaswamy, S. (2019). Clinical practice guidelines for child sexual abuse. *Indian Journal of Psychiatry, 61*(Suppl 2), 317–332. Retrieved from doi:10.4103/psychiatry.IndianJPsychiatry_502_18

Shackelford, T. K., & Hansen, R. D. (Eds.). (2015). *Evolutionary psychology. The evolution of sexuality.* Cham, CH: Springer International Publishing.

Shand, G. (2013). Culture and the self: A comparison of attitudes to study among English and Japanese students in state secondary education. *Compare: A Journal of Comparative and International Education, 43,* 857–858. http://dx.doi.org/10.1080/03057925.2012.752623

Shang, S. S. C., Wu, Y.-L., & Sie, Y.-J. (2017). Generating consumer resonance for purchase intention on social network sites. *Computers in Human Behavior, 69,* 18–28. http://dx.doi.org/10.1016/j.chb.2016.12.014

Shannon, P. J., Wieling, E., McCleary, J. S., & Becher, E. (2015). Exploring the mental health effects of political trauma with newly arrived refugees. *Qualitative Health Research, 25,* 443–457. http://dx.doi.org/10.1177/1049732314549475

Shao, R., & Wang, Y. (2019). The relation of violent video games to adolescent aggression: An examination of moderated mediation effect. *Frontiers in Psychology, 10,* 384. Retrieved from doi:10.3389/fpsyg.2019.00384

Shapiro, S. L., & Carlson, L. E. (2017). *The art and science of meditation: Integrating mindfulness into psychology and the helping professions* (2rd ed.). Washington, DC: American Psychological Association.

Sharma, S. (2017). The epigenetics of intrauterine smoke exposure: Can maternal vitamin C supplementation prevent neonatal respiratory disease? *American Journal of Respiratory and Critical Care Medicine, 196*(6), 672–674. doi:10.1164/rccm.201705-0856ED

Shaw, A. M., Timpano, K. R., Tran, T. B., & Joormann, J. (2015). Correlates of Facebook usage patterns: The relationship between passive Facebook use, social anxiety symptoms, and brooding. *Computers in Human Behavior, 48,* 575–580. http://dx.doi.org/10.1016/j.chb.2015.02.003

Shaw, J., & Porter, S. (2015). Constructing rich false memories of committing crime. *Psychological Science, 26,* 291–301. http://dx.doi.org/10.1177/0956797614562862

Shaw, N. D., Butler, J. P., McKinney, S. M., Nelson, S. A., Ellenbogen, J. M., & Hall, J. E. (2012). Insights into puberty: The relationship between sleep stages and pulsatile LH secretion. *Journal of Clinical Endocrinology & Metabolism, 97,* E2055–E2062. http://dx.doi.org/10.1210/jc.2012-2692

Shepherd, S. V. (2017). *The Wiley handbook of evolutionary neuroscience.* Hoboken, NJ; Wiley-Blackwell.

Sherif, M. (1966). *In common predicament: Social psychology of intergroup conflict and cooperation.* Boston, MA: Houghton Miff lin.

Sherif, M. (1998). Experiments in group conflict. In J. M. Jenkins, K. Oatley, & N. L. Stein (Eds.), *Human emotions: A reader* (pp. 245–252). Malden, MA: Blackwell.

Sher, L., Fisher, A. M., Kelliher, C. H., Penner, J. D., Goodman, M., Koenigsberg, H. W., . . . Hazlett, E. A. (2016). Clinical features and psy-chiatric comorbidities of borderline personality disorder patients with versus without a history of suicide attempt. *Psychiatry Research, 246,* 261–266. http://dx.doi.org/10.1016/j.psy-chres.2016.10.003

Sherlock, M., & Wagstaff, D. L. (2019). Exploring the relationship between frequency of Instagram use, exposure to idealized images, and psychological well-being in women. *Psychology of Popular Media Culture, 8*(4), 482–490. http://dx.doi.org/10.1037/ppm0000182

Sherman, R. A., Rauthmann, J. F., Brown, N. A., Serfass, D. G., & Jones, A. B. (2015). The independent effects of personality and situations on real-time expressions of behavior and emotion. *Journal of Personality and Social Psychology, 109,* 872–888. http://dx.doi.org/10.1037/pspp0000036

Shigemura, J., & Chhem, R. K. (Eds.) (2016). *Mental health and social issues following a nuclear accident: The case of Fukushima.* Tokyo, JP: Springer. http://dx.doi.org/10.1007/978-4-431-55699-2

Shi, Z., Wang, A. L., Aronowitz, C. A., Cappella, J. N., Romer, D., & Langleben, D. D. (2019). Connectivity between visual and auditory cortices mediates the influence of argument strength on the effectiveness of smoking-cessation videos among smokers low in sensation seeking. *Psychology Research and Behavior Management, 12,* 531–542. doi:10.2147/PRBM.S183394

Short, F., & Thomas, P. (2015). *Core approaches in counselling and psychotherapy.* New York, NY: Routledge/Taylor & Francis Group.

Shukla, A. K., Khaitan, T., Gupta, P., & Vaik, S. R. (2019). Smokeless tobacco and its adverse effects on hematological parameters: A cross-sectional study. *Advances in Preventive Medicine.* Article ID 3182946. https://doi.org/10.1155/2019/3182946

Shweder, R. A. (2011). Commentary: Ontogenetic cultural psychology. In L. A. Jensen (Ed.), *Bridging cultural and developmental approaches to psychology: New syntheses in theory, research, and policy* (pp. 303–310). New York, NY: Oxford University Press.

Siegel, J. M. (2000, January). Narcolepsy. *Scientific American,* 76–81. http://dx.doi.org/10.1038/scientificamerican0100-76.

Sierksma, J., Thijs, J., & Verkuyten, M. (2015). In-group bias in children's intention to help can be overpowered by inducing empathy. *British Journal of Developmental Psychology, 33,* 45–56. http://dx.doi.org/10.1111/bjdp.12065

Sievert, L., Morrison, L. A., Reza, A. M., Brown, D. E., Kalua, E., & Tefft, H. T. (2007). Age-related differences in health complaints: The Hilo women's health study. *Women & Health, 45,* 31–51. http://dx.doi.org/10.1300/J013v45n03-03

Sifferlin, A. (2017, January 5). Eleven surprising uses for Botox. *Time.* http://time.com/4501839/botoxinection-wrinkles-migraine-depression/?xid=newsletter-brief

Silberner, J. (2019). Ketamine based drug should be available for treatment resistant depression, says FDA panel. *BMJ, 364:*1858.

Silver, L. (2019, May 13). Misinformation and fears about its impact are pervasive in 11 emerging economies. *FactTank.* Retrieved May 14, 2019 from https://www.pewresearch.org/fact-tank/2019/05/13/misinformation-and-fears-about-its-impact-are-pervasive-in-11-emerging-economies/

Silverstein, M. L. (2013). *Personality and clinical psychology. Personality assessment in depth: A casebook.* New York, NY: Routledge.

Silvia, P. J., Delaney, P. F., & Marcovitch, S. (2017). *What psychology majors could (and should) be doing: A guide to research experience, professional skills, and your options after college* (2nd ed.). Washington, DC: American Psychological Association.

Simm, A., & Klotz, L.-O. (2015). Stress and biological aging: A double-edged sword. *Zeitschrift für Gerontologie und Geriatrie, 48,* 505–510. http://dx.doi.org/10.1007/s00391-015-0928-6

Simmons, R. (2019, May 23). We tell our kids that hard work always pays off. What happens when they fail anyway? *Time.* Retrieved June 8, 2019 from http://time.com/5593706/hard-work-achievement-mindset/?utm_source=time.com&utm_medium=email&utm_campaign=the-brief&utm_content=2019052512pm&xid=newsletter-brief

Simons, D. J., & Chabris, C. F. (1999). Gorillas in our midst: Sustained inattentional blindness for dynamic events. *Perception, 28,* 1059–1074. http://dx.doi.org/10.1068/p2952

Simons, L. G., Wickrama, K. A. S., Lee, T. K., Landers-Potts, M., Cutrona, C., & Conger, R. D. (2016). Testing family stress and family investment explanations for conduct problems among African American adolescents. *Journal of Marriage and Family, 78,* 498–515. http://dx.doi.org/10.1111/jomf.12278

Sinatra, R., Wang, D., Deville, P., Song, C., & Barabási, A.-L. (2016). Quantifying the evolution of individual scientific impact. *Science, 354*(6312). http://dx.doi.org/10.1126/science.aaf5239

Singh, A., & Kar, S. K. (2017). How electroconvulsive therapy works?: Understanding the neurobiological mechanisms. *Clinical*

Psychopharmacology and Neuroscience, 15(3), 210–221. doi:10.9758/cpn.2017.15.3.210

Singh, M. (2017, September 21). Macho man, little princess: How gender norms can harm kids everywhere. *NPR*. Retrieved from https://www.npr.org/sections/goatsandsoda/2017/09/21/552573637/macho-man-little-princess-how-gender-norms-can-harm-kids-everywhere

Sisk, V. F., Burgoyne, A. P., Sun, J., Butler, J. L., & Macnamara, B. N. (2018). To what extent and under which circumstances are growth mind-sets important to academic achievement? Two meta-analyses. *Psychological Science, 29*(4), 549–571. https://doi.org/10.1177/0956797617739704

Situala, S., Amador, A., & Burris, T. P. (2016). The circadian clock as a drug target. In M. L. Gumz (Ed.), *Circadian clocks: Role in health and disease* (pp. 335–366). New York, NY: Springer Science + Business Media. http://dx.doi.org/10.1007/978-1-4939-3450-8_12

Skinner, B. F. (1956). A case history in the scientific method. *American Psychologist, 11*, 221–233. http://dx.doi.org/10.1037/h0047662

Skinner, B. F. (1958). Diagramming schedules of reinforcement. *Journal of the Experimental Analysis of Behavior, 1*, 67–68. https://doi.org/10.1901/jeab.1958.1-67

Skoglund, C., Tiger, A., Rück, C., Petrovic, P., Asherson, P., Hellner, C., . . . Kuja-Halkola, R. (2019). Familial risk and heritability of diagnosed borderline personality disorder: A register study of the Swedish population. Molecular Psychiatry. Retrieved from https://www.nature.com/articles/s41380-019-0442-0#article-info

Smalheiser, N. R., Zhang, H., & Dwivedi, Y. (2014). Enoxacin elevates microRNA levels in rat frontal cortex and prevents learned helplessness. *Frontiers in Psychiatry, 5*, 6. http://dx.doi.org/10.3389/fpsyt.2014.00006

Smarandescu, L., & Shimp, T. (2015). Drink Coca-Cola, eat popcorn, and choose Powerade: Testing the limits of subliminal persuasion. *Marketing Letters, 26*, 715–726. doi:10.1007/s11002-014-9294-1

Smiley, P. A., Tan, S. J., Goldstein, A., & Sweda, J. (2016). Mother emotion, child temperament, and young children's helpless responses to failure. *Social Development, 25*, 285–303. http://dx.doi.org/10.1111/sode.12153

Smith, A. M., Floerke, V. A., & Thomas, A.K. (2016). Retrieval practice protects memory against acute stress. *Science, 354*, 1046–1048. http://dx.doi.org/10.1126/science.aah5067

Smith, D., Smith, R., & Misquitta, D. (2016). Neuroimaging and violence. *Psychiatric Clinics of North America, 39*(4), 579–597. http://dx.doi.org/10.1016/j.psc.2016.07.006

Smith, K. Z., Smith, P. H., Cercone, S. A., McKee, S. A., & Homish, G. G. (2016). Past year non-medical opioid use and abuse and PTSD diagnosis: Interactions with sex and associations with symptom clusters. *Addictive Behaviors, 58*, 167–174. http://dx.doi.org/10.1016/j.addbeh.2016.02.019

Smith, L. S. (2016). Family-based therapy for parent-child reunification. *Journal of Clinical Psychology, 72*, 498–512. http://dx.doi.org/10.1002/jclp.22259

Smith, M. L., & Glass, G. V. (1977). Meta-analysis of psychotherapy outcome studies. *American Psychologist, 32*, 752–760. http://dx.doi.org/10.1037/0003-066X.32.9.752

Smith, M. L., Glass, G. V., & Miller, T. I. (1980). *The benefits of psychotherapy.* Baltimore, MD: Johns Hopkins University Press.

Smith, M., Robinson, L., & Segal, R. (2012). How much sleep do you need? Sleep cycles and stages, lack of sleep, and getting the hours you need. *HelpGuide.Org.* Retrieved from http://helpguide.org/life/sleeping.htm

Smith, N. K., Madeira, J., & Millard, H. R. (2015). Sexual function and fertility quality of life in women using in vitro fertilization. *Journal of Sexual Medicine, 12,* 985–993. http://dx. doi.org/10.1111/jsm.1282

Smith, O. (2018. February 7). Which nationalities work the longest hours? *The Telegraph*. Retrieved from https://www.telegraph.co.uk/travel/maps-and-graphics/nationalities-that-work-the-longest-hours/

Smith, P. K., & Robinson, S. (2019). How does individualism-collectivism relate to bullying victimisation? *International Journal of Bullying Prevention, 1*(1), 3–13. https://doi.org/10.1007/s42380-018-0005-y

Smit, L., Knoors, H., Hermans, D., Verhoeven, L., & Vissers, C. (2019). The interplay between theory of mind and social emotional functioning in adolescents with communication and language problems. *Frontiers in Psychology, 10*(1488). doi:10.3389/fpsyg.2019.01488

Snider, S. E., Quisenberry, A. J., & Bickel, W. K. (2016). Order in the absence of an effect: Identifying rate-dependent relationships. *Behavioural Processes, 127*, 18–24. http://dx.doi.org/10.1016/j.beproc.2016.03.012

Social Work Guide. (2019). How to Become a Social Worker: A Quick Guide. *Social Work Guide.* Retrieved from https://www.socialwork-guide.org/

Sohal, S. S., Eapen, M. S., Naidu, V. G. M., & Sharma, P. (2019). IQOS exposure impairs human airway cell homeostasis: Direct comparison with traditional cigarette and e-cigarette. *ERJ Open Research, 5*(1): 00159-2018. doi:10.1183/23120541.00159-2018

Soh, D. W. (2017, April 25). Cross-cultural evidence for the genetics of homosexuality. *Scientific American*. Retrieved from https://www.scientificamerican.com/article/cross-cultural evidence for the genetics of homosexuality/&content Placement=2&pgtype=-collection &_r=0

Solms, M. (1997). *The neuropsychology of dreams.* Hillsdale, NJ: Erlbaum.

Solnit, R. (2009). *A paradise built in hell: The extraordinary communities that arise in disaster.* New York, NY: Penguin.

Soloff, P. H., Abraham, K., Burgess, A., Ramaseshan, K., Chowdury, A., & Diwadkar, V. A. (2017). Impulsivity and aggression mediate regional brain responses in borderline personality disorder: An fMRI study. *Psychiatry Research: Neuroimaging, 260*, 76–85. http://dx.doi.org/10.1016/j.pscychresns.2016.12.009

Solomon, A., Turunen, H., Ngandu, T., Peltonen, M., Levälahti, E., Helisalmi, S., . . . Kivipelto, M. (2018). Effect of the apolipoprotein E genotype on cognitive change during a multidomain lifestyle intervention: A subgroup analysis of a randomized clinical trial. *JAMA Neurology, 75*(4), 462–470. doi:10.1001/jamaneurol.2017.4365

Song, H., Fang, F., Arnberg, F. K., Mataix-Cols, D., Fernández de la Cruz, L., Almqvist, C., . . . Valdimarsdóttir, U. A. (2019). Stress related disorders and risk of cardiovascular disease: Population based, sibling controlled cohort study. *BMJ (Clinical Research Ed.), 365*, l1255. doi:10.1136/bmj.l1255

Song, M. J., & Bharti, K. (2016). Looking into the future: Using induced pluripotent stem cells to build two and three dimensional ocular tissue for cell therapy and disease modeling. *Brain Research, 1638*(Pt A), 2–14. http://dx.doi.org/10.1016/j.brainres.2015.12.011

Sörman, D. E., Hansson, P., & Ljungberg, J. K. (2019). Different features of bilingualism in relation to executive functioning. *Frontiers in Psychology, 10*, 269. doi:10.3389/fpsyg.2019.00269

Sorokowska, A., Sorokowski, P., Hilpert, P., Cantarero, K., Frackowiak, T., Ahmadi, K., . . . Pierce, J. D. (2017). Preferred interpersonal distances: A global comparison. *Journal of Cross-Cultural Psychology, 48*(4), 577–592. doi:10.1177/0022022117698039

Sotomayor, S. (2014). *My beloved world.* New York, NY: Vintage.

Souza, A. L., Conroy-Beam, D., & Buss, D. M. (2016). Mate preferences in Brazil: Evolved desires and cultural evolution over three decades. *Personality and Individual Differences, 95,* 45–49. http://dx.doi.org/10.1016/j.paid.2016.01.053

Spearman, C. (1923). *The nature of "intelligence" and the principles of cognition.* London, UK: Macmillan.

Speed, B. C., Goldstein, B. L., & Goldfried, M. R. (2019). Assertiveness training: A forgotten evidence-based treatment. *Clinical Psychology Science and Practice, 25,* 1–20. Retrieved from https://onlinelibrary.wiley.com/doi/abs/10.1111/cpsp.12216

Sperling, G. (1960). The information available in brief visual presentations. *Psychological Monographs, 74,* 1–29. http://dx.doi.org/10.1037/h0093759

Spiegel, D. (2015). Hypnosis and pain control. In T. R. Deer, M. S. Leong, & A. L. Ray (Eds.), *Treatment of chronic pain by integrative approaches: The American Academy of Pain Medicine textbook on patient management* (pp. 115–122). New York, NY: Springer. doi:10.1007/978-1-4939-1821-8

Spiegler, M. (2016). *Contemporary behavior therapy* (6th ed.). Boston, MA: Cengage.

Spinazzola, J., Hodghon, H., Liang, L. J., Ford, J. D., Layne, C. M., Pynoos, R. S., . . . Kisiel, C. (2014). Unseen wounds: The contribution of psychological maltreatment to child and adolescent mental health and risk outcomes. *Psychological Trauma: Theory, Research, Practice, and Policy, 6,* S18–S28. http://dx.doi.org/10.1037/a0037766

Spindle, T. R., Cone, E. J., Schlienz, N. J., Mitchell, J. M., Bigelow, G. G., Flegel, R., . . . Vandrey, R. (2018, November 30). Acute effects of smoked and vaporized cannabis in healthy adults who infrequently use cannabis: A crossover trial. *JAMA Network Open, 1*(7):e184841. Retrieved from doi:10.1001/jamanetworkopen.2018.4841

Spitz, R. A., & Wolf, K. M. (1946). The smiling response: A contribution to the ontogenesis of social relations. *Genetic Psychology Monographs, 34,* 57–123.

Sprecher, S., Felmlee, D., Metts, S., & Cupach, W. (2015). Relationship initiation and development. In M. Mikulincer, P. R. Shaver, J. A. Simpson, & J. F. Dovidio (Eds.), *APA handbook of personality and social psychology, Vol. 3. Interpersonal relations* (pp. 211–245). Washington, DC: American Psychological Association. http://dx.doi.org/10.1037/14344-008

Srienc, A., Narang, P., Sarai, S., Xiong, Y., & Lippmann, S. (2018). Is electroconvulsive therapy a treatment for depression following traumatic brain injury? *Innovations in Clinical Neuroscience, 15*(3–4), 43–46. https://www.ncbi.nlm.nih.gov/pubmed/29707426

Srinivasan, V., Singh, J., Brzezinski, A., Zakaria, R., Shillcutt, S. D., & Brown, G. M. (2014). Jet lag: Use of melatonin and melatonergic drugs. In V. Srinivasan, A. Brzezinski, S. Oter, & S. Shillcutt (Eds.), *Melatonin and melatonergic drugs in clinical practice* (pp. 367–378). Tamilnadu, IN: Springer. doi:10.1007/978-81-322-0825-9_26

Srivastava, D., Torquati, J., de Guzman, M. R. T., & Dev, D. A. (2019). Understanding parental ethnotheories and practices about healthy eating: Exploring the developmental niche of preschoolers. *American Journal of Health Promotion, 33*(5), 727–735. doi:10.1177/0890117118810247.

Sriwilai, K., & Charoensukmongkol, P. (2016). Face it, don't Facebook it: Impacts of social media addiction on mindfulness, coping strategies and the consequence on emotional exhaustion. *Stress and Health: Journal of the International Society for the Investigation of Stress, 32*(4), 427–434. http://dx.doi.org/10.1002/smi.2637

Stadler, M., Aust, M., Becker, N., Niepel, C., & Greiff, S. (2016). Choosing between what you want now and what you want most: Self-control explains academic achievement beyond cognitive

ability. *Personality and Individual Differences, 94,* 168–172. http://dx.doi.org/10.1016/j.paid.2016.01.029

Staff, R. T., Hogan, M. J., Williams, D. S., & Whalley, L. J. (2018). Intellectual engagement and cognitive ability in later life (the "use it or lose it" conjecture): Longitudinal, prospective study. *BMJ, 363:*k4925. https://www.bmj.com/content/363/bmj.k4925

Stamatakis, A. M., Van Swieten, M., Basiri, M. L., Blair, G. A., Kantak, P., & Stuber, G. D. (2016). Lateral hypothalamic area glutamatergic neurons and their projections to the lateral habenula regulate feeding and reward. *The Journal of Neuroscience, 36,* 302–311. http://dx.doi.org/10.1523/JNEUROSCI.1202-15.2016

Stam, D., Huang, Y.-A., & Van den Stock, J. (2019). Non-overlapping and inverse associations between the sexes in structural brain-trait associations. *Frontiers in Psychology, 10:*904. Retrieved from doi:10.3389/fpsyg.2019.00904

Stange, M., Graydon, C., & Dixon, M. J. (2016). "I was that close": Investigating players' reactions to losses, wins, and near-misses on scratch cards. *Journal of Gambling Studies, 32,* 187–203. http://dx.doi.org/10.1007/s10899-015-9538-x

Stanley, I. H., Boffa, J. W., & Joiner, T. E. (2019). PTSD from a suicide attempt: Phenomenological and diagnostic considerations. *Psychiatry, 82*(1), 57–71. doi:10.1080/00332747.2018.1485373

Stanley, I. H., Hom, M. A., & Joiner, T. E. (2016). A systematic review of suicidal thoughts and behaviors among police officers, firefighters, EMTs, and paramedics. *Clinical Psychology Review, 44,* 25–44. http://dx.doi.org/10.1016/j.cpr.2015.12.002

Stanovich, K. E. (2015). Rational and irrational thought: The thinking that IQ tests miss. *Scientific American, 23,* 12–17. http://dx.doi.org/10.1038/scientificamericangenius0115-12

Starr, C. R., & Zurbriggen, E. L. (2017). Sandra Bem's gender schema theory after 34 years: A review of its reach and impact. *Sex Roles, 76*(9), 566–578. http://dx.doi.org/10.1007/s11199-016-0591-4

State of American Jobs, The. (2016, October 6). *Pew Research Center.* Retrieved June 9, 2019 from https://www.pewsocialtrends.org/2016/10/06/the-state-of-american-jobs/

Steele, C. M., & Aronson, J. (1995). Stereotype threat and the intellectual test performance of African Americans. *Journal of Personality and Social Psychology, 69,* 797–811.

Steel, P., Schmidt, J., Bosco, F., & Uggerslev, K. (2019). The effects of personality on job satisfaction and life satisfaction: A meta-analytic investigation accounting for bandwidth–fidelity and commensurability. *Human Relations, 72*(2), 217–247. https://doi.org/10.1177/0018726718771465

Stefanek, E., Strohmeier, D., Fandrem, H., & Spiel, C. (2012). Depressive symptoms in native and immigrant adolescents: The role of critical life events and daily hassles. *Anxiety, Stress and Coping: An International Journal, 25,* 201–217. http://dx.doi.org/10.1080/10615806.2011.605879

Stefanovics, E. A., He, H., Cavalcanti, M., Neto, H., Ofori-Atta, A., Leddy, M., Ighodaro, A., & Rosenheck, R. (2016). Witchcraft and biopsychosocial causes of mental illness: Attitudes and beliefs about mental illness among health professionals in five countries. *Journal of Nervous and Mental Disease, 204*(3), 169–174. http://dx.doi.org/10.1097/NMD.0000000000000422

Steiner, K. L., Pillemer, D. B., Thomsen, D. K., & Minigan, A. P. (2014). The reminiscence bump in older adults' life story transitions. *Memory, 22,* 1002–1009. http://dx.doi.org/10.1080/09658211.2013.86335

Steinert, C., Munder, T., Rabung, S., Hoyer, J., & Leichsenring, F. (2017). Psychodynamic therapy: As efficacious as other empirically supported treatments? A meta-analysis testing equivalence of outcomes. *American Journal of Psychiatry, 174*(10), 943–953. https://doi.org/10.1176/appi.ajp.2017.17010057

Steinmayr, R., & Kessels, U. (2017). Good at on the job? Explaining gender differences in scholastic and vocational success. *Personality and Individual Differences, 105*, 107–115. http://dx.doi.org/10.1016/j.paid. 2016.09.032

Stein, S. J., & Deonarine, J. M. (2015). Current concepts in the assessment of emotional intelligence. In S. Goldstein, D. Princiotta, & J. A. Naglieri (Eds.), *Handbook of intelligence: Evolutionary theory, historical perspective, and current concepts* (pp. 381–402). New York, NY: Springer. http://dx.doi.org/10.1007/978-1-4939-1562-0_24

Stephenson, E., Watson, P. J., Chen, Z. J., & Morris, R. J. (2018). Self-compassion, self-esteem, and irrational beliefs. *Current Psychology, 37*, 809–815. http://dx.doi.org/10.1007/s12144-017-9563-2

Sterley, T. L., Baimoukhametova, D., Fuzesi, T., Zurek, A. A., Daviu, N., Rashiah, N. P., Rosenegger, D., & Bains, J. S. (2018). Social transmission and buffering of synaptic changes after stress. *Nature Neuroscience, 21*, 393–403. doi:10.1038/s41593-017-0044-6

Sternberg, K. (2014). *Psychology of love 101.* New York, NY: Springer.

Sternberg, R. J. (1985). *Beyond IQ: A triarchic theory of human intelligence.* New York, NY: Cambridge University Press.

Sternberg, R. J. (1986). A triangular theory of love. *Psychological Review, 93*, 119–135.

Sternberg, R. J. (1988). *The triangle of love.* New York, NY: Basic Books.

Sternberg, R. J. (2006). A duplex theory of love. In R. J. Sternberg & K. Weis (Eds.), *The new psychology of love* (pp. 184–199). New Haven, CT: Yale University Press.

Sternberg, R. J. (2014). Teaching about the nature of intelligence. *Intelligence, 42*, 176–179. http://dx.doi.org/10.1016/j.intell.2013.08.010

Sternberg, R. J. (2015). Multiple intelligences in the new age of thinking. In S. Goldstein, D. Princiotta, & J. A. Naglieri (Eds.), *Handbook of intelligence: Evolutionary theory, historical perspective, and current concepts* (pp. 229–241). New York, NY: Springer. http://dx.doi.org/10.1007/978-1-4939-1562-0_16

Sternberg, R. J. (2017). *Career paths in psychology: Where your dreams can take you* (3rd ed.). Washington, DC: American Psychological Association.

Stets, J. E., & Carter, M. J. (2012). A theory of the self for the sociology of morality. *American Sociological Review, 77*, 120–140. doi:10.1177/0003122411433762

Steullet, P. (2019). Thalamus-related anomalies as candidate mechanism-based biomarkersfor psychosis. *Schizophrenia Research.* doi:10.1016/j.schres.2019.05.027

Steullet, P. (2019). Thalamus-related anomalies as candidate mechanism-based biomarkers for psychosis. *Schizophrenia Research.* http://dx.doi:10.1016/j.schres.2019.05.027

Stiles, N. R. B., Zheng, Y., & Shimojo, S. (2015). Length and orientation constancy learning in 2-dimensions with auditory sensory substitution: The importance of self-initiated movement. *Frontiers in Psychology, 6,* Article 842.

Stone, M. H. (2014). The spectrum of borderline personality disorder: A neurophysiological view. *Current Topics in Behavioral Neurosciences, 21*, 23–46. http://dx.doi.org/10.1007/7854_2014_308

Stoner, J. A. (1961). A comparison of individual and group decisions involving risk. Unpublished master's thesis, School of Industrial Management, MIT, Cambridge, MA.

Storm, B. C., Stone, S. M., & Benjamin, A. S. (2017). Using the Internet to access information inflates future use of the Internet to access other information. *Memory, 25*(6), 717–723. http://dx.doi.org/10.1080/09658211.2016.1210171

Strachan, E., Duncan, G., Horn, E., & Turkheimer, E. (2017). Neighborhood deprivation and depression in adult twins: Genetics and gene×environment interaction. *Psychological Medicine, 47*(4), 627–638. http://dx.doi.org/10.1017/S0033291716002622

Strack, F. (2016). Reflection on the smiling registered replication report. *Perspectives on Psychological Science, 11*, 929–930. http://dx.doi.org/10.1177/1745691616674460

Strack, F., Martin, L. L., & Stepper, S. (1988). Inhibiting and facilitating conditions of the human smile: A nonobstrusive test of the facial feedback hypothesis. *Journal of Personality and Social Psychology, 54*, 768–777.

Strassberg, D. S., Mackaronis, J. E., & Perelman, M. A. (2015). Sexual dysfunctions. In P. H. Blaney, R. F. Krueger, & T. Millon (Eds.), *Oxford textbook of psychopathology* (3rd ed., pp. 421–462). New York, NY: Oxford University Press.

Stratton, G. M. (1896). Some preliminary experiments on vision without inversion of the retinal image. *Psychological Review, 3*, 611–617. http://dx.doi.org/10.1037/h0072918

Straub, R. O. (2014). *Health psychology* (4th ed.). New York, NY: Worth.

Stress in College Students for 2019. (2019, February 14). *Western Governors University.* Retrieved from https://www.wgu.edu/blog/stress-college-students-2019-how-to-cope1902.html

Stricker, L. J., & Rock, D. A. (2015). An "Obama effect" on the GRE General Test? *Social Influence, 10*, 11–18. http://dx.doi.org/10.1080/15534510.2013.878665

Stringer, H. (2017). Boosting productivity. *Monitor on Psychology, 48*(8), 54. Retrieved from https://www.apa.org/monitor/2017/09/boosting-productivity

Sturdy, C. B., & Nicoladis, E. (2017). How much of language acquisition does operant conditioning explain? *Frontiers in Psychology, 8*, 1918. doi:10.3389/fpsyg.2017.01918

Sue, D., Sue, D., Sue, S., & Sue, D. (2016). *Understanding abnormal behavior* (11th ed.). Stamford, CT: Cengage.

Suerken, C. K., Reboussin, B. A., Egan, K. L., Sutfin, E. L., Wagoner, K. G., Spangler, J., & Wolfson, M. (2016). Marijuana use trajectories and academic outcomes among college students. *Drug and Alcohol Dependence, 162*, 137–145. http://dx.doi.org/10.1016/j.drugalcdep.2016.02.041

Sugar, J. A., Rieske, R. J., Holstege, H., & Faber, M. A. (2014). *Introduction to aging: A positive, interdisciplinary approach.* New York, NY: Springer.

Sugarman, H., Impey, C., Buxner, S., & Antonellis, J. (2011). Astrology beliefs among undergraduate students. *Astronomy Education Review, 10.* http://dx.doi.org/10.3847/AER2010040

Suhay, E. (2015). Explaining group influence: The role of identity and emotion in political conformity and polarization. *Political Behavior, 37*, 221–251. http://dx.doi.org/10.1007/s11109-014-9269-1

Suher, J., Raj, R., & Hoyer, W. (2016). Eating healthy or feeling empty? How the "Healthy = Less Filling" intuition influences satiety. *The Journal of the Association for Consumer Research, 1*, 26–40. https://doi.org/10.1086/684393

Suissa, A. J. (2015). Cyber addictions: Toward a psychosocial perspective. *Addictive Behaviors, 43*, 28–32. doi:10.1016/j.addbeh.2014.09.020

Suizzo, M-A., Rackley, K. R., Robbins, P. A., Jackson, K. M., Rarick, J. R. D., & McClain, S. (2017). The unique effects of fathers' warmth on adolescents' positive beliefs and behaviors: Pathways to resilience in low-income families. *Sex Roles, 77*(1), 46–58. http://dx.doi.org/10.1007/s11199-016-0696-9

Sullivan, K. (2019, August 6). Mental illness isn't a major risk factor for gun violence, but here's what is. *NBC News*. Retrieved from https://www.nbcnews.com/health/health-news/mental-illness-isn-t-major-risk-factor-gun-violence-here-n1039666

Sullivan, T. A. (2014). Greedy institutions, overwork, and work-life balance. *Sociological Inquiry, 84*, 1–15. http://dx.doi.org/10.1111/soin.12029

Sumter, S. R., & Vandenbosch, L. (2019). Dating gone mobile: Demographic and personality-based correlates of using smartphone-based dating applications among emerging adults. *New Media & Society, 21*(3), 655–673. https://doi.org/10.1177/1461444818804773

Sung, J., Beijers, R., Garstein, M. A., de Weerth, C., & Putnam, S. P. (2015). Exploring temperamental differences in infants from the USA and the Netherlands. *European Journal of Developmental Psychology, 12*, 15–28.

Sun, H., Huang, H., Ji, S., Chen, X., Xu, Y., Zhu, F., & Wu, J. (2019). The efficacy of cognitive behavioral therapy to treat depression and anxiety and improve quality of life among early-stage breast cancer patients. *Integrative Cancer Therapies, 18*, 1534735419829573. doi:10.1177/1534735419829573

Sun, H., Liu, Z., & Ma, X. (2016). Interactions between astrocytes and neurons in the brainstem involved in restraint water immersion stress-induced gastric mucosal damage. *NeuroReport: For Rapid Communication of Neuroscience Research, 27*, 151–159. http://dx.doi.org/10.1097/WNR.0000000000000515.

Super, C., & Harkness, S. (2015). Charting infant development: Milestones along the way. In L. A. Jensen (Ed.), *The Oxford handbook of human development and culture: An interdisciplinary perspective* (pp. 79–93). New York, NY: Oxford University Press.

Survey: Americans Becoming More Open. (2019, May 1). *American Psychological Association*. https://www.apa.org/news/press/releases/2019/05/mental-health-survey

Sussman, T. J., Szekely, A., Hajcak, G., & Mohanty, A. (2016). It's all in the anticipation: How perception of threat is enhanced in anxiety. *Emotion, 16*, 320–327. doi:10.1037/emo0000098

Sutin, A. R., Stephan, Y., Carretta, H., & Terracciano, A. (2015). Perceived discrimination and physical, cognitive, and emotional health in older adulthood. *The American Journal of Geriatric Psychiatry, 23*, 171–179. http://dx.doi.org/10.1016/j.jagp.2014.03.007

Sutin, R., Terracciano, A., Milaneschi, Y., An, Y., Ferrucci, L., & Zonderman, A. B. (2013). The effect of birth cohort on well-being: The legacy of economic hard times. *Psychological Science, 24*, 379–385. doi:10.1177/0956797612459658

Suvilehto, J. T., Nummenmaa, L., Harada, T., Dunbar, R., Hari, R., Turner, R., . . . Kitada, R. (2019). Cross-cultural similarity in relationship-specific social touching. *Proceedings. Biological Sciences, 286*(1901), 20190467. doi:10.1098/rspb.2019.0467

Suwabe, K., Byun, K., Hyodo, K., Reagh, Z. M., Roberts, J. M., Matsushita, A., . . . Soya, H. (2018). Rapid stimulation of human dentate gyrus function with acute mild exercise. *Proceedings of the National Academy of Sciences of the United States of America, 115*(41), 10487–10492. doi:10.1073/pnas.1805668115

Suzuki, H., & Lucas, L. R. (2015). Neurochemical correlates of accumbal dopamine d2 and amygdaloid 5-ht1b receptor densities on observational learning of aggression. *Cognitive, Affective & Behavioral Neuroscience, 15*, 460–474. doi:10.3758/s13415-015-0337-8

Suzuki, L. A., Naqvi, S., & Hill, J. S. (2014). Assessing intelligence in a cultural context. In F. T. L. Leong, L. Comas-Díaz, G. C. Nagayama Hall, V. C. McLoyd, & J. E. Trimble (Eds.), *APA handbook of multicultural psychology, Vol. 1: Theory and research* (pp. 247–266).

Washington, DC: American Psychological Association. http://dx.doi.org/10.1037/14189-013

Svetkey, B. (2017, January 26). Emma Stone's battle with shyness, panic attacks, and phobias on the way to the Oscars. *Hollywood Reporter*. Retrieved from https://www.hollywoodreporter.com/features/emma-stones-battle-shyness-panic-attacks-phobias-way-os-cars-968543

Swain, J. E., & Ho, S. S. (2012). What's in a baby-cry? Locationist and constructionist frameworks in parental brain responses. *Behavior and Brain Sciences, 35*, 167–168. http://dx.doi.org/10.1017/S0140525X11001762

Sweeney, S., Air, T., Zannettino, L., & Galletly, C. (2015). Gender differences in the physical and psychological manifestation of childhood trauma and/or adversity in people with psychosis. *Frontiers in Psychology, 6*, Article 1768. doi:10.3389/fpsyg.2015.0176

Sylvestre, A., & Mérette, C. (2010). Language delay in severely neglected children: A cumulative or specific effect of risk factors? *Child Abuse & Neglect, 34*, 414–428. http://dx.doi.org/10.1016/j.chiabu.2009.10.003

Sztachańska, J., Krejtz, I., & Nezlek, J. B. (2019). Using a gratitude intervention to improve the lives of women with breast cancer: A daily diary study. *Frontiers in Psychology, 10*, 1365. doi:10.3389/fpsyg.2019.01365

Takahashi, M. (2019). Sociomedical problems of overwork-related deaths and disorders in Japan. *Journal of Occupational Health, 61*(4), 269–277. doi:10.1002/1348-9585.12016.

Takarangi, M. K. T., & Loftus, E. F. (2016). Suggestion, placebos, and false memories. In A. Raz & C. S. Harris (Eds.), *Placebo talks: Modern perspectives on placebos in society* (pp. 204–226). New York, NY: Oxford University Press.

Talamas, S. N., Mavor, K. I., & Perrett, D. I. (2016). The influence of intelligence on the endorsement of the intelligence–attractiveness halo. *Personality and Individual Differences, 95*, 162–167. http://dx.doi.org/10.1016/j.paid.2016.02.053

Tamir, M., Bigman, Y. E., Rhodes, E., Salerno, J., & Schreier, J. (2015). An expectancy-value model of emotion regulation: Implications for motivation, emotional experience, and decision making. *Emotion, 15*, 90–103. doi:10.1037/emo0000021

Tamnes, C. K., Herting, M. M., Goddings, A. L., Meuwese, R., Blakemore, S. J., Dahl, R. E., . . . Mills, K. L. (2017). Development of the cerebral cortex across adolescence: A multisample study of inter-related longitudinal changes in cortical volume, surface area, and thickness. *The Journal of Neuroscience, 37*(12), 3402–3412. doi:10.1523/JNEUROSCI.3302-16.2017

Tang, Y., Newman, L. S., & Huang, L. (2014). How people react to social-psychological accounts of wrongdoing: The moderating effects of culture. *Journal of Cross-Cultural Psychology, 45*, 752–763. http://dx.doi.org/10.1177/0022022114527343

Tang, Y. Y., Posner, M. I., & Rothbart, M. K. (2014). Meditation improves self-regulation over the life span. *Annals of the New York Academy of Sciences, 1307*, 104–111. http://dx.doi.org/10.1111/nyas.12227

Tannen, D. (1990). *You just don't understand: Women and men in conversation*. New York, NY: HarperCollins.

Tannen, D. (2007). Power maneuvers and connection maneuvers in family interaction. In D. Tannen, S. Kendall, & C. Gordon (Eds.), *Family talk: Discourse and identity in four American families* (pp. 27–48). Oxford, UK: Oxford University Press.

Tannen, D. (2011). Turn-taking and intercultural discourse and communication. In C. B. Paulston, S. Kiesling, & E. Rangel (Eds.), *The handbook of intercultural discourse and communication* (pp. 133–157). Hoboken, NJ: Wiley.

Tan, X., Alén, M., Cheng, S. M., Mikkola, T. M., Tenhunen, J., Lyytikäinen, A., . . . Cheng, S. (2015a). Associations of disordered sleep with body fat distribution, physical activity and diet among overweight middle-aged men. *Journal of Sleep Research, 24*, 414–424. http://dx.doi.org/10.1111/jsr.12283

Tarr, B., Launay, J., & Dunbar, R. I.M. (2016). Silent disco: Dancing in synchrony leads to elevated pain thresholds and social closeness. *Evolution and Human Behavior, 37*, 343–349. http://dx.doi.org/10.1016/j.evolhumbehav. 2016.02.004

Tasci, G., Baykara, S., Gurok, M. G., & Atmaca, M. (2018). Effect of exercise on therapeutic response in depression treatment. *Psychiatry and Clinical Psychopharmacology, 29*(2), 137–143. doi:10.1080/24750573.2018.1426159

Tashani, O. A., Burnett, D., & Phillips, G. (2017). The effect of brief mindfulness meditation on cold-pressor induced pain responses in healthy adults. *Pain Studies and Treatment, 5*, 11–19. https://doi.org/10.4236/pst.2017.52002

Taub, E. (2004). Harnessing brain plasticity through behavioral techniques to produce new treatments in neurorehabilitation. *American Psychologist, 59*, 692–704. http://dx.doi.org/10.1037/0003-066X.59.8.692

Taub, E., Uswatte, G., & Mark, V. W. (2014). The functional significance of cortical reorganization and the parallel development of CI therapy. *Frontiers in Human Neuroscience, 8*, Article 396. doi:10.3389/fnhum.2014.00396

Tavassolie, T., Dudding, S., Madigan, A. L., Thorvardarson, E., & Winsler, A. (2016). Differences in perceived parenting style between mothers and fathers: Implications for child outcomes and marital conflict. *Journal of Child and Family Studies, 25*, 2055–2068. http://dx.doi.org/10.1007/s10826-016-0376-y

Tavernier, R., Choo, S. B., Grant, K., & Adam, E. K. (2016). Daily affective experiences predict objective sleep outcomes among adolescents. *Journal of Sleep Research, 25*, 62–69. http://dx.doi.org/10.1111/jsr.12338

Tayama, J., Li, J., & Munakata, M. (2016). Working long hours is associated with higher prevalence of diabetes in urban male Chinese workers: The Rosai Karoshi study. *Stress and Health, 32*, 84–87. http://dx.doi.org/10.1002/smi.2580

Tay, L., & Diener, E. (2011). Needs and subjective well-being around the world. *Journal of Personality and Social Psychology, 101*, 354–365. http://dx.doi.org/10.1037/a0023779

Taylor, B., Miller, E., Farrington, C. P., Petropoulos, M. C., Favot-Mayaud, I., Li, J., & Waight, P. A. (1999). Autism and measles, mumps, and rubella vaccine: No epidemiologic evidence for a causal association. *Lancet, 353*, 2026–2029.

Taylor-Clift, A., Holmgreen, L., Hobfoll, S. E., Gerhart, J. I., Richardson, D., Calvin, J. E., & Powell, L. H. (2016). Traumatic stress and cardiopulmonary disease burden among low-income, urban heart failure patients. *Journal of Affective Disorders, 190*, 227–234. http://dx.doi.org/10.1016/j.jad.2015.09.023

Taylor, K. N., & Abba, N. (2015). Mindfulness meditation in cognitive-behavioral therapy for psychosis. In B. A. Gaudiano (Ed.), *Incorporating acceptance and mindfulness into the treatment of psychosis: Current trends and future directions* (pp. 170–200). New York, NY: Oxford University Press.

Taylor, L., Chrismas, B. C. R., Dascombe, B., Chamari, K., & Fowler, P. M. (2016). Sleep medication and athletic performance—The evidence for practitioners and future research directions. *Frontiers in Physiology, 7*, 83. http://doi.org/10.3389/fphys.2016.00083

Taylor, S. E. (2006). Tend and befriend: Biobehavioral bases of affiliation under stress. *Current Directions in Psychological Science, 15*, 273–277. http://dx.doi.org/10.1111/j.1467-8721.2006.00451.x

Taylor, S. E. (2012). Tend and befriend theory. In P. A. M. Van Lange, A. W. Kruglanski, & E. T. Higgins (Eds.), *Handbook of theories of social psychology* (Vol 1., pp. 32–49). Thousand Oaks, CA: Sage.

Tedeschi, R. G., & Blevins, C. L. (2015). From mindfulness to meaning: Implications for the theory of posttraumatic growth. *Psychological Inquiry, 26*, 373–376. http://dx.doi.org/10.1080/1047840X.2015.1075354

Tefft, B. C. (2018). Acute sleep deprivation and culpable motor vehicle crash involvement. *Sleep, 41*(10). doi:10.1093/sleep/zsy144

Teicher, M. H., & Samson, J. A. (2016). Annual research review: Enduring neurobiological effects of childhood abuse and neglect. *Journal of Child Psychology and Psychiatry, 57*, 241–266. http://dx.doi.org/10.1111/jcpp.12507

Teitelbaum, P., & Stellar, E. (1954). Recovery from the failure to eat produced by hypothalamic lesions. *Science, 120*, 894–895. http://dx.doi.org/10.1126/science.120.3126.894

Tellegen, A. (1985). Structures of mood and personality and their relevance to assessing anxiety with an emphasis on self-report. In A. H. Tuma & J. D. Maser (Eds.), *Anxiety and the anxiety disorders* (pp. 681–706). Hillsdale, NJ: Erlbaum.

Templeton, J. A., Dixon, M. J., Harrigan, K. A., & Fugelsang, J. A. (2015). Upping the reinforcement rate by playing the maximum lines in multi-line slot machine play. *Journal of Gambling Studies, 31*, 949–964. http://dx.doi.org/10.1007/s10899-014-9446-5

Templin, C., Hänggi, J., Klein, C., Topka, M. S., Hiestand, T., Levinson, R. A., . . . Jäncke, L. (2019). Altered limbic and autonomic processing supports brain-heart axis in Takotsubo syndrome. *European Heart Journal, 40*(15), 1183–1187. doi:10.1093/eurheartj/ehz068

Tennen, H., Suls, J., & Weiner, I. B. (Eds.). (2013). *Handbook of psychology, Vol. 5. Personality and social psychology* (2nd ed.). Hoboken, NJ: Wiley.

Terman, L. M. (1916). *The measurement of intelligence.* Boston, MA: Houghton Mifflin.

Terman, L. M. (1925). *Genetic studies of genius: Vol. 1. Mental and physical traits of a thousand gifted children.* Palo Alto, CA: Stanford University Press.

Terman, L. M. (1954). Scientists and nonscientists in a group of 800 gifted men. *Psychological Monographs, 68*, 1–44.

Terrace, H. S. (1979, November). How Nim Chimpsky changed my mind. *Psychology Today*, 65–76.

Tesarz, J., Schuster, A. K., Hartmann, M., Gerhardt, A., & Eich, W. (2012). Pain perception in athletes compared to normally active controls: A systematic review with meta-analysis. *Pain, 153*, 1253–1262. doi:10.1016/j.pain.2012.03.005

Tetrick, L. E., & Peiró, J. M. (2016). Health and safety: Prevention and promotion. In M. J. Grawitch & D. W. Ballard (Eds.), *The psychologically healthy workplace: Building a win-win environment for organizations and employees* (pp. 199–229). Washington, DC: American Psychological Association. http://dx.doi.org/10.1037/14731-010

Teunissen, H. A., Spijkerman, R., Prinstein, M. G., Cohen, G. L., Engles, R. C., & Scholte, R. H. (2012). Adolescents' conformity to their peers' pro-alcohol and anti-alcohol norms: The power of popularity. *Alcoholism: Clinical and Experimental Research, 36*, 1257–1267.

Thair, H., Holloway, A. L., Newport, R., & Smith, A. D. (2017). Transcranial direct current stimulation (tDCS): A beginner's guide for design and implementation. *Frontiers in Neuroscience, 11*, 641. doi:10.3389/fnins.2017.00641

Thalmann, M., Souza, A. S., & Oberauer, K. (2019). How does chunking help working memory? *Journal of Experimental Psychology: Learning, Memory, and Cognition, 45*(1), 37–55.

Tharmaratnam, T., Iskandar, M. A., Tabobondung, T. C., Tobbia, I., Gopee-Ramanan, P., & Tabobondung, T. A. (2018). Chronic traumatic encephalopathy in professional American football players: Where are we now? *Frontiers in Neurology, 9,* 445. doi:10.3389/fneur.2018.00445

The Amazing Meeting. (2011). The amazing one: James Randi. Retrieved from http://www.amaz- ingmeeting.com/speakers#randi

The Global Gender Gap Report. (2018). *World Economic Forum.* Retrieved from http://www3.weforum.org/docs/WEF_GGGR_2018.pdf

Thieme, H., Morkisch, N., Rietz, C., Dohle, C., & Borgetto, B. (2016). The efficacy of movement representation techniques for treatment of limb pain—A systematic review and meta-analysis. *The Journal of Pain, 17,* 167–180. http://dx.doi.org/10.1016/j.jpain.2015.10.015

Thomas, A., & Chess, S. (1977). *Temperament and development.* New York, NY: Brunner/Mazel.

Thomas, A., & Chess, S. (1987). Round-table: What is temperament: Four approaches. *Child Development, 58,* 505–529.

Thomas, A., & Chess, S. (1991). Temperament in adolescence and its functional significance. In R. M. Lerner, A. C. Petersen, & J. Brooks-Gunn (Eds.), *Encyclopedia of adolescence* (Vol. 2). New York, NY: Garland.

Thomason, T. (2014). Issues in the diagnosis of Native American culture-bound syndromes. *Arizona Counseling Journal.* Retrieved from http://works.bepress.com/cgi/viewcontent.cgi?article=1181&context=timothy_thomason

Thomassin, K., Guérin Marion, C., Venasse, M., & Shaffer, A. (2017). Specific coping strategies moderate the link between emotion expression deficits and nonsuicidal self-injury in an inpatient sample of adolescents. *Child and Adolescent Psychiatry and Mental Health, 11,* 21. http://doi.org/10.1186/s13034-017-0158-3

Thompson, D. (1997, March 24). A boy without a penis. *Time,* 83. Tosh, J. (2016). *Psychology and gender dysphoria: Feminist and transgender perspective.* New York, NY: Routledge.

Thompson, E. (2015). *Waking, dreaming, being: Self and consciousness in neuroscience, meditation, and philosophy.* New York, NY: Columbia University Press.

Thorndike, E. L. (1898). Animal intelligence. *Psychological Review Monograph, 2*(8).

Thorndike, E. L. (1911). *Animal intelligence.* New York, NY: Macmillan.

Thorn, R. (2013). 12 tips for surviving personal crisis. *Huffington Post.* Retrieved from http://www.huffingtonpost.com/rayanne-thorn/mindfulness-practice_b_4026593.html

Thrailkill, E. A., & Bouton, M. E. (2015). Contextual control of instrumental actions and habits. *Journal of Experimental Psychology: Animal Learning and Cognition, 41,* 69–80. http://dx.doi.org/10.1037/xan0000045

Thrasher, C., & LoBue, V. (2016). Do infants find snakes aversive? Infants' physiological responses to "fear-relevant" stimuli. *Journal of Experimental Child Psychology, 142,* 382–390. Retrieved from https://doi.org/10.1016/j.jecp.2015.09.013/

Thurstone, L. L. (1938). *Primary mental abilities.* Chicago, IL: University of Chicago Press.

Tillmann, S., Tobin, D., Avison, W., & Gilliland, J. (2018). Mental health benefits of interactions with nature in children and teenagers: A systematic review. *Journal of Epidemiology and Community Health, 72,* 958–966. https://jech.bmj.com/content/72/10/958

Todd, P. M., & Gigerenzer, G. (2000). Precis of simple heuristics that make us smart. *Behavioral and Brain Sciences, 23,* 727–741. http://dx.doi.org/10.1017/S0140525X00003447

Tolman, E. C., & Honzik, C. H. (1930). Introduction and removal of reward and maze performance in rats. *University of California Publications in Psychology, 4,* 257–275.

Tomash, J. J., & Reed, P. (2013). The generalization of a conditioned response to deception across the public/private barrier. *Learning and Motivation, 44,* 196–203. http://dx.doi.org/10.1016/j.lmot.2012.12.001

Tonnaer, F., Cima, M., & Arntz, A. (2019). Explosive matters: Does venting anger reduce or increase aggression? Differences in anger venting effects in violent offenders. *Journal of Aggression, Maltreatment & Trauma.* doi:10.1080/10926771.2019.1575303

Topper, M., Emmelkamp, P. M. G., Watkins, E., & Ehring, T. (2017). Prevention of anxiety disorders and depression by targeting excessive worry and rumination in adolescents and young adults: A randomized controlled trial. *Behaviour Research and Therapy, 90,* 123–136. http://dx.doi.org/10.1016/j.brat.2016.12.015

Torborg, L. (2019, March 29). Mayo clinic Q and A: Tanning beds raise risk for skin cancer. *Mayo Clinic.* Retrieved from https://newsnetwork.mayoclinic.org/discussion/mayo-clinic-q-and-a-tanning-beds-raise-risk-for-skin-cancer/

Tornquist, M., & Chiappe, D. (2015). Effects of humor production, humor receptivity, and physical attractiveness on partner desirability. *Evolutionary Psychology, 13*(4), 1–13. http://dx.doi.org/10.1177/1474704915608744

Torrens, M., & Rossi, P. (2015). Mood disorders and addiction. In G. Dom & F. Moggi (Eds.), *Co-occurring addictive and psychiatric disorders: A practice-based handbook from a European perspective* (pp. 103–117). New York, NY: Springer-Verlag. http://dx.doi.org/10.1007/978-3-642-45375-5_8

Tosh, J. (2016). *Psychology and gender dysphoria: Feminist and transgender perspective.* New York, NY: Routledge.

Trafton, A. (2017, January 10). A glimpse into the workings of the baby brain. *MIT News.* Retrieved from http://news.mit.edu/2017/mri-scans-baby-brain-visual-cortex-0110

Trail, S. M. (2015). Sexual disorders. In L. Sperry, J. Carlson, J. D. Sauerheber, & J. Sperry (Eds.), *Psychopathology and psychotherapy: DSM-5 diagnosis, case conceptualization, and treatment* (3rd ed., pp. 265–283). New York, NY: Routledge/Taylor & Francis Group.

Tran, D. M., & Westbrook, R. F. (2015). Rats fed a diet rich in fats and sugars are impaired in the use of spatial geometry. *Psychological Science, 26,* 1947–1957. http://dx.doi.org/10.1177/0956797615608240

Trautmann-Lengsfeld, S. A., & Herrmann, C. S. (2014). Virtually simulated social pressure influences early visual processing more in low compared to high autonomous participants. *Psychophysiology, 51,* 124–135. http://dx.doi.org/10.1111/psyp.12161

Travers, K. M., Creed, P. A., & Morrissey, S. (2015). The development and initial validation of a new scale to measure explanatory style. *Personality and Individual Differences, 81,* 1–6. http://dx.doi.org/10.1016/j.paid.2015.01.045

Trayhurn, P. (2018). Brown adipose tissue-A therapeutic target in obesity? *Frontiers in Physiology, 9,* 1672. Retrieved from doi:10.3389/fphys.2018.01672

Traynor, K. (2019). Esketamine nasal spray approved for treatment-resistant depression. *American Journal of Health-System Pharmacy, 76*(9), 573. https://doi.org/10.1093/ajhp/zxz065

Treffert, D. A. (2014). Savant syndrome: Realities, myths and misconceptions. *Journal of Autism and Developmental Disorders, 44,* 564–571. http://dx.doi.org/10.1007/s10803-013-1906-8

Triantafillou, S., Saeb, S., Lattie, E. G., Mohr, D. C., & Kording, K. P. (2019). Relationship between sleep quality and mood: Ecological momentary assessment study. *Journal of Medical Internet Research, 6*(3):e12613. doi:10.2196/12613

Trofimova, I., & Robbins, T. W. (2016). Temperament and arousal systems: A new synthesis of differential psychology and functional neurochemistry. *Neuroscience and Biobehavioral Reviews, 64,* 382–402. http://dx.doi.org/10.1016/j.neubiorev.2016.03.008

Trumbo, M. C., Leiting, K. A., McDaniel, M. A., & Hodge, G. K. (2016). Effects of reinforcement on test-enhanced learning in a large, diverse introductory college psychology course. *Journal of Experimental Psychology: Applied, 22*(2), 148–160. http://dx.doi.org/10.1037/xap0000082

Trust for America's Health. (2019). Pain in the nation: Building a national resilience strategy. *WellBeingTrust.* Retrieved June 10, 2019 from https://wellbeingtrust.org/wp-content/uploads/2019/06/TFAH-2019-YoundAdult-Pain-Brief-FnlRv.pdf?utm_source=STAT+Newsletters&utm_campaign=d90ea217be-MR_COPY_01&utm_medium=email&utm_term=0_8cab1d7961-d90ea217be-150444909

Tsai, Y., Lu, B., Ljubimov, A. V., Girman, S., Ross-Cisneros, F. N., Sadun, A. A., . . . Wang, S. (2014). Ocular changes in TgF344-AD rat model of Alzheimer's disease. *Investigative Ophthalmology & Visual Science, 55*, 521–534. http://dx.doi.org/10.1167/iovs.13-12888

Tsien, J. Z. (2000, April). Building a brainier mouse. *Scientific American, 282*, 62–68. http://dx.doi.org/10.10789248

Tskhay, K. O., Clout, J. M., & Rule, N. O. (2017). The impact of health, wealth, and attractiveness on romantic evaluation from photographs of faces. *Archives of Sexual Behavior, 46*(8), 2365–2376. http://dx.doi.org/10.1007/s10508-017-0963-z

Tsoukalas, I. (2012). The origin of REM sleep: A hypothesis. *Dreaming, 22*, 253–283.

Tucker, S., Pek, S., Morrish, J., & Ruf, M. (2015). Prevalence of texting while driving and other risky driving behaviors among young people in Ontario, Canada: Evidence from 2012 and 2014. *Accident Analysis and Prevention, 84*, 144–152. http://dx.doi.org/10.1016/j.aap.2015.07.011

Tulving, E., & Thompson, D. M. (1973). Encoding specificity and retrieval processes in episodic memory. *Psychological Review, 80*, 352–373. http://dx.doi.org/10.1037/h0020071

Turkheimer, E., Pettersson, E., & Horn, E. E. (2014). A phenotypic null hypothesis for the genetics of personality. *Annual Review of Psychology, 65*, 515–540. http://dx.doi.org/10.1146/annurev-psych-113011-143752

Turner, M. J. (2016). Rational Emotive Behavior Therapy (REBT), irrational and rational beliefs, and the mental health of athletes. *Frontiers in Psychology, 7*, Article 1423.

Turner, R. (2019). Myelin and modeling: Bootstrapping cortical microcircuits. *Frontiers in Neural Circuits, 13*(34). http://dx.doi:10.3389/fncir.2019.00034

Tuulari, J. J., Tuominen, L., de Boer, F. E., Hirvonen, J., Helin, S., Nuutila, P., & Nummenmaa, L. (2017). Feeding releases endogenous opioids in humans. *The Journal of Neuroscience, 37*(34): 8284. https://doi.org/10.1523/JNEUROSCI.0976-17.2017

Tuwani, R., Wadhwa, S., & Bagler, G. (2019). BitterSweet: Building machine learning models for predicting the bitter and sweet taste of small molecules. *Scientific Reports, 9*(1), 7155. doi:10.1038/s41598-019-43664-y

Tversky, A., & Kahneman, D. (1974). Judgment under uncertainty: Heuristics and biases. *Science, 185*, 1124–1131. http://dx.doi.org/10.1126/science.185.4157.1124

Tversky, A., & Kahneman, D. (1993). Probabilistic reasoning. In A. I. Goldman (Ed.), *Readings in philosophy and cognitive science* (pp. 43–68). Cambridge, MA: MIT Press.

Twenge, J. M., Martin, G. N., & Campbell, W. K. (2018). Decreases in psychological well-being among American adolescents after 2012 and links to screen time during the rise of smartphone technology. *Emotion, 18*(6), 765–780. http://dx.doi.org/10.1037/emo0000403

Tyner, S., Brewer, A., Helman, M., Leon, Y., Pritchard, J., & Schlund, M. (2016). Nice doggie! Contact desensitization plus reinforcement decreases dog phobias for children with autism. *Behavior Analysis in Practice, 9*(1), 54–57. http://dx.doi.org/10.1007/s40617-016-0113-4

Tyson, P. J., Jones, D., & Elcock, J. (2011). *Psychology in social context: Issues and debates.* Malden, MA: Wiley-Blackwell.

Ulrich, R. E., Stachnik, T. J., & Stainton, N. R. (1963). Student acceptance of generalized personality interpretations. *Psychological Reports, 13*, 831–834. http://dx.doi.org/10.2466/pr0.1963.13.3.831

Underwood, M. K., & Ehrenreich, S. E. (2017). The power and pain of adolescents' digital communication: Cyber victimization and the perils of lurking. *American Psychologist, 72*(2), 144–158. http://www.americanpsychologist-digital.org/americanpsychologist/20170203?folio=144&pg=74#pg74

UNESCO. (2019). I'd blush if I could: Closing gender divides in digital skills through education. *EQUALS.* Retrieved from https://unesdoc.unesco.org/ark:/48223/pf0000367416.page=1

Unnava, V., Singh, A. S., & Unnava, H. R. (2018). Coffee with co-workers: role of caffeine on evaluations of the self and others in group settings. *Journal of Psychopharmacology, 32*(8), 943–948. https://doi.org/10.1177/0269881118760665

Urban, L. A. (2016). Alternative treatments. In A. M. Matthews & J. C. Fellers (Eds.), *Treating comorbid opioid use disorder in chronic pain* (pp. 25–33). Cham, CH: Springer International Publishing. http://dx.doi.org/10.1007/978-3-319-29863-4_3

Urbanová, L., Vyhnánková, V., Krisová, Š., Pacík, D., & Nečas, A. (2015). Intensive training technique utilizing the dog's olfactory abilities to diagnose prostate cancer in men. *Acta Veterinaria Brno, 84*, 77–82. doi:10.2754/avb201585010077

Urriza, J., Arranz-Arranz, B., Ulkatan, S., Téllez, M.J., & Deletis, V. (2016). Integrative action of axonal membrane explored by trains of subthreshold stimuli applied to the peripheral nerve. *Clinical Neurophysiology, 127*, 1707–1709. doi:10.1016/j.clinph.2015.07.024

Urzúa, A., Ferrer, R., Canales Gaete, V., Núñez Aragón, D., Ravanal Labraña, I., & Tabilo Poblete, B. (2017). The influence of acculturation strategies in quality of life by immigrants in Northern Chile. *Quality of Life Research: An International Journal of Quality of Life Aspects of Treatment, Care & Rehabilitation, 6*(3), 717–726. http://dx.doi.org/10.1007/s11136-016-1470-8

U.S. Bureau of Labor Statistics, U.S. Department of Labor. (2019). Psychologists. *Occupational outlook handbook, 2018–2019 edition.* Retrieved from https://www.bls.gov/ooh/life-physical-and-social-science/psychologists.htm

U.S. Department of Justice. (2019). Sexual assault. Retrieved from https://www.justice.gov/ovw/sexual-assault

U.S. Equal Employment Opportunity Commission. (2019). Sexual harassment. Retrieved from https://www.eeoc.gov/laws/types/sexual_harassment.cfm

Vaccarino, V., Badimon, L., Bremner, J. D., Cenko, E., Cubedo, J., Dorobantu, M., . . . ESC Scientific Document Group Reviewers. (2019). Depression and coronary heart disease: 2018 ESC position paper of the working group of coronary pathophysiology and microcirculation developed under the auspices of the ESC Committee for Practice Guidelines. *European Heart Journal.* https://doi.org/10.1093/eurheartj/ehy913

Vacharkulksemsuk, T., Reit, E., Khambatta, P., Eastwick, P. W., Finkel, E. J., & Carney, D. R. (2016). Dominant, open nonverbal displays are attractive at zero-acquaintance. *Proceedings of the National Academy of Sciences of the United States of America, 113*, 4009–4014. http://dx.doi.org/10.1073/pnas.1508932113

Vachon-Presseau, E., Berger, S. E., Abdullah, T. B., Huang, L., Cecchi, G., Griffith, J. W., . . . Apkarian, V. (2018). Brain and psychological determinants of placebo pill response in chronic pain patients. *Nature Communications, 9,* Article number: 3397. doi:10.1038/s41467-018-05859-1

Vaiserman, A., & Lushchak, O. (2019). Prenatal malnutrition-induced epigenetic dysregulation as a risk factor for type 2 diabetes. *International Journal of Genomics,* 3821409. doi:10.1155/2019/3821409

Valdez, P. (2019). Circadian rhythms in attention. *The Yale Journal of Biology and Medicine, 92*(1), 81–92. https://www.ncbi.nlm.nih.gov/pmc/articles/PMC6430172/

Valentine, K. A., Li, N. P., Penke, L., & Perrett, D. I. (2014). Judging a man by the width of his face: The role of facial ratios and dominance in mate choice at speed-dating events. *Psychological Science, 25,* 806–811. http://dx.doi.org/10.1177/0956797613511823

Vallejo-Medina, P., & Sierra, J. C. (2013). Effect of drug use and influence of abstinence on sexual functioning in a Spanish male drug dependent sample: A multisite study. *The Journal of Sexual Medicine, 10*(2), 333–341. http://dx.doi.org/10.1111/j.1743-6109.2012.02977.x.

Vallejo-Torres, L., Castilla, I., González, N., Hunter, R., Serrano-Pérez, P., & Perestelo-Pérez, L. (2015). Cost-effectiveness of electroconvulsive therapy compared to repetitive transcranial magnetic stimulation for treatment-resistant severe depression: A decision model. *Psychological Medicine, 45,* 1459–1470. http://dx.doi.org/10.1017/S0033291714002554

Van Bavel, J. J., Mende-Siedlecki, P., Brady, W. J., & Reinero, D. A. (2016). Contextual sensitivity in scientific reproducibility. *Proceedings of the National Academy of Sciences of the United States of America, 113*(23), 6454–6459. doi:10.1073/pnas.1521897113

Van de Carr, F. R., & Lehrer, M. (1997). *While you are expecting: Your own prenatal classroom.* New York, NY: Humanics.

van de Kamp, M.-T., Admiraal, W., van Drie, J., & Rijlaarsdam, G. (2015). Enhancing divergent thinking in visual arts education: Effects of explicit instruction of metacognition. *British Journal of Educational Psychology, 85,* 47–58. http://dx.doi.org/10.1111/bjep.12061

Vandeleur, C. L., Rothen, S., Lustenberger, Y., Glaus, J., Castelao, E., & Preisig, M. (2015). Inter-informant agreement and prevalence estimates for mood syndromes: Direct interview vs. family history method. *Journal of Affective Disorders, 171,* 120–127. doi:10.1016/j.jad.2014.08.048

van den Akker, K., Havermans, R. C., & Jansen, A. (2015). Effects of occasional reinforced trials during extinction on the reacquisition of conditioned responses to food cues. *Journal of Behavior Therapy and Experimental Psychiatry, 48,* 50–58. http://dx.doi.org/10.1016/j.jbtep.2015.02.001

van den Berg, S. M., de Moor, M. H. M., Verweij, K. J. H., Krueger, R. F., Luciano, M., Arias Vasquez, A., . . . Boomsma, D. I. (2016). Meta-analysis of genome-wide association studies for extraversion: Findings from the genetics of personality consortium. *Behavior Genetics, 46,* 170–182. http://dx.doi.org/10.1007/s10519-015-9735-5

van der Hoek, M., Groeneveld, S., & Kuipers, B. (2018). Goal setting in teams: Goal clarity and team performance in the public sector. *Review of Public Personnel Administration, 38*(4), 472–493. doi:10.1177/0734371X16682815

van der Lely, S., Frey, S., Garbazza, C., Wirz-Justice, A., Jenni, O. G., Steiner, R., . . . Schmidt, C. (2015). Blue blocker glasses as a countermeasure for alerting effects of evening light-emitting diode screen exposure in male teenagers. *Journal of Adolescent Health, 56,* 113–119. http://dx.doi.org/10.1016/j.jadohealth.2014.08.002

van der Pligt, J., & Vliek, M. (2016). *The psychology of influence.* New York, NY: Psychology Press.

van Dijk, S. J., Molloy, P. L., Varinli, H., Morrison, J. L., Muhlhausler, B. S., Buckley, M., . . . Tellam, R. L. (2015). Epigenetics and human obesity. *International Journal of Obesity, 39,* 85–97. http://dx.doi.org/10.1038/ijo.2014.34

van IJzendoorn, M. H., & Bakermans-Kranenburg, M. J. (2010). Invariance of adult attachment across gender, age, culture, and socioeconomic status? *Journal of Social and Personal Relationships, 27,* 200–208. http://dx.doi.org/10.1177/0265407509360908

van Lenthe, F. J., Jansen, T., & Kamphuis, C. (2015). Understanding socio-economic in equalities in food choice behaviour: Can Maslow's pyramid help? *British Journal of Nutrition, 113,* 1139–1147. http://dx.doi.org/10.1017/S0007114515000288

van Ommen, M. M., van Beilen, M., Cornelissen, F. W., Smid, H. G. O. M., Knegtering, H., Aleman, A., . . . & GROUP Investigators. (2016). The prevalence of visual hallucinations in non-affective psychosis, and the role of perception and attention. *Psychological Medicine, 46,* 1735–1747. doi:10.1017/S0033291716000246

Van Tilburg, W. A., & Igou, E. R. (2014). From Van Gogh to Lady Gaga: Artist eccentricity increases perceived artistic skill and art appreciation. *European Journal of Social Psychology, 44,* 93–103. doi:10.1002/ejsp.1999

Vasileva, O. & Balyasnikova, N. (2019). (Re)Introducing Vygotsky's thought: From historical overview to contemporary psychology. *Frontiers in Psychology, 10:*1515. doi:10.3389/fpsyg.2019.01515

Vasiljevic, M., Couturier, D.-L., Frings, D., Moss, A. C., Albery, I. P., & Marteau, T. M. (2018). Impact of lower strength alcohol labeling on consumption: A randomized controlled trial. *Health Psychology, 37*(7), 658–667. http://dx.doi.org/10.1037/hea0000622

Vecchione, M., Dentale, F., Alessandri, G., Imbesi, M. T., Barbaranelli, C., & Schnabel, K. (2017). On the applicability of the big five implicit association test in organizational settings. *Current Psychology, 36*(3), 665–674. http://dx.doi.org/10.1007/s12144-016-9455-x

Venables, P. H., & Raine, A. (2016). The impact of malnutrition on intelligence at 3 and 11 years of age: The mediating role of temperament. *Developmental Psychology, 52,* 205–220. http://dx.doi.org/10.1037/dev0000046

Vendantam, S., Lu, T., Boyle, T., & Vargas-Restrepo, C. (2018, October 8). Nature, nurture, and your politics. *NPR.* Retrieved from https://www.npr.org/2018/10/03/654127241/nature-nurture-and-your-politics

Ventriglio, A., Ayonrinde, O., & Bhugra, D. (2016). Relevance of culture-bound syndromes in the 21st century. *Psychiatry and Clinical Neurosciences, 70,* 3–6. http://dx.doi.org/10.1111/pcn.12359

Vezzali, L., Stathi, S., Giovannini, D., Capozza, D., & Trifiletti, E. (2015). The greatest magic of Harry Potter: Reducing prejudice. *Journal of Applied Social Psychology, 45,* 105–121. http://dx.doi.org/10.1111/jasp.12279

Villa-Alcázar, M., Aboitiz, J., Bengoechea, C., Martinez-Romera, I., Martinez-Naranjo, C., & Lopez-Ibor, B. (2019). Coping with incongruence: Mirror therapy to manage the phantom limb phenomenon in pediatric amputee patients. *Journal of Pain and Symptom Management, 57*(1), e1–e3. https://www.jpsmjournal.com/article/S0885-3924(18)31009-1/fulltext

Villa, V. (2019, March 19). Five facts about vaccines in the U.S. *FactTank Pew Research Center.* Retrieved April 4, 2019 from https://www.pewresearch.org/fact-tank/2019/03/19/5-facts-about-vaccines-in-the-u-s/

Villines, Z. (2018, June 22). Overcoming the stigma of sexual assault: Know the facts. *Good Therapy.* Retrieved April 16, 2019 from https://www.goodtherapy.org/blog/overcoming-stigma-of-sexual-assault-know-the-facts-0622187

Vinall, J., & Grunau, R. E. (2014). Impact of repeated procedural pain-related stress in infants born very preterm. *Pediatric Research, 75,* 584–587. http://dx.doi.org/10.1038/pr.2014.16

Vincent, J. (2019, January 28). The state of AI in 2019. *The Verge.* Retrieved from https://www.theverge.com/2019/1/28/18197520/ai-artificial-intelligence-machine-learning-computational-science

Vis, B. (2019). Heuristics and political elites' judgment and decision-making. *Political Studies Review, 17*(1), 41–52. https://doi.org/10.1177/1478929917750311

Visintin, E., De Panfilis, C., Amore, M., Balestrieri, M., Wolf, R. C., & Sambataro, F. (2016). Mapping the brain correlates of borderline personality disorder: A functional neuro imaging meta-analysis of resting state studies. *Journal of Affective Disorders, 204,* 262–269. http://dx.doi.org/10.1016/j.jad.2016.07.025

Vissia, E. M., Giesen, M. E., Chalavi, S., Nijenhuis, E. R. S., Draijer, N., Brand, B. L., & Reinders, A. A. T. S. (2016). Is it Trauma- or Fantasy-based? Comparing dissociative identity disorder, post-traumatic stress disorder, simulators, and controls. *Acta PsychiatricaScandinavica, 134,* 111–128. http://dx.doi.org/10.1111/acps.12590

Vlaeyen, J. W., Morley, S., & Crombez, G. (2016). The experimental analysis of the interruptive, interfering, and identity-distorting effects of chronic pain. *Behaviour Research and Therapy, 86,* 23–34. http://dx.doi.org/10.1016/j.brat.2016.08.016

Vokey, J. R., & Read, J. D. (1985). Subliminal messages: Between the devil and the media. *American Psychologist, 40,* 1231–1239. http://dx.doi.org/10.1037/0003-066X.40.11.1231

Volbert, R., May, L., Hausam, J., & Lau, S. (2019). Confessions and denials when guilty and innocent: forensic patients' self-reported behavior during police interviews. *Frontiers in Psychiatry, 10,* 168. doi:10.3389/fpsyt.2019.00168

Volz, B. D. (2017). Race and quarterback survival in the National Football League. *Journal of Sports Economics, 18*(8), 850–866. https://doi.org/10.1177/1527002515609659

von Dawans, B., Fischbacher, U., Kirschbaum, C., Fehr, E., & Heinrichs, M. (2012). The social dimension of stress reactivity: Acute stress increases prosocial behavior in humans. *Psychological Science, 23,* 651–660. http://dx.doi.org/10.1177/0956797611431576

von Eye, A., Lősel, F., & Mayzer, R. (2003). Is it all written in the stars? A methodological commentary on Sachs' astrology monograph and re-analysis of his data on crime statistics. *Psychology Science, 45,* 78–91.

von Hofsten, C. (2013). Action in infancy: A foundation for cognitive development. In W. Prinz, M. Beisert, & A. Herwig (Eds.), *Action science foundation of an emerging discipline* (pp. 255–280). New York, NY: Oxford University Press.

Von Stumm, S., & Plomin, R. (2015). Socioeconomic status and the growth of intelligence from infancy through adolescence. *Intelligence, 48,* 30–36. http://dx.doi.org/10.1016/j.intell.2014.10.002

Vorster, A. P., & Born, J. (2015). Sleep and memory in mammals, birds and invertebrates. *Neuroscience and Biobehavioral Reviews, 50,* 103–119. http://dx.doi.org/10.1016/j.neubiorev.2014.09.020

Vosoughi, S., Roy, D., & Aral, S. (2018). The spread of true and false news online. *Science,* 09 Mar, 1146–1151. doi:10.1126/science.aap9559.

Vrij, A., Granhag, P. A., & Porter, S. (2010). Pitfalls and opportunities in nonverbal and verbal lie detection. *Psychological Science in the Public Interest, 11,* 89–121. doi:10.1177/1529100610390861

Vrolijk-Bosschaart, T. F., Brilleslijper-Kater, S. N., Benninga, M. A., Lindauer, R. J. L., & Teeuw, A. H. (2018). Clinical practice: Recognizing child sexual abuse—what makes it so difficult? *European Journal of Pediatrics, 177,* 1343–1350. https://doi.org/10.1007/s00431-018-3193-z

Vygotsky, L. S. (1962). *Thought and language.* Cambridge, MA: MIT Press.

Wagener, D. (2019, July 17). What is the success rate of AA? *American Addiction Centers.* Retrieved from https://americanaddictioncenters.org/rehab-guide/12-step/whats-the-success-rate-of-aa

Wagenmakers, E. J., Beek, T., Dijkhoff, L., Gronau, Q. F., Acosta, A., Adams Jr. R. B., . . . Zwaan, R. (2016). Registered replication report: Strack, Martin, & Stepper (1988). *Perspectives on Psychological Science, 11,* 917–928. https://doi.org/10.1177/1745691616674458

Wagner, D. A. (1982). Ontogeny in the study of culture and cognition. In D. A. Wagner & H. W. Stevenson (Eds.), *Cultural perspectives on child development* (pp. 105–123). San Francisco, CA: Freeman.

Wagner, F. L., Rammsayer, T. H., Schweizer, K., & Troche, S. J. (2014). Relations between the attentional blink and aspects of psycho-metric intelligence: A fixed-links modeling approach. *Personality and Individual Differences, 58,* 122–127. http://dx.doi.org/10.1016/j.paid.2013.10.023

Wågström, G. (2018, November 21). Is social media addiction worse than cigarettes? *Forbes.* Retrieved March 21, 2018 from https://www.forbes.com/sites/forbestechcouncil/2018/11/21/is-social-media-addiction-worse-than-cigarettes/#4bdfe35b5d64

Waite, T. (2019, April 21). Prince fans are remembering the singer three years on from his death. *Dazed.* Retrieved from https://www.dazeddigital.com/music/article/44127/1/prince-fans-remembering-the-singer-three-years-on-from-his-death

Wakefield, A. J., Murch, S. H., Anthony, A., Linnell, J., Casson, D. M., Malik, M., . . . Walker-Smith, J. A. (1998). Ileal-lymphoid-nodular hyperplasia, non-specific colitis, and pervasive developmental disorder in children. *Lancet, 351,* 637–641.

Waldinger, R. J., & Schulz, M. S. (2016). The long reach of nurturing family environments: Links with midlife emotion-regulatory styles and late-life security in intimate relationships. *Psychological Science, 27*(11), 1443–1450. https://doi.org/10.1177/0956797616661556

Waldron, J. C., Wilson, L. C., Patriquin, M. A., & Scarpa, A. (2015). Sexual victimization history, depression, and task physiology as predictors of sexual revictimization: Results from a 6-month prospective pilot study. *Journal of Interpersonal Violence, 30,* 622–639. http://dx.doi.org/10.1177/0886260514535258

Walker, A. K., Rivera, P. D., Wang, Q., Chuang, J. C., Tran, S., Osborne-Lawrence, S., . . . Zigman, J. M. (2015). The P7C3 class of neuroprotective compounds exerts antidepressant efficacy in mice by increasing hippocampal neurogenesis. *Molecular Psychiatry, 20,* 500–508. http://dx.doi.org/10.1038/mp.2014.34

Walker, H. M., & Gresham, F. M. (2016). *Handbook of evidence-based practices for emotional and behavioral disorders* (Reprint edition). New York, NY: Guilford.

Walker, J. V., III, & Lampropoulos, G. K. (2014). A comparison of self-help (homework) activities for mood enhancement: Results from a brief randomized controlled trial. *Journal of Psychotherapy Integration, 24,* 46–64. http://dx.doi.org/10.1037/a0036145

Wallack, L., & Thornburg, K. (2016). Developmental origins, epigenetics, and equity: Moving upstream. *Maternal and Child Health Journal, 20,* 935–940. http://dx.doi.org/10.1007/s10995-016-1970-8

Walsh, E., Blake, Y., Donati, A., Stoop, R., & von Gunten, A. (2019). Early secure attachment as a protective factor against later cognitive decline and dementia. *Frontiers in Aging Neuroscience, 11*, 161. doi:10.3389/fnagi.2019.00161

Walsh, K., & Cross, W. (2013). Depression: Classification, culture and the westernization of mental illness. In N. Kocabasoglu (Ed.), *Mood Disorders.* Retrieved from http://cdn.intechopen.com/pdfs/42233/InTech-Depression_classification_culture_and_the_westernisation_of_mental_illness.pdf

Walsh, K., Zwi, K., Woolfenden, S., & Shlonsky, A. (2015). School-based education programmes for the prevention of child sexual abuse. *Cochrane Database of Systematic Reviews,* Issue 4. http://dx.doi.org/10.1002/14651858.CD004380.pub3

Wamsley, E. J., & Stickgold, R. (2010). Dreaming and offline memory processing. *Current Biology, 20,* 1010–1013. http://dx.doi.org/10.1016/j.cub.2010.10.045

Wang, H., & Hall, N. C. (2018). A systematic review of teachers' causal attributions: Prevalence, correlates, and consequences. *Frontiers in Psychology, 9,* 2305. doi:10.3389/fpsyg.2018.02305

Wang, L., Luo, P., Zhang, F., Zhang, Y., Wang, X., Chang, F., . . . Xia, Z. (2017). Toll-like receptor 4 protects against stress-induced ulcers via regulation of glucocorticoid production in mice. *Stress: The International Journal on the Biology of Stress, 20*(1), 2–9. http://dx.doi.org/10.1080/10253890.2016.1224843

Wang, M.-T., & Kenny, S. (2014). Longitudinal links between fathers' and mothers' harsh verbal discipline and adolescents' conduct problems and depressive symptoms. *Child Development, 85,* 908–923. http://dx.doi.org/10.1111/cdev.12143

Wang, Q. (2011). Autobiographical memory and culture. *Online Readings in Psychology and Culture, 5.* http://dx.doi.org/10.9707/2307-0919.1047

Wang, S. H., Hsiao, P-C., Yeh, L. L., Liu, C. M., Liu, C. C., Hwang, T-J., . . . Chen, W. J. (2019). Advanced paternal age and early onset of schizophrenia in sporadic cases: Not confounded by parental polygenic risk for schizophrenia. *Biological Psychiatry, 86*(1), 55–64. doi:10.1016/j.biopsych.2019.01.023

Wang, T.-C., Tyler, R. S., Chang, T.-Y., Chen, J.-C., Lin, C.-D., Chung, H.-K., & Tsou, Y.-A. (2018). Effect of transcranial direct current stimulation in patients with tinnitus: A meta-analysis and systematic review. *Annals of Otology, Rhinology & Laryngology, 127*(2), 79–88. https://doi.org/10.1177/0003489417744317

Wang, Y., Zhang, L., Kong, X., Hong, Y., Cheon, B., & Liu, J. (2016). Pathway to neural resilience: Self-esteem buffers against deleterious effects of poverty on the hippocampus. *Human Brain Mapping, 37*(11), 3757–3766. http://dx.doi.org/10.1002/hbm.23273

Wan, L., Crookes, K., Dawel, A., Pidcock, M., Hall, A., & McKone, E. (2017). Face-blind for other-race faces: Individual differences in other-race recognition impairments. *Journal of Experimental Psychology: General, 146,* 102–122. http://dx.doi.org/10.1037/xge0000249

Ward, A. F., Duke, K., Gneezy, A., & Bos, M. W. (2017). Brain drain: The mere presence of one's own smartphone reduces available cognitive capacity. *Journal of the Association for Consumer Research, 2*(2):140. doi:10.1086/691462

Wassing, R., Benjamins, J. S., Dekker K., Moens, S., Spiegelhalder, K., Feige, B., . . . Van Someren, E. J. W. (2016). Slow dissolving of emotional distress contributes to hyperarousal. *Proceedings of the National Academy of Sciences of the United States of America, 113,* 2538–2543. http://dx.doi.org/10.1073/pnas.1522520113

Watsky, R. E., Ludovici Pollard, K., Greenstein, D., Shora, L., Dillard-Broadnax, D., Gochman, P., . . . Ordóñez, A. E. (2016). Severity of cortical thinning correlates with schizophrenia spectrum

symptoms. *Journal of the American Academy of Child & Adolescent Psychiatry, 55,* 130–136. http://dx.doi.org/10.1016/j.jaac.2015.11.008

Watson, J. B. (1913). Psychology as the behaviorist views it. *Psychological Review, 20,* 158–177. http://dx.doi.org/10.1037/h0074428

Watson, J. B., & Rayner, R. (1920). Conditioned emotional reactions. *Journal of Experimental Psychology, 3,* 1–14. http://dx.doi.org/10.1037/h0069608

Watson, J. C., & Greenberg, L. S. (2017). Working with worry: Anxiety splits. In J. C. Watson & L. S. Greenberg (Eds.), *Emotion-focused therapy for generalized anxiety* (pp. 135–163). Washington, DC: American Psychological Association. http://dx.doi.org/10.1037/0000018-007

Watson, J. C., & Watson, A. A. (2016). Coping self-efficacy and academic stress among Hispanic first-year college students: The moderating role of emotional intelligence. *Journal of College Counseling, 19,* 218–230. doi:10.1002/jocc.12045

Watts, B. V., Zayed, M. H., Llewellyn-Thomas, H., & Schnurr, P. P. (2016). Understanding and meeting information needs for patients with posttraumatic stress disorder. *BMC Psychiatry, 16,* Article 21. http://dx.doi.org/10.1186/s12888-016-0724-x

Watts, T. W., Duncan, G. J., & Quan, H. (2018). Revisiting the marshmallow test: A conceptual replication investigating links between early delay of gratification and later outcomes. *Psychological Science, 29*(7), 1159–1177. https://doi.org/10.1177/0956797618761661

Webb, B., Hine, A. C., & Bailey, P. E. (2016). Difficulty in differentiating trustworthiness from untrustworthiness in older age. *Developmental Psychology, 52,* 985–995. http://dx.doi.org/10.1037/dev0000126

Webber, D., Schimel, J., Faucher, E. H., Hayes, J., Zhang, R., & Martens, A. (2015). Emotion as a necessary component of threat-induced death thought accessibility and defensive compensation. *Motivation and Emotion, 39,* 142–155. doi:10.1007/s11031-014-9426-1

Webb, S. (2016). Schizophrenia. In A. Breland-Noble, C. S. Al-Mateen, & N. N. Singh (Eds.), *Handbook of mental health in African American youth. Springer series on child and family* studies (pp. 249–259). Cham, CH: Springer International Publishing. http://dx.doi.org/10.1007/978-3-319-25501-9_15

Wechsler, D. (1944). *The measurement of adult intelligence* (3rd ed.). Baltimore, MD: Williams & Wilkins.

Wechsler, D. (1977). *Manual for the Wechsler Intelligence Scale for Children* (Rev.). New York, NY: Psychological Corporation.

Wedow, R., Zacher, M., Huibregtse, B. M., Mullan Harris, K., Domingue, B. W., & Boardman, J. D. (2018). Education, smoking, and cohort change: Forwarding a multidimensional theory of the environmental moderation of genetic effects. *American Sociological Review, 83*(4), 802–832. https://doi.org/10.1177/0003122418785368

Weeks, B. E., & Garrett, R. K. (2014). Electoral consequences of political rumors: Motivated reasoning, candidate rumors, and vote choice during the 2008 US presidential election. *International Journal of Public Opinion Research, 26,* 401–422. http://dx.doi.org/10.1093/ijpor/edu005

Weems, C. F., Scott, B. G., Banks, D. M., & Graham, R. A. (2012). Is TV traumatic for all youths? The role of preexisting posttraumatic stress symptoms in the link between disaster coverage and stress. *Psychological Science, 23,* 1293–1297. http://dx.doi.org/10.1177/0956797612446952

Weger, U. W., Wagemann, J., & Tewes, C. (2019). The challenges and opportunities of introspection in psychology: Theory and method. *Frontiers in Psychology, 10*:2196. doi:10.3389/fpsyg.2019.02196

Wegmann, E., & Brand, M. (2016). Internet-communication disorder: It's a matter of social aspects, coping, and Internet-use expectancies. *Frontiers in Psychology, 7:*1747.

Wegrzyn, M., Garlichs, A., Woermann, F. G., & Labudda, K. (2019). The hidden identity of faces: A case of lifelong prosopagnosia. *BMC Psychology, 7*(1), 4. doi:10.1186/s40359-019-0278-z

Weimer, A. A., Dowds, S. J. P., Fabricius, W. V., Schwanenflugel, P. J., & Suh, G. W. (2017). Development of constructivist theory of mind from middle childhood to early adulthood and its relation to social cognition and behavior. *Journal of Experimental Child Psychology, 154,* 28–45. http://dx.doi.org/10.1016/j. jecp.2016.10.002

Weinberg, B. A., & Galenson, D. W. (2019). Creative careers: The life cycles of Nobel laureates in economics. *De Economist.* Retrieved from doi:10.1007/s10645-019-09339-9

Weiner, B. (1972). *Theories of motivation.* Chicago, IL: Rand-McNally.

Weiner, B. (2015). On the cross-cultural trail, searching for (non)-replication. *International Journal of Psychology, 50,* 303–307. http://dx. doi.org/10.1002/ijop.12156

Weinstein, D., Launay, J., Pearce, E., Dunbar, R. I. M., & Stewart, L. (2016). Singing and social bonding: Changes in connectivity and pain threshold as a function of group size. *Evolution and Human Behavior, 37,* 152–158. http://dx.doi.org/10.1016/j.evolhumbehav.2015. 10.002

Weinstein, N., Campbell, R., & Vansteenkiste, M. (2018). Linking psychological need experiences to daily and recurring dreams. *Motivation and Emotion, 42*(1), 50–63. http://dx.doi.org/10.1007/s11031-017-9656-0

Weinstein, N., Ryan, W. S., DeHaan, C. R., Przybylski, A. K., Legate, N., & Ryan, R. M. (2012). Parental autonomy support and discrepancies between implicit and explicit sexual identities: Dynamics of self acceptance and defense. *Journal of Personality and Social Psychology, 102,* 815–832. http://dx.doi.org/10.1037/a0026854

Weintraub, K. (2016). Young and sleep deprived. *Monitor on Psychology, 47,* 46. Retrieved from http://www.apa.org/monitor/2016/02/sleep-deprived.aspx

Weir, K. (2018, December). The future of psychobiotics. *Monitor on Psychology.* Retrieved from https://www.apa.org/monitor/2018/12/cover-psychobiotics

Weir, K. (2019, March). Worrying trends in U.S. suicide rates. *Monitor on Psychology.* Retrieved from http://www.apamonitor-digital.org/apamonitor/201903/MobilePagedArticle. action?articleId=1466310#articleId1466310

Weiss, A., Gartner, M. C., Gold, K. C., & Stoinski, T. S. (2013). Extraversion predicts longer survival in gorillas: An 18-year longitudinal study. *Proceedings. Biological sciences, 280*(1752), 20122231. doi:10.1098/rspb.2012.2231

Weiss, A., Staes, N., Pereboom, J. J., Inoue-Murayama, M., Stevens, J. M., & Eens, M. (2015). Personality in bonobos. *Psychological Science, 26,* 1430–1439. http://dx.doi. org/10.1177/0956797615589933

Weitlauf, J. C., Cervone, D., Smith, R. E., & Wright, P. M. (2001). Assessing generalization in perceived self-efficacy: Multi domain and global assessments of the effects of self defense training for women. *Personality and Social Psychology Bulletin, 27,* 1683–1691. http://dx. doi.org/10.1177/01461672012712011

Welch, A. (2019, April 30). Teen suicide increased after Netflix's "13 Reasons Why" premiered, study finds. *CBS News.* Retrieved from https://www.cbsnews.com/news/teen-suicide-increased-after-netflixs-13-reasons-why-premiered-study-finds/

Welsch, R., von Castell, C., & Hecht, H. (2019). The anisotropy of personal space. *PLoS ONE, 14*(6): e0217587. https://doi.org/10.1371/journal.pone.0217587

Wergård, E.-M., Westlund, K., Spångberg, M., Fredlund, H., & Forkman, B. (2016). Training success in group-housed longtailed macaques (Macaca fascicularis) is better explained by personality than by social rank. *Applied Animal Behaviour Science, 177,* 52–58. http://dx.doi.org/10.1016/j.applanim.2016.01.017

Werner, K. H., Roberts, N. A., Rosen, H. J., Dean, D. L., Kramer, J. H., Weiner, M. W., . . . Levenson, R. W. (2007). Emotional reactivity and emotion recognition in frontotemporal lobar degeneration. *Neurology, 69,* 148–155.

Wertz, J., Caspi, A., Belsky, D. W., Beckley, A. L., Arseneault, L., Barnes, J. C., . . . Moffitt, T. E. (2018). Genetics and crime: Integrating new genomic discoveries into psychological research about antisocial behavior. *Psychological Science, 29*(5), 791–803. https://doi.org/10.1177/0956797617744542

Westen, D. (1998). The scientific legacy of Sigmund Freud: Toward a psychodynamically informed psychological science. *Psychological Bulletin, 124,* 333–371.

Westfall, J., Van Boven, L., Chambers, J. R., & Judd, C. M. (2015). Perceiving political polarization in the United States: Party identity strength and attitude extremity exacerbate the perceived partisan divide. *Perspectives on Psychological Science, 10,* 145–158. http://dx. doi.org/10.1177/1745691615569849

Weston, G., Zilanawala, A., Webb, E., Carvalho, L. A., & McMunn, A. (2019). Long work hours, weekend working and depressive symptoms in men and women: Findings from a UK population-based study. *Journal of Epidemiology and Community Health, 73,* 465–474. Retrieved from https://jech.bmj.com/content/73/5/465.citation-tools

West, T. V., Magee, J. C., Gordon, S. H., & Gullett, L. (2014). A little similarity goes a long way: The effects of peripheral but self-revealing similarities on improving and sustaining interracial relationships. *Journal of Personality and Social Psychology, 107,* 81–100. http://dx. doi.org/10.1037/a0036556

Weyandt, L. L., Oster, D. R., Gudmundsdottir, B. G., DuPaul, G. J., & Anastopoulos, A. D. (2017). Neuropsychological functioning in college students with and without ADHD. *Neuropsychology, 31,* 160–172. http://dx.doi.org/10.1037/neu0000326

Weyrich, A., Lenz, D., & Fickel, J. (2018). Environmental change-dependent inherited epigenetic response. *Genes, 10*(1), 4. doi: 10.3390/genes10010004

Whealin, J., & Barnett, E. (2014). Child sexual abuse. *National Center for Post Traumatic Stress Disorder, U.S. Department of Veterans Affairs.* Retrieved from http://www.ptsd.va.gov/professional/trauma/other/child_sexual_abuse.asp

Wheeler, R. L., & Gabbert, F. (2017). Using self-generated cues to facilitate recall: A narrative review. *Frontiers in Psychology, 8:*1830. doi:10.3389/fpsyg.2017.01830

Whillans, A., Macchia, L., & Dunn, E. (2019). Valuing time over money predicts happiness after a major life transition: A preregistered longitudinal study of graduating students. *Science Advances, 5*(9):eeax2615. https://advances.sciencemag.org/content/5/9/eaax2615

Whillans, A. V., Weidman, A. C., & Dunn, E. W. (2016). Valuing time over money is associated with greater happiness. *Social Psychological and Personality Science, 7,* 213–222. doi:10.1177/1948550615623842

White, D., Sutherland, C., & Burton, A. L. (2017). Choosing face: The curse of self in profile image selection. *Cognitive Research: Principles and Implications, 2*(1), 23. doi:10.1186/s41235-017-0058-3

White, J. B. (2018, April 7). Robert Kennedy Jr. warns of vaccine-linked 'holocaust.' *Sacramento Bee.* Retrieved April 4, 2019 from https://www.sacbee.com/news/politics-government/capitol-alert/article17814440.html

White, T., Andreasen, N. C., & Nopoulos, P. (2002). Brain volumes and surface morphology in monozygotic twins. *Cerebral Cortex, 12,* 486–493. http://dx.doi.org/10.1093/cercor/12.5.486

Whorf, B. L. (1956). *Language, thought, and reality.* New York, NY: Wiley.

Wieman, C., & Welsh, A. (2016). The connection between teaching methods and attribution errors. *Educational Psychology Review, 28*(3), 645–648. http://dx.doi.org/10.1007/s10648-015-9317-3

Wiggin, K. L., & Yalch, R. F. (2015). Whose fault is it? Effects of relational self-views and outcome counterfactuals on self-serving attribution biases following brand policy changes. *Journal of Consumer Psychology, 25,* 459–472. doi:10.1016/j.jcps.2015.02.004

Wilkie, G., Sakr, B., & Rizack, T. (2016). Medical marijuana use in oncology: A review. *JAMA Oncology, 2,* 670–675. http://dx.doi.org/10.1001/jamaoncol.2016.0155.

Wilkins, C. L., Wellman, J. D., Babbitt, L. G., Toosi, N. R., & Schad, K. D. (2015). You can win but I can't lose: Bias against high status groups increases their zero-sum beliefs about discrimination. *Journal of Experimental Social Psychology, 57,* 1–14. http://dx.doi.org/10.1016/j.jesp.2014.10.008

Wilkins, C. L., Wellman, J. D., Flavin, E. L., & Manrique, J. A. (2018). When men perceive anti-male bias: Status-legitimizing beliefs increase discrimination against women. *Psychology of Men & Masculinity, 19*(2), 282–290. http://dx.doi.org/10.1037/men0000097

Willen, R. M., Mutwill, A., MacDonald, L. J., Schiml, P. A., & Hennessy, M. B. (2017). Factors determining the effects of human interaction on the cortisol levels of shelter dogs. *Applied Animal Behaviour Science, 186,* 41–48. http://dx.doi.org/10.1016/j.applanim.2016.11.002

Williams, C. L., & Lally, S. J. (2017). MMPI-2, MMPI-2-RF, and MMPI-A administrations (2007–2014): Any evidence of a "new standard?" *Professional Psychology: Research and Practice, 48*(4), 267–274. http://dx.doi.org/10.1037/pro0000088

Williams, D. L. (2014). Neural integration of satiation and food reward: Role of GLP-1 and orexin pathways. *Physiology & Behavior, 136,* 194–199.

Williams, K. J., Lee, K. E., Hartig, T., Sargent, L. D., Williams, N. S., & Johnson, K. A. (2018). Conceptualising creativity benefits of nature experience: Attention restoration and mind wandering as complementary processes. *Journal of Environmental Psychology, 59,* 36–45. doi:10.1016/j.jenvp.2018.08.005

Williams, K. M., Bentham, G. C. G., Young, I. S., McGinty, A., McKay, G. J., Hogg, R., . . . Fletcher, A. E. (2017). Association between myopia, ultraviolet B radiation exposure, serum vitamin D concentrations, and genetic polymorphisms in vitamin D metabolic pathways in a multicountry European study. *JAMA Ophthalmology, 135*(1), 47–53. doi:10.1001/jamaophthalmol.2016.4752

Williamson, J. M., Lounsbury, J. W., & Han, L. D. (2013). Key personality traits of engineers for innovation and technology development. *Journal of Engineering Technology Management, 30,* 157–168.

Williamson, J. N., & Williamson, D. G. (2015). Sleep-wake disorders. In L. Sperry, J. Carlson, J. D. Sauerheber, & J. Sperry (Eds.), *Psychopathology and psychotherapy: DSM-5 diagnosis, case conceptualization, and treatment* (3rd ed., pp. 243–264). New York, NY: Routledge/Taylor & Francis Group.

Williams, S. S. (2001). Sexual lying among college students in close and casual relationships. *Journal of Applied Social Psychology, 31*(11), 2322–2338.

Willis, M. (2018, March 01). Gender and sexuality in two non-western cultures. *Society for Personality and Social Psychology.* Retrieved from http://spsp.org/news-center/blog/mate-competition-nonwestern- cultures

Wills, M. (2019, February 26). The strange story behind your breakfast cereal. *JSTOR Daily.* Retrieved from https://daily.jstor.org/the-strange-backstory-behind-your-breakfast-cereal/

Willyard, C. (2011). Men: A growing minority. *grad-PSYCH, 9,* 40–44. http://dx.doi.org/10.1037/e669902010-010

Wilmot, M. P., Wanberg, C. R., Kammeyer-Mueller, J. D., & Ones, D. S. (2019). Extraversion advantages at work: A quantitative review and synthesis of the meta-analytic evidence. *Journal of Applied Psychology.* http://dx.doi.org/10.1037/apl0000415

Wilson, D. S. (2015). *Does altruism exist? Culture, genes, and the welfare of others.* New Haven, CT: Yale University Press.

Wilson, E. O. (1975). *Sociobiology: The new synthesis.* Cambridge, MA: Harvard University Press.

Wilson, E. O. (1978). *On human nature.* Cambridge, MA: Harvard University Press.

Wilson, M. (2015, June 5). A Manhattan fortune teller cost him fortune after fortune. *The New York Times.* Retrieved from http://www.nytimes.com/2015/06/06/nyregion/he-went-to-thefortuneteller-now-his-fortune-is-gone.html?

Wilson, P. A., Stadler, G., Boone, M. R., & Bolger, N. (2014). Fluctuations in depression and well-being are associated with sexual risk episodes among HIV-positive men. *Health Psychology, 33*(7), 681–685. doi:10.1037/a0035405

Wilson, V., Guenther, A., Øverli, Ø., Seltmann, M. W., & Altschul, D. (2019). Future directions for personality research: Contributing new insights to the understanding of animal behavior. *Animals: An Open Access Journal From MDPI, 9*(5), 240. doi:10.3390/ani9050240

Wimmer, H., & Perner, J. (1983). Beliefs about beliefs: Representation and constraining function of wrong beliefs in young children's understanding of deception. *Cognition, 13,* 103–128.

Winston, C. N., Maher, H., & Easvaradoss, V. (2017). Needs and values: An exploration. *The Humanistic Psychologist, 45*(3), 295–311. http://dx.doi.org/10.1037/hum0000054

Witelson, S. F., Kigar, D. L., & Harvey, T. (1999). The exceptional brain of Albert Einstein. *The Lancet, 353,* 2149–2153. http://dx.doi.org/10.1016/S0140-6736(05)70590-0

Witt, W. P., Mandell, K. C., Wisk, L. E., Cheng, E. R., Chatterjee, D., Wakeel, F., . . . Zarak, D. (2016). Infant birthweight in the US: The role of preconception stressful life events and substance use. *Archives of Women's Mental Health, 19*(3), 529–542. http://dx.doi.org/10.1007/s00737-015-0595-z

Wixted, J. T., Mickes, L., Clark, S. E., Gronlund, S. D., & Roediger, H. L. III. (2015). Initial eyewitness confidence reliably predicts eyewitness identification accuracy. *American Psychologist, 70,* 515–526. http://dx.doi.org/10.1037/a0039510

Wofford, N., Defever, A. M., & Chopik, W. J. (2019). The vicarious effects of discrimination: How partner experiences of discrimination affect individual health. *Social Psychological and Personality Science, 10*(1), 121–130. https://doi.org/10.1177/1948550617746218

Wölfer, R., Christ, O., Schmid, K., Tausch, N., Buchallik, F. M., Vertovec, S., & Hewstone, M. (2019). Indirect contact predicts direct contact: Longitudinal evidence and the mediating role of intergroup anxiety. *Journal of Personality and Social Psychology, 116*(2), 277–295. http://dx.doi.org/10.1037/pspi0000146

Wolff, M., & Vann, S. D. (2019). The cognitive thalamus as a gateway to mental representations. *Journal of Neuroscience, 39*(1), 3–14. https://doi.org/10.1523/JNEUROSCI.0479-18.2018

Wolgast, S., Björklund, F., & Bäckström, M. (2018). Applicant ethnicity affects which questions are asked in a job interview: The role of expected fit. *Journal of Personnel Psychology, 17*(2), 66–74. http://dx.doi.org/10.1027/1866-5888/a000197

Wollan, M. (2015, August 16). How to brush a gorilla's teeth. *The New York Times Magazine,* p. 25. https://www.nytimes.com/2015/08/16/magazine/how-to-brush-a-gorillas-teeth.html

Wollan, M. (2015). How to beat a polygraph test. *The New York Times Magazine.* Retrieved from http://www.nytimes.com/2015/04/12/magazine/how-to-beat-apolygraph-test.html?_r=0

Wolpe, J., & Plaud, J. J. (1997). Pavlov's contributions to behavior therapy. *American Psychologist, 52,* 966–972.

Wong, Y. J., Ho, M.-H. R., Wang, S.-Y., & Miller, I. S. K. (2017). Meta-analyses of the relationship between conformity to masculine norms and mental health-related outcomes. *Journal of Counseling Psychology, 64*(1), 80–93. http://dx.doi.org/10.1037/cou0000176

Wood, A., Lupyan, G., Sherrin, S., & Niedenthal, P. (2016). Altering sensorimotor feedback disrupts visual discrimination of facial expressions. *Psychonomic Bulletin & Review, 23*(4), 1150–1156. http://dx.doi.org/10.3758/s13423-015-0974-5

Woodin, E. M., Sukhawathanakul, P., Caldeira, V., Homel, J., & Leadbeater, B. (2016). Pathways to romantic relational aggression through adolescent peer aggression and heavy episodic drinking. *Aggressive Behavior, 42*(6), 563–576. doi:10.1002/ab.21651

Wood, J. T., & Fixmer-Oraiz, N. (2019). *Gendered lives* (13th ed.). Boston, MA: Cengage.

Woodley of Menie, M. A., & Madison, G. (2015). The association between g and K in a sample of 4246 Swedish twins: A behavior genetic analysis. *Personality and Individual Differences, 74,* 270–274. http://dx.doi.org/10.1016/j.paid.2014.10.027

Woodley of Menie, M. A., Peñaherrera, M. A., Fernandes, H. B. F., Becker, D., & Flynn, J. R. (2016). It's getting bigger all the time: Estimating the Flynn effect from secular brain mass increases in Britain and Germany. *Learning and Individual Differences, 45,* 95–100. http://dx.doi.org/10.1016/j.lindif.2015.11.004

Woods, R. J., & Wilcox, T. (2013). Posture support improves object individuation in infants. *Developmental Psychology, 49*(8), 1413–1424. http://dx.doi.org/10.1037/a0030344

Wooley, K., & Fishbach, A. (2019). Shared plates, shared minds: Consuming from a shared plate promotes cooperation. *Psychological Science, 30*(4), 541–552. https://doi.org/10.1177/0956797619830633

Workman, L., & Reader, W. (2014). *Evolutionary psychology: An introduction* (3rd ed.). New York, NY: Cambridge University Press.

World Health Organization. (2018a). Schizophrenia and other psychoses. *WHO.* Retrieved from https://www.who.int/en/news-room/fact-sheets/detail/mental-disorders

World Health Organization. (2018b). Autism spectrum disorders. *World Health Organization.*

World Health Organization. (2018c). Suicide data. *WHO.* Retrieved from https://www.who.int/mental_health/prevention/suicide/suicideprevent/en/

World Health Organization. (2019). Gender and women's mental health. *WHO.* Retrieved from https://www.who.int/mental_health/prevention/genderwomen/en/

World Health Organization. (2019). Suicide. *WHO.* Retrieved from https://www.who.int/news-room/fact-sheets/detail/suicide

World Health Organization (n.d.). Risks to mental health: An overview of vulnerabilities and risk factors. *WHO.* Retrieved from https://www.who.int/mental_health/mhgap/risks_to_mental_health_EN_27_08_12.pdf

World Health Organization (WHO). (2011). Depression. *World Health Organization.* Retrieved from February 12, 2011 from http://www.who.int/topics/depression/en/

World Health Organization (WHO). (2017). Mental health. *World Health Organization.* Retrieved February 27, 2017 from http://www.who.int/mental_health/prevention/genderwomen/en/

Worthington, E. L., Jr., Berry, J. W., Hook, J. N., Davis, D. E., Scherer, M., Griffin, B. J., . . . Campana, K. L. (2015). Forgiveness reconciliation and communication-conflict resolution interventions versus retested controls in early married couples. *Journal of Counseling Psychology, 62,* 14–27. http://dx.doi.org/10.1037/cou0000045

Wright, T. J., Boot, W. R., & Brockmole, J. R. (2015). Functional fixedness: The functional significance of delayed disengagement based on attention set. *Journal of Experimental Psychology: Human Perception and Performance, 41,* 17–21. http://dx.doi.org/10.1037/xhp0000016

Wrzesniewski, A., Schwartz, B., Cong, X., Kane, M., Omar, A., & Kolditz, T. (2014). Multiple types of motives don't multiply the motivation of West Point cadets. *Proceedings of the National Academy of Sciences of the United States of America, 111,* 10990–10995. http://dx.doi.org/10.1073/pnas.1405298111

Wu, C., & Chao, R. K. (2011). Intergenerational cultural dissonance in parent–adolescent relationships among Chinese and European Americans. *Developmental Psychology, 47*(2), 493–508.

Wu, C. C., Hsu, T. Y., Chang, J. C., Ou, C. Y., Kuo, H. C., Liu, C. A., . . . Yang, K. D. (2019). Paternal tobacco smoke correlated to offspring asthma and prenatal epigenetic programming. *Frontiers in Genetics, 10*:471. doi:10.3389/fgene.2019.00471

Wufong, W., Rhodes, P., & Conti, J. (2019). "We don't really know what else we can do": Parent experiences when adolescent distress persists after the Maudsley and family-based therapies for anorexia nervosa. *Journal of Eating Disorders, 7*(5). https://jeatdisord.biomedcentral.com/articles/10.1186/s40337-019-0235-5

Wu, J., Perry, D. C., Bupp, J. E., Jiang, F., Polgar, W. E., Toll, L., & Zaveri, N. T. (2014). [125I] AT-1012, a new high affinity radioligand for the α3β4 nicotinic acetylcholine receptors. *Neuropharmacology, 77,* 193–199. http://dx.doi.org/10.1016/j.neuropharm.2013.09.023

Wu, X. N., Zhang, T., Qian, N. S., Guo, X. D., Yang, H. J., Huang, K. B., . . . Pan, S. Y. (2015). Antinociceptive effects of endomorphin-2: Suppression of substance P release in the inflammatory pain model rat. *Neurochemistry International, 82,* 1–9. doi:10.1016/j.neuint.2015.01.004

Wyman, A. J., & Vyse, S. (2008). Science versus the stars: A double-blind test of the validity of the NEO Five Factor Inventory and computer generated astrological natal charts. *Journal of General Psychology, 135,* 287–300. doi:10.3200/GENP.135.3.287-300

Wynn, K., Bloom, P., Jordan, A., Marshall, J., & Sheskin, M. (2018). Not noble savages after all: Limits to early altruism. *Current Directions in Psychological Science, 27*(1), 3–8. doi:10.1177/0963721417734875

Xavier, M. J., Roman, S. D., Aitken, R. J., & Nixon, B. (2019). Transgenerational inheritance: How impacts to the epigenetic and genetic information of parents affect offspring health. *Human Reproduction Update, 25*(5), 519–541. https://doi.org/10.1093/humupd/dmz017

Xiao, N., Yang, B. F., Shi, J. Z., Yu, Y. G., Zhang, F., Miao, Q., & Li, D. R. (2019). Karoshi may be a consequence of overwork-related malignant arrhythmia. *Medical Science Monitor: International Medical Journal of Experimental and Clinical Research, 25,* 357–364. doi:10.12659/MSM.911685

Xie, L., Kang, H., Xu, Q., Chen, M. J., Liao, Y., Thiyagarajan, M., . . . Nedergaard, M. (2013). Sleep drives metabolite clearance from the human brain. *Science, 342,* 373–377. http://dx.doi.org/10.1126/science.1241224

Xi, J., Lee, M., LeSuer, W., Barr, P., Newton, K., & Poloma, M. (2016). Altruism and existential wellbeing. *Applied Research in Quality of Life, 12*(1), 67–88. http://dx.doi.org/10.1007/s11482-016-9453-z

Xue, S. W., Tang, Y. Y., Tang, R., & Posner, M. I. (2014). Short-term meditation induces changes in brain resting EEG theta networks. *Brain and Cognition, 87,* 1–6. http://dx.doi.org/10.1016/j.bandc.2014.02.008

Xu, L., Becker, B., & Kendrick, K. M. (2019). Oxytocin facilitates social learning by promoting conformity to trusted individuals. *Frontiers in Neuroscience, 13*(56). http://dx.doi:10.3389/fnins.2019.00056

Yadollahpour, A., Hosseini, S. A., & Shakeri, A. (2016). Rtms for the treatment of depression: A comprehensive review of effective protocols on right dlpfc. *International Journal of Mental Health and Addiction, 14,* 539–549. http://dx.doi.org/10.1007/s11469-016-9669-z

Yamada, H. (1997). *Different games, different rules: Why Americans and Japanese misunderstand each other.* London, UK: Oxford University Press.

Yamaguchi, K., Inoue, Y., Ohki, N., Satoya, N., Inoue, F., Maeda, Y., . . . Nagai, A. (2014). Gender-specific impacts of apnea, age, and BMI on parasympathetic nerve dysfunction during sleep in patients with obstructive sleep apnea. *PLoS ONE, 9,* 1–11. http://dx.doi.org/10.1371/journal.pone.0092808

Yanes, J. A., McKinnell, Z. E., Reid, M. A., Busler, J. N., Michel, J. S., Pangelinan, M. M., . . . Robinson, J. L. (2019). Effects of cannabinoid administration for pain: A meta-analysis and meta-regression. *Experimental and Clinical Psychopharmacology, 27*(4), 370–382. http://dx.doi.org/10.1037/pha0000281

Yang, C-L. (2019). The relationships between personality and Facebook photographs: A study in Taiwan. *Cogent Business & Management, 6:*1. doi:10.1080/23311975.2019.1577521

Yang, J., Hou, X., Wei, D., Wang, K., Li, Y., & Qiu, J. (2016). Only-child and non-only-child exhibit differences in creativity and agreeableness: Evidence from behavioral and anatomical structural studies. *Brain Imaging and Behavior, 11*(2), 493–502. http://dx.doi.org/10.1007/s11682-016-9530-9

Yang, J., Watanabe, J., Kanazawa, S., Nishida, S.'y., & Yamaguchi, M. K. (2015). Infants' visual system nonretinotopically integrates color signals along a motion trajectory. *Journal of Vision, 15,* Article ID 25. doi:10.1167/15.1.25

Yang, T. (2016). Image schemas in verb–particle constructions: Evidence from a behavioral experiment. *Journal of Psycholinguistic Research, 45,* 379–393. http://dx.doi.org/10.1007/s10936-015-9354-6

Yannis, G., Laiou, A., Papantoniou, P., & Gkartzonikas, C. (2016). Simulation of texting impact on young drivers' behavior and safety on motorways. *Transportation Research Part F: Traffic Psychology and Behaviour, 41,* 10–18. http://dx.doi.org/10.1016/j.trf.2016.06.003

Yapko, M. D. (2015). *Essentials of hypnosis* (2nd ed.). New York, NY: Routledge/Taylor & Francis Group.

Yasnitsky, A. (2015). *Vygotsky: An intellectual biography.* Boca Raton, FL: Taylor & Francis Group.

Yetish, G., Kaplan, H., Gurven, M., Wood, B., Pontzer, H., Manger, P. R., . . . Siegel, J. M. (2015). Natural sleep and its seasonal variations in three pre-industrial societies. *Current Biology, 25,* 2862–2868. http://dx.doi.org/10.1016/j.cub.2015.09.046

Yogman, M., Garner, A., Hutchinson, J., Hirsh-Pasek, K., & Golinkoff, R. M. (2018). The power of play: A pediatric role in enhancing development in young children. *Pediatrics, 142*(3), e20182058. doi:10.1542/peds.2018-2058

Yong, E. (2018). Psychology's replication crisis is running out of excuses. *The Atlantic.* Retrieved from https://www.theatlantic.com/science/archive/2018/11/psychologys-replication-crisis-real/576223/

Yoo, J., Miyamoto, Y., Rigotti, A., & Ryff, C. D. (2017). Linking positive affect to blood lipids: A cultural perspective. *Psychological Science, 28*(10), 1468–1477. https://doi.org/10.1177/0956797617713309

Yoshikawa, Y., Ohmaki, E., Kawahata, H., Maekawa, Y., Ogihara, T., Morishita, R., & Aoki, M. (2018). Beneficial effect of laughter therapy on physiological and psychological function in elders. *Nursing Open, 6*(1), 93–99. doi:10.1002/nop2.190

Yoshimoto, S., Imai, H., Kashino, M., & Takeuchi, T. (2014). Pupil response and the subliminal mere exposure effect. *PLoS ONE, 9,* e90670. http://dx.doi.org/10.1371/journal.pone.0090670

Yoshimura, S. M., & Berzins, K. (2017). Grateful experiences and expressions: The role of gratitude expressions in the link between gratitude experiences and well-being. *Review of Communication, 17,* 106–118. http://dx.doi.org/10.1080/15358593.2017.1293836

Yoshinaga, N., Kubota, K., Yoshimura, K., Takanashi, R., Ishida, Y., Iyo, M., . . . Shimizu, E. (2019). Long-term effectiveness of cognitive therapy for refractory social anxiety disorder: One-year follow-up of a randomized controlled trial. *Psychotherapy and Psychosomatics, 88,* 244–246. doi:10.1159/000500108

Yoshinaga, Y., Kubota, K., Yoshimura, K., Takanashi, R., Ishida, Y., Iyo, M., . . . Shimizu, E. (2019). Long-term effectiveness of cognitive therapy for refractory social anxiety disorder: One-year follow-up of a randomized controlled trial. *Psychotherapy and Psychosomatics, 88*(4), 244–246. doi:10.1159/000500108

Young, A., & Wimmer, R. D. (2017). Implications for the thalamic reticular nucleus in impaired attention and sleep in schizophrenia. *Schizophrenia Research, 180,* 44–47. http://dx.doi.org/10.1016/j.schres.2016.07.011

Young, S. G., Brown, C. M., & Ambady, N. (2012). Priming a natural or human-made environment directs attention to context congruent threatening stimuli. *Cognition & Emotion, 26,* 927–933. http://dx.doi.org/10.1080/02699931.2011.625399

Young, T. (1802). On the theory of light and colours. *Philosophical Transactions of the Royal Society, 92,* 12–48.

Yousafzai, M. (2019). *We are displaced: My journey and stories from refugee girls.* Boston, MA: Little Brown.

Youyou, W., Kosinski, M., & Stillwell, D. (2015). Computer-based personality judgments are more accurate than those made by humans. *Proceedings of the National Academy of Sciences of the United States of America, 112,* 1036–1040. http://dx.doi.org/10.1073/pnas.1418680112

Youyou, W., Stillwell, D., Schwartz, H. A., & Kosinski, M. (2017). Birds of a feather do flock together. *Psychological Science, 28*(3), 276–284. http://dx.doi.org/10.1177/0956797616678187

Yücel, M., Carter, A., Harrigan, K., van Holst, R. J., & Livingstone, C. (2018). Hooked on gambling: A problem of human or machine design? *The Lancet Psychiatry, 5*(1), 20–21. http://dx.doi.org/10.1016/S2215-0366(17)30467-4

Yu, J., Zhu, L., & Leslie, A. M. (2016). Children's sharing behavior in mini-dictator games: The role of in-group favoritism and theory of mind. *Child Development, 87*(6), 1747–1757. http://dx.doi.org/10.1111/cdev.12635

Yuki, M., Maddux, W.W., & Masuda, T. (2007). Are the windows to the soul the same in the East and West? Cultural differences in using the eyes and mouth as cues to recognize emotions in Japan and the United States. *Journal of Experimental Social Psychology, 43,* 303–311.

Zajonc, R. B. (1965). Social facilitation. *Science, 149* (Whole No. 3681), 269–274. http://dx.doi.org/10.1126/science.149.3681.269

Zeanah, C. H., & Gleason, M. M. (2015). Annual research review: Attachment disorders in early childhood—clinical presentation, causes, correlates, and treatment. *Journal of Child Psychology and Psychiatry, 56,* 207–222. http://dx.doi.org/10.1111/jcpp.12347

Zemestani, M., & Fazeli, N. Z. (2019). Effectiveness of mindfulness-based cognitive therapy for comorbid depression and anxiety in pregnancy: A randomized controlled trial. *Archives of Women's Mental Health.* doi:10.1007/s00737-019-00962-8.

Zhang, B., Tian, D., Yu, C., Zhang, J., Tian, X., von Deneen, K. M., . . . Liu, Y. (2015). Altered baseline brain activities before food intake in obese men: A resting state fMRI study. *Neuroscience Letters, 584,* 156–161. doi:10.1016/j.neulet.2014.10.020

Zhang, E. J., Chughtai, A. A., Heywood, A., & MacIntyre, C. R. (2019). Influence of political and medical leaders on parental perception of vaccination: A cross-sectional survey in Australia. *BMJ Open, 9:*e025866. doi:10.1136/bmjopen-2018-025866

Zhang, H. (2015). Moderate tolerance promotes tag-mediated cooperation in spatial Prisoner's dilemma game. *Physica A: Statistical Mechanics and its Applications, 424,* 52–61. http://dx.doi.org/10.1016/j.physa.2015.01.005

Zhang, M. W., Harris, K. M., & Ho, R. C. (2016). Is off-label repeat prescription of ketamine as a rapid antidepressant safe? Controversies, ethical concerns, and legal implications. *BMC Medical Ethics, 17,* Article 4. http://dx.doi.org/10.1186/s12910-016-0087-3

Zhang, Q.-F., Yuan, Y.-T., Ren, Q.-T., & Lu, Y.-Z. (2014). A randomized single-blind controlled trial of combination of Naikan and Morita therapy (NMT) in patients with generalized anxiety. *Chinese Mental Health Journal, 28,* 651–656.

Zhang, W., Liu, H., Jiang, X., Wu, D., & Tian, Y. (2014). A longitudinal study of posttraumatic stress disorder symptoms and its relationship with coping skill and locus of control in adolescents after an earthquake in China. *PLoS ONE, 9,* e88263. http://dx.doi.org/10.1371/journal.pone.0088263

Zhang, Y., Haddad, E., Torres, B., & Chen, C. (2011). The reciprocal relationships among parents' expectations, adolescents' expectations, and adolescents' achievement: A two-wave longitudinal analysis of the NELS data. *Journal of Youth and Adolescence, 40*(4), 479–489.

Zhang, Z., & Chen, W. (2019). A systematic review of the relationship between physical activity and happiness. *Journal of Happiness Studies, 20*(4), 1305–1322. doi:10.1007/s10902-018-9976-0

Zhao, J., & Wood, J. N. (2015). Glycine at the gate—from model to mechanism. *Neuron, 85,* 152–1154. doi:10.1016/j.neuron.2015.03.012

Zhong, W., Li, Y., Li, P., Xu, G., & Mo, L. (2015). Short-term trained lexical categories produce preattentive categorical perception of color: Evidence from ERPs. *Psychophysiology, 52,* 98–106. http://dx.doi.org/10.1111/psyp.12294

Zhong, Y., Auchincloss, A. H., Lee, B. K., & Kanter, G. P. (2018). The short-term impacts of the Philadelphia beverage tax on beverage consumption. *American Journal of Preventive Medicine, 55*(1), 26–34. doi:10.1016/j.amepre.2018.02.01

Zhou, X., & Wu, X. (2016). The relationship between rumination, posttraumatic stress disorder, and posttraumatic growth among Chinese adolescents after earthquake: A longitudinal study. *Journal of Affective Disorders, 193,* 242–248. http://dx.doi.org/10.1016/j.jad.2015.12.076

Zhu, B., Chen, C., Loftus, E. F., He, Q., Chen, C., Lei, D., . . . Dong, Q. (2012). Brief exposure to misinformation can lead to long-term false memories. *Applied Cognitive Psychology, 26,* 301–307. http://dx.doi.org/10.1002/acp.1825

Zilioli, S., Slatcher, R. B., Chi, P., Li, X., Zhao, J., & Zhao, G. (2017). The impact of daily and trait loneliness on diurnal cortisol and sleep among children affected by parental HIV/AIDS. *Psychoneuroendocrinology, 75,* 64–71. http://dx.doi.org/10.1016/j.psyneuen.2016.10.012

Zimbardo, P. G. (2007). *The Lucifer effect: Understanding how good people turn evil.* New York, NY: Random House.

Zinik, G., & Padilla, J. (2016). Rape and paraphilic coercive disorders. In A. Phenix & H. M. Hoberman (Eds.), *Sexual offending: Predisposing antecedents, assessments and management* (pp. 45–66). New York, NY: Springer Science + Business Media. http://dx.doi.org/10.1007/978-1-4939-2416-5_4

Zinzow, H. M., & Thompson, M. (2015). Factors associated with use of verbally coercive, incapacitated, and forcible sexual assault tactics in a longitudinal study of college men. *Aggressive Behavior, 41,* 34–43. doi:10.1002/ab.21567

Zuberbühler, K. (2015). Linguistic capacity of non-human animals. *WIREs Cognitive Science, 6,* 313–321. http://dx.doi.org/10.1002/wcs.1338

Zuckerman, M. (1978, February). The search for high sensation. *Psychology Today,* 38–46.

Zuckerman, M. (1979). *Sensation seeking: Beyond the optimal level of arousal.* Hillsdale, NJ: Erlbaum.

Zuckerman, M. (1994). *Behavioral expressions and biosocial bases of sensation seeking.* New York, NY: Cambridge University Press.

Zuckerman, M. (2004). The shaping of personality: Genes, environments, and chance encounters. *Journal of Personality Assessment, 82,* 11–22.

Zuckerman, M. (2014). Sensation seeking, impulsivity and the balance between behavioral approach and inhibition. *Personality and Individual Differences, 60,* S4. http://dx.doi.org/10.1016/j.paid.2013.07.150

Zuckerman, M., & Aluja, A. (2015). Measures of sensation seeking. In G. J. Boyle, D. H. Saklofske, & G. Matthews (Eds.), *Measures of personality and social psychological constructs* (pp. 352–380). San Diego, CA: Elsevier Academic Press. http://dx.doi.org/10.1016/B978-0-12-386915-9.00013-9

Zvolensky, M. J., Jardin, C., Garey, L., Robles, Z., & Sharp, C. (2016). Acculturative stress and experiential avoidance: Relations to depression, suicide, and anxiety symptoms among minority college students. *Cognitive Behaviour Therapy, 45,* 501–517. http://dx.doi.org/10.1080/16506073.2016.1205658

Zysberg, L., Orenshtein, C., Gimmon, E., & Robinson, R. (2017). Emotional intelligence, personality, stress, and burnout among educators. *International Journal of Stress Management, 24*(Suppl 1), 122–136. http://dx.doi.org/10.1037/str0000028

Name Index

Page numbers followed by f and t refer to figures and tables, respectively.